Managing Diversity This third AACSB-mandated topic is covered thoroughly in Chapters 3 and 11 as well as being integrated throughout the text. These boxes also draw attention to the importance of valuing diversity in the contemporary workplace.

Islam's Growth Affects Workplace Policies (Ch. 4)
Diversity Boosts Allstate's Bottom Line (Ch. 7)
Native Americans No Longer "Silent Minority" (Ch. 11)
Exabyte: Where Nonverbal Communication, Diversity, and Ethics Come Together (Ch. 12)
Writing His Own Prescription for Self-Actualization at Age 55 (Ch. 13)
For These Successful Women, Empowerment Began at Home (Ch. 15)

Skills & Tools This text puts a big emphasis on skill development and preparing students to be tomorrow's managers. This end-of-chapter feature is just one of many places students will find how-to tips and instructions.

Career Tips for Today's and Tomorrow's Managers (Ch. 1)
Recommended Periodicals for Staying Current in the Field of Management (Ch. 2)
How Business Leaders Can Help Women Break the Glass Ceiling (Ch. 3)
Twelve Tips for Safe International Business Trips (Ch. 4)
An International Code of Ethics (Ch. 5)
Ten Common Errors to Avoid When Writing a Plan for a New Business (Ch. 6)
Reengineering: Strong Medicine for Strategic Ills (Ch. 7)
How to Construct a Fishbone Diagram (Ch. 8)
How to Build Your Organization's Learning Capability (Ch. 9)
If You Want to Be Delegated Important Duties, Then Demonstrate a Lot of Initiative (Ch. 10)
How to Handle the Job Interview Successfully (Ch. 11)
Harvard's Sarah McGinty Tells How to Develop Your Speaking Style (Ch. 12)
Stress Management 101 (Ch. 13)
How to Use Cooperative Conflict to Avoid Groupthink (Ch. 14)
Putting the Empowerment Puzzle Together (Ch. 15)
How to Express Anger (Ch. 16)
Pros and Cons of ISO 9000 (Ch. 17)

Like The Chapter-Opening **Closing Case** feature at the beginning of each chapter, these cases give students additional real-world examples as a context for solving problems.

"If I'm in Charge, Why Am I Working So Hard?" (Ch. 1)
Russia's New Management Style (Ch. 2)
Welcome to the World of Younger Bosses and Older Workers (Ch. 3)
Tell the Kids We're Moving to Kenya (Ch. 4)
Waste Not, Want Not: A Real Fish Story (Ch. 5)
Profitable Planning at Emerson Electric (Ch. 6)
Can Dell Computer Make It in China? (Ch. 7)
Creativity Helps Hallmark "Send the Very Best" (Ch. 8)
Hard Times for PeopleSoft's People-Centered Culture (Ch. 9)
Bean Counters' Revenge: "Tear Down the Walls" (Ch. 10)
It Takes More than a Great Résumé to Impress Amazon.com (Ch. 11)
The Case of the Errant Messenger (Ch. 12)
Sharon Allred Decker: "We Had to Recognize That People Have Lives" (Ch. 13)
Thirteen Time Zones Can't Keep Lucent's Virtual Team from Succeeding (Ch. 14)
Empowerment Has a Full-Time Job at This Temporary Staffing Company (Ch. 15)
The Unstoppable Entrepreneur (Ch. 16)
When Coca-Cola's Control Systems Fizzled in Europe (Ch. 17)

VIDEO SKILL BUILDER Following up on the skill-building theme, these video-based end-of-part features provide additional how-to advice for effectively handling management situations and problems.

Karen Sand: A Manager in Action (Part 1A)
Recycling Pays at Kodak (Part 1B)
Mary Guerrero-Pelzel, Contractor (Part 2A)
A Florida Hot Sauce Goes International (Part 2B)
Organizational Culture: Three Profiles (Part 3A)
T.G.I. Friday's Organizes for Global Expansion (Part 3B)
Motivation at World Book Publishing (Part 4A)
Entrepreneurial Leadership (Part 4B)
Gulfstream Aircraft Flies on Quality (Part 5)

Management

Management

Eighth Edition

Robert Kreitner

ARIZONA STATE UNIVERSITY

Houghton Mifflin Company   Boston   New York

With lots of love and respect to my wife, Margaret—
from the managerial trenches at Intel to the top of Mount Kilimanjaro—
simply the best.

Executive Editor: George Hoffman
Senior Associate Editor: Susan M. Kahn
Senior Project Editor: Cathy Labresh Brooks
Senior Production/Design Coordinator: Carol Merrigan
Senior Manufacturing Coordinator: Marie Barnes
Marketing Manager: Melissa Russell

Cover design: Harold Burch
Photo credits appear on page I26.

Printed in the U.S.A.

Library of Congress Catalog Card Number: 00-132081
ISBN: 0-618-05638-6

1 2 3 4 5 6 7 8 9–VH–04 03 02 01 00

Brief Contents

Contents

3 The Changing Environment of Management 69

4 International Management and Cross-Cultural Competence 100

---

5 Management's Social and Ethical Responsibilities   134

THE CHANGING WORKPLACE: *A Canadian Logger
Goes Against the Grain*   135

Social Responsibility: Definition and Perspectives   136
What Does Social Responsibility Involve?   137
What Is the Role of Business in Society?   139
MANAGEMENT ETHICS: *Clara Conti Gets Back
What She Gives*   141

6 The Basics of Planning and Project Planning   164

THE CHANGING WORKPLACE: *In a Fast-Paced World,
How Three Managers Plan on the Run*   165

7 Strategic Management 197

8 Decision Making and Creative Problem Solving 226

14 Group Dynamics and Teamwork   427

15 Influence Processes and Leadership   456

Today's managers face a complex web of difficult and exciting challenges. A global economy in which world-class quality is the ticket to ride, increased diversity in the work force, the proliferation of technology and e-commerce, and demands for more ethical conduct promise to keep things interesting. As trustees of society's precious human, material, financial, and informational resources, today's and tomorrow's managers hold the key to a better world. A solid grounding in management is essential to successfully guiding large or small, profit or nonprofit, organizations into the twenty-first century. *Management*, Eighth Edition, represents an important step toward managerial and personal success in an era of rapid change. It is a comprehensive, up-to-date, and highly readable introduction to management theory, research, and practice. This eighth edition is the culmination of my twenty-eight years in management classrooms and management development seminars around the world. Its style and content have been shaped by interaction with literally thousands of students, instructors, reviewers, and managers. All have taught me valuable lessons about organizational life, management, and people in general. Organized along a time-tested functional/process framework, *Management*, Eighth Edition, integrates classical and modern concepts with a rich array of contemporary real-world examples and cases.

New Topics and Research Insights

In response to feedback from students, colleagues, and managers who read the previous edition, and reflecting the latest trends in management thinking, more than 50 new topics can be found in this edition. Among the new topics are the Internet and e-commerce revolution, transnational companies, North American women on foreign assignments, perception of declining moral values in the United States, real versus realizable goals, project-management software, Internet strategy, e-commerce strategy lessons, the myth and reality of workplace creativity, balancing authority and ambition, avoiding layoffs with job banks, customer service as a corporate value, employee orientation programs, organizational culture and digital storytelling, improving cross-functional coordination, how reengineering got a bad name, virtual organizations, hiring at Internet speed, employee retention in diversity programs, the business case for diversity, behavioral interviewing, message overload, media selection in cross-cultural settings, coaching and feedback, upward communication via Internet chat rooms, profanity in the workplace, e-mail policy guidelines, how to compose a clear e-mail message, new tips for preparing for and conducting meetings, how to develop your speaking style, Pfeffer's seven people-centered practices, worker attitudes and company results, new research findings on realistic job previews, employees who are motivated by passion for their work, trophy value of cash, open-book management, transparent organizations, employee wellness programs, stress management 101, group maturity and increased productivity, political in-fighting at Internet start-ups, virtual teams, trust builders and trust busters, successful female executives empowered by their mothers, envisioning the leader of the future, building a mentor mosaic, making change happen, 5P checklist for change agents, disagreeing without being disagreeable, curbing workplace incivility, how to negotiate a pay raise, the illusion of control, and crisis management.

To make room for these new topics and research insights, outdated material and unnecessary wording were studiously identified and eliminated. The net result is an efficient and very up-to-date introduction to the field of management.

Structural Changes

As part of the ongoing process of keeping this book in tune with the times, the following significant structural changes have been made:

- This edition has seventeen chapters, as opposed to eighteen chapters in the prior edition.
- Chapter 17 now contains a natural marriage of material on organizational control and product/service quality improvement. Material on operations management has been eliminated because it typically is covered in a separate course.
- In tune with students' desire for shorter, more concise textbooks, this eighth edition is 32 pages shorter than the already streamlined prior edition.

Complete Coverage of AACSB/IAME Topics

Though concepts have been expanded, relocated, or refined according to new directions in the discipline, the eighth edition continues to offer complete and comprehensive treatment of the following topics recommended by the AACSB/International Association for Management Education:

- Interpersonal and administrative skill development
- The changing environment of management—social, political/legal, economic, and technological dimensions
- Management history
- International management and the global economy
- The Internet and e-commerce
- Managing diversity
- Corporate social responsibility and business ethics
- Strategic management, with special emphasis on implementation and speed
- Staffing and human resource management
- Organizational cultures
- Teams and teamwork
- Change and conflict
- Leadership and communication
- Service organizations and service quality
- Total quality management and quality improvement concepts and techniques

Major Themes

The study of management takes in a great deal of territory, both conceptually and geographically. Therefore, it is important for those being introduced to the field to have reliable guideposts to help them make sense of it all. Six major themes guiding our progress through the fascinating world of management are change, skill development, global economy, the Internet revolution, diversity, and ethics.

An Overriding Focus on Change

It may be a cliché to say "the only certainty today is change," but it is nonetheless true. The challenge for today's and especially tomorrow's managers is to be aware of *specific* changes, along with the factors contributing to them and their likely impact on the practice of management. Change has been woven into the fabric of this edition in the following ways:

- Under the heading of "The Changing Workplace," each chapter-opening case introduces students to real-world changes at large and small, domestic and foreign, and profit and nonprofit organizations.
- Chapter 1 profiles the twenty-first-century manager and ten major changes in the practice of management.
- Chapter 1 focuses on the Internet and e-commerce revolution by tracing the history of the Internet and providing a helpful glossary of common Internet terms.
- Chapter 3 is entirely devoted to the changing social, political/legal, economic, and technological environment that management faces. Workplace demographics document the changing face of the work force.
- Chapter 4 discusses the growth of global and transnational corporations and how to adapt to cross-cultural situations.
- Chapter 7 has an entirely new major section titled "Strategy.com," covering such things as "sticky" Web sites, ethical standards in e-commerce, and six e-commerce strategy lessons.
- Chapter 9 includes an updated discussion of learning organizations as well as how to detect and avoid the ever-present problem of organizational decline.
- Chapter 10 describes the new virtual organizations and shows a global virtual organization in action.
- Chapter 12 discusses how to fight e-mail overload with organizational e-mail policy guidelines and practical tips on how to compose effective e-mail messages.
- Chapter 13 introduces Pfeffer's seven people-centered practices.
- Chapter 14 covers virtual teams and how to build them.
- Chapter 16 introduces a practical new 5P checklist for change agents.
- Chapter 17 now covers the timely topic of crisis management.
- Completely new **Internet Exercises** at the end of each chapter help the reader stay in touch with recent changes in the world of management.

Emphasis on Skill Development

Managers tell us they want job applicants who know more than just management theory. They value people who can communicate well, solve problems, see the big picture, and work cooperatively in teams. Consequently, this edition has a very strong skills orientation.

- **Skills & Tools** sections at the end of each chapter teach students how to manage their career, stay current with management literature, help women break the glass ceiling, have a safe foreign business trip, behave ethically around the world, write a new business plan, reengineer the organization, construct a fishbone diagram (for problem finding), build an organization's learning capability, demonstrate initiative, successfully handle a job interview, develop a more effective speaking style, manage stress, use cooperative conflict to avoid groupthink, empower employees, constructively express anger, and improve product/service quality.
- **How-to-do-it instructions** are integrated into the text for the following skills and tasks: preparing employees for foreign assignments, examining the ethics of a business decision, writing a good objective, using management by objectives (MBO), constructing flow charts and Gantt charts, building a PERT network, performing a break-even analysis, performing a strategic situational (SWOT) analysis, writing planning scenarios, making decisions, avoiding decision-making traps, managing creative people, avoiding layoffs, delegating, interviewing, discouraging sexual harassment, communicating via e-mail, participating in a videoconference, listening, writing effectively, running a meeting, using rewards, making employee participation programs work, curbing organizational politics, preventing groupthink, building trust, modifying behavior, managing change, overcoming resistance to change, managing conflict, negotiating, using Deming's Plan-Do-Check-Act cycle, and improving product and service quality.
- **Video Skill Builders,** following each major part of the text, emphasize the development of essential management skills; and focus on topics such as managing customer service, being an entrepreneur, taking a business international, shaping organizational culture, motivating, leading, and managing quality.

Emphasis on Globalism

For managers, the world is shrinking rapidly. Foreign assignments are becoming a standard part of a well-rounded and successful career in management. Cross-cultural skills are a must. Even employees who stay at home stand a good chance of working for a foreign-owned company. With an eye toward preparing tomorrow's global managers, we have included the following global coverage and themes:

- There is an international selection of cases from the United States, China, Russia, Kenya, Europe, Germany, Norway, Canada, India, and the Netherlands.
- **The Global Manager** and **Management Ethics** boxes throughout the text feature people and companies from the United States, Canada, Britain, China, India, Ireland, Italy, Singapore, and Mexico.
- Many examples from a wide variety of countries are woven into the text discussion.
- Chapter 1 emphasizes the global economy and global skills.
- Chapter 2 describes the historical contributions of a worldwide cast of management pioneers.
- Chapter 3 includes a major section on the global economy and how it affects each of us.
- Chapter 4 is completely devoted to international and cross-cultural management.

Emphasis on the Internet and E-commerce Revolution

The Internet has changed *everything* for many individuals, companies, and entire industries in just a few short years. Problems and opportunities flash by with lightning speed.

It is no longer a joke to say "If you snooze, you lose." Today's and tomorrow's managers need to be "Internet-ready" if they are to win in this new age of e-commerce. A concerted effort has been made to *integrate* the realities and promises of the Internet into both the content and pedagogy of this eighth edition. Specific topics and features include:

- Eight of the chapter-opening and -closing cases focus on high-tech companies and Internet-related companies.
- Chapter 1 frames the importance of the Internet and e-commerce revolution by tracing the history of the Internet, citing relevant facts and figures, and providing a handy **glossary of key Internet terms.**
- **Strategy.com** is a new major section in Chapter 7 covering the following areas: different ways to make money on the Web, creating "sticky" Web sites that hold fickle customers, the "clicks-and-mortar" approach to e-commerce, how cannibalism can pay in e-commerce, maintaining strategic control and ethical standards in e-commerce, and six e-commerce strategy lessons.
- Among the high-tech and Internet-related companies discussed throughout the eighth edition in the cases, boxes, and in-text examples are Yahoo!, eBay, Intel, Microsoft, Amazon.com, America Online, e-Schwab, IBM, Dell Computer, Cisco Systems, Motorola, EMC Corp., Hewlett-Packard, Sun Microsystems, E*Trade, Della.com, General Electric, Lucent, Barnesandnoble.com, Honeywell, EarthLink/MindSpring, Medtronic, PeopleSoft, Egghead Software, Planet-Intra.com, Silicon Graphics, Autodesk, Calico Technologies, and WisdomWare.
- Important Internet-related topics and issues covered in this new eighth edition include international legal issues for the Internet, the troubling "digital divide" between technology haves and have nots, the Internet as Earth's "electronic skin," the Internet as a common language for China and the world, and "Will bugs eat up the U.S. lead in software?"
- Every chapter is followed by a completely new set of **Internet Exercises.** These step-by-step exercises include thoroughly tested Web sites complete with reliable URLs. However, because URLs and specific Web site content can change over time, these exercises are repeated on the text's Web site, and will be updated there as necessary. Each exercise comes complete with specific and challenging questions to sharpen the learning process. The Internet Exercises are intended to be both instructive and fun.

Emphasis on Diversity

Labor forces and customers around the globe, particularly in the United States, are becoming more diverse in terms of national origin, race, religion, gender, predominant age categories, and personal preferences. Managers are challenged to manage diversity effectively to tap the *full* potential of *every* individual's unique combination of abilities and traits. The following diversity coverage and themes can be found in this edition:

- Six new boxed features titled **Managing Diversity** focus needed attention on the growth of Islam in the United States, how Allstate makes diversity pay, Native Americans, deaf and hearing-disabled employees, self-actualization over the age of 55, and how successful female executives got help from Mom.
- Women play the central managerial roles in the chapter-opening cases for Chapters 1, 3, 6, 8, and 15 and the chapter-closing case for Chapter 13.
- A diverse selection of individuals is featured in cases, boxes, examples, and photos.
- Chapter 1 describes the demand for multilingual and multicultural managers.
- Chapter 3 includes a section on managing diversity.

- Chapter 4 discusses managing across cultures and emphasizes the importance of learning foreign languages. Chapter 4 also describes the work goals and leadership styles in different cultures.
- Chapter 5 discusses different value systems.
- Chapter 8 describes different information-processing styles and how to manage creative individuals.
- Chapter 11 discusses moving from tolerance to appreciation when managing diversity. It also covers equal employment opportunity, affirmative action, and the Americans with Disabilities Act (ADA); how to foster union-management cooperation; and how to develop policies for sexual harassment; and substance abuse.
- Chapter 13 discusses how to motivate a diverse work force and provides coverage of the U.S. Family and Medical Leave Act (FMLA).
- Chapter 14 includes major coverage of teamwork.
- Chapter 15 discusses women and the use of power as well as different leadership styles.
- Chapter 16 discusses *cooperative* conflict and describes different conflict resolution styles.

Emphasis on Ethics

Simply put, society wants managers to behave better. Ethical concerns are integrated throughout this edition, as well as featured in Chapter 5. Ethical coverage is evidenced by:

- Eight **Management Ethics** boxes throughout the text
- Discussion of management's ethical reawakening in Chapter 1
- Chapter 5, in Part One, entirely devoted to management's social and ethical responsibilities, providing an ethical context for the entire book
- Ethical aspects of e-commerce
- Value judgments in decision making in Chapter 8
- Ethics of downsizing and layoffs in Chapter 9
- Ethical implications of group norms and avoiding groupthink in Chapter 14
- Greenleaf's ethical "servant leader" in Chapter 15
- Covey's ethical win-win negotiating style in Chapter 16

Interactive Annotations

This unique feature was introduced in the prior edition. The idea was to link the textbook and the Internet to create a dynamic, instructive, and interesting learning tool. In short, to make the textbook come alive. This pedagogical experiment was a great success. Consequently, there are 165 interactive annotations in this eighth edition (105 are new; 3 updated) that integrate timely facts, provocative ideas, discussion questions, and back-to-the-opening-case questions into the flow of the book. The annotations make reading this eighth edition an active, rather than passive, learning process.

Answers and interpretations for the annotations are provided in the *Instructor's Resource Manual* and on the Internet at our Web site (**http://college.hmco.com**).

At the instructor's discretion, many of the annotations provide stimulating opportunities for cooperative learning. Valuable new insights are gained and interpersonal skills are developed when students work together in groups and teams.

Successful Pedagogical Structure for Students

As with the previous edition, pedagogical features of the text, along with student ancillaries, make *Management*, Eighth Edition, a complete and valuable learning tool—one that will satisfy the needs of both students and professors. This is demonstrated by the following:

- Chapter objectives at the beginning of each chapter focus the reader's attention on key concepts.
- Chapter objectives are repeated at appropriate locations, in the text margin, to pace the reader's progress.
- Key terms are emphasized in bold, where first defined, repeated in marginal notes, and listed at the close of each chapter to reinforce important terminology and concepts.
- A stimulating photo/art program and an inviting, user-friendly layout make the material in this edition visually appealing, accessible, and interesting. Captioned color photographs of managers in action and organizational life enliven the text discussion.
- In-text examples and boxes with three different themes—The Global Manager, Management Ethics, Managing Diversity—provide students with extensive, interesting real-world illustrations to demonstrate the application and relevance of topics important to today's managers.
- Clear, comprehensive chapter summaries refresh the reader's memory of important material.
- Cases at the beginning and end of each chapter provide a real-world context for handling management problems. Twenty-six (76 percent) of the cases in this edition are new.
- A Skills & Tools section follows each chapter to give today's and tomorrow's managers practical tools for the twenty-first-century workplace.
- Internet exercises at the end of each chapter challenge the reader to learn more about relevant managerial topics and problems.
- Video Skill Builders at the end of each part foster experiential learning by providing how-to-do-it instruction on key managerial skills.
- An end-of-text glossary (with chapter annotations) of all key terms provides a handy reference for the study of management.
- A student Web site (**http://college.hmco.com**) provides comments on the text annotations, links to the sites discussed in the Internet exercises and any necessary updates to the exercises, links to the companies highlighted in each chapter's boxes and cases, a description of and additional links to sites of interest, and ACE self-tests.
- A management game called *Manager: A Simulation*, Third Edition, prepared by Jerald R. Smith and Peggy Golden, Florida Atlantic University, offers students the chance to act as managers themselves. The game simulates a business environment in which student management teams produce and market a product. Players make various management decisions and learn from the positive or negative outcomes.
- A *Study Guide* (with answers) helps students to measure their understanding of the terms and concepts in each chapter of the text and to prepare for tests and exams.
- A free CD, *Real Deal Upgrade,* contains a variety of review materials as well as tips on improving study habits.

Complete Teaching Package

Management, Eighth Edition, also includes a comprehensive package of teaching materials:

- An instructor's Web site, accessed via a password, provides teaching tips, links to online publications and professional organizations, electronic lecture notes from the *Instructor's Resource Manual*, and PowerPoint® slides for previewing.
- The *Instructor's Resource Manual*, prepared by Maria Muto, contains the chapter objectives, a lecture outline, case interpretation/solutions, interpretations for the Interactive Annotations, discussion/essay questions, a key issue expansion, a decision case and answers to discussion questions, a cooperative learning tool, and transparency masters for every chapter.
- The completely updated *Test Bank* includes nearly 3,000 true/false, multiple-choice, scenario multiple-choice, and short-answer essay questions with page references and answers. Information about the learning level and the degree of difficulty of each multiple-choice item is also included.
- The *Computerized Test Bank* is an electronic version of the *Test Bank* that allows instructors to generate and change tests easily on the computer. The program will print an answer key appropriate to each version of the test you have devised, and it lets you customize the printed appearance of the test. A call-in test service is also available. The program also includes the Online Testing System and Gradebook. This feature allows instructors to administer tests via a network system, modem, or personal computer. It also includes a grading function that lets instructors set up a new class, record grades, analyze grades, and produce class and individual statistics.
- An Instructor's CD-ROM containing over 300 PowerPoint slides provides an effective presentation tool for lectures. The slides highlight key textual material and provide interesting exercises and discussion questions.
- A Blackboard Course Cartridge and a WebCT Courselet that include chapter review materials, PowerPoint slides, Internet exercises, discussion questions, online quizzes, and hyperlinks allow instructors to customize content for online/distance learning courses.
- Close to 100 color transparencies include figures both from within and outside the text.
- The video package includes nine videos for the Skill Builders that follow each part of the text. Four bonus videos supplement various chapters and focus on the global economy, ethics and social responsibility, organizational values and culture, diversity, conflict, and change.

Acknowledgments

Countless people, including colleagues, students, and relatives, have contributed in many ways to the eight editions of this book. For me, this project has been a dream come true; it is amazing where life's journey leads when you have a clear goal, the support of many good people, and a bone-deep belief in the concept of continuous improvement. Whether critical or reinforcing, everyone's suggestions and recommendations have been helpful and greatly appreciated.

While it is impossible to acknowledge every contributor here, some key people need to be identified and sincerely thanked. I particularly appreciate the help and thoughtful comments of my colleague, co-author, and good friend, Professor Angelo Kinicki. My colleagues on the Management 301 team at Arizona State University—John Lea, Angelo Kinicki, and George Bohlander—have been very supportive of my work through the years; I thank them for that as well as for their dedication to good teaching. I am proud to be a long-standing member of that teaching team. I am grateful for the cornerstone reviews of earlier editions by Professors Jack L. Mendleson and Angelo Kinicki. A hearty thank you to Professor Amit Shah, Frostburg State University, for a top-quality job on the *Test Bank*. Sincere thanks also to Maria Muto for her usually outstanding and creative work on the *Instructor's Resource Manual*.

Warmest thanks are also extended to the following colleagues who have provided valuable input for this and prior editions by serving as content advisers or manuscript reviewers:

Teshome Abebe
University of Southern Colorado

Benjamin Abramowitz
University of Central Florida

Raymond E. Alie
Western Michigan University

Stephen L. Allen
Northwest Missouri State University

Douglas R. Anderson
Ashland University

Mark Anderson
Point Loma Nazarene College

Eva Beer Aronson
Interboro Institute

Debra A. Arvanites
Villanova University

Robert Ash
Rancho Santiago College

Seymour Barcun
St. Frances College

R. B. Barton Jr.
Murray State University

Andrew J. Batchelor
Ohio University—Chillicothe

Walter H. Beck Sr.
Kennesaw State University and
Reinhardt College

Roger Best
Louisiana College

Gerald D. Biby
Sioux Falls College

Glenn M. Blair
Baldwin-Wallace College

Bob Bowles
Cecils College

Barbara Boyington
Brookdale Community College

Steve Bradley
Austin Community College

Molly Burke
Rosary College

Marie Burkhead
University of Southwestern Louisiana

John Cantrell
Cleveland State Community College

Thomas Carey
Western Michigan University

Elaine Adams Casmus
Chowan College

David Chown
Mankato State University

Anthony A. Cioffi
Lorain County Community College

George M. Coggins
High Point College

Naomi Berger Davidson
California State University—Northridge

Pamela Davis
Eastern Kentucky University

Richard A. Davis
Rosary College

Thomas Daymont
Temple University—Philadelphia

Tim Donahue
Sioux Falls College

Thomas Duda
S.U.N.Y. Canton Tech College

Deborah J. Dwyer
University of Toledo

Gary Ernst
North Central College

Janice Feldbauer
Macomb Community College

Jacque Foust
University of Wisconsin—River Falls

Ellen Frank
Southern Connecticut State University

Phyllis Goodman
College of DuPage

Sue Granger
Jacksonville State University

John Hall
University of Florida

Susan C. Hanlon
University of Akron

Nell Hartley
Robert Morris College

Lindle Hatton
University of Wisconsin—Oshkosh

Rick Hebert
East Carolina University

Brian R. Hinrichs
Illinois Wesleyan University

Jerome Hufnagel
Horry Georgetown Tech

Cathy Jensen
University of Nebraska—Lincoln

Marvin Karlins
University of South Florida

Velta Kelly
University of Cincinnati

Sylvia Keyes
Bridgewater State College

Mary Khalili
Oklahoma City University

John Lea
Arizona State University

Charles Lee
Baldwin-Wallace College

Roger D. Lee
Salt Lake Community College

Bob Lower
Minot State University

James L. Mann
Ashland Community College

Irvin Mason
Herkimer County Community College

Fredric L. Mayerson
CUNY—Kingsboro Community College

Ann McClure
Ft. Hays State University

Barbara McIntosh
University of Vermont

Debra Miller
Ashland Community College

Peggy M. Miller
Ohio University—Athens

John Nagy
Cleary College

James Nead
Vincennes University

Joan Nichols
Emporia State University

Alice E. Nuttall
Kent State University

Darlene Orlov
New York University

Robert Ottemann
University of Nebraska—Omaha

Clyde A. Painter
Ohio Northern University

Herbert S. Parker
Kean College of New Jersey

Gus Petrides
Borough of Manhattan Community College

J. Stephen Phillips
Ohio University—Chillicothe

Allen H. Pike
Ferrum College

Khush Pittenger
Ashland University

Jyoti N. Prasad
Eastern Illinois University

Lynn J. Richardson
Fort Lewis College

Robert W. Risteen
Ohio University—Chillicothe

Ralph Roberts
University of West Florida

Jake Robertson
Oklahoma State University

Robert Rowe
New Mexico State University–Alamogordo and *Park College, Holloman Air Force Base*

Wendell J. Roye
Franklin Pierce College

Doug Rymph
Emporia State University

Nestor St. Charles
Dutchess County Community College

John T. Samaras
Central State University

Roger C. Schoenfeldt
Murray State University

C. L. Scott III
Indiana University NW—Gary

Kathryn Severance
Viterbo College

Jane Shuping
Western Piedmont Community College

Marc Siegall
California State University—Chico

G. David Sivak
Westmoreland County Community College

Mick Stahler
Stautzenberger College

Jacqueline Stowe
McMurray University

Sharon Tarnutzer
Utah State University

Margo Underwood
Brunswick College

John Valentine
Kean College of New Jersey

Joe F. Walenciak
John Brown University

Dorothy Wallace
Chowan College

Stanley Welaish
Kean College of New Jersey

Richard A. Wells
Aiken Technical College

Ty Westergaard
Lincoln University

Timothy Wiedman
Ohio University—Lancaster

James Wittman
Rock Valley College

My partnership with Houghton Mifflin through the years has been productive and enjoyable. Many Houghton Mifflin Company people have contributed enormously to this project. I would like to offer a hearty thank you to everyone by acknowledging the following key contributors: George Hoffman, Melissa Russell, Susan Kahn, Cathy Brooks, Marcy Kagan, Lauren Gagliardi, David Cunningham, Carol Merrigan, Marie Barnes, and Ryan Vine.

The discussion of mentoring in Chapter 15 is dedicated once again to Professor Fred Luthans, University of Nebraska—Lincoln, for getting me into the textbook business. To Margaret—my wife, best friend, and hiking buddy—thanks for being my center of gravity and for keeping the spirit of the dancing bears alive. Once again, I must thank our cat, Amaranth, for supervising my every move during the last fifteen years from his cozy napping places in my home office.

Finally, I would like to thank the thousands of introductory management students I have had the pleasure of working with through the years for teaching me a great deal about tomorrow's managers. Best wishes for a rewarding career in management.

Bob Kreitner

Management

"IF YOU HAVE BUILT CASTLES IN THE AIR,
YOUR WORK NEED NOT BE LOST;
THAT IS WHERE THEY SHOULD BE.
NOW PUT THE FOUNDATIONS
UNDER THEM."
henry david thoreau

Part One

The MANAGEMENT CHALLENGE

MANAGERS and ENTREPRENEURS

CHAPTER OBJECTIVES

When you finish studying this chapter, you should be able to

1 Define the term *management* and explain the managerial significance of the terms *effectiveness* and *efficiency*.

2 Identify and summarize five major sources of change for today's managers.

3 Contrast the functional and role approaches to explaining what managers do.

4 Summarize the ten facts of managerial life.

5 Explain the basic formula for managerial success ($S = A \times M \times O$).

6 Explain how managers learn to manage.

7 Challenge two myths about small businesses and describe entrepreneurs.

"WHEN I THINK ABOUT WHAT IT TAKES TO MAKE A SUCCESSFUL STARTUP, I ASK THREE QUESTIONS: WHAT AM I DOING TO BUILD VALUE? DO I HAVE THE RIGHT TEAM IN PLACE? AND—IN TERMS OF USING MY OWN TIME AND ENERGY— AM I THE RIGHT PERSON FOR MY PARTICULAR TEAM?"

mary furlong

"Neither Rain nor Fear Can Stop Deborah Rosado Shaw"

Gangs attacked her on the way to school. They beat her up in the hallways between classes. They snatched her books, money and homework at will.

Things became so bad that she had to ride the elevators with her teachers to avoid the violence at Taft High School in the South Bronx. But Deborah Rosado Shaw was lucky. The studious minister's daughter from New York's Spanish Harlem was determined to survive.

Today, 26 years later, that courage has helped her become an entrepreneur worth $1 million.

"I confronted enormous fear back then, and there's not a lot that could scare me as much today," says Rosado Shaw, 38. "In business, I believe if you're not doing something that makes you shake in your shoes, you're not doing enough."

Over the past decade, she's done plenty. Starting with $300,000, the Hispanic executive has built her New Jersey-based company, Umbrellas Plus, into a $10 million enterprise with a client list that includes such powerful retailers as Wal-Mart, Costco and Toys "R" Us.

"There's nothing sexy about our business," says Rosado Shaw. "We sell beach umbrellas, sand chairs and tote bags, the portable stuff you take to the beach."

But it's a brutal business, with shrinking margins and ferocious competitors that dwarf Umbrellas Plus.

"They'd love to remove me from the landscape," says Rosado Shaw. "But I'm not going anywhere. I've always played in a game that's too big for me."

Hard Knocks

That kind of passion and pride has inspired many up-and-coming entrepreneurs in the USA.

"Deborah's story is one of those positive, land-of-opportunity stories," says Manuel Mirabal, president of the National Puerto Rican Coalition. "She started with nothing, and then she used lots of her energy and intelligence to end up where she is."

The land of opportunity seemed far away when Rosado Shaw entered elite Wellesley College at the age of 16.

During her first week on campus, her roommate's parents wanted to toss her out of the dorm room.

"I was devastated," says Rosado Shaw. "I had fought so hard for this dream."

The dream was in tatters after Rosado Shaw dropped out of Wellesley and returned to New York in search of a job.

"I had no skills or experience," she says. "And I didn't know anyone in business except the corner bodega owner, and he was a thief."

Commuting from New Jersey, Rosado Shaw formed a tenants' group to make sure her apartment building had heat and hot water. The group's attorney introduced Rosado Shaw to his wife, who worked at a company that made umbrellas and tote bags.

Rosado Shaw was hired and quickly fell in love with business.

"It was incredible," she says. "The orders came in. The stuff got made. I was creating something out of nothing."

Rosado Shaw wanted to be a salesperson, but the company wouldn't let her sell. So, the 19-year-old dynamo took a sick day and called on marketers at the Museum of Natural History.

She came away with a $140,000 order.

"I went to the president of the company after that," recalls Rosado Shaw, "and I asked him, 'Are you guys going to let me sell now, or what?'"

They did, but two years later, at age 21, she defected to a rival firm. Soon after, she moved to California to expand her new employer's umbrella business.

Dreaming Big

In 1987, Rosado Shaw scratched together $300,000 to buy a controlling interest in the company.

By then, she was married and the mother of two children.

"I was in shock," says Rosado Shaw. "All of a sudden, I was an entrepreneur without a salary. But I didn't have a choice. There was no way, no how, that a large corporation would ever let me do what I wanted."

Freedom didn't translate into easy profits. Rosado Shaw had never seen a balance sheet before. She had no idea how to calculate her return on investment. And she lost money on late deliveries.

"I was one of those seat-of-the-pants, didn't-know-what-I-was-doing entrepreneurs," she says. "Most people think success is a straight line. It's not."

When orders finally started raining down, however, Rosado Shaw was able to get Umbrellas Plus cranking.

And to better serve her retail customers, the entrepreneur re-tooled her company and moved it to New Jersey three years ago.

Instead of creating a line of beach gear ahead of time, sticking it in a warehouse and then waiting for orders to arrive before distributing the merchandise, Umbrellas Plus now custom manufactures its products for large retail chains after lengthy consultations with them.

This new business model cuts way back on inventory and killer overhead costs, but it doesn't eliminate risk altogether. If Rosado Shaw's products don't sell at retail, she must take them back and swallow the cost.

That hasn't been a problem in her dealings with Wal-Mart, which purchased and sold about $1 million worth of merchandise from Umbrellas Plus last year.

"They are an entrepreneurial mecca," says Rosado Shaw. "And they have supported me and opened a lot of doors."

The relationship began two years ago when Rosado Shaw, then an unknown at Wal-Mart, was invited to address the chain's top 1,500 executives at one of their weekly Saturday morning meetings. The experience was intimidating. But she performed.

And Wal-Mart vice chairman Don Soderquist was impressed.

"(Rosado Shaw) is the kind of person you'd like to have as a friend or neighbor," he says. "There are unlimited opportunities for her."

All those opportunities may not be in the umbrella business.

"I've made so much money," says Rosado Shaw, "that I can exit at any time."

Indeed, the entrepreneur is in the process of becoming a much-sought-after inspirational speaker.

Coca-Cola, for example, has asked her to deliver a series of motivational talks to children. Rosado Shaw also wants to start a foundation called Dream Big, which would impart skills for entrepreneurial success.

"I want to tell people they have the same power I have, that they can live a dignified life, too," she says.

In the end, however, perhaps the best advice Rosado Shaw can give appears on her PC as a screen saver: "Don't let fear stop you."

Source: Bill Meyers, "Umbrella Made Skies Brighter," *USA Today* (January 14, 1999): 8B. Copyright 1999, USA Today. Reprinted with permission.

Deborah Rosado Shaw is a typical modern manager in action. Her overriding goal is to do whatever it takes to achieve her organization's mission in a highly competitive world. Relative to our present challenge to learn more about management, Rosado Shaw's inspiring story underscores four key realities of managing today:

1. The only certainty today is *change*. Challenging *goals* motivate people to strive for improvement and overcome obstacles and resistance to change.
2. Successful corporate giants like Wal-Mart have learned to partner with small entrepreneurial ventures. Sheer size alone no longer ensures success. *Customer service, teamwork, speed,* and *flexibility* are the orders of the day.
3. Product/service quality cannot be an afterthought; quality must be the *driving force* in the battle to stay competitive.
4. Without *lifelong learning*, there can be no true economic progress for individuals and organizations alike.

Keep these managerial realities in mind as you explore the world of management in this book.

Every one of us—whether as an employee, a customer, or a stockholder—has a direct stake in the quality of management. As an everyday example, consider the positive connection Hyatt Hotels has found between good management, customer satisfaction, and profitability.

Hyatt Hotels has been surveying all employees at its 106 hotels in North America for 15 years. Although its questionnaire includes some 100 items, the answers to seven key queries—one of which is "Tell us what you think of management"—make up the general morale index, or GMI, that Hyatt's top officers watch most closely. The company has just finished developing a computer program that compares employees' attitudes in each location with what guests say on those how-did-you-like-your-stay postcards in Hyatt's hotel rooms. Guess what: The hotels with the highest GMI scores also rack up the highest ratings from customers—and, not coincidentally, the highest sales and gross operating profits.[1]

Conversely, bad management is a serious threat to our quality of life. In fact, "studies . . . show the single biggest source of stress is poorly trained and inept supervisors."[2]

Effective management is the key to a better world, but mismanagement squanders our resources and jeopardizes our well-being. Every manager, regardless of level or scope of responsibility, is either part of the solution or part of the problem. Management or mismanagement—the choice is yours. A basic knowledge of management theory, research, and practice will help prepare you for productive and gainful employment in a highly organized world in which virtually everything is managed.

Management Defined

We now need to define management, in order to highlight the importance, relevance, and necessity of studying it. **Management** is the process of working with and through others to achieve organizational objectives in a changing environment. Central to this process is the effective and efficient use of limited resources.

Five components of this definition require closer examination: (1) working with and through others, (2) achieving organizational objectives, (3) balancing effectiveness and efficiency, (4) making the most of limited resources, and (5) coping with a changing environment (see Figure 1.1).

1 Define the term *management* and explain the managerial significance of the terms *effectiveness* and *efficiency*.

management *the process of working with and through others to achieve organizational objectives in a changing environment*

Working with and Through Others

Management is, above all else, a social process. Many collective purposes bring individuals together—building cars, providing emergency health care, publishing books, and on and on. But in all cases, managers are responsible for getting things done by working with and through others.

Aspiring managers who do not interact well with others hamper their careers. This was the conclusion two experts reached following interviews with 62 executives from the United States, United Kingdom, Belgium, Spain, France, Germany, and Italy. Each of the executives was asked to describe two managers whose careers had been *derailed*. Derailed managers were those who had not lived up to their peers' and superiors' high expectations. The derailed managers reportedly had these shortcomings:

- Problems with interpersonal relationships.
- Failure to meet business objectives.
- Failure to build and lead a team.
- Inability to change and adapt during a transition.[3]

Figure 1.1

Key Aspects of the Management Process

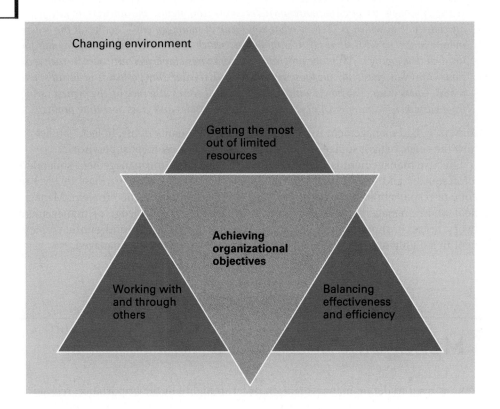

Significantly, the first and third shortcomings involve failure to work effectively with and through others. The derailed managers experienced a number of interpersonal problems; among other things they were perceived as manipulative, abusive, untrustworthy, demeaning, overly critical, not team players, and poor communicators.[4]

Even managers who make it all the way to the top often have interpersonal problems, according to management consultant Richard Hagberg. His study of 511 chief executive officers led to this conclusion about why managers often fail to inspire loyalty in employees:

Many are also hobbled by self-importance, which keeps them from hearing feedback about their own strengths and weaknesses. The head of one large company recently told me about an incident that occurred as he and his wife waited in line to get his driver's license renewed. He was frustrated at how long it was taking and grumbled to his wife, "I have a lot to do. Don't they know who I am?" She replied, "Yeah, you're a plumber's son who got lucky." Her remark really got to him. It drove home how far he had gotten caught up in his sense of self-importance.[5]

Achieving Organizational Objectives

An objective is a target to be strived for and, one hopes, attained. Like individuals, organizations are usually more successful when their activities are guided by challenging, yet achievable, objectives. From an individual perspective, scheduling a course load becomes more systematic and efficient when a student sets an objective, such as graduating with a specific degree by a given date.

How to Deal with a Boss Who Is a Bully   1A

Psychologist Hara Estroff Marno recently offered this practical advice:

- Confront the bully boss about *specific behavior* and its consequences *in private* (bullies don't back down in public).
- Get support from your coworkers.
- Inform a trustworthy person in the human resources department about the problem.
- As a risky last resort, go to your boss's boss (bullies don't like people going over their heads). But, as Marno concluded, "The unemployment line may be preferable to life eternal with a bully boss."

Source: Adapted and quoted from "Dealing with a Bully Boss," *Training*, 33 (February 1996): 14.

Questions: *What is your personal experience with abusive, manipulative, or overly critical managers? What did you do (or not do)? What lessons in how* not *to manage did you learn?*

For further information about the interactive annotations in this chapter, visit our Web site (**www.hmco.com/college**).

Although personal objectives are typically within the reach of individual effort, organizational objectives or goals always require collective action. For example, Texas entrepreneur John Mackey has a very precise objective for his nationwide chain of natural-food supermarkets, Whole Food Market, Inc. As *Business Week* reported in 1998, Mackey's "aim is to reach 200 stores and more than triple sales to $4.5 billion by 2003."[6] That is a long way from 87 stores and $1.4 billion in sales. Mackey cannot do it alone. But he hopes that his clear and challenging strategic objective will energize his growing workforce to band together to get the job done.

Organizational objectives also serve later as measuring sticks for performance. Without organizational objectives, the management process, like a trip without a specific destination, would be aimless and wasteful.

Balancing Effectiveness and Efficiency

Distinguishing between effectiveness and efficiency is much more than an exercise in semantics. The relationship between these two terms is important, and it presents managers with a never-ending dilemma. **Effectiveness** entails promptly achieving a stated objective. Swinging a sledgehammer against the wall, for example, would be an effective way to kill a bothersome fly. But given the reality of limited resources, effectiveness alone is not enough. **Efficiency** enters the picture when the resources required to achieve an objective are weighed against what was actually accomplished. The more favorable the ratio of benefits to costs, the greater the efficiency. Although a sledgehammer is an effective tool for killing flies, it is highly inefficient when the wasted effort and smashed walls are taken into consideration. A fly swatter is both an effective and an efficient tool for killing a single housefly.

Managers are responsible for balancing effectiveness and efficiency (see Figure 1.2). Too much emphasis in either direction leads to mismanagement. On the one hand, managers must be effective, although those who are too stingy with resources will not get the job done.

On the other hand, managers need to be efficient by containing costs as much as possible and conserving limited resources. Boeing, for example, is presently waging a

effectiveness *a central element in the process of management that entails achieving a stated organizational objective*

efficiency *a central element in the process of management that balances the amount of resources used to achieve an objective against what was actually accomplished*

Figure 1.2

Balancing Effectiveness and Efficiency

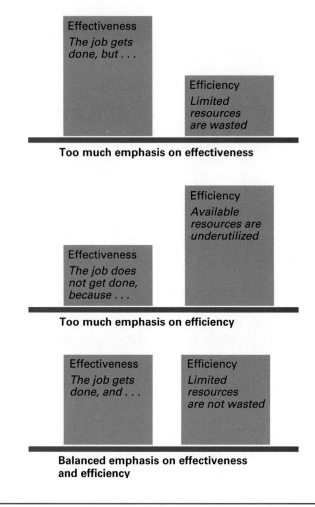

Too much emphasis on effectiveness

Too much emphasis on efficiency

Balanced emphasis on effectiveness and efficiency

mighty war against inefficiency at its huge Everett, Washington, factory, where four 747 jumbo jets are custom-made each month.

What the customer wants, the customer gets, with no seeming end to the possible permutations: Boeing offers 747 buyers as many choices of paint colors as Elton John has outfits, including no fewer than 109 shades of white. The factory is surprisingly quiet and low tech. There are no flashing lasers or whizzing robots. Just small teams of workers, many wielding nothing more sophisticated than hand tools. It looks, in fact, like a giant version of the repair bay in your neighborhood service station.

Boeing's problem—and it's a big one—is that your humble service station probably operates more efficiently than the largest aerospace company on the planet. Boeing's fusty production techniques carry an enormous price tag. Every alteration, even a seemingly minor one like moving the location of an emergency flashlight holder, consumes thousands of hours of engineering time, requires hundreds of pages of detailed drawings, and costs hundreds of thousands, if not millions, of dollars to execute.[7]

Stiffer competition from Europe's Airbus Industrie means that Boeing's executives can no longer afford to indulge this sort of inefficiency. Managers who waste resources may get the job done, but they risk bankruptcy in the process. A balance between effectiveness and efficiency is the key to competitiveness today.

Making the Most of Limited Resources

We live in a world of scarcity. Those who are concerned with such matters worry not only about running out of nonrenewable energy and material resources but also about the lopsided use of those resources. The United States, for example, with slightly more than 4 percent of the world's population, is currently consuming about 25 percent of the world's annual oil production and generating 23 percent of the greenhouse gases linked to global warming.[8]

Although experts and nonexperts alike may quibble over exactly how long it will take to exhaust our nonrenewable resources or come up with exotic new technological alternatives, one bold fact remains. Our planet is becoming increasingly crowded.

Demographers who collect and study population statistics like to be very precise. Accordingly, by their count, the world's population reached six billion (that's 6,000,000,000) people on July 16, 1999.[9] Taking deaths into account, planet Earth gains a net 160 new human passengers every minute, 1,609,325 every week, and 83,684,897 each year.[10]

Approximately 83 percent of the world's population in the year 2020 will live in relatively poor and less-developed countries (see Figure 1.3). Developed and industrialized nations, consequently, will experience increasing pressure to divide the limited resource pie more equitably.

Because of their common focus on resources, economics and management are closely related. Economics is the study of how limited resources are distributed among alternative uses. In productive organizations, managers are the trustees of limited resources, and it is their job to see that the basic factors of production—land, labor, and capital—are used efficiently as well as effectively. Management could be called "applied economics."

↗↙ 1B

Efficient, or Just Plain Cheap?

When Bob Kierlin, CEO of Fastenal Co., recently had to dash out to California from company headquarters in Winona, Minn., he didn't even think about flying first class. Or coach, for that matter. Kierlin, who owns $234 million of Fastenal stock, did what he always does: drove the entire 5,000-mile roundtrip in one of the company's Dodge Caravan minivans. Along the way Kierlin and CFO Dan Florness dined at Burger King, Subway, and Arby's, largely because the company doesn't reimburse employees for road meals. "You have to eat whether you're traveling or not," reasons the soft-spoken Kierlin . . .

All this would be of only passing interest except for one fact: Kierlin presides, in his curious way, over one white-hot sizzler of a growth company. Profits have risen 38.1% annually over the past five years.

Source: Richard Teitelbaum, "Who Is Bob Kierlin—And Why Is He So Successful?" *Fortune* (December 8, 1997): 245–246.

Question: *What do you think about Kierlin's approach to balancing effectiveness and efficiency? Explain.*

Coping with a Changing Environment

Successful managers are the ones who anticipate and adjust to changing circumstances rather than being passively swept along or caught unprepared. Employers today are hiring managers who can take unfamiliar situations in stride. For instance, an AT&T recruiter recently said:

We're seeking out people who have learned how to learn and can adapt to changing situations . . . We're not really looking for people who have a dogmatic approach. That might

Figure 1.3

**World Population
Growth Projections**

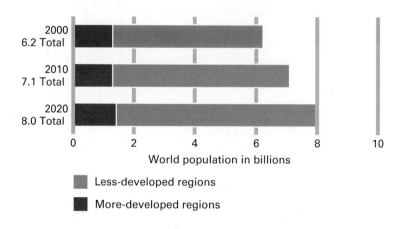

Source: Scott Pendleton, in *The Christian Science Monitor*, October 21, 1992. © 1992 The Christian Science Publishing Society.

have been attractive in the days when AT&T was a regulated monopoly, but today's market and technology are changing so rapidly, if you're hiring people who don't like surprises, you're probably not hiring the right people.[11]

2 Identify and summarize five major sources of change for today's managers.

Chapter 3 provides detailed coverage of important changes and trends in management's social, political-legal, economic, and technological environments. At this point, it is instructive to preview major changes for managers doing business in the twenty-first century[12] (see Table 1.1). This particular collection of changes is the product of five overarching sources of change: globalization, the evolution of product quality, environmentalism, an ethical reawakening, and the Internet revolution. Together, these factors are significantly reshaping the practice of management.

Globalization.   Figuratively speaking, the globe is shrinking in almost every conceivable way. Networks of transportation, communication, computers, music, and economics have tied the people of the world together as never before. Companies are having to become global players just to survive, let alone prosper. Coca-Cola is a leader in this regard. The Atlanta-based soft drinks giant derives over 75 percent of its profits from foreign sales in nearly 200 countries.[13] In a recent American Management Association survey, 1,797 executives from 36 countries were asked to look ten years into the future. "Globalization and foreign markets" was ranked the likely number one issue for managers in ten years.[14] Business and job opportunities show little regard for international borders these days.

On the negative side, some worry about giant global corporations eclipsing the economic and political power of individual nations and their citizens. Indeed, "half of the hundred largest budgets in the world now belong to corporations, not nations."[15]

Today's model manager is one who is comfortable transacting business in multiple languages and cultures. A prime example is Jacques Nasser, the new CEO of Ford Motor Company:

His background . . . makes him one of that rare breed in Detroit: an import—and therefore an unusual candidate to run an American icon. In fact, he's as close to zero percent American as you can get. Born in a mountain village in Lebanon and raised in Australia from

It's party time at a Colorado resort for the extended corporate family called Internet Capital Group. Although the Wayne, Pennsylvania, startup only employs 42 people, it owns stakes in 36 different companies specializing in business-to-business (B2B) Internet commerce. B2B has rapidly become the 800-pound gorilla in the e-commerce revolution because businesses presently buy much more over the Web than individual consumers do.

Table 1.1

The Twenty-First Century Manager: Ten Major Changes		
	Moving away from ➝	**Moving toward**
Administrative role	Boss/superior/leader	Team member/facilitator/teacher/sponsor/advocate/coach
Cultural orientation	Monocultural/monolingual	Multicultural/multilingual
Quality/ethics/ environmental impacts	Afterthought (or no thought)	Forethought (unifying themes)
Power bases	Formal authority; rewards and punishments	Knowledge; relationships; rewards
Primary organizational unit	Individual	Team
Interpersonal dealings	Competition; win-lose	Cooperation; win-win
Learning	Periodic (preparatory; curriculum-driven)	Continuous (lifelong; learner-driven)
Problems	Threats to be avoided	Opportunities for learning and continuous improvement
Change and conflict	Resist/react/avoid	Anticipate/seek/channel
Information	Restrict access/hoard	Increase access/share

Potholes in the Road to a Global Economy?   1C

... spreading capitalism is not simply an exercise in economic engineering. It is an assault on other nations' culture and politics that almost guarantees a collision. Even when countries adopt some trappings of capitalism, they may not embrace the basic values that make the system work.

Source: Robert J. Samuelson, "Global Capitalism, R.I.P.?", *Newsweek* (September 14, 1998): 42.

Questions: *What does the term* capitalism *mean to you? What cultural values are necessary to make capitalism succeed? How likely is a capitalist global economy to prevail in 20 years? Explain.*

the age of 4, he speaks five languages, . . . loves opera, and holds an Australian passport.

But Nasser has one distinctly American characteristic, other than his obsession with cars: a highly entrepreneurial, impatient, can-do mentality.[16]

Unusual? No. There is a rapidly growing army of global managers from all corners of the world, and you can become a member of it through diligent effort and a clear sense of purpose. Chapter 4 is devoted to the topic of international management. The international cases and The Global Manager features throughout the text are intended to broaden your awareness of international management.

The Evolution of Product Quality.   Managers have been interested in the quality of their products, at least as an afterthought, since the Industrial Revolution. But thanks to U.S. and Japanese quality gurus such as W. Edwards Deming and Kaoru Ishikawa[17] (more about them in Chapter 2), product/service quality has become both a forethought and a driving force in effective organizations of all kinds. Today's hospitals, hotels, universities, and government agencies are as interested in improving product/service quality as are factories, mines, airlines, and railroads.

In its most basic terms, the emphasis on quality has evolved through four distinct stages since World War II—from "fix it in" to "inspect it in" to "build it in" to "design it in." Progressive managers are moving away from the first two approaches and toward the build-it-in and design-it-in approaches.[18] Here are the key differences:

- *The fix-it approach to quality.* Rework any defective products identified by quality inspectors at the end of the production process.
- *The inspect-it-in approach to quality.* Have quality inspectors sample work in process and prescribe machine adjustments to avoid substandard output.
- *The build-it-in approach to quality.* Make *everyone* who touches the product responsible for spotting and correcting defects. Emphasis is on identifying and eliminating *causes* of quality problems.
- *The design-it-in approach to quality.* Intense customer and employee involvement drives the entire design-production cycle. Emphasis is on *continuous improvement* of personnel, processes, and product.

Notice how each stage of this evolution has broadened the responsibility for quality, turning quality improvement into a true team effort. Also, the focus has shifted from reactively fixing product defects to proactively working to prevent them and to satisfy the customer completely. Today's quality leaders strive to *exceed*, not just meet, the customer's expectations.

A popular label for the build-it-in and design-it-in approaches to quality is *total quality management* (TQM).[19] TQM is discussed in detail in Chapter 17.

Environmentalism.   Environmental issues such as deforestation; global warming; depletion of the ozone layer; toxic waste; and pollution of land, air, and water are no longer strictly the domain of campus radicals. Mainstream politicians and managers around the world have picked up the environmental banner. The so-called green

The Global Manager

A Society That Reuses Almost Everything

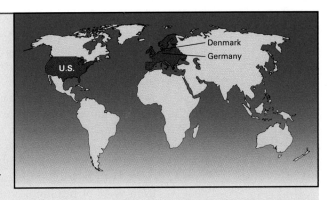

Corporate America's traditional response to pollution concerns and regulations has been to clean up the mess that spews from smokestacks and waste pipes. More than two-thirds of the billions of dollars industry spends on the environment goes for such costly "end-of-pipe" controls.

Now, some companies are adopting a more sophisticated approach. They are considering the environmental impact of products and services over their entire lifetimes. That might mean using one industry's dross as another's raw material—such as turning power-plant ash into gypsum board. Or it might mean redesigning products to make them easier to reuse, recycle, or incinerate. Or substituting cleaner technologies, such as telecommuting for car travel. "One can imagine a society that reuses almost everything," says Jesse H. Ausubel, director of the human environment program at Rockefeller University.

Elusive Savings

The approach is called "industrial ecology," and some companies are beginning to find that it makes sense. At an innovative site in Kalundborg, Denmark, four industrial facilities—an oil refinery, a coal power plant, a gypsum wallboard factory, and a pharmaceutical plant—pass energy, wastewater, and some products back and forth, says Massachusetts Institute of Technology researcher John R. Ehrenfeld. In the U.S., Ford Motor Co. began a program to recycle plastic bumpers into taillight housings and new bumpers—saving money in the process.

Perhaps the best example of industrial ecology in action is Xerox Corp. In the early 1990s, copiers coming off lease were piling up in its warehouses. Several European countries were floating proposals, some later enacted into law, to require companies to take back packaging and discarded products. And archrival Canon Inc. began recycling toner cartridges.

Xerox responded with an "asset recycle management" plan to cut factory waste and reuse or recycle more parts. Engineers now design copiers to last longer and use more

parts in common. Designers have cut the number of chemicals they use from 500 to 50 to facilitate recycling. Print and toner cartridges come with prepaid return labels, boosting reuse rates to as much as 60%. The effort saves Xerox more than $200 million a year, estimates Patricia A. Calkins, manager of environmental products and technology.

Often, however, savings are more elusive. Germany's BMW is a leader in designing cars that can be easily disassembled and recycled. But so far, the costs of collecting and disposing of the nonmetal parts of discarded cars outweigh the benefits, executives say. In the U.S., IBM promotes eco-friendly products, such as its RAMAC disk drives, made with less energy and fewer materials. But the recycled plastics that are used to make them cost more than virgin materials. Turning eco-friendliness into a cost advantage "will be the next big step," concedes Diana J. Bendz, IBM's director of environmentally conscious products.

Computer Dilemma

Another challenge is figuring out the best eco-friendly strategy. Is it better to recycle obsolete computers or to dump them and save on energy and transportation costs? Researchers don't always have the answers. Indeed, academics still argue about whether paper or plastic grocery bags are "greener."

But few doubt that there is plenty of room for improvement. Right now, estimates Rockefeller's Ausubel, the U.S. and other developed nations use materials and energy with only 5% efficiency. With innovative industrial ecology measures, that percentage could be boosted dramatically.

Source: John Carey, "A Society That Reuses Almost Everything." Reprinted from the November 10, 1997 issue of *Business Week* by special permission. Copyright © 1997 by McGraw-Hill, Inc.

movement has spawned successful political parties in Europe and is gaining a foothold in North America and elsewhere.[20] Managers are challenged to develop creative ways to make a profit without unduly harming the environment in the process. Terms such as "industrial ecology" and "eco-efficiency" are heard today under the general umbrella of sustainable development.[21] Also, cleaning up the environment promises to generate whole new classes of jobs and robust profits in the future. The debate over jobs versus the environment has been rendered obsolete by the need for both a healthy economy *and* a healthy environment.[22] (See The Global Manager.)

An Ethical Reawakening.   Managers are under strong pressure from the public, elected officials, and respected managers to behave better. This pressure has resulted from years of headlines about discrimination, illegal campaign contributions, price fixing, insider trading, selling unsafe products, and other unethical practices.

Traditional values such as honesty are being reemphasized in managerial decision making and conduct. This conclusion is supported by the results of a nationwide survey of executives who were asked to rank the desired characteristics of superior leaders. The number one choice was *honest* (87 percent).[23] Ethics and honesty are everyone's concern: *mine, yours,* and *ours.* Every day we have countless opportunities to be honest or dishonest. One survey of over 4,000 employees uncovered the following ethical problems in the workplace (the percentage of employees observing the problem during the past year appears in parentheses):

- Lying to supervisors (56 percent)
- Lying on reports or falsifying records (41 percent)
- Stealing and theft (35 percent)
- Sexual harassment (35 percent)
- Abusing drugs or alcohol (31 percent)
- Conflict of interest (31 percent)[24]

Because of closer public scrutiny, ethical questions can no longer be shoved aside as irrelevant. The topic of managerial ethics is covered in depth in Chapter 5 and explored in the Management Ethics boxes throughout the text.

The Internet and E-Commerce Revolution.   Like a growing child, the Internet first crawled, then walked, and eventually ran. In concept, the Internet began as a U.S. Department of Defense (DOD) research project during the Cold War era of the 1960s. The plan was to give university scientists a quick and inexpensive way to share their DOD research data. Huge technical problems such as getting incompatible computers to communicate in a fail-safe network were solved in 1969 at UCLA when researchers succeeded in getting two linked computers to exchange data. The Internet was born. Other universities were added to the Internet during the 1970s, and gradually applications such as e-mail emerged. By 1983, technology made it possible to link computer networks into one global network called the World Wide Web. Time passed and improvements were made. During the early 1990s, individuals and businesses began to log on to the "Web" to communicate via e-mail and to buy and sell things. (See the Internet glossary in Table 1.2).

Internet *global network of servers and personal and organizational computers*

Recent growth of the **Internet**—the worldwide network of personal computers, powerful servers, and organizational computer systems—has been explosive. No one owns the Web, and anyone with a computer modem can be part of it. Within its digital recesses are both trash and treasure. In 1999, about 159 million people had access to the Internet. "By 2003, International Data estimates 510 million people will be online worldwide."[25] The implications of this massive interconnectedness for managers are

		Table 1.2
Browser	Software, such as Microsoft Internet Explorer or Netscape Navigator, that enables computer users to search for, display, and download multimedia information that appears on the Internet.	**An Internet Glossary**
Cookie	A text file that is stored on your computer to identify you when you visit a particular Web site, so you can use personalized services like virtual shopping carts.	
ISP	Internet service provider; a company that offers Internet access, usually for a monthly fee. ISPs can be local operators, specialists like America Online, or companies like AT&T and Gateway.	
Link, hyperlink	A highlighted word or image on a Web page that connects to another Web page when clicked on with a mouse.	
Portal	A term for the many multiservice sites such as Excite and Yahoo that act as gateways to the Internet. Originally only a search engine and some suggested links, portals now present an ever-growing selection of features and services.	
Search engine	A tool for finding Web sites on the topics of your choice. No one engine can find everything on the Web, and each one displays information differently, so it pays to check out several.	
URL	Uniform Resource Locator. The standard format for the address of any computer or resource on the Internet. It contains information about the server to be contacted and the method and path of access, e.g., **www.apple.com/imac.**	

Source: Excerpted and combined from "A Power User's Guide to the Internet," *Fortune* Technology Buyer's Guide (Summer 1998): 219 and "The Great Portal Race," *Fortune* Technology Buyer's Guide (Winter 1999): 234. Reprinted by permission.

profound and truly revolutionary. Legal, ethical, and privacy issues, however, remain largely unresolved.

In a manner of speaking, e-commerce (short for electronic commerce) over the Internet is turning many different kinds of businesses into pizza delivery shops. Pizza customers place their orders by phone. Each pizza is tailor-made to the customer's specifications and promptly delivered. Dell Computer Corp. refined and extended this "pizza shop" model of business, called *mass customization*, first with toll-free telephone service and then with the Internet. As *The Wall Street Journal* recently observed:

> *Dell has bypassed traditional distribution channels and gone directly to customers. Most important, perhaps, like Amazon.com Inc., Cisco Systems Inc. and a few other companies, Dell helped pioneer the almost end-to-end use of digital networks to communicate with its customer, take orders then and pull together products from suppliers.[26]*

Unlike Boeing's cumbersome made-to-order system, discussed earlier, Dell's e-commerce model is lean, efficient, and *fast.*

1D

Seeking Privacy in a Wired World

By slapping high prices on personal information, e-business adds a frightening new dimension to the privacy debate. That fear extends across society. Hospitals and schools, for example, are constructing vast national databases with everything from your child's fourth-grade report card to the unique twists and turns of your DNA. Businesses want that information, and in the online world—where virtually every piece of data is for sale—they will probably get it. "You already have zero privacy. Get over it," Sun Microsystems Inc. CEO Scott G. McNealy glibly noted at a recent computer-fest.

Source: Edward C. Baig, Marcia Stepanek, and Neil Gross, "Privacy," *Business Week* (April 5, 1999): 84.

Question: *How would you respond to McNealy? Explain your reasoning.*

The immense scope of the e-commerce revolution becomes apparent when we realize that direct links between companies and individual customers are merely the tip of the iceberg. Consider these figures published in 1999:

Consumer sales over the Internet were about $10 billion last year and are expected to top $100 billion by 2003. Business-to-business commerce over the Internet was $43 billion last year and is expected to be $1.3 trillion in 2003.[27]

No wonder Jack Welch, General Electric's very successful CEO, was quoted as saying: "I don't think there's been anything more important or more widespread in all my years at GE. . . . Where does the Internet rank in priority? It's No. 1, 2, 3, and 4."[28] Aspects and implications of the Internet and e-commerce revolution are explored throughout this book.

Considering the variety of these sources of change in the environment, managers are challenged to keep abreast of them and adjust and adapt as necessary.

What Do Managers Do?

3 Contrast the functional and role approaches to explaining what managers do.

Although nearly all aspects of modern life are touched at least indirectly by the work of managers, many people do not really understand what the management process involves. Management is much more, for example, than the familiar activity of telling employees what to do. Management is a complex and dynamic mixture of systematic techniques and common sense. As with any complex process, the key to learning about management lies in dividing it into readily understood subprocesses. Currently, there are two different approaches to dividing the management process for study and discussion. One approach, dating back to the early part of the past century, is to identify managerial functions. A second, more recent approach focuses on managerial roles.

managerial functions *general administrative duties that need to be carried out in virtually all productive organizations to achieve desired outcomes*

managerial roles *specific categories of managerial behavior*

Managerial functions are general administrative duties that need to be carried out in virtually all productive organizations. **Managerial roles** are specific categories of managerial behavior. A British management scholar clarified this distinction by pointing out that managerial functions involve "desired outcomes." Those outcomes are achieved through the performance of managerial roles (actual behavior).[29] Stated another way, roles are the *means* and functions are the *ends* of the manager's job. We shall examine both approaches more closely and then have a frank discussion of some managerial facts of life.

Managerial Functions

For most of the past century, the most popular approach to describing what managers do has been the functional view. It has been popular because it characterizes the management process as a sequence of rational, logical steps. Henri Fayol, a French industrialist turned writer, became the father of the functional approach in 1916 when he identified five managerial functions: planning, organizing, command, coordination, and control.[30] Fayol claimed that these five functions were the common denominators of all managerial jobs, whatever the purpose of the organization. Over the years Fayol's original list of managerial functions has been updated and expanded by management

Figure 1.4

Identifiable Functions in the Management Process

scholars. This book, even though it is based on more than just Fayol's approach, is organized around eight different managerial functions: planning, decision making, organizing, staffing, communicating, motivating, leading, and controlling (see Figure 1.4). A brief overview of these eight managerial functions will describe what managers do and will preview what lies ahead in this text.

Planning.   Commonly referred to as the primary management function, planning is the formulation of future courses of action. Plans and the objectives on which they are based give purpose and direction to the organization, its subunits, and contributing individuals.

Decision Making.   Managers choose among alternative courses of action when they make decisions. Making intelligent and ethical decisions in today's complex world is a major management challenge.

Organizing.   Structural considerations such as the chain of command, division of labor, and assignment of responsibility are part of the organizing function. Careful organizing helps ensure the efficient use of human resources.

Staffing.   Organizations are only as good as the people in them. Staffing consists of recruiting, training, and developing people who can contribute to the organized effort.

Communicating.   Today's managers are responsible for communicating to their employees the technical knowledge, instructions, rules, and information required to get the job done. Recognizing that communication is a two-way process, managers should be responsive to feedback and upward communications.

Motivating.   An important aspect of management today is motivating individuals to pursue collective objectives by satisfying needs and meeting expectations with meaningful work and valued rewards. Flexible work schedules can be motivational for today's busy employees.

Leading.   Managers become inspiring leaders by serving as role models and adapting their management style to the demands of the situation. The idea of visionary leadership is popular today.

Controlling.   When managers compare desired results with actual results and take the necessary corrective action, they are keeping things on track through the control function. Deviations from past plans should be considered when formulating new plans.

Managerial Roles

During the 1970s, a researcher named Henry Mintzberg criticized the traditional functional approach as unrealistic. From his firsthand observation of top-level managers and similar studies conducted by others, he concluded that functions "tell us little about what managers actually do. At best they indicate some vague objectives managers have when they work."[31]

Those who agree with Mintzberg believe that the functional approach portrays the management process as far more systematic and rational and less complex than it really is. Even the most casual observation reveals that managers do not plan on

Gary White, CEO of fast-growing Gymboree, isn't just playing around in the children's clothing and play center market. As a top-level manager he performs many functions and roles. He recently expanded the company's retail base of outlets in the United States and Canada to Britain and Ireland. Gymboree's core value of "celebrating childhood" is reflected in White's volunteer work with the March of Dimes and Kids in Distressed Situations (K.I.D.S.).

Monday, organize on Tuesday, coordinate on Wednesday, and so on, as the functional approach might lead one to believe. Moreover, according to the Mintzberg view, the average manager is not the reflective planner and precise "orchestra leader" that the functional approach suggests. Mintzberg characterizes the typical manager as follows: "The manager is overburdened with obligations; yet he cannot easily delegate his tasks. As a result, he is driven to overwork and is forced to do many tasks superficially. Brevity, fragmentation, and verbal communication characterize his work."[32]

In addition, according to Mintzberg's research, constant interruptions are the order of the day. A recent study supported Mintzberg's view and provided a somewhat surprising insight into the reality of nonstop interruptions. Stephanie Winston interviewed 48 top U.S. executives, including Katharine Graham, the former chief executive of *The Washington Post*, and discovered that constant interruptions are not a threat to successful top executives. Indeed, interruptions are what the work of top managers is all about and actually constitute a valuable resource. Winston concluded, "They use a fluid time style to make abundant connections and draw in streams of information. . . . The torrent of questions, comments, updates, requests, and expectations is a rich resource to be mined."[33]

Mintzberg and his followers have suggested that a more fruitful way of studying what managers do is to focus on the key roles they play. Using a method called "structured observation," which entailed recording the activities and correspondence of five top-level executives, Mintzberg isolated ten roles he believes are common to all managers.[34] These roles (see Figure 1.5) have been grouped into three major categories: interpersonal, informational, and decisional roles.

Interpersonal Roles. Because of their formal authority and superior status, managers engage in a good deal of interpersonal contact, especially with people who report to them and peers. The three interpersonal roles that managers play are those of figurehead, leader, and liaison.

Informational Roles. Every manager is a clearinghouse for information relating to the task at hand. Informational roles are important because information is the lifeblood of organizations. Typical roles include acting as nerve center, disseminator, and spokesperson.

Decisional Roles. In their decisional roles, managers balance competing interests and make choices. Through decisional roles, strategies are formulated and put into action. Four decisional roles are those of entrepreneur, disturbance handler, resource allocator, and negotiator.

Merging Functions and Roles

Both the functional approach and the role approach to explaining management are valuable to the student of management. Managerial functions are a useful categorization of a manager's tasks. It is important for future managers to realize that planning and staffing, for example, require different techniques and perspectives. The role approach is valuable because it injects needed realism, emphasizing that the practice of management is less rational and systematic than the functional approach implies. This text merges the functional and role approaches by explaining how the important roles are played within each functional category.

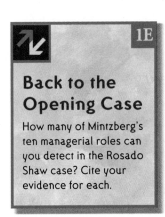

1E

Back to the Opening Case

How many of Mintzberg's ten managerial roles can you detect in the Rosado Shaw case? Cite your evidence for each.

Figure 1.5

Mintzberg's Managerial Roles

Category	Role	Nature of Role
Interpersonal roles	1. Figurehead	As a symbol of legal authority, performing certain ceremonial duties (*e.g., signing documents and receiving visitors*)
	2. Leader	Motivating subordinates to get the job done properly
	3. Liaison	Serving as a link in a horizontal (*as well as vertical*) chain of communication
Informational roles	4. Nerve center	Serving as a focal point for nonroutine information; receiving all types of information
	5. Disseminator	Transmitting selected information to subordinates
	6. Spokesperson	Transmitting selected information to outsiders
Decisional roles	7. Entrepreneur	Designing and initiating changes within the organization
	8. Disturbance handler	Taking corrective action in nonroutine situations
	9. Resource allocator	Deciding exactly who should get what resources
	10. Negotiator	Participating in negotiating sessions with other parties (*e.g., vendors and unions*) to make sure the organization's interests are adequately represented

Source: Adapted from Henry Mintzberg, "Managerial Work: Analysis from Observation," *Management Science,* 18 (October 1971): B97–B110.

Some Managerial Facts of Life (with No Sugar Coating)

Managing is a tough and demanding job today. The hours are long and, at first anyway, the pay may not be generous. Worse yet, managers are visible authority figures who get more than their fair share of criticism and ridicule from politicians and Scott Adams's Dilbert cartoons.[35] Nevertheless, managing can be a very rewarding occupation for those who develop their skills and persist, as evidenced by recent American Management Association (AMA) research findings:

Figure 1.6

Cartoonist Scott Adams, a former cubicle dweller at a phone company, gets lots of laughs at the pointy-haired boss's expense. Readers tell Adams this is their favorite Dilbert cartoon.

Dilbert reprinted by permission of United Feature Syndicate, Inc.

- Forty-six percent of U.S. managers say they feel more overwhelmed at work today than two years ago, and 22 percent more say they're "somewhat" more overwhelmed.
- Half of U.S. managers say they experience stress every day, but an even greater share—63 percent—say they feel enthusiasm for their jobs.[36]

A Hectic Pace.   Mintzberg is right. The typical manager's day follows a hectic schedule, with lots of brief and mostly verbal interactions. Interruptions and fragmentation are the norm. Extended quiet periods for contemplation simply don't exist. A landmark observational study by the Center for Creative Leadership gives a realistic picture of managerial life (see Table 1.3). An even quicker pace is in store for future managers.

4 Summarize the ten facts of managerial life.

Managers Lose Their Right to Do Many Things.   Mention the word *manager*, and the average person will probably respond with terms like *power, privilege, authority, good pay,* and so on. Although many managers eventually do enjoy some or all of these good things, they pay a significant price for stepping to the front of the administrative parade. According to one management expert, when you accept a supervisory or managerial position you lose your right to:

- Lose your temper.
- Be one of the gang.
- Bring your personal problems to work.
- Vent your frustrations and express your opinion at work.
- Resist change.
- Pass the buck on tough assignments.
- Get even with your adversaries.
- Play favorites.
- Put your self-interests first.
- Ask others to do what you wouldn't do.
- Expect to be immediately recognized and rewarded for doing a good job.[37]

Table 1.3

Ten Facts of Managerial Life (from direct observation and diaries)

1. **Managers work long hours.** The number of hours worked tends to increase as one climbs the managerial ladder.

2. **Managers are busy.** The typical manager's day is made up of hundreds of brief incidents or episodes. Activity rates tend to decrease as rank increases.

3. **A manager's work is fragmented; episodes are brief.** Given managers' high activity level, they have little time to devote to any single activity. Interruptions and discontinuity are the rule.

4. **The manager's job is varied.** Managers engage in a variety of activities (paperwork, phone calls, scheduled and unscheduled meetings, and inspection tours/visits), interact with a variety of people, and deal with a variety of content areas.

5. **Managers are "homebodies."** Managers spend most of their time pursuing activities within their own organizations. As managerial rank increases, managers spend proportionately more time outside their work areas and organizations.

6. **The manager's work is primarily oral.** Managers at all levels spend the majority of their time communicating verbally (by personal contact or telephone).

7. **Managers use a lot of contacts.** Consistent with their high level of verbal communication, managers continually exchange information with superiors, peers, subordinates, and outsiders on an ongoing basis.

8. **Managers are not reflective planners.** The typical manager is too busy to find uninterrupted blocks of time for reflective planning.

9. **Information is the basic ingredient of the manager's work.** Managers spend most of their time obtaining, interpreting, and giving information.

10. **Managers don't know how they spend their time.** Managers consistently overestimate the time they spend on production, reading and writing, phone calls, thinking, and calculating and consistently underestimate the time spent on meetings and informal discussions.

Source: Adapted from Morgan W. McCall, Jr., Ann M. Morrison, and Robert L. Hannan, *Studies of Managerial Work: Results and Methods* (Greensboro, N.C.: Center for Creative Leadership, 1978), Technical Report No. 9, pp. 6–18. Used by permission of the authors.

We tell you this not to scare you away from what could be a financially and emotionally rewarding career, but rather to present a realistic picture so you can choose intelligently. Management is not for everyone—it is not for the timid, the egomaniacal, or the lazy. Management requires clear-headed individuals who can envision something better and turn it into reality by working with and through others.

What Does It Take to Become a Successful Manager?

5 Explain the basic formula for managerial success (S = A × M × O).

Successful managers come from a wide variety of backgrounds and possess an equally wide variety of traits and skills. No sure-fire formula exists for getting to the top of the managerial ladder, but three general preconditions for achieving lasting success as a manager are: ability (A), motivation to manage (M), and opportunity (O). Together, they constitute a basic formula for managerial success (S): $S = A \times M \times O$. Notice that success depends on a balanced combination of ability, motivation to manage, and opportunity. A total absence of one factor can cancel out strength in the other two. (Hence, the use of multiplication rather than addition signs.) For example, high ability and motivation are useless without opportunity.

Ability

As used here, the term **managerial ability** is the demonstrated capacity to achieve organizational objectives with specific skills and competencies.[38] Actually, today's successful manager needs a whole package of conceptual, technical, administrative, and interpersonal abilities. According to work done by the AACSB/International Association for Management Education, an accrediting agency, business school graduates should be able to demonstrate certain skills and possess managerial characteristics.

AACSB's package of skills and characteristics can help everyone better understand the term *ability to manage*. They include:

1. Leadership.
2. Oral communication and presentation skills.
3. Written communication.
4. Planning and organizing.
5. Information gathering and problem analysis.
6. Decision making.
7. Delegation and control.
8. Self-objectivity (being aware of one's strengths and limitations).
9. A willingness and desire to lead others in new directions.[39]

managerial ability *the demonstrated capacity to achieve organizational objectives with specific skills and competencies*

Motivation to Manage

Uplifting stories about disabled persons and adventurers who succeed despite seemingly insurmountable odds are often summed up in one word: *desire*. The same force drives successful managers. All the ability in the world will not help a future manager succeed if he or she does not possess a persistent desire to move ahead. Linda Wachner, chief executive officer of a *Fortune* 1000 company, garment maker Warnaco, is an inspiring case in point. *Fortune* magazine called her America's most successful businesswoman:

> *From the time she was 11 and growing up in Forest Hills, New York, Wachner knew she wanted to run something. That was the year she lay flat on her back, encased in a plaster cast from her head to her knees, the first step in a surgical procedure to correct severe scoliosis. Hardly able to move and facing the possibility that she would never walk again, Linda became determined that whatever she did in life, she would call the shots—not doctors, or parents, or physical therapists. "The focus I have today comes from when I was sick," she says. "When you want to walk again, you have to learn how to focus on that with all your might, and you don't stop until you do it."*
>
> *That brand of determination was evident from the first day Wachner hit the job market in 1966. After graduating at age 20 from the University of Buffalo with a bachelor's degree in business administration, she landed at Associated Merchandising Corp., the New York*

A Billionaire's Take on Success and Happiness

Warren Buffett, the legendary Omaha investor:

> . . . *success is getting what you want and happiness is wanting what you get.*

Source: As quoted in Brent Schlender, "The Bill and Warren Show," *Fortune* (July 20, 1998): 52.

Question: *How do you define success and happiness?*

City buying arm of Federated and other department stores. Her pay: $90 a week. . . . [A former boss] remembers her: "Linda used to come flying through my door every morning hitting me with ideas on how we could run the business better. She wanted to tell our manufacturers how they could do more business with the stores."[40]

Until the mid-1960s, this kind of desire was an intangible trait that could be measured only subjectively. Then a management researcher named John B. Miner developed a psychometric instrument to measure objectively an individual's **motivation to manage.** Miner's test, in effect, measures one's desire to be a manager.

motivation to manage

desire to succeed in performing managerial functions and roles; one of the three elements of the basic formula for managerial success

The Seven Dimensions of Motivation to Manage.   Miner's measure of motivation to manage is anchored to the following seven dimensions:

1. Favorable attitude toward those in positions of authority, such as superiors.
2. Desire to engage in games or sports competition with peers.
3. Desire to engage in occupational or work-related competition with peers.
4. Desire to assert oneself and take charge.
5. Desire to exercise power and authority over others.
6. Desire to behave in a distinctive way, which includes standing out from the crowd.
7. Sense of responsibility in carrying out the routine duties associated with managerial work.[41]

Joy Covey's motto could be "work hard, play hard, and blaze your own trail." Indeed! She passed the California high school-equivalency exam as a sophomore. Her 173 IQ then propelled her to a college degree and CPA certification at age 19. After a stint at accounting firm Arthur Young, she earned MBA and law degrees from Harvard. As chief financial officer and strategist at Amazon.com, she has helped blaze new trails in e-commerce and built a personal stake worth $150 million.

The higher the individual scores on each trait, the greater is the motivation to manage. (Although the complete instrument is not given here, you can readily gauge your own motivation to manage as low, moderate, or high). Miner's research indicates that this concept can accurately predict how fast and how far one will move up the hierarchy.

Motivation to Manage Among Business Students.   Miner and his colleagues went on to track motivation-to-manage scores for business students at two major U.S. universities over a 20-year period and came to some interesting conclusions.[42] First, although the steady decline of motivation to manage during the 1960s and early 1970s had stopped, students' motivation to manage still was very low. Generally speaking, students continued to show a distaste for authority, competitiveness, assertiveness, and routine managerial duties. Miner believed this situation foreshadowed a shortage of managerial talent over the coming years (which is now indeed the case).[43] A second conclusion was that female students no longer lagged behind their male counterparts in motivation to manage.

More recently, Miner's research has focused on international differences in motivation to manage. His student samples from Mexico, Japan, China, Korea, and Taiwan all scored consistently higher than did his samples from the United States. Miner sees this as a potential threat to America's global competitiveness.[44]

Opportunity to Manage

There are plenty of opportunities around the world for those seeking a managerial position. Take the United States, for example. As indicated in Figure 1.7, according to the U.S. Bureau of Labor Statistics, nearly 15 million people were employed as executives, administrators, or managers in 1999—11 percent more than in 1992.[45] Figure 1.7 also shows that women are approaching an equal footing with men in this important segment of the labor force.

Bill Gates, Microsoft Cofounder and World's Richest Person—and *Very* Competitive Guy   1G

Those who know Gates understand that the traits most evident at work—a driving competitiveness, an omnivorous intelligence and an impatience with ego tripping—are equally prominent at play....

The same applies at the home of Melinda and Bill Gates. Guests are sometimes partitioned into teams, each group given a shrink-wrapped jigsaw puzzle to open and solve at a designated signal. Then there are charades, Pictionary, trivia contests and campfire songs, when people make up new verses. On vacation, it's the same routine. Leroy Hood, a biologist whose lab received funding from Gates, went with Bill and Melinda on a trip to Africa in 1993—and played games: "There was even a contest on how fast you could build a fire," he says. "Bill was fiercely competitive, and he did very well—better, on average, than any of us."

Source: Steven Levy, "Behind the Gates Myth," *Newsweek* (August 30, 1999): 46.

Question: *How well does this glimpse of Bill Gates validate Miner's motivation to manage concept? Explain.*

Figure 1.7

Executives, Administrators, and Managers in the U.S. Civilian Labor Force in 1999

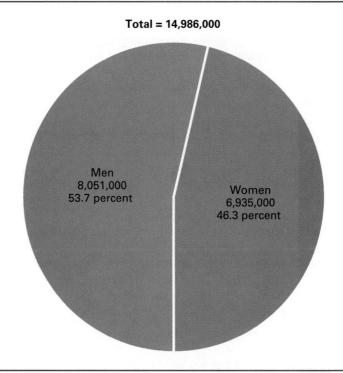

Total = 14,986,000

Men
8,051,000
53.7 percent

Women
6,935,000
46.3 percent

Source: U.S. Bureau of Labor Statistics (**http://stats.bls.gov/news.release/wkyeng.t03.htm**).

Significantly, these statistics tell only part of the story for managerial job seekers. Not counted among the managers in Figure 1.7 are the millions of administrators and managers in military, government, and nonprofit organizations. Also, there is the mushrooming small-business sector. One quick way to become a manager is to start your own business. Additionally, foreign assignments involving managerial duties beckon the more adventuresome.

Despite periodic ups and downs in job markets, there will continue to be a worldwide need for those with the right combination of ability and motivation to manage. The time to start working out your own S = A × M × O formula is now.[46]

Learning to Manage

6 Explain how managers learn to manage.

Students of management are left with one overriding question: "How do I acquire the ability to manage?" This question has stimulated a good deal of debate among those interested in management education. What is the key, theory or practice? Some contend that future managers need a solid background in management theory acquired through formal education. Others argue that managing, like learning to ride a bicycle, can be learned only by actually doing it.[47] We can leapfrog this debate by looking at how managers learn to manage, understanding how students learn about management, and considering how you can blend the two processes to your best advantage.

Figure 1.8

The Honeywell Study: How Managers Learn to Manage

Job assignments ("the school of hard knocks") 50 percent

Relationships 30 percent

Formal training and education 20 percent

Source: Data from Ron Zemke, "The Honeywell Studies: How Managers Learn to Manage," *Training,* 22 (August 1985): 46–51.

They say cream rises to the top. But sometimes it needs a little help, particularly at huge companies. At Best Buy, the large retailer of computers and electronics, it took a Gallup poll. Best Buy commissioned a poll of its employees to find the company's *great* managers. Mary Garey, pictured here on the left having fun with her Florida employees, made the list. Best Buy has asked Garey to act as a mentor so others can acquire her excellent people-management skills.

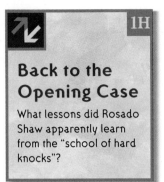

Back to the Opening Case

What lessons did Rosado Shaw apparently learn from the "school of hard knocks"?

How Do Managers Learn to Manage?

We have an answer to this simple but intriguing question, thanks to the Honeywell study, which was conducted by a team of management development specialists employed by Honeywell.[48] In a survey, they asked 3,600 Honeywell managers: "How did you learn to manage?" Ten percent of the respondents were then interviewed for additional insights. Successful Honeywell managers reportedly acquired 50 percent of their management knowledge from job assignments (see Figure 1.8). The remaining 50 percent of what they knew about management reportedly came from relationships with bosses, mentors, and coworkers (30 percent) and from formal training and education (20 percent).

Fully half of what the Honeywell managers knew about managing came from the so-called school of hard knocks. To that extent, at least, learning to manage is indeed like learning to ride a bike. You get on, you fall off and skin your knee, you get back on a bit smarter, and so on, until you're able to wobble down the road. But in the minds of aspiring managers, this scenario raises the question of what classes are held in the school of hard knocks. A second study, this one of British managers, provided an answer. It turns out that the following are considered *hard knocks* by managers:

- Making a big mistake.
- Being overstretched by a difficult assignment.
- Feeling threatened.
- Being stuck in an impasse or dilemma.
- Suffering an injustice at work.
- Losing out to someone else.
- Being personally attacked.[49]

These situations are traumatic enough to motivate managers to learn how to avoid repeating the same mistakes.

Figure 1.9

Acquiring the Ability to Manage by Merging Theory and Practice

Theory	→	Acquiring the ability to manage	←	Practice

Theory
- Definitions
- Relevant facts
- Concepts
- Techniques
- Guidelines

Source:
Textbooks, audiovisual presentations, and formal classroom instruction

Acquiring the ability to manage
Systematic integration of theory and practice into personally meaningful and useful ways of managing
Source: *Self*

Imitating managerial role models
Source: *Practicing managers*

Practice
Simulated experience: Participating in instructor-aided experiential exercises, case studies, and role-playing
Source: *Semistructured classroom experience*

Real experience: Actually managing an organized endeavor
Source: *Part-time or full-time employment as a manager*

How Can Future Managers Learn to Manage?

As indicated in Figure 1.9, students can learn to manage by integrating theory and practice and observing role models. Theory can help you systematically analyze, interpret, and internalize the managerial significance of practical experience and observations. Although formal training and education contributed only 20 percent to the Honeywell managers' knowledge, they nonetheless represent a needed conceptual foundation. Returning to our bicycle example, a cross-country trip on a high-tech bike requires more than the mere ability to ride a bike. It requires a sound foundation of knowledge about bicycle maintenance and repair, weather and road conditions, and road safety. So, too, new managers who have a good idea of what lies ahead can go farther and faster with fewer foolish mistakes. The school of hard knocks is inevitable. But you can foresee and avoid at least some of the knocks.[50]

Ideally, an individual acquires theoretical knowledge and practical experience at the same time, perhaps through work-study programs or internships. Usually, though, full-time students get a lot of theory and little practice. This is when simulated and real experience become important. If you are a serious management student, you will put your newly acquired theories into practice wherever and whenever possible (for example, in organized sports; positions of leadership in fraternities, sororities, or clubs; and part-time and summer jobs). What really matters is your personal integration of theory and practice.

Small-Business Management

Small businesses have been called the "engine" of the U.S. economy. They have produced the vast majority of both new jobs and innovations during the last 20 years. But a reality check shows that these accomplishments have come amid great turbulence and nonstop change. According to the most recent data from the U.S. Small Business Administration: "Between 1989 and 1995, . . . 2.9 million companies were born, and 2.6 million died."[51] Free-enterprise capitalism is a rough-and-tumble arena where anyone can play, but only the very best survive. As Deborah Rosado Shaw discovered in the case study at the beginning of this chapter, the only guaranteed result for those starting their own business is that they will be tested to their limit.

Few would dispute the facts and claims cited above, but agreement on the definition of a small business is not so easily reached. Some of the many yardsticks used to distinguish small from large businesses include the number of employees, level of annual sales, amount of owner's equity, and total assets. For our present purposes, a **small business** is defined as an independently owned and managed profit-seeking enterprise employing fewer than 100 people. (If the small business is incorporated, the owner/manager owns a significant proportion of the firm's stock.)

Statistics for this particular slice of the U.S. economy are mind-boggling. The 5.8 million companies with fewer than 100 employees constitute 98 percent of the country's employers. They generate 40 percent of the nation's output.[52] Small businesses are an indispensable part of both the U.S. and the global economies.

The health of every nation's economy depends on how well its small businesses are managed. To get a better grasp of the realm of small-business management, we will clear up two common misconceptions, explore small-business career options, and discuss entrepreneurship.

7 **Challenge two myths about small businesses and describe entrepreneurs.**

small business *an independently owned and managed profit-seeking enterprise with fewer than 100 employees*

The School of Hard Knocks

Harry V. Quadracci, founder and president of Quad/Graphics, a $600-million-a-year printing company in Peewaukee, Wisconsin:

Mistakes are the tuition for learning management. You only learn management by doing, by making mistakes. If you don't make any mistakes, how are you going to learn what was wrong? If people are afraid of making mistakes, then nothing new will happen.

Source: Craig Cox, "Interview: Harry V. Quadracci," *Business Ethics,* 7 (May–June 1993): 21.

Questions: *What important life lessons have you learned by making mistakes? Do you tend to accept and deal with mistakes or try to avoid them at all costs? What are the managerial implications of your behavior?*

Exploding Myths About Small Businesses

Mistaken notions can become accepted facts if they are repeated often enough. Such is the case with failure rates and job creation for small businesses. Fortunately, recent research sets the record straight.

The 80-Percent-Failure-Rate Myth.   An often-repeated statistic says that four out of five small businesses will fail within five years. This 80 percent casualty rate is a frightening prospect for anyone thinking about starting a business. But a recent study by Bruce A. Kirchhoff of the New Jersey Institute of Technology found the failure rate for small businesses to be *only 18 percent during their first eight years.*[53] Why the huge disparity? It turns out that studies by the U.S. government and others defined business failures much too broadly. Any closing of a business, whether because someone died, sold the business, or retired, was recorded as a business failure. In fact, only 18 percent of the 814,000 small businesses tracked by Kirchhoff for eight years went out of business with unpaid bills. This should be a comfort to would-be entrepreneurs.

The Low-Wage-Jobs Myth.   When it came to creating jobs during the 1980s and 1990s, America's big businesses were put to shame by their small and mid-size counterparts. Eighty percent of the new job growth was generated by the smaller companies; massive layoffs were the norm at big companies.[54] Critics, meanwhile, claimed that most of the new jobs in the small-business sector went to low-paid clerks and hamburger flippers. Such was not the case, according to a Cambridge, Massachusetts, study by researcher David Birch.

After analyzing new jobs created in the United States between 1987 and 1992, Birch found that businesses with fewer than 100 employees had indeed created most new jobs. Surprisingly, however, only 4 percent of those small firms produced 70 percent of that job growth.[55] Birch calls these rapidly growing small companies "gazelles," as opposed to the "mice" businesses that tend to remain very small. For the period studied, the gazelles added more high-paying jobs than big companies eliminated. Gazelles are not mom-and-pop operations. They tend to be computer software, telecommunications, and specialized engineering or manufacturing firms.[56] So, while small businesses do in fact pay on average less than big companies do, they are not low-wage havens.[57]

Again, as in the case of failure rates, the truth about the prospects of starting or working for a small company is different—and brighter—than the traditional fallacy suggests.

Career Opportunities in Small Business

Among the five small-business career options listed in Table 1.4, only franchises require definition. The other four are self-defining.[58] A franchise is a license to sell another company's products and/or to use another company's name in business.

Familiar franchise operations include McDonald's, the National Basketball Association, and Holiday Inn.[59] Notice how each of the career options in Table 1.4 has positive and negative aspects. There is no one best option. Success in the small-business sector depends on the right combination of money, talent, hard work, luck, and opportunity.[60] Fortunately, career opportunities in small business are virtually unlimited.

Entrepreneurship

According to experts on the subject, **"entrepreneurship** is the process by which individuals—either on their own or inside organizations—pursue opportunities without regard to the resources they currently control."[61] In effect, entrepreneurs look beyond current resource constraints when they envision new possibilities. Entrepreneurs are preoccupied with "how to," rather than "why not." Conversations about entrepreneurship these days invariably turn to tales of Internet billionaires. Actual statistics offer a more sobering outlook: "A 1999 study by ActivMedia found 47% of revenue-generating Web sites produce less than $10,000."[62] But who is to say *your* $10,000 Web site won't become your ticket to the billionaires' club? Entrepreneurs, as we discuss next, are risk takers—and all they want is a chance.

In Chapter 3, we refer to entrepreneurs in large companies as *intrapreneurs*. Although intrapreneurs are needed to pump new blood into large organizations, our focus here is on entrepreneurs who envision, start, and operate whole new businesses. Entrepreneurship is thriving today from Argentina to Poland to Malaysia to China, thanks to the global swing toward market-based economies.[63]

> **1J**
> ## Got a Good Business Idea? You've Got 45 Seconds
>
> According to new-venture expert Elton B. Sherwin Jr., entrepreneurs who are trying to raise venture capital should be able to answer these "Seven Sacred Questions" in 45 seconds:
>
> 1. What is your product?
> 2. Who is the customer?
> 3. Who will sell it?
> 4. How many people will buy it?
> 5. How much will it cost to design and build?
> 6. What is the sales price?
> 7. When will you break even?
>
> *Source:* Marc Ballon, "Hot Tips," *Inc.*, 21 (April 1999): 104.
>
> **Question:** *Can you pass this 45-second test with your new business idea? Give details.*

entrepreneurship *process of pursuing opportunities without regard to resources currently under one's control*

Table 1.4	**Career Opportunities in Small Business**			
Small-business career options	**Capital requirements**	**Likelihood of steady paycheck**	**Degree of personal control**	**Ultimate financial return**
1. Become an independent contractor/consultant	Low to moderate	None to low	Very high	Negative to high
2. Take a job with a small business	None	Moderate to high	Low to moderate	Low to moderate
3. Join or buy a small business owned by your family	Low to high	Low to high	Low to high	Moderate to high
4. Purchase a franchise	Moderate to high	None to moderate	Moderate to high	Negative to high
5. Start your own small business	Moderate to high	None to moderate	High to very high	Negative to very high

Table 1.5

Contrasting Trait Profiles for Entrepreneurs and Administrators

Entrepreneurs tend to	Administrators tend to
Focus on envisioned futures	Focus on the established present
Emphasize external/market dimensions	Emphasize internal/cost dimensions
Display a medium-to-high tolerance for ambiguity	Display a low-to-medium tolerance for ambiguity
Exhibit moderate-to-high risk-taking behavior	Exhibit low-to-moderate risk-taking behavior
Obtain motivation from a need to achieve	Obtain motivation from a need to lead others (i.e., social power)
Possess technical knowledge and experience in the innovative area	Possess managerial knowledge and experience

Source: Philip D. Olson, "Choices for Innovation-Minded Corporations," *The Journal of Business Strategy*, 11 (January–February 1990): Exhibit 1, p. 44. Reprinted from *Journal of Business Strategy* (New York: Warren, Gorham & Lamont). © 1990 Warren, Gorham & Lamont Inc. Used with permission.

A Trait Profile for Entrepreneurs.   Exactly how do entrepreneurs differ from general managers or administrators? According to the trait profiles in Table 1.5, entrepreneurs tend to be high achievers who focus more on future possibilities, external factors, and technical details. Also, compared with general administrators, entrepreneurs are more comfortable with ambiguity and risk taking. It is important to note that entrepreneurs are not necessarily better or worse than other managers—they are just different.[64]

Entrepreneurship Has Its Limits.   Many successful entrepreneurs have tripped over a common stumbling block. Their organizations outgrow the entrepreneur's ability to manage them. Entrepreneurs generally feel stifled by cumbersome and slow-paced bureaucracies. A prime example is Victor Kiam, who became famous with his television advertisements proclaiming that he liked his Remington electric razor so much that he bought the company. In 1991, Kiam admitted, "The company got too big for my entrepreneurial style. . . . A lot of things were falling through the cracks."[65] Remington's costs got out of control and the company lost 25 percent of its U.S. market share for men's electric shavers. Kiam eventually turned the day-to-day management of his company over to David J. Ferrari, a corporate turnaround specialist.[66] Kiam's case is not unique. Entrepreneurs who launch successful and growing companies face a tough dilemma: either grow with the company[67] or have the courage to step aside and turn the reins over to professional managers who possess the administrative traits needed, such as those listed in Table 1.5.

Summary

1.   Formally defined, *management* is the process of working with and through others to achieve organizational objectives in a changing environment. Central to this process is the effective and efficient use of limited resources. An inability to work

with people, not a lack of technical skills, is the main reason some managers fail to reach their full potential. A manager is *effective* if he or she reaches a stated objective and *efficient* if limited resources are not wasted in the process. Five overarching sources of change affecting the way management is practiced today are globalization, the evolution of product quality, environmentalism, an ethical reawakening, and e-commerce on the Internet.

2. Two ways to answer the question, "What do managers do?" are the functional approach and role approach. *Managerial functions* relate to the desired outcomes of managerial action, whereas *managerial roles* categorize managers' actual behavior. This text is organized around eight managerial functions: planning, decision making, organizing, staffing, communicating, motivating, leading, and controlling. Having criticized the functional approach for making management appear to be more orderly than it really is, Henry Mintzberg concluded from his observation of managers that management is best explained in terms of roles. Three managerial role categories, according to Mintzberg, are interpersonal, informational, and decisional.

3. The ten facts of managerial life, derived from direct observation, characterize managers as hard-working and busy people who engage in many and varied, primarily oral, interactions with others. Interestingly, managers do not have an accurate self-perception of how they spend their time.

4. The basic formula for managerial success is $S = A \times M \times O$ (managerial success = ability × motivation to manage × opportunity). *Managerial ability* results when theory and practice are systematically integrated. John Miner identified seven dimensions of *motivation to manage* that predict how far and how fast managers move up through the ranks. A 20-year study of motivation to manage in college business students indicated that, although the decline in motivation to manage has stopped, it still remains very low. Recent international research by Miner has negative implications for America's future competitiveness because American business students consistently score lower on motivation to manage than do their foreign counterparts.

5. Honeywell researchers found that managers learned 50 percent of what they know about managing from job assignments (or the school of hard knocks). The remaining 50 percent of their management knowledge came from relationships (30 percent) and formal training and education (20 percent). A good foundation in management theory can give management students a running start and help them avoid foolish mistakes.

6. *Small businesses* (independently owned and managed profit-seeking companies with fewer than 100 employees) are central to a healthy economy. Contrary to conventional wisdom, 80 percent of new businesses do not fail within five years. In fact, one large study found only an 18 percent failure rate during the first eight years. The belief that small businesses create only low-wage jobs also has been shown to be a myth. Five career opportunities in the small business sector include (1) becoming an independent contractor/consultant; (2) going to work for a small business; (3) joining or buying your family's business; (4) buying a franchise; and (5) starting your own business. Compared with general administrators, entrepreneurs tend to be high achievers who are more future-oriented, externally focused, ready to take risks, and comfortable with ambiguity.

Terms to Understand

Management (p. 5)

Effectiveness (p. 7)

Efficiency (p. 7)

Internet (p. 14)

Managerial functions (p. 16)

Managerial roles (p. 16)

Managerial ability (p. 23)

Motivation to manage (p. 24)

Small business (p. 29)

Entrepreneurship (p. 31)

Skills & Tools

Career Tips for Today's and Tomorrow's Managers

How to Find the *Right Job*

1. **Assess yourself.** "Job seekers need to emphasize the things they do best" says Diane Wexler of Career Transition Management in Palo Alto, California. Wexler takes clients through a process of examining goals, interests, skills, and resources. Questions include: What are the 20 things you love to do, both alone and with others? What are the roles you fill, and which aspects would you like to incorporate into a career?

2. **Draft a mission statement.** Just as a company writes and adheres to a mission statement, create one for yourself. Thinking about your mission and putting it on paper will help define your job search.

3. **Brainstorm**. Ask others about what your ideal job would be, and how you should go about landing that position. Nancy Nagel invited eight people with a variety of interests and careers to dinner. "I got these great ideas, ranging from being a talk show host to leading adventure travel" she says. "I ended up tossing most of them out, but the session reminded me that there was a great big world out there."

4. **Network**. Conduct informational interviews. Yes, call those friends-of-friends and ask them for a few minutes of their time. Be prepared with some thoughtful questions.

5. **Research companies.** Job seekers often accept positions without adequately researching their employers, says Valerie Frankel, co-author of the *I Hate My Job Handbook*. "Inevitably, after a year or two, the job becomes intolerable" she says. Before talking to anyone at a company, research its history, values, and priorities.

6. **Be aware of your abilities and the realities of work.** "We have this entitlement problem, that we expect to be completely satisfied with our jobs," says Frankel. "I help people be humble when it comes to their job search," adds Elissa Sheridan of BSR. "You can't walk in with a BA or even an MBA and expect someone to be excited by your background without practical experience."

Source: Excerpted from Mary Scott, "Finding the Perfect Job," *Business Ethics*, 10 (March–April 1996): 16. Reprinted with permission from *Business Ethics Magazine*, 52 South 10th Street, #110, Minneapolis, Minn. 55403 (612-962-4700).

How to *Supercharge* Your Career After You've Found the Right Job

1. Love what you do, which entails first figuring out who you are.

2. Never stop learning about new technologies and new management skills.

3. Try to get international experience even if it means only a short stint overseas.

4. Create new business opportunities—it could lead to a promotion.

5. Expect more raises but fewer titles and fewer people reporting to you.

6. Be really outstandingly terrific at what you're doing now, this week, this month.

Source: Excerpted from Anne Fisher, "Six Ways to Supercharge Your Career," *Fortune* (January 13, 1996): 47.
© 1996 Time Inc. All rights reserved.

Internet Exercises

1. **Free Internet research tutorial:** Internet experience varies greatly today. Some people are heavy users, others barely have their toe in the water, and still others either fear it or just have not tried it. This tutorial can help both experienced and novice Web surfers get needed information more efficiently. Go to the Internet site **www.intellifact.com** and click on the heading "business research tutorials" in the section titled "Intellifact.com Business Research Portal." Next, click on the link titled "Free Online Business Tutorial." If you are a novice or an experienced Internet user who could use some skill development, study the sections on using basic and advanced search engines. Otherwise, explore the links in the second and third main menu sections: "Finding Company Information" and "Following Business News."

   Learning Points: 1. What useful tips for using the Internet did you pick up? 2. What interesting or useful things did you learn about specific companies, industries, or current events?

2. **Want to start and run your own business?** When surveyed, nearly two-thirds of Americans say they either own their own business or have dreamed of being their own boss. If you are in that category, here is a must-visit on the Internet. Go to the home page of **www.morebusiness.com.** If your business is already up and running, explore the entire site for useful information and updates. If you are thinking of starting your own business, click on the main menu item "Start Up" and then select the link "Small Business Primer." Work your way through relevant parts of the primer.

   If you are hungry for more information about starting your own business, get down to details with the Web site **www.tannedfeet.com.** Select "Table of Contents" from the main menu and click on "A. Master Checklist for Starting a Business." Scroll through the checklist, reading relevant material.

   Learning Points: 1. Does starting your own business entail more than you expected? Explain. 2. Are you more or less inclined to start your own business after this Web exercise? Explain. 3. What legal form will your new business take (sole proprietorship, partnership, C corporation, etc.)? Why? If you are already in business, do you have the right legal form? Explain.

3. **Good source for quick management readings and practical tips:** Call up the home page of the Briefings Publishing Group (**www.briefings.com**) and click on the navigation tab "Advice for Managers." Scan the short articles from the most recent issue of *Managers Edge* and check out archive topics such as "Leadership," "Employee Motivation," and "Teamwork."

   Learning Points: 1. What was the most useful piece of management information you acquired? 2. How does what you read relate to topics in Chapter 1 of this text? Be specific.

4. **Check it out:** The U.S. Small Business Administration provides a gold mine of free information for small business owners and future entrepreneurs (**www.sba.gov**).

   For updates to these exercises, visit our Web site (**www.hmco.com/college**).

"If I'm in Charge, Why Am I Working So Hard?"

Midway through another 14-hour day, depleted after six meetings, an employee pep rally, eight stock-price updates and more than a dozen expletives, Allan Schuman rubs his eyes.

"My wife says to me, 'This is crazy! You're the CEO. You're in charge. Why do you work so hard?'" says the 64-year-old Mr. Schuman, who heads Ecolab Inc., a $1.9 billion maker of commercial cleaning supplies. "But you're constantly pushing. It never ends. You can never let up."

The grueling workplace has reached the top floor. Not so long ago, being chief executive officer often meant being principal business strategist and corporate ambassador to the outside world. These days, amid the uncertainties created by globalization and rapid technological change, CEOs are expected to be hands-on managers. And those who don't manage to deliver growth and higher stock prices often face the ax. . . .

Like many of his peers, Mr. Schuman has flattened his company's hierarchy, eliminating senior executive positions—including his old post of operating chief—to put himself in closer touch with operations. As president and CEO, "I'm everything," he says. "There is nothing going on here that I don't know about."

Mr. Schuman waited nearly 40 years for his chance to be chief. The son of a Bronx, N.Y., butcher, he began work as an Ecolab salesman in 1957—becoming one of the company's first Jewish employees, he says, in what was then a workforce of 1,000; Ecolab now employs 12,000 worldwide. In 1995, he was named CEO, at 60, an age when many of his contemporaries are contemplating retirement or already on the golf course. . . .

Since he took over the company, profits are up more than 55%, and Ecolab's stock price has quadrupled. But Mr. Schuman—who earned almost $2 million in salary and bonuses last year and holds more than $75 million in Ecolab stock and options—worries that he will miss analysts' profit estimates by a penny a share and that his company's stock will take a pounding.

Though Ecolab now dominates its U.S. market, Mr. Schuman worries about being surpassed by a global rival, such as Anglo-Dutch giant Unilever Group, or taken over

by Henkel KGaA, Ecolab's German joint-venture partner. He worries the company will make a bad acquisition, as it did in 1987 when it bought ChemLawn Services Corp., which it later sold at a loss. "I can't afford to be surprised," he says.

Mr. Schuman cuts an unusual figure for a Midwestern CEO, with his Bronx accent, rough humor, and conversation peppered with curses and Yiddish expressions. On a shelf in his vast office sits a black-and-white picture of himself as a teenager and his immigrant father, in the family butcher shop. "I've always felt like an outsider," he says.

And everyone wants a piece of him. Mr. Schuman used to send the chairman and chief financial officer to meet with Wall Street analysts, but analysts now insist on hearing directly from him, so he flies to New York himself. He meets regularly with customers and fields their phone calls because they expect to go right to the top if they have a complaint. At Christmas, he dresses as Santa Claus to distribute toys to the children of the nearly 2,000 employees at Ecolab's headquarters here.

Mr. Schuman serves on only one outside corporate board, because he can't spare the time. Last year, he stopped reading his e-mail himself because he was being flooded by 75 to 100 messages a day.

At times, Mr. Schuman finds his schedule daunting: "I say to my secretary, 'Give me an hour, give me an hour and a half. I want to read.'"

On a recent chilly, rainy morning, his workday begins at 6:30 A.M. He arrives before almost everyone except the security guard in the lobby. Mr. Schuman meets with his "skunkworks"—a team of middle managers working on their own time to come up with product ideas.

Investing Time

The topic today is the Internet, which barely mattered to businesses when he became CEO four years ago. Mr. Schuman has been cruising the Internet and has directed this team—most of them at least 20 years his junior—to see how Ecolab might use it to sell a new line of consumer products. "We've got to make this screen come up faster," he says as he watches a demonstration. Looking at a potential cleaning product, he bangs the table. "Let's get going on this," he says. "We've been futzing around with it."

The meeting lasts 90 minutes, but Mr. Schuman considers the time a good investment. Ecolab must keep

Source: Republished with permission of The Wall Street Journal, from Jonathan Kaufman, "For Latter-Day CEO, 'All in a Day's Work' Often Means Just That" (May 3, 1999). Permission conveyed through Copyright Clearance Center, Inc.

coming up with new products to stay competitive; 35% of its product lineup has been developed in the past five years, including a water-filtration system for coffee machines and a product for food-service operations to use for washing fruits and vegetables.

As he heads back to his office, his secretary hands him a note on Ecolab's early stock price—down an eighth. Mr. Schuman was in New York the previous day meeting with analysts. "Damn, maybe I didn't do so well yesterday," he says.

"That's OK; it's early," his secretary reassures him.

Mr. Schuman heads downstairs to meet with a group of $35,000-a-year salesmen visiting headquarters for a training session. They wouldn't have met the CEO in years past; Mr. Schuman didn't meet the chief until he had been at the company 10 years.

The salesmen deluge Mr. Schuman with questions, including how often the transmission of their company vans should be checked. He barks out orders to assistants: "Make a note of that." Later, the salesmen will get a note signed by Mr. Schuman following up on their questions. Mr. Schuman closes with a rousing speech on their importance to the company. The salesmen give him a standing ovation. One snaps a picture.

"You're always on stage," Mr. Schuman says.

But he believes a motivated sales force is crucial. "It's not rocket science here," he says. "We're selling soap." . . .

Over the past decade, Ecolab's international business has expanded sharply, with 55% of its sales and 20% of profits coming from overseas, drawing it into competition with multinationals like Unilever. Two summers ago, Mr. Schuman got a call from his international vice president informing him that turmoil in Asia would hurt the company's bottom line. A few months ago he received another call when Brazil's economy sagged. "It happened like that," says Mr. Schuman, banging the table. "When you get global, things can get away from you."

Mr. Schuman now keeps a closer eye on international operations. On the way to a meeting he looks over the proposed salary and benefits for a new Brazilian manager. He pops his head into the office of his international vice president. "What kind of a car is he going to get? A BMW?," he asks, concerned about costs. "I don't

want any more BMWs." (He is assured that the new manager will get an American car.) . . .

As the day winds down, Ecolab's stock price moves up more than a point. Mr. Schuman greets senior executives, all of whom hold stock options, with a jovial, "So, you made a lot of money today!" Michael Monahan, Ecolab's vice president of investor relations, meets with Mr. Schuman to discuss coming meetings with analysts. "Do you think I need to make the pitch in person?" Mr. Schuman asks.

"So much depends on you as the personality of the company," says Mr. Monahan. "Hearing from you helps reassure them." Mr. Schuman agrees to more analysts' meetings, including flying back and forth to London for a day to meet with European analysts.

His 65th birthday is nearing, but Mr. Schuman, who has two grown sons and several grandchildren, doesn't plan to retire anytime soon. "What am I going to do, play tennis, play golf every day?" he asks. He rubs his eyes again. "The other day my son called me and said, 'Dad, you work as hard today as you did coming up.' You know what I told him? There's no difference. No damn difference."

FOR DISCUSSION

1. Which of the five major changes mangers face today (globalization, quality, environmentalism, ethics, and the Internet/e-commerce) are evident in this case? Cite specific evidence. Which area is Allan Schuman's biggest challenge? Explain.

2. What managerial functions (see Figure 1.4) did Allan Schuman play in this case? Cite specific evidence for each function identified.

3. How well do you think Mintzberg's managerial roles (see Figure 1.5) approach explains what has taken place in this case? What particular roles can you identify?

4. Do you think Allan Schuman is a good manager? Present your evidence and explain your reasoning.

5. If you were in Allan Schuman's place, what would you have done differently? Why?

The EVOLUTION of MANAGEMENT THOUGHT

CHAPTER OBJECTIVES

When you finish studying this chapter, you should be able to

1 Identify two key assumptions supporting the universal process approach and briefly describe Henri Fayol's contribution.

2 Discuss Frederick W. Taylor's approach to improving the practice of industrial management.

3 Identify at least four key quality improvement ideas from W. Edwards Deming and the other quality advocates.

4 Describe the general aim of the human relations movement and explain the circumstances in which it arose.

5 Explain the significance of applying open-system thinking to management.

6 Explain the practical significance of adopting a contingency perspective.

7 Identify and explain the nature of at least four of Thomas J. Peters and Robert H. Waterman Jr.'s eight attributes of excellence.

"IN THE RENEWING SOCIETY
THE HISTORIAN CONSULTS THE PAST
IN THE SERVICE OF THE PRESENT
AND THE FUTURE."
john w. gardner

Berry Gordy Jr.'s Motown Musical Assembly Line

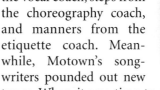

"Imagine a world without the Supremes, Smokey Robinson, Marvin Gaye, Stevie Wonder, Diana Ross, Michael Jackson, Lionel Richie, the Temptations, and the Four Tops," someone once said, "and you've just imagined a world without Berry Gordy."

Gordy, who worked on the Ford assembly line and sold cookware door to door, submitted in the end to his passion for songwriting and transforming no-names into stars.

As a songwriter, Gordy found early success with hits like "Lonely Teardrops," sung by Jackie Wilson. But Gordy soon realized he wanted more control. "To protect my songs, which are my loves, I had to find singers who could sing and record them like I heard them in my head."

At 29, with an $800 loan from his family, Gordy founded Motown. He leased a two-story house at 2648 West Grand Boulevard in Detroit. "Everything was makeshift," he says. We used the bathroom as an echo chamber."

Gordy borrowed from his assembly-line experience in refining Motown acts. The kids learned harmony from the vocal coach, steps from the choreography coach, and manners from the etiquette coach. Meanwhile, Motown's songwriters pounded out new tunes. When it was time to perform, the kids—Diana, Marvin, Stevie, Smokey, and the rest—piled into the Motown Revue bus and headed out on the road, competing to see who could win the most applause.

By 1975, Motown had become the biggest black-owned business in America, with activities spanning several record labels, film, and television. "I had no idea that Diana Ross would become an industry or that Michael Jackson would become an industry or that the Temptations would become an industry," Gordy says. "While I say I'm a songwriter and businessman, really, deep down, I think I'm a teacher, like my father."

For an interesting history of Motown, see: **www.motownat40.com.**

Berry Gordy Jr. became a music industry legend by relying on the right blend of talent, hard work, ingenuity, and lessons from the past. He fittingly sees himself as a teacher, someone who collects wisdom and passes it on to future generations. In a parallel sense, that is what this chapter is all about. Management historians believe that a better knowledge of the past will lead to a more productive future. They contend that students of management who fail to understand the evolution of management thought are destined to repeat past mistakes. Moreover, historians and managers alike believe that one needs to know where management has been if one is to understand where it is going. For example, while participating in a Harvard Business School round-table discussion on the value of management history, a top-level executive summarized:

> It is always hard to communicate any sort of abstract idea to someone else, let alone get any acceptance of it. But when there is some agreement on the factual or historical background of that idea, the possibilities for general agreement expand enormously.[1]

Historians draw a distinction between history and historical perspective. According to one management scholar:

> Historical perspective is the study of a subject in light of its earliest phases and subsequent evolution. Historical perspective differs from history in that the object of historical perspective is to sharpen one's vision of the present, not the past.[2]

This chapter qualifies as a historical perspective because it is part historical fact and part modern-day interpretation. Various approaches in the evolution of management thought are discussed relative to the lessons each can teach today's managers. The term *evolution* is appropriate here because management theory has developed in bits and pieces through the years. Moreover, pioneering contributors to management theory and practice have come from around the globe (see Figure 2.1). A historical perspective puts these pieces together.

The Practice and Study of Management

The systemic study of management is relatively new. As an area of academic study, management is essentially a product of the twentieth century. Only three universities—Pennsylvania, Chicago, and California—offered business management courses before 1900.[3]

But the actual practice of management has been around for thousands of years. The pyramids of Egypt, for example, stand as tangible evidence of the ancient world's ability to manage. It took more than 100,000 individuals 20 years to construct the great pyramid of Cheops. This remarkable achievement was the result of systematically managed effort. Although the Egyptians' management techniques were crude by modern standards, many problems they faced are still around today. They, like today's managers, had to make plans, obtain and mobilize human and material resources, coordinate interdependent jobs, keep records, report their progress, and take corrective action as needed.

Information Overload

Since the building of the pyramids, entire civilizations have come and gone. In one form or another, management was practiced in each. Sadly, during those thousands of years of management experience, one modern element was missing: a systematically recorded body of management knowledge. In early cultures management was something one learned by word of mouth and trial and error—not something one studied in school, read about in textbooks and on the Internet, theorized about, experimented with, or wrote about.

Thanks to modern print and electronic media, the collective genius of thousands of management theorists and practitioners has been compressed into a veritable mountain of textbooks, journals, research monographs, microfilms, movies, audio- and videotapes, and computer files. Never before have present and future managers had so much relevant information at their fingertips, often as close as the nearest Internet-linked computer or library. As an indication of what is available, a 1990 study identified 54 journals dealing with just the behavioral side of management.[4] There are many, many others (see Skills & Tools at the end of this chapter). In fact, so much information on management theory and practice exists today that it is difficult, if not impossible, to keep abreast of all of it.

Figure 2.1

Management Is a Global Affair: Selected Contributors to Management Theory

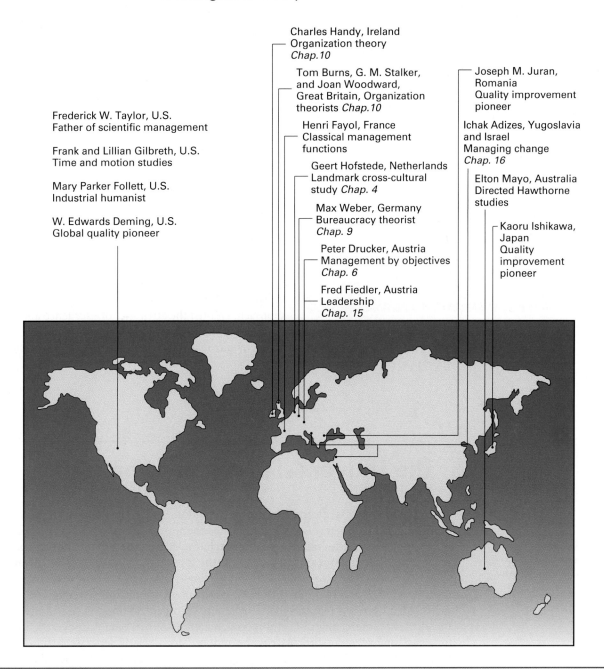

Charles Handy, Ireland
Organization theory
Chap. 10

Tom Burns, G. M. Stalker, and Joan Woodward, Great Britain, Organization theorists *Chap. 10*

Henri Fayol, France
Classical management functions

Geert Hofstede, Netherlands
Landmark cross-cultural study *Chap. 4*

Max Weber, Germany
Bureaucracy theorist
Chap. 9

Peter Drucker, Austria
Management by objectives
Chap. 6

Fred Fiedler, Austria
Leadership
Chap. 15

Joseph M. Juran, Romania
Quality improvement pioneer

Ichak Adizes, Yugoslavia and Israel
Managing change
Chap. 16

Elton Mayo, Australia
Directed Hawthorne studies

Kaoru Ishikawa, Japan
Quality improvement pioneer

Frederick W. Taylor, U.S.
Father of scientific management

Frank and Lillian Gilbreth, U.S.
Time and motion studies

Mary Parker Follett, U.S.
Industrial humanist

W. Edwards Deming, U.S.
Global quality pioneer

An Interdisciplinary Field

A principal cause of the information explosion in management theory is its interdisciplinary nature. Scholars from several fields—including psychology, sociology, cultural anthropology, mathematics, philosophy, statistics, political science, economics, logistics, computer science, ergonomics, history, and various fields of engineering—have, at one

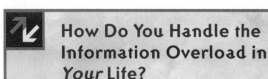

time or another, been interested in management. In addition, administrators in business, government, church, health care, and education all have drawn from and contributed to the study of management. Each group of scholars and practitioners has interpreted and reformulated management according to its own perspective. With each new perspective have come new questions and assumptions, new research techniques, different technical jargon, and new conceptual frameworks.[5]

No Universally Accepted Theory of Management

We can safely state that no single theory of management is universally accepted today.[6] To provide a useful historical perspective that will guide our study of modern management, we shall discuss six different approaches to management: (1) the universal process approach, (2) the operational approach, (3) the behavioral approach, (4) the systems approach, (5) the contingency approach, and (6) the attributes of excellence approach. Understanding these general approaches to the theory and practice of management can help you appreciate how management has evolved, where it is today, and where it appears to be headed.

The Universal Process Approach

The universal process approach is the oldest and one of the most popular approaches to management thought. It is also known as the universalist or functional approach. According to the **universal process approach,** the administration of all organizations, public or private or large or small, requires the same rational process. The universalist approach is based on two main assumptions. First, although the purpose of organizations may vary (for example, business, government, education, or religion), a core management process remains the same across all organizations. Successful managers, therefore, are interchangeable among organizations of differing purpose. Second, the universal management process can be reduced to a set of separate functions and related principles. Early universal process writers emphasized the specialization of labor (who does what), the chain of command (who reports to whom), and authority (who is ultimately responsible for getting things done).

universal process approach *assumes all organizations require the same rational management process*

1 Identify two key assumptions supporting the universal process approach and briefly describe Henri Fayol's contribution.

Henri Fayol's Universal Management Process

In 1916, at the age of 75, Henri Fayol published his now classic book *Administration Industrielle et Générale,* though it did not become widely known in Britain and the

United States until an English translation became available in 1949.[7] Despite its belated appearance in the English-speaking world and despite its having to compete with enthusiastic scientific management and human relations movements in the United States, Fayol's work has left a permanent mark on twentieth-century management thinking.

Fayol was first an engineer and later a successful administrator in a large French mining and metallurgical concern, which is perhaps why he did not resort to theory in his pioneering management book. Rather, Fayol was a manager who attempted to translate his broad administrative experience into practical guidelines for the successful management of all types of organizations.

As we mentioned in the previous chapter, Fayol believed that the manager's job could be divided into five functions, or areas, of managerial responsibility—planning, organizing, command, coordination, and control—which are essential to managerial success. (Some educators refer to them as the POC[3] functions.) His 14 universal principles of management, as listed in Table 2.1, were intended to show managers how to carry out their functional duties. Fayol's functions and principles have withstood the test of time because of their widespread applicability. In spite of years of reformulation, rewording, expansion, and revision, Fayol's original management functions still can be found in nearly all management texts. In fact, after an extensive review of studies of managerial work, a pair of management scholars concluded:

The classical functions still represent the most useful way of conceptualizing the manager's job, especially for management education, and perhaps this is why it is still the most favored description of managerial work in current management textbooks. The classical functions provide clear and discrete methods of classifying the thousands of different activities that managers carry out and the techniques they use in terms of the functions they perform for the achievement of organizational goals.[8]

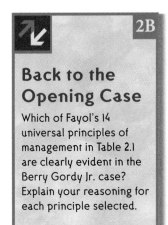

2B

Back to the Opening Case

Which of Fayol's 14 universal principles of management in Table 2.1 are clearly evident in the Berry Gordy Jr. case? Explain your reasoning for each principle selected.

Table 2.1

Fayol's 14 Universal Principles of Management

1. **Division of work.** Specialization of labor is necessary for organizational success.
2. **Authority.** The right to give orders must accompany responsibility.
3. **Discipline.** Obedience and respect help an organization run smoothly.
4. **Unity of command.** Each employee should receive orders from only one superior.
5. **Unity of direction.** The efforts of everyone in the organization should be coordinated and focused in the same direction.
6. **Subordination of individual interests to the general interest.** Resolving the tug of war between personal and organizational interests in favor of the organization is one of management's greatest difficulties.
7. **Remuneration.** Employees should be paid fairly in accordance with their contribution.
8. **Centralization.** The relationship between centralization and decentralization is a matter of proportion; the optimum balance must be found for each organization.
9. **Scalar chain.** Subordinates should observe the formal chain of command unless expressly authorized by their respective superiors to communicate with each other.
10. **Order.** Both material things and people should be in their proper places.
11. **Equity.** Fairness that results from a combination of kindliness and justice will lead to devoted and loyal service.
12. **Stability and tenure of personnel.** People need time to learn their jobs.
13. **Initiative.** One of the greatest satisfactions is formulating and carrying out a plan.
14. **Esprit de corps.** Harmonious effort among individuals is the key to organizational success.

Source: Adapted from Henri Fayol, *General and Industrial Management*, trans. Constance Storrs (London: Isaac Pitman & Sons, 1949). Copyright 1949 by Lake Publishing Company. Reprinted by permission.

Lessons from the Universal Process Approach

Fayol's main contribution to management thought was to show how the complex management process can be separated into interdependent areas of responsibility, or functions. Fayol's contention that management is a continuous process beginning with planning and ending with controlling also remains popular today. Contemporary adaptations of Fayol's functions offer students of management a useful framework for analyzing the management process. But as we mentioned in Chapter 1, this sort of rigid functional approach has been criticized for creating the impression that the management process is more rational and orderly than it really is. Fayol's functions, therefore, form a skeleton that needs to be fleshed out with concepts, techniques, and situational refinements from more modern approaches. The functional approach is useful because it specifies what managers *should* do, but the other approaches help explain *why* and *how*.

The Operational Approach

operational approach
production-oriented field of management dedicated to improving efficiency and cutting waste

The term **operational approach** is a convenient description of the production-oriented area of management dedicated to improving efficiency, cutting waste, and improving quality. Since the turn of the century, it has had a number of labels, including scientific management, management science, operations research, production management, and operations management. Underlying this somewhat confusing evolution of terms has been a consistent purpose: to make person-machine systems work as efficiently as possible. Throughout its historical development, the operational approach has been technically and quantitatively oriented.

Frederick W. Taylor's Scientific Management

2 Discuss Frederick W. Taylor's approach to improving the practice of industrial management.

Born in 1856, the son of a Philadelphia lawyer, Frederick Winslow Taylor was the epitome of the self-made man. Because a temporary problem with his eyes kept him from attending Harvard University, Taylor went to work as a common laborer in a small Philadelphia machine shop. In just four years he picked up the trades of pattern maker and machinist.[9] Later, Taylor went to work at Midvale Steel Works in Philadelphia, where he quickly moved up through the ranks while studying at night for a mechanical engineering degree. As a manager at Midvale, Taylor was appalled at industry's unsystematic practices. He observed little, if any, cooperation between the managers and the laborers. Inefficiency and waste were rampant. Output restriction among groups of workers, which Taylor called "systematic soldiering," was widespread. Ill-equipped and inadequately trained workers were typically left on their own to determine how to do their jobs. Hence, the father of scientific management committed himself to the relentless pursuit of "finding a better way."[10] Taylor sought nothing less than what he termed a "mental revolution" in the practice of industrial management.[11]

scientific management
developing performance standards on the basis of systematic observation and experimentation

According to an early definition, **scientific management** is "that kind of management which *conducts* a business or affairs by *standards* established by facts or truths gained through *systematic* observation, experiment, or reasoning."[12] The word *experiment* deserves special emphasis because it was Taylor's trademark. While working at Midvale and later at Bethlehem Steel, Taylor started the scientific management movement in industry in four areas: standardization, time and task study, systematic selection and training, and pay incentives.

Standardization.   By closely studying metal-cutting operations, Taylor collected extensive data on the optimum cutting-tool speeds and the rates at which stock should be fed into the machines for each job. The resulting standards were then posted for quick reference by the machine operators. He also systematically cataloged and stored the expensive cutting tools that usually were carelessly thrown aside when a job was completed. Operators could go to the carefully arranged tool room, check out the right tool for the job at hand, and check it back in when finished. Taylor's approach caused productivity to jump and costs to fall.

Frederick W. Taylor, 1856–1915

Time and Task Study.   According to the traditional rule-of-thumb approach, there was no "science of shoveling." But after thousands of observations and stopwatch recordings, Taylor detected a serious flaw in the way various materials were being shoveled—each laborer brought his own shovel to work. Taylor knew the company was losing, not saving, money when a laborer used the same shovel for both heavy and light materials. A shovel load of iron ore weighed about 30 pounds, according to Taylor's calculations, whereas a shovel load of rice coal weighed only 4 pounds. Systematic experimentation revealed that a shovel load of 21 pounds was optimum (permitted the greatest movement of material in a day). Taylor significantly increased productivity by having workers use specially sized and shaped shovels provided by the company—large shovels for the lighter materials and smaller ones for heavier work.

Systematic Selection and Training.   Although primitive by modern standards, Taylor's experiments with pig iron handling clearly reveal the intent of this phase of scientific management. The task was to lift a 92-pound block of iron (in the steel trade, a "pig"), carry it up an incline (a distance of about 36 feet), and drop it into an open railroad car. Taylor observed that on the average, a pig iron handler moved about $12\frac{1}{2}$ tons in a ten-hour day of constant effort. After careful study, Taylor found that if he selected the strongest men and instructed them in the proper techniques of lifting and carrying the pigs of iron, he could get each man to load 47 tons in a ten-hour day. Surprisingly, this nearly fourfold increase in output was achieved by having the pig iron handlers spend only 43 percent of their time actually hauling iron. The other 57 percent was spent either walking back empty-handed or sitting down. Taylor reported that the laborers liked the new arrangement because they were less fatigued and took home 60 percent more pay.

Pay Incentives.   According to Taylor, "What the workmen want from their employers beyond anything else is high wages."[13] This "economic man" assumption led Taylor to believe that piece rates were important to improved productivity. Under traditional piece-rate plans, an individual received a fixed amount of money for each unit of output. Thus, the greater the output, the greater the pay. In his determination to find a better way, Taylor attempted to improve the traditional piece-rate scheme with his differential piece-rate plan.

Figure 2.2 illustrates the added incentive effect of Taylor's differential plan. (The amounts are typical rates of pay in Taylor's time.) Under the traditional plan, a worker would receive a fixed amount (for example, 5 cents) for each unit produced. Seventy-five cents would be received for producing 15 units and $1.00 for 20 units. In contrast, Taylor's plan required that a time study be carried out to determine the company's idea of a fair day's work. Two piece rates were then put into effect. A low rate would be paid if the worker finished the day below the company's standard, and a high rate when the day's output met or exceeded the standard. As the lines in Figure 2.2 indicate, a hard worker who produced 25 units would earn $1.25 under the traditional plan and $1.50 under Taylor's plan.

Taylor's Followers

Among the many who followed in Taylor's footsteps, Frank and Lillian Gilbreth and Henry L. Gantt stand out.

Frank and Lillian Gilbreth. Inspired by Taylor's time studies and motivated by a desire to expand human potential, the Gilbreths turned motion study into an exact science. In so doing, they pioneered the use of motion pictures for studying and streamlining work motions. They paved the way for modern work simplification by cataloging 17 different hand motions, such as "grasp" and "hold." These they called "therbligs" (actually the name *Gilbreth* spelled backward with the *t* and *h* reversed). Their success stories include the following:

> *In laying brick, the motions used in laying a single brick were reduced from eighteen to five—with an increase in output, from one hundred and twenty bricks an hour to three hundred and fifty an hour, and with a reduction in the resulting fatigue. In folding cotton cloth, twenty to thirty motions were reduced to ten or twelve, with the result that instead of one hundred and fifty dozen pieces of cloth, four hundred dozen were folded, with no added fatigue.*[14]

Frank and Lillian Gilbreth were so dedicated to the idea of finding the one best way to do every job that two of their 12 children wrote *Cheaper by the Dozen*, a humorous recollection of scientific management and motion study applied to the Gilbreth household.[15]

Figure 2.2

Taylor's Differential Piece-Rate Plan

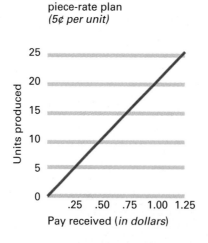

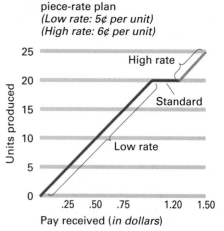

Lillian M. Gilbreth, 1878–1972, at right, and Frank B. Gilbreth, 1868–1924, at left, with eleven of their dozen children

Henry L. Gantt. Gantt, a schoolteacher by training, contributed to scientific management by refining production control and cost control techniques. As illustrated in Chapter 6, variations of Gantt's work-scheduling charts are still in use today.[16] He also humanized Taylor's differential piece-rate system by combining a guaranteed day rate (minimum wage) with an above-standard bonus. Gantt was ahead of his time in emphasizing the importance of the human factor and in urging management to concentrate on service rather than profits.[17]

The Quality Advocates

Today's managers readily attach strategic importance to quality improvement. The road to this enlightened view, particularly for U.S. managers, was a long and winding one. It started in factories and eventually made its way through service businesses, nonprofit organizations, and government agencies. An international cast of quality advocates took much of the twentieth century to pave the road to quality. Not until 1980, when NBC ran a television documentary titled "If Japan Can . . . Why Can't We?" did Americans begin to realize fully that *quality* was a key to Japan's growing dominance in world markets. Advice from the following quality advocates finally began to sink in during the 1980s.[18]

Henry L. Gantt, 1861–1919

3 **Identify at least four key quality improvement ideas from W. Edwards Deming and the other quality advocates.**

Walter A. Shewhart. A statistician for Bell Laboratories, Shewhart introduced the concept of statistical quality control in his 1931 landmark text, *Economic Control of Quality of Manufactured Product.*

Kaoru Ishikawa. The University of Tokyo professor advocated quality before World War II and founded the Union of Japanese Scientists and Engineers (JUSE), which became the driving force behind Japan's quality revolution. Ishikawa proposed a preventive approach to quality. His expanded idea of the customer included both *internal and external customers.* Ishikawa's fishbone diagrams, discussed in Chapter 8, remain a popular problem-solving tool to this day.

W. Edwards Deming.   This Walter Shewhart understudy accepted an invitation from JUSE in 1950 to lecture on his principles of statistical quality control. His ideas, detailed later in Chapter 17, went far beyond what his Japanese hosts expected from a man with a mathematics Ph.D. from Yale. Japanese manufacturers warmly embraced Deming and his unconventional ideas about encouraging employee participation and striving for continuous improvement. His 1986 book *Out of the Crisis* is "a guide to the 'transformation of the style of American management,' which became a bible for Deming disciples."[19]

Joseph M. Juran.   Juran's career bore a striking similarity to Deming's. Both were Americans (Juran was a naturalized U.S. citizen born in Romania) schooled in statistics, both strongly influenced Japanese managers via JUSE, and both continued to lecture on quality into their nineties. Thanks to extensive training by the Juran Institute, the concept of internal customers is well established today.[20] Teamwork, partnerships with suppliers, problem solving, and brainstorming are all Juran trademarks. "A specific term associated with Juran is *Pareto analysis,* a technique for separating major problems from minor ones. A Pareto analysis looks for the 20 percent of possible causes that lead to 80 percent of all problems."[21] (The 80/20 rule is discussed in Chapter 6 under the heading of priorities.)

W. Edwards Deming,
1900–1993

Armand V. Feigenbaum.   While working on his doctorate at MIT, Feigenbaum developed the concept of *total quality control.* He expanded upon his idea of an organizationwide program of quality improvement in his 1951 book, *Total Quality Control.* He envisioned all functions of the business cycle—from purchasing and engineering, to manufacturing and finance, to marketing and service— as necessarily involved in the quest for quality. The *customer,* according to Feigenbaum, is the one who ultimately determines quality.[22]

Philip B. Crosby.   The author of the 1979 best-seller *Quality Is Free,* Crosby learned about quality improvement during his up-from-the-trenches career at ITT (a giant global corporation in many lines of business). His work struck a chord with top managers because he documented the huge cost of having to rework or scrap poor-quality products. He promoted the idea of *zero defects,* or doing it right the first time.[23]

Lessons from the Operational Approach

Scientific management often appears rather unscientific to those who live in a world of genetic engineering, manned space flight, industrial robots, the Internet, and laser technology. *Systematic management* might be a more accurate label. Within the context of haphazard,

---

↗↙ Juran on Quality   **2D**

Just before his ninety-fourth birthday in 1998, Joseph M. Juran made this observation in a *Fortune* magazine interview:

There's a lot of confusion as to whether quality costs money or whether it saves money. In one sense, quality means the features of some product or service that make people willing to buy it. So it's income-oriented—has an effect on income. Now to produce features, ordinarily you have to invest money. In that sense, higher quality costs more. Quality also means freedom from trouble, freedom from failure. This is cost-oriented. If things fail internally, it costs the company. If they fail externally, it also costs the customer. In these cases, quality costs less.

Source: Thomas A. Stewart, "A Conversation with Joseph Juran," *Fortune* (January 11, 1999): 170.

Questions: *What sorts of product and/or service quality problems have you observed lately? How could they have been prevented?*

turn-of-the-century industrial practices, however, scientific management was indeed revolutionary. Heading the list of its lasting contributions is a much-needed emphasis on promoting production efficiency and combating waste. Today, dedication to finding a better way is more important than ever in view of uneven productivity growth and diminishing resources.

Nevertheless, Taylor and the early scientific management proponents have been roundly criticized for viewing workers as unidimensional economic beings interested only in more money. These critics fear that scientific management techniques have dehumanized people by making them act like mindless machines. Not all would agree. According to one respected management scholar who feels that Taylor's work is widely misunderstood and unfairly criticized, Taylor actually improved working conditions by reducing fatigue and redesigning machines to fit people. A systematic analysis of Taylor's contributions led this same management scholar to conclude: "Taylor's track record is remarkable. The point is not, as is often claimed, that he was 'right in the context of his time' but is now outdated, but that *most of his insights are still valid today.*"[24]

Contributions by the quality advocates are subject to less debate today. The only question is, Why didn't we listen to them earlier? (See Chapter 17.)

An important post–World War II outgrowth of the operational approach is operations management. Operations management, like scientific management, aims at promoting efficiency through systematic observation and experimentation. However, operations management (sometimes called production/operations management) tends to be broader in scope and application than scientific management was. Whereas scientific management was limited largely to hand labor and machine shops, operations management specialists apply their expertise to all types of production and service operations, such as the purchase and storage of materials, energy use, product and service design, work flow, safety, quality control, and data processing. Thus, **operations management** is defined as the process of transforming raw materials, technology, and human talent into useful goods and services.[25] Operations managers could be called the frontline troops in the battle for productivity growth.

operations management
the process of transforming material and human resources into useful goods and services

The Behavioral Approach

Like the other approaches to management, the behavioral approach has evolved gradually over many years. Advocates of the behavioral approach to management point out that people deserve to be the central focus of organized activity. They believe that successful management depends largely on a manager's ability to understand and work with people who have a variety of backgrounds, needs, perceptions, and aspirations. The progress of this humanistic approach from the human relations movement to modern organizational behavior has greatly influenced management theory and practice.

4 Describe the general aim of the human relations movement and explain the circumstances in which it arose.

The Human Relations Movement

The **human relations movement** was a concerted effort among theorists and practitioners to make managers more sensitive to employee needs. It came into being as a

human relations movement *an effort to make managers more sensitive to their employees' needs*

result of special circumstances that occurred during the first half of this century. As illustrated in Figure 2.3, the human relations movement may be compared to the top of a pyramid. Just as the top of a pyramid must be supported, so too the human relations movement was supported by three very different historic influences: (1) the threat of unionization, (2) the Hawthorne studies, and (3) the philosophy of industrial humanism.

Threat of Unionization. To understand why the human relations movement evolved, one needs first to appreciate its sociopolitical background. From the late 1800s to the 1920s, American industry grew by leaps and bounds as it attempted to satisfy the many demands of a rapidly growing population. Cheap immigrant labor was readily available, and there was a seller's market for finished goods. Then came the Great Depression in the 1930s, and millions stood in bread lines instead of pay lines. Many held business somehow responsible for the depression, and public sympathy swung from management to labor. Congress consequently began to pass prolabor legislation. When the Wagner Act of 1935 legalized union-management collective bargaining, management began searching for ways to stem the tide of all-out unionization. Early human relations theory proposed an enticing answer: satisfied employees would be less inclined to join unions. Business managers subsequently began adopting morale-boosting human relations techniques as a union-avoidance tactic.

The Hawthorne Studies. As the sociopolitical climate changed, a second development in industry took place. Behavioral scientists from prestigious universities began to conduct on-the-job behavior studies. Instead of studying tools and techniques in the scientific management tradition, they focused on people. Practical behavioral research such as the famous Hawthorne studies stirred management's interest in the psychological and sociological dynamics of the workplace.

Figure 2.3

The Human Relations Movement Pyramid

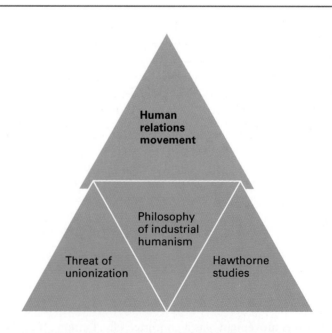

The Hawthorne studies began in 1924 in a Western Electric plant near Chicago as a small-scale scientific management study of the relationship between light intensity and productivity. Curiously, the performance of a select group of employees tended to improve no matter how the physical surroundings were manipulated. Even when the lights were dimmed to moonlight intensity, productivity continued to climb! Scientific management doctrine could not account for what was taking place, and so a team of behavioral science researchers, headed by Elton Mayo, was brought in from Harvard to conduct a more rigorous study.

By 1932, when the Hawthorne studies ended, over 20,000 employees had participated in one way or another. After extensive interviewing of the subjects, it became clear to researchers that productivity was much less affected by changes in work conditions than by the attitudes of the workers themselves. Specifically, relationships between members of a work group and between workers and their supervisors were found to be more significant. Though the experiments and the theories that evolved from them are criticized today for flawed methodology and statistical inaccuracies, the Hawthorne studies can be credited with turning management theorists away from the simplistic "economic man" model to a more humanistic and realistic view, the "social man" model.[26]

The Philosophy of Industrial Humanism.   Although unionization prompted a search for new management techniques and the Hawthorne studies demonstrated that people were important to productivity, a philosophy of human relations was needed to provide a convincing rationale for treating employees better. Elton Mayo, Mary Parker Follett, and Douglas McGregor, although from very different backgrounds, offered just such a philosophy.

Born in Australia, Elton Mayo was a Harvard professor specializing in psychology and sociology when he took over the Hawthorne studies. His 1933 book, *The Human Problems of an Industrial Civilization*, inspired by what he had learned at Hawthorne, cautioned managers that emotional factors were a more important determinant of productive efficiency than physical and logical factors were. Claiming that employees create their own unofficial yet powerful workplace culture complete with norms and sanctions, Mayo urged managers to provide work that fostered personal and subjective satisfaction. He called for a new social order designed to stimulate individual cooperation.[27]

Elton Mayo, 1880–1949

Mary Parker Follett's experience as a management consultant and her background in law, political science, and philosophy produced her strong conviction that managers should be aware that each employee is a complex collection of emotions, beliefs, attitudes, and habits. To get employees to work harder, she believed, managers had to recognize the individual's motivating desires. Accordingly, Follett urged managers to motivate performance rather than simply demand it. Cooperation, a spirit of unity, and self-control were seen as the keys to both productivity and a democratic way of life.[28] Historians credit Follett, who died in 1933, with being decades ahead of her time in terms of behavioral and systems management theory.[29]

A third philosophical rallying point for industrial humanism was provided by an American scholar named Douglas McGregor. In his 1960 classic, *The Human Side of Enterprise*, McGregor outlined a set of highly optimistic assumptions about human nature. McGregor viewed the typical employee as an energetic and creative individual who could achieve great things if given the opportunity. He labeled the set of assumptions for this optimistic perspective **Theory Y.** McGregor's Theory Y assumptions are listed in Table 2.2, along with what he called the traditional Theory X assumptions. These two sets of assumptions about human nature enabled

Mary Parker Follett, 1868–1933

Theory Y *McGregor's optimistic assumptions about working people*

Table 2.2

McGregor's Theories X and Y

Theory X: Some traditional assumptions about people	Theory Y: Some modern assumptions about people
1. Most people dislike work, and they will avoid it when they can.	1. Work is a natural activity, like play or rest.
2. Most people must be coerced and threatened with punishment before they will work. They require close direction.	2. People are capable of self-direction and self-control if they are committed to objectives.
3. Most people prefer to be directed. They avoid responsibility and have little ambition. They are interested only in security.	3. People will become committed to organizational objectives if they are rewarded for doing so.
	4. The average person can learn to both accept and seek responsibility.
	5. Many people in the general population have imagination, ingenuity, and creativity.

Douglas McGregor,
1906–1964

organizational behavior
a modern approach seeking to discover the causes of work behavior and develop better management techniques

McGregor to contrast the modern or enlightened view he recommended (Theory Y) with the prevailing traditional view (Theory X), which he criticized for being pessimistic, stifling, and outdated. Because of its relative recency (compared with Mayo's and Follett's work), its catchy labels, and its intuitive appeal, McGregor's Theory X/Y philosophy has left an indelible mark on modern management thinking. Some historians have credited McGregor with launching the field of organizational behavior.

Organizational Behavior

Organizational behavior is a modern approach to management that attempts to determine the causes of human work behavior and translate the results into effective management techniques. As such, it has a strong research orientation. Organizational behaviorists have borrowed an assortment of theories and research techniques from all of the behavioral sciences and applied them to people at work in modern organizations. The result is an interdisciplinary field in which psychology predominates. In spite of its relatively new and developing state, organizational behavior has had a significant impact on modern management thought by helping to explain why employees behave as they do. Because human relations has evolved into a practical, how-to-do-it discipline for supervisors, organizational behavior amounts to a scientific extension of human relations. Many organizational behavior findings will be examined in Part Four of this text.

Lessons from the Behavioral Approach

Above all else, the behavioral approach makes it clear to present and future managers that *people* are the key to productivity. According to advocates of the behavioral approach, technology, work rules, and standards do not guarantee good job performance. Instead, success depends on motivated and skilled individuals who are committed to organizational objectives.[30] Only a manager's sensitivity to individual concerns can foster the cooperation necessary for high productivity.

2E

↗↙ Leadership Tips from *Star Trek*

According to one management writer, here's why Jean-Luc Picard, captain of the starship *Enterprise*, is a good leader:

If you watch the character of Picard, even in a crisis he opts for consensus and asks for other people's opinions.

Even when the ship is about to blow up, he remains calm and effectively says, "Hey, I need your help here." In other words, what he's saying to these people is that "if you're good enough to be in your position, you're good enough for me to listen to." That's something I think senior managers in all corporations can learn from.

. . . And the other thing about Picard is he doesn't always act on (his crew's) advice. He still may decide he wants to do what he had originally intended to do.

But his people know they'll be listened to and therefore they're not offended. They don't feel like they're neglected. They don't feel like their opinions mean nothing.

Source: Excerpted from "Management Tips Aren't Science Fiction," *USA Today* (September 29, 1995): 14B.

Questions: *Would Mary Parker Follett approve of Picard's style? Explain. Is Picard a Theory X or Theory Y manager? Explain.*

On the negative side, traditional human relations doctrine has been criticized as vague and simplistic. According to these critics, relatively primitive on-the-job behavioral research does not justify such broad conclusions. For instance, critics do not believe that supportive supervision and good human relations will lead automatically to higher morale and hence to better job performance. Also, recent analyses of the Hawthorne studies, using modern statistical techniques, have generated debate about the validity of the original conclusions.[31]

Fortunately, organizational behavior, as a scientific extension of human relations, promises to fill some of the gaps left by human relationists while at the same time retaining an emphasis on people. Today, organizational behaviorists are trying to piece together the multiple determinants of effective job performance in various work situations and across cultures.

The Systems Approach

A **system** is a collection of parts operating interdependently to achieve a common purpose. Working from this definition, the systems approach represents a marked departure from the past; in fact, it requires a completely different style of thinking.

Universal process, scientific management, and human relations theorists studied management by taking things apart. They assumed that the whole is equal to the sum of its parts and can be explained in terms of its parts. Systems theorists, in contrast, study management by putting things together and assume that the whole is greater than the sum of its parts. The difference is analytic versus synthetic thinking. According to one management systems expert, "Analytic thinking is, so to speak, outside-in thinking; synthetic thinking is inside-out. Neither negates the value of the

system *a collection of parts that operate interdependently to achieve a common purpose*

other, but by synthetic thinking we can gain understanding that we cannot obtain through analysis, particularly of collective phenomena."[32]

Systems theorists recommend synthetic thinking because management is not practiced in a vacuum. Managers affect, and are in turn affected by, many organization and environmental variables. Systems thinking has presented the field of management with an enormous challenge: to identify all relevant parts of organized activity and to discover how they interact. Two management writers predicted that systems thinking offers "a basis for understanding organizations and their problems which may one day produce a revolution in organizations comparable to the one brought about by Taylor with scientific management."[33]

Chester I. Barnard's Early Systems Perspective

In one sense, Chester I. Barnard followed in the footsteps of Henri Fayol. Like Fayol, Barnard established a new approach to management on the basis of his experience as a top-level manager. But the former president of New Jersey Bell Telephone's approach differed from Fayol's. Rather than isolating specific management functions and principles, Barnard devised a more abstract systems approach. In his landmark 1938 book, *The Functions of the Executive*, Barnard characterized all organizations as cooperative systems: "A cooperative system is a complex of physical, biological, personal, and social components which are in a specific systematic relationship by reason of the cooperation of two or more persons for at least one definite end."[34]

According to Barnard, willingness to serve, common purpose, and communication are the principal elements in an organization (or cooperative system).[35] He felt that an organization did not exist if these three elements were not present and working interdependently. As illustrated in Figure 2.4, Barnard viewed communication as an energizing force that bridges the natural gap between the individual's willingness to serve and the organization's common purpose.

Barnard's systems perspective has encouraged management and organization theorists to study organizations as complex and dynamic wholes instead of piece by piece. Significantly, he was also a strong advocate of business ethics in his speeches and writings.[36] (See Management Ethics for a profile of another business ethics pioneer.) Barnard opened some important doors in the evolution of management thought.

Figure 2.4

Barnard's Cooperative System

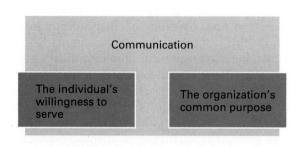

General Systems Theory

General systems theory is an interdisciplinary area of study based on the assumption that everything is part of a larger, interdependent arrangement. According to Ludwig von Bertalanffy, a biologist and the founder of general systems theory, "In order to understand an organized whole we must know the parts and the relations between them."[37] This interdisciplinary perspective was eagerly adopted by Barnard's followers because it categorized levels of systems and distinguished between closed and open systems.

general systems theory *an area of study based on the assumption that everything is part of a larger, interdependent arrangement*

Levels of Systems.   Envisioning the world as a collection of systems was only the first step for general systems theorists. One of the more important recent steps has been the identification of hierarchies of systems, ranging from very specific systems to general ones. Identifying systems at various levels has helped translate abstract general systems theory into more concrete terms.[38] A hierarchy of systems relevant to management is the seven-level scheme of living systems shown in Figure 2.5. Notice that each system is a subsystem of the one above it.

5 **Explain the significance of applying open-system thinking to management.**

Closed Versus Open Systems.   In addition to identifying hierarchies of systems, general systems theorists have distinguished between closed and open systems. A **closed system** is a self-sufficient entity, whereas an **open system** depends on the surrounding environment for survival. In reality, these two kinds of systems cannot be completely separated from each other. The key to classifying a system as relatively closed or relatively open is to determine the amount of interaction between the system and its environment. A battery-powered digital watch, for example, is a relatively closed system; after the battery is in place, it runs without help from the outside environment. In contrast, a solar-powered clock is a relatively open system; it cannot operate without a continuous supply of outside energy. The human body is a highly open system because life depends on the body's ability to import oxygen and energy and to export waste. In other words, the human body is highly dependent on the environment for survival.

closed system   *a self-sufficient entity*

open system   *something that depends on its surrounding environment for survival*

Figure 2.5

Levels of Living Systems

System level	General	Practical examples
Supranational		United Nations
National		United States, Canada
Organizational	↑	AT&T, Wal-Mart
Group		Family, work group
Organismic		Human being
Organic		Heart
Cellular	Specific	Blood cell

Management Ethics

Rebecca Webb Lukens (1794–1854): America's First Female Chief Executive Officer

As America's first female CEO of an industrial company, Rebecca Lukens was a woman more than a century ahead of her time. For her, the critical year was 1825. Lukens, a devout Quaker, was raising three children and was pregnant with another in Coatesville, Pennsylvania, when her husband became mortally ill. On his deathbed, he urged Rebecca to take over his job of operating the Brandywine Iron Works and Nail Factory, founded by her late father.

She agreed and went on to run it for 24 years. Lukens not only rescued the mill from near bankruptcy but also built it into the country's premier manufacturer of boilerplate, high-quality iron essential to the making of steam boilers in what was the dawn of the age of steam. Her ironworks survives today as Lukens Inc., . . . [a *Fortune* 1000 company with over $1 billion in sales in 1995] and the oldest continuously operating steel mill in the U.S.

Lukens was an unusual woman from the start. Her father taught her to ride and often took her to his ironworks. A book lover, she sometimes read secretly in her room until dawn. When she was a teenager, her parents sent her to a boarding school in Wilmington, Delaware, where she developed a love of chemistry. About that time, she recalled later, "vanity began to whisper to me that I was of some importance, and my beloved tutor often warned me against its siren power." Fortunately, she listened to the whisper and ignored the tutor.

A hands-on executive, Lukens made many purchases and sales. When revenues slumped during the panic of 1837, she laid in a little inventory and then assigned her employees to do maintenance on the factory or gave them work on her farm. She laid off no one. When cash flow ran dry, she paid workers with farm produce. Near the end of her business career, she wrote: "There was difficulty and danger on every side. Now I look back and wonder at my daring."

Source: Excerpted from Peter Nulty, "The National Business Hall of Fame," *Fortune* (April 4, 1994): 126. *Fortune* 1,000 data from "*Fortune* 1,000 Ranked Within Industries,*" *Fortune* (April 29, 1996): F-57. © 1994, 1996 Time, Inc. All rights reserved.

Back to the Opening Case

Did Berry Gordy run his music company like a closed system or an open system? Explain.

Along the same lines, general systems theorists tell us that all organizations are open systems because organizational survival depends on interaction with the surrounding environment. Just as no person is an island, no organization or organizational subsystem is an island, according to this approach.

New Directions: Organizational Learning and Chaos Theory

Two very different streams of thought are taking systems thinking in interesting new directions today. No one knows for sure where these streams will lead, but they promise to stimulate creative ideas about modern organizations. The first, called organizational learning, portrays the organization as a living and *thinking* open system. Like the human mind, organizations rely on feedback to adjust to changing environmental conditions. In short, organizations are said to learn from experience, just as humans and higher animals do. Organizations thus engage in complex mental processes—such as anticipating, perceiving, envisioning, and problem solving. According to two organization theorists:

Some forms of organizational learning occur regularly in many organizations. Human resource development activities, strategic and other planning activities, and the introduction and mastering of new technologies for doing work are three common learning processes. They often do not fulfill their potential for true organizational learning, however.

Organizational learning is more than the sum of the learning of its parts—more than cumulative individual learning. The training and development of individuals with new skills, knowledge bases, theories, and frameworks does not constitute organizational learning unless such individual learning is translated into altered organizational practices, policies, or design features. Individual learning is necessary but not sufficient for organizational learning.[39]

You will find more about organizational learning in Chapter 9.

Chaos theory, meanwhile, has one idea in common with organizational learning: systems are influenced by feedback. Work in the 1960s and 1970s by mathematicians Edward Lorenz and James Yorke formed the basis of modern chaos theory. So-called chaologists are trying to find order among the seemingly random behavior patterns of everything from weather systems to organizations to stock markets.[40] Behind all this is the intriguing notion that every complex system has a life of its own, with its own rule book. The challenge for systems researchers is to discover "the rules" in seemingly chaotic systems. Margaret Wheatley offered this hopeful perspective:

A system is defined as chaotic when it becomes impossible to know where it will be next. There is no predictability; the system never lands in the same place twice. But as chaos theory shows, if we look at such a system long enough, with the perspective of time, the system always demonstrates its inherent orderliness. The most chaotic of systems never goes beyond certain boundaries. . . . Within chaos lies order, and the shape of chaos is often strikingly beautiful.[41]

Lessons from the Systems Approach

Because of the influence of the systems approach, managers now have a greater appreciation for the importance of seeing the whole picture. Open-systems thinking does not permit the manager to become preoccupied with one aspect of organizational management while ignoring other internal and external realities. The manager of a business, for instance, must consider resource availability, technological developments, and market trends when producing and selling a product or service. Another positive aspect of the systems approach is that it tries to integrate various management theories. Although quite different in emphasis, both operations management and organizational behavior have been strongly influenced by systems thinking.

There are critics of the systems approach, of course. Some management scholars see systems thinking as long on intellectual appeal and catchy terminology and short on verifiable facts and practical advice. Even two staunch advocates of a management systems perspective are wary: "Recognizing that the social organization is a contrived system cautions us against making an exact analogy between it and physical and biological systems."[42] At the present time, the systems approach is an instructive way of thinking about managing modern organizations rather than a collection of final answers.[43]

The Contingency Approach

A comparatively new line of thinking among management theorists has been labeled the contingency approach. Contingency management advocates are attempting to take a step away from universally applicable principles of management and toward situational appropriateness. In the words of Fred Luthans, a noted contingency management writer, "The traditional approaches to management were not necessarily wrong, but today they are no longer adequate. The needed breakthrough for management theory and practice can be found in a contingency approach."[44] Formally defined, the **contingency approach** is an effort to determine through research which managerial practices and techniques are appropriate in specific situations. Imagine using Taylor's approach with a college-educated computer engineer! Different situations require different managerial responses, according to the contingency approach.

contingency approach
research effort to determine which managerial practices and techniques are appropriate in specific situations

Generally, the term *contingency* refers to the choice of an alternative course of action. For example, roommates may have a contingency plan to move their party indoors if it rains. Their subsequent actions are said to be contingent (or dependent) on the weather. In a management context, contingency has become synonymous with situational management. As one contingency theorist put it, "The effectiveness of a given management pattern is contingent upon multitudinous factors and their interrelationship in a particular situation."[45] This means the application of various management tools and techniques must be appropriate to the particular situation because each situation presents to the manager its own problems. A contingency approach is applicable in intercultural dealings in which customs and habits cannot be taken for granted.

6 **Explain the practical significance of adopting a contingency perspective.**

In real-life management, the success of any given technique is dictated by the situation. For example, researchers have found that rigidly structured organizations with many layers of management function best when environmental conditions are relatively stable. Unstable surroundings dictate a more flexible and streamlined organization that can adapt quickly to change. Consequently, traditional principles of management that call for rigidly structured organizations, regardless of the situation, have come into question.

Contingency Characteristics

Some management scholars are attracted to contingency thinking because it is a workable compromise between the systems approach and what can be called a purely situational perspective. Figure 2.6 illustrates this relationship. The systems approach is often criticized for being too general and abstract, although the purely situational view, which assumes that every real-life situation requires a distinctly different approach, has been called hopelessly specific. Contingency advocates have tried to take advantage of common denominators without getting trapped into simplistic generalization. Three characteristics of the contingency approach are (1) an open-system perspective, (2) a practical research orientation, and (3) a multivariate approach.

An Open-System Perspective.   Open-system thinking is fundamental to the contingency view. Contingency theorists are not satisfied with focusing on just the

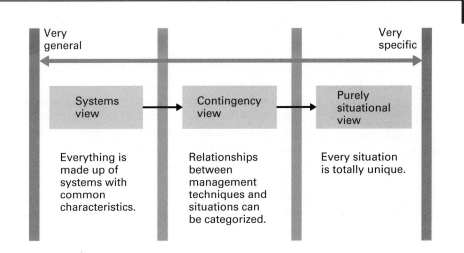

Figure 2.6

**The Contingency View:
A Compromise**

internal workings of organizations. They see the need to understand how organizational subsystems combine to interact with outside social, political, and economic systems.

A Practical Research Orientation.   Practical research is that which ultimately leads to more effective on-the-job management. Contingency researchers attempt to translate their findings into tools and situational refinements for more effective management.

A Multivariate Approach.   Traditional closed-system thinking prompted a search for simple one-to-one causal relationships. This approach is called bivariate analysis. For example, the traditional human relations assumption that higher morale leads automatically to higher productivity was the result of bivariate analysis. Only one variable, morale, was seen as the sole direct cause of changes in a second variable, productivity. Subsequent multivariate analysis has shown that many variables, including the employee's personality, the nature of the task, rewards, and job and life satisfaction, collectively account for variations in productivity. **Multivariate analysis** is a research technique used to determine how a combination of variables interacts to cause a particular outcome. For example, if an employee has a conscientious personality, the task is highly challenging, and the individual highly satisfied with his or her life and job, then analysis might show that productivity could be expected to be high. Contingency management theorists strive to carry out practical and relevant multivariate analyses.

multivariate analysis
research technique used to determine how a combination of variables interacts to cause a particular outcome

Lessons from the Contingency Approach

Although still not fully developed, the contingency approach is a helpful addition to management thought because it emphasizes situational appropriateness. People, organizations, and problems are too complex to justify rigid adherence to universal principles of management. Too, contingency thinking is a practical extension of the systems approach. Assuming that systems thinking is a unifying synthetic force in management

Career Implications of the Contingency Approach

Harry Pearce, vice chairman of General Motors:

We don't have the luxury of having functional experts who do nothing but their function anymore. They have to wear multiple hats. Because real world problems don't crop up as a safety problem, an environmental problem, a PR [public relations] problem. It's a mix. The most valued employee is one who can evaluate a variety of issues. We've got to educate and train people to do that.

Source: Excerpted from Micheline Maynard, "GM's New Vice Chairman Wants to See Walls Fall," *USA Today* (January 8, 1996): 6B.

Question: *What education and skills training do you need to become this kind of employee?*

thought, the contingency approach promises to add practical direction.

The contingency approach, like each of the other approaches, has its share of critics. One has criticized contingency theory for creating the impression that the organization is a captive of its environment.[46] If such were strictly the case, attempts to manage the organization would be in vain. In actual fact, organizations are subject to a combination of environmental forces and management practices.

Whether the contingency management theorists have bitten off more than they can chew remains to be seen. At present they appear to be headed in a constructive direction. But it is good to keep in mind that the contingency approach is a promising step rather than the end of the evolution of conventional management thought.

Attributes of Excellence: A Modern Unconventional Approach

In 1982, Thomas J. Peters and Robert H. Waterman Jr., a pair of management consultants, wrote a book that took the management world by storm. It topped the nonfiction best-seller lists for months, was translated into several foreign languages, and later appeared in paperback. By late 1987, an astounding 5 million copies had been sold worldwide.[47] *In Search of Excellence* attempted to explain what makes America's best-run companies successful. Many respected corporate executives hailed Peters and Waterman's book as the remedy for America's productivity problems. Certain management scholars, however, called the book simplistic and accused the authors of pandering to management's desire for a quick fix. If for no reason other than its widespread acceptance in the management community, *In Search of Excellence* deserves discussion in any historical perspective of management thought.[48]

Peters and Waterman's approach to management was unconventional for three reasons. First, they attacked conventional management theory and practice for being too conservative, rationalistic, analytical, unemotional, inflexible, negative, and preoccupied with bigness. Second, they replaced conventional management terminology (such as planning, management by objectives, and control) with catch phrases gleaned from successful managers (for example, "Do it, fix it, try it" and "management by wandering around"). Third, they made their key points with stories and anecdotes rather than with objective, quantified data and facts. All this added up to a challenge to take a fresh new look at management. In this section we explore that challenge by discussing the eight attributes of excellence uncovered by Peters and Waterman. Subsequent interpretations of their approach are also examined.

Thomas J. Peters

Robert H. Waterman Jr.

2H

Is the Customer *Always* Right?

Doctors no longer have "patients," teachers no longer have "students," magazines no longer have "readers." Instead, everyone has "customers," people who pay for a commodity and expect satisfaction. Or else.

Or else *what*? Or else they'll take their business across the street, is the implication. What the word "customers" does is to change the locus of power in the relationship.

Source: Rebecca Ganzel, "Shut Up and Fly," *Training*, 35 (September 1998): 8.

Question: *Can this sort of "customer orientation" be taken too far? Explain.*

Eight Attributes of Excellence

Peters and Waterman employed a combination of subjective and objective criteria to identify 62 of the best-managed companies in the United States. Among the final subsample of 36 "excellent" companies that boasted 20-year records of innovation and profitability were such familiar names as Boeing, Caterpillar, Delta Air Lines, Eastman Kodak, IBM, Johnson & Johnson, McDonald's, and 3M. Extensive interviews were conducted at half of these firms and less extensive interviewing took place at the rest.[49] After analyzing the results of their interviews, Peters and Waterman isolated the eight attributes of excellence summarized in Table 2.3. Importantly, the authors noted: "not all eight attributes were present or conspicuous to the same degree in all of the excellent companies we studied. But in every case at least a preponderance of the eight was clearly visible, quite distinctive."[50]

A Critical Appraisal of the Excellence Approach

Critics took Peters and Waterman to task for giving managers more questions than answers, ignoring the contingency approach to management, and relying too heavily on unsupported generalizations. They also criticized them for taking an overly narrow viewpoint of organizational success. According to one skeptical management consultant:

> *The authors fail to position management effectiveness among the several nonmanagement variables that are also important to sustained corporate excellence. Technology, finances, government policy, raw materials, and others must be acknowledged, if only to forestall unreasonable expectations of and for management.*[51]

In fact, after reviewing research evidence that 14 of Peters and Waterman's "excellent" companies had fallen on hard times by 1984, *Business Week* observed:

7 Identify and explain the nature of at least four of Thomas J. Peters and Robert H. Waterman Jr.'s eight attributes of excellence.

Table 2.3

Peters and Waterman's Eight Attributes of Excellence

Attributes of excellence	Key indicators
1. A bias for action	Small-scale, easily managed experiments to build knowledge, interest, and commitment.
	Managers stay visible and personally involved in all areas through active, informal communication and spontaneous MBWA ("management by wandering around").
2. Close to the customer	Customer satisfaction is practically an obsession.
	Input from customers is sought throughout the design/production/marketing cycle.
3. Autonomy and entrepreneurship	Risk taking is encouraged; failure is tolerated.
	Innovators are encouraged to "champion" their pet projects to see them through to completion.
	Flexible structure permits the formation of "skunk works" (small teams of zealous innovators working on a special project).
	Lots of creative "swings" are encouraged to ensure some "home runs" (successful products).
4. Productivity through people	Individuals are treated with respect and dignity.
	Enthusiasm, trust, and a family feeling are fostered.
	People are encouraged to have fun while getting something meaningful accomplished.
	Work units are kept small and humane.
5. Hands-on, value driven	A clear company philosophy is disseminated and followed.
	Personal values are discussed openly, not buried.
	The organization's belief system is reinforced through frequently shared stories, myths, and legends.
	Leaders are positive role models, not "Do-as-I-say, not-as-I-do" authority figures.
6. Stick to the knitting	Management sticks to the business it knows best.
	Emphasis is on internal growth, not mergers.
7. Simple form, lean staff	Authority is decentralized as much as possible.
	Headquarters staffs are kept small; talent is pushed out to the field.
8. Simultaneous loose-tight properties	Tight overall strategic and financial control is counterbalanced by decentralized authority, autonomy, and opportunities for creativity.

Source: "Eight Attributes of Excellence" from *In Search of Excellence* by Thomas J. Peters and Robert H. Waterman Jr. Copyright © 1982 by Thomas J. Peters and Robert H. Waterman Jr. Reprinted by permission of HarperCollins Publishers, Inc.

One major lesson from all this is that the excellent companies of today will not necessarily be the excellent companies of tomorrow. But the more important lesson is that good management requires much more than following any one set of rules. In Search of Excellence *was a response to an era when management put too much emphasis on number-crunching. But companies can also get into trouble by overemphasizing Peters' and Waterman's principles.*[52]

Subsequent research has reinforced the foregoing criticisms of the excellence approach. Unlike Peters and Waterman, Michael Hitt and Duane Ireland conducted a *comparative* analysis of "excellent" companies and industry norms. Companies that satisfied all of Peters and Waterman's excellence criteria turned out to be no more effective than a random sample of *Fortune* 1000 companies.[53] This outcome prompted Hitt and Ireland to offer five tips for avoiding what they termed "the quick-fix mentality"[54] (see Table 2.4).

Lessons from the Excellence Approach

Certainly more than anything else, Peters and Waterman did a good job of reminding managers to pay closer attention to *basics* such as customers, employees, and new ideas. While reviewing their findings, they noted:

The project showed, more clearly than could have been hoped for, that the excellent companies were, above all, brilliant on the basics. Tools didn't substitute for thinking. Intellect didn't overpower wisdom. Analysis didn't impede action. Rather, these companies worked hard to keep things simple in a complex world. They persisted. They insisted on top quality. They fawned on their customers. They listened to their employees and treated them like adults. They allowed their innovative product or service "champions" long tethers. They allowed some chaos in return for quick action and regular experimentation.[55]

	Table 2.4
Our research suggests that practicing managers should embrace appealing ideas when appropriate, but anticipate that solutions typically are far more complex than the type suggested by Peters and Waterman's search for excellence. To avoid the quick-fix mentality, managers should: 1. Remain current with literature in the field, particularly with journals that translate research into practice. 2. Ensure that concepts applied are based on science or, at least, on some form of rigorous documentation, rather than purely on advocacy. 3. Be willing to examine and implement new concepts, but first do so using pilot tests with small units. 4. Be skeptical when simple solutions are offered; analyze them thoroughly. 5. Constantly anticipate the effects of current actions and events on future results.	**How to Avoid the Quick-Fix Mentality in Management**

Source: Michael A. Hitt and R. Duane Ireland, "Peters and Waterman Revisited: The Unended Quest for Excellence," *Academy of Management Executive*, vol. 2, no. 2, May 1987, p. 96. Reprinted by permission.

Management Wisdom: Beyond Quick Fixes

21

. . . if you look hard at the history of the Fortune 500 over the past 40 years, there emerges through all the static a set of golden management rules that have surviving power. They don't have labels—once you stick a name on something, it's fast on its way to becoming a flavor-of-the-month disappointment—but are broad management principles. They are (1) Management is a practice. (2) People are a resource. (3) Marketing and innovation are the key functions of a business. (4) Discover what you do well. (5) Quality pays for itself.

Source: Excerpted from Brian Dumaine, "Distilled Wisdom: Buddy, Can You Paradigm?" *Fortune* (May 15, 1995): 205.

Question: *What lesson does each of these broad management principles teach you?*

Although discussion of these basics may strike some as a tedious review of the obvious, it is precisely neglect of the basics that keeps many organizations and individuals from achieving excellence.[56]

Despite Peters and Waterman's subjective research methodology, they deserve credit for reminding managers of the importance of on-the-job experimentation. All the planning in the world cannot teach the practical lessons that one can learn by experimentally rearranging things and observing the results, trying an improved approach, observing, and so on.[57]

A concluding comment is in order to help put the foregoing historical overview into proper perspective. The theoretical tidiness of this chapter, although providing a useful conceptual framework for students of management, generally does not carry over to the practice of management. As the excellence approach makes clear, managers are, first and foremost, pragmatists. They use whatever works. Instead of faithfully adhering to a given school of management thought, successful managers tend to use a "mixed bag" approach. This chapter is a good starting point for you to begin building your own personally relevant and useful approach to management by blending theory, the experience and advice of others, and your own experience.

Summary

1. Management is an interdisciplinary and international field that has evolved in bits and pieces over the years. Six approaches to management theory are (1) the universal process approach, (2) the operational approach, (3) the behavioral approach, (4) the systems approach, (5) the contingency approach, and (6) the attributes of excellence approach. Useful lessons have been learned from each approach.

   Henry Fayol's universal approach assumes that all organizations, regardless of purpose or size, require the same management process. Furthermore, it assumes that this rational process can be reduced to separate functions and principles of management. The universal approach, the oldest of the various approaches, is still popular today.

2. Dedicated to promoting production efficiency and reducing waste, the operational approach has evolved from scientific management to operations management. Frederick W. Taylor, the father of scientific management, and his followers revolutionized industrial management through the use of standardization, time and motion study, selection and training, and pay incentives.

3. The quality advocates taught managers about the strategic importance of high-quality goods and services. Shewhart pioneered the use of *statistics* for quality control. Japan's Ishikawa emphasized *prevention* of defects in quality and drew management's attention to *internal* as well as external *customers*. Deming sparked the Japanese quality revolution with calls for *continuous improvement* of the entire

production process. Juran trained many U.S. managers to improve quality through *teamwork, partnerships with suppliers,* and *Pareto analysis* (the 80/20 rule). Feigen-baum developed the concept of *total quality control,* thus involving all business functions in the quest for quality. He believed that the *customer* determined quality. Crosby, a champion of *zero defects,* emphasized how costly poor-quality products could be.

4. Management has turned to the human factor in the human relations movement and organizational behavior. Emerging from such influences as unionization, the Hawthorne studies, and the philosophy of industrial humanism, the human rela-tions movement began as a concerted effort to make employees' needs a high management priority. Today, organizational behavior tries to identify the multiple determinants of job performance.

5. Advocates of the systems approach recommend that modern organizations be viewed as open systems. Open systems depend on the outside environment for survival, whereas closed systems do not. Chester I. Barnard stirred early interest in systems thinking in 1938 by suggesting that organizations are cooperative systems energized by communication. General systems theory, an interdiscipli-nary field based on the assumption that everything is systematically related, has identified a hierarchy of systems and has differentiated between closed and open systems. New directions in systems thinking are organizational learning and chaos theory.

6. A comparatively new approach to management thought is the contingency approach, which stresses situational appropriateness rather than universal princi-ples. The contingency approach is characterized by an open-system perspective, a practical research orientation, and a multivariate approach to research. Contin-gency thinking is a practical extension of more abstract systems thinking.

7. *In Search of Excellence,* Peters and Waterman's best-selling book, challenged managers to take a fresh, unconventional look at managing. They isolated eight attributes of excellence after studying many of the best-managed and most successful companies in America. Generally, the excellent companies were found to be relatively decentralized and value-driven organizations dedicated to humane treatment of employees, innovation, experimentation, and customer satisfaction. Critics of the excellence approach caution managers to avoid the quick-fix mentality, in which organizational problems and solutions are oversim-plified.

Terms to Understand

Universal process approach (p. 42)	System (p. 53)
Operational approach (p. 44)	General systems theory (p. 55)
Scientific management (p. 44)	Closed system (p. 55)
Operations management (p. 49)	Open system (p. 55)
Human relations movement (p. 49)	Contingency approach (p. 58)
Theory Y (p. 51)	Multivariate analysis (p. 59)
Organizational behavior (p. 52)	

Skills & Tools

Recommended Periodicals for Staying Current in the Field of Management

**Academic Journals
(with a research orientation)**

Academy of Management Journal
Academy of Management Review
Administrative Science Quarterly
Human Relations
Journal of Applied Psychology
Journal of Management
Journal of World Business
Nonprofit Management & Leadership

**Scholarly Journals
(with a practical orientation)**

Academy of Management Executive
Business Horizons
California Management Review
Harvard Business Review
National Productivity Review
Organizational Dynamics
Public Administration Review

**Practitioner Journals
(general audience)**

HR Magazine
Management Review
Personnel Journal
Supervision
Training

General Periodicals

Business Week
Canadian Business
The Economist
Fast Company
Forbes
Fortune
Industry Week
International Management (Europe)
Nation's Business
The Wall Street Journal
Wired (business with an attitude)

Practitioner Journals (special interest)

Black Enterprise
Business Ethics
Entrepreneur
Executive Female
Hispanic Business
Inc. (small business)
Macworld (Apple computer users)
Money (personal finance and investing)
Nonprofit World (not-for-profit organizations)
PC World (personal computing and Internet)
Public Management (public sector)
Purchasing
Technology Review (new technology)
Web Bound (Internet)
Working Mother (work/family issues)
Working Woman

Internet Exercises

1. **Managerial shortcuts to the information superhighway:** Busy managers typically cannot afford the luxury of spending hours surfing the Internet for needed information. Fortunately, Web sites have been built for managers who need good information quickly. Two useful ones are **www.ceoexpress.com** and **www.bizvillage.com.** Visit each of these sites and spend some time sampling their links. If you are presently a manager, how can these sites help you use the Internet more efficiently? Otherwise, put yourself in the place of a busy manager who needs to tap the power of the Internet. Think of this exercise as a comparison shopping trip for a good general business Internet site.

Learning Points: 1. Which site do you like better? Why? 2. Which site would you recommend to a parent or friend who is a manager? Why? *Note:* If you find a better general business Internet site, be sure to tell your instructor and friends. Useful new things pop up on the Web all the time.

2. **Check it out:** A growing segment of the U.S. population speaks Spanish. An excellent bilingual Web site is **www.quepasa.com.** At the home page, select either "in English" or "*en Español*" and then click on the main menu category "Business & Finance." This is a useful Internet tool for those learning to read and speak Spanish and for finding out what is happening in the Hispanic and Latino communities.

For updates to these exercises, visit our Web site (**www.hmco.com/college**).

Russia's New Management Style

Closing Case

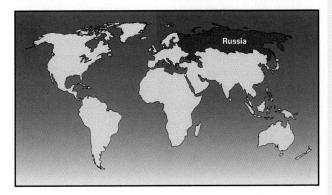

Moscow—The rise of Russian capitalism is giving birth to a uniquely Russian brand of business management.

Helping with the delivery is a small but growing cadre of Russian management consultants, homegrown counterparts to the horde of organizational experts who advise Corporate America.

But what Russian consultants are preaching isn't exactly what they teach at the Harvard Business School. In a country still reeling from the collapse of socialism, they're blending Western practices—such as Total Quality Management—with Russian techniques, including some inherited from Soviet days.

"We have our own ideas and our own theories, even though no one in the West knows about them," says Anatoli Levenchuk, director of the Institute for Commercial Engineering, a Russian consulting firm.

The idea that the Soviet era might yield useful management insights is startling, to say the least. The conventional view is that under communism, Russian managers were little more than glorified foremen, blindly obeying production plans handed down by the Soviet bureaucracy.

The truth is more complex. Most Soviet factories were inefficient nightmares, producing refrigerators that didn't refrigerate and washing machines that didn't wash. But the fact the system functioned at all is a tribute to the resourcefulness of Russian managers.

Source: Bill Montague, "Russia's New Management Style," *USA Today* (August 12, 1996): 7B. Copyright 1996, USA Today. Reprinted with permission.

"Given the realities of centralized planning, state monopoly and constant shortage, a remarkable number of Soviet enterprises produce usable, sophisticated products," economists Paul Lawrence and Charalambos Vlachoutsicos concluded in a 1990 study.

Communism also didn't prevent Russian managers from developing shrewd bargaining skills. Unworkable central plans forced them to craft elaborate barter deals to obtain crucial components. Just-in-time inventories were routine—out of necessity, not choice. Those survival skills have grown even sharper in the post-communist era, as managers have wrestled with the economic chaos, crime and corruption unleashed by the breakup of the Soviet Union.

But harnessing all that ingenuity to the profit motive hasn't been easy. Many Russian managers remain deeply suspicious of the free market. While some have become owners, most still believe their main loyalty should be to their workers and fellow managers, not to company shareholders.

Levenchuk is trying to change that mentality by stressing the cooperative aspects of capitalism. He encourages his clients to view suppliers, customers—even competitors—as potential strategic partners, to use the Western buzzword.

"We're trying to teach people that they can work together as a team," Levenchuk says.

His theory draws heavily on the work of Ronald Coase, a Nobel Prize–winning economist at the University of Chicago who emphasized the need to lower "transactional costs"—the social, legal and personal barriers that impede efficiency.

But Levenchuk also makes wide use of games and role-playing exercises developed in the 1970s by a Soviet sociologist, Georgi Shedrovitski.

"If anything, the need for such techniques was greater under socialism," Levenchuk says, "because the system itself was so inefficient."

Many Western analysts remain pessimistic about the possibility of converting Soviet-era managers into modern business executives. Bringing modern management to Russia, they say, will take time—and the rise of a new generation free of the psychological baggage of communism.

That process is happening, but slowly. "There is a cadre of trained executives, but they can't churn them out fast enough," says Phil Cronin, vice president in the Moscow office of A. T. Kearney, a U.S. consulting firm. "The pool of talent is still very small, relative to the size of the Russian economy."

Levenchuk is more optimistic. "We *can* change because our past does not define our future. And it will not define the future of our country."

FOR DISCUSSION

1. What does Henri Fayol's work tell Russian managers about making the transition from the old Soviet system to modern capitalism?

2. What advice would Mary Parker Follett probably give Russia's managers?

3. What advice about building successful businesses would Chester I. Barnard probably offer to Russian managers?

4. If you were asked to make a guest presentation to a group of Russian managers, which of the eight attributes of excellence in Table 2.3 would you urge them to focus on when making the transition from communism to capitalism? Why?

5. Do you think it is a good idea for Russian managers to blend Western management practices with Russian techniques? Explain.

The CHANGING ENVIRONMENT of MANAGEMENT

Diversity, Global Economy, and Technology

CHAPTER OBJECTIVES

When you finish studying this chapter, you should be able to

1 Identify and briefly highlight seven major changes shaping the twenty-first-century workplace.

2 Summarize the demographics of the new workforce.

3 Define the term *managing diversity* and explain why it is particularly important today.

4 Discuss how the changing political-legal environment is affecting the practice of management.

5 Discuss why business cycles and the global economy are vital economic considerations for modern managers.

6 Describe the three-step innovation process and define the term *intrapreneur.*

"EARLY IDENTIFICATION OF EMERGING TRENDS WILL ALLOW...ORGANIZATIONS TO PREPARE APPROPRIATE RESPONSES AND, IN SOME CASES, MAY EVEN ENABLE THOSE WITH INTERESTS AFFECTED BY A TREND TO INFLUENCE ITS DEVELOPMENT."

maureen minehan

A "No Limits" Attitude Helped Carleton (Carly) Fiorina Reach the Top

No doubt about it: Carly Fiorina runs a good meeting. Six months ago, a small group of executives at Lucent Technologies gathered in her office to celebrate a third straight year of record profits. "So, where do we go from here?" she asked, amid the good-natured banter. "I know you won't want to rest on your laurels." It was a telling demonstration of her leadership, according to one of those present. The boss didn't say, "Great job, but I'm not satisfied." Instead, it was: "You're wonderful, and I know you want to do even better."

Hewlett-Packard, struggling to find its way in the Internet age, also wants to "do even better." That's why it snared Fiorina . . . [in 1999] to be its new chief executive. She was already one of the most powerful women in corporate America, president of the global services group at Lucent, the $30 billion telecom giant. But her appointment as head of mighty HP, the world's second-largest computermaker and the 13th-biggest company in the country, puts her into a league of her own. No wonder her face was all over the business pages: the 44-year-old exec is the first woman to head a Fortune 100 company, and one of only three in the entire top 500. Many hailed the news as a victory for equal opportunity in the workplace; Fiorina herself shrugged off the gender question. Women, she told reporters bluntly, face "no limits whatsoever. There is not a glass ceiling."

Right or not, Fiorina clearly has never been bounded by limits. The iconoclastic daughter of an abstract painter and a California judge, she graduated from Stanford with a degree in medieval history, dropped out of law school after concluding she was averse to precedents, then began working her way through the male-dominated ranks of AT&T. Along the way she went through one marriage, taught English in Italy, picked up business degrees from the University of Maryland and MIT and then married a fellow AT&Ter, with whom she has raised two stepdaughters and who happily stays home as a "house husband" and volunteer firefighter. At Lucent, she was legendary for her crushing travel schedule, as well as her deft human touch—late-night phone calls to those burning the midnight oil, flowers and balloons for jobs well done. "She has a gift for taking account of people's very diverse desires, goals and abilities," says Dan Plunkett at Delta Consulting Group, who worked with her at Lucent. "In her mind, there is no space between defining a problem and solving it."

For Hewlett-Packard, her arrival marks a watershed. Never before has it filled a top spot from outside. (The runner-up for the job, incidentally, was another woman at the company.) But transforming Hewlett-Packard from a slow-moving engineering company into a nimble Internet player will require more than aggressive marketing, Fiorina's forte at Lucent. Getting new products to market quickly will take a wholesale change in culture. For Fiorina, that's another mold to be broken.

Source: Michael Meyer, "In a League of Her Own," from *Newsweek* (August 2, 1999). © 1999 Newsweek Inc. All rights reserved. Reprinted by permission.

Now that Carly Fiorina has reached the top rung of the corporate ladder, she will face a steady diet of change. Nothing new for her.[1] Like many successful managers today, Fiorina has learned to do more than merely cope with change; she has learned to thrive on it. Consequently, present and future managers need to be aware of *how* things are changing in the world around them.

Ignoring the impact of general environmental factors on management makes about as much sense as ignoring the effects of weather and road conditions on high-speed driving. The general environment of management includes social, political-legal, economic, and technological dimensions. Changes in each area present managers with unique opportunities and obstacles that will shape not only the organization's strategic

Figure 3.1

What Managers Want from Today's Employees

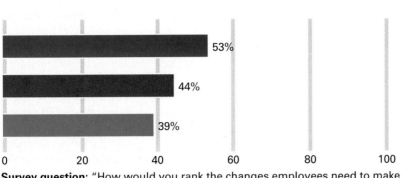

Survey question: "How would you rank the changes employees need to make to achieve today's business goals?"
(Ranking procedure caused responses to total more than 100%)

▓ Adaptability/openness to change
▓ More teamwork
▓ Ability to see the "Big Picture"

Source: Data adapted from "HR Data Files," *HRMagazine*, 40 (June 1995): 65.

direction but also the course of daily operations. This challenge requires forward-thinking managers who can handle change and see the greater scheme of things. A survey of American Management Association members underscored the need for improvement in these areas. Managers were asked to rank changes employees need to make to achieve today's business goals. As illustrated in Figure 3.1, *adaptability and openness to change* ranked number one, while *ability to see the big picture* came in third. *Teamwork*, discussed in Chapter 14 and elsewhere in this book, finished a strong second.

The purpose of this chapter, then, is to prepare you for constant change and help you see the big picture by identifying key themes in the changing environment of management.

The Twenty-First-Century Workplace: Seven Major Changes

Predictions about everything under the sun are plentiful with the dawn of the new millennium. Our immediate concern is how the workplace will change in the twenty-first century. After all, the workplace is where you will spend half (or more) of your nonsleep life in the years to come. Management consultant and futurist Robert Barner foresees seven major changes that promise to challenge managers and employees.[2] As a departure point for this chapter, let us highlight each of Barner's major workplace changes.

1. *The virtual organization.* Thanks to modern telecommunications and computer network technology, centralized workplaces where employees gather each workday for face-to-face interaction are being dispersed. Yes, many people will continue to

commute to factories and offices. But many more will set up shop *wherever* they are—on a plane, at home, in a customer's office, or in a moving vehicle—and communicate with their coworkers via cellular phones, e-mail, fax machines, and personal digital assistants. Virtual organizations will be faster and more flexible. Meanwhile, they will present managers with new challenges regarding information overload, organization structure, teamwork, communication, decision making, and career development. Barner notes: "To meet these challenges, workers will need to develop skills in network-based decision making, including the use of such specialized tools as group-decision-support software."[3]

2. *The just-in-time workforce.* The trends toward using part-time or temporary workers and outsourcing organizational tasks and functions to other companies will pick up speed. But how can part-time employees be motivated to do their best and be committed employees? Human resource practices such as hiring, training, and compensation will need to be refined.

3. *The ascendancy of knowledge workers.* We are moving from an industrial economy to an information economy. Information-age technologies require sharp minds, not strong backs. Lifelong learning will be the key to fighting the rapid obsolescence of technical skills. According to Barner, "The rapid growth of knowledge workers will require organizations to rethink their traditional approaches to directing, coaching, and motivating employees." Instead of doing nothing but manage, ". . . managers will be expected to contribute technical expertise to their jobs and to be willing to roll up their sleeves and contribute when necessary."[4]

4. *Computerized coaching and electronic monitoring.* Computers will continue to be a mixed blessing in the workplace. Computer-assisted learning, decision making, and performance monitoring can trim costs and boost productivity. However, we can anticipate a backlash from employees who feel manipulated and deprived of their privacy rights.

1 Identify and briefly highlight seven major changes shaping the twenty-first-century workplace.

What do you see here? Someone at work in a factory? Production engineers at DaimlerChrysler's factory in Indiana see much more: a productive unit consisting of a skilled employee and computer-controlled tools. The benefits of this futuristic marriage of human and technology are greater speed, less waste, and higher quality.

5. *The growth of worker diversity.* Growing minority and immigrant populations will contribute to increased racial and ethnic diversity in North America. A multicultural and multilingual workforce will slowly evolve as managers learn how to compete in the global economy where cross-cultural dealings are constant. Products and services will be customized to accommodate individual tastes. Women and minorities will occupy a greater proportion of executive positions. Labor unions will attempt to exploit the proliferation of special-interest groups and technology-based grievances.

6. *The aging workforce.* As the leading edge of the post–World War II baby-boom generation reaches retirement age, our preoccupation with youth is giving way to greater sophistication, realism, and responsibility. College education is no longer just for the young. Older workers will be viewed as a vital and reliable economic resource. Attempts will be made to reverse the trend toward early retirement in the United States as employees pay more into the Social Security retirement system, while collecting less at an older age.

7. *The birth of the dynamic workforce.* Information-age managers will question traditional assumptions about employees, organizations, competitors, and customers. Boundaries between the private (business) and public (government) sectors will blur as social problems such as educational reform and child care are tackled by business leaders. Whole new industries, such as the one surrounding the Internet, will emerge. As Barner sees it: "managers will be increasingly judged on their ability to identify and implement improvements and to encourage innovative thinking from team members, while professionals will be judged on their ability to adapt quickly to widely different work environments."[5] Rapid redeployment of employees from one project team to another will be the norm.

These seven major changes promise to reshape our world significantly, both for better and for worse. Whether one likes or dislikes them is another matter. Progressive managers must heed them as early warning signals of change in their social, political-legal, economic, and technological environments.

3A

Calling All Optimists!

The United States will elect an African American president and people routinely will live past 100 in the twenty-first century, Americans predict. But they also say a series of major problems, from crime and terrorism to violations of personal privacy and freedom, will get worse.

A *USA Today* poll focused on the future finds that a 53% majority say they're optimistic that the quality of life for average Americans will be better by 2025.

But the survey shows a mixture of high hopes and deep pessimism in predictions about personal lives, social trends, international relations and the future of the Earth.

Source: Excerpted from Susan Page, "Americans Expect Good, Bad and Catastrophic," *USA Today* (October 13, 1998): 1A.

Questions: *Globally and nationally, what do you see happening by 2025? Are you optimistic about your personal future? Explain.*

For further information about the interactive annotations in this chapter, visit our Web site (**www.hmco.com/college**).

The Social Environment

According to sociologists, society is the product of a constant struggle between the forces of stability and change. Cooperation promotes stability, whereas conflict and competition upset the status quo. The net result is an ever-changing society. Keeping this perspective in mind, we shall discuss four important dimensions of the social environment: demographics, the new social contract, inequalities, and managing diversity. Each presents managers with unique challenges.

Demographics of the New Workforce

demographics *statistical profiles of population changes*

2 Summarize the demographics of the new workforce.

Demographics—statistical profiles of population characteristics—are a valuable planning tool for managers. Foresighted managers who study demographics can make appropriate adjustments in their human resources and marketing plans. Selected demographic shifts reshaping the U.S. workforce are presented in Figure 3.2. (Other countries have their own demographic trends.) The projections in Figure 3.2 are not "blue sky" numbers. They are based on people already born, more than two-thirds of whom are presently working. In short, the U.S. workforce is getting older, more diverse, and increasingly female.

Needed: Remedial Education.   The U.S. labor force is growing much more slowly between 1996 and 2006 than it did between 1976 and 1986, when postwar baby boomers were flooding the job market.[6] This trend foretells possible labor shortages in the near term. The picture for employers grows worse when the issue of labor force *quality* is put on the table. In the United States, the numbers are not encouraging. At present, the U.S. workforce is at a competitive disadvantage globally because of deficient reading, writing, science, and basic math skills. According to the American Management Association, "36% of job applicants failed some version of a basic-skills test"[7] in 1998, sharply up from 19 percent in 1997.

Experts say about 20 percent of working adults in the United States are *functionally illiterate*, which means that they have difficulty with basic life skills such as reading a newspaper, completing a job application, or interpreting a bus schedule. In other words, 23 to 27 million U.S. workers could not comprehend the paragraph you are now reading. Another 12 million would struggle to do so.[8] Consequently, many businesses,

Andy Grove (seated in the middle), the legendary chairman of Intel, is a strong advocate of life-long learning. While performing his executive chores at the computer chip giant, he has penned a couple of best-selling books on management. At this recent gathering of industry heavyweights in Sun Valley, Idaho, Grove took time to tutor a group of CEOs and their spouses on personal computer technology.

Figure 3.2

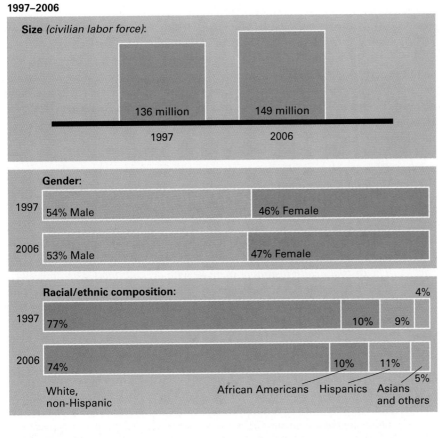

1997–2006

Size *(civilian labor force)*:

136 million — 1997
149 million — 2006

Gender:

1997 54% Male   46% Female
2006 53% Male   47% Female

Racial/ethnic composition:

1997 77%   10% 9%   4%
2006 74%   10% 11% 5%

White, non-Hispanic   African Americans   Hispanics   Asians and others

1990–2005

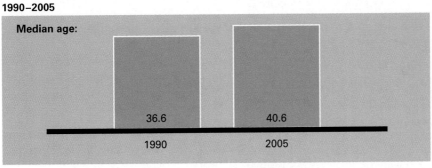

Median age:

36.6 — 1990
40.6 — 2005

Sources: Data from U.S. Bureau of Labor Statistics, September 1999 (**stats.bls.gov/emplab1.htm**); and from U.S. Bureau of Labor Statistics, *Occupational Outlook Handbook,* 1992–93 edition, pp. 8–9.

often in partnership with local schools and colleges, have launched remedial education programs.[9] A *Training* magazine survey of 1,456 companies with 100 or more employees found a broad corporate commitment to remedial education: 47 percent taught basic math/arithmetic; 46 percent taught English as a second language; 40 percent taught writing; and 38 percent taught reading.[10] These remedial programs typically involve an intensive schedule of small group sessions emphasizing practical, work-related instruction in reading, writing, and basic math. Knowledge is the entry ticket to today's computerized service economy.

Myths About Older Workers.   The U.S. workforce is getting older.[11] But how old is old? According to a nationwide survey of 2,503 Americans between the ages of 18 and 75, the answer depends on how old you are. "Among those over 65, only 8 percent think of people under 65 as old, while 30 percent of those under 25 say 'old' is anywhere from 40 to 64."[12] Older workers, defined by the U.S. Department of Labor as those aged 55 and up, tend to be burdened by a negative image in America's youth-oriented culture.[13] Researchers have identified and disproved five stubborn myths about older workers:

Myth: *Older workers are less productive than the average worker.*

Fact: *Research shows that productivity does not decline with a worker's age. Older employees perform as well as younger workers in most jobs. Moreover, older workers meet the productivity expectations. . . .*

Myth: *The costs of employee benefits outweigh any possible gain from hiring older workers.*

Fact: *The costs of health insurance increase with age, but most other fringe benefits do not since they are tied to length of service and level of salary. A study at The Travelers Companies found that it was not safe to assume that older workers cost more or less than younger workers. . . .*

Myth: *Older workers are prone to frequent absences because of age-related infirmities and above-average rates of sickness.*

Fact: *Data show that workers age 65 and over have attendance records that are equal to or better than most other age groups of workers. Older people who are not working may have dropped out of the workforce because of their health. Older workers who stay in the labor force may well represent a self-selected healthier group of older people.*

Myth: *Older workers have an unacceptably high rate of accidents at work.*

Fact: *Data show that older workers account for only 9.7 percent of all workplace injuries while they make up 13.6 percent of the labor force. . . .*

Myth: *Older workers are unwilling to learn new jobs and [are] inflexible about the hours they will work.*

Fact: *The truth depends on the individual. Studies of older employees' interest in alternative work arrangements found that many were interested in altering their work hours and their jobs. They were particularly interested in part-time work.*[14]

Enlightened employers view older workers as an underutilized and valuable resource in an aging society facing a labor shortage. Like all employees, older workers need to be managed according to their individual abilities, not as members of a demographic group.

3B

What Is Your Attitude Toward Older Workers?

Research Insight: In a study of 179 employees in the southeastern United States, researchers made the following discovery. The more younger employees interacted with older workers (50 and older), the more *positively* they perceived their older coworkers. So instead of familiarity breeding contempt, familiarity bred respect.

Source: Data from Barbara L. Hassell and Pamela L. Perrewe, "An Examination of Beliefs About Older Workers: Do Stereotypes Still Exist?", *Journal of Organizational Behavior*, 16 (September 1995): 457–468.

Questions: *What are your feelings about older employees? Do these feelings reflect cultural stereotypes or personal experience? How has firsthand experience with older workers affected your attitude toward them?*

A New Social Contract Between Employer and Employee

Between World War II and the 1970s there was an implicit cultural agreement, a social contract, in the United States between employers and employees: "Be loyal to the company and the company will take care of you until retirement." But then the 1980s brought restructuring, downsizing, and layoffs. Between 1989 and 1996, major U.S. companies laid off more than 3 million employees.[15] The traditional social contract between employers and employees had been broken. In its place is a new social contract, framed in these terms:

> *In short, the rules of the game have changed, and they go something like this: Your career depends on you, and you had better work at increasing your own long-term value, because nobody is going to do it for you. Employers, in turn, have accepted this reality: In the new marketplace for talent, we must provide opportunities, resources, and rewards for the continual development of our workforce or risk losing our greatest competitive asset.*[16]

Thus, the **new social contract** is based not on the notion of lifetime employment with a single employer but rather on shorter-term relationships of convenience and mutual benefit.[17] The senior vice president of human resources at AT&T, Harold Burlingame, put it more bluntly:

new social contract *assumption that employer-employee relationship will be a shorter-term one based on convenience and mutual benefit, rather than for life*

> *There was a time when someone would come to the front door of AT&T and see an invisible sign that said,* AT&T: A JOB FOR LIFE. . . . *That's over. Now it's a shared kind of thing. Come to us. We'll invest in you, and you invest in us. Together, we'll face the market, and the degree to which we succeed will determine how things work out.*[18]

Nagging Inequalities in the Workplace

Can the United States achieve full and lasting international competitiveness if a large proportion of its workforce suffers nagging inequalities?[19] Probably not. Unfortunately, women, minorities, and part-timers often encounter barriers in the workplace. Let us open our discussion by focusing on women because their plight is shared by all minorities to varying degrees.

Under the Glass Ceiling. As a large and influential minority, women are demanding—and getting—a greater share of workplace opportunities and rewards. Women occupy over 46 percent of the managerial and administrative positions in the U.S. civilian workforce, as documented in Chapter 1 (see Figure 1.7). But a large inequity remains. In 1999, the median weekly salary for those women managers was $659, compared with $954 for their male counterparts (a 31 percent shortfall).[20] Across all job categories, the same sort of gender pay gap persists (see Figure 3.3). As the trend line in Figure 3.3 indicates, it is appropriate to characterize the male-female pay gap in the United States as *slowly shrinking but still large.* Comparatively well-paid men can grasp the significance of the gender wage gap by pondering the impact on their standard of living of a 23.3 percent pay cut. Moreover, men who share household expenses with a woman wage earner are also penalized by the gender wage gap.

In addition to suffering a wage gap, women (and other minorities) bump up against the so-called glass ceiling when climbing the managerial ladder.[21] "The **glass ceiling** is a concept popularized in the 1980s to describe a barrier so subtle that it is transparent, yet so strong that it prevents women and minorities from moving up in the management hierarchy."[22] It is not unique to the United States.

glass ceiling *the transparent but strong barrier keeping women and minorities from moving up the management ladder*

3C

Back to the Opening Case

Carly Fiorina certainly doesn't shy away from controversy. Upon being named CEO of computer maker Hewlett-Packard, she declared "There is not a glass ceiling."

Question: Does her comment help or hinder women's progress toward equal opportunity and pay? Explain.

Consider the situation as recently as early 2000:

- The *Fortune* 500, America's largest corporations, were headed by 497 men and 3 women (Hewlett-Packard's Carly Fiorina; Avon Products' Andrea Jung; and Marion Sandler, co-CEO of Golden West Financial).
- African Americans and Hispanics combined occupied fewer than 2 percent of executive positions.[23] Two African Americans headed *Fortune* 500 companies (Franklin Raines, CEO of financial giant Fannie Mae; and Maytag CEO Lloyd D. Ward. Kenneth I. Chenault is scheduled to become CEO of American Express in 2001).
- There were "only 63 women (2.7) percent among the 2,320 top-earning corporate officers in *Fortune* 500 companies."[24]
- As *Fortune* magazine reported in 1998, ". . . in Europe and Asia, the ceiling may as well be concrete. In Britain, women hold a mere 5% of board seats in its top 200 companies."[25]

Why is there a glass ceiling? According to *Working Woman* magazine, women are being held back by "the lingering perception of women as outsiders, exclusion from informal networks, male stereotyping and lack of experience."[26]

Another force is also at work here, siphoning off some of the best female executive talent part way up the corporate ladder. Many women are leaving the corporate ranks to start their own businesses. By 1999, the 9.1 million U.S. businesses (38 percent of the total) owned by women generated almost $4 trillion dollars in annual revenue.[27]

Figure 3.3

The Persistent Gender Pay Gap in the United States

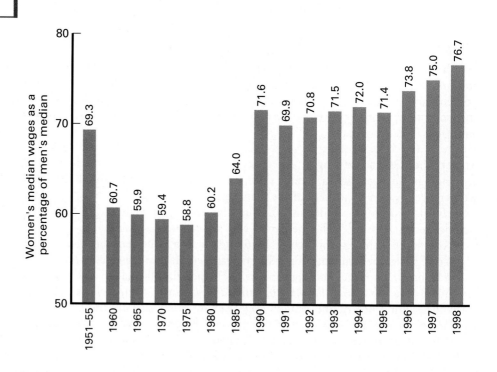

Source: Marc Adams, "Fair and Square," *HRMagazine*, 44 (May 1999): 44. Reprinted with the permission of *HRMagazine*, published by the Society for Human Resource Management, Alexandria, Virginia.

Continuing Pressure for Equal Opportunity.   Persistent inequality between whites and blacks is underscored by the fact that unemployment among blacks has been more than twice that for whites in recent years. This, despite a strong economy and low unemployment. *Black Enterprise* pointed out another lopsided situation.

> *Thanks to the ringing endorsements of superstar athletes and hip-hop fashion statements of black entertainers, African-Americans accounted for 22.6 percent of the $2.7 billion basketball shoe market, according to American Sports Data Inc. of Hartsdale, N.Y.*
>
> *Yet, best estimates are that blacks represent less than 3 percent of the industry's professional work force nationwide.*[28]

Women, African Amerians, Hispanics, Native Americans, the physically challenged, and other minorities who are overrepresented in either low-level, low-paying jobs or the unemployment line can be expected to press harder to become full partners in the world of work. Equal employment opportunity (EEO) and affirmative action are discussed in Chapter 11.

Part-Timer Promises and Problems.   An increasing percentage of the U.S. labor force is now made up of **contingent workers.** Estimates vary widely. A recently cited figure was 8 million (5.7 percent of the U.S. workforce).[29] This "just-in-time" or "flexible" workforce includes a diverse array of part-timers, temporary workers, and self-employed persons. "Their common denominator is that they do not have a long-term implicit contract with their ultimate employers, the purchasers of the labor and services they provide."[30] Employers are relying more on part-timers for two basic reasons. First, because they are paid at lower rates and typically do not receive employer-paid benefits, part-timers are much less costly to employ than full-time employees. Second, as a flexible workforce, they can be let go when times are bad, without the usual repercussions of a general layoff.

contingent workers *part-timers and other employees who do not have a long-term implicit contract with their ultimate employers*

On the down side, research indicates that part-time employees tend to have more negative work attitudes than their full-time coworkers. In addition, part-timers express less organizational loyalty and quit more readily than full-timers.[31] Also, critics warn of the risk of creating a permanent underclass of employees. Indeed, health insurance and retirement benefits are a rarity for contingent workers. While some highly skilled professionals enjoy good pay and greater freedom by working part-time, most part-timers do not.[32]

> *. . . the fact is that contingent work dooms a great many people to a much lower standard of living than they enjoyed as core workers. Even discounting the lower wages that many of them earn and the fact that they have no fringe benefits, such as health care or disability insurance, to buoy them in case of disaster, the very precariousness of their work situation makes it hard for them to get ahead. A low-income worker, for instance, will find it especially hard to qualify for a home loan if he is employed on a contingent basis, subject to layoff at any time.*[33]

The plight of part-timers promises to become a major social and political issue worldwide in the years to come.[34]

Is the Software King Playing Hardball with Its Temps?

3D

Microsoft is perhaps the leading practitioner of the trend, employing about 5,000 temps, including 1,500 long-term ones, who have worked for the software colossus for at least a year. These temps work next to Microsoft's 17,000 permanent employees.

Some prefer the flexibility and the higher take-home pay that temp status affords, but many assail temping as a back-door way to create a two-tier workforce. . . .

"It's a system of having two classes of people and instilling fear and inferiority and loathing," said Rebecca Hughes, who was a temp at Microsoft for three years, helping edit its CD-ROM on health care.

With work lives strung together by three-month contracts, some temps have worked at Microsoft for more than five years and have seized on an awkward term to describe their awkward status: permatemps.

Source: Excerpted from Steven Greenhouse, "Debate Swirls Around Hiring Temps," *The Arizona Republic* (April 5, 1998): D11.

Question: *Is this just good business or an unethical labor practice? Explain.*

Managing Diversity

The United States, a nation of immigrants, is becoming even more racially and ethnically diverse. The evidence is compelling:

- Out of every 100 new U.S. residents, 64 are native born and 34 are *legal* immigrants.[35]
- "By the year 2005, Latinos are projected to be the largest minority in the country, passing non-Hispanic blacks for the first time. By 2050, nearly one quarter of the population will be Latino."[36]
- "Los Angeles is now the second largest Spanish-speaking city in the world, after Mexico City, before Madrid and Barcelona."[37]

3 **Define the term** *managing diversity* **and explain why it is particularly important today.**

Accordingly, the U.S. workforce is becoming more culturally diverse. For example, the employees at some Marriott Hotels speak 30 different languages.[38] Some Americans decry what they consider to be an invasion of "their" national and organizational "territories." But many others realize that America's immigrants and minorities have always been a vitalizing, creative, hardworking force.[39] Progressive organizations are taking steps to better accommodate and more fully utilize America's more diverse workforce. **Managing diversity** is the process of creating an organizational culture that enables *all* employees, including women and minorities, to realize their full potential.[40]

managing diversity *process of helping all employees, including women and minorities, reach their full potential*

More than EEO.   Managing diversity builds upon equal employment opportunity (EEO) and affirmative action programs (discussed in Chapter 11). EEO and affirmative action are necessary to get more women and minorities into the workplace. But getting them in is not enough. Comprehensive diversity programs are needed to create more *flexible* organizations where *everyone* has a fair chance to thrive and succeed.[41] These programs have to include white males who have sometimes felt slighted or ignored by EEO and affirmative action; they, too, have individual differences (opinions, lifestyles, age, and schedules) that deserve fair accommodation. Managing diversity requires many of us to adjust our thinking. According to sociologist Jack McDevitt, "We don't want to have as a goal just tolerating people. We have to *value* them."[42] In addition to being the ethical course of action, managing diversity is a necessity; a nation cannot waste human potential and remain globally competitive.

Promising Beginnings.   Among the diversity programs in use today are:

- Teaching English as a second language.
- Creating mentor programs (an experienced employee coaches and sponsors a newcomer).
- Providing immigration assistance.
- Fostering the development of support groups for minorities.
- Training minorities for managerial positions.
- Training managers to value and skillfully manage diversity.
- Actively recruiting minorities.[43]

The scope of managing diversity is limited only by management's depth of commitment and imagination.[44] For example, a supervisor learns sign language to communicate with a hearing-impaired employee. Or a married male manager attends a diversity workshop and becomes aware of the difficulties of being a single working mother. Perhaps a younger manager's age bias is blunted after reading a research report documenting that older employees tend to be absent less often and have lower accident rates than younger ones.[45] Maybe other companies begin to follow Corning's diversity policy, whereby "new employees are no longer encouraged to adopt the dress, style, and social activities of the white male majority."[46]

The Political-Legal Environment

In its broadest terms, *politics* is the art (or science) of public influence and control. Laws are an outcome of the political process that differentiate good and bad conduct. An orderly political process is necessary because modern society is the product of an evolving consensus among diverse individuals and groups, often with conflicting interests and objectives. Although the list of special-interest groups is long and still growing, not everyone can have his or her own way. The political system tries to balance competing interests in a generally acceptable manner.

Ideally, elected officials pass laws that, when enforced, control individual and collective conduct for the general good. Unfortunately, as we all know, variables such as hollow campaign promises, illegal campaign financing, and voter apathy throw sand into a democracy's political gears. A prime example is Russia's experiment with democracy. In its 1993 multiparty election, the first since 1917, the combination of wild promises and low voter turnout helped give control of its Parliament to radical antireformers.[47] Managers, as both citizens and caretakers of socially, politically, and economically powerful organizations, have a large stake in the political-legal environment. Two key pressure points for managers in this area are the politicization of management and increased personal legal accountability.

4 **Discuss how the changing political-legal environment is affecting the practice of management.**

The Politicization of Management

Prepared or not and willing or not, today's managers often find themselves embroiled in issues with clearly political overtones.[48] (See The Global Manager.) Just ask Walt Disney Company. In 1994 Disney abandoned plans to build a history-oriented theme park in Virginia in the face of public outcry about dishonoring nearby Civil War battlefields.[49] Another political bombshell exploded in 1996. "The Southern Baptist Convention, 16 million members strong, threatened ... to boycott Walt Disney's parks, movies and products to protest Disney's departure from its 'family-values image.' The chief complaint: Disney gives health benefits to companions of gay employees."[50] This time, Disney did not give in to pressure. Disney's official response: "We question any group that demands that we deprive people of health benefits."[51] This sort of political pressure has spurred the growth of a practice called *issues management*.

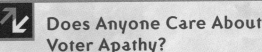

Does Anyone Care About Voter Apathy?   3E

For the November 1998 congressional and state elections in the United States, "turnout among first-time voters ages 18–19 was only about 11%. The rate was 15% among the broader age group 18–24.... Total turnout was put at 36.06%, the lowest since 1942, when millions of Americans were overseas fighting in World War II."

Source: "Voter Apathy," *USA Today* (February 10, 1999): 11A.

Questions: *Why is voter apathy a problem in a democracy? Why do young people have such a dismal voting record? What needs to be done to increase voter turnout?*

issues management
ongoing process of identifying, evaluating, and responding to important social and political issues

Issues Management.   **Issues management** (IM) is defined as the ongoing organizational process of identifying, evaluating, and responding to relevant and important social and political issues. According to a pair of experts on the subject:

> *The purpose of IM is twofold. First, it attempts to minimize "surprises" which accompany social and political change by serving as an early warning system for potential environment threats and opportunities. IM analyzes the past development of an issue and assesses its importance for the firm. Second, IM attempts to prompt more systematic and effective responses to particular issues by serving as a coordinating and integrating force within the corporation. Once the issue has been analyzed, IM constructs alternative responses to deal with competing internal and external demands.*[52]

IM is not an exact science. It has been carried out in various ways in the name of strategic planning, public relations, community affairs, and corporate communications, among others. IM's main contribution to good management is its emphasis on systematic preparedness for social and political action. With this background in mind, let us turn our attention to three general political responses and four specific political strategies.

General Political Responses.   The three general political responses available to management can be plotted on a continuum, as illustrated in Figure 3.4. Managers who are politically inactive occupy the middle neutral zone and have a "wait and see" attitude. But few managers today can afford the luxury of a neutral political stance. Those on the extreme left of the continuum are politically active in defending the status quo. In contrast, politically active managers on the right end of the continuum try to identify and respond to emerging public wishes.

Although the companies on this banner were not responsible for the accidental bombing of the Chinese embassy in Belgrade by NATO jets in 1999, they were a handy target for angry protesters in Beijing. Like it or not and ready or not, managers of highly visible multinational companies often find themselves embroiled in political and legal issues and conflicts. They need to be vigilant to avoid being caught off guard.

The Global Manager

Watch Out for Legal Traps in a Wired World

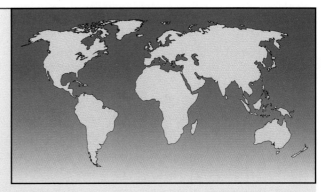

If your company is hooked up to the Internet, it has automatically entered the international marketplace. Once there, language, culture and international legal issues become entwined. Issues that have no legal consequence for businesses in one country can be illegal in another. For example, let's assume that your company uses comparative advertising—the "We try harder" theme of Avis Rent-a-Car, for instance—or that an advertisement on your Web page has a tendency to incite racial hatred. Both would be banned in Germany, and your company could be in a legal bind for transmitting them. International legal disputes surrounding Internet commerce will increase tremendously over the next few years. Two steps can help you avoid these disputes: First, contact a lawyer familiar with Internet commerce and international cultural issues to determine what problems you may encounter because of a message's content and the technique used to convey it. Second, have the lawyer determine what technology is available to limit link-ups to the sites in question.

Source: Teresa Brady, "Internet Legal Watch: 'When in Rome, Do As the Romans . . .'" *Management Review*, 87 (March 1998): 7. Reprinted by permission of the author.

In recent years, more and more business managers have noticeably swung from being reactive to proactive. Why? In short, they view prompt action as a way to avoid additional governmental regulation. A program at 3M Company is illustrative.

> *Minnesota Mining & Manufacturing . . . [went] beyond the call of duty and government deadlines. For example, new federal regulations require[d] replacement or improvement by 1998 of underground storage tanks for liquids and gases. The company decided to comply by 1992 instead, and to have all tanks worldwide in compliance. Cost: more than $80 million. "Regulations are about to overwhelm us," says Robert Bringer, 3M staff vice president for environmental engineering and pollution control. "The only way we see to deal with that is to reduce the number of materials we emit that trigger regulation."*[53]

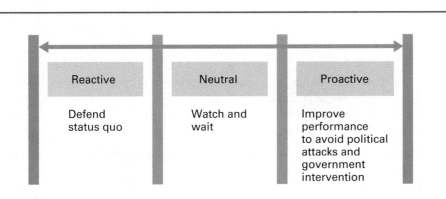

Figure 3.4

Management's Political Response Continuum

Bill Versus the Bullies

Microsoft cofounder Bill Gates, on the U.S Justice Department's prosecution of his company for monopolistic practices:

The people who compete with us are a lot more sophisticated about spending money on politicians than we are. I've been very naive. I thought just sitting here and writing great products was enough. I've been criticized for not realizing that's how the world works, and maybe I made a big mistake. I wasn't back there [in Washington] like they were. And now that we've done tiny things in that direction, the headlines are: "Microsoft Buying Influence." You're damned if you get involved and damned if you don't. It's an awful situation to be sued by the government. It certainly is bad for our reputation.

Source: Steve Hamm, "Gates on Bullies, Browsers—and the Future," *Business Week* (January 19, 1998): 67. Also see Joseph Nocera, "Spin City," *Fortune* (December 21, 1998): 159–166.

Question: *What advice would you give Bill Gates about dealing effectively with lawmakers and government regulators?*

Specific Political Strategies. Whether acting reactively or proactively, managers can employ four major strategies.[54]

1. *Campaign financing.* Although federal law prohibits U.S. corporations from backing a specific candidate or party with the firm's name, funds, or free labor, a legal alternative is available. Corporations can form political action committees (PACs) to solicit volunteer contributions from employees biannually for the support of preferred candidates and parties. Importantly, PACs are registered with the Federal Election Commission and are required to keep detailed and accurate records of receipts and expenditures. Some criticize corporate PACs for having too great an influence over federal politics. But legislators are reluctant to tamper with a funding mechanism that tends to favor those already in office.[55]
2. *Lobbying.* Historically, lobbying has been management's most popular and successful political strategy. Secret and informal meetings between hired representatives and key legislators in smoke-filled rooms have largely been replaced by a more forthright approach. Today, formal presentations by well-prepared company representatives are the preferred approach to lobbying for political support. Despite lobbying reform legislation from the U.S. Congress in 1995 in response to abuses, loop-holes, and weak penalties for inappropriate gifts, it is pretty much business as usual for corporate lobbyists.[56]
3. *Coalition building.* In a political environment of countless special-interest groups, managers are finding that coalitions built around common rallying points are required for political impact.
4. *Indirect lobbying.* Having learned a lesson from unions, business managers now appreciate the value of grassroots lobbying. Members of legislative bodies tend to be more responsive to the desires of their constituents than to those of individuals who vote in other districts. Employee and consumer letter-writing, telephone, and e-mail campaigns have proved effective. **Advocacy advertising,** the controversial practice of promoting a point of view along with a product or service, is another form of indirect lobbying that has grown in popularity in recent years.[57]

advocacy advertising
promoting a point of view along with a product or service

Increased Personal Legal Accountability

Recent changes in the political and legal climate have made it increasingly difficult for managers to take refuge in the bureaucratic shadows when a law has been broken. Managers in the United States who make illegal decisions stand a good chance of being held personally accountable in a court of law. Consider this recent news item:

Federal prosecutors are asking courts to give white-collar criminals longer stretches in tougher prisons for price-fixing and bid-rigging.

The average jail term for those crimes has more than doubled, from five months in 1994 to 11 months in 1996, the latest figures available show. . . .

"There's nothing like a jail sentence to send a clear message to corporate executives that antitrust crimes should not be treated as a cost of doing business," says Gary Spratling,

enforcement chief in Justice's antitrust division. "There's no accounting category or line on a corporate balance sheet to cover the president spending 11 months in jail."[58]

This shows a clear pattern of managers being held *personally responsible* for the illegal actions of their companies. The trend is spreading to other countries as well.

Political-Legal Implications for Management

Managers will continue to be forced into becoming more politically astute, whether they like it or not. Support appears to be growing for the idea that managers can and should try to shape the political climate in which they operate.[59] And the vigilant media and a wary public can be expected to keep a close eye on the form and substance of managerial politics to ensure that the public interest is served. Managers who abuse their political power and/or engage in criminal conduct while at work will increasingly be held accountable.

On the legal side, managers are attempting to curb the skyrocketing costs of litigation. U.S. businesses spend more than $20 billion annually on court-related legal fees.[60] One promising approach is the legal audit. A **legal audit** reviews all aspects of a firm's operations to pinpoint possible liabilities and other legal problems.[61] For example, a company's job application forms need to be carefully screened by the human resources department to eliminate any questions that could trigger a discriminatory hiring lawsuit. Another approach, called **alternative dispute resolution** (ADR), strives to curb courtroom costs by settling disagreements out of court through techniques such as arbitration and mediation.

> *The modern ADR phenomenon has led to much greater use of older methods such as arbitration and mediation, as well as the creation of many new methods such as mini-trial, summary jury trial, private judging, neutral evaluation, and regulatory negotiation. Variations and hybrids of these techniques are also commonly found today.*[62]

As a technical point, a third-party arbitrator makes a binding decision, whereas a mediator helps the parties reach their own agreement.

legal audit *review of all operations to pinpoint possible legal liabilities or problems*

alternative dispute resolution *avoiding courtroom battles by settling disputes with less costly methods, including arbitration and mediation*

The Economic Environment

As stated in Chapter 1, there is a close relationship between economics and management. Economics is the study of how scarce resources are used to create wealth and how that wealth is distributed. Managers, as trustees of our resource-consuming productive organizations, perform an essentially economic function.

Three aspects of the economic environment of management deserving special consideration are jobs, business cycles, and the global economy.

The Job Outlook in Today's Service Economy Where Education Counts

As in other important aspects of life, you have no guarantee of landing your dream job. However, as you move through college and into the labor force, one assumption is safe:

3G

Getting a Good Job

Chad Baldwin may not have done his career any favors studying liberal arts at Miami of Ohio. But between Spanish classes, he hung around the computer lab. When he won an internship at Chicago ad agency J. Walter Thompson, he used his summer to look into the future. "I figured interactive advertising was going to be a hot area," he concluded. The CD-ROM he produced for his senior project helped persuade J. Walter Thompson/*Interactive Enterprise* in San Francisco to snap him up at premium pay. Now Baldwin spends his days—and nights—designing the Web sites companies erect to tout themselves online. It's a job that didn't exist in an industry that didn't exist when the 22-year-old started college.

Source: Marc Levinson, "Not Everyone Is Downsizing," *Newsweek* (March 18, 1996): 44.

Questions: *What valuable lessons does Chad's experience teach you about finding a good job?*

you will probably end up with a service-producing job. Why? "By 2006 manufacturing jobs will account for just 12 percent of the [U.S.] labor force, down 5 percentage points in the last 20 years."[63]

The traditional notion of the service sector as a low-wage haven of nothing but hamburger flippers and janitors is no longer valid. Well-paid doctors, lawyers, airline pilots, engineers, scientists, consultants, and other professionals are all service-sector employees enjoying the fruits of a good education. According to the U.S. Bureau of Labor Statistics: "Occupations that require a bachelor's degree are projected to grow the fastest, nearly twice as fast as the average for all occupations. All of the 20 occupations with the highest earnings require at least a bachelor's degree. . . . Education is essential in getting a high paying job."[64]

Coping with Business Cycles

business cycle *the up-and-down movement of an economy's ability to generate wealth*

The **business cycle** is the up-and-down movement of an economy's ability to generate wealth; it has a predictable structure but variable timing. Historical economic data from industrialized economies show a clear pattern of

Meet Tracey A. Adams, an assistant vice president at Citibank, specializing in business and professional lending. Unlike her predecessors who sat in cushy offices and said yes or no to loan applicants, Adams serves her more than 100 clients on their turf. Her presentations and seminars in New York's North Bronx and Harlem areas help spawn real economic power where it is most needed. Aside from financing, she helps her clients get whatever it takes to be successful—such as business contacts, computers, and telephone service.

alternating expansions and recessions. In between have been peaks and troughs of varying magnitude and duration. According to economist Paul Samuelson, the four phases are like the changing seasons: "Each phase passes into the next. Each is characterized by different economic conditions: for example, during expansion we find that employment, production, prices, money, wages, interest rates, and profits are usually rising, with the reverse true in recession."[65]

5 Discuss why business cycles and the global economy are vital economic considerations for modern managers.

Cycle-Sensitive Decisions.   Important decisions depend on the ebb and flow of the business cycle (see Figure 3.5). These decisions include ordering inventory, borrowing funds, increasing staff, and spending capital for land, equipment, and energy. Decision making in preparation for a recession is especially difficult. Costs need to be cut, but not so deeply or in such places as to jeopardize the organization's mission or reputation. Delta Air Lines's experience is instructive:

> *In the last slump, Delta Air Lines tried to save money by serving pretzels rather than peanuts. Passengers hated it. One told a stewardess, "You're so cheap, you won't even spring for peanuts." It also sent the wrong signal to flight attendants, who assumed the airline was more interested in costs than service.*[66]

Delta, proud of its strong reputation for service, won't make that mistake again. Managers attempt to make the right decisions at the right time by responding appropriately to valid economic forecasts.

Benefiting from Economic Forecasts.   *Timing* is everything when it comes to making good cycle-sensitive decisions. Just as a baseball batter needs to start swinging before the ball reaches home plate, managers need to make appropriate cutbacks prior to the onset of a recession. Failure to do so, in the face of decreasing sales, leads to bloated inventories and idle productive resources—both costly situations. On the other hand, managers cannot afford to get caught short during a period of rapid expansion. Prices and wages rise sharply when everyone is purchasing inventories and

Figure 3.5

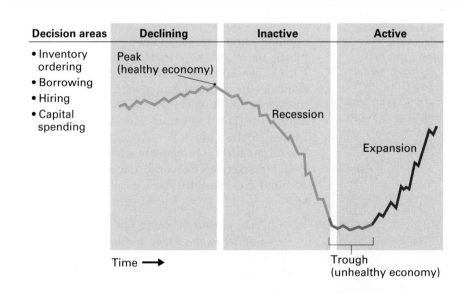

Business Cycles Affect Managerial Decisions

Decision areas	Declining	Inactive	Active
• Inventory ordering • Borrowing • Hiring • Capital spending	Peak (healthy economy)	Recession	Expansion

Time ➡

Trough (unhealthy economy)

hiring at the same time. The trick is to stay slightly ahead of the pack. This is where accurate economic forecasts are a necessity.

In view of the fact that Congress's economic advisers accurately predicted the U.S. economy's output only one-third of the time between 1980 and 1994,[67] economic forecasting has come under fire lately.[68] One wit chided economic forecasters by claiming they have predicted eight out of the last four recessions! How can managers get some value from the hundreds of economic forecasts they encounter each year?

A pair of respected forecasting experts recommends a *consensus approach*.[69] They urge managers to survey a wide variety of economic forecasts, taking the forecasters' track records into consideration, and to look for a consensus or average opinion. Cycle-sensitive decisions can then be made accordingly, and slavish adherence to a single forecast avoided. One sure formula for failure is naively to assume that the future will simply be a replication of the past. In spite of their imperfection, professional economic forecasts are better than no forecasts at all. One economist puts it this way: "Forecasters are very useful, in fact indispensable, because they give you plausible scenarios to help you think about the future in an organized way."[70]

The Challenge of a Global Economy

The global economy is expanding today as international trade increases. By 2006, according to U.S. Department of Labor projections, nearly 20 percent of America's economic output will be exported to other countries (slightly less than the amount expected to be imported).[71] Each of us is challenged to understand the workings and implications of the global economy better in light of its profound impact on our lives and work.

A Single Global Marketplace.   Money spent on imported Japanese cars, French perfumes, Colombian coffee, New Zealand meat and produce, German beers, and Italian shoes may be evidence of a global economy. Deeper analysis, however, reveals more profound changes. First, according to John Naisbitt and Patricia Aburdene's book *Megatrends 2000*, "The new global economy cannot be understood if it is thought to be merely more and more trade among 160 countries; it must be viewed as the world moving from trade among countries to a single economy. One economy. One marketplace."[72] Both the North American Free Trade Agreement (NAFTA) among Mexico, Canada, and the United States and the 134-nation World Trade Organization (WTO) represent steps toward that single global marketplace. Second, the size of the global economy has expanded dramatically. *Fortune* explains why:

> ... the commercial world has been swelled by the former Soviet empire, China, India, Indonesia, and much of Latin America—billions of people stepping out from behind political and economic walls. This is the most dramatic change in the geography of capitalism in history.[73]

Some See a Globalized Economy as a Threat   3H

When World Trade Organization (WTO) representatives met in Seattle in 1999, beginning a three-year program of trade talks, observers were stunned by the bloody street riots:

"There's never been an event in American history that has brought together so many disparate groups," said consumer activist Ralph Nader. . . . Disparate isn't the word; those on the streets included steelworkers, animal-rights activists, the Sisters of Perpetual Indulgence, Pat Buchanan, French makers of Roquefort cheese, anarchists, fans of a Free Tibet, students against sweatshopped sweatshirts, grandmas, and a fine turnout of local folk, too. When they had all gone home, America started to wonder what had brought them together, and what, if anything, Seattle meant for the future.

Source: Michael Elliott, "The New Radicals," *Newsweek* (December 13, 1999): 36.

Questions: *What are your feelings about a globalized economy? Explain. Will it likely impact your life positively or negatively? Explain.*

Globalization Is Personal.   Economic globalization is a huge concept, stretching the limits of the imagination. For instance, try to grasp what it means that more than $1 trillion moves through the global banking network in a single day![74] Ironically, globalization is also a very personal matter affecting where we work, how much we're paid, what we buy, and how much we pay. Let us explore two personal aspects of the global economy:

1. *Working for a foreign-owned company.* One of the most visible signs of a global economy is the worldwide trend toward foreign ownership. As *The Wall Street Journal* observed in 1993, "foreign-owned businesses employ 4.7 million people in the U.S., or 5.2 percent of U.S. employment."[75] Has the rapid growth of these figures since then been a positive or a negative? Recent research shows a positive impact on paychecks:

   Foreign direct investment into the U.S. has tripled over the past two years, leading to a heated debate over the pluses and minuses of foreign ownership. Do foreign companies set up low-paying operations in the U.S., or does foreign investment create new opportunities that benefit workers? . . .

   [Researchers] discovered that in Mexico, Venezuela, and the U.S., workers employed by foreign-owned businesses tend to have higher wages than other workers in the same industry.

   In the U.S., this wage differential comes to about 10 percent.[76]

2. *Meeting world standards.* One does not have to work for a foreign-owned company to be personally impacted by the global economy. Many people today complain of having to work harder for the same (or perhaps less) money. Whether they realize it or not, they are being squeezed by two global economic trends: higher quality and lower wages. Only companies striking the right balance between quality and costs can be globally competitive. For example, the 1,600 employees at Cargill's Schuyler, Nebraska, meatpacking plant enjoy good job security by doing a better job for less. "Japan's growing taste for American beef more than makes up for Americans' declining appetite: whereas U.S. customers buy huge slabs of meat, Japanese importers want labor-intensive trimming work done at the plant to avoid high wage costs at home."[77]

The Technological Environment

Technology is a term that ignites passionate debates in many circles these days. Some blame technology for environmental destruction and cultural fragmentation. Others view technology as the key to economic and social progress. No doubt there are important messages in both extremes. See Table 3.1 for major technologies likely to have a significant impact on our lives in the near future.[78]

For our purposes, **technology** is defined as all the tools and ideas available for extending the natural physical and mental reach of humankind. A central theme in technology is the practical application of new ideas, a theme that is clarified by the following distinction between science and technology: "Science is the quest for more or less abstract knowledge, whereas technology is the application of organized knowledge to help solve problems in our society."[79] According to the following

technology *all the tools and ideas available for extending the natural physical and mental reach of humankind*

Table 3.1	Scientists and technology experts at the Battelle Memorial Institute in Columbus, Ohio, predict that these ten technologies will most significantly impact our lives by 2005.
Scientists Forecast These Top Ten Technologies by the Year 2005	1. Mapping of the human genome for gene-based personal identification and diagnostics. The intent is to treat diseases before they occur.
	2. Super materials: high-performance materials designed at molecular level for transportation, computers, energy and communications.
	3. Compact, long-lasting and highly portable energy sources, including fuel cells and batteries.
	4. Digital high-definition television for entertainment as well as better computer modeling and imaging.
	5. Miniaturization of electronics for personal use: interactive, wireless data centers in a unit the size of a pocket calculator.
	6. Cost-effective systems that integrate power, sensors and controls: smart systems that will control manufacturing processes from beginning to end.
	7. Anti-aging products and services: from genetic code manipulation to aging creams.
	8. Medical treatments, with highly accurate sensors and problem locators, and drug delivery systems that will be highly specific to precisely targeted parts of the body.
	9. Hybrid fuel vehicles capable of using several types of fuels to reduce emissions and increase performance.
	10. Edutainment—educational games and computer simulations for school and business.

Source: Excerpted from Dayton Fandray, "Ideas with a Future," *Alaska Airlines Magazine,* 19 (August 1995): 28–29. Reprinted with permission of the author.

historical perspective, technology is facilitating the evolution of the industrial age into the information age, just as it once enabled the agricultural age to evolve into the industrial age.

> *Stephen R. Barley, a professor at Cornell's School of Industrial and Labor Relations, builds on the work of others to argue that until recently, "the economies of the advanced industrial nations revolved around electrical power, the electric motor, the internal combustion engine, and the telephone." The development of these "infrastructural technologies" made possible the shift from an agricultural to a manufacturing economy, in the process precipitating "urbanization, the growth of corporations, the rise of professional management. . . ."*
>
> *Now, Barley writes, the evidence suggests that another shift is taking place, with implications likely to be just as seismic: "Our growing knowledge of how to convert electronic and mechanical impulses into digitally encoded information (and vice versa) and how to transmit such information across vast distances is gradually enabling industry to replace its electromechanical infrastructure with a computational infrastucture."*[80]

Consequently, *information* has become a valuable strategic resource. Organizations using appropriate information technologies to get the right information to the right people at the right time will enjoy a competitive advantage. According to *Business Week*: "The ubiquity of the Internet and the rapid drop in the cost and complexity of networking equipment is bringing such sophisticated applications as electronic commerce, electronic data interchange, telecommuting, groupware, and the World Wide Web to businesses with just a handful of employees."[81] Cisco Systems Inc., for example, which manufactures Internet switching and routing gear, is a leader in the e-commerce revolution discussed in Chapter 1. The company reportedly saved $1.5 billion during a recent three-year period by selling 78 percent of its equipment directly over the Internet.[82]

Two aspects of technology with important implications for managers are the innovation process and intrapreneurship.

The Innovation Process

Technology comes into being through the **innovation process,** defined as the systematic development and practical application of a new idea.[83] A great deal of time-consuming work is necessary to develop a new idea into a marketable product or service. And many otherwise good ideas do not become technologically feasible, let alone marketable and profitable. According to one innovation expert, "only one of every 20 or 25 ideas ever becomes a successful product—and of every 10 or 15 new products, only one becomes a hit."[84] A better understanding of the innovation process can help improve management's chances of turning new ideas into profitable goods and services.

A Three-Step Process.   The innovation process has three steps (see Figure 3.6). First is the conceptualization step, when a new idea occurs to someone. Development of a working prototype is the second step, called **product technology**. This involves actually creating a product that will work as intended. The third and final step is developing a production process to create a profitable quantity-quality-price relationship. This third step is labeled **production technology.** Successful innovation depends on the right combination of new ideas, product technology, and production technology. A missing or deficient step can ruin the innovation process.

Innovation Lag.   The time it takes for a new idea to be translated into satisfied demand is called **innovation lag.** The longer the innovation lag, the longer society must wait to benefit from a new idea. For example, fax machines came into wide use in the early 1990s. But the fax concept was patented by a Scottish clockmaker named Alexander Bain in 1843—an innovation lag of nearly a century and a half.[85] Over the years, the trend has been toward shorter innovation lags. For example, Britain's Imperial Chemical Industries has "slashed the time it takes to commercialize a technology from the industry norm of more than a decade to only five years."[86]

innovation process *the systematic development and practical application of a new idea*

6 Describe the three-step innovation process and define the term *intrapreneur.*

product technology *second stage of innovation process involving the creation of a working prototype*

production technology *third stage of innovation process involving the development of a profitable production process*

innovation lag *time it takes for a new idea to be translated into satisfied demand*

Figure 3.6

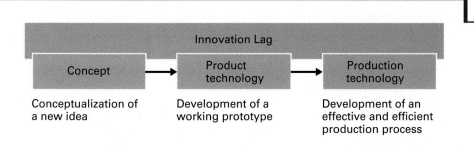

The Three-Step Innovation Process

Concern over the "Digital Divide" Between Technology Haves and Have-Nots

31

Much is made these days of the "digital divide"—that growing chasm between the haves and the have-nots in the new economy that's being driven at warp speed by computers and computing. The concern is a familiar one and an honest one: Technology creates change—economic change, certainly. But, even more than economic change, technology drives social change, and it does that less visibly. And, just as the Industrial Revolution threatened to unravel the social compact of the United States at the beginning of this century, so the Information Revolution is threatening to undo society in the century's waning years. Those with access to computers and with skills at computing—and their children, and, perhaps, their children's children—stand a chance of cashing in on an economy that amply rewards the techno-educated, and relentlessly punishes the techno-illiterate.

Sources: Sara Terry, "Across the Great Divide," *Fast Company*, no. 26 (July–August 1999): 194. Also see Michael Dertouzos, "The Rich People's Computer?" *Technology Review*, January–February 1999 (**www.techreview.com**); and Jonathan Alter, "Bridging the Digital Divide," *Newsweek* (September 20, 1999): 55.

Questions: *Why should managers be concerned about the digital divide? Why should you be concerned about it? What can be done to narrow it?*

Shortening Innovation Lag.   Reducing innovation lags should be a high-priority goal for modern managers. Prior to his retirement as chief executive officer of Hewlett-Packard (H-P), John Young made shorter innovation lags a strategic goal for the computer and scientific instrument company. His aim was to cut 50 percent off H-P's average product innovation lag by the year 2000. This is a particularly important goal, considering that H-P generates 50 percent of its annual sales from products developed within the prior three years.[87]

Another step in the right direction is a practice called *concurrent engineering*. Also referred to as parallel design, **concurrent engineering** is a team approach to product design. This approach lets research, design, production, finance, and marketing specialists have a direct say in the product design process from the very beginning.[88] This contrasts with the traditional, and much slower, practice of having a product move serially from research to design, from design to manufacturing, and so on down the line toward the marketplace. The time to hear about possible marketing problems is while a product is still in the conceptualization stage, not after it has become a warehouse full of unsold goods.

concurrent engineering
team approach to product design involving specialists from all functional areas including research, production, and marketing

Promoting Innovation Through Intrapreneurship

When we hear someone called an entrepreneur, we generally think of a creative individual who has risked everything while starting his or her own business. Indeed, entrepreneurs are a vital innovative force in the economy.[89] A lesser-known but no less important type of entrepreneur is the so-called intrapreneur.

Gifford Pinchot, author of the book *Intrapreneuring*, defines an **intrapreneur** as an employee who takes personal "hands-on responsibility" for pushing any type of innovative idea, product, or process through the organization. Pinchot calls intrapreneurs "dreamers who do." But unlike traditional entrepreneurs, who tend to leave the organizational confines to pursue their dreams, intrapreneurs strive for innovation *within* existing organizations.[90] Intrapreneurs tend to have a higher need for security than

intrapreneur   *an employee who takes personal responsibility for pushing an innovative idea through a large organization*

What's this? A cure for cancer? No, but it may help medical science take big steps in that direction someday. Actually, Monty Denneau (left) and his IBM colleagues are intent on turning a $100 million investment into the world's fastest computer, code named Blue Gene. Their 1000-processor supercomputer is expected to crunch one quadrillion (that's 15 zeros) bits of data per second. Think of a computer that is 2 million times more powerful than your PC and you have an idea of the innovative leap involved.

entrepreneurs, who strike out on their own. They pay a price for being employees rather than owners. Pinchot explains:

> *Corporate entrepreneurs [or intrapreneurs], despite prior successes, have no capital of their own to start other ventures. Officially, they must begin from zero by persuading management that their new ideas are promising. Unlike successful independent entrepreneurs, they are not free to guide their next ventures by their own intuitive judgments; they still have to justify every move.*[91]

Kathleen Synnott, a division marketing manager for Pitney Bowes Inc., is the classic intrapreneur. After seeing the potential of the versatile new Mail Center 2000, a computerized mail-handling and stamping machine, Synnott became its enthusiastic champion. Just two things stood in her way: change-resistant managers and satisfied customers.

⇄ Advice for Future Intrapreneurs   3J

Among Gifford Pinchot's ten commandments for intrapreneurs are the following:

- "Come to work each day willing to be fired."
- "Do any job needed to make your project work, regardless of your job description."
- "Remember it is easier to ask for forgiveness than for permission."

Source: Excerpted from Gifford Pinchot III, *Intrapreneuring: Why You Don't Have to Leave the Corporation to Become an Entrepreneur* (New York: Harper & Row, 1985), 22.

Questions: *How can these ideas enhance innovation in large organizations? Is this advice a formula for career success or sudden unemployment?*

During the design process, for instance, Synnott helped protect the original blueprint from execs who wanted to break up the Mail Center 2000 and sell it as upgrading components to Pitney's existing mail-metering machines. She also guided it through a technical maze, insisting on 22 simulations to make sure potential customers liked what they saw. "There were naysayers who didn't think we were ready" for such a system, says Synnott. . . . "But they got religion."[92]

If today's large companies are to achieve a competitive edge through innovation, they need to foster a supportive climate for intrapreneurs like Synnott. According to experts on the subject, an organization can foster intrapreneurship if it:

- Focuses on results and teamwork.
- Rewards innovation and risk taking.
- Tolerates and learns from mistakes.
- Remains flexible and change-oriented.[93]

Our discussions of creativity, participative management, and organizational cultures in later chapters contain ideas about how to encourage intrapreneurship of all types.

Summary

1. Seven major changes reshaping the workplace at the dawn of the twenty-first century are (1) *the virtual organization* with greater reliance on computer networks, (2) *the just-in-time workforce* with more part-timers, (3) *the ascendancy of knowledge workers* as we pursue lifelong learning in the information age, (4) *computerized coaching and electronic monitoring* with enhanced learning and decision making, as well as privacy concerns, (5) *the growth of worker diversity* in an evolving multicultural and multilingual workforce, (6) *the aging workforce* with a greater appreciation of older workers and less emphasis on early retirement, and (7) *the birth of the dynamic workforce* with an emphasis on innovation and adaptability.

2. Demographically, the U.S. workforce is becoming older, more culturally diverse, and increasingly female. Remedial education programs are needed to improve the quality of the U.S. workforce. Researchers have disproved persistent myths that older workers are less productive and more accident-prone than younger coworkers. A new social contract between employers and employees is taking shape because the tradition of lifetime employment with a single organization is giving way to shorter-term relationships of convenience and mutual benefit.

3. The persistence of opportunity and income inequalities (and the so-called glass ceiling) among women and minorities is a strong stimulus for change. With part-timers playing a greater role in the U.S. workforce, there is genuine concern about creating a disadvantaged underclass of employees. Managing-diversity programs attempt to go a step beyond equal employment opportunity. The new goal is to tap *every* employee's *full* potential in today's diverse workforce.

4. Because of government regulations and sociopolitical demands from a growing list of special-interest groups, managers are becoming increasingly politicized. More and more believe that if they are going to be affected by political forces, they should be more active politically. Some organizations rely on issues management to systematically identify, evaluate, and respond to important social and political issues. Managers can respond politically in three ways: by being reactive, neutral, or proactive. Four political strategies that managers have found useful for pursuing active or reactive political goals are campaign financing, lobbying, coalition building, and indirect lobbying. In a number of recent court cases managers have

been held personally accountable for the misdeeds of their organizations. Alternative dispute resolution tactics such as arbitration and mediation can help trim management's huge litigation bill.

5. Managers can make timely decisions about inventory, borrowing, hiring, and capital spending during somewhat unpredictable business cycles by taking a consensus approach to economic forecasts. Business is urged to compete actively and creatively in the emerging global economy. By influencing jobs, prices, quality standards, and wages, the global economy affects virtually *everyone*.

6. Including conceptualization, product technology, and production technology, a healthy innovation process is vital to technological development. Innovation lags must be shortened. An organizational climate that fosters intrapreneurship can help. An intrapreneur is an employee who champions an idea or innovation by pushing it through the organization.

Terms to Understand

Demographics (p. 74)

New social contract (p. 77)

Glass ceiling (p. 77)

Contingent workers (p. 79)

Managing diversity (p. 80)

Issues management (p. 82)

Advocacy advertising (p. 84)

Legal audit (p. 85)

Alternative dispute resolution (p. 85)

Business cycle (p. 86)

Technology (p. 89)

Innovation process (p. 91)

Product technology (p. 91)

Production technology (p. 91)

Innovation lag (p. 91)

Concurrent engineering (p. 92)

Intrapreneur (p. 92)

How Business Leaders Can Help Women Break the Glass Ceiling

Skills & Tools

Businesses need as much leadership, talent, quality, competence, productivity, innovation, and creativity as possible as they face more effective worldwide competition. Following are ten actions companies can take to ensure maximum use of women's business capability:

1. **Provide feedback on job performance.** Give frequent and specific appraisals. Women need and want candid reviews of their work. Clearly articulated suggestions for improvement, standards for work performance and plans for career advancement will make women feel more involved in their jobs and help make them better employees.

2. **Accept women.** Welcome them as valued members of your management team. Include women in every kind of communication. Listen to their needs and concerns and encourage their contributions.

3. **Ensure equal opportunities.** Give women the same chances you give to talented men to grow, develop, and contribute to company profitability. Give them the responsibility to direct major projects, to plan and implement systems and programs. Expect them to travel and relocate and to make the same commitment to the company as do men who aspire to leadership positions.

4. **Provide career counseling.** Give women the same level of counseling on professional career advancement opportunities as you give to men.

5. **Identify potential.** Identify women as possible future managers early in their employment and encourage their advancement through training and other developmental activities.

6. **Encourage assertiveness.** Assist women in strengthening their assertion skills. Reinforce strategic career planning to encourage women's commitment to their careers and long-term career plans.

7. **Accelerate development.** Provide "fast track" programs for qualified women. Either formally or informally, these programs will give women the exposure, knowledge and positioning they need for career advancement.

8. **Offer mentoring opportunities.** Give women the chance to develop mentoring relationships with other employees. The overall goal should be to provide advice, counsel, and support to promising female employees from knowledgeable, senior-level men and women.

9. **Encourage networking.** Promote management support systems and networks among employees of both genders. Sharing experiences and information with other men and women who are managers provides invaluable support to peers. These activities give women the opportunity to meet and learn from men and women in more advanced stages of their careers—a helpful way of identifying potential mentors or role models.

10. **Increase women's participation.** Examine the feasibility of increasing participation of women in company-sponsored planning retreats, use of company facilities, social functions, and so forth. With notable exceptions, men are still generally more comfortable with other men, and as a result, women miss many of the career and business opportunities that arise during social functions. In addition, women may not have access to information about the company's informal political and social systems. Encourage male managers to include women when socializing with other business associates.

Source: Excerpted from Rose Mary Wentling, "Breaking Down Barriers to Women's Success," *HRMagazine,* 40 (May 1995). Reprinted with the permission of *HRMagazine,* published by the Society for Human Resource Management, Alexandria, Virginia.

Internet Exercises   ⇧

1. **Current events online:** Today's managers need to follow worldwide current events to track new markets, customer preferences, competitors, new technology, and investment opportunities. The Internet stands ready to fill this need 24 hours a day, seven days a week. For example, select one of the following three general news Web sites and search it for a news story that updates one of the topical areas in this chapter (social/demographic, political/legal, economic, and technological). Read the news story and be prepared to take a copy of it to class if your instructor requests.

- Go to the home page of the Cable News Network (**www.cnn.com**) and select one or more of the following main menu items: "World," "Politics," "Business," or "Technology."
- At the home page of MSNBC (**www.msnbc.com**), start by clicking on the last heading on the navigation bar: "Quick News." After that, you may want to move on to the "Business" and "Technology" pages.
- The BBC, Britain's publicly funded and noncommercial radio, television, and Internet broadcaster (known in the U.K. as "The Beeb"), is a good source for news from around the world (**www.bbc.co.uk**). Alternative language versions—including Russian, Spanish for Latin America, and Cantonese—are available at the click of a mouse. Select "News" at the home page main menu, and then "World," "Business," or "Sci/Tech" from the BBC News page.

2. **Diversity on the Web:** (The objective here is to acquire five or more instructive facts or insights, from a managerial perspective, about people whose backgrounds are different from your own.) Internet offerings mirror the planet's gender, racial, ethnic, and cultural diversity. Select one of those recommended Web sites and do some exploratory reading:

- **Women:** At the home page of **www.women.connect.com,** click on the main menu section "Business" and explore some of the many areas of interest. On the "Career" page, you will find especially useful information and tips under the headings "Career Toolbox" and "Career Coach."
     The AFL-CIO, the principal U.S. labor union organization, has a very strong Internet offering on working women (**www.aflcio.org**). Click on the home page menu item "Working Women" and then select the topic "Facts About Working Women" for a well-documented presentation. The "Working Women" page also links to interesting surveys and reports.
- **African Americans:** Black Entertainment Television's Web site (**www.betnetworks.com**) is a good source for job hunters and businesspeople. Click on the home page menu item "Business & Career" and explore the areas titled "Business and Management," "Careers and Work," "Black Enterprise Online," and "MSBET Career Builder."
- **Hispanics/Latinos:** The National Council of *La Raza* has an Internet site with the stated goal of "making a difference for Hispanic Americans" (**www.nclr.org**). Review its broad range of offerings.

3. **Check it out:** A treasure chest of free career information is available at *The Wall Street Journal*'s Internet site (**www.wsj.com**). Simply scroll to the bottom of the home page and click on the "Careers" link under the heading "Visit Our Other Sites." Be sure to review the helpful readings in the section titled "Job-Hunting Advice."

     For updates to these exercises, visit our Web site (**www.hmco.com/college**).

Welcome to the World of Younger Bosses and Older Workers

Closing Case

They're young corporate climbers, full of brash attitude and rogue ideas. And suddenly, they're in charge.

Better get used to it. As Generation X matures and job promotions no longer depend on seniority, the baby-faced boss is here to stay.

Source: Excerpted from Stephanie Armour, "The Challenge: Mix Energy, Experience," *USA Today* (April 20, 1999): 1A–*/2A. Copyright 1999, USA Today. Reprinted with permission.

That means more managers are in their 20s or 30s and overseeing employees who are older, a twist on the typical manager-employee relationship. The age reversal is causing a shake-up. Employers are more vulnerable to age-discrimination lawsuits, and workers are facing generation gaps never before tackled on the job.

"We've always had older and younger workers, but they never mixed. You were ghettoized with your own age group," says Ron Zemke, co-author of the soon-to-be-released *Generations At Work*. "Now it's the first time they're together. It's a new kind of diversity and a new kind of challenge."

In a tight labor market, the trend has swept across industries. Youthful managers are cropping up in manufacturing plants and white-collar offices. When striking General Motors workers in Flint, Mich., took to the picket lines last year, many complained that supervisors were too young and inexperienced.

The discord is coming in part because the number of workers age 20–34 in the managerial category increased from 4.8 million in 1994 to 5.2 million last year, the Department of Labor reports.

The ranks of young bosses are expected to surge as the 52.4 million people who make up Generation X—born from 1965 through 1978—assume more supervisory roles. Already, 14% of top executives such as CEOs, presidents and company owners are in their 30s or 20s, according to Dun & Bradstreet, which provides financial management services.

The age difference is bringing a values clash. Raised on a diet of MTV and video games, Generation X bosses are generally quick to roam from job to job, hungry for quick results, willing to do things differently and intolerant of technophobes. All this can be a bit bewildering to baby boomers widely considered more loyal to employers and less likely to bend rules.

"I say 'dude' a lot, which people have to get used to," says Ryan Deutsch, 27, vice president of operations at Sidney Printing Works in Cincinnati, who directs employees in their 40s. "The experience gap is the biggest challenge. You're never going to know or have as much experience as the people you work with, so it's important to give the proper respect."

Says Richard Autzen, 43, a plant manager and his employee: "I enjoy his energy. I get to explain a lot of things to him."

A New Breed of Boss

More young bosses are coming in part because employers are seeking a different type of supervisor no longer molded solely by seniority and experience.

They want a new breed of boss who can provide strong leadership, handle technology, inspire teamwork, cope with constant change and handle never-ending uncertainty. Many older workers have such attributes. But such characteristics are widely considered to be traits learned in college business programs or picked up from employees who hop scotch from job to job—attributes strongly linked to younger workers and newly minted graduates.

And employers are willing to pay. Managers' salaries can range from the mid-$20,000 a year in the service sector on up into six figures. It's no longer safe to assume that the silver-haired worker earns more than a new hire.

Companies are showering young managers with fat signing bonuses, cars, stock options and generous salaries. Some MBA graduates are easily landing salaries topping $100,000.

But making it work once they've started the job is easier said than done. Younger bosses can contend with plenty of resistance.

Older workers may think a young boss who is still single can't understand family demands. They may chafe at taking commands from someone with less job experience. And they can be less tolerant of a younger person's management mistakes.

"There are huge value differences among generations," says Ben Rosen, a management professor at the University of North Carolina. "So many companies have focused on diversity, but they've overlooked age, and it's such a prevalent issue. There are potential problems."

No age group is immune from the friction. In today's tight labor market, even 20-something employees have found themselves dealing with younger supervisors.

"She was terrible," says Ali Friedman, 26, who once had a boss who was just out of college. Friedman now works for a record label in Boston. "When someone has no mentors, how are they supposed to mentor someone else? I had to manage her managing me." . . .

Some young workers burst onto the scene full of flashy new ideas without the experience or proof to back them up.

"The signing bonuses and intense recruitment sets up younger managers to think they're pretty hot," says Sharon McFarland, a management professor at the University of Cincinnati. "They're highly prized and groomed to feel elite."

But newer isn't necessarily better. Hagberg Consulting Group of Foster City, Calif., researched results of more than 3,000 executives who were rated by coworkers and found that as an executive's age increases, he or she becomes more thorough and better at planning.

Stereotyping Problems

Blame many of the problems on stereotyping. Young workers may see their older counterparts as ill at ease with technology, unable to make snap decisions, and set in their ways.

"People tend to look on older people as if they can only do so much," says Mary Barbour, 73, an administrative assistant in Washington, D.C., whose supervisor is roughly 20 years younger. "But believe it or not, our memory does not leave us. You're never really too old to learn."

Older workers, on the other hand, may see their younger managers as inferior. They may doubt their loyalty to the company, think they're favored because of their youth.

"You have to work harder to prove yourself," says Lyle Lininger, 31, at Sandia National Laboratories in Albuquerque. "Especially when I was new in this job, it was really awkward to feel like I was giving instructions to someone as old as my parents. I just say, 'You know what, I don't have all the answers.'". . .

And there is hope for younger managers and their older counterparts. Many such pairings work.

They've relied on patience, mutual understanding and an ability to look beyond age-defined stereotypes, drawing on each other's strengths instead [of] focusing on their differences.

Take Russ McFee, 40. He is a manager at GHS Strings, a company in Battle Creek Mich., that makes guitar strings. He says he doesn't let age become an issue.

"Age is irrelevant," McFee says. "It's the person."

It's a good thing he sees it that way. One of his employees, John Mally, is still working as an engineer at the age of 90.

"It's wonderful," Mally quips. "You never know what he's going to do next. It's a very big pleasure. He's a very nice fellow to work for."

FOR DISCUSSION

1. (Some people do not like to have a group label attached to them.) Are you opposed to terms such as "generation X" and "baby boomers"? Explain.

2. Honestly, how do you typically characterize older workers? How do you generally characterize younger workers?

3. Would you be uncomfortable reporting to a manager who is younger than you? Explain.

4. If you worked for Ryan Deutsch, the Sidney Printing Works vice president in Cincinnati, and he called you "dude" all the time, how would you respond?

5. What is an older employee entitled to at the end of a long career at the same company? Explain.

INTERNATIONAL MANAGEMENT and CROSS-CULTURAL COMPETENCE

CHAPTER OBJECTIVES

When you finish studying this chapter, you should be able to

1 Describe the six-step internationalization process, and explain how to make an international joint venture a success.

2 Distinguish between a global company and a transnational company.

3 Contrast ethnocentric, polycentric, and geocentric attitudes toward foreign operations.

4 Explain from a cross-cultural perspective the difference between high-context and low-context cultures, and distinguish between monochronic and polychronic time.

5 Discuss what Geert Hofstede's research has to say about the applicability of U.S. management theories in foreign cultures.

6 Identify important comparative management lessons learned from William Ouchi's Theory Z research and international studies of work goals and leadership styles.

7 Discuss the nature and importance of cross-cultural training in international management.

8 Summarize the position of women on foreign assignments.

> "THE BOUNDARIES OF OUR COUNTRIES CAN NO LONGER BE THE BORDERS OF OUR MINDS."
>
> dean c. barnlund

Detroit Gears Up on Its German

Welcome to DaimlerChrysler!

Most executives' offices are decorated with family photos, award plaques, and artwork.

But these days, Tom Stallkamp's suite features flash cards with phrases like "*Guten Tag*." The Daimler-Chrysler president spends four hours a week in German lessons—a consequence of Chrysler's newly formed merger with Germany's Daimler-Benz.

"It's about 35 years too late, but it's coming," quips silver-haired Stallkamp.

He's not alone. Across DaimlerChrysler's U.S. head-quarters and, in fact, across the Motor City, business ties to Germany have never been stronger—and an interest in all things Teutonic has never been greater.

German auto suppliers such as Thyssen, Robert Bosch and Siemens have expanded their Detroit opera-tions, transferring hundreds of employees who have nestled in northern suburbs such as Troy and Rochester. . . .

Lots of Interest

But the DaimlerChrysler deal, announced in May [1998], sent Chrysler employees searching for keys to under-standing their new colleagues. Requests flooded in for language classes and cultural seminars, transfers to Stuttgart, and offers to host German families, spokes-woman Megan Giles says.

With so many people interested in learning more, the company had to prioritize: While cultural training will be widely available, those who are moving overseas or who will work directly with Germans from Daimler have first dibs on German lessons, Giles says.

Along with Stallkamp, that includes James Donlon, DaimlerChrysler controller who held the same job at Chrysler. In a few weeks, he becomes the first American to move from Auburn Hills to Stuttgart. Donlon expressed interest early on: "It was something short of walking in with my hand raised, but I said, 'Sure, I'll go,'" Donlon says.

Some Differences

Donlon and hundreds of other Chrysler employees, including DaimlerChrysler co-CEO Robert Eaton, have

been tipped by cultural experts to obvious differences in dealing with their German counterparts. Among them:

- *Precision.* To Germans, the phrase "I'm working on it" means you really are, while to an American, it often means "I haven't gotten to it yet." Promptness is a priority and schedules—often called "the program" at German companies—are all important. Itineraries are followed closely, even if it means cutting short a meeting just when ideas are flowing or key points are being made.
- *Small talk and socializing.* Although Americans like to break the ice by chatting about children or sports, Germans avoid it during business hours, getting right to the point with presentations and appointments. But they don't want to talk business during purely social occasions, when U.S. executives often don't want to discuss anything else. Meanwhile, everyone from boss to assistant celebrates birthdays with workplace festivities.
- *Sundays.* Considered just an extension of the weekend in the United States, Sunday in Germany is generally reserved for family, exercise, and cultural pursuits, not simply an extra day to run errands or visit the mall.

In fact, GM Europe general counsel Michael Millikin's cultural training included where to find groceries on Sunday, when most stores are closed. The answer: Food shops in airports and convenience stores at gas stations. It was among many adjustments Millikin, who moved from Detroit headquarters last year, was told to expect.

"They teach you that what you will experience is not what you have to come to know at home," Millikin says.

He is one of 2,500 expatriates—officially called Inter-national Service Personnel or ISPs—that GM has posted around the world, says international human resources chief Cheri Alexander. Equally divided between U.S.-born and foreign-born, many of these ISPs are engineers who trade jobs between GM's Warren, Mich., technical center and its engineering base at Opel in Russelsheim. That's largely because GM is developing global car chassis, called platforms, that will be shared primarily between North America and Europe. "You hear a lot of different languages now," says Jay Wetzel, GM's chief engineer for North America.

Language Skills

GM stresses language skills for all of its vagabonds, many of whom undergo immersion training—as much as eight hours a day, five days a week for a month before they leave home. The reason: "Once you hit the ground, [bosses] want you to work," and employees are often too busy to listen to tapes and study grammar, Alexander says.

Former Chrysler vice chairman Robert Lutz, a Swiss native who speaks English, German, and French, agrees. "Language unlocks everything. And the other guys will respect you more if they see you making an effort in their language, rather than just assuming you will do [business] in English," says Lutz. . . .

Going Overboard?

But Lutz, who worked for GM, BMW, and Ford in Europe before joining Chrysler in 1986, thinks the frenzied focus on cultural training at his former company, at least, is misplaced.

The Germans in charge at Daimler are a sophisticated, post–World War II breed who grew up with McDonald's, Coca-Cola, IBM computers, and MTV, Lutz contends. Dealing with them won't be difficult for his former Chrysler colleagues.

However, GM's Alexander, who has been posted to France and Switzerland, argues strongly for trying to get beneath cultural skins. "It may look the same on the surface, but underlying habits and customs are not the same. We simply will not see one culture around the world," she says.

Case update: Stallcamp and Eaton have since left DaimlerChrysler.

Source: Excerpted from Micheline Maynard, "Detroit Gears Up on Its German," *USA Today* (November 30, 1998): 3B. Copyright 1998, USA Today. Reprinted with permission.

Managers, such as those at DaimlerChrysler,[1] are moving from country to country as never before, meeting the challenges of international competition. They are carrying on a business tradition dating back farther than one might think:

> *In the antique shops of Shanghai's old French quarter, amid the German cameras, American radios, Russian crystal and other relics of a vanished past, lie tarnished reminders of just how long the world economy has been a global economy: rough-cast taels of South American silver and smooth-worn Mexican silver dollars.*
>
> *It was in 1571 that modern global commerce began, argues Dennis O. Flynn, head of the economics department of the University of the Pacific in Stockton, Calif. That year, the Spanish empire founded the city of Manila in the Philippines to receive its silver-laden galleons that made their way across the vast Pacific Ocean from the New World. The metal was bound not for Spain, but for imperial China. For the first time, all of the world's populated continents were trading directly—Asia with the Americas, Europe and Africa, and each with the others. They were highly interdependent: when silver depreciated in later decades, world-wide inflation ensued.*
>
> *"Some economists think the global economy is a post–World War II thing," says Prof. Flynn. "That just demonstrates an ignorance of history."[2]*

Both air travel and modern information technology have made the world a seemingly smaller place. A third globe-shrinking force steadily gaining momentum is *corporate globalism*. By creating global organizations, this third force promises to be the main contributor to a smaller world in which similarities prevail.

Striking evidence of the modern global marketplace is everywhere. Consider these recent examples:

- *Japan and North America:* Japan's Honda Motor Company earns 85 percent of its operating profits in North America.[3]
- *Germany and Mexico:* ". . . in the city of Puebla, 15,000 Mexican workers churn out Volkswagen's new Beetle for export to the world, including Germany."[4]
- *North America, Europe, and Asia:* Forte Cashmere, based in the state of Rhode Island, "owns a cashmere processing plant in Mongolia, one of the leading suppliers of the soft goat's hair used in sweaters. . . . Mills and manufacturers in Scotland and other European countries buy 80% of Forte's cashmere. Many, in turn, sell their garments to U.S. retailers such as Neiman Marcus."[5]
- *Russia, North America, and Europe:* In 1996, Russia launched a U.S.-made communications satellite for a French company.[6]
- *North and Central America:* "The major-league baseball, that most American of icons, is made exclusively in Costa Rica."[7]

This dizzying array of international commerce is simply business as usual in our global economy, which is projected to grow from $26 trillion in 1994 to $48 trillion in 2010. Over the same period, world trade is expected to quadruple, from $4 trillion to $16.6 trillion![8]

Like any other productive enterprise, an international corporation must be effectively and efficiently managed. Consequently, **international management,** the pursuit of organizational objectives in international and intercultural settings, has become an important discipline. The purpose of this chapter is to define and discuss multinational and global corporations, stimulate global and cultural awareness, explore comparative management, and discuss the need for cross-cultural training.

international management
pursuing organizational objectives in international and intercultural settings

Global Organizations for a Global Economy

Many labels have been attached to international business ventures over the years. They have been called international companies, multinational companies, global companies, and transnational companies. This section clarifies the terminology confusion by reviewing the six-stage internationalization process as a foundation for contrasting global and transnational companies.

The Internationalization Process

There are many ways to do business across borders. At either extreme, a company may merely buy goods from a foreign source or actually buy the foreign company itself. In between is an internationalization process with identifiable stages. Companies may skip steps when pursuing foreign markets, so the following sequence should *not* be viewed as a lockstep sequence.

1 **Describe the six-step internationalization process, and explain how to make an international joint venture a success.**

Stage I: Licensing.   Companies in foreign countries are authorized to produce and/or market a given product within a specified territory in return for a fee. For example, under the terms of a recent ten-year licensing agreement, South Korea's

4A

The Global Economy in Your Own Backyard

Team up with two or three other people and have a five-minute brainstorming session to come up with as many answers to the following question as possible.

Question: *What evidence of the global economy is there in your city, region, or state? Hint: Think of foreign-made products sold in local stores, foreign-owned companies, and local companies that export goods or services.*

For further information about the interactive annotations in this chapter, visit our Web site (**www.hmco.com/college**).

Samsung Electronics will get to use Texas Instruments' patented semiconductor technology for royalty payments exceeding $1 billion.[9]

Stage 2: Exporting.   Goods produced in one country are sold to customers in foreign countries. As documented in Chapter 3, exports amount to a large and growing slice of the U.S. economy.[10]

Stage 3: Local Warehousing and Selling.   Goods produced in one country are shipped to the parent company's storage and marketing facilities located in one or more foreign countries.

Stage 4: Local Assembly and Packaging.   Components, rather than finished products, are shipped to company-owned assembly facilities in one or more foreign countries for final assembly and sales.

Stage 5: Joint Ventures.   A company in one country pools resources with one or more companies in a foreign country to produce, store, transport, and market products with resulting profits/losses shared appropriately. Joint ventures, also known as *strategic alliances* or *strategic partnerships*, have become very popular in recent years.[11] Fuji Xerox is a prime example of a successful international joint venture.

> *Joint ventures are usually formed to ensure a fast and convenient entry into a complex foreign market. That's particularly the case in Japan, where convoluted distribution systems, tightly knit supplier relationships and close business-government cooperation have long encouraged foreign companies to link up with knowledgeable local partners.*
>
> *But in truth, these joint ventures don't often last long. And they sometimes flop, occasionally spectacularly. The reason for failure can include disagreements over strategy, struggles over operational control or even simple spats over each partner's level of effort.*
>
> *But Fuji Xerox, a 34-year-old joint venture between Xerox Corp., Stamford, Conn., and Tokyo-based Fuji Photo Film Co., has avoided all that. In contrast to the turmoil at many other joint ventures, Fuji Xerox not only has been bedrock stable, but also has grown into what Xerox Chairman Paul Allaire sometimes calls "Xerox's most important strategic asset."[12]*

International joint ventures/strategic alliances have tended to be fruitful for Japanese companies but disappointing for American and European partners.

> *Gary Hamel, a professor at the London Business School, regards partnerships as "a race to learn": The partner that learns fastest comes to dominate the relationship and can then rewrite its terms. Thus, an alliance becomes a new form of competition. The Japanese excel at learning from others, Hamel says, while Americans and Europeans are not so good at it.[13]*

Experts offer the following recommendations for successful international joint ventures/strategic alliances. First, exercise *patience* when selecting and building trust with a partner that has compatible (but not directly competitive) products and markets. Second, *learn* as fast and as much as possible without giving away core technologies and secrets. Third, establish firm *ground rules* about rights and responsibilities at the outset.[14]

Stage 6: Direct Foreign Investments.   Typically, a company in one country produces and markets products through wholly owned subsidiaries in foreign countries. Global corporations are expressions of this last stage of internationalization.

As second-generation farmer Terry L. Wolf inspects his corn crop in Illinois, he is figuratively standing in the middle of the global economy. Despite the prospects of a good crop, reduced exports due to a global slowdown will depress the prices he receives for his corn and soybeans. He will have to use every trick in the book just to keep farming.

Cross-border mergers are an increasingly popular form of direct foreign investment.[15] A cross-border merger occurs when a company in one country buys an entire company in another country. For example, European companies purchased $280 billion worth of U.S. companies in 1998 and 1999, creating new global giants such as DaimlerChrysler and British Petroleum-Amoco.[16] Unfortunately, cross-border mergers are not a quick and easy way to go global.

> *On top of the usual challenges of acquiring a company—paying a fair price, melding two management teams, and capturing the elusive "synergy" that's supposed to light up the bottom line—special risks and costs attach to cross-border mergers. They often involve wide differences in distance, language, and culture that can lead to serious misunderstandings and conflicts. . . .*
>
> *According to a study of cross-border mergers among large companies by consultants McKinsey & Co., nearly 40% end in total failure, with the acquiring company never earning back its cost of capital.[17]*

Back to the Opening Case

At which stage of the six-stage internationalization process is DaimlerChrysler? How can you tell?

From Global Companies to Transnational Companies

The difference between these two types of international ventures is the difference between actual and theoretical. That is to say, transnational companies are evolving and represent a futuristic concept. Meanwhile, global companies, such as the giants in Table 4.1, do business in many countries simultaneously. They have global strategies for product design, financing, purchasing, manufacturing, and marketing. By

2 **Distinguish between a global company and a transnational company.**

Table 4.1

Corporate Giants Worldwide

Company	Home country	Industry	1998 Sales (U.S. $, billions)
AMP	Australia	Insurance	17
Banco do Brasil	Brazil	Banking	25
Bank of China	China	Banking	21
BP Amoco	Britain	Petroleum refining	68
DaimlerChrysler	Germany	Motor vehicles	155
ENI	Italy	Petroleum refining	32
General Electric	United States	Electrical equipment	100
ING Group	Netherlands	Insurance	56
L'Oréal	France	Cosmetics and soaps	13
Nestlé	Switzerland	Food products	50
Nokia	Finland	Electronics	15
Northern Telecom	Canada	Electrical equipment	18
PDVSA	Venezuela	Petroleum refining	26
Petróleos Mexicanos	Mexico	Crude oil production	21
Samsung	South Korea	Trading	29
Telefónica	Spain	Telecommunications	19
Toyota Motor	Japan	Motor vehicles	100
Volvo	Sweden	Motor vehicles	27

Source: Adapted from data in Jeremy Kahn, "The *Fortune* Global 500: The World's Largest Corporations," *Fortune* (August 2, 1999): 144, 146; and F1–F24.

global company *a multinational venture centrally managed from a specific country*

definition, a **global company** is a multinational venture centrally managed from a specific country.[18] For example, even though Coca-Cola earns most of its profits outside the United States, it is viewed as a U.S. company because it is run from a powerful headquarters in Atlanta, Georgia.[19] The same goes for McDonald's, Ford, IBM, and Wal-Mart, with their respective U.S. headquarters.

transnational company *a futuristic model of a global, decentralized network with no distinct national identity*

A **transnational company,** in contrast, is a global network of productive units with a decentralized authority structure and no distinct national identity.[20] Transnationals rely on a blend of global and local strategies, as circumstances dictate. Local values and practices are adopted whenever possible because, in the end, all *customer contacts* are local. Ideally, managers of transnational organizations "think globally, but act locally." Managers of foreign operations are encouraged to interact freely with their colleagues from around the world. Once again, this type of international business venture exists mostly in theory, although some global companies are moving toward transnationalism. For example, consider L. M. Ericsson, the Swedish telecommunications equipment manufacturer. As reported recently in *Business Week,* "Ericsson . . . moved its European headquarters to London to escape Sweden's high personal-income taxes, and to be closer to investors and customers."[21] Ericsson's decision to relocate its headquarters was not constrained by national identity, but rather guided by business and financial considerations.

Significantly, many experts are alarmed at the prospect of immense "stateless" transnational companies because of unresolved political, economic, and tax implications. If transnational companies become more powerful than the governments of even the largest countries in which they do business, who will hold them accountable in cases of human rights violations and environmental mishaps?[22]

"Made Right *Where*?"   4C

For years, Wal-Mart shoppers in the United States have been greeted by big signs proclaiming such things as MADE RIGHT HERE and SUPPORT AMERICAN MADE.

[But in 1998,] the National Labor Committee (NLC) found that 85 percent of the company's private-label merchandise was manufactured abroad. Racks hung under red, white, and blue banners were filled with clothes and accessories made in Asian and South American sweatshops. . . .

   The company does have a code of conduct for overseas labor. But in Honduran factories, the NLC found workers producing garments for Wal-Mart under conditions that directly violated that code—including forced unpaid overtime; blocked fire exits; denial of sick days and health care; wages drastically below subsistence levels; and the employment of minors. None of the workers interviewed knew anything about Wal-Mart's "commitment to assuring respect for human and worker rights."

Source: Keri Hayes, "Made in the U.S.A. (Sort of . . .)," *Business Ethics*, 13 (March–April 1999): 6.

Questions: *Is Wal-Mart misleading its shoppers? Explain. What would be an ethical course of action for Wal-Mart in the situation reported above?*

Toward Greater Global Awareness and Cross-Cultural Competence

Americans in general and American business students and managers in particular are often considered too narrowly focused for the global stage. Boris Yavitz, former dean of Columbia University's Graduate School of Business, observed that, "unlike European and Asian managers, who grow up expecting to see international service, U.S. executives are required to prepare only for domestic experience, with English as their only language."[23] This state of affairs is slowly changing amid growth of international business and economic globalization. To compete successfully in a dynamic global economy, present and future managers need to develop their international and cross-cultural awareness. In this section we distinguish between travelers and settlers, examine attitudes toward international operations, and explore key sources of cultural diversity.

Travelers Versus Settlers

One or more short visits to a foreign country do not make a person competent to transact business deals there. Accordingly, cross-cultural management experts distinguish between travelers and settlers. Travelers visit foreign countries, whether for work or pleasure, on a short-term basis (a few days to several weeks). They tend to have limited knowledge of the local history, culture, and customs. Their local language skills typically vary from none to few. In contrast, settlers take foreign assignments lasting from two to five years or more.

The Settler has to deal with a variety of challenges, starting from pre-departure training to the hassles of relocating, transitional challenges to acclimatization, to culture shock to re-entry shock . . . [because] the Settler must receive more in-depth insights into the host country's customs and culture. The language skills must be much more than conversational and a solid knowledge of the country's religion, politics, history, meaning of nature, morals, social structure, education, food and table manners, roles of man and woman, business ethics, negotiation techniques, humor and values is highly important. . . . The Settler should be extremely open-minded, flexible, friendly and honest . . . adaptability is a valuable asset.[24]

Contrasting Attitudes Toward International Operations

3 Contrast ethnocentric, polycentric, and geocentric attitudes toward foreign operations.

Can a firm's degree of internationalization be measured? Some observers believe it can, and they claim a true global company must have subsidiaries in at least six nations. Others say that, to qualify as a multinational or global company, a firm must have a certain percentage of its capital or operations in foreign countries. However, Howard Perlmutter insisted that these measurable guidelines tell only part of the story and suggested it is management's *attitude* toward its foreign operations that really counts.

The more one penetrates into the living reality of an international firm, the more one finds it is necessary to give serious weight to the way executives think about doing business around the world. The orientation toward "foreign people, ideas, resources," in headquarters and subsidiaries, and in host and home environments, becomes crucial in estimating the multi-nationality of a firm.[25]

This symbolic handshake between Hong Kong's chief executive, Tung Chee Hwa, and Mickey Mouse sealed the deal on Walt Disney's fifth amusement park. Experience in France and Japan taught Disney the value of balancing American-style Disney magic with local tastes and traditions. For example, unlike Americans who prefer to buy meals at the park, the French tend to pack a lunch when visiting Euro-Disney. Rest assured, Mickey and his friends will be up to Chinese standards when the new park opens in 2005.

Perlmutter identified three managerial attitudes toward international operations, which he labeled ethnocentric, polycentric, and geocentric.[26] Each attitude is presented here in its pure form, but all three are likely to be found in a single multinational or global corporation (see Table 4.2). The key question is, "Which attitude predominates?"

Ethnocentric Attitude.   Managers with an **ethnocentric attitude** are home-country-oriented. Home-country personnel, ideas, and practices are viewed as inherently superior to those from abroad. Foreign nationals are not trusted with key decisions or technology. Home-country procedures and evaluation criteria are applied worldwide without variation. Proponents of ethnocentrism say that it makes for a simpler and more tightly controlled organization. Critics believe this attitude makes for poor planning and ineffective operations because of inadequate feedback, high turnover of subsidiary managers, reduced innovation, inflexibility, and social and political backlash.

    In U.S.-Japanese business relations, ethnocentrism cuts both ways. Procter & Gamble failed to do its cultural homework when it ran a series of advertisements for Pampers in Japan. Japanese customers were bewildered by the ads, in which a stork carried a baby, because storks have no cultural connection to birth in Japan.[27] Similarly, Japanese companies operating in the United States seem to be out of touch with the expectations of American managers. In a survey of American managers employed by 31 such companies, the common complaint was too few promotions and too little responsibility.[28] Ethnocentric attitudes can also cause problems in ethnically diverse countries, such as the United States, where Hispanics/Latinos are projected to be the largest minority by 2005 and nearly one-quarter of the population by 2050.[29]

ethnocentric attitude
view that assumes the home country's personnel and ways of doing things are best

Table 4.2

Three Different Attitudes Toward International Operations			
Organization design	**Ethnocentric**	**Polycentric**	**Geocentric**
Identification	Nationality of owner	Nationality of host country	Truly international company but identifying with national interests
Authority; decision making	High in headquarters	Relatively low in headquarters	Aim for a collaborative approach between headquarters and subsidiaries
Evaluation and control	Home standards applied for person and performance	Determined locally	Find standards that are universal and local
Communication; information flow	High volume to subsidiaries; orders, commands, advice	Little to and from headquarters; little between subsidiaries	Both ways and between subsidiaries; heads of subsidiaries part of management team
Perpetuation (recruiting, staffing, development)	Recruit and develop people of home country for key positions everywhere in the world	Develop people of local nationality for key positions in their own country	Develop best people everywhere in the world for key positions everywhere in the world

Source: Excerpted from Howard V. Perlmutter, "The Tortuous Evolution of the Multinational Corporation," *Columbia Journal of World Business,* 4 (January–February 1969): 12. Used with permission.

When it comes to Hispanic marketing, a little knowledge is a dangerous thing . . . Tropicana advertised jugo de china in Miami. China means orange to Puerto Ricans, but Miami's Cubans thought it was juice from the Orient. Jack in the Box goofed with a commercial featuring a band of Mexican mariachis accompanying a Spanish flamenco dancer. "That's like having Willie Nelson sing while Michael Jackson does the moonwalk," says Bert Valencia, a marketing professor at the American Graduate School of International Management in Glendale, Arizona.

Why do companies sometimes end up looking like idiotas? Because learning this market takes more than a few lessons at Berlitz. An occasional blunder is forgivable. But many companies are designing advertising for the nation's . . . [more than 31] million Hispanics without understanding the differences among Mexicans, Puerto Ricans, Cubans, and the rich array of the other nationalities that make up the U.S. Hispanic population.[30]

Indeed, U.S. Hispanics and Latinos trace their roots to 22 different countries.

Polycentric Attitude.   This host-country orientation is based on the assumption that, because cultures are so different, local managers know what is best for their operations. A **polycentric attitude** leads to a loose confederation of comparatively independent subsidiaries rather than to a highly integrated structure. Because foreign operations are measured in terms of ends (instead of means), methods, incentives, and training procedures vary widely from location to location.

On the negative side, wasteful duplication of effort occurs at the various units within the confederation precisely because they are independent. Such duplication can erode the efficiency of polycentric organizations. Moreover, global objectives can be undermined by excessive concern for local traditions and success. But there is a positive side: "The main advantages are an intensive exploitation of local markets, better sales since local management is often better informed, more local initiative for new products, more host-government support, and good local managers with high morale."[31]

polycentric attitude *view that assumes local managers in host countries know best how to run their own operations*

geocentric attitude *world-oriented view that draws upon the best talent from around the globe*

Geocentric Attitude.   Managers with a **geocentric attitude** are world-oriented. "As Sue Evens, senior manager of international human resources consulting at KPMG, New York, says, thinking globally means 'taking the best other cultures have to offer and blending that into a third culture.'"[32] Skill, not nationality, determines who gets promoted or transferred to key positions around the globe. In geocentric companies, local and worldwide objectives are balanced in all aspects of operation. Collaboration between headquarters and subsidiaries is high, but an effort is made to maintain a balance between global standards and local discretion. Thus, a geocentric attitude is essential in the transnational model discussed earlier. Bausch & Lomb, the Rochester, New York, maker of Ray-Ban sunglasses, fosters a geocentric attitude by telling its managers to "think globally, but act locally." Says international division senior vice president Ronald Zarella: "What we try to do today is set strategic goals and let local manage-

---

4D

McDonald's Rethinks Its Global Strategy

Jack M. Greenberg, who became McDonald's CEO in 1998:

Q. *You've said McDonald's must adopt a "global mindset." What do you mean?*

A. *We've run our business as two distinct operations. The United States was predominant; international was a concept of trying to export the idea of McDonald's. It made sense, but we haven't taken enough opportunity to borrow ideas across borders. McFlurries [a new ice cream dessert] was an idea being tested in Toronto that we just tripped over by accident. Here's a good idea from Canada that took several years for us to discover. We're going to be more rigorous about sharing people and best practices.*

Source: Craig Matters, "Remaking an Icon—and a Burger," *Money*, 27 (Year-End 1998): 40.

Question: *In terms of the ethnocentric, polycentric, and geocentric distinction, what sort of attitude shift seems to be taking place here? Explain.*

ment take advantage of nuances in their market."[33] This has enabled Bausch & Lomb to satisfy European demand for more styles and costly sunglasses than is typical in the United States. "In Asia the company redesigned them to better suit the Asian face—with its flatter bridge and higher cheek bones—and sales took off."[34]

Of these three contrasting attitudes, only a geocentric attitude can help management take a long step toward success in today's vigorously competitive global marketplace (see The Global Manager).

The Cultural Imperative

Culture has a powerful impact on people's behavior. For example, consider the everyday activity of negotiating a business contract.

> *To Americans, a contract signals the conclusion of negotiations; its terms establish the rights, responsibilities, and obligations of the parties involved. However, to the Japanese, a company is not forever bound to the terms of the contract. In fact, it can be renegotiated whenever there is a significant shift in the company's circumstances. For instance, an unexpected change in governmental tax policy, or a change in the competitive environment, are considered legitimate reasons for contract renegotiation. To the Chinese, a signatory to an agreement is a partner with whom they can work, so to them the signing of a contract is just the beginning of negotiations.*[35]

Those doing business in foreign countries often encounter strikingly different cultural traditions and practices. Complicating matters is the blending of culture, politics, and religion. In Afghanistan, for example, things have changed dramatically for women in recent years. Strict Islamic traditions were liberalized after the 1960s when women gained voting rights. But when fundamentalist Taliban leaders took power, women's rights were radically curbed. Today they are banned from school and forced to conceal their entire bodies with traditional chadri when in public. At great physical risk to themselves, some women in Afghanistan are publicizing and protesting their brutal oppression over the Internet.

The Global Manager

A Trip to India for the Pillsbury Doughboy

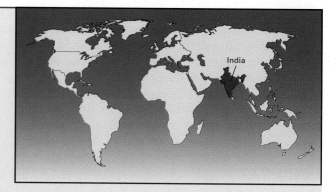

The Pillsbury Doughboy has landed in India to pitch a product that he had just about abandoned in America: plain old flour.

Pillsbury, the Diageo PLC unit behind the pudgy character, has a raft of higher-margin products such as microwave pizzas in other parts of the world but discovered that in this tradition-bound market, it needs to push the basics.

Even so, selling packaged flour in India is almost revolutionary, because most Indian housewives still buy raw wheat in bulk, clean it by hand, store it in huge metal hampers, and every week carry some to a neighborhood mill, or *chakki*, where it is ground between two stones.

To help reach those housewives, the Doughboy himself has gotten a makeover. In TV spots, he presses his palms together and bows in the traditional Indian greeting. He speaks six regional languages.

Pillsbury is onto a potentially huge business. India consumes about 69 million tons of wheat a year, second only to China. (The United States consumes about 26 million tons.) Much of India's wheat ends up as *roti*, a flat bread prepared on a griddle that accompanies almost every meal. In a nation where people traditionally eat with their hands, roti is the spoon. But less than 1 percent of all wholewheat flour, or *atta*, is sold prepackaged. India's climatic extremes and deplorable roads make it difficult to maintain freshness from mill to warehouse, let alone on store shelves.

Then there are the standards of the Indian housewife, who is determined to serve only the softest, freshest roti to her family. "Packaged flour sticks to your stomach and is bad for the intestines," says Poonam Jain, a New Delhi housewife.

Pillsbury knows that ultimately it won't make fistfuls of dough from packaged flour. Its aim is to establish its flour business and then introduce new products to carry its customers up to more lucrative products.

That payoff may take a decade or two. "As a food company, we have to be where the mouths are," says Robert Hancock, marketing director for Europe and Eurasia. "We'll get our rewards later."

Starting a flour operation meant turning back the clock for Pillsbury. Though it was born as a U.S. flour-milling company 130 years ago, the Diageo unit all but exited from that business in the early 1990s to focus on products such as frozen baked goods and ice cream. The food giant thought of introducing high-value products when it first explored India. But it quickly learned that most Indians don't have enough disposable income for such fare. Many lack refrigerators and ovens, too.

Pillsbury is betting that flour will generate sales volumes to compensate for the razor-thin profit margins. "We wanted a product with huge and widespread mainstream appeal," Mr. Hancock says.

Pitching packaged flour meant overcoming thousands of years of tradition. "I'd never met women so intimately involved with the food they prepare," recalls Bill Barrier, who led a Pillsbury team that spent 18 months trying to decode Indian wheat and consumers.

Marketing managers climbed into the attics where housewives store their wheat and accompanied them to their tiny neighborhood flour mills. "Anywhere else, flour is flour," says Samir Behl, vice president of marketing for Pillsbury International. "In India, the color, aroma, feel between the fingers, and mouth feel are all crucial."

Pillsbury had hoped to establish contracts with existing mills, but inspectors found hygiene and safety at some to be appalling. Pillsbury scouts visited 40 plants, where they encountered mice, rotting wheat and treacherous machinery. They often left coated in fine flour dust, whose presence is a severe fire hazard. In fact, when the electricity went out during a visit to one mill, Pillsbury executives were dumbfounded to see one worker light a match in the dark.

Pillsbury eventually found two mills capable of the required standards. But even then, their rollout was delayed by several months because the company rejected 40 percent of the wheat delivered to the mills after the 1998 harvest.

Many focus groups and lab tests later, Pillsbury came up with its packaged wheat blend, Pillsbury Chakki Fresh Atta. Godrej-Pillsbury Ltd., its joint venture here, launched the flour in southern and western India last year. The blue package, which features the Doughboy hoisting a roti, has become the market leader in Bombay, India's largest city. . . .

Source: Republished with permission of *The Wall Street Journal,* from Miriam Jordan, "Pillsbury Presses Flour Power in India," (May 5, 1999): B1. Permission conveyed through Copyright Clearance Center, Inc.

Cross-cultural business negotiators who ignore or defy cultural traditions do so at their own risk. That means the risk of not making the sale or of losing a contract or failing to negotiate a favorable deal. Therefore, a sensitivity to cross-cultural differences is imperative for people who do business in other countries.

In this section, we define the term *culture* and discuss a cultural profile of U.S. managers. Then, drawing primarily from the work of pioneering cultural anthropologist Edward T. Hall, we explore key sources of cross-cultural differences.

Culture Defined.   **Culture** is the pattern of taken-for-granted assumptions about how a given collection of people should think, act, and feel as they go about their daily affairs.[36] Regarding the central aspect of this definition—taken-for-granted assumptions—Hall noted:

> *Much of culture operates outside our awareness; frequently, we don't even know what we know. . . . This applies to all people. The Chinese or the Japanese or the Arabs are as unaware of their assumptions as we are of our own. We each assume that they're part of human nature. What we think of as "mind" is really internalized culture.[37]*

In Chapter 9, *organizational* culture is called the social glue binding members of an organization together. Similarly, at a broader level, societal culture acts as a social glue. That glue is made up of norms, values, attitudes, role expectations, taboos, symbols, heroes, beliefs, morals, customs, and rituals. Cultural lessons are imparted from birth to death via role models, formal education, religious teachings, and peer pressure.

Cultural undercurrents make international dealings immensely challenging. According to Fons Trompenaars and Charles Hampden-Turner, the Dutch and English authors of the landmark book, *Riding the Waves of Culture*:

> *International managers have it tough. They must operate on a number of different premises at any one time. These premises arise from their culture of origin, the culture in which they are working, and the culture of the organization which employs them.*
>
> *In every culture in the world such phenomena as authority, bureaucracy, creativity, good fellowship, verification, and accountability are experienced in different ways. That we use the same words to describe them tends to make us unaware that our cultural biases and our accustomed conduct may not be appropriate, or shared.[38]*

A Cultural Profile of American Managers.   A good way to become more aware of cross-cultural differences is to look at oneself through the eyes of people from other cultures. One study based on interviews with 40 managers from many different countries has given American managers a revealing look in the cultural mirror.[39] All of the managers had professional experience in more than one country. Only three of the interviewees were American. Each manager was asked to characterize the "American style" of management. Results of the study are presented in Table 4.3.

Two sets of characteristics of the American style of managing turned out to be clearly positive. International managers generally like Americans' informality, creativity, open-mindedness, and related traits. At the other end of the scale, American managers were roundly criticized for being educationally and professionally narrow. Between the extremes, representing a mix of

culture *a population's taken-for-granted assumptions, values, beliefs, and symbols that foster patterned behavior*

↙ The Cultural Mirror   **4E**

Sometimes it's hard to appreciate one's own culture because it is dictated by *taken-for-granted assumptions* (generally unspoken) about how we should think and act. Here is an opportunity to step back and objectively analyze one aspect of your own culture.

Questions: *What cultural assumptions influence student behavior in the typical American college classroom? Which behaviors are okay? Which are not okay? How is the student classroom culture enforced? How does the student classroom culture affect what professors can and cannot do?*

Table 4.3

How Do International Managers Characterize American Managers?

Frequently mentioned features that distinguish the U.S. from other nations	
Positive	**Negative**
Informal, frank, trustworthy	
Innovative, open-minded, objective, pragmatic, flexible	
Work harder than Europeans	But less than many Asians. Often "spinning wheels"
Impatient; get things done; hands-on mentality	Short-term orientation
Materialistic; profit-oriented; business is a valid, worthy profession	Judge persons' worth by their wealth; shun low-pay manufacturing jobs
Individualistic; entrepreneurial	Loyal to division, not firm
Aggressive, hard-nosed, pragmatic	Overlook simpler, diplomatic means
	Not well rounded educationally; parochial

Source: Ashok Nimgade, "American Management as Viewed by International Professionals," November–December 1989, Figure 4, p. 102. Reprinted from *Business Horizons*, November–December 1989. Copyright 1989 by the Foundation for the School of Business at Indiana University. Used with permission.

positives and negatives, were five other sets of characteristics. In this middle zone, strengths such as impatience and individualism, when taken to extreme, became weaknesses. In sum, American managers have a lot going for themselves. But a number of their basic cultural tendencies can cause problems in cross-cultural dealings. Self-awareness and cultural adaptations are required.

4 Explain from a cross-cultural perspective the difference between high-context and low-context cultures, and distinguish between monochronic and polychronic time.

High-Context and Low-Context Cultures.   People from European-based cultures typically assess people from Asian cultures such as China and Japan as quiet and hard to figure out. Conversely, Asians tend to view Westerners as aggressive, insensitive, and even rude.[40] True, language differences are a significant barrier to mutual understanding. But something more fundamental is involved, something cultural. Anthropologist Hall prompted better understanding of cross-cultural communication by distinguishing between high- and low-context cultures.[41] The difference centers on how much meaning one takes from what is actually said or written versus who the other person is.

In **high-context cultures,** people rely heavily on nonverbal and subtle situational messages when communicating with others. The other person's official status, place in society, and reputation say a great deal about the person's rights, obligations, and trustworthiness. In high-context cultures, people do not expect to talk about such "obvious" things. Conversation simply provides general background information about the other person. Thus, in high-context Japan, the ritual of exchanging business cards is a social necessity, and failing to read a card you have been given is a grave insult. The other person's company and position determine what is said and how. Arab, Chinese, and Korean cultures also are high-context.

People from **low-context cultures** convey essential messages and meaning primarily with words. Low-context cultures in Germany, Switzerland, Scandinavia, North America, and Great Britain expect people to communicate their precise intended

high-context cultures
cultures in which nonverbal and situational messages convey primary meaning

low-context cultures
cultures in which words convey primary meaning

meaning. While low-context people do read so-called body language, its messages are secondary to spoken and written words. Legal contracts with precisely worded expectations are important in low-context countries such as the United States. However, according to international communications experts, "in high-context cultures the process of forging a business relationship is as important as, if not more important than, the written details of the actual deal."[42] This helps explain why Americans tend to be frustrated with the apparently slow pace of business dealings in Japan. For the Japanese, the many rounds of meetings and social gatherings are necessary to collect valuable contextual information as a basis for judging the other party's character. For the schedule-driven American, anything short of actually signing the contract is considered a pointless waste of time. *Patience* is a prime virtue for low-context managers doing business in high-context cultures.

Back to the Opening Case

Have DaimlerChrysler's "low-context" and "monochronic" American employees met their match in their German counterparts? Explain.

Other Sources of Cultural Diversity.   Managers headed for a foreign country need to do their homework on the following cultural variables to avoid awkwardness and problems.[43] There are no rights or wrongs here, only cross-cultural differences.

■ *Time.* Hall referred to time as a silent language of culture. He distinguished between monochronic and polychronic time.[44] **Monochronic time** is based on the perception that time is a unidimensional straight line divided into standard units, such as seconds, minutes, hours, and days. In monochronic cultures, including North America and Northern Europe, everyone is assumed to be on the same clock and time is treated as money. The general rule is to use time efficiently, and above all, to be on time. In contrast, **polychronic time** involves the perception of time as flexible, elastic, and multidimensional. Latin American, Mediterranean,

monochronic time *a perception of time as a straight line broken into standard units*

polychronic time *a perception of time as flexible, elastic, and multidimensional*

Look out, Latin America—here comes a new wave of Spanish conquistadors! Only this time they're wearing business suits and selling telephones. Spain's recently privatized telephone giant, Telefónica, has invested nearly $11 billion in its Latin American expansion. Antonio Viana-Baptista (pictured here), head of Telefónica's international operations, will likely experience more language barriers than North Americans might expect. The Spanish spoken in various Latin American countries is very different from that spoken in Madrid, and the national language of Brazil is Portuguese.

and Arab cultures are polychronic. Managers in polychronic cultures such as Mexico see no problem with loosely scheduled, overlapping office visits. A mono-chronic American, arriving ten minutes early for an appointment with a Mexican official, resents having to wait another 15 minutes. The American perceives the Mexican official as slow and insensitive. The Mexican believes the American is self-centered and impatient.[45] Different perceptions of time are responsible for this collision of cultures.

- *Interpersonal space.* People in a number of cultures prefer to stand close when conversing. Both Arabs and Asians fall into this group. An interpersonal distance of only six inches is very disturbing to a Northern European or an American who is accustomed to conversing at arm's length. Cross-cultural gatherings in the Middle East often involve an awkward dance as Arab hosts strive to get closer while their American and European guests shuffle backwards around the room to maintain what they consider to be a proper distance.

- *Language.* Foreign language skills are the gateway to true cross-cultural under-standing. Translations are not an accurate substitute for conversational ability in the local language.[46] Consider, for example, the complexity of the Japanese language:

> *Japanese is a situational language and the way something is said differs with the rela-tionship between speaker, listener, or the person about whom they are speaking; their respective families, ages, professional statuses, and companies all affect the way they express themselves.*

> *In this respect, Japanese isn't one language but a group of them, changing with a dizzying array of social conventions with which Americans have no experience. Japanese people are raised dealing with the shifting concepts of in group/out group, male and female speech patterns, appropriate politeness levels, and humble and honorific forms of speech. An unwary student, armed only with a few years of classroom Japanese, can pile up mistakes in this regard very quickly.[47]*

Foreign language instructors who prepare Ameri-cans for foreign assignments have noted these recent trends: an increase in demand for Brazilian Portuguese and Mandarin Chinese and a decrease in demand for Japanese. Spanish remains the most widely studied foreign language, followed by French and German.[48]

- *Religion.* Awareness of a business colleague's reli-gious traditions is essential for building a lasting relationship. (See Managing Diversity.) Those traditions may dictate dietary restrictions, religious holidays, and Sabbath schedules, which are impor-tant to the devout and represent cultural mine-fields for the uninformed. For instance, the official day of rest in Iran is Thursday; in Kuwait and Pakistan it is Friday.[49] In Israel, where the official day off is Saturday, "Burger King restaurants— unlike McDonald's— do not offer cheeseburgers in order to conform to Jewish dietary laws forbidding mixing milk products and meat."[50]

↗↙ **4G**
Foreign Language Skills

Learning a foreign language is easier for some than for others. International business experts say it is worth the time and effort in order to

- Enhance the traveler's sense of mastery, self-confidence, and safety.
- Show respect for foreign business hosts or guests.
- Help build rapport and trust with foreign hosts or guests.
- Improve the odds of a successful foreign business venture.
- Build a base of confidence for learning other languages.
- Promote a deeper understanding of other cultures.
- Help travelers obtain the best possible medical care during emergencies.
- Minimize culture shock and the frustrations of being an outsider.

Source: Adapted from Gary P. Ferraro, "The Need for Linguistic Proficiency in Global Business," *Business Horizons*, 39 (May–June 1996): 39–46.

Questions: *Could you conduct a business meeting in one or more foreign languages? What has been your experience with trying to learn foreign languages? How strong is your desire to speak a foreign language? Which language(s)? Why? Would a strong second language help you get a better job? Explain.*

Managing Diversity

Islam's Growth Affects Workplace Policies

With more than 5 million adherents, Islam is expected to soon surpass Judaism as the second-most commonly practiced religion in the United States (Christianity being the first). As a result, human resource professionals will need to ensure that their organizations consider both Muslim employees and customers when designing policies and programs.

An initial challenge for employers will be to overcome anti-Muslim sentiment in the workplace. Distrust and limited understanding often characterize Americans' perceptions of Islam. Surveys have shown that terrorist activity involving Islamic groups, such as the recent U.S. embassy attacks in Kenya and Tanzania, frequently lead Americans to link Islam with violent behavior. In a recent Roper poll, for example, more than half of the respondents indicated that Islam was, by definition, anti-American, anti-Western, or supportive of terrorism.

Several organizations, such as the American Muslim Council (**www.amermuslim.org**) and the Council on American-Islamic Relations (CAIR) (**www.cair-net.org**), are trying to counter these perceptions. CAIR recently explained that through education and sensitization, it hopes to reduce the negative impact of Islamophobia. "This impact is manifest in actions as diverse as discrimination in the workplace, the singling out of American Muslims in airports, harassment of our children and even threats against Islamic institutions."

Employers cannot afford to ignore the growing influence of Muslims, both as consumers and employees. In 1997, for example, after it received complaints, Nike recalled a shoe line imprinted with a logo that resembled the Arabic script for Allah. The company offered refunds for returned shoes, issued a public apology, implemented sensitivity training for employees, and provided financial support for a Muslim elementary school in the United States.

In another example, the July issue of US Airways' *Attache* magazine contained a picture of the Prophet Muhammad. After receiving letters and phone calls saying that it is both inappropriate and offensive to Muslims to attempt to portray the Prophet Muhammad, the company issued an apology in the magazine.

Religious discrimination cases are likely to increase as Muslims become more willing to assert their rights in the workplace. Many of the cases filed to date relate to disagreements over religious dress, daily prayers, or derogatory remarks by coworkers. Misunderstandings seem to occur frequently over the issues of head scarves worn by women and facial hair for men.

HR professionals should educate themselves and their employees about Islam to ensure that their organizations work appropriately with Muslim employees and customers. A recent publication, *An Employer's Guide to Islamic Religious Practices* (CAIR, 202-659-2247), provides information on the legal protections of religious rights and explains practices such as daily prayers, washing, prayer space, dietary requirements, holidays, clothing, and grooming. The guide offers tips for scheduling accommodations and explains social customs involving work-related requirements for eye contact, handshaking, and socializing.

Source: Maureen Minehan, "Islam's Growth Affects Workplace Policies," *HRMagazine*, 43 (November 1998): 216. Reprinted with the permission of *HRMagazine,* published by the Society for Human Resource Management, Alexandria, Virginia.

Comparative Management Insights

Comparative management is the study of how organizational behavior and management practices differ across cultures. In this comparatively new field of inquiry, as in other fields, there is disagreement about theoretical frameworks and research methodologies.[51] Nevertheless, some useful lessons have been learned. In this section, we focus

comparative management
study of how organizational behavior and management practices differ across cultures

on (1) the applicability of American management theories in other cultures, (2) Ouchi's Theory Z, which contrasts American and Japanese management practices, (3) a cross-cultural study of work goals, and (4) an international contingency model of leadership.

Applying American Management Theories Abroad

5 **Discuss what Geert Hofstede's research has to say about the applicability of American management theories in foreign cultures.**

The results of a unique study indicate that management theories may not be universally applicable. Geert Hofstede, a Dutch organizational behavior researcher, surveyed 116,000 IBM employees from 40 different countries.[52] Hofstede classified each of his 40 national samples according to four different cultural dimensions, each of which probed an important question about the prevailing culture:

- *Power distance.* How readily do individuals accept the unequal distribution of power in organizations and institutions?
- *Uncertainty avoidance.* How threatening are uncertain and ambiguous situations, and how important are rules, conformity, and absolute truths?
- *Individualism-collectivism.* Are people responsible for their own welfare within a loosely knit social framework, or does the group look out for individuals in exchange for loyalty?
- *Masculinity-femininity.* How important are masculine attitudes (assertiveness, money and possessions, and performance) versus feminine attitudes (concern for people, the quality of life, and the environment)?

Hofstede scored the 40 countries in his sample from low to high on each of the four cultural dimensions. The United States ranked moderately low (15 out of 40) on power

American companies are slowly tiptoeing back into Vietnam. Memories of a disastrous war and failed business ventures linger. The cultural differences are immense. Made-in-America management theories and practices will have to be adapted to Vietnamese culture.

Security	Security and social	Social	Self-actualization	Table 4.4
Switzerland	Iran	Singapore	Hong Kong**	**Top-Ranking Needs Vary from Country to Country**
Germany*	Thailand	Denmark	Great Britain	
Austria	Taiwan	Sweden	India	
Italy	Brazil	Norway	United States	
Venezuela	Israel	Netherlands	Philippines	
Mexico	France	Finland	Canada	
Colombia	Spain		New Zealand	
Argentina	Turkey		Australia	
Belgium	Peru		South Africa	
Japan	Chile		Ireland	
Greece	Yugoslavia			
Pakistan	Portugal			

*At the time of this study, East and West Germany were separate countries. East Germany was not one of the 40 countries surveyed.

**Now reunited with China.

Source: Paraphrased with permission from Geert Hofstede, "Motivation, Leadership, and Organization: Do American Theories Apply Abroad?" in *Organizational Dynamics,* 9, no. 1 (Summer 1980): 54–56. This article summarizes Dr. Hofstede's research published in the book *Culture's Consequences: International Differences in Work-Related Values* (Beverly Hills, Calif.: Sage Publications, 1980).

distance, low (9 out of 40) on uncertainty avoidance, very high (40 out of 40) on individualism, and moderately high (28 out of 40) on masculinity.

The marked cultural differences among the 40 countries led Hofstede to recommend that American management theories should be adapted to local cultures rather than imposed on them. As we saw in Chapter 2, many popular management theories were developed within the U.S. cultural context. Hofstede believes that it is naive to expect those theories to apply automatically in significantly different cultures. For example, American-made management theories that reflect Americans' preoccupation with individualism are out of place in countries such as Mexico, Brazil, and Japan, where individualism is discouraged. Moreover, as Hofstede discovered, the need ranked highest differs from culture to culture (see Table 4.4).

Hofstede's research does not attempt to tell international managers *how* to apply various management techniques in different cultures. However, it does provide a useful cultural typology and presents a convincing case for the cultural adaptation of American management theory and practice.[53]

Ouchi's Theory Z: The Marriage of American and Japanese Management

6 Identify important comparative management lessons learned from William Ouchi's Theory Z research and international studies of work goals and leadership styles.

The work of UCLA management scholar William Ouchi highlighted a type of U.S. company that successfully melded the American way of managing with some aspects of management in another culture. Ouchi began his study by identifying the

Back to the Opening Case

Based on the different need profiles for Germany and the United States in Table 4.4, what sort of cross-cultural conflict might occur between Daimler-Chrysler's German and American executives? (*Note:* See the discussion of Maslow's need hierarchy theory in Chapter 13.)

contrasting characteristics of Japanese and American companies.[54] During the course of his research, he discovered that certain then-successful U.S.-based companies—including IBM, Intel, Hewlett-Packard, Eastman Kodak, and Eli Lilly—exhibited a style of management that effectively combined the traits of typical American and Japanese companies. He called these hybrid companies *Theory Z* organizations (see Figure 4.1). Interestingly, Ouchi's Theory Z companies did not simply imitate the Japanese. Instead, each firm's Theory Z qualities evolved from a desire to improve upon the typical American way of managing. Each Theory Z company was strictly American in origin, but American and Japanese in conduct and appearance.

The Japanese-like qualities of Theory Z organizations are identified as long-term employment, slower promotions, cross-functional career paths, greater emphasis on self-control, participative decision making, and a concern for the whole employee. Unlike Japanese organizations, Theory Z organizations emphasize *individual* responsibility, a distinctly American trait. Ouchi's work not only gives us a better understanding of Japanese management,[55] it also shows that American organizations can benefit from thoughtful incorporation of the experience of managers in other cultures.

Too much emphasis on one country's cultural management practices can cause problems. For example, *Business Week* recently described how the Japanese style of management has been a hindrance to change-minded leaders at Mitsubishi, Toshiba, and Toyota during Japan's prolonged 1990s recession:

> [They] are among the best corporate chiefs on the planet. But they have been cruelly misplaced in a Japan that cannot tolerate the unemployment and social upheaval that wholesale restructuring would entail. And because Japanese corporate culture places so much stress on building consensus and saving face, even world-class bosses often struggle vainly to impose their visions on the organizations they theoretically run.
>
> As competition grows increasingly global, these executives are at a huge disadvantage compared with rivals in America and Europe.[56]

The principal lesson from this example and from Hofstede's and Ouchi's research is clear. *Successful geocentric managers are not prisoners of their own culture.* They create (and constantly update) a workable blend of management concepts and practices from around the world.

A Cross-Cultural Study of Work Goals

What do people want from their work? A survey of 8,192 employees from seven countries found general disagreement about the relative importance of 11 different work goals.[57] Respondents to the survey represented a broad range of professions and all levels of the organizational hierarchy. They were asked to rank 11 work goals. Those work goals are listed in Table 4.5, along with the average rankings for five countries. "Interesting work" got a consistently high ranking. "Opportunity for promotion" and "working conditions" consistently were at or very near the bottom of each country's rankings. Beyond those few consistencies, general disagreement prevailed.

The main practical implication of these findings is that managers need to adapt their motivational programs to local preferences.[58] Throughout this text, we consistently stress the importance of the contingency approach to management. In this case,

Figure 4.1 | The Evolution of Theory Z Organizations

Japanese Organizations	+	American Organizations	=	Theory Z Organizations
Lifetime employment		Short-term employment		Long-term employment (Large training investment encourages company to retain personnel through good and bad times.)
Slow evaluation and promotion		Rapid evaluation and promotion		Relatively slow evaluation and promotion (Promotions are tied to skills and contributions rather than to the calendar.)
Nonspecialized career paths		Specialized career paths		Cross-functional career paths (Companywide skills are acquired through varied and nonspecialized experience.)
Implicit control mechanisms (self-control)		Explicit control mechanisms (control through policies and rules)		Balanced explicit and implicit control mechanisms (Bureaucratic control is supplemented by personal judgments and feelings about what is right or wrong, appropriate or inappropriate.)
Collective decision making		Individual decision making		Consensual, participative decision making (Decisions are derived through democratic process involving all affected employees.)
Collective responsibility		Individual responsibility		Individual responsibility (Ultimate responsibility for decisions remains with relevant individuals.)
Holistic concern		Segmented concern		Holistic concern for employees (There is a willingness to deal with the "whole" person rather than fragmented organizational role players.)

Source: From *Theory Z: How American Business Can Meet the Japanese Challenge* by William Ouchi. Copyright © 1981. Reprinted by permission of Perseus Books Publishers, a member of Perseus Books, L.L.C.

an international contingency approach to motivation is called for. For instance, pay is relatively less important in Japan than in the other four countries. And job security is much less important to Israelis than it is to American, British, German, and Japanese employees.

Table 4.5

Work Goals Vary from Country to Country

Work goals	Means rankings (by country)				
	U.S.	Britain	Germany*	Israel	Japan
Interesting work	1	1	3	1	2
Pay	2	2	1	3	5
Job security	3	3	2	10	4
Match between person and job	4	6	5	6	1
Opportunity to learn	5	8	9	5	7
Variety	6	7	6 **	11	9
Interpersonal relations	7	4	4	2	6
Autonomy	8	10	8	4	3
Convenient work hours	9	5	6 **	7	8
Opportunity for promotion	10	11	10	8	11
Working conditions	11	9	11	9	10

* Formerly West Germany.
** Two goals tied for sixth rank.
Source: Data from Itzhak Harpaz, "The Importance of Work Goals: An International Perspective," *Journal of International Business Studies*, 21 (First Quarter 1990): 81. Reprinted with permission.

Table 4.6

An International Contingency Model of Leadership: Culturally Appropriate Path-Goal Leadership Styles

Country	Directive	Supportive	Participative	Achievement-oriented
Australia		X	X	X
Brazil	X		X	
Canada		X	X	X
France	X		X	
Germany		X	X	X
Great Britain		X	X	X
Hong Kong*	X	X	X	X
India	X		X	X
Italy	X	X	X	
Japan	X	X	X	
Philippines	X	X	X	X
Sweden			X	X
Taiwan	X	X	X	
United States		X	X	X

*Now reunited with China.
Sources: Adapted from Carl A. Rodrigues, "The Situation and National Culture as Contingencies for Leadership Behavior: Two Conceptual Models," in *Advances in International Comparative Management*, 5, ed. S. Benjamin Prasad (Greenwich, Conn.: JAI Press, 1990), pp. 51–68; and Geert Hofstede and Michael Harris Bond, "The Confucius Connection: From Cultural Roots to Economic Growth," *Organizational Dynamics* (Spring 1988): 4–21.

An International Contingency Model of Leadership

Like motivational programs, leadership styles must be adapted to the local culture. This conclusion is based on a new international contingency model of leadership, which is the product of two separate but overlapping studies. As indicated in Table 4.6, the four path-goal leadership styles have varying applicability in selected countries. (Refer to our discussion of path-goal leadership theory in Chapter 15 for definitions of the four styles.) Importantly, the model in Table 4.6 is intended to be a general guideline for international managers, not a set of hard-and-fast rules.

According to the model, participative leadership is the most broadly applicable style. Participative leadership is not necessarily the *best* style; it simply is culturally acceptable in many different countries. Interestingly, in a more recent study of employees in Russia's largest textile factory, participative leadership triggered a *decrease* in output. Why? The researchers felt the Russians had a lack of faith in participative schemes found to be untrustworthy during the communist era.[59] It takes time for people in new democracies to get used to participative management. For example, American entrepreneur Michael Smolens has taken it one step at a time at Danube Knitware Ltd., the textile mill he cofounded in Hungary. It has been a learning experience for all involved at the 950-employee company that recently opened a sewing factory in neighboring Romania.

> *The first step was getting workers used to high Western production standards and motivating them to accept the company's priorities. Hungary's low wage base was seen as a big plus when the company was being formed, but absenteeism has been an ongoing problem. . . . Smolens realized he'd have to strengthen his wage structure to keep his workers from abandoning the company for the family farms or the black market. He also moved from awarding attendance bonuses to providing other job incentives—in particular, cultivating a more comfortable, open work environment.*

 ## Democracy and Participative Leadership   4I

Call it the democratic dilemma: A historic number of people this year are selecting their governments by ballot, yet the process has made many of their countries more turbulent than ever. . . .

For the U.S. and other Western countries, the triumph of the hallowed one-person, one-vote system is a testament to their ideals and virtues. . . .

Yet this is a deeply anxious time for the nations scorched by the brushfire of democracy spreading around the post–Cold War globe. For all its desirability, democracy has drawbacks. While the developed world is moving toward borderless economic integration, elections in upstart democracies sometimes favor hotheaded nationalists and demagogues. One result: Democracy still takes limited forms in some countries. Another: Resistance to democracy and its ideals is mounting among many remaining authoritarian states.

Source: Excerpted from Marcus W. Brauchli, "More Nations Embrace Democracy—And Find It Often Can Be Messy," *The Wall Street Journal* (June 25, 1996): A1.

Questions: *Is there a connection between democracy and participative leadership in the workplace? Is it possible for managers to use participative leadership in a country where democracy does not exist or does not work? How strong is your personal commitment to participative leadership in the workplace? Explain.*

"We're actively soliciting comments from the workers day to day," says [cofounder Phil] Lightly. "They know what the problems are, but because of the way things used to be in this country, they're not always comfortable sharing them."

"It's a good approach," Smolens adds, "and we do see progress. They're starting to realize that what they say is being taken seriously." [60]

Relative to the countries listed in Table 4.6, directive leadership turned out to be the *least* appropriate leadership style. Hong Kong and the Philippines, probably because of their rich cultural diversity, are unique in their receptiveness to all four leadership styles. International managers need a full repertoire of leadership styles in a culturally diverse world. [61]

Staffing Foreign Positions

In today's global economy, successful foreign experience is becoming a required stepping-stone to top management. *Fortune* magazine's Marshall Loeb recently observed, "An assignment abroad, once thought to be a career dead end, has become a ticket to speedy advance. And an increasingly necessary one." [62]

Unfortunately, owing largely to the sink-or-swim approach to foreign assignments, too many Americans find it very difficult to become competent global managers. [63] "According to the Centre for International Briefing, roughly 25 percent of American managers fail overseas. That's three to four times higher than failure rates experienced by European and Asian companies." [64] Failure in this context means that foreign-posted employees perform so poorly they are either fired or sent home early. This problem can be very costly in view of the following data: "Each year, U.S. firms send an estimated 100,000 Americans on foreign assignments. With an average stay of four years, the investment in an expatriate—including salary, housing allowances, and moving expenses—can easily run over $1 million." [65] Predeparture training for the employee and education allowances for children can drive the bill much higher. Managers are challenged not to waste this sort of investment. They need to do a much better job of preparing employees for foreign assignments. Toward that end, let us examine why such a high proportion of American managers fail abroad and what can be done about it.

Why Is the U.S. Expatriate Failure Rate So High?

Although historically a term for banishment or exile to a foreign country, *expatriate* today refers to those who live and work abroad. A survey of 80 U.S.-based multinational companies uncovered some important facts about the reasons for corporate expatriate failures (see Table 4.7). *Family and personal adjustment problems* head the list, whereas technical incompetence ranks near the bottom. Expatriate American managers tend to be technically competent, but they and/or their families too often are at a disadvantage in cross-cultural settings. [66] This state of affairs is not surprising in view of the following:

[Recent research] underscores the woeful lack of preparation many U.S. executives receive for assignments overseas. Of some 100 high-level U.S. executives (average income $172,000)

	Table 4.7
1. Inability of the manager's spouse to adjust to a different physical or cultural environment	**Why U.S. Employees Fail in Foreign Assignments (in descending order of importance)**
2. The manager's inability to adapt to a different physical or cultural environment	
3. Other family-related problems	
4. The manager's personality or emotional immaturity	
5. The manager's inability to cope with the responsibilities posed by overseas work	
6. The manager's lack of technical competence	
7. The manager's lack of motivation to work overseas	

Source: Ranking based on responses to a survey of 80 U.S. MNCs. Rosalie L. Tung, "Expatriate Assignments: Enhancing Success and Minimizing Failure," *Academy of Management Executive,* 1 (May 1987): 117. Reprinted by permission.

> working in Western Europe, 84 percent received no corporate briefing on management practices in their host countries, and 77 percent didn't even get factual information on the new country. Only 15 percent received language training. And over 75 percent of the companies failed to communicate with their employee's spouses about the new assignments and to offer them job assistance overseas.[67]

Twenty percent of the polled executives desired a transfer home, and 9 percent actually went home early.

Cross-Cultural Training

In line with our earlier definition, culture is the unique system of values, beliefs, and symbols that foster patterned behavior in a given population. It is difficult to distinguish the individual from his or her cultural context. Consequently, people tend to be very protective of their cultural identity. Careless defiance of cultural norms or traditions by outsiders can result in grave personal insult and put important business dealings at risk.[68] Cultural sensitivity can be learned, fortunately, through cross-cultural training.[69]

7 Discuss the nature and importance of cross-cultural training in international management.

Specific Techniques.   **Cross-cultural training** is defined as any form of guided experience aimed at helping people live and work comfortably in another culture. Following is a list of five basic cross-cultural training techniques, ranked in order of increasing complexity and cost.

cross-cultural training
guided experience that helps people live and work in foreign cultures

- *Documentary programs.* Trainees read about a foreign country's history, culture, institutions, geography, and economics. Videotaped presentations also are often used.
- *Culture assimilator.* Cultural familiarity is achieved through exposure to a series of simulated intercultural incidents, or typical problem situations. This technique has been used to quickly train those who are given short notice of a foreign assignment.
- *Language instruction.* Conversational language skills are taught through a variety of methods. Months, sometimes years, of study are required to master difficult languages. But as a cross-cultural communications professor noted, "To speak more than one language is no longer a luxury, it is a necessity."[70] A good role

What do these Chinese college students studying at the China Europe International Business School in Shanghai have in common with their counterparts around the world? Hopes, dreams, and visions for a brighter future. With one-fifth of the world's population and a burgeoning business sector, China promises to become a dominant player in the global economy. These talented and multilingual students are poised to play key roles in that transformation.

model is Tupperware's top management team, made up of nine executives (all with foreign experience) who speak from two to four languages each.[71]

- *Sensitivity training.* Experiential exercises teach awareness of the impact of one's actions on others.
- *Field experience.* Extensive firsthand exposure to ethnic subcultures in one's own country or to foreign cultures heightens awareness.[72]

Is One Technique Better than Another?   A study of 80 (63 male, 17 female) managers from a U.S. electronics company attempted to compare the relative effectiveness of different training techniques.[73] A documentary approach was compared with an interpersonal approach. The latter combined sensitivity training and local ethnic field experience. Both techniques were judged equally effective at promoting cultural adjustment, as measured during the managers' three-month stay in South Korea. The researchers recommended a *combination* of documentary and interpersonal training. The importance of language training was diminished in this study because the managers dealt primarily with English-speaking Koreans.

Considering that 57 percent of U.S. companies have no formal expatriate training programs,[74] the key issue is not which type of training is better, but whether companies have any systematic cross-cultural training at all.

An Integrated Expatriate Staffing System.   Cross-cultural training, in whatever form, should not be an isolated experience. Rather, it should be part of an integrated, selection-orientation-repatriation process focused on a distinct career path.[75] The ultimate goal should be a positive and productive experience for the employee and his or her family and a smooth professional and cultural reentry back home.

During the selection phase, the usual interview should be supplemented with an orientation session for the candidate's family. This session gives everyone an opportunity to "select themselves out" before a great deal of time and money has been invested. Experience has shown that, upon arrival at the foreign assignment, family sponsors or assigned mentors are effective at reducing culture shock. Sponsors and mentors ease the expatriate family through the critical first six months by answering naive but important questions and by serving as cultural translators.

Finally, repatriation should be a forethought rather than an afterthought.[76] Candidates for foreign assignments deserve a firm commitment from their organization that a successful tour of duty will lead to a step up the career ladder upon return. Expatriates who spend their time worrying about being leapfrogged while they are absent from headquarters are less likely to succeed.

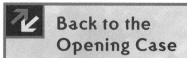

Back to the Opening Case
4J

Put yourself in the place of a U.S.-born human resources manager working in Michigan for DaimlerChrysler. Your German vocabulary is limited to greetings and selecting items from a German restaurant menu. You have been given the assignment to help ten German managers prepare to live and work in the United States for three years. What do you need to do to help them avoid culture shock and have their families enjoy a smooth transition to living in America? (*Note:* Good resource articles for this assignment are David Stamps, "Welcome to America: Watch Out for Culture Shock," *Training*, 33 (November 1996): 22–30; and Daniel McGinn and Stefan Theil, "Hands on the Wheel," *Newsweek* (April 12, 1999): 49–52.)

What About North American Women on Foreign Assignments?

Historically, companies in Canada and the United States have sent very few women on foreign assignments. Between the early 1980s and late 1990s, the representation of women among North American expatriates grew from 3 percent to a still small 14 percent.[77] Conventional wisdom—that women could not be effective because of foreign prejudice—has turned out to be a myth. Recent research and practical experience have given us these insights:

8 **Summarize the position of women on foreign assignments.**

- North American women have enjoyed above-average success on foreign assignments.
- The greatest barriers to foreign assignments for North American women have been self-disqualification and prejudice among *home-country* managers. A recent survey led to this conclusion: "We found that American women in management and executive roles in foreign countries can do just as well as American men. Their biggest problem was convincing their companies to give them the assignments."[78]
- Culture is a bigger hurdle than gender. In other words, North American women on foreign assignments are seen as North Americans first and women second.[79]

Testimonial evidence suggests these last two factors are also true for African Americans, many of whom report smoother relations abroad than at home.[80] Thus, the best career advice for *anyone* seeking a foreign assignment is this: Carefully prepare yourself, *go for it*, and don't take "no" for an answer!

Relying on Local Managerial Talent

In recent years, the expensive expatriate failure problem and general trends toward geocentrism and globalism have resulted in a greater reliance on managers from host countries. Foreign nationals already know the language and culture and do not require huge relocation expenditures.[81] In addition, host-country governments tend to look favorably on a greater degree of local control. On the negative side, local managers may have an inadequate knowledge of home-office goals and procedures. The staffing of foreign positions is necessarily a case-by-case proposition.

Summary

1. The study of international management is more important than ever as the huge global economy continues to grow. Doing business internationally typically involves much more than importing and/or exporting goods. The six stages of the internationalization process are licensing, exporting, local warehousing and selling, local assembly and packaging, joint ventures, and direct foreign investments. There are three main guidelines for success in international joint ventures: (a) be patient while building trust with a carefully selected partner; (b) learn as much and as fast as possible without giving away key secrets; and (c) establish clear ground rules for rights and responsibilities.

2. The main distinction between global companies and transnational companies is the difference between reality and a futuristic vision. A global company does business simultaneously in many countries but pursues global strategies administered from a strong home-country headquarters. In contrast, a transnational company is envisioned as a decentralized global network of productive units with no distinct national identity. There is growing concern about the economic and political power of these stateless enterprises as they eclipse the power and scope of their host nations.

3. Experts, noting that American managers generally are prepared only for domestic service, recommend that present and future managers begin to think globally and cross-culturally. According to Howard Perlmutter, management may have any of three general attitudes about international operations: an ethnocentric attitude (home-country-oriented), a polycentric attitude (host-country-oriented), or a geocentric attitude (world-oriented). Perlmutter claims that a geocentric attitude will lead to better product quality, improved use of resources, better local management, and more profit than the other attitudes.

4. Communication in high-context cultures such as Japan is based more on nonverbal and situational messages than it is in low-context cultures such as the United States. People in monochronic time cultures perceive time to be linear and divided into standard units. They believe time should be used efficiently. In contrast, people in cultures based on polychronic time consider time to be flexible and multidimensional. International managers need to be aware of cultural differences in interpersonal space, agreements, language, and religion.

5. Comparative management is a new field of study concerned with how organizational behavior and management practices differ across cultures. A unique study by Geert Hofstede of 116,000 IBM employees in 40 nations classified each country by its prevailing attitude toward power distance, uncertainty avoidance, individualism-collectivism, and masculinity-femininity. In view of significant international differences on these cultural dimensions, Hofstede suggests that American management theory and practice be adapted to local cultures rather than imposed on them.

6. Ouchi's Theory Z describes a hybrid type of American company that exhibits a combination of typical American and Japanese characteristics. Theory Z firms rely heavily on Japanese-style consensus and participation during decision making. But Theory Z organizations prefer an American-style emphasis on individual responsibility. Cross-cultural studies of work goals and leadership styles uncovered a great deal of diversity. Thus international contingency approaches to motivation and leadership are recommended.

7. Compared with European and Japanese companies, U.S. multinationals have a much higher expatriate failure rate. Family and personal adjustment problems to foreign cultures, not lack of technical expertise, are the leading causes of this failure. Systematic cross-cultural training is needed to help solve this costly problem, though use of local managerial talent is also a possible solution, depending on the situation.

8. North American women fill a growing but still small share of foreign positions. The long-standing assumption that women will fail on foreign assignments because of foreigners' prejudice has turned out to be false. Women from the United States and Canada have been successful on foreign assignments but face two major hurdles at *home:* self-disqualification and prejudicial managers. Culture, not gender, is the primary challenge for women on foreign assignments. The situation for African Americans parallels that of women.

Terms to Understand

International management (p. 103)

Global company (p. 106)

Transnational company (p. 106)

Ethnocentric attitude (p. 109)

Polycentric attitude (p. 110)

Geocentric attitude (p. 110)

Culture (p. 113)

High-context cultures (p. 114)

Low-context cultures (p. 114)

Monochronic time (p. 115)

Polychronic time (p. 115)

Comparative management (p. 117)

Cross-cultural training (p. 125)

Twelve Tips for Safe International Business Trips

Skills & Tools

1. Before leaving home, discuss with your family what to do in case of an emergency. Upon arrival at your destination, register with the U.S. Embassy or Consulate and inform them of your travel plans. This approach will enable a relative to find you quickly in an emergency. It will also enable State Department officials to quickly contact you if conditions in the country deteriorate and require evacuation of U.S. citizens.

2. Listen to the ubiquitous television commercials touting the benefits of traveler's checks. They're as good as cash in most places and much safer. If you don't have traveler's checks, convert as much money as possible into local currency to spend during your stay. Flashing Yankee dollars is a dead giveaway of your identity.

3. At the airport, keep hand luggage in sight at all times. Experienced thieves know carry-on bags are likely to contain valuables such as cameras, computers, jewelry, or cash.

4. Don't put a sign in your car window advertising yourself as a traveler. Tuck the car rental agreement into the glove compartment. It's like a beacon to drug addicts and petty thieves who assume you have money in your pocket, and expensive clothes, cameras, and other valuables in the trunk.

5. Stick to main roads when leaving the airport. Never take shortcuts or turnoffs unless you know exactly where they lead. Drive with the windows up and lock the doors.

6. Don't pull off the road or stop if another motorist attempts to alert you that something is wrong with your car. It's a favorite ruse of carjackers from Moscow to Miami. Also, don't get out of your car to examine the damage when a vehicle rear ends you. Drive to a busy, well-lighted intersection and wait for the police.

7. Take taxis instead of hiring limousines. Those big, block-long luxury liners attract the wrong kind of attention, particularly in countries where the poverty and crime rates are high. Cabdrivers know their way around and can park freely at stands near office buildings, stores, embassies, and concert halls without attracting the attention of panhandlers, pickpockets, and professional criminals.

8. When making a hotel reservation, book a room between the second and eighth floor because fire apparatus can't go higher and the first floor is usually an invitation to burglars. Check all valuables and keep your door locked at all times. Never admit anyone to your room who isn't expected—including room service. Also, be suspicious of a call from the front desk just after checking in requesting verification of your credit card number because the imprint was unreadable. A thief may have watched you enter the hotel and called from the guest phone in the lobby.

9. Travel with friends, colleagues, or an escort whenever possible. A lone person is always a more tempting target.

10. Stay away when you see trouble developing. Riots, civil disturbances, and political demonstrations are common in many foreign countries, and you can literally get run over or caught in the cross-fire. Travel security reports frequently can alert you to avoid certain unsafe areas based on advanced information about where and when dangerous demonstrations may occur.

11. Don't fight a "hostile takeover." If confronted by bandits or street thugs, surrender your valuables and/or vehicle without a struggle. Comply with instructions, act calm, keep your self-control, and hide your fear. Pleading for mercy, cringing, crying, or other actions that diminish your dignity in the eyes of your captors can actually provoke gratuitous violence.

12. Avoid fatal attractions. Stay away from districts known for gambling, pornography, or prostitution. Aside from the physical danger, your presence or an embarrassing photograph of you in an unsavory surrounding can lead to extortion attempts. When planning to visit historic or scenic locations, never hire street guides to show you the sites. Ask the hotel concierge to recommend a licensed tour agent.

By observing these simple precautions you'll greatly minimize the risks involved with international travel. So next time someone tells you to have a safe trip, smile and say "thanks."[82]

Source: Excerpted from J. Antonio Tijerino, "12 Tips for Business Travel." Reprinted from *Management Review*, 85 (December 1995). © 1995, American Management Association International. Reprinted by permission of American Management Association International, New York, NY. All rights reserved. **http://www.amanet.org**

Internet Exercises

1. **Using the Internet to prepare for a foreign assignment (or travel adventure).** When your author was in graduate school, he was offered the chance to teach for six months in Micronesia. He accepted—and then ran to the university library to find out where Micronesia was (it turned out to be 2,200 islands in the Western Pacific, just north of the Equator). To make a long story short, he soon found himself standing at the airport in a pool of sweat on a tiny coral atoll in the Marshall Islands with his books, virtually no knowledge of the local culture, and a big lump in his throat. Six months, lots of mistakes and lessons, countless mosquito bites, and five islands later, he boarded a plane back to the United States, a grateful and wiser person. Thanks to the Internet, you can get to the grateful and wiser stage a lot more efficiently.

   Log on to the Internet and go to *The Wall Street Journal*'s home page (**www.wsj.com**). Scroll down to the bottom of the home page and click on "Careers," under the heading "Visit Our Other Sites." From the main menu on the Careers page, click on "Working Globally." At that page, select "Country Profiles." Pick one of the more than two dozen countries where you would like to visit, take a job, or just learn more about. (*Note:* You may want to print a copy of your selected country profile for class discussion or future reference.)

   An excellent second source of national and cultural information about your selected country (or one not on the *Journal*'s list) comes from the publishers of the somewhat offbeat *Lonely Planet* travel guides (**www.lonelyplanet.com**). From the top of the home page menu, click on "Destinations." On this page, follow the prompts to tap into useful information about the country you have in mind.

   If the local language for your selected country is not your native language, the Internet can get you headed in the right direction. At the home page of **www.travlang.com,** follow steps one and two. Next, at your selected country page, click on the option "Basic Words." Practice your new vocabulary of essential greetings and questions. The quiz option is a good learning tool.

   Learning Points: 1. Does your selected country appear to be high-context or low-context? Monochronic or polychronic? How can you tell? 2. How much culture shock are you likely to experience in your chosen country? Explain. 3. How well will your native language serve you? What language will you have to know to do business in your selected country? 4. If it is not your native language, how do you say "Yes," "No," "Hello," "Thank you," and "Goodbye" in the language of your selected country? 5. Based on your Internet studies, how strong is your desire to visit or work in the country you selected? Explain.

2. **Check it out:** Take a trip to Europe without ever leaving your keyboard via **www.europages.com.** Navigate in any one of six languages: German, English, Spanish, French, Italian, or Dutch. Be sure to click on the "Europe Online" button beneath the "About Europages" menu. This opens a treasure chest of information about Europe.

   For updates to these exercises, visit our Web site (**www.hmco.com/college**).

| Closing Case | **Tell the Kids We're Moving to Kenya** |

D ale Pilger, General Motors Corp.'s new managing
director for Kenya, wonders if he can keep his
Kenyan employees from interrupting his paper
work by raising his index finger.

"The finger itself will offend," warns Noah Midamba,
a Kenyan. He urges that Mr. Pilger instead greet a worker
with an effusive welcome, offer a chair and request that he
wait. It can be even trickier to fire a Kenyan, Mr. Midamba
says. The government asked one German auto executive
to leave Kenya after he dismissed a man—whose brother
was the East African country's vice president.

Mr. Pilger, his adventurous wife and their two
teenagers, miserable about moving, have come to . . .
[Boulder, Colorado,] for three days of cross-cultural
training. The Cortland, Ohio, family learns to cope with
being strangers in a strange land as consultants Moran,
Stahl & Boyer International give them a crash immersion
in African political history, business practices, social
customs and nonverbal gestures. The training enables
managers to grasp cultural differences and handle
culture-shock symptoms such as self-pity.

Cross-cultural training is on the rise everywhere
because more global-minded corporations moving fast-
track executives overseas want to curb the cost of failed
expatriate stints. . . .

But as cross-cultural training gains popularity, it
attracts growing criticism. A lot of the training is
garbage, argues Robert Bontempo, assistant professor of
international business at Columbia University. Even
customized family training offered by companies like
Prudential Insurance Co. of America's Moran Stahl—
which typically costs $6,000 for three days—hasn't been
scientifically tested. "They charge a huge amount of
money, and there's no evidence that these firms do any
good" in lowering foreign-transfer flops, Prof. Bontempo
contends.

"You don't need research," to prove that cross-cultural
training works because so much money has been wasted
on failed overseas assignments, counters Gary Weder-
spahn, director of design and development at Moran Stahl.

General Motors agrees. Despite massive cost cutting
lately, the auto giant still spends nearly $500,000 a year on

cross-cultural training for about 150 Americans and their
families headed abroad. "We think this substantially
contributes to the low [premature] return rate" of less than
1 percent among GM expatriates, says Richard Rachner,
GM general director of international personnel. . . .

The Pilgers' experience reveals the benefits and drawbacks of such training. Mr. Pilger, a 38-year-old engineer
employed by GM for 20 years, sought an overseas post
but never lived abroad before. He finds the sessions
"worthwhile" in readying him to run a vehicle-assembly
plant that is 51 percent owned by Kenya's government.
But he finds the training "horribly empty . . . in helping
us prepare for the personal side of the move."

Dale and Nancy Pilger have just spent a week in
Nairobi. But the executive's scant knowledge of Africa
becomes clear when trainer Jackson Wolfe, a former
Peace Corps official, mentions Nigeria. "Is that where Idi
Amin was from?" Mr. Pilger asks. The dictator ruled
Uganda. With a sheepish smile, Mr. Pilger admits, "We
don't know a lot about the world."

The couple's instructors don't always know everything about preparing expatriates for Kenyan culture,
either. Mr. Midamba, an adjunct international-relations
professor at Kent State University and son of a Kenyan
political leader, concedes that he neglected to caution
Mr. Pilger's predecessor against holding business dinners
at Nairobi restaurants.

As a result, the American manager "got his key people
to the restaurant and expected their wives to be there,"
Mr. Midamba recalls. But "the wives didn't show up."
Married women in Kenya view restaurants "as places
where you find prostitutes and loose morals," notes
Mungai Kimani, another Kenyan trainer.

The blunder partly explains why Mr. Midamba goes
to great lengths to teach the Pilgers the art of enter-

Source: Republished with permission of *The Wall Street Journal,* from
Joann S. Lublin, "Companies Use Cross-Cultural Training to Help Their
Employees Adjust Abroad" (Aug. 4, 1992). Permission conveyed by Copy-
right Clearance Center, Inc.

taining at home. Among his tips: Don't be surprised if guests arrive an hour early, an hour late or announce their departure four times.

The Moran Stahl program also zeros in on the family's adjustment (though not to Mr. Pilger's satisfaction). A family's poor adjustment causes more foreign-transfer failures than a manager's work performance. That is the Pilgers' greatest fear because 14-year-old Christy and 16-year-old Eric bitterly oppose the move. The lanky, boyish-looking Mr. Pilger remembers Eric's tearful reaction as: "You'll have to arrest me if you think you're going to take me to Africa."

While distressed by his children's hostility, Mr. Pilger still believes living abroad will be a great growth experience for them. But he says he promised Eric that if "he's miserable" in Kenya, he can return to Ohio for his last year of high school next year.

To ease their adjustment, Christy and Eric receive separate training from their parents. The teens' activities include sampling Indian food (popular in Kenya) as well as learning how to ride Nairobi public buses, speak a little Swahili and juggle, of all things.

By the training's last day, both youngsters grudgingly accept being uprooted from friends, her swim team and his brand-new car. Going to Kenya "no longer seems like a death sentence," Christy says. Eric mumbles that he may volunteer at a wild-game reserve.

But their usually upbeat mother has become increasingly upset as she hears more about a country troubled by drought, poverty, and political unrest—where foreigners live behind walled fortresses. Now, at an international parenting session, she clashes with youth trainer Amy Kaplan over whether her offspring can safely ride Nairobi's public buses, even with Mrs. Pilger initially accompanying them.

"All the advice we've gotten is that it's deadly" to ride buses there, Mrs. Pilger frets. Ms. Kaplan retorts, "It's going to be hard" to let teenagers do their own thing in Kenya, but then they'll be less likely to rebel. The remark fails to quell Mrs. Pilger's fears that she can't handle life abroad. "I'm going to let a lot of people down if I blow this," she adds, her voice quavering with emotion.

FOR DISCUSSION

1. Does the Pilgers' son, Eric, seem to have an ethnocentric, polycentric, or geocentric attitude? Explain.

2. Would you label Kenya a monchronic or polychronic culture, based on the evidence in this case? Explain.

3. What were the positive and negative aspects of the Pilgers' predeparture training?

4. Do you think the Pilger family will end up having a productive and satisfying foreign assignment? Explain.

MANAGEMENT'S
SOCIAL & ETHICAL
RESPONSIBILITIES

CHAPTER OBJECTIVES

When you finish studying this chapter, you should be able to

1 Define corporate social responsibility and summarize the arguments for and against it.

2 Identify and describe the four social responsibility strategies.

3 Explain the role of enlightened self-interest in social responsibility.

4 Summarize the three practical lessons from business ethics research.

5 Distinguish between instrumental and terminal values and explain their relationship to business ethics.

6 Identify and describe at least four of the ten general ethical principles.

7 Discuss what management can do to improve business ethics.

"I FIND A UNIVERSAL BELIEF
IN FAIRNESS, KINDNESS, DIGNITY,
CHARITY, INTEGRITY, HONESTY,
QUALITY, AND PATIENCE."
stephen r. covey

A Canadian Logger Goes Against the Grain

Viewed from a helicopter, there appears to be no shortage of trees in British Columbia. Douglas firs, hemlocks, alders, and other species cover the hills of Vancouver Island like a thick carpet.

But the frequent patches of bare earth—reddish at first, then gray-brown after they have weathered—attest to the fact that clear-cutting of old-growth forests continues in this resource-dependent Canadian province. In fact, it has been an article of faith within the forest-products industry here—which accounts for half of the province's exports—that clear-cutting is the only truly cost-effective and safe way to log.

Until now.

MacMillan Bloedel Ltd. [MacBlo], based in Vancouver, British Columbia, sent shock waves through the Canadian forest-products industry last month when it announced that it would phase out clear-cutting in old growth forests in the province over the next five years.

It is clear, says William Beese, a forest ecologist at MacBlo, "that if we don't clean up our act, we risk losing our social license."

The forest-products industry here has changed dramatically over the past several years. Foresters in both the private sector and in government have heard the warnings in new research about the value of biodiversity.

"I can't think of any other term or concept that has had such an impact in such a short time," Mr. Beese says.

And a new statutory Forest Practices Code has been introduced. But, Beese says, "We've seen that the social agenda is moving faster than the law." Practices such as clear-cutting may still be legal but are becoming less acceptable to consumers, particularly affluent, educated Europeans.

These buyers want to know how a piece of wood was harvested before they buy it. They are particularly important customers right now when Japan is in a slump and lumber exports to the United States are constrained by a trade agreement.

Mimicking Nature's Harvest

MacBlo is switching to "variable-retention logging," which calls for leaving a portion of the trees in a tract standing. When a fire or a windstorm or an insect infestation rips through a forest, the destruction is never complete; some trees survive. By means of these, the entire ecosystem can regenerate itself. Variable-retention logging seeks to mimic nature's "harvesting" of trees.

Foresters have several techniques for leaving trees standing, depending on whether the emphasis is on preserving habitat, maximizing the tree harvest, or simply maintaining old-growth trees. A shared goal is to maintain forest structure; that is, ensuring that what is left standing is as complete as possible a microcosm of the original woods.

Forest-products companies don't usually win kudos from environmental groups, but MacBlo has on this one: The Rainforest Action Network in San Francisco called the decision "courageous." . . .

MacBlo is somewhat sensitive about being seen as knuckling under to environmentalists.

"We'd like to say we're not reacting to pressure from lobby groups. We'd like to say we're being proactive," says Craig Neeser, senior vice president of the company's solid-wood group.

But what MacBlo brass call the "market access" issue is much on their minds. The very changes in practices that are making the companies better eco-citizens have also driven up costs, which makes it all the more imperative for MacBlo and its competitors to do whatever it takes to win ecology-minded consumers. . . .

Safety and Cost Issues

New technologies, such as the use of helicopter logging, or the reintroduction of old technologies, such as use of horse-drawn wagons, have helped make variable retention more economical.

Safety is also an issue. The industry has traditionally argued that clear-cutting is safer for loggers, and MacBlo has said it will not compromise safety to undertake variable-retention logging.

Some observers point out that MacBlo's decision represents a certain amount of enlightened self-interest. A giant within its industry, it has the resources to try a new approach. The company has been in business long enough, and has been reforesting long enough, that it has alternatives to old-growth clear-cutting that other companies don't. Higher costs—about 10 to 15 percent—may be offset by getting premium prices for the "environmentally correct" timber.

Case update: MacBlo was recently purchased by industry giant Weyerhaeuser. Will MacBlo's progressive approach to lumbering survive?

Change is never easy. MacMillan Bloedel Ltd.'s search for a profitable alternative to clear-cutting is bound to stir passionate debate in the Canadian timber industry. Only time will tell if the company can live up to its good intentions now that it has joined Weyerhaeuser. Meanwhile, important questions beg for answers. Is this just a public relations gimmick? Or is the firm wisely ensuring its survival in the face of stiffening global competition? Is this sort of corporate social responsibility an expedient luxury or a nonnegotiable necessity? What is the appropriate balance between profits and the public good? This chapter will help you tackle these tough questions.

As the social, political, economic, and technological environments of management have changed, the practice of management itself has changed. This is especially true for managers in the private business sector. Today, more than ever, it is far less acceptable for someone in business to stand before the public and declare that his or her only job is to make as much profit as possible.[1] The public is wary of the abuse of power and the betrayal of trust, and business managers—indeed, managers of all types of organizations—are expected to make a wide variety of economic and social contributions. Demands on business that would have been considered patently unreasonable 30 years ago have become normal today. The purpose of this chapter is to examine management's social and ethical responsibilities.

Social Responsibility: Definition and Perspectives

When John D. Rockefeller was at the zenith of his power as the founder of Standard Oil Company, he handed out dimes to rows of eager children who lined the street. Rockefeller did this on the advice of a public relations expert who believed the dime campaign would counteract his widespread reputation as a monopolist who had ruthlessly eliminated his competitors in the oil industry. The dime campaign was not a complete success, however, because Standard Oil was broken up under the Sherman Antitrust Act of 1890.[2] Conceivably, Rockefeller believed he was fulfilling some sort of social responsibility by passing out dimes to hungry children. Since Rockefeller's time, the concept of social responsibility has grown and matured to the point where many of today's companies are intimately involved in social programs that have no direct connection with the bottom line. These programs include everything from support of the arts and urban renewal to environmental protection. But like all aspects of management, social responsibility needs to be carried out in an effective and efficient manner.

What Does Social Responsibility Involve?

Social responsibility, as defined in this section, is a relatively new concern of the business community. Like a child maturing through adolescence on the way to adulthood, the idea of corporate social responsibility is evolving. Business writer Susan Gaines recently offered this perspective:

> Analysts predict that what was once known as "the socially responsible business movement" will from this point forward grow more slowly as its appeal broadens and takes root in the mainstream business community. "The low-hanging fruit has already been picked for the most part," says Bill Shireman, CEO and president of California Futures, a research and consulting firm that helps resolve conflicts between the business and environmental communities. "The businesses that very easily and eagerly call themselves socially responsible are already in the arena. Mainstream businesses will get there, too, but they are very, very cautious." Eventually, most businesses will begin to understand that they are maximizing profits to pursue higher values, he adds.[3]

A wide-ranging disagreement remains over the exact nature and scope of management's social responsibilities.

Voluntary Action.   One expert defined **corporate social responsibility** as "the notion that corporations have an obligation to constituent groups in society other than stockholders and beyond that prescribed by law or union contract."[4] A central feature of this definition is that an action must be *voluntary* to qualify as a socially responsible action. For example, when Malden Mills in Lawrence, Massachusetts, was nearly destroyed by a huge fire in December 1995, threatening the jobs of its 3,000 employees, owner Aaron Feuerstein made a decision that has been both celebrated and ridiculed. He could have taken the insurance money and eased into a long overdue retirement. Alternatively, he could have used the fire as an excuse to escape America's high wages and moved production to a low-wage country. Instead, he amazed everyone by rebuilding the mill and keeping all his employees on the payroll for three months during reconstruction. An interviewer probed his beliefs and motivation:

> "I consider our workers an asset, not an expense," he told me. Indeed, he believes his job goes beyond just making money for shareholders, even though the only shareholders of Malden Mills are Feuerstein and his family.
>
> "I have a responsibility to the worker, both blue-collar and white-collar," Feuerstein added, his voice taking an edge of steely conviction. "I have an equal responsibility to the community. It would have been unconscionable to put 3,000 people on the streets and deliver a death blow to the cities of Lawrence and Methuen. Maybe on paper our company is worth less to Wall Street, but I can tell you it's worth more. We're doing fine."[5]

According to our definition and the ten commandments listed in Table 5.1, Aaron Feuerstein's decision was socially responsible because it went above and beyond the stockholders' needs and was carried out *voluntarily*, without government or union coercion.

When lawsuits must be initiated or court orders issued before a company will respond to societal needs, that company is not being socially responsible. A prime

1 **Define corporate social responsibility and summarize the arguments for and against it.**

corporate social responsibility *idea that business has social obligations above and beyond making a profit*

Table 5.1

Ten Commandments of Corporate Social Responsibility

I.	Thou Shall Take Corrective Action Before It Is Required.
II.	Thou Shall Work with Affected Constituents to Resolve Mutual Problems.
III.	Thou Shall Work to Establish Industrywide Standards and Self-Regulation.
IV.	Thou Shall Publicly Admit Your Mistakes.
V.	Thou Shall Get Involved in Appropriate Social Programs.
VI.	Thou Shall Help Correct Environmental Problems.
VII.	Thou Shall Monitor the Changing Social Environment.
VIII.	Thou Shall Establish and Enforce a Corporate Code of Conduct.
IX.	Thou Shall Take Needed Public Stands on Social Issues.
X.	Thou Shall Strive to Make Profits on an Ongoing Basis.

Source: Excerpted from Larry D. Alexander and William F. Matthews, "The Ten Commandments of Corporate Social Responsibility," *Business and Society Review*, 50 (Summer 1984): 62–66.

example of this type of foot-dragging behavior was the manner in which Beech-Nut Nutrition Corporation, a subsidiary of Switzerland's Nestlé, responded to charges that it had adulterated its supposedly 100 percent apple juice for babies between 1981 and 1983.

Federal and state officials later charged that Beech-Nut's strategy—executed very effectively—was to avoid publicity and stall their investigations until it could unload its $3.5 million inventory of tainted apple juice products. "They played a cat-and-mouse game with us," says one investigator. When the FDA [U.S. Food and Drug Administration] would identify a specific apple juice lot as tainted, Beech-Nut would quickly destroy it before the

Ray Anderson is the founder and CEO of Interface, a $1-billion-a-year maker of carpet tile based in Atlanta. Many would be more than satisfied if they were in his place. Yet Anderson wants more—not more money or power; he wants to make his company "sustainable." By that he means no fossil fuels, no pollution, no waste, and no damage to the earth. A pipe dream? Not technically feasible? Anderson passionately vows to find a way.

FDA could seize it, an act that could have created negative publicity.[6]

In 1988, two top Beech-Nut officials who had pleaded guilty to 215 felony charges were sentenced to a year and a day in jail and fined $100,000 apiece.[7] Endless court battles and reluctant compliance do not exemplify corporate social responsibility; neither does the use of hollow public relations ploys in lieu of meaningful action.

An Emphasis on Means, Not Ends.   Another key feature of this definition of corporate social responsibility is its emphasis on means rather than ends:

> *Corporate behavior should not, in most cases, be judged by the decisions actually reached, but by the process by which they were reached. Broadly stated, corporations need to analyze the social consequences of their decisions before they make them and take steps to minimize the social costs of these decisions when appropriate. The appropriate demand to be made of those who govern large corporations is that they incorporate into their decision-making process means by which broader social concerns are given full consideration. This is corporate social responsibility as a means, not as a set of ends.*[8]

Unfortunately, social consequences are too often shortchanged in the heat of competitive battle.

5A

Corporate Social Responsibility or Crass Commercialism?

It's a kid marketer's dream: a huge audience with great demographics and a willingness to pay full attention. No, it's not Cartoon Network or *Beavis & Butt-Head*. It's America's classrooms, where advertisers have been descending in droves, angling for the chance to display their logos before a truly captive audience.

These days, teachers find themselves deluged with lessons-in-a-box, videos, and other teaching aids courtesy of some familiar brand names, including Nike Inc., and McDonald's Corp. But not all gifts are of equal value.

Source: Pat Wechsler, "This Lesson Brought to You By . . . ," *Business Week* (June 30, 1997): 68.

Question: *From a societal perspective, what are the pros and cons of commercialism in the classroom? What is your personal stance on this issue? Explain.*

For further information about the interactive annotations in this chapter, visit our Web site (**www.hmco.com/college**).

What Is the Role of Business in Society?

Much of the disagreement over what social responsibility involves can be traced to a fundamental debate about the exact purpose of a business. Is a business an economic entity responsible only for making a profit for its stockholders? Or is it a socioeconomic entity obligated to make both economic and social contributions to society?[9] Depending on one's perspective, social responsibility can be interpreted either way.

The Classical Economic Model.   The classical economic model can be traced to the eighteenth century, when businesses were owned largely by entrepreneurs or owner-managers. Competition was vigorous among small operations, and short-run profits were the sole concern of these early entrepreneurs. Of course, the key to attaining short-run profits was to provide society with needed goods and services. According to Adam Smith, father of the classical economic model, an "invisible hand" promoted the public welfare. Smith believed the efforts of competing entrepreneurs had a natural tendency to promote the public interest when each tried to maximize short-run profits. In other words, Smith believed the public interest was served by individuals pursuing their own economic self-interests.[10]

This model has survived into modern times. For example, *Business Week* quoted Robert J. Eaton, chairman of Chrysler Corporation prior to the creation of Daimler-Chrysler, as saying, "The idea of corporations taking on social responsibility is

Figure 5.1

A Sample Stakeholder Audit for an Automobile Company

absolutely ridiculous. . . . You'll simply burden industry to a point where it's no longer competitive."[11] Thus, according to the classical economic model of business, short-run profitability and social responsibility are the same thing.

stakeholder audit *identifying all parties possibly impacted by the organization*

Back to the Opening Case

Using the model in Figure 5.1 as guide, conduct a stakeholder audit for MacBlo. How many different stakeholders can you identify?

The Socioeconomic Model.   Reflecting society's broader expectations for business (for example, safe and meaningful jobs, clean air and water, charitable donations, safe products), many think the time has come to revamp what they believe to be an obsolete, classical economic model. Oligopolistic industries such as autos, rubber, and brewing, in which a handful of corporate giants dominate the market, are cited as evidence that the classical economic model is outdated. In its place its opponents propose a socioeconomic model, in which business is seen as one subsystem among many in a highly interdependent society.[12]

Advocates of the socioeconomic model point out that many groups in society besides stockholders have a stake in corporate affairs. Creditors, current and retired employees, customers, suppliers, competitors, all levels of government, the community, and society in general have expectations, often conflicting, for management. Some companies go so far as to conduct a **stakeholder audit.**[13] This growing practice involves systematically identifying all parties that could possibly be impacted by the company's performance (for an example, see Figure 5.1). According to the socioeconomic view, business has an obligation to respond to the needs of all stakeholders while pursuing a profit. (See Management Ethics.)

Management Ethics

Clara Conti Gets Back What She Gives

"Running a business is like having a mirror in front of your face," says Clara Conti, founder of Aurora Enterprise Solutions. Based in Reston, Va., Aurora is solidly profitable on $4 million in annual revenue, mostly from government contracts. Now the firm is completing its first commercial product: a system for managing the security of health records. Where did Ms. Conti get the vision? Helping the Red Cross test a blood database.

Ms. Conti, 37, is living proof that in business, as in love or parenting, you get back what you give. She serves on the board of a local homeless shelter—invaluable experience, she says, for when she puts together an outside board of her own. Her engineers build databases for charities and provide computer training for the poor, activities that drive them from their cubicles into the real world.

Most startling of all, her firm tithes 10 percent of its pretax profits to charity. "We do it faithfully every month," she says. One Christmas, she and her staff purchased 200,000 meals for Feed the Children in Reston and Orlando, Florida—then helped dish out the food.

Now seeking its first outside investment, Aurora will have to explain its charitable policies to investors with a narrower concept of payback. "They'll have to accept it as the culture of the company," says Tom McHale, who recently joined Aurora from a senior position at Platinum Technology. "If you're buying intellectual equity, the culture of the company is everything."

In Aurora's case, says Ms. Conti, the culture of giving "is the glue that holds everything together."

Source: Republished with permission of *The Wall Street Journal,* from Thomas Petzinger Jr., "New Business Leaders Find Greater Profit Mixing Work, Caring," (April 2, 1999): B1. Permission conveyed through Copyright Clearance Center, Inc.

Arguments for and Against Corporate Social Responsibility

As one might suspect, the debate about the role of business has spawned many specific arguments both for and against corporate social responsibility.[14] A sample of four major arguments on each side reveals the principal issues.

Arguments For. Convinced that a business should be more than simply a profit machine, proponents of social responsibility have offered these arguments:

1. *Business is unavoidably involved in social issues.* As social activists like to say, business is either part of the solution or part of the problem. There is no denying that private business shares responsibility for such societal problems as unemployment, inflation, and pollution. Like everyone else, corporate citizens must balance their rights and responsibilities.

2. *Business has the resources to tackle today's complex societal problems.* With its rich stock of technical, financial, and managerial resources, the private business sector can play a decisive role in solving society's more troublesome problems. After all, without society's support, business could not have built its resource base in the first place.

3. *A better society means a better environment for doing business.* Business can enhance its long-run profitability by making an investment in society today. Today's problems can turn into tomorrow's profits.

4. *Corporate social action will prevent government intervention.* As evidenced by waves of antitrust, equal employment opportunity, and pollution-control legislation, government will force business to do what it fails to do voluntarily.

Arguments like the above four give business a broad socioeconomic agenda.

Arguments Against.   Remaining faithful to the classical economic model, opponents of corporate social responsibility rely on the first two arguments below. The third and fourth arguments have been voiced by those who think business is already too big and powerful.

1. *Profit maximization ensures the efficient use of society's resources.* By buying goods and services, consumers collectively dictate where assets should be deployed. Social expenditures amount to theft of stockholders' equity.
2. *As an economic institution, business lacks the ability to pursue social goals.* Gross inefficiencies can be expected if managers are forced to divert their attention from their pursuit of economic goals.
3. *Business already has enough power.* Considering that business exercises powerful influence over where and how we work and live, what we buy, and what we value, more concentration of social power in the hands of business is undesirable. In fact, in a *Business Week*/Harris Poll of 1,247 American adults, 69 percent agreed with the statement, "Business has gained too much power over too many aspects of American life."[15]
4. *Because managers are not elected, they are not directly accountable to the people.* Corporate social programs can easily become misguided. The market system effectively controls business's economic performance but is a poor mechanism for controlling business's social performance.

These arguments are based on the assumption that business should stick to what it does best—pursuing profit by producing marketable goods and services. Social goals

---

⇄ A South African Company on a Mission   5C

The Freeplay Group, a young $30 million company based in Cape Town, makes colorful plastic wind-up flashlights and radios. Self-powered computers and global-positioning systems are on the drawing board. The company's name comes from the "free" electricity generated by unique spring-coil mechanisms and solar cells. Radios leaving the two Cape Town factories, staffed largely by disadvantaged and disabled people and ex-convicts, go in very different directions, economically speaking. Some are sold for nearly $80 apiece in the United States and other rich countries. Tens of thousands of others, sold to charities at a deep discount, are given to people in the poorest reaches of Africa. This allows villagers to listen to educational programs, learn about health care and AIDS, and get agricultural tips.

"We're not just a business," says [co-CEO Rory] Stear. "We're a business with a soul." It would be easy for Freeplay to leverage its popularity with First World consumers by postponing its plans to distribute radios throughout the Third World. If it did, the company would be more profitable—and even more attractive to investors. But it would lose something valuable as a result—its mission.

Source: Cheryl Dahle, "We're Creating a Whole New Industry That Can Improve People's Lives," *Fast Company*, no. 23 (April 1999): 171. (Read this fascinating article online at **www.fastcompany.com**.)

Question: *Is this good business or naive idealism run wild? Explain.*

should be handled by other institutions such as the family, school, religious organizations, or government.

Toward Greater Social Responsibility

Is it inevitable that management will assume greater social responsibility? Some scholars believe so. It has been said that business is bound by an **iron law of responsibility,** which states that "in the long run, those who do not use power in a way that society considers responsible will tend to lose it." [16] This is an important concept, considering that cynicism about business runs deep today, despite a more probusiness political climate worldwide. In the *Business Week*/Harris Poll just mentioned, only 3 percent of the respondents gave American corporations an "excellent" performance rating. Fifty-six percent rated them "pretty good" and 32 percent "only fair." [17] The demand for business to act more responsibly is clear. If this challenge is not met voluntarily, government reform legislation will probably force business to meet it. In this section we look at four alternative social responsibility strategies and some contrasting expressions of corporate social responsibility.

iron law of responsibility
those who do not use power in a socially responsible way will eventually lose it

Social Responsibility Strategies

Similar to management's political response continuum, discussed in Chapter 3, is its social responsibility continuum (see Figure 5.2), marked by four strategies: reaction, defense, accommodation, and proaction. [18] Each involves a distinctly different approach to demands for greater social responsibility.

Reaction. A business that follows a **reactive social responsibility strategy** will deny responsibility while striving to maintain the status quo. A case in point involves

2 Identify and describe the four social responsibility strategies.

reactive social responsibility strategy *denying responsibility and resisting change*

Figure 5.2

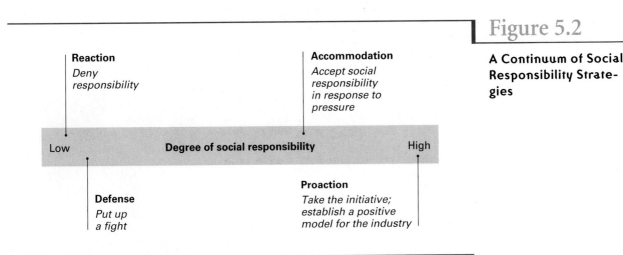

A Continuum of Social Responsibility Strategies

charges of "environmental racism" made by local residents against the many petrochemical plants along the Mississippi River near Baton Rouge, Louisiana. Their complaint centers on the fact that industrial pollution tends to be worst in the poorest, typically minority-populated neighborhoods. In response, a Louisiana Chemical Association spokesman said: "There has been a big emphasis on minority training, recruiting, and hiring. . . . We are trying to reach out to the minority community, to those who live near our plants, to find out what their concerns are. I just think we need to talk more and build up some trust."[19] Widespread mistrust in the affected minority communities presages a wave of lawsuits against the chemical companies.

defensive social responsibility strategy *resisting additional responsibilities with legal and public relations tactics*

Defense.   A **defensive social responsibility strategy** uses legal maneuvering and/or a public relations campaign to avoid assuming additional responsibilities. This strategy has been a favorite one for the tobacco industry, intent on preventing any legal liability linkage between smoking and cancer. When European countries showed signs of adopting U.S.-style bans on secondhand smoke, Philip Morris launched a rather odd defensive strategy:

> *In a Western European ad campaign that backfired, Philip Morris suggested that inhaling secondhand smoke is less dangerous than eating a cookie or drinking milk. The campaign was banned from France after the National Union of Biscuit Makers and the National Committee Against Tobacco Use filed separate suits against Philip Morris.*[20]

accommodative social responsibility strategy *assuming additional responsibilities in response to pressure*

Accommodation.   The organization must be pressured into assuming additional responsibilities when it follows an **accommodative social responsibility strategy.** Some outside stimulus, such as pressure from a special-interest group or threatened government action, is usually required to trigger an accommodative strategy.[21] A prime example is Texaco's 1996 response to media broadcasts of embarrassing audiotapes of

It's not easy being the richest guy on earth. Just ask Microsoft cofounder and chairman, Bill Gates. He gets lots of mixed signals: praise—for building an entirely new industry in just a few years; criticism—for being greedy and not giving away enough money. He was even chided for being self-serving when he donated software to schools, as pictured here in a Washington, D.C., community center. As Bill and Melinda Gates pour *billions* of dollars into their charitable foundations, critics still howl. Perhaps they should dig into their own pockets and follow his lead.

top executives making racist remarks. Only after civil rights leader Jesse Jackson threatened to call for a boycott of Texaco products did the company settle a long-standing discrimination lawsuit and announce an ambitious plan for hiring minorities.[22] In the end, Texaco took appropriate action, but only in response to bad publicity and outside pressure.

Proaction.   A **proactive social responsibility** strategy involves formulating a program that serves as a role model for the industry. Proaction means aggressively taking the initiative. Consider, for example, Herman Miller's actions:

> . . . the furniture maker in Zeeland, Michigan, no longer uses tropical woods, such as rosewood, from endangered rain forests in its office desks and tables. Instead it uses cherry, which does not come from the tropics. Says CEO Richard Ruch: "We thought first about the environmental aspect and then wondered if the switch would impact sales." In fact, the switch has not hurt sales. . . . And it has added more luster to Herman Miller's already fine reputation. Inspired by Herman Miller's decision, the Business and Institutional Furniture Manufacturers Association now urges all its members not to use tropical wood from endangered forests.[23]

Such creative and trend-setting action qualifies as proactive social responsibility. But because today's solution often becomes tomorrow's problem, furniture makers may have to adjust once again if and when cherry trees become endangered.

Corporate social responsibility proponents would like to see proactive strategies become management's preferred response in both good times and bad.[24]

5D

Whiplash for GM?

General Motors is arguing against recalling nearly 280,000 1999 Chevrolet Tahoes and GMC Yukons to replace air bags even though the sport-utility vehicles failed a federal safety test in February.

The automaker deemed the test failure serious enough to switch to new-design air bags in those vehicles two months ago.

The head of an adult male-size dummy went through the bag and hit the windshield frame. Then the unbelted dummy's neck was thrown back enough to cause an injury some experts say could be serious.

But GM is making an unusual pitch to regulators to avoid a recall: The company says the test failure is "inconsequential" to safety.

Source: Jayne O'Donnell, "GM Fights Recall After Air Bags Fail Test," *USA Today* (July 6, 1999): 1B.

Question: *Which of the four social responsibility strategies does this represent? Explain.*

---

proactive social responsibility strategy *taking the initiative with new programs that serve as models for the industry*

Who Benefits from Corporate Social Responsibility?

Is social responsibility the old theory of home medicine, "It has to taste bad to be good"? In other words, does social responsibility have to be a hardship for the organization? Those who answer yes believe that social responsibility should be motivated by **altruism,** an unselfish devotion to the interests of others.[25] This implies that businesses that are not socially responsible are motivated strictly by self-interest. In short-run economic terms, Beech-Nut's cover-up saved it millions of dollars. In contrast, Aaron Feuerstein's decision to rebuild Malden Mills and pay his temporarily unemployed workers cost him more than $300 million.[26] On the basis of these facts alone, one would be hard pressed to say that social responsibility pays. But recent research paints a brighter picture.

altruism *unselfish devotion to the interests of others*

- A study of 243 companies for two years found a positive correlation between industry leadership in environmental protection/pollution control and profitability. The researchers concluded: "It pays to be green."[27]
- A second study found a good reputation for corporate social responsibility to be a competitive advantage in recruiting talented people.[28]

3 Explain the role of
enlightened self-interest
in social responsibility.

enlightened self-interest
*a business ultimately helping itself
by helping to solve societal problems*

corporate philanthropy
*charitable donation of company
resources*

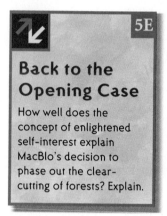

**Back to the
Opening Case**

How well does the
concept of enlightened
self-interest explain
MacBlo's decision to
phase out the clear-
cutting of forests? Explain.

Enlightened Self-Interest.   **Enlightened self-interest,** the realization that business ultimately helps itself by helping to solve societal problems, involves balancing
short-run costs and long-run benefits.[29] Advocates of enlightened self-interest contend
that social responsibility expenditures are motivated by profit. Research into
corporate philanthropy, the charitable donation of company resources ($8.2 billion
in the United States in 1997),[30] supports this contention.

After analyzing Internal Revenue Service statistics for firms in 36 industries,
researchers concluded that corporate giving is a form of *profit-motivated advertising.*
They went on to observe that "it would seem ill-advised to use philanthropy data to
measure altruistic responses of corporations."[31] This profit-motivated advertising
thesis was further supported by a study of 130 large manufacturing firms in the
United States. Companies that had committed significant crimes but donated a good
deal of money had better responsibility ratings than companies that had committed
no crimes and donated very little money.[32] Still more evidence of corporate philanthropy being profit-motivated advertising is the tactic called *cause-related marketing.*
This is an offshoot of advocacy advertising, discussed in Chapter 3. Only in this
instance, instead of promoting a point of view or opinion along with their products,
advertisers support a worthy cause. Typically, customers are urged to buy a product
or service because a portion of the proceeds will go to a specified charity. For
example, "Use of American Express credit cards generated $22 million for Share Our
Strength, a poverty-relief charity, over the four-year life of the Charge Against Hunger
program."[33] Clearly, this win-win situation was an act of enlightened self-interest by
American Express because it polished the company's reputation while fighting
poverty.

An Array of Benefits for the Organization.   In addition to the advertising
effect, other possible long-run benefits for the socially responsible organizations
include:

- Tax-free incentives to employees (such as buying orchestra tickets and giving
  them to deserving employees).
- Retention of talented employees by satisfying their altruistic motives.
- Help in recruiting talented and socially conscious personnel.
- Swaying public opinion against government intervention.
- Improved community living standards for employees.
- Attracting socially conscious investors.
- A nontaxable benefit for employees in which company funds are donated to their
  favorite causes. Many companies match employees' contributions to their college
  alma maters, for example.

Social responsibility can be a "win-win" proposition; both society and the socially
responsible organization can benefit in the long run.[34]

The Future of Corporate Social Responsibility

As pointed out repeatedly in this text, the success of organizational programs and
changes hinges on top-management support. Proactive social responsibility is no
exception. As shown in Figure 5.3, pollsters found strong support in 1990 among
present and future executives for the concept of corporate social responsibility.[35] It
is important to note that the MBA students in this study are part of an age group
now moving into executive decision-making positions. This bodes well for corpo-

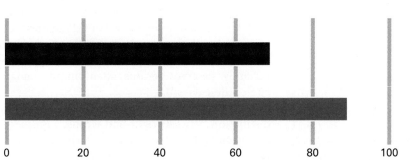

Figure 5.3

**Present and Future
Executives Support the
Concept of Corporate
Social Responsibility**

Source: Data from Mark N. Vamos and Christopher Power, "A Kinder, Gentler Generation of Executives?", *Business Week* (April 23, 1990): 86–87.

rate social responsibility, as do the results of surveys of today's students. Recent evidence:

- According to UCLA's extensive annual survey of college freshmen in 1998, students "show a strong interest in volunteering—which suggests they are trying to help their own communities even if they're turned off by national politics."[36]
- When it comes to boycotting companies, in a recent survey 63 percent of those aged between 18 and 24 said that they would refuse to buy a product from a company embroiled in a lawsuit.[37]

The American social conscience seems to be alive and well among tomorrow's managers.

The Ethical Dimension of Management

Highly publicized accounts of corporate misconduct in recent years have led to widespread cynicism about business ethics. In 1996 alone, "companies doing business in the United States (or American companies doing business abroad and covered by U.S. ethics statutes) paid the federal government more than $1.3 billion in fines and assessments."[38] When a Gallup Poll asked Americans to rate the ethical standards of various professions, only 18 percent scored business executives either high or very high on honesty and ethical standards. Other professions rated as follows: druggists/pharmacists, 66 percent; medical doctors, 52 percent; police officers, 42 percent; funeral directors, 35 percent; journalists, 27 percent; stockbrokers, 13 percent; members of

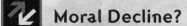

Moral Decline?   5F

In a recent survey for Shell Oil Company, 60 percent of adults ranked "declining moral values" as the most serious problem in the United States. In turn, 88 percent said "Families not teaching children good moral values" was the leading cause of that moral decline.

Source: Adapted and quoted from "Causes of Moral Decline," *USA Today* (August 2, 1999): 1D.

Questions: *Do you agree with these findings? Explain. If you perceive a general decline in moral values, what additional causes are to blame? What needs to be done to improve the situation? What specific constructive steps can managers take?*

ethics *study of moral obligation involving right versus wrong*

Congress, 11 percent; and car salespeople, 5 percent.[39] Indeed, a 1999 survey of 1,000 executives yielded this finding: "As many as one-third of U.S. senior-level executives lie on their résumés."[40] What sort of role models will these powerful people make? The subject of ethics certainly deserves serious attention in management circles these days.[41]

Ethics is the study of moral obligation involving the distinction between right and wrong.[42] *Business ethics*, sometimes referred to as management ethics or organizational ethics, narrows the frame of reference to productive organizations.[43] But, as a pair of ethics experts recently noted, business ethics is not a simple matter:

Just being a good person and, in your own way, having sound personal ethics may not be sufficient to handle the ethical issues that arise in a business organization. Many people who have limited business experience suddenly find themselves making decisions about product quality, advertising, pricing, hiring practices, and pollution control. The values they learned from family, church, and school may not provide specific guidelines for these complex business decisions. For example, is a particular advertisement deceptive? Should a gift to a customer be considered a bribe, or is it a special promotional incentive? . . . Many business ethics decisions are close calls. Years of experience in a particular industry may be required to know what is acceptable.[44]

With this realistic context in mind, we turn to a discussion of business ethics research, personal values, ethical principles, and steps that management can take to foster ethical business behavior.

Practical Lessons from Business Ethics Research

Empirical research is always welcome in a socially relevant and important area such as business ethics.[45] It permits us to go beyond mere intuition and speculation to determine more precisely who, what, and why. On-the-job research of business ethics has produced three practical insights for managers: (1) ethical hot spots, (2) pressure from above, and (3) discomfort with ambiguity.

4 Summarize the three practical lessons from business ethics research.

Ethical Hot Spots.   In a recent survey of 1,324 U.S. employees from all levels across several industries, 48 percent admitted to at least one illegal or unethical act (during the prior year) from a list of 25 questionable practices. The list included everything from calling in sick when feeling well to cheating on expense accounts, forging signatures, and giving or accepting kickbacks, to ignoring violations of environmental laws. Also uncovered in the study were the top ten workplace hot spots responsible for triggering unethical and illegal conduct:

- Balancing work and family.
- Poor internal communications.
- Poor leadership.
- Work hours, work load.

- Lack of management support.
- Need to meet sales, budget, or profit goals.
- Little or no recognition of achievements.
- Company politics.
- Personal financial worries.
- Insufficient resources.[46]

Pressure from Above.   A number of studies have uncovered the problem of perceived pressure for results. As discussed later in Chapter 14, pressure from superiors can lead to blind conformity. How widespread is the problem? Very widespread, according to the ethical hot spots survey just discussed:

- Most workers feel some pressure to act unethically or illegally on the job (56 percent), but far fewer (17 percent) feel a high level of pressure to do so. . . .
- Mid-level managers most often reported a high level of pressure to act unethically or illegally (20 percent). Employees of large companies cited such pressure more than those at small businesses (21 percent versus 14 percent).
- High levels of pressure were reported more often by those with a high school diploma or less (21 percent) versus college graduates (13 percent).[47]

By being aware of this problem of pressure from above, managers can (1) consciously avoid putting undue pressure on others and (2) prepare to deal with excessive organizational pressure.

A prime case in point is the overselling scandal at Sears, Roebuck & Company's automotive centers. According to investigations by the California attorney general's office and a U.S. Senate subcommittee, between 1990 and 1992 Sears systematically pressured auto customers to buy parts and services they didn't need. Many customers across the country complained of having paid hundreds of dollars for

Location: U.S.–Mexico border in Nogales, Arizona. *Problem:* The FBI wants to know how a U.S. Immigration and Naturalization Service (INS) officer earning $30,000 a year happens to have $300,000 in cash lying around the house. They claim three INS officers collected nearly $800,000 from smugglers for letting 20 tons of cocaine pass through. *Ethical dilemma:* Who is primarily to blame: overworked and underpaid public servants tempted by lottery-size payoffs or Americans who buy illegal drugs?

unnecessary repair work. Roy Liebman, a California deputy attorney general, told *Business Week*, "There was a deliberate decision by Sears management to set up a structure that made it totally inevitable that the customer would be oversold."[48] Indeed, former Sears employees claimed that intense pressure to boost revenue, a commission pay system tied to actual sales, and unrealistic sales goals forced them to oversell. Sears reworked the goal-setting and commission structure in its auto repair shops only to see similar problems crop up among overzealous bill collectors in its credit card operations. The situation led to a two-year FBI investigation and culminated in a record $60 million fine for bankruptcy fraud in 1999.[49] Excessive pressure to achieve results is a serious problem, because it can cause otherwise good and decent people to take ethical shortcuts just to keep their jobs. The challenge for managers is to know where to draw the line between motivation to excel and undue pressure.[50]

Ambiguous Situations.   Surveys of purchasing managers and field sales personnel have uncovered discomfort with ambiguous situations in which there are no clear-cut ethical guidelines. One result of this kind of research is the following statement: "A striking aspect of the responses to the questionnaire is the degree to which the purchasing managers desire a stated policy."[51] In other words, those who often face ethically ambiguous situations want formal guidelines to help sort things out. Ethical codes, discussed later, can satisfy this need for guidelines.

A Call to Action.   Corporate misconduct and the foregoing research findings underscore the importance of the following call to action. It comes from Thomas R. Horton, former president and chief executive officer of the American Management Association:

> *In my view, this tide can be turned only by deliberate and conscious actions of management at all levels. Each manager needs to understand his or her own personal code of ethics: what is fair; what is right; what is wrong? Where is the ethical line that I draw, the line beyond which I shall not go? And where is the line beyond which I shall not allow my organization to go?*[52]

Horton's call is *personal*. His words suggest each of us can begin the process of improving business ethics by looking in a mirror.

A survey of 2,856 college students from 28 schools across the United States revealed that female students were more concerned about business ethics than were their male counterparts.[53] In view of the proportional growth in the number of female managers in recent years, this finding might foretell a needed boost for business ethics. Managers—women or men—who have a well-developed value system are better equipped to confront tough ethical questions.

Personal Values as Ethical Anchors

Values are too often ignored in discussions of management. This oversight is serious because personal values play a pivotal role in managerial decision making and ethics.[54] Contemporary social observers complain that many managers have turned their backs on ethical values such as honesty. But others, including management consultant Michael Blondell, detect a change in the wind: "I think we're going back to basic, fundamental values—issues of trust, respect, dignity, commitment, integrity, and accountability. The world is crying out for these things to become more important."[55] Defined broadly, **values** are abstract ideals that shape an individual's thinking and behavior.[56] Let us

values *abstract ideals that shape one's thinking and behavior*

explore two different types of values that act as anchors for our ethical beliefs and conduct.

Instrumental and Terminal Values. Each manager, indeed each person, values various means and ends in life. Recognizing this means-ends distinction, behavioral scientists have identified two basic types of values. An **instrumental value** is an enduring belief that a certain way of behaving is appropriate in all situations. For example, the time-honored saying, "Honesty is the best policy" represents an instrumental value. A person who truly values honesty will probably behave in an honest manner. A **terminal value,** in contrast, is an enduring belief that a certain end-state of existence is worth striving for and attaining.[57] Whereas one person may strive for eternal salvation, another may strive for social recognition and admiration. Instrumental values (modes of behavior) help achieve terminal values (desired end-states).

Because a person can hold a number of different instrumental and terminal values in various combinations, individual value systems are somewhat like fingerprints: each of us has a unique set. No wonder managers who face the same ethical dilemma often differ in their interpretations and in their acts.

Identifying Your Own Values. To help you discover your own set of values, refer to the Rokeach value survey in Table 5.2. Take a few moments now to complete this survey. (As a reliability check between your intentions and your actual behavior, have a close friend or spouse evaluate you later with the Rokeach survey.)

If your results surprise you, it is probably because we tend to take our basic values for granted. We seldom stop to arrange them consciously according to priority. For the sake of comparison, compare your top five instrumental and terminal values with the value profiles uncovered in a survey of 220 eastern U.S. managers. On average, those managers ranked their instrumental values as follows: (1) honest, (2) responsible, (3) capable, (4) ambitious, and (5) independent. The most common terminal value rankings were (1) self-respect, (2) family security, (3) freedom, (4) a sense of accomplishment, and (5) happiness.[58] These managerial value profiles are offered for purposes of comparison only; they are not necessarily an index of desirable or undesirable priorities. When addressing specific ethical issues, managers need to consider each individual's personal values.

> **Back to the Opening Case** 5G
>
> What do you suppose forest ecologist William Beese's top two or three instrumental and terminal values are, according to the Rokeach Value Survey in Table 5.2? Using the same method, what do you suppose the top-ranked values are for logging industry managers who want to continue clear-cutting forests? Why is conflict inevitable with this issue? How does your *own* value profile influence your view of the clear-cutting controversy?

5 **Distinguish between instrumental and terminal values and explain their relationship to business ethics.**

instrumental value *enduring belief in a certain way of behaving*

terminal value *enduring belief in the attainment of a certain end-state*

General Ethical Principles

Like your highly personalized value system, your ethical beliefs have been shaped by many factors, including family and friends, the media, culture, schooling, religious instruction, and general life experiences. This section brings taken-for-granted ethical beliefs, generally unstated, out into the open for discussion and greater understanding. It does so by exploring ten general ethical principles. Even though we may not necessarily know how ethics scholars label them, we use ethical principles both consciously and unconsciously when dealing with ethical dilemmas. Each of the ten ethical principles is followed by a brief behavioral guideline.*

6 **Identify and describe at least four of the ten general ethical principles.**

---

*Source: Excerpted from Hosmer, *Moral Leadership in Business*, pp. 39–41, © 1994, McGraw-Hill. Reprinted with permission of The McGraw-Hill Companies.

Table 5.2

The Rokeach Value Survey

Instructions: Study the two lists of values presented below. Then rank the instrumental values in order of importance to you (1 = most important, 18 = least important). Do the same with the list of terminal values.

Instrumental values	Terminal values
Rank	**Rank**
___ Ambitious (hardworking, aspiring)	___ A comfortable life (a prosperous life)
___ Broadminded (open-minded)	___ An exciting life (a stimulating active life)
___ Capable (competent, effective)	
___ Cheerful (lighthearted, joyful)	___ A sense of accomplishment (lasting contribution)
___ Clean (neat, tidy)	
___ Courageous (standing up for your beliefs)	___ A world at peace (free of war and conflict)
___ Forgiving (willing to pardon others)	___ A world of beauty (beauty of nature and the arts)
___ Helpful (working for the welfare of others)	___ Equality (brotherhood, equal opportunity for all)
___ Honest (sincere, truthful)	
___ Imaginative (daring, creative)	___ Family security (taking care of loved ones)
___ Independent (self-sufficient)	
___ Intellectual (intelligent, reflective)	___ Freedom (independence, free choice)
___ Logical (consistent, rational)	___ Happiness (contentedness)
___ Loving (affectionate, tender)	___ Inner harmony (freedom from inner conflict)
___ Obedient (dutiful, respectful)	
___ Polite (courteous, well-mannered)	___ Mature love (sexual and spiritual intimacy)
___ Responsible (dependable, reliable)	
___ Self-controlled (restrained, self-disciplined)	___ National security (protection from attack)
	___ Pleasure (an enjoyable, leisurely life)
	___ Salvation (saved, eternal life)
	___ Self-respect (self-esteem)
	___ Social recognition (respect, admiration)
	___ True friendship (close companionship)
	___ Wisdom (a mature understanding of life)

Source: Copyright, 1967, by Milton Rokeach, and reproduced by permission of Halgren Tests, 873 Persimmon Avenue, Sunnyvale, Calif. 94087.

1. *Self-interests.* "Never take any action that is not in the *long-term* self-interests of yourself and/or of the organization to which you belong."
2. *Personal virtues.* "Never take any action that is not honest, open, and truthful and that you would not be proud to see reported widely in national newspapers and on television."
3. *Religious injunctions.* "Never take any action that is not kind and that does not build a sense of community, a sense of all of us working together for a commonly accepted goal."
4. *Government requirements.* "Never take any action that violates the law, for the law represents the minimal moral standards of our society."
5. *Utilitarian benefits.* "Never take any action that does not result in greater good than harm for the society of which you are a part."
6. *Universal rules.* "Never take any action that you would not be willing to see others, faced with the same or closely similar situation, also be free to take."

7. *Individual rights.* "Never take any action that abridges the agreed-upon and accepted rights of others."
8. *Economic efficiency.* "Always act to maximize profits subject to legal and market constraints, for maximum profits are the sign of the most efficient production."
9. *Distributive justice.* "Never take any action in which the least [fortunate people] among us are harmed in some way."
10. *Contributive liberty.* "Never take any action that will interfere with the right of all of us for self-development and self-fulfillment." [59]

Which of these ethical principles appeals most to you in terms of serving as a guide for making important decisions? Why? The best way to test your ethical standards and principles is to consider a *specific* ethical question and see which of these ten principles is most likely to guide your *behavior*. Sometimes, in complex situations, a combination of principles would be applicable.

Will Your Ethical Principles Go Up in Smoke?   **5H**

Fact: In 1996, "the World Health Organization reported that tobacco-related deaths would triple by 2020, turning the leaf into the world's No. I cause of death."

1999 Data: ". . . 28 percent more college students smoke than just six years ago." That's about 4 million college students, or almost 30 percent.

Situation: You are interviewing for a postgraduate job. You have bills outstanding and a hefty student loan to repay. You will be the sole supporter of your poverty-stricken and invalid mother. She has terminal lung cancer from 45 years of heavy cigarette smoking. A major tobacco company that makes cigarettes for both domestic and foreign markets has offered you a sales position that will pay 50 percent more than anything you have been offered. This offer is beyond your wildest expectations.

Sources: Mike France, "The World War on Tobacco," *Business Week* (November 11, 1996): 99; and Aaron Davis and Bree Fowler, "Smoke-Free Zones Spreading Across Nation's Campuses," *USA Today* (March 4, 1999): 1A.

Questions: *Will you take the job? Which of the ten ethical principles could you use to justify your decision. Explain your ethical reasoning. Has your own use or nonuse of tobacco products influenced your decision? Explain.*

Encouraging Ethical Conduct

Simply telling managers and other employees to be good will not work. Both research evidence and practical experience tell us that words must be supported by action. Four specific ways to encourage ethical conduct within the organization are ethics training, ethical advocates, ethics codes, and whistle-blowing. Each can make an important contribution to an integrated ethics program.

7 Discuss what management can do to improve business ethics.

Ethics Training

amoral managers
*managers who are neither moral
nor immoral, but ethically lazy*

Managers lacking ethical awareness have been labeled *amoral* by ethics researcher Archie B. Carroll. **Amoral managers** are neither moral nor immoral, but indifferent to the ethical implications of their actions. Carroll contends that managers in this category far outnumber moral or immoral managers.[60] If his contention is correct, there is a great need for ethics training, a need that too often is not adequately met. According to annual surveys by *Training* magazine, the use of ethics training programs has increased, but remains disappointingly low. For companies with more than 100 employees, figures for 1988, 1990, and 1997 were 20 percent, 37 percent, and 46 percent, respectively.[61]

Some say ethics training is a waste of time because ethical lessons are easily shoved aside in the heat of competition.[62] For example, Dow Corning's model ethics program included ethics training but did not keep the company from getting embroiled in charges of selling leaky breast implants.[63] Ethics training is often halfhearted and intended only as window dressing.[64] Hard evidence that ethics training actually improves behavior is lacking. Nonetheless, carefully designed and administered ethics training courses can make a positive contribution. Key features of effective ethics training programs include the following:

- Top-management support.
- Open discussion of realistic ethics cases or scenarios.
- A clear focus on ethical issues specific to the organization.
- Integration of ethics themes into all training.
- A mechanism for anonymously reporting ethical violations. (Companies have had good luck with telephone hot lines.)
- An organizational climate that rewards ethical conduct.[65]

Ethical Advocates

ethical advocate *ethics
specialist who plays a role in top-
management decision making*

An **ethical advocate** is a business ethics specialist who sits as a full-fledged member of the board of directors and acts as the board's social conscience.[66] This person may also be asked to sit in on top-management decision deliberations. The idea is to assign someone the specific role of critical questioner (see Table 5.3 for recommended questions). Problems with groupthink and blind conformity, discussed in Chapter 14, are less likely when an ethical advocate tests management's thinking about ethical implications during the decision-making process.

Codes of Ethics

An organizational code of ethics is a published statement of moral expectations for employee conduct. Some codes specify penalties for offenders. As with the case of ethics training, growth in the adoption of company codes of ethics has stalled in recent years. Again, *Training* magazine's annual survey of industry practices shows that 53 percent of the responding 1,456 companies in 1996 reported having a formal code of ethics. *Training* reported exactly the same figure in its 1992 survey.[67]

Recent experience has shown codes of ethics to be a step in the right direction, but not a cure-all.[68] To encourage ethical conduct, formal codes of ethics for organization members must satisfy two requirements. First, they should refer to specific

	Table 5.3
1. Have you defined the problem accurately? 2. How would you define the problem if you stood on the other side of the fence? 3. How did this situation occur in the first place? 4. To whom and to what do you give your loyalty as a person and as a member of the corporation? 5. What is your intention in making this decision? 6. How does this intention compare with the probable results? 7. Whom could your decision or action injure? 8. Can you discuss the problem with the affected parties before you make your decision? 9. Are you confident that your position will be as valid over a long period of time as it seems now? 10. Could you disclose without qualm your decision or action to your boss, your CEO, the board of directors, your family, society as a whole? 11. What is the symbolic potential of your action if understood? If misunderstood? 12. Under what conditions would you allow exceptions to your stand?	**Twelve Questions for Examining the Ethics of a Business Decision**

Source: Reprinted by permission of the *Harvard Business Review.* Exhibit from "Ethics Without the Sermon," by Laura L. Nash (November–December 1981). Copyright © 1981 by the President and Fellows of Harvard College; all rights reserved.

practices such as kickbacks, payoffs, receiving gifts, record falsification, and misleading claims about products. For example, Xerox Corporation's 15-page ethics code says: "We're honest with our customers. No deals, no bribes, no secrets, no fooling around with prices. A kickback in any form kicks anybody out. Anybody." [69] General platitudes about good business practice or professional conduct are ineffective—they do not provide specific guidance and they offer too many tempting loopholes.

The second requirement for an organizational code of ethics is that it be firmly supported by top management and equitably enforced through the reward-and-punishment system.[70] Selective or uneven enforcement is the quickest way to kill the effectiveness of an ethics code. The effective development of ethics codes and monitoring of compliance are more important than ever in today's complex global economy.[71]

Whistle-Blowing

Detailed ethics codes help managers deal swiftly and effectively with employee misconduct. But what should a manager do when a superior or an entire organization is engaged in misconduct? Yielding to the realities of organizational politics, many managers simply turn their backs or claim they were "just following orders." (Nazi war criminals who based their defense at the Nuremberg trials on the argument that they were following orders ended up with ropes around their necks.) Managers with leadership and/or political skills may attempt to work within the organizational system for positive change.[72] Still others will take the boldest step of all, whistle-blowing. **Whistle-blowing** is the practice of reporting perceived unethical practices to outsiders such as the news media, government agencies, or public interest groups.[73]

Not surprisingly, whistle-blowing is a highly controversial topic among managers, many of whom believe that whistle-blowing erodes their authority and

whistle-blowing *reporting perceived unethical organizational practices to outside authorities*

decision-making prerogatives. Because loyalty to the organization is still a cherished value in some quarters, whistle-blowing is criticized as the epitome of disloyalty. Consumer advocate Ralph Nader disagrees, "The willingness and ability of insiders to blow the whistle is the last line of defense ordinary citizens have against the denial of their rights and the destruction of their interests by secretive and powerful institutions."[74] Still, critics worry that whistle-blowers may be motivated by revenge.

Whistle-blowing generally means putting one's job and/or career on the line, even though the federal government and many states have passed whistle-blower protection acts.[75] The challenge for today's management is to create an organizational climate in which the need to blow the whistle is reduced. Constructive steps include the following:

- Encourage the free expression of controversial and dissenting viewpoints.
- Streamline the organization's grievance procedure so that problems receive a prompt and fair hearing.
- Find out what employees think about the organization's social responsibility policies and make appropriate changes.
- Let employees know that management respects and is sensitive to their individual consciences.
- Recognize that the harsh treatment of a whistle-blower will probably lead to adverse public opinion.[76]

In the final analysis, individual behavior makes organizations ethical or unethical. Organizational forces can help bring out the best in people by clearly identifying and rewarding ethical conduct.

Lawyer Richard Scruggs from Mississippi led the charge as major tobacco companies recently agreed to a $240 billion settlement of health-related claims. Scruggs, seen here with his assistant Charlene Bosarge amid boxes and boxes of evidence, had a secret weapon. Jeffrey Wigand, a tobacco industry insider turned whistle-blower, provided the "smoking gun" regarding Big Tobacco's knowledge of the health risks of smoking.

An Uphill Battle?   5I

After a study of the ethical principles and ethical behavior of 674 business students at a U.S. university, a pair of researchers drew this rather somber conclusion:

While ethical behavior can be taught to our business students in the classroom, their resolve will be challenged on the job. Faced with pressure from above, platitudinous ethical codes, spotty enforcement, and no discernible link to the reward system many will revert to expedience.

Recent news item:

When San Diego State University instructor Brian Cornforth received an anonymous tip in March that students were cheating in his undergraduate business-ethics course, he decided to make a case study of his own class. The tipster said students in one class had obtained answer keys for the multiple-choice quizzes from earlier test-takers, so Cornforth scrambled the questions for the later class. "I was horrified," Cornforth says: 25 of 75 students simply cribbed the pirated test key, even though many answers were clearly nonsense. Punishment came swiftly. He flunked all 25, and several management majors won't graduate until they retake the required course. "Students really want that piece of paper and apparently they are willing to do anything to get it," says Julie Logan, the school's judicial officer.

Sources: Larry R. Watts and Joseph G. Ormsby, "Ethical Frameworks and Ethical Behavior: A Survey of Business Students," *International Journal of Value-Based Management*, 73, no. 3 (1994): 233; and Jamie Reno, "Need Someone in Creative Accounting?" *Newsweek* (May 17, 1999): 51.

Questions: *Is it a waste of time to teach business ethics to college students? Explain. How can colleges and universities do a better job of improving business ethics? What does the business community need to do to improve ethics in the workplace?*

Summary

1. Corporate social responsibility is the idea that management has broader responsibilities than just making a profit. A strict interpretation holds that an action must be voluntary to qualify as socially responsible. Accordingly, reluctant submission to court orders or government coercion is not an example of social responsibility. The debate over the basic purpose of the corporation is long-standing. Those who embrace the classical economic model contend that business's social responsibility is to maximize profits for stockholders. Proponents of the socioeconomic model disagree, saying that business has a responsibility, above and beyond making a profit, to improve the general quality of life. The arguments *for* corporate responsibility say businesses are members of society with the resources and motivation to improve society and avoid government regulation. Those arguing *against* call for profit maximization because businesses are primarily economic institutions run by unelected officials who have enough power already.

2. Management scholars who advocate greater corporate social responsibility cite the iron law of responsibility. This law states that if business does not use its socioeconomic power responsibly, society will take away that power. A continuum of social responsibility includes four strategies: reaction, defense, accommodation, and proaction. The reaction strategy involves *denying* social responsibility, whereas

the defense strategy involves actively *fighting* additional responsibility with political and public relations tactics. Accommodation occurs when a company must be *pressured into* assuming additional social responsibilities. Proaction occurs when a business *takes the initiative* and becomes a positive model for its industry.

3. In the short run, proactive social responsibility usually costs the firm money. But, according to the notion of enlightened self-interest, both society and the company will gain in the long run. Research indicates that corporate philanthropy actually is a profit-motivated form of advertising. The future looks promising for corporate social responsibility because of broad acceptance of the concept by present and future executives.

4. Business ethics research has taught these three practical lessons: (1) 48 percent of surveyed workers reported engaging in illegal or unethical practices; (2) perceived pressure from above can erode ethics; and (3) employees desire clear ethical standards in ambiguous situations. The call for better business ethics is clearly a *personal* challenge.

5. Managers cannot afford to overlook each employee's personal value system; values serve as anchors for one's beliefs and conduct. Instrumental values relate to desired behavior, whereas terminal values involve desired end-states. Values provide an anchor for one's ethical beliefs and conduct.

6. The ten general ethical principles that consciously and unconsciously guide behavior when ethical questions arise are self-interests, personal virtues, religious injunctions, government requirements, utilitarian benefits, universal rules, individual rights, economic efficiency, distributive justice, and contributive liberty.

7. The typical manager is said to be *amoral*—neither moral nor immoral—just ethically lazy or indifferent. Management can encourage ethical behavior in the following four ways: conduct ethics training; use ethical advocates in high-level decision making; formulate, disseminate, and consistently enforce specific codes of ethics; and create an open climate for dissent in which whistle-blowing becomes unnecessary.

Terms to Understand

Corporate social responsibility (p. 137)	Altruism (p. 145)
Stakeholder audit (p. 140)	Enlightened self-interest (p. 146)
Iron law of responsibility (p. 143)	Corporate philanthropy (p. 146)
Reactive social responsibility strategy (p. 143)	Ethics (p. 148)
Defensive social responsibility strategy (p. 144)	Values (p. 150)
Accommodative social responsibility strategy (p. 144)	Instrumental value (p. 151)
Proactive social responsibility strategy (p. 145)	Terminal value (p. 151)
	Amoral managers (p. 154)
	Ethical advocate (p. 154)
	Whistle-blowing (p. 155)

An International Code of Ethics

Developed in 1994 by the Caux Round Table in Switzerland, these Principles for Business are believed to be the first international ethics code created from a collaboration of business leaders in Europe, Japan, and the United States.

Principle 1. *The Responsibility of Businesses: Beyond Shareholders Toward Stakeholders.* The value of a business to society is the wealth and employment it creates and the marketable products and services it provides to consumers at a reasonable price commensurate with quality. To create such value, a business must maintain its own economic health and viability, but survival is not a sufficient goal.

Businesses have a role to play in improving the lives of all their customers, employees, and shareholders by sharing with them the wealth they have created. Suppliers and competitors as well should expect businesses to honor their obligations in a spirit of honesty and fairness. As responsible citizens of the local, national, regional, and global communities in which they operate, businesses share a part in shaping the future of those communities.

Principle 2. *The Economic and Social Impact of Business: Toward Innovation, Justice, and World Community.* Businesses established in foreign countries to develop, produce, or sell should also contribute to the social advancement of those countries by creating productive employment and helping to raise the purchasing power of their citizens. Businesses also should contribute to human rights, education, welfare, and vitalization of the countries in which they operate.

Businesses should contribute to economic and social development not only in the countries in which they operate, but also in the world community at large, through effective and prudent use of resources, free and fair competition, and emphasis upon innovation in technology, production methods, marketing, and communications.

Principle 3. *Business Behavior: Beyond the Letter of Law Toward a Spirit of Trust.* While accepting the legitimacy of trade secrets, businesses should recognize that sincerity, candor, truthfulness, the keeping of promises, and transparency contribute not only to their own credibility and stability but also to the smoothness and efficiency of business transactions, particularly on the international level.

Principle 4. *Respect for Rules.* To avoid trade frictions and to promote freer trade, equal conditions for competition, and fair and equitable treatment for all participants, businesses should respect international and domestic rules. In addition, they should recognize that some behavior, although legal, may still have adverse consequences.

Principle 5. *Support for Multilateral Trade.* Businesses should support the multilateral trade systems of the GATT/World Trade Organization and similar international agreements. They should cooperate in efforts to promote the progressive and judicious liberalization of trade, and to relax those domestic measures that unreasonably hinder global commerce, while giving due respect to national policy objectives.

Principle 6. *Respect for the Environment.* A business should protect and, where possible, improve the environment, promote sustainable development, and prevent the wasteful use of natural resources.

Principle 7.   *Avoidance of Illicit Operations.* A business should not participate in or condone bribery, money laundering, or other corrupt practices: indeed, it should seek cooperation with others to eliminate them. It should not trade in arms or other materials used for terrorist activities, drug traffic, or other organized crime.

Source: Excerpted from "Principles for Business," *Business Ethics,* 10 (May–June 1996): 16–17. Reprinted with permission from *Business Ethics Magazine,* 52 South 10th Street, #110, Minneapolis, Minn. 55403, 612-962-4700.

Internet Exercises

1. **In search of socially responsible companies.** One of *Fortune* magazine's annual features is its list of "America's Most Admired Companies." Eight criteria, including "Social Responsibility," are used to screen candidates for the list. Our purpose here is to learn more about the top ten socially responsible companies in America. What makes them stand out from the crowd? To find out, go to *Fortune*'s home page (**www.pathfinder.com/fortune**) and click on "Careers" in the main menu. Scroll down the Career Resource Center page and select the heading "Most Admired Companies Search." Under the heading "Custom Rankings: Basic," select the option "Social Responsibility" and follow the prompts to rank the top ten. Print a copy of your search results for the next stage of this exercise. Next, pick one of the top ten companies, either at random or based on your interests, and do either a standard library search or Web search for more information on that company. A good research tool for the Internet is *The Wall Street Journal*'s interactive edition (**www.wsj.com**): Click on the link **dowjones.com** and follow the prompts to learn more about your selected company. Be sure to make notes of the company's social responsibility and ethics initiatives.
   Learning Points: 1. What are the top ten socially responsible companies? Which one did you pick? Why? 2. What does this company do to earn its top ranking? 3. Is it a profitable company as well? 4. Does its high ranking in this category make you want to work for the company? Why or why not?

2. **Check it out:** The Ethics Center for Engineering and Science has created an excellent Web resource (**http://onlineethics.org**). Be sure to scan the main menu headings: "Corporate Settings" and "Ethical Codes." You will find loads of good material and practical advice for tough ethical situations.

   For updates to these exercises, visit our Web site (**www.hmco.com/college**).

Closing Case | # Waste Not, Want Not—A Real Fish Story

" I was out there on the deck throwing these big, perfectly good fish—15-pound chinook salmon—over the rail," recalls Tuck Donnelly of the day in 1991 when inspiration hit, just out of Dutch Harbor, Alaska. At the time, Donnelly was the operations manager of a boat that was licensed to catch only pollack and cod. A small number of salmon and other fish were routinely caught by accident, and federal law, to prevent their being sold, required such fish, though dead, to be

dumped over the side. The waste "was really aggravating," says Donnelly. "I was talking to a deckhand, and he said, 'Man, this is nuts.'"

Donnelly agreed—and did something about it. After a two-year fight to convince skeptical industry and government officials, Donnelly obtained a special permit to collect salmon caught out of season—known as bycatch—and give them to food banks across the country. In 1996 he won a fight to do the same with halibut. With 55 Alaskan fishing vessels and 30 seafood processors pitching in, his nonprofit Northwest Food Strategies has donated a whopping 3 million pounds of fish since 1994.

Source: Excerpted from Samantha Miller and Johnny Dodd, "Net Benefit," *People Weekly* (March 29, 1999): 105–106. © 1999 Time Inc.

"Other than the federal government," the 49-year-old father of two says proudly, "we're the single largest source of protein for hunger relief in this country."

Initially, Donnelly, who quit his seafaring job to run the nonprofit group, was swimming upstream. Industry members feared he might create, he says, "a secret black market for prohibited fish." Such a market might cause fishermen to chase out-of-season salmon and halibut and damage the breeding populations. Donnelly argued that the risks could be managed and that the potential rewards were great. "The by-catch rate for a vessel fishing for pollack is probably less than 1 percent," Donnelly says. "But when we're talking about catching a million fish a day, that's a lot of fish."

In 1993, Donnelly was granted an experimental permit to test his idea and persuaded boats, processors, cold-storage operators and transporters to donate their services. Second Harvest, the nation's largest food-bank network, agreed to distribute the frozen fish steaks to shelters, soup kitchens and food pantries. Undercover federal agents made sure Donnelly ran a tight ship. "They went to food banks trying to buy fish, trying to find holes in the system," he says he later learned.

They found none, and Northwest Food Strategies—which Donnelly and one assistant run from a tiny office near Donnelly's Bainbridge Island, Wash., home—won permanent permission to harvest by-catch fish soon after. Food banks, increasingly strapped by welfare reform and an increase in the number of working poor, welcome the fish bonanza—far healthier than staple proteins such as government surplus cheese, peanut butter and low-grade meat. "The nutritional boost is phenomenal," says Linda Nageotte, executive director of Seattle's Food Lifeline. "This literally has the potential to change the face of hunger in the nation."

Now, Donnelly often travels the country to teach food-bank employees and food recipients how to cook fish ("The simplest preparation is the best," he says).

Donnelly took a pay cut to run his donation-fueled organization, which is now expanding to Washington, Oregon, and California. His family doesn't mind—[his wife] Jax recently heard their kids chatting with some friends: "One boy said, 'My dad's a lawyer, and he makes a lot of money,'" she recalls. "Another child said, 'My dad's a doctor, and he makes a lot of money.' And [ten-year-old daughter] Rachel said, 'My dad feeds hungry people.' That felt really neat."

FOR DISCUSSION

1. What type of social responsibility strategy was this: reaction, defense, accommodation, or proaction? Explain.

2. Is Donnelly motivated more by altruism or enlightened self-interest? Explain. What else could have motivated him to blaze a new trail in the commercial fishing industry?

3. According to the Rokeach Value Survey in Table 5.2, what are Donnelly's likely top-ranking instrumental and terminal values? Explain.

4. Is Donnelly a good role model for business ethics? Why or why not?

5. Can business ethics instruction foster the type of behavior exhibited in this case? Explain.

VIDEO SKILL BUILDERS

Karen Sand, a customer service supervisor for Southwest Airlines, talks about her key role in making her employer an industry leader in customer service. Karen's job is to orchestrate a complex symphony of factors including tight schedules, employees, special customer needs, facilities, computers, problems, and emergencies.

1A Karen Sand: A Manager in Action

Learning objective: To learn more about day-to-day management by observing and hearing from a supervisor in action.

Links to textual material: *Chapter 1:* Management defined; The twenty-first century manager; Managerial functions and roles; Motivation to manage

Discussion questions

1. How does Karen Sand exemplify the definition of management?
2. Which characteristics of the twenty-first century manager (see Table 1.1) are evident in this video profile?
3. Which of the eight managerial functions (Figure 1.4) and Mintzberg's ten managerial roles (Figure 1.5) are evident in this video case?
4. How would you rate Karen Sand's motivation to manage, using Miner's seven factors?

Kodak's Funsaver cameras are a big hit with consumers who like the convenience of not having to load and unload film; the entire camera is returned for photo processing. But what about the potential mountain of waste from the used cameras? Kodak has "closed the loop" and created jobs with a recycling program.

1B Recycling Pays at Kodak

Learning objectives: To better appreciate the complex environment in which today's organizations and managers operate. To demonstrate how the concepts of corporate social responsibility and enlightened self-interest can be brought to life through an innovative program.

Links to textual material: *Chapter 3:* The general environment of management *Chapter 5:* Corporate social responsibility; Enlightened self-interest; General ethical principles

Discussion questions

1. What evidence of management's social, political/legal, economic, and technological environments can you detect in this video case?
2. Which social responsibility strategy has Kodak exhibited (see Figure 5.2)? Explain.
3. What role, if any, does enlightened self-interest play in this case? Explain.
4. Which of the ten general ethical principles are evident in this video case? Explain.

Part Two

PLANNING and DECISION MAKING

The **BASICS** of **PLANNING** and PROJECT PLANNING

CHAPTER OBJECTIVES

When you finish studying this chapter, you should be able to

1 Distinguish among state, effect, and response uncertainty.

2 Identify and define the three types of planning.

3 Write good objectives and discuss the role of objectives in planning.

4 Describe the four-step management by objectives (MBO) process and explain how it can foster individual commitment and motivation.

5 Discuss project planning within the context of the project life cycle.

6 Compare and contrast flow charts and Gantt charts, and discuss the value of PERT networks.

7 Explain how break-even points can be calculated.

> "MANAGEMENT IS A BALANCING ACT BETWEEN THE SHORT TERM AND THE LONG TERM, BETWEEN DIFFERENT OBJECTIVES AT DIFFERENT TIMES."
> peter f. drucker

In a Fast-Paced World, How Three Managers Plan on the Run

More than ever before, people in the business world are scrambling to control this elusive thing called time. The pace of marketplace change has become dizzying, making it difficult for executives to get beyond the day-to-day travails and grasp the bigger picture.

Indeed, the corporate world is experiencing the greatest calamity of its history as millions of corporate souls suffer from a phenomenon known as "time famine." It's not about having too little time to manage what you have to *do* on a daily basis; it is about not having time to *think* strategically. This inability to engage in long-range thinking affects the majority of executives today. They are in such a survival mode, always reacting to what's urgent, that they maneuver the bumps in the road rather than make decisions that will guide their company's futures. . . .

Name: Bobby Yazadani

Title: President and founder, Saba Software Inc., Redwood Shores, California

Who has time to think? "You have to create a business plan [for this]. It's something that not only I have to do, it's something my management team has to do. I have to manage the space for thinking."

How do you find the space/time to think? "I try to do two sets of disciplines for myself. One discipline is to communicate to the staff what they'll do and what I'll do. This communication truly empowers the executives; by doing that I have more space. I've done that in the past two years, and I have gained more and more time and space. I actually have time to follow research and spend time doing some planning work."

"Secondly, I am involved with the advisory board and board directors on a biweekly basis, so I can get away from my business. That has helped me to clear my mind, to make sound [decisions]."

Name: Maria D. Chevalier

Title: Director of special projects, HQ Global Workplaces, Atlanta, Georgia

Who has time to think? "I have the time to react but not enough time to spend on strategic planning. That is probably one of my biggest challenges and frustrations that I've ever had."

How do you find the space/time to think? "I have started to literally put it on my calendar and make it part of my tasks that I have scheduled. I find that's the only way I can do it because if not, the days and weeks get away from me. The best time I have found to think strategically is to come in as early as possible in the morning when it is quieter. I find that at the end of the day, you are too exhausted. And during the course of the day, too many things are occurring."

Name: Joe Crace

Title: Executive vice president and COO, Gaylord Entertainment Co., Nashville, Tennessee

Who has time to think? "You have to almost schedule time to think. Not only do you have to have time to think, but you have to have time where people are free to express their ideas and let their minds run without any restrictions."

How do you find the space/time to think? "From time to time, once or twice a quarter, Terry London, our CEO, and myself, or other key people in the management group, go off-site somewhere where everybody locks themselves indoors. There are no interruptions; we just schedule time to blend some fun and some time to sit and go through each of our businesses. We also think of any other distribution outlets, products or services, people and talent that we are not touching on."

Source: Reprinted from *Management Review,* January 2000. © 2000 American Management Association International. Reprinted by permission of American Management Association International, New York, NY. All rights reserved. **http://www.amanet.org**

I n the age of Internet speed, more and more managers are finding they have a lot in common with Yazadani, Chevalier, and Crace. Small and large, public and private organizations are struggling to stay relevant and responsive. A standing joke among managers is that they are responsible for "doing the impossible by yesterday!" Indeed, virtually all of today's managers are asked to do a lot with limited budgets, resources, and time. All this takes thoughtful planning and a healthy dose of courage in the face of nerve-wracking uncertainty.

planning *coping with uncertainty by formulating courses of action to achieve specified results*

Planning is the process of coping with uncertainty by formulating future courses of action to achieve specified results. Planning enables humans to achieve great things by envisioning a pathway from concept to reality. The greater the mission, the longer and more challenging the pathway. For example, Timothy A. Koogle, the CEO of Yahoo! Inc., recently stated this wide-eyed goal: "to be the largest media company in the world."[1] It will take an incredible amount of planning, creativity, money, and market growth to make Koogle's vision come true. And this Internet portal company will surely encounter many surprises along the way as it strives to overtake the likes of Walt Disney, AOL-Time Warner, and Viacom. Planning is a never-ending process because of constant change, uncertainty, new competition, unexpected problems, and emerging opportunities.[2]

Because planning affects all downstream management functions (see Figure 6.1), it has been called the primary management function. With this model in mind, we shall discuss uncertainty, highlight five essential aspects of the planning function, and take a close look at management by objectives and project planning. We shall also introduce four practical tools (flow charts, Gantt charts, PERT networks, and break-even analysis).

Figure 6.1   Planning: The Primary Management Function

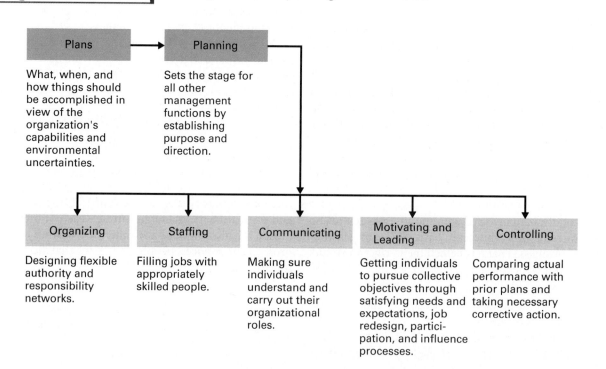

Coping with Uncertainty

Ben Franklin said that the only sure things in life are death and taxes. Although this is a gloomy prospect, it does capture a key theme of modern life: We are faced with a great deal of uncertainty. Organizations, like individuals, are continually challenged to accomplish something in spite of general uncertainty. Organizations meet this challenge largely through planning. As a context for our discussion of planning in this and the following chapter, let us explore environmental uncertainty from two perspectives: (1) types of uncertainty and (2) organizational responses to environmental uncertainty.

Three Types of Uncertainty

Through the years, *environmental uncertainty* has been a catch-all term among managers and researchers. However, research indicates that people actually perceive three types of environmental uncertainty: state uncertainty, effect uncertainty, and response uncertainty. **State uncertainty** occurs when the environment, or a portion of the environment, is considered unpredictable. A manager's attempt to predict the *effects* of specific environmental changes or events on his or her organization involves **effect uncertainty**. **Response uncertainty** relates to being unable to predict the *consequences* of a particular decision or organizational response.[3]

A simple analogy can help us conceptually sort out these three types of uncertainty. Suppose you are a golfer and on your way to the course you wonder if it is going to rain; this is *state uncertainty*. Next, you experience *effect uncertainty* because you are not sure it will rain hard enough, if it does rain, to make you quit before finishing nine holes. You begin weighing your chances of making par if you have to adjust your choice of golf clubs to poor playing conditions; now you are experiencing *response uncertainty*. Each of the three types of perceived uncertainty could affect your golfing attitude and performance. Similarly, managers are affected by their different perceptions of environmental factors. Their degree of uncertainty may vary from one type of uncertainty to another. A manager may, for example, be unsure about the timing of a labor strike (state uncertainty) but certain that a strike would ruin profits (effect uncertainty).

1 Distinguish among state, effect, and response uncertainty.

state uncertainty *unpredictable environment*

effect uncertainty *impacts of environmental changes are unpredictable*

response uncertainty *consequences of decisions are unpredictable*

Organizational Responses to Uncertainty

Some organizations do a better job than others of planning amid various combinations of uncertainty. This is due in part to differing patterns of response to environmental factors beyond the organization's immediate control. As outlined in Table 6.1, organizations cope with environmental uncertainty by adopting one of four positions vis-à-vis the environment in which they operate. These positions are defenders, prospectors, analyzers, and reactors,[4] each with its own characteristic impact on planning.

Defenders.   A defender can be successful as long as its primary technology and narrow product line remain competitive. Defenders can become stranded on a dead-end road if their primary market seriously weakens. A prime example of a defender is Harley-Davidson, which recently sold its recreational vehicle division and other nonmotorcycle businesses to get back to basics.

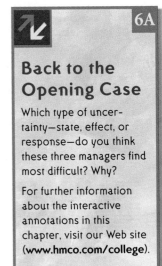

Back to the Opening Case

Which type of uncertainty—state, effect, or response—do you think these three managers find most difficult? Why?

For further information about the interactive annotations in this chapter, visit our Web site (**www.hmco.com/college**).

Table 6.1

Different Organizational Responses to an Uncertain Environment	
Type of organizational response	**Characteristics of response**
1. Defenders	Highly expert at producing and marketing a few products in a narrowly defined market
	Opportunities beyond present market not sought
	Few adjustments in technology, organization structure, and methods of operation because of narrow focus
	Primary attention devoted to efficiency of current operations
2. Prospectors	Primary attention devoted to searching for new market opportunities
	Frequent development and testing of new products and services
	Source of change and uncertainty for competitors
	Loss of efficiency because of continual product and market innovation
3. Analyzers	Simultaneous operations in stable and changing product market domains
	In relatively stable product/market domain, emphasis on formalized structures and processes to achieve routine and efficient operation
	In changing product/market domain, emphasis on detecting and copying competitors' most promising ideas
4. Reactors	Frequently unable to respond quickly to perceived changes in environment
	Make adjustments only when finally forced to do so by environmental pressures

Source: Adapted from *Organizational Strategy, Structure, and Process,* by Raymond E. Miles and Charles C. Snow. Copyright © 1978, McGraw-Hill Book Company, p. 29. Used with permission of McGraw-Hill Book Company.

"With worldwide demand for our motorcycles far outweighing supply and growth in our motorcycle business expected to continue, we've made the decision to focus our resources on our core business," Harley CEO Richard Teerlink said in a press release. Harley hopes to double motorcycle production by 2003, its 100th anniversary.

Analysts say the move makes sense. Customers often have to wait months for a new Hog, as Harley's bikes are known.

Also, the return to basics comes just as Harley has begun selling overseas, where Hogs are hot.[5]

Harley-Davidson enjoys such a fierce brand loyalty among Hog riders that many sport a tattoo of the company's logo. Can you imagine Coca-Cola, McDonald's, Nike, and Honda tattoos?

Prospectors.   Prospector organizations are easy to spot because they have a reputation for aggressively making things happen rather than waiting for them to happen. But life is not easy for prospectors such as Capital One. The credit card issuer has to run faster and faster to stay a step ahead of competitors:

Capital One scored some early victories in the credit-card game by changing the rules. Its founders invented the "teaser rate"—the banking equivalent of a cheap mortgage that gets adjusted up after a certain period. The teaser attracted millions of customers, and eventually competitors began to mimic the idea. The result was a merry-go-round of so-called teaser hoppers. People would move their balance to a low-introductory-rate card; as soon as the rate expired, they would switch to another card. Over time, Cap One was being eaten alive because of customer attrition.

Talk about uncertainty! Why would people shop at a store specializing in things they really don't need? Worse yet, the store's name is OOP. For co-owners Jennifer Neuguth (pictured here) and David Riordan, the answer is finding out what visitors to their Rhode Island gift and novelty store really *want*, rather than need. Their secret weapon is a customer database built through countless surveys that they pay people to complete. With annual revenues of $1.3 million, they must be asking the right questions.

The lesson: Companies that thrive on change can never rest. Competitors are quick to copy good ideas. The way to compete on innovation is to keep innovating.

That's the hard part. And that's why Capital One is so obsessed with making its own innovations obsolete.[6]

A study of 1,452 business units shed some light on the comparative effectiveness of these first two strategies. "Specifically, in every type of environment examined, defenders outperformed prospectors in terms of current profitability and cash flow. The costs and risks of product innovation appear significant."[7] Prospectors in the business sector need to pick their opportunities very carefully, selecting those with the best combination of feasibility and profit potential. This is especially true for entrepreneurs starting small businesses.[8]

Analyzers.   An essentially conservative strategy of following the leader marks an organization as an analyzer. It is a "me too" response to environmental uncertainty. Analyzers let the market leader take expensive R&D risks and then imitate what works. For example, VF Corporation, maker of Wrangler and Lee jeans, does very nicely following in the footsteps of trendsetter Levi Strauss & Company:

Letting others take the lead may be outré at Paris salons, but it's a winning style at VF. By sticking mostly to timeless apparel staples, finely honing its "second-to-the-market" approach, and bringing high technology to the nitty-gritty details of distribution, VF, based in Wyomissing, Pa., has avoided the financial gyrations that beset many clothing makers. Says VF CEO Lawrence R. Pugh: "Clearly, there is less risk."[9]

Although analyzers may not get a lot of respect, they do perform the important economic function of breaking up monopolistic situations. Customers appreciate the resulting lower prices.[10]

Reactors.   The reactor is the exact opposite of the prospector. Reactors wait for adversity, such as declining sales, before taking corrective steps. They are slow to develop new products to supplement their tried-and-true ones. Their strategic responses to changes in the environment are often late. An interesting example in this area is Joseph E. Seagram & Sons, Inc. The Canadian firm grew into the world's largest distiller by specializing in brown liquors such as Seagram's 7 Crown. But drinking habits have changed in recent years. Consequently, white liquors such as Bacardi rum and Smirnoff vodka pushed Seagram's 7 Crown from first place to third. Moreover, with more North Americans drinking wine, the public outcry against drunk driving, and higher excise taxes on liquor, Seagram's sales dropped. By the time Seagram reacted by bolstering its wine business in the 1980s, the wine market was glutted because of European imports and overplanted vineyards in California.[11]

According to one field study, reactors tended to be less profitable than defenders, prospectors, and analyzers.[12]

Balancing Planned Action and Spontaneity in the Twenty-First Century

In the obsolete command-and-control management model, plans were considered destiny. Top management formulated exacting plans for every aspect of operations and then kept everything under tight control to "meet the plan." All too often, however, plans were derailed by unanticipated events and success was dampened by organizational inflexibility. Today's progressive managers see plans as general guidelines for action, based on imperfect and incomplete information. Planning is no longer the exclusive domain of top management; it now typically involves those who carry out the plans because they are closer to the customer. Planning experts say managers need to balance planned action with the flexibility to take advantage of surprise events and unexpected opportunities. A good analogy is to an improvisational comedy act.[13] The stand-up comic has a plan for the introduction, structure of the act, some tried-and-true jokes, and closing remarks. Within this planned framework, the comic will play off the audience's input and improvise as necessary. Accordingly, 3M Corporation had a plan for encouraging innovation that allowed it to capitalize on the spontaneous success of the Post-it Note. Planning should be a springboard to success, not a barrier to creativity.

The Chaos Theory of Planning   6B

Andy Grove, Chairman of Intel Corporation, the world's leading computer chip maker:

> You need to try to do the impossible, to anticipate the unexpected. And when the unexpected happens, you should double your efforts to make order from the disorder it creates in your life. The motto I'm advocating is, Let chaos reign, then rein in chaos. Does that mean that you shouldn't plan? Not at all. You need to plan the way a fire department plans. It cannot anticipate fires, so it has to shape a flexible organization that is capable of responding to unpredictable events.

Source: Andrew S. Grove, "A High-Tech CEO Updates His Views on Managing and Careers," *Fortune* (September 18, 1995): 229.

Questions: *How well does Grove's approach to planning agree with what you just read about the need to balance planned action with creative spontaneity? Do either of these new perspectives of planning go against your assumptions about why or how companies should plan? What do you think of Grove's philosophy?*

The Essentials of Planning

Planning is an ever-present feature of modern life, although there is no universal approach. Virtually everyone is a planner, at least in the informal sense. We plan leisure activities after school or work; we make career plans. Personal or informal plans give

Apple Computer's iMac has been called the VW Beetle of computers. It's cute, functional, user friendly, and moves fast (off the store shelves, that is). The driving force behind this winner is Apple's CEO Steve Jobs. It's actually his second turn at heading the company he cofounded, having been nudged aside during a mid-'80s power struggle. Jobs has always been a man on a mission. Dating back to his earliest days at Apple, Jobs has been possessed with computerizing the masses. First came the Mac; now the iMac. Mission accomplished!

purpose to our lives. In a similar fashion, more formalized plans enable managers to mobilize their intentions to accomplish organizational purposes. A **plan** is a specific, documented intention consisting of an objective and an action statement. The objective portion is the end, and the action statement represents the means to that end. Stated another way, objectives give management targets to shoot at, whereas action statements provide the arrows for hitting the targets. Properly conceived plans tell *what, when,* and *how* something is to be done.

plan *an objective plus an action statement*

In spite of the wide variety of formal planning systems that managers encounter on the job, we can identify some essentials of sound planning. Among these common denominators are organizational mission, types of planning, objectives, priorities, and the planning/control cycle.

Organizational Mission

To some, defining an organization's mission might seem an unnecessary exercise. But exactly the opposite is true. Some organizations drift along without a clear mission. Others lose sight of their original mission. Sometimes an organization, such as the U.S. Army Corps of Engineers, finds its original mission no longer acceptable to key stakeholders (see Management Ethics). Periodically redefining an organization's mission is both common and necessary in an era of rapid change.

A clear, formally written, and publicized statement of an organization's mission is the cornerstone of any planning system that will effectively guide the organization through uncertain times. The satirical definition by Scott Adams, the Dilbert cartoonist, tells us how *not* to write an organizational mission statement: "A Mission

A Sample Mission Statement   6C

The staff of St. Mary's Food Bank in Phoenix, Arizona, recently drafted this mission statement:

St. Mary's Food Bank—the world's first food bank—is a non-sectarian, non-profit organization that alleviates hunger by efficiently gathering and distributing food to agencies that serve the hungry. We are committed to volunteerism, building community relationships, and improving the quality of life for our entire community.

Questions: *Based on what you have just read, is this a well-written mission statement? How can you tell?*

Management Ethics

A New Mission for the U.S. Army Corps of Engineers

Ask most environmentalists about the U.S. Army Corps of Engineers and you're likely to get an unprintable reply. Traditionally, the Corps has viewed nature as "the enemy": it dammed rivers, drained swamps, and made marshes into farmland, destroying the nesting and feeding grounds of thousands of animal species. But for both philosophical and practical reasons, the Corps has changed with the times, sometimes reworking what it built just a few years ago.

Under pressure from its many stakeholders, who include Audubon Society members as well as agribusinesses, the new Corps knows its own future is tied to attempts to improve the environment. The Corps's basic values and purpose have been adapted to the country's rediscovery of the value of nature, and the Corps has been using its planning and engineering skills for very different ends. Recognizing that programs aimed at improving the environment almost always need engineers, the Corps's new leaders want to supply those engineers. As part of its new focus, the Corps has been working with the Environmental Protection Agency and local communities to develop wastewater treatment plants and to handle solid wastes. Instead of draining wetlands, it now tries to save them in areas like the Mississippi Delta.

The Corps's most important about-face to date occurred in southern Florida. Historically, summer rains would fill Lake Okeechobee and drain slowly south, creating a rich natural environment that supported the wide variety of plant and animal species for which the Everglades became famous. But Florida's big cities wanted to use the water, and farmers and land developers didn't like the unpredictable floods. At the state's request, the Corps built 1,500 miles of canals and levees and turned the winding Kissimmee River into a straight channel half its original length. Florida's cities and farms prospered, but nature suffered dramatically. The population of the area's wading birds alone has declined by 90 percent since the 1930s.

So Florida asked the Corps to undo its work, tear down the levees, let the Kissimmee take its natural course, and bring water back into the Everglades. After eight years of study, the Corps's Everglades plan emerged in 1999 as a 20-year project with a nearly $8 billion price tag. Political wrangling was intense. Environmentalists remain suspicious, but the Corps may in time earn the title it now desires: "friend of the environment."

Sources: Based on "Everglades Plan," *USA Today* (October 14, 1998): 3A; John Bacon, "Corps Hopes to Reverse Everglades Damage," *USA Today* (April 8, 1999): 7A; and Laura Parker, "Big Plan Seeks Everglades Revival," *USA Today* (July 1, 1999): 3A.

Statement is defined as a long, awkward sentence that demonstrates management's inability to think clearly."[14] This sad state of affairs, too often true, can be avoided by a well-written mission statement that does the following things:

1. *Defines* your organization for key stakeholders.
2. Creates an *inspiring vision* of what the organization can be and can do.
3. Outlines *how* the vision is to be accomplished.
4. Establishes key *priorities*.
5. States a *common goal* and fosters a sense of togetherness.
6. Creates a *philosophical anchor* for all organizational activities.
7. Generates *enthusiasm* and a "can do" attitude.
8. *Empowers* present and future organization members to believe that *every* individual is the key to success.[15]

A good mission statement provides a focal point for the entire planning process. When Vincent A. Sarni took the top job at PPG, the large glass and paint company, he created a document he called "Blueprint for the Decade." In it, he specified the company's mission and corporate objectives for such things as service, quality, and financial performance.

> *Sarni . . . trudged from plant to plant preaching the virtues in his Little Blue Book. "My first two or three years I always started with a discussion of the Blueprint," he says. "I don't have to do that anymore. The Blueprint's on the shop floor, and it has meaning."*[16]

Types of Planning

Ideally, planning begins at the top of the organizational pyramid and filters down. The rationale for beginning at the top is the need for coordination. It is top management's job to state the organization's mission, establish strategic priorities, and draw up major policies. After these statements are in place, successive rounds of strategic, intermediate, and operational planning can occur. Figure 6.2 presents an idealized picture of the three types of planning, as carried out by different levels of management.

2 Identify and define the three types of planning.

Strategic, Intermediate, and Operational Planning.   **Strategic planning** is the process of determining how to pursue the organization's long-term goals with the resources expected to be available. A well-conceived strategic plan communicates much more than general intentions about profit and growth. It specifies *how* the organization will achieve a competitive advantage, with profit and growth as necessary by-products. **Intermediate planning** is the process of determining the contributions subunits can make with allocated resources. Finally, **operational planning** is the process of determining how specific tasks can best be accomplished on time with

strategic planning *determining how to pursue long-term goals with available resources*

intermediate planning *determining subunits' contributions with allocated resources*

operational planning *determining how to accomplish specific tasks with available resources*

Figure 6.2

Types of Planning

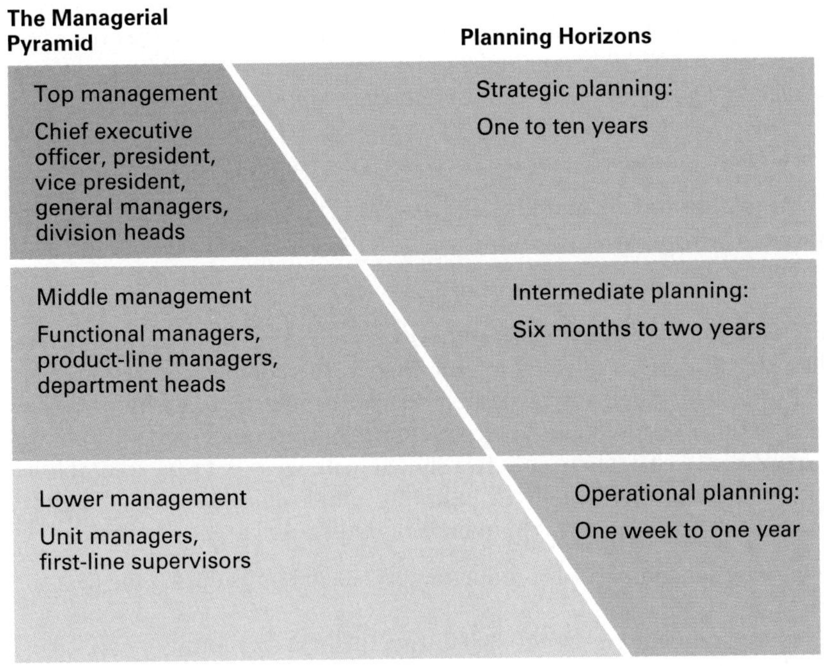

The Managerial Pyramid	Planning Horizons
Top management Chief executive officer, president, vice president, general managers, division heads	**Strategic planning:** One to ten years
Middle management Functional managers, product-line managers, department heads	**Intermediate planning:** Six months to two years
Lower management Unit managers, first-line supervisors	**Operational planning:** One week to one year

available resources. Each level of planning is vital to an organization's success and cannot effectively stand alone without the support of the other two levels.

Planning Horizons.   As Figure 6.2 illustrates, planning horizons vary for the three types of planning. The term **planning horizon** refers to the time that elapses between the formulation and the execution of a planned activity. As the planning process evolves from strategic to operational, planning horizons shorten, and plans become increasingly specific. Naturally, management can be more confident and hence more specific about the near future than it can about the distant future.

Notice, however, that the three planning horizons overlap, their boundaries being elastic rather than rigid. The trend today is toward involving employees from all levels in the strategic planning process. Also, it is not uncommon for top and lower managers to have a hand in formulating intermediate plans. Middle managers often help lower managers draw up operational plans as well. So, Figure 6.2 is an ideal model with countless variations in the workplace.

planning horizon *elapsed time between planning and execution*

Objectives

Just as a distant port is the target or goal for a ship's crew, objectives are targets that organizational members steer toward. Although some theorists distinguish between goals and objectives, managers typically use the terms interchangeably. A goal or an **objective** is defined as a specific commitment to achieve a measurable result within a given time frame. Many experts view objectives as the single most important feature of the planning process. They help managers and entrepreneurs build a bridge between their dreams, aspirations, and visions and an achievable *reality*. Dan Sullivan, a consultant for entrepreneurs, explains:

objective *commitment to achieve a measurable result within a specified period*

> [Objectives and goals] should be achievable by definition. If you are setting functional goals, at useful increments, they should be both real and realizable. The distance between where you actually are now and your goal can be measured objectively, and when you achieve your goal, you know it. Think of the distinction this way: no matter how fast you run toward the horizon, you'll never get there, but if you run more quickly toward a goalpost, you will get there faster. Sounds simplistic, but I'm constantly amazed at how many people—and entrepreneurs in particular—confuse their goals with their ideals.[17]

3 Write good objectives and discuss the role of objectives in planning.

It is important for present and future managers to be able to write good objectives, to be aware of their importance, and to understand how objectives combine to form a means-ends chain.

Writing Good Objectives.   An authority on objectives recommends that "as far as possible, objectives are expressed in quantitative, measurable, concrete terms, in the form of a written statement of desired results to be achieved within a given time period."[18] In other words, objectives represent a firm commitment to accomplish something specific. A well-written objective should state what is to be accomplished and when it is to be accomplished. In the following sample objectives, note that the desired results are expressed *quantitatively*, in units of output, dollars, or percentage of change.

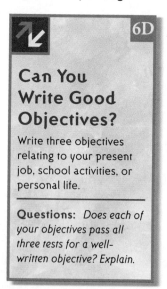

Can You Write Good Objectives?

Write three objectives relating to your present job, school activities, or personal life.

Questions: *Does each of your objectives pass all three tests for a well-written objective? Explain.*

- To increase subcompact car production by 240,000 units during the next production year.
- To reduce bad-debt loss by $50,000 during the next six months.
- To achieve an 18 percent increase in Brand X sales by December 31 of the current year.

The following is a handy three-way test to judge how well objectives are written:

- *Test 1:* Does this objective tell me exactly *what* the intended result is?
- *Test 2:* Does this objective specify *when* the intended result is to be accomplished?
- *Test 3:* Can the intended result be *measured?*

Statements of intention that fail one or more of these three tests do not qualify as objectives and will tend to hinder rather than help the planning process.

The Importance of Objectives.   From the standpoint of planning, carefully prepared objectives benefit managers by serving as targets and measuring sticks, fostering commitment, and enhancing motivation.[19]

- *Targets.* As mentioned earlier, objectives provide managers with specific targets. Without objectives, managers at all levels would find it difficult to make coordinated decisions. People quite naturally tend to pursue their own ends in the absence of formal organizational objectives.
- *Measuring sticks.* An easily overlooked, after-the-fact feature of objectives is that they are useful for measuring how well an organizational subunit or individual has performed. When appraising performance, managers need an established standard against which they can measure performance. Concrete objectives enable managers to weigh performance objectively on the basis of accomplishment rather than subjectively on the basis of personality or prejudice.
- *Commitment.* The very process of getting an employee to agree to pursue a given objective gives that individual a personal stake in the success of the enterprise. Thus objectives can be helpful in encouraging personal commitment to collective ends. Without individual commitment, even well-intentioned and carefully conceived strategies are doomed to failure.
- *Motivation.* Good objectives represent a challenge—something to reach for. As such, they have a motivational aspect. People usually feel good about themselves and what they do when they successfully achieve a challenging objective. Moreover, objectives give managers a rational basis for rewarding performance. Employees who believe they will be equitably rewarded for achieving a given objective will be motivated to perform well.

The Means-Ends Chain of Objectives.   Like the overall planning process, objective setting is a top-to-bottom proposition. Top managers set broader objectives with longer time horizons than do successively lower levels of managers. In effect, this downward flow of objectives creates a means-ends chain. Working from bottom to top in Figure 6.3, supervisory-level objectives provide the means for achieving middle-level objectives (ends) that, in turn, provide the means for achieving top-level objectives (ends).

The organizational hierarchy in Figure 6.3 has, of course, been telescoped and narrowed at the middle and lower levels for illustrative purposes. Usually, two or three layers of management would separate the president and the product-line managers. Another layer or two would separate product-line managers from area sales managers. But the telescoping helps show that lower-level objectives provide the means for accomplishing higher-level ends or objectives.

Priorities

Defined as a ranking of goals, objectives, or activities in order of importance, **priorities** play a special role in planning. By listing long-range organizational objectives in order of their priority, top management prepares to make later decisions regarding the

priorities *ranking goals, objectives, or activities in order of importance*

Figure 6.3

A Typical Means-Ends Chain of Objectives

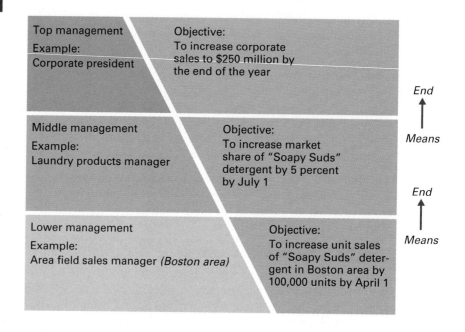

allocation of resources. Limited time, talent, and financial and material resources need to be channeled proportionately into more important endeavors and away from other areas. Establishment of priorities is a key factor in managerial and organizational effectiveness.[20] Strategic priorities give both insiders and outsiders answers to the questions, "Why does the organization exist?" and "Where is it headed?"

Despite time-management seminars, day planners, and computerized "personal digital assistants," establishing priorities remains a subjective process affected by organizational politics and value conflicts.[21] Although there is no universally acceptable formula for carrying out this important function, the following A-B-C priority system is helpful.

A: "Must do" objectives critical *to successful performance.* They may be the result of special demands from higher levels of management or other external sources.

B: "Should do" objectives necessary *for improved performance.* They are generally vital, but their achievement can be postponed if necessary.

C: "Nice to do" objectives desirable *for improved performance, but not critical to survival or improved performance.* They can be eliminated or postponed to achieve objectives of higher priority.[22]

Another priority-setting tool used by many managers is Pareto analysis (the 80/20 principle mentioned in other chapters). A business that focuses its attention on the 20 percent of its customers responsible for about 80 percent of its orders can stay a step ahead of competitors that do otherwise. These simple yet

---

6F

Meg Whitman Avoids the Busyness Trap by Getting Her Priorities Straight

Margaret C. Whitman, CEO of eBay Inc., the online auction site:

Again, it's this notion of choosing what you're going to focus on. And I have this philosophy that you really need to do things 100 percent. Better to do five things at 100 percent than ten things at 80 percent. And while we have to move very, very fast, I think you are not well served by moving incredibly rapidly and not doing things that well.

Source: As quoted in Linda Himelstein, "Meg Whitman: eBay," *Business Week* (May 31, 1999): 134.

Questions: *Are you caught in the busyness trap? How can you tell? What can you do to improve the situation?*

effective tools for establishing priorities can help managers avoid the so-called *busyness trap.*[23] In these fast-paced times, managers should not confuse being busy with being effective and efficient. *Results* are what really count. Activities and speed, without results, are an energy-sapping waste of time. By slowing down a bit, having clear priorities, and taking a strategic view of daily problems, busy managers can be successful *and* "get a life."

Finally, managers striving to establish priorities amid lots of competing demands would do well to heed management expert Peter Drucker's advice—that the most important skill for setting priorities and managing time is simply learning to say no.

The Planning/Control Cycle

To put the planning process in perspective, it is important to show how it is connected with the control function. Figure 6.4 illustrates the cyclical relationship between planning and control. Planning gets things headed in the right direction, and control keeps them headed in the right direction. (Because of the importance of the control function, it is covered in detail in Part Five.) Basically, each of the three levels of planning is a two-step sequence followed by a two-step control sequence.

The initial planning/control cycle begins when top management establishes strategic plans. When those strategic plans are carried out, intermediate and operational plans are formulated, thus setting in motion two more planning/control cycles. As strategic, intermediate, and operational plans are carried out, the control function begins. Corrective action is necessary when either the preliminary or the final results deviate from plans. For planned activities still in progress, the corrective action can get things back on track before it is too late. Deviations between final results and plans, on the other hand, are instructive feedback for the improvement of future plans. The dotted lines in Figure 6.4 represent the important sort of feedback that makes the planning/control cycle a dynamic and evolving process. Our attention now turns to some practical planning tools.

Figure 6.4

**The Basic
Planning/Control Cycle**

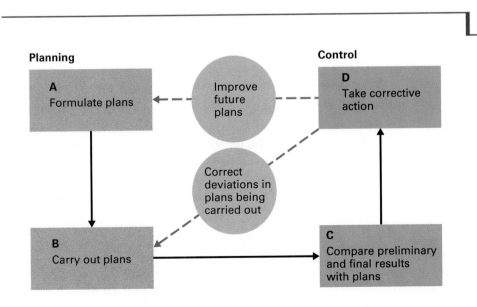

Management by Objectives and Project Planning

In this section we examine a traditional planning technique and a modern planning challenge. Valuable lessons about planning can be learned from each.

Management by Objectives

management by objectives (MBO) *comprehensive management system based on measurable and participatively set objectives*

Management by objectives (MBO) is a comprehensive management system based on measurable and participatively set objectives. MBO has come a long way since it was first suggested by Peter Drucker in 1954 as a way of promoting managerial self-control.[24] MBO theory[25] and practice subsequently mushroomed and spread around the world. In one form or another, and under various labels, MBO has been adopted by most public and private organizations of any significant size. For example, at Cypress Semiconductor Corporation, the San Jose, California, electronics firm, computerization paved the way for high-tech MBO. T. J. Rodgers, the company's founder and chief executive officer, explains:

> All of Cypress's 1,400 employees have goals, which, in theory, makes them no different from employees at most other companies. What makes our people different is that every week they set their own goals, commit to achieving them by a specific date, enter them into a database, and report whether or not they completed prior goals. Cypress's computerized goal system is an important part of our managerial infrastructure. It is a detailed guide to the future and an objective record of the past. In any given week, some 6,000 goals in the database come due. Our ability to meet those goals ultimately determines our success or failure. . . .
>
> I developed the goal system long before personal computers existed. It has its roots in management-by-objectives techniques I learned in the mid-1970s at American Microsystems.[26]

The common denominator that has made MBO programs so popular in both management theory and practice is the emphasis on objectives that are both *measurable* and *participatively set*.

4 Describe the four-step management by objectives (MBO) process and explain how it can foster individual commitment and motivation.

The MBO Cycle.   Because MBO combines planning and control, the four-stage MBO cycle corresponds to the planning/control cycle outlined in Figure 6.4. Steps 1 and 2 make up the planning phase of MBO, and steps 3 and 4 are the control phase.

Step 1: Setting Objectives. A hierarchy of challenging, fair, and internally consistent objectives is the necessary starting point for the MBO cycle and serves as the foundation for all that follows. All objectives, according to MBO theory, should be reduced to writing and put away for later reference during steps 3 and 4. Consistent with what was said earlier about objectives, objective setting in MBO begins at the top of the managerial pyramid and filters down, one layer at a time.

MBO's main contribution to the objective-setting process is its emphasis on the participation and involvement of people at lower levels. There is no place in MBO for the domineering manager ("Here are the objectives I've written for you") or for the passive manager ("I'll go along with whatever objectives you set"). MBO calls for a give-and-take negotiation of objectives between the manager and those who report directly to him or her.

Step 2: Developing Action Plans. With the addition of action statements to the participatively set objectives, the planning phase of MBO is complete. Managers at each level develop plans that incorporate objectives established in step 1. Higher managers are responsible for ensuring that their direct assistants' plans complement one another and do not work at cross-purposes.

Step 3: Periodic Review. As plans turn into action, attention turns to step 3, monitoring performance. Advocates of MBO usually recommend face-to-face meetings between a manager and his or her people at three-, six-, and nine-month intervals. (Some organizations, such as Cypress, rely on shorter cycles.) These periodic checkups permit those who are responsible for a particular set of objectives to reconsider them, checking their validity in view of unexpected events—added duties or the loss of a key assistant—that could make them obsolete. If an objective is no longer valid, it is amended accordingly. Otherwise, progress toward valid objectives is assessed. Periodic checkups also give managers an excellent opportunity to give their people needed and appreciated feedback.

Step 4: Performance Appraisal. At the end of one complete cycle of MBO, typically one year after the original goals were set, final performance is matched with the previously agreed-upon objectives. The pairs of superior and subordinate managers who mutually set the objectives one year earlier meet face-to-face once again to discuss how things have turned out. MBO emphasizes results, not personalities or excuses.[27] The control phase of the MBO cycle is completed when success is rewarded with promotion, merit pay, or other suitable benefits and when failure is noted for future corrective action.

After one round of MBO, the cycle repeats itself, with each cycle contributing to the learning process. A common practice in introducing MBO is to start at the top and to

Meet the X-Force. They're a hot bunch of computer wizards who work for Atlanta-based Internet Security Systems. Everything they do is focused on a top-priority problem for major companies willing to pay big bucks for their services. Their job is to beat so-called crackers (short for criminal hackers) at their own game. Corporate bottom lines and consumer privacy hang in the balance in this cyberspace cowboy cliffhanger.

Making MBO Work

Questions: *What is your experience with MBO-type programs in the workplace? What was the program called? Was the program effective? Why or why not? Referring back to McGregor's Theory X and Theory Y distinction in Chapter 2, why does a Theory Y manager have a better chance of administering an MBO program?*

pull in a new layer of management to the MBO process each year. Experience has shown that plunging several layers of management into MBO all at once often causes confusion, dissatisfaction, and failure. In fact, even a moderate-size organization usually takes five or more years to evolve a full-blown MBO system that ties together such areas as planning, control, performance appraisal, and the reward system. MBO programs can be facilitated by using software programs such as ManagePro® from Avantos. Such programs offer helpful spreadsheet formats for goal setting, time lines, at-a-glance status boards, and performance reports. MBO proponents believe that effective leadership and greater motivation—through the use of realistic objectives, more effective control, and self-control—are the natural by-products of a proper MBO system.[28]

Strengths and Limitations of MBO.   Any widely used management technique is bound to generate debate about its relative strengths and weaknesses, and MBO is no exception.[29] Present and future managers will have more realistic expectations for MBO if they are familiar with both sides of this debate. The four primary strengths of MBO and four common complaints about it are compared in Figure 6.5.

This debate will probably not be resolved in the near future. Critics of MBO, such as the late quality expert W. Edwards Deming, point to both theoretical and methodological flaws.[30] Meanwhile, MBO advocates are quick to point out that the misapplication of MBO, not the MBO concept itself, leads to problems. In the final analysis, MBO will probably work when organizational conditions are favorable and will probably fail when those conditions are unfavorable. A favorable climate for MBO includes top-management commitment, openness to change, Theory Y management, and employees who are willing and able to shoulder greater responsibility.[31] Research justifies putting *top-management commitment* at the top of the list. In a review of 70 MBO studies, researchers found that "when top-management commitment was high, the average gain in productivity was 56 percent. When commitment was low, the average

Figure 6.5

MBO's Strengths and Limitations

Strengths	Limitations
• MBO blends planning and control into a rational system of management.	• MBO is too often sold as a cure-all.
• MBO forces an organization to develop a top-to-bottom hierarchy of objectives.	• MBO is easily stalled by authoritarian (Theory X) managers and inflexible bureaucratic policies and rules.
• MBO emphasizes end results rather than good intentions or personalities.	• MBO takes too much time and effort and generates too much paperwork.
• MBO encourages self-management and personal commitment through employee participation in setting objectives.	• MBO's emphasis on measurable objectives can be used as a threat by overzealous managers.

gain in productivity was only 6 percent."[32] A strong positive relationship also was found between top-management commitment to MBO program success and employee job satisfaction.[33] The greater management's commitment, the greater the satisfaction.

Project Planning

Project-based organizations are becoming the norm today. Why? Drawing-board-to-market times are being honed to the minimum in today's technology-driven world.[34] Typically, cross-functional teams of people with different technical skills are brought together on a temporary basis to complete a specific project as swiftly as possible. When the job is done, they disband and move on to other projects or return to their usual work routines.[35] For example, imagine yourself having to manage the following situation at Hewlett-Packard (take note of how the project managers balanced planned action and creativity, as discussed earlier):

> HP's North American distribution organization handles billions of dollars in products, from PCs to toner cartridges, from order to delivery. But there was a problem: On average, it took a languid 26 days for a product to reach the customer. . . . The job of reengineering the process fell to two seasoned managers, Mei-Lin Cheng, 44, and Julie Anderson, 46.
>
> They came up with an extraordinary strategy. Assigned to create entirely new processes, they bought freedom from their bosses at HP by agreeing to produce significant and measurable improvements in customer satisfaction—in less than nine months. Failure would mean a cut-off of funding. They assembled a team of 35 people from HP and two other companies, explained the ground rules—and then vigorously refused to tell anyone what to do. Result: They met the deadline and achieved their goal.[36]

When dealing with less talented employees or those who do not take the initiative, project managers must rely on specific job assignments and detailed schedules.

Project management is the usual thing on Hollywood movie sets and at construction companies building homes, roads, and skyscrapers. But it is new to manufacturers, banks, insurance companies, hospitals, and government agencies. Unfortunately, much of this Internet-age project management leaves a lot to be desired. For example, consider the dismal track record for information technology (IT) projects, typically involving conversion of an old computer system to new hardware, software, and work methods.

> Most large IT projects are delivered late and over budget because they are inefficiently managed. A study by the Hackett Group, a Hudson, Ohio-based benchmarking firm, found that the average company completes only 37 percent of large IT projects on time and only 42 percent on budget.[37]

A broader and deeper understanding of project management is in order.

Project managers face many difficult challenges. First and foremost, they work outside the normal organizational hierarchy or chain of command because projects are ad hoc and temporary. So they must rely on excellent "people management skills" instead of giving orders. Those skills include, but are not limited to, communication, motivation, leadership, conflict resolution, and negotiation[38] (see Chapters 12–16).

Project *planning* deserves special attention in this chapter because project managers have the difficult job of being both intermediate/tactical and operational planners. They are responsible for both the big picture and the little details of their project. A project that is not well planned is a project doomed to failure. So let us take a look at the project life cycle, project management software, and planning guidelines for project managers.

6H

A Work of Art

At a conference this week I ran into a high-school classmate I hadn't seen in 26 years. I remember her winning all the art awards. Now she's in satellite communications. "Still painting?" I asked. "No," she said, "but managing a complex project uses the same creativity."

Source: Thomas Petzinger Jr., "Some Thoughts on All I've Learned from You As New Fronts Beckon," *The Wall Street Journal* (May 21, 1999): B1.

Question: *What do you think she meant?*

The Project Life Cycle.   Every project, from developing a new breakfast cereal to staging a benefit rock concert, has a predictable four-stage life cycle. As shown in Figure 6.6, the four stages are conceptualization, planning, execution, and termination. Although equally spaced in Figure 6.6, the four stages typically involve varying periods of time. Sometimes the borders between stages blur. For example, project goal setting actually begins in the conceptualization stage and often carries over to the planning stage. During this stage project managers turn their attention to facilities and equipment, personnel and task assignments, and scheduling. Work on the project begins in the execution stage, and additional resources are acquired as needed. Budget demands are highest during the execution stage because everything is in motion. To some, the label "termination" in stage 4 might suggest a sudden end to the project. But more typically, the completed project is turned over to an end user (e.g., a new breakfast cereal is turned over to manufacturing) and project resources are phased out.[39]

5 **Discuss project planning within the context of the project life cycle.**

Figure 6.6   The Project Life Cycle and Project Planning Activities

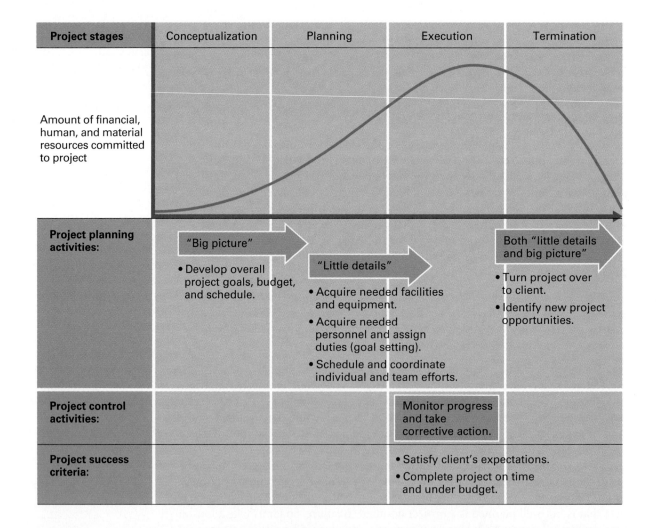

Source: Adapted in part from Figure 1.2 and discussion in Jeffrey K. Pinto and O. P. Kharbanda, *Successful Project Managers: Leading Your Team to Success* (New York: Van Nostrand Reinhold, 1995), pp. 17–21.

Project Management Software.   Recall from our earlier discussion of the basic planning/control cycle (Figure 6.4) how planning and control are intertwined. One cannot occur without the other. The same is true for project planning. Making sure planned activities occur when and where appropriate and taking corrective action when necessary can be an overwhelming job for the manager of a complex project. Fortunately, a host of computer software programs can make the task manageable. But which one of the many available programs should a project manager use? Thanks to a recent survey of 159 project managers from across the United States, we have a handy screening tool (see Table 6.2). Notice how the most widely used program, Microsoft Project, did not have a high user satisfaction rating; that honor went to the less widely used Project Scheduler.

Project Planning Guidelines.   Project managers need a working knowledge of basic planning concepts and tools, as presented in this chapter. Beyond that, they need to be aware of the following special planning demands of projects.[40]

Table 6.2

How Do the Leading Project Management Software Programs Stack Up?

Software package	Extent of use	User satisfaction ranking*	Brief description
Microsoft Project	48.8%	7	Complete planning/control tool for projects of all sizes.
Primavera Project Planner	13.8%	2	Plan, schedule, and control large, complex multi-projects.
Microsoft Excel	8.5%	4	Spreadsheet for budgeting and tracking costs.
Project Workbench	8.1%	3	Complete package for projects of all sizes.
Time Line	6.1%	10	Plan, track, and schedule small and medium projects.
Primavera Sure Trak	6.1%	5	Schedule, allocate resources, and control single and multiple projects of all sizes.
CA-SuperProject	2.8%	6	Plan, schedule, track, and monitor training for projects of all sizes.
Project Scheduler	2.8%	1	Schedule, budget, allocate resources, and track multi-projects.
Artemis Prestige	2%	8	Plan, schedule, analyze costs, and track multi-projects.
FasTracs	2%	9	Gantt charts and schedule presentations for small projects.

*Ranked on a scale of 1 to 10, 1 being the highest.
Source: Data adapted from Terry L. Fox and J. Wayne Spence, "Tools of the Trade: A Survey of Project Management Tools," *Project Management Journal,* 29 (September 1998): 20–27.

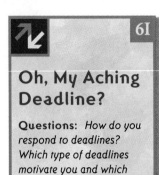

Oh, My Aching Deadline?

Questions: *How do you respond to deadlines? Which type of deadlines motivate you and which types do not? Why are deadlines such a powerful motivational tool?*

- *Projects are schedule-driven and results-oriented.* By definition, projects are created to accomplish something specific by a certain time. Project managers require a positive attitude about making lots of quick decisions and doing things in a hurry. They tend to value results more than process.
- *The big picture and the little details are of equal importance.* Project managers need to keep the overall project goal and deadline in mind when attending to day-to-day problems and personnel issues. This is difficult because distractions are constant.
- *Project planning is a necessity, not a luxury.* Novice project managers tend to get swept away by the pressure for results and fail to devote adequate time and resources to project planning.
- *Project managers know the motivational power of a deadline.* A challenging (but not impossible) project deadline is the project manager's most powerful motivational tool. The final deadline serves as a focal point for all team and individual goal setting.[41]

Graphic Planning/Scheduling/ Control Tools

6 **Compare and contrast flow charts and Gantt charts, and discuss the value of PERT networks.**

Management science specialists have introduced needed precision to the planning/ control cycle through graphics analysis. Three graphics tools for planning, scheduling, and controlling operations are flow charts, Gantt charts, and PERT networks. They can be found in the project management software programs reviewed in Table 6.2.

Sequencing with Flow Charts

Flow charts have been used extensively by computer programmers for identifying task components and by TQM teams for *work simplification* (eliminating wasted steps and activities). Beyond that, flow charts are a useful sequencing tool with broad application.[42] Sequencing is simply arranging events in the order of their actual or desired occurrence. For instance, this book had to be purchased before it could be read. Thus the event "purchase book" would come before the event "read book" in flow-chart sequence.

A sample flow chart is given in Figure 6.7. Notice that the chart consists of boxes and diamonds in addition to the start and stop ovals. Each box contains a major event, and each diamond contains a yes-or-no decision.

Managers at all levels and in all specialized areas can identify and properly sequence important events and decisions with flow charts of this kind. User-friendly computer programs, such as ABC Flow Charter from Micrografx,[43] make flow-charting fun and easy today. Flow charts force people to consider all relevant links in a particular endeavor as well as their proper sequence. This is an advantage because it encourages analytical thinking. But flow charts have two disadvantages. First, they do not indicate the time dimension, that is, the varying amounts of time required to complete each step and make each decision. Second, flow charts are not practical for complex situations in which several activities take place at once.

Figure 6.7   A Sample Flow Chart

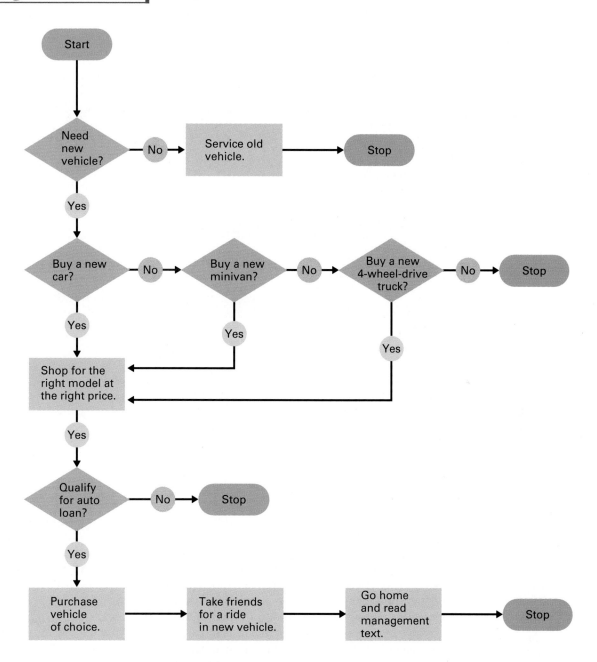

Scheduling with Gantt Charts

Scheduling is an important part of effective planning. When later steps depend on the successful completion of earlier steps, schedules help managers determine when and where resources are needed. Without schedules, inefficiency creeps in as equipment

Figure 6.8

A Sample Gantt Chart

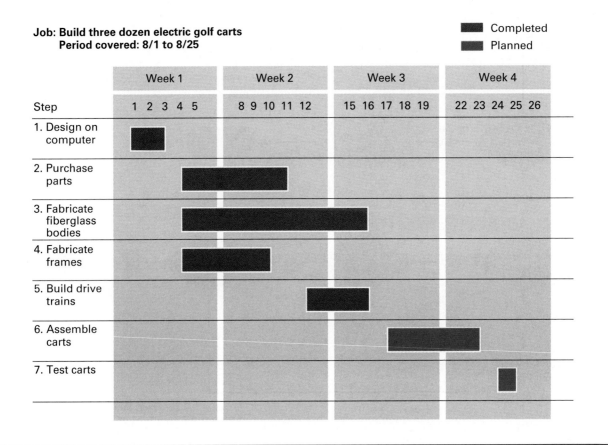

Job: Build three dozen electric golf carts
Period covered: 8/1 to 8/25

■ Completed
■ Planned

Step	Week 1 1 2 3 4 5	Week 2 8 9 10 11 12	Week 3 15 16 17 18 19	Week 4 22 23 24 25 26
1. Design on computer				
2. Purchase parts				
3. Fabricate fiberglass bodies				
4. Fabricate frames				
5. Build drive trains				
6. Assemble carts				
7. Test carts				

Gantt chart *graphic scheduling technique*

6J

Gantt Chart Exercise

Construct a Gantt chart for a project you are presently working on or might be working on soon. For example, a Gantt chart can help you plan for a major school project such as a term paper or team project. Workplace projects are fair game, too.

and people stand idle. Also, like any type of plan or budget, schedules provide management with a measuring stick for corrective action. Gantt charts, named for Henry L. Gantt, who developed the technique, are a convenient scheduling tool for managers.[44] Gantt worked with Frederick W. Taylor at Midvale Steel beginning in 1887 and, as discussed in Chapter 2, helped refine the practice of scientific management. A **Gantt chart** is a graphic scheduling technique historically used in production operations. Things have changed since Gantt's time, and so have Gantt chart applications. Updated versions like the one in Figure 6.8 are widely used today for planning and scheduling all sorts of organizational activities. They are especially useful for large projects such as moving into a new building or installing a new computer network.[45]

Figure 6.8 also shows how a Gantt chart can be used for more than just scheduling the important steps of a job. By filling in the time lines of completed activities, *actual* progress can be assessed at a glance. Like flow charts, Gantt charts force managers to be analytical as they reduce jobs or projects to separate steps. Moreover, Gantt charts improve on flow charts by allowing the planner to specify the time to be spent on each activity. A disadvantage Gantt charts share with flow charts is that overly complex situations are cumbersome to chart.

PERT Networks

The more complex the project, the greater the need for reliable sequencing and scheduling of key activities. Simultaneous sequencing and scheduling amounts to programming. One of the most widely recognized programming tools used by managers is a technique referred to simply as PERT. An acronym for Program Evaluation and Review Technique, **PERT** is a graphic sequencing and scheduling tool for large, complex, and nonroutine projects.

PERT (Program Evaluation and Review Technique) *graphic sequencing and scheduling tool for complex projects*

History of PERT.   PERT was developed in 1958 by a team of management consultants for the U.S. Navy Special Projects Office. At the time, the navy was faced with the seemingly insurmountable task of building a weapon system that could fire a missile from the deck of a submerged submarine. PERT not only contributed to the development of the Polaris submarine project but was also credited with helping to bring the system to combat readiness nearly two years ahead of schedule. News of this dramatic administrative feat caught the attention of managers around the world. But, as one user of PERT reflected, "No management technique has ever caused so much enthusiasm, controversy, and disappointment as PERT."[46] Realizing that PERT is not a panacea, but rather a specialized planning and control tool that can be appropriately or inappropriately applied, helps managers accept it at face value.[47]

PERT Terminology.   Because PERT has its own special language, four key terms must be understood.

- *Event.* A **PERT event** is a performance milestone representing the start or finish of some activity. Handing in a difficult management exam is an event.
- *Activity.* A **PERT activity** represents work in process. Activities are time-consuming jobs that begin and end with an event. Studying for a management exam and taking the exam are activities.
- *Time.* **PERT times** are estimated times for the completion of PERT activities. PERT times are weighted averages of three separate time estimates: (1) *optimistic time* (T_o)—the time an activity should take under the best of conditions; (2) *most likely time* (T_m)—the time an activity should take under normal conditions; and (3) *pessimistic time* (T_p)—the time an activity should take under the worst possible conditions. The formula for calculating estimated PERT time (T_e) is:

$$T_e = \frac{T_o + 4T_m + T_p}{6}$$

PERT event *performance milestone; start or finish of an activity*

PERT activity *work in process*

PERT times *weighted time estimates for completion of PERT activities*

- *Critical path.* The **critical path** is the most time-consuming chain of activities and events in a PERT network. In other words, the longest path through a PERT network is critical because if any of the activities along it are delayed, the entire project will be delayed accordingly.[48]

critical path *most time-consuming route through a PERT network*

PERT in Action.   A PERT network is shown in Figure 6.9. The task in this example, the design and construction of three dozen customized golf carts for use by physically challenged adults, is relatively simple for instructional purposes. PERT networks are usually reserved for more complex projects with dozens or even hundreds of activities. PERT events are coded by circled letters, and PERT activities, shown by the arrows connecting the PERT events, are coded by number. A PERT time (T_e) has been calculated and recorded for each PERT activity.

See if you can pick out the critical path in the PERT network in Figure 6.9. By calculating which path will take the most time from beginning to end, the critical path turns

Figure 6.9

A Sample PERT Network

**Task: Build three dozen customized golf carts
for use by physically challenged adults.**

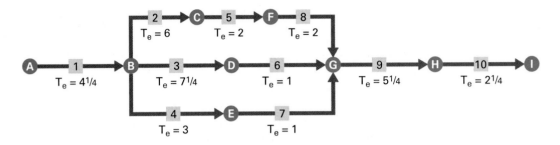

PERT events		PERT activities and times				
		Activities	T_o	T_m	T_p	T_e*
A. Receive contract.		1. Prepare final design.	3	4	6	$4\frac{1}{4}$
B. Begin construction.		2. Purchase parts.	4	5	12	6
C. Receive parts.		3. Fabricate bodies.	5	$7\frac{1}{2}$	9	$7\frac{1}{4}$
D. Bodies ready for testing.		4. Fabricate frames.	$2\frac{1}{2}$	3	4	3
E. Frames ready for testing.		5. Build drive trains.	$1\frac{1}{2}$	2	3	2
F. Drive trains ready for testing.		6. Test bodies.	$\frac{1}{2}$	1	$1\frac{1}{2}$	1
G. Components ready for assembly.		7. Test frames.	$\frac{1}{2}$	1	$1\frac{1}{2}$	1
H. Carts assembled.		8. Test-drive trains.	1	$1\frac{1}{2}$	5	2
I. Carts ready for shipment.		9. Assemble carts.	3	5	9	$5\frac{1}{4}$
		10. Test carts.	1	2	5	$2\frac{1}{4}$

* Rounded to nearest $\frac{1}{4}$ workday

out to be *A-B-C-F-G-H-I*. This particular chain of activities and events will require an estimated 21.75 workdays to complete. The overall duration of the project is dictated by the critical path, and a delay in any of the activities along this critical path will delay the entire project.

Positive and Negative Aspects of PERT.   During the more than 40 years that PERT has been used in a wide variety of settings, both its positive and negative aspects have become apparent.

On the plus side, PERT is an excellent scheduling tool for large, nonroutine projects, ranging from constructing an electric generation station to launching a space vehicle. PERT is a helpful planning aid because it forces managers to envision projects in their entirety. It also gives them a tool for predicting resource needs, potential problem areas, and the impact of delays on project completion. If an activity runs over or under its estimated time, the ripple effect of lost or gained time on downstream activities can be calculated. PERT also gives managers an opportunity, through the calculation of optimistic and pessimistic times, to factor in realistic uncertainties about planning horizons.

On the minus side, PERT is an inappropriate tool for repetitive assembly-line operations in which scheduling is dictated by the pace of machines. PERT also shares with other planning and decision-making aids the disadvantage of being only as good as its underlying assumptions. False assumptions about activities and events and miscalculations of PERT times can render PERT ineffective. Despite the objective impression of numerical calculations, PERT times are derived rather subjectively. Moreover, PERT's critics say it is too time-consuming: A complex PERT network prepared by hand may be obsolete by the time it is completed, and frequent updates can tie PERT in knots. Project management software with computerized PERT routines is essential for complex projects because it can greatly speed the graphic plotting process and updating of time estimates.

Break-Even Analysis

In well-managed businesses, profit is a forethought rather than an afterthought. A widely used tool for projecting profits relative to costs and sales volume is break-even analysis. In fact, break-even analysis is often referred to as cost-volume-profit analysis. By using either the algebraic method or the graphic method, planners can calculate the **break-even point,** the level of sales at which the firm neither suffers a loss nor realizes a profit. In effect, the break-even point is the profit-making threshold. If sales are below that point, the organization loses money. If sales go beyond the break-even point, it makes a profit. Break-even points, as discussed later, are often expressed in units. For example, consider these clips from the business press: "Chrysler needs to sell only 1.6 million cars and trucks to break even on its operations, down from a break-even point of 2 million in 1989, when it launched its cost-reduction drive."[49] Carlo De Benedetti, the CEO of Italy's Olivetti, lowered his company's break-even point on computers from 1 million units annually to 900,000 by cutting his workforce 50 percent.[50]

From a procedural standpoint, a critical part of break-even analysis is separating fixed costs from variable costs.

7 Explain how break-even points can be calculated.

break-even point *level of sales at which there is no loss or profit*

Fixed Versus Variable Costs

Some expenses, called fixed costs, must be paid even if a firm fails to sell a single unit. Other expenses, termed variable costs, are incurred only as units are produced and sold. **Fixed costs** are contractual costs that must be paid regardless of the level of output or sales. Typical examples include rent, utilities, insurance premiums, managerial and professional staff salaries, property taxes, and licenses. **Variable costs** are costs that vary directly with the firm's production and sales. Common variable costs include costs of production (such as labor, materials, and supplies), sales commissions, and product delivery expenses. As output/sales increase, fixed costs remain the same but variable costs accumulate. Looking at it another way, fixed costs are a function of *time*, and variable costs are a function of *volume*. You can now calculate the break-even point.

fixed costs *contractual costs that must be paid regardless of output or sales*

variable costs *costs that vary directly with production and sales*

The Algebraic Method

Relying on the following labels,

$$FC = \text{total fixed costs}$$
$$P = \text{price (per unit)}$$
$$VC = \text{variable costs (per unit)}$$
$$BEP = \text{break-even point}$$

the formula for calculating break-even point (in units) is

$$BEP \text{ (in units)} = \frac{FC}{P - VC}$$

contribution margin
selling price per unit minus variable costs per unit

The difference between the selling price *P* and per unit variable costs *VC* is referred to as the **contribution margin.** In other words, the contribution margin is the portion of the unit selling price that falls above and beyond the variable costs and that can be applied to fixed costs. Above the break-even point, the contribution margin contributes to profits.

Variable costs are normally expressed as a percentage of the unit selling price. As a working example of how the break-even point (in units) can be calculated, assume that a firm has total fixed costs of $30,000, a unit selling price of $7, and variable costs of 57 percent (or $4 in round numbers):

$$BEP \text{ (in units)} = \frac{30,000}{7 - 4} = 10,000$$

This calculation shows that 10,000 units must be produced and sold at $7 each if the firm is to break even on this particular product.

Price Planning.   Break-even analysis is an excellent "what if" tool for planners who want to know what impact price changes will have on profit. For instance, what would the break-even point be if the unit selling price were lowered to match a competitor's price of $6?

$$BEP \text{ (in units)} = \frac{30,000}{6 - 4} = 15,000$$

In this case, the $1 drop in price to $6 means that 15,000 units must be sold before a profit can be realized.

Fily and Madeline Keita run a successful African art and clothing shop in an exclusive location in Marina del Rey, California. Factored into their break-even calculation for their store, Fara Fina Collection, are some high fixed costs. Three times each year, Fily travels to his native Mali and other African nations such as Cameroon, Tanzania, and Zimbabwe to buy native art, crafts, and fabrics. Annual travel expenses approaching $20,000 are an unavoidable cost of doing business first-hand with village crafts-people. Of course, the love they have for their business is incalculable.

Profit Planning.   Planners often set profit objectives and then work backward to determine the required level of output. Break-even analysis greatly assists such planners. The modified break-even formula for profit planning is:

$$BEP \text{ (in units)} = \frac{FC + \text{desired profit}}{P - VC}$$

Assuming that top management has set a profit objective for the year at $30,000 and that the original figures above apply, the following calculation would result:

$$BEP \text{ (in units)} = \frac{30,000 + 30,000}{7 - 4} = 20,000$$

To meet the profit objective of $30,000, the company would need to sell 20,000 units at $7 each.

The Graphic Method

If you place the dollar value of costs and revenues on a vertical axis and unit sales on a horizontal axis, you can calculate the break-even point by plotting fixed costs, total costs (fixed + variable costs), and total revenue. As illustrated in Figure 6.10, the break-even point is where the total costs and the total sales revenue lines intersect. Although the algebraic method does the same job as the graphic method, some planners prefer

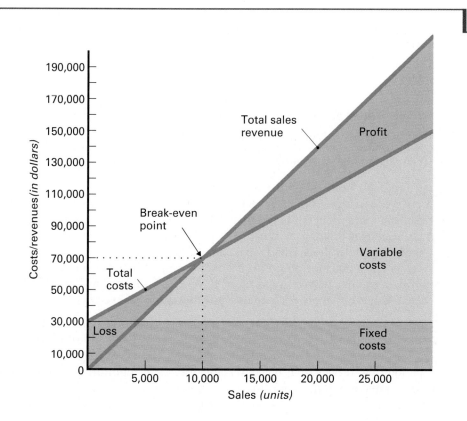

Figure 6.10

Graphic Break-Even Analysis

the graphic method because it presents in a convenient visual aid the various cost-volume-profit relationships at a glance.

Break-Even Analysis: Strengths and Limitations

Like the other planning tools discussed in this chapter, break-even analysis is not a cure-all. It has both strengths and limitations.

On the positive side, break-even analysis forces planners to interrelate cost, volume, and profit in a realistic way. All three variables are connected so that a change in one sends ripples of change through the other two. As mentioned earlier, break-even analysis allows planners to ask "what if" questions concerning the impact of price changes and varying profit objectives.

The primary problem with break-even analysis is that a neat separation of fixed and variable costs can be very difficult. General managers should get the help of accountants to isolate relevant fixed and variable costs. Moreover, because of complex factors in supply and demand, break-even analysis is not a good tool for setting prices. It serves better as a general planning and decision-making aid.

Summary

1. Planning has been labeled the primary management function because it sets the stage for all other aspects of management. Along with many other practical reasons for planning, managers need to plan in order to cope with an uncertain environment. Three types of uncertainty are state uncertainty ("What will happen?"), effect uncertainty ("What will happen to our organization?"), and response uncertainty ("What will be the outcome of our decisions?"). To cope with environmental uncertainty, organizations can respond as defenders, prospectors, analyzers, or reactors.

2. A properly written plan tells what, when, and how something is to be accomplished. A clearly written organizational mission statement tends to serve as a useful focus for the planning process. Strategic, intermediate, and operational plans are formulated by top, middle, and lower-level management, respectively.

3. Objectives have been called the single most important feature of the planning process. Well-written objectives spell out in measurable terms what should be accomplished and when it is to be accomplished. Good objectives help managers by serving as targets, acting as measuring sticks, encouraging commitment, and strengthening motivation. Objective setting begins at the top of the organization and filters down, thus forming a means-ends chain. Priorities affect resource allocation by assigning relative importance to objectives. Plans are formulated and executed as part of a more encompassing planning/control cycle.

4. Management by objectives (MBO), an approach to planning and controlling, is based on measurable and participatively set objectives. MBO basically consists of four steps: (1) setting objectives participatively, (2) developing action plans, (3) periodically reevaluating objectives and plans and monitoring performance, and (4) conducting annual performance appraisals. Objective setting in MBO flows from top to bottom. MBO has both strengths and limitations and requires a supportive climate favorable to change, participation, and the sharing of authority.

5. Project planning occurs throughout the project life cycle's four stages: conceptualization, planning, execution, and termination. "Big picture" tactical planning—project goal, budget, and schedule—occurs during stage 1 and into stage 2. During stage 2 and into the execution phase in stage 3, project planning deals with the "little details" of facilities and equipment, personnel and job assignments, and scheduling. Starting near the end of stage 3 and carrying into the termination stage, both little details and big picture planning are required to pass the project along and identify new project opportunities. Planning is central to project success because projects are schedule-driven and results-oriented. Project planners need to keep constantly abreast of both the big picture and the little details. Novice project managers too often shortchange planning. Challenging but realistic project deadlines are project managers' most powerful motivational tool.

6. Flow charts, Gantt charts, and PERT networks, found in project management software packages, are three graphics tools for more effectively planning, scheduling, and controlling operations. Flow charts visually sequence important events and yes-or-no decisions. Gantt charts, named for Frederick W. Taylor's disciple Henry L. Gantt, are a graphic scheduling technique used in a wide variety of situations. Both flow charts and Gantt charts have the advantage of forcing managers to be analytical. But Gantt charts realistically portray the time dimension, whereas flow charts do not. PERT, which stands for Program Evaluation and Review Technique, is a sequencing and scheduling tool appropriate for large, complex, and nonroutine projects. Weighted PERT times enable management to factor in their uncertainties about time estimates.

7. Break-even analysis, or cost-volume-profit analysis, can be carried out algebraically or graphically. Either way, it helps planners gauge the potential impact of price changes and profit objectives on sales volume. A major limitation of break-even analysis is that specialized accounting knowledge is required to identify relevant fixed and variable costs.

Terms to Understand

Ten Common Errors to Avoid When Writing a Plan for a New Business

Here are errors in business-plan preparation that almost certainly will result in denial of a loan application by a bank:

■ Submitting a "rough copy," perhaps with coffee stains on the pages and crossed-out words in the text, tells the banker that the owner doesn't take his idea seriously.

■ Outdated historical financial information or industry comparisons will leave doubts about the entrepreneur's planning abilities.

■ Unsubstantiated assumptions can hurt a business plan; the business owner must be prepared to explain the "whys" of every point in the plan.

■ Too much "blue sky"—a failure to consider prospective pitfalls—will lead the banker to conclude that the idea is not realistic.

■ A lack of understanding of the financial information is a drawback. Even if an outside source is used to prepare the projections, the owner must fully comprehend the information.

■ Absence of any consideration of outside influences is a gap in a business plan. The owner needs to discuss the potential impact of competitive factors as well as the economic environment prevalent at the time of the request.

■ No indication that the owner has anything at stake in the venture is a particular problem. The lender will expect the entrepreneur to have some equity capital invested in the business.

■ Unwillingness to personally guarantee any loans raises a question: If the business owner isn't willing to stand behind his or her company, then why should the bank?

■ Introducing the plan with a demand for unrealistic loan terms is a mistake. The lender wants to find out about the viability of the business before discussing loan terms.

■ Too much focus on collateral is a problem in a business plan. Even for a cash-secured loan, the banker is looking toward projected profits for repayment of the loan. The emphasis should be on cash flow.

Source: J. Tol Broome, Jr., "Mistakes to Avoid in Drafting a Plan," *Nation's Business,* 81 (February 1993): 30. Reprinted by permission, *Nation's Business,* February 1993. Copyright 1993, U.S. Chamber of Commerce.

Internet Exercises

1. **All about project management.** Project management software, as covered in this chapter, belongs in virtually every modern manager's tool kit. The purpose of this exercise is to explore the different features of the most widely used project management software package: Microsoft Project. The journey begins at Microsoft's home page (**www.microsoft.com**), where you need to click on the main menu heading "Product Families." In the submenu that appears, select "Office" (because Microsoft Project is part of the Microsoft Office suite of software for businesses). At the Microsoft Office page, click on "Product Details" under the heading "Office Product Guide." Scroll down to the bottom of the Product Details page and click on "Microsoft Project." At the Microsoft Project page, select the heading "Tour of Microsoft Project 98." (*Note:* By the time you read this, a new version of Microsoft Project may have been released.) Take the tour by reading "Introduction," "Controlling the Details," and "Communicating the Plan."

    Learning Points: 1. Have you ever used project management software? Was it Microsoft Project? If you used something else, does Microsoft Project appear to be superior or inferior? Explain. 2. If you have never

used project management software, which of the features of Microsoft Project do you like best? Why?
   3. Why is project management software essential for today's complex projects?

2. **Check it out:** Thinking of starting your own business? If so, you will need a business plan to get financing. Visit **www.bplans.com** and learn what is involved in business planning by selecting the "Table-by-Table" option under the heading "Planning Spreadsheet Glossary." This site has many other valuable resources for business planners.

   For updates to these exercises, visit our Web site (**www.hmco.com/college**).

Profitable Planning at Emerson Electric

If a professional sports team had not lost a game in 41 years, you'd surely know about it. Emerson Electric Co. has chalked up the business equivalent of a 41-year winning streak, but many have never heard of the company. The St. Louis-based maker of motors, compressors, air conditioner parts, and many other industrial components has enjoyed 41 straight years of profit growth, making it one of America's most respected manufacturers.[51] In recent years, Emerson has become a major global player. The company, which was ranked 318th on the 1999 *Fortune* Global 500 list, has 111,800 employees and annual sales in excess of $13 billion.[52]

What is Emerson's secret? What makes Emerson tick? Chief executive officer Charles F. Knight provided some answers in a *Harvard Business Review* article. Here are some excerpts from that article.

Simply put, what makes us "tick" at Emerson is an effective management process. We believe we can shape our future through careful planning and strong follow-up. Our managers plan for improved results and execute to get them. Driving this process is a set of shared values, including involvement, intensity, discipline, and persistence. We adhere to few policies or techniques that could be called unique or even unusual. But we do act on our policies, and that may indeed make us unusual.

. . . Through our Best Cost Producer Strategy, we have spent more than a quarter of a billion dollars on restructuring and now have best cost positions in all of our major product lines. We've moved from an export-led to an invest-

ment-led international strategy, resulting in a rise of international sales from about 20 percent to about 40 percent in the past five years. As a result of a $1.6 billion investment in technology during the 1980s, new products—those introduced in the past five years—as a percentage of sales have increased from 9 percent to 20 percent. All the while, we've adhered to the discipline of constantly increasing earnings, earnings per share, and dividends per share. . . .

The driving force behind all that change is a simple management process that emphasizes setting targets, planning carefully, and following up closely. The process is supported by a long-standing history of continuous cost reduction and open communication and is fueled by annual dynamic planning and control cycles. Finally, it is nourished by strongly reinforced cultural values and an approach to organizational planning that is as rigorous as our approach to business planning. It is an environment in which people at all levels can and do make a difference. . . .

The first step is to "set financial targets," since almost everything we do is geared toward reaching our financial objectives. . . .

Consistent high performance requires ambitious and dynamic targets. Every year we reexamine our growth targets to see whether they remain valid, and we have recalibrated our growth objectives several times because the business environment has changed, or Emerson has changed, or we've learned something that causes us to see the world a little differently. . . .

These elements of strategy are not especially new or original. We think the key to success is closely tracking performance along these dimensions and attacking deviations immediately. Ten years ago, Emerson was not globally competitive in all its major product lines. Today we are, thanks to the intensity of our manufacturing approach and to the management process through which we make it work.

At Emerson, rigorous planning has been essential to the company's success since the 1950s; it's no coincidence that our long record of improved annual earnings dates from the same period. As CEO, more than half my time each year is blocked out strictly for planning. Emerson President and Chief Operating Officer Al Suter and other senior managers spend even more time in planning sessions. We devote so much time to planning because that is when we identify business investment opportunities in detail—and because good planning takes time.

Each fiscal year, from November through June, selected corporate officers, Al Suter, and I meet with the management of every division for a one- or two-day planning conference, usually held off-site. These division conferences are the culmination of our planning cycle. The mood is confrontational—by design. Though we're not trying to put anyone on the spot, we do want to challenge assumptions and conventional thinking and give ample time to every significant issue. We want proof that a division is stretching to reach its goals, and we want to see the details of the actions division management believes will yield improved results. Our expectations are high, and the discussions are intense. A division president who comes to a planning conference poorly prepared has made a serious mistake.

Corporate management sets the stage. We require only a few standard exhibits. . . . While the list is short, it takes substantial planning and backup data to develop these exhibits. To prepare properly requires that division presidents really understand their business. Every piece of data we ask for is something division management needs to know itself. . . .

Beyond the required exhibits, the planning conference belongs to the division presidents. We're there to help them improve their plans and their results. We want to hear division management's views of customers and markets; its plans for new products; its analysis of the competition; and the status of such manufacturing issues as quality, capacity, productivity, inventory levels, and compensation.

We also believe in the logic of illogic. Often, a manager will give a logical presentation on why we should approve a plan. We may challenge that logic by questioning underlying assumptions illogically. The people who know their strategies in detail are the ones who, after going through that, are able to stand up for the merits of their proposal. In the end, the test of a good planning conference is whether it results in managers taking actions that will have a significant impact on the business.

Since operating managers carry out the planning, we effectively establish ownership and eliminate the artificial distinction between strategic and operating decisions. Managers on the line do not—and must never—delegate the understanding of the business. To develop a plan, operating managers work together for months. They often tell me that the greatest value of the planning cycle lies in the teamwork and discipline that the preparation phase requires. . . .

The measure of Emerson's managers is whether they achieve what they say they will in a planning conference. We track the implementation of our plans through a tight control system. That system starts at the top, with a corporate board of directors that meets regularly and plays an active role in overseeing our business. Management of the company is directed by the office of the chief executive (OCE), which presently consists of me, Al Suter, Vice Chairman Bob Staley, Vice Chairman Jan Ver Hagen, the seven other business leaders, and three additional corporate officers. The OCE meets from 10 to 12 times a year to review and discuss issues facing the divisions individually as well as the corporation as a whole.

Input from the divisions arrives in the form of their president's operating reports (PORs), monthly submissions that summarize the divisions' results and immediate prospects. . . . We view the budget process used by many companies as static. In contrast, the POR is a dynamic tool: we update expected annual results each month and make rolling comparisons against historical and projected performance. . . .

Emerson's annual planning and control cycles provide important advantages in addition to good plans and tight controls; the process fosters teamwork, communication, understanding of the business and the marketplace, improved management skills, and focus on the fundamentals; it serves as an ongoing mechanism to identify and assess management talent; and it helps assimilate new acquisitions into the company.

FOR DISCUSSION

1. Is Emerson Electric a defender, prospector, analyzer, or reactor? How can you tell?

2. What would you say is the key to Emerson's impressive record of profitability? Explain.

3. Using Figure 6.4 as a guide, decide whether Emerson does a good job of linking planning and control. Why or why not?

4. What evidence of MBO can you find in this case?

STRATEGIC MANAGEMENT

Planning for Long-Term Success

CHAPTER OBJECTIVES

When you finish studying this chapter, you should be able to

1 Define the term *strategic management* and explain its relationship to strategic planning, implementation, and control.

2 Explain the concept of synergy and identify four kinds of synergy.

3 Describe Porter's model of generic competitive strategies.

4 Identify and explain the major contribution the business ecosystems model makes to strategic thinking.

5 Identify and discuss at least four strategic lessons from the e-commerce revolution.

6 Identify and descibe the four steps in the strategic management process.

7 Explain the nature and purpose of a SWOT analysis.

8 Describe the three types of forecasts.

"THE ONLY SUSTAINABLE COMPETITIVE
ADVANTAGE ANY BUSINESS HAS
IS ITS REPUTATION."
laurel cutler

Burger King Seeks New Sizzle

A twenty-first-century Burger King is opening . . . [in Reno, Nevada.] It embodies the most sweeping changes in the chain's 45-year history, from how a Burger King looks and cooks to how it hooks children. The overhaul was so extensive that an existing Burger King had to be razed here just to construct the prototype.

Dumping the dated tan-and-brick color scheme, the designers highlighted the new restaurant in cobalt blue. The exterior is brighter, with yellow and red stripes. Inside, walls are mustard-yellow, countertops are gray, and waste containers are tomato-red. Even the Burger King-in-a-bun logo has been updated, with tilted letters to give it more zing. Much of the kitchen is open for viewing so those waiting in line can see flames flickering in the broiler, emphasizing a key Burger King attribute.

A "virtual fun center" is designed for one important customer—children. In addition to the usual playground equipment, the restaurant features electronic kiosks loaded with interactive games. The machines have video-conferencing capability so kids at one restaurant can eventually chat with those at a similarly equipped Burger King miles away.

Management predicts the prototype eventually could boost average unit sales to $1.6 million annually from $1.15 million currently. That would surpass the $1.5 million average tally of a McDonald's Corp. restaurant in the United States.

Yet transformation is expensive—at least 15,000 dollars more than the current cost of building a new Burger King—so skepticism is detectable among franchisees gathered here for the chain's annual convention.

"We need to see what the return is," says Don White, whose store was torn down to make room for the prototype. "But if we get the kind we think we're going to get, we're going to be warming up the bulldozers."

In the first real test of the upgrade, Burger King will begin converting 40 company-owned restaurants in Orlando, Fla. A full rollout across Burger King's chain may take two to three years.

The prototype doesn't have new menu items, but its new cooking system could facilitate some. Until now, Burger King has been able to cook at only one speed. But the new system features three computer-controlled broiler chambers that can heat more slowly, allowing for thicker patties like a planned half-pound burger, tentatively called the Great American.

The restaurant-upgrade program may further a run that Burger King, a unit of Britain's Diageo PLC, has had much of this decade. Since 1993, its share of the U.S. quick-serve hamburger market has grown to 21.9 percent from 17.2 percent, the company says. It has about 7,800 restaurants in the United States. Market leader McDonald's, meanwhile, has nearly 13,000 U.S. restaurants and about 44 percent of the market.

Despite the progress, some Burger King franchisees say a dramatic overhaul was needed. "Some stores are 40 years old and have been modified to the 'nth,'" says Steven Lewis, a longtime Blue Bell, Pa., franchisee and president of the chain's franchisee association. . . .

A recent McKinsey & Co. study commissioned by Diageo revealed "tremendous upside potential in the brand," says the restaurant chain's chief executive, Dennis Malamatinas. And after years of losses, Burger King's European operations recently started making money. Now "Diageo's pretty excited," says Mr. Malamatinas, who sits on the board of the parent company.

Indeed, management will announce that Burger King is quadrupling its company-owned restaurants to 2,000 from 500, buying some from franchisees, building the rest. And to help franchisees pay for their own upgrades, Burger King is considering offering a combination of "investments and incentives," Mr. Malamatinas says.

Some options from the prototype focus on the drive-through customer, who accounts for about half of sales. Mobile patrons can see electronic screens that show them exactly what they've ordered and how much it will cost. There is also a speaker beyond the food-delivery window to report any problems. To help quickly check orders, the new restaurant places takeout items in transparent bags.

The drive-through counter also has its own kitchen to speed up service. "We'll get the food to the window before the car" arrives, says Tulin Tuzel, research-and-development head at Miami-based Burger King.

The ultimate verdict, of course, lies with consumers. If they fail to recognize or approve the restaurant's new look—or to like the food put out by its new high-tech kitchens—the initiative could prove a costly miscalculation.

Before building the prototype, Burger King asked what customers wanted in the ideal fast-food place. "A stress-free experience" was their response, says Jacqueline McCook, company head of strategic planning.

At Burger King in particular, patrons complained about hard-to-read menu boards, crowded eating areas, and tables bolted to the floor. Their overall impression of the chain? "'Boring' would be the right word—but they love the food," Ms. McCook says, adding that their message was: "If you make it a more pleasant environment, we'd come more often."

Source: Republished with permission of *The Wall Street Journal*, from Richard Gibson, "Burger King Seeks New Sizzle" (Aug. 14, 1999). Permission conveyed through Copyright Clearance Center, Inc.

Strategic management serves as the cutting edge for the entire management process. Organizations like Burger King and McDonald's that are guided by a coherent strategic framework tend to execute even the smallest details of their mission in a coordinated fashion. Indeed, McDonald's operations manual is 600 pages long.[1] Without the guidance of a strategic management orientation, organization members tend to work at cross-purposes, and important things do not get accomplished.[2] In fact, a statistical analysis of 26 published studies documented the positive impact of strategic planning on business performance.[3]

Many people automatically assume that strategy is the exclusive domain of top-level management, but that is simply not true. Its relevance for those lower in the organization may not be as apparent, but it is equally important. A management student who is 10 to 20 years away from a top-level executive position might ask, "If top managers formulate strategies and I'm headed for a supervisory or staff position, why should I care about strategic management?" There are three good reasons why staff specialists and managers at all levels need a general understanding of strategic management.

First, in view of widespread criticism that American managers tend to be shortsighted, a strategic orientation encourages farsightedness[4] (see Table 7.1). Second, employees who think in strategic terms tend to understand better how top managers think and why they make the decisions they do. In other words, the rationale behind executive policies and decisions is more apparent when things are put into a strategic perspective.

A third reason for promoting a broader understanding of strategic management relates to a recent planning trend. Specifically, greater teamwork and cooperation throughout the planning/control cycle are eroding the traditional distinction between those who plan and those who implement plans. In terms of

---

7A A Mickey Mouse Approach to Strategy Making at Disney?

The company has grown so big and its problems are so far-reaching—ranging from the phenomenon of "age compression" to the explosion of media choices—that they can't be fixed by a couple of hit movies or TV shows or more Disney stores. The other scary thing is this: Disney seems less able than ever to cope with adversity. That's because [CEO Michael] Eisner, for all his creativity and charisma and grand plans, presides over an insular—some say arrogant—corporate culture where decision making is hierarchical, centralized, and slow. It's an utter mismatch for the Internet age. "This isn't Mickey's house anymore," says a former Disney insider. "It's a multibillion-dollar company."

Source: Marc Gunther, "Eisner's Mouse Trap," *Fortune* (September 6, 1999): 108.

Questions: *Which strategy-making model in Table 7.2 appears to be in use at Disney? Explain. What implications does this have for Disney's long-term success?*

For further information about the interactive annotations in this chapter, visit our Web site (**www.hmco.com/college**).

Table 7.1

Key Dimensions of Strategic Farsightedness		
	Shortsighted	**Farsighted**
1. Organizational strategy	No formally documented strategies.	A formally written and communicated statement of long-term organizational mission.
2. Competitive advantage	"Follow the leader." No attention devoted to long-term competitive edge.	"Be the leader." Emphasis on gaining and holding a strategic competitive edge.
3. Organizational structure	Rigid structure emphasizing status quo, downward communication, and predictability.	Flexible structure encouraging change, upward and lateral communication, adaptability, and speed.
4. Research and development	Emphasis on applying competitors' good ideas.	Heavy emphasis on developing new products and services and on innovations in production, marketing, and human resource management.
5. Return	Emphasis on short-term profits.	Emphasis on increased market share, growth, and future profit potential.
6. Human resources	Emphasis on stopgap hiring and training. Labor viewed as a commodity. Layoffs common.	Emphasis on long-term development of employees. Labor viewed as a valuable human resource. Layoffs seen as a last resort.
7. Problem solving	Emphasis on chasing symptoms and blaming scapegoats.	Emphasis on finding solutions to problems.
8. Management style	Emphasis on day-to-day firefighting, owing to short-term orientation.	Multilevel strategic thinking that encourages managers to consider long-term implications of their actions and decisions.

the five strategy-making modes shown in Table 7.2, there is a clear trend *away from* the command, symbolic, and rational modes and *toward* the transactive and generative modes. In other words, the traditional idea of top-management strategists as commanders, coaches, or bosses is giving way to a view of them more as participative facilitators and sponsors. In each of the traditional modes, people below the top level must be obedient, passive, and reactive. In the *transactive* strategy-making mode, continuous improvement is the order of the day, as middle- and lower-level managers and staff specialists actively participate in the process. They go a step further, becoming risk-taking entrepreneurs, in the *generative* mode.[5] Here is a recent example:

J. M. Smucker Co., the Ohio-based maker of jams and jellies, . . . enlisted a team of 140 employees—7 percent of its workforce—who devoted nearly 50 percent of their time to a major strategy exercise for more than six months. "Instead of having just 12 minds working it, we really used the team of 140 as ambassadors to solicit input from all 2,000 employees," says President Richard K. Smucker. "It gave us a broader perspective, and it brought to the surface a lot of people with special talents." The company, which has struggled to grow in a mature market, now has a dozen viable initiatives that could double its $635 million revenues over the next five years.[6]

Table 7.2

Five Different Strategy-Making Modes				
Traditional modes			**Modern modes**	
Command	**Symbolic**	**Rational**	**Transactive**	**Generative**
Style *Imperial* Strategy driven by leader or small top team	*Cultural* Strategy driven by mission and a vision of the future	*Analytical* Strategy driven by formal structure and planning systems	*Procedural* Strategy driven by internal process and mutual adjustment	*Organic* Strategy driven by organizational actors' initiative
Role of Top Management *Commander* Provide direction	*Coach* Motivate and inspire	*Boss* Evaluate and control	*Facilitator* Empower and enable	*Sponsor* Endorse and support
Role of Organizational Members *Soldier* Obey orders	*Player* Respond to challenge	*Subordinate* Follow the system	*Participant* Learn and improve	*Entrepreneur* Experiment and take risks

Source: Adapted from Stuart L. Hart, "An Integrative Framework for Strategy-Making Processes," *Academy of Management Review,* 17 (April 1992): 334. Reprinted by permission.

Thus, you, today's management student, are not as far away from the strategic domain as you may think. The time to start thinking strategically is *now.* This chapter defines strategic management, looks at ways to think strategically, explores the strategic management process, and discusses forecasting.

Strategic Management = Strategic Planning + Implementation + Control

Strategic management is the ongoing process of ensuring a competitively superior fit between an organization and its changing environment.[7] In a manner of speaking, strategic management is management on a grand scale, management of the "big picture." Accordingly, **strategy** has been defined by MIT strategy scholar Arnoldo C. Hax as "the pattern of decisions a firm makes."[8] Hax's definition is instructive because it reminds us that strategy is the product of *actions* and *results,* not just of good intentions. The strategic management perspective is the product of a historical evolution and is now understood to include budget control, long-range planning, and strategic planning.[9]

Significantly, strategic management does not do away with earlier, more restricted approaches. Instead, it synthesizes and coordinates them all in a more systematic fashion. For example, consider the relationship between strategic planning, as defined in Chapter 6, and strategic management. Recall that *strategic planning* is the process of determining how to pursue the organization's long-term goals with the resources expected to be available. Notice that nothing is said in this definition about adjustment

1 Define the term *strategic management* and explain its relationship to strategic planning, implementation, and control.

strategic management *seeking a competitively superior organization-environment fit*

strategy *the pattern of decisions a firm makes*

Wal-Mart became the world's largest retailer without venturing into foreign markets until 1991, when it opened a store in Mexico. Although 90 percent of the firm's sales still come from stores in the United States, Wal-Mart's global strategy has kicked into high gear. The German Wal-Mart pictured here is one of 95 in that key European market, thanks to the acquisition of two German retail chains. British and French retailers are revamping their strategies in anticipation of Wal-Mart invasions of their countries.

or control. But just as astronauts and space scientists need to make mid-flight corrections to ensure that space shuttles reach their distant destinations, strategic adjustment and control are necessary. The more encompassing strategic management concept is useful today because it effectively blends strategic planning, implementation, and control.

Today's competitive pressures necessitate a dynamic strategic management process. According to *Fortune:*

> *The old methods won't do. At too many companies strategic planning has become overly bureaucratic, absurdly quantitative, and largely irrelevant. In executive suites across America, countless five-year plans, updated annually and solemnly clad in three-ring binders, are gathering dust—their impossibly specific prognostications about costs, prices, and market share long forgotten.*[10]

Managers who adopt a strategic management perspective appreciate that strategic plans are living documents. They require updating and fine tuning as conditions change. They also need to draw upon all available talent in the organization.

The strategic management process is discussed in greater detail later in this chapter. But first we need to consider alternative ways to encourage strategic thinking.

Thinking Strategically

Effective strategic management involves more than just following a few easy steps. It requires *every* employee, on a daily basis, to consider the "big picture" and think strategically about gaining and keeping a competitive edge.[11] A pair of experts on the subject recently framed the issue in terms of *innovation:*

Strategy innovation is not simply about extending a product line or pouring money into long-term, theoretical R&D projects. It is about rethinking the basis of competition for any company in any industry. Innovation cannot be a one-time event in the race to the future; it must be a continuous theme that extends throughout the entire company. . . .

It is a deliberate process by which daring companies question the business model that may have brought them success in the first place. Although obviously needed when the economic chips are down, this type of thinking is equally critical for companies riding a wave of success. That's precisely when they may feel exempt from the need for radical innovation. "Why tinker," the reasoning goes, "with a proven formula?". . .

What's needed is a built-in capacity to challenge orthodoxies, develop foresight, build innovation-oriented processes, and continuously regenerate the strategy.[12]

This section presents four alternative perspectives for thinking innovatively about strategy in today's fast-paced global economy: synergies, Porter's generic strategies, business ecosystems, and e-commerce strategy.

Synergy

Although not necessarily a familiar term, *synergy* is a well-established and valuable concept. **Synergy** occurs when two or more variables (for example, chemicals, drugs, people, organizations) interact to produce an effect greater than the sum of the effects of the variables acting independently. Some call this the $1 + 1 = 3$ effect; others prefer to say that with synergy, the whole is greater than the sum of its parts. Either definition is acceptable as long as one appreciates the bonus effect in synergistic relationships. In strategic management, managers are urged to achieve as much *market, cost, technology,* and *management synergy*[13] as possible when making strategic decisions. Those decisions may involve mergers, acquisitions, new products, new technology or production processes, or executive replacement. When Germany's Daimler Benz and Detroit's Chrysler merged in 1998 to form DaimlerChrysler, *Business Week* trumpeted the potential synergies:

> *. . . if ever a merger had the potential for that elusive quality—synergy—this could be the one. Mercedes-Benz passenger cars are synonymous with luxury and sterling engineering. Chrysler is renowned for its low-cost production of trucks, minivans, and sport-utility vehicles. Chrysler is almost wholly domestic, and Mercedes is increasing global sales—albeit within the confines of the luxury-car market. By spreading Chrysler's production expertise to Daimler operations and merging both product-development forces, the new company could cut costs by up to $3 billion annually—including $1.1 billion in purchasing costs, analysts say.[14]*

The next decade will tell if these potential synergies were fact or fantasy.

Market Synergy.   When one product or service fortifies the sales of one or more other products or services, market synergy has been achieved. Examples of market synergy abound in the business press:

- Amazon.com, originally an online bookstore, leveraged its name recognition and huge customer base to become a one-stop Web site for books, music, videos, toys, and electronics.[15]
- AT&T recently went on a buying spree for cable TV, wireless telephone, and Internet service companies to create a *bundle* of communications services and the convenience of a single monthly bill for customers.[16]

2 Explain the concept of synergy and identify four kinds of synergy.

synergy   *the concept that the whole is greater than the sum of its parts*

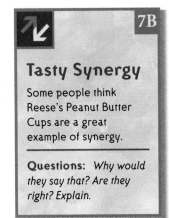

7B

Tasty Synergy

Some people think Reese's Peanut Butter Cups are a great example of synergy.

Questions: *Why would they say that? Are they right? Explain.*

How's this for a giant combination of market, cost, technological, and management synergy? Sotheby's is known for auctioning art and other treasures. Amazon.com is known for selling, well, just about anything on the Internet. Sotheby's CEO Diana Brooks and Amazon.com's founder and Chairman Jeff Bezos recently formed a joint venture to sell antiques, art, and other collectibles through an online auction site. Going once. Going twice. Sold . . . on a great idea.

Cost Synergy.   This second type of synergy can occur in almost every dimension of organized activity. When two or more products can be designed by the same engineers, produced in the same facilities, distributed through the same channels, or sold by the same salespeople, overall costs will be lower than if each product received separate treatment. In an interesting example of cost synergy, major hotels are trying to squeeze more value from their costly real estate. "At Miami Airport, Marriott has three hotels on the same plot of land. There's the Marriott Hotel, a full-service hotel. Behind the hotel are a Courtyard by Marriott, a midprice hotel, and a Fairfield Inn, an economy brand."[17]

Cost synergy also can be achieved by recycling by-products that would normally be thrown away. Human imagination is the only limit to creating cost synergies through recycling. For example, researchers in Ireland have found a potentially profitable use for free chicken feathers by making feather quilts that soak up oil spills very efficiently.[18] Meanwhile, researchers in Idaho have found a way to turn used vegetable cooking oil into an economical substitute for diesel fuel. This is good news for J. R. Simplot Co., McDonald's French fries supplier. "Currently, the used oil gets carted off to landfills. That's expensive, so Simplot would like nothing better than to turn that cooking oil into fuel for its fleet of trucks."[19] Cost synergy through waste recycling is good business ethics, too.

Technological Synergy.   The third variety of synergy involves transferring technology from one application to another, thus opening up new markets. For example, Alfa-Laval, a Swedish manufacturing company specializing in centrifugal separators, broadened its market base through technological synergy.

Alfa designed a separator to remove yeast particles from beer. Brewers were uninterested, but genetic researchers were fascinated; with some modifications, the same equipment is well-suited for preparing cells and harvesting bacteria in genetic research.[20]

Thanks to this sort of technological synergy, profitable new markets can be tapped without the expense of developing totally new products.

Management Synergy.   This fourth type of synergy occurs when a management team is more productive because its members have complementary rather than identical skills. A productive match was made in 1994 when America Online (AOL) purchased Redgate Communications, a maker of CD-ROM shopping guides. The well-connected and creative founder of Redgate, Ted Leonsis, multiplied the effectiveness of Steve Case, the low-key head of AOL.[21]

You may find it difficult, if not impossible, to take advantage of all four types of synergy when developing new strategies. Nonetheless, your strategies are more likely to be realistic and effective if you give due consideration to all four types of synergy as early as possible.

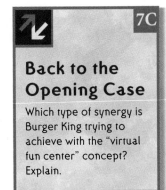

Back to the Opening Case

Which type of synergy is Burger King trying to achieve with the "virtual fun center" concept? Explain.

Porter's Generic Competitive Strategies

In 1980, Michael Porter, a Harvard University economist, developed a model of competitive strategies. During a decade of research, Porter's model evolved to encompass these four generic strategies: (1) cost leadership, (2) differentiation, (3) cost focus, and (4) focused differentiation.[22] As shown in Figure 7.1, Porter's model combined two variables, *competitive advantage* and *competitive scope.*

On the horizontal axis is competitive advantage, which can be achieved via low costs or differentiation. A competitive advantage based on low costs, which means lower prices, is self-explanatory. **Differentiation,** according to Porter, "is the ability to provide unique and superior value to the buyer in terms of product quality, special features, or after-sale service.[23] Differentiation helps explain why consumers willingly pay more for branded products such as Sunkist oranges or Crest toothpaste.[24] On the vertical axis is competitive scope. Is the firm's target market broad or narrow? IBM, which sells many types of computers all around the world, serves a very broad market. A neighborhood pizza parlor that offers one type of food in a small geographical area has a narrow target market.

3 Describe Porter's model of generic competitive strategies.

differentiation *buyer perceives unique and superior value in a product*

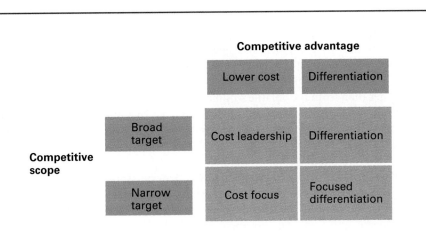

Figure 7.1

Porter's Generic Competitive Strategies

		Competitive advantage	
		Lower cost	Differentiation
Competitive scope	Broad target	Cost leadership	Differentiation
	Narrow target	Cost focus	Focused differentiation

Source: Reprinted with permission of The Free Press, a Division of Simon & Schuster, Inc. from *The Competitive Advantage of Nations* by Michael E. Porter. Copyright © 1990, 1998 by Michael E. Porter.

Like the concept of synergy, Porter's model helps managers think strategically: it enables them to see the big picture as it affects the organization and its changing environment. Each of Porter's four generic strategies deserves a closer look.

Cost Leadership Strategy.   Managers pursuing this strategy have an overriding concern for keeping costs, and therefore prices, lower than those of competitors. Normally, this means extensive production or service facilities with efficient economies of scale (low unit costs of making products or delivering services). Productivity improvement is a high priority for managers following the cost leadership strategy. Wal-Mart Stores, Inc., is a prime example of the cost leadership strategy.

> *The Wal-Mart formula is deceptively simple: Sell good-quality, name-brand, modestly-priced merchandise in a clean, no-frills setting that offers one-stop family shopping. Rather than entice shoppers with an ever-changing array of discounts and sales, Wal-Mart operates from an "everyday low price" philosophy.*[25]

Wal-Mart's computerized warehousing network gives it an additional cost advantage over its less efficient competitors.

In manufacturing firms, the preoccupation with minimizing costs flows beyond production into virtually all areas: purchasing, wages, overhead, R&D, advertising, and selling. A relatively large market share is required to accommodate this high-volume, low-profit margin strategy.

Differentiation Strategy.   For this strategy to succeed, a company's product or service must be considered unique by most of the customers in its industry. Advertising and promotion help the product to stand out from the crowd. Specialized design (BMW automobiles), a widely recognized brand (Diet Coke), leading-edge technology (Intel), or reliable service (Caterpillar) also may serve to differentiate a product in the industry. Because customers with brand loyalty will usually spend more for what they perceive to be a superior product, the differentiation strategy can yield larger profit margins than the low-cost strategy.[26] When brand loyalty erodes, as it did in the early 1990s for Compaq Computer Corp. because clones became available for 30 percent less,[27] prices need to be lowered to meet the competition. This step necessitates a switch to a cost leadership or a cost focus strategy. For businesses sticking to a differentiation strategy, it is important to note that cost reduction is not ignored; it simply is not the highest priority.

Cost Focus Strategy.   Organizations with a cost focus strategy attempt to gain a competitive edge in a narrow or regional market by exerting strict control. Atlantic Richfield Company (ARCO), the Los Angeles-based oil company, adopted this strategy in the 1980s, when it sold all of its 1,100 gas stations east of the Rocky Mountains. The idea was to serve the fast-growing western states better. By getting most of its oil from Alaska, rather than from the volatile Middle East, pruning its payroll by 12,000 people, and refusing to accept credit cards, ARCO managed to undersell its competitors by about 6 cents a gallon.[28] We are left to wonder if ARCO's pending merger with BP Amoco will alter this strategy.[29]

Focused Differentiation Strategy.   This generic strategy involves achieving a competitive edge by delivering a superior product and/or service to a limited audience. The Mayo Clinic's world-class health care facilities in Rochester, Minnesota; Jacksonville, Florida; and Scottsdale, Arizona, are an expression of this strategy.

A contingency management approach is necessary for determining which of Porter's generic strategies is appropriate. Research on Porter's model indicates a positive relationship between long-term earnings growth and a good strategy/environment fit.[30]

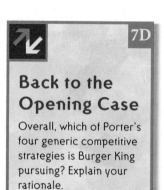

Back to the Opening Case

Overall, which of Porter's four generic competitive strategies is Burger King pursuing? Explain your rationale.

Business Ecosystems

Researchers recently have given new meaning to the saying, "It's a jungle out there." They have extended the concept of ecosystems from nature to business. In his best-seller, *The Death of Competition: Leadership and Strategy in the Age of Business Ecosystems*, James F. Moore writes: "It is my view that executives need to think of themselves as part of organisms participating in an ecosystem in much the same way that biological organisms participate in a biological ecosystem."[31] A **business ecosystem** is an economic community of organizations and all their stakeholders, including suppliers and customers.[32] This evolving model makes one very important contribution to modern strategic thinking: *organizations need to be as good at cooperating as they are at competing if they are to succeed.*

A Business Ecosystem in Action.   Within a dominant business ecosystem, key organizations selectively cooperate and compete to achieve both their individual and collective goals. A prime example is the relationship between Microsoft and Intel. In fact, the so-called Wintel technology (the combination of Microsoft Windows software and Intel microprocessors) dominates the personal computer market. Yet make no mistake about it, Microsoft and Intel are competitors in all other respects.[33] In the language of business ecosystems, Microsoft and Intel have *coevolved* to a dominant position in the personal computer ecosystem. Meanwhile, according to Moore: "Larry Ellison at Oracle is promoting $500 Internet-access devices as substitutes for personal computers, hoping to steal the future from Intel and Microsoft."[34] The Wintel ecosystem has responded by slashing the cost of personal computers and saying PCs are not obsolete in the Internet age.[35] In ten years, will the Wintel ecosystem, with its reliance on personal computers packed with expensive software, still be dominant? Or will Ellison be able to pull together a successful community of organizations and individuals to create a new dominant ecosystem in which inexpensive information appliances are used to pull low-cost software applications off the Internet on an as-needed basis? Only time will tell; an epic battle is on in the business jungle.

Needed: More Strategic Cooperation.   Through the years, the terms *strategy* and *competition* have become synonymous.[36] Business ecologists now call for greater cooperation, even among the toughest of competitors. Moore puts it this way: "The major factor today limiting the spread of realized innovation is not a lack of good ideas, technology, or capital. It is the inability to command cooperation across broad, diverse communities of players who must become intimate parts of a far-reaching process of coevolution."[37] So Oracle's Ellison will need to team up with organizations that can provide high-speed, high-volume, and reliable Internet access (not yet widely available at reasonable cost) if he is to realize his vision.[38] In ecosystem terms, he will have to coevolve with key strategic partners because his company cannot do it alone.[39]

4 Identify and explain the major contribution the business ecosystems model makes to strategic thinking.

business ecosystem
economic community of organizations and all their stakeholders

---

7E

Intel on the Prowl

News item: Intel agreed to buy wireless telephone-chip maker DSP Communications for $1.6 billion, the latest in a series of aggressive moves by Intel to move beyond its traditional microprocessor business. Intel said it was interested in DSP because cellular phones are increasingly being used to connect to the Internet.

Source: "Intel Purchase," USA Today (October 15, 1999): 1B.

Question: *In terms of business ecosystems, what does Intel appear to be doing? Explain.*

Strategy.com

As you will recall from our discussion of the e-commerce revolution in Chapter 1, no one owns the entire Internet, and its complexity and scope are difficult to comprehend. *Business Week* explains:

> *It's a ready-made marketplace—essentially $1 trillion worth of network connections, computer power, and limitless databases full of information. And it's available largely free*

to anyone with a phone line and a personal computer. Anywhere in the world. Anytime, day or night. In short, the Net offers an entry point to all comers in every market and industry.[40]

5 Identify and discuss at
least four strategic
lessons from the
e-commerce revolution.

This vision of hundreds of millions of people being connected to a global computer network generates both excitement and fear among corporate strategists today. The prospect of doing business directly and inexpensively with countless new customers is exciting. For example, according to banking industry data, it costs a bank $1.07 to process a single transaction when a customer deals with a teller at a branch bank. The same transaction costs 27 cents when an automated teller machine (ATM) is used and only *one penny* when the customer uses the Internet.[41] On the other hand, the fear of getting run over or being left behind by what experts call a "disruptive technology" is daunting. Traditional business models, asset valuations, time frames, and profit calculations are all being tossed out the window by the e-commerce revolution. To echo President Franklin Delano Roosevelt's famous phrase, "the thing to fear the most is *fear* itself." Instead, the Internet and e-commerce revolution need to be studied and exploited in a measured fashion.

This section explores key realities and challenges for developing strategy in the Internet age. Circumstances are too new and changing too rapidly to yield a cookbook approach to building an Internet strategy. We have to settle for some general signposts, pointing the way toward competitive advantage in e-commerce.

When 46-year-old Rick Inatome was introduced as the new CEO of ZapMe, an Internet education company, he sported an impressive high-tech résumé and a fine business suit. The only question he could tease out of the assembled 111 employees was: "Why are you wearing a tie?" This apparently superficial question probed the deeper issue of whether or not Inatome "got it," meaning—did he really understand e-commerce on a gut level? Indeed, aside from shedding his tie, Inatome has had to do a lot of learning and unlearning to figure out the new rules of doing business at Internet speed. But he's "getting it."

There Are Lots of Ways to Make Money on the Web.

A business can make money via the Internet through one or a combination of the following revenue sources: collecting fees from subscribers (e.g., online newsletters), selling advertising space, selling goods and services directly to other businesses or end consumers, collecting transaction fees (e.g., online banks and stockbrokers), and collecting commissions for bringing together buyers and sellers (e.g., auctions and real estate).[42]

> *E-commerce strategy lesson.*   Different types and combinations of revenue sources will require different business models.[43]

Customer Loyalty Is Built with Reliable Brand Names and "Sticky" Web Sites.

Web surfers have proved to have very short attention spans. Apparently attractive Web sites can have many visitors ("hits"), but few or no sales. When doing business at Internet speed, Web sites need to satisfy three criteria: (1) high-quality layout and graphics; (2) fast, responsive service; and (3) complete and up-to-date information.[44] A trusted brand name can further enhance what e-commerce people call the *stickiness* of a Web site, that is, the ability to draw the same customer back again and again. "Web surfers aren't going to invest time to register and trust you with personal data unless they have a clear idea of who you are."[45] Internet pioneers such as Yahoo! have loyal customers because they stay relevant, give things away, personalize their offerings, and facilitate interaction among their customers.[46] Dell Computer achieves stickiness in a different, but equally effective, manner:

Dell's main weapon is its Premier Page program, which serves over 5,000 U.S. companies. When Dell wins a corporate customer with more than 400 employees, it will build that customer a Premier Page. The Page is little more than a set of smaller Web pages, often linked to the customer's intranet, which let approved employees go online to configure PCs, pay for them, and track their delivery status—about 5 million dollars of Dell PCs are ordered this way every day. Premier Pages provide access to instant technical support (no more waiting on hold!) and Dell sales reps.

"We often set up Premier Pages for prospective customers before we've won their business. It blows them away," says Chris Halligan, who runs business-to-business e-commerce.[47]

> ***E-commerce strategy lesson.***   Even though e-commerce might appear to be a quick-and-easy and impersonal process, loyal customers still expect a personal touch and some "hand holding" when they have questions, problems, or suggestions.

Bricks and Mortar Must Earn Their Keep.   Popular accounts of e-commerce conjure up visions of "virtual organizations" where an entrepreneur and a handful of employees run a huge business with little more than an Internet hookup and a coffee maker. Everything—including product design, production, marketing, shipping, billing, and accounting—is contracted out. As discussed in Chapter 10, these network or virtual organizations *do* exist, but they are more the exception than the rule. More typically, companies with bricks-and-mortar facilities such as factories, warehouses, retail stores, and showrooms are blending e-commerce into their traditional business models. A prime example is Gap, the owner of Gap, Banana Republic, and Old Navy clothing stores. Gap seeks to gain a competitive advantage with its *clicks*-and-mortar vision of an integrated experience for those who shop at one of its 2,600 stores and browse its Web site.

> *What's Gap's secret? The same sort of compelling marketing and customer focus that has brought it success in the off-line world. The Web site is promoted at every cash register and, recently, in window displays with the slogan "surf.shop.ship." Clerks are trained to refer shoppers to Gap's Web site. And in eight high-traffic Gap and GapKids stores, the retailer has recently installed "Web lounges" that lure buyers with comfortable couches and sleek gray computer terminals hooked up to gap.com. Meanwhile, online customers can return items purchased on the Net the old-fashioned way, by walking into any neighborhood Gap.[48]*

In contrast, Egghead Software closed all its stores in 1998 in favor of Internet sales.

> ***E-commerce strategy lesson.***   Strategists need to identify their company's *core competencies* to determine which bricks-and-mortar assets and tasks give them a distinct competitive advantage. No one can afford the luxury of inefficient or unproductive assets in the Internet age. For example, why own a fleet of trucks and warehouses when FedEx or United Parcel Service can handle your shipments faster, better, and less expensively?[49]

Cannibalism Can Pay.   Over the years, one article of faith in management classrooms and offices has been that you should never get into a line of business or sell a product that cannibalizes your present sales. One early lesson from the e-commerce front directly contradicts this rule. However, as David Pottruck discovered at Charles Schwab, this e-commerce strategy is not for the faint-hearted:

> *In 1996 the co-CEO of discount broker Charles Schwab established a separate online unit, e.Schwab, with its own staff, own offices, and own sense of mission. Then he did the unthinkable: He let e.Schwab eat Schwab.*
>
> *The moment of truth came in late 1997, just as demand for e.Schwab's $29.95 online trades was booming beyond anyone's expectations. Problem was, customers with Charles Schwab's traditional brokerage still had to pay an average of $65 per trade. The two-tiered pricing system was clearly awkward: Some customers were keeping small sums of money with Charles Schwab to maintain access to live brokers, then executing their trades through e.Schwab. So Pottruck came to a radical decision: All trades would be priced at $29.95. In essence, all of Schwab would become e.Schwab.*
>
> *Employees in the company's branch offices were skittish. "All of them thought they would have no more business and were going to lose their jobs," Pottruck says. "It attacked our old business." Schwab's board had its doubts too. The price cut would shave an estimated $125*

7F

Smile for the Computer, Please

Research insight:

. . . research from Jupiter Communications shows that 90 percent of online customers prefer human interaction.

Source: Bill Meyers, "Service with an E-Smile," *USA Today* (October 12, 1999): 1B.

Questions: *Would you count yourself among the 90 percent? Explain. What is your personal experience with e-commerce service? In your opinion, what does it take to make a commercial Web site sticky?*

million off revenues, and the company's stock would clearly take a pummeling. Even Pottruck himself wasn't quite sure of what he was doing. "I can't tell you honestly that I didn't lose a lot of sleep about it," he says now. . . .

In January 1998 the price cut took effect. Schwab's stock lost almost a third of its value. But the short-term pain yielded outsized long-term gain: Total accounts climbed from three million to 6.2 million; the stock recovered; $51 billion in new assets poured in during the first six months of [1999].[50]

E-commerce strategy lesson.   E-commerce sometimes requires a quick revolution, rather than slow evolution. A separate e-commerce unit can start with a blank sheet of paper when building a new business model, as opposed to encountering the stubborn resistance to change found in existing business units. Managers and employees are typically reluctant to turn their backs on comfortably familiar assumptions, tools, techniques, facilities, and work habits.

E-Commerce Partnering Should Not Dilute Strategic Control or Ethical Standards.   If uncompetitive assets are sold and tasks contracted out, care needs to be taken to maintain ethical and quality standards. Do both domestic and foreign subcontractors follow applicable labor laws and ethical labor practices, or do sweat shop conditions prevail? Are subcontractors ruining the natural environment to reduce costs? Is a product designed properly before it is manufactured by an outside contractor? Are product quality standards faithfully met? These ethical and technical questions can be answered only through systematic monitoring and strategic oversight. Tough sanctions are also needed.[51]

E-commerce strategy lesson.   Increasingly, informed consumers are holding the sellers of goods and services to higher standards. And in doing so, they include a company's *entire* supply chain, foreign and domestic. Sweatshop-produced goods sold via sophisticated e-commerce networks are still dirty business.

Everyone Is a Potential Competitor.   One major consequence of the e-commerce revolution is a blurring of traditional boundaries between industries. Microsoft is getting into car sales and the travel reservation business. E*Trade, the online stockbroker, is venturing into banking.

E-commerce strategy lesson.   Intel's chairman Andy Grove put a sharp point on it by saying, "Only the paranoid survive."[52] Apt words for e-commerce strategists.

The Strategic Management Process

6 Identify and describe the four steps in the strategic management process.

Strategic plans are formulated during an evolutionary process with identifiable steps. In line with the three-level planning pyramid covered in Chapter 6, the strategic management process is broader and more general at the top and filters down to narrower and more specific terms. Figure 7.2 outlines the four major steps of the strategic management process: (1) formulation of a grand strategy, (2) formulation

Figure 7.2

The Strategic Management Process

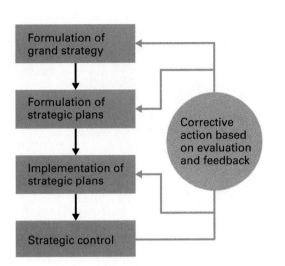

of strategic plans, (3) implementation of strategic plans, and (4) strategic control. Corrective action based on evaluation and feedback takes place throughout the entire strategic management process to keep things headed in the right direction.

Of important note, this model represents an ideal approach. Because of organizational politics, as discussed in Chapter 14, and different planning orientations among managers, a somewhat less systematic process typically results. Nevertheless, it is helpful to study the strategic management process as a systematic and rational sequence to better understand what it involves. Although noting that rational strategic planning models should not be taken literally, Henry Mintzberg acknowledged their profound instructional value. They teach necessary vocabulary and implant the notion "that strategy represents a fundamental congruence between external opportunity and internal capability."[53]

Formulation of a Grand Strategy

As pointed out in Chapter 6, a clear statement of organizational mission serves as a focal point for the entire planning process. Key stakeholders inside and outside the organization are given a general idea of why the organization exists and where it is headed. Working from the mission statement, top management formulates the organization's **grand strategy,** a general explanation of *how* the organization's mission is to be accomplished. Grand strategies are not drawn out of thin air. They are derived from a careful *situational analysis* of the organization and its environment. A clear vision of where the organization *is* headed and where it *should be* headed is the gateway to competitive advantage.[54]

grand strategy *how the organization's mission will be accomplished*

Situational Analysis. A **situational analysis** is a technique for matching organizational strengths and weaknesses with environmental opportunities and threats to determine the organization's right niche (see Figure 7.3). Many strategists refer to this process as a SWOT analysis (SWOT stands for *Strengths, Weaknesses, Opportunities,* and *Threats*).[55] Every organization should be able to identify the purpose for which it is best suited. But this matching process is more difficult than it may at first appear. Strategists are faced not with snapshots of the environment and the organization but

situational analysis
finding the organization's niche by performing a SWOT analysis

7 **Explain the nature and purpose of a SWOT analysis.**

Figure 7.3

Determining Strategic Direction Through Situational (SWOT) Analysis

with a movie of rapidly changing events. As one researcher said: "The task is to find a match between opportunities that are still unfolding and resources that are still being acquired."[56] For example, Citibank, whose headquarters are in New York City, has set its strategic sights on a greater share of emerging Asian markets:

> *. . . most foreign banks still shy away from developing countries such as India, Indonesia, and Thailand. Their rationale is that these markets are too small and that consumers lack experience in handling personal debt. . . .*
>
> *Citi, however, is gambling that such Asian economies won't remain backward. Consider India, with a population of [998] million. The growing middle class still rides mopeds. But within a decade, Citi bets they'll be buying BMWs. To take advantage of that possibility, Citi has positioned itself as one of the country's leading moped-loan originators.*[57]

Forecasting techniques, such as those reviewed later in this chapter, help managers cope with uncertainty about the future while conducting situational analyses.

Strategic planners, whether top managers, key operating managers, or staff planning specialists, have many ways to scan the environment for opportunities and threats. They can study telltale shifts in the economy, recent innovations, growth and movement among competitors, market trends, labor availability, and demographic shifts.

Back to the Opening Case 7G

Based on the facts of this case and any reasonable assumptions you might make about Burger King, what would a situational (SWOT) analysis suggest Burger King's strategic direction should be? *Hint:* First arrange your evidence under these four headings: organizational strengths, organizational weaknesses, environmental opportunities, and environmental threats.

Unfortunately, according to a recent survey of executives at 100 U.S. corporations, not enough time is spent looking outside the organization: "Respondents said they spend less than half of their planning time (44 percent) evaluating external factors—competition and markets—compared with 48 percent on internal analysis—budget, organizational factors, human resources. 'That's the corporate equivalent of contemplating one's navel,' "[58] says the researcher.

Environmental opportunities and threats need to be sorted out carefully. A perceived threat may turn out to be an opportunity, or vice versa. Steps can be taken to turn negatives into positives.[59]

Capability Profile.   After scanning the external environment for opportunities and threats, management's attention turns inward to identifying the organization's strengths and weaknesses.[60] This subprocess is called a **capability profile.** Key capabilities for today's companies are

capability profile *identifying the organization's strengths and weaknesses*

- Quick response to market trends.
- Rapid product development.
- Rapid production and delivery.

- Continuous cost reduction.
- Continuous improvement of processes, human resources, and products.
- Greater flexibility of operations.[61]

Diversity initiatives are an important way to achieve continuous improvement of human resources (for example, see Managing Diversity). Also, notice the clear emphasis on *speed* in this list of key organizational capabilities.

The Strategic Need for Speed.   Speed has become an important competitive advantage. For example, product development time at General Electric's Medical Systems unit has been cut from two years to one. Says Jack Welch, GE's respected chief executive officer: "Faster, in almost every case, is better. From decision-making to deal-making to communications to product introduction, speed, more often than not, ends up being the competitive [edge]. . . ."[62]

Significantly, the new strategic emphasis on speed involves more than doing the same old things, only faster. It calls for rethinking and radically redesigning the entire business cycle, a process called **reengineering**[63] (see Skills & Tools). The idea is to have cross-functional teams develop a whole new—and better—production process, one that does not let time-wasting mistakes occur in the first place. (The related topic of horizontal organizations is covered in Chapter 10.)

reengineering *radically redesigning the entire business cycle for greater strategic speed*

Formulation of Strategic Plans

In the second major step in the strategic management process, general intentions are translated into more concrete and measurable strategic plans, policies, and budget allocations.[64] This translation is the responsibility of top management, though input from staff planning specialists and middle managers is common. From our discussion in the last chapter we recall that a well-written plan consists of both an objective and an action

"I'm not sure where we're going, but at least I know where we've been!" While this camel may be a bit confused, management experts generally laud Toyota for knowing where it's going. The Japanese car and truck maker, consistently ranked among the world's best run companies, is said to have a 100-year plan. Now that's thinking strategically!

Managing Diversity

Diversity Boosts Allstate's Bottom Line

A number of progressive companies that had a head start in elevating diversity to a strategic priority are starting to see the results, from better customer satisfaction to increased sales. Allstate Insurance Co. is one of those leaders (**www.allstate.com**). Since 1993, the Northbrook, Illinois, insurance company has been managing diversity as a central business issue closely connected to its overall corporate objectives. The focus is to drive greater levels of employee and customer satisfaction by taking an integrated approach to diversity in the workplace and the market.

Joan Crockett, senior vice president for human resources at Allstate, stresses that the company's diversity initiative isn't a nice-to-do, social conscience program. "It's a compelling business strategy," she says. . . .

An Integrated Approach

For Allstate, the concept of diversity is not limited to ethnicity and gender. It is based on a wider perspective that includes diversity in age, religion, sexual orientation, disability, etc.

Diversity at Allstate is rooted in the company's culture, which has embodied inclusiveness and equal opportunity since the 1960s. But it wasn't until 1993 that it became a strategic initiative. Carlton Yearwood, director of diversity management, says that programs in the 1960s and 1970s were geared toward assimilating cultural differences into Allstate's culture. Today, the focus is on accepting these differences. The question thus becomes: "How do you take this workforce of differences and bring them together in a more powerful way so that it can impact business results?" asks Yearwood.

The answer was to incorporate differences into all business processes, such as decision making and product innovation. Once Allstate began this process, it started to see an increase in its customer base and greater levels of customer satisfaction as well.

"Diversity has become an initiative that has clear business outcomes," Yearwood says. "If you start by having customers say they want to interact with knowledge workers who are like themselves, that gives the customers absolute best services and products. . . . Through the diversity initiative, we demonstrate our commitment to a diverse marketplace."

Just as a company would inject financial goals in its daily operations, Allstate is resolved to penetrate its day-to-day functions with the concept of diversity. A number of processes have been established to bring the concept and strategy alive. These processes go beyond recruiting a diverse mix of employees to encompass a proactive retention strategy, ongoing training and education, a rigorous feedback mechanism, and community outreach. . . .

Sensitivity to Customers

Allstate's leading position in market share among minorities reflects its commitment to local communities consisting of many ethnic backgrounds. The key to success is that local agents, with backing from Allstate's relationship marketing managers and staff, have learned over the years how to relate to the specific needs of their respective communities.

Allstate's director of relationship marketing, Andre Howell, says that learning from customers is the best way to develop products and services which serve their specific needs. "Education, education and education will be my primary lead," he says. "We need to be continuously in a learning mode from customers."

Howell works with a team of six to create community outreach programs whose ultimate aim is to capture a larger market share. These programs include financial and expert contributions to ethnic, local, and other organizations.

The company also works with community groups and homeowner associations to accelerate urban revitalization projects through its Neighborhood Partnership Program (NPP). There are currently 33 NPPs operating in 26 cities, including Chicago, Cleveland, Los Angeles, New York and Philadelphia. By establishing a good relationship with residents of the communities, Allstate has been able to accelerate its customer acquisitions. In many cases, the company's businesses in inner cities that used to lose money are now profitable, says Ron McNeil, senior vice president for product operations.

"Our diverse workforce has allowed us to establish relationships in communities and allowed us to shorten the acquisition curves for new customers," he says. The partnership program in Philadelphia, for example, boosted Allstate's market share in the city from 7.3 percent in 1993 to 33 percent in 1997.

Source: Excerpted from Louisa Wah, "Diversity at Allstate: A Competitive Weapon." Reprinted from *Management Review,* July–August 1999. © 1999 American Management Association International. Reprinted by permission of American Management Association International, New York, NY. All rights reserved. **http://www.amanet.org**

statement. Plans at all levels should specify who, what, when, and how things are to be accomplished and for how much. Many managers prefer to call these specific plans "action plans" to emphasize the need to turn good intentions into action. Even though strategic plans may have a time horizon of one or more years, they must meet the same criteria that shorter-run intermediate and operational plans meet. They should:

1. Develop clear, results-oriented objectives in measurable terms.
2. Identify the particular activities required to accomplish the objectives.
3. Assign specific responsibility and authority to the appropriate personnel.
4. Estimate times to accomplish activities and their appropriate sequencing.
5. Determine resources required to accomplish the activities.
6. Communicate and coordinate the above elements and complete the action plan.[65]

All of this does not happen in a single quick-and-easy session. Specific strategic plans usually evolve over a period of months as top management consults with key managers in all areas of the organization to gather their ideas and recommendations and, one hopes, to win their commitment.

Strategic Implementation and Control

As illustrated earlier in Figure 7.2, the third and fourth stages of the strategic management cycle involve implementation and control. The entire process is only as strong as these two traditionally underemphasized areas.

Implementation of Strategic Plans

Because strategic plans are too often shelved without adequate attention to implementation, top managers need to do a better job of facilitating the implementation process and building middle-manager commitment.

A Systematic Filtering-Down Process.   Because planning is a filtering-down process, strategic plans require further translation into successively lower-level plans. Top-management strategists can do some groundwork to ensure that the filtering-down process occurs smoothly and efficiently. Planners need answers to four questions, each tied to a different critical organizational factor:

1. *Organizational structure.* Is the organizational structure compatible with the planning process, with new managerial approaches, and with the strategy itself?
2. *People.* Are people with the right skills and abilities available for key assignments, or must attention be given to recruiting, training, management development, and similar programs?
3. *Culture.* Is the collective viewpoint on "the right way to do things" compatible with strategy, must it be modified to reflect a new perspective, or must top management learn to manage around it?
4. *Control systems.* Is the necessary apparatus in place to support the implementation of strategy and to permit top management to assess performance in meeting strategic objectives?[66]

Strategic plans that successfully address these four questions have a much greater chance of helping the organization achieve its intended purpose than those that do not. In addition, field research indicates the need to *sell* strategies to all affected parties. New strategies represent change, and people tend to resist change for a variety of reasons. "The strategist thus faces a major selling job; that is, trying to build and maintain support among key constituencies for a plan that is freshly emerging."[67] This brings us to the challenge of obtaining commitment among middle managers.

Building Middle-Manager Commitment.   Resistance among middle managers can kill an otherwise excellent strategic management program. A study of 90 middle managers who wrote 330 reports about instances in which they had resisted strategic decisions documented the scope of this problem. It turned out that, to protect their own self-interests, the managers in the study frequently derailed strategies. This finding prompted the researchers to conclude as follows:

> *If general management decides to go ahead and impose its decisions in spite of lack of commitment, resistance by middle management can drastically lower the efficiency with which the decisions are implemented, if it does not completely stop them from being implemented. Particularly in dynamic, competitive environments, securing commitment to the strategy is crucial because rapid implementation is so important.*[68]

Participative management (see Chapter 13) and influence tactics (see Chapter 15) can foster middle-management commitment.[69]

Strategic Control

Strategic plans, like our more informal daily plans, can go astray. But a formal control system helps keep strategic plans on track. Strategic control systems need to be carefully designed ahead of time, not merely tacked on as an afterthought.[70] Before strategies are translated downward, planners should set up and test channels for information on progress, problems, and strategic assumptions about the environment or organization that have proved to be invalid. If a new strategy varies significantly from past ones, new production, financial, or marketing reports will probably have to be drafted and introduced.

The ultimate goal of a strategic control system is to detect and correct downstream problems in order to keep strategies updated and on target, without stifling creativity and innovation in the process. A survey of 207 planning executives found that in high-performing companies there was no trade-off between strategic control and creativity. Both were delicately balanced.[71]

High-Speed Strategic Driving

7H

"The pace of change is stunning," says Dr. W. Allen Schaffer, head of managed care at CIGNA Healthcare Inc. "We have to reevaluate our strategic assumptions every six months."

Source: Keith H. Hammonds, "The Patient Is Stable—For Now," *Business Week* (January 8, 1996): 102.

Question: *"Strategic planning is a waste of time for CIGNA when things are changing so fast." How would you answer a manager who made this statement?*

Corrective Action Based on Evaluation and Feedback

As illustrated in Figure 7.2, corrective action makes the strategic management process a dynamic cycle. A rule of thumb is that negative feedback should prompt corrective action at the step immediately before. Should the problem turn out to be more deeply rooted, then the next earlier step also may require corrective action. The key is to detect problems and initiate corrective action, such as updating strategic assumptions, reformulating plans, rewriting policies, making personnel changes, or modifying budget allocations, as soon as possible. In the absence of prompt corrective action, problems can rapidly worsen.

Let us turn to forecasting. Without the ability to obtain or develop reliable environmental forecasts, managerial strategists have a minimal chance of successfully negotiating their way through the strategic management process.

Forecasting

An important aspect of strategic management is anticipating what will happen. **Forecasts** may be defined as predictions, projections, or estimates of future events or conditions in the environment in which the organization operates.[72] Forecasts may be little more than educated guesses or may be the result of highly sophisticated statistical analyses. They vary in reliability. (Consider the track record of television weather forecasters!)[73] They may be relatively short run—a few hours to a year—or long run—five or more years. A combination of factors determines a forecast's relative sophistication, time horizon, and reliability. These factors include the type of forecast required, management's knowledge of forecasting techniques, and the money that management is willing to invest.[74]

forecasts *predictions, projections, or estimates of future situations*

Types of Forecasts

There are three types of forecasts: (1) event outcome forecasts, (2) event timing forecasts, and (3) time series forecasts.[75] Each type answers a different general question (see Table 7.3). **Event outcome forecasts** are used when strategists want to predict the outcome of highly probable future events. Examples are: "What will be the first year's sales for a new product?"[76] or "How will an impending strike affect output?" Information bases for reliably answering these two questions could be built by, respectively, conducting market tests and interviewing other strike victims in the industry.

8 Describe the three types of forecasts.

event outcome forecasts *predictions of the outcome of highly probable future events*

Type of forecast	General question	Example	Table 7.3
1. **Event outcome forecast**	"What will happen when a given event occurs?"	"Who will win the next World Series?"	**Types of Forecasts**
2. **Event timing forecast**	"When will a given event occur?"	"When will the United States have a permanently manned space station?"	
3. **Time series forecast**	"What value will a series of periodic data have at a given point in time?"	"What will the closing Dow Jones Industrial Average be on January 5, 2004?"	

event timing forecasts
predictions of when a given event will occur

Event timing forecasts predict when, if ever, given events will occur. Strategic questions in this area might include, "When will the prime interest rate begin to fall?" or, "When will our primary competitor introduce a certain product?" Timing questions like these typically can be answered by identifying leading indicators that historically have preceded the events in question. For instance, a declining inflation rate often prompts major banks to lower their prime interest rate, or a competitor may flag the introduction of a new product by conducting market tests or ordering large quantities of a new raw material.

time series forecasts
estimates of future values in a statistical sequence

Time series forecasts seek to estimate future values in a sequence of periodically recorded statistics. For example, to gauge the availability of labor, strategists may want to forecast future values in a time series of quarterly unemployment data for a region. Trend analysis, discussed below, helps chart the future course of a time series.

Forecasting Techniques

Modern managers may use one or a combination of four techniques to forecast future outcomes, timing, and values. These techniques are informed judgment, scenario analysis, surveys, and trend analysis.

Informed Judgment.   Limited time and money often force strategists to rely on their own intuitive judgment when forecasting. Judgmental forecasts are both fast and inexpensive, but their accuracy depends greatly on how well informed the strategist is. Frequent visits with employees—in sales, purchasing, and public relations, for example—who regularly tap outside sources of information are a good way of staying informed. A broad reading program to stay in touch with current events and industry trends and refresher training through management development programs are also helpful. Additionally, customized news clipping services (delivered by e-mail), spreadsheet forecasting software, and a competitive intelligence-gathering operation can help keep strategic decision makers up-to-date.

The hugely-profitable Pokémon craze traces to this intuitive approach to making important decisions:

> In 1997, Nintendo of America President Minoru Arakawa made the biggest bet of his career. Everyone said he was nuts to import a strange Japanese video game featuring 150 tiny collectible monsters. Research showed that American kids hated it, and employees dismissed the game as too confusing. But Arakawa persisted—and hit the Pokémon jackpot.[77]

Of course, informed judgment is no panacea. It generally needs to be balanced with data from other forecasting techniques.

scenario analysis
preparing written descriptions of equally likely future situations

Scenario Analysis.   This technique also relies on informed judgment, but it is more systematic and disciplined than the approach just discussed. **Scenario analysis** is the preparation and study of written descriptions of *alternative* but *equally likely* future conditions. Scenarios are visions of what "could be." The late futurist Herman Kahn is said to have first used the term *scenario* in conjunction with forecasting during the 1950s. The two types of scenarios are longitudinal and cross-sectional. **Longitudinal scenarios** describe how the present is expected to evolve into the future. **Cross-sectional scenarios,** the most common type, simply describe possible future situations at a given time.

longitudinal scenarios
describing how the future will evolve from the present

cross-sectional scenarios
describing future situations at a given point in time

While noting that *multiple forecasts* are the cornerstone of scenario analysis, one researcher offered the following perspective:

As you might expect for a banker, June Yee Felix goes by the numbers. The senior vice president at Chase Manhattan recently was picked to create an online bill-paying service for corporate clients. But market forecasts for this and other Web-based ventures with no track records need to be interpreted *very* cautiously. Time will tell if this new project adds up.

Scenario writing is a highly qualitative procedure. It proceeds more from the gut than from the computer, although it may incorporate the results of quantitative models. Scenario writing is based on the assumption that the future is not merely some mathematical manipulation of the past, but the confluence of many forces, past, present and future that can best be understood by simply thinking about the problem.[78]

The same researcher recommends developing two to four scenarios (three being optimal) for narrowly defined topics.[79] Likely candidates for scenario analysis are specific products, industries, or markets. For example, a grain-exporting company's strategists might look five years into the future by writing scenarios for three different likely situations: (1) above-average grain harvests, (2) average harvests, and (3) below-average harvests. These scenarios could serve as focal points for strategic plans concerning construction of facilities, staffing and training, and so on. As the future unfolds, the strategies accompanying the more realistic scenario would be followed.

This approach has been called "no surprise" strategic planning. As *Business Week* recently explained while offering up scenarios for the twenty-first century:

If you envision multiple versions of the future and think through their implications, you will be better prepared for whatever ends up happening. In effect, you won't be seeing the future for the first time. You'll be remembering it. The alternative won't cut it: Those who cannot remember the future are condemned to be taken by surprise.[80]

The key to good scenario writing is to focus on the few readily identifiable but unpredictable factors that will have the greatest impact on the topic in question. Because scenarios look far into the future, typically five or more years, they need to be written in general and rather imprecise terms.[81]

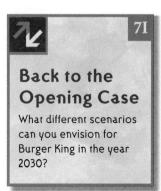

71

Back to the Opening Case

What different scenarios can you envision for Burger King in the year 2030?

Surveys.   Surveys are a forecasting technique that involves face-to-face or telephone interviews and mailed or Internet questionnaires. They can be used to pool expert opinion or fathom consumer tastes, attitudes, and opinions. When carefully constructed and properly administered to representative samples, surveys can give management comprehensive and fresh information. They suffer the disadvantages, however, of being somewhat difficult to construct, time-consuming to administer and interpret, and expensive. Although costs can be trimmed by purchasing an off-the-shelf or "canned" survey, standardized instruments too often either fail to ask precisely the right questions or ask unnecessary questions.[82]

trend analysis *hypothetical extension of a past series of events into the future*

Trend Analysis.   Essentially, a **trend analysis** is the hypothetical extension of a past pattern of events or time series into the future. An underlying assumption of trend analysis is that past and present tendencies will continue into the future.[83] Of course, surprise events such as the October 1987 stock market crash can destroy that assumption. Trend analysis can be fickle and cruel to reactive companies. As a case in point, Chrysler's commitment to fuel-efficient, four-cylinder cars in the early 1980s was based on the assumption that the 1970s trend toward higher gas prices would continue. However, when the price of gasoline stabilized during the 1980s, Chrysler came up short as U.S. car buyers demanded more horsepower.[84] By the time Chrysler had geared up its production of more powerful V-6 engines, Iraq's 1990 invasion of Kuwait sent the price of gasoline skyward and car buyers scrambling for four-cylinder cars. Again Chrysler tripped over a faulty trend analysis. If sufficient valid historical data are readily available, trend analysis can, barring disruptive surprise events, be a reasonably accurate, fast, and inexpensive strategic forecasting tool (see cartoon). An unreliable or atypical database, however, can produce misleading trend projections.

Each of these forecasting techniques has inherent limitations. Consequently, strategists are advised to validate one source of forecast information with one or more additional sources.

Summary

1. Strategic management sets the stage for virtually all managerial activity. Managers at all levels need to think strategically and to be familiar with the strategic management process for three reasons: farsightedness is encouraged, the rationale behind top-level decisions becomes more apparent, and strategy formulation and implementation are more decentralized today. Strategic management is defined as the ongoing process of ensuring a competitively superior fit between the organization and its ever-changing environment. Strategic management effectively merges strategic planning, implementation, and control.

2. Strategic thinking, the ability to look ahead and spot key organization/environment interdependencies, is necessary for successful strategic management and planning. Four perspectives that can help managers think strategically are synergy, Porter's model of competitive strategies, the concept of business ecosystems, and e-commerce strategic signposts. Synergy has been called the 1 + 1 = 3 effect because it focuses on situations where the whole is greater than the sum of its parts. Managers are challenged to achieve four types of synergy: market synergy, cost synergy, technological synergy, and management synergy.

3. According to Porter's generic competitive strategies model, four strategies are (1) cost leadership, (2) differentiation, (3) cost focus, and (4) focused differentiation. Porter's model helps managers create a profitable organization-environment "fit."

4. Contrary to the traditional assumption that strategy automatically equates to competition, the business ecosystems model emphasizes that organizations need to be as good at *cooperating* as they are at competing. By balancing competition and cooperation, competitors can *coevolve* into a dominant economic community (or business ecosystem).

5. The Internet is a disruptive technology that has managers scrambling to create successful e-commerce strategies. E-commerce pioneers have taught us these six lessons: (1) ways to make money on the Web include subscriptions, advertising space, sales to businesses and consumers, transaction fees, and commissions; (2) reliable brand names and sticky Web sites, integrated with a personal touch and hand holding, are required to build customer loyalty; (3) existing bricks-and-mortar assets such as factories and stores are useful in the Internet age only if they relate to core competencies that provide a competitive advantage; (4) contrary to the traditional rule against cannibalizing one's own sales, e-commerce sometimes requires a strategic revolution; (5) informed consumers will not tolerate the use of sophisticated e-commerce partnerships, both domestic and foreign, to mask unethical labor practices and poor product quality; and (6) in the e-commerce world, new competitors can pop up from practically anywhere.

6. The strategic management process consists of four major steps: (1) formulation of grand strategy, (2) formulation of strategic plans, (3) implementation of strategic plans, and (4) strategic control. Corrective action based on evaluation of progress and feedback helps keep the strategic management process on track. Results-oriented strategic plans that specify what, when, and how are then formulated and translated downward into more specific and shorter-term intermediate and operational plans. Participative management can build needed middle-manager commitment during implementation. Problems encountered along the way should be detected by the strategic control mechanism or by ongoing evaluation and subjected to corrective action.

7. Strategists formulate the organization's grand strategy after conducting a SWOT analysis. The organization's key capabilities and appropriate niche in the marketplace become apparent when the organization's strengths (S) and weaknesses (W) are cross-referenced with environmental opportunities (O) and threats (T). Strategic speed has become an important capability today, sometimes necessitating radical reengineering of the entire business cycle.

8. Event outcome, event timing, and time series forecasts help strategic planners anticipate and prepare for future environmental circumstances. Popular forecasting techniques among today's managers are informed judgment, scenario analysis, surveys, and trend analysis. Each technique has its own limitations, so forecasts need to be crosschecked against one another.

Terms to Understand

Strategic management (p. 201)	Forecasts (p. 217)
Strategy (p. 201)	Event outcome forecasts (p. 217)
Synergy (p. 203)	Event timing forecasts (p. 218)
Differentiation (p. 205)	Time series forecasts (p. 218)
Business ecosystem (p. 207)	Scenario analysis (p. 218)
Grand strategy (p. 211)	Longitudinal scenarios (p. 218)
Situational analysis (p. 211)	Cross-sectional scenarios (p. 218)
Capability profile (p. 212)	Trend analysis (p. 220)
Reengineering (p. 213)	

Skills & Tools

Reengineering: Strong Medicine for Strategic Ills

Reengineering, a.k.a. process innovation and core process redesign, is the search for, and implementation of, radical change in business processes to achieve breakthrough results. Its chief tool is a clean sheet of paper. Most change efforts start with what exists and fix it up. Reengineering, adherents emphasize, is not tweaking old procedures and certainly not plain-vanilla downsizing. Nor is it a program for bottom-up continuous improvement. Reengineers start from the future and work backward, as if unconstrained by existing methods, people, or departments. In effect they ask, "If we were a new company, how would we run this place?" Then, with a meat ax and sandpaper, they conform the company to their vision.

That's how GTE looks at its telephone operations, which account for four-fifths of the company's $20 billion in annual revenues. Facing new competitive threats, GTE figured it had to offer dramatically better customer service. Rather than eke out steady gains in its repair, billing, and marketing departments, the company examined its operations from the outside in. Customers, it concluded, wanted one-stop shopping—one number to fix an erratic dial tone, question a bill, sign up for call waiting, or all three, at any time of day.

GTE set up its first pilot "customer care center" in Garland, Texas, late last year and began to turn vision into fact. The company started with repair clerks, whose job had been to take down information from a customer, fill out a trouble ticket, and send it on to others who tested lines and switches until they found and fixed the problem. GTE wanted that done while the customer was still on the phone—something that happened just once in 200 calls. The first step was to move testing and switching equipment to the desks of the repair clerks—now called "front-end technicians"—and train them to use it. GTE stopped measuring how fast they handled calls and instead tracked how often they cleared up a problem without passing it on. Three out of ten now, and GTE is shooting for upward of seven.

The next step was to link sales and billing with repair, which GTE is doing with a push-button phone menu that allows callers to connect directly to any service. It has given operators new software so their computers can get into databases that let the operators handle virtually any customer request. In the process, says GTE vice president Mark Feighner, "we eliminated a tremendous amount of work—in the pilots, we've seen a 20 percent or 30 percent increase in productivity so far."

GTE's rewired customer-contact process—one of eight similar efforts at the company—displays most of the salient traits of reengineering: It is occurring in a dramatically altered competitive landscape; it is a major change, with big results; it cuts across departmental lines; it requires hefty investment in training and information technology; and layoffs result. . . .

It ain't cheap, and it ain't easy. At Blue Cross of Washington and Alaska, where redesigning claims processing raised labor productivity 20 percent in 15 months, CEO Betty Woods says the resource she drew on most was courage: "It was more difficult than we ever imagined, but it was worth it."

Therein lies the most important lesson from business's experience with reengineering: Don't do it if you don't have to. Says Thomas H. Davenport, head of research for Ernst & Young: "This hammer is incredibly powerful, but you can't use it on everything." Don't reengineer your buggy whip business; shut it. If you're in decent shape but struggling with cost or quality problems or weak brand recognition, by all means juice up your quality program and fire your ad agency, but don't waste money and energy on reengineering. Save reengineering for big processes that really matter, like new-product development or customer service, rather than test the technique someplace safe and insignificant.

Source: Excerpted from Thomas A. Stewart, "Reengineering: The Hot New Managing Tool," *Fortune* (August 23, 1993): 41–42. © 1993 Time, Inc. All rights reserved.

Internet Exercises

1. **Get the BIG Picture with BIG Ideas:** Strategic management is all about looking forward and thinking big. Busy students and managers can stretch their minds and jump-start their imaginations by going online. A good place to begin is at *Fast Company* magazine's excellent Web site. Any article published in paper by the magazine can be found in its Internet archive. Log on, go to **www.fastcompany.com,** and click on the home page heading "Core Themes." At the Themes and Ideas page, scroll down and select the topic "The Big Ideas." (*Note:* Because Web sites are often redesigned, you may have to access the *Fast Company* archives with other relevant headings.) Scan the list of articles to find any relating to key words used in this chapter, such as *strategy, strategic planning, synergy, e-commerce, forecasting,* and *scenarios.* Flag any article dealing with the *future* of business or management. *Change* is another relevant theme. Read two or three of the articles you have selected to identify a BIG idea about strategic management and/or making sense of an uncertain future. Your instructor may want you to print a hard copy of your key article if it is part of a formal assignment or class presentation.

Learning Points: 1. What is the BIG idea you selected and how is it relevant to strategic management? 2. How should managers respond appropriately to your BIG idea (understand, exploit, avoid, etc.)? 3. Is your BIG idea a threat or opportunity? Explain. 4. Does your BIG idea represent an opportunity to start a new business? Explain.

2. **Check it out:** Go to the home page of the World Future Society (**www.wfs.org**) and search for forecasts and predictions. The main menu lists good search options. Make sure you click on the society's publication, *The Futurist*, to scan article titles past and present.

Do you want to make strategic decisions as the CEO of a troubled medical products company? For a challenging interactive business simulation, go to Ernst & Young's Web site (**www.ey.com**) and click on the "Strategy Zone."

For updates to these exercises, visit our Web site (**www.hmco.com/college**).

| Closing Case | # Can Dell Computer Make It in China?

It's a wet morning in old Shanghai, and Dell salesman Peter Chan is selling hard. As the Yangtze River flows by the Bund district a few floors below, Chan is getting a flow of his own. His subject: computers and the unique benefits of Dell's direct-selling model. His customer: Xiao Jian Yi, deputy general manager of China Pacific Insurance, a fast-growing, state-owned insurance company. The audience: three of Xiao's subordinates.

China Pacific, a potentially big account, is in the process of computerizing its entire billing system. It already has about 400 desktops and about 70 servers, mainly from IBM and Hewlett-Packard. But Xiao needs more hardware. Much more.

Though Xiao's sleep-heavy eyes suggest he's heard it all before, Chan excitedly says that "direct selling" means China Pacific can order PCs directly through the Internet, the telephone, or salesmen like himself. At the mention of the Internet, still a rare marketing tool in China, the fustily dressed bureaucrat visibly perks up.

Chan goes on to explain that direct selling not only eliminates middlemen—saving Xiao and China Pacific a chunk of change—but also means that Dell can build China Pacific's computers to the firm's exact requirements, from the hardware on the outside to the software on the inside. A murmur of approval ripples through Xiao's subordinates. By the time Chan finishes with a description of Dell's convenient after-sales service, the rain has stopped and Xiao is smiling. "All salesmen from computer compa-

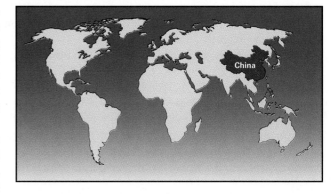

nies are aggressive," he says. Then Xiao whispers to *Fortune:* "But the Dell guys are even more aggressive." . . .

The point of Dell's push into China seems so obvious as to be a cliché: China is becoming too big a PC market for Dell, or anyone, to ignore. "If we're not in what will soon be the second-biggest PC market in the world," asks John Legere, president of Dell Asia-Pacific, "then how can Dell possibly be a global player?"

China is already the fifth-largest PC market, behind the United States, Japan, Germany, and Britain. But if PC shipments in China continue to grow at an average annual rate of 30 percent—as they have over the past three years—China's PC market will surpass Japan's in only five years. . . .

Though the competition is intense, Dell is confident it has a strategy that will pay off. First, it has decided not to target retail buyers, who account for only about 10 percent of Dell's China sales. That way Dell avoids going head to head against entrenched local market leaders like Legend. "It takes nearly two years of a person's savings to buy a PC in

Source: Excerpted from Neel Chowdhury, "Dell Cracks China," *Fortune,* (June 21, 1999): 120–124. © 1999 Time Inc. Reprinted by permission.

China," notes Mary Ma, the chief financial officer of Legend. "And when two years of savings is at stake, the whole family wants to come out to a store to touch and try the machine." Dell just isn't set up to make that kind of sale yet.

Instead, the company thinks it can make big inroads by selling directly to corporations. Established American PC makers in China—Hewlett-Packard, IBM, and Compaq—depend largely on resellers. Because of the cost savings derived from cutting out the middleman, Dell believes it can sell computers at lower prices than its competitors can—and thus steal market share. Already the gambit seems to be working: At the end of last year Dell's market share tripled to 1.2 percent, while Compaq's fell from 3.5 percent to 2.7 percent.

The outlook wasn't always so rosy. When Dell set up its first Asian factory in Malaysia in 1996 [Dell now has a factory in China], there were serious doubts as to whether its direct-selling model would work. Skeptics fretted that Asia's low Internet penetration and the value Asians put on personal relationships with distributors would punish the Dell model. But in practice Dell has managed to pump up sales during one of Asia's worst economic crises. That has silenced most of the critics.

In fact, the direct-selling model has almost certainly been a boon, not a barrier, to Dell's plans. "With low-priced, entry-level PCs shaving traditional profit margins, the direct-order model is gaining popularity across Asia," says Archana Gidwani, an analyst with the Gartner Group in Singapore. She figures that starting in 1998, direct sellers like Dell saw shipments in Asia jump 15 percent, while Hewlett-Packard, IBM, Compaq, and other PC makers that go through resellers saw shipments decline 3 percent. And she expects 40 percent of Asia's PC shipments to be ordered directly this year, up from roughly 30 percent last year. "Dell," she concludes, "is changing the way computers are being sold in Asia."

... Dell is starting to rattle Chinese PC makers like Legend and Founder by nibbling into their most valuable client base: state-owned enterprises. These bureaucratic behemoths may seem an odd fit with Dell's fast-as-lightning direct model, but somehow it works. Two-thirds of Dell's corporate customers in China are state-owned enterprises, up from next to none ten months ago. The rest of Dell's customers are multinationals like Ericsson, Nortel, Motorola, and Ford. Dell hopes to keep signing up more Chinese companies—not easy, given the price-slashing tactics of the small shops that sell cheap PCs with bootlegged software. But if it does, then Dell will do something few U.S. companies in China ever manage to do: turn a profit without investing a fortune in manufacturing and without sharing the booty with a Chinese partner or middleman.

Why is Dell's direct model winning in China? First, look at the way Dell is selling to the Chinese. Shredding the myth that to sell in China requires padding the egos (and wallets) of capricious bureaucrats—usually during long and boring banquets—Dell is winning over the chief information officers of state-owned companies the American way: with speed, convenience, and service. "We don't have to change the formula," insists Dell salesman Peter Chan. "It will work in the U.S., China, India, or even in space."

At the heart of that "formula" is the simple tenet that the customer knows best. When Dell's Chan pauses for breath after his sales pitch at China Pacific, for example, the newly awakened Xiao peppers him with questions. How quickly will the computers arrive? Can Excel be loaded onto the hard drive? What kind of service does Dell offer? And, ahem, how much?

What is powerfully clear is that Xiao knows computers. He knows what he needs from Dell. He knows how much he wants to pay. Critically, Xiao knows enough that he does not need to see or touch the machine, or even raise a few glasses of Tsingtao beer with a honey-tongued distributor, before he orders it. All Xiao needs is a phone or, better yet, an Internet connection, to buy what he needs.

Such tech savviness and straightforwardness is increasingly common in China, and that is a terrific advantage for Dell, whose biggest perceived shortcoming was that it lacked the kind of service network that Hewlett-Packard or IBM has. These service networks can provide companies like China Pacific with technical advice and long-term system consultancy. But as Xiao makes clear, Chinese managers are growing more and more tech savvy on their own. They simply don't need that kind of babysitting—and they don't want to pay for it. "We may still need some consulting services, but in our own front offices we know how to choose our equipment," says Xiao. "Dell provides exactly what we need, and with Dell we can choose exactly what we want."

FOR DISCUSSION

1. What, if any, synergies has Dell achieved in this case? Explain.

2. Which of Porter's generic competitive strategies does Dell seem to be employing? Explain your rationale.

3. How does Dell's e-commerce strategy give it a competitive edge?

4. Will Dell's e-commerce strategy likely create or prevent ethical problems in its China operation? Explain.

5. How important to Dell's strategy is speed?

DECISION MAKING
and CREATIVE
PROBLEM SOLVING

CHAPTER OBJECTIVES

When you finish studying this chapter, you should be able to

1 Specify at least five sources of decision complexity for modern managers.

2 Explain what a *condition of risk* is and what managers can do to cope with it.

3 Define and discuss the three decision traps: framing, escalation of commitment, and overconfidence.

4 Discuss why programmed and non-programmed decisions require different decision-making procedures.

5 Explain the need for a contingency approach to group-aided decision making.

6 Identify and briefly describe five of the ten "mental locks" that can inhibit creativity.

7 List and explain the four basic steps in the creative problem-solving process.

8 Describe how causes of problems can be tracked down with fishbone diagrams.

"IF YOUR INSTINCT IS TO WAIT, PONDER,
AND PERFECT, THEN YOU'RE DEAD.
        IN PRACTICE, THAT MEANS THAT
LEADERS HAVE TO HIT THE UNDO KEY
        WITHOUT FLINCHING."
                ruthann quindlen

Three Women in Pursuit of an Internet Dream

Background: Fortune *magazine ran into Erin Gershon, Stacy Sukov, and Nicole Ginsburg in June 1999 shortly after they received their MBA degrees from the Kellogg Graduate School of Management at Northwestern University in Evanston, Illinois. "Erin, Stacy, and Nicole were packing up their stuff and moving to San Francisco to launch WebWisher, an Internet company they had dreamed up while at Kellogg. WebWisher was conceived as an online gift registry for kids. For competitive reasons, the women couldn't say much in June about the company and its plans; they wouldn't even discuss details when WebWisher joined forces with another startup. Erin, Stacy, and Nicole reported for their first day of work just a week after graduation." In early 2000,* Fortune *reported the following update.*

It used to be that entrepreneurs Erin Gershon, Stacy Sukov, and Nicole Ginsburg worked together closely, huddled in the living room of Stacy's Evanston, Illinois, apartment. They shared a phone line and made big decisions about their startup, WebWisher, as they sat on the floor and nibbled on tossed salads from the Whole Foods Market down the street. When they needed a break, someone would run out and pick up Milano cookies.

The women still work together, still socialize as a group, and live within a few blocks of each other on San Francisco's Russian Hill. But now when they go for munchies, they walk to a large communal kitchen, where they grab fistfuls of Tootsie Rolls out of a huge basket. Free sodas are in the Coke machine on the left. These days WebWisher is called Della Kidz; when it was barely more than a business plan, it was absorbed into a larger gift-registry company called Della.com.

Della.com is a startup, just like WebWisher was. But—and this is a key difference—it is a startup that recently got more than $45 million in venture backing and also has a product out the gate. Almost a hundred people work at Della.com, most of them women in their 20s with stylish clothes and lots of energy, just like Erin, Stacy, and Nicole. Della Kidz is still the grads' baby—and they are still jazzed about it—but now they are part of a larger enterprise. The women sit in far-flung corners of the cavernous, open office. They often pick up the phone when they want to talk with each other.

Not that there's a lot of time for that. One Wednesday morning in October, Erin sits at her desk near the others in Della.com's retail-relations group. It seems like she's having a tough day. She fires up her computer and sees four e-mails from Nicole, who had been on her honeymoon in the South Pacific. "She got back at midnight last night," Erin says, "and she's already called every phone number I have." Erin also has a couple of messages from clients—account management has become a big part of her job.

Erin is in charge of developing partnerships with retailers who list their products on Della Kidz. Some of the work is glamorous—like powwows with Internet executives at national retailers—but she spends a good portion of her day fielding calls. She also surfs the Web to research prospects. She's read about a mall-based store for teens that doesn't yet have an e-commerce outlet. She types their URL into her Web browser and surfs around until she finds a phone number for the company's corporate offices in Texas. She picks up her phone and punches in the numbers.

"Hello," she says. "I was wondering when you were going to have e-commerce on your site. . . . My name is Erin Gershon, and I'm calling from Della.com. . . . Who's the correct contact? . . . Okay, I'll try again tomorrow."

She hangs up. "You make a random call, you wait a few days, you call back and dig a little deeper," she explains. "I'll do phone calls like this for three weeks. If I'm lucky, the retailer will be interested, and I'll get a meeting." She says that a lot of retailers already know about Della.com, which makes her job a little easier.

Della Kidz is supposed to be up and running sometime in mid-December so that children will be able to set up their "wish lists" just in time for Christmas. (In fact, Della Kidz went online December 17.) In her four months as a startup entrepreneur, Erin has contacted between 30 and 40 companies, both for Della Kidz and for the general registry at Della.com. She's closed three deals and is bearing down on four more. "Everyone I talk to has 15 deals on their plate," she sighs. "One more deal is a lot for them to look at. I'm asking people to change their marketing model, change their resource allocation, change their Web site, and then give us money. It can seem like a lot to ask."

She glances at the pile of magazines on her desk—on top is a *Newsweek* with "Tweens" on the cover—and shifts in her chair. "I've got to get a sales grid done by 4:30. I've also got a meeting at 11. I've got to crank," she says.

I take the hint and walk to Stacy's desk across the room. As product manager for Della Kidz, she approves all design and engineering decisions for the site, making sure everybody involved—from programmers to attorneys to designers to Della.com's top marketing people—stays on track.

Stacy does market research too. She has a collection of kids across the country whom she e-mails and visits regularly (the "kid crew"). She has even parked herself outside F.A.O. Schwarz from time to time to fire questions at kids walking by.

Today, partly for my benefit, she grills Yana, a shy 10-year-old whose mom works in the office. "Where do you think you should click?" Stacy asks her. "Do you know what a wish list is? Does this look like it was made for you? Do you like American Girl dolls? Do you like books?"

Yana squirms in her chair. Stacy tries again. She moves the cursor to an animated bee on the site. "What do you think of the bee?" she asks.

"It's funny looking," Yana replies.

"Um . . . okay." Stacy says. She writes something in a notebook and seems amused.

These interviews are sometimes less than revealing. The kids often contradict all the "expert" advice Della Kidz gets from consultants. But, happily, Stacy doesn't have to agonize over the conflicts. "We work on gut here," says her boss, Della.com CEO Rebecca Patton. "This business is not about rigorous analysis. You can't do huge research projects. You go by what seems reasonable."

Later in the day Stacy and Erin have their weekly meeting with Rebecca. (Nicole, whose job is to forge alliances with Web portals like Disney's GO Network, joins in on speakerphone from Dallas.) Since everything is on track for the Christmastime launch, Rebecca wants the women to think about the "game over"—what they need to do to be sure Della Kidz emerges as the leading kids' registry online. She pushes the women to come up with concrete goals and reminds Erin that her strategy presentation needs to be ready by the end of the week. Erin, who's been too busy to even start her sales grid, nods stoically.

"Let's get back to the WebWisher days!" Nicole says as Rebecca ducks out of the meeting. "What's the perfect company? Once we have an idea, we can back off from that. . . ."

So Della Kidz isn't perfect yet. The work environment can be chaotic, job roles can shift, deadlines are unforgiving. Still, Erin, Stacy, and Nicole are happy with the decisions they've made, happy to be in San Francisco in the midst of the Internet startup scene, even happy with having sacrificed some of their autonomy. "By coming here we made it ten times easier on ourselves," says Stacy. Erin agrees. "I don't think Stacy, Nicole, and I could have sold GapKids a registry on our own," she says.

---

decision making *identifying and choosing alternative courses of action*

Decision making is the process of identifying and choosing alternative courses of action in a manner appropriate to the demands of the situation. The act of choosing implies that alternative courses of action must be weighed and weeded out. Many tough choices face entrepreneurs Erin, Stacy, and Nicole amid huge uncertainties. They are making important decisions at a rapid pace, despite incomplete information. Reason and judgment are required. Thus judgment and discretion are fundamental to decision making. This chapter highlights major challenges for decision makers, introduces a general decision-making model, discusses group-aided decision making, and examines creativity and problem solving.

Challenges for Decision Makers

Though decision making has never been easy, it is especially challenging for today's managers. In an era of accelerating change, the pace of decision making has also accelerated. No one knows this better than AT&T's chief executive officer, C. Michael

The $178 billion handshake. In a complex stream of decisions creating the biggest corporate marriage in history, America Online's founder and CEO Steve Case (left) bought Time Warner in early 2000. Time Warner's CEO Gerald Levin (right) will become CEO of AOL Time Warner, while Case will assume the position of chairman. AOL, only one-fifth the size of Time Warner (in terms of annual sales), could afford to purchase the much larger company because of the boom in Internet stocks. Timing, uncertainty, and luck—although difficult to quantify—can play crucial roles in key decisions.

Armstrong. Within only a year of being hired for the top job at the telecommunications giant, Armstrong had announced $70 billion worth of mergers and deals. After the concept had languished for years, "Armstrong approved AT&T's hit wireless offering, Digital One Rate, after a 20-minute meeting"[1] in 1998. In addition to having to cope with this acceleration, today's decision makers face a host of tough challenges. Ones we will discuss here include (1) complex streams of decisions, (2) uncertainty, (3) information-processing styles, and (4) perceptual and behavioral decision traps.

Dealing with Complex Streams of Decisions

Above all else, today's decision-making contexts are not neat and tidy. A pair of experts recently lent realism to the subject by using the analogy of a stream:

> *If decisions can be viewed as streams—streams containing countless bits of information, events, and choices—then how should decision makers be viewed? . . . The streams flowing through the organization do not wait for them; they flow around them. The streams do not serve up problems neatly wrapped and ready for choice. Rather, they deliver the bits and pieces, the problems and choices, in no particular order. . . .*
>
> *In short, decision makers in an organization are floating in the stream, jostled capriciously by problems popping up, and finding anchors through action at a given time in a given place.*[2]

Importantly, the foregoing is a recognition of complexity, *not* an admission of hopelessness. A working knowledge of seven intertwined factors contributing to decision complexity can help decision makers successfully navigate the stream (see Figure 8.1). They include the following:

1 **Specify at least five sources of decision complexity for modern managers.**

1. *Multiple criteria.* Typically, a decision today must satisfy a number of often conflicting criteria representing the interests of different groups. For example, the new Denver International Airport was designed and built with much more than airplanes in mind:

   > *Denver's is the first airport to be built for maximum accessibility for the disabled. During construction, the city took blind people, deaf people and those who use wheelchairs and canes through the terminal and concourses to road-test the layout.*

Figure 8.1

Sources of Complexity for Today's Managerial Decision Makers

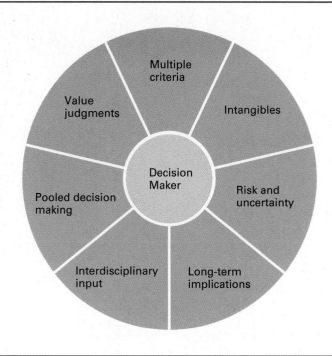

> *"They wanted to make sure a sign wasn't too low or a drinking fountain sticking out too far," says Thom Walsh, project manager at Fentress Bradburn. "It's a completely accessible building and uses Braille and voice paging."*[3]

Identifying stakeholders and balancing their conflicting interests is a major challenge for today's decision makers.

2. *Intangibles.* Factors such as customer goodwill, employee morale, increased bureaucracy, and aesthetic appeal (for example, a billboard on a scenic highway), although difficult to measure, often determine decision alternatives.

3. *Risk and uncertainty.* Along with every decision alternative goes the chance that it will fail in some way. Poor choices can prove costly. Yet the right decision, as illustrated in this legendary example, can open up whole new worlds of opportunity:

> *In 1967, seven dry holes on Alaska's harsh North Slope had left Atlantic Richfield Chairman Robert O. Anderson facing a costly choice. Should he try one more? The consummate wildcatter, Anderson pushed ahead, making one of the strategic decisions in U.S. oil history.*
>
> *The day after Christmas, oil historian Daniel Yergin recounts, a sound like four jumbo jets flying just overhead announced a plume of spewing natural gas. Prudhoe Bay turned out to be the largest petroleum discovery ever in North America.*[4]

Because of the importance of this particular aspect of decision complexity, we shall devote special attention to it in the next section.

4. *Long-term implications.* Managers are becoming increasingly aware that their decisions have not only intended short-term impact but also unintended long-term impact. For example, Chrysler's management responded to lower sales during the 1974–1975 recession by cutting capital spending and laying off engineers and designers. Although these cost-cutting decisions helped Chrysler reduce its short-run losses, the firm's long-term competitiveness was nearly destroyed because of obsolete facilities and a shortage of creative talent.[5]

To millions of adoring music fans, she's known simply as Brandy. Her debut album sold more than 4 million copies and a promising career in modeling, television, and movies lies ahead. Meanwhile, behind the scenes, her mother Sonja Norword (right) teamed with agents, accountants, lawyers, and industry contacts to make sure her daughter received favorable contracts. This interdisciplinary input prepared Sonja for the jump from her job as an H&R Block district manager to forming her own talent management company. Of course, the only future certainty for Sonja and Brandy is lots of hard work.

5. *Interdisciplinary input.* Decision complexity is greatly increased when technical specialists such as lawyers, consumer advocates, tax advisers, accountants, engineers, and production and marketing experts are consulted before making a decision. This also is a time-consuming process.

6. *Pooled decision making.* Rarely is a single manager totally responsible for the entire decision process. For example, consider the approach of Brian Ruder, the successful president of Heinz's U.S. unit:

> [He] has collected a number of mentors and advisers over the course of his career. Ruder, in fact, has elected a group of people, including his father, to a personal board of directors. He canvasses them whenever he's faced with a major decision, such as introducing plastic ketchup bottles. . . . "I rely on them," he says, "for total frankness and objectivity." Obviously, it's helped.[6]

After pooled input, complex decisions wind their way through the organization, with individuals and groups interpreting, modifying, and sometimes resisting. Minor decisions set the stage for major decisions, which in turn are translated back into local decisions. Typically, many people's fingerprints are on final decisions in the organizational world.

7. *Value judgments.* As long as decisions are made by people with differing backgrounds, perceptions, aspirations, and values, the decision-making process will be marked by disagreement over what is right or wrong, good or bad, and ethical or unethical.[7]

 The Key to Effective Decisions?   8A

"In business as in politics, the effectiveness of a decision is the quality of the decision multiplied by the acceptance of it."

Source: Marshall Loeb, "Where Leaders Come From," *Fortune* (September 19, 1994): 241.

Questions: *What important lesson does this quote teach about being an effective decision maker? What are some other keys to effective organizational decisions?*

For further information about the interactive annotations in this chapter, visit our Web site (**www.hmco.com/college**).

Coping with Uncertainty

Among the valuable contributions of decision theorists are classification schemes for types and degrees of uncertainty. (Recall our discussion in Chapter 6 about state, effect, and response uncertainty.) Unfortunately, life is filled with varying degrees of these types of uncertainties. Managers are continually asked to make the best decisions they can, despite uncertainties about both present and future circumstances. Imagine yourself as a manager in Canada's pulp and paper industry facing this complex web of uncertainties, as described by a business writer during the 1990s:

> *Battered by slack demand and production overcapacity, hounded by environmentalists, and hit with regulations forcing costly new pollution controls, Canada's paper manufacturers are under siege. . . .*
>
> *To the recession, add unfavorable exchange rates, tougher competition abroad, and a shift toward recycled newsprint in the crucial United States market. . . .*[8]

Managers who are able to assess the degrees of certainty in a situation—whether conditions are certain, risky, or uncertain—are able to make more effective decisions. As illustrated in Figure 8.2, there is a negative correlation between uncertainty and the decision maker's confidence in a decision. In other words, the more uncertain a manager is about the principal factors in a decision, the less confident he or she will be about the successful outcome of that decision. The key, of course, lies not in eliminating uncertainty, which is impossible, but rather in learning to work within an acceptable range of uncertainty.

condition of certainty
solid factual basis allows accurate prediction of decision's outcome

Certainty.   A **condition of certainty** exists when there is no doubt about the factual basis of a particular decision and its outcome can be predicted accurately. Much like the economic concept of pure competition, the concept of certainty is useful mainly as a theoretical anchor point for a continuum. In a world filled with uncertainties, certainty is relative rather than absolute. For example, the decision to order more rivets for a manufacturing firm's fabrication department is based on the relative certainty that the current rate of use will exhaust the rivet inventory on a specific date.

Figure 8.2

The Relationship Between Uncertainty and Confidence

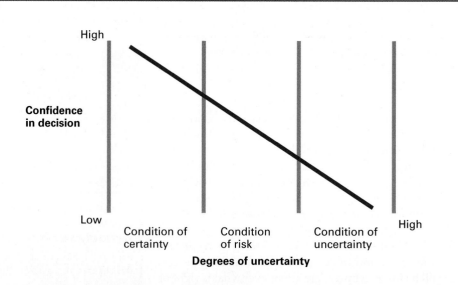

But even in this case, uncertainties about the possible misuse or theft of rivets creep in to reduce confidence. Because nothing is truly certain, conditions of risk and uncertainty are the general rule for managers, not the exception.

Risk.   A **condition of risk** is said to exist when a decision must be made on the basis of incomplete but reliable factual information.[9] Reliable information, though incomplete, is still useful to managers coping with risk because they can use it to calculate the probability that a given event will occur and then to select a decision alternative with favorable odds.

The two basic types of probabilities are objective and subjective. **Objective probabilities** are derived mathematically from reliable historical data, whereas **subjective probabilities** are estimated from past experience or judgment. Decision making based on probabilities is common in all areas of management today. For instance, laundry product manufacturers would not think of launching a new detergent without determining its probability of acceptance by means of consumer panels and test marketing. A number of inferential statistical techniques can help managers objectively cope with risks.[10]

Uncertainty.   A **condition of uncertainty** exists when little or no reliable factual information is available. Although there is no data base from which to calculate objective probabilities, judgmental or subjective probabilities can still be estimated. Decision making under conditions of uncertainty can be both rewarding and nerve-racking for managers. Just ask the folks at Wisconsin's Northland Cranberries. After a recent fall harvest, management had to decide whether to process the cranberries right away or keep them in storage for more profitable sale as fresh berries at Thanksgiving. A decision was made to hold off processing. But Mother Nature had other plans. An unpredictable early frost followed by a heat wave increased the likelihood of spoilage. Northland was stuck with tons of rotted cranberries by mid-November.[11] Decision confidence is lowest when a condition of uncertainty prevails because decisions are then based on educated guesses rather than on hard factual data.[12]

2 Explain what a *condition of risk* is and what managers can do to cope with it.

condition of risk *decision made on basis of incomplete but reliable information*

objective probabilities *odds derived mathematically from reliable data*

subjective probabilities *odds based on judgment*

condition of uncertainty *no reliable factual information available*

Information-Processing Styles

Thinking is one of those activities we engage in constantly, yet seldom pause to examine systematically. But within the context of managerial decision making and problem solving, it is important that one's thinking does not get into an unproductive rut. The quality of our decisions is a direct reflection of how we process information.

Researchers have identified two general information-processing styles: the thinking style and the intuitive style.[13] One is not superior to the other. Both are needed during organizational problem solving. Managers who rely predominantly on the *thinking* style tend to be logical, precise, and objective. They prefer routine assignments requiring attention to detail and systematic implementation. Conversely, managers who are predominantly *intuitive* find comfort in rapidly changing situations in which they can be creative and

---

8B

Back to the Opening Case

Jonathan Bulkeley, CEO, **Barnesandnoble.com:**

. . . at our last directors' meeting, I handed out copies of my favorite business book—Harold and the Purple Crayon. The plot is simple: A little baldheaded kid with a big purple crayon draws himself into and out of various situations. If he's on a path that's too long, he draws a shortcut. If he gets hungry, he draws some pies. If he finds himself in deep water, he draws a boat. The point is, Harold creates the solutions he needs as he proceeds through an uncertain landscape. Harold has the kind of creativity and nimbleness that we need to win in the Net market. The lesson that the book teaches is key—and so is the fact that it takes only five minutes to read!

Source: Excerpted from "Jonathan Bulkeley," *Fast Company*, no. 25 (June 1999): 96.

Question: *How could Erin, Stacy, and Nicole use this approach to refine and advance their vision for Della Kidz?*

Figure 8.3 | Two General Information-Processing Styles

Brain skill emphasized	Type of organization where predominant	Task preference	Problem-solving/ decision-making style	Example applications	Sample occupational specialty
Thinking	• Traditional • Pyramid	• Routine • Precision • Detail • Implementation • Repetitive	• Deductive • Objective • Prefers solving problems by breakdown into parts, then approaching the problem sequentially using logic.	• Model building • Projection	• Planning • Management science • Financial management • Engineering • Law enforcement • Military
Intuitive	• Open • Temporary • Rapidly changing	• Nonroutine • Broad issues • General policy options • Constant new assignments	• Inductive • Subjective • Prefers solving problems by looking at the whole, then approaching the problem through hunches.	• Brain-storming • Challenging traditional assumptions	• Personnel • Marketing • Organization development • Intelligence

Source: Weston H. Agor, "Managing Brain Skills: The Last Frontier," *Personnel Administrator,* 32 (October 1987): 58, Figure 1. Reprinted by permission of the author.

follow their hunches and visions. Intuitive managers see things in complex patterns rather than as logically ordered bits and pieces.[14] Of course, not everyone falls neatly into one of these two categories; many people process information through a combination of the two styles (see Figure 8.3).

The important thing to recognize here is that managers approach decision making and problem solving in very different ways, depending on their information-processing styles.[15] Their approaches, perceptions, and recommendations vary because their minds work differently. In traditional pyramid work organizations, where the thinking style tends to prevail, intuitive employees may be criticized for being imprecise and rocking the boat. A concerted effort needs to be made to tap the creative skills of "intuitives" and the implementation abilities of "thinkers." An appreciation for alternative information-processing styles needs to be cultivated because they complement one another.

Avoiding Perceptual and Behavioral Decision Traps

Behavioral scientists have identified some common human tendencies capable of eroding the quality of decision making. Three well-documented ones are framing, escalation, and overconfidence. Awareness and conscious avoidance of these traps can give decision makers a competitive edge.

Framing Error.   One's judgment can be altered and shaped by how information is presented or labeled. In other words, labels create frames of reference with the power to bias our interpretations. **Framing error** is the tendency to evaluate positively presented information favorably and negatively presented information unfavorably.[16] Those evaluations, in turn, influence one's behavior. A study with 80 male and 80 female University of Iowa students documented the framing-interpretation-behavior linkage. Half of each gender group was told about a cancer treatment with a 50 percent success rate. The other two groups heard about the same cancer treatment but were told it had a 50 percent failure rate. The researchers summed up results of the study as follows:

> *Describing a medical treatment as having a 50 percent success rate led to higher ratings of perceived effectiveness and higher likelihood of recommending the treatment to others, including family members, than describing the treatment as having a 50 percent failure rate.*[17]

Framing thus influenced both interpretations and intended behavior. Given the importance of the information in this study (cancer treatment), ethical questions arise about the potential abuse of framing error.

In organizations, framing error can be used constructively or destructively. Advertisers, for instance, take full advantage of this perceptional tendency when attempting to sway consumers' purchasing decisions. A leading brand of cat litter boasts of being 99 percent dust free. Meanwhile, a shampoo claims to be fortified with 1 percent natural protein. Thanks to framing error, we tend to perceive very little dust in the cat litter and a lot of protein in the shampoo. Managers who couch their proposals in favorable terms hope to benefit from framing error. And who can blame them? On the negative side, prejudice and bigotry thrive on framing error. A male manager who believes women can't manage might frame interview results so that John looks good and Mary looks bad.

Escalation of Commitment.   Why are people slow to write off bad investments? Why do companies stick to unprofitable strategies? And why has the government typically continued to fund over-budget and behind-schedule weapons systems? Escalation of commitment is a possible explanation for these diverse situations.[18] **Escalation of commitment** is the tendency of individuals and organizations to get locked into losing courses of action because *quitting is personally and socially difficult.* This decision-making trap has been called the "throwing good money after bad" dilemma. Those victimized by escalation of commitment often are heard talking about "sunk costs" and "too much time and money invested to quit now." Within the context of management, psychological, social, and organizational factors conspire to encourage escalation of commitment[19] (see Figure 8.4).

The model in Figure 8.4 can be brought to life by using it to analyze a highly unusual decision by the Pentagon in 1991. Two giant defense contractors, McDonnell Douglas and General Dynamics, were under contract to design and build the A-12 attack plane. All told, 620 of the aircraft carrier-based bombers were to be built for the U.S. Navy at a cost of $60 billion. With the A-12 program 18 months behind schedule

3 Define and discuss the three decision traps: framing, escalation of commitment, and overconfidence.

framing error *how information is presented influences one's interpretation of it*

escalation of commitment *people get locked into losing courses of action to avoid embarrassment of quitting or admitting error*

Figure 8.4

Why Escalation of Commitment Is So Common

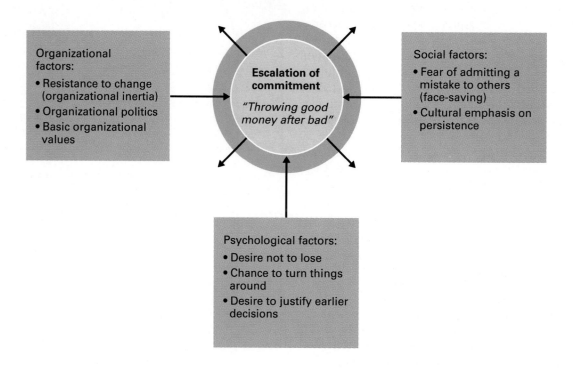

Organizational factors:
- Resistance to change (organizational inertia)
- Organizational politics
- Basic organizational values

Escalation of commitment

"Throwing good money after bad"

Social factors:
- Fear of admitting a mistake to others (face-saving)
- Cultural emphasis on persistence

Psychological factors:
- Desire not to lose
- Chance to turn things around
- Desire to justify earlier decisions

Source: Adapted from discussion in Barry M. Staw and Jerry Ross, "Understanding Behavior in Escalation Situations," *Science,* 246 (October 13, 1989): 216–220.

and $2.7 billion over budget, then Secretary of Defense Richard Cheney terminated the contract. It was the Pentagon's biggest cancellation ever. An appreciation of the contributing factors shown in Figure 8.4 underscores how truly unusual Cheney's decision was. Psychologically, his termination decision flew in the face of three possible motives for throwing good money after bad. Cheney went against the social grain as well by publicly admitting the Defense Department's mistake and doing something culturally distasteful to Americans, giving up. (American folk heroes tend to be persistent to the bitter end.) Finally, Cheney had to overcome bureaucratic resistance in the defense establishment. He also had to withstand political opposition from the contractors about their having to lay off 8,000 A-12 project employees. Nevertheless, despite many pressures to continue the program, Cheney refused to let the forces of escalation carry the day.

Reality checks, in the form of comparing actual progress with effectiveness and efficiency standards, are the best way to keep escalation in check.[20] In Cheney's case, he concluded: "No one can tell me exactly how much more it will cost to keep this [A-12] program going. And I do not believe that a bailout is in the national interest. If we cannot spend the taxpayers' money wisely, we will not spend it."[21] This is an instructive lesson for all potential victims of escalation.[22]

Overconfidence.   The term *overconfidence* is commonplace and requires no technical definition. We need to comprehend the psychology of overconfidence because it can expose managers to unreasonable risks. For instance, overconfidence proved costly for Boeing in 1998. As *Business Week* reported at the time:

Boeing's prized new Delta III rocket blew up on its maiden flight on Aug. 26, taking with it a $225 million PanAmSat Corp. satellite. Overconfidence lured Boeing into taking the risky step of carrying a live payload on the maiden voyage.[23]

Ironically, researchers have found a positive relationship between overconfidence and task difficulty. In other words, the more difficult the task, the greater the tendency for people to be overconfident.[24] Easier and more predictable situations foster confidence, but generally not unrealistic overconfidence. People may be overconfident about one or more of the following: accuracy of input data; individual, team, or organizational ability; and the probability of success. There are various theoretical explanations for this research evidence. One likely reason is that overconfidence is often necessary to generate the courage needed to tackle difficult situations.

As with the other decision traps, managerial awareness of this problem is the important first step toward avoiding it. Careful analysis of situational factors, critical thinking about decision alternatives, and honest input from stakeholders can help managers avoid overconfidence.[25]

8D

Here's a Hot Tip for the Stock Market

With the advent of around-the-clock online stock trading, research by Professor Terry Odean is setting off alarm bells in investment circles:

The unifying theme of Odean's work in behavioral finance—an area of study that focuses on the psychology of investing—is the peril that overconfidence brings. He's examined topics ranging from the different ways men and women invest to the performance of investment clubs, and in every case, one conclusion rings louder than all others: Overconfident investors trade excessively—and excessive trading torpedoes returns.

Source: Amy Feldman, "A Finance Professor for the People," *Money,* 28 (November 1999): 173.

Questions: *Why would novice investors be prone to overconfidence? Are you a likely candidate for overconfidence? Why or why not?*

Making Decisions

It stands to reason that if the degree of uncertainty varies from situation to situation, there can be no single way to make decisions.[26] A second variable with which decision makers must cope is the number of times a particular decision is made. Some decisions are made frequently, perhaps several times a day. Others are made infrequently or just once. Consequently, decision theorists have distinguished between programmed and nonprogrammed decisions.[27] Each of these types of decisions requires a different procedure.

4 Discuss why programmed and nonprogrammed decisions require different decision-making procedures.

Making Programmed Decisions

Programmed decisions are those that are repetitive and routine. Examples include hiring decisions, billing decisions in a hospital, supply reorder decisions in a purchasing department, consumer loan decisions in a bank, and pricing decisions in a university bookstore. Managers tend to devise fixed procedures for handling these everyday decisions. Most decisions made by the typical manager on a daily basis are of the programmed variety.

At the heart of the programmed decision procedure are decision rules. A **decision rule** is a statement that identifies the situation in which a decision is required and spec-

programmed decisions *repetitive and routine decisions*

decision rule *tells when and how programmed decisions should be made*

The Global Manager

Programmed for Ethical Decision Making at Citizens Bank of Canada

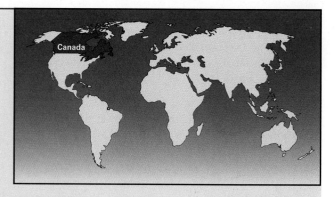

It's a marvelous prototype for businesses in the new millennium: Citizens Bank of Canada, launched in 1997, has no branches—offering services through telephone, automated tellers, and the Internet. *And* it's designed specifically as a socially responsible bank. Recently, for example, the bank announced its new Ethical Policy, and made a commitment to performing an annual third-party audit of compliance.

"We are a bank that believes we are, in fact, *stewards* of the funds we hold," the Ethical Policy says. "And we demonstrate our leadership by being responsible and conscientious about where our money comes from and what we do with it." The Ethical Policy prohibits the bank from investing in or doing business with companies that violate human rights, produce nuclear energy or tobacco products, harm the environment, or have a poor employee relations record, as well as other criteria.

The bank's goal is to make social responsibility a part of everyday practices, not an after-profit "giving-back" exercise. In its 1999 mortgage campaign, for example, the bank advertised mortgage rates alongside an eye-opening social statistic—giving free advertising to selected social change organizations, like the National Anti-Poverty Organization.

Source: Gilian Dusting, "A Bank with Ethics, Without Branches," *Business Ethics*, 13 (July–August 1999): 7. Reprinted with permission from *Business Ethics*, P.O. Box 8439, Minneapolis, Minn. 55408. (612) 879-0695.

---

ifies how the decision will be made. Behind decision rules is the idea that standard, recurring problems need to be solved only once. Decision rules permit busy managers to make routine decisions quickly without having to go through comprehensive problem solving over and over again. Generally, decision rules should be stated in "if-then" terms. A decision rule for a consumer loan officer in a bank, for example, might be: *If* the applicant is employed, has no record of loan default, and can put up 20 percent collateral, *then* a loan not to exceed $10,000 can be authorized." Carefully conceived decision rules can streamline the decision-making process by allowing lower-level managers to shoulder the responsibility for programmed decisions and freeing higher-level managers for relatively more important, nonprogrammed decisions (see The Global Manager).

Making Nonprogrammed Decisions

nonprogrammed decisions
decisions made in complex and nonroutine situations

Nonprogrammed decisions are those made in complex, important, and nonroutine situations, often under new and largely unfamiliar circumstances. This kind of decision is made much less frequently than are programmed decisions. Examples of nonprogrammed decisions include deciding whether to merge with another company, how to replace an executive who died unexpectedly, whether a foreign branch should be opened, and how to market an entirely new kind of product or service. The following six questions need to be asked prior to making a nonprogrammed decision:

1. What decision needs to be made?
2. When does it have to be made?

"It's a bird. It's a plane. No, it's Superkid!" This youngster and millions of others are the focal point of lots of nonprogrammed decision making at Toys "R" Us these days. The one-time undisputed leader in toy sales has lost some of its luster in recent years. Its huge warehouse stores, like this one in Georgia, are being refurbished and made more interactive. After all, how can a child decide which toy is best without some hands-on experience?

3. Who will decide?
4. Who will need to be consulted prior to the making of the decision?
5. Who will ratify or veto the decision?
6. Who will need to be informed of the decision?[28]

The decision-making process becomes more sharply focused when managers take the time to answer these questions.

One respected decision theorist has described nonprogrammed decisions as follows: "There is no cut-and-dried method for handling the problem because it hasn't arisen before, or because its precise nature and structure are elusive or complex, or because it is so important that it deserves a custom-tailored treatment."[29]

Nonprogrammed decision making calls for creative problem solving. The four-step problem-solving process introduced later in this chapter helps managers make effective and efficient nonprogrammed decisions.

8E

Back to the Opening Case

What evidence of programmed and nonprogrammed decision making can you detect in this case?

A General Decision-Making Model

Although different decision procedures are required for different situations, it is possible to construct a general decision-making model. Figure 8.5 shows an idealized, logical, and rational model of organizational decision making. Importantly, it describes how decisions can be made, but it does not portray how managers actually make decisions.[30] In fact, on-the-job research found managers did not follow a rational and logical series of steps when making decisions.[31] Why, then, should we even consider a rational, logical model? Once again, as in the case of the strategic management process in Chapter 7, a rational descriptive model has instructional value because it identifies key components of a complex process. It also suggests a better way of doing things.

Figure 8.5

A General Decision-Making Model

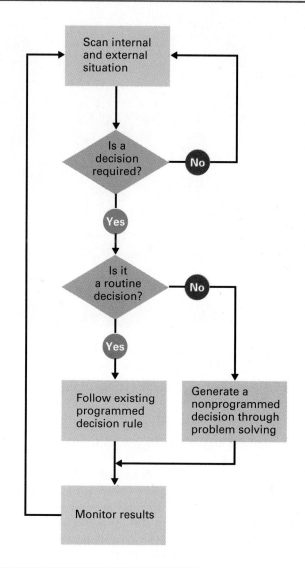

The first step, a scan of the situation, is important, although it is often underemphasized or ignored altogether in discussions of managerial decision making. Scanning answers the question "How do I know a decision should be made?" More than 60 years ago, Chester I. Barnard gave one of the best answers to this question, stating that "the occasions for decision originate in three distinct fields: (a) from authoritative communications from superiors; (b) from cases referred for decision by subordinates; (c) from cases originating in the initiative of the [manager] concerned."[32] In addition to signaling when a decision is required, scanning reveals the degree of uncertainty and provides necessary information for pending decisions.

When the need for a decision has been established, the manager must determine whether the situation is routine. If it is routine and there is an appropriate decision rule, the rule is applied. But if it turns out to be a new situation demanding a nonprogrammed decision, comprehensive problem solving begins. In either case, the results of the final decision need to be monitored to see if any follow-up action is necessary.

Group-Aided Decision Making: A Contingency Perspective

Decision making, like any other organizational activity, does not take place in a vacuum. Typically, decision making is a highly social activity with committees, study groups, review panels, or project teams contributing in a variety of ways.

Collaborative Computing

Computer networks, the Internet, and the advent of **collaborative computing** guarantee even broader participation in the decision-making process.

collaborative computing
teaming up to make decisions via a computer network programmed with groupware

> *Collaborative computing is a catchphrase for a new body of software and hardware that helps people work better together. A collaborative system creates an environment in which people can share information without the constraints of time and space.*
>
> *Network groupware applications link workgroups across a room or across the globe. The software gives the group a common, online venue for meetings, and it lets all members labor on the same data simultaneously.*
>
> *Collaborative applications include calendar management, video teleconferencing, computer teleconferencing, integrated team support, and support for business meetings and group authoring. Messaging and e-mail systems represent the most basic type of groupware.*[33]

Unfortunately, according to a recent survey, groupware is typically plagued by low-quality implementation. Sixty-five percent of the survey respondents used it simply as a communication tool, to send and receive e-mail, which is analogous to using a personal computer for word processing only. Groupware users need to be taught how to *collaborate* via computer (for instance, jointly identifying and solving problems). "When implemented correctly, the benefits are astounding. Groupware had twice the impact on individual job performance and nearly three times the impact on customer satisfaction at the organizations with the highest-quality implementation compared with the organization with the lowest."[34]

Group Involvement in Decisions

Whether the situation is a traditional, face-to-face committee meeting or a global computer network, at least five aspects of the decision-making process can be assigned to groups:

1. Analyzing the problem.
2. Identifying components of the decision situation.
3. Estimating components of the decision situation [for example, determining probabilities, feasibilities, time estimates, and payoffs].
4. Designing alternatives.
5. Choosing an alternative.[35]

Assuming that two (or more) heads may be better than one and that managers can make better use of their time by delegating various decision-making chores, there is a strong case for turning to groups when making decisions. But before bringing others into the decision process, managers need to be aware of the problem of dispersed accountability and

What Does *Consensus* Mean?

8F

A consensus requires unity but not unanimity and concurrence but not consistency. . . .

A consensus is reached when all members can say they either agree with the decision or have had their "day in court" and were unable to convince the others of their viewpoint. In the final analysis, everyone agrees to support the outcome. It is not a majority because that implies a vote, and voting is *verboten* [taboo] for teams using the consensus method. Voting tends to split the group into winners and losers, thereby creating needless divisions. Consensus does not require unanimity since members may still disagree with the final result but are willing to work toward its success. This is the hallmark of a team player.

Source: Glenn M. Parker, *Team Players and Teamwork: The New Competitive Business Strategy* (San Francisco: Jossey-Bass, 1990), p. 44.

Questions: *Are you surprised by any of this information? Why is it so important not to submit an issue to a vote when trying to reach a consensus? In today's organizations, why is it often better to strive for a consensus rather than insist upon unanimous support? What are the major drawbacks of the consensus approach?*

consider the trade-off between the advantages and disadvantages of group-aided decision making. In view of these problems and of research evidence comparing individual and group performance, a contingency approach is recommended.

The Problem of Dispersed Accountability

There is a critical difference between group-aided decision making and group decision making. In the first instance, the group does everything except make the final decision. In the second instance, the group actually makes the final decision. Managers who choose the second route face a dilemma. Although a decision made by a group probably will reflect the collective experience and wisdom of all those involved, personal accountability is lost. Blame for a joint decision that fails is too easily passed on to others. For example, Robert Palmer, hired to turn Digital Equipment around, inherited the following situation: "This was a company run by committee, by consensus. No one actually made a decision. When things went well, there would be a number of people willing to take credit. But when things went wrong, it was impossible to fix responsibility on anyone."[36] This legacy of dispersed accountability proved too much for Palmer, and Digital was sold to Compaq Computer.

The traditional formula for resolving this problem is to make sure that a given manager is personally accountable for a decision when the responsibility for it has to be traced. According to this line of reasoning, even when a group is asked to recommend a decision, the responsibility for the final outcome remains with the manager in charge. For managers who want to maintain the integrity of personal accountability, there is no such thing as group decision making; there is only group-*aided* decision making. There are three situations in which individual accountability for a decision is necessary.

- The decision will have significant impact on the success or failure of the unit or organization.
- The decision has legal ramifications (such as possible prosecution for price-fixing, antitrust, or product safety violations).
- A competitive reward is tied to a successful decision. (For example, only one person can get a promotion.)

In less critical areas, the group itself may be responsible for making decisions.[37]

Advantages and Disadvantages of Group-Aided Decision Making

5 Explain the need for a contingency approach to group-aided decision making.

Various combinations of positive and negative factors are encountered when a manager brings others into the decision-making process. The advantages and disadvantages are listed in Table 8.1. If there is a conscious effort to avoid or at least minimize the disadvantages, managers can gain a great deal by sharing the decision-making process with peers, outside consultants, and team members.[38] However, some important contingency factors need to be taken into consideration.

A Contingency Approach Is Necessary

Are two or more heads actually better than one? The answer depends on the nature of the task, the ability of the contributors, and the form of interaction (see Figure 8.6). An analysis of dozens of individual-versus-group performance studies conducted over a 61-year period led one researcher to the following conclusions: (1) groups tend to do quantitatively and qualitatively better than the *average* individual; and (2) *exceptional* individuals tend to outperform the group, particularly when the task is complex and the group is made up of relatively low-ability people.[39]

Consequently, busy managers need to delegate aspects of the decision-making process (specified earlier) according to the contingencies in Figure 8.6. More is said about delegation in Figure 8.6. More is said about delegation in Chapter 10.

Advantages	Disadvantages	Table 8.1
1. **Greater pool of knowledge.** A group can bring much more information and experience to bear on a decision or problem than can an individual acting alone.	1. **Social pressure.** Unwillingness to "rock the boat" and pressure to conform may combine to stifle the creativity of individual contributors.	**Advantages and Disadvantages of Group-Aided Decision Making and Problem Solving**
2. **Different perspectives.** Individuals with varied experience and interests help the group see decision situations and problems from different angles.	2. **Domination by a vocal few.** Sometimes the quality of group action is reduced when the group gives in to those who talk the loudest and longest.	
3. **Greater comprehension.** Those who personally experience the give-and-take of group discussion about alternative courses of action tend to understand the rationale behind the final decision.	3. **Logrolling.** Political wheeling and dealing can displace sound thinking when an individual's pet project or vested interest is at stake.	
4. **Increased acceptance.** Those who play an active role in group decision making and problem solving tend to view the outcome as "ours" rather than "theirs."	4. **Goal displacement.** Sometimes secondary considerations such as winning an argument, making a point, or getting back at a rival displace the primary task of making a sound decision or solving a problem.	
5. **Training ground.** Less experienced participants in group action learn how to cope with group dynamics by actually being involved.	5. **"Groupthink."** Sometimes cohesive "in groups" let the desire for unanimity override sound judgment when generating and evaluating alternative courses of action. (Groupthink is discussed in Chapter 14.)	

Figure 8.6

Individual Versus Group Performance: Contingency Management Insights from 61 Years of Research

Nature of task	Insights from research
Problem-solving task	Individuals are faster, but groups tend to produce better results
Complex task	Best results achieved by polling the contributions of individuals working alone
Brainstorming task	Same as for complex task
Learning task	Groups consistently outperform individuals
Concept mastery/ creative task	Contributions from average-ability group members tend to improve when they are teamed with high-ability group members

Source: Based in part on research conclusions found in Gayle W. Hill, "Group Versus Individual Performance: Are N + 1 Heads Better than One?", *Psychological Bulletin,* 91 (May 1982): 517–539.

Managerial Creativity

Demands for creativity and innovation make the practice of management endlessly exciting (and sometimes extremely difficult). Nearly all managerial problem solving requires a healthy measure of creativity as managers mentally take things apart, rearrange the pieces in new and potentially productive configurations, and look beyond normal frameworks for new solutions. This process is like turning the kaleidoscope of one's mind. Thomas Edison used to retire to an old couch in his laboratory to do his creative thinking. Henry Ford reportedly sought creative insights by staring at a blank wall in his shop. Although the average manager's attempts at creativity may not be as dramatically fruitful as Edison's or Ford's, workplace creativity needs to be understood and nurtured.[40] As a steppingstone for the next section on creative problem solving, this section defines creativity, discusses the management of creative people, and identifies barriers to creativity.

What Is Creativity?

creativity *the reorganization of experience into new configurations*

Creativity is a rather mysterious process known chiefly by its results and is therefore difficult to define. About as close as we can come is to say that **creativity** is the reorganization of experience into new configurations.[41] According to a management consultant specializing in creativity:

Creativity is a function of knowledge, imagination, and evaluation. The greater our knowledge, the more ideas, patterns, or combinations we can achieve. But merely having the knowledge does not guarantee the formation of new patterns; the bits and pieces must be shaken up and interrelated in new ways. Then, the embryonic ideas must be evaluated and developed into usable ideas.[42]

Creativity is often subtle and may not be readily apparent to the untrained eye. But the combination and extension of seemingly insignificant day-to-day breakthroughs lead to organizational progress.

Identifying general types of creativity is easier than explaining the basic process. One pioneering writer on the subject isolated three overlapping domains of creativity: art, discovery, and humor.[43] These have been called the "ah!" reaction, the "aha!" reaction, and the "haha!" reaction, respectively.[44]

The discovery ("aha!") variation is the most relevant to management. Entirely new businesses can spring from creative discovery. A prime example is Donald L. Beaver Jr.'s low-tech discovery that grew into a thriving multimillion-dollar business.[45] He found that nylon stockings stuffed with ground-up corncobs could soak up oil and grease spills faster than any known technique and at much less cost. Machine shops and gas stations, where slippery oil spills are a costly occupational hazard, clamored for Beaver's new product. Beaver's creativity did not stop there. It extended to the company's name: New PIG Corp. According to Beaver, PIG stands for "Partners in Grime." Creative ideas spring from unexpected places and unlikely people.

Workplace Creativity: Myth and Modern Reality

Recent research has shattered a long-standing myth about creative employees. According to the myth, creative people are typically nonconformists. But Alan Robinson's field research paints a very different picture:

"We went to 450 companies in 13 countries and spoke to 600 people who'd done highly creative things, from big new innovations to tiny improvements," he explains. Only three

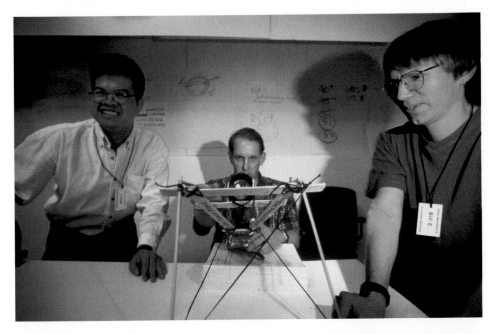

Okay, fire up your creativity. Your team has 90 minutes to build a contraption to propel a steel cannonball farther than those of competing teams. Lots of fun, but nonetheless serious business at Silicon Valley's Ideo, a product design company offering one-day creativity and innovation training sessions. Called Ideo U., the program helps trainees from the corporate world refine their brainstorming, teamwork, and implementation skills. Stand back! The slingshot rig pictured here just might work.

out of the 600 were true nonconformists. The rest were more like your average corporate Joe, much more "plodding and cautious" than most managers would expect. Other creativity studies have had similar results, he says.

One reason for the mismatch between popular perception and reality, he believes, is that so many steps are needed to bring most new ideas to fruition. Those who succeed must be able to build support for the idea among other team members, and they sometimes need a lot of patience as well. Corporate nonconformists may not have a great deal of either.[46]

Thus, creative self-expression through unconventional dress and strange behavior does not necessarily translate into creative work.

Today's managers are challenged to create an organizational culture and climate capable of surfacing the often hidden creative talents of *every* employee. In the Internet age, where intellectual capital is the number one resource, the emphasis is on having fun in high-energy work environments. For example, Theresa Garza, a vice president and general manager at Dell Computer, seeks to make the workplace "hum":

Not the whirling white noise emanating from your computer, but the very tangible sense of fully engaged people, channeling unbounded energy into their work. "You know it as soon as you enter a building," says Garza, general manager of Dell's large corporate-accounts group. "You can tell when a company feels dead just by walking through its halls. We try to create the hum. It's people who have momentum, who are working hard, and who are excited to be here."

To get hum, Garza has flung herself onto Velcro walls and had fellow employees dunk her in a water tank—all in the name of generating enthusiasm and encouraging accessibility.[47]

Learning to Be More Creative

Some people naturally seem to be more creative than others. But that does not mean that those who feel the need cannot develop their creative capacity. It does seem clear that creative ability can be learned, in the sense that our creative energies can be released from the bonds of convention, lack of self-confidence, and narrow thinking. We all have the potential to be more creative.[48]

The best place to begin is by trying consciously to overcome what creativity specialist Roger von Oech calls *mental locks.* The following mental locks are attitudes that get us through our daily activities but tend to stifle our creativity:

6 Identify and briefly describe five of the ten "mental locks" that can inhibit creativity.

1. *Looking for the "right" answer.* Depending on one's perspective, a given problem may have several right answers.
2. *Always trying to be logical.* Logic does not always prevail, given human emotions and organizational inconsistencies, ambiguity, and contradictions.
3. *Strictly following the rules.* If things are to be improved, arbitrary limits on thinking and behavior need to be questioned.
4. *Insisting on being practical.* Impractical answers to "what-if" questions can become steppingstones to creative insights.
5. *Avoiding ambiguity.* Creativity can be stunted by too much objectivity and specificity.
6. *Fearing and avoiding failure.* Fear of failure can paralyze us into not acting on our good ideas. This is unfortunate because we learn many valuable and lasting lessons from our mistakes.[49]

↗↘ Creativity and MTV   **8G**

Bob Pittman, who created MTV and VH-1 prior to becoming president of America Online, the Internet service giant:

My first piece of advice is to ignore conventional wisdom. Today when it comes to building companies, if you want to win big, you have to think different. A case in point: "Music is meant to be heard, not seen." My colleagues and I heard that over and over as we building MTV. Imagine if we had listened!

Source: "Bob Pittman," *Fast Company,* no. 27 (September 1999): 124.

Question: *When working on a creative new idea, how can you separate good advice from bad advice?*

Figure 8.7 | How Creative Are You?

Exercise: Assume that a steel pipe is embedded in the concrete floor of a bare room as shown below. The inside diameter is .06" larger than the diameter of a ping-pong ball (1.50") which is resting gently at the bottom of the pipe. You are one of a group of six people in the room, along with the following objects:

- *100' of clothesline*
- *Carpenter's hammer*
- *Chisel*
- *Box of Wheaties*
- *File*
- *Wire coat hanger*
- *Monkey wrench*
- *Light bulb*

List as many ways you can think of (in five minutes) to get the ball out of the pipe without damaging the ball, tube, or floor.

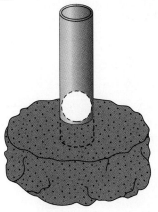

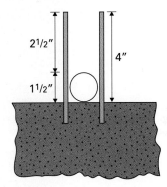

Source: From *Conceptual Blockbusting* by James L. Adams. © 1986 by James L. Adams. Reprinted by permission of Perseus Books Publishers, a member of Perseus Books, L.L.C.

7. *Forgetting how to play.* The playful experimentation of childhood too often disappears by adulthood.[50]
8. *Becoming too specialized.* Cross-fertilization of specialized areas helps in defining problems and generating solutions.
9. *Not wanting to look foolish.* Humor can release tensions and unlock creative energies. Seemingly foolish questions can enhance understanding.
10. *Saying "I'm not creative."* By nurturing small and apparently insignificant ideas we can convince ourselves that we are indeed creative.[51] (Try the creativity exercise in Figure 8.7.)

If these mental locks are conquered, the creative problem-solving process discussed in the next section can be used to its full potential.

Creative Problem Solving

We are all problem solvers. But this does not mean that all of us are good problem solvers or even, for that matter, that we know how to solve problems systematically. Most daily problem solving is done on a haphazard, intuitive basis. A difficulty arises, we look around for an answer, jump at the first workable solution to come along, and move on to other things. In a primitive sense, this sequence of events qualifies as a problem-solving process, and it works quite well for informal daily activities. But in the

7 List and explain the four basic steps in the creative problem-solving process.

Figure 8.8

The Problem-Solving Process

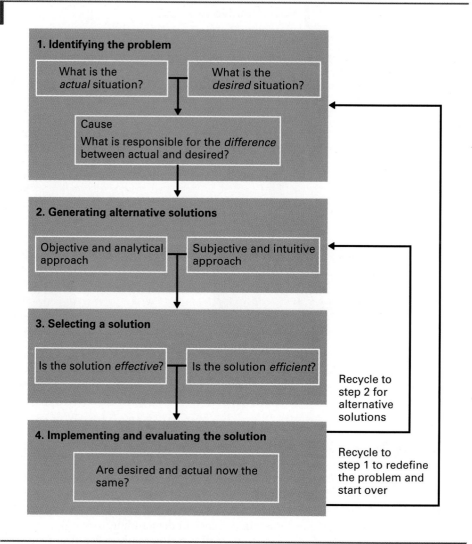

problem solving *conscious process of closing the gap between actual and desired situations*

world of management, a more systematic problem-solving process is required for tackling difficult and unfamiliar nonprogrammed decision situations. In the context of management, **problem solving** is the conscious process of bringing the actual situation closer to the desired situation.[52] Managerial problem solving consists of a four-step sequence: (1) identifying the problem, (2) generating alternative solutions, (3) selecting a solution, and (4) implementing and evaluating the solution (see Figure 8.8).

Identifying the Problem

As strange as it may seem, the most common problem-solving difficulty lies in the identification of problems. Busy managers have a tendency to rush into generating and selecting alternative solutions before they have actually isolated and understood the real problem. According to Peter Drucker, a respected management scholar, "the most common source of mistakes in management decisions is emphasis on finding the right answers rather than the right questions."[53] As problem finders, managers should probe for the right questions.[54] Only then can the right answers be found.

Problem finding can be a great career booster, too, as Michael Iem has discovered. It all started with his love of tough challenges.

> *This bricklayer's son has no formal job title and no office, but his career at Tandem Computers is on a tear. He personifies the advice that executive recruiter Robert Horton offers all who want to advance: "Find the biggest business problem your employer faces for which you and your skills are the solution.".... [Iem's problem-solving ability] made him known throughout Tandem, bringing promotions and a doubling of his $32,000 starting salary. . . . The company lets him decide what projects to take on, making him the youngest of perhaps a dozen employees with the broad mandate.*[55]

What Is a Problem?   Ask a half-dozen people how they identify problems and you are likely to get as many answers. Consistent with the definition given earlier for problem solving, a **problem** is defined as the difference between an actual state of affairs and a desired state of affairs. In other words, a problem is the gap between where one is and where one wants to be. Problem solving is meant to close this gap. For example, a person in New York who has to make a presentation in San Francisco in 24 hours has a problem. The problem is not being in New York (the actual state of affairs), nor is it presenting in San Francisco in 24 hours (the desired state of affairs). Instead, the problem is the distance between New York and San Francisco. Flying would be an obvious solution. But, thanks to modern communications technology such as videoconferencing, there are ways to overcome the 2,934-mile gap without having to travel.

Managers need to define problems according to the gaps between the actual and the desired situations. A production manager, for example, would be wise to concentrate on the gap between the present level of weekly production and the desired level. This focus is much more fruitful than complaining about the current low production or wishfully thinking about high production. The challenge is discovering a workable alternative for closing the gap between actual and desired production.[56]

problem *the difference between actual and desired states of affairs*

Stumbling Blocks for Problem Finders.   There are three common stumbling blocks for those attempting to identify problems:

1. *Defining the problem according to a possible solution.* One should be careful not to rule out alternative solutions in the way one states a problem. For example, a manager in a unit plagued by high absenteeism who says, "We have a problem with low pay," may prevent management from discovering that tedious and boring work is the real cause. By focusing on how to close the gap between actual and desired attendance, instead of simply on low pay, management stands a better chance of finding a workable solution.
2. *Focusing on narrow, low-priority areas.* Successful managers are those who can weed out relatively minor problems and reserve their attention for problems that really make a difference. Formal organizational goals and objectives provide a useful framework for determining the priority of various problems. Don't be concerned with waxing the floor when the roof is caving in.
3. *Diagnosing problems in terms of their symptoms.* As a short-run expedient, treating symptoms rather than underlying causes may be appropriate. A bottle of aspirin is cheaper than trying to find a less stressful job, for example. In the longer run, however, symptoms tend to reappear and problems tend to get worse. There is a two-way test for discovering whether one has found the cause of a problem: "If I *introduce* this variable, will the problem (the gap) disappear?" or "If I *remove* this variable, will the problem (the gap) disappear?" **Causes,** then, are variables that, because of their presence or absence from the situation, are primarily responsible

causes *variables responsible for the difference between actual and desired conditions*

for the difference between the actual and the desired conditions. For example, the *absence* of a key can cause a problem with a locked door, and the *presence* of a nail can cause a problem with an inflated tire.[57]

8 Describe how causes of problems can be tracked down with fishbone diagrams.

Pinpointing Causes with Fishbone Diagrams.   Fishbone diagrams, discussed in Chapter 17 as a TQM process improvement tool, are a handy way to track down causes of problems. They work especially well in group problem-solving situations. Construction of a fishbone diagram begins with a statement of the problem (the head of the fish skeleton). "On the bones growing out of the spine one lists possible causes of . . . problems, in order of possible occurrence. The chart can help one see how various separate problem causes might interact. It also shows how possible causes occur with respect to one another, over time, helping start the problem-solving process."[58] (A sample fishbone diagram is illustrated in Skills & Tools at the end of this chapter.)

Generating Alternative Solutions

After the problem and its most probable cause have been identified, attention turns to generating alternative solutions. This is the creative step in problem solving. Unfortunately, as the following statement points out, creativity is often shortchanged.

> *The natural response to a problem seems to be to try to get rid of it by finding an answer—often taking the first answer that occurs and pursuing it because of one's reluctance to spend the time and mental effort needed to conjure up a rich storehouse of alternatives from which to choose.*[59]

It takes time, patience, and practice to become a good generator of alternative solutions: a flexible combination of analysis and intuition is helpful. A good sense of humor can aid the process as well.[60] Several popular and useful techniques can stimulate individual and group creativity. Among them are the following approaches:

- *Brainstorming.* A group technique in which any and all ideas are recorded, in a *nonjudgmental* setting, for later critique and selection.[61] Computerized brainstorming on computer network systems is proving worthwhile now that sophisticated "groupware" is available.[62]
- *Free association.* Analogies and symbols are used to foster unconventional thinking. For example, think of your studies as a mountain requiring special climbing gear and skills.
- *Edisonian.* Named for Thomas Edison's tedious and persistent search for a durable light bulb filament, this technique involves trial-and-error experimentation.
- *Attribute listing.* Ideal characteristics of a given object are collected and then screened for useful insights.
- *Scientific method.* Systematic hypothesis testing, manipulation of variables, situational controls, and careful measurement are the essence of this rigorous approach.

↗↙ **Something to *Think* About**   8H

Joey Reiman, an Atlanta-based creativity consultant:

Coming up with an idea requires investigation, incubation, illumination and illustration. We always forget about incubation. . . . Business is full of people who are crashing and burning because there is a tremendous pressure to constantly be producing. If you're just sitting at your desk thinking when someone asks what you are doing, what do you say? 'I was just thinking.' People devalue themselves by apologizing for thinking. . . .

Yet incubation is the most important step in the idea process. It's no surprise that great ideas come to us at unexpected times: when you go for a run, when you're in the shower. Those are some of the rare times in most people's busy days when their minds are free to explore. Great thinking is always simmering just below the surface.

Source: As quoted in Echo Montgomery Garrett, "Joey Reiman, Idea Man," *Management Review,* 88 (October 1999): 64.

Questions: *When and where do you usually do most of your creative thinking? How could you do a better job of "incubating" creative ideas?*

- *Creative leap.* This technique involves thinking up idealistic solutions to a problem and then working back to a feasible solution.[63]

Selecting a Solution

Simply stating that the best solution should be selected in step 3 (refer to Figure 8.8) can be misleading. Because of time and financial constraints and political considerations, *best* is a relative term. Generally, alternative solutions should be screened for the most appealing balance of effectiveness and efficiency in view of relevant constraints and intangibles. Russell Ackoff, a specialist in managerial problem solving, contends that three things can be done about problems: they can be resolved, solved, or dissolved.[64]

Resolving the Problem.   When a problem is resolved, a course of action that is good enough to meet the minimum constraints is selected. The term **satisfice** has been applied to the practice of settling for solutions that are good enough rather than the best possible.[65] A badly worn spare tire may satisfice as a replacement for a flat tire for the balance of the trip, although getting the flat repaired is the best possible solution. According to Ackoff, most managers rely on problem resolving. This nonquantitative, subjective approach is popular because managers claim they do not have the necessary information or time for the other approaches. Satisficing, however, has been criticized as a shortsighted and passive technique emphasizing expedient survival instead of improvement and growth.

satisfice *settling for a solution that is good enough*

optimize *systematically identifying the solution with the best combination of benefits*

idealize *changing the nature of a problem's situation*

Solving the Problem.   A problem is solved when the best possible solution is selected. Managers are said to **optimize** when through scientific observation and quantitative measurement they systematically research alternative solutions and select the one with the best combination of benefits.

Dissolving the Problem.   A problem is dissolved when the situation in which it occurs is changed so that the problem no longer exists. Problem dissolvers are said to **idealize** because they actually change the nature of the system in which a problem resides. Managers who dissolve problems rely on whatever combination of nonquantitative and quantitative tools is needed to get the job done. The replacement of automobile assembly-line welders with robots, for instance, has dissolved the problem of costly absenteeism among people in that job category.

Whatever approach a manager chooses, the following advice from Ackoff should be kept in mind: "Few if any problems . . . are ever permanently resolved, solved, or dissolved; every treatment of a problem generates new problems."[66] A Japanese manager at the General Motors–Toyota joint venture auto plant in California put it this way: "No problem is a problem."[67] However, as pointed out by the cofounder of a successful import business, an administrative life made up of endless problems is cause for optimism, not pessimism:

> **8I**
>
> ## Resolving, Solving, or Dissolving?
>
> Executives at Deere & Co. had a novel plan back in 1985. Concerned about runaway health-care costs, Deere founded its own health-maintenance organization. The company hoped that its Heritage National Healthplan could control spending while still providing adequate services to employees.
>
> As it turned out, Deere's HMO proved far more successful than executives at the company's Moline (Illinois) headquarters ever imagined. Besides putting the brakes on costs, it was a hit with Deere employees. Before long, Deere even began selling its HMO service to other companies. Today, only 22 percent of the HMO's 290,000 members have any relation to the agricultural-equipment manufacturer.
>
> *Source:* Kevin Kelly, "Deere's Surprising Harvest in Health Care," *Business Week* (July 11, 1994): 107.
>
> **Question:** *In this particular case, has a problem been resolved, solved, or dissolved? Explain.*

"Spare yourself some grief. Understand that, in business, you will always have problems. They are where the opportunities lie."[68] Hence the need for continuous improvement.

Implementing and Evaluating the Solution

Time is the true test of any solution. Until a particular solution has had time to prove its worth, the manager can rely only on his or her judgment concerning its effectiveness and efficiency. Ideally, the solution selected will completely eliminate the difference between the actual and the desired in an efficient and timely manner. Should the gap fail to disappear, two options are open. If the manager remains convinced that the problem has been correctly identified, he or she can recycle to step 2 to try another solution that was identified earlier. This recycling can continue until all feasible solutions have been given a fair chance or until the nature of the problem changes to the extent that the existing solutions are obsolete. If the gap between actual and desired persists in spite of repeated attempts to find a solution, then it is advisable to recycle to step 1 to redefine the problem and engage in a new round of problem solving.

Summary

1. Decision making is a fundamental part of management because it requires choosing among alternative courses of action. In addition to having to cope with an era of accelerating change, today's decision makers face the challenges of dealing with complexity, uncertainty, the need for flexible thinking, and decision traps. Seven factors contributing to decision complexity are multiple criteria, intangibles, risk and uncertainty, long-term implications, interdisciplinary input, pooled decision making, and value judgments.

2. Managers must learn to assess the degree of certainty in a situation—whether conditions are certain, risky, or uncertain. Confidence in one's decisions decreases as uncertainty increases. Managers can respond to a condition of risk—incomplete but reliable factual information—by calculating objective or subjective probabilities. Today's managers need to tap the creative potential of intuitive employees and the implementation skills of those who process information as thinkers.

3. Researchers have identified three perceptual and behavioral decision traps that can hamper the quality of decisions. Framing error occurs when people let labels and frames of reference sway their interpretations. People are victimized by escalation of commitment when they get locked into losing propositions for fear of quitting and looking bad. Oddly, researchers find overconfidence tends to grow with the difficulty of the task.

4. Decisions, generally, are either programmed or nonprogrammed. Because programmed decisions are relatively clear-cut and routinely encountered, fixed decision rules can be formulated for them. In contrast, nonprogrammed decisions require creative problem solving because they are novel and unfamiliar.

5. Managers may choose to bring other people into virtually every aspect of the decision-making process. However, when a group rather than an individual is responsible for making the decision, personal accountability is lost. Dispersed accountability is undesirable in some key decision situations. Group-aided decision making has both advantages and disadvantages. Because group performance does not always exceed individual performance, a contingency approach to group-aided decision making is advisable.

6. Creativity requires the proper combination of knowledge, imagination, and evaluation to reorganize experience into new configurations. The domains of creativity may be divided into art, discovery (the most relevant to management), and humor. Contrary to myth, researchers have found a weak link between creativity and nonconformity. A fun and energizing workplace climate can tap *every* employee's creativity. By consciously overcoming ten mental locks, we can become more creative.

7. The creative problem-solving process consists of four steps: (1) identifying the problem, (2) generating alternative solutions, (3) selecting a solution, and (4) implementing and evaluating the solution. Inadequate problem finding is common among busy managers. By seeing problems as gaps between an actual situation and a desired situation, managers are in a better position to create more effective and efficient solutions. Depending on the situation, problems can be resolved, solved, or dissolved. It is important to remember that today's solutions often become tomorrow's problems.

8. After making a problem the head of the fishlike skeleton in a fishbone diagram, "bones" can be added for clusters of related causes. Earlier causes are charted farther away from the head; later causes are charted closer to the head. Fishbone diagrams are particularly well suited to problem solving in groups, such as TQM teams.

Terms to Understand

Decision making (p. 228)

Condition of certainty (p. 232)

Condition of risk (p. 233)

Objective probabilities (p. 233)

Subjective probabilities (p. 233)

Condition of uncertainty (p. 233)

Framing error (p. 235)

Escalation of commitment (p. 235)

Programmed decisions (p. 237)

Decision rule (p. 237)

Nonprogrammed decisions (p. 238)

Collaborative computing (p. 241)

Creativity (p. 244)

Problem solving (p. 248)

Problem (p. 249)

Causes (p. 249)

Satisfice (p. 251)

Optimize (p. 251)

Idealize (p. 251)

How to Construct a Fishbone Diagram

Tips

- Reduce complex web of problems to a distinct, high-priority problem.
- Create fishbones for main categories of causes.
- Chart most recent causes nearest the head (problem).
- Fill in specific causes.

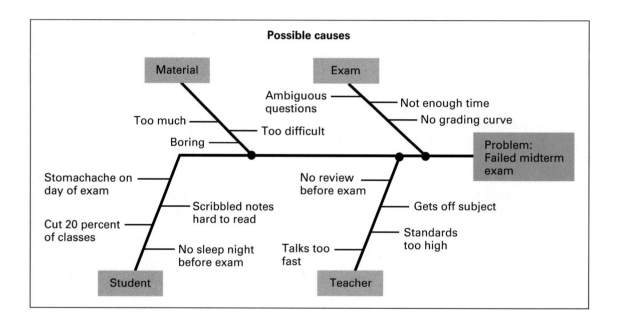

Internet Exercises

1. **Creativity in action:** 3M Company enjoys a worldwide reputation as an innovative company. Among its thousands of products are familiar items such as Scotch tape and Post-it notes as well as less familiar ones like surgical staplers and traffic signal lenses. According to the firm's cultural values, creativity generates new ideas and innovation turns those ideas into reality. The purpose of this exercise is to learn how 3M creates and exploits new ideas. 3M has prospered from new ideas in some interesting and unexpected ways.

   Log on to 3M's home page (**www.mmm.com/index.html**) and click on "More . . ." under the heading "About 3M." On the next two pages, select "Our Pioneers" and then "Innovation Chronicles." From the collection of 21 short stories about 3M innovators, find a product category that interests you and read the story. You may want to read three or four different stories to find a particularly interesting and/or instructive one. Three recommended stories are "Dick Drew and the invention of masking tape," "Art Fry and the invention of Post-it notes," and "How Harry Heltzer and his glass beads produced 3M's first reflective sheeting." As you read your selected stories, keep the following questions in mind.

   Learning Points: 1. What was the creative idea that got things going? 2. What barriers or obstacles did the innovator encounter? How were they avoided or overcome? 3. Did the innovator get help from others? What sorts of help? 4. How did 3M foster a good climate for creativity and innovation? 5. How important was plain old persistence? Explain.

2. **Check it out:**   Sometimes our creativity needs a boost and our inspiration needs a jump start. A good departure point is **www.queendom.com,** a richly stocked Web site created by and for women, but equally valuable to men. Get your creativity cranked up by selecting the section "Mind-Stretching" from the main menu. Among the fun and challenging mind-stretching exercises are lots of trivia quizzes (*Warning:* the "Sexuality & Health" category may be a bit too frank for some, but the rest are fine), jigsaw puzzles, and puzzles. *Note:* This Internet resource also has a great selection of automatically scored self-assessment and personality tests under the main menu heading "Tests, Tests, Tests. . . ."

For updates to these exercises, visit our Web site (**www.hmco.com/college**).

Creativity Helps Hallmark "Send the Very Best"

Closing Case

For 54 years, Hallmark cards has cared "enough to send the very best," in the process becoming the fourth leading brand in America outranking Chiquita, Disney and Levi's, according to Equitrend's annual ranking of the top ten world-class brands. The slogan itself, penned by a Hallmarker in 1944, has become its own American icon repeated in Hallmark print and television advertising for more than 50 years.

Producing greeting cards that have expressed emotions from joy to sorrow and everything in between, this family-owned company, started by J. C. Hall in 1910, really took off during the Depression when the average American might have been able to afford a card but not much else to mark a special occasion.

While most Hallmark cards disappear from radar after two years, at least two have lasted over the decades with a combined sales record of more than 64 million copies.

One of these, a 19-year-old card called "Three Little Angels," has delivered Christmas greetings over 36 million times, bringing in the equivalent of $22 million over the years. Not bad for an average $2 sale.

A 90-cent friendship card featuring a cart full of purple pansies that reads, "To let you know I am thinking of you . . . Pansies always stand for thoughts—at least that's what folks say. So this just comes to show my thoughts are there with you today," has sold 28 million since its inception in 1939. It still sells to the tune of 500,000 cards each year.

A business founded on the basic human need for nurturing relationships, Hallmark's best sales strategy remains creating brand insistence. Get card customers to

insist on nothing but Hallmark. And get the Hallmark creative staff to think about what will touch the hearts of consumers.

It takes 740 creative people to produce 18,000 new Hallmark greeting cards each year. To manage that creative energy, CEO Irv Hockaday says, "We have the largest creative staff in the world. If you mismanage, it's like a sack full of cats. You have to strike a balance between defining for them generally what you want and then giving them a lot of running room to try ways to respond to it. You don't overmanage, but you anchor them in well-articulated consumer needs. Then allow them exposure to all kinds of trends going on. We encourage them to travel and we support their traveling. They follow fashion trends, go to museums, look at what the automotive industry is doing in terms of design and color pallets. We have a wonderful pastoral environment, a retreat where they can go and reflect." Hockaday also understands why people buy cards, saying, "We help our customers create a more enduring bond in a time when relationships are fleeting and allegiances are brief."

FOR DISCUSSION

1. Can you motivate employees to be creative? How? Explain.

2. What do you suppose is Hallmark's greatest problem in managing such a large creative staff?

3. Which aspect of Hallmark's creative environment would most effectively stimulate *your* creativity?

4. What else could Hallmark do to foster a supportive climate for creativity?

Source: "Caring Enough," *Selling Power,* 19 (June 1999): 18. Copyright 1999–2000 by *Selling Power.* Reprinted by permission of the publisher.

VIDEO SKILL BUILDERS

Since 1982, when Mary Guerrero-Pelzel became a general contractor in Austin, Texas, Pelzel Construction has faced tough challenges. Heavy construction historically has been a male-dominated field, but Guerrero-Pelzel has thrived because her suppliers, subcontractors, and customers trust her to get the job done properly and on time. She earned that trust by carefully watching costs, keeping her employee teams motivated, and maintaining tight control.

2A Mary Guerrero-Pelzel, Contractor

Learning objectives: To learn more about the marriage of planning and control. To appreciate how a project manager needs to balance the little details and the big picture.

Links to textual material: *Chapter 6:* Planning/control cycle; Project planning *Chapter 7:* Porter's generic competitive strategies *Chapter 8:* Decision complexity

Discussion questions

1. Using Figure 6.4 as a guide, how is the planning/control cycle demonstrated in this video case?
2. Relative to Figure 6.6, why is Guerrero-Pelzel an effective project manager?
3. Which of Porter's generic competitive strategies (see Figure 7.1) is Pelzel Construction using?
4. Which sources of decision complexity (see Figure 8.1) are evident in this video case? Explain your choices.

Hot sauce maker Dat'l Do-It has a unique strategic competitive advantage: The fiery datil peppers from which its sauces and relishes are made grow only in the company's home region of St. Augustine, Florida. Founder Christopher Way enlists the help of Kodo Matsumoto to penetrate foreign markets in Japan and possibly elsewhere.

2B A Florida Hot Sauce Goes International

Learning objective: To learn more about international strategic management.

Links to textual material: *Chapter 4:* The internationalization process *Chapter 7:* Strategy-making modes; Synergy; E-commerce; SWOT analysis

Discussion questions

1. Which step in the six-step internationalization process would be most appropriate for Dat'l Do-It at this time? Why?
2. What strategy-making mode is evident here? What are its advantages and drawbacks?
3. What types of synergy are evident in this video case? Explain.
4. What sort of e-commerce strategy would you recommend for Dat'l Do-It?
5. What does your SWOT analysis of this case tell you about the firm's direction?

Part Three

ORGANIZING, MANAGING HUMAN RESOURCES, and COMMUNICATING

ORGANIZATIONS

Structure, Effectiveness, and Cultures

CHAPTER OBJECTIVES

When you finish studying this chapter, you should be able to

1 Identify and describe four characteristics common to all organizations.

2 Identify and explain the two basic dimensions of organization charts.

3 Contrast the traditional and modern views of organizations.

4 Describe a business organization in terms of the open-system model.

5 Explain the term *learning organization*.

6 Explain the time dimension of organizational effectiveness.

7 Explain the role of complacency in organizational decline and discuss the ethics of downsizing.

8 Describe at least three characteristics of organizational cultures and explain the cultural significance of stories.

**"EQUIP PEOPLE TO MAKE DECISIONS
BY CLEARLY DEFINING THE CULTURE."**
kevin and jackie freiberg

THE CHANGING WORKPLACE

Dave Neenan's *Learning* Organization

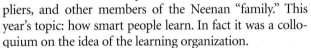

Disaster struck Dave Neenan in 1978 when his new and struggling construction business lost $1 million on a single project. With his net worth hovering in the neighborhood of $90,000, Chapter 11 [bankruptcy] seemed the only option. His financial advisers encouraged him to hang it up. Only his handful of remaining employees urged him to keep going.

Neenan found that he had no stomach for attempting a turnaround if the only goal would be a return to business as usual in an industry rife with litigation, interpersonal conflict, and too many win-loss situations between stakeholders. Dragging his firm back from the brink would be worth the struggle, he decided, only if the company emerged as something quite new and different. "Somehow or another," says Neenan, "we had to figure out how to [keep] our souls and make money with dignity."

Today, Denver-based Neenan Construction is a healthy, 150-employee outfit. CEO Neenan calls it an "archistruction" company. The term is meant to refer not only to the fact that the operation handles both architecture and construction, but also to a particular way of doing business. Neenan Construction uses concurrent-engineering principles to develop its projects, bringing together customers, architects, subcontractors and financial backers to work cooperatively from the start.

In 1990, with the publication of Peter Senge's *The Fifth Discipline*, a new term gained national currency, one that seemed to capture the spirit of what Neenan meant by "keeping our souls and making money with dignity." Neenan's goal now, he says, is to create a "learning organization."

His own role in this organization? Teacher. He has done a lot of prepping for the part. In the early '80s, he set out to learn everything he could about doing business. "You name it, I took it," says Neenan of the wide variety of educational courses in which he participated. He finally developed a public seminar of his own, called "Business and You," which he delivers six to eight times a year, mostly in Eastern Europe and in the Pacific Rim. From time to time he also consults with private companies. But most of the training he conducts is for his own employees.

Every Monday morning Neenan meets with about 60 of his employees in a session that usually evolves into a learning event. He questions people about the projects they're working on, pressing for details and fishing for better ideas. One recent meeting turned into a discussion about how every employee can serve to inspire others to do their best work.

Once a year, Neenan sponsors a two-day conference on the concept of archistruction. He estimates that he pumps $30,000 to $50,000 into each event, inviting employees, customers, subcontractors, suppliers, and other members of the Neenan "family." This year's topic: how smart people learn. In fact it was a colloquium on the idea of the learning organization.

Neenan also pays about $5,000 a month to a personal coach who helps him and his core team of six people. The coach (a CEO from a *Fortune* 500 company) sends weekly assignments to Neenan's team via e-mail. A typical assignment might include questions such as, "What's the difference between defensive and productive reasoning?" or, "How should you intervene with an employee who isn't making the grade?"

Neenan plans to launch a program next year in which all employees can take ten days out of the year to work on their improvement. "I am totally committed to [building] a learning organization," he vows.

Neenan is not dewy-eyed about the fuzzy, glowing rapture of "learning," however. In his experience, he says, the most powerful learning experiences also tend to be the most painful. He includes depression, anxiety, fear and sadness in the emotional baggage that accompanies learning. He warns that creating a learning organization is not about making people comfortable. Indeed, a key question is, "What can we do organizationally to create a context for learning, given the fact that learning sometimes isn't the most pleasant thing that people go through?"

As far as Neenan is concerned, the "learning organization" concept is ultimately about personal accountability. The real challenge, he says, is to help his employees become accountable for their work, their careers and, on a broader level, their lives. "What kind of training program or what kind of learning organization [will it take] to get all employees to accept responsibility for their own experience within the firm?" he asks. He doesn't claim to have found the answer yet. But he's looking.

Organizations are an ever-present feature of modern industrial society. We look to organizations for food, clothing, education, employment, entertainment, health care, transportation, and protection of our basic rights. Nearly every aspect of modern life is influenced in one way or another by organizations. As Dave Neenan's struggle to achieve greater competitiveness demonstrates, the management of modern organizations requires bold and imaginative action.

In Chapter 1 we said the purpose of the management process is to achieve *organizational* objectives in an effective and efficient manner. Organizations are social entities that enable people to work together to achieve objectives they normally could not achieve working alone. This chapter explores the organizational context in which managers operate. It serves as an introduction, laying the foundation for the discussion of organization design alternatives in Chapter 10. Specifically, this chapter defines the term *organization* and discusses different types of organizations and organization charts. It contrasts traditional and modern (open-system) views in the evolution of organization theory and introduces the concept of the learning organization. The chapter also examines organizational effectiveness as a backdrop for a discussion of organizational decline. Finally, it explores organizational cultures.

What Is an Organization?

organization *cooperative and coordinated social system of two or more people with a common purpose*

An **organization** is defined as a cooperative social system involving the coordinated efforts of two or more people pursuing a shared purpose.[1] In other words, when people gather and formally agree to combine their efforts for a common purpose, an organization is the result.

There are exceptions, of course, as when two individuals agree to push a car out of a ditch. This task is a one-time effort based on temporary expediency. But if the same two people decide to pool their resources to create a towing service, an organization would be created. The "coordinated efforts" portion of our definition, which implies a degree of formal planning and division of labor, is present in the second instance but not in the first.

Common Characteristics of Organizations

1 **Identify and describe four characteristics common to all organizations.**

According to Edgar Schein, a prominent organizational psychologist, all organizations share four characteristics: (1) coordination of effort, (2) common goal or purpose, (3) division of labor, and (4) hierarchy of authority.[2]

Coordination of Effort.   As discussed in the last chapter, two heads are sometimes better than one. Individuals who join together and coordinate their mental and/or physical efforts can accomplish great and exciting things. Building the great pyramids, conquering polio, sending manned flights to the moon—all these achievements far exceeded the talents and abilities of any single individual. Coordination of effort multiplies individual contributions.

Common Goal or Purpose.   Coordination of effort cannot take place unless those who have joined together agree to strive for something of mutual interest. A common goal or purpose gives the organization focus and its members a rallying point.

Division of Labor.   By systematically dividing complex tasks into specialized jobs, an organization can use its human resources efficiently. Division of labor permits each organization member to become more proficient by repeatedly doing the same specialized task. (But, as is discussed in Chapter 13, overspecialized jobs can cause boredom and alienation.)

The advantages of dividing labor have been known for a long time. One of its early proponents was the pioneering economist Adam Smith. While touring an eighteenth-century pin-manufacturing plant, Smith observed that a group of specialized laborers could produce 48,000 pins a day. This was an astounding figure, considering that each laborer could produce only 20 pins a day when working alone.[3]

Hierarchy of Authority.   According to traditional organization theory, if anything is to be accomplished through formal collective effort, someone should be given the authority to see that the intended goals are carried out effectively and efficiently. Organization theorists have defined **authority** as the right to direct the actions of others. Without a clear hierarchy of authority, coordination of effort is difficult, if not impossible, to achieve. Accountability also is enhanced by having people serve in what is often called, in military language, the *chain of command*. For instance, a grocery store manager has authority over the assistant manager, who has authority over the produce department head, who in turn has authority over the employees in the produce department. Without such a chain of command, the store manager would have the impossible task of directly overseeing the work of every employee in the store.

9A

Back to the Opening Case

What sort of message does Dave Neenan's strategic goal of creating "a learning organization" send to the company's employees, suppliers, and customers?

For further information about the interactive annotations in this chapter, visit our Web site (**www.hmco.com/college**).

authority   *right to direct the actions of others*

Although the definition and common characteristics of organizations are identical the world around, the same cannot be said for organizational life. Americans, for example, wrestled with the insecurity of restructurings and layoffs, while their Japanese counterparts traditionally enjoyed the security of lifetime employment. Because of global competition, however, things are changing in Japan. Some of these Japanese factory workers may find themselves out of work as automaker Nissan cuts its workforce in an attempt to pull out of a losing skid.

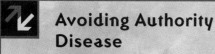

Avoiding Authority Disease   9B

Donald G. Smith, retired manager:

One of the most difficult things that a new boss must do is to back off and leave things alone. For people who are actively engaged in climbing the corporate ladder, it means they must do battle with their own ambition. I have seen such people make the most superficial of unnecessary changes: rearranging the furniture, making lateral personnel switches. Employees recognize these silly charades for what they are, namely futile exercises in demonstrating authority.

Source: Donald G. Smith, "Fighting the Ego Monster," *Training*, 36 (February 1999): 84.

Questions: *Why do new managers often get carried away with their authority? What sort of response do authoritarian managers generally get in today's workplaces? Explain. How do effective managers handle their authority?*

The idea of hierarchy has many critics, particularly among those who advocate flatter organizations with fewer levels of management.[4] An organization theorist answered those critics as follows:

> *At first glance, hierarchy may seem difficult to praise. Bureaucracy is a dirty word even among bureaucrats, and in business there is a widespread view that managerial hierarchy kills initiative, crushes creativity, and has therefore seen its day. Yet 35 years of research have convinced me that managerial hierarchy is the most efficient, the hardiest, and in fact the most natural structure ever devised for large organizations. Properly structured, hierarchy can release energy and creativity, rationalize productivity, and actually improve morale.[5]*

Putting All the Pieces Together.   All four of the foregoing characteristics are necessary before an organization can be said to exist. Many well-intentioned attempts to create organizations have failed because something was missing. In 1896, for example, Frederick Strauss, a boyhood friend of Henry Ford, helped Ford set up a machine shop, supposedly to produce gasoline-powered engines. But while Strauss was busy carrying out his end of the bargain by machining needed parts, Ford was secretly building a horseless carriage in a workshop behind his house.[6] Although Henry Ford eventually went on to become an automobile-industry giant, his first attempt at organization failed because not all of the pieces of an organization were in place. Ford's and his partner's efforts were not coordinated, they worked at cross-purposes, their labor was vaguely divided, and they had no hierarchy of authority. In short, they had organizational intentions, but no organization.

Classifying Organizations

Because organizations are created to pursue particular purposes, they can be classified accordingly. The classification by organizational purpose discussed here has four categories: business, nonprofit service, mutual-benefit, and commonweal organizations.[7] Some of today's large and complex organizations overlap categories. For example, religious organizations are both nonprofit service organizations and mutual-benefit organizations. Nevertheless, classifying organizations by their purpose helps clarify the variety of roles they play in society and the similar problems shared by organizations with similar purposes (see Table 9.1).

Business Organizations.   Business organizations such as General Mills, United Airlines, and the Washington Post all have one underlying purpose: to make a profit in a socially acceptable manner. Businesses cannot survive, let alone grow, without earning a profit, and profits are earned by efficiently satisfying demand for products and services. This economic production function is so important to society that many think immediately of business when the word *management* is mentioned.

Table 9.1

Classifying Organizations by Their Intended Purpose

Purpose	Primary beneficiary	Common examples	Overriding management problem
Business	Owners	Computer manufacturers Newspapers Railroads Fast-food restaurant chains	Must make a profit
Nonprofit service	Clients	Universities Welfare agencies Hospitals (nonprofit)	Must selectively screen large numbers of potential clients
Mutual-benefit	Members	Unions Clubs Political parties Trade associations Cooperatives	Must satisfy members' needs
Commonweal	Public at large	U.S. Postal Service Police departments Fire departments Public schools	Must provide standardized services to large groups of people with diverse needs

Nonprofit Service Organizations. Unlike businesses, many organizations survive and even grow, without making any profits at all. They need to be solvent, of course, but they measure their success not in dollars and cents but by how well they provide a specific service for some segment of society. The American Heart Association, Notre Dame University, and Massachusetts General Hospital are examples of nonprofit service organizations. Because the services of such organizations are usually in great demand, one of their biggest problems lies in screening large numbers of applicants to determine who qualifies for service. Another problem for most nonprofit service organizations is securing a reliable stream of funds through fees, donations, grants, or appropriations. Given today's limited resources, both private-sector and public-sector nonprofit service organizations are under pressure to operate more efficiently.[8]

Mutual-Benefit Organizations. Often, as in the case of labor unions or political parties, individuals join together strictly to pursue their own self-interests. In other cases—the National Association of Manufacturers, for example—organizations may feel compelled to join together in an umbrella organization. Mutual-benefit organizations, like all other types of organizations, must be effectively and efficiently managed if they are to survive. In this instance, survival depends on satisfying members' needs.

9C

Peter Drucker Sees a Nonprofit in Your Future

For the first time in human history, people can expect to outlive the organizations that they work for. As we live longer and work for more years, we risk becoming "too good" at what we do. Work that felt challenging when we were in our thirties may feel dull when we reach our fifties—at which point we have 20 years left in our careers.

So we need new ways to manage the "second half" of our work lives. That might mean retraining yourself for a different kind of job. It might mean developing a "parallel career"—for example, working in a nonprofit organization that interests you while cutting back on your regular job. It might mean doing the same kind of work that you've done, but in a different setting.

Source: "Peter Drucker," *Fast Company,* no. 27 (September 1999): 112.

Questions: *What particular nonprofit organization would likely offer you new challenge and meaning later in your career? Explain. Does Drucker's concept of a parallel career appeal to you? Explain.*

Commonweal Organizations.   Like nonprofit service organizations, commonweal organizations offer public services without attempting to earn a profit. But unlike nonprofit service organizations, which serve some *segment* of society, a **commonweal organization** offers standardized service to *all* members of a given population. The Canadian Army, for example, protects everyone within Canada's borders, not just a select few. The same can be said for local police and fire departments. Commonweal organizations generally are large, and their great size makes them unwieldy and difficult to manage. Competing demands from a diverse array of clients also complicate matters. Phoenix, Arizona, Fire Department Chief Alan Brunacini makes sure his firefighters have their priorities straight as they stand ready to do everything from fighting fires to administering emergency medical treatment to rescuing pets. "Brunacini expresses his philosophy in a succinct, five-word mission statement: 'Prevent harm; survive; be nice.'"[9]

commonweal organization
nonprofit organization serving all members of a given population

Organization Charts

An **organization chart** is a diagram of an organization's official positions and formal lines of authority. In effect, an organization chart is a visual display of an organization's structural skeleton. With their familiar pattern of boxes and connecting lines, these

organization chart *visual display of organization's positions and lines of authority*

Excuse me, anyone smell something burning? These Oregon firefighters are not being inattentive; they've just finished putting out repeated blazes in this condemned house. While these firefighters may share a common profession, they could work for very different types of organizations. Volunteer firefighters generally work for nonprofit service organizations. Reflecting the trend toward privatization of public agencies, others might work for profit-seeking businesses. Those employed by local governments work for commonweal organizations.

charts (called tables by some) are a useful management tool because they are an organizational blueprint for deploying human resources. Organization charts are common in both profit and nonprofit organizations.

Vertical and Horizontal Dimensions

Every organization chart has two dimensions, one representing *vertical hierarchy* and one representing *horizontal specialization*. Vertical hierarchy establishes the chain of command, or who reports to whom. Horizontal specialization establishes the division of labor. A short case tracing the growth of a new organization helps demonstrate the relationship between vertical hierarchy and horizontal specialization.

2 Identify and explain the two basic dimensions of organization charts.

A Case Study: The Growth of an Organization

For years, George Thomas was an avid trout fisherman.[10] The sight of George loading up his old camper with expensive fly-casting gear and heading out to the nearest trout stream was familiar to his family and neighbors. About six years ago, George tried his hand at the difficult task of tying his own trout flies. Being a creative individual and a bit of a handyman, George soon created a fly that trout seemingly fought over to bite. Word spread rapidly among local and regional fishing enthusiasts. Eventually, George was swamped with orders for his newly patented Super Flies at $3.50 each. What had started out as a casual hobby turned into a potentially lucrative business bringing in roughly $500 per week. George no longer found any time to fish; all his time was taken up tying and selling Super Flies. An organization chart at that point would have looked like the one in Figure 9.1A on page 266. George was the entire operation, and technically, an organization did not yet exist. There was no vertical hierarchy or horizontal specialization at that early stage.

George soon found it impossible to tie more than a couple hundred flies a week and still visit fishing-tackle retailers who might carry his Super Flies. To free some time, George hired and trained a family friend named Amy to help him run the operation in a small building he had leased. An organization chart could have been drawn up at that time because an organization came into existence when Amy was hired. (Remember that it takes at least two people to make an organization.) The chart would have resembled the one in Figure 9.1B. Vertical hierarchy had been introduced since Amy was George's subordinate. However, there still was no horizontal specialization because Amy did many different things.

As business picked up, George had to hire and train four full-time employees to work under Amy tying flies. He also hired Fred, a sharp salesman and an old fishing buddy, to head the marketing operation and recruit and train two regional sales representatives. Shortly afterward, an accountant was brought into the organization to set up and keep the books. Today, Super Fly, Inc., is recording annual sales in excess of $2.5 million. George has finally gotten around to formally organizing the company he built in patchwork fashion through the years. His current organization chart is displayed in Figure 9.1C.

Notice that the company now has three layers in the vertical hierarchy and three distinct forms of horizontal specialization. The three specialized directors now do separately what George used to do all by himself. George's job of general management will become progressively more difficult as additional vertical layers and horizontal specialists are added. Coordination is essential; the "right hand" must operate in concert with the "left hand." *Generally, specialization is achieved at the expense of*

Figure 9.1 | The Evolution of an Organization Chart

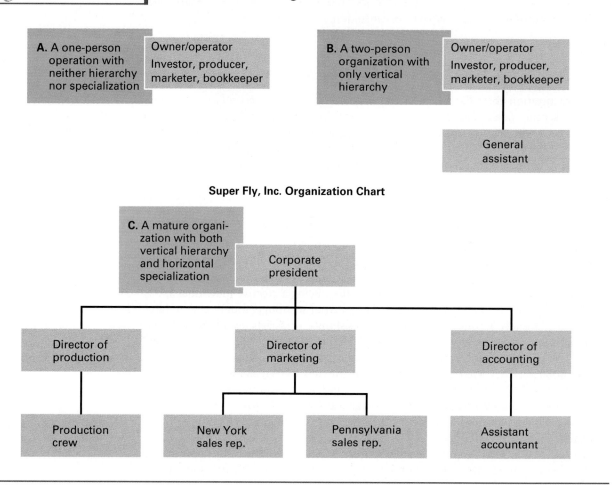

A. A one-person operation with neither hierarchy nor specialization

Owner/operator
Investor, producer, marketer, bookkeeper

B. A two-person organization with only vertical hierarchy

Owner/operator
Investor, producer, marketer, bookkeeper

General assistant

Super Fly, Inc. Organization Chart

C. A mature organization with both vertical hierarchy and horizontal specialization

Corporate president

Director of production

Director of marketing

Director of accounting

Production crew

New York sales rep.

Pennsylvania sales rep.

Assistant accountant

coordination when designing organizations. A workable balance between specialization and coordination can be achieved through contingency design, as discussed in the next chapter.

Contrasting Theories of Organization

3 Contrast the traditional and modern views of organizations.

The study of organization theory is largely a twentieth-century development. As one organization theorist philosophically observed, "The study of organizations has a history but not a pedigree."[11] This history is marked by disagreement rather than uniformity of thinking. A useful way of approaching the study of organization theory is to contrast the traditional view with a modern view, two very different ways of thinking about organizations.

	Traditional view	Modern view	Table 9.2
General perspective	Closed-system thinking	Open-system thinking	**Contrasting Theories of Organization**
Primary goal of organization	Economic efficiency	Survival in an environment of uncertainty and surprise	
Assumption about surrounding environment	Predictable	Generally uncertain	
Assumptions about organizations	All causal, goal-directed variables are known and controllable. Uncertainty can be eliminated through planning and controlling.	The organizational system has more variables than can be comprehended at one time. Variables often are subject to influences that cannot be controlled or predicted.	

Source: Adapted, by permission, from James D. Thompson, *Organizations in Action* (New York: McGraw-Hill, 1967), pp. 4–7.

In the traditional view, the organization is characterized by closed-system thinking. This view assumes the surrounding environment is fairly predictable and uncertainty within the organization can be eliminated through proper planning and strict control. An organization's primary goal is seen to be economic efficiency. In contrast, a prevailing modern view characterizes the organization as an open system interacting continuously with an uncertain environment. Both the organization and its surrounding environment are assumed to be filled with variables that are difficult to predict or control. As the open-system theorists see it, the organization's principal goal is survival in an environment of uncertainty and surprise. These contrasting approaches are summarized in Table 9.2.

The Traditional View

Let us explore the evolution of traditional organization theory by reviewing the contributions of the early management writers, Max Weber's concept of bureaucracy, and challenges to these traditional models. This will prepare the way for our examination of the modern open-system model of organizations.

The Early Management Writers.   Early contributors to management literature, such as Henri Fayol and Frederick W. Taylor, treated organizing as a subfield of management. You will recall from Chapter 1 that organizing was among Fayol's five universal functions of management. Taylor's narrow task definitions and strict work rules implied a tightly structured approach to organization design.

In general, Fayol and the other pioneering management writers who followed in his footsteps endorsed closely controlled authoritarian organizations. For instance, managers were advised to have no more than six immediate subordinates. Close supervision and obedience were the order of the day. Emphasis in these organizations was on the unrestricted downward flow of authority in the form of orders

Table 9.3

Traditional Principles of Organization

1. **A well-defined hierarchy of authority.** This principle was intended to ensure the coordinated pursuit of organizational goals by contributing individuals.
2. **Unity of command.** It was believed that the possibility of conflicting orders, a serious threat to the smooth flow of authority, could be avoided by making sure that each individual answered to only one superior.
3. **Authority equal to responsibility.** *Authority* was defined as the right to get subordinates to accomplish something. *Responsibility* was defined as the obligation to accomplish something. The traditionalists cautioned against holding individuals ultimately accountable for getting something done unless they were given formal authority to get it done.
4. **Downward delegation of authority but not of responsibility.** Although a superior with the requisite authority and responsibility can pass along the *right* to get something accomplished to subordinates, the *obligation* for getting it done remains with the superior. This arrangement was intended to eliminate the practice of "passing the buck."

and rules. Four traditional principles of organization that emerged were (1) a well-defined hierarchy of authority, (2) unity of command,[12] (3) authority equal to responsibility, and (4) downward delegation of authority but not of responsibility (see Table 9.3).

Max Weber's Bureaucracy.   Writing a hundred years ago, a German sociologist named Max Weber described what he considered to be the most rationally efficient form of organization, to which he affixed the label **bureaucracy.** According to Weber's model, bureaucracies are efficient because of the following characteristics: (1) division of labor, (2) hierarchy of authority, (3) a framework of rules, and (4) impersonality.[13] By *impersonality*, Weber meant hiring and promoting people on the basis of *what* they know, not *who* they know. It is important to realize that Weber's ideas about organizations were shaped by prevailing circumstances. In the late 1800s, Germany was a semifeudal state struggling to adjust to the pressures of the Industrial Revolution. Weber was appalled at the way public administrators relied on subjective judgment, emotion, fear tactics, and nepotism (the hiring and promotion of one's relatives) rather than on sound management practices.[14] He used the widely respected and highly efficient Prussian army as the model for his bureaucratic form of organization.

> **bureaucracy** *Weber's model of a rationally efficient organization*

In theory, Weber's bureaucracy was supposedly the epitome of efficiency. But experience with bureaucracies has shown that they can be slow, insensitive to individual needs, and grossly inefficient.[15] Today, the term *bureaucracy* has a strongly negative connotation. This bureaucratic paradox can be reconciled somewhat by viewing bureaucracy as a matter of degree.

Every systematically managed organization, regardless of its size or purpose, is to some extent a bureaucracy. Bureaucratic characteristics are simply more pronounced or advanced in some organizations than in others.[16] Trying to eliminate bureaucracy is impractical. The real challenge is keeping bureaucratic characteristics within functional limits. As Table 9.4 indicates, a moderate degree of bureaucratization can enhance organizational efficiency, but, taken too far, each dimension of bureaucracy can hinder efficiency. Managers who learn to read and retreat from the symptoms of dysfunction can reap the benefits of functional bureaucracy.[17]

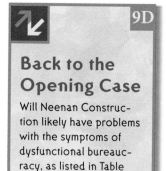

9D

Back to the Opening Case

Will Neenan Construction likely have problems with the symptoms of dysfunctional bureaucracy, as listed in Table 9.4, as it continues to grow? Explain.

Table 9.4

	Functional Versus Dysfunctional Bureaucracy: A Matter of Degree	
	Indications of functional bureaucracy	**Symptoms of dysfunctional bureaucracy**
Degree of bureaucratization	Moderate	High
Division of labor	More work, of higher quality, can be completed faster because complex tasks are separated into more readily mastered jobs.	Grievances, absenteeism, and turnover increase as a result of overly fragmented jobs that people find boring and dehumanizing. Poor-quality performance leads to customer complaints.
Hierarchy of authority	A generally accepted chain of command serves to direct individuals' efforts toward organizational goal accomplishment.	Due to a fear of termination, a climate of blind obedience to authority, whether right or wrong, exists.
Framework of rules	Individual contributions to the collective effort are directed and coordinated by rules that answer important procedural questions.	Pursuit of the organization's mission is displaced by the practice of formulating and enforcing self-serving rules that protect, create unnecessary work, hide, or disperse accountability.
Impersonality	Hiring, promotion, and other personnel decisions are made on the basis of objective merit rather than favoritism or prejudice.	Employees and clients complain about being treated like numbers by bureaucrats who fail to respond to the full range of human needs.

Challenges to the Traditional View of Organizations

Because the traditionalists' rigid recommendations for organizing and managing did not work in all situations, their recommendations were eventually challenged. Prescriptions for machinelike efficiency that worked in military units and simple shop operations often failed to work in complex organizations. Fayol's universal functions and principles turned out to be no guarantee of success. Similarly, experience proved that organizing was more than just the strict obedience to authority that Taylor had emphasized. In spite of Weber's rationally efficient organizational formula, bureaucracy in practice often became the epitome of inefficiency. In addition, challenges to traditional thinking about organizations arose from two other sources.

Bottom-Up Authority.   Traditionalists left no doubt about the origin of authority in their organizational models. Authority was inextricably tied to property ownership and therefore naturally flowed from the top of the organization to the bottom. In businesses, those farthest removed from the ownership of stock were entitled to the least amount of authority. Naturally, this notion appealed strongly to those interested in maintaining the power base of society's more fortunate members. But when Chester I. Barnard described organizations as cooperative systems, he questioned the traditional assumption about the automatic downward flow of authority. Instead, he proposed a

acceptance theory of authority   *Barnard's theory that authority is determined by subordinates' willingness to comply*

more democratic **acceptance theory of authority.** According to Barnard's acceptance theory, a leader's authority is determined by his or her subordinates' willingness to comply with it. Barnard believed that a subordinate recognizes a communication from above as being authoritative and decides to comply with it only when

1. The message is understood.
2. The subordinate believes it is consistent with the organization's purpose.
3. It serves the subordinate's interest.
4. The subordinate is able to comply.[18]

Barnard's acceptance theory opened the door for a whole host of ideas, such as upward communication and the informal organization that is based on friendship rather than work rules. Prior to Barnard's contribution, such concepts had been discussed only by human relationists. In effect, Barnard humanized organization theory by characterizing subordinates as active controllers of authority, not mere passive recipients. Interestingly, Barnard's empowerment theme has resulted in a distaste for the term *subordinate*, regarded today by many as a demeaning label.

Environmental Complexity and Uncertainty.   Although traditionalists liked to believe that rigid structure and rational management were important to organizational effectiveness and efficiency, environmental complexity and uncertainty often intervened to upset them. As Charles Perrow observed in writing about the history of organization theory, "The increasing complexity of markets, variability of products, increasing number of branch plants, and changes in technology all required more adaptive organizations."[19] Plans usually have to be made on the basis of incomplete or imperfect information and, consequently, things do not always work out according to plan. Similarly, many of the traditional principles of organization, such as the number of people a manager can effectively manage, have proved to be naive.

The net result of these and other challenges to traditional thinking was a desire to look at organizations in some new ways. When open-system thinking appeared on the management horizon, as discussed in Chapter 2, many eagerly embraced it because it emphasized the need for flexibility and adaptability in organization structure.

Organizations as Open Systems: A Modern View

Open-system thinking fosters a more realistic view of the interaction between an organization and its environment.[20] Traditional closed-system perspectives—such as Fayol's universal process approach, scientific management, and bureaucracy—largely ignored environmental influences. Today's managers cannot afford that luxury. Intense competition in a fast-changing world prompted Andy Grove, chairman of Intel Corp., to offer this view: "A corporation is a living organism, and it has to continue to shed its skin."[21]

Organizations are systems made up of interacting subsystems. Organizations are themselves subsystems that interact with larger social, political-legal, and economic systems. Those who take an open-system perspective realize that system-to-system interactions are often as important as the systems themselves. Among these interactions are movements of people in and out of the labor force (for example, unemployment), movements of capital (for example, stock exchanges and corporate borrowing), and movements of goods and services (for example, international trade). A highly

organized and vigorously interactive world needs realistically dynamic models. In this area, particularly,
open-system thinking can make a contribution to
organization theory.

Some Open-System Characteristics.   According
to general systems theory, all open systems—whether the
human body, an organization, a society, or the solar
system—share certain characteristics. At the same time,
the theory recognizes significant differences among the
various kinds of open systems. Four characteristics that
emphasize the adaptive and dynamic nature of all open
systems are (1) interaction with the environment, (2)
synergy, (3) dynamic equilibrium, and (4) equifinality.

- *Interaction with the environment.* Open systems have
  permeable boundaries, whereas closed systems do
  not. Open systems, like the human body, are not self-
  sufficient. Life-sustaining oxygen, nutrients, and
  water must be imported from the surrounding environment, and waste must be exported. Similarly,
  organizations depend on the environment for
  survival.
- *Synergy.* As discussed in Chapter 7, synergy is the
  1 + 1 = 3 effect. In other words, an open system
  adds up to more than the sum of its parts. A
  winning athletic team is more than its players,
  coaches, plays, and equipment. Only when all parts

are in place and working in concert can the winning edge be achieved. Likewise,
a successful business is more than the traditional factors of production—land,
labor, and capital. Synergistic thinking emphasizes that a firm's competitive edge
is dictated as much by how the factors of production are mobilized as by what
those factors are.

- *Dynamic equilibrium.* In open systems, **dynamic equilibrium** is the process of
  maintaining the internal balance necessary for survival by importing needed
  resources from the environment. Proper blood chemistry in the human body is
  maintained through dynamic equilibrium. When a person's blood sugar drops
  below normal, a craving for sugar prompts the ingestion of something sweet, thus
  increasing the blood-sugar level. Similarly, management can take out a loan when
  operations have drained the organization's cash reserves.
- *Equifinality.* Open systems are made up of more than fixed cause-and-effect link-
  ages. **Equifinality** means reaching the same result by different means. In their landmark book *Organization and Management*, Fremont Kast and James Rosenzweig
  summarize: "The concept of equifinality suggests that the manager can utilize a
  varying bundle of inputs into the organization, can transform them in a variety of
  ways, and can achieve satisfactory output."[22] For example, Nucor, a rapidly growing
  and highly profitable steel producer, is almost totally unlike traditional steel companies. Nucor builds its own mills, avoids debt, makes steel from scrap rather than
  ore, uses the latest energy-saving technology, and ties its nonunion employees'
  weekly bonuses to productivity.[23] Whereas America's steel giants have had to
  retrench in the face of stiff foreign competition, Nucor has thrived because of equifinality. In short, Nucor found a different (and better) way of getting the job done.

dynamic equilibrium
*process whereby an open system
maintains its own internal
balances with help from its environment*

equifinality   *open systems can
achieve similar ends through
different means*

Figure 9.2

Open-System Model of a Business

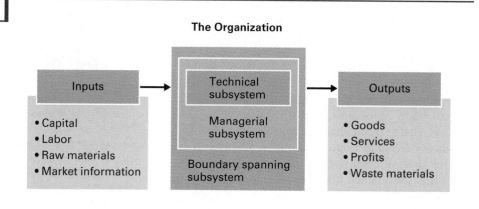

Developing an Open-System Model.   An open-system model encourages managers to think about organization-environment interaction (see Figure 9.2). A business must acquire various *inputs:* capital, either through selling stock or borrowing; labor, through hiring people; raw materials, through purchases; and market information, through research. On the *output* side of the model, goods and services are marketed, profits (or losses) are realized, and waste materials are discarded (if not recycled). There are other inputs and outputs as well. This open-system model, although descriptive of a business organization, readily generalizes to all types of organizations.

By using the open-system premise that systems are made up of interacting subsystems, we can identify three prominent organizational subsystems: technical, boundary-spanning, and managerial. Sometimes called the production function, the technical subsystem physically transforms raw materials into finished goods and services. But the ability to turn out a product does not in itself guarantee organizational survival. Other supporting subsystems working in concert are also needed.

Whereas technical subsystems may be viewed as being at an organization's very core, boundary-spanning subsystems are directed outward toward the general environment. Most boundary-spanning jobs, or interface functions, as they are sometimes called, are easily identified by their titles. Purchasing agents are responsible for making sure that the organization has a steady and reliable flow of raw materials and subcomponents. Public relations staff are in charge of developing and maintaining a favorable public image of the organization. Strategic planners have the responsibility of surveying the general environment for actual or potential opportunities and threats. Sales personnel probe the environment for buyers for the organization's goods or services. Purchasing agents, public relations staff, strategic planners, and sales personnel have one common characteristic: they all facilitate the organization's interaction with its environment. Each, so to speak, has one foot inside the organization and one foot outside.

Although the technical and boundary-spanning subsystems are important and necessary, one additional subsystem is needed to tie the organization together. As Figure 9.2 indicates, the managerial subsystem serves as a bridge between the other two subsystems. The managerial subsystem controls and directs the other subsystems in the organization. It is within this subsystem that the subject matter of this book is practiced as a blend of science and art.

4 **Describe a business organization in terms of the open-system model.**

According to the open-system concept of equifinality, there is more than one way to get the job done. Dramatic evidence of equifinality was spotted by race fans in 1989 at the Golden Gate Fields track in Albany, California. As Nate Hubbard, a 19-year-old apprentice jockey, guided Sweetwater Oak into the final stretch, the filly stumbled on the muddy track and Hubbard lurched out of the saddle, holding on to the horse's mane. Hubbard finished second. Officials declared it a legal ride because the jockey remained aboard the horse.

Extending the Open-System Model: The Learning Organization.   The idea of organizational learning, as briefly introduced in Chapter 2, dates back to the 1970s.[24] It took Peter Senge's 1990 best-seller, *The Fifth Discipline*, to popularize this extension of open-system thinking.[25] Many management writers and consultants then jumped on the bandwagon and confusion prevailed.

Fortunately, Harvard's David A. Garvin did a good job of sorting things out. According to Garvin, "A **learning organization** is an organization skilled at creating, acquiring, and transferring knowledge, and at modifying its behavior to reflect new knowledge and insights."[26] One could view Garvin and the others as having extended the open-system model of organizations by putting a human head on the biological (open-system) model. Garvin believes that organizational learning, just like human learning, involves three stages (see Figure 9.3 on page 274): (1) cognition (learning new concepts), (2) behavior (developing new skills and abilities), and (3) performance (actually getting something done). All three stages are required to erase the famous gap between theory and practice.

Also illustrated in Figure 9.3 are five organizational skills Garvin claims are needed to turn new ideas into improved organizational performance. Each skill is important if today's organizations are to *thrive*, not just survive.

- *Solving problems.* Problems, as discussed in Chapter 8, are the gap between actual and desired situations. Everyone in the organization needs to be skilled at finding problems and creatively solving them.

- *Experimenting.* W. Edwards Deming's plan-do-check-act (PDCA) cycle, covered in Chapter 17, is an excellent tool for learning through systematic experimentation.

5 Explain the term *learning organization.*

learning organization
one that turns new ideas into improved performance

↗↙ Back to the Opening Case   **9F**

Jim Collins, co-author of the best-selling book, *Built to Last: Successful Habits of Visionary Companies:*

. . . sadly, as we add years to our lives, it becomes increasingly difficult to remain dedicated learners. We become experts in our field and cease asking as many questions. We're all born as learning people, but most of us lose our innate curiosity and love of learning as we age. The more we know, the less we learn.

Source: Jim Collins, "The Learning Person," *Training*, 36 (March 1999): 84.

Question: *How does Neenan Construction keep the learning spark alive?*

Figure 9.3

Garvin's Model of the Learning Organization

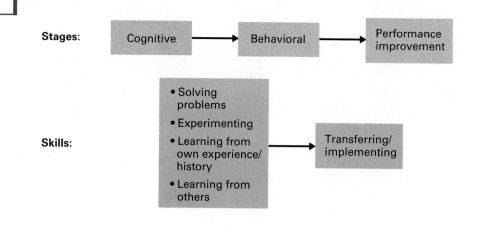

Source: Adapted from discussion in David A. Garvin, "Building a Learning Organization," *Harvard Business Review*, 71 (July–August 1993): 78–91.

- *Learning from organizational experience/history.* Role models and often-told stories of success and failure embedded in the organization's culture teach vital lessons. Also, as recently pointed out, creating an organization "that can concurrently harness innovation, initiative, and competence-building is a difficult task that often requires significant 'unlearning' of previous organizational practices."[27]
- *Learning from others.* Two prime sources of valuable knowledge in this regard are benchmarking, also discussed in Chapter 17, and customer input and feedback.
- *Transferring and implementing.* All the other skills are for naught if actions are not taken to make the organization perform better. Training (Chapter 11) and effective communication (Chapter 12) are key bridges spanning the gap between ideas and skills and superior organizational performance.

The concept of learning organizations is a valuable addition to organization theory because it explains how managers can deal with today's only certainty—*change*.[28] (For more, see Skills & Tools at the end of this chapter.)

Organizational Effectiveness

The practice of management, as defined in Chapter 1, challenges managers to use organizational resources effectively and efficiently. Effectiveness is a measure of whether or not organizational objectives are accomplished. In contrast, efficiency is the relationship between outputs and inputs. Only monopolies can get away with being effective but not efficient. Moreover, in an era of diminishing resources and increasing concern about civil rights, society is reluctant to label "effective" any organization that wastes scarce resources or tramples on civil rights. Management's definition of organizational effectiveness therefore needs to be refined. The related issue of organizational decline also needs to be understood and skillfully managed.

No Silver Bullet

According to one management scholar, "no single approach to the evaluation of effectiveness is appropriate in all circumstances or for all organizational types."[29] More and more, the effectiveness criteria for modern organizations are being prescribed by society in the form of explicit expectations, regulations, and laws. In the private sector, profitability is no longer the sole criterion of effectiveness.[30] Winslow Buxton, CEO of Pentair, Inc., a Minnesota manufacturing company with $2 billion in annual revenue and 10,000 employees, recently offered this perspective:

> *One of the most challenging aspects of my job is balancing the differing expectations of employees, management, customers, financial analysts, and investors. The common denominator for all these groups is growth. But this seemingly simple term has different connotations for each constituency, and a successful company must satisfy all of those meanings.*[31]

Moreover, today's managers are caught up in an enormous web of laws and regulations covering employment practices, working conditions, job safety, pensions, product safety, pollution, and competitive practices. To be truly effective, today's productive organizations need to strike a generally acceptable balance between organizational and societal goals. Direct conflicts, such as higher wages for employees and lower prices for customers, are inevitable. Therefore, the process of determining the proper weighting of organizational effectiveness criteria is an endless one requiring frequent review and updating.[32]

Assessing organizational effectiveness can be a tricky proposition, depending upon whose criteria are used. Take New York City developer Douglas Durst, for instance. His 48-story Times Square skyscraper has been lauded by environmentalists for including nontoxic building materials, solar-energy panels, on-site electricity generation, and other environmentally responsible features. Meanwhile, two deaths and a dozen injuries among construction crew members followed by assorted startup mishaps prompted the nickname "Times Square Titanic." Durst steadfastly claims to have taken architecture in a needed "green" direction.

Figure 9.4

The Time Dimension of Organizational Effectiveness

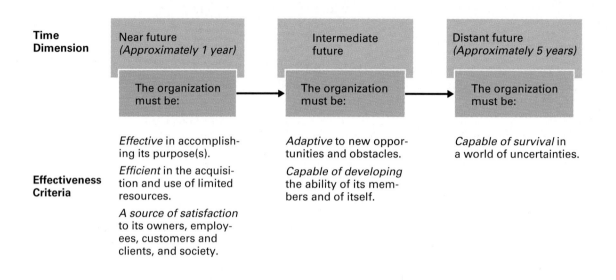

Time Dimension	Near future (Approximately 1 year)	Intermediate future	Distant future (Approximately 5 years)
	The organization must be:	The organization must be:	The organization must be:
Effectiveness Criteria	*Effective* in accomplishing its purpose(s). *Efficient* in the acquisition and use of limited resources. *A source of satisfaction* to its owners, employees, customers and clients, and society.	*Adaptive* to new opportunities and obstacles. *Capable of developing* the ability of its members and of itself.	*Capable of survival* in a world of uncertainties.

Source: Adapted from James L. Gibson, John M. Ivancevich, and James H. Donnelly Jr., *Organizations: Behavior, Structure, Processes*, 5th ed. (Homewood, Ill.: Richard D. Irwin, Inc.), p. 37. © 1991.

A Time Dimension

6 Explain the time dimension of organizational effectiveness.

organizational effectiveness *being effective, efficient, satisfying, adaptive and developing, and ultimately surviving*

To build a workable definition of organizational effectiveness, we shall introduce a time dimension. As indicated in Figure 9.4, the organization needs to be effective in the near, intermediate, and distant future. Consequently, **organizational effectiveness** can be defined as meeting organizational objectives and prevailing societal expectations in the near future, adapting and developing in the intermediate future, and surviving in the distant future.[33]

Most people think only of the near future. It is in the near future that the organization has to produce goods or render services, use resources efficiently, and satisfy both insiders and outsiders with its activity. But this is just the beginning, not the end. To grow and be effective, an organization must adapt to new environmental demands and mature and learn in the intermediate future (two to four years).[34]

Organizational Decline

Prior to the mid-1970s, North American managers sped along a one-way street to growth. Fueled by strong demand, corporations mushroomed in size and diversity of operations as they achieved ever-greater market shares. In recent years, however, unsteady economic growth, resource shortages, mismanagement, global competition, and the end of the cold war have taken their toll among industrial giants. Layoffs, retrenchments, cutbacks, and plant closings have become commonplace in the United States, despite a tightening labor market. The figures are stunning. Between 1995 and 1997, alone, an estimated 7.9 million U.S. workers received layoff notices.[35] Europe and Asia appear to be next in line as companies such as the British

Broadcasting Corporation and Japanese automaker Nissan announce unprecedented layoffs.

Turnaround specialists, hired to restore companies to health, have come to use terms like *downsizing, demassing,* and *reengineering* when shrinking and breaking up companies. This organizational revolution points up a fundamental short-coming of modern management theory and practice: We know a lot about striving for growth when times are good, but precious little about retreating when times are bad. Logic says what goes up must come down. According to a pair of experts on the subject, "Corporate performance almost always declines following a period of success."[36] These experts believe that *management complacency* is largely responsible for turning success into decline (see Figure 9.5). If allowed to persist, organizational decline can mean failure and bankruptcy. Today's managers must be adept at expanding, remaking, and sometimes shrinking their organizations, as conditions warrant.

Organizational decline is a weakened condition resulting from resource or demand restrictions and/or mismanagement. It typically involves a reduction in the size or scope of the organization.[37] For example, Lee Iacocca's turnaround team had to reduce Chrysler's size by 50 percent during its 1979–1981 brush with bankruptcy. Because that management era was preoccupied with growth, Iacocca had no textbook models, research base, or collection of proven techniques from which to learn. Thanks to recent interest in the management of organizational decline, an instructive body of theory, research, and practice is taking shape. Let us review that body of knowledge to better understand how managers can steer their organizations through the bad times that typically follow the good times.

> **7** Explain the role of complacency in organizational decline and discuss the ethics of downsizing.

> **organizational decline**
> *organization is weakened by resource or demand restrictions and/or mismanagement*

Figure 9.5 | Complacency Can Lead to Organizational Decline

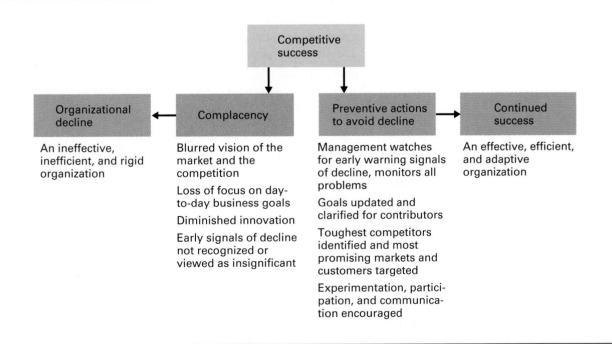

How to Kill Organizational Complacency   9G

Six Ways to Raise the Heat

- Create a crisis by allowing a financial loss to occur or an error to blow up.
- Eliminate obvious examples of excess like corporate jet fleets and gourmet dining rooms.
- Set targets like income, productivity, and cycle time so high that they can't be reached by doing business as usual.
- Share more information about customer satisfaction and financial performance with employees.
- Insist that people talk regularly to unsatisfied customers, unhappy suppliers, and disgruntled shareholders.
- Put more honest discussions of the firm's problems in company newspapers and management speeches. Stop senior management happy talk.

Source: John P. Kotter, "Kill Complacency," *Fortune* (August 5, 1996): 170.

Questions: *Which one of these tips is the best advice? Why? Which is the worst? Why? Do any of these tips raise any ethical problems? Explain.*

Characteristics of Organizational Decline

What are the characteristics or indicators of an organization in decline? A partial answer to this question came from a survey of 3,406 administrators at 334 four-year colleges in the United States.[38] Kim Cameron and his colleagues used six years of revenue data to divide the schools into three categories: growing, stable, and declining. They found that nine attributes (listed in Table 9.5) were statistically significant characteristics of organizational decline. The researchers were surprised to find that the same characteristics were associated with stable organizations, suggesting that all organizations are actually in one of two phases—either growth or decline. In short, an organization that has entered a period of stability has taken the first step toward decline.

Decline Dilemmas.   Of the nine characteristics of organizational decline presented in Table 9.5, five particularly troublesome dilemmas emerge. First, the leaders most needed by the organization tend to be the first to leave. For example, Apple Computer lost many key players as it slumped in 1996 and 1997.[39] Second, control is achieved at the expense of employee participation and morale. Third, when management needs to take long-term risks, short-term thinking and risk avoidance prevail. Fourth, conflict intensifies when teamwork is most needed. Finally, at precisely the time when changes are required, resistance to change is the greatest. Organizational decline is a cycle that feeds on itself and only gets worse if left unmanaged.

Decline Is a Never-Ending Challenge.   More research is required in this important area.[40] Meanwhile, to avoid being caught by surprise, managers need to anticipate and counteract the characteristics of decline (refer again to Figure 9.5). Seeds of decline are sown during periods of success, when management is most likely to become overconfident, arrogant, and complacent. At these times, Peter Drucker actually recommends stirring things up.

Characteristic	Description
Centralization	Decision making is passed upward, participation decreases, control is emphasized.
No long-term planning	Crisis and short-term needs drive out strategic planning.
Innovation curtailed	No experimentation, risk aversion, and skepticism about noncore activities.
Scapegoating	Leaders are blamed for the pain and uncertainty.
Resistance to change	Conservatism and turf protection lead to rejection of new alternatives.
Turnover	The most competent leaders tend to leave first, causing leadership anemia.
Low morale	Few needs are met, and infighting is predominant.
Nonprioritized cuts	Attempts to ameliorate conflict lead to attempts to equalize cutbacks.
Conflict	Competition and in-fighting for control predominate when resources are scarce.

Table 9.5

Nine Characteristics of Organizational Decline

Source: Characteristics and descriptions excerpted from Kim S. Cameron, David A. Whetten, and Myung U. Kim, "Organizational Dysfunction of Decline," *Academy of Management Journal*, 30 (March 1987): 128. Reprinted by permission.

One strategy is practically infallible: Refocus and change the organization when you are successful. *When everything is going beautifully. When everybody says, "Don't rock the boat. If it ain't broke, don't fix it." At that point, let's hope, you have some character in the organization who is willing to be unpopular by saying, "Let's* improve *it." If you don't improve it, you will go downhill pretty fast.*[41]

Kaizen, the Japanese philosophy of continuous improvement, is the best weapon against organizational decline.[42] Just ask the people at Boeing, the world's number-one manufacturer of commercial jet aircraft. The president of Boeing's Commercial Airplane Group is clear about the challenge: "We are dedicated to not doing what IBM, Sears Roebuck, and General Motors have done—which is to get to the top, be the best, and then get fat and lazy."[43] Boeing is reinventing itself by shortening product development cycles, shrinking inventories, and training *every* employee to be a world-class competitor.[44]

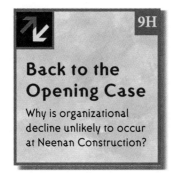

9H

Back to the Opening Case

Why is organizational decline unlikely to occur at Neenan Construction?

Downsizing: An Ethical Perspective

Downsizing has been defined simply as "the planned elimination of positions or jobs."[45] While generally associated with organizations in decline, mergers and acquisitions also can prompt downsizing, especially when jobs and/or facilities become redundant. For example, when Bank of America merged with neighboring Security Pacific Bank, unnecessary branches had to be closed. Whether due to decline or merger, the net result is the same—people lose their jobs. Ethical implications abound.

downsizing *planned elimination of positions or jobs*

Does Downsizing Work?   Based on recent research, the short answer is: *not nearly as well as expected.* An analysis of annual nationwide surveys by the American Management Association revealed the following:

. . . only 30 percent of companies implementing job cuts since 1990 reported an increase in worker productivity over the next year, and only 40 percent report an increase in subsequent years.

Similarly, just 45 percent of job-cutters experienced a rise in operating profits in either the year following a workforce reduction or over the longer term.[46]

Another survey of 1,000 companies found that downsizings yielded the expected savings only 34 percent of the time. This was the case because the companies tended to go through cycles of overstaffing, laying off, overstaffing, laying off, and so on.[47] If this scenario reminds you of the unhealthy weight control strategy of overeating and then crash dieting, you understand the problem.

Critics remind us that layoffs are traumatic for *everyone*—those who lose their jobs, the managers who must decide who stays and who goes, the community, and the survivors.[48] Managers who see their employees as a commodity to be hired when times are good and fired when times are bad are rightfully criticized for being shortsighted and unethical. The preferred model today views employees as valuable human resources requiring careful nurturing and career assistance in the event of a last-resort layoff[49] (see The Global Manager).

Making Layoffs a Last Resort.   Managers who view employees as valuable human resources have several progressive alternatives to sudden, involuntary layoffs.

- *Redeployment.* Displaced employees are retrained and/or transferred.[50] This approach amounts to a recycling program for human resources.
- *Downgrading.* To prevent a layoff, the organization moves displaced employees to unstaffed, lower-level jobs, avoiding pay cuts if possible.
- *Work sharing.* Instead of laying off a portion of its workforce, management divides the available work among all employees, who take proportional cuts in hours and pay. This approach has been called "share the gain, share the pain."
- *Job banks.* Work that would normally be out-sourced is kept in-house for employees caught in a downturn. For example, Harman International Industries, the Washington, D.C., maker of JBL and Infinity audio systems, calls its job bank program Off-Line Enterprises (OLÉ). At any time, a total of 15 to 20 jobs are available through OLÉ in four general categories:
  1. Manufacturing products usually purchased by external suppliers.
  2. Providing services such as security, which usually is contracted out.
  3. Converting waste by-products into marketable products, such as making clocks from scrap wood.
  4. Training and employing plant employees in Harman's nearby retail outlet.[51]
- *Voluntary early retirement and voluntary layoffs.* Employees are induced to leave the organization with offers of accelerated retirement benefits, severance pay, bonuses, and/or prepaid health insurance. This tactic can backfire if valued

9I

Is Training the Secret to Improving Productivity After a Layoff?

According to a 1998 survey by the American Management Association, companies that increase long-term training activity after downsizing are

- 80 percent more likely to increase worker productivity.
- More than twice as likely to report improvements in quality.
- 75 percent more likely to increase operating profits.
- 80 percent more likely to increase the value of their stock.

Unfortunately, training budgets typically are among the first items to be cut when times get tough.

Source: Marc Adams, "Training Employees as Partners," *HRMagazine,* 44 (February 1999): 66.

Questions: *Based on this information and what you have just read about the ethics of downsizing, what would you say to a top executive who is thinking about resorting to a big layoff?*

The Global Manager

Well-Managed Singapore Airlines Avoids Layoffs in Turbulent Times

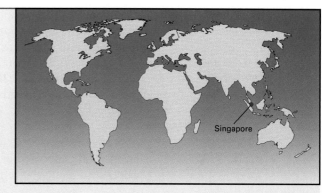

To fly Singapore Airlines, you'd never guess that these are difficult times for one of the world's most renowned airlines.

Even in economy class, complimentary champagne is flowing, and the menu features sautéed salmon with asparagus.

Never mind that operating profit plunged 42 percent in the April-September period, the latest for which results have been reported. Singapore has chopped $158 million out of its expenses, primarily by deferring delivery of 11 Boeing jets. The CEO and most of the airline's executives have frozen their salaries.

Yet in the passenger cabin, where Singapore has made its reputation as one of the world's best airlines for international travel, there's no sign of scrimping. In fact, the airline won 23 awards for its service from international tourism groups last year. . . .

"We have a reputation for service that we believe is unrivaled, and we want to keep it that way, so we must be ready to invest," says Singapore Airlines CEO Cheong Choong Kong. . . .

Singapore's strategy for tough times stands in contrast to what other airlines have done when they have faced financial difficulties.

Consider Delta Air Lines' actions in 1994. Its earnings had slumped after it bought some of Pan Am's routes, it struggled to compete against new low-cost airlines like ValuJet, and the U.S. economy faltered in the early 1990s. So the company announced it would cut 15,000 jobs and $2 billion or 16 percent from its annual operating costs. By 1997, Delta restored profits to record levels, but along the way, it lost its reputation for stellar service, employee morale suffered, and then CEO Ronald W. Allen was ousted. Airline officials admitted they had taken cost cutting too far.

How does Singapore do it?

One key point is Singapore Airlines was in strong financial shape, fortified with $1.1 billion in cash, when Asia's financial crisis started in Thailand in 1997. . . .

"Singapore Airlines has weathered this extremely well. They've suffered diminished profits but they are still very much in the black," says Peter Harbison, managing director of the Centre for Asia Pacific Aviation.

Other Asian airlines have had more difficulty. Philippine Airlines was forced to temporarily suspend operations, Indonesia's ailing Garuda airlines slashed its flight schedule, and Australia's Qantas stopped flying to South Korea. The Centre for Asia Pacific Aviation says 15 Asian airlines, including Korean Air, Air India, and Thai Airways, are seeking equity investors.

Unlike some of its competition, Singapore Airlines has avoided layoffs because it previously kept costs under control, Cheong says. In the past five years, the airline's flying capacity has increased 50 percent, but its administrative staff has stayed constant.

"We're emerging from this crisis better than the others because we have always been lean," he says.

Source: Excerpted from Sara Nathan, "Singapore Air Soars Through Asian Financial Crisis," *USA Today* (March 16, 1999): 10E. Copyright © 1999, USA Today. Reprinted with permission.

employees leave and poor performers stay. For example, "Eastman Kodak had to scurry to refill the jobs of 2,000 of the 8,300 workers who unexpectedly took its 1991 buyout offer."[52]

■ *Early warning of facility closings.* Imagine the pain of an unsuspecting employee who goes to work only to find a permanently locked gate. Several state legislatures in the United States have passed laws requiring companies to provide employees with some sort of advance warning of factory or office closings.[53] The Worker Adjustment and Retraining Notification Act, a federal law that went into effect in

1989, requires U.S. companies with 100 or more employees to give 60 days' notice of a closing or layoff.[54] Early warnings give displaced employees time to prepare financially and emotionally for a job change.

outplacement *the ethical practice of helping displaced employees find new jobs*

■ *Outplacement.* The practice of **outplacement** involves helping laid-off workers polish their job-seeking skills to increase their chances of finding suitable employment promptly.[55] This ethical practice can be costly.

■ *Helping layoff survivors.* The needs of these people have traditionally been ignored because, after all, they are the "lucky ones who still have their jobs." But research indicates that layoff survivors are stressed by overwork, uncertainty about future layoffs, and guilt over not suffering the same fate as their friends. Psychological and career counseling and retraining are appropriate and ethical options.[56]

Our discussions of organizational structure, effectiveness, and decline teach valuable lessons about the functioning of modern organizations. But the picture is not complete. A more subtle yet influential dimension of organizations remains to be explored. Managers who ignore this key dimension of organizations have little chance of success. So let's turn our attention to the interesting topic of organizational cultures to see what makes otherwise static structures come alive.

Organizational Cultures

organizational culture *shared values, beliefs, and language that create a common identity and sense of community*

The notion of organizational culture is rooted in cultural anthropology.[57] **Organizational culture** is the collection of shared (stated or implied) beliefs, values, rituals, stories, myths, and specialized language that foster a feeling of community among organization members.[58] Culture, although based largely on taken-for-granted or "invisible" factors, exerts a powerful influence on behavior. For example, a six-year study of more than 900 newly hired college graduates found significantly lower turnover among those who joined public accounting firms with cultures emphasizing respect for people and teamwork. New hires working for accounting firms whose cultures emphasized detail, stability, and innovation tended to quit 14 months sooner than their counterparts in the more people-friendly organizations. According to the researcher's estimate, the companies with people-friendly cultures saved $6 million in human resources expenses because of lower turnover rates.[59]

Some call organizational (or corporate) culture the "social glue" that binds an organization's members together. Accordingly, this final section binds together all we have said about organizations in this chapter. Without an appreciation for the cultural aspect, an organization is just a meaningless collection of charts, tasks, and people. An anthropologist-turned-manager offered these cautionary words:

> *Corporate culture is not an ideological gimmick to be imposed from above by management or management consulting firms but a stubborn fact of human social organization that can scuttle the best of corporate plans if not taken into account.[60]*

8 Describe at least three characteristics of organizational cultures and explain the cultural significance of stories.

Characteristics of Organizational Cultures

Given the number of variables involved, organizational cultures can vary widely from one organization to the next. Even so, authorities on the subject have identified six

Culture is what gives an organization its unique look and feel. Small companies, such as Evolution Film & Tape Inc. of North Hollywood, California, have an advantage over large companies because they tend to be more flexible. Owner Doug Ross wanted to hang on to his valued television production employees, so he created an employee-friendly company. Among his offerings: dress as you like, bring your kids, create your own work schedule, enjoy free health insurance, and here's a 401(k) retirement plan for contract workers. "Where do we sign?"

common characteristics.[61] Let us briefly examine these common characteristics to gain a fuller understanding of organizational cultures.

1. *Collective.* Organizational cultures are *social* entities. While an individual may exert a cultural influence, it takes collective agreement and action for an organization's culture to take on a life of its own. Organizational cultures are truly synergistic $(1 + 1 = 3)$.

2. *Emotionally charged.* People tend to find their organization's culture a comforting security blanket that enables them to deal with (or sometimes mask) their insecurities and uncertainties. Not surprisingly, people can develop a strong emotional attachment to their cultural security blanket. They will fight to protect it, often refusing to question its basic values. Corporate mergers often get bogged down in culture conflicts.[62]

3. *Historically based.* Shared experiences, over extended periods of time, bind groups of people together. We tend to identify with those who have had similar life experiences. Trust and loyalty, two key components of culture, are earned by consistently demonstrating predictable patterns of words and actions.

4. *Inherently symbolic.* Actions may speak louder than words. But some words or slogans can have great symbolic meaning that shapes an organization's entire culture and identity. Ford Motor Company's famous slogan, "Quality Is Job #1," is an instructive case in point. *Fortune* magazine's Thomas A. Stewart explains:

9J

Serious Fun at Sun Microsystems

At Sun's Mountain View (California) headquarters, . . . [Scott McNealy, the firm's ice hockey–playing CEO is] building a corporate culture based on his own motto: "Kick butt and have fun." The company has become equally famous for its aggressive marketing and the juvenile antics staged around its headquarters. Each April Fools' Day, scores of photographers now arrive to record the elaborate pranks Sun engineers play on McNealy and other execs. Once, the company's engineers built a golf course hole in McNealy's office, complete with green and water hazard.

Source: Robert D. Hof, "Scott McNealy's Rising Sun," *Business Week* (January 22, 1996): 70.

Questions: *Which of the six characteristics of organizational culture are evident in this situation? Would you like to work for Sun Microsystems? Why or why not?*

. . . one day Philip Caldwell, then CEO, simply wrote on a piece of paper, "Quality is the No. 1 job of the Ford Motor Co.," and it grew from there. I like it for three reasons: First, it's local. "Job 1" is industry slang for the first car of a new model coming off the assembly line. For car people, it said, "This is about us," whereas something like "Quality in everything we do" could apply equally to banking or cookie making. Second, it's commercial. Ford could and does use it as an advertising slogan. This tied it to business success: Make good cars because that's what sells. (It also meant that whenever a Ford employee clicked on his TV, he saw the value affirmed.) Most important, these are words to live by. If you faced a choice—should I okay this dashboard design? Accept this box of parts?— "Quality Is Job #1" gave you a way to decide. Every day.[63]

5. *Dynamic.* In the long term, organizational cultures promote predictability, conformity, and stability. Just beneath this apparently stable surface, however, change boils as people struggle to communicate and comprehend subtle cultural clues. A management trainee who calls the president by her first name after being invited to do so may be embarrassed to learn later that "no one actually calls the president by her first name, even if she asks you to."

6. *Inherently fuzzy.* Ambiguity, contradictions, and multiple meanings are fundamental to organizational cultures. Just as a photographer cannot capture your typical busy day in a single snapshot, it takes intense and prolonged observation to capture the essence of an organization's culture.

Forms and Consequences of Organizational Cultures

Figure 9.6 lists major forms and consequences of organizational cultures. To the extent that people in an organization share symbols, a common language, stories, and practices, they will tend to experience the four consequences. The degree of sharing and intensity of the consequences determine whether the organization's culture is strong or weak.

organizational values
shared beliefs about what the organization stands for

Shared values stand out as a pivotal factor in Figure 9.6. Unlike instrumental and terminal values, discussed in Chapter 5 as *personal* beliefs, **organizational values** are *shared* beliefs about what the organization stands for.[64] For example, prior to its merger with EarthLink in 2000, Internet service provider MindSpring took great pride in superior customer service. MindSpring's founder, Charles Brewer, drove home his customer service ethic with strong corporate values. As *Fast Company* magazine reported at the time:

MindSpring has nine "core values and beliefs" that govern how it operates. The principles are posted on office walls and on the backs of business cards. MindSpringers even recite them before their weekly all-hands meeting. "Work is an important part of life," declares one principle, "and it should be fun. Being a good business person does not mean being stuffy and boring." Another declares, "We make commitments with care, and then live up to them."[65]

Now that Brewer is chairman of EarthLink, it will be interesting so see how successful he has been in transplanting MindSpring's cherished values. The proof will be in the quality of EarthLink's customer service.

The Organizational Socialization Process

organizational socialization
process of transforming outsiders into accepted insiders

Organizational socialization is the process through which outsiders are transformed into accepted insiders.[66] In effect, the socialization process shapes newcomers to fit the organizational culture.

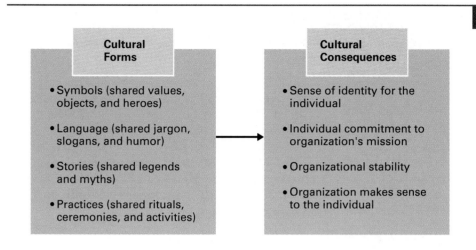

Figure 9.6

Forms and Conse-quences of Organiza-tional Cultures

Source: Forms adapted from Harrison M. Trice and Janice M. Beyer, *The Cultures of Work Organizations* (Englewood Cliffs, N.J.: Prentice-Hall, 1993), pp. 77–128. Consequences adapted from Linda Smircich, "Concepts of Culture and Organizational Analysis," *Administrative Science Quarterly*, 28 (September 1983): 339–358.

The culture asserts itself when the taken-for-granted cultural assumptions are in some way violated by the uninitiated and provoke a response. As the uninitiated bump into one after another taken-for-granted assumption, more acculturated employees respond in a variety of ways (tell stories, offer advice, ridicule, lecture, shun, and so forth) that serve to mold the way in which the newcomer thinks about his or her role and about "how things are done around here."[67]

Orientations.   *Orientation programs*—in which newly hired employees learn about their organization's history, culture, competitive realities, and compensation and benefits—are an important first step in the socialization process. Too often today, however, orientations are hurried or nonexistent and new employees are left to "sink or swim." This is a big mistake, according to recent workplace research:

One study at Corning Glass Works (in Corning, New York) found that new employees who went through a structured orientation program were 69 percent more likely to be with the company after three years than those who were left on their own to sort out the job. A similar two-year study at Texas Instruments concluded that employees who had been carefully oriented to both the company and their jobs reached full productivity two months sooner than those who weren't.[68]

Storytelling.   *Stories* deserve special attention here because, as indicated in Figure 9.6, they are a central feature of organizational socialization and culture. Company stories about heroic or inspiring deeds let newcomers know what "really counts."[69] For example, 3M's eleventh commandment—"Thou shalt not kill a new product idea"—has been ingrained in new employees through one inspiring story about the employee who invented transparent cellophane tape.

According to the story, an employee accidentally discovered the tape but was unable to get his superiors to buy the idea. Marketing studies predicted a relatively small demand for the new material. Undaunted, the employee found a way to sneak into the

Here Comes Digital Storytelling

9K

Consultant Dana Winslow Atchley III thinks most corporate storytelling is boring. His "digital storytelling" relies on modern technology including video, computers, and scanners. He sells corporate clients on his approach with a story of his own life titled "Next Exit":

The show is a remarkable blend of performance art, memoir, stand-up comedy, and documentary film. Here's how "Next Exit" works: Atchley strides onstage and sits on a tree stump. Beside him is a monitor surrounded by logs. He blows on the screen and—poof—a video campfire begins to crackle. On a wall behind him, tethered to a computer, is a screen of roughly the same size as one that you'd find at a multiplex. Atchley puts on a headset microphone à la Garth Brooks, grabs his wireless mouse, and begins. With the mouse, he opens an on-screen suitcase containing about 70 stories, most of them short digital videos that he has crafted from home movies, still photos, and videotapes. With the audience's help, he selects 12 to 18 stories for the evening.

It's a wacky and poignant narrative.

Source: Daniel H. Pink, "What's Your Story?" *Fast Company*, no. 21 (January 1999): 32.

Question: *Would this be a good tool for socializing employees and strengthening an organization's culture today? Explain.*

board room and tape down the minutes of board members with his transparent tape. The board was impressed enough with the novelty to give it a try and experienced incredible success.[70]

Upon hearing this story, a 3M newcomer has believable, concrete evidence that innovation and persistence pay off at 3M. It has been said that stories are "social roadmaps" for employees, telling them where to go and where not to go and what will happen when they get there. Moreover, stories are remembered longer than abstract facts or rules and regulations. How many times have you recalled a professor's colorful story but forgotten the rest of the lecture?

Strengthening Organizational Cultures

Given the inherent fuzziness of organizational cultures, how can managers identify cultural weak spots needing improvement? Symptoms of a weak organizational culture include the following:

- *Inward focus.* Have internal politics become more important than real-world problems and the marketplace?
- *Morale problems.* Is there chronic unhappiness and high turnover?
- *Fragmentation/inconsistency.* Is there a lack of "fit" in the way people behave, communicate, and perceive problems and opportunities?
- *Ingrown subcultures.* Is there a lack of communication among subunits?
- *Warfare among subcultures.* Has constructive competition given way to destructive conflict?
- *Subculture elitism.* Have organizational units become exclusive "clubs" with restricted entry? Have subcultural values become more important than the organization's values?[71]

Evidence of these symptoms may encourage a potential recruit to look elsewhere. Each of these symptoms of a weak organizational culture can be a formidable barrier to organizational effectiveness. Organizations with strong cultures do a good job of avoiding these symptoms.[72]

Summary

1. Organizations need to be understood and intelligently managed because they are an ever-present feature of modern life. Whatever their purpose, all organizations have four characteristics: (1) coordination of effort, (2) common goal or purpose,

(3) division of labor, and (4) hierarchy of authority. If even one of these characteristics is absent, an organization does not exist. One useful way of classifying organizations is by their intended purpose. Organizations can be classified as business, nonprofit service, mutual-benefit, or commonweal.

2. Organization charts are helpful visual aids for managers. Representing the organization's structural skeleton, organization charts delineate vertical hierarchy and horizontal specialization. Vertical hierarchy is the so-called chain of command. Horizontal specialization involves the division of labor.

3. There are both traditional and modern views of organizations. Traditionalists such as Fayol, Taylor, and Weber subscribed to closed-system thinking and ignored the impact of environmental forces. Modern organization theorists tend to prefer open-system thinking because it realistically incorporates organizations' environmental dependency. Early management writers proposed tightly controlled authoritarian organizations. Max Weber, a German sociologist, applied the label *bureaucracy* to his formula for the most rationally efficient type of organization. When bureaucratic characteristics, which are present in all organizations, are carried to an extreme, efficiency gives way to inefficiency. Chester I. Barnard's acceptance theory of authority and growing environmental complexity and uncertainty questioned traditional organization theory.

4. Open-system thinking became a promising alternative because it was useful in explaining the necessity of creating flexible and adaptable rather than rigid organizations. Although the analogy between natural systems and human social systems (organizations) is imperfect, there are important parallels. Organizations, like all open systems, are unique because of their (1) interaction with the environment, (2) synergy, (3) dynamic equilibrium, and (4) equifinality. In open-system terms, business organizations are made up of interdependent technical, boundary-spanning, and managerial subsystems.

5. Harvard's David A. Garvin characterizes learning organizations as those capable of turning new ideas into improved performance. Five skills required to do this are (1) solving problems, (2) experimenting, (3) learning from organizational experience and history, (4) learning from others, and (5) transferring and implementing knowledge for improved performance.

6. Because there is no one criterion for organizational effectiveness, for-profit as well as nonprofit organizations need to satisfy different effectiveness criteria in the near, intermediate, and distant future. Effective organizations are effective, efficient, and satisfying in the near term. They are adaptive and developing in the intermediate term. Ultimately, in the long term, effective organizations survive.

7. The management of organizational decline has only recently received the attention it deserves. Decline is often attributable to managerial complacency. The characteristics of decline are interlocking dilemmas that foster organizational self-destruction. To avoid decline as much as possible, or at least lessen its frequency, organizations should adopt preventive safeguards that counteract complacency. Continuous improvement is the primary tool for fighting decline. Downsizing tends to yield disappointing results. Among the ethical alternatives to layoffs are redeployment and work sharing.

8. Organizational culture is the "social glue" binding people together through shared symbols, language, stories, and practices. Organizational cultures can commonly be characterized as collective, emotionally charged, historically based, inherently symbolic, dynamic, and inherently fuzzy (or ambiguous). Diverse outsiders are transformed into accepted insiders through the process of organizational socialization. Orientations and stories are powerful and lasting socialization techniques. Systematic observation can reveal symptoms of a weak organizational culture.

Terms to Understand

Organization (p. 260)

Authority (p. 261)

Commonweal organization (p. 264)

Organization chart (p. 264)

Bureaucracy (p. 268)

Acceptance theory of authority (p. 270)

Dynamic equilibrium (p. 271)

Equifinality (p. 271)

Learning organization (p. 273)

Organizational effectiveness (p. 276)

Organizational decline (p. 277)

Downsizing (p. 279)

Outplacement (p. 282)

Organizational culture (p. 282)

Organizational values (p. 284)

Organizational socialization (p. 284)

Skills & Tools

How to Build Your Organization's Learning Capability

"**Learning capability** represents the capacity of managers within an organization to generate and generalize ideas with *impact*."

Managerial Actions to Ensure Learning Capability

Step 1: Build a commitment to learning capability.

- Make learning a visible and central element of the strategic intent.
- Invest in learning.
- Publicly talk about learning.
- Measure, benchmark, and track learning.
- Create symbols of learning.

Step 2: Work to generate ideas with impact.

- Continuous improvement (improve it).
- Competence acquisition (buy or hire it).

- Experimentation (try it).
- Boundary spanning (adapt it).

Step 3: Work to generalize ideas with impact.

- Teach leaders to coach.
- Teach leaders to facilitate.
- Select leaders who teach.
- Select leaders with vision.
- Walk the talk.

Source: Adapted from Dave Ulrich, Todd Jick, and Mary Ann Von Glinow, "High-Impact Learning: Building and Diffusing Learning Capability." Reprinted from *Organizational Dynamics,* Autumn 1993. © 1993 American Management Association International. Reprinted by permission of American Management Association International, New York, NY. All rights reserved. **http://www.amanet.org**

Internet Exercises

1. **Applying organizational effectiveness criteria:** (*Note:* This is a variation of the Internet exercise for Chapter 5.) Organizational effectiveness criteria can be used by job seekers, customers, and investors for making important decisions. The point of this exercise is to give you a Web-based tool for evaluating America's corporate giants. *Fortune* magazine's online version of its annual "America's Most Admired Companies" survey can be found at **www.pathfinder.com/fortune.** Click on "Careers" in the main menu. Scroll down the Career Resource Center page and select the heading "Most Admired Companies Search." Under the heading "Advanced," respond to prompt number 1 by typing in 10, respond to prompt number 2 by selecting "All Industries," and respond to prompt number 3 by doing your own rating of the eight organizational attributes. Click on "List Companies" and print your list for possible class discussion and/or later reference. You may want to click on some or all of the companies on your list to learn more about them.
   Learning Points: 1. Are you surprised by the top-ranked company? Why? Are you surprised a particular company is *not* on your top ten? 2. What is your rationale for the ratings you gave the eight attributes? 3. How do your attribute ratings compare with your classmates' ratings? How does your top ten compare with theirs? 4. Do you like/dislike *Fortune*'s list of corporate attributes as effectiveness criteria? How would you amend their list?

2. **The power of organizational stories:** As discussed in this chapter, stories can be a powerful way to socialize newcomers and reinforce the organization's cultural values. Giant retailer Wal-Mart's Web site (**www.wal-mart.com**) includes some insightful company stories. On the home page, click on the main heading "Company." Next, select the category "Wal-Mart Culture" to find an interesting collection of brief stories about Wal-Mart, founder Sam Walton, and its employees. Read two or three of these stories (print a copy if they are to be discussed in class).
   Learning Points: 1. What specific cultural values are communicated by the Wal-Mart stories you read? 2. Would reading these stories help socialize a new Wal-Mart employee? Explain. 3. Have you heard any stories about Wal-Mart that create a different impression? 4. Why is a well-told story such a powerful cultural tool?

3. **Check it out:** Follow the instructions in exercise 1 above to get to *Fortune*'s online Career Resource Center. Scroll down until you find the heading "Best Companies to Work For" (for the most recent year). By clicking on that feature, you will uncover lots of interesting bits of corporate culture information about many highly respected companies. Who knows . . . you may even find your next employer.

   For updates to these exercises, visit our Web site (**www.hmco.com/college**).

Hard Times for PeopleSoft's People-Centered Culture

[In January 1999,] a dozen managers at PeopleSoft Inc. met to plan layoffs. First, they wept.

"How do you feel?" Larry Butler, vice president of human resources, asked them. One manager outlined firing strategies, but the boss cut him off. "No," Mr. Butler said, "how do you *feel*?" Half the room dissolved in tears.

Most people thought layoffs "could never happen at PeopleSoft," recalls Tina Cox, PeopleSoft's manager of employee communications, who was at the meeting. "We are a family." Three weeks later, President and Chief Executive Officer David A. Duffield announced to employees that layoffs were coming—in a companywide e-mail headed with his initials, DAD.

"We will agonize over the departure of some valued coworkers," Mr. Duffield wrote. There was agony, all right. One longtime staffer was called on her vacation and told not to come back. Others among the 430 casualties say they got the word on their voice mail, or were given no explanation of why they were chosen.

The cuts, part of a huge restructuring under way at once-highflying PeopleSoft, were in some ways more surprising than the 78 percent stock dive over the past year, or the disappointing acquisitions, or the other problems that set the stage for the layoffs—and not just because one of PeopleSoft's main businesses is creating software to help manage personnel issues.

Even by the standards of Silicon Valley, PeopleSoft is famous for an aggressively informal and sensitive corporate culture. Its staff routinely worked 70-hour weeks, but for more than the stock options. There was a payoff in PeopleSoft's in-house jokes and clubby code words—in company lingo, employees are "PeoplePeople," they feast on company-funded "PeopleSnacks," which causes them to gain "PeoplePounds."

They fed, too, off the exploits of Mr. Duffield, a sometimes flamboyant, good-time guy who has lately given more than $200 million to help stray dogs and cats. PeopleSoft, Mr. Duffield preached, was about more than money—it was about having fun and having a heart.

In sum, it was the kind of company often idealized in today's high-tech world: an emotional, empathetic workplace that contrasts with the industry's highly rational products and often cutthroat tactics. And for a long time, it worked. Revenue in 1998 hit $1.3 billion, up 12-fold since 1994, and the stock had risen 32-fold over six years

before beginning to slide last summer. But now, PeopleSoft's remaining 6,600 employees are struggling with the suspicion that their special enterprise is really just another company, fallen on hard times.

PeopleSoft "is a living organism and a phenomenon," insists David Ogden, an in-house writer and the company historian, who says it attracted "the kind of person who is willing to work 14 hours a day—not in a culty way, but because 'this is what I *want* to do.'" Only these days, he says, "there is uncertainty about the future." He feels litigation and bad press aimed at the company lately are bad raps.

At the center of the doubt is Mr. Duffield, the 58-year-old founder. He has for months quietly searched for a replacement as president. He has seen friends from the early days peel off, including his brother, Al, the head of sales, who resigned as of April 1. In another company-wide e-mail, Al declared that he was leaving in part because "I'm rich." Many employees, their own stock options now underwater, found that in poor taste.

In an interview, David Duffield is unflappable. "The entire industry didn't see this slowdown, not one of us," the energetic, white-haired Mr. Duffield says. Rather than mope over the $2 billion drop in the value of his own PeopleSoft holdings over the past year (his current stake is worth about $800 million), he talks about possible acquisitions and Internet plans. If some firings were needed, well, "life is brutal," he notes. "Overall, they were beautifully handled."

But he also knows that this is no time for DAD to scare the family. When news of his replacement search shook up staff, he assured them that he would still be CEO, "the big Kahuna." As PeopleSoft's stock was tumbling last fall, Mr. Duffield still found time to judge a company pumpkin-carving contest. He also told a meeting of about 3,000 employees that the company's new mission is to double the value of the stock in one year. He regrets saying that now.

Mr. Duffield's sense of his own centrality to People-Soft seems well-placed. Cindy Denny, who calls her February layoff while on holiday in Australia "unprofessional," still openly worships Mr. Duffield. "I still think, 'What a guy,'" she says. "He's done his best to keep it a family, but it's out of control now."

Yet there are signs Mr. Duffield's commitment may be tempered by growing outside interests. During an interview, his nearby spokesman blanches at Mr. Duffield's mention that board member Edgar Codd, another old friend, will also resign, and that Mr. Duffield is selling his house near Pleasanton in order to spend more time at a mansion near Lake Tahoe. Both were news to the spokesman. Besides establishing a $200 million foundation to end the euthanasia of stray dogs and cats in America, Mr. Duffield has in the past four years adopted five children, to go with three kids of his own. . . .

But PeopleSoft is distinct, and so are some of its problems. In the mid-1980s, Mr. Duffield, a former International Business Machines Corp. sales executive, sensed that there was a coming boom in so-called client-server systems, which tie workers' personal computers to a bigger computer serving a whole office. To tap it, he founded PeopleSoft in 1987 with software designer Ken Morris.

They had a product by 1989, just as client-server computing was about to sweep corporate America. They also worked hard on developing a culture that would bind workers to the mission. Mr. Duffield leavened the merciless pace with beer blasts and parties at his house. At bigger company bashes, employees wore shirts they had been issued that bore their employee number. Some workers still talk enviously of the "double digits," the pioneers who joined before there were 100 PeoplePeople.

The money was fantastic. PeopleSoft had $113 million in revenue by 1994, and sales roughly doubled for several years running. For all their internal touchy-feeliness, PeopleSoft salesmen and other workers were take-no-prisoners competitors. The stock surged, peaking at $57.44 last May; it had gone public in 1992 at an adjusted $1.81 a share. The company was minting stock-option millionaires. The family grew rapidly, too, from 914 employees in 1994 to 7,032 before the layoffs this year.

Mr. Duffield seemed to have the magic touch, and he became a mythic figure within the company. The company band called itself "The Raving Daves." Employees gave birth to "PeopleBabies," who received their own numbers. There was shopping at the company "PeopleStore," which offers all sorts of knickknacks with

Source: Republished with permission of *The Wall Street Journal* from "A Software Star Sees Its 'Family' Culture Turn Dysfunctional," by Quentin Hardy. *The Wall Street Journal* (May 5, 1999); permission conveyed through Copyright Clearance Center, Inc.

the PeopleSoft logo and sells luggage called a "Duffield bag." In company newsletters, the CEO was called "the legendary Dave Duffield." . . .

If the atmosphere struck some newcomers as strange, most quickly adapted. "When I first interviewed there, I thought it was weird," says Ellen Brout, laid off from PeopleSoft's public-relations department in February. She recalls waiting for her interview next to a big pile of coins bearing Mr. Duffield's image—the "PeopleDollars" that PeopleSoft marketers gave to clients to help determine where the customers wanted PeopleSoft to "spend" its time in their companies. "After you were there awhile, things like that seemed normal," she says.

Mr. Duffield says he never liked the attention, but felt it was important for building up a strong company culture. "I will do what's right for the company," he says. "If I'm 'the legendary,' so be it."

Some found the persona a problem. "Dave would start joking at the meetings about how people from Oracle might be double agents," says Rick Hess, a former head of PeopleSoft's international sales, who came to PeopleSoft from Oracle in 1992. "A lot of us concluded that experienced businesspeople from outside PeopleSoft would have a hard time becoming part of the family. . . . They never trusted outsiders." Mr. Hess left in 1994. . . .

PeopleSoft says it has hot new products in the works that will restore its luster. It has high hopes for its Internet offering, the PeopleSoft Business Network, which is a portal, or entry to the Internet, for a business user. Further out, the company has secret projects under way involving electronic commerce and software systems for smaller companies.

FOR DISCUSSION

1. Which of the characteristics of organizational decline in Table 9.5 are evident in this case?

2. What alternatives to layoffs could PeopleSoft have used?

3. Which of the six common characteristics of organizational cultures are evident in this case?

4. How did PeopleSoft's efforts to build a very strong organizational culture backfire?

5. Was CEO Duffield wise to encourage his employees to worship him as a hero and a legend? Explain.

ORGANIZING in the TWENTY-FIRST CENTURY

CHAPTER OBJECTIVES

When you finish studying this chapter, you should be able to

1 Explain the concept of contingency organization design.

2 Distinguish between mechanistic and organic organizations.

3 Discuss the roles that differentiation and integration play in organization structure.

4 Identify and briefly describe the five basic departmentalization formats.

5 Describe how a highly centralized organization differs from a highly decentralized one.

6 Define the term *delegation* and list at least five common barriers to delegation.

7 Explain how the traditional pyramid organization is being reshaped.

"YOU HAVE TO
 THINK SMALL
TO GROW BIG."
sam walton

Microsoft's CEO,* Steve Ballmer: "I'm Trying to Let Other People Dive in Before I Do"

teven A. Ballmer's explosive temper is legendary. Back in his bad old days, before being appointed Microsoft Corp.'s president nine months ago, Ballmer would shout himself hoarse if a lieutenant didn't do his bidding fast enough. His motivational techniques drew heavily from Attila the Hun. When he directed the company's Windows product group, he put the fear of God into engineers by bellowing at them and pounding a baseball bat into his palm. And don't forget his outburst last May after the Justice Dept. sued Microsoft for antitrust law violations. "To heck with Janet Reno!" he blurted out.

Today, you'll find a tamer Ballmer. Since he took over running Microsoft's day-to-day operations, the 19-year veteran has worked hard to fashion a leadership style that's diplomatic rather than bullying—more Eisenhower than Patton. He still has the booming voice, but what he does with it is more constructive. "I'm trying to temper myself. I don't think I've mellowed. But I try to redirect my energy," he says, bursting into a raucous laugh. The difference is obvious to people who know Ballmer well. "He's certainly changed. He's calmer," says Microsoft board member Jon A. Shirley.

The fact is, Ballmer, 43, is coming into his own as Microsoft's president—and putting his mark on the company to boot. Since Ballmer got the job, he hasn't been content just to make the trains run on time. He's spearheading the effort to reshape Microsoft. He dreamed up a plan—which he calls Vision Version 2—for energizing employees, focusing them on customers, and broadening their outlook far beyond the narrow confines of the PC and Windows.

Wild Cheers

It's quite a different role for Ballmer. He has long played loyal sidekick to Chairman William H. Gates III. The two met as undergraduates at Harvard in 1973. Both were math whizzes, but Ballmer was more outgoing. He managed the college football team, the *Harvard Crimson* newspaper, and the student literary magazine. Ballmer also was more firmly rooted in day-to-day tasks than the absent-minded Gates. Once, after Gates left his dorm door and window open to weather and burglars when he departed for Christmas vacation, a watchful Ballmer battened down the place for him.

Gates eventually dropped out of Harvard to form Microsoft. But he didn't forget Ballmer. In 1980, he coaxed his pal to leave Stanford business school to join the fledgling company and whip into shape its chaotic business operations. The offer: A $50,000 salary and 7 percent of the company—a stake now worth nearly $20 billion. Later, Gates called on Ballmer to goose delivery of Microsoft's crucial Windows operating system. Then he relied on his friend to build a sales organization to compete with IBM in large corporate accounts.

Ballmer was always the passionate heart of the company. He led wild cheers at company meetings—leaping around on stage like a burly Mick Jagger. On a dare, he once dove into a pond on the company's Redmond (Wash.) campus in November. Charismatic as he was, Ballmer always remained in Gates's shadow. Now Gates is sharing the limelight. "Of the upper management at Microsoft, Steve's the one that gets it," says a former company executive.

Not only does Ballmer get it, but he's doing something about it. As part of Vision 2, he hopes to transform a culture where he and Gates made too many decisions themselves. Now, he's pushing authority down into the ranks. And he's more inclined to listen to subordinates before he speaks. At a review of the Consumer Windows Div.'s product plans on April 30, for instance, he made polite suggestions to managers, rather than quickly telling them what they ought to do. "I see him coaching more than in the past—as opposed to pushing," says Bill Veghte, the group's general manager. Ballmer admits his biggest challenge is delegating, "I'm used to diving in deeply," he says. "Now I'm trying to let other people dive in before I do."

---

*Ballmer was promoted from president to chief executive officer in January 2000.

Ballmer's getting atta-boys for his efforts. Gates praises the way he shepherded Microsoft's new e-commerce strategy. The company hopes to get 1 million businesses to use its software to create electronic stores linked to the MSN Web portal. "I think it's a brilliant idea," says Gates. Others say Ballmer has notched up the level of teamwork in the company by forming a Business Leadership Team—14 managers who meet monthly to coordinate strategies across the operating units. "Early days, but signs are good," says Paul A. Maritz, executive vice president in charge of the Developer Group.

Ballmer appears willing to do whatever it takes to make Microsoft successful. And that includes giving up his beloved baseball bat. In late March, when marketing vice president Deborah N. Willingham spotted him with the bat in a hallway and urged him to be careful, he handed it over to her. "He was saying you're the leaders—the bat swingers. It's a new world," Willingham says. Ballmer still unleashes his famous temper now and then—but at least he isn't swinging a bat anymore.

Source: Steve Hamm, "'I'm Trying to Let Other People Dive in Before I Do.'" Reprinted from the May 17, 1999 issue of *Business Week* by special permission. Copyright © 1999 by McGraw-Hill, Inc.

W e've probably all been to picnics where everyone brings a bottle of ketchup but no one brings the mustard. Although too much of one thing and too little of another may be laughable at a picnic, such disorganized situations can spell disaster for an organization that needs to manage human and material resources effectively and efficiently in order to survive. In the case of Microsoft, where there is intense pressure to shorten the product development cycle, disorganization would be a major liability.[1] At such times, the organizing function becomes crucial.

organizing *creating a coordinated authority and task structure*

Organizing is the structuring of a coordinated system of authority relationships and task responsibilities. By spelling out who does what and who reports to whom, organizational structure can translate strategy into an ongoing productive operation. Structure always follows strategy in well-managed organizations. Tasks and interrelationships cannot be realistically and systematically defined without regard for the enterprise's overall direction. Furthermore, strategy determines the technologies that are required and the resources that will probably be available.[2]

As mentioned in the previous chapter, traditional closed-system prescriptions for designing organizations have proved inadequate in recent years. In the face of rapid change and increasing complexity, traditional authoritarian bureaucracies are now seen as unwieldy structural dinosaurs. *Business Week* issued the following blunt warning back in 1990: "Americans, in short, must revolutionize the way they organize, manage, and carry out work, or their jobs will disappear in the fast-paced global economy."[3] The challenge to do things differently has triggered an organizational revolution, as you will see in this chapter.

The modern open-system view, with its emphasis on organization-environment interaction and learning organizations, has helped underscore the need for more flexible organization structures. These more flexible organizations are adaptable to sudden changes and are also interesting and challenging for employees. Traditional principles of organization are severely bent or broken during the design of flexible and adaptive organizations, and managers need new formulas for drawing up these designs. This is where the contingency approach enters the picture. The contingency approach permits the custom tailoring of organizations to meet unique external and internal situational demands.[4]

In this chapter we introduce and discuss organizational design alternatives that enhance situation appropriateness and, hence, organizational effectiveness. We also explore the dramatic reshaping of today's organizations.

Contingency Design

Recall from our discussion in Chapter 2 that contingency thinking amounts to situational thinking. Specifically, the contingency approach to organizing involves taking special steps to make sure the organization fits the demands of the situation. In direct contrast to traditional bureaucratic thinking, contingency design is based on the assumption that there is no single best way to structure an organization. **Contingency design** is the process of determining the degree of environmental uncertainty and adapting the organization and its subunits to the situation. This does not necessarily mean that all contingency organizations will differ from each other. Instead, it means that managers who take a contingency approach select from a number of standard design alternatives to create the most situationally effective organization possible. Contingency managers typically start with the same basic collection of design alternatives but end up with unique combinations of them as dictated by the demands of their situations.

The contingency approach to designing organizations boils down to two questions: (1) How much environmental or state uncertainty is there? (See Table 10.1 for a handy way to answer this question.) (2) What combination of structural characteristics is most appropriate? We will examine two somewhat different contingency models to establish the validity of the contingency approach. Each model presents a scheme for systematically matching structural characteristics with environmental demands.

1 Explain the concept of contingency organization design.

contingency design *fitting the organization to its environment*

The Burns and Stalker Model

Tom Burns and G. M. Stalker, both British behavioral scientists, proposed a useful typology for categorizing organizations by structural design.[5] They distinguished between mechanistic and organic organizations. **Mechanistic organizations** tend to be rigid in design and have strong bureaucratic qualities. In contrast, **organic organizations** tend to be quite flexible in structure and adaptive to change.[6] Actually, these two organizational types are the extreme ends of a single continuum. Pure types are difficult to find, but it is fairly easy to check off the characteristics listed in Table 10.2

2 Distinguish between mechanistic and organic organizations.

mechanistic organizations *rigid bureaucracies*

organic organizations *flexible, adaptive organization structures*

	Low	Moderate	High
1. How strong are social, political, and economic pressures on the organization?	Minimal	Moderate	Intense
2. How frequent are technological breakthroughs in the industry?	Infrequent	Occasional	Frequent
3. How reliable are resources and supplies?	Reliable	Occasional, predictable shortages	Unreliable
4. How stable is the demand for the organization's product or service?	Highly stable	Moderately stable	Unstable

Table 10.1

Determining Degree of Environmental Uncertainty

Table 10.2

Mechanistic Versus Organic Organizations

Characteristic	Mechanistic organizations	Organic organizations
1. Task definition for individual contributors	Narrow and precise	Broad and general
2. Relationship between individual contribution and organization purpose	Vague	Clear
3. Task flexibility	Low	High
4. Definition of rights, obligations, and techniques	Clear	Vague
5. Reliance on hierarchical control	High	Low (reliance on self-control)
6. Primary direction of communication	Vertical (top to bottom)	Lateral (between peers)
7. Reliance on instructions and decisions from superior	High	Low (superior offers information and advice)
8. Emphasis on loyalty and obedience	High	Low
9. Type of knowledge required	Narrow, technical, and task-specific	Broad and professional

Source: Adapted from Tom Burns and G. M. Stalker, *The Management of Innovation* (London: Tavistock, 1961), pp. 119–125. Reprinted by permission.

to determine whether a particular organization (or subunit) is relatively mechanistic or relatively organic. It is notable that a field study found distinctly different communication patterns in mechanistic and organic organizations. Communication tended to be the formal command-and-control type in the mechanistic factory and participative in the organic factory.[7]

Telling the Difference.   Here is a quick test of how well you understand the distinction between mechanistic and organic organizations. Read the following description of McDonald's operating system and decide if it describes a mechanistic or organic situation:

> *In the kitchens of his restaurants, [founder Ray] Kroc set up an industrial system based on mass production and absolute uniformity, so a Big Mac would taste the same in Bangkok or Boston. Dressing a hamburger, for example, is always done in unvarying order: mustard first, then ketchup, onions, and two pickles. In this much admired fast-food ballet, customers played a crucial part. With few choices, they sped service along by ordering promptly.*[8]

If you labeled the McDonald's system mechanistic, you're right. Using Table 10.2 as a guide, we see evidence in the McDonald's restaurant of narrow task definition, low task flexibility, clear definition of techniques, high reliance on instructions, and narrow knowledge requirements. An organic organization would have precisely the opposite characteristics.[9]

Situational Appropriateness.   Burns and Stalker's research uncovered distinct organization-environment patterns indicating the relative appropriateness of both mechanistic and organic organizations. They discovered that *successful organizations in*

Organic organizations, where employees have a great deal of latitude in how they perform their jobs, are popular today. But mechanistic characteristics, such as precise task definition, still have a place in some situations. For example, human lives may ultimately depend on how precisely and properly this Rocketdyne employee deburrs the engine combustion chamber before it is attached to the rocket nozzle unit in the background. Real "rocket science" isn't as glamorous as the proverbial kind.

relatively stable and certain environments tended to be mechanistic. Conversely, they also discovered that *relatively organic organizations tended to be the successful ones when the environment was unstable and uncertain.*

For practical application, this means that mechanistic design is appropriate for environmental stability, and organic design is appropriate for high environmental uncertainty. Today, the trend necessarily is toward more organic organizations because uncertainty is the rule. *Management Review* recently summed up the situation this way:

> *Products, companies, and industries all have shorter life cycles, which means that product launches, corporate realignments, and other initiatives may take place in months rather than years. The global span of today's companies, which have employees, customers, and suppliers throughout the world, also multiplies the complexities of change. And let us not forget another complicator—technology. Companies must constantly upgrade systems, evaluate new technology, and adopt new ways of doing business.*[10]

This is not to say that organic is good and mechanistic is bad. Some fledgling organizations, for example, are too organic and require the discipline of mechanistic qualities. Indeed, Paul Brainerd, the founder of Aldus

Corporation, a software start-up in Seattle, discovered he could no longer run the company as a one-man show. He then created and staffed the new position of chief operating officer to achieve some administrative order.[11]

Woodward's Study.   Since Burns and Stalker's pioneering study, several different contingency models have been proposed. Some, such as Joan Woodward's study of the relationship among technology, structure, and organizational effectiveness, focused on a single environmental variable rather than on general environmental certainty-uncertainty. Applying her own scale of technological complexity to 100 British firms, Woodward found distinctly different patterns of structure in effective and ineffective organizations. When technological complexity was either low or high, Woodward found that effective organizations tended to have organic structure. Mechanistic structure was associated with effectiveness when technological complexity was moderate.[12] In spite of criticism of weak methodology, Woodward's study added to the case against the traditional notion of a universally applicable organization design.

The Lawrence and Lorsch Model

3 **Discuss the roles that differentiation and integration play in organization structure.**

differentiation *tendency of specialists to think and act in restricted ways*

integration *collaboration needed to achieve a common purpose*

Paul R. Lawrence and Jay W. Lorsch, researchers from Harvard University, made a valuable contribution to contingency design theory by documenting the relationship between two opposing structural forces and environmental complexity. The opposing forces they isolated were labeled *differentiation* and *integration*. **Differentiation** is the tendency among specialists to think and act in restricted ways. This structural force results from division of labor and technical specialization. Differentiation tends to fragment and disperse the organization (see Figure 10.1). **Integration,** in opposition to differentiation, is the collaboration among specialists that is needed to achieve a common purpose.[13] Integration can be partially achieved through a number of mechanisms, including hierarchical control, standard policies and procedures, departmentalization, computer networks, cross-functional teams and committees, better human relations, and liaison individuals and groups. As illustrated in Figure 10.1, integration is a unifying and *coordinating* force.

According to Lawrence and Lorsch, every organization requires an appropriate *dynamic equilibrium* (an open-system term) between differentiation and integration. Moreover, their comparison of successful and unsuccessful firms in three different industries demonstrated that in the successful firms *both differentiation and integration increased as environmental complexity increased.* These findings applied not only to the overall organization but also to organizational subunits such as departments or divisions. Lawrence and Lorsch also found that "the more differentiated an organization, the more difficult it is to achieve integration."[14]

These findings suggest that organizational failure in the face of environmental complexity probably results from a combination of high differentiation and inadequate integration.[15] Under these conditions, specialists in different areas within the organization work at cross-purposes and get embroiled in counterproductive jurisdictional conflicts. Greater integration (coordination) certainly was on the minds of 360 senior executives in the United States during a recent survey. Among the four key ways to boost profits, according to the executives, was to: "Implement cross-functional coordination throughout the organization to increase customer retention."[16] Such action could prove fruitful, because in another study of 39 companies, productivity increased when organizational integration was improved. One source of improvement involved increased contact and coordination between product design and manufacturing specialists.[17] Today's advanced computer networks make cross-functional cooperation easier than ever before.

10B

Back to the Opening Case

Using Figure 10.1 as a guide, what evidence of organizational integration can you find at Microsoft?

Figure 10.1 | Differentiation and Integration: Opposing Organizational Forces

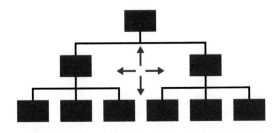
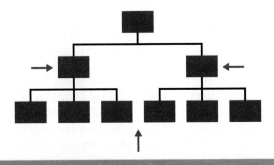

Differentiation (Fragmentation)	Integration (Coordination)	
Differentiating Mechanisms: Forces pushing the organization apart • Division of labor • Technical specialization	Integrating Mechanisms: Forces pulling the organization together • Formal hierarchy (chain of command) • Standard policies, rules, and procedures • Departmentalization • Computer networks	• Cross-functional teams and committees • Human relations training for managers (to help avoid interpersonal conflict) • Liaison individuals and groups (to bridge gaps between specialists)

Although contingency design models may differ in perspective and language, two conclusions stand out. First, research has proved time and time again that *there is no single best organization design*. Second, research generally supports the idea that the more uncertain the environment, the more flexible and adaptable the organization structure must be[18] (see Management Ethics on page 300). With this contingency perspective in mind, we now consider five structural formats.

Basic Structural Formats

As we noted earlier, differentiation occurs in part through division of labor. When labor is divided, complex processes are reduced to distinct and less complex jobs. But because differentiation tends to fragment the organization, some sort of integration must be introduced to achieve the necessary coordination. Aside from the hierarchical chain of command, one of the most common forms of integration is departmentalization. It is through **departmentalization** that related jobs, activities, or processes are grouped into major organizational subunits. For example, all jobs involving staffing activities such as recruitment, hiring, and training are often grouped into a human resources department. Grouping jobs through the formation of departments, according to management author James D. Thompson, "permits coordination to be handled in the least costly manner."[19] A degree of coordination is achieved through departmentalization because

departmentalization
grouping related jobs or processes into major organizational subunits

Management Ethics

A Globe-Trotting Organizational Thinker Looks at the Future of Work Organizations

About Charles Handy: A native of Dublin, Ireland, he is the author of well-regarded books such as *The Age of Unreason* and, most recently, *The Hungry Spirit.* His diverse background includes being the executive of an oil company and a London Business School professor. He and his wife, a professional photographer, shuttle between residences in England and Italy.

Here are excerpts from an interview by Barbara Ettorre, senior editor of *Management Review:*

Q. The corporation as we know it is approximately 100 years old. Will it survive the twenty-first century?

HANDY: Not in its present form. The twentieth century will be known as the century of the organization. The next one will not be known as that. We are seeing the withering of the employment organization. It won't totally disappear, but it will be reduced to an organizing core. Organizations will live up to the name—they will organize. [They won't] have to employ everybody being organized, only the organizers. So my formula is half-by-two-by-three: Half the workers paid twice as well, producing three times as much.

The other half will be outside the organization. And because those on the inside are working very hard to be paid twice as well, they will have short lives in the organization, 20 or 30 years, instead of 50 years. It could be 15.

It's a hell of a reduction. I try not to frighten people too much. But I would say 15 to 20.

This upper half of society, those with competent skills, will become independent workers, selling back into the organization for the most part, but also into several organizations at the same time. At the bottom level you will still need people because most of the jobs for the less skilled will be in the service world, giving people food and drink, keeping places clean, [taking care of old] folks. They will probably be organized by what I call intermediary employers.

Q. If the future consists of virtual corporations, portfolio workers, and knowledge as the competitive edge, what of the vast majority that cannot be a part of this? Are we creating an even larger underclass, large groups without salable portfolios?

HANDY: To some extent, there's no way out of that. Wealth doesn't trickle down as it used to. If you don't make the poor rich, the rich are not going to have any customers before long.

Source: Excerpted from Barbara Ettorre, "The Handy Reference to the Future." Reprinted from *Management Review,* July 1996. © 1996 American Management Association International. Reprinted by permission of American Management Association International, New York, NY. All rights reserved. **http://www.amanet.org**

---

4 **Identify and briefly describe the five basic departmentalization formats.**

members of the department work on interrelated tasks, obey the same departmental rules, and report to the same department head. It is important to note that although the term *departmentalization* is used here, it does not always literally apply; managers commonly use labels such as *division, group,* or *unit* in large organizations.

Five basic types of departmentalization are functional departments, product-service departments, geographic location departments, customer classification departments, and work flow process departments.[20]

Functional Departments

Functional departments categorize jobs according to the activity performed. Among profit-making businesses, variations of the functional production-finance-marketing arrangement in Figure 10.2A are the most common forms of departmentalization.

Figure 10.2 | Alternative Departmentalization Formats

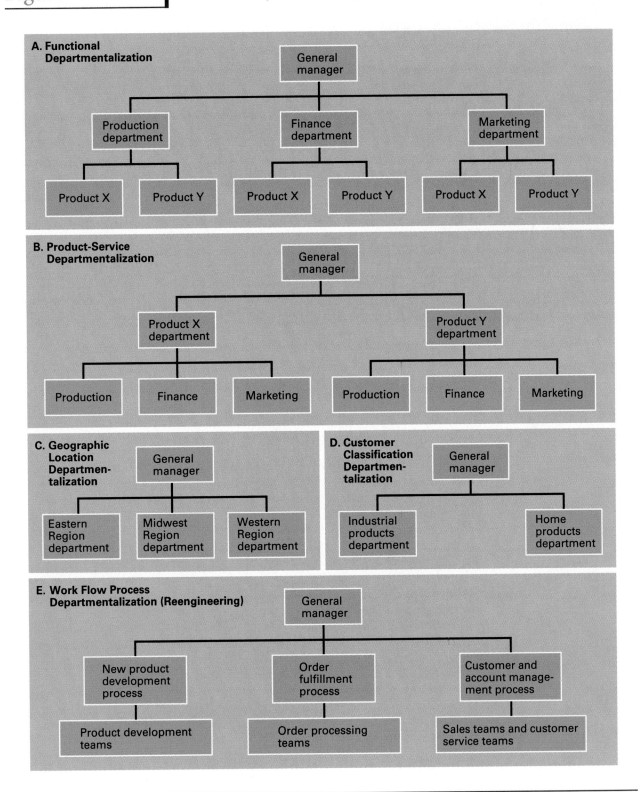

Functional departmentalization is popular because it permits those with similar technical expertise to work in a coordinated subunit.[21] Of course, functional departmentalization is not restricted to profit-making businesses. Functional departments in a nonprofit hospital might be administration, nursing, housekeeping, food service, laboratory and x-ray, admission and records, and accounting and billing.

A negative aspect of functional departmentalization is that it creates "technical ghettos," in which local departmental concerns and loyalties tend to override strategic organizational concerns. For example, look what Bruce L. Claflin, head of IBM's new mobile computing division, ran into when he called a planning meeting for the Think-Pad 700C.

> Everybody cared more about how their own area—say, marketing—would fare than for what was best for IBM. The marketing people knew [the 700C] would be competitive, but they had made commitments to sell only 6,000 worldwide. They didn't believe the development group would build it anyway. The development people knew they could design it, but they said, "Well, marketing won't sell it, and anyway, manufacturing can't build it." And manufacturing figured it would never be developed. It was complete gridlock.[22]

Situations like this prompted the recent overhaul of IBM.[23]

Product-Service Departments

Because functional departmentalization has been criticized for encouraging differentiation at the expense of integration, a somewhat more organic alternative has evolved. It is called product-service departmentalization because a product (or service), rather than a functional category of work, is the unifying theme. As diagrammed in Figure 10.2B, the product-service approach permits each of, say, two products to be managed as semiautonomous businesses. Organizations that render a service instead of turning out a tangible product might find it advantageous to organize around service categories. For example, reflecting its greater interest in the fast-growing casino gambling area, Hilton Hotels Corp. reorganized its worldwide operations into two units: gaming and lodging.[24] Ideally, those working in this sort of product-service structure have a broad "business" orientation rather than a narrow functional perspective. As Figure 10.2B shows, it is the general manager's job to ensure that these minibusinesses work in a complementary fashion. Such was *not* the case at Motorola, where the two-way radio, paging, and cellular phone units were constantly at war with one another. A recent reorganization combined these products into a single network-equipment division.[25] This created a more productive balance between the forces of differentiation and integration, discussed earlier.

Geographic Location Departments

Sometimes, as in the case of organizations with nationwide or worldwide markets, geography dictates structural format (see Figure 10.2C). Geographic dispersion of resources (for example, mining companies), facilities (for example, railroads), or

Should the customer come to you, or should you go to the customer? Computer-maker Gateway has organized itself around the latter approach. Its Gateway Country Stores offer local retail outlets for convenient hands-on shopping. Once inside the store, the focus shifts from geographic location to customer classification, as customers find special niches for business computing, home computing, and children's applications. This particular organizational structure sets Gateway apart from the herd—Compaq, Dell, Hewlett-Packard, and IBM.

customers (for example, chain supermarkets) may encourage the use of a geographic format to put administrators "closer to the action." One can imagine that drilling engineers in a Houston-based petroleum firm would be better able to get a job done in Alaska if they actually went up there. Similarly, a department-store marketing manager would be in a better position to judge consumer tastes in Florida if working out of a regional office in Orlando rather than a home office in Salt Lake City or Toronto.

Long lines of communication among organizational units have traditionally been a limiting factor with geographically dispersed operations. But space-age telecommunications technology has created some interesting regional advantages. One interesting case in point is Omaha, Nebraska. Its central location, along with the absence of a distinct regional accent among Nebraskans, has made Omaha the 1-800 capital of the country. Every major hotel chain and most of the big telemarketers have telephone service centers in Omaha.[26]

Global competition is pressuring managers to organize along geographical lines. This structure allows multinational companies to serve local markets better.

Customer Classification Departments

A fourth structural format centers on various customer categories (see Figure 10.2D). Aircraft maker Boeing, for example, was reorganized in 1998 into three units: commercial, defense, and space.[27] The rationale was to better serve the distinctly different needs of those three sets of customers. Customer classification departmentalization shares a weakness with the product-service and geographic location approaches: all three can create costly duplication of personnel and facilities. Functional design is the answer when duplication is a problem.

Work Flow Process Departments in Reengineered Organizations

In Chapter 7, we introduced the concept of reengineering, which involves starting with a clean sheet of paper and radically redesigning the organization into cross-functional teams that speed up the entire business process. The driving factors behind reengineering are lower costs, better quality, greater speed, better use of modern information technology, and improved customer satisfaction.[28] Organizations with work flow process departments are called *horizontal organizations* because emphasis is on the smooth and speedy horizontal flow of work between two key points: (1) identifying customer needs and (2) satisfying the customer.[29] This is a distinct *outward* focus, as opposed to the inward focus of functional departments. Here is what happens inside the type of organization depicted in Figure 10.2E:

> *Rather than focusing single-mindedly on financial objectives or functional goals, the horizontal organization emphasizes customer satisfaction. Work is simplified and hierarchy flattened by combining related tasks—for example, an account-management process that subsumes the sales, billing, and service functions—and eliminating work that does not add value. Information zips along an internal superhighway. The knowledge worker analyzes it, and technology moves it quickly across the corporation instead of up and down, speeding up and improving decision making.*[30]

Each of the preceding design formats is presented in its pure form, but in actual practice hybrid versions occur frequently. For example, to make Hewlett-Packard more responsive, then CEO John A. Young "divided the computer business into two main groups: One handles personal computers, printers, and other products sold through dealers, and the second oversees sales of workstations and minicomputers to big customers."[31] H-P's new structure amounted to a combination of the product-service and customer classification formats. Large organizations that serve broad markets may find it useful to combine central production and finance departments with several geographic marketing departments instead of having a single marketing department. From a contingency perspective, the five design formats are useful starting points rather than final blueprints for organizers. A number of structural variations show how the basic formats can be adapted to meet situational demands.

10D

How Reengineering Got a Bad Name

A manager reportedly told James Champy, co-author of the landmark book on reengineering:

We don't really know how to do reengineering in our company; so what we do is, we regularly downsize and leave it to the three people who are left to figure out how to do their work differently.

Source: As quoted in "Anything Worth Doing Is Worth Doing from Scratch," *Inc.* 20th Anniversary Issue, 21 (May 18, 1999): 51–52.

Questions: *Does the term* reengineering *have a positive or negative connotation for you? Explain. How often do you think misapplication or misinterpretation gives otherwise sound management practices a bad name? Explain.*

Contingency Design Alternatives

Contingency design requires managers to select from a number of situationally appropriate alternatives instead of blindly following fixed principles of organization.[32] Managers who face a relatively certain environment can enhance their effectiveness by drawing on comparatively mechanistic alternatives. Those who must cope with high uncertainty will do better to select organic alternatives. Design alternatives include span of control, decentralization, line and staff, and matrix design.

Span of Control

The number of people who report directly to a manager represents that manager's **span of control.** (Some scholars and managers prefer the term *span of management.*) Managers with a narrow span of control oversee the work of a few people, whereas those with a wide span of control have many people reporting to them (see Figure 10.3). Generally, narrow spans of control foster tall organizations (many levels in the hierarchy). In contrast, flat organizations (few hierarchical levels) have wide spans of control. Everything else being equal, it stands to reason that an organization with narrow spans of control needs more managers than one with wide spans. Management theorists and practitioners have devoted a good deal of time and energy through the years attempting to answer the question, "What is the ideal span of control?"[33] Ideally, the right span of control strikes an efficient balance between too little and too much supervision, important considerations in the era of lean organizations.

span of control *number of people who report directly to a given manager*

Is There an Ideal Span of Control?

Early management theorists confidently specified exactly how many individuals should be in a manager's span of control. In the words of one early management scholar, "No superior can supervise directly the work of more than five or, at the most, six subordinates whose work interlocks."[34]

As time went by, research results began to supersede strictly intuitive judgments and evidence supported wider spans of control. James C. Worthy, a vice president of Sears, Roebuck and Co., reported that his company had gotten good results with spans of control far in excess of six. Specifically, Worthy found morale and effectiveness were

---

10E

Wider Is Better, for the Head of Cisco Systems

Says John Chambers, CEO of Cisco Systems Inc.: "I learned a long time ago that a team will always defeat an individual. And if you have a team of superstars, then you have a chance to create a dynasty." That's one reason Chambers has two to three times as many people reporting to him as does the average executive in his company: It forces him to empower those directly under him with greater autonomy, because he can't possibly keep up with every detail of their work.

Source: John Byrne, "The Global Corporation Becomes the Leaderless Corporation," *Business Week* (August 30, 1999): 90.

Question: *What is the key to making Chambers's wide span of control work?*

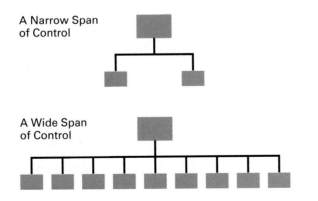

Figure 10.3

Narrow and Wide Spans of Control

A Narrow Span of Control

A Wide Span of Control

higher in one department store in which 36 department managers reported to a single manager than in a second store in which the span of control averaged only five.[35]

Today's emphasis on contingency organization design, combined with evidence that wide spans of control can be effective, has made the question of an ideal span obsolete. The relevant question is no longer how wide spans of control *should* be but instead, "How wide *can* one's span of control be?" Wider spans of control mean less administrative expense and more self-management, both popular notions today.

The Contingency Approach to Spans of Control.   Both overly narrow and overly wide spans of control are counterproductive. Overly narrow spans create unnecessarily tall organizations plagued by such problems as oversupervision; long lines of communication; slow, multilevel decision making; limited initiative due to minimal delegation of authority; restricted development among managers who devote most of their time to direct supervision; and increased administrative cost.[36] In contrast, overly wide spans can erode efficiency and inflate costs due to workers' lack of training, behavioral problems among inadequately supervised workers, and lack of coordination. Clearly, a rationale is needed for striking a workable balance.

Situational factors such as those listed in Figure 10.4 are a useful starting point. The narrow, moderate, and wide span of control ranges in Figure 10.4 are intended to be illustrative benchmarks rather than rigid limits. Each organization must do its own on-the-job experimentation. At Federal Express, for example, the span of control varies with different areas of the company. Departments that employ many people doing the same or very similar jobs—such as customer service agents, handlers/sorters, and couriers—usually have a span of control of 15 to 20 employees per manager. Groups performing

Figure 10.4   Situational Determinants of Span of Control

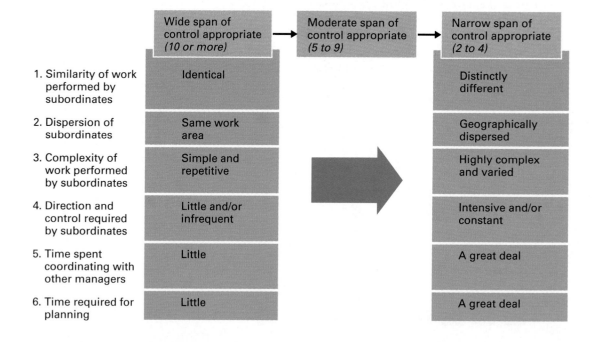

	Wide span of control appropriate (10 or more)	Moderate span of control appropriate (5 to 9)	Narrow span of control appropriate (2 to 4)
1. Similarity of work performed by subordinates	Identical		Distinctly different
2. Dispersion of subordinates	Same work area		Geographically dispersed
3. Complexity of work performed by subordinates	Simple and repetitive		Highly complex and varied
4. Direction and control required by subordinates	Little and/or infrequent		Intensive and/or constant
5. Time spent coordinating with other managers	Little		A great deal
6. Time required for planning	Little		A great deal

multiple tasks, or tasks that require only a few people, are more likely to have spans of control of five or fewer.[37] No ideal span of control exists for all kinds of work.

Centralization and Decentralization

Where are the important decisions made in an organization? Are they made strictly by top management or by middle- and lower-level managers? These questions are at the heart of the decentralization design alternative. Centralization is at one end of a continuum and at the other end is decentralization. **Centralization** is defined as the relative retention of decision-making authority by top management. Almost all decision-making authority is retained by top management in highly centralized organizations. In contrast, **decentralization** is the granting of decision-making authority by management to lower-level employees. Decentralization increases as the degree, importance, and range of lower-level decision making *increases* and the amount of checking up by top management *decreases* (see Figure 10.5).

The Need for Balance.   When we speak of centralization or decentralization, we are describing a comparative degree, not an absolute. The challenge for managers, as a management consultant observed, is to strike a workable balance between two extremes.

The modern organization in transition will recognize the pull of two polarities: a need for greater centralization to create low-cost shared resources; and, a need to improve market responsiveness with greater decentralization. Today's winning organizations are the ones that can handle the paradox and tensions of both pulls. These are the firms that analyze the optimum organizational solution in each particular circumstance, without prejudice for

5 **Describe how a highly centralized organization differs from a highly decentralized one.**

centralization *the retention of decision-making authority by top management*

decentralization *management shares decision-making authority with lower-level employees*

Figure 10.5 | Factors in Relative Centralization/Decentralization

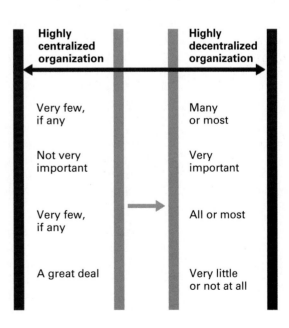

	Highly centralized organization	Highly decentralized organization
• How many decisions are made at lower levels in the hierarchy?	Very few, if any	Many or most
• How important are the decisions that are made at lower levels (i.e., do they impact organizational success or dollar values)?	Not very important	Very important
• How many different functions (e.g., production, marketing, finance, personnel) rely on lower-level decision making?	Very few, if any	All or most
• How much does top management monitor or check up on lower-level decision making?	A great deal	Very little or not at all

People who shop at Abercrombie & Fitch want a certain look. Stylish, comfortable, socially appealing, and functional—you know—"the look." Unknown to customers, the driving force behind Abercrombie's look is CEO Michael Jeffries. He maintains centralized control over what he calls Abercrombie's "movies"—carefully orchestrated themes running through the firm's stores, Web site, and catalogs.

one type of organization over another. The result is, almost invariably, a messy mixture of decentralized units sharing cost-effective centralized resources.[38]

For example, put yourself in the shoes of Johnson & Johnson's chief executive officer. Ralph S. Larsen's New Brunswick, New Jersey, health care products corporation is made up of 166 separate companies. Each is responsible for its own research and development, production, and marketing. Yet, the structure Larsen has put in place effectively orchestrates J&J's far-flung empire, making it a feared and profitable competitor.

> *Directly overseeing the 166 operating companies are 19 company group chairmen, a few of whom work out of Europe. Strategy flows up from the bottom as individual companies set their plans and review them with group chairmen. Above the group leaders are three sector chairmen, representing J&J's pharmaceutical, professional, and consumer sectors. They report to Larsen. The CEO also hatches broad strategic plans with a seven-member executive committee. . . .*[39]

Support for greater decentralization in the corporate world has come and gone over the years in faddish waves. Today, the call is for the type of balance Larsen continually strives for at J&J.[40] The case against extreme decentralization can be summed up in three words: *lack of control*. Balance helps neutralize this concern. Again, the contingency approach dictates which end of the continuum needs to be emphasized.[41] Centralization, because of its mechanistic nature, generally works best for organizations in relatively stable situations.[42] A more organic, decentralized approach is appropriate for firms in complex and changing conditions.

Decentralization Through Strategic Business Units.   Because of their growing popularity, particularly among very large businesses attempting to become more entrepreneurial, strategic business units deserve special mention. A **strategic business unit (SBU)** is an organizational subunit that acts like an independent business in all major respects, including the formulation of its own strategic plans. To qualify as a full-fledged SBU, an organizational unit must meet four criteria:

1. It must serve a specific market outside the parent organization, rather than being simply an internal supplier.
2. It must face outside competitors.
3. It should be in a position of controlling its own destiny, especially through strategic planning and new product development. However, SBUs may choose to share the parent organization's resources, such as manufacturing facilities or sales personnel. The important point here is that the SBU, not the parent organization, makes the key choices.
4. It should be a profit center, with its effectiveness measured in terms of profit and loss.[43]

Like the underlying concept of decentralization, SBUs vary in degree. Units that fail to meet the above criteria are still called SBUs by some managers. A true SBU is highly decentralized from the parent organization.

In addition to encouraging organizational units to take greater entrepreneurial risk, SBUs can foster customer-centeredness. Xerox Corporation is a good case in point:

[Until 1992,] Xerox was set up in the usual functions—R&D, manufacturing, sales, and the like. The new design creates nine businesses aimed at markets such as small businesses and individuals, office document systems, and engineering systems. Each business will have an income statement and a balance sheet, and an identifiable set of competitors. New manufacturing layouts will permit so-called focused factories dedicated to specific businesses. . . .

Teams lead the businesses, whose building blocks are what CEO Paul Allaire calls "microenterprise units": complete work processes or subprocesses. Says Allaire: "We've given everyone in the company a direct line of sight to the customer."[44]

Interference by the parent organization is the surest way to render SBUs ineffective. Research shows that the more decentralized SBUs are from the parent organization, the more effective they are.[45] Ironically, to succeed, SBUs need the freedom to fail.

strategic business unit
organizational subunit that acts like an independent business

Line and Staff Organizations

Through the years, managers of large mechanistic organizations have struggled to strike a balance between technical specialization and unity of command. Remember that unity of command was emphasized by traditional management theorists. According to the unity-of-command principle, people should have only one immediate superior to avoid receiving conflicting orders. Unfortunately, in highly differentiated organizations there is often a mismatch between technical expertise and authority. For example, a production manager with the appropriate authority to take constructive action may not perceive sloppy inventory control as the source of runaway production costs. But an assistant accounting manager who has the technical expertise to identify and solve the inventory problem does not have the authority to take direct action in the production area. This is a common and frustrating situation. Line and staff organization design helps management apply technical expertise where it is most needed while maintaining relative unity of command.

line and staff organization
organization in which line managers make decisions and staff personnel provide advice and support

Line Versus Staff.   In a **line and staff organization,** a distinction is made between line positions, those in the formal chain of command, and staff positions, those serving in an advisory capacity outside the formal chain of command. Line managers have the authority to make decisions and give orders to those lower in the chain of command. In contrast, those who occupy staff positions merely advise and support line managers. Staff authority is normally restricted to immediate assistants. The line-staff distinction is relatively clear in mechanistic organizations but tends to blur in organic organizations.

As one might suspect, line and staff distinctions are a natural setting for conflict. Disagreement and conflict, as discussed in Chapter 16, are inevitable when two groups have different backgrounds, goals, and perspectives of the organization. For instance, line managers tend to emphasize decisiveness and deadlines, whereas staff members prefer to analyze problems systematically and thoroughly. Thus, line managers often criticize staff for taking too much time, and staff in turn complain of line managers' impatience and hasty decisions. A study of 207 Israeli police officers found yet another potential source of line-versus-staff conflict. Line employees were found to have greater job commitment than their staff coworkers.[46] The differing levels of commitment could cause line managers to question staff members' loyalty to the organization's mission. Teamwork and trust could become casualties in the conflict over loyalties. Fortunately, the recent emphasis on *internal service,* often in conjunction with total quality management, promises to reduce line-staff conflict. According to a pair of respected organization theorists, ". . . it is reasonable to expect that as the line operations of organizations develop and perfect their own concepts of how to deliver high quality, they will in turn demand high-quality service from their staff organizations. Line managers are likely to expect staff organizations to treat them as customers."[47]

Personal Versus Specialized Staff.   There are two general types of staff, personal and specialized.[48] Personal staff are individuals assigned to a specific manager to provide research support, specialized technical expertise, and counsel. For example, in Figure 10.6, the strategic planning specialist and legal counsel are on the president's personal staff. But unlike the president's line authority, which extends to all functions, the authority of personal staff is normally limited to those working in their technical areas.

In contrast, specialized staff are "a reservoir of special knowledge, skills, and experience which the entire organization can use."[49] Consider the organization in Figure 10.6. Because it is primarily a manufacturing firm, manufacturing is a line function, whereas research and development, marketing, finance-accounting, and personnel are specialized staff functions. Notice that each of the four specialized staff functions supports but does not directly control the manufacturing function.

functional authority
gives staff temporary and limited authority for specified tasks

Functional Authority.   Strict distinctions between line and staff tend to disappear in relatively organic organizations. A device called functional authority helps prevent the collapse of unity of command. **Functional authority** is an organic design alternative that gives staff personnel temporary, limited line authority for specified tasks. In Figure 10.6, for example, the president's personal legal counsel may be given functional authority for negotiating a new union contract with factory personnel. When acting in that capacity, the legal counsel's authority would override that of cooperating line managers such as the manufacturing and personnel/human resource directors. By giving knowledgeable staff the direct authority to get something done, functional authority can reduce bureaucratic delays and enhance organizational flexibility.[50]

Figure 10.6 | A Line and Staff Organization

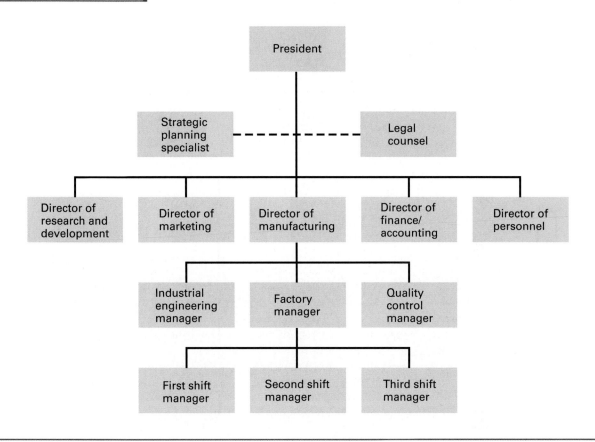

Matrix Organization

This last design alternative is sometimes called *project management.*[51] In a **matrix organization,** vertical and horizontal lines of authority are combined in checkerboard fashion. Authority flows both down and across the organization structure.

matrix organization *a structure with both vertical and horizontal lines of authority*

Matrix design originally became popular in the construction and aerospace industries. Imagine how difficult it would be for a construction firm to complete, simultaneously and in a cost-effective manner, several huge projects such as hydroelectric dams. (Recall our discussion of project planning in Chapter 6.)[52] Because each major project has its own situational and technical demands, mechanistic bureaucracies have not worked out well as principal contractors of airports and other large projects. A more organic alternative had to be found. Likewise, aerospace giants such as Lockheed, Grumman, and General Dynamics had to turn to a more organic structure to build complex weapons systems and space vehicles for the federal government. Consequently, the matrix format evolved.[53]

Take a moment to study the matrix organization chart in Figure 10.7. Notice the checkerboard configuration. In effect, the project managers borrow specialists from the line managers in charge of engineering, manufacturing, and contract administration. Technical needs dictate the number of specialists who will be borrowed from a given functional area at a given time. It is important to note that project managers have only limited (project-related) authority over the specialists, who otherwise report to their line managers. Matrix design has both advantages and disadvantages (see Table 10.3).

Figure 10.7

A Simplified Matrix Organization Chart

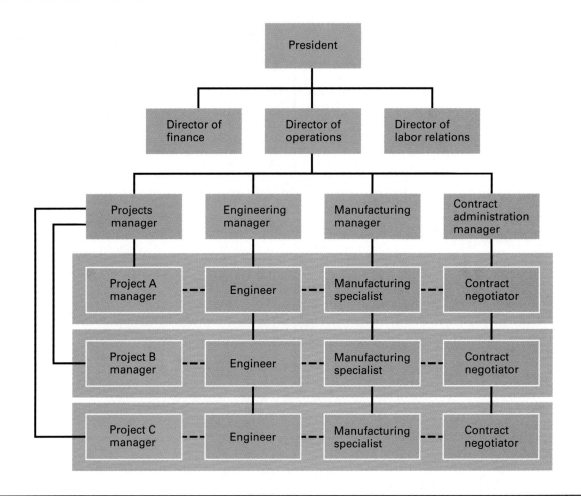

Advantages.   Increased *coordination* is the overriding advantage of matrix design. The matrix format places a project manager in a good position to coordinate the many interrelated aspects of a particular project, both inside and outside the organization.[54] In mechanistic organizations, the various aspects of a project normally would be handled in a fragmented fashion by functional units, such as production and marketing, with no single person being in charge of the project.

Improved information flow, the third advantage listed in Table 10.3, needs to be interpreted carefully. Research has found that matrix design increases the *quantity* of communication but decreases its *quality*.[55]

Disadvantages.   First and foremost, matrix design flagrantly violates the traditional unity-of-command principle. A glance at Figure 10.7 reveals that an engineer, for instance, actually has two supervisors at the same time. This special arrangement can and sometimes does cause power struggles and conflicts of interest. Only frequent and comprehensive communication between functional and project managers (integration) can minimize unity-of-command problems. A corollary of the unity-of-command problem is the "authority gap" facing project managers who must complete

Advantages	Disadvantages	Table 10.3
Efficient use of resources: Individual specialists as well as equipment can be shared across projects.	**Power struggles:** Conflict occurs because boundaries of authority and responsibility overlap.	**Advantages and Disadvantages of Matrix Organizations**
Project integration: There is a clear and workable mechanism for coordinating work across functional lines.	**Heightened conflict:** Competition over scarce resources occurs especially when personnel are being shared across projects.	
Improved information flow: Communication is enhanced both laterally and vertically.	**Slow reaction time:** Heavy emphasis on consultation and shared decision making retards timely decision making.	
Flexibility: Frequent contact between members from different departments expedites decision making and adaptive responses.	**Difficulty in monitoring and controlling:** Multidiscipline involvement heightens information demands and makes it difficult to evaluate responsibility.	
Discipline retention: Functional experts and specialists are kept together even though projects come and go.	**Excessive overhead:** Double management by creating project managers.	
Improved motivation and commitment: Involvement of members in decision making enhances commitment and motivation.	**Experienced stress:** Dual reporting relations contribute to ambiguity and role conflict.	

Source: From Erik W. Larson and David H. Gobeli, "Matrix Management: Contradictions and Insights." Copyright © 1987 by the Regents of the University of California. Reprinted from the *California Management Review*, vol. 29, no. 4, by permission of the Regents.

projects in spite of a lack of formal line authority. Research has shown that project managers tend to use negotiation, persuasive ability, technical competence, and the exchange of favors to compensate for their lack of authority.[56] All of these challenges might explain why project managers, in a recent study of a matrix organization, reported significantly higher job satisfaction than did their line-manager colleagues.[57]

Finally, matrix organizations have turned out to be too complex and cumbersome for some organizations. After years of serving as a model for matrix design, Texas Instruments scrapped its complex matrix structure in favor of a more decentralized arrangement approximating strategic business units.[58] However, to conclude that matrix design was a passing fad of the 1970s and early 1980s, as some have done, would be a mistake. According to a study reported in the late 1980s, 89 percent of 387 U.S. and Canadian companies with matrix management experience said they would continue using it.[59]

Effective Delegation

6 Define the term *delegation* and list at least five common barriers to delegation.

Delegation is an important common denominator that runs through virtually all relatively organic design alternatives. It is vital to successful decentralization. Formally defined, **delegation** is the process of assigning various degrees of decision-making authority to lower-level employees.[60] As this definition implies, delegation is

delegation *assigning various degrees of decision-making authority to lower-level employees*

Figure 10.8

The Delegation Continuum

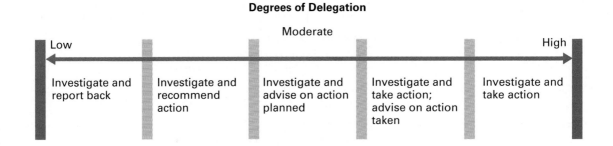

Degrees of Delegation

Moderate

Low   High

| Investigate and report back | Investigate and recommend action | Investigate and advise on action planned | Investigate and take action; advise on action taken | Investigate and take action |

not an all-or-nothing proposition. There are at least five different degrees of delegation[61] (see Figure 10.8).

A word of caution about delegation is necessary because there is one thing it does not include. Former President Harry Truman is said to have had a little sign on his White House desk that read, "The Buck Stops Here!"[62] Managers who delegate should keep this idea in mind because, although authority may be passed along to people at lower levels, ultimate responsibility cannot be passed along. Thus delegation is the sharing of authority, not the abdication of responsibility. Chrysler's former CEO Lee Iacocca admittedly fell victim to this particular lapse:

> *When the company started to make money, it spent its cash on stock buybacks and acquisitions. For his part, Iacocca was distracted by nonautomotive concerns.*
>
> *[Iacocca] concedes that while he kept his finger on finance and marketing, he should have paid closer attention to new model planning. "If I made one mistake," he says now, "it was delegating all the product development and not going to one single meeting."*[63]

Iacocca corrected this mistake prior to his retirement, and customers liked Chrysler's bold new designs.

The Advantages of Delegation

Managers stand to gain a great deal by adopting the habit of delegating. By passing along well-defined tasks to lower-level people, managers can free more of their time for important chores like planning and motivating. Regarding the question of exactly *what* should be delegated, Intel's chairman, Andy Grove, made the following recommendation: "Because it is easier to monitor something with which you are familiar, if you have a choice you should delegate those activities you know best."[64] Grove cautions that delegators who follow his advice will experience some psychological discomfort because they will quite naturally want to continue doing what they know best.[65]

In addition to freeing valuable managerial time,[66] delegation is also a helpful management training and development tool. Moreover, lower-level managers who desire more challenge generally become more committed and satisfied when they are given the opportunity to tackle significant problems. Conversely, a lack of delegation can stifle initiative. Consider the situation of a California builder:

> [The founder and chairman] personally negotiates every land deal. Visiting every construction site repeatedly, he is critical even of details of cabinet construction. "The building business is an entrepreneurial business," he says. "Yes, you can send out people. But you better follow them. You have to manage your managers."
>
> Says one former . . . executive: "The turnover there's tremendous. He hires bright and talented people, but then he makes them eunuchs. He never lets them make any decisions."[67]

Perfectionist managers who avoid delegation have problems in the long run when they become overwhelmed by minute details.

Barriers to Delegation

There are several reasons why managers generally do not delegate as much as they should:

- Belief in the fallacy, "If you want it done right, do it yourself."
- Lack of confidence and trust in lower-level employees.
- Low self-confidence.
- Fear of being called lazy.
- Vague job definition.
- Fear of competition from those below.
- Reluctance to take the risks involved in depending on others.
- Lack of controls that provide early warning of problems with delegated duties.
- Poor example set by bosses who do not delegate.[68]

Managers can go a long way toward effective delegation by recognizing and correcting these tendencies both in themselves and in their fellow managers.[69] Since successful delegation is habit forming, the first step usually is the hardest. Properly trained and motivated people who know how to take initiative in challenging situations (see Skills & Tools at the end of this chapter) often reward a delegator's trust with a job well done.[70]

Once managers have developed the habit of delegating, they need to remember this wise advice from Peter Drucker: "Delegation . . . requires that delegators follow up. They rarely do—they think they have delegated, and that's it. But they are still accountable for performance. And so they have to follow up, have to make sure that the task gets done—and done right."[71]

Back to the Opening Case 10G

Dawn Gould Lepore, Chief Information Officer, Charles Schwab & Co.:

Having my son has made me a more balanced leader. I'm trying hard to cut back on my usual 60- to 70-hour workweek. I'm much less tolerant of activities that aren't a good use of my time, and I'm a better delegator. I frequently ask myself, Do I really have to do this? Does my organization need me to follow up on every detail? My answer often is, "No, it doesn't." Now I focus on what's important: providing inspiration and emotional support for my organization.

Source: Anna Muoio, "Balancing Acts," *Fast Company*, no. 22 (February–March 1999): 84.

Questions: *Could Steve Ballmer learn something from this executive mother? What do priorities have to do with Lepore's management style? Explain.*

Initiative by Any Other Name 10H

Taking initiative is defined differently by star performers and average performers. Frequently what average workers see as initiative, star performers see as part of the job.

Source: Catherine Romano, "A Star Is Made," *Management Review*, 84 (February 1995): 6.

Questions: *From the average employee's viewpoint, what is wrong with demonstrating a lot of initiative? How important is employee initiative to managerial delegation? Based on what you have just read, plus the tips in the Skills & Tools box at the end of this chapter, what must managers do to get employees to demonstrate greater initiative?*

The Changing Shape of Organizations

7 Explain how the traditional pyramid organization is being reshaped.

Management scholars have predicted the death of traditional pyramid-shaped bureaucracies for more than 30 years.[72] Initial changes were slow in coming and barely noticeable. Observers tended to dismiss the predictions as naive and exaggerated. However, the pace and degree of change has picked up dramatically since the 1980s. All of the social, political-legal, economic, and technological changes discussed in Chapter 3 threaten to make traditional organizations obsolete. Why? Because they are too slow, unresponsive, uncreative, costly, and hard to manage. It is clear today that no less than a reorganization revolution is under way. Traditional pyramid organizations, though still very much in evidence, are being questioned as never before. General Electric's Jack Welch put it this way:

> *The old organization was built on control, but the world has changed. The world is moving at such a pace that control has become a limitation. It slows you down. You've got to balance freedom with some control, but you've got to have more freedom than you ever dreamed of.*[73]

Consequently, to be prepared for tomorrow's workplace, we need to take a look at how organizations are being reshaped.

Characteristics of the New Organizations

Three structural trends, already well established, are paving the way for new and different organizations. Layers are being eliminated, teamwork is becoming the norm, and size is being compartmentalized. Let us explore each of these exciting and sometimes troublesome trends.

Fewer Layers.   As documented in the last chapter, the dramatic downsizing of large U.S. businesses continues. Well-paid middle managers have been particularly hard hit. The plain truth is that companies can no longer afford layer upon layer of costly managerial talent in today's global economy. *Fortune* magazine offered this instructive historical perspective:

> *Middle managers have always handled two main jobs: supervising people, and gathering, processing, and transmitting information. But in growing numbers of companies, self-managed teams are taking over such standard supervisory duties as scheduling work, maintaining quality, even administering pay and vacations. Meanwhile, the ever-expanding power and dwindling cost of computers have transformed information handling from a difficult, time-consuming job to a far easier and quicker one. Zap! In an instant, historically speaking, the middle manager's traditional functions have vaporized.*
>
> *That's bad enough. At the same time, competition is forcing many companies to squeeze costs without mercy. Guess who looks like a big, fat target?*[74]

The so-called delayering of corporate America during the past decade has been remarkable. General Electric stripped away six layers of management, from ten to four.[75] W. R. Grace & Co., a chemical company, also sliced out six layers of management.[76] America's second biggest copper company, Asarco, compressed 13 layers of management down to only five, thus helping to save the company $100 million.[77] Does delayering mean that hierarchies are unnecessary? According to motivation expert Edward Lawler, hierarchies are necessary, but less hierarchy is better:

Hierarchies perform some very important organizational functions that must be done in some way if coordinated, organized behavior is to take place. On the other hand, if an organization design is adopted that includes work teams, new reward systems, extensive training, and . . . various other practices . . ., organizations can operate effectively with substantially less hierarchy.[78]

Some organizations already have proved Lawler's point. Federal Express, for example, created a whole new overnight delivery industry with only five layers of management.[79]

More Teams.   Envisioning tomorrow's organizations, Peter Drucker mentions three characteristics: fewer layers, information-based, and structured around teams.[80] Common team formats include quality circles, cross-functional teams, and self-managed teams. We pay close attention to each of these in later chapters. Greater emphasis on teamwork demands more effective communication, greater interpersonal trust, negotiating skills, and efficient conflict management. These topics also are discussed in later chapters.

> **You Call That Teamwork?**   10I
>
> Michael Schrage, author of the book, *No More Teams!*:
>
> *Somehow, we have to get past this idea that all we have to do is join hands and sing Kum Ba Yah and say, 'We've moved to teamwork.' . . . It's just not that easy. Anyone who's ever been on a team knows that. . . .*
>
> *Source:* As quoted in Ellen Neuborne, "Companies Save, but Workers Pay," *USA Today* (February 25, 1997): 1B.
>
> **Questions:** *Does Schrage have a good point or is he being overly negative? Explain. What is your own experience with real teamwork? What does management have to do to promote real teamwork?*

Smallness Within Bigness.   When it comes to organizations, how big is too big? Is small beautiful? Is bigger better? These questions continue to stir lively debate in management circles. Research has not produced clear-cut answers.[81] Today, however, many have come to realize the issue is not the size of the organization. Rather, *complexity* seems to be the key issue. As organizations grow, they tend to become more complex and unmanageable. The trick for managers is to strike a balance to jointly reap the benefits of large size and small scale. A prime example is Cleveland's Parker Hannifin Corporation, the successful maker of hydraulics and other heavy equipment.

> *"When a division gets to a point where its general manager can't know and understand the business and be close to the customer, we split it off," says Chief Executive Paul G. Schloemer. Typically, that means plants of 300 to 400 workers, but there is no hard-and-fast rule on size. It has more to do with how well managers can deal with the organization's complexity. Parker Hannifin now has more than 200 plants in some 80 divisions.*[82]

We can expect to see many attempts to create entrepreneurial units within the financial security blanket of big companies in the years ahead. General Electric's Jack Welch observed: "Well, in the end, that's what it's all about, trying to create a small-company soul in a big-company body. If you can do that and use the leverage and power, the global reach and human resources of a big company, you can create massive amounts of opportunity."[83]

New Organizational Configurations

Figure 10.9 illustrates three different ways in which the traditional pyramid organization is being reshaped.[84] They are the hourglass organization, the cluster organization, and the virtual organization. In various combinations, these three configurations embody the characteristics just discussed. They also may overlap, as when an hourglass organization relies extensively on teams. The new structures have important

Figure 10.9

Reshaping the Traditional Pyramid Organization

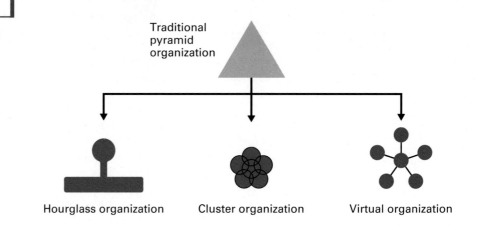

implications for both the practice of management and your quality of work life. Let us examine them and take an imaginary peek into the not-too-distant future of work organizations.

hourglass organization
a three-layer structure with a constricted middle layer

Hourglass Organizations.   The **hourglass organization** consists of three layers, with the middle layer distinctly pinched. A strategic elite is responsible for formulating a vision for the organization and making sure it becomes reality. A significantly shrunken middle-management layer carries out a coordinating function for diverse lower-level activities. Thanks to computer networks that flash information directly from the factory floor or retail outlet to the executive suite and back again, middle managers are no longer simply conduits for warmed-over information. Also unlike traditional middle managers, hourglass middle managers are generalists rather than narrow specialists. They are comfortable dealing with complex interfunctional problems. A given middle manager might deal with an accounting problem one day, a product design issue the next, and a marketing dilemma the next—all within cross-functional team settings.

At the bottom of the hourglass is a broad layer of technical specialists who act as their own supervisors much of the time. Consequently, the distinction between supervisors and rank-and-file personnel is blurred. Employees at this operating level complain about a very real lack of promotion opportunities. Management tries to keep them motivated with challenging work assignments, lateral transfers, skill-training opportunities, and pay-for-performance schemes. Union organizers attempt to exploit complaints about employees "having to act like managers, but not being paid like managers."

cluster organization
collaborative structure in which teams are the primary unit

Cluster Organizations.   Another new configuration shown in Figure 10.9 is the **cluster organization.** This label is appropriate because teams are the primary structural unit. This is how Harvard's Rosabeth Moss Kanter envisions what she calls the new collaborative organization:

> *The new, collaborative organization is predicated on a logic of flexible work assignments, not of fixed job responsibilities. To promote innovation and responsiveness, two of today's competitive imperatives, managers need to see this new organization as a cluster of activity sets, not as a rigid structure.*[85]

Imagining ourselves working in a cluster organization, we see multiskilled people moving from team to team as projects dictate. Pay for knowledge is a common practice. Motivation seems to be high, but some complain about a lack of job security because things are constantly changing. Stress levels rise when the pace of change quickens. Special training efforts, involving team-building exercises, are aimed at enhancing everyone's communication and group involvement skills.[86]

Virtual Organizations.   From the time of the industrial revolution until the Internet age, the norm was to build an organization capable of designing, producing, and marketing products. Bigger was assumed to be better. And this approach worked as long as large batches of look-alike products were acceptable to consumers. But along came the Internet, e-commerce, and mass customization, discussed in Chapters 1 and 7. *Speed*—in the form of faster market research, faster product development, faster production, and faster delivery—became more important than size. Meanwhile, global competition kept a lid on prices. Suddenly, consumers realized they could get exactly what they wanted, at a good price, and fast. Lumbering organizational giants of the past were not up to the task. Enter **virtual organizations,** flexible networks of value-adding subcontractors, linked by the Internet, e-mail, fax machines, and telephones.[87] *Business Week* recently offered this perspective:

> *The sea change flowing from the Net is so profound that owning a factory is increasingly regarded as a liability. Hewlett-Packard, IBM, Silicon Graphics, and others have sold plants to contract producers such as Solectron, SCI Systems, Flextronics, and Celestica—then signed up these manufacturing specialists as suppliers. Some experts imagine that many enterprises will ultimately become tripartite virtual partnerships. One arm will handle*

virtual organizations
Internet-linked networks of value-adding subcontractors

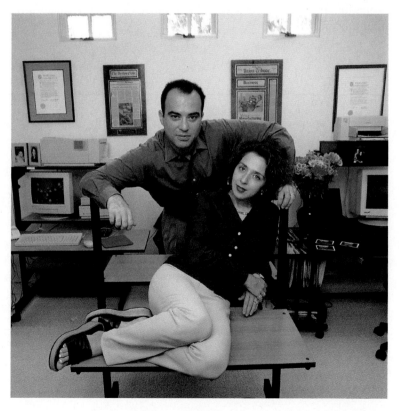

Husband-and-wife team Mahmoud (Max) Ladjevardi and Bibi Kasrai run a thriving $8-million-a-year ergonomic office furniture business out of their home office. La Jolla, California–based Soho Inc. is a virtual organization with no factory, no warehouses, and no delivery trucks. Two employees in Massachusetts handle orders and record keeping. Wood components shipped in from North Carolina, metal parts from Georgia, and brackets from Ohio are boxed into ready-to-assemble units in Chicago and shipped to Soho's catalog and retail customers. The biggest job for these entrepreneurs was lining up reliable suppliers, a two-year "virtual headache."

⇗⇘ A Virtual Global Organization   **10J**

    Consider Planet-Intra.com Ltd., a year-old software company that is nominally based in Mountain View, California. Alan J. McMillan, the 37-year-old founder and CEO, is a Canadian who had been working in Hong Kong. The company's product was written by a software team in Croatia. The vice president for technology is Russian, while the VP of international sales is a German living in Tokyo. They use the Internet—in fact, their own product—to collaborate across borders. "We live and breathe the Internet," says McMillan.

Source: John Byrne, "The Search for the Young and Gifted," *Business Week* (October 4, 1999): 110.

Questions: *What are the positives and negatives of this type of organization? Would you like to work in this sort of virtual organization? Explain.*

---

product development and engineering, another will take care of marketing, and the third will do the production chores.[88]

From a personal perspective, life in virtual organizations is *hectic.* Everything moves at Internet speed. Change and learning are constant. Cross-functional teams are the norm, and job reassignments are frequent. Project specialists rarely see a single project to completion because they are whisked off to other projects. Unavoidable by-products of constant change are stress and burnout. Unexpectedly, the need for face-to-face contact increases as geographically dispersed team members communicate via e-mail and voice mail. Only face-to-face interaction, both on and off the job, can build the rapport and trust necessary to get something done quickly with people you rarely see. The growing gap between information haves and have-nots produces resentment and alienation among low-paid workers employed by factory, data-processing, and shipping subcontractors.

Summary

1. Contingency organization design has grown in popularity as environmental complexity has increased. The idea behind contingency design is structuring the organization to fit situational demands. Consequently, contingency advocates contend that there is no one best organizational setup for all situations. Diagnosing the degree of environmental uncertainty is an important first step in contingency design. Field studies have validated the assumption that organization structure should vary according to the situation.

2. Burns and Stalker discovered that mechanistic (rigid) organizations are effective when the environment is relatively stable and that organic (flexible) organizations are best when unstable conditions prevail.

3. Lawrence and Lorsch found that differentiation (division of labor) and integration (cooperation among specialists) increased in successful organizations as environmental complexity increased. Today's organizations tend to suffer from excessive differentiation and inadequate integration.

4. There are five basic departmentalization formats, each with its own combination of advantages and disadvantages. Functional departmentalization is the most common approach. The others are product-service, geographic location, customer classification, and work flow process departmentalization. In actual practice, these pure types of departmentalization usually are combined in various ways.

5. Design variables available to organizers are span of control, decentralization, line and staff, and matrix. As organizers have come to realize that situational factors dictate how many people a manager can directly supervise, the notion of an ideal span of control has become obsolete. Decentralization, the delegation of decision authority to lower-level managers, has been praised as being democratic and criticized for reducing top management's control. Strategic business units foster a high degree of decentralization. Line and staff organization helps balance specialization and unity of command. Functional authority serves to make line and staff organizations more organic by giving staff specialists temporary and limited line authority. Matrix organizations are highly organic because they combine vertical and horizontal lines of authority to achieve coordinated control over complex projects.

6. Delegation of authority, although generally resisted for a variety of reasons, is crucial to decentralization. Effective delegation permits managers to tackle higher-priority duties while helping train and develop lower-level managers. Although delegation varies in degree, it never means abdicating primary responsibility. Successful delegation requires plenty of initiative from lower-level managers.

7. Many factors, with global competition leading the way, are forcing management to reshape the traditional pyramid bureaucracy. These new organizations are characterized by fewer layers, extensive use of teams, and manageably small subunits. Three emerging organizational configurations are the hourglass organization, the cluster organization, and virtual organizations. Each has its own potentials and pitfalls.

Terms to Understand

Organizing (p. 294)

Contingency design (p. 295)

Mechanistic organizations (p. 295)

Organic organizations (p. 295)

Differentiation (p. 298)

Integration (p. 298)

Departmentalization (p. 299)

Span of control (p. 305)

Centralization (p. 307)

Decentralization (p. 307)

Strategic business unit (p. 309)

Line and staff organization (p. 310)

Functional authority (p. 310)

Matrix organization (p. 311)

Delegation (p. 313)

Hourglass organization (p. 318)

Cluster organization (p. 318)

Virtual organizations (p. 319)

Skills & Tools

If You Want to Be Delegated Important Duties, Then Demonstrate a Lot of *Initiative*

Instructions: Assess yourself with this checklist for taking initiative. What areas need improvement?

Going Beyond the Job

- I make the most of my present assignment.
- I do more than I am asked to do.
- I look for places where I might spot problems and fix them.
- I fix bugs that I notice in programs or at least tell someone about them.
- I look for opportunities to do extra work to help the project move along more quickly.

New Ideas and Follow-Through

- I try to do some original work.
- I look for places where something that's already done might be done better.
- I have ideas about new features and other technical projects that might be developed.
- When I have an idea, I try to make it work and let people know about it.
- I try to document what my idea is and why it's a good idea.
- I think about and try to document how my idea would save the company money or bring in new business.
- I seek advice from people who have been successful in promoting ideas.
- I construct a plan for selling my idea to people in the company.

Dealing Constructively with Criticism

- I tell colleagues about my ideas to get their reactions and criticisms.
- I use their comments and criticisms to make my ideas better.
- I consult the sources of criticisms to help find solutions.
- I continue to revise my ideas to incorporate my colleagues' concerns.

Planning for the Future

- I spend time planning what I'd like to work on next.
- I look for other interesting projects to work on when my present work gets close to the finish line.
- I talk to people to find out what projects are coming up and will need people.

Source: Reprinted by permission of *Harvard Business Review*. An exhibit from "How Bell Labs Creates Star Performers," by Robert Kelly and Janet Caplan, 71 (July–August 1993). Copyright © 1993 by the President and Fellows of Harvard College; all rights reserved.

Internet Exercises

1. **Let's get really organic:** Safe to say, there's probably no other company quite like W. L. Gore & Associates (**www.gore.com**). The maker of Gore-Tex fabrics, popular among sportspeople, consistently makes the "100 Best Companies to Work for in America" list. This exercise gives you a peek inside an extraordinarily organic organization. Select the main menu heading "About Gore." Also, the Profile and Careers pages provide additional insights.

   Learning Points: 1. Using Table 10.2 as a guide, try to figure out what organic organization features are evident at Gore. 2. What types of people would and would not be comfortable working at W. L. Gore? Would you like to work at Gore? 3. What are the main risks of being too organic?

2. **Achieving "integration" at General Electric:** Differentiation and integration, as discussed in this chapter and illustrated in Figure 10.1, are opposing organizational forces requiring proper balance. Typically, the forces of differentiation (caused by division of labor and technical specialization) overpower the forces of integration (coordinating mechanisms). GE (**www.ge.com/index.htm**) studiously encourages integration so that the organization will be a true coordinated learning organization that grows and prospers. This exercise reveals a couple of GE's "secret weapons" in the battle against unchecked differentiation. Go to GE's home page and select "Inside GE" from the menu bar at the top. At the Inside GE page, click on the subheading "Horizontal Learning" in the "Learning Culture" category. Read the short piece on horizontal learning. (*Note:* Additional relevant information can be obtained by clicking on the following at the Inside GE page: "Values;" "Careers"; and "Leadership Dev.")

   Learning Points: 1. Why do GE's "Work-Outs" qualify as integrating mechanisms? 2. How does GE's concept of "horizontal learning" foster integration in the giant company? 3. Why is integration so important at GE (the world's ninth largest corporation, with nearly 300,000 employees worldwide)?[89]

   For updates to these exercises, visit our Web site (**www.hmco.com/college**).

Bean Counters' Revenge: "Tear Down the Walls"

Closing Case

Anton Hendler, a certified public accountant, is deep into a phone conversation with a longtime client whose $10-million textile business unexpectedly found itself without a controller a couple of days ago. Hendler speedily dispatched a fellow accountant to fill in for a while, and now his client is going into raptures over the way the arrangement's working out. "That's wonderful news," Hendler booms into the telephone. "WON-DAH-FULL!" Half a dozen heads whirl around as his baritone reverberates like a sonic wave through the wide-open work environment (there are no private offices, no cubicles, no secrets) owned and occupied by Lipschultz, Levin & Gray, Certified Public Accountants, in Northbrook, Illinois, just north of Chicago.

If LLG were your basic run-of-the-mill CPA practice, Hendler would be squirreled away in a sound-sucking windowless warren of bank-teller-size cubes near the elevators. Happy news straight from paying customers would never reach him or any other staff accountant unless it had been vetted by senior heavyweights and handed down the chain of command in dignified order. No, Hendler would be as far removed as possible from real live clients and unfiltered feedback, until the day he finally hit the big time and moved up into the lonely grandeur and complex networks of privileged communication that mark partnership territory.

Then again, Lipschultz, Levin & Gray (or "The Bean Counters," as the firm likes to be called) is way out of the range of what anyone who's halfway familiar with accounting firms is used to. Not one of the firm's 26 employees (called "team members") or five partners (called "members") has an office or a desk to call his or her own—or even a regular location. Instead, everyone who works there is part of a nomadic tribe of people who tote their gear (files, phones, laptops) to a new spot every day, a chore made easier than it sounds because each piece of furniture is mounted on casters and locomotes at a touch.

The foundation of LLG's novel approach is everywhere you look in this building: evidence of versatility, comfort, and eccentricity in a fizzy, constantly metamorphosing space that makes even a hot new concept like "flexible workplace" seem drab and worn-out. True, the top people had to give up some executive ego candy, like private offices and reserved parking and pinstriped suits, but in exchange for roughing it, they got this jaw dropper of an office, as beautiful as it is revolutionary.

The firm's nickname is really what started it. In the early 1990s, when LLG surveyed its clients to find out what they thought of accountants in general, the thing that kept turning up was the phrase *bean counter*, the rude but ubiquitous term that disses accountants as uncommunicative, shortsighted penny pinchers who are obsessed with the smallest of financial details. Maybe these accountants couldn't do much to alter the negative perceptions that dogged their whole profession—which, as everybody kept telling them, is as boring as airline food—but that didn't stop them from poking fun at it. Why not liberate themselves from the confines of the green-eyeshade mentality to pursue a bigger, zippier way of working, where souped-up skills and distinctive service to clients are far more important than the size of partners' offices?

The Bean Counters have since unleashed a whole slew of changes that are wonderfully entrepreneurial and also sort of nuts. Every telltale remnant of dreary CPA-ness

has been purged. Today the firm still delivers traditional accounting, audit, and tax services, but it also has just launched four new business-consulting offshoots. Income has tripled and client referrals have doubled over the past ten years. More than anything else, LLG has paid careful attention to developing the creativity, talent, and diversity of its staffers so that new knowledge can be acquired and passed around without getting hung up on the thorns of reporting relationships or stuck in out-of-the-way corner offices. That is an accomplishment that could be brought about only by time, a deep and durable dissatisfaction with the way things were, accidental discoveries, and the kind of leader who is bold and funny and idealistic and a natural at figuring stuff out. . . .

"We always followed the pattern of the big firms," says Steve Siegel, LLG's 47-year-old managing member, a CPA/lawyer who joined the firm full-time in 1976 and was named to his current post in 1991. "We threw more and more people at problems and built big offices and a big wonderful pyramid," he says. Ask Siegel about the business preoccupation back then, and he gets a little hyper. "Why aren't we making any money? Where's our money?' That was it," he says, chuckling.

He can laugh about it now, but back in those dark pre–Bean Counter megapyramid days, it was no joke. LLG employed some 55 people, who occupied nearly 17,000 square feet of standard-issue chopped-up office space. The firm spent a fortune on salaries and most of the rest of its revenues on rent. Partners, whose take-home pay is traditionally about a third of a firm's profits, were making about one-sixth of LLG's profits. . . .

Since new clients weren't exactly clamoring for LLG's services, the firm didn't kick up enough work to keep everybody busy. Staffers—bored, discouraged, and underpaid—headed for the green in other pastures. Recruiting new people became a regular, though dismal, feature of life at the firm. "We kept saying we wanted top-notch people, but who the hell would come to us? So we ended up with everybody else's dregs," says Siegel. . . .

Siegel's eyes were opened when he cornered Scottish-born-and-trained partner Bill Finestone. "Are you a really good accountant in Scotland?" he wanted to know, and, "Are there others of you?" When Finestone replied he thought that among Scottish accountants he was about average, it came as a shock. Here was this Scot who'd scored in the top 100 in the United States when he sat for his CPA exam, who is everything you'd want in a partner and an accountant—and he says, well, I'm about average. That convinced Siegel he should look outside the United States for talent, a search that has paid off handsomely. Of the 26 current team members, four are from Scotland, two are English, two are South Africans, one is Russian, and one is from France.

Source: Republished with permission of *Inc., The Magazine for Growing Companies* from "Tear Down the Walls," by Nancy K. Austin. *Inc.*, 21 (April 1999). Permission conveyed through Copyright Clearance Center, Inc.

FOR DISCUSSION

1. Using Table 10.2 as a guide, is LLG a mechanistic or organic organization? Site specific supporting evidence.

2. Would you call LLG a centralized or decentralized organization? Explain.

3. Is LLG a good or bad climate for delegation? Explain.

4. Which of the new organizational configurations—hourglass, cluster, or virtual—apparently fits LLG? Explain.

HUMAN RESOURCE MANAGEMENT

CHAPTER OBJECTIVES

When you finish studying this chapter, you should be able to

1 Explain what human resource management involves.

2 Describe the human resource planning process.

3 Distinguish among equal employment opportunity, affirmative action, and managing diversity.

4 Explain how managers can be more effective interviewers.

5 Discuss how performance appraisals can be made legally defensible.

6 Compare and contrast the ingredients of good training programs for both skill and factual learning.

7 Explain how *enterprise compacts* can foster union-management cooperation.

8 Specify the essential components of an organization's policies for dealing with sexual harassment and alcohol and drug abuse.

"PEOPLE ARE
THE COMMON DENOMINATOR
OF PROGRESS."
john kenneth galbraith

THE CHANGING WORKPLACE

Is Texaco Free of Corporate Racism?

It's known as "The Crisis" around Texaco's sprawling office headquarters in a leafy suburb north of New York City, which is certainly apropos. It was the embarrassing and expensive saga that forced the oil giant to cut a hefty $175 million check nearly three years ago to settle a racial discrimination lawsuit filed by some of the company's African-American employees, the largest such settlement ever. As the drama evolved both before and after the settlement in November 1996, details emerged that exposed blatant acts of racism by Texaco managers and employees. There was the dicey taped discussion among company executives that included racist language and talk of destroying key evidence, and the vile occasion when a white employee stopped outside a coveted two-window office inhabited by an African-American woman and said, ". . . [expletive], I never thought I'd live to see the day when a black woman had an office at Texaco." Moments like these—along with several examples of institutional racism, such as hundreds of minority employees being paid less than the minimum salary for their job category—caused Texaco to be branded the worst of corporate rogues.

So, here's the shocker: Texaco, still perceived by many as a chamber of horrors for minorities, is in the midst of a remarkable transformation, one that just may turn the company into a bastion of equal opportunity for people of color. In time, it may even become a model for any corporation that wants to learn how to become more hospitable to employees of all races.

Just how far has Texaco come? Here are a few numbers worth noting: Last year minorities accounted for nearly four in ten new hires at Texaco and more than 20 percent of promotions. During the first six months of 1999, minorities accounted for 44 percent of new hires and 22 percent of promotions. In 1996 company officials vowed to spend at least $1 billion with minority- and women-owned vendors—or about 15 percent of overall spending—before 2001. They passed the halfway mark two years into the program, spending $528 million with minority- and women-owned vendors during 1997 and 1998. (Black and Hispanic firms received $135 million of that total.) Also, *all* employees are now required to attend diversity training; managers and supervisors are shipped to change-management communications courses, as well. CEO Peter Bijur, an aggressive, fast-talking, 33-year company veteran, also made several high-profile hires at

key executive positions, a clear signal that Texaco's leadership—the "top of the house," in industry parlance—was not immune to dramatic change. Yet Bijur isn't ready to declare victory (white men, after all, still account for nearly 80 percent of company executives), though he's clearly satisfied with what he sees as concrete signs of a cultural shift. "Now," he says, "we treat all people with the utmost respect—that is a real achievement."

Here's another telling note: Company officials were feeling good enough about themselves earlier this year to apply for inclusion in *Fortune*'s 1999 list of America's 50 Best Companies for Asians, Blacks, and Hispanics. . . . Texaco didn't make the cut, but the very fact the firm aspired to make the list (and actually believed it had a chance) says plenty about how some folks there are feeling about themselves these days on matters of race. And at least one diversity expert says their new attitude may indeed be warranted. "I have never seen a company be so creative and so dedicated to change," says Weldon Latham, a senior partner at the Washington, D.C., law firm Shaw Pittman and a prominent racial-harassment litigator. "They are absolutely a model for how to approach one of the biggest problems facing this country." . . .

. . . [Bijur] recruited African-American heavyweights to Texaco and gave them key jobs. Ira D. Hall, director of global business development at IBM, came over to manage Texaco's joint ventures around the world—entities that are expected to generate about one-third of company earnings in 1999. Then came Angela E. Vallot, a hotshot Washington, D.C., attorney, to head up the company's diversity programs. Finally, Deval L. Patrick, a Boston attorney and former Justice Department official who had led the independent task force studying Texaco's diversity efforts, signed on as vice president and general counsel.

You might think Bijur would have had a rough time recruiting such talent in the wake of the settlement. But by that time, Texaco was in an unusual position in corporate America: It was under a court order to improve its diversity record. Says Patrick: "There's often a lot of noise created by employers about what they're going to do about diversity. This was a situation where they couldn't just get away with noise. I detected a very unusual desire to solve [the] problem."

Certainly Bijur needed to do some arm-twisting, but his obvious personal interest in enacting change at Texaco was often a key factor in negotiations. "It's obvious that top-of-the-house commitment is there, and it will remain there," says Vallot. For Hall in particular, a powerful selling point was the presence of a comprehensive, well-scripted plan for changing the company's culture. "It suggested that they had a systematic approach, which you need for success," he says. "There was a sufficient risk-reward profile for me to want to come work here."

It's hard to quarrel with Texaco's strategy and—at least in the short term—its results. But you still have to wonder if what's going on at Texaco represents essential, fundamental change or merely cosmetic alterations. Some company officials still seem to be in denial about the true state of racial affairs at Texaco prior to The Crisis. . . .

Perhaps the best way to assess change at Texaco is to look at how the residue of past grievances is filtering through the system, and how managers and workers are dealing with each other daily. As Vallot puts it: "You're not going to change the way people think, but you can change the way people behave." By that standard, the company's transformation has indeed been significant—though not perfect. Consider this: Patrick, the new general counsel, had expected to be involved in frequent discrimination litigation, but new cases have dwindled to near zero. Instead, Patrick mostly works on meatier matters, such as Texaco's recent proposed merger with Chevron. Says Patrick: "It's a seismic change."

---

1 **Explain what human resource management involves.**

human resource management *planning, acquisition, and development of human resources*

Staffing has long been an integral part of the management process. Like other traditional management functions, such as planning and organizing, the domain of staffing has grown throughout the years. This growth reflects increasing environmental complexity and greater organizational sophistication, as the Texaco case clearly illustrates. Early definitions of staffing focused narrowly on hiring people for vacant positions. Today, the traditional staffing function is just one part of the more encompassing human resource management process. **Human resource management** involves the planning, acquisition, and development of human resources necessary for organizational success.[1] This broader definition underscores the point that people are valuable *resources* requiring careful nurturing. In fact, what were once called personnel departments are now called human resource departments. In a more folksy manner, the top human resources executive at Wal-Mart is called the "senior vice president of people."[2] This people-centered human resource approach emphasizes the serious moral and legal issues involved in viewing labor simply as a commodity to be bought, exploited to exhaustion, and discarded when convenient. Moreover, global competitive pressures have made the skillful management of human resources more important than ever.[3]

Progressive and successful organizations treat all employees as valuable human resources. Frederick W. Smith, founder and chairman of Federal Express Corporation, has helped his company prosper by putting his employees first. Smith reportedly spends one-third of his week handling personnel matters, including worker-grievance appeals.[4] Field research indicates that employees tend to return the favor when they are treated with dignity and respect. For instance, one recent study compared steel mills with either "control" or "commitment" human resource systems. Emphasis at the control-oriented steel mills was on cost cutting, rule compliance, and efficiency. Meanwhile, the other steel mills encouraged psychological commitment to the company with a climate of trust and participation. "The mills with commitment systems had higher productivity, lower scrap rates, and lower employee turnover than those with control systems."[5]

A particularly promising development in the staffing area is the linkage of the human resource perspective with strategic management.[6] Such linkage is evident in the following statement by Kathryn Connors, vice president of human resources at clothing retailer Liz Claiborne.

> *Human resources is part of the strategic planning process. . . . It's part of policy development, line extension planning and the merger and acquisition processes. Little is done in the company that doesn't involve us in the planning, policy or finalization stages of any deal.*[7]

In a recent survey of senior human resource managers, 37 percent said they "always" participated in corporate strategic planning. Another 42 percent said they "sometimes" had a hand in company strategy.[8]

Figure 11.1 presents a model for the balance of this chapter; it reflects this strategic orientation. Notice how a logical sequence of human resource management activities—human resource planning, selection, performance appraisal, and training—all derive from organizational strategy and structure. Without a strategic orientation, the management of people becomes haphazardly inefficient and ineffective. Also, as indicated in Figure 11.1, an ongoing process following selection involves identifying and solving human resource problems. Three contemporary human resource problems, explored in the last section of this chapter, are fostering union-management cooperation, sexual harassment, and alcohol and drug abuse.

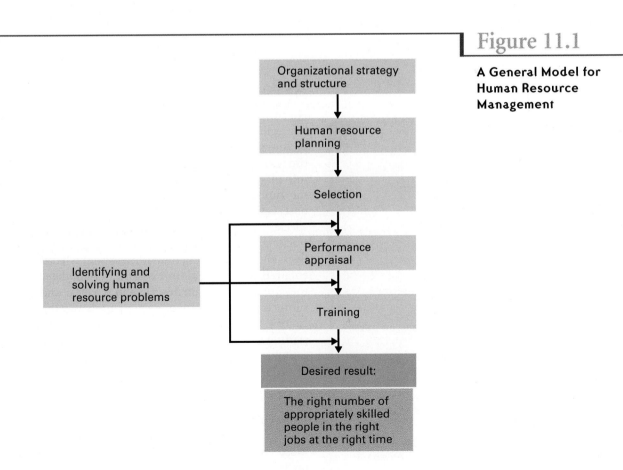

Figure 11.1

A General Model for Human Resource Management

Human Resource Planning

2 **Describe the human resource planning process.**

human resource planning *meeting future human resource needs with a comprehensive staffing strategy*

Human resource planning helps management find the right people for the right jobs at the right time. Formally defined, **human resource planning** is the development of a comprehensive staffing strategy for meeting the organization's future human resource needs.[9]

A Systems Perspective

Human resource planning requires a systematic approach to staffing. Staffing has suffered from a lack of continuity as people are hired and trained on an "as needed" basis. With today's rapidly changing conditions, organizations need a foresighted, systematic approach that provides specific answers to this overriding question: "How can the organization assure that it will have people of the right types and numbers, organized appropriately, managed effectively, and focused on customer satisfaction?"[10] Answers to this question can be obtained through a systematic approach such as the one shown in Figure 11.2. First, current staffing needs are assessed. Next, the future needs of human resources are forecast. Third, a comprehensive staffing strategy is formulated. Finally, evaluation and updating of the system are achieved by continually recycling through the process.

job analysis *determining fundamental elements of jobs through systematic observation*

job description *summary of duties and qualifications for a specific position*

Assessing Current Needs

No meaningful forecasting and formulation of staffing strategies can take place until management has a clear picture of the organization's current staffing situation. A time-consuming procedure called job analysis comes into play here. **Job analysis** is the process of determining the fundamental elements of jobs through systematic observation and analysis.[11] Usually, a team of trained specialists isolates specific jobs by analyzing work flows, tracking procedures for accomplishing subunit objectives, and interviewing individuals about what their jobs entail. If job descriptions exist, they are updated. If not, they are written. A **job description** is a clear and concise summary of the duties of a specific job and the qualifications for holding it.[12] Job descriptions are a useful staffing tool for achieving productive individual-organization matches. But keeping job descriptions up-to-date in today's fast-paced, project-driven organizations can be hectic because they are often obsolete by the time the ink is dry.

By comparing updated job descriptions with the qualifications and duties of the individuals currently holding those jobs, management can determine whether the organization is appropriately staffed. Overstaffing can be wastefully expensive, but understaffing can block the

---

11A

How Important Are People?

Jack Welch, legendary CEO of General Electric:

"We spend all our time on people. The day we screw up the people thing, this company is over."

Scott Adams, cartoonist whose Dilbert comic strip "runs in more than 1,000 newspapers with a readership of some 60 million people":

"The First Great Lie of Management: 'Employees are our most valuable asset.'"

Sources: As quoted in Thomas A. Stewart, "The Contest for Welch's Throne Begins: Who Will Run GE?" *Fortune* (January 11, 1999): 27; and Scott Adams, "Dilbert's Management Handbook," *Fortune* (May 13, 1996): 99, 108.

Questions: *What is wrong with an organizational world where managers say Welch is right while many employees say Adams is telling it straight? Explain.*

For further information about the interactive annotations in this chapter, visit our Web site (**www.hmco.com/college**).

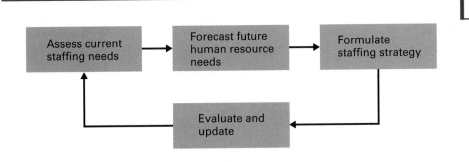

Figure 11.2

A Basic Model for Human Resource Planning Systems

achievement of organizational objectives. An appropriately staffed organization has the right number of people working in jobs best suited to their talents.

Organizations are finding computerized personnel inventories invaluable. *Human resource information systems* can be compiled most conveniently during the initial assessment of human resources. By keying or scanning each present employee's name, identification number, and biographical summary into a computer data base along with such pertinent data as seniority, pay status, promotion record, skills, and training experience, a time-saving human resource decision tool is created.[13] Privacy-protected access to the organization's human resource data base via computer networks or the Internet helps managers and empowers employees. For example,

A robust economy and record low unemployment in recent years have fostered some creative staffing strategies in the United States. For example, shoemaker Allen-Edmonds reversed the usual order of things. Instead of trying to attract people to its factories, it opened a factory where people needed good jobs. When Allen-Edmonds moved into downtown Milwaukee's Hispanic community, these local residents signed on for pay that was much higher than usual. Now that's a win-win situation to smile about.

Federal Express' PRISM system was specifically developed to help grow and track employee capabilities. It ensures that employees are well trained and that growth opportunities are available to them. Employees can access information online and view all job vacancies in the company, then bid on those that interest them . . . and the computer verifies that their experience meets the needs of the job.[14]

Forecasting Future Needs

This second phase of the human resource planning cycle compares projected demand and projected supply. Many environmental and organizational factors need to be considered (see Table 11.1).[15] It is often helpful for managers to envision human resources as flowing into, through, and out of the organization. Like any other resource, human resources are subject to subtle erosion: employees leave the organization for a wide variety of reasons, and they must be replaced. Management should explore both internal and external sources of supply for these replacements. If, for instance, enough people are studying computer programming in schools and colleges, data-processing firms may not need to train so many of their own computer programmers in the future.

The net result of human resource demand and supply forecasting is a detailed list of future staffing requirements. This list will tell management how many people with what sorts of abilities will be needed at specific future points in time.

Formulating a Staffing Strategy

To satisfy future staffing requirements, management has two sets of options. First, it can rely on current employees or hire new ones. Second, employees can be trained or not trained. Combined, these two sets of options yield four staffing strategies: (1) do not train current employees, (2) train current employees, (3) hire but do not

Table 11.1

Factors in Forecasting the Demand for and Supply of Human Resources

Forecast demand	Expected growth of the organization.
	Budget constraints.
	Turnover resulting from resignations, terminations, transfers, retirement, and death.
	Introduction of new technology.
	Minority-hiring goals.
Forecast supply	Number of employees willing and able to be trained.
	Promotable employees.
	Availability of required talent in local, regional, national, and international labor markets.
	Competition for talent within the industry and in general.
	Demographic trends (such as in Ireland, where the population is increasingly young and well educated).
	Enrollment trends in government training programs, trade schools, and colleges and universities.

train outsiders, and (4) hire and train outsiders. In today's larger organizations all four strategies are usually used simultaneously, according to situational requirements.

Evaluation and Update

Like many other systems, human resource planning requires a feedback loop, or a means of monitoring the system. Comparisons of the actual performance of the system with previously formulated plans allow necessary corrections to be made. Unexpected shortages or excesses of qualified people signal a defect in the planning system. Sometimes management discovers it has overlooked critical demand or supply considerations. Whatever the problem, prompt corrective action will help the human resource planning cycle work more smoothly and effectively each time it is repeated.

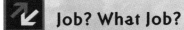

Job? What Job?   11B

Euclid, Ohio: Andre Miles has applied for a job at Lincoln Electric Co. three times in the past three years, but he never got past a screening interview.

"It is frustrating that I don't even have a chance," says the 22-year-old construction worker. He isn't alone. More than 20,000 applications have been submitted to Lincoln in the past 18 months, and most were rejected. Yet the maker of motors and welding products says it still has positions to fill and can't find the workers it needs.

Source: Raju Narisetti, "Manufacturers Decry a Shortage of Workers While Rejecting Many," *The Wall Street Journal* (September 8, 1995): A1.

Questions: *From a human resource planning perspective, what is the meaning of this situation? What changes need to be made to improve this situation?*

Selection

Management finds qualified people to fill available jobs through the employee selection process. Because researchers have documented "very large" differences in individual job performance, careful employee selection is more important than ever.[16] In a manner of speaking, employee selection serves as the organization's human resource gatekeeper. Today's managers are challenged to find the best available talent without unfairly discriminating against any segment of society.

A person who has applied for a particular job is not necessarily qualified to hold it. Thus, a screening mechanism is required to separate those who are qualified from those who are not. Human resource management experts commonly compare the screening process to a hurdle race. Typical hurdles job applicants have to clear are psychological tests, work sampling tests, reference checks, interviews, and physical examinations. Many companies have added preemployment drug tests to this list. Importantly, Equal Employment Opportunity (EEO) legislation in the United States and elsewhere delineates what managers can and cannot do when screening job applicants.[17] As indicated in Figure 11.3, there is no perfect screening device; each has the potential for adversely affecting one or more protected minorities.

Caution: Don't Hire at Internet Speed   11C

Alan Naumann, CEO of Calico Technologies, a California e-commerce firm:

Despite all of our focus on speed, we consciously slow down for one thing: hiring people. That's tough to do when you're growing as fast as we are, but it's the one aspect of business today in which the cost of mistakes is greater than the advantage of acting in real time. Within the hiring process, we do spend a good deal of time defining a job's requirements and checking an applicant's references. That way, we can build a better partnership when an employee does come on board.

Source: "Alan Naumann," *Fast Company*, no. 25 (June 1999): 106.

Questions: *Why is careful hiring a key to strategic success today? What problems are associated with hiring the wrong person?*

Figure 11.3

Adverse Impact of Screening Techniques on Minorities

	African Americans	Females	Elderly	Physically challenged
Cognitive ability tests	●	★	◓	✕
Work-sample tests	★	○	○	○
Interview	○	◓	◓	◓
Educational requirements	●	★	◓	✕
Physical ability tests (height, weight, etc.)	★	●	✕	●

● = Fairly established evidence of adverse impact

◓ = Some evidence of adverse impact

✕ = No data that bear direct evidence, but adverse impact seems likely depending on type of disability or type of test

○ = Little or no evidence to indicate one way or the other

★ = Evidence indicates that particular minority group does as well or even better than majority members

Source: Richard D. Arvey and Robert H. Faley, *Fairness in Selecting Employees* (Figure 9.1 from p. 323), © 1988 by Addison-Wesley Publishing Company, Inc. Reprinted by permission of Addison Wesley Longman, Inc.

Equal Employment Opportunity

3 Distinguish among equal employment opportunity, affirmative action, and managing diversity.

Although earlier legislation selectively applies, the landmark EEO law in the United States is Title VII of the Civil Rights Act of 1964. Subsequent amendments, presidential executive orders, and related laws have expanded EEO's coverage. EEO law now provides a broad umbrella of employment protection for certain categories of disadvantaged individuals:

> *The result of this legislation has been that in virtually all aspects of employment, it is unlawful to discriminate on the basis of race, color, sex, religion, age, national origin, . . . [disabilities], being a disabled veteran, or being a veteran of the Vietnam Era.*[18]

What all this means is that managers cannot refuse to hire, promote, train, or transfer employees simply on the basis of the characteristics listed above. Nor can they lay off or discharge employees on these grounds. Sexual preference has been added to the list in some local jurisdictions.[19] Selection and all other personnel decisions must be made solely on the basis of objective criteria such as ability to perform or seniority. Lawsuits and fines by agencies such as the Equal Employment Opportunity Commission (EEOC) are powerful incentives to comply with the EEO laws.

Affirmative Action.   A more rigorous refinement of EEO legislation is affirmative action. An **affirmative action program (AAP)** is a plan for actively seeking out, employing, and developing the talents of those groups traditionally discriminated against in employment.[20] Affirmative action amounts to a concerted effort to make up for *past* discrimination. EEO, in contrast, is aimed at preventing *future* discrimination. Typical AAPs attack employment discrimination with the following four methods: (1) *active* recruitment of women and minorities, (2) elimination of prejudicial questions on employment application forms, (3) establishment of specific goals

affirmative action program *making up for past discrimination by actively seeking and employing minorities*

It is a tragic waste of human potential when disabled people are not given a fair chance to contribute in the workplace. We are reminded once again to emphasize *ability* in the word *disability*. Just ask the Wal-Mart customers in Kingston, New York, who rely on greeter Ginny Lockwood to answer their questions and point them in the right direction. Lockwood may be just one of Wal-Mart's nearly one million employees, but to her customers she's one of a kind.

and timetables for minority hiring, and (4) statistical validation of employment testing procedures.

Like any public policy with legal ramifications, the EEO/AAP area is fraught with complexity.[21] Varying political and legal interpretations and inconsistent court decisions have sometimes frustrated and confused managers.[22] Researchers have uncovered both negative and positive findings about affirmative action. On the negative side, "people believed to be hired through affirmative action programs carry a stigma of incompetence no matter how qualified they are for the job."[23] On the positive side, a study based on nationwide U.S. Census Bureau data found that affirmative action had helped the promotion opportunities of black workers in both government and business organizations. In fact, according to the researcher, "with the exception of women in the public sector, women and blacks enjoyed better promotion opportunities than equally qualified and situated white male workers."[24] These findings disturb some white males, who claim to be the victims of "reverse discrimination."[25] At the same time, some minority employees complain of swapping one injustice for another when they take advantage of affirmative action. Legislated social change, however necessary or laudable, is not without pain. Much remains to be accomplished to eliminate the legacy of unfair discrimination in the workplace.

From Affirmative Action to Managing Diversity.   As discussed in Chapter 3, the "managing diversity" movement promises to raise the discussion of equal employment opportunity and affirmative action to a higher plane. One authority on the subject, R. Roosevelt Thomas Jr., put it this way:

Managers usually see affirmative action and equal employment opportunity as centering on minorities and women, with very little to offer white males. The diversity I'm talking about includes not only race, gender, creed, and ethnicity but also age, background, education, function, and personality differences. The objective is not to assimilate minorities and women into a dominant white male culture but to create a dominant heterogeneous culture.[26]

In short, diversity advocates want to replace all forms of bigotry, prejudice, and intolerance with tolerance and, ideally, *appreciation* of interpersonal differences.[27] They also want to broaden the focus on minorities to include recruitment *and retention*. Don Richards, senior vice president and director of human resource development at Leo Burnett Company, the Chicago-based advertising agency, offered this hopeful perspective of managing diversity:

"As an African-American, when I was graduated from college in 1960, there was little effort made by private industries to recruit minority students," Richards said. "I'm encouraged by the changes I've seen in the past 30 years. We have a long way to go, but my hope is that one day diversity will not be a special effort but the norm—just part of doing business."[28]

Periodically, as in the case of Texaco, we are reminded of just how much remains to be done (see Managing Diversity).

Accommodating the Needs of People with Disabilities.   From the perspective of someone in a wheelchair, the world can be a very unfriendly place. Curbs, stairways, and inward-swinging doors in small public toilet stalls all symbolically say, "You're not welcome here; you don't fit in." Human disabilities vary widely, but historically, disabled people have had one thing in common—unemployment. Consider this telling statistic: the unemployment rate among 750,000 blind Americans has been 70 percent in recent years.[29] Reducing the unemployment rate for people with disabilities is not just about jobs and money. It is about self-sufficiency, hopes, and dreams.[30] With enactment of the Americans with Disabilities Act of 1990 (ADA), 43 million disabled Americans hoped to get a real chance to take their rightful place in the workforce.[31] But according to recent data, this hope remains unfulfilled. In fact, added government regulation reportedly has discouraged some employers from hiring disabled people. The disappointing findings: "analysis of Census Bureau survey data from 1987 to 1996 indicates that the act's impact on employment of the disabled was negative."[32]

The ADA, enforced by the EEOC, requires employers to make *reasonable* accommodations to the needs of present and future employees with physical and mental disabilities. As the ADA was being phased in to cover nearly all employers, many feared that their businesses would be saddled with burdensome expenses and many lawsuits. Since then, there has been some creative problem solving. According to *Business Week:*

The difficulty isn't cost, as most experts had anticipated. In fact, employers have found that many problems are easily solved. To help workers in wheelchairs, Greiner Engineering Inc. in Irving, Tex., installed a lighter-weight door on the women's restroom and raised a drafting table by putting bricks under its legs. "You don't have to do sophisticated structural designs and spend lots of money to be accommodating," says Tom R. Smith, Greiner's vice president for human resources.[33]

Managing Diversity

Native Americans No Longer "Silent Minority"

For a long time Tom Smith, a Cherokee, considered Native Americans to be "lost in the shadows" of corporate America—widely overlooked by recruiters and purchasing managers. His own people didn't help the cause either by being "a silent minority" while other ethnic groups lobbied for greater portions of the corporate pie. But Smith, president of a five-year-old advocacy group, the Native American Business Alliance, and CEO of a $15 million plastic-molding firm in Englewood, Ohio, says American Indians are slowly rising to join the chorus calling for major companies to recognize and embrace the talents among all minorities. "We have become more vocal in telling corporations that it's time to bring us into the mainstream," he says.

Some companies appear to be listening: Native American representation in the total workforce of the companies in our [1999 *Fortune* magazine] survey rose from 0.67 percent last year to 0.72 percent this year, though it must be added that the companies in that pool have excellent diversity records. The 1999 figure corresponds with the proportion of Native Americans in the United States at large, indicating that these companies, at least, are headed in the right direction.

Yet Smith and his colleagues aren't exactly cheering. After all, Native Americans are historically and legally isolated from the rest of America by tribal sovereignty laws. The unique laws governing Indian reservations have enabled some tribes to establish lucrative gambling oper-ations, though only 8 percent of Native Americans, in fact, gain from casino revenues. Little wonder progress has come slowly for the only people indigenous to this nation. "Most students in Indian country consider working for the *Fortune* 500 a very remote idea," says Dean Chavers, director of the Native American Scholar-ship Fund, an Albuquerque-based organization that urges Indian students to pursue business careers. Alas, only one of the fund's 198 former students works for a *Fortune* 500 firm—most have returned to their reservations.

To ease the transition, some companies are taking real steps to assure Native Americans that they don't have to leave their culture at the door. At Lucent, around 250 American Indian employees are members of Luna, an affinity group that holds monthly conference calls connecting employees from across the country; hosts an annual meeting on an Indian reservation; provides updates on job openings; and helps address career concerns. Luna members regularly advise Lucent recruiters on seeking applicants in Native American strongholds like New Mexico. And the company has forged a strong bond with the American Indian Scientific and Engineering Society in Albuquerque. "You never know, you may miss hiring a talented person if you don't recruit from as many sources as possible," says Ralph Bazhaw, Luna's president.

Source: Edward Robinson, "What About *Native* Americans?" *Fortune* (July 19, 1999): 56. © 1999 Time Inc. Reprinted by permission.

Indeed, a 1998 White House–sponsored survey "determined that the mean cost of helping disabled workers to overcome their impairments was a mere $935 per person."[34]

New technology also is making accommodation easier. Large-print computer screens for the partially blind, braille keyboards and talking computers for the blind, and tele-phones with visual readouts for the deaf are among today's helpful technologies.[35] Here are some general policy guidelines for employers from experts on the subject:

- Audit all facilities, policies, work rules, hiring procedures, and labor union contracts to eliminate barriers and bias.
- Train all managers in ADA compliance and all employees in how to be sensitive to coworkers and customers with disabilities.
- Do not hire anyone who cannot safely perform the basic duties of a particular job with reasonable accommodation.

With lots of low-tech ingenuity, a touch of high-tech, and support from coworkers, millions of disabled people can help their employers win the battle of global competition.

Employment Selection Tests

employment selection test *any procedure used in the employment decision process*

EEO guidelines in the United States have broadened the definition of an **employment selection test** to include any procedure used as a basis for an employment decision. This means that, in addition to traditional pencil-and-paper tests, unscored application forms; informal and formal interviews; performance tests; and physical, educational, or experience requirements all qualify as tests.[36] This definition of an employment test takes on added significance when you realize that the federal government requires all employment tests to be statistically valid and reliable predictors of job success.[37] Historically, women and minorities have been victimized by invalid, unreliable, and prejudicial employment selection procedures. Similar complaints have been voiced about the use of polygraphs, drug tests, and AIDS and DNA screening during the hiring process[38] (see Table 11.2).

Table 11.2

Employment Testing Techniques: An Overview		
Type of test	**Purpose**	**Comments**
Pencil-and-paper psychological and personality tests	Measure attitudes and personality characteristics such as emotional stability, intelligence, and ability to deal with stress.	Renewed interest based on claims of improved validity. Can be expensive when scoring and interpretations are done by professionals. Validity varies widely from test to test.
Pencil-and-paper honesty tests (integrity testing)	Assess candidate's degree of risk for engaging in dishonest behavior.	Inexpensive to administer. Promising evidence of validity. Growing in popularity since recent curtailment of polygraph testing. Women tend to do better than men.
Job skills tests (clerical and manual dexterity tests, math and language tests, assessment centers, and simulations)	Assess competence in actual "hands-on" situations.	Generally good validity if carefully designed and administered. Assessment centers and simulations can be very expensive.
Polygraph (lie detector) tests	Measure physical signs of stress, such as rapid pulse and perspiration.	Growing use in recent years severely restricted by federal (Employee Polygraph Protection Act of 1988), state, and local laws. Questionable validity.
Drug tests	Check for controlled substances through urine, blood, or hair samples submitted to chemical analysis.	Rapidly growing in use despite strong employee resistance and potentially inaccurate procedures.
Handwriting analysis (graphoanalysis)	Infer personality characteristics and styles from samples of handwriting.	Popular in Europe and growing in popularity in United States. Sweeping claims by proponents leave validity in doubt.
AIDS/HIV antibody tests	Find evidence of AIDS virus through blood samples.	An emerging area with undetermined legal and ethical boundaries. Major confidentiality issue.
Genetic/DNA screening	Use tissue or blood samples and family history data to identify those at risk of costly diseases.	Limited but growing use strongly opposed on legal and moral grounds. Major confidentiality issue.

Ethical Hot Spots.   Busy managers often seek quick, inexpensive, and supposedly sure-fire ways to make hiring decisions. Consequently, the area of employee selection and testing is plagued by unethical claims and practices. *Handwriting analysis* (also called graphoanalysis and graphology) is a good case in point. Proponents of this technique make generous claims about its ability to identify personality characteristics and predict job performance.[39] However, a statistical analysis of 17 graphology studies raised serious doubts about the practice. In fact, psychologists, who were untrained in graphology, actually did a better job of predicting future performance from handwritten scripts than did graphologists.[40] Hiring people strictly on the basis of their handwriting is an open invitation to a costly lawsuit.

Both giving and seeking references for job seekers have become legal and ethical hot spots as well.[41] The best practice when *giving* references is to focus solely on job performance and respect the person's privacy rights. Increasingly, employers are protecting themselves by having employees sign reference release forms.[42] When you are *seeking* references, it is a good practice to check all references, seek multiple references, and stick to discussing job performance.

No Quick Fixes.   In the final analysis, there are no really good shortcuts when screening job applicants. At the very least, vendors of screening techniques should be asked for objective, third-party validation evidence. Library and Internet searches can turn up academic studies such as the one on graphology cited earlier. Companies conducting validation studies of their own screening techniques have an obvious conflict of interest problem. A *multimethod approach* to employee selection is most desirable. For example, a manager might weigh a particular job candidate's employability on the basis of education and experience, one or more interviews, a performance test, and a reference check.

> **11F**
>
> ### ⤵ Testing, Testing
>
> **Fact:** Microsoft, the Redmond, Washington, software giant, receives about 12,000 résumés each month.
>
> *Fortune* magazine interviewed David Pritchard, Microsoft's director of recruiting, and came up with this provocative insight:
>
> *What about your approach to testing? Lots of companies conduct psychological tests. Does that interest you?*
>
> *It doesn't really interest me much. In the end, you end up with a bunch of people who answer the questions correctly, and that's not always what you want. How can a multiple-choice test tell whether someone is creative or not?*
>
> *Source:* Ron Lieber, "Wired for Hiring: Microsoft's Slick Recruiting Machine," *Fortune* (February 5, 1996): 124.
>
> ―――――――――――――――――――
>
> **Questions:** *Do you agree or disagree with this position? Why? How can a recruiter determine if a job applicant is creative?*

Effective Interviewing

Interviewing warrants special attention here because it is the most common employee selection tool.[43] Line managers at all levels are often asked to interview candidates for job openings and promotions and should be aware of the weaknesses of the traditional unstructured interview. The traditional unstructured or informal interview, which has no fixed question format or systematic scoring procedure, has been criticized on grounds such as the following:

4 Explain how managers can be more effective interviewers.

- It is highly susceptible to distortion and bias.
- It is highly susceptible to legal attack.
- It is usually indefensible if legally contested.
- It may have apparent validity, but no real validity.
- It is rarely totally job-related and may incorporate personal items that infringe on privacy.

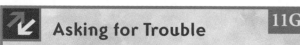

Asking for Trouble   11G

Research fact: "Job seekers asked an illegal interview question pertaining to race, age, marital status, religion, ethnicity: 39 percent."

Source: "Footnotes," *Business Week* (May 10, 1999): 8.

Questions: *What inappropriate and/or illegal interview questions have you ever been asked? How did it make you feel about the interviewer and the organization? Explain.*

- It is the most flexible selection technique, thereby being highly inconsistent.
- There is a tendency for the interviewer to look for qualities he or she prefers, and then to justify the hiring decision based on these qualities.
- Often the interviewer does not hear about the selection mistakes.
- There is an unsubstantiated confidence in the traditional interview.[44]

The Problem of Cultural Bias.   Traditional unstructured interviews are notorious for being culturally insensitive. Evidence of this problem surfaced in a study of the interviewing practices of 38 general managers employed by nine different fast-food chains. According to the researcher:

> *Considering the well-known demographics of today's workforce, it's amazing that 9 percent of those receiving a negative hiring decision are turned down for inappropriate eye contact. To give a firm handshake and look someone straight in the eyes is a very important lesson taught by Dad to every middle-class male at a tender age. Not only do nonmainstream groups miss the lesson from Dad, some are taught that direct eye contact is rude or worse. Girls are frequently taught that direct eye contact is unbecoming in a female. In reality, having averted or shifty eyes may indicate mostly that the job applicant is not a middle-class male.[45]*

Managers can be taught, however, to be aware of and to overcome cultural biases when interviewing. This is particularly important in today's era of managing diversity and greater sensitivity to disabled people.

structured interview *a set of job-related questions with standardized answers*

Structured Interviews.   Structured interviews are the recommended alternative to traditional unstructured or informal interviews.[46] A **structured interview** is defined as a set of job-related questions with standardized answers applied consistently across all interviews for a specific job.[47] Structured interviews are constructed, conducted, and scored by a committee of three to six members to try to eliminate individual bias. The systematic format and scoring of structured interviews eliminate the weaknesses inherent in unstructured interviews. Interviews via the Internet, a growing practice, can enhance the discipline of structured interviews.[48] Four types of questions typically characterize structured interviews: (1) situational, (2) job knowledge, (3) job sample simulation, and (4) worker requirements (see Table 11.3). The growing practice of determining competencies with *behavioral interviewing*, by asking job applicants to explain what they actually did (or would do) in a specific job-related situation, makes use of the situational type of question.[49]

Performance Appraisal

Annual performance appraisals are such a common part of modern organizational life that they qualify as a ritual. As with many rituals, the participants repeat the historical pattern without really asking the important questions, "Why?" and "Is there a better way?" Both appraisers and subjects tend to express general dissatisfaction with

Table 11.3 — Types of Structured Interview Questions

Type of question	Method	Information sought	Sample question
Situational	Oral	Can the applicant handle difficult situations likely to be encountered on the job?	"What would you do if you saw two of your people arguing loudly in the work area?"
Job knowledge	Oral or written	Does the applicant possess the knowledge required for successful job performance?	"Do you know how to search the Internet?"
Job sample simulation	Observation of actual or simulated performance	Can the applicant actually do essential aspects of the job?	"Can you show us how to compose and send an e-mail message?"
Worker requirements	Oral	Is the applicant willing to cope with job demands such as travel, relocation, or hard physical labor?	"Are you willing to spend 25 percent of your time on the road?"

Source: "Structured Interviewing: Avoiding Selection Problems," by Elliott D. Pursell, Michael A. Campion, and Sarah R. Gaylord, copyright November 1980. Reprinted with permission of *Personnel Journal*, Costa Mesa, California; all rights reserved.

performance appraisals. In fact, nearly 75 percent of the companies responding to a recent survey expressed major dissatisfaction with their performance appraisal system.[50] This is not surprising, in view of the following research evidence:

> Only 25 percent of managers who do performance appraisals receive training for it. When there is training it often goes little further than to explain how to use the form, administrative procedures, and deadlines for submitting and getting the forms approved.[51]

Considering that experts estimate the average cost of a *single* performance appraisal to be $1,500, the waste associated with poorly administered appraisals is mind boggling![52]

Performance appraisal can be effective and satisfying if systematically developed and implemented techniques replace haphazard methods. For our purposes, **performance appraisal** is the process of evaluating individual job performance as a basis for making objective personnel decisions.[53] This definition intentionally excludes occasional coaching, in which a supervisor simply checks an employee's work and gives immediate feedback. Although personal coaching is fundamental to good management, formally documented appraisals are needed both to ensure equitable distribution of opportunities and rewards and to avoid prejudicial treatment of protected minorities.[54]

In this section, we will examine two important aspects of performance appraisal: (1) legal defensibility and (2) alternative techniques.

performance appraisal
evaluating job performance as a basis for personnel decisions

Making Performance Appraisals Legally Defensible

Lawsuits challenging the legality of specific performance appraisal systems and resulting personnel actions have left scores of human resource managers asking themselves, "Will my organization's performance appraisal system stand up in court?" From the standpoint of limiting legal exposure, it is better to ask this question when developing a formal appraisal system rather than after it has been implemented. Managers

5 **Discuss how perform-ance appraisals can be made legally defensible.**

need specific criteria for legally defensible performance appraisal systems. Fortunately, researchers have discerned some instructive patterns in court decisions.

After studying the verdicts in 66 employment discrimination cases in the United States, one pair of researchers found that employers could successfully defend their appraisal systems if they satisfied four criteria:

1. A *job analysis* was used to develop the performance appraisal system.
2. The appraisal system was *behavior-oriented*, not trait-oriented.
3. Performance evaluators followed *specific written instructions* when conducting appraisals.
4. Evaluators *reviewed the results* of the appraisals with the ratees.[55]

Each of these conditions has a clear legal rationale. Job analysis, discussed earlier relative to human resource planning, anchors the appraisal process to specific job duties, not to personalities. Behavior-oriented appraisals properly focus management's attention on *how* the individual actually performed his or her job.[56] Performance appraisers who follow specific written instructions are less likely to be plagued by vague performance standards and/or personal bias. Finally, by reviewing performance appraisal results with those who have been evaluated, managers provide the feedback necessary for learning and improvement. Managers who keep these criteria for legal defensibility in mind are better equipped to select a sound appraisal system from alternative approaches and techniques.

Alternative Performance Appraisal Techniques

The list of alternative performance appraisal techniques is long and growing. Appraisal software programs also are proliferating.[57] Unfortunately, many are simplistic, invalid, and unreliable. In general terms, an *invalid* appraisal instrument does not accurately measure what it is supposed to measure. *Unreliable* instruments do not measure criteria in a consistent manner. Many other performance appraisal techniques are so complex that they are impractical and burdensome to use. But armed with a working knowledge of the most popular appraisal techniques, a good manager can distinguish the strong from the weak. Once again, the strength of an appraisal technique is gauged by its conformity to the criteria for legal defensibility discussed previously. Following are some of the techniques used through the years:

- *Goal setting.* Within an MBO framework, performance is typically evaluated in terms of formal objectives set at an earlier date. This is a comparatively strong technique if desired outcomes are clearly linked to specific behavior. For example, a product design engineer's "output" could be measured in terms of the number of product specifications submitted per month.
- *Written essays.* Managers describe the performance of employees in narrative form, sometimes in response to predetermined questions. Evaluators often criticize this technique for consuming too much time. This method is also limited by the fact that some managers have difficulty expressing themselves in writing.
- *Critical incidents.* Specific instances of inferior and superior performance are documented by the

Your Job's on the Line   11H

Recent advice to managers: "If you're relying on some formal system of evaluations to tell you how you're really doing, you're probably taking a big risk. At most companies your actual standing is seldom revealed through formal channels."

Source: Anne Fisher, "Hey, Hotshot, Take a Good Look at Yourself," *Fortune* (November 11, 1996): 211.

Questions: *What is the truth behind this bit of advice? Which approach to performance appraisal would best neutralize this problem of less-than-honest feedback? Why?*

supervisor when they occur. Accumulated incidents then provide an objective basis for evaluations at appraisal time. The strength of critical incidents is enhanced when evaluators document specific behavior in specific situations and ignore personality traits.[58]

- *Graphic rating scales.* Various traits or behavior are rated on incremental scales. For example, "initiative" could be rated on a 1(= low)—2—3—4—5(= high) scale. This technique is among the weakest when personality traits are employed. However, **behaviorally anchored rating scales (BARS),** defined as performance rating scales divided into increments of observable job behavior determined through job analysis, are considered to be one of the strongest performance appraisal techniques[59] (see Figure 11.4).

- *Weighted checklists.* Evaluators check appropriate adjectives or behavioral descriptions that have predetermined weights. The weights, which gauge the relative

behaviorally anchored rating scales *performance appraisal scales with notations about observable behavior*

Figure 11.4

A Sample Behaviorally Anchored Rating Scale for a College Professor

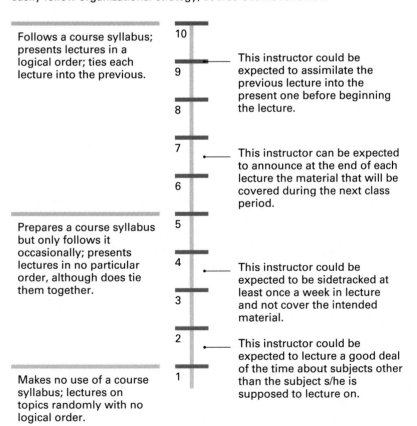

Organizational skills:
A good constructional order of material slides smoothly from one topic to another; design of course optimizes interest; students can easily follow organizational strategy; course outline followed.

Follows a course syllabus; presents lectures in a logical order; ties each lecture into the previous. — 10, 9 — This instructor could be expected to assimilate the previous lecture into the present one before beginning the lecture.

8

7 — This instructor can be expected to announce at the end of each lecture the material that will be covered during the next class period.

6

Prepares a course syllabus but only follows it occasionally; presents lectures in no particular order, although does tie them together. — 5, 4 — This instructor could be expected to be sidetracked at least once a week in lecture and not cover the intended material.

3

2 — This instructor could be expected to lecture a good deal of the time about subjects other than the subject s/he is supposed to lecture on.

Makes no use of a course syllabus; lectures on topics randomly with no logical order. — 1

Source: Adapted from *Performance Appraisal: Assessing Human Behavior At Work* by Bernardin, Beatty. Copyright © 1984. By permission of South-Western College Publishing, a division of Thomson Learning. Fax 800-730-2215.

importance of the randomly mixed items on the checklist, are usually unknown to the evaluator. Following the evaluation, the weights of the checked items are added or averaged to permit interpersonal comparisons. As with the other techniques, the degree of behavioral specificity largely determines the strength of weighted checklists.

■ *Rankings/comparisons.* Coworkers in a subunit are ranked or compared in head-to-head fashion according to specified accomplishments or job behavior. A major shortcoming of this technique is that the absolute distance between ratees is unknown. For example, the employee ranked number one may be five times as effective as number two, who in turn is only slightly more effective than number three. Rankings/comparisons are also criticized for causing resentment among lower-ranked, but adequately performing, coworkers. This technique can be strengthened by combining it with a more behavioral technique, such as critical incidents or BARS.

■ *Multirater appraisals.* This is a general label for a diverse array of nontraditional appraisal techniques involving more than one rater for the focal person's performance. The rationale for multirater appraisals is that "two or more heads are less biased than one." One approach enjoying faddish popularity in recent years is 360-degree feedback. In a **360-degree review,** a manager is evaluated by his or her boss, peers, and subordinates. The results may or may not be statistically pooled and are generally fed back anonymously.[60] Although 360-degree feedback is best suited for use in management development programs, some companies have turned it into a performance appraisal tool, with predictably mixed results.[61] If 360-degree appraisals are to be successful, they need to be carefully designed and skillfully implemented.[62]

360-degree review
pooled, anonymous evaluation by one's boss, peers, and subordinates

Training

No matter how carefully job applicants are screened, typically a gap remains between what employees *do* know and what they *should* know. Training is needed to fill this knowledge gap. In 1999, U.S. companies with 100 or more employees spent nearly $62.5 billion on training, according to *Training* magazine's annual industry survey.[63] Huge as this number sounds, it still is not nearly enough. How the $62.5 billion was spent is also a problem. Most of it was spent by big companies training already well-educated managers and professionals.

Clearly, American managers need to rethink the country's training priorities. Remedial education and basic skills training for nonmanagement personnel are good for both the employer and the employee.

> *At Borden Foodservice, 71 percent of those who received basic skills certification remained employed five years later, despite downsizing and the sale of the company. Of those who received other training, but not basic skills, only 54 percent are still with the company. In the same period and among the same groups of employees, 21 percent of basic-skills trainees were promoted, while not a single promotion was made from among those who had not received the training.[64]*

Given that 47 percent of all American adults are not literate enough to read this page, the need for more extensive worker training is inescapable.[65]

"Let me get this straight. I need to get a good education and a college degree. You hire me as a consultant to work with well-known companies. But first I have to go back to the classroom?" That's precisely what is happening in today's "learning organizations" where so-called knowledge workers experience nonstop training and development. These new hires at Boston consulting firm Viant are undergoing a three-week training program. The company's goal: "What one person knows, everybody knows."

Formally defined, **training** is the process of changing employee behavior and/or attitudes through some type of guided experience. We now focus on the content and delivery of modern training, the ingredients of a good training program, and the important distinction between skill and factual learning.

training *using guided experience to change employee behavior/attitudes*

Modern Training: Content and Delivery

A 1999 survey by *Training* magazine, which covered 1,097 U.S. companies with 100 or more employees, shed instructive light on today's training practices. The companies surveyed represented all major industries. Small (at least 100 employees), medium, and large firms responded.[66] Figure 11.5 presents the top ten training content areas and the most frequently used methods of instruction. In the number one content spot was training in computer applications. In a similar survey nine years before, computer training was fifth. So has modern technology completely redirected workplace training? Not as much as one would expect. Yes, computer-based training (and Internet training) are used by the companies surveyed.[67] But the old standbys—classroom presentations, workbooks/manuals, videotapes, and seminars—are still the norm. For better or for worse, the typical college classroom is still a realistic preview of what awaits you in the world of workplace training.

Which instructional method is best? There probably are as many answers to this question as there are trainers. Given variables such as interpersonal differences, budget limitations, and instructor capabilities, it is safe to say that there is no one best training technique.[68] For example, the lecture method, though widely criticized for being dull and encouraging learner passivity, is still on top in the study just discussed. Whatever method is used, trainers need to do their absolute best because they are key facilitators for people's hopes and dreams.

Figure 11.5

The Content and Delivery of Today's Training

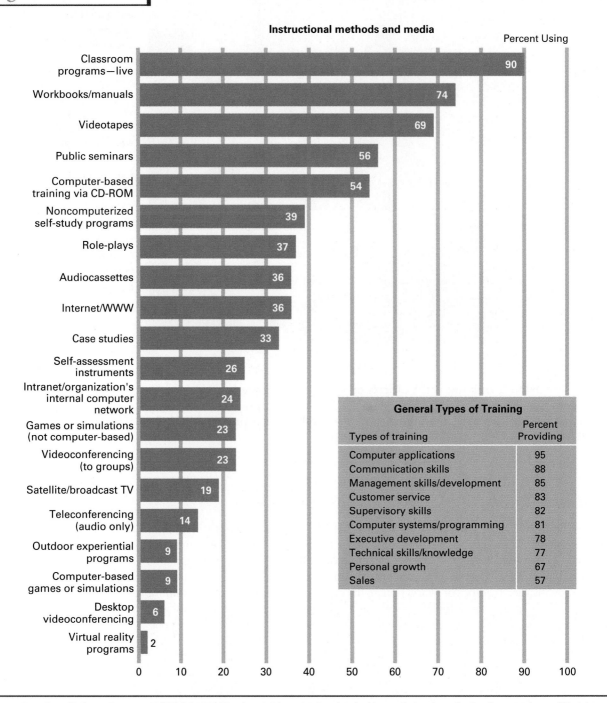

Instructional methods and media

Percent Using

Method	Percent
Classroom programs—live	90
Workbooks/manuals	74
Videotapes	69
Public seminars	56
Computer-based training via CD-ROM	54
Noncomputerized self-study programs	39
Role-plays	37
Audiocassettes	36
Internet/WWW	36
Case studies	33
Self-assessment instruments	26
Intranet/organization's internal computer network	24
Games or simulations (not computer-based)	23
Videoconferencing (to groups)	23
Satellite/broadcast TV	19
Teleconferencing (audio only)	14
Outdoor experiential programs	9
Computer-based games or simulations	9
Desktop videoconferencing	6
Virtual reality programs	2

General Types of Training	
Types of training	Percent Providing
Computer applications	95
Communication skills	88
Management skills/development	85
Customer service	83
Supervisory skills	82
Computer systems/programming	81
Executive development	78
Technical skills/knowledge	77
Personal growth	67
Sales	57

Source: Data from "Industry Report 1999," *Training*, 36 (October 1999): 54, 56. Reprinted with permission from the October 1999 issue of *Training* magazine. Copyright 1999, Bill Communications, Minneapolis, Minn. All rights reserved. Not for resale.

The Ingredients of a Good Training Program

Although training needs and approaches vary, managers can get the most out of their training budgets by following a few guidelines. According to two training specialists, every training program should be designed along the following lines to maximize retention and transfer learning to the job:

1. Maximize the similarity between the training situation and the job situation.
2. Provide as much experience as possible with the task being taught.
3. Provide for a variety of examples when teaching concepts or skills.
4. Label or identify important features of a task.
5. Make sure that general principles are understood before expecting much transfer.
6. Make sure that the trained behaviors and ideas are rewarded in the job situation.
7. Design the training content so that the trainees can see its applicability.
8. Use adjunct questions to guide the trainee's attention.[69]

Skill Versus Factual Learning

The ingredients of a good training program vary according to whether skill learning or factual learning is involved.

> *Effective skill learning should incorporate four essential ingredients: (1) goal setting, (2) modeling, (3) practice, and (4) feedback. Let's take as an example the task of training someone to ride horseback. How would you do it? It basically must entail telling someone specifically what you want them to do (goal setting), showing them how you want them to do it (modeling), giving them the opportunity to try out what you have told them and shown them (practice), and then telling them what they are doing correctly (feedback).*[70]

When factual learning is involved, the same sequence is used, except that in step 2, "meaningful presentation of the materials" is substituted for modeling. Keep in mind that the object of training is *learning*. Learning requires thoughtful preparation, carefully guided exposure to new ideas or behavior, and motivational support.[71] Let us turn our attention to some modern human resource management problems that have serious implications for the well-being of today's organizations and employees.

11I

Back to the Opening Case

If you were a diversity training consultant for Texaco, what sort of skill and/or factual training program would you recommend? How would you suggest it should be implemented?

6 Compare and contrast the ingredients of good training programs for both skill and factual learning.

Contemporary Human Resource Challenges and Problems

Modern organizations are a direct reflection of society in general. People take societal influences to work (such as attitudes toward labor unions and the opposite sex). Along with these predispositions, they take their social, emotional, behavioral, and health-related problems to work. Like it or not and prepared or not, managers face potential union opposition and problems such as sexual harassment and alcohol and drug abuse. Today's challenge to foster union-management cooperation and deal effectively with human resource problems of this nature cannot be ignored because organizational competitiveness is at stake.

Fostering Union-Management Cooperation

An adversarial relationship between management and organized labor has been the historical norm in the United States. The Reagan-Bush era of conservative, promanagement politics was unkind to the American labor movement. In addition to politics, international competition, deregulation, and automation have exacted a toll on industrial unions in the United States. Consider this statistical picture: Less than 15 percent of employees in the United States belong to labor unions today, down from the 1953 high of 33 percent. The United Auto Workers union saw its membership cut in half—from 1.5 million to 750,000—between 1979 and 1998. Only 10 percent of private-sector employees in the United States are unionized.[72] "The one area where labor has prospered is the public sector. Unionization among government workers is at 38 percent, and public employees, in fact, now make up 42 percent of U.S. union members."[73] Unions responded to the loss of jobs because of downsizing and outsourcing to foreign and nonunion firms by agreeing to wage cuts and more flexible work rules. In return they received selective job security pledges, better training, and a greater say in organizational affairs. From this mix of social, political, and economic realities grew the U.S. union-management cooperation movement.

The Verdict Is Still Out.   Some enthusiasts claim that a new age of union-management cooperation is here to stay.[74] But that is a generous overstatement, in view of recent research. In a study of 584 U.S. manufacturers, researchers correlated efficiency (in terms of output per employee) with the degree of employee participation. Contrary to the volumes written about the benefits of participative management, the unionized companies with no employee participation programs were the most efficient. Unionized plants with participation came in second, while nonunionized firms with participation were the least efficient.[75] Predictably, those who oppose union-management cooperation are happy with the study, while proponents discredit it. Regardless of one's attitude toward unions, this study serves as a reminder that the traditionally adversarial union-management relationship in the United States is down but not out.

Not too many years ago, Continental Airlines was in a major tailspin. It was losing money, service was terrible, and management and labor were constantly at war. Enter Gordon Bethune, chairman. First to go was Continental's bureaucratic, confrontational culture. Next, he encouraged all employees to use their judgment to improve operations and rewarded everyone with cash bonuses for improvements in on-time performance. He then built trust with union members by telling them the truth and promising only what he could deliver. As Berthune told *Fortune* magazine, "You can't continue to be at war with your employees—it's got to stop."

Making Union-Management Cooperation Work.   Some envision a closer partnership among government, business, and labor, similar to that found in Europe. A more union-oriented political climate would undoubtedly bolster unions, but union members still disagree over the importance and value of cooperating with management. One longtime union advocate for more cooperation with management is Irving Bluestone, a former United Auto Workers of America vice president. Now a labor studies professor at Detroit's Wayne State University, Bluestone calls for union-management "enterprise compacts" based on these seven principles:

1. Productivity growth goals jointly determined by union and management.
2. Linking of wages and productivity growth for global competitiveness.
3. Prices jointly set by union and management.
4. The right of union members to strike to ensure world-class quality.
5. Guaranteed employment security.
6. Profit-sharing and gain-sharing incentives.
7. Joint labor-management decision making at all levels, including union representation on the board of directors.[76]

Bluestone's win-win prescription is provocative and controversial. Bitter opposition from both sides can be expected. Managers are reluctant to give up their exclusive control over strategy and product pricing. They also find employment guarantees too confining. For their part, many union officials ridicule the idea of "playing manager." After all, they are "not paid to manage." Bluestone's list of principles is nonetheless valuable because it provides fuel for constructive dialogue between management and organized labor. If union-management cooperation is to thrive in the United States, traditional methods will have to give way to new thinking.[77]

7 Explain how *enterprise compacts* can foster union-management cooperation.

Discouraging Sexual Harassment

A great deal of misunderstanding surrounds the topic of sexual harassment because of sexist attitudes, vague definitions, and inconsistent court findings. **Sexual harassment,** defined generally as unwanted sexual attention or conduct, has both behavioral and legal dimensions[78] (see Table 11.4). Important among these are the following:

8 Specify the essential components of an organization's polices for dealing with sexual harassment and alcohol and drug abuse.

sexual harassment
unwanted sexual attention that creates an offensive or intimidating work environment

What exactly is sexual harassment? The Equal Employment Opportunity Commission (EEOC) says that unwelcome sexual advances, requests for sexual favors, and other verbal or physical conduct of a sexual nature constitute sexual harassment when submission to such conduct is made a condition of employment; when submission to or rejection of sexual advances is used as a basis for employment decisions; or when such conduct creates an intimidating, hostile, or offensive work environment. These EEOC guidelines interpreting Title VII of the Civil Rights Act of 1964 further state that employers are responsible for the actions of their supervisors and agents and that employers are responsible for the actions of other employees if the employer knows or should have known about the sexual harassment.

Table 11.4

Behavioral and Legal Dimensions of Sexual Harassment

Source: "Sexual Harassment, 1: Discouraging It in the Work Place," by B. Terry Thornton. Reprinted, by permission of the publisher, from *Personnel*, April 1986, © 1986. American Management Association, New York, N.Y. All rights reserved.

- Although typically it is female employees who are the victims of sexual harassment, both women and men (in the United States) are protected under Title VII of the Civil Rights Act of 1964.
- Sexual harassment includes, but is not limited to, unwanted physical contact. Gestures, displays, joking, and language also may create a sexually offensive or intimidating work environment.
- It is the manager's job to be aware of and correct cases of sexual harassment. Ignorance of such activity is not a valid legal defense.[79]

Research evidence indicates that sexual harassment is commonplace. In a nationwide survey of 2,765 employees, "45 percent of women and 19 percent of men said they have been sexually harassed at work."[80] Employees using computer e-mail systems and computer networks must also contend with problems of sexual harassment in the form of rape threats and obscene words and graphics.[81] Sexual harassment begins early, with 83 percent of high school girls and 60 percent of high school boys reportedly experiencing it.[82] Researchers find people generally agree that unwanted sexual propositions, promises or threats tied to sexual favors, lewd comments/gestures/jokes, and touching/grabbing/brushing qualify as sexual harassment. Beyond that, opinions differ.[83] Personal tastes and sensibilities vary widely from individual to individual. In view of the foregoing evidence, corrective action needs to be taken by both the victims of sexual harassment and management.

What Can the Victim Do?   Employees who believe they are victims of sexual harassment can try to live with it, fight back, complain to higher-ups, find another job, or sue their employer. Those who choose to file a lawsuit need to know how to put the odds in their favor. An analysis of sexual harassment cases revealed the following five factors likely to lead to success. Victims of sexual harassment tended to win their lawsuits when

- The harassment was severe.
- There were witnesses.
- Management had been notified.
- There was supporting documentation.
- Management had failed to take action.[84]

The higher the number of these factors that apply, the greater the chances a sexual harassment lawsuit will be successful. Courtrooms are the last line of defense for victims of sexual harassment. Preventive and remedial actions also are needed. Harassers need to be told by their victims, coworkers, and supervisors that their actions are illegal, unethical, and against company policy. As more organizations develop and enforce sexual harassment policies, the problem can be greatly reduced without costly court battles and the loss of valued employees.

What Can the Organization Do?   Starting with top management, an organizationwide commitment to eliminating sexual harassment should be established. A clear policy statement, with behavioral definitions of sexual harassment and associated penalties, is essential. As with all policies, sexual harassment policies need to be disseminated and uniformly enforced if they are to have the desired impact. Appropriate training, particularly for new employees, can alert people to the problem and consequences of sexual harassment. Finally, in accordance with EEOC guidelines, management can remain adequately informed of any sexual harassment in the organization by establishing a grievance procedure. Harassed employees should be able to get a fair hearing of their case without fear of retaliation.[85]

Back to the Opening Case

Survey data: Among U.S. companies with 100 or more employees, 81 percent provide training about sexual harassment.

Source: Data from "Industry Report 1999: Where the Training Dollars Go," *Training,* 36 (October 1999): 58.

Question: *Should a sexual harassment awareness-and-prevention program be part of Texaco's diversity efforts? Explain.*

Controlling Alcohol and Drug Abuse

Statistics tell a grim story about the number one drug problem—alcohol. In the United States, 70 percent of adults consume alcohol and 43 percent of the population claim to have an alcoholic spouse or blood relative.[86] Once believed to be a character disorder, **alcoholism** is now considered a disease in which an individual's normal social and economic roles are disrupted by the consumption of alcohol. Very few alcoholics are actually the skid-row-bum type; the vast majority are average citizens with jobs and families. Alcoholism cuts across all age, gender, and racial and ethnic categories. Experts say a glance in the mirror shows what the average alcoholic looks like.[87]

alcoholism *a disease in which alcohol abuse disrupts one's normal life*

Close on the heels of employee alcoholism is workplace drug abuse.

> *Although alcohol is the nation's most abused drug, an increasingly greater number of Americans are also abusing mood-altering drug substances apart from, and in addition to, the usage of alcohol. These other drug substances can be described as "illegal"—heroin, cocaine, marijuana, morphine, and so on—or "legal"—prescription drugs such as amphetamines, tranquilizers, and barbiturates.[88]*

Experts say 8 to 12 percent of the general population is at risk of drug addiction. Seventy percent of drug users in the United States are employed full time.[89] Compared with nonabusers, alcoholic employees and drug abusers are significantly less productive, ten times more likely to be absent, and three times more likely either to have or to cause an accident.[90] In terms of lost productivity due to absenteeism, accidents, shoddy work, sick leave, and theft of organizational resources, employee drug abuse costs the U.S. economy an estimated $100 billion a year.[91] Employers can play a key role in curbing this tragic and costly erosion of our human resources.

The Legal Side of Workplace Substance Abuse.   Businesses doing contract work for the U.S. government are squeezed on two sides by the law. On one side, alcoholics and drug addicts are protected from employment discrimination by the Vocational Rehabilitation Act of 1973. They are presumed to have the same employment rights as any disabled person.[92] On the other side, employers with federal contracts exceeding $25,000 are subject to the Federal Drug-Free Workplace Act of 1988. These employers "must certify that they will maintain a drug-free workplace."[93] The idea is to rid federal contractors' workplaces of the production, distribution, and possession of controlled substances. Alcohol is not considered a controlled substance by the 1988 act. Companies found to be in violation of the act may lose their right to do business with the U.S. government.

Do these two legal thrusts work in opposite directions? Actually, the two laws work in combination because they make *rehabilitation* the best option.

Referral and Rehabilitation.   Alcoholism or drug abuse typically reveals itself to the manager in the form of increased absenteeism, tardiness, sloppy work, and complaints from coworkers. As soon as a steady decline in performance is observed, the manager should confront the individual with his or her poor performance record. Experts advise supervisors *not* to make accusations about alcohol or drug abuse. It is the employee's challenge to admit having such a problem. Management's job is to refer troubled employees to appropriate sources of help.[94] Managers are cautioned

11K

Drug Testing in the Workplace

Fact: In 1998, 74 percent of U.S. employers tested for drugs, up from 52 percent in 1990.

Fact: A workplace drug-testing company recorded a 5 percent positive rate in 1997, versus 18.1 percent in 1987.

Sources: Data from "1998 AMA Survey: Workplace Testing and Monitoring," *Management Review*, 87 (October 1998): 33; and Leon Rubis, "Positive Drug Tests Hit 11-Year Low," *HRMagazine*, 43 (June 1998): 20.

Question: *What is your opinion about drug testing for job applicants and employees? Explain your reasoning.*

against "playing doctor" when trying to help the alcohol- or drug-abusing employee. If the organization has an *employee assistance program (EAP)*,[95] counselors, or a company doctor, an in-house referral can be made. One study, "which tracked 25,000 employees over a four-year period, showed that the company's EAP saved $4 in health claims and absentee rates for every dollar it spent."[96]

Managers in small organizations without sophisticated employee services can refer the alcoholic employee to community resources such as Alcoholics Anonymous. Similar referral agencies for drug abusers exist in most communities. The overriding objective for the manager is to put troubled employees in touch with trained rehabilitation specialists as soon as possible.

Summary

1. Human resource management involves human resource planning, acquisition, and development. Four key human resource management activities necessarily linked to organizational strategy and structure are (1) human resource planning, (2) selection, (3) performance appraisal, and (4) training. After an employee has joined the organization, part of the human resource management process involves dealing with unionization and human resource problems such as sexual harassment and alcohol and drug abuse.

2. A systems approach to human resource planning will help management devise staffing strategies for future human resource needs. As the organization's gatekeeper for vital human resources, employee selection should be more than a haphazard process of looking around for people to fill vacancies.

3. Federal equal employment opportunity laws require managers to make hiring and other personnel decisions on the basis of ability to perform rather than personal prejudice. Affirmative action, making up for past discrimination, is evolving into managing diversity. Appreciation of interpersonal differences within a heterogeneous organizational culture is the goal of managing-diversity programs. The Americans with Disabilities Act of 1990 (ADA) requires employers to make reasonable accommodations so that disabled people can enter the workforce.

4. All employment tests must be valid predictors of job performance. Because interviews are the most popular employee screening device, experts recommend structured rather than traditional, informal interviews.

5. Legally defensible performance appraisals enable managers to make objective personnel decisions. Four key legal criteria are job analysis, behavior-oriented appraisals, specific written instructions, and evaluation of results with ratees. Seven common performance appraisal techniques are goal setting, written essays, critical incidents, graphic rating scales, weighted checklists, rankings/comparisons, and 360-degree reviews.

6. Today, training is a huge business in itself. Unfortunately, most training dollars are being spent where they are least needed, to train well-educated managers and professionals. Managers can ensure that their training investment pays off by using techniques appropriate to the situation. Training programs should be designed with an eye toward maximizing the retention and transfer of learning to the job. Successful skill learning and factual learning both depend on goal setting, practice, and feedback. But skills should be modeled, whereas factual information should be presented in a logical and meaningful manner.

7. The American labor movement has undergone major changes in recent years. Union membership has fallen significantly in the private sector and grown in the public sector. Both unions and management are calling for greater union-management cooperation and teamwork. Irving Bluestone recommends win-win enterprise compacts between unions and management. The principles behind this concept call for joint decisions on productivity goals and pricing, wages linked to productivity growth, profit sharing, strikes to protest poor quality, employment guarantees, and union representation at all levels of decision making.

8. Sexual harassment and alcohol and drug abuse are contemporary human resource problems that require top-management attention and strong policies. A sexual harassment policy needs to define the problem behaviorally, specify penalties, and be disseminated and enforced. Referral to professional help and rehabilitation are the keys to fighting substance abuse in the workplace.

Terms to Understand

Human resource management (p. 328)

Human resource planning (p. 330)

Job analysis (p. 330)

Job description (p. 330)

Affirmative action program (p. 334)

Employment selection test (p. 338)

Structured interview (p. 340)

Performance appraisal (p. 341)

Behaviorally anchored rating scales (p. 343)

360-degree review (p. 344)

Training (p. 345)

Sexual harassment (p. 349)

Alcoholism (p. 351)

How to Handle the Job Interview Successfully

Skills & Tools

1. **Thoroughly pre-scout the employer.** Spy discreetly on the company to learn about its activities, characteristics, strengths, trends, and market position. Review newsletters, product literature, financial and annual reports, brochures, news articles, and anything else you can find about the company in the library or on the Internet. For personal accounts, visit the company on a pre-interview day or arrive early for your appointment and casually converse with departing or arriving employees. . . .

2. **Ask permission to take notes.** Your interviewer won't refuse this request, so have paper and a pen handy for jotting down important facts during the meeting. Not only will this help you make a good impression, but it also will provide ammunition for your interview summary and follow-up letter.

   Examples of what you should write down include the final hiring deadline, details about the job description, information about the company and its policies, the name of your prospective manager, product information, and advice on next steps you can take.

3. **Ask pertinent questions.** This underutilized strategy may, in fact, be the most valuable of all to candidates. By asking questions, you'll show what you've learned about

the company and find out more about the job requirements and where you stand. Questions you might want to ask include the following:

"Would you take a few moments to give me a more comprehensive description of the job requirements?"

"What do you think are the most important qualities that candidates for this job should have?"

"What opportunities exist in the future for someone who performs successfully in this position?". . .

4. **Ask the interviewer to rate your qualifications for the job.** From this reply, you'll learn which way the wind is blowing and possibly uncover a potentially fatal problem or weakness the interviewer didn't plan to discuss with you. . . .

You've made an impression, gained information, and set the stage to politely and briefly summarize the strengths and assets you'd bring to the job. This is where the notes you've taken during the interview come in handy.

Quoting the interviewer's job description and specifications whenever possible, repeat each requirement for the position as you understand them. Then cite the strengths, experience, and values you'd bring to each area. Candidly admit to any weaknesses, but promise to embark on a vigorous training program to overcome them. State that the company's training strengths and your attitude are a winning combination.

As you finish your summary, be sure to ask for the job confidently and pleasantly. If you're enthusiastic and polite, you won't be labeled as overly aggressive. Employers prefer you to be results-oriented because they think you'll act the same way on the job. . . .

5. **Always follow up.** Write and mail a follow-up letter to the interviewer within 12 to 24 hours of your meeting, with a copy to any other executives who are involved in the decision. [An e-mail can get lost in the clutter.]

Your letter should state:

- What you liked most about the company.
- The assets you'd bring to the position.
- Your availability and enthusiasm.
- Your hope of meeting other decision-makers as soon as possible.

Source: Republished with permission of *The Wall Street Journal.* Excerpted from Milton Gralla, "Interview Success Tips from an Old Pro," *The College Edition of the National Business Employment Weekly* (Winter/Spring 1997): 15, 18–19, 30. Permission conveyed through Copyright Clearance Center, Inc.

Internet Exercises

1. **Making diversity come to life:** Ernst & Young, one of the Big Five accounting, tax, and consulting companies, takes managing diversity very seriously. In addition to having an active recruiting and retention program for women and minorities, E&Y strives to accommodate the special lifestyle needs of today's diverse working population. This Internet exercise gives you a real-life model of various diversity initiatives.

Go to Ernst & Young's home page (**www.ey.com**) and click on the main menu category "Careers." Recommended topics from the Career page menu are "Diversity" and "Life Balance." Keep the following questions in mind when exploring all the subtopics at these two sites.

Learning Points: 1. How many different ways of accommodating employee diversity can you detect? What are they? 2. Which particular diversity initiative appeals most to you? Why? 3. Why does Ernst & Young work so hard on its diversity strategy? 4. Would you like to work for Ernst & Young? Why or why not?

2. **Interviewing: "Watch your behavior":** The purpose of this exercise is to give you realistic practice writing behavioral interview questions. Ernst & Young makes no secret about its use of behavioral interviewing. Go to E&Y's Career page by following the instructions above. Click on the menu heading "Career Resources" and read the section "Interview Cheat Sheet." Write one generic behavioral interview question for at least four of the skill/ability categories (e.g., leadership, team spirit, communication).
   Learning Points: 1. Is each of your questions situationally and behaviorally specific? 2. Would any of your questions put a candidate at a disadvantage because of his or her gender, race, ethnicity, religion, or marital status? 3. When you try your questions on someone else, are they judged to be fair questions?

3. **Check it out:** A great way to keep up on the field of human resources is to go to the Society for Human Resources Management Web site (**www.shrm.org**) and select the main menu item "HR Magazine." Scan the full-text online versions of articles in the current issue of *HRMagazine*. Also explore the "Articles from Previous Issues." You'll find a rich supply of recent full-text articles on all key human resource topics.

For updates to these exercises, visit our Web site (**www.hmco.com/college**).

It Takes More Than a Great Résumé to Impress Amazon.com

Closing Case

In just four years, Amazon.com Inc. has gone from being an idea to being an industry giant with a staff of 3,000. From its origins as a bookseller, it continues to gobble up acquisitions and race into new markets at a staggering pace.

A company like this needs the right staff to achieve its lofty goals, but getting in the door isn't easy. Chief Executive Jeff Bezos wants stars on his staff, not the merely competent.

So how does this company go about hiring?

Mr. Bezos exhorts his managers to discover the person behind the résumé during job interviews—and to be brave enough to choose those who are more skilled and talented than they themselves are. Managers who feel threatened by hiring superstars "have to understand that if they don't hire them, they'll be working for them down the road," says Mr. Bezos.

He believes his company's success depends on constantly improving the workforce, raising standards for entry. He plans to add more staff this year, although

Source: Republished with permission of *The Wall Street Journal* from "How Amazon.com Staffs a Juggernaut: It's Not About Résumés," by Carol Hymowitz, *The Wall Street Journal* (May 4, 1999). Permission conveyed through Copyright Clearance Center, Inc.

he won't say how many positions are open. Five years from now, he says, employees hired today should be saying, "I'm glad I got hired when I did, because I wouldn't get hired now." . . .

Beyond superstar performers, Mr. Bezos urges managers to hire people who have some special talent or quality that may not be connected to work. Job candidates are interviewed by several Amazon.com employees, who then meet to share their impressions of the person's strengths and weaknesses. One central question at the meeting: "What do you admire about this candidate?"

"Maybe they were a spelling champion" in elementary school or are passionate about Baroque music or are avid mountain climbers, says Mr. Bezos. "When you are working very hard and very long hours, you want to be around people who are interesting and fun to be with."

David Risher, senior vice president of Amazon.com, was first exposed to Mr. Bezos's hiring philosophy when he was working at Microsoft several years ago. He received a call for a reference from Mr. Bezos, who was thinking about hiring a colleague of Mr. Risher's. The two men talked for more than an hour, with Mr. Bezos asking an array of questions from "What is he terrible at?" to "How would he handle such and such a situation?"

A year later, Mr. Bezos called again to say he was looking for a vice president of marketing. He wondered if Mr. Risher could suggest some candidates.

"I started thinking I should apply and threw my hat into the ring," says Mr. Risher, who is 33 years old. He interviewed at Amazon.com but, instead of getting the marketing post, was hired as vice president of product development. "I was employee No. 183," says Mr. Risher.

That was in January 1997, and since then he has learned to approach hiring with the same investigative fervor as his boss. When doing reference checks, "we have at least 23 questions," he says, from "'Tell me this candidate's greatest strength' to worst mistake."

The goal is to learn not just what a candidate has done "but how he has done it," Mr. Risher says.

When he interviews candidates, Mr. Risher tries to avoid drilling them about their job histories, preferring instead to foster an exchange about values, personal interests, and approaches to work problems.

"I might ask, 'How would you design a car for a deaf person?'" he says. "Some people freeze when they get a question like that—others say they'd talk to people who are deaf. But the best candidates say they'd plug their ears and drive around in their cars to experience what it feels like to be a deaf driver. They put themselves right into the customer's mind and body, to find out what they need."

Mr. Risher also has learned that there are no hard-and-fast rules to successful hiring. Rather, it is akin to dating, with some seemingly certain fix-ups going bust on an initial meeting and other, less likely prospects forming a lasting fit.

Since so much depends on the right fit, Mr. Risher says, it is natural to recruit employees one has worked with before. The problem is, "we don't like to poach."

For that reason, he waited a year after joining Amazon.com to woo Christopher Payne from Microsoft. He said he first tried to get Mr. Payne's wife for a public-relations job and, when he couldn't, went after her husband instead.

"He'd worked for me before and is one of the most customer-focused people I know," he says of Mr. Payne, now Amazon.com's general manager of videos.

Six months ago, he hired Allen Olivo, then Apple Computer's director of marketing, as Amazon.com's new vice president of marketing. He was intrigued by the fact that Mr. Olivo had worked for Steve Jobs, a temperamental boss, and "for a company that had been on top of the world and then lost its way and then came back to the top again" with the launch of the iMac computer. "I wanted to know how he had pulled it all off," says Mr. Risher.

"No one can do something like this alone," Mr. Olivo told him. "My job is to get the best out of people."

That response delighted Mr. Risher, who says Mr. Olivo wasn't like "a lot of smart people I've met who think they alone have the right answers." Moreover, in addition to his teamwork skills, Mr. Olivo collects guitars and knows a lot about music. "I felt I could learn a lot from him," Mr. Risher says.

FOR DISCUSSION

1. Does staffing appear to have strategic importance at Amazon.com? Explain.

2. What do you like or dislike about Amazon.com's approach to hiring?

3. What type of interview question, according to Table 11.3, is popular at Amazon.com? What are the main positive and negative aspects of this approach to assessing job applicants?

4. If you were applying for a job at Amazon.com, would you be bothered or intimidated by seemingly off-beat questions such as how to design a car for a deaf person? Explain.

5. If you were an interviewer for Amazon.com, what questions would you ask applicants?

COMMUNICATING
in the INTERNET AGE

CHAPTER OBJECTIVES

When you finish studying this chapter, you should be able to

1 Identify each major link in the communication process.

2 Explain the concept of media richness and the Lengel-Daft contingency model of media selection.

3 Discuss why it is important for managers to know about grapevine and nonverbal communication.

4 Explain ways in which management can encourage upward communication.

5 Identify and describe four barriers to communication.

6 Discuss how e-mail, videoconferences, and telecommuting are affecting organizational communication.

7 List at least three practical tips for improving each of the following communication skills: listening, writing, and running a meeting.

> **"IT IS A LUXURY TO BE UNDERSTOOD."**
> ralph waldo emerson

Fun and Profits at Uncle Herb's Southwest Airlines

Do you have to be a cold-hearted tyrant to run an efficient and profitable business? Not if you're Herb Kelleher, chief executive officer and cofounder of Dallas-based Southwest Airlines. Southwest's strategy of using fuel-efficient 737s for low-fare, short-haul flights between secondary airports has made it a feared competitor and the fourth largest airline in the United States. With the addition of Providence, Rhode Island, in 1996, Southwest spread its wings coast to coast, encompassing 29 states. The airline's more than 27 straight years of growth and profitability, service awards, and cooperative relationships with its unions have made it the envy of an industry that was awash in red ink during the early 1990s. Although Herb Kelleher may not be a household name, the flying public owes him a personal thanks for low air fares. U.S. Transportation Department officials say fares drop by 50 percent and passenger traffic more than doubles when Southwest Airlines moves into an area. Cities compete vigorously for a spot on Southwest's route map. According to Kelleher: "We've created a solid niche—our main competition is the automobile. We're taking people away from Toyota and Ford."[1]

To Southwest's employees, the CEO is not a distant Mr. Kelleher but "Uncle Herb" or "Herbie." In fact, Kelleher does not fit the top executive stereotype in most ways. His fast-and-loose style has fostered a productive blend of hard work and fun. In one legendary move, Uncle Herb helped celebrate the opening of San Antonio's Sea World by having one of the firm's Boeing 737 jets painted to resemble a black-and-white killer whale. And he's been known to spend time on baggage duty or behind the ticket counter, and even to show up for a flight in a jungle-print outfit. Friends say it's unlikely his 1999 battle with prostate cancer will slow him down. Southwest's more than 29,000 employees take their cue from the boss and share a few laughs among themselves and with passengers. For instance, on one Southwest flight, the author and his fellow passengers were told by the flight attendant to "put your seats in the upright and uncomfortable position before landing." On other occasions flight crews have recognized passengers with the biggest holes in their socks. If it's Friday, Southwest's "fun uniform" day, Herb may wear a clown suit or dress up as Elvis—even for business meetings.

Yet Kelleher is no fool when it comes to running a profitable airline. Southwest frustrates competitors by keeping its operating costs about 20 percent below the industry average. Southwest's no-frills approach pleases both customers, who like the low fares, and stockholders, who like steady profits. In fact, the airline receives up to 3,500 complimentary letters from customers every month. It keeps maintenance, parts, and training costs below average by having only Boeing 737s in the fleet. First-time Southwest flyers may be surprised at the unassigned seats and lack of in-flight meals. Peanuts have become Southwest's informal symbol. No wonder, considering an incredible 87 million bags of peanuts were handed out to passengers in 1998! But the low fares and friendly service keep them coming back. The company's profit sharing and no-layoff policies keep employees happy and working hard.

Southwest enjoys an unusually low (10 percent) turnover rate, and although 85 percent of its employees are unionized, both management and employees sign new contracts without any fuss. At the heart of this teamwork is the willingness of Southwest's employees to do whatever job is necessary to ensure an on-time takeoff. Pilots may help clean up a plane, flight attendants and ramp crew may sell tickets, ticket agents may help with baggage, and so on. Up to 80 percent of promotions come from within the company, and the airline's employees commonly express a family feeling toward their company.

Many companies would like their employees to feel and perform as Southwest's do. So why does Southwest Airlines succeed so much more than the rest? Besides having an eccentric, fun-loving CEO, the key is communication. Although many of Kelleher's antics may be spontaneous improvisations, all consistently communicate to customers and employees alike a sense of what the company is all about. His stunts demonstrate that good service and good fun are not incompatible—efficient does not have to mean boring. The president of the Flight Attendants Union Local 556, Kay Wallace, has said: "Herb's fun is infectious. . . . Everyone enjoys what they're doing and realizes they've got to make an extra effort."[2]

That extra effort translates into turning a plane around from arrival at the gate to departure in 15 minutes with crews 50 percent smaller than the competition. Southwest boasts an 85 percent success rate for that dizzying feat, thanks to teamwork and communication.

Southwest relies on quick-hitting, often humorous ads featuring Kelleher to get across its message of fun and value. In response to a competitor's ad that said people should be embarrassed to fly on a no-frills airline like Southwest, Kelleher filmed a commercial with a bag over his head, offering the bag to anyone who was ashamed to be seen on Southwest. He coyly added that perhaps they could use the bag to carry the money they'd save flying Southwest.

Building upon Uncle Herb's showmanship, management uses various media to tell its employees about Southwest's way of doing business. It believes in treating its employees with the same care and attention companies usually reserve for their best customers. Most new recruits see Kelleher first on a training film, strutting like a chicken, flapping his chicken-wing arms, singing "The Southwest Shuffle; Shuffle Down, Down." Kelleher is known for making unexpected flights on Southwest planes to see firsthand how things are going. He's also willing to listen and encourages employees to drop in anytime. The CEO's "open door" is located in the company's Dallas headquarters, a building dedicated to its employees.

Like a family, the airline has its traditions, including cookouts and an annual awards dinner at which Kelleher personally hands out the prizes. Southwest's newsletter also is a family affair, passing on information about employees' awards, acts of community service, or recent illnesses. And Southwest's top human resources executive says that what it looks for in job applicants is, logically enough, a sense of humor. Even Southwest's quarterly report is different. Instead of the usual slick brochure, the airline sends out a video.

Kelleher's unique style has yet to catch on among his larger and less profitable rivals, but he's trying to change that, too. After hearing about Southwest's killer whale 737, Robert L. Crandall, the usually stern former CEO of American Airlines, called Kelleher to congratulate him on his clever marketing and asked what he planned to do with all that killer whale waste. On the following Monday, during a staff meeting at American, a messenger appeared with Kelleher's response: a huge bowl of chocolate mousse and a spoon.

One of the most difficult challenges for management is getting individuals to understand and voluntarily pursue organizational objectives. Effective communication, of the sort seen at Southwest Airlines, is vital to meeting this challenge. Organizational communication takes in a great deal of territory—virtually every management function and activity can be considered communication in one way or another. Planning and controlling require a good deal of communicating, as do organization design and development, decision making and problem solving, leadership, and staffing. Organizational cultures would not exist without communication. Studies have shown that both organizational and individual performance improve when managerial communication is effective.[3] Given today's team-oriented organizations where things need to be accomplished with and through people over whom a manager has no direct authority, communication skills are more important than ever.

Thanks to modern technology, we can communicate more quickly and less expensively. But the ensuing torrent of messages (see Figure 12.1) has proved to be a mixed blessing for managers and nonmanagers, alike. Complaints of information overload are common today.[4] Worse yet, managers have a growing suspicion that more

12A

Some Information About Information Overload

Fact: Two-thirds of business managers surveyed report tension with colleagues, loss of job satisfaction, and strained personal relationships as a result of information overload.

Fact: While 61 percent of adults in one survey believed society suffers from information overload, a much lower 37 percent saw themselves as suffering the same fate.

Sources: Excerpted from David Shenk, "Why You Feel the Way You Do," *Inc.*, 21 (January 1999): 59; and adapted from "Too Much Information?" *USA Today* (February 5, 1999): 1A.

Questions: *Are you suffering from information overload? If so, how is it affecting your life and personal productivity? What could you do to avoid or deal more effectively with information overload?*

For further information about the interactive annotations in this chapter, visit our Web site (**www.hmco.com/college**).

Figure 12.1

The World of Communication Overload (average daily number of messages sent and received by office workers)

	United States	United Kingdom	Germany
Telephone	52	46	50
E-mail	36	27	20
Voice mail	23	11	6
Postal mail	18	19	26
Interoffice mail	18	15	27
Fax	14	11	15
Cell phone	4	9	10
TOTAL =	165	138	154

Source: Data from "Message Overload?" *USA Today* (September 13, 1999): 1B.

communication is not necessarily better. Recent research validates this suspicion: "Executives say 14 percent of each 40-hour workweek is wasted because of poor communication between staff and managers. . . . That amounts to a staggering seven workweeks of squandered productivity a year."[5] The challenge to improve this situation is both immense and immediate. But before managers, or anyone else for that matter, can become more effective communicators they need to appreciate that communication is a complex process subject to a great deal of perceptual distortion and many problems. This is especially true for the apparently simple activity of communicating face to face.

1 **Identify each major link in the communication process.**

communication *interpersonal transfer of information and understanding*

The Communication Process

Management scholar Keith Davis defined **communication** as "the transfer of information and understanding from one person to another person."[6] Communication is inherently a social process. Whether one communicates face to face with a single

Figure 12.2

**The Basic Communica-
tion Process**

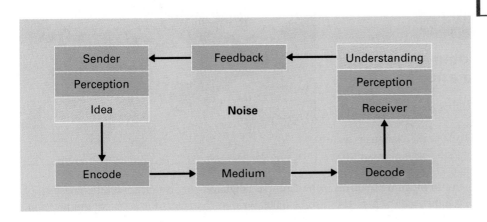

person or with a group of people via television, it is still a social activity involving two or more people. By analyzing the communication process, one discovers that it is a chain made up of identifiable links (see Figure 12.2). Links in this process include sender, encoding, medium, decoding, receiver, and feedback.[7] The essential purpose of this chainlike process is to send an idea from one person to another in a way that will be understood by the receiver. Like any other chain, the communication chain is only as strong as its weakest link.[8]

Encoding

Thinking takes place within the privacy of your brain and is greatly affected by how you perceive your environment. But when you want to pass along a thought to someone else, an entirely different process begins. This second process, communication, requires that you, the sender, package the idea for understandable transmission. Encoding starts at this point. The purpose of encoding is to translate internal thought patterns into a language or code that the intended receiver of the message will probably understand.

Managers usually rely on words, gestures, or other symbols for encoding. Their choice of symbols depends on several factors, one of which is the nature of the message itself. It is technical or nontechnical, emotional or factual? Perhaps it could be expressed better with colorful PowerPoint slides than with words, as in the case of a budget report. To express skepticism, merely a shrug might be enough.

Greater cultural diversity in the workplace also necessitates careful message encoding. Trudy Milburn, an American Management Association program coordinator, recently offered this perspective:

> *Communication . . . becomes problematic when organizations adopt a narrow perspective of communication that focuses on a single normative standard. Some African-American employees, for example, may be discouraged from speaking in a dialect defined as "black English" and may be mandated to adopt proper business grammar. When companies deem their standard to be the only acceptable one, they will not be able to appreciate different ways of interacting.*[9]

In the global marketplace, where language barriers hamper communication, the Internet promises to make the encoding process a bit easier (see The Global Manager).

The Global Manager

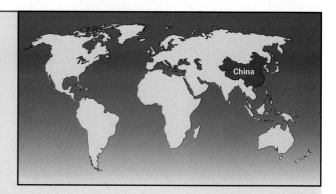

The Internet as a Common Language for China and the World

George Wang, director of IBM's China Research Laboratory in Beijing:

In China, though we have only one written language, we have many spoken ones. It might be hard, in a country of one language like the United States, to realize how much this can impede progress. But to the more than 1.2 billion people of my country—roughly one-fifth of the world's population—this language incompatibility can blunt the success of communication and halt progress.

That's why, to me, the greatest advance of this century is the set of fundamental agreements collectively known as Internet Standards. While not commonly thought of as a "technology," these protocols provide the first real opportunity for people across my country to communicate—to exchange information, to transact business—with each other and the rest of the world, regardless of what language they speak.

For China, this is no luxury. Historically, we have alternated between periods of openness to the outside world and times of prolonged introspection. As a scientist, I know that little progress can be made in a hermetic environment. For us, these agreements on protocol mean access to global technological discourse.

Although "agreements" might sound more akin to the world of diplomacy than technology, these Internet Standards have engendered a revolution dwarfing the so-called information revolution. Some of them, such as TCP/IP (Transfer Control Protocol, which governs the sending of packets of information over the global network) date back to work done in the United States in the 1970s as government, academic, and military research facilities looked for ways to be linked and share information across an open environment. Others, like the World Wide Web, were developed in Europe in the early 1990s and quickly caught on as a dynamic and exciting way to exchange all types of information.

But significantly, beyond linking computers and computer users, the one language of these standards has prompted a shift away from the computer to the network itself—the Internet—as the focus of attention, a shift that will redefine how we all think of information technology....

This, in turn, is driving efforts to overcome an impediment to computing unique to Asia: the keyboard. Since the Chinese language, for instance, requires mastery of some 6,000 written characters for basic communication, a 101-key keyboard is hardly user-friendly for us.

At the IBM China Research Laboratory, we develop speech recognition systems and handwriting recognition systems for Chinese languages, which are being ported to hand-held devices. Suddenly, entering information into a computer or accessing information on the Internet is as easy for us as for the rest of the world.

Chinese language search engines we have developed allow us to use our one written language to obtain information easily. We are also working to perfect machine translation programs, since there are potentially billions of users across the globe seeking to access information—and each other—in a variety of tongues.

Throughout history, China has flourished by absorbing and assimilating outside influences and applying them in a uniquely Chinese way. What began as a series of protocol agreements to connect scientific and government computers in the United States and Europe will provide the basis for my country at the very end of the twentieth century to leapfrog to technological parity with the rest of the industrialized world.

It will also enable all of us in China to communicate with each other as never before. We have reached, in a sense, a solution to an age-old problem: We will have moved beyond finding just one tongue for China, and instead have found one tongue for the entire world.

Note: George Wang, 51, became director of IBM China Research and Development Laboratory in Beijing in January 1999. His primary research focus these days is on Chinese language and speech processing and how to apply it to electronic commerce.

Source: Excerpted from George Wang, "Net Brings a Common Language," *USA Today* (June 22, 1999): 6E. Reprinted by permission of the author.

Larry Johnston, who works for General Electric Medical Systems in Europe, has a tough communication job. Oddly enough, it took a sophisticated quality improvement initiative called Six Sigma—that strives for no more than 3.4 defects per million units of output—to help Johnston and his colleagues succeed despite language and cultural differences. This "language of quality" allowed GE's European customers to create the specifications for a completely digital mammography machine. GE engineers worked out the technical details and made the innovative product a reality.

Selecting a Medium

Managers can choose among a number of media: face-to-face conversations, telephone calls, e-mails, memos, letters, computer reports and networks, photographs, bulletin boards, meetings, organizational publications, and others. Communicating with those outside the organization opens up further possibilities, such as news releases, press conferences, and advertising on television and radio or in magazines, newspapers, and the Internet.

Media Selection in Cross-Cultural Settings.   The importance of selecting an appropriate medium is magnified when one moves from internal to cross-cultural dealings. Recalling the distinction we made in Chapter 4, managers moving from low-context cultures to high-context cultures need to select communication media with care.

> *The United States, Canada, and northern European nations are defined as low-context cultures, meaning that the verbal content of a message is more important than the medium—the setting through which the message is delivered. In such cultures, a videoconference or an e-mail is usually accepted as an efficient substitute for an in-person meeting.*
>
> *But in other countries—including many in Asia and the Middle East—context, or setting, with its myriad nonverbal cues, can convey far more meaning than the literal words of a given message. In such high-context cultures, business transactions are ritualized, and the style in which the rituals are carried out matters more than the words. A high value is placed on face-to-face interaction, and after-hours socialization with customers and colleagues is almost a daily occurrence.*[10]

2 Explain the concept of media richness and the Lengel-Daft contingency model of media selection.

A Contingency Approach.   A contingency model for media selection has been proposed by Robert Lengel and Richard Daft.[11] It pivots on the concept of media richness. **Media richness** describes the capacity of a given medium to convey information

media richness *a medium's capacity to convey information and promote learning*

Figure 12.3

The Lengel-Daft Contingency Model of Media Selection

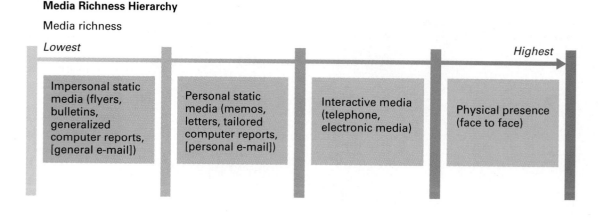

Media Richness Hierarchy

Media richness

Lowest			*Highest* →

| Impersonal static media (flyers, bulletins, generalized computer reports, [general e-mail]) | Personal static media (memos, letters, tailored computer reports, [personal e-mail]) | Interactive media (telephone, electronic media) | Physical presence (face to face) |

Media Selection Framework

Management problem

Media richness	*Routine*	*Nonroutine*
Rich	Communication failure Data glut. Rich media used for routine messages. Excess cues cause confusion and surplus meaning.	Effective communication Communication success because rich media match nonroutine messages.
Lean	Effective communication Communication success because media low in richness match routine messages.	Communication failure Data starvation. Lean media used for nonroutine messages. Too few cues to capture message complexity.

Source: Robert H. Lengel and Richard L. Daft, "The Selection of Communication Media as an Executive Skill," *Academy of Management Executive,* 2 (August 1988): 226, 227, exhibits 1 and 2. Reprinted by permission.

and promote learning. As illustrated in the top portion of Figure 12.3, media vary in richness from high (or rich) to low (or lean). Face-to-face conversation is a rich medium because it (1) simultaneously provides *multiple information cues,* such as message content, tone of voice, facial expressions, and so on; (2) facilitates immediate *feedback;* and (3) is *personal* in focus. In contrast, bulletins and general computer reports are lean media, that is, they convey limited information and foster limited learning. Lean media, such as general e-mail bulletins, provide a single cue, do not facilitate immediate feedback, and are impersonal.

Management's challenge, indicated in the bottom portion of Figure 12.3, is to match media richness with the situation. Nonroutine problems are best handled with such rich media as face-to-face, telephone, or video interactions.[12] Lean media are appropriate for routine problems. Examples of mismatched media include reading a corporate annual report at a stockholders' meeting (data glut) or announcing a massive layoff with an impersonal e-mail (data starvation).

A Call for More Media Richness

12B

Edward M. Hallowell, psychiatry instructor at Harvard:

[When communicating, managers] need to experience what I call the human moment: an authentic psychological encounter that can happen only when two people share the same physical space. I have given the human moment a name because I believe that it has started to disappear from modern life—and I sense that we all may be about to discover the destructive power of its absence.

The human moment has two prerequisites: people's physical presence and their emotional and intellectual attention. That's it. Physical presence alone isn't enough; you can ride shoulder-to-shoulder with someone for six hours in an airplane and not have a human moment the entire ride. And attention alone isn't enough either. You can pay attention to someone over the telephone, for instance, but somehow phone conversations lack the power of true human moments.

Source: Edward M. Hallowell, "The Human Moment at Work," *Harvard Business Review*, 77 (January–February 1999): 59–60.

Question: *Do you agree or disagree with this approach to improving organizational communication? Explain.*

Decoding

Even the most expertly fashioned message will not accomplish its purpose unless it is understood. After physically receiving the message, the receiver needs to comprehend it. If the message has been properly encoded, decoding will take place rather routinely. But perfect encoding is nearly impossible to achieve in our world of many languages and cultures.[13] (In fact, India alone has 17 official languages!)[14] The receiver's willingness to receive the message is a principal prerequisite for successful decoding. The chances of successful decoding are greatly enhanced if the receiver knows the language and terminology used in the message. It helps too if the receiver understands the sender's purpose and background situation. Effective listening is given special attention later in this chapter.

Feedback

Some sort of verbal or nonverbal feedback from the receiver to the sender is required to complete the communication process. Appropriate forms of feedback are determined by the same factors governing the sender's encoding decision. Without feedback, senders have no way of knowing whether their ideas have been accurately understood. Knowing whether others understand us significantly affects both the form and content of our follow-up communication.

Employee surveys consistently underscore the importance of timely and personal feedback from management. For example, one recent survey of 500,000 employees from more than 300 firms contrasted satisfaction with "coaching and feedback from boss" for two groups of employees: (1) committed employees who planned to stay with their employer for at least five years and (2) those who intended to quit within a year. Satisfaction with coaching and feedback among the committed employees averaged 64 percent, while it dropped to 34 percent among those ready to quit.[15]

12C

Back to the Opening Case

Does Herb Kelleher do an effective or ineffective job with media selection? Why is Kelleher likely to get honest feedback from Southwest's employees?

Noise

noise *any interference with*
normal flow of communication

Noise is not an integral part of the chainlike communication process, but it may influence the process at any or all points. As the term is used here, **noise** is any interference
with the normal flow of understanding from one person to another. This is a very
broad definition. Thus, a speech impairment, garbled technical transmission, negative
attitudes, lies,[16] misperception, illegible print or pictures, telephone static, partial loss
of hearing, and poor eyesight all qualify as noise.[17] Understanding tends to diminish
as noise increases. In general, the effectiveness of organizational communication can
be improved in two ways. Steps can be taken to make verbal and written messages
more understandable. At the same time, noise can be minimized by foreseeing and
neutralizing sources of interference.[18]

Dynamics of Organizational Communication

As a writer on the subject pointed out, "civilization is based on human cooperation
and without communication, no effective cooperation can develop."[19] Accordingly,
effective communication is essential for cooperation within productive organizations.
At least four dynamics of organizational communication—structural considerations,
the grapevine, nonverbal communication, and upward communication—largely
determine the difference between effectiveness and ineffectiveness in this important
area.

Needed: More Coordinated Communication

As we mentioned earlier, the term *organizational communication* takes in a lot of territory. Research on major companies has identified seven categories of organizational
communication: advertising and promotion, employee communications, media relations, shareholder relations, consumer affairs, community relations, and government
relations.[20]

In the early 1980s, there was a clear trend toward centralized communication departments. The idea was to manage various facets of organizational communication in a
coordinated and cost-effective way. Then came the era of downsizing and corporate reorganization, along with lots of new communication technologies. Recent research has
revealed corporate communication programs to be disjointed and wasteful, precisely the
opposite of what managers envisioned in the early 1980s. A 1996 survey of 10,000 U.S.
companies by the American Management Association led to this conclusion:

> *Although senior managers cite communications as a top business priority that they plan to
> devote more time to, they are focusing on technological solutions (for example, electronic
> mail and Internet connections) when the answers have more to do with words and thoughts
> than tools.*[21]

A more specific indication of just how far things have gotten out of control came in a
survey of 100 *Fortune* 500 companies by Pitney Bowes Management Services. A

surprising 73 percent "did not have established policies governing the form of communication appropriate for specific circumstances."[22] This lack of oversight led to the following picture of disorganization:

> . . . 72 percent of the respondents could not quantify their annual expenditures for mail, fax, e-mail and overnight/express services. Only 8 percent had a single department coordinating all these costs, and most companies (58 percent) divided these responsibilities among three or more departments.[23]

The message for managers is clear: Don't be dazzled by new communication technologies to the point of losing control of costs. A strategic approach to organizational communication is sorely needed today.

The Grapevine

In every organization, large or small, there are actually two communication systems, one formal, and the other informal. Sometimes these systems complement and reinforce one another; at other times they come into direct conflict. Although theorists have found it convenient to separate the two, distinguishing one from the other in real life can be difficult. Information required to accomplish official objectives is channeled throughout the organization via the formal system. Official or formal communication by definition flows in accordance with established lines of authority and structural boundaries. Media for official communication include all of those discussed earlier. But superimposed on this formal network is the **grapevine,** the unofficial and informal communication system. The term *grapevine* can be traced back to Civil War days, when vinelike telegraph wires were strung from tree to tree across battlefields.

3 Discuss why it is important for managers to know about grapevine and nonverbal communication.

grapevine *unofficial and informal communication system*

Grapevine Patterns.   An authority on grapevine communication has offered the following vivid description:

> The grapevine operates fast and furiously in almost any work organization. It moves with impunity across departmental lines and easily bypasses superiors in chains of command. It flows around water coolers, down hallways, through lunch rooms, and wherever people get together in groups. It performs best in informal social contacts, but it can operate almost as effectively as a sideline to official meetings. Wherever people congregate, there is no getting rid of the grapevine. No matter how management feels about it, it is here to stay.[24]

Since this description originally was written, computer networks and e-mail have become commonplace in the workplace. These new electronic grapevines, along with the more traditional telephone, have made grapevine communication more vibrant than ever.[25]

Regardless of the medium used, an important point needs to be made about grapevine communication. It is not a formless, haphazard process: close study has uncovered definite orderly patterns (see Figure 12.4), the most common of which is the cluster configuration. When the cluster pattern is operating, only select individuals repeat what they hear; others do not.[26] Those who consistently pass along what they hear to others serve as grapevine liaisons or gatekeepers.

> About 10 percent of the employees on an average grapevine will be highly active participants. They serve as liaisons with the rest of the staff members who receive information but spread it to only a few other people. Usually these liaisons are friendly, outgoing people who are in positions that allow them to cross departmental lines. For example, secretaries tend to be liaisons because they can communicate with the top executive, the janitor, and everyone in between without raising eyebrows.[27]

Figure 12.4

Grapevine Patterns

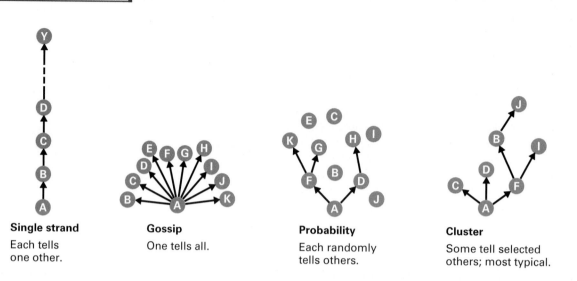

Single strand
Each tells
one other.

Gossip
One tells all.

Probability
Each randomly
tells others.

Cluster
Some tell selected
others; most typical.

Source: John W. Newstrom and Keith Davis, *Organizational Behavior: Human Behavior at Work*, 9th ed. (New York: McGraw-Hill, 1993), p. 445. Reproduced with permission of the McGraw-Hill Companies.

Alert managers can keep abreast of grapevine communication by regularly conversing with known gatekeepers.

Managerial Attitudes Toward the Grapevine.   One survey of 341 participants in a management development seminar uncovered predominantly negative feelings among managers toward the grapevine. Moreover, first-line supervisors perceived the grapevine to be more influential than did middle managers. This second finding led the researchers to conclude that "apparently the grapevine is more prevalent, or at least more visible, at lower levels of the managerial hierarchy where supervisors can readily feel its impact."[28] Finally, the survey found that employees of relatively small organizations (fewer than 50 people) viewed the grapevine as less influential than did those from larger organizations (more than 100 people). A logical explanation for this last finding is that smaller organizations are usually more informal.

In spite of the negative attitude that many managers have toward it, the grapevine does have a positive side. In fact, experts estimate that grapevine communication is about 75 percent accurate.[29] Though the grapevine has a reputation among managers as a bothersome source of inaccurate information and gossip, it helps satisfy a natural desire to know what is really going on and gives employees a sense of belonging. The grapevine also serves as an emotional outlet for employee fears and apprehensions.[30] Consider, for example, what happened when investor Laurence A. Tisch became chairman of CBS:

> *Tisch's reputation as a ferocious cost cutter, which he despises, forces him to watch every word and gesture. Simple questions—such as why a department needs so many people—are sometimes interpreted as orders to slash. One day Tisch and [the CBS News department head] were talking outside CBS's broadcast center on Manhattan's West 57th Street when Tisch pointed to a tower atop the building, asking what it was. Apparently staffers at a window saw him pointing in their general direction, and the next day newspaper reporters called CBS checking out a rumor that Tisch planned to sell the building.*[31]

Nevertheless, grapevine communication can carry useful information through the organization with amazing speed. Moreover, grapevine communication can help management learn how employees truly feel about policies and programs.[32]

Coping with the Grapevine.   Considering how the grapevine can be an influential and sometimes negative force, what can management do about it? First and foremost, the grapevine *cannot be extinguished.* In fact, attempts to stifle grapevine communication may serve instead to stimulate it. Subtly monitoring the grapevine and officially correcting or countering any potentially damaging misinformation is about all any management team can do. "Management by walking around" is an excellent way to monitor the grapevine in a nonthreatening manner. Some managers selectively feed information into the grapevine. For example, a health care administrator has admitted: "Sure, I use the grapevine. Why not? The employees sure use it. It's fast, reaches everyone, and employees believe it—no matter how preposterous. I limit its use, though."[33] Rumor-control hot lines have proved useful for neutralizing disruptive and inaccurate grapevine communication.[34]

> **12D**
>
> ↗↙ **Have You Heard About the Rumor Formula?**
> **Uncertainty + Anxiety = Rumors**
>
> *Source:* Inspired by discussion in Nicholas Difonzo, Prashant Bordia, and Ralph L. Rosnow, "Reining in Rumors," *Organizational Dynamics*, 23 (Summer 1994): 47–62.
>
> **Questions:** *What does this formula tell you about how organizational grapevine rumors get started? What does it suggest managers can do to avoid destructive rumors?*

Nonverbal Communication

In today's hurried world, our words often have unintended meanings. Facial expressions and body movements that accompany our words can worsen matters. This nonverbal communication, sometimes referred to as **body language,** is an important part of the communication process. In fact, one expert contends that only 7 percent of the impact of our face-to-face communication comes from the words we utter; the other 93 percent comes from our vocal intonations, facial expressions, posture, and appearance.[35] The whole idea of "dressing for success" is an attempt to send a desired nonverbal message about oneself.[36] Image consultants have developed a thriving business helping aspiring executives look the part:

body language *nonverbal communication based on facial expressions, posture, and appearance*

> *Vanda Sachs had a problem. The 35-year-old senior marketing executive for a well-known fashion magazine had her sights set on the publisher's office. Her trouble? Projecting enough authority to be considered for the job. "I'm petite and blonde and I'm baby-faced," she says, "none of which goes over very well in a world of 45-year-old men who are 6-foot-2." Being short, in particular, is a "major liability," she adds, "more so than being a woman."*
>
> *Beyond wearing high heels, Sachs (a pseudonym) couldn't do much about her height, but she decided she could improve on her appearance. The first step was to hire a personal image consultant. Her choice: Emily Cho, founder of New Image, a respected New York City personal-image shopping service that for 19 years has been helping women choose clothes compatible with their private and professional aspirations. Four days and $3,000 later, Sachs had a knockout wardrobe and a newly acquired savvy that would help her look the part of a publisher. "Like it or not," she explains, "we're a society that's built on first impressions."[37]*

Types of Body Language.   There are three kinds of body language: facial, gestural, and postural.[38] Without the speaker or listener consciously thinking about it, seemingly insignificant changes in facial expressions, gestures, and posture send various messages. A speaker can tell whether a listener is interested by monitoring a

Imagine you're sitting in your cubicle enjoying a lively phone chat and suddenly a red foam block comes flying over the wall and lands on your desk after ricocheting off your head. Do you angrily toss it back? If you work for a company using Protoblocs, you take the not-so-subtle hint and quiet down. A green foam pyramid would send a different message altogether; something along the lines of "come on over!" A yellow foam ball perched on an officemate's wall would be a gentle reminder to "do not disturb." In a couple of departments at America Online, where these nonverbal aids are part of the culture, foam sometimes speaks louder than words.

combination of nonverbal cues, including an attentive gaze, an upright posture, and confirming or agreeing gestures. Unfortunately, many people in positions of authority—parents, teachers, and managers—ignore or misread nonverbal feedback. When this happens, they become ineffective communicators.

Receiving Nonverbal Communication.   Like any other interpersonal skill, sensitivity to nonverbal cues can be learned (see Table 12.1). Listeners need to be especially aware of subtleties, such as the fine distinctions between an attentive gaze and a glaring stare and between an upright posture and a stiff one. Knowing how to interpret a nod, a grimace, or a grin can be invaluable to managers. If at any time the response seems inappropriate to what one is saying, it is time to back off and reassess one's approach. It may be necessary to explain things more clearly, adopt a more patient manner, or make other adjustments.

Nonverbal behavior can also give managers a window on deep-seated emotions. For example, consider the situation Michael C. Ruettgers encountered shortly after joining EMC Corp., a leading manufacturer of computer data storage equipment:

> *Four months into Ruettgers' new job as head of operations and customer service, EMC's product quality program erupted into a full-blown crisis. Every piece of equipment the company sold was crashing because EMC engineers [had] failed to detect faulty disk drives supplied by NEC Corp. Ruettgers made a series of marathon swings across the country to meet personally with customers. In Denver and Salt Lake City, he came face to face with the scope of the catastrophe when managers broke down in tears because their computer operations were in shambles. "Nothing can really prepare you for that," Ruettgers says.*[39]

Since his promotion to CEO, Ruettgers has helped make EMC a leader in product quality and profitability. No doubt his face-to-face interaction with frustrated

Unspoken message	Behavior	**Table 12.1**
"I want to be helpful."	Uncrossing legs Unbuttoning coat or jacket Unclasping hands Moving closer to other person Smiling face Removing hands from pockets Unfolding arms from across chest	**Reading Body Language**
"I'm confident."	Avoiding hand-to-face gestures and head scratching Maintaining an erect stance Keeping steady eye contact Steepling fingertips below chin	
"I'm nervous."	Clearing throat Expelling air (such as "Whew!") Placing hand over mouth while speaking Hurried cigarette smoking	
"I'm superior to you."	Peering over tops of eyeglasses Pointing a finger Standing behind a desk and leaning palms down on it Holding jacket lapels while speaking	

Source: Adapted from William Friend, "Reading Between the Lines," *Association Management*, 36 (June 1984): 94–100. Reprinted by permission of the publisher.

customers, who conveyed powerful nonverbal emotional messages, drove home the need for improvement.

Giving Nonverbal Feedback.   What about the nonverbal feedback that managers give rather than receive? A research study carried out in Great Britain suggests that nonverbal feedback from authority figures significantly affects employee behavior. Among the people who were interviewed, those who received nonverbal approval from the interviewers in the form of smiles, positive head nods, and eye contact behaved quite differently from those who received nonverbal disapproval through frowns, head shaking, and avoidance of eye contact. Those receiving positive nonverbal feedback were judged by neutral observers to be significantly more relaxed, more friendly, more talkative, and more successful in creating a good impression.[40]

Positive nonverbal feedback to and from managers is a basic building block of good interpersonal relations. A smile or nod of the head in the appropriate situation tells the individual that he or she is on the right track and to keep up the good work. Such feedback is especially important for managers, who must avoid participating in the subtle but powerful nonverbal discrimination experienced by women in leadership positions.[41] When samples of men and women leaders in one study offered the same arguments and suggestions in a controlled setting, the women leaders received more negative and less positive nonverbal feedback than did the men.[42] Managing-diversity workshops target this sort of "invisible barrier" to

Back to the Opening Case   **12E**

Research finding: "A little corporate horseplay goes right to the bottom line. A gag to take the edge off a busted project, a funny story to bring people around to your point of view, a good laugh—any and all relieve stress, fuel creativity, and contribute to better performance.... In short, good managers are funny managers."

Source: "Get Funny, Make Money," *Training*, 33 (July 1996): 14–15.

Questions: *How would you respond to a manager who made the following statement: "Herb Kelleher's humorous style encourages employees to slack off and be disrespectful to management"? What sort of humorous communication should managers not use in today's organizations?*

Managing Diversity

Exabyte: Where Nonverbal Communication, Diversity, and Ethics Come Together

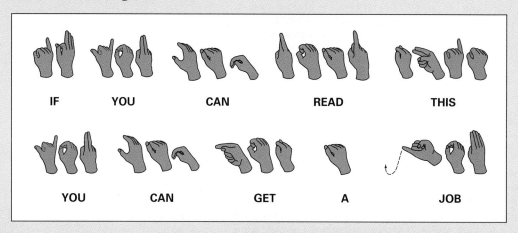

IF	YOU	CAN	READ	THIS
YOU	CAN	GET	A	JOB

In 1989, Exabyte, a Boulder, Colorado, manufacturer of computer storage tape drives, hired Mike Kirchner, who is deaf, to work in its assembly plant. Any fears the company had about Kirchner's abilities were quickly dispelled. Says human resources manager Dan Peters: "We became interested in hiring someone else like Mike, not because he was deaf, but because he had great organizational skills."

. . . two months after Kirchner signed on, he urged a deaf friend from high school, John Martinez, to apply for a job. He got it.

Four more deaf employees have come aboard since, accounting for 0.5 percent of the workforce, twice the U.S. average. Exabyte also scores as a hirer of nonwhites, who make up 12 percent of 1,150 employees, versus 6 percent of the local population.

Today, Kirchner helps coordinate production and Martinez supervises five "hearing" workers, who have learned the hand signs for "Good!" and even for "Put on your antistatic jacket."

The company thinks diversity is worth the cost, which includes hiring a translator for meetings and offering sign language classes to other staffers. Says human resources boss Richard Shinton: "The accommodations are things you'd have to be a Scrooge not to do. And other employees know that if they have an issue, they'll be treated fairly. It's a morale booster all around."

So it is. Says Martinez, 32, talking through a translator, "Exabyte's done a lot more for me than other places." Adds Monte Way, who has worked under him: "We used to communicate by notes, but my spelling's terrible, so I learned to sign. It didn't slow us down at all."

Source: Jennifer Reese, "If You Can Read This You Can Get a Job," *Fortune* (July 12, 1993): 11. © 1993 Time Inc. All rights reserved.

women and minorities. Similarly, cross-cultural training alerts employees bound for foreign assignments to monitor their nonverbal gestures carefully. For example, the familiar thumbs-up sign tells American employees to keep up the good work. Much to the embarrassment of poorly informed expatriates, that particular nonverbal message does not travel well. The same gesture would be a vulgar sign in Australia, would say "I'm winning" in Saudi Arabia, and would signify the number one in Germany and the number five in Japan. Malaysians use the thumb, instead of their forefinger, for pointing.[43]

Two other trends in nonverbal communication are etiquette classes for students and management trainees[44] and teaching sign language to coworkers of deaf employees (see Managing Diversity).

Upward Communication

As used here, the term **upward communication** refers to a process of systematically encouraging employees to share with management their feelings and ideas.[45] Upward communication has become increasingly important in recent years as employees have demanded—and, in some cases, received—a greater say in their work lives. A role model in this regard is Ingram Micro, number 68 on *Fortune* magazine's 1999 list of "The 100 Best Companies to Work for in America":

> . . . *Chairman Jerre Stead maintains his own 24-hour 800-number phone line—yes, he really answers it—to take calls from employees. "If we are doing something right, I love to hear about it," says Stead, who has also supplied his home phone number to all 13,000 IMers. "If there's something we should be doing differently, I want to know that too."*[46]

At least seven different options are open to managers who want to improve upward communication.

Formal Grievance Procedures.   When unions represent rank-and-file employees, provisions for upward communication are usually spelled out in the collective bargaining agreement. Typically, unionized employees utilize a formal grievance procedure for contesting managerial actions and oversights. Grievance procedures usually consist of a series of progressively more rigorous steps. For example, union members who have been fired may talk with their supervisor in the presence of the union steward. If the issue is not resolved at that level, the next step may be a meeting with the department head. Sometimes the formal grievance process includes as many as five or six steps, with a third-party arbitrator as the last resort. Formal grievance procedures are also found in nonunion situations.[47]

A promising alternative to the traditional grievance process is the *peer review* program. Originally developed in the early 1980s by General Electric at its Appliance Park factory in Columbia, Maryland, peer reviews have been adopted by a growing number of organizations. At GE, the three specially trained coworkers and two managers on the panel listen to the grievance, conduct a majority-rule secret ballot, and render a final decision. Certain issues, including those involving work rules, performance appraisal results, and pay rates, are not handled by GE's peer review panels. GE created this process as a union avoidance tactic, and the Appliance Park facility is still union-free.[48]

Employee Attitude and Opinion Surveys.   Both in-house and commercially prepared surveys can bring employee attitudes and feelings to the surface. Thanks to commercial software packages, time-saving and paperless electronic surveys are popular in today's workplaces.[49] Employees usually will complete surveys if they are convinced meaningful changes will result. Du Pont, for example, took the right approach:

> *Du Pont surveyed 6,600 of its people, including some at Towanda, [Pennsylvania,] and found that flexible work hours were a top priority. Working mothers and single parents said it was hard to cope with the kids while keeping to a rigid plant schedule. A team at Towanda got together and devised a novel solution: Take vacation time by the hour. During slack times when three of the four [task] team members could easily handle the job, one could take off a few hours in the afternoon to go to a school play or bring a sick kid to the doctor. Today other Du Pont workers and managers visit Towanda to learn about flextime. A few have already borrowed it for their own plants.*[50]

Surveys with no feedback or follow-up action tend to alienate employees, who feel they are just wasting their time.[51] For example, American Airlines recently conducted its first

upward communication
encouraging employees to share their feelings and ideas

4 Explain ways in which management can encourage upward communication.

Fair Play with Employee Suggestions 12F

Fact: "The National Association of Suggestion Systems estimates that member companies, government agencies and other organizations save $2 billion or more annually while spending more than $150 million in cash or other awards to implement suggestion systems."

Actual situation: Jodie Kavanagh, a paint shop employee at one of Honda's Ohio facilities, suggested a design modification in the bumpers of the Honda Civic to reduce painting time. She persisted and prevailed, after an initial disappointing response. "Honda's annual savings: $1.2 million in the U.S. alone."

Sources: David I. Shair, "An Economical Way to Track Employee Suggestions," *HRMagazine*, 38 (August 1993): 39; and Edith Hill Updike and David Woodruff, "Honda's Civic Lesson," *Business Week* (September 18, 1995): 76.

Questions: *What would be a fair reward for Jodie? What are the implications of your decision for Jodie's coworkers?*

---

employee satisfaction survey in five years and discovered only 30 percent believed morale to be good. Said new CEO Donald Carty, "Doing a survey like this probably hurts morale in a company unless it leads to some changes."[52] He's right. On the other hand, a researcher found unionized companies conducting regular attitude surveys were less likely to experience a labor strike than companies failing to survey their employees.[53]

Suggestion Systems. Who knows more about a job than someone who performs that job day in and day out? This rhetorical question is the primary argument for suggestion systems. According to Ohio Bell manager Cynthia McCabe, president of the Employee Involvement Association, "The best we can estimate, in the United States there are approximately 6,000 formal suggestion programs and possibly an equal number of semi-formal ones."[54] Fairness and prompt feedback are keys to successful suggestion systems. Monetary incentives can help, too. IBM, for example, pays from $50 to $5,000, depending on the financial impact of the suggestion.[55] Other companies are a bit more creative. Paul Orfalea, the founder and CEO of Kinko's, developed a team-oriented reward to prompt employee suggestions at the chain of 24-hour copy centers bearing his nickname: "The best suggestion of the year wins that entire store a Disney vacation—while Orfalea and his VPs man the counters and run the machines."[56] A study of U.S. government employees found a positive correlation between suggestions and productivity.[57]

Open-Door Policy. The open-door approach to upward communication has been both praised and criticized.[58] Proponents say problems can be nipped in the bud when managers keep their doors open and employees feel free to walk in at any time and talk with them. But critics contend that an open-door policy encourages employees to leapfrog the formal chain of command (something that happens a lot these days because of e-mail). They argue further that it is an open invitation to annoying interruptions when managers can least afford them.[59] A limited open-door policy—afternoons only, for example—can effectively remedy this last objection.

Informal Meetings. Employees may feel free to air their opinions and suggestions if they are confident management will not criticize or penalize them for being frank.[60] James Halpin, CEO of CompUSA, America's largest PC retailer, casts it in cultural terms:

> Culture's a big deal for us. We send out a broadcast to our team members four or five times a week. Every Friday when I'm in the office we have coffee and donuts with the boss for anybody in the company who wants to talk to me about whatever's on their mind. We also do lunch with the boss regularly where we take 12 of our employees to lunch and talk about what's going on in our business. With 20,000 team members, you've somehow got to make a bond between them so that they feel like they know you.[61]

Internet Chat Rooms. In the Internet age, a convenient way for management to get candid feedback is to host a meeting place on the Web. These so-called "virtual water coolers" give employees unprecedented freedom of speech. Dave Barram, head of the huge General Services Administration (GSA) in Washington, D.C., offered this assessment:

. . . GSA has set up a Web-based "chat line," in which employees exchange uncensored thoughts and ideas. "If we have honest conversations about what's working and what isn't, we can become really good," Barram says. "If we don't, we'll never help each other." [62]

This approach takes lots of managerial courage, if the rough-and tumble "cyber-venting" on unauthorized Web sites aimed at specific companies are any indication. [63]

Exit Interviews.   An employee leaving the organization, for whatever reason, no longer fears possible recrimination from superiors and so can offer unusually frank and honest feedback, obtained in a brief, structured **exit interview.** [64] On the other hand, exit interviews have been criticized for eliciting artificially negative feedback because the employee may have a sour-grapes attitude toward the organization.

> **exit interview** *brief structured interview with a departing employee*

In general, attempts to promote upward communication will be successful only if employees truly believe that their contributions will have a favorable impact on their employment. Halfhearted or insincere attempts to get employees to open up and become involved will do more harm than good.

Communication Problems and Promises in the Internet Age

Because communication is a complex, give-and-take process, problems will occur. Managers who are aware of common barriers to communication and who are sensitive to the problems of sexist and racist communication are more likely to be effective communicators. In addition, managers who want to be effective communicators need to be aware of opportunities and obstacles in Internet-age communication systems.

Barriers to Communication

Do intended messages actually have the desired impact on employee behavior? This is the true test of organizational communication. Emerson Electric, the successful maker of electric motors profiled in the Closing Case for Chapter 6, has a simple but effective way of testing how well its organizational communication is working. According to the head of the company, Charles F. Knight:

> **5** Identify and describe four barriers to communication.

As a measure of communication at Emerson, we claim that every employee can answer four essential questions about his or her job:

1. What cost reduction are you currently working on?
2. Who is the "enemy" (who is the competition)?
3. Have you met with your management in the past six months?
4. Do you understand the economics of your job?

When I repeated to a business journalist the claim that every employee can answer these questions, he put it to the test by randomly asking those questions of different employees at one of our plants. Each employee provided clear and direct answers, passing both the journalist's test and ours. [65]

Emerson Electric evidently has done a good job of overcoming the four main types of communication barriers: (1) process barriers, (2) physical barriers, (3) semantic barriers, and (4) psychosocial barriers.

Process Barriers.   Every step in the communication process is necessary for effective communication. Blocked steps become barriers. Consider the following situations:

- *Sender barrier.* A management trainee with an unusual new idea fails to speak up at a meeting for fear of criticism.
- *Encoding barrier.* This is a growing problem in today's culturally diverse workplace:

  > *William D. Fleet, human-resources director at the Seattle Marriott, where employees speak 17 languages, once fired a Vietnamese kitchen worker for wrongly accusing a chef of assault. Only after another employee was attacked by a kitchen worker did Fleet figure out that the Vietnamese employee had used the word "chef" to refer to all kitchen workers with white uniforms. The misunderstanding had led to the firing of a good staffer and delayed the arrest of a dangerous one. . . .*
  >
  > *That's why. . . [Fleet] instituted a comprehensive ESL [English as a second language] program for staffers to take on company time. After all, workers who know English interact better with guests.*[66]

- *Medium barrier.* After getting no answer three times and a busy signal twice, a customer concludes that a store's consumer hot line is a waste of time.
- *Decoding barrier.* A restaurant manager does not understand unfamiliar computer jargon during a sales presentation for laptop computers.
- *Receiver barrier.* A manager who is preoccupied with the preparation of a budget asks a team member to repeat an earlier statement.
- *Feedback barrier.* During on-the-job training, the failure of the trainee to ask any questions causes a manager to wonder if any real understanding has taken place.

The complexity of the communication process itself is a potentially formidable barrier to communication. Malfunctions anywhere along the line can singly or collectively block the transfer of understanding.

Physical Barriers.   Sometimes a physical object blocks effective communication. For example, a riveter who wears ear protectors probably could not hear someone yelling "Fire!" Distance is another physical barrier. Thousands of miles and differing time zones traditionally made international business communication difficult. So today's global managers appreciate how the Internet and modern telecommunications technology have made the planet a seemingly smaller place. Although people often take physical barriers for granted, they can sometimes be removed. For example, an inconveniently positioned wall in an office can be torn out. Architects and office layout specialists called "organizational ecologists" are trying to redesign buildings and offices with more effective communication in mind. They seek to make offices more like the home. "Advocates of the domesticated office emphasize social spaces rather than individual turf, in keeping with business's emphasis on teamwork. That makes communication and exchanging ideas important."[67] Choosing an appropriate medium is especially important for managers who must overcome physical barriers. A manager with a soft voice can reach hundreds of people by using a sound system.

semantics *study of the meaning of words*

Semantic Barriers.   Formally defined, **semantics** is the study of the meaning of words. Words are indispensable, though they can sometimes cause a great deal of trouble. In a well-worn army story, a growling drill sergeant once ordered a frightened recruit to go out and paint his entire jeep. Later, the sergeant was shocked to find that the private had painted

Some call it downtown San Francisco. Others refer to it as SOMA (South of Market Area; as in Market Street). Still others call it Multimedia Gulch. Whatever you call it, it's an epicenter of the Internet age. Bright, ambitious people gravitate to SOMA to work hard and party hard and maybe get rich in the process. Open work spaces without walls, as seen here in one SOMA Internet company, are the rule because communication needs to occur at Web speed.

his *entire* jeep, including the headlights, windshield, seats, and dashboard gauges. Obviously, the word *entire* meant something different to the recruit than it did to the sergeant.

In today's highly specialized world, managers in such fields as accounting, computer science, or advertising may become so accustomed to their own technical language that they forget that people outside their field may not understand them. Unexpected reactions or behavior by others may signal a semantic barrier. It may become necessary to reencode the message using more familiar terms. Sometimes, if the relationship among specialists in different technical fields is an ongoing one, remedial steps can be taken. For example, hospital administrators often take a special course in medical terminology so that they can better understand the medical staff.

Psychosocial Barriers.   Psychological and social barriers are probably responsible for more blocked communication than any other type of barrier.[68] People's backgrounds, perceptions, values, biases, needs, and expectations differ. Childhood experiences may result in negative feelings toward authority figures (such as supervisors), racial prejudice, distrust of the opposite sex, or lack of self-confidence. Family and personal problems, including poor health, alcoholism, and emotional strain, may be so upsetting that an employee is unable to concentrate on work. Experience on present or past jobs may have created anger, distrust, and resentment that speak more loudly in the employee's mind than any work-related communication. Sincere sensitivity to the receiver's needs and personal circumstances goes a long way toward overcoming psychosocial barriers to communication.

Watch Your #@~&*$% Language!   12G

While the latitude of acceptable language varies across companies, managers should know that there are legal implications to cursing in the workplace. Anna Segobia Masters, chair of the labor and employment practice at McKenna and Cuneo LLP, Los Angeles, says that profane words uttered in the context of sex, race, age, or religion could be considered a form of harassment. If left unchecked, such language could be the basis of an employee complaint about a hostile work environment....

To minimize the risks of lawsuits, Masters suggests creating a written policy stating that harassment can be verbal and establishing procedures for employees who want to seek corrective action.

Source: Excerpted from Louisa Wah, "Profanity in the Workplace," *Management Review*, 88 (June 1999): 8.

Questions: *Do you hear more profanity in the workplace today? Is it a problem? Does it create a hostile work environment? Explain.*

Sexist and Racist Communication

In recent years the English language has been increasingly criticized for being sexist and racist.[69] Words like *he, chairman, brotherhood, mankind,* and the like have traditionally been used in reference to both men and women. The usual justification is that everyone understands that these words refer to both sexes, and it is simpler to use the masculine form. Critics maintain that wholly masculine wording subtly denies women a place and image worthy of their equal status and importance in society.[70] This criticism is largely based on psychological and sociological considerations. Calling the human race *mankind,* for instance, is seldom a real barrier to understanding. But a Stanford University researcher found that "males appear to use 'he' in response to male-related imagery, rather than in response to abstract or generic notions of humanity."[71] In other words, *he* is commonly interpreted to mean literally *he* (a man), not *they* (men and women).

These same cautions carry over to the problem of racist communication for both ethical and legal reasons.

> *Words spoken at work that aren't literally racist—such as "you people," "poor people," and "that one in there"—now can be grounds for employment discrimination lawsuits [in the United States].*
>
> *They're called "code words.". . .*
>
> *It's not just the words, says Herman Cain, the black CEO of Godfather's Pizza and author of* Leadership Is Common Sense. *"It's body language. Tone of voice. How people talk to you. Over the years you can develop a sixth sense."*[72]

Progressive and ethical managers are weeding sexist and racist language out of their vocabularies and correspondence to eliminate the intentional and inadvertent demeaning of women and racial minorities.

Communicating in the Online Workplace

Computers speak a simple digital language of 1s and 0s. Today, every imaginable sort of information is being converted into a digital format, including text, numbers, still and moving pictures, and sound. This process means nothing short of a revolution for the computer, telecommunications, consumer electronics, publishing, and entertainment industries. Organizational communication, already significantly reshaped by computer technology, promises its own revolutionary change. This section does *not* attempt the impossible task of describing all the emerging communication technologies, which range from voice recognition computers to multimedia computers to virtual reality. Rather, it explores the impact of some established Internet-age technologies on workplace communications. Our goal is to appreciate how new and yet unknown technologies will change the way we communicate.

6 Discuss how e-mail, videoconferences, and telecommuting are affecting organizational communication.

Getting a Handle on E-mail.   E-mail via the Internet has precipitated a communication revolution akin to those brought about by the printing press, telephone, radio, and television. The numbers are astonishing. If you are on the Internet, you are ultimately linked to each of the 225 million people on earth capable of sending and receiving e-mail.[73] By 1998, "the volume of e-mail in the United States surpassed the volume of hand-delivered mail."[74] According to a recent survey of executives, "76 percent said they spend at least an hour each day reading and responding to e-mail, with 12 percent spending three hours a day."[75] (This, on top of the one hour 42 percent reportedly spend each day on voice mail.) E-mail is a two-headed beast: easy and efficient, while at the same time grossly abused and mismanaged. By properly managing e-mail, the organiza-

Concise. A brief message in simple conversational language is faster for you to write and more pleasant for your readers to read.

Table 12.2

How to Compose a CLEAR E-mail Message

Concise. A brief message in simple conversational language is faster for you to write and more pleasant for your readers to read.

Logical. A message in logical steps, remembering to include any context your readers need, will be more easily understood.

Empathetic. When you identify with your readers, your message will be written in the right tone and in words they will readily understand.

Action-oriented. When you remember to explain to your readers what you want them to do next, they are more likely to do it.

Right. A complete message, with no important facts missing, with all the facts right, and with correct spelling, will save your readers having to return to you to clarify details.

Source: Joan Tunstall, *Better, Faster Email: Getting the Most Out of Email* (St. Leonards, Australia: Allen & Unwin, 1999), p. 37. Reprinted by permission.

tion can take a big step toward properly using the Internet. An organizational e-mail policy, embracing these recommendations from experts, can help:

■ The e-mail system belongs to the company, which has the legal right to monitor its use. (*Never* assume privacy with company e-mail.)
■ Workplace e-mail is for business purposes only.
■ Harassing and offensive e-mail will not be tolerated.
■ E-mail messages should be concise (see Table 12.2). As in all correspondence, grammar and spelling count because they reflect on your diligence and credibility. Typing in all capital letters makes the message hard to read and amounts to SHOUTING in cyberspace. (All capital letters can be appropriate, for contrast purposes, when adding comments to an existing document.)
■ Lists of bullet items (similar to the format you are reading now) are acceptable because they tend to be more concise than paragraphs.
■ Long attachments defeat the quick-and-easy nature of e-mail.
■ Recipients should be told when a reply is *unnecessary*.
■ An organization-specific priority system should be used for sending and receiving all e-mail. *Example:* "At Libit, a company in Palo Alto, Calif., that makes silicon products for the cable industry, e-mail is labeled as either informational or action items to avoid time wasting."[76]
■ "Spam" (unsolicited and unwanted e-mail) that gets past filters should be deleted without being read.
■ To avoid file clutter, messages unlikely to be referred to again should not be saved.[77]

Videoconferences.   A **videoconference** is a live television exchange between people in different locations. The decreasing cost of steadily improving videoconferencing technologies and the desire to reduce costly travel time have fostered the wider use of this approach to organizational communication.[78] Experts say videoconferencing is cost-effective, but not cheap. For example, Apple Computer saved $28 million in travel expenses by creating and staffing a companywide videoconferencing system for $6 million.[79]

With the development of Internet-linked multimedia computers, "desktop videoconferencing" promises to make videoconferencing much more convenient and dramatically less expensive. *Fortune* recently observed:

Long an ungainly form of communication that required over $30,000 worth of bulky, room-size equipment, videoconferencing is finally evolving into a more practical, desktop creature.

videoconference *live television exchange between people in different locations*

"On the Internet, nobody knows you're a dog."

It is also becoming more versatile: Multiple participants from many locations can share data such as spreadsheets and documents while conversing through video links.[80]

Communication pointers for videoconference participants include the following:

- Test the system before the meeting convenes.
- Dress for the occasion. The video image is distorted by movement of wild patterns and flashy jewelry. Solid white clothing tends to "glow" on camera.
- Make sure everyone is introduced.
- Check to make sure everyone can see and hear the content of the meeting.
- Do not feel compelled to direct your entire presentation to the camera or monitor. Directly address those in the same room.
- Speak loudly and clearly. Avoid slang and jargon in cross-cultural meetings where translations are occurring.
- Avoid exaggerated physical movements that tend to blur on camera.
- Adjust your delivery to any transmission delay, pausing longer than usual when waiting for replies.
- Avoid side conversations, which are disruptive.
- Do not nervously tap the table or microphone or shuffle papers.[81]

Telecommuting.   Futurist Alvin Toffler used the term *electronic cottage* to refer to the practice of working at home on a personal computer connected—typically by telephone—to an employer's place of business. More recently, this practice has been labeled **telecommuting** because work, rather than the employee, travels between a

telecommuting *sending work to and from one's office via computer modem while working at home*

Promises	Potential problems	Table 12.3
1. Significantly boosts individual productivity.	1. Can cause fear of stagnating at home.	**Telecommuting: Promises and Problems**
2. Saves commuting time and travel expenses (lessens traffic congestion).	2. Can foster sense of isolation, due to lack of social contact with coworkers.	
3. Taps broader labor pool (such as mothers with young children, disabled and retired persons, and prison inmates).	3. Can result in competition or interference with family duties, thus causing family conflict.	
4. Eliminates office distractions and politics.	4. Can disrupt traditional manager-employee relationship.	
5. Reduces employer's cost of office space.	5. Can cause fear of being "out of sight, out of mind" at promotion time.	

central office and the employee's home, reaching the computer via telephone modem. The advent of overnight delivery services, low-cost facsimile (fax) machines, e-mail, and high-speed modems, combined with traditional telephone communication, has broadened the scope of telecommuting. An estimated 16 million Americans telecommute, a fourfold increase during the 1990s.[82] Worldwide, that figure is much higher. Despite some compelling advantages, telecommuting has enough drawbacks to make it unsuitable for many employees as well as employers (see Table 12.3). Telecommuting seriously disrupts the normal social and communication patterns in the workplace. Telecommuting will not become the prevailing work mode anytime soon, but it certainly is more than a passing fad.[83]

12H

Is Telecommuting for You?

Survey finding (103 U.S. white-collar employees): "73 percent claim they operate more efficiently at home."
Survey finding (British Telecom study): "The average work-at-homer puts in 11 percent more hours than his office-bound counterpart."

Sources: Lesley Alderman, "You Can Achieve More in a Lot Less Time by Following Five Key Steps," *Money,* 24 (October 1995): 37; and Thomas A. Stewart, "A Thought in the Shower," *Fortune* (May 15, 1995): 124.

Questions: *What portion of your typical workweek would you like to devote to telecommuting? Why? Why is telecommuting not for everyone?*

Becoming a Better Communicator

Three communication skills especially important in today's highly organized world are listening, writing, and running meetings. Managers who master these skills usually have relatively few interpersonal relations problems. Moreover, effective communicators tend to move up the hierarchy faster than poor ones do. According to *Fortune* magazine:

> *Management experts say that communicating often and clearly with workers will be among every manager's key skills in coming years, while in an interconnected world, skillful communication outside one's company becomes steadily more important. Yet just as these trends take hold, many managers are becoming worse communicators. If you doubt it, a look at the standard of memo writing around your shop will probably persuade you.*[84]

7 List at least three practical tips for improving each of the following communication skills: listening, writing, and running a meeting.

Effective Listening

Almost all training in oral communication in high school, college, and management development programs is in effective speaking. But what about listening, the other half of the communication equation? Listening is the forgotten stepchild in communication skills training. This is unfortunate because the most glowing oration is a waste of time if it is not heard. Interestingly, a Cornell University researcher asked 827 employees in the hospitality industry to rate their managers' listening ability. Managers considered to be good listeners by employees tended to be female, under 45 years of age, and relatively new to their position.[85]

Listening takes place at two steps in the communication process. First, the receiver must listen in order to decode and understand the original message. Then the sender becomes a listener when attempting to decode and understand subsequent feedback. Identical listening skills come into play at both ends.

We can hear and process information much more quickly than the normal speaker can talk. According to researchers our average rate of speaking is about 125 words per minute, whereas we are able to listen to about 400 to 600 words a minute.[86] Thus, listeners have up to 75 percent slack time during which they can daydream or alternatively analyze the information and plan a response. Effective listeners know how to put that slack time to good use. Here are some practical tips for more effective listening:

- Tolerate silence. Listeners who rush to fill momentary silences cease being listeners.
- Ask stimulating, open-ended questions, ones that require more than merely a yes or no answer.
- Encourage the speaker with attentive eye contact, alert posture, and verbal encouragers such as "umhum," "yes," and "I see." Occasionally repeating the speaker's last few words also helps.

Listen to this! Native American tradition calls for giving each person in a "talking circle" an uninterrupted opportunity to speak. It is referred to as "passing the rock." The person holding the object speaks without interference, then passes the rock and shifts into a listening mode. Here a group of Xerox employees in Rochester, New York, pass the rock in their talking circle. Of course, you don't have to work for Xerox to copy this tradition.

- Paraphrase. Periodically restate in your own words what you have just heard.
- Show emotion to demonstrate that you are a sympathetic listener.
- Know your biases and prejudices and attempt to correct for them.
- Avoid premature judgments about what is being said.
- Summarize. Briefly highlight what the speaker has just finished saying to bring out possible misunderstandings.[87]

Wal-Mart has developed an admired "culture of listening." All of Wal-Mart's senior managers, including CEO David D. Glass, try to devote two days each week to visiting stores across the United States and listening to employees' concerns.[88] The valuable information gathered more than makes up for the Wal-Mart managers' hectic travel schedules.

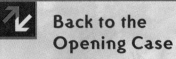

Back to the Opening Case   **12I**

Listening demands openness, trust, and respect, qualities difficult to maintain and seldom exhibited in any uniform way even by the most experienced listeners. It is more an attitude than a skill. The best kind of listening comes not from technique but from being genuinely interested in what really matters to the other person. Listening is much more than patiently hearing people out.

Source: Richard Farson, *Management of the Absurd: Paradoxes in Leadership* (New York: Simon & Schuster, 1996), p. 62.

Questions: *Is Herb Kelleher a good role model for this approach to listening? Explain. How does it help him maintain a good relationship with Southwest's unionized employees?*

Effective Writing

Managers often complain about college graduates' poor writing skills.[89] Writing difficulties stem from an educational system that requires students to do less and less writing. Essay tests have given way in many classes to the multiple-choice variety, and term papers are being pushed aside by team activities and projects. Quick-and-dirty computer e-mail correspondence at home, school, and the workplace also have contributed to the erosion of writing quality in recent years. Moreover, computerized "spelling checkers" used by those who compose at the computer keyboard do little to improve grammar. (There is no substitute for careful proofreading.) As a learned skill, effective writing is the product of regular practice.[90] Students who do not get the necessary writing practice in school are at a disadvantage when they step onto the managerial firing line.

Good writing is clearly part of the encoding step in the basic communication process. If it is done skillfully, potentially troublesome semantic and psychosocial barriers can be surmounted. Caterpillar Company's publications editor offered four helpful reminders:

1. *Keep words simple.* Simplifying the words you use will help reduce your thoughts to essentials; keep your readers from being "turned off" by the complexity of your letter, memo, or report; and make it more understandable.
2. *Don't sacrifice communication to rules of composition.* Most of us who were sensitized to the rules of grammar and composition in school never quite recovered from the process. As proof, we keep trying to make our writing conform to rigid rules and customs without regard to style or the ultimate purpose of the communication. (Of course, managers need to be sensitive to the stylistic preferences of their bosses.)
3. *Write concisely.* This means expressing your thoughts, opinions, and ideas in the fewest number of words consistent with composition and smoothness. But don't confuse conciseness with mere brevity; you may write briefly without being clear or complete.
4. *Be specific.* Vagueness is one of the most serious flaws in written communication because it destroys accuracy and clarity, leaving the reader to wonder about your meaning or intent.[91]

Also, avoid irritating your readers with useless phrases such as "to be perfectly honest," "needless to say," "as you know," and "please be advised that."[92]

Running a Meeting

Meetings are an ever-present feature of modern organizational life.[93] Whether they are convened to find facts, devise alternatives, or pass along information, meetings typically occupy a good deal of a manager's time. Meetings are the principal format for committee action. Too often, as illustrated by this recent research insight, meetings are a waste of valuable time. "The typical professional attends more than 60 meetings per month—and more than one-third are rated unproductive."[94] Whatever the reason for a meeting, managers who chair meetings owe it to themselves and their organization to use everyone's time and talent efficiently. Some useful pointers for conducting successful meetings are the following*:

- Prepare ahead of time.
- Have a reason for the meeting. Don't get together just because of tradition.
- Distribute an agenda to participants before the meeting.
- Give participants at least one day's notification.
- Participants should ask themselves what is expected of them, what they can read to prepare.
- Limit attendance and designate a leader.
- Keep a clock in the meeting room and have a specific start and end time.
- Encourage everyone to talk while keeping with the agenda.
- Foster rigorous debate and brainstorming while respecting each person's opinion.
- Use visual aids. Presentations with visual aids are 43 percent more persuasive than those without such presentations.
- Follow up. Meeting leader should let participants know any outcome.[95]

With practice, these guidelines will become second nature. Running a meeting brings into focus all the components of the communication process, including coping with noise and barriers. Effective meetings are important to organizational communication and, ultimately, to organizational success.

↙ This Meeting Is Called to Order. Stand Up!   12J

Research finding: The effects of meeting format (standing or sitting) on meeting length and the quality of group decision making were investigated by comparing meeting outcomes for 56 five-member groups that conducted meetings in a standing format with 55 five-member groups that conducted meetings in a seated format. Sit-down meetings were 34 percent longer than stand-up meetings, but they produced no better decisions than stand-up meetings.

Source: Allen C. Bluedorn, Daniel B. Turban, and Mary Sue Love, "The Effects of Stand-Up and Sit-Down Meeting Formats," *Journal of Applied Psychology*, 84 (April 1999): 277.

Questions: *What is your opinion about stand-up meetings? What are the potential drawbacks?*

---

*Stephanie Armour, "Team Efforts, Technology Add New Reasons to Meet," *USA Today* (December 8, 1997): 2A. Copyright 1997, USA Today. Reprinted with permission.

Summary

1. Modern technology has made communicating easier and less costly, with the unintended side effect of information overload. Managers are challenged to improve the *quality* of their communication because it is a core process for everything they do. Communication is a social process involving the transfer of information and understanding. Links in the communication process include sender, encoding, medium, decoding, receiver, and feedback. Noise is any source of interference.

2. According to the Lengel-Daft contingency model, media richness is determined by the amount of information conveyed and learning promoted. Rich media such as face-to-face communication are best for nonroutine problems. Lean media such as impersonal bulletins are suitable for routine problems.

3. The unofficial and informal communication system that sometimes complements and sometimes disrupts the formal communication system has been labeled the grapevine. A sample of managers surveyed had predominantly negative feelings toward it. Recognizing that the grapevine cannot be suppressed, managers are advised to monitor it constructively. Nonverbal communication, including facial, gestural, and postural body language, accounts for most of the impact of face-to-face communication. Managers can become more effective communicators by doing a better job of receiving and giving nonverbal communications.

4. Upward communication can be stimulated by using formal grievance procedures, employee attitude and opinion surveys, suggestion systems, an open-door policy, informal meetings, Internet chat rooms, and exit interviews.

5. Managers need to identify and overcome four barriers to communication. Process barriers can occur at any one of the basic links in the communication process. Physical barriers, such as walls and distance between two points, can block the transfer of understanding. Semantic barriers are encountered when there is confusion about the meaning of words. Psychosocial barriers to communication involve the full range of human perceptions, prejudices, and attitudes that can block the transfer of understanding. Care needs to be taken to eliminate subtle forms of sexist and racist communication.

6. E-mail, supposedly a real time saver, has quickly become a major time waster. Organizations need to create and enforce a clear e-mail policy to improve message quality and curb abuses. Videoconferencing restricts how people communicate because televised contacts are more mechanical than face-to-face meetings. While telecommuting can reduce travel time and expense and offer employment to nontraditional employees, it severely restricts normal social contact and face-to-face communication in the workplace.

7. Listening does not get sufficient attention in communications training. Active, cooperative listening is to be encouraged. Writing skills are no less important in the computer age. Written messages need to be specific, simply worded, and concise. Meetings, an ever-present feature of organizational life, need to be agenda-driven if time is to be used wisely.

Terms to Understand

Communication (p. 360)	Upward communication (p. 373)
Media richness (p. 363)	Exit interview (p. 375)
Noise (p. 366)	Semantics (p. 376)
Grapevine (p. 367)	Videoconference (p. 379)
Body language (p. 369)	Telecommuting (p. 380)

Skills & Tools

Harvard's Sarah McGinty Tells How to Develop Your Speaking Style

Popular discussion of communication style in recent years has centered on differences between the sexes. The subject has been fodder for TV talk shows, corporate seminars, and best-sellers, notably Deborah Tannen's *You Just Don't Understand* and John Gray's *Men Are from Mars, Women Are from Venus*. But Sarah McGinty, a teaching supervisor at Harvard University's School of Education, believes language style is based more on power than on gender—and that marked differences distinguish the powerful from the powerless loud and clear. As a consultant, she is often called on to help clients develop more effective communication styles. *Fortune*'s Justin Martin spoke with McGinty about her ideas:

What style of speaking indicates that someone possesses power?
A person who feels confident and in control will speak at length, set the agenda for conversation, stave off interruptions, argue openly, make jokes, and laugh. Such a person is more inclined to make statements, less inclined to ask questions. They are more likely to offer solutions or a program or a plan. All this creates a sense of confidence in listeners.

What about people who lack power? How do they speak?
The power deficient drop into conversations, encourage other speakers, ask numerous questions, avoid argument, and rely on gestures such as nodding and smiling that suggest agreement. They tend to offer empathy rather than solutions. They often use unfinished sentences. Unfinished sentences are a language staple for those who lack power.

How do you figure out what style of communication you lean toward?
It's quite hard to do. We're often quite ignorant about our own way of communicating. Everyone comes home at night occasionally and says, "I had that idea, but no one heard me, and everyone thinks it's Harry's idea." People like to pin that on gender and a lot of other things as well. But it's important to find out what really did happen. Maybe it was the volume of your voice, and you weren't heard. Maybe you overexplained, and the person who followed up pulled out the nugget of your thought.

But it's important to try to get some insight into what your own language habits are so that you can be analytical about whether you're shooting yourself in the foot. You can tape your side of phone calls, make a tape of a meeting, or sign up for a communications workshop. That's a great way to examine how you conduct yourself in conversations and in meetings.

Does power language differ from company to company?

Certainly. The key is figuring out who gets listened to within your corporate culture. That can make you a more savvy user of language. Try to sit in on a meeting as a kind of researcher, observing conversational patterns. Watch who talks, who changes the course of the discussion, who sort of drops in and out of the conversation. Then try to determine who gets noticed and why.

One very effective technique is to approach the person who ran the meeting a couple of days after the fact and ask for an overall impression. What ideas were useful? What ideas might have a shot at being implemented?

How can you get more language savvy?

You can start by avoiding bad habits, such as always seeking collaboration in the statements you make. Try to avoid "as Bob said" and "I pretty much agree with Sheila." Steer clear of disclaimers such as "I may be way off base here, but . . ." All these serve to undermine the impact of your statements.

The amount of space you take up can play a big part in how powerful and knowledgeable you appear. People speaking before a group, for instance, should stand with their feet a little bit apart and try to occupy as much space as possible. Another public-speaking tip: Glancing around constantly creates a situation in which nobody really feels connected to what you're saying.

Strive to be bolder. Everyone tends to worry that they will offend someone by stating a strong opinion. Be bold about ideas, tentative about people. Saying "I think you're completely wrong" is not a wise strategy. Saying "I have a plan that I think will solve these problems" is perfectly reasonable. You're not attacking people. You're being bold about an idea.

Source: Justin Martin, "How to Speak Shows Where You Rank," *Fortune* (February 2, 1998): 156. © 1998 Time Inc. Reprinted by permission.

Internet Exercises   ⇧

1. **Assessing your communication style and skills:** Communication is such a common everyday activity we seldom pause to review how we're actually doing. Here's an opportunity to systematically evaluate your communication style and skills, with the goal of becoming a more effective communicator. Once again, as we did in Chapters 8 and 13, let's visit Mind-Body QueenDom's unique Web site (**www.queendom.com**) and take advantage of the excellent collection of free self-assessment questionnaires. At the home page, select the main menu category "Tests, Tests, Tests . . ." Then select "Communication Skills Test," under the heading Relationships. This 34-item assessment instrument is designed to take about 15 to 20 minutes to complete. It is self-paced, so you might complete it in less time. Score the test and read the interpretation. Next, back at the "Tests, Tests, Tests . . ." page, click on the "Assertiveness Test," under the heading Career/Job. This 32-item assessment test also uses a multiple-choice format and should take ten to 15 minutes to complete. Score the test and read the interpretation.

   Learning Points: 1. Are you surprised by the results of these assessment tests? Explain. 2. What are your communication strengths? 3. What are your communication weaknesses or limitations? 4. What do you need to do to improve? 5. How motivated are you to improve your communication skills? Explain.

2. **Some timeless advice on good writing:** Most literary scholars say the best primer on English composition ever written was William Strunk Jr.'s *The Elements of Style*. This masterful little book was originally published in 1918. More than 80 years later, after revision by E. B. White and countless reprintings, it is still essential reading for college students. The current 105-page paperback version is William Strunk Jr. and E. B. White, *The Elements of Style*, 4th ed. (Boston: Allyn & Bacon, 1999.) Thanks to the miracle of the Internet, the original version is available free online. Go to (**www.bartleby.com**), scroll down the list of

authors and titles, and click on Strunk. Browse through the topics in Part III, Elementary Principles of Composition, with the objective of answering the following questions.

Learning Points: 1. Is this 80-year-old book instructive for e-mail users? How? 2. According to Strunk's standards, which principles of composition are your strengths? 3. What elements of composition do you need to improve? 4. How important are writing skills in the Internet age? Explain.

3. **Check it out:** Interested in telecommuting? Want to know more, from the organization's standpoint? Go to the home page of the International Telework Association & Council (**www.telecommute.org**) and check out the ten workshops for employers wanting to start a telecommuting program. The first workshop, Getting Educated, provides good background information.

For updates to these exercises, visit our Web site (**www.hmco.com/college**).

| Closing Case | # The Case of the Errant Messenger |

The following case study has been reported by Robert I. Stevens, a systems consultant and writer.

Whenever anyone on the executive floor wanted to tease Henry Reeves, they would ask him, "Are you sure you don't have any messages for me from the president?" Hank would become somewhat flustered and ignore the question. This byplay, which lasted for a year or so, was the result of the following incident—known by many, but not including the president.

The president of the company was a grizzled, dour army veteran who ran the operation as if he was still commanding a unit in the service. He made all major decisions and was almost always right in his judgment. I had seen him join a meeting of top staff just after a policy decision had been reached and ask a few big questions that resulted in a complete reversal of the original decision. The only executive who contested the president, usually at meetings where the president was not present, was vice president James Dubler, who was almost always wrong.

The president believed in "seeing what the troops were doing" and spent a good portion of his time visiting the many dispersed locations of the company. . . . Whenever the president wanted to inform an officer of the company who was not present of a decision, request for

information, or at times a reprimand, he would turn to a member of his traveling party and give him an oral message to deliver to the appropriate person. Usually, the selected messenger was Henry Reeves, a shy, introverted MBA, recently hired.

On one trip that I attended just before Reeves was hired, a situation developed that displeased the president. He turned to me and said, "You tell Jim Dubler, he better get this problem corrected before it blows up in his face." Although I was only a senior analyst, it would never have occurred to me to question the president's order to deliver such a message to a vice president.

When I delivered the president's message to Mr. Dubler, he became very agitated and gave me the type of verbal thrashing that a vice president can give an analyst. I finally blurted out, "Mr. Dubler, I'm only the messenger." He immediately calmed down and told me to leave.

From what we pieced together later, the first time Hank Reeves delivered a message to Mr. Dubler, he received the same type of tongue-lashing from Dubler without being able to withdraw from the confrontation. Evidently, the occasion so traumatized Reeves that when the president gave him other messages to be relayed to Dubler, he never delivered them. The situation of Reeves not delivering the president's messages to Dubler went on for several months without Reeves telling anyone about his problem. During that time, the president was heard to grumble about Dubler not reacting too fast to various situations.

Source: "The Case of the Errant Messenger," *Journal of Systems Management*, 35 (July 1984): 42. Reprinted by permission of the author, Robert I. Stevens.

Then one Friday afternoon the president asked Reeves to get Dubler to prepare a report over the weekend that he wanted on his desk Monday morning. Reeves again did not deliver the message. Monday morning, when the president arrived at his office and no report was present, he checked with his secretary if Dubler had left a message as to why he had not finished the report. He muttered to me (I had just entered his office as requested), "Well, this is the last straw." He then called the personnel office on the phone and said, "Fire Dubler. Give him whatever severance benefits you think he should have, but get him off the property—and I don't want him coming up to see me."

As in most corporations, such situations become common knowledge in short order—and that's why Reeves was asked occasionally if he had any messages to deliver from the president.

FOR DISCUSSION

1. Who is primarily to blame for Dubler's firing: the president, Reeves, or Dubler himself? Why?

2. Did the grapevine have a positive or negative impact in this case? Explain.

3. Considering what you now know about organizational communication, what advice would you give the president? Reeves? Dubler?

VIDEO SKILL BUILDERS

This video contrasts the cultures of three very different organizations: (1) At UOP, a large and profitable petroleum refining company, emphasis is on globalization, innovation, and loyalty; (2) Von Maur, a chain of upscale department stores, directs its training and motivation programs toward excellent customer service; (3) The culture of Alligator Records is informal, participative, and sharply focused on promoting the blues.

3A Organizational Culture: Three Profiles

Learning objective: To gain a fuller understanding of organizational culture, values, and socialization.

Links to textual material: *Chapter 9:* Organizational culture; Organizational values; Organizational socialization

Discussion questions

1. Which of the six common characteristics of organizational cultures are evident in these three video profiles? Explain your evidence.
2. How would you briefly summarize the organizational values (or shared beliefs) for each of the three companies?
3. How does each of the three companies "socialize" its new employees to fit its culture?
4. Which organizational culture best suits your own style and way of doing things? Why?

T.G.I. Friday's recently reorganized into smaller and more manageable units as it continues to grow internationally. The reorganization, along geographic lines, has divided the business into five U.S. regions and an international region. The international division (with 75 restaurants in 35 countries), in turn, is organized into geographic regions. T.G.I. Friday's works hard to create a distinctly American dining experience wherever it does business.

3B T.G.I. Friday's Organizes for Global Expansion

Learning objective: To learn more about mechanistic/organic design, departmentalization, and centralization/decentralization in a global company.

Links to textual material: *Chapter 10:* Mechanistic versus organic organizations; Departmentalization; Centralization and decentralization

Discussion questions

1. In terms of Table 10.2, is T.G.I. Friday's relatively mechanistic or organic? Explain.
2. Is a geographic organization structure best for T.G.I. Friday's? Explain.
3. How does the company strike a balance between centralization and decentralization?

Part Four

MOTIVATING and LEADING

MOTIVATING JOB
PERFORMANCE

CHAPTER OBJECTIVES

When you finish studying this chapter, you should be able to

1 Explain the motivational lessons taught by Maslow's theory, Herzberg's theory, and expectancy theory.

2 Describe how goal setting motivates performance.

3 Discuss how managers can improve the motivation of routine-task personnel.

4 Explain how job enrichment can be used to enhance the motivating potential of jobs.

5 Distinguish extrinsic rewards from intrinsic rewards and list four rules for administering extrinsic rewards effectively.

6 Discuss the contributions quality control circles and self-managed teams can make to participative management.

7 Explain how companies are striving to motivate an increasingly diverse workforce.

"THERE ARE NO
SIMPLE, COOKBOOK FORMULAS
FOR WORKING WITH PEOPLE."
keith davis

THE CHANGING WORKPLACE

Seeking Proper Balance at Norway's Norsk Hydro

On the surface, Norway seems to be a moderate place. The climate can be intemperate, but the people and the lifestyle are just the opposite—the picture of restraint and judiciousness. Oh, there are some unassuming little oddities: Norwegians eat fish for breakfast, and often for lunch and for dinner. Caviar is so common that it comes in tubes, just like toothpaste. Very few people are overweight.

All of which seems charmingly unusual—but hardly alien.

The workplace, too, seems familiar: computers, cubicles, bullet-point slides. Familiar, that is, until you look more closely.

Every weekday at 6:10 A.M., Morten Lingelem boards a train at Sandefjord for the 90-minute ride to his job in Oslo. Lingelem, 42, a process-technology manager, has a standing reservation in the train's "office car," where he can power up his laptop and work in quiet comfort. That office car serves a purpose that's exactly the opposite of what it would be in the United States: It enables Lingelem to hold down a demanding engineering-management job, to spend more than three hours a day commuting, and still to be home by 6 P.M.

Atle Tærum, a colleague of Lingelem's, lives on a farm 90 minutes west of Oslo. And, two days a week, that's where he is, taking care of his 10-month-old daughter. Tærum is never without his cell-phone. On those days, customers—perhaps calling from Africa or from the Middle East—often reach him while he's plowing his fields, or chaperoning his son's kindergarten class.

Norway is, in fact, a sort of alternative universe of work. The inhabitants, the setting, the language, and the profit imperative all seem familiar. But Norwegians have a very different attitude about work—and a singular view of what work can become.

That vision is rooted in the notion that balance is healthy. The argument: work can be redesigned to promote balance. More than that, balance can become a source of corporate and national competitive advantage. Working less can, in fact, mean working better.

Norsk Hydro, the company that employs both Lingelem and Tærum, is one of Norway's dominant institutions. It's the world's second-largest producer of oil from the Norwegian North Sea, and the single-largest salmon farmer. Hydro fertilizer feeds Florida tomatoes and Arizona golf courses. Hydro metals toughen Cadillac Seville bumpers and Nokia cell-phones.

Hydro operates in 70 countries and employs 39,000 people, many of whom live and work outside of Norway. But it remains emphatically Norwegian—an organization not easily understood in American terms. As excess defines American culture, so balance shapes life for Norwegians, who long ago discovered sane responses to the tension between work and family. Norway is a place, after all, where people typically leave work between 4 P.M. and 4:30 P.M. Working women get at least 38 weeks of paid maternity leave; men get as many as 4 weeks of paid leave. Norway's answer to "How much is enough?" is found in the way the nation operates. Balance is the place where conversations about work and life begin.

In its 94 years of operation, "Hydro has created and nurtured industry in Norway," says Roald Nomme, a consultant and former manager at Hydro. "What is deep in the culture of Hydro is to think in the long term, to think more holistically—to think about the connections between employees, the company, and society."

Now Hydro is reexamining these connections. In a series of experiments across the company, it is testing a much more ambitious vision of balance. The two-year-old project, known as Hydroflex, has given hundreds of employees varying combinations of flexible hours, home offices, new technology, and redesigned office space.

What has Hydro learned?

Hydro believes that it can help employees find a better balance by redesigning physical work spaces—and by redesigning work itself. It can free people from old restrictions on where and when they work. That flexibility makes workers more productive and jobs more appealing, and more appealing jobs attract more talented people.

Linked to the push for flexibility are new notions of diversity. Hydro believes that diversity goes beyond race or gender. Diversity has to do with *perspective*—and it exists *within* individuals: each of us is many different people at different times in our lives. Cultivate that diversity, and greater creativity will follow.

These workplace initiatives come at a critical time for Hydro. Because of weak commodity and oil prices, profits dropped by 4 percent between 1994 and 1998, even as revenues increased by 40 percent. In most American companies, such performance would be enough to end any grand experiments in work redesign, diversity, and balance. But at Hydro, those projects persist and even thrive—because, to Hydro, these initiatives are not indulgences. They are critical strategic elements for survival.

Yes, Hydro must go head-to-head with competitors in the United States—and in Germany, in Singapore, and in Mexico. As it fights these global battles, Hydro is up against relentless freneticism. We Americans pay lip service to sanity, but when the going gets tough, we readily abandon balance and work even harder.

Norwegians believe that such mania is not sustainable. In the end, they say, balance will win out. . . .

Indeed, Norwegian culture—the prism through which Hydro's efforts at balance must be viewed—takes some fundamental American attitudes about work and turns them upside down.

In the United States, for instance, working long hours is seen as admirable, even heroic. At Hydro, the standard workday, even for professionals, is seven and a half hours. If you're still sitting at your desk at 6 P.M., people wonder why you can't get your work done.

Work in Norway is also shaped by a tradition of cooperation between unions and management that's unheard of in the United States. Labor and management typically work together to change processes and structures for greater efficiency. Unions believe that higher productivity brings more jobs and higher pay. Management wants higher profits—but satisfied employees aren't bad either.

All this allows—and perhaps requires—Norwegians to consider balance in fundamental terms. A rich life is a diverse collection of compelling experiences, some of which involve work. Work that is all-consuming is unhealthy—for the individual, for the organization, and for the community. Time spent away from work is restorative. More to the point: Time spent outside work fuels work itself.

Source: Charles Fishman, "The Way to Enough." Reprinted from July/August 1999 issue of *Fast Company* magazine. All rights reserved. To subscribe, please call (800) 688-1545.

Norsk Hydro's workplace initiatives give real meaning to the frequently made statement: "people are our most valuable resource." By tapping the full potential of each individual employee, Norsk Hydro hopes to boost motivation and improve its global competitiveness. Research support for this approach comes from Stanford's Jeffrey Pfeffer, who recently reported a strong connection between *people-centered practices* and higher profits and lower employee turnover. Pfeffer identified seven people-centered practices:

- Protection of job security
- Rigorous hiring process
- Employees empowered through decentralization and self-managed teams
- Compensation linked to performance
- Comprehensive training
- Reduction of status distinctions
- Sharing of key information

Pfeffer sees these practices as an integrated package and cautions against implementing them piecemeal. Unfortunately, according to Pfeffer's calculations, only about 12 percent of today's organizations qualify as systematically people-centered.[1] Clearly, employee motivation is not what it could be. As used here, the term **motivation** refers to the psychological process that gives behavior purpose and direction. By appealing to this process, managers attempt to get individuals to willingly pursue organizational objectives. Motivation theories are generalizations about the "why" and "how" of purposeful behavior.[2]

Figure 13.1 is an overview model for this chapter. The final element in this model, job performance, is the product of a combination of an individual's motivation and

motivation *psychological process giving behavior purpose and direction*

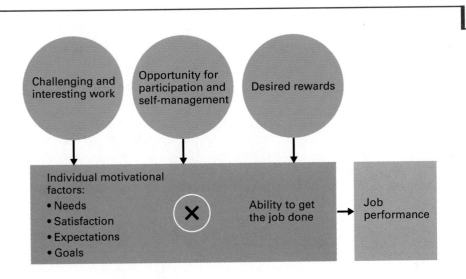

Figure 13.1

**Individual Motivation
and Job Performance**

ability. Both are necessary. All the motivation in the world, for example, will not enable a computer-illiterate person to sit down and create a computer spreadsheet. Ability and skills, acquired through training and/or on-the-job experience, also are required. The individual's motivational factors—needs, satisfaction, expectations, and goals—are affected by challenging work, rewards, and participation.[3] We need to take a closer look at each key element in this model. A review of four basic motivation theories is a good starting point.

Motivation Theories

Although there are dozens of different theories of motivation, four have emerged as the most influential: Maslow's needs hierarchy theory, Herzberg's two-factor theory, expectancy theory, and goal-setting theory. Each approaches the motivation process from a different angle, each has supporters and detractors, and each teaches important lessons about motivation to work.

1 **Explain the motivational lessons taught by Maslow's theory, Herzberg's theory, and expectancy theory.**

Maslow's Needs Hierarchy Theory

In 1943 psychologist Abraham Maslow proposed that people are motivated by a predictable five-step hierarchy of needs.[4] Little did he realize at the time that his tentative proposal, based on an extremely limited clinical study of neurotic patients, would become one of the most influential concepts in the field of management. Perhaps because it is so straightforward and intuitively appealing, Maslow's theory has strongly influenced those interested in work behavior. Maslow's message was simply this: people always have needs, and when one need is relatively fulfilled, others emerge in a predictable sequence to take its place. From bottom to top, Maslow's needs hierarchy

Figure 13.2

Maslow's Hierarchy of Needs Theory

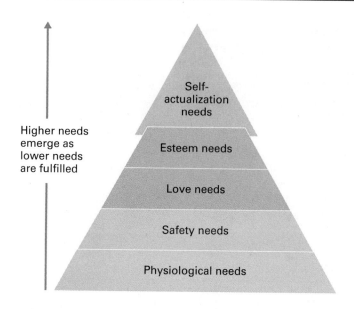

Higher needs emerge as lower needs are fulfilled

- Self-actualization needs
- Esteem needs
- Love needs
- Safety needs
- Physiological needs

Source: Data for diagram drawn from A. H. Maslow, "A Theory of Human Motivation," *Psychological Review,* 50 (July 1943): 370–396.

includes physiological, safety, love, esteem, and self-actualization needs (see Figure 13.2). According to Maslow, most individuals are not consciously aware of these needs; yet we all supposedly proceed up the hierarchy of needs, one level at a time.

Physiological Needs.   At the bottom of the hierarchy are needs based on physical drives, including the need for food, water, sleep, and sex. Fulfillment of these lowest-levels needs enables the individual to survive, and nothing else is important when these bodily needs have not been satisfied. As Maslow observed, "It is quite true that man lives by bread alone—when there is no bread."[5] But today the average employee experiences little difficulty in satisfying physiological needs. Figuratively speaking, the prospect of eating more bread is not motivating when one has plenty of bread to eat.

Safety Needs.   After our basic physiological needs have been relatively well satisfied, we next become concerned about our safety from the elements, enemies, and other threats. Most modern employees, by earning a living, achieve a high degree of fulfillment in this area. Unemployment assistance is a safety net for those between jobs. Insurance also helps fulfill safety needs, a point not lost on Coca-Cola Femsa, Mexico's primary bottler of Coke:

> *Many of the store owners in Mexico, Coke's second-biggest market, turned out to be single mothers and retirees who couldn't afford health insurance. Armed with that intelligence, Fensa was able to create an incentive program that rewards shopkeepers who sell enough Cokes with access to group insurance—a move that helped boost Coke's sales volume in Mexico 13 percent last year.[6]*

Love Needs.   A physiologically satisfied and secure person focuses next on satisfying needs for love and affection. This category is a powerful motivator of human behavior. People typically strive hard to achieve a sense of belonging with others. As with the first two levels of needs, relative satisfaction of love needs paves the way for the emergence of the next, higher level.

Esteem Needs.   People who perceive themselves as worthwhile are said to possess high self-esteem.[7] Self-respect is the key to esteem needs. Much of our self-respect, and therefore our esteem, comes from being accepted and respected by others. It is important for those who are expected to help achieve organizational objectives to have their esteem needs relatively well fulfilled. But esteem needs cannot emerge if lower-level needs go unattended.

Self-Actualization Needs.   At the top of Maslow's hierarchy is the open-ended category *self-actualization needs*. It is open-ended because it relates to the need "to become more and more what one is, to become everything that one is capable of becoming."[8] One may satisfy this need by striving to become a better homemaker, plumber, rock singer, or manager (see Managing Diversity). According to one management writer, the self-actualizing manager has the following characteristics:

1. Has warmth, closeness, and sympathy.
2. Recognizes and shares negative information and feelings.

Billionaire Investor Warren Buffett on Self-Actualization   13A

"I can certainly define happiness, because happy is what I am," Buffett told students at the University of Washington. "I get to do what I like to do every single day of the year. I get to do it with people I like, and I don't have to associate with anybody who causes my stomach to churn. I tap-dance to work . . . I'd advise you that when you go out to work, work for an organization of people you admire, because it will turn you on. I always worry about people who say, 'I'm going to do this for ten years; I really don't like it very well. And then I'll do this . . .' That's a little like saving up sex for your old age. Not a very good idea."

Source: Steve Nearman, "The Simple Billionaire," *Selling Power*, 19 (June 1999): 48.

Questions: *How do you interpret Buffett's remarks to the students? What would it take to help you achieve self-actualization? Is it possible that once you reach your "mountaintop" you will set your sights on a higher peak? Explain.*

For further information about the interactive annotations in this chapter, visit our Web site (**www.hmco.com/college**).

Self-actualization, becoming all that one can become, sometimes means getting reacquainted with one's cultural heritage. David Rocky Mountain, a 13-year-old Lakota, surveys a traditional campsite constructed by troubled teens from the Cheyenne River Sioux tribe in South Dakota. This "spiritual boot camp" bonds the youngsters with their elders who offer many valuable life lessons. Funding is provided by the Robert Wood Johnson Foundation.

Managing Diversity

Writing His Own Prescription for Self-Actualization at Age 55

Robert Lopatin's prescription for a fulfilling, no-regrets life: Don't be afraid of change, and never pass up an opportunity to try something new.

He's taken a healthy dose of his own medicine. At 55, Lopatin is fresh out of medical school, one of the oldest first-year residents in the country.

He works 100-hour weeks, including exhausting overnight calls, alongside colleagues young enough to be his children, while physicians his own age may ponder retirement.

"It's like nirvana," he said. "I feel like I died and was born again."

Lopatin dreamed as a boy of becoming a doctor but put his interest in medicine aside during college and eventually went into business with his father. The two ran a women's clothing company for 27 years.

A year or so after they sold it in the early 1990s, Lopatin decided it wasn't too late to fulfill his longtime dream.

At age 51, he began studying at the Albert Einstein College of Medicine.

Now half a year out of medical school, Lopatin has just started a four-year residency at Montefiore Medical Center in the Bronx. Lopatin admits the hours are tough.

A 6:30 A.M.-to-midnight workday is common, and graveyard shifts are required four times a month.

But he believes his maturity helps him practice better medicine, and colleagues and patients agree.

"He's a fabulous intern because he has a true devotion to what he's doing," says his supervisor, Lawrence Brandt. "Being older, he sees things from a different perspective. Patients immediately . . . see someone who they can trust."

Lopatin's late leap to medicine was completely in character.

After long days working as a garment industry executive, he studied art history at Columbia University at night, completing all the requirements for a doctorate except his dissertation. He studied clothing production at the Fashion Institute of Technology and took classes in Spanish, French, Italian, German, and Yiddish.

"I've never been out of school," he explained. "It just makes me feel alive; that's who I am."

He studied Shakespeare and Latin, took calculus, and enrolled in a U.N. training program for Spanish-language interpreters.

Then, at a friend's wedding in Zurich, he happened to sit near a young man who'd just finished medical school. Talking with him reminded Lopatin of his own boyhood dream.

"How many times is a person . . . genuinely free to be able to restart their life?" he asked. "I said to myself, 'I have to at least pursue it . . . because if I don't, I will be forever filled with self-reproach. I will have failed myself.'"

Source: Beth Gardiner, "At 55, New York Man Writes a New Prescription for His Life," *USA Today* (October 11, 1999): 5A. Copyright 1999, USA Today. Reprinted with permission.

3. Exhibits trust, openness, and candor.
4. Does not achieve goals by power, deception, or manipulation.
5. Does not project own feelings, motivations, or blame onto others.
6. Does not limit horizons; uses and develops body, mind, and senses.
7. Is not rationalistic; can think in unconventional ways.
8. Is not conforming; regulates behavior from within.[9]

Granted, this is a rather tall order to fill. It has been pointed out that "a truly self-actualized individual is more of an exception than the rule in the organizational context."[10] Whether productive organizations need more self-actualized individuals is subject to debate. On the positive side, self-actualized employees might help break down barriers to creativity and steer the organization in new directions. On the negative side, too many unconventional nonconformists could wreak havoc with the typical administrative setup dedicated to predictability.

Relevance of Maslow's Theory for Managers. Behavioral scientists who have attempted to test Maslow's theory in real life claim it has some deficiencies.[11] Even Maslow's hierarchical arrangement has been questioned. Practical evidence points toward a two-level rather than a five-level hierarchy. In this competing view, physiological and safety needs are arranged in hierarchical fashion, as Maslow contends. But beyond that point, any one of a number of needs may emerge as the single most important need, depending on the individual. Edward Lawler, a leading motivation researcher, observed, "Which higher-order needs come into play after the lower ones are satisfied and in which order they come into play cannot be predicted. If anything, it seems that most people are simultaneously motivated by several of the same-level needs."[12]

Although Maslow's theory has not stood up well under actual testing, it teaches managers one important lesson: a *fulfilled* need does not motivate an individual. For example, the promise of unemployment benefits may partially fulfill an employee's need for economic security (the safety need). But the added security of additional unemployment benefits will probably not motivate fully employed individuals to work any harder. Effective managers try to anticipate each employee's personal need profile and to provide opportunities to fulfill *emerging* needs. Because challenging and worthwhile jobs and meaningful recognition tend to enhance self-esteem, the esteem level presents managers with the greatest opportunity to motivate better performance.

Herzberg's Two-Factor Theory

During the 1950s, Frederick Herzberg proposed a theory of employee motivation based on satisfaction.[13] His theory implied that a satisfied employee is motivated from within to work harder and that a dissatisfied employee is not self-motivated. Herzberg's research uncovered two classes of factors associated with employee satisfaction and dissatisfaction (see Table 13.1). As a result, his concept has come to be called Herzberg's two-factor theory.

Dissatisfiers and Satisfiers. Herzberg compiled his list of dissatisfiers by asking a sample of about 200 accountants and engineers to describe job situations in which they felt exceptionally bad about their jobs. An analysis of their responses revealed a consistent pattern. Dissatisfaction tended to be associated with complaints about the job context or factors in the immediate work environment.

Herzberg then drew up his list of satisfiers, factors responsible for self-motivation, by asking the same accountants and engineers to describe job situations in which they had felt exceptionally good about their jobs. Again, a patterned response emerged, but this time different factors were described: the opportunity to experience achievement, receive recognition, work on an interesting job, take responsibility, and experience advancement and growth. Herzberg observed that these satisfiers centered on the nature of the task itself. Employees appeared to be motivated by *job content*—that is, by what they actually did all day long. Consequently, Herzberg concluded that

> **13B**
> ### Is Everybody Happy?
> . . . Do happy workers improve corporate performance? The Gallup Organization recently surveyed 55,000 workers in an attempt to match employee attitudes with company results. The survey found that four attitudes, taken together, correlate strongly with higher profits. The attitudes: Workers feel they are given the opportunity to do what they do best every day; they believe their opinions count; they sense that their fellow workers are committed to quality; and they've made a direct connection between their work and the company's mission.
>
> *Source:* Linda Grant, "Happy Workers, High Returns," *Fortune* (January 12, 1998): 81.
>
> **Questions:** *What would Herzberg likely say about this evidence? Is your own job performance affected by your job satisfaction? Explain.*

Table 13.1

Herzberg's Two-Factor Theory of Motivation

Dissatisfiers: Factors mentioned most often by dissatisfied employees	Satisfiers: Factors mentioned most often by satisfied employees
1. Company policy and administration	1. Achievement
2. Supervision	2. Recognition
3. Relationship with supervisor	3. Work itself
4. Work conditions	4. Responsibility
5. Salary	5. Advancement
6. Relationship with peers	6. Growth
7. Personal life	
8. Relationship with subordinates	
9. Status	
10. Security	

Source: Adapted and reprinted by permission of the *Harvard Business Review.* An exhibit from "One More Time: How Do You Motivate Employees?" by Frederick Herzberg (January–February 1968). Copyright © 1968 by the President and Fellows of Harvard College, all rights reserved.

enriched jobs were the key to self-motivation. The work itself—not pay, supervision, or some other environmental factor—was the key to satisfaction and motivation.

Implications of Herzberg's Theory. By insisting that satisfaction is not the opposite of dissatisfaction, Herzberg encouraged managers to think carefully about what actually motivates employees. According to Herzberg, "the opposite of job satisfaction is not job dissatisfaction, but rather *no* job satisfaction; and similarly, the opposite of job dissatisfaction is not job satisfaction, but *no* dissatisfaction,"[14] Rather, the dissatisfaction-satisfaction continuum contains a zero midpoint at which both dissatisfaction and satisfaction are absent. An employee stuck on this midpoint, though not dissatisfied with pay and working conditions, is not particularly motivated to work hard because the job itself lacks challenge. Herzberg believes that the most managers can hope for when attempting to motivate employees with pay, status, working conditions, and other contextual factors is to reach the zero midpoint. But the elimination of dissatisfaction is not the same as truly motivating an employee. To satisfy and motivate employees, an additional element is required: meaningful, interesting, and challenging work. Herzberg believed that money is a weak motivational tool because, at best, it can only eliminate dissatisfaction.

Like Maslow, Herzberg triggered lively debate among motivation theorists. His assumption that job performance improves as satisfaction increases has been criticized for its weak empirical basis. For example, one researcher, after reviewing 20 studies that tested this notion, concluded that the relationship, though positive, was too weak to have any theoretical or practical significance.[15] Others have found that one person's dissatisfier may be another's satisfier (for example, money).[16] Nonetheless, Herzberg made a useful contribution to motivation theory by emphasizing the motivating potential of enriched work. (Job enrichment is discussed in detail in the next section.)

Expectancy Theory

Both Maslow's and Herzberg's theories have been criticized for making unsubstantiated generalizations about what motivates people. Practical experience tells us that the same people are motivated by different things at different times and that different people are motivated by different things at the same time. Fortunately, expectancy theory, which is based largely on Victor H. Vroom's 1964 classic *Work and Motivation*, effectively deals with the highly personalized rational choices that individuals make when faced with the prospect of having to work to achieve rewards. Individual perception, though secondary in the Maslow and Herzberg models, is central to expectancy theory. Accordingly, **expectancy theory** is a motivation model based on the assumption that motivational strength is determined by perceived probabilities of success. The term **expectancy** refers to the subjective probability (or expectation) that one thing will lead to another. Work-related expectancies, like all other expectancies, are shaped by ongoing personal experience. For instance, an employee's expectation of a raise, diminished after being turned down, later rebounds when the supervisor indicates a willingness to reconsider the matter.

A Basic Expectancy Model. Although Vroom and other expectancy theorists developed their models in somewhat complex mathematical terms, the descriptive model in Figure 13.3 is helpful for basic understanding. In this model, one's motivational strength increases as one's perceived effort-performance and performance-reward probabilities increase. All this is not as complicated as it sounds. For example, estimate your motivation to study if you expect to do poorly on a quiz no matter how hard you study (low effort-performance probability) and you know the quiz will not be graded (low performance-reward probability). Now contrast that estimate with

expectancy theory *model that assumes motivational strength is determined by perceived probabilities of success*

expectancy *one's belief or expectation that one thing will lead to another*

Lu Cordova (bottom, center), CEO of Internet startup TixToGo, is betting her young company on expectancy motivation theory. She has lured several high-talent professionals to the San Francisco–based Web site for special events with stock that will be worthless until the company is bought out or goes public with a stock offering to investors. Working long hours for deferred compensation is a real gamble requiring people who can survive without a paycheck in hopes of cashing in big later. Any takers?

Figure 13.3

A Basic Expectancy Model

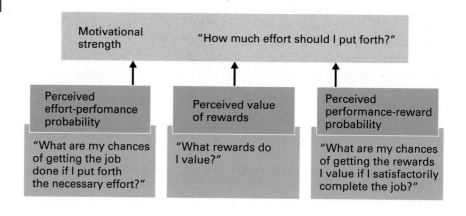

your motivation to study if you believe you can do well on the quiz with minimal study (high effort-performance probability) and that by doing well on the quiz your course grade will significantly improve (high performance-reward probability). Like students, employees are motivated to expend effort when they believe it will ultimately lead to rewards they themselves value. This expectancy approach not only appeals strongly to common sense, it has received encouraging empirical support from researchers.[17]

Relevance of Expectancy Theory for Managers. According to expectancy theory, effort → performance → reward expectations determine whether motivation will be high or low. Although these expectations are in the mind of the employee, they can be influenced by managerial action and organizational experience. Training, combined with challenging but realistic objectives, helps give people the idea that they can get the job done if they put forth the necessary effort. But perceived effort-performance probabilities are only half the battle. Listening skills enable managers to discover each individual's perceived performance-reward probabilities. Employees tend to work harder when they believe they have *a good chance* of getting *personally meaningful* rewards. Both sets of expectations require managerial attention. Each is a potential barrier to work motivation.

Back to the Opening Case   13C

Results of a *Fast Company* Roper Starch online survey of 1,122 college-educated employees:

When you started to work for your current employer, did you think that your job would be . . . ?

Mostly just a way to make money	12%
Meaningful, but not as meaningful as the rest of your life	37%
Just as meaningful as family life and other activities	46%
The most meaningful thing in your life	5%

Think about your job *today*. Do you think that your job is . . . ?

Mostly just a way to make money	18%
Meaningful, but not as meaningful as the rest of your life	52%
Just as meaningful as family life and other activities	26%
The most meaningful thing in your life	4%

Overall, do you think that your job has . . . ?

Exceeded your expectations	16%
Met your expectations	52%
Fallen short of your expectations	28%
Been completely disappointing	4%

Source: Excerpted from "FC Roper Starch Survey," *Fast Company,* no. 29 (November 1999): 214–222.

Questions: *What would Norsk Hydro managers probably say about the results of this survey? How do your met and unmet job expectations influence your job performance?*

Goal-Setting Theory

Think of the three or four most successful people you know personally. Their success may have come via business or professional achievement, politics, athletics, or community service. Chances are they got where they are today by being goal-oriented. In other words, they committed themselves to (and achieved) progressively more challenging goals in their professional and personal affairs. Biographies and autobiographies of successful people in all walks of life generally attest to the virtues of goal setting. Accordingly, goal setting is acknowledged today as a respected and useful motivation theory.

Within an organizational context, **goal setting** is the process of improving individual or group job performance with formally stated objectives, deadlines, or quality standards.[18] Management by objectives (MBO), discussed in Chapter 6, is a specific application of goal setting that advocates participative and measurable objectives. Also, recall from Chapter 6 how managers tend to use the terms *goal* and *objective* interchangeably.

goal setting   *process of improving performance with objectives, deadlines, or quality standards*

A General Goal-Setting Model.

Thanks to motivation researchers such as Edwin A. Locke, there is a comprehensive body of knowledge about goal setting.[19] Goal setting has been researched more rigorously than the three motivation theories just discussed.[20] Important lessons from goal-setting theory and research are incorporated in the general model in Figure 13.4. This model shows how properly conceived goals trigger a motivational process that improves performance. Let us explore the key components of this goal-setting model.

2 Describe how goal setting motivates performance.

Personal Ownership of Challenging Goals.

In Chapter 6, the discussion of MBO and writing good objectives stressed that goal effectiveness is enhanced by *specificity, difficulty*, and *participation*. Measurable and challenging goals encourage an individual or group to stretch while trying to attain progressively more difficult levels of achievement. For instance, parents who are paying a college student's tuition and expenses are advised to specify a challenging grade point goal rather than to simply tell their son or daughter, "Just do your best." Otherwise, the student could show up at the end of the semester with two Cs and three Ds, saying, "Well, I did my best!" It is important to note that goals need to be difficult enough to be challenging but not impossible. Impossible goals hamper performance; they are a handy excuse for not even trying.[21]

Participation in the goal-setting process gives the individual *personal ownership*. From the employee's viewpoint, it is "something I helped develop, not just my boss's wild idea." Feedback on performance operates in concert with well-conceived goals. Feedback lets the

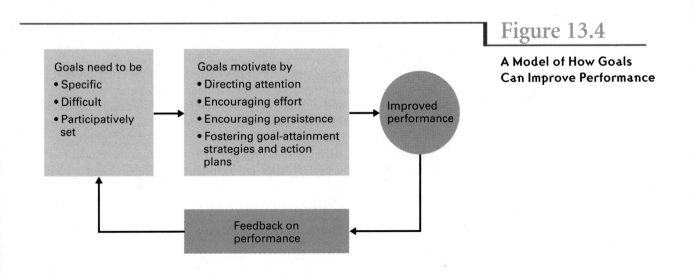

Figure 13.4

A Model of How Goals Can Improve Performance

person or group know if things are on track or if corrective action is required to reach the goal. An otherwise excellent goal-setting program can be compromised by lack of timely and relevant feedback from managers. Researchers have documented the motivational value of matching *specific goals* with *equally specific feedback.*[22] Sam Walton, the founder of Wal-Mart, was a master of blending goals and feedback. For example, consider this exchange between Sam Walton and an employee during one of his regular visits:

A manager rushes up with an associate in tow.

"Mr. Walton, I want you to meet Renee. She runs one of the top ten pet departments in the country."

"Well, Renee, bless your heart. What percentage of the store [sales] are you doing?"

"Last year it was 3.1 percent," Renee says, "but this year I'm trying for 3.3 percent."

"Well, Renee, that's amazing," says Sam. "You know our average pet department only does about 2.4 percent. Keep up the great work."[23]

How Do Goals Actually Motivate?   Goal-setting researchers say goals perform a motivational function by doing the four things listed in the center of Figure 13.4. First, a goal is an exercise in selective perception because it directs one's *attention* to a specific target. Second, a goal encourages one to exert *effort* toward achieving something specific. Third, because a challenging goal requires sustained or repeated effort, it encourages *persistence*. Fourth, because a goal creates the problem of bridging the gap between actual and desired, it fosters the creation of *strategies and action plans*. Consider, for example, how all these motivational components were activated by the following program at Marriott's hotel chain.

For years, Marriott's room-service business didn't live up to its potential. But after initiating a 15-minute-delivery guarantee for breakfast in 1985, Marriott's breakfast business—the biggest portion of its room-service revenue—jumped 25 percent. [Hotel guests got their breakfast free if it was delivered late.] Marriott got employees to devise ways to deliver the meals on time, including having deliverers carry walkie-talkies so they [could] receive instructions more quickly.[24]

Marriott's goal, increased room-service revenue, was the focal point for this program. In effect, the service-guarantee program told Marriott employees that prompt room service was important, and they rose to the challenge with persistent and creative effort. Clear, reasonable, and challenging goals, reinforced by specific feedback and meaningful rewards, are indeed a powerful motivational tool.

Practical Implications of Goal-Setting Theory.   Because the model in Figure 13.4 is a generic one, the performance environment may range from athletics to academics to the workplace. The motivational mechanics of goal setting are the same, regardless of the targeted performance. If you learn to be an effective goal setter in school, that ability will serve you faithfully throughout life.

Anyone tempted to go through life without goals should remember the smiling Cheshire Cat's good advice to Alice when she asked him to help her find her way through Wonderland:

"Would you tell me, please, which way I ought to walk from here?"
"That depends a good deal on where you want to get to," replied the Cat.
"I don't much care where—" said Alice.
"Then it doesn't matter which way you walk," said the Cat.
"—so long as I get somewhere," Alice added as an explanation.
"Oh, you're sure to do that," said the Cat, "if you only walk long enough." [25]

Motivation Through Job Design

A job serves two separate but related functions. It is a productive unit for the organization and a career unit for the individual. Thus **job design,** the delineation of task responsibilities as dictated by organizational strategy, technology, and structure, is a key determinant of individual motivation and ultimately of organizational success. Considering that the average adult spends about half of his or her waking life at work, jobs are a central feature of modern existence. A challenging and interesting job can add zest and meaning to one's life. Boring and tedious jobs, on the other hand, can become a serious threat to one's motivation to work hard, not to mention the effect on one's physical and mental health.[26] Concern about uneven productivity growth, product quality, and declining employee satisfaction has persuaded managers to consider two job design strategies.[27]

job design *creating task responsibilities based upon strategy, technology, and structure*

Strategy One: Fitting People to Jobs

For technological or economic reasons, work sometimes must be divided into routine and repetitive tasks. Imagine, for example, doing Paula Villalta's job at Chung's Gourmet Foods in Houston, Texas:

3 **Discuss how managers can improve the motivation of routine-task personnel.**

> *Quickly wrapping one egg roll after another, Paula Villalta becomes rapt herself.*
>
> *Her fingers move with astonishing speed, placing a glutinous vegetable mixture on a small sheet of pastry before rolling it closed in one smooth stroke. But the secret to her swiftness lies not just in her nimble hands.*
>
> *The real key, says Ms. Villalta, pointing to her head, is staying completely focused throughout an eight-hour shift. . . .*
>
> *The results are stunning. The average wrapper at Chung's Gourmet churns out about 4,000 shrimp, pork, vegetable, or chicken egg rolls per shift. Ms. Villalta typically tops 6,000.*[28]

In routine-task situations, steps can be taken to avoid chronic dissatisfaction and bolster motivation.[29] Three proven alternatives include realistic job previews, job rotation, and limited exposure. Each involves adjusting the person rather than the job in the person-job match. Hence each entails creating a more compatible fit between an individual and a routine or fragmented job. (In line with this approach is the use of mentally disadvantaged workers, often in sheltered workshops.)

Realistic Job Previews.   Unrealized expectations are a major cause of job dissatisfaction, low motivation, and turnover. Managers commonly create unrealistically

Here's a case of do-it-yourself job design. Skilled in sign language, Wendy Thompson (in purple) realized a few years ago that her deaf friends would be able to enjoy the music in music videos if it was communicated via sign language. From this simple beginning, Thompson built a successful company, Kuumba Inc., serving the entertainment needs of deaf and hearing-impaired people. In addition to teaching ASL (American Sign Language) courses, the Bronx, New York, company provides interpreters and deaf entertainers to a wide range of clients.

high expectations in recruits to entice them to accept a position. This has proved particularly troublesome with regard to routine tasks. Dissatisfaction too often sets in when lofty expectations are brought down to earth by dull or tedious work. **Realistic job previews** (RJPs), honest explanations of what a job actually entails, have been successful in helping to avoid employee dissatisfaction resulting from unrealized expectations. On-the-job and laboratory research have demonstrated the practical value of giving a realistic preview of both positive and negative aspects to applicants for highly specialized and/or difficult jobs.

realistic job previews
honest explanations of what a job actually entails

A recent statistical analysis of 40 different RJP studies revealed these patterns: fewer dropouts during the recruiting process, lower initial expectations, and lower turnover and higher performance once on the job. The researcher recommended a contingency approach regarding the form and timing of RJPs. *Written* RJPs are better for reducing the dropout rate during the recruiting process, whereas *verbal* RJPs more effectively reduce post-hiring turnover (quitting). "RJPs given just *before* hiring are advisable to reduce attrition [dropouts] from the recruitment process and to reduce . . . turnover, but organizations wishing to improve employee performance should provide RJPs *after* job acceptance, as part of a realistic socialization effort."[30]

job rotation *moving people from one specialized job to another*

Job Rotation.   As the term is used here, **job rotation** involves periodically moving people from one specialized job to another. Such movement prevents stagnation. Other reasons for rotating personnel include compensating for a labor shortage, safety, and preventing fatigue. *Carpal tunnel syndrome* and other painful and disabling injuries stemming from repetitive motion tasks can be reduced significantly through job rotation.[31] (The FBI rotates its agents off the drug squad periodically to discourage corruption.[32]) If highly repetitive and routine jobs are unavoidable, job rotation, by introducing a modest degree of novelty, can help prevent boredom and resulting alienation. Of course, a balance needs to be achieved—people should be rotated often enough to fight boredom and injury but not so often that they feel unfairly manipulated or disoriented.

Limited Exposure.   Another way of coping with the need to staff a highly fragmented and tedious job is to limit the individual's exposure to it. A number of organizations have achieved high productivity among routine-task personnel by allowing them to earn an early quitting time.[33] This technique, called **contingent time off** (CTO) or earned time off, involves establishing a challenging yet fair daily performance standard, or quota, and letting employees go home when it is reached. The following CTO plan was implemented at a large manufacturing plant where the employees were producing about 160 units a day with 10 percent rejects:

> *If the group produced at 200 units with three additional good units for each defective unit, then they could leave the work site for the rest of the day. Within a week of implementing this CTO intervention, the group was producing 200+ units with an average of 1.5 percent rejects. These employees, who had formerly* put in *an 8-hour day, were now* working *an average of 6.5 hours per day and, importantly, they increased their performance by 25 percent.*[34]

Some employees find the opportunity to earn eight hours of pay for six hours of steady effort extremely motivating.

Companies that use contingent time off report successful results. Impressive evidence comes from a large-scale survey of 1,598 U.S. companies employing about 10 percent of the civilian workforce. Among nine nontraditional reward systems, "earned time off" ranked only eighth in terms of use (5 percent of the companies). But among those using it, earned time off ranked *second* in terms of positive impact on job performance—an 85 percent approval rating.[35] Thus, the use of contingent time off has not yet reached its excellent potential as a motivational tool.

> ### A Production Ballet at Honda
> **13E**
>
> As a nearly completed StepWGN moves down the line, a worker jumps into the front compartment and pats carpeting into place around the front console. Then he uses an electric screwdriver to bolt the back seats to the floor, first fastening screws in front of the seat, then scurrying around to the back to fasten two more. Finally, he hops out of the vehicle again to affix two plastic pieces to the rear taillights and glues the nameplate onto the tailgate. This incredible ballet takes him all of 60 seconds—and if he's doing his job properly, he repeats it 60 times an hour.
>
> *Source:* Alex Taylor III, "The Man Who Put Honda Back on Track," *Fortune* (September 9, 1996): 98, 100.
>
> **Questions:** *How can management effectively motivate this repetitive-task employee? What would motivate you to accept this job at Honda?*

contingent time off
rewarding people with early time off when they get the job done

Strategy Two: Fitting Jobs to People

The second job-design strategy calls for managers to consider changing the job instead of the person. Two job-design experts have proposed that managers address the question, "How can we achieve a fit between persons and their jobs that fosters *both* high work productivity and a high-quality organizational experience for the people who do the work?"[36] Two techniques for moving in this direction are job enlargement and job enrichment.

Job Enlargement.   As used here, **job enlargement** is the process of combining two or more specialized tasks in a work flow sequence into a single job. Aetna used this technique to give some of its office employees a measure of relief from staring into a video display terminal (VDT) all day:

> *Aetna Life & Casualty in Hartford last year reorganized its payroll department to combine ten full-time data-entry jobs with ten jobs that involve paperwork and telephoning. Now*

job enlargement *combining two or more specialized tasks to increase motivation*

nobody in the department spends more than 70 percent of [the] day on a VDT. Morale and productivity have gone up dramatically since the change, says Richard Assunto, Aetna's payroll services manager.[37]

A moderate degree of complexity and novelty can be introduced in this manner. But critics claim that two or more potentially boring tasks do not necessarily make one challenging job. Furthermore, organized labor has criticized job enlargement as a devious ploy for getting more work for the same amount of money. But if pay and performance are kept in balance, boredom and alienation can be pushed aside a bit by job enlargement.

job enrichment *redesigning jobs to increase their motivational potential*

Job Enrichment. In general terms, **job enrichment** is redesigning a job to increase its motivating potential.[38] Job enrichment increases the challenge of one's work by reversing the trend toward greater specialization. Unlike job enlargement, which merely combines equally simple tasks, job enrichment builds more complexity and depth into jobs by introducing planning and decision-making responsibility normally carried out at higher levels. For example, "Montgomery Ward . . . has authorized 7,700 sales clerks to approve checks and handle merchandise-return problems—functions that once were reserved for store managers."[39] Ward's customers like the resulting speedier service. Thus, enriched jobs are said to be *vertically loaded*, whereas enlarged jobs are *horizontally loaded*.

Jobs can be enriched by upgrading five core dimensions of work: (1) skill variety, (2) task identity, (3) task significance, (4) autonomy, and (5) job feedback. Each of these core dimensions deserves a closer look.

4 Explain how job enrichment can be used to enhance the motivating potential of jobs.

- *Skill variety.* The degree to which a job requires a variety of different activities in carrying out the work, involving the use of a number of different skills and talents of the person.

A Call for More Passion and Less Dilbert 13F

Eric S. Raymond, programmer, high-tech author, and open-source software advocate:

You cannot motivate the best people with money. Money is just a way to keep score. The best people in any field are motivated by passion. That becomes more true the higher the skill level gets. . . .

People are happiest when they're the most productive. People enjoy tasks, especially creative tasks, when the tasks are in the optimal-challenge zone: not too hard and not too easy. To some extent, that has always been true. But it becomes even more true as work becomes more about brains and creativity.

The flip side is that when people are frustrated with their work environments—when they don't trust the institutions they work for—it is virtually impossible for them to do great work. . . . "Why do even top executives hang 'Dilbert' cartoons on their office doors?" There's nothing funny about the popularity of "Dilbert." Companies should take that more seriously than they seem to.

Source: William C. Taylor, "Inspired by Work," *Fast Company,* no. 29 (November 1999): 202.

Questions: *What sort of work would ignite your passion? Relative to your ideal job, how important is money? What would your ideal job have in the way of the five core job characteristics? Explain.*

Figure 13.5 | How Job Enrichment Works

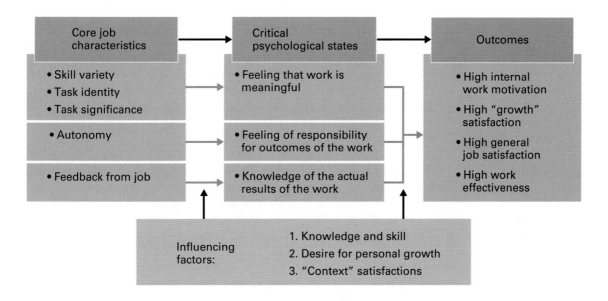

Source: J. Richard Hackman and Greg R. Oldham, *Work Redesign* (Figure 4.6). © 1980 by Addison-Wesley Publishing Company, Inc. Reprinted by permission of Addison Wesley Longman, Inc.

- *Task identity.* The degree to which a job requires completion of a "whole" and identifiable piece of work; that is, doing a job from beginning to end with a visible outcome.
- *Task significance.* The degree to which the job has a substantial impact on the lives of other people, whether those people are in the immediate organization or in the world at large.
- *Autonomy.* The degree to which the job provides substantial freedom, independence, and discretion to the individual in scheduling the work and in determining the procedures to be used in carrying it out.
- *Job feedback.* The degree to which carrying out the work activities required by the job provides the individual with direct and clear information about the effectiveness of his or her performance.[40]

Figure 13.5 shows the theoretical connection between enriched core job characteristics and high motivation and satisfaction. At the heart of this job-enrichment model are three psychological states that highly specialized jobs usually do not satisfy: meaningfulness, responsibility, and knowledge of results.

It is important to note that not all employees will respond favorably to enriched jobs. Personal traits and motives influence the connection between core job characteristics and desired outcomes. Only those with the necessary knowledge and skills plus a desire for personal growth will be motivated by enriched work. Furthermore, in keeping with Herzberg's two-factor theory, dissatisfaction with factors such as pay, physical working conditions, or supervision can neutralize enrichment efforts. Researchers have reported that fear of failure, lack of confidence, and lack of trust in management's intentions can stand in the way of effective job enrichment. But job enrichment can and does work when it is carefully thought out, when management is committed to its long-term success, and when employees desire additional challenge.[41]

Motivation Through Rewards

rewards *material and psychological payoffs for working*

All workers, including volunteers who donate their time to worthy causes, expect to be rewarded in some way for their contributions. **Rewards** may be defined broadly as the material and psychological payoffs for performing tasks in the workplace. Managers have found that job performance and satisfaction can be improved by properly administered rewards. Today, rewards vary greatly in both type and scope, depending on one's employer and geographical location. In fact, a popular book among managers is titled *1001 Ways to Reward Employees.*[42]

In this section, we distinguish between extrinsic and intrinsic rewards, review alternative employee compensation plans, and discuss the effective management of extrinsic rewards.

5 Distinguish extrinsic rewards from intrinsic rewards and list four rules for administering extrinsic rewards effectively.

Extrinsic Versus Intrinsic Rewards

extrinsic rewards *payoffs, such as money, that are granted by others*

intrinsic rewards *self-granted and internally experienced payoffs, such as a feeling of accomplishment*

There are two different categories of rewards. **Extrinsic rewards** are payoffs granted to the individual by other people. Examples include money, employee benefits, promotions, recognition, status symbols, and praise. The second category is called **intrinsic rewards,** which are self-granted and internally experienced payoffs. Among intrinsic rewards are a sense of accomplishment, self-esteem, and self-actualization.[43] Usually, on-the-job extrinsic and intrinsic rewards are intermingled. For instance, employees often experience a psychological lift when they complete a big project in addition to reaping material benefits.

Pensions are an important part of today's sophisticated compensation plans. Until recently, small companies like Kosola & Associates Inc., an Albany, Georgia, aircraft parts maker with only 27 employees, could not afford a decent pension plan. This put them at a disadvantage when trying to recruit top talent. Thanks to growing competition in the financial services industry, Kosola's comptroller, Carmella Owens (lower center), recently was able to offer her co-workers a 401(k) pension plan. The Internet-based plan from Principal Financial Group required only $650 in start-up costs and an annual administrative fee of $1,100. Now there's a deal you can take to the bank!

Employee Compensation

Compensation plans deserve special attention at this point because money is the universal extrinsic reward.[44] Employee compensation is a complex area fraught with legal and tax implications. Although an exhaustive treatment of employee compensation plans is beyond our present purpose, we can identify major types. Table 13.2 lists and briefly describes ten different pay plans. Two are nonincentive plans, seven qualify as incentive plans, and one plan is in a category of its own. Each type of pay plan has

Table 13.2	Guide to Employee Compensation Plans		
Pay plan	**Description/calculation**	**Main advantage**	**Main disadvantage**
Nonincentive			
Hourly wage	Fixed amount per hour worked	Time is easier to measure than performance	Little or no incentive to work hard
Annual salary	Contractual amount per year	Easy to administer	Little or no incentive to work hard
Incentive			
Piece rate	Fixed amount per unit of output	Pay tied directly to personal output	Negative association with sweatshops and rate-cutting abuses
Sales commission	Fixed percentage of sales revenue	Pay tied directly to personal volume of business	Morale problem when sales personnel earn more than other employees
Merit pay	Bonus granted for outstanding performance	Gives salaried employees incentive to work harder	Fairness issue raised when tied to subjective appraisals
Profit sharing	Distribution of specified percentage of bottom-line profits	Individual has a personal stake in firm's profitability	Profits affected by more than just performance (for example, by prices and competition)
Gain sharing	Distribution of specified percentage of productivity gains and/or cost savings	Encourages employees to work harder *and* smarter	Calculations can get cumbersome
Pay-for-knowledge	Salary or wage rates tied to degrees earned or skills mastered	Encourages life-long learning	Tends to inflate training and labor costs
Stock options	Selected employees earn right to acquire firm's stock free or at a discount	Gives individual a personal stake in firm's financial performance	Can be resented by ineligible personnel; morale tied to stock price
Other			
Cafeteria compensation (life-cycle benefits)	Employee selects personal mix of benefits from an array of options	Tailored benefits package fits individual needs	Can be costly to administer

advantages and disadvantages. Therefore, there is no single best plan suitable for all employees. Indeed, two experts at the U.S. Bureau of Labor Statistics say the key words in compensation for the next 25 years will be "flexible" and "varied."[45] A diverse work-force will demand an equally diverse array of compensation plans.

Improving Performance with Extrinsic Rewards

Extrinsic rewards, if they are to motivate job performance effectively, need to be administered in ways that (1) satisfy operative needs, (2) foster positive expectations, (3) ensure equitable distribution, and (4) reward results. Let us see how these four criteria can be met relative to the ten different pay plans in Table 13.2.

Rewards Must Satisfy Individual Needs.   Whether it is a pay raise or a pat on the back, a reward has no motivational impact unless it satisfies an operative need. Not all people need the same things, and one person may need different things at different times. Money is a powerful motivator for those who seek security through material wealth. But the promise of more money may mean little to a financially secure person who seeks ego gratification from challenging work. People's needs concerning when and how they want to be paid also vary.

Because cafeteria compensation is rather special and particularly promising, we shall examine it more closely. **Cafeteria compensation** (also called life-cycle benefits) is a plan that allows each employee to determine the make-up of his or her benefit package.[46] Because today's nonwage benefits are a significant portion of total compensation,[47] the motivating potential of such a privilege can be sizable.

> *Under these plans, employers provide minimal "core" coverage in life and health insurance, vacations, and pensions. The employee buys additional benefits to suit [his or her] own needs, using credit based on salary, service, and age.*
>
> *The elderly bachelor, for instance, may pass up the maternity coverage he would receive, willy-nilly, under conventional plans and "buy" additional pension contributions instead. The mother whose children are covered by her husband's employee health insurance policy may choose legal and dental care insurance instead.*[48]

Although some organizations have balked at installing cafeteria compensation because of added administrative expense, the number of programs in effect in the United States has grown steadily.[49] Cafeteria compensation enhances employee satisfaction, according to at least one study,[50] and represents a revolutionary step toward fitting rewards to people, rather than vice versa.

Employees Must Believe Effort Will Lead to Reward.   According to expectancy theory, an employee will not strive for an attractive reward unless it is perceived as being attainable. For example, the promise of an expenses-paid trip to Hawaii for the leading salesperson will prompt additional efforts at sales only among those who feel they have a decent chance of winning. Those who believe they have little chance of winning will not be motivated to try any harder than usual. Incentive pay plans, especially merit pay, profit sharing, gain sharing, and stock options, need to be designed and communicated in a way that will foster believable effort-reward link-ages.[51]

Rewards Must Be Equitable.   Something is equitable if people perceive it to be fair and just. Each of us carries in our head a pair of scales upon which we weigh equity.[52] Figure 13.6 shows one scale for *personal equity* and another for *social equity*. The personal

Figure 13.6 | Personal and Social Equity

Personal Equity

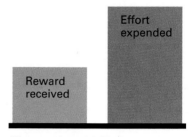

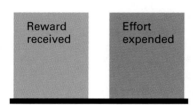

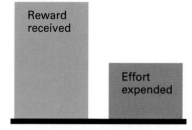

"I am underpaid. That's unfair. I'm going to take it easy from now on."

"I am paid what I deserve. That's fair."

"I am overpaid. I feel guilty about getting more than I deserve."

Social Equity

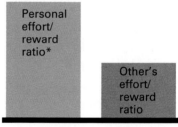

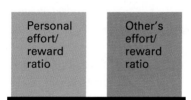

"Joe and I have the same job but he is paid more than I. That's unfair. I'm going to take it easy. Is Joe special?"

"Joe and I have the same job and we are paid the same. That's fair."

"Joe and I have the same job but he is paid less than I. That's unfair. He's going to wonder why I receive special treatment."

* The lower the effort/reward ratio, the greater the motivation.

equity scale tests the relationship between effort expended and rewards received. The social equity scale, in contrast, compares our own effort-reward ratio with that of someone else in the same situation. We are motivated to seek personal and social equity and to avoid inequity.[53] An interesting aspect of research on this topic has demonstrated that inequity is perceived by those who are *overpaid* as well as by those who are underpaid.[54] Since perceived inequity is associated with feelings of dissatisfaction and anger, jealousy, or guilt, inequitable reward schemes tend to be counterproductive and are ethically questionable. Record-setting executive pay in recent years of painful downsizings and massive layoffs has been roundly criticized as inequitable and unfair.[55]

Rewards Must Be Linked to Performance.   Ideally, there should be an if-then relationship between task performance and extrinsic rewards. Traditional hourly wage and annual salary pay plans are weak in this regard. They do little more than reward the person for showing up at work. Managers can strengthen motivation to work by making sure that those who give a little extra get a little extra. In addition to piece-rate and sales-commission plans, merit pay, profit sharing, gain sharing, and stock option plans are popular ways of linking pay and performance.[56] The concept of team-based incentive

Cash Bonus? How About a TV?

13G

Staci Fleener, marketing consultant:

A problem with cash is that it has no trophy value. It can be spent on gas, groceries, or the electric bill. Will they remember that tank of gas or that stub from the month's utilities bill and associate it with the program? Probably not. But merchandise items or travel have trophy value— they give you bragging rights. Every time you look at that TV you remember where it came from. Or your memories of the Bahamas you associate with the company that provided you with the trip. That's what we call mind share, which is the ultimate goal of an incentive program.

Source: Staci Fleener, "All That Inspires Isn't Green," *Selling Power,* 19 (June 1999): 33.

Questions: *Do you agree or disagree with this line of reasoning? Explain. Which incentive would you work harder for: cash or merchandise? Explain.*

pay as a way of rewarding teamwork and cooperation has been slow to take hold in the United States for two reasons: (1) it goes against the grain of an individualistic culture; and (2) poorly conceived and administered plans have given team-based pay a bad reputation.[57]

All incentive pay plans should be carefully conceived because undesirable behavior may inadvertently be encouraged. Consider, for example, what the head of Nucor Corporation, a successful minimill steel company, had to say about his firm's bonus system:

[Nucor's] bonus system . . . is very tough. If you're late even five minutes, you lose your bonus for the day. If you're late more than 30 minutes, or you're absent because of sickness or anything else, you lose your bonus for the week. Now, we do have what we call four "forgiveness" days during the year when you can be sick or you have to close on a house or your wife is having a baby. But only four. We have a melter, Phil Johnson, down in Darlington, and one of the workers came in one day and said that Phil had been in an automobile accident and was sitting beside his car off of Route 52, holding his head. So the foreman asked, "Why didn't you stop and help him?" And the guy said, "And lose my bonus?"[58]

Like goals, incentive plans foster selective perception.[59] Consequently, managers need to make sure goals and incentives point people in ethical directions.

Motivation Through Employee Participation

While noting that the term *participation* has become a "stewpot" into which every conceivable kind of management fad has been tossed, one management scholar has helpfully identified four key areas of participative management. Employees may participate in (1) setting goals, (2) making decisions, (3) solving problems, and (4) designing and implementing organizational changes.[60] Thus, **participative management** is defined as the process of empowering employees to assume greater control of the workplace.[61] When personally and meaningfully involved, above and beyond just doing assigned tasks, employees are said to be more motivated and productive. *Open-book management,* forming a partnership with nonmanagement personnel by sharing key financial information with them, is an emerging expression of participative management. "By sharing detailed operating information and educating employees about how to use it, management provides its workers with the opportunity to contribute to the success of the enterprise."[62]

This section focuses on two team-oriented approaches to participation. They are quality control circles and self-managed teams. The former are typically found in manufacturing operations, whereas the latter are found in both factory and office settings. These two approaches to employee participation have been singled out for

participative management
empowering employees to assume greater control of the workplace

three reasons. First, they mesh well with the trend toward team-based organizations. Second, when executed properly, they have a good track record. Third, they have broad applicability. This section concludes with a discussion of four keys to successful employee participation programs.

Quality Control Circles

Developed in Japan during the early 1960s, this innovation took the U.S. industrial scene by storm during the late 1970s and early 1980s. Today, thousands of quality control circles can be found in hundreds of North American and European companies. **Quality control circles,** commonly referred to as QC circles or simply quality circles, are voluntary problem-solving groups of five to ten employees from the same work area who meet regularly to discuss quality improvement and ways to reduce costs.[63] A weekly one-hour meeting, during company time, is common practice. By relying on *voluntary* participation, QC circles attempt to tap the creative potential every employee possesses. Although QC circles do not work in every situation, benefits such as direct cost savings, improved worker-management relations, and greater individual commitment have been reported.[64]

> **quality control circles**
> *voluntary problem-solving groups committed to improving quality and reducing costs*

QC circles should be introduced in evolutionary fashion rather than by management edict. As the following description of Northrop Corporation's successful QC circle program illustrates, training, supportive supervision, and team building are all part of this evolutionary development:

> **6** Discuss the contributions quality control circles and self-managed teams can make to participative management.

> *In a well-managed program like Northrop's, team members are given a good dose of training in the basic techniques of problem solving. They learn to gather and analyze data, weed out trivial issues to focus on major ones, generate innovative ideas in brainstorming sessions, forge consensus decisions, and communicate effectively. At least one team member—usually though not always the supervisor—gets extra training in leadership. And any well-run program has one or more people trained as "facilitators," who help the leader organize groups and get people who were accustomed to performing isolated jobs on an assembly line to begin thinking, talking, listening, and caring as members of a team.[65]*

The idea is to give those who work day in and day out at a specific job the tools, group support, and opportunity to have a say in nipping quality problems in the bud. Each QC circle is responsible not only for recommending solutions but also for actually implementing and evaluating those solutions. According to one observer, "The invisible force behind the success of QC's is its ability to bring the psychological principles of Maslow, McGregor, and Herzberg into the workplace through a structured process."[66]

QC circles foster employee participation within the confines of the existing power structure. In contrast, self-managed teams create a whole new decentralized power structure.

Self-Managed Teams

According to the logic of this comprehensive approach to participation, because it taps people's full potential, self-management is the best management. Advocates say self-management fosters creativity, motivation, and productivity. **Self-managed teams,** also known as autonomous work groups or high-performance work teams, take on traditional managerial tasks as part of their normal work routine.[67] They can have anywhere from five to more than 30 members, depending on the job. Unlike QC circles, which are staffed with volunteers, employees are assigned to self-managed teams. Cross-trained team members

> **self-managed teams**
> *high-performance teams that assume traditional managerial duties such as staffing and planning*

Figure 13.7

Research Insight: What Do Self-Managed Teams Manage?

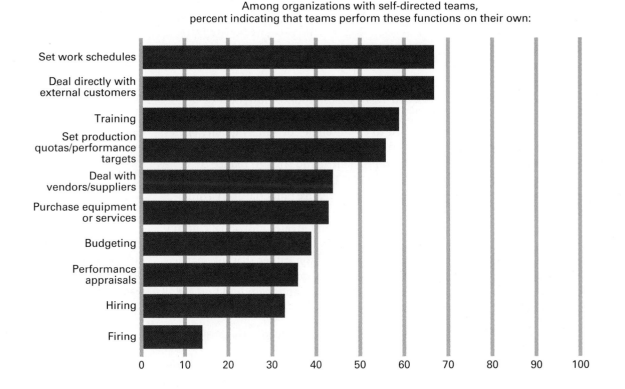

Among organizations with self-directed teams,
percent indicating that teams perform these functions on their own:

typically rotate jobs as they turn out a complete product or service. Any supervision tends to be minimal, with managers acting more as *facilitators* than as order givers.[68] Self-managed teams are a central feature of Total Quality Management (TQM) programs.

Vertically Loaded Jobs.   In the language of job enrichment, team members' jobs are vertically loaded. This means nonmanagerial team members assume duties traditionally performed by managers. But specifically which duties? *Training* magazine's 1996 annual survey of industry practices answered this question. The profile of traditional managerial duties performed by self-managing teams in Figure 13.7 was derived from a sample of 1,456 U.S. companies with 100 or more employees. Significantly, the researchers observed: "For all the talk of self-directed teams, fewer than one-third [31 percent] of our respondents say they let teams call the shots."[69] Thus, self-managed teams are still in the early growth stage.

General Mills has extended the idea of self-managed teams to the point that the night shift in its cereal plant in Lodi, California, runs with no managers at all. Other progressive organizations such as General Foods, Texas Instruments, Corning, General Electric, Boeing, Procter & Gamble, and Volvo have operations built around self-managed teams. *Fortune* quoted the head of Texas Instruments as saying, "No matter what your business, these teams are the wave of the future"[70] (see The Global Manager).

The Global Manager

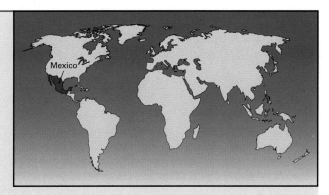

Culturally Adapting Self-Managed Teams in Mexico

Background

During a management seminar, Spanish-language versions of a self-managed teams survey were completed by 243 Mexican executives, jointly responding in 32 discussion groups.

Self-Managed Teams	Mexican Business Culture
Norms	**Value Expectations**
Individualism	*Collectivism*
Personal accountability	Shared responsibility
Individual responsibility	Moral obligation
Confidence in ability	Paternalistic management
Confrontation and debate	Harmony
Low uncertainty avoidance	*High uncertainty avoidance*
Take self-initiative	Resist change
Low power distance	*High power distance*
Self-leadership	Respect status roles
Bottom-up decision making	Top-down hierarchical structure
Required Behaviors	**Expected Behaviors**
Team members solve problems, resolve conflicts, set goals, assess performance, initiate change, and communicate upward. Managers delegate, provide information, and encourage open communication.	Workers follow instructions, respect managers, receive feedback, avoid conflict and criticism, and save face. Managers make decisions, direct, control, and discipline.

Contrasting Cultures

"Although a team-based work design would seem to appeal to the collectivist values of the Mexican culture, the behavioral requirements of the North American concept of teamwork reflect individualist values, as well as value placed on low power distance and individual risk tolerance."

Source: Excerpted and adapted with permission of *Academy of Management Executive* from Chantell E. Nicholls, Henry W. Lane, and Mauricio Brehm Brechu, "Taking Self-Managed Teams to Mexico," *Academy of Management Executive*, 13 (August 1999): 15–25. Permission conveyed through Copyright Clearance Center, Inc.

Conclusions

". . . it would be feasible to implement self-managed teams in Mexico, but the process of implementation will take longer than expected; training will be required for more basic skills necessary for effective work teams (e.g., holding meetings, setting goals, and solving problems) than would be required in Canada or the United States; and clear instruction and endorsement from the top will be necessary to legitimize changes, even those involving a participatory style of work design."

Transparent Organizations

13H

Peter Janson, CEO of AGRA Inc., a Canadian construction services company, says the three keys to excellence are speed, simplicity, and transparency:

Transparency is the atmosphere of openness and trust that helps turn a simple, speedy organization into an excellent company. It means letting go of command-and-control methods. It also means addressing problems openly so that they can be identified, analyzed, and dealt with early on. In a transparent culture, relevant information is shared with customers, employees, and shareholders, enabling these essential decision makers to make good, informed decisions.

Source: Peter Janson, "Three Keys to Excellence," *Management Review*, 88 (September 1999): 9.

Questions: *What does transparency have to do with participative management and open-book management? What are the major positives and negatives of organizational transparency?*

Managerial Resistance.   Not surprisingly, managerial resistance is the number one barrier to self-managed teams. More than anything else, self-managed teams represent *change*, and lots of it.

> *Adopting the team approach is no small matter; it means wiping out tiers of managers and tearing down bureaucratic barriers between departments. Yet companies are willing to undertake such radical changes to gain workers' knowledge and commitment—along with productivity gains that exceed 30 percent in some cases.[71]*

Traditional authoritarian supervisors view autonomous teams as a threat to their authority and job security. For this reason, *new* facilities built around the concept of self-managed teams, so-called greenfield sites, tend to fare better than reworked existing operations.

Managers who take the long view and switch to self-managed teams are finding it well worth the investment of time and money. Self-managed teams even show early promise of boosting productivity in the huge service sector.[72] (Teamwork is discussed in the next chapter.)

Keys to Successful Employee Participation Programs

According to researchers, four factors build the *employee* support necessary for any sort of participation program to work:

1. A profit-sharing or gain-sharing plan.
2. A long-term employment relationship with good job security.
3. A concerted effort to build and maintain group cohesiveness.
4. Protection of the individual employee's rights.[73]

Working in combination, these factors help explain motivational success stories such as that of Norsk Hydro in the chapter opening case.

It should be clear by now that participative management involves more than simply announcing a new program, such as open-book management. To make sure a supportive climate exists, a good deal of background work often needs to be done.[74] This is particularly important in view of the conclusion drawn by researchers who analyzed 41 participative management studies:

> *Participation has . . . [a positive] effect on both satisfaction and productivity, and its effect on satisfaction is somewhat stronger than its effect on productivity. . . . Our analysis indicates specific organizational factors that may enhance or constrain the effect of participation. For example, there is evidence that a participative climate has a more substantial effect on workers' satisfaction than participation in specific decisions.[75]*

In the end, effective participative management is as much a managerial attitude about sharing power as it is a specific set of practices. In some European countries, such as Germany, the supportive climate is reinforced by government-mandated participative management.[76]

Other Motivation Techniques for a Diverse Workforce

Workforce diversity has made "flexibility" a must for managers today. This chapter concludes with a look at ways of accommodating emerging employee needs. By meeting these needs in creative ways, such as flexible work schedules, family support services, wellness programs, and sabbaticals, managers can hope to enhance motivation and job performance.

7 Explain how companies are striving to motivate an increasingly diverse workforce.

Flexible Work Schedules

The standard 8 A.M. to 5 P.M., 40-hour workweek has come under fire as dual-income families, single parents, and others attempt to juggle hectic schedules. Taking its place is **flextime,** a work-scheduling plan that allows employees to determine their own arrival and departure times within specific limits.[77] All employees must be present during a fixed core time (see the center portion of Figure 13.8). If an eight-hour day is required, as in Figure 13.8, an early bird can put in the required eight hours by arriving at 7:00 A.M., taking a half-hour for lunch, and departing at 3:30 P.M. Alternatively, a late starter can come in at 9:00 A.M. and leave at 5:30 P.M. According to the U.S. Bureau of Labor Statistics, almost 28 percent of full-time employees in the U.S. determined their own arrival and departure times in 1997. That was nearly double the 1991 figure.[78] This trend will likely continue, in view of a recent survey showing a 92 percent approval rating for flexible hours among workers caring for dependents.[79]

flextime   *allows employees to choose their own arrival and departure times within specified limits*

Benefits.   In addition to many anecdotal reports citing the benefits of flextime, research studies have uncovered promising evidence. Flextime has several documented benefits:

- Better employee-supervisor relations.
- Reduced absenteeism.

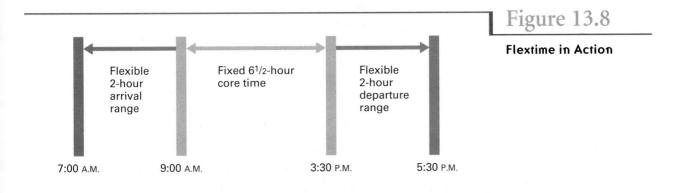

Figure 13.8

Flextime in Action

- Selective positive impact on job performance (a 24 percent improvement for computer programmers over a two-year period but no effect on the performance of data-entry workers).[80]

Flextime, though very popular among employees because of the degree of freedom it brings, is not appropriate for all situations. Problems reported by adopters include greater administrative expense, supervisory resistance, and inadequate coverage of jobs.

Alternatives.   Other work-scheduling innovations include *compressed workweeks* (40 or more hours in fewer than five days)[81] and *permanent part-time* (workweeks with fewer than 40 hours). *Job sharing* (complementary scheduling that allows two or more part-timers to share a single full-time job), yet another work-scheduling innovation, is growing in popularity among employers of working mothers. Steelcase Inc., the Grand Rapids, Michigan, office furniture maker, responded favorably to a joint résumé from Anne Saliers and Peggy Hoogerhyde. Both women have preschoolers at home and wanted to work two or three days a week.

> *Saliers and Hoogerhyde each work two days a week and alternate Fridays, preparing presentations for customer groups and working with sales representatives from the field. "We do most of our coordination by phone, or leave messages for each other," says Saliers.*[82]

A recent European study suggests employees may be paying a price for the freedom of flexible work scheduling. Compared with a control group of employees on fixed schedules, employees with compressed workweeks, rotating shifts, irregular schedules, and part-time jobs experienced significantly more health, psychological, and sleeping problems.[83]

"... AM I INTERESTED IN AN ALTERNATIVE WORK ARRANGEMENT?... YES,... I'D LIKE TO TELECOMMUTE FROM A COMPUTER EQUIPPED HOT TUB ON FLEX TIME..."

	Table 13.3
The Federal Family and Medical Leave Act:	**The 1993 Family and Medical Leave Act (FMLA) in Brief**

The Federal Family and Medical Leave Act:

- Guarantees workers up to 12 weeks a year off, unpaid, for births, adoptions, the care of sick children, spouses or parents, or to recover from an illness themselves.
- Affects businesses with 50 or more workers living within a 75-mile radius of work.
- Covers employees who have spent at least 1,250 hours on the job the last 12 months.
- Allows employers to exclude the top-paid 10 percent of their employees.
- Allows employers to require workers to use vacation or other leave first.
- Allows companies to restrict couples employed at the same place to 12 weeks total leave a year.
- Requires workers to provide employers with 30 days' notice when practical, such as for birth or adoption.
- Requires employers to continue to provide health insurance during an employee's leave.
- Guarantees workers the same or equivalent job upon return.
- Affects 5 percent of U.S. employers and 57 percent of workers.

Companies found in violation of the family leave act can be found liable for back wages, reinstatement, promotions, and monetary damages. Damage claims must be filed within two years of the alleged violation, unless state law says otherwise.

The family leave law doesn't overrule state laws with more generous provisions, such as a state statute providing for more than 12 weeks of unpaid leave.

Source: Mimi Hall and Blair S. Walker, "Federal Family Leave Act: Provisions at a Glance," *USA Today* (August 5, 1993): 2B. Copyright 1993, USA Today. Reprinted with permission.

Family Support Services

With dual-income families and single parents caught between obligations to family and the job, both the government and companies are coming to the rescue. On the federal government front, the Family and Medical Leave Act (FMLA) took effect in the United States in 1993 after years of political debate.[84] As indicated in Table 13.3, FMLA has significant holes and limitations. First, only companies with 50 or more employees are required to comply with the law mandating up to 12 weeks of unpaid leave per year for family events such as births, adoptions, or sickness. Because the vast majority of U.S. businesses (95 percent) employ fewer than 50 people, millions of working Americans (43 percent) are left unprotected by FMLA. Second, employees can be required by their employer to exhaust their sick leave and vacation allotments before taking FMLA leave. Fortunately, states and businesses can plug some of the holes in FMLA.

At least 35 states have equivalent or more generous parental and family leave laws. Eligible employees can choose the more generous option when both federal and state laws apply.[85] Meanwhile, on the business front, a few companies go so far as to grant *paid* parental and family sickness leaves. Many other exciting corporate family support service initiatives are cropping up. A growing but still very small number of companies in the United States (11 percent in 1999) provide on-site day-care facilities. About 15 percent provide emergency child-care services.[86] Elder-care centers, for employees' elderly relatives who cannot be left home alone, are starting to appear.[87] Some companies have banded together to form reduced-rate day-care cooperatives for their employees. Emergency child care is a welcome corporate benefit for working parents.

13I   Sorting Out the Work–Family Dilemma

Companies are trying to help. To their credit, many offer flexible schedules, job sharing, and personal leaves. Some have gone the extra mile to establish on-site day care; others provide personal valet services to buy groceries, birthday presents—even plan the birthday party. While all that relieves some symptoms of the work and family dilemma, it doesn't alleviate the structural problems: the hierarchical and often unforgiving way in which work is organized; the pace of the managerial career path, which requires the highest investment of time just when child rearing is most intense; the emphasis on face time as a measure of dedication and commitment.

Source: Betsy Morris, "Is Your Family Wrecking Your Career? (and Vice Versa)," *Fortune* (March 17, 1997): 73.

Questions: *What has been your experience with work and family conflicts (either firsthand or indirectly through your parents)? Acting as a management consultant, explain what recommendations you would make for alleviating the "structural problems" mentioned above.*

Wellness Programs

13J   Back to the Opening Case

What is the relationship between Norsk Hydro's idea of proper balance and stress/burnout?

Stress and burnout are inevitable consequences of modern work life.[88] (See Skills & Tools, page 424.) Family-versus-work conflict, long hours, overload, hectic schedules, deadlines, frequent business travel, and accumulated workplace irritations are taking their toll. Progressive companies are coming to the rescue with *wellness programs* featuring a wide range of offerings. Among them are stress reduction, healthy eating and living clinics, quit smoking and weight loss programs, exercise facilities, massage breaks, behavioral health counseling, and health screenings.[89] The ultimate objective is to help employees achieve a sustainable balance between their personal lives and work lives, with win-win benefits all around.

Sabbaticals

Several companies, including IBM, Wells Fargo, and McDonald's, give selected employees paid sabbaticals after a certain number of years of service. Two to six months of paid time off gives the employee time for family, recreation, and travel. At Intel, which offers an eight-week break with pay every seven years, more than 2,000 employees from all levels took sabbaticals in 1998.[90] The idea is to refresh long-term employees and hopefully bolster their motivation and loyalty in the process.[91]

Summary

1. Maslow's five-level needs hierarchy, although empirically criticized, makes it clear to managers that people are motivated by emerging rather than fulfilled needs. Assuming that job satisfaction and performance are positively related,

Herzberg believes that the most that wages and working conditions can do is eliminate sources of dissatisfaction. According to Herzberg, the key to true satisfaction, and hence motivation, is an enriched job that provides an opportunity for achievement, responsibility, and personal growth. Expectancy theory is based on the idea that the strength of one's motivation to work is the product of perceived probabilities of acquiring personally valued rewards. Both effort-performance and performance-reward probabilities are important to expectancy theory.

2. Goals can be an effective motivational tool when they are specific, difficult, participatively set, and accompanied by feedback on performance. Goals motivate performance by directing attention, encouraging effort and persistence, and prompting goal-attainment strategies and action plans.

3. Managers can counteract the boredom associated with routine-task jobs through realistic job previews, job rotation, and limited exposure. This third alternative involves letting employees earn early time off.

4. Job enrichment vertically loads jobs to meet individual needs for meaningfulness, responsibility, and knowledge of results. Personal desire for growth and a supportive climate must exist for job enrichment to be successful.

5. Both extrinsic (externally granted) and intrinsic (self-granted) rewards, when properly administered, can have a positive impact on performance and satisfaction. There is no single best employee compensation plan. A flexible and varied approach to compensation will be necessary in the coming years because of workforce diversity. The following rules can help managers maximize the motivational impact of extrinsic rewards: (1) rewards must satisfy individual needs, (2) one must believe that effort will lead to reward, (3) rewards must be equitable, and (4) rewards must be linked to performance. Gain-sharing plans have great motivational potential because they emphasize participation and link pay to actual productivity.

6. Participative management programs foster direct employee involvement in one or more of the following areas: goal setting, decision making, problem solving, and change implementation. Quality control circles and self-managed teams are appropriate participative techniques in today's team-based organizations. Profit sharing or gain sharing, job security, cohesiveness, and protection of employee rights are keys to building crucial employee support for participation programs.

7. A diverse workforce requires diverse motivational techniques. Flextime, a flexible work-scheduling scheme that allows employees to choose their own arrival and departure times, has been effective in improving employee-supervisor relations while reducing absenteeism. Employers are increasingly providing family support services such as child care, elder care, parental leaves, and adoption benefits. Employee wellness programs and sabbaticals are offered by some companies.

Terms to Understand

Motivation (p. 394)

Expectancy theory (p. 401)

Expectancy (p. 401)

Goal setting (p. 403)

Job design (p. 405)

Realistic job previews (p. 406)

Job rotation (p. 406)

Contingent time off (p. 407)

Job enlargement (p. 407)

Job enrichment (p. 408)

Rewards (p. 410)

Extrinsic rewards (p. 410)

Intrinsic rewards (p. 410)

Cafeteria compensation (p. 412)

Participative management (p. 414)

Quality control circles (p. 415)

Self-managed teams (p. 415)

Flextime (p. 419)

Skills & Tools

Stress Management 101

Feeling burned out? You're not alone. According to a survey of 7,000 senior executives in the United States and 12 other countries, burnout is on the rise in the executive ranks, and many companies fail to handle the problem properly.

"All leaders are at risk for burnout, but too often companies are embarrassed by the phenomenon and have no idea how to address it," says Andrew Kakabadse, director of the survey and professor of management at the Cranfield University School of Management, Bedford, UK.

Even if companies aren't addressing the issue of burnout, there are some steps individuals can take on their own. Lois Tamir, vice president of Personnel Decisions International in Minneapolis, Minnesota, offers a number of suggestions for the busy executive who needs to stay focused during a tough time (see list). In a nutshell, managers can reduce stress by thinking big and treating themselves better.

How to Avoid Burnout

Pace yourself. Don't put in extra hours because you probably won't get much done anyway.

Laugh more. Humor relieves a great deal of physiological and psychological stress.

Be good to yourself. Do something that you enjoy, such as going to the movies.

Keep it simple. Separate your work into small tasks that can be accomplished easily. It's important to feel a sense of achievement.

Stay true to your values. Think about the larger values in your work and personal life. Integrity, family priorities, and kindness to others will keep you grounded and put things in perspective.

Keep expectations in check. Forget about changing the world or achieving your greatest goal at work. Some things will have to be postponed until you are better equipped to handle your own situation.

Don't try to be perfect. Everyone experiences difficult times in his or her professional and personal life.

```
┌─────────────────────────────────────────────────────────────────────────────────────┐
│ ▢                        Internet Exercises                                       ⇧ │
├─────────────────────────────────────────────────────────────────────────────────────┤
```

1. **In search of a truly people-centered company:** Practical work experience makes it clear that many companies claiming to put their people first do not live up to their high-sounding words. Hewlett-Packard (HP) has a widespread reputation as an innovative company and a good place to work. Let's put HP to the test. Specifically, how well does HP measure up to the seven people-centered practices listed in the introductory paragraph of this chapter?

   At HP's home page (**www.hp.com**), click on the main menu item "Company Information." Then select the following sequence of headings: "About HP" and "Corporate Objectives & the HP Way." Read the material in the sections "Our People," "Management," and "HP Way."

   Learning Points: 1. What *specific* evidence did you find for any or all of the seven people-centered practices? 2. On a scale of 1 (low) to 10 (high), how would you rate HP's people-centeredness? 3. How confident are you that HP lives up to its intentions about managing people? Explain. 4. Would you like to work for HP? Why or why not?

2. **Check it out:** Are you under stress? Are you suffering burnout? What is your potential for stress and your ability to cope with it? You can get answers to these questions by taking the self-awareness tests at **www.queendom.com.** Select the category "Tests, Tests, Tests . . ." from the home page main menu. Recommended automatically scored tests include "Coping Skills Test" under the heading Intelligence, "Type A Personality Test" under the heading Personality, and "Burnout Test" under the heading Career/Job.

   For updates to these exercises, visit our Web site (**www.hmco.com/college**).

```
│                                                                                   ⇩ │
└─────────────────────────────────────────────────────────────────────────────────────┘
```

Closing Case

Sharon Allred Decker: "We Had to Recognize That People Have Lives"

In 1990, Duke Power Co. in Charlotte, N.C., gave Sharon Allred Decker a critical assignment: consolidate the customer-service functions of its 98 local offices and make the once-sheltered monopoly more responsive to customers. Decker jumped at the chance. She launched a service center that operates 24 hours a day, seven days a week. But Decker quickly realized that for Duke Power to be more responsive to customers, it had to become more responsive to employees, too. "I saw an opportunity to create an environment I wanted to work in," says the vice president for customer service. "We needed to recognize that people have lives."

"They're Adults."

Decker sought to bring about an atmosphere where the 500-person staff could handle family matters more easily. Her first move: getting her bosses to combine with other local employers, such as IBM and Allstate Insurance Co., to build a child-care center. She also campaigned successfully for a fitness center.

Early on, Decker got an earful from employees who hated working swing shifts: days one week, evenings the next, and then nights. So she came up with 22 separate schedules and let workers bid on them yearly, based on seniority. Some are traditional weeks of five 8-hour days, but there also are weekly schedules of four 10-hour days and three 12-hour days. She did away with swing shifts, making it easier to arrange care for children—and parents: The staff is 75 percent female, 33 years old on average, and earns starting pay of $19,000 a year. Decker dropped the requirement that supervisors—called coaches—had to give approval before staff swapped shifts. "They're adults," she says. "They know they're responsible for someone being here."

Decker, 36, knows how tough juggling work and family can be. At her last peer review, colleagues remarked that she was working too hard—and not practicing what she preached. The mother of two boys, 7 and

4, and a 2-year-old daughter (an adopted son, 24, is no longer at home) says she got the message.

Decker's boss, Executive Vice President William A. Coley, has nothing but praise for her work. Why not? The employee-to-manager ratio has gone from 12 to 1 to 20 to 1. And even though turnover in telephone-call centers nationwide usually runs at 40 percent a year, Decker says her center's attrition is running at only 12 percent annually—and 75 percent of those transfer within the utility. Her moral is fairly simple: "As I treat my team, that's how they're going to treat the customer."

Source: Chuck Hawkings, "Sharon Allred Decker: 'We Had to Recognize That People Have Lives.'" Reprinted from the June 28, 1993, issue of *Business Week* by special permission. Copyright © 1993 by The McGraw-Hill Companies, Inc.

FOR DISCUSSION

1. How would you explain Sharon Allred Decker's motivation to work so hard at Duke Power Co.?

2. How would you answer a manager who made the following statement: "Decker should have fired or transferred the employees who didn't like working a swing shift. Lots of unemployed people would be happy to replace them"?

3. Is Decker's role as a working mother a distinct advantage when it comes to managing a predominantly female department? Explain.

4. From a motivational standpoint, how important were the changes in work schedules?

GROUP DYNAMICS and TEAMWORK

CHAPTER OBJECTIVES

When you finish studying this chapter, you should be able to

1 Define the term *group*.

2 Explain the significance of cohesiveness, roles, norms, and ostracism in regard to the behavior of group members.

3 Identify and briefly describe the six stages of group development.

4 Define organizational politics and summarize relevant research insights.

5 Explain how groupthink can lead to blind conformity.

6 Define and discuss the management of virtual teams.

7 Discuss the criteria and determinants of team effectiveness.

8 Explain why trust is a key ingredient of teamwork and discuss what management can do to build trust.

"IT TAKES TIME, EFFORT, AND CONSIDERABLE RESOURCES TO BUILD AND MAINTAIN UNCONDITIONAL TRUST."

gareth r. jones
& jennifer m. george

THE CHANGING WORKPLACE

Lear Team Takes Quality Problems Personally

A chance conversation over lunch launched one of the biggest cost-saving accomplishments at Lear's auto supplier plant . . . [in Strasburg, Virginia].

A nine-member team of workers, the Eliminators, had been looking for ways to reduce the number of parts rejected for poor paint quality.

The plant builds interior parts for General Motors, Ford Motor, Chrysler, and Nissan vehicles. Specifically, the Eliminators sought to improve the performance of the No. 2 paint line, where workers paint about 3.5 million door-pulls a year.

The problem: how to keep water that catches paint-gun overspray from leaving spots on parts.

Too many spots and the part must be repainted or rejected. Lear was repainting more than 35,000 parts a year.

Different paint nozzles, brighter lights, employee training, and other potential solutions helped, but none solved the problem.

To visualize the problem, imagine a worker standing in front of a moving rack of parts that looks similar to the overhead clothes rack found in most dry cleaners. The worker uses a paint gun to blast each part with paint.

Behind the rack is a waterfall. The water catches the overspray from the paint gun, keeping potentially harmful fumes from entering the atmosphere. But after months of research, meetings, and frustration, the team was hitting a dead end. Then one day during a lunch break, team members asked paint technician Rick Edge, who worked on another paint line, whether he had similar problems.

"I said no," Edge says. "I don't have a waterfall."

Edge's paint line, which handles armrests in a building across the street from the No. 2 paint line—uses vacuum air to suck the overspray onto a cardboardlike filter that is burned. Nancy Lloyd, the former continuous improvement coordinator for Lear, says it's common in a high-output, just-in-time production plant for workers not to communicate with others outside their work areas. "That's where the cross-functional team really helped us to bring people from different departments together."

The Eliminators began calling vendors, visiting other paint plants, and analyzing costs, savings, potential benefits, and the environmental impact of eliminating the waterfall.

After a few glitches (initially, the air filters clogged every hour), the team came up with a plan that lowered the plant's scrap rate by 16 percent and defects by 25 percent while improving productivity by 33 percent and saving Lear $112,000 this year.

The successful solution won the team the 1999 RIT/*USA Today* Quality Cup for manufacturing.

"What I thought was unusual, (Lear) allowed the team players to call up suppliers to get price quotes," says Chuck Blevins, a quality cup judge and CEO of his own company.

"And the team players were determined not to waste any of the company's money, like it was their personal company."

Source: Earl Eldridge, "After Spotting Paint Glitch, Lear Workers Eliminate It," *USA Today*, (May 7,1999): 6B. Copyright 1999, USA Today. Reprinted with permission.

A s in daily life itself, relationships rule in modern organizations. The more managers know about building and sustaining good working relationships, the better. A management consultant recently put it this way:

At the end of the day, a company's only sustainable competitive advantage is its relationships with customers, business partners, and employees. After all, we provide products and services to people, not to companies. A commitment to developing effective relationships strengthens the fabric of the organization in the long run.[1]

At Lear, effective working relationships both within the Eliminators team and between teams created a winning formula for the company, its employees, and its customers. The purpose of this chapter is to build a foundation of understanding in regard to how groups and teams function in today's organizations.

Fundamental Group Dynamics

According to one organization theorist, "All groups may be collections of individuals, but all collections of individuals are not groups."[2] This observation is more than a play on words; mere togetherness does not automatically create a group. Consider, for example, this situation. A half-dozen people who worked for different companies in the same building often shared the same elevator in the morning. As time passed, they introduced themselves and exchanged pleasantries. Eventually, four of the elevator riders discovered that they all lived in the same suburb. Arrangements for a car pool were made, and they began to take turns picking up and delivering one another. A group technically came into existence only when the car pool was formed. To understand why this is so, we must examine the definition of the term *group*.

What Is a Group?

From a sociological perspective, a **group** can be defined as two or more freely interacting individuals who share a common identity and purpose.[3] Careful analysis of this definition reveals four important dimensions (see Figure 14.1). First, a group must be made up of two or more people if it is to be considered a social unit. Second, the individuals must freely interact in some manner. An organization may qualify as a sociological group if it is small and personal enough to permit all its members to interact regularly with each other. Generally, however, larger organizations with bureaucratic tendencies are made up of many overlapping groups. Third, the interacting individuals must share a common identity. Each must recognize himself or herself as a member of the group. Fourth, interacting individuals who have a common identity must also have a common purpose. That is, there must be at least a rough consensus on why the group exists.

1 **Define the term** *group*.

group *two or more freely interacting individuals with a common identity and purpose*

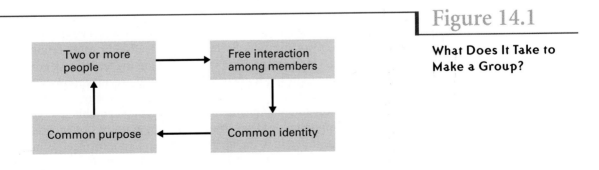

Figure 14.1

What Does It Take to Make a Group?

Types of Groups

Human beings belong to groups for many different reasons. Some people join a group as an end in itself. For example, an accountant may enjoy the socializing that is part of belonging to a group at a local health club. That same accountant's membership in a work group is a means to a professional end. Both the exercise group and the work group satisfy the sociological definition of a group, but they fulfill very different needs. The former is an informal group, and the latter is a formal group.

Informal Groups.   As Abraham Maslow pointed out, a feeling of belonging is a powerful motivator. People generally have a great need to fit in, to be liked, to be one of the gang. Whether the group meets at work or during leisure time, it is still an **informal group** if the principal reason for belonging is friendship.[4] Informal groups usually evolve spontaneously. They serve to satisfy esteem needs because one develops a better self-image when accepted, recognized, and liked by others. Sometimes, as in the case of a group of friends forming a service club, an informal group may evolve into a formal one.

informal group *collection of people seeking friendship*

Managers cannot afford to ignore informal groups because grassroots social networks can either advance or threaten the organization's mission.[5] As experts on the subject explained:

> *These informal networks can cut through formal reporting procedures to jump-start stalled initiatives and meet extraordinary deadlines. But informal networks can just as easily sabotage companies' best-laid plans by blocking communication and fomenting opposition to change unless managers know how to identify and direct them. . . .*
>
> *If the formal organization is the skeleton of a company, the informal is the central nervous system driving the collective thought processes, actions, and reactions of its business units. Designed to facilitate standard modes of production, the formal organization is set up to handle easily anticipated problems. But when unexpected problems arise, the informal organization kicks in. Its complex web of social ties form[s] every time colleagues communicate and solidif[ies] over time into surprisingly stable networks. Highly adaptive, informal networks move diagonally and elliptically, skipping entire functions to get work done.[6]*

formal group *collection of people created to do something productive*

Formal Groups.   A **formal group** is a group created for the purpose of doing productive work. It may be called a team, a committee, or simply a work group. Whatever its name, a formal group is usually formed for the purpose of contributing to the success of a larger organization. Formal groups tend to be more rationally structured and less fluid than informal groups. Rather than joining formal task groups, people are assigned to them according to their talents and the organization's needs. One person normally is granted formal leadership responsibility to ensure that the members carry out their assigned duties. Informal friendship groups, in contrast, generally do not have officially appointed leaders, although informal leaders often emerge by popular demand.[7] For the individual, the formal group and an informal group at the place of employment may or may not overlap. In other words, one may or may not be friends with one's coworkers.

The line between formal and informal groups can blur when you're working long hours on a project with a looming deadline. Here at a tropical camp in Peru—where the Andes Mountains give way to the Amazon River—botanist Bruce Holst, mammalogist Louise Emmons, and ornithologist Tom Schulenberg document their findings. With the help of their Peruvian colleagues, this team from the Rapid Assessment Program of Conservation International recently spent a month surveying the endangered rain forest.

Attraction to Groups

What attracts a person to one group but not to another? And why do some groups' members stay whereas others leave? Managers who can answer these questions can take steps to motivate others to join and remain members of a formal work group. Individual commitment to either an informal or formal group hinges on two factors. The first is *attractiveness*, the outside-looking-in view.[8] A nonmember will want to join a group that is attractive and will shy away from a group that is unattractive. The second factor is **cohesiveness**, the tendency of group members to follow the group and resist outside influences. This is the inside-looking-out view. In a highly cohesive group, individual members tend to see themselves as "we" rather than "I." Cohesive group members stick together.[9]

Factors that either enhance or destroy group attractiveness and cohesiveness are listed in Table 14.1. It is important to note that each factor is a matter of degree. For example, a group may offer the individual little, moderate, or great opportunity for prestige and status. Similarly, group demands on the individual may range from somewhat disagreeable to highly disagreeable. What all this means is that both the decision to join a group and the decision to continue being a member depend on a net balance of the factors in Table 14.1. Naturally, the resulting balance is colored by one's perception and frame of reference, as it was in the case of Richard Dale, a former manager of distribution at Commodore International, during his first meeting with the company's founder, Jack Tramiel:

> *Dale's first meeting with Tramiel began with a summons to appear at Tramiel's office. Dale flew from his office in Los Angeles to Santa Clara . . . , only to find that Tramiel had decided to visit him instead.*
>
> *Terrified, Dale caught a plane back to find his secretary shaking in her shoes and the burly Tramiel sitting at his desk. For an hour Tramiel grilled Dale on his philosophy of business, pronounced it all wrong, and suggested a tour of the warehouse. When they passed boxes of . . . [computers] waiting for shipment, recalls Dale, Tramiel seemed to "go crazy," pounding the boxes with his fists and yelling, "Do you think this is bourbon? Do you think it gets better with age?"[10]*

2 Explain the significance of cohesiveness, roles, norms, and ostracism in regard to the behavior of group members.

cohesiveness *tendency of group to stick together*

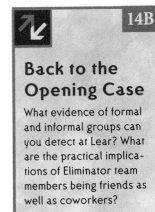

14B

Back to the Opening Case

What evidence of formal and informal groups can you detect at Lear? What are the practical implications of Eliminator team members being friends as well as coworkers?

Table 14.1	Factors that enhance	Factors that detract
Factors That Enhance or Detract from Group Attractiveness and Cohesiveness	1. Prestige and status 2. Cooperative relationship 3. High degree of interaction 4. Relatively small size 5. Similarity of members 6. Superior public image of the group 7. A common threat in the environment	1. Unreasonable or disagreeable demands on the individual 2. Disagreement over procedures, activities, rules, and the like 3. Unpleasant experience with the group 4. Competition between the group's demands and preferred outside activities 5. Unfavorable public image of the group 6. Competition for membership by other groups

Source: Table adapted from *Group Dynamics: Research and Theory*, 2nd ed., by Dorwin Cartwright and Alvin Zander. New York: HarperCollins Publishers, Inc.

Dale's departure within a few months of this episode is not surprising in view of the fact that Tramiel's conduct destroyed work group attractiveness and cohesiveness.

Roles

role *socially determined way of behaving in a specific position*

According to Shakespeare, "All the world's a stage, and all the men and women merely players." In fact, Shakespeare's analogy between life and play-acting can be carried a step further—to organizations and their component formal work groups. Although employees do not have scripts, they do have formal positions in the organizational hierarchy, and they are expected to adhere to company policies and rules. Furthermore, job descriptions and procedure manuals spell out how jobs are to be done. In short, every employee has one or more organizational roles to play. An organization that is appropriately structured, in which everyone plays his or her role(s) effectively and efficiently, will have a greater chance for organizational success.

A social psychologist has described the concept of *role* as follows:

> *The term role is used to refer to (1) a set of expectations concerning what a person in a given position must, must not, or may do, and (2) the actual behavior of the person who occupies the position. A central idea is that any person occupying a position and filling a role behaves similarly to anyone else who could be in that position.*[11]

A **role,** then, is a socially determined prescription for behavior in a *specific* position. Roles evolve out of the tendency for social units to perpetuate themselves, and roles are socially enforced. Role models are a powerful influence. They are indispensable to those trying to resolve the inherent conflicts between work and family roles, for example.[12]

<table>
<tr><td>↗↘</td><td>**Toward a Sense of Com-
munity in the Workplace**</td><td>14C</td></tr>
</table>

Carolyn Schaffer and Kristin Anundsen, authors of the book, *Creating Community Anywhere: Finding Support and Connection in a Fragmented World*:

Community is a dynamic whole that emerges when a group of people:

- *Participate in common practices;*
- *Depend upon one another;*
- *Make decisions together;*
- *Identify themselves as part of something larger than the sum of their individual relationships; and*
- *Commit themselves for the long term to their own, one another's, and the group's well-being.*

Source: Quoted in Ron Zemke, "The Call of Community," *Training,* 33 (March 1996): 27.

Questions: *How important is it to build this sense of community in today's work groups and organizations? Explain. What is your personal experience with a genuine feeling of community? Are we naive to expect a sense of community in today's hurried and rapidly changing workplace? Explain.*

Norms

Norms define "degrees of acceptability and unacceptability."[13] More precisely, **norms** are general standards of conduct that help individuals judge what is right or wrong or good or bad in a given social setting (such as work, home, play, or religious organization). Because norms are culturally derived, they vary from one culture to another. For example, public disagreement and debate, which are normal in Western societies, are often considered rude in Eastern countries such as Japan.

Norms have a broader influence than do roles, which focus on a specific position. Although usually unwritten, norms influence behavior enormously.[14]

Every mature group, whether informal or formal, generates its own pattern of norms that constrains and directs the behavior of its members. Norms are enforced for at least four different reasons:

1. To facilitate survival of the group.
2. To simplify or clarify role expectations.
3. To help group members avoid embarrassing situations (protect self-images).
4. To express key group values and enhance the group's unique identity.[15]

As illustrated in Figure 14.2, norms tend to go above and beyond formal rules and written policies. Compliance is shaped with social reinforcement in the form of attention, recognition, and acceptance.[16] Those who fail to comply with the norm may be criticized or ridiculed. For example, consider the pressure Gwendolyn Kelly experienced in medical school:

> *The word among students is that if you've got any brains, "tertiary" medicine—which involves complex diagnostic procedures and comprehensive care—is where it's at. Instructors often*

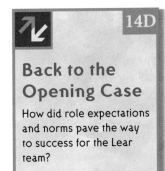

Back to the Opening Case

How did role expectations and norms pave the way to success for the Lear team?

norms *general standards of conduct for various social settings*

Figure 14.2 — Norms Are Enforced for Different Reasons

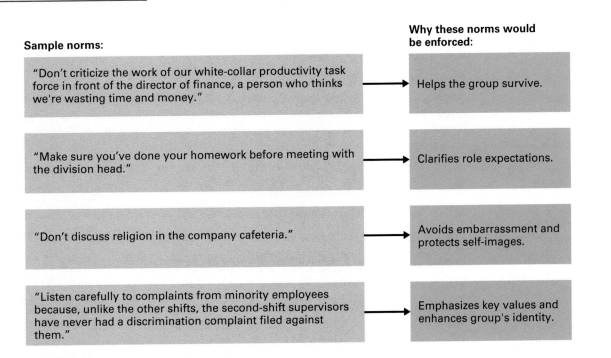

Sample norms:

"Don't criticize the work of our white-collar productivity task force in front of the director of finance, a person who thinks we're wasting time and money."

"Make sure you've done your homework before meeting with the division head."

"Don't discuss religion in the company cafeteria."

"Listen carefully to complaints from minority employees because, unlike the other shifts, the second-shift supervisors have never had a discrimination complaint filed against them."

Why these norms would be enforced:

Helps the group survive.

Clarifies role expectations.

Avoids embarrassment and protects self-images.

Emphasizes key values and enhances group's identity.

Team sports offer many instructive lessons in group dynamics. Pictured here are the Michigan State Spartans on their way to beating the defending national champion, the University of Connecticut Huskies, 85–66 toward the end of the 1999–2000 season. Referees made sure players on both basketball teams followed the rules. For example, UConn was called for charging on this play. But largely unseen by referees and fans are the subtle yet powerful pressures team members put on each other—to enforce norms about being a team player and always giving your best effort. Michigan State ultimately captured the national title.

refer to the best students as "future surgeons" and belittle the family-practice specialty. These attitudes trickle down. I've heard my peers say the reason so many women choose pediatrics is that "they want to be mommies." And students who take a family-practice residency may be maligned by colleagues who say the choice is a sign of subpar academic credentials.[17]

Reformers of the U.S. health care system, who want to increase the number of primary care (family practice) doctors from one-third to one-half, need to begin by altering medical school norms.

ostracism *rejection from a group*

Worse than ridicule is the threat of being ostracized. **Ostracism,** or rejection from the group, is figuratively the capital punishment of group dynamics. Informal groups derive much of their power over individuals through the ever-present threat of ostracism. Thus, informal norms play a pivotal role in on-the-job ethics.[18] Police officers, for example, who honor the traditional "code of silence" norm that demands *total* loyalty to one's fellow officers, face a tough moral dilemma (see Management Ethics).

Group Development

Like inept youngsters who mature into talented adults, groups undergo a maturation process before becoming effective. We have all experienced the uneasiness associated with the first meeting of a new group, be it a class, club, or committee. Initially, there is little mutual understanding, trust, and commitment among the new group

Management Ethics

A Cop-Turned-Professor Takes Aim at the Code of Silence

Several factors enable the code to infect even the most well-intentioned officers. The way a law enforcement organization describes its mission can influence how much misbehavior officers will tolerate from peers. Many police managers and politicians portray officers as a thin line of warriors standing between civilization and the barbarian hordes.

This unrealistic expectation that cops, rather than communities, control crime increases the zeal with which many officers approach their job. When one participates in a crusade, it is easy to rationalize extreme measures.

The patrol environment is also important. We often have unrealistic expectations of patrol officers in high-crime areas, who regularly handle several adrenaline-pumping incidents a shift. Moreover, they often do so while exhausted from overtime assignments, off-duty court appearances, and job-related activities such as attending college. This combination of environmental stressors and fatigue magnifies perceptions of threats, degrades decision-making, and increases the tendency to overreact....

Combining institutionally fostered zealousness with unrealistic physical and emotional expectations is a recipe for misconduct.

Take the case of a normally diligent and professional officer who erupts and strikes that one person too many who screams in his face at the end of an arduous night. Acting out of anger rather than fear for his safety, he has committed a felony. If he is truthful, the career that defines him is over. He could go to prison. If he chooses to lie, he must obtain his partner's complicity. They both know he was wrong, but they also know that any person who repeatedly dealt with the same situation would blow it eventually. Recognizing that the system makes impossible demands and offers impossible choices, they choose to submit a false report and, if necessary, perjure themselves.

The code of silence is reborn each time this decision is made.

Later, when his partner uses excessive force, our officer reciprocates. Eventually, even the most idealistic officers can be infected by the code. As this erodes an officer's moral fiber, self-interest and continued stress make future compromises easier. Since police agencies promote mostly from within, many supervisors and managers are tainted by past misdeeds. This hardly leaves them in a position to control the behavior of subordinates.

The code of silence can undermine even determined attempts at police reform. If we want to control the conduct of our police and strengthen their ability to work with communities to control crime, we need to inhibit the code. How? First, we should debunk the demagoguery of the "thin blue line" myth. Our inner cities need calm professional officers, not exhausted crusaders.

More fundamentally, we must ensure that officers are emotionally and physically fit for duty each time they hit the streets, just as the military must ensure the reliability of those who control nuclear weapons. For decades, the military has accomplished this via personnel reliability programs combining cooperative self-regulation with active monitoring by health-care professionals.

Exhausted or otherwise debilitated cops should be encouraged to excuse themselves from duty. Good cops protect one another. Supervisors and peers need to learn that protection includes convincing unfit officers to stay off the streets. As a final safety check, a trained professional should have the authority to immediately remove unfit officers from duty. Personnel reliability program costs would be offset by fewer lawsuits and accidents.

Steps such as these would neither condone nor excuse police misbehavior. But they would attack the source of the awful silence that allows it to persist.

Source: Excerpted from Bryan Vila, "The Cops' Code of Silence," *The Christian Science Monitor* (August 31, 1992): 18. Reprinted by permission of the author.

---

members, and their uncertainty over objectives, roles, and leadership doesn't help. The prospect of cooperative action seems unlikely in view of defensive behavior and differences of opinion about who should do what. Someone steps forward to assume a leadership role, and the group is off and running toward eventual maturity (or perhaps premature demise). A working knowledge of the characteristics of a mature group can help managers envision a goal for the group development process.

Characteristics of a Mature Group

If and when a group takes on the following characteristics, it can be called a mature group:

1. Members are aware of their own and each other's assets and liabilities vis-à-vis the group's task.
2. These individual differences are accepted without being labeled as good or bad.
3. The group has developed authority and interpersonal relationships that are recognized and accepted by the members.
4. Group decisions are made through rational discussion. Minority opinions and dissension are recognized and encouraged. Attempts are not made to force decisions or a false unanimity.
5. Conflict is over substantive group issues such as group goals and the effectiveness and efficiency of various means for achieving those goals. Conflict over emotional issues regarding group structure, processes, or interpersonal relationships is at a minimum.
6. Members are aware of the group's processes and their own roles in them.[19]

Effectiveness and productivity should increase as the group matures. Recent research with groups of school teachers found positive evidence in this regard. The researchers concluded: "Faculty groups functioning at higher levels of development have students who perform better on standard achievement measures."[20] This finding could be fruitful for those seeking to reform and improve the American education system.

A hidden but nonetheless significant benefit of group maturity is that individuality is strengthened and not extinguished.[21] Protecting the individual's right to dissent is particularly important in regard to the problem of blind obedience, which we shall consider later in this chapter.

Six Stages of Group Development

3 Identify and briefly describe the six stages of group development.

Experts have identified six distinct stages in the group development process[22] (see Figure 14.3). During stages 1 through 3, attempts are made to overcome the obstacle of uncertainty over power and authority. Once this first obstacle has been surmounted, uncertainty over interpersonal relations becomes the challenge. This second obstacle must be cleared during stages 4 through 6 if the group is to achieve maturity. Each stage confronts the group's leader and contributing members with a unique combination of problems and opportunities.

Stage 1: Orientation.   Attempts are made to "break the ice." Uncertainty about goals, power, and interpersonal relationships is high. Members generally want and accept any leadership at this point. Emergent leaders often misinterpret this "honeymoon period" as a mandate for permanent control.

Stage 2: Conflict and Challenge.   As the emergent leader's philosophy, objectives, and policies become apparent, individuals or subgroups advocating alternative courses of action struggle for control. This second stage may be prolonged while members strive to clarify and reconcile their roles as part of a complete redistribution of power and authority. Many groups never continue past stage 2 because they get bogged down due to emotionalism and political infighting. Committees within the organization often bear the brunt of jokes because their frequent failure to mature beyond stage 2 prevents them from accomplishing their goals. (As one joke goes, a camel is a horse designed by a committee.)

Figure 14.3

Group Development from Formation to Maturity

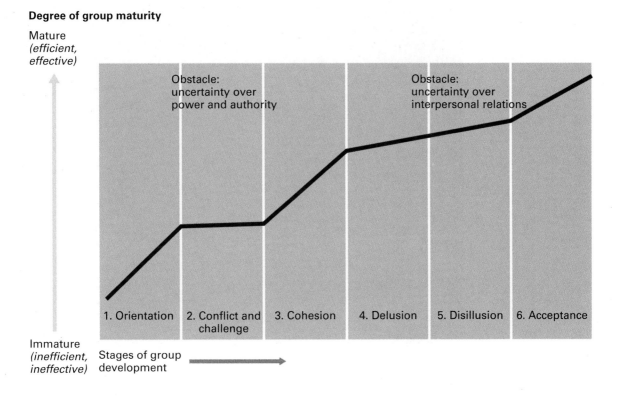

Degree of group maturity

Mature (efficient, effective)

Obstacle: uncertainty over power and authority

Obstacle: uncertainty over interpersonal relations

1. Orientation   2. Conflict and challenge   3. Cohesion   4. Delusion   5. Disillusion   6. Acceptance

Immature (inefficient, ineffective)   Stages of group development

Source: Group Effectiveness in Organizations, by Linda N. Jewell and H. Joseph Reitz, p. 20. Used with permission of the authors.

Stage 3: Cohesion.   The shifts in power started in stage 2 are completed, under a new leader or the original leader, with a new consensus on authority, structure, and procedures. A "we" feeling becomes apparent as everyone becomes truly involved. Any lingering differences over power and authority are resolved quickly. Stage 3 is usually of relatively short duration. If not, the group is likely to stall.

Stage 4: Delusion.   A feeling of "having been through the worst of it" prevails after the rather rapid transition through stage 3. Issues and problems that threaten to break this spell of relief are dismissed or treated lightly. Members seem committed to fostering harmony at all costs. Participation and camaraderie run high as members believe that all the difficult emotional problems have been solved.

Stage 5: Disillusion.   Subgroups tend to form as the delusion of unlimited goodwill wears off, and there is a growing disenchantment with how things are turning out. Those with unrealized expectations challenge the group to perform better and are prepared to reveal their personal strengths and weaknesses if necessary. Others hold back. Tardiness and absenteeism are symptomatic of diminishing cohesiveness and commitment.

Stage 6: Acceptance.   It usually takes a trusted and influential group member who is concerned about the group to step forward and help the group move from conflict to cohesion. This individual, acting as the group catalyst, is usually someone

Developing a work group into an effective and efficient team sometimes can be a life-and-death matter. Following the devastating earthquakes in Turkey in 1999, search-and-rescue teams from around the world joined in a race against the clock. This nine-year-old girl, buried in rubble for 100 hours, was rescued by an Israeli military team.

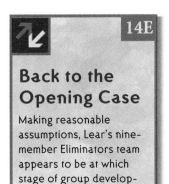

14E

Back to the Opening Case

Making reasonable assumptions, Lear's nine-member Eliminators team appears to be at which stage of group development? How can you tell?

other than the leader. Members are encouraged to test their self-perceptions against the reality of how others perceive them. Greater personal and mutual understanding helps members adapt to situations without causing problems. Members' expectations are more realistic than ever before. Since the authority structure is generally accepted, subgroups can pursue different matters without threatening group cohesiveness. Consequently, stage 6 groups tend to be highly effective and efficient.

Time-wasting problems and inefficiencies can be minimized if group members are consciously aware of this developmental process. Just as it is impossible for a child to skip being a teenager on the way to adulthood, committees and other work groups will find that there are no short cuts to group maturity. Some emotional stresses and strains are inevitable along the way.[23]

Organizational Politics

4 **Define organizational politics and summarize relevant research insights.**

Only in recent years has the topic of organizational politics (also known as impression management) begun to receive serious attention from management theorists and researchers.[24] But as we all know from practical experience, organizational life is often highly charged with political wheeling and dealing. A corporate executive has underscored this point by asking:

Have you ever done a very satisfactory piece of work only to have it lost in the organizational shuffle? Have you ever come up with a new idea only to have your boss take credit for it? Have you ever faced a situation where someone else made a serious mistake and somehow engineered it so you got the blame?[25]

Workplace surveys reveal that organizational politics can hinder effectiveness and be an irritant to employees. A recent three-year study of 46 companies attempting to establish themselves on the Internet "found that poor communication and political infighting were the No. 1 and No. 2 causes, respectively, for slowing down change."[26] Meanwhile, 44 percent of full-time employees and 60 percent of independent contractors listed "freedom from office politics" as extremely important to their job satisfaction.[27]

Whether politically motivated or not, managers need to be knowledgeable about organizational politics because their careers will be affected by it.[28] New managers, particularly, should be aware of the political situation in their organization. As "new kids on the job" they might be more easily taken advantage of than other more experienced managers.[29] Certain political maneuvers also have significant ethical implications[30] (see Table 14.2).

Table 14.2   How Do You Feel About "Hard Ball" Organizational Politics?

Circle one number for each item, total your responses, and compare your score with the scale below:

	Unacceptable attitude/conduct			Acceptable attitude/conduct	
1. The boss is always right.	1	2	3	4	5
2. If I were aware that an executive in my company was stealing money, I would use that information against him or her in asking for favors.	1	2	3	4	5
3. I would invite my boss to a party in my home even if I didn't like that person.	1	2	3	4	5
4. Given a choice, take on only those assignments that will make you look good.	1	2	3	4	5
5. I like the idea of keeping a "blunder (error) file" about a company rival for future use.	1	2	3	4	5
6. If you don't know the correct answer to a question asked by your boss, bluff your way out of it.	1	2	3	4	5
7. Why go out of your way to be nice to any employee in the company who can't help you now or in the future?	1	2	3	4	5
8. It is necessary to lie once in a while in business in order to look good.	1	2	3	4	5
9. Past promises should be broken if they stand in the way of one's personal gain.	1	2	3	4	5
10. If someone compliments you for a task that is another's accomplishment, smile and say thank you.	1	2	3	4	5

Scale

10–20 = Straight arrow with solid ethics.   Total score = _____
21–39 = Closet politician with elastic ethics.
40–50 = Hard ball politician with no ethics.

Source: From *Winning Office Politics* by Andrew Dubrin. Copyright © 1990. Reprinted with permission of Prentice-Hall Direct.

What Does Organizational Politics Involve?

organizational politics
the pursuit of self-interest in response to real or imagined opposition

As the term implies, self-interest is central to organizational politics. In fact, **organizational politics** has been defined as "the pursuit of self-interest at work in the face of real or imagined opposition."[31] Political maneuvering is said to encompass all self-serving behavior above and beyond competence, hard work, and luck.[32] Although the term organizational politics has a negative connotation, researchers have identified both positive and negative aspects:

> *Political behaviors widely accepted as legitimate would certainly include exchanging favors, "touching bases," forming coalitions, and seeking sponsors at upper levels. Less legitimate behaviors would include whistle-blowing, revolutionary coalitions, threats, and sabotage.*[33]

Recall our discussion of whistle-blowing in Chapter 5.

Employees resort to political behavior when they are unwilling to trust their career solely to competence, hard work, or luck. One might say that organizational politicians help luck along by relying on political tactics. Whether employees will fall back on political tactics has a lot to do with an organization's climate or culture. A culture that presents employees with unreasonable barriers to individual and group success tends to foster political maneuvering. Consider this situation, for example: "A cadre of Corvette lovers inside General Motors lied, cheated, and stole to keep the legendary sports car from being eliminated during GM's management turmoil and near-bankruptcy in the late 1980s and early 1990s."[34] The redesigned Corvette finally made it to market in 1997, thanks in part to the Corvette team giving high-level GM executives thrilling unauthorized test rides in the hot new model.

Research on Organizational Politics

Researchers in one widely cited study of organizational politics conducted structured interviews with 87 managers employed by 30 electronics firms in southern California. Included in the sample were 30 chief executive officers, 28 middle managers, and 29 supervisors. Significant results included the following:

- The higher the level of management, the greater the perceived amount of political activity.
- The larger the organization, the greater the perceived amount of political activity.
- Personnel in staff positions were viewed as more political than those in line positions.
- People in marketing were the most political; those in production were the least political.
- "Reorganization changes" reportedly prompted more political activity than any other type of change.
- A majority (61 percent) of those interviewed believed organizational politics helps advance one's career.
- Forty-five percent believed that organizational politics distracts from organizational goals.[35]

Regarding the last two findings, it was clear that political activities were seen as helpful to the individual. On the other hand, the interviewed managers were split on the question of the value of politics to the organization. Managers who believed political behavior had a positive impact on the organization cited the following reasons: "gaining visibility for ideas, improving coordination and communication, developing teams and groups, and increasing *esprit de corps*. . . ."[36] As listed above, the most often cited negative effect of politics was its distraction of managers from organizational goals. Misuse of resources and conflict were also mentioned as typical problems.

Political Tactics

As defined earlier, organizational politics takes in a lot of behavioral territory. The following six political tactics are common expressions of politics in the workplace:

- *Posturing.* Those who use this tactic look for situations in which they can make a good impression. "One-upmanship" and taking credit for other people's work are included in this category.
- *Empire building.* Gaining and keeping control over human and material resources is the principal motivation behind this tactic. Those with large budgets usually feel more safely entrenched in their positions and believe they have more influence over peers and superiors.
- *Making the supervisor look good.* Traditionally referred to as "apple polishing," this political strategy is prompted by a desire to favorably influence those who control one's career ascent. Anyone with an oversized ego is an easy target for this tactic.
- *Collecting and using social IOUs.* Reciprocal exchange of political favors can be done in two ways: (1) by helping someone look good or (2) by preventing someone from looking bad by ignoring or covering up a mistake. Those who rely on this tactic feel that all favors are coins of exchange rather than expressions of altruism or unselfishness.

How Political Are You?   14F
Characteristics of Political Behaviors

Characteristics	Naive	Sensible	Sharks
Underlying Attitude	Politics is unpleasant	Politics is necessary	Politics is an opportunity
Intent	Avoid at all costs	Further departmental goals	Self-serving and predatory
Techniques	Tell it like it is	Network; expand connections; use system to give and receive favors	Manipulate; use fraud and deceit when necessary
Favorite Tactics	None—the truth will win out	Negotiate, bargain	Bully; misuse information; cultivate and use "friends" and other contacts

Source: Model from Jeffrey K. Pinto and Om P. Kharbanda, "Lessons for an Accidental Profession." Reprinted with permission from *Business Horizons*, 38 (March–April 1995): 45. Copyright © 1995 by the Board of Trustees at Indiana University, Kelley School of Business.

Questions: *Based on your responses to the quiz in Table 14.2 and your review of the above model, are you politically naive, politically sensible, or a political shark? Thinking of people you know who fit into the different categories, how well are their careers progressing? What are the personal and organizational implications of your political tendencies? What are the ethical implications of your orientation toward organizational politics?*

- *Creating power and loyalty cliques.* Because there is power in numbers, the idea here is to face superiors and competitors as a cohesive group rather than alone.
- *Destructive competition.* As a last-ditch effort, some people will resort to character assassination through suggestive remarks, vindictive gossip, or outright lies. This tactic also includes sabotaging the work of a competitor.[37]

Obvious illegalities notwithstanding, one's own values and ethics and organizational sanctions are the final arbiters of whether or not these tactics are acceptable. (See Table 14.3 for a practicing manager's advice on how to win at office politics.)

Antidotes to Political Behavior

Each of the foregoing political tactics varies in degree. The average person will probably acknowledge using at least one of these strategies. But excessive political maneuvering can become a serious threat to productivity when self-interests clearly override the interests of the group or organization. Organizational politics can be kept within reasonable bounds by applying the following five tips:

- Strive for a climate of openness and trust.
- Measure performance results rather than personalities.
- Encourage top management to refrain from exhibiting political behavior that will be imitated by employees.
- Strive to integrate individual and organizational goals through meaningful work and career planning.[38]
- Practice job rotation to encourage broader perspectives and understanding of the problems of others.[39]

Table 14.3 **One Manager's Rules for Winning at Office Politics**	
	1. Find out what the boss expects.
	2. Build an information network. Knowledge is power. Identify the people who have power and the extent and direction of it. Title doesn't necessarily reflect actual influence. Find out how the grapevine works. Develop good internal public relations for yourself.
	3. Find a mentor. This is a trusted counselor who can be honest with you and help train and guide you to improve your ability and effectiveness as a manager.
	4. Don't make enemies without a very good reason.
	5. Avoid cliques. Keep circulating in the office.
	6. If you must fight, fight over something that is really worth it. Don't lose ground over minor matters or petty differences.
	7. Gain power through allies. Build ties that bind. Create IOUs, obligations, and loyalties. Do not be afraid to enlist help from above.
	8. Maintain control. Don't misuse your cohorts. Maintain the status and integrity of your allies.
	9. Mobilize your forces when necessary. Don't commit your friends without their approval. Be a gracious winner when you do win.
	10. Never hire a family member or a close friend.

Source: Adapted from David E. Hall, "Winning at Office Politics," *Credit & Financial Management*, 86 (April 1984): 23. Reprinted with permission from *Credit & Financial Management*, copyright April 1984, published by the National Association of Credit Management, 475 Park Avenue South, New York, NY 10016.

Conformity and Groupthink

Conformity means complying with the role expectations and norms perceived by the majority to be appropriate in a particular situation. Conformity enhances predictability, generally thought to be good for rational planning and productive enterprise. How can anything be accomplished if people cannot be counted on to perform their assigned duties? On the other hand, why do so many employees actively participate in or passively condone illegal and unethical organizational practices involving discrimination, environmental degradation, and unfair competition? The answers to these questions lie along a continuum with anarchy at one end and blind conformity at the other. Socially responsible management is anchored to a point somewhere between them.

conformity *complying with prevailing role expectations and norms*

Research on Conformity

Social psychologists have discovered much about human behavior by studying individuals and groups in controlled laboratory settings. One classic laboratory study conducted by Solomon Asch was designed to answer the question, How often will an individual take a stand against a unanimous majority that is obviously wrong?[40] Asch's results were both intriguing and unsettling.

The Hot Seat.   Asch began his study by assembling groups of seven to nine college students, supposedly to work on a perceptual problem. Actually, though, Asch was studying conformity. All but one member of each group were Asch's confederates, and Asch told them exactly how to behave and what to say. The experiment was really concerned with the reactions of the remaining student—called the naive subject—who didn't know what was going on.

All the students in each group were shown cards with lines similar to those in Figure 14.4. They were instructed to match the line on the left with the one on the right that was closest to it in length. The differences in length among the lines on the right were obvious. Each group went through 12 rounds of the matching process, with a different set of lines for every round. The researcher asked one group member at a time to announce to the group his or her choice. Things proceeded normally for the first two rounds as each group member voiced an opinion. Agreement was unanimous. Suddenly, on the third round only one individual, the naive subject, chose the correct pair of lines.

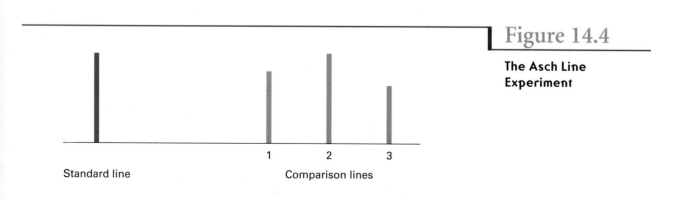

Figure 14.4

The Asch Line Experiment

Standard line   1   2   3

Comparison lines

All the other group members chose a different (and obviously wrong) pair. During the rounds in which there was disagreement, all of Asch's confederates conspired to select an incorrect pair of lines. It was the individual versus the rest of the group.

Following the Immoral Majority.   Each of the naive subjects was faced with a personal dilemma. Should he or she fight the group or give in to the obviously incorrect choice of the overwhelming majority? Among 31 naive subjects who made a total of 217 judgments, two-thirds of the judgments were correct. The other one-third were incorrect; that is, they were consistent with the majority opinion. Individual differences were great, with some subjects yielding to the incorrect majority opinion more readily than others. *Only 20 percent of the naive subjects remained entirely independent in their judgments.* All the rest turned their backs on their own perceptions and went along with the group at least once. In other words, 80 percent of Asch's subjects knuckled under to the pressure of group opinion at least once, even though they knew the majority was dead wrong.

Replications of Asch's study in the Middle East (Kuwait) and in Japan have demonstrated that this tendency toward conformity is not unique to American culture.[41] Indeed, a recent statistical analysis of 133 Asch conformity studies across 17 countries concluded that blind conformity is a greater problem in collectivist ("we") cultures than in individualist ("me") cultures. Japan is strongly collectivist, whereas the United States and Canada are highly individualistic cultures.[42] (You may find it instructive to ponder how you would act in such a situation.)

Because Asch's study was a contrived laboratory experiment, it failed to probe the relationship between cohesiveness and conformity. Asch's naive subjects were outsiders. But more recent research on "groupthink" has shown that a cohesive group of insiders can fall victim to blind conformity.

Groupthink

5 Explain how groupthink can lead to blind conformity.

groupthink   *Janis's term for blind conformity in cohesive in-groups*

After studying the records of several successful and unsuccessful American foreign policy decisions, psychologist Irving Janis uncovered an undesirable byproduct of group cohesiveness. He labeled this problem **groupthink** and defined it as a "mode of thinking that people engage in when they are deeply involved in a cohesive in-group, when the members' strivings for unanimity override their motivation to realistically appraise alternative courses of action."[43] Groupthink helps explain how intelligent policymakers, in both government and business, can sometimes make incredibly unwise decisions.

One dramatic result of groupthink in action was the Vietnam War. Strategic advisors in three successive administrations unwittingly rubber-stamped battle plans laced with false assumptions. Critical thinking, reality testing, and moral judgment were temporarily shelved as decisions to escalate the war were enthusiastically railroaded through. Although Janis acknowledges that cohesive groups are not inevitably victimized by groupthink, he warns group decision makers to be alert for the signs of groupthink—the risk is always there.

Symptoms of Groupthink.   According to Janis, the onset of groupthink is foreshadowed by a definite pattern of symptoms. Among these are excessive optimism, an assumption of inherent morality, suppression of dissent, and an almost desperate quest for unanimity.[44] Given such a decision-making climate, the probability of a poor decision is high. Managers face a curious dilemma here. While a group is still in stage 1 or stage 2 of development, its cohesiveness is too low to get much accomplished because of emotional and time-consuming power struggles. But by the time the group achieves enough cohesiveness in stage 3 to make decisions promptly, the risk of groupthink is high. The trick is to achieve needed cohesiveness without going to the extreme of groupthink.

Preventing Groupthink.   According to Janis, one of the group members should periodically ask, "Are we allowing ourselves to become victims of groupthink?"[45] More fundamental preventive measures include the following:

- Avoiding the use of groups to rubber-stamp decisions that have already been made by higher management.[46]
- Urging each group member to be a critical evaluator.
- Bringing in outside experts for fresh perspectives.
- Assigning to someone the role of devil's advocate to challenge assumptions and alternatives.[47]
- Taking time to consider possible side effects and consequences of alternative courses of action.[48]

> ## 14G   Fighting Groupthink with Diversity
>
> *Because group cohesiveness is directly related to degree of homogeneity, and because groupthink only occurs in highly cohesive groups, the presence of cultural diversity in groups should reduce the probability of groupthink.*
>
> *Source:* Taylor Cox Jr., *Cultural Diversity in Organizations: Theory, Research, and Practice* (San Francisco: Berrett–Koehler, 1993), p. 34.
>
> **Questions:** *Is groupthink likely to be more or less of a problem in a group whose members are both women and men of varying ages from different cultures and with different backgrounds and life experiences? Explain.*

Ideally, decision quality will improve when these steps become second nature in cohesive groups. Dayton Hudson Corp. has structured its board of directors to avoid groupthink and effectively monitor the performance of its chief executive officer. Lots of outside advice keeps the Minneapolis-based owner of Marshall Field's and Target department stores on track:

> *Twelve out of 14 directors are outsiders. A vice chairman chosen from among the outside directors serves as a special liaison between the board and the CEO. The result is a powerful, independent group of directors—a rare species in boardrooms today.*[49]

Managers who cannot imagine themselves being victimized by blind conformity are prime candidates for groupthink. Dean Tjosvold of Canada's Simon Fraser University recommends "cooperative conflict" (see Skills & Tools at the end of this chapter). The constructive use of conflict is discussed further in Chapter 16.

Teams, Teamwork, and Trust

Ask Gordon Bethune, CEO of Continental Airlines, about the secret to success in his highly competitive industry today and he zeros in on *teamwork:*

> *Running an airline is the biggest team sport there is. It's not an approach, it's not reorganization, and it's not a daily team plan. We are like a wristwatch—lots of different parts, but the whole has value only when we all work together. It has no value when any part fails. So we are not a cross-functional team, we're a company of multi functions that has value when we all work cooperatively—pilots, flight attendants, gate agents, airport agents, mechanics, reservation agents. And not to understand that about doing business means you're going to fail. Lots of people failed because they don't get it.*[50]

Thus, teams and teamwork are vital group dynamics in the modern workplace.[51] Unfortunately, team skills in today's typical organization tend to lag far behind technical

You want the finest hand-tailored Italian suit? Ciro Paone, founder of Kiton in Naples, Italy, has the right formula. A team of master tailors + 24 hours of labor + lots of passion + love + the finest materials = one suit costing up to $5,000. World-class quality takes incredible talent, teamwork, and dedication to craft. And in this case, it doesn't come cheap!

skills.[52] It is one thing to be a creative software engineer, for example. It is quite another for that software specialist to be able to team up with other specialists in accounting, finance, and marketing to beat the competition to market with a profitable new product. In this final section, we explore teams and teamwork by discussing cross-functional teams, virtual teams, a model of team effectiveness, and the importance of trust.

Cross-Functional Teams

cross-functional team
task group staffed with a mix of specialists pursuing a common objective

A **cross-functional team** is a task group staffed with a mix of specialists focused on a common objective. This structural innovation deserves special attention here because cross-functional teams are becoming commonplace.[53] They may or may not be self-managed, although self-managed teams generally are cross-functional. Cross-functional teams are based on assigned rather than voluntary membership. Quality control (QC) circles made up of volunteers, discussed in Chapter 13, technically are in a different category. Cross-functional teams stand in sharp contrast to the tradition of lumping specialists into functional departments, thereby creating the problem of integrating and coordinating those departments. Boeing, for example, relies on cross-functional teams to integrate its various departments to achieve important strategic goals. The giant aircraft manufacturer thus accelerated its product development process for the Boeing 777 jetliner. Also, Boeing engineer Grace Robertson turned to cross-functional teams for faster delivery of a big order of customized jetliners to United Parcel Service:

When UPS ordered 30 aircraft, Boeing guaranteed that it could design and build a new, all-cargo version of the 767 jet in a mere 33 months—far faster than the usual cycle time of 42 months. The price it quoted meant slashing development costs dramatically.

Robertson's strategy has been to gather all 400 employees working on the new freighter into one location and organize them into "cross-functional" teams. By combining people from the design, planning, manufacturing, and tooling sectors, the teams speed up development and cut costs by enhancing communication and avoiding rework.[54]

This teamwork approach helped Robertson's group stay on schedule and within its budget, both vitally important achievements in Boeing's quest to remain the world's leading aircraft maker.

Cross-functional teams have exciting potential. But they present management with the immense challenge of getting technical specialists to be effective boundary spanners.

Virtual Teams

Along with the move toward virtual organizations, discussed in Chapter 10, have come virtual teams. A **virtual team** is a physically dispersed task group linked electronically.[55] Face-to-face contact usually is minimal or nonexistent. E-mail, voice mail, videoconferencing, and other forms of electronic interchange allow members of virtual teams from anywhere on the planet to accomplish a common goal. It is commonplace today for virtual teams to have members from different organizations, different time zones, and different cultures.[56] Because virtual organizations and teams are so new, paced as they are by emerging technologies, managers are having to learn from the school of hard knocks rather than from established practice.

As discussed in Chapter 10 relative to virtual organizations, one reality of managing virtual teams is clear. *Periodic face-to-face interaction, trust building, and team building are more important than ever when team members are widely dispersed in time and space.* While faceless interaction may work in Internet chat rooms, it can doom a virtual team

6 **Define and discuss the management of virtual teams.**

virtual team *task group members from dispersed locations who are electronically linked*

Call it new millennium motherhood. When Joanna Dapkevich got pregnant in 1997, her boss at IBM okayed her proposal to retain a part-time portion of her job as the manager of 50 software sales representatives. Here she steers her "virtual team" in Raleigh, North Carolina, from her home ten miles away. Dapkevich's long-distance management requires just the right combination of teamwork and trust. Her toddler seems to be very pleased with the arrangement.

with a crucial task and pressing deadline. Additionally, special steps need to be taken to clearly communicate role expectations, performance norms, goals, and deadlines (see Table 14.4). Virtual teamwork may be faster than the traditional face-to-face kind, but it is by no means easier (see Closing Case).

What Makes Workplace Teams Effective?

7 **Discuss the criteria and determinants of team effectiveness.**

Widespread use of team formats—including QC circles, self-managed teams, cross-functional teams, and virtual teams—necessitates greater knowledge of team effectiveness.[57] A model of team effectiveness criteria and determinants is presented in Figure 14.5. This model is the product of two field studies involving 360 new-product development managers employed by 52 high-tech companies.[58] Importantly, it is a generic model, applying equally well to all workplace teams.[59]

Table 14.4 | It Takes More than E-mail to Build a Virtual Team

Teams need a structure to work successfully across time and distance. In *Mastering Virtual Teams: Strategies, Tools, and Techniques That Succeed*, authors Deborah Duarte and Nancy Tennant Snyder list six steps for creating a virtual team, of which each acts as a support beam that helps uphold the structure.

  1. Identify the team's sponsors, stakeholders, and champions. These are the people who connect the team to the power brokers within the organizations involved.

  2. Develop a team charter that includes its purpose, mission, and goals. The authors say it's best to do this in a face-to-face meeting that includes the team's leader, management, and other stakeholders.

  3. Select team members. Most virtual teams have at least three types of members: *core* members who regularly work on the project; *extended* members who provide support and advice; and *ancillary* members who review and approve work.

  4. Contact team members and introduce them to each other. During this initial meeting, team leaders should make sure members understand why they've been selected, use computers that are compatible, and have a forum in which to ask and get answers to questions. Duarte says leaders should use this time to find out what other projects members are working on. "It's easy to put people on a team when you can't see them," she says. "People don't say 'no,' but then they find themselves on five or six teams and don't have time for any of them."

  5. Conduct a team-orientation session. This is one of the most important steps. Duarte says an eyeball-to-eyeball meeting is essential, unless team members are working on a very short task or have worked together in another capacity and know each other. "This forms the basis for more natural dialogue later if problems arise," she says. At this getting-to-know-you session, which often includes some type of team-building activity, the leader should provide an overview of the team's charter so members understand the task they are charged with and their roles in achieving it.

  Leaders also should provide guidance in developing team norms. This includes discussing telephone, audio- and video-conference etiquette; establishing guidelines for sending and replying to e-mail and returning phone calls; determining which meetings members must attend in person and which can be done by audio- or videoconference; outlining how work will be reviewed; and discussing how meetings will be scheduled.

  Team leaders also can use this session to decide which technologies the team will use and discuss how members will communicate with each other, with the leader, and with management.

  6. Develop a team process. Leaders should explain how the team's work will be managed, how information will be stored and shared, and who will review documents and how often.

  Duarte says teams that follow these steps often have a better sense of clarity about their goals, the roles of each member, how the work will get done, and how the team will communicate. "They don't feel as though they've been left floating."

Source: Kim Kiser, "Building a Virtual Team," *Training*, 36 (March 1999): 34. Reprinted with permission from the March 1999 issue of *Training* magazine. Copyright 1999, Bill Communications, Minneapolis, Minn. All rights reserved. Not for resale.

Figure 14.5

A Model of Team
Effectiveness

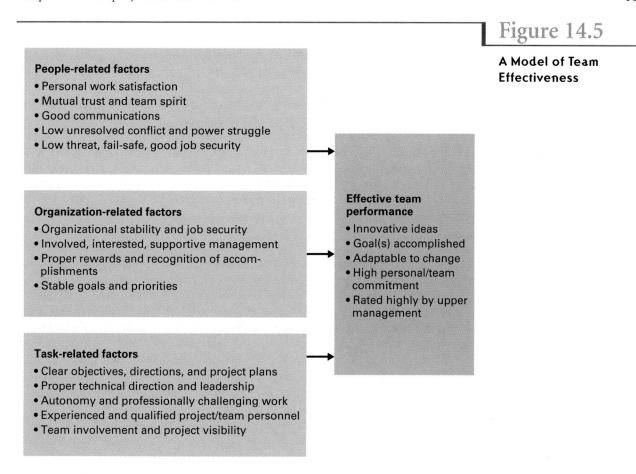

People-related factors
• Personal work satisfaction
• Mutual trust and team spirit
• Good communications
• Low unresolved conflict and power struggle
• Low threat, fail-safe, good job security

Organization-related factors
• Organizational stability and job security
• Involved, interested, supportive management
• Proper rewards and recognition of accomplishments
• Stable goals and priorities

Task-related factors
• Clear objectives, directions, and project plans
• Proper technical direction and leadership
• Autonomy and professionally challenging work
• Experienced and qualified project/team personnel
• Team involvement and project visibility

Effective team performance
• Innovative ideas
• Goal(s) accomplished
• Adaptable to change
• High personal/team commitment
• Rated highly by upper management

Source: Reprinted from *Journal of Product Innovation Management,* 7, Hans J. Thamhain, "Managing Technologically Innovative Team Efforts Toward New Product Success," pp. 5–18. Copyright 1990, with permission from Elsevier Science, Inc.

The five criteria for effective team performance in the center of Figure 14.5 parallel the criteria for organizational effectiveness discussed in Chapter 9. Thus, team effectiveness feeds organizational effectiveness. For example, if the Boeing 777 product development teams had not been effective, the entire corporation could have stumbled.

Determinants of team effectiveness, shown in Figure 14.5, are grouped into people-, organization-, and task-related factors. Considered separately, these factors involve rather routine aspects of good management. But the collective picture reveals each factor to be part of a complex and interdependent whole. Managers cannot maximize just a few of them, ignore the rest, and hope to have an effective team. In the spirit of the Japanese concept of *kaizen*, managers and team leaders need to strive for "continuous improvement" on all fronts. Because gains on one front will inevitably be offset by losses in another, the pursuit of team effectiveness and teamwork is an endless battle with no guarantees of success.[60]

Let us focus on trust, one of the people-related factors in Figure 14.5 that can make or break work teams.

Trust: A Key to Team Effectiveness

trust *belief in the integrity, character, or ability of others*

8 Explain why trust is a key ingredient of teamwork and discuss what management can do to build trust.

Trust, a belief in the integrity, character, or ability of others, is essential if people are to achieve anything together in the long run.[61] Participative management programs are very dependent on trust.[62] Sadly, trust is not one of the hallmarks of the current U.S. business scene. Back in 1966, 55 percent of Americans had a "great deal of confidence" in major companies. By 1994, that general barometer of trust had plunged to 19 percent.[63] By all accounts, the situation has worsened since. This "trust gap," as *Fortune* magazine labeled it, exists in other developed countries as well. "A 1998 Watson Wyatt Worldwide survey of 2,004 workers in all sectors across Canada concluded that three out of four Canadian employees do not trust the people they work for."[64] To a greater extent than they may initially suspect, managers determine the level of trust in the organization and its component work groups and teams.

Zand's Model of Trust.   Trust is not a free-floating variable. It affects, and in turn is affected by, other group processes. Dale E. Zand's model of work group interaction puts trust into proper perspective (see Figure 14.6). Zand believes that trust is the key to establishing productive interpersonal relationships.[65]

Primary responsibility for creating a climate of trust falls on the manager. Team members usually look to the manager, who enjoys hierarchical advantage and greater access to key information, to set the tone for interpersonal dealings. Threatening or intimidating actions by the manager will probably encourage the group to bind together in cohesive resistance. Therefore, trust needs to be developed right from the beginning, when team members are still receptive to positive managerial influence.

Trust is initially encouraged by a manager's openness and honesty. Trusting managers talk *with* their people rather than *at* them. A trusting manager, according to Zand's model, demonstrates a willingness to be influenced by others and to change if the facts show that a change is appropriate. Mutual trust between a manager and team members encourages *self-control*, as opposed to control through direct supervision. Hewlett-Packard, for example, has carefully nurtured an organizational culture based on trust.

> *The faith that HP has in its people is conspicuously in evidence in the corporate "open lab stock" policy. . . . The lab stock area is where the electrical and mechanical components are kept. The open lab stock policy means that not only do the engineers have free access to this equipment, but they are actually encouraged to* take it home for their personal use![66]

HP's rationale for this trusting policy is that the company will reap innovative returns no matter how the engineers choose to work with the valuable lab equipment.

Paradoxically, managerial control actually expands when committed group or team members enjoy greater freedom in pursuing consensual goals. Those who trust each other generally avoid taking advantage of others' weaknesses or shortcomings.[67]

Six Ways to Build Trust.   Trust is a fragile thing. As most of us know from personal experience, trust grows at a painfully slow pace, yet can be destroyed in an

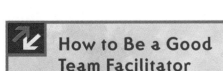

How to Be a Good Team Facilitator   `14H`

The ability to facilitate comprises a collection of skills. Expert facilitators do the following tasks:

- manage meetings
- help teams agree on clear goals, roles, and procedures
- ensure that all team members contribute
- discourage disruptive behaviors
- manage conflict
- guide teams' decision-making processes
- communicate clearly with all team members
- observe and accurately interpret group dynamics.

Source: Greg Burns, "The Secrets of Team Facilitation," *Training & Development,* 49 (June 1995): 46.

Questions: *Is it better today to use the term* team facilitator *rather than* team manager *or* team leader? *Why or why not? Which of the above team facilitation skills are the most important to team success? Explain. Which of your team facilitation skills need development? How?*

Figure 14.6

Trust and Effective Group Interaction

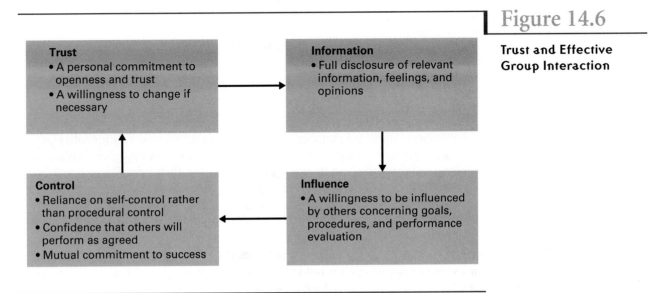

Trust
- A personal commitment to openness and trust
- A willingness to change if necessary

Information
- Full disclosure of relevant information, feelings, and opinions

Control
- Reliance on self-control rather than procedural control
- Confidence that others will perform as agreed
- Mutual commitment to success

Influence
- A willingness to be influenced by others concerning goals, procedures, and performance evaluation

Source: Reprinted from "Trust and Managerial Problem Solving," by Dale E. Zand and published in *Administrative Science Quarterly*, 17, no. 2 (June 1972) by permission of *Administrative Science Quarterly*. © 1972 by Cornell University.

instant with a thoughtless remark. Mistrust can erode the long-term effectiveness of work teams and organizations. According to management professor and consultant Fernando Bartolomé, managers need to concentrate on six areas: communication, support, respect, fairness, predictability, and competence.

- *Communication:* Keep your people informed by providing accurate and timely feedback and explaining policies and decisions. Be open and honest about your own problems. Do not hoard information or use it as a political device or reward.
- *Support:* Be an approachable person who is available to help, encourage, and coach your people. Show an active interest in their lives and be willing to come to their defense.
- *Respect:* Delegating important duties is the sincerest form of respect, followed closely by being a good listener.
- *Fairness:* Evaluate your people fairly and objectively and be liberal in giving credit and praise.
- *Predictability:* Be dependable and consistent in your behavior and keep all your promises.
- *Competence:* Be a good role model by exercising good business judgment and being technically and professionally competent.[68]

Managers find that trust begets trust. In other words, those who feel they are trusted tend to trust others in return.[69]

14I   Trust Me!

Survey of 500 professionals who had quit their jobs:

Nearly 95 percent of the respondents said the primary factor for deciding to leave was whether or not they were able to develop a trusting relationship with their manager.

Survey of 215 executives:

Trust builders: Maintain integrity (58 percent)
Openly communicate vision and values (51 percent)
Show respect for fellow employees as equal partners (47 percent)

Trust busters: Act inconsistently in what they say and do (69 percent)
Seek personal gain above shared gain (41 percent)
Withhold information (34 percent)

Sources: "Good Relationship with Boss a Key to Retention," *HRMagazine*, 44 (October 1999): 28; and Jenny C. McCune, "That Elusive Thing Called Trust," *Management Review*, 87 (July–August 1998): 13.

Questions: *How important is a trusting relationship with your boss? Explain. What makes you trust (or distrust) your manager? Your coworkers? Your family and friends?*

Summary

1. Managers need a working understanding of group dynamics because groups are the basic building blocks of organizations. Both informal (friendship) and formal (work) groups are made up of two or more freely interacting individuals who have a common identity and purpose.

2. After someone has been attracted to a group, cohesiveness—a "we" feeling— encourages continued membership. Roles are social expectations for behavior in a specific position, whereas norms are more general standards for conduct in a given social setting. Norms are enforced because they help the group survive, clarify role expectations, protect self-images, and enhance the group's identity by emphasizing key values. Compliance with role expectations and norms is rewarded with social reinforcement; noncompliance is punished by criticism, ridicule, and ostracism.

3. Mature groups that are characterized by mutual acceptance, encouragement of minority opinion, and minimal emotional conflict are the product of a developmental process with identifiable stages. During the first three stages—orientation, conflict and challenge, and cohesion—power and authority problems are resolved. Groups are faced with the obstacle of uncertainty over interpersonal relations during the last three stages—delusion, disillusion, and acceptance. Committees have a widespread reputation for inefficiency and ineffectiveness because they tend to get stalled in an early stage of group development.

4. Organizational politics centers on the pursuit of self-interest. Research shows greater political activity to be associated with higher levels of management, larger organizations, staff and marketing personnel, and reorganizations. Political tactics such as posturing, empire building, making the boss look good, collecting and using social IOUs, creating power and loyalty cliques, and destructive competition need to be kept in check if the organization is to be effective.

5. Although a fairly high degree of conformity is necessary if organizations and society in general are to function properly, blind conformity is ultimately dehumanizing and destructive. Research shows that individuals have a strong tendency to bend to the will of the majority, even if the majority is clearly wrong. Cohesive decision-making groups can be victimized by groupthink when unanimity becomes more important than critical evaluation of alternative courses of action.

6. Teams are becoming the structural format of choice. Today's employees generally have better technical skills than team skills. Cross-functional teams are particularly promising because they enable greater strategic speed. Although members of virtual teams by definition collaborate via electronic media, there is still a need for periodic face-to-face interaction and team building. Three sets of factors—relating to people, organization, and task—combine to determine the effectiveness of a work team.

7. Trust, a key ingredient of effective teamwork, is disturbingly low in the American workplace today. When work group members trust one another, there will be a more active exchange of information, more interpersonal influence, and hence greater self-control. Managers can build trust through communication, support, respect (primarily in the form of delegation), fairness, predictability, and competence.

Terms to Understand

How to Use *Cooperative Conflict* to Avoid Groupthink

Skills & Tools

Guides for Action

- Elaborate positions and ideas.
- List facts, information, and theories.
- Ask for clarification.
- Clarify opposing ideas.
- Search for new information.
- Challenge opposing ideas and positions.
- Reaffirm your confidence in those who differ.
- Listen to all ideas.
- Restate opposing arguments that are unclear.
- Identify strengths in opposing arguments.
- Change your mind only when confronted with good evidence.
- Integrate various information and reasoning.
- Create alternative solutions.
- Agree to a solution responsive to several points of view.
- Use a new round of cooperative conflict to develop and refine the solution.

Pitfalls to Avoid

- Assume your position is superior.
- Prove your ideas are right and must be accepted.
- Interpret opposition to your ideas as a personal attack.
- Refuse to admit weaknesses in your position.
- Pretend to listen.
- Ridicule to weaken the others' resolve to disagree.
- Try to win over people to your position through charm and exaggeration.
- See accepting another's ideas as a sign of weakness.

Source: Reprinted from *Learning to Manage Conflict: Getting People to Work Together Productively* by Dean Tjosvold. Copyright © 1993 Dean Tjosvold. First published by Lexington Books. All rights reserved. All correspondence should be sent to Lexington Books, 4720 Boston Way, Lanham, Md., 20706.

Internet Exercises

1. **What's new with teams and teamwork?** Things are changing rapidly in this area because teams have become such an important part of organizational life. Lots of new ideas can be found on the Internet for those willing to search a bit. Here is a way to jump-start your Web search for updates on teams and teamwork. Go to *Fast Company* magazine's excellent Web site (**www.fastcompany.com**) and click on the main menu heading "Core Themes." At the themes and ideas page, select the category "Teamwork." Read at least two of the full-text articles, with the goal of picking up at least three good ideas about managing workplace teams. You may have to select and read additional articles if you don't find enough good ideas right away. *Note:* You may want to make hard copies of the articles you selected and notes of your good ideas for possible class discussion.

   Learning Points: 1. Why did you select those particular articles? 2. Among your "good ideas" about managing teams, which idea stands out as the best? Why? 3. Did other class members tend to focus on the same (or different) articles and ideas as you? 4. When comparing notes with your classmates, which of their "good ideas" are superior to the ones on your list?

2. **Getting "street smart" about organizational politics:** Ethical managers today play clean in the game of business but are street smart enough to avoid getting hurt by those who fight dirty. For good background reading, go back to *Fast Company* magazine's home page and click on the main menu heading "Archives." Select the heading "The Archives" and scroll down to the April–May 1998 issue (no. 14). From the table of contents for that issue, select and read the articles titled "The Bad Guy's (and Gal's) Guide to Office Politics" and "The Good Guy's (and Gal's) Guide to Office Politics." While you're in *Fast Company*'s online archives, you may want to search recent issues for articles relating to organizational and office politics.

   Learning Points: 1. Why is it fair to say organizational politics can be both good and bad? 2. What new ideas or useful tips did you learn about workplace politics? 3. Is political maneuvering an inescapable part of life on the job? Explain. 4. Is organizational politics a fun (or distasteful) aspect of organizational life for you? Explain. 5. Why is it important to know about political tactics in the workplace even if you don't enjoy engaging in them?

3. **Check it out:** The Briefings Publishing Group Web site (**www.briefings.com**) has a section titled "Team Management" containing a regularly updated collection of practical ideas about the exciting area of workplace teams. Be sure to explore the site's other management topics as well.

   For updates to these exercises, visit our Web site (**www.hmco.com/college**).

| Closing Case | # Thirteen Time Zones Can't Keep Lucent's Virtual Team from Succeeding |

Imagine designing the most complex product in your company's history. You need 500 engineers for the job. They will assemble the world's most delicate hardware and write more than a million lines of code. In communicating, the margin for error is minuscule.

Now, scatter those 500 engineers over 13 time zones. Over three continents. Over five states in the United States alone. The Germans schedule to perfection. The Americans work on the fly. In Massachusetts, they go to work early. In New Jersey, they stay late.

Now you have some idea of what Bill Klinger and Frank Polito have been through in the past 18 months. As

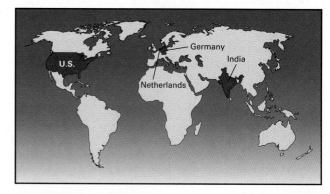

top software-development managers in Lucent Technologies' Bell Labs division, they played critical roles in creating a new fiber-optic phone switch called the Bandwidth Manager, which sells for about $1 million, the kind of global product behind the company's surging earnings. The high-stakes development was Lucent's most complex undertaking by far since its spin-off from AT&T in 1996.

Managing such a far-flung staff ("distributed development," it's called) is possible only because of technology. But as the two Lucent leaders painfully learned, distance still magnifies differences, even in a high-tech age. "You lose informal interaction—going to lunch, the water cooler," Mr. Klinger says. "You can never discount how many issues get solved that way."

The product grew as a hybrid of exotic, widely dispersed technologies: "lightwave" science from Lucent's Merrimack Valley plant, north of Boston, where Mr. Polito works; "cross-connect" products here in New Jersey, where Mr. Klinger works; timing devices from the Netherlands; and optics from Germany.

Development also demanded multiple locations because Lucent wanted a core model as a platform for special versions for foreign and other niche markets. Involving overseas engineers in the flagship product would speed the later development of spin-offs and impress foreign customers.

And rushing to market meant tapping software talent wherever it was available—ultimately at Lucent facilities in Colorado, Illinois, North Carolina, and India. "The scary thing, scary but exciting, was that no one had really pulled this off on this scale before," says Mr. Polito.

Communication technology was the easy part. Lashing together big computers in different cities assured everyone was working on the same up-to-date software version. New project data from one city were instantly available on Web pages everywhere else. Test engineers in India could tweak prototypes in New Jersey. The project never went to sleep.

Technology, however, couldn't conquer cultural problems, especially acute between Messrs. Klinger's and Polito's respective staffs in New Jersey and Massachusetts. Each had its own programming traditions and product histories. Such basic words as "test" could mean different things. A programming chore requiring days in one context might take weeks in another. Differing work schedules and physical distance made each location suspect the other of slacking off. "We had such clashes," says Mr. Klinger.

Personality tests revealed deep geographic differences. Supervisors from the sleek, glass-covered New Jersey office,

principally a research facility abounding in academics, scored as "thinking" people who used cause-and-effect analysis. Those from the old, brick facility in Massachusetts, mainly a manufacturing plant, scored as "feeling" types who based decisions on subjective, human values. Sheer awareness of the differences ("Now I know why you get on my nerves!") began to create common ground.

Amid much cynicism, the two directors hauled their technical managers into team exercises—working in small groups to scale a 14-foot wall and solve puzzles. It's corny, but such methods can accelerate trust building when time is short and the stakes are high. At one point Mr. Klinger asked managers to show up with the product manuals from their previous projects—then, in a ritualistic break from technical parochialism, instructed everyone to tear the covers to pieces.

More than anything else, it was sheer physical presence—face time—that began solidifying the group. Dozens of managers began meeting fortnightly in rotating cities, socializing as much time as their technical discussions permitted. (How better to grow familiar than over hot dogs, beer, and nine innings with the minor league Durham Bulls?) Foreign locations found the direct interaction especially valuable. "Going into the other culture is the only way to understand it," says Sigrid Hauenstein, a Lucent executive in Nuremberg, Germany. "If you don't have a common understanding, it's much more expensive to correct it later."

Eventually the project found its pace. People began wearing beepers to eliminate time wasted on voice-mail tag. Conference calls at varying levels kept everyone in the loop. Staffers posted their photos in the project's Web directory. Many created personal pages. "It's the ultimate democracy of the Web," Mr. Klinger says.

The product is now shipping—on schedule, within budget, and with more technical versatility than Lucent expected. Distributed development "paid off in spades," says Gerry Butters, Lucent optical-networking chief.

Even as it helps build the infrastructure of a digitally connected planet, Lucent is rediscovering the importance of face-to-face interaction. All the bandwidth in the world can convey only a fraction of what we are.

FOR DISCUSSION

1. Which team effectiveness criteria in Figure 14.5 are apparent in this case?

2. How big a problem do you suppose organizational politics was during this project? Explain.

3. What practical lessons does this case teach managers about managing a virtual team?

4. Would you be comfortable working on this sort of global virtual team? Explain.

Source: Republished with permission of *The Wall Street Journal* from "With the Stakes High, a Lucent Duo Conquers Distance and Culture," by Thomas Petzinger Jr., *The Wall Street Journal* (April 23, 1999). Permission conveyed through Copyright Clearance Center, Inc.

INFLUENCE PROCESSES
and LEADERSHIP

CHAPTER OBJECTIVES

When you finish studying this chapter, you should be able to

1 Identify and describe eight generic influence tactics used in modern organizations.

2 Identify the five bases of power and explain what it takes to make empowerment work.

3 Summarize what the Ohio State model and the Leadership Grid® have taught managers about leadership.

4 Describe the path-goal theory of leadership and explain how the assumption on which it is based differs from the assumption on which Fiedler's contingency theory is based.

5 Explain how the Vroom/Yetton/Jago and transformational leadership theories can help managers deal with decision making and change, respectively.

6 Explain Greenleaf's philosophy of the servant leader.

7 Identify the two key functions that mentors perform and explain how a mentor can develop a junior manager's leadership skills.

8 Explain the management of antecedents and consequences in behavior modification.

> "PEOPLE ARE HUNGRY FOR LEADERSHIP. THEY'LL GRAVITATE TOWARD LEADERS WHO HAVE A VISION. WHEN PEOPLE SEE THAT YOU LOVE YOUR WORK, THEY WANT TO CATCH YOUR ENERGY."
> lorraine monroe

Canada's Cynthia Trudell Steers Saturn into the Twenty-First Century

Cynthia Trudell, Saturn's new president and one of the few women with influence in the auto industry, enjoys a challenge.

As a child growing up in Moncton, New Brunswick, her objective was to earn enough pins and badges to land the Girl Guides' gold cord—the equivalent of Eagle Scout for boys.

Later, it was blasting through chemical engineering studies in three years at respected Acadia University and landing a sought-after Canadian Research Council scholarship and a place in the University of Windsor's Ph.D. program.

Most recently, Trudell stepped in to make sure a new diesel engine was ready on time for the latest version of the Frontera sport utility, which General Motors sells across Europe.

Next up: jump-starting GM's Saturn, whose cute, quirky image has been overshadowed in recent years by slower sales and labor unhappiness.

It will be a tough task, but Trudell is undaunted.

"I've always been the kind of person who asks, 'Why do things have to be this way?' And I can be tenacious," says Trudell, tall and lean with short blond hair.

That determination "gains her respect very quickly," says Nick Reilly, Trudell's boss at IBC Vehicles, the British GM subsidiary where she was president before her Saturn appointment last month.

It's been the case in just a few weeks in Spring Hill, Tennessee, where Trudell's first stop was Saturn's sprawling factory floor on December 14, the day her appointment was announced.

GM manufacturing chief Donald Hackworth accompanied her on a plant tour that saw Trudell strolling along the assembly line to chat with workers.

"She's definitely a people person," says Hackworth, who first noticed Trudell during her early manufacturing jobs that included a stint as GM plant manager in Wilmington, Del.

Says Saturn union leader Mike Bennett: "I think she's going to be good for Saturn."

An Outgoing Child

Trudell's personality took root during her childhood in New Brunswick, the picturesque but remote maritime province north of Maine.

Her mother, Jean Owens, recalls an extroverted child who liked to sing, dance, and play piano, got good grades, and occasionally misbehaved.

"She wasn't perfect, mind you," says Owens, a retired physiotherapist. But she was persuasive: Trudell loved Girl Guides so much that she persuaded her mother to be a leader.

Trudell says that through Girl Guides and her schoolwork, she became fascinated by "why things work the way they work."

Science became a passion, leading to her original field of photochemistry, which explores how gases affect objects. That led to the study of automotive emissions, and ultimately, a job in 1979 as a Ford Motor chemical process engineer at its operations in Windsor. Two years later, GM named her a supervisor at its Windsor plant, launching a career that took her from Canada to Detroit and into GM's factories.

Trudell sees manufacturing as "not just a matter of equipment. It's a holistic system," combining man with machine, that "takes an understanding not only technically but of people."

That attitude came in handy during her stint in Wilmington, where Trudell helped transform an inefficient plant that GM wanted to close into a factory that now builds Chevrolet Malibu and soon will produce Saturn LS.

Her philosophy served her even better at IBC, initially a joint venture between GM and Japanese automaker Isuzu that soon will begin producing vans for French automaker Renault.

In the course of a day, Trudell routinely dealt with executives from the three different companies, representatives of English labor unions, customers from 17 European countries, and suppliers from around the world. Says Trudell: "One of the assets I bring to Saturn is my experience with different kinds of relationships."

Key Time for Saturn

Trudell, who considers Saturn founder Skip LeFauve a mentor, has wanted to work there for years. She arrives with the division at a crossroads.

Famous throughout the 1990s for its dealers' customer-friendly service, quality small cars, and partnership with the United Auto Workers, Saturn hit troubled times recently. Sales dropped 10 percent the past two years, slicing workers' bonuses and prompting a first-ever strike vote.

But GM, which starved Saturn of products until it could pay back some of its initial $3 billion investment, now plans to beef up the lineup with the bigger LS and a sport-utility vehicle.

"Saturn, to go forward, needs to grow," Trudell says.

And GM wants that to happen more efficiently. Spring Hill, which built about 280,000 cars last year, is set to produce 500,000 a year by early next decade, using modular assembly with pre-assembled components.

Meanwhile, Wilmington is expected to be declared a Saturn plant, putting it under Trudell's purview, but with workers still covered by the national UAW contract, which is more restrictive than Saturn's teamwork-focused labor pact.

None of this is likely to go smoothly, but that's what challenge-seeking Trudell says makes Saturn appealing.

"It has always appeared to me that embracing change and innovation are natural to (Saturn). If there was ever an organization that was poised for the twenty-first century, from raw material to sales to the customer, this is it," she says.

Source: Micheline Maynard, "She's Jump-Starting Saturn," *USA Today,* (March 9, 1999): 3B. Copyright 1999, USA Today. Reprinted with permission.

What do the following situations have in common?

- An employee praises her supervisor's new outfit immediately before asking for the afternoon off.
- A milling-machine operator tells a friend that he will return the favor if his friend will watch out for the supervisor while he takes an unauthorized cigarette break.
- An office manager attempts to head off opposition to a new e-mail policy by carefully explaining how it will make everyone's job easier.

Aside from the fact that all of these situations take place on the job, the common denominator is "influence." In each case, someone is trying to get his or her own way by influencing someone else's behavior. Cynthia Trudell's professional life at Saturn is all about influence, power, and leadership because she faces a job too big to do alone. She spends her days influencing employees and suppliers to do their best and, through marketing and advertising, influencing the public to buy Saturn automobiles. Her efforts to influence also focus on getting parent company General Motors to boost its investment in Saturn.

influence *any attempt to change another's behavior*

Influence is any attempt by a person to change the behavior of superiors, peers, or subordinates. Influence is not inherently good or bad. As the foregoing situations illustrate, influence can be used for purely selfish reasons, to subvert organizational objectives, or to enhance organizational effectiveness. Managerial success is firmly linked to the ability to exercise the right sort of influence at the right time.[1]

The purpose of this chapter is to examine different approaches to influencing others. We focus specifically on influence tactics, power, leadership, mentoring, and behavior modification.

Influence Tactics in the Workplace

Identify and describe eight generic influence tactics used in modern organizations.

A replication and refinement of an earlier groundbreaking study provides useful insights about on-the-job influence.[2] Both studies asked employees basically the same question: "How do you get your boss, coworker, or subordinate to do something you want?" The following eight generic influence tactics emerged:

1. *Consultation.* Seeking someone's participation in a decision or change.
2. *Rational persuasion.* Trying to convince someone by relying on a detailed plan, supporting information, reasoning, or logic.
3. *Inspirational appeals.* Appealing to someone's emotions, values, or ideals to generate enthusiasm and confidence.
4. *Ingratiating tactics.* Making someone feel important or good before making a request; acting humble or friendly before making a request.
5. *Coalition tactics.* Seeking the aid of others to persuade someone to agree.
6. *Pressure tactics.* Relying on intimidation, demands, or threats to gain compliance or support.
7. *Upward appeals.* Obtaining formal or informal support of higher management.
8. *Exchange tactics.* Offering an exchange of favors; reminding someone of a past favor; offering to make a personal sacrifice.[3]

15A

Back to the Opening Case

Which influence tactics will Trudell likely rely on most heavily at Saturn? What are the advantages and disadvantages of these particular tactics?

For further information about the interactive annotations in this chapter, visit our Web site (www.hmco.com/college).

These influence tactics are *generic* because they are used by various organizational members to influence lower-level employees (downward influence), peers (lateral influence), or superiors (upward influence). Table 15.1 indicates what the researchers found out about patterns of use for the three different directions of influence. Notice how consultation, rational persuasion, and inspirational appeals were the three most popular tactics, regardless of the direction of influence. Meanwhile, pressure tactics, upward appeals, and exchange tactics consistently were the least used influence tactics. Ingratiating and coalition tactics fell in the midrange of use. This is an encouraging pattern from the standpoint of getting things done through problem solving rather than through intimidation and conflict.

Table 15.1

Use of Generic Organizational Influence Tactics

	Rank order (by direction of influence)		
Tactic	**Downward**	**Lateral**	**Upward**
Consultation	1	1	2
Rational persuasion	2	2	1
Inspirational appeals	3	3	3
Ingratiating tactics	4	4	5
Coalition tactics	5	5	4
Pressure tactics	6	7	7
Upward appeals	7	6	6
Exchange tactics	8	8	8

Source: Adapted from discussion in Gary Yukl and Cecilia M. Falbe, "Influence Tactics and Objectives in Upward, Downward, and Lateral Influence Attempts," *Journal of Applied Psychology,* 75 (April 1990): 132–140.

Management has been called a team sport. No one knows this better than Earvin "Magic" Johnson (pictured center). As a dazzling player in the National Basketball Association for 13 years and a victim of HIV, Magic Johnson knows that tough challenges require a great team effort. His team these days runs a $25-million-a-year business called Johnson Development Corp. He uses a finely polished set of influence skills in his role as "urban entrepreneur" to guide the Los Angeles company in a wide variety of ventures including movies, music, and retailing. In business, as in sport, Magic Johnson always plays to win.

Do women and men tend to rely on different influence tactics? Available research evidence reveals no systematic gender-based differences relative to influencing others.[4] In contrast, influence tactics used by employees to influence their bosses were found to vary with different leadership styles. Employees influencing authoritarian managers tended to rely on ingratiating tactics and upward appeals. Rational persuasion was used most often to influence participative managers.[5]

Power

Power is inevitable in modern organizations. According to one advocate of the positive and constructive use of power:

> *Power must be used because managers must influence those they depend on. Power also is crucial in the development of managers' self-confidence and willingness to support subordinates. From this perspective, power should be accepted as a natural part of any organization. Managers should recognize and develop their own power to coordinate and support the work of subordinates; it is powerlessness, not power, that undermines organizational effectiveness.*[6]

As a manager, if you understand power, its bases, and empowerment, you will have an advantage when it comes to getting things accomplished with and through others.[7]

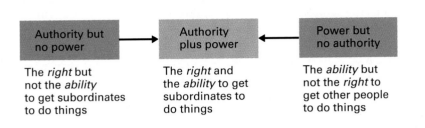

Figure 15.1

The Relationship Between Authority and Power

The relationship diagram shows:

Authority but no power	→	Authority plus power	←	Power but no authority
The *right* but not the *ability* to get subordinates to do things		The *right* and the *ability* to get subordinates to do things		The *ability* but not the *right* to get other people to do things

What Is Power?

Power is "the ability to marshal the human, informational, and material resources to get something done."[8] Power affects organizational members in the following three areas:

1. *Decisions.* A packaging engineer decides to take on a difficult new assignment after hearing her boss's recommendations.
2. *Behavior.* A hospital lab technician achieves a month of perfect attendance after receiving a written warning about absenteeism from his supervisor.
3. *Situations.* The productivity of a product design group increases dramatically following the purchase of computerized workstations.[9]

Another instructive way of looking at power is to distinguish between "power over" (ability to dominate), "power to" (ability to act freely), and "power from" (ability to resist the demands of others).[10]

By emphasizing the word *ability* in our definition and discussion of power, we can contrast power with authority. As defined in Chapter 9, authority is the "right" to direct the activities of others.[11] Authority is an officially sanctioned privilege that may or may not get results. In contrast, power is the demonstrated *ability* to get results. As illustrated in Figure 15.1, one may possess authority but have no power, possess no authority yet have power, or possess both authority and power. The first situation, authority but no power, was experienced by Albanian police in 1997, when Europe's poorest nation fell into anarchy over dissatisfaction with a corrupt government. According to *Newsweek,* "An angry mob surrounded one group of police, stripped them to their underpants, and burned their gear."[12] At the other end of the model in Figure 15.1, power but no authority can occur. For example, employees may respond to the wishes of the supervisor's spouse.[13] Finally, a manager who gets employees to work hard on an important project has both authority and power.

The Five Bases of Power

Essential to the successful use of power in organizations is an understanding of the various bases of power. One widely cited classification of power bases identifies five types of power: reward, coercive, legitimate, referent, and expert.[14]

Reward Power.   One's ability to grant rewards to those who comply with a command or request is the key to **reward power.** Management's reward power can be strengthened by linking pay raises, merit pay, and promotions to job performance. Sought-after expressions of friendship or trust also enhance reward power.

---

2 **Identify the five bases of power and explain what it takes to make empowerment work.**

power *ability to marshal resources to get something done*

reward power *gaining compliance through rewards*

15B

Authority to Do What?

The secret of today's most successful power players: They are candid about what their formal authority is, bring it out into the open, and give it away.

Source: Thomas A. Stewart, "Get with the *New* Power Game," *Fortune* (January 13, 1997): 60.

Questions: *How does this perspective differ from traditional beliefs about managerial power? Why wouldn't a manager who adopted this approach to power be considered weak and ineffective?*

coercive power *gaining compliance through threats or punishment*

Coercive Power.

Rooted in fear, **coercive power** is based on threatened or actual punishment. For example, a manager might threaten a habitually tardy employee with a demotion if he or she is late one more time.

legitimate power *compliance based on one's formal position*

Legitimate Power.

Legitimate power is achieved when a person's superior position alone prompts another person to act in a desired manner. This type of power closely parallels formal authority, as discussed above. Parents, teachers, religious leaders, and managers who demand obedience by virtue of their superior social position are attempting to exercise legitimate power. Note, however, the following warning about legitimate power:

> *Trying to control others solely by directing them and on the basis of the power associated with one's position simply will not work—first, because managers are always dependent on some people over whom they have no formal authority, and second, because virtually no one in modern organizations will passively accept and completely obey a constant stream of orders from someone just because he or she is the "boss."*[15]

One might reasonably conclude that legitimate power has been eroded by its frequent abuse (or overuse) through the years.[16]

referent power *compliance based on charisma or personal identification*

Referent Power.

An individual has **referent power** over those who identify with him or her if they comply on that basis alone. Personal attraction is an elusive thing to define, let alone consciously cultivate. *Charisma* is a term often used in conjunction with referent power. Although leaders with the personal magnetism of Abraham Lincoln, John Kennedy, or Martin Luther King Jr., are always in short supply, charisma in the workplace can be problematic. *Fortune* magazine recently offered this perspective:

expert power *compliance based on ability to dispense valued information*

> *Used wisely, it's a blessing. Indulged, it can be a curse. Charismatic visionaries lead people ahead—and sometimes astray. They can be impetuous, unpredictable, and exasperating to work for, like [media mogul Ted] Turner. [Donald] Trump. Steve Jobs. Ross Perot. Lee Iacocca. "Often what begins as a mission becomes an obsession," says John Thompson, president of Human Factors, a leadership consulting service in San Rafael, California. "Leaders can cut corners on values and become driven by self-interest. Then they may abuse anyone who makes a mistake."*
>
> *Like pornography, charisma is hard to define. But you know it when you see it. And you don't see much of it in the* Fortune 500.[17]

Empowerment in Action   15C

Ron Ferner, former Campbell's Soup Co. vice president:

One time a packaging team in Sacramento was having problems with boxes breaking. Some of us managers started talking to them about what the problems were and realized they really had a good handle on what was wrong. So we said, "Why don't you guys call the supplier?" Then we called the supplier to tell them they would be hearing from our crew, and they said, "Why not have them talk directly to our hourly employees?"

If the managers alone had tried to solve this problem, it would have gone on forever. Instead, we rented a van, sent our people over, and solved the whole thing. Afterward, we had a party. It gave the workers great confidence.

Source: As quoted in Thea Singer, "Share It All with Employees, Soup to Nuts," *Inc.* Tech, no. 1 (1999): 48.

Questions: *Why do many managers who say they believe in empowering employees fail to do it? Can empowerment be carried too far? Explain.*

Still, as we will see in our discussion of transformational leadership later in this chapter, charisma does have its positive side.

Expert Power.

Those who possess and can dispense valued information generally exercise **expert power** over those in need of such information. Information technology experts, for instance, are in a position today to wield a great deal of expert power. Anyone who has ever been taken advantage of by an unscrupulous automobile mechanic knows what expert power in the wrong hands can mean.[18]

Managing Diversity

For These Successful Women, Empowerment Began at Home

The Ivy League degree, the Harvard MBA, and the fast-track management-training program are all useful accoutrements. But what does a powerful woman need most? A larger-than-life mother. When we asked the women in our Power 50 to describe their childhoods, we heard a lot about kind, supportive fathers. But the women talked much more about unusual, influential mothers who became their role models and biggest fans.

Some of these older women were highly creative, like Carly Fiorina's mother, Madelon Sneed. She was an artist who "had an unbelievable zest for life," says Fiorina. "She taught me the power of keeping a positive attitude." Her mother began her career painting oil portraits and later moved to abstract work, using bold strokes and vibrant colors. Three years ago, when Fiorina was directing the Lucent Technologies spinoff at AT&T, she chose the Lucent logo—the bright-red ring of hand-drawn brush strokes—partly because it reminded her of her mother's paintings. Sneed died . . . [in 1998] at 77. She saw her daughter make the cover of *Fortune* . . . as the most powerful woman in business, but didn't live to see her become CEO of Hewlett-Packard.

Other mothers of Power 50 women are pioneers. Avon . . . [CEO] Andrea Jung's mother immigrated to the United States from Shanghai to study and then went on to a successful career as a chemical engineer. Jung, who has a younger brother, says her parents (her dad is an architect) urged both of their children to have careers. "They told me I could do everything my brother could," says Jung.

Meg Whitman's mother used to pile her children—Meg and her older sister and brother—into a Ford Econoline van and drive coast to coast or up the Alaskan highway during summer vacations. "We camped for three months. No hotels," says the CEO of eBay. In 1973, when Whitman was in high school, her mother traveled to China with actress Shirley MacLaine. Margaret Whitman was the Boston housewife in a delegation of "ordinary" American women whom MacLaine featured in a documentary, *The Other Half of the Sky: A China Memoir.* "Before the China trip, my mother told my sister to get a teaching degree—in case her husband couldn't support her," Whitman says. "When she came back from China, her perspective on women had changed completely. She told me, 'Go figure out what you want to do, and do it.'"

These mothers tended to be bold and unafraid to stand out. Pattie Dunn's mom, a former Las Vegas showgirl, "is a redhead in every way—mercurial, feisty, extremely funny, wacky," says the chairman of Barclays Global Investors. Her mother imposed no specific expectations on Pattie, except that she go to college, which neither Dunn's mother nor her late father, a vaudevillian, had done. Pattie graduated from Berkeley.

When Debby Hopkins was a girl growing up outside Detroit, her mother wrote the weekly social column for the Birmingham-Bloomfield *Eccentric* newspaper. Tagging along as photographer, Debby schmoozed at an early age with Henry Ford II and Lee Iacocca. "My mother loves to party, loves people," says the gregarious CFO [Chief Financial Officer] of Boeing*. As children, "we never had a box drawn around us like most kids do. We had no restrictions, not even curfews." Today, in her office, Hopkins displays a photo of her mother riding an alligator. "Whenever I feel like I'm up to my ass in alligators, I look at that picture and think, Just go for it," Hopkins says.

*Now with Lucent Technologies.

Source: Excerpted from Patricia Sellers, "Behind Every Successful Woman There Is . . . a Woman," *Fortune* (October 25, 1999): 129–130. © Time Inc. Reprinted by permission.

Empowerment

Empowerment occurs when employees are adequately trained, provided with all relevant information and the best possible tools, fully involved in key decisions, and fairly rewarded for results.[19] Those who endorse this key building block of progressive management view power as an unlimited resource. Frances Hesselbein, a widely respected former head of the Girl Scouts of the USA, offered this perspective: "The more power you give away, the more you have."[20] This can be a difficult concept to grasp for traditional authoritarian managers who see empowerment as a threat to their authority and feeling of being in control. Today, the issue is not empowerment versus

empowerment *making employees* full *partners in the decision-making process and giving them the necessary tools and rewards*

As the co-founders of a fast-growing company with 175 employees, Ron and Paula Lawlor (second and third from left) wield power skillfully. Their company, Medi-Health, headquartered in King of Prussia, Pennsylvania, handles the record-keeping for hospitals and health-care companies on a contract basis. The Lawlors' answer to meeting the demands of fast growth is *empowerment*. Division heads are set free to run their own operations, including drawing up their own budgets. Paula's dynamo personality also is a power booster as she challenges everyone to remove the word "no" from their vocabularies.

no empowerment. Rather, the issue is how empowerment should take place. As indicated in Skills & Tools at the end of this chapter, employee empowerment is like a seed requiring favorable growing conditions (see Managing Diversity). Notice how much of the burden for successful empowerment falls on the *individual*. No amount of empowerment and supportive management can overcome dishonesty, untrustworthiness, selfishness, and inadequate skills.[21] Once again, rigorous employee selection and training and ethics training, as discussed in Chapters 5 and 11, come to the forefront.

Leadership

Leadership has fascinated people since the dawn of recorded history. References to both good and bad leadership in the literature of every age give testimony to the search for good leaders that has been a common thread running through human civilization.[22] In view of research evidence that effective leadership is associated with both better performance and more ethical performance, the search for ways to identify (or develop) good leaders needs to continue.[23]

Leadership Defined

leadership *social influence process of inspiring and guiding others in a common effort*

Research on leadership has produced many definitions of the term. Much of the variation is semantic; the definition offered here is a workable compromise. **Leadership** is the process of inspiring, influencing, and guiding others to participate in a common effort.[24] To encourage participation, leaders supplement any authority and power they possess with their personal attributes, visions, and social skills. As a wit once observed, a good leader is someone who can tell you to go to hell and make you look forward to the trip!

Formal Versus Informal Leaders

Experts on leadership distinguish between formal and informal leadership. **Formal leadership** is the process of influencing relevant others to pursue official organizational objectives. **Informal leadership,** in contrast, is the process of influencing others to pursue unofficial objectives that may or may not serve the organization's interests. Formal leaders generally have a measure of legitimate power because of their formal authority, whereas informal leaders typically lack formal authority. Beyond that, both types rely on expedient combinations of reward, coercive, referent, and expert power. Informal leaders who identify with the job to be done are a valuable asset to an organization. Conversely, an organization can be brought to its knees by informal leaders who turn cohesive work groups against the organization.

Like the study of management, the study of leadership has evolved as theories were developed and refined by successive generations of researchers.[25] Something useful has been learned at each stage of development. We now turn to significant milestones in the evolution of leadership theory by examining the trait, behavioral styles, situational, and transformational approaches (see Figure 15.2).

formal leadership *the process of influencing others to pursue official objectives*

informal leadership *the process of influencing others to pursue unofficial objectives*

Trait Theory

During most of recorded history the prevailing assumption was that leaders are born and not made. Leaders such as Alexander the Great, Napoleon Bonaparte, and George Washington were said to have been blessed with an inborn ability to lead. This so-called great-man approach to leadership[26] eventually gave way to trait theory.

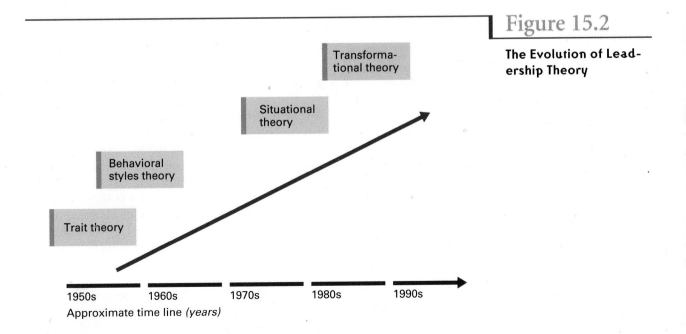

Figure 15.2

The Evolution of Leadership Theory

Sometimes the most difficult challenge for hard-working entrepreneurs is *success.* Just ask Pamela Barefoot (center), founder and president of Blue Crab Bay Co. As the Virginia specialty foods and gifts company she started in her home grew and prospered, she feared it had eclipsed her leadership abilities. That's when she began to polish her CAT leadership skills: Communication, Accountability, and Trust. With two dozen employees and a new 12,500-square-foot facility, Pamela Barefoot is able to lead her company to greater heights because she has grown along with the business.

According to one observer, "under the influence of the behavioristic school of psychological thought, the fact was accepted that leadership traits are not completely inborn but can also be acquired through learning and experience. Attention turned to the search for universal traits possessed by leaders."[27]

As the popularity of the trait approach mushroomed during the second quarter of the twentieth century, literally hundreds of physical, mental, and personality traits were said to be the key determinants of successful leadership. Unfortunately, few theorists agreed on the most important traits of a good leader. The predictive value of trait theory was severely limited because traits tend to be a chicken-and-egg proposition: Was George Washington a good leader because he had self-confidence, or did he have self-confidence because he was thrust into a leadership role at a young age? In spite of inherent problems, trait profiles provide a useful framework for examining what it takes to be a good leader.

An Early Trait Profile.   Not until 1948 was a comprehensive review of competing trait theories conducted. After comparing more than 100 studies of leader traits and characteristics, the reviewer uncovered moderate agreement on only five traits. In the reviewer's words, "the average person who occupies a position of leadership exceeds the average member of his group in the following respects: (1) intelligence, (2) scholarship, (3) dependability in exercising responsibilities, (4) activity and social participation, and (5) socioeconomic status."[28]

Renewed Interest in Leader Traits.   Interest in the trait approach to leadership has been stirred recently on two fronts. First, James M. Kouzes and Barry Z. Posner surveyed over 7,500 managers from across the

---

Envisioning the Leader of the Future   15D

The leader of the past ... is a doer; of the present, a planner; of the future, a teacher. Her job is to develop capabilities: not to plan the company's actions but to increase its capacity to act, its responsiveness, and its repertoire; to create intellectual capital rather than deploy other assets. This kind of leader doesn't need to know everything; on the contrary, she'll want to be surrounded by people who know a whole lot more but trust her to weigh their competing claims.

Source: Thomas A. Stewart, "Have You Got What It Takes?" *Fortune* (October 11, 1999): 322.

Questions: *Do you agree or disagree with this vision? Explain. Does exclusive use of a female perspective bother you in any way? Explain.*

United States during the 1980s to determine the traits they admired in superior leaders. *Honesty* was selected by 87 percent of the respondents, easily outdistancing *competent* (74 percent), *forward-looking* (67 percent), *inspiring* (61 percent), and *intelligent* (46 percent).[29] This sequence could be a positive sign from the standpoint of business ethics.

The Controversy of Female and Male Leadership Traits.   A second source of renewed interest in leadership traits is the ongoing debate about female versus male leadership traits. In an often-cited survey by Judy B. Rosener, female leaders were found to be better at sharing power and information than were their male counter-parts.[30] Critics have chided Rosener for reinforcing this traditional feminine stereo-type.[31] Actually, a comprehensive review of 162 different studies found *no significant difference* in leadership styles exhibited by women and men. In real-life organizational settings, women did *not* fit the feminine stereotype of being more relationship-oriented and men did *not* fit the masculine stereotype of being more task-oriented.[32] As always, it is bad practice to make prejudicial assumptions about individuals based on their membership in some demographic category.

Behavioral Styles Theory

During World War II, the study of leadership took on a significant new twist. Rather than concentrating on the personal traits of successful leaders, researchers working with the military began turning their attention to patterns of leader behavior (called leadership styles). In other words, attention turned from who the leader was to how the leader actually behaved. One early laboratory study of leader behavior demonstrated that followers overwhelmingly preferred managers who had a democratic style to those with an authoritarian style or a laissez-faire (hands-off) style.[33] An updated review of these three classic leadership styles can be found in Table 15.2.

For a number of years, theorists and managers hailed democratic leadership as the key to productive and happy employees. Eventually, however, their enthusiasm was dampened when critics pointed out that the original study relied on children as

Table 15.2   The Three Classic Styles of Leadership

	Authoritarian	Democratic	Laissez-faire
Nature	Leader retains all authority and responsibility	Leader delegates a great deal of authority while retaining ultimate responsibility	Leader grants responsibility and authority to group
	Leader assigns people to clearly defined tasks	Work is divided and assigned on the basis of participatory decision making	Group members are told to work things out themselves and do the best they can
	Primarily a downward flow of communication	Active two-way flow of upward and downward communication	Primarily horizontal communication among peers
Primary strength	Stresses prompt, orderly, and predictable performance	Enhances personal commitment through participation	Permits self-starters to do things as they see fit without leader interference
Primary weakness	Approach tends to stifle individual initiative	Democratic process is time-consuming	Group may drift aimlessly in the absence of direction from leader

Figure 15.3

Basic Leadership Styles from the Ohio State Study

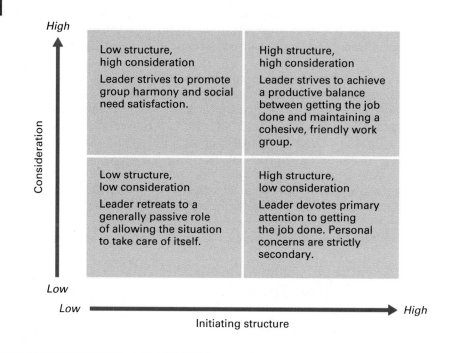

subjects and virtually ignored productivity. Although there is a general agreement that these basic styles exist, debate has been vigorous over their relative value and appropriateness. Practical experience has shown, for example, that the democratic style does not always stimulate better performance. Some employees prefer to be told what to do rather than to participate in decision making.[34]

3 Summarize what the Ohio State model and the Leadership Grid® have taught managers about leadership.

The Ohio State Model.   While the democratic style of leadership was receiving attention, a slightly different behavioral approach to leadership emerged. This second approach began in the late 1940s when a team of Ohio State University researchers defined two independent dimensions of leader behavior.[35] One dimension, called "initiating structure," was the leader's efforts to get things organized and get the job done. The second dimension, labeled "consideration," was the degree of trust, friendship, respect, and warmth that the leader extended to subordinates. By making a matrix out of these two independent dimensions of leader behavior, the Ohio State researchers identified four styles of leadership (see Figure 15.3).

This particular scheme proved to be fertile ground for leadership theorists, and variations of the original Ohio State approach soon appeared.[36] Leadership theorists began a search for the "one best style" of leadership. The high-structure, high-consideration style was generally hailed as the best all-around style. This "high-high" style has intuitive appeal because it embraces the best of both categories of leader behavior. But one researcher cautioned in 1966 that, although there seemed to be a positive relationship between consideration and subordinate satisfaction, a positive link between the high-high style and work group performance had not been proved conclusively.[37]

The Leadership Grid®.   Developed by Robert R. Blake and Jane S. Mouton, and originally called the Managerial Grid®, the Leadership Grid® is a trademarked and widely recognized typology of leadership styles.[38] Today, amid the growing popularity

Figure 15.4

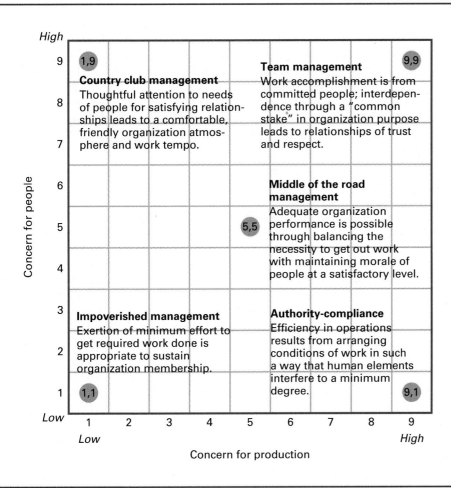

Source: Reproduced by permission from *Leadership Dilemmas—Grid Solutions* by Robert R. Blake and Anne Adams McCanse. Copyright © 1991, Gulf Publishing Company, Houston, Texas, 800-231-6275. All rights reserved.

of situational and transformational leadership theories, Blake and his colleagues remain convinced that there is one best style of leadership.[39] As we will see, they support this claim with research evidence.

As illustrated in Figure 15.4, the Leadership Grid® has "concern for production" on the horizontal axis and "concern for people" on the vertical axis. Concern for production involves a desire to achieve greater output, cost-effectiveness, and profits in profit-seeking organizations. Concern for people involves promoting friendship, helping coworkers get the job done, and attending to things that matter to people, like pay and working conditions. By scaling each axis from 1 to 9, the grid is highlighted by five major styles:

9,1 style: primary concern for production; people secondary

1,9 style: primary concern for people; production secondary

1,1 style: minimal concern for either production or people

5,5 style: moderate concern for both production and people to maintain the status quo

9,9 style: high concern for both production and people as evidenced by personal commitment, mutual trust, and teamwork

15E

Back to the Opening Case

Where would you plot Saturn's Trudell on Blake and McCanse's Leadership Grid®? Why? Is this particular style the best for her present situation? Why or why not?

Although they stress that managers and leaders need to be versatile enough to select the courses of action appropriate to the situation, Blake and his colleagues contend that a 9,9 style correlates positively with better results, better mental and physical health, and effective conflict resolution. They believe there *is* one best leadership style. As they see it, the true 9,9 style has never been adequately tested by the situationalists. In a more recent study by Blake and Mouton, 100 experienced managers overwhelmingly preferred the 9,9 style, regardless of how the situation varied.[40] Consequently, Blake's management training and organization development programs are designed to help individuals and entire organizations move into the 9,9 portion of the Leadership Grid®.

Situational Theory

Convinced that no one best style of leadership exists, a number of management scholars have advocated situational or contingency thinking. Although a number of different situational-leadership theories have been developed, they all share one fundamental assumption: successful leadership occurs when the leader's style matches the situation. Situational-leadership theorists stress the need for flexibility. They reject the notion of a universally applicable style. Research is under way to determine precisely when and where various styles of leadership are appropriate. Fiedler's contingency theory, the path-goal theory, and the Vroom/Yetton/Jago decision-making model are introduced and discussed here because they represent distinctly different approaches to situational leadership.

Fiedler's Contingency Theory.   Among the various leadership theories proposed so far, Fiedler's is the most thoroughly tested. It is the product of more than 30 years of research by Fred E. Fiedler and his associates. Fiedler's contingency theory gets its name from the following assumption:

> *The performance of a leader depends on two interrelated factors: (1) the degree to which the situation gives the leader control and influence—that is, the likelihood that [the leader] can successfully accomplish the job; and (2) the leader's basic motivation—that is, whether [the leader's] self-esteem depends primarily on accomplishing the task or on having close supportive relations with others.*[41]

Regarding the second factor, the leader's basic motivation, Fiedler believes leaders are either task-motivated or relationship-motivated. These two motivational profiles are roughly equivalent to initiating structure (or concern for production) and consideration (or concern for people).

A consistent pattern has emerged from the many studies of effective leaders carried out by Fiedler and others.[42] As illustrated in Figure 15.5, task-motivated leaders seem to be effective in extreme situations when they have either very little control or a great deal of control over situational variables. In moderately favorable situations, however, relationship-motivated leaders tend to be more effective. Consequently, Fiedler and one of his colleagues summed up their findings by noting that "everything points to the conclusion that there is no such thing as an ideal leader."[43] Instead, there are leaders, and there are situations. The challenge, according to Fiedler, is to analyze a leader's basic motivation and then match that leader with a suitable situation to form a productive combination. He believes it is more efficient to move leaders to a suitable situation than to tamper with their personalities by trying to get task-motivated leaders to become relationship-motivated, or vice versa.

Path-Goal Theory.   Another situational leadership theory is the path-goal theory, a derivative of expectancy motivation theory (see Chapter 13). Path-goal theory gets its name from the assumption that effective leaders can enhance employee motivation by

Figure 15.5 | Fiedler's Contingency Theory of Leadership

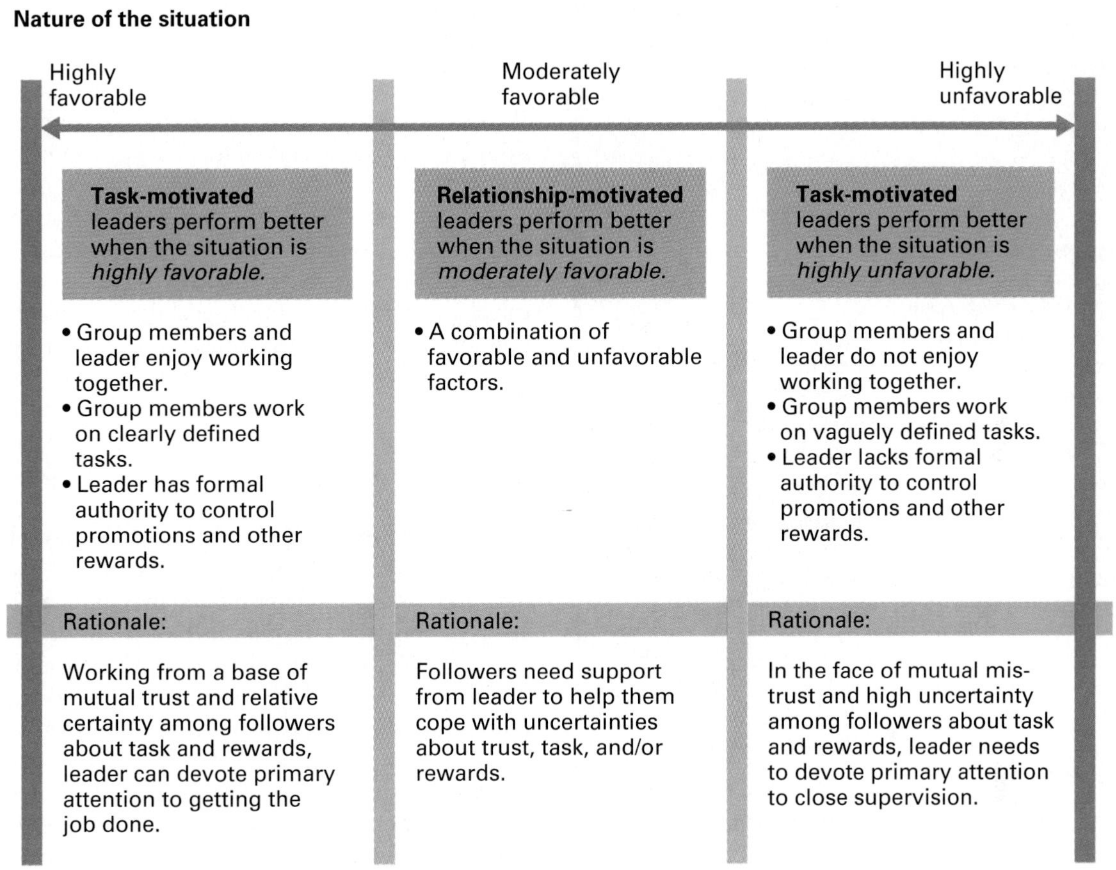

Nature of the situation

Highly favorable	Moderately favorable	Highly unfavorable
Task-motivated leaders perform better when the situation is *highly favorable.*	**Relationship-motivated** leaders perform better when the situation is *moderately favorable.*	**Task-motivated** leaders perform better when the situation is *highly unfavorable.*
• Group members and leader enjoy working together. • Group members work on clearly defined tasks. • Leader has formal authority to control promotions and other rewards.	• A combination of favorable and unfavorable factors.	• Group members and leader do not enjoy working together. • Group members work on vaguely defined tasks. • Leader lacks formal authority to control promotions and other rewards.
Rationale:	Rationale:	Rationale:
Working from a base of mutual trust and relative certainty among followers about task and rewards, leader can devote primary attention to getting the job done.	Followers need support from leader to help them cope with uncertainties about trust, task, and/or rewards.	In the face of mutual mistrust and high uncertainty among followers about task and rewards, leader needs to devote primary attention to close supervision.

(1) clarifying the individual's perception of work goals, (2) linking meaningful rewards with goal attainment, and (3) explaining how goals and desired rewards can be achieved. In short, leaders should motivate their followers by providing clear goals and meaningful incentives for reaching them. Path-goal theorists believe that motivation is essential to effective leadership.

According to two path-goal theorists, leaders can enhance motivation by "increasing the number and kinds of personal payoffs to subordinates for work-goal attainment and making paths to these payoffs easier to travel by clarifying the paths, reducing road blocks and pitfalls, and increasing the opportunities for personal satisfaction en route."[44] Personal characteristics of employees, environmental pressures, and demands on employees will all vary from situation to situation. Thus, path-goal proponents believe managers need to rely contingently on four different leadership styles:

4 Describe the path-goal theory of leadership and explain how the assumption on which it is based differs from the assumption on which Fiedler's contingency theory is based.

- *Directive:* Tell people what is expected of them and provide specific guidance, schedules, rules, regulations, and standards.[45]
- *Supportive:* Treat employees as equals in a friendly manner while striving to improve their well-being.
- *Participative:* Consult with employees to seek their suggestions and then seriously consider those suggestions when making decisions.

■ *Achievement-oriented:* Set challenging goals, emphasize excellence, and seek continuous improvement while maintaining a high degree of confidence that employees will meet difficult challenges in a responsible manner.[46]

The assumption that managers can and do shift situationally from style to style clearly sets path-goal theory apart from Fiedler's model. Recall that Fiedler claims managers cannot and do not change their basic leadership styles.

Limited research on the path-goal model has produced mixed results.[47] So far, though, some enlightening contingency relationships have surfaced (see Table 15.3). One valuable contribution of path-goal theory is its identification of the achievement-oriented leadership style. As managers deal with an increasing number of highly educated and self-motivated employees in advanced-technology industries, they will need to be-come skilled facilitators rather than just order givers or hand holders.

The Vroom/Yetton/Jago Decision-Making Model. A model originally proposed by Victor H. Vroom and Philip W. Yetton and later refined by Vroom and Arthur G. Jago portrays leadership as a *decision-making* process.[48] (Recall from Chapter 13 that Vroom helped develop the expectancy theory of motivation.) Their model qualifies as a situational-leadership theory because they prescribe different decision styles for varying situations managers typically encounter.

The Vroom model identifies five distinct decision-making styles (see Figure 15.6), each of which requires a different degree of subordinate participation. Two styles are autocratic (AI and AII). Two others are consultative (CI and CII). The fifth style, group-directed (GII), involves

Table 15.3	Leadership style	Effect in various situations
Contingency Relationships in the Path-Goal Leadership Model	**Directive**	Positively affects satisfaction and expectancies of subordinates working on ambiguous tasks.
		Negatively affects satisfaction and expectancies of subordinates working on clearly defined tasks.
	Supportive	Positively affects satisfaction of subordinates working on dissatisfying, stressful, or frustrating tasks.
	Participative	Positively affects satisfaction of subordinates who are ego involved with nonrepetitive tasks.
	Achievement-oriented	Positively affects confidence that effort will lead to effective performance of subordinates working on ambiguous and nonrepetitive tasks.

Source: From *Managerial Process and Organizational Behavior*, by Alan C. Filley, Robert J. House, and Steven Kerr. Copyright © 1976 Scott, Foresman and Company. Reprinted by permission of the publisher.

Degree of subordinate participation	Symbol	Decision-making style
		Autocratic leader
None	AI	You solve the problem or make the decision yourself, using information available to you at that time.
Low	AII	You obtain the necessary information from your subordinate(s), then decide on the solution to the problem yourself. You may not tell your subordinates what the problem is in getting the information from them. The role played by your subordinates in making the decision is clearly one of providing the necessary information to you, rather than generating or evaluating alternative solutions.
		Consultative leader
Moderate	CI	You share the problem with relevant subordinates individually, getting their ideas and suggestions without bringing them together as a group. Then you make a decision that may or may not reflect your subordinates' influence.
Moderate	CII	You share the problem with your subordinates as a group, collectively obtaining their ideas and suggestions. Then you make a decision that may or may not reflect your subordinates' influence.
		Group directed
High	GII	You share a problem with your subordinates as a group. Together you generate and evaluate alternatives and attempt to reach agreement (consensus) on a solution. Your role is much like that of a chairman. You do not try to influence the group to adopt "your" solution and you are willing to accept and implement any solution that has the support of the entire group.

Source: Reprinted from *Leadership and Decision-Making*, by Victor H. Vroom and Philip W. Yetton, by permission of the University of Pittsburgh Press. © 1973 by University of Pittsburgh Press.

decisions based on group consensus. In addition, the Vroom model gives managers tools for matching styles with various individual and group situations. One tool is a user-friendly computer software program,[49] the other is a set of four decision trees for hand calculations. Both the computerized and decision-tree versions are based on a series of diagnostic questions about the situation. (See the eight questions at the top of Figure 15.7.) Vroom and Jago are quick to point out, however, that the computer program and the decision trees are not adequate substitutes for managerial judgment:

The program, like the model itself, is intended to provide nothing more than a standard against which one's choices or intended choices can be compared. Sometimes such a standard is not

5 Explain how the Vroom/Yetton/Jago and transformational leadership theories can help managers deal with decision making and change, respectively.

Figure 15.7

The Vroom/Jago Decision Tree for Dealing with a Group Problem When Time Is Limited

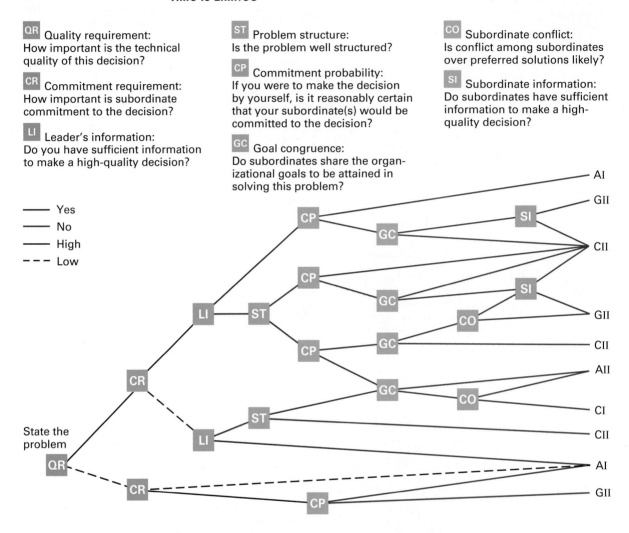

QR Quality requirement: How important is the technical quality of this decision?

CR Commitment requirement: How important is subordinate commitment to the decision?

LI Leader's information: Do you have sufficient information to make a high-quality decision?

ST Problem structure: Is the problem well structured?

CP Commitment probability: If you were to make the decision by yourself, is it reasonably certain that your subordinate(s) would be committed to the decision?

GC Goal congruence: Do subordinates share the organizational goals to be attained in solving this problem?

CO Subordinate conflict: Is conflict among subordinates over preferred solutions likely?

SI Subordinate information: Do subordinates have sufficient information to make a high-quality decision?

Source: Reprinted from *The New Leadership: Managing Participation in Organizations* by Victor H. Vroom and Arthur G. Jago, 1988, Englewood Cliffs, N.J.: Prentice-Hall. Copyright 1987 by V. H. Vroom and A. G. Jago. Used with permission of the authors.

required. An awareness of the benefits and liabilities of participation and an understanding of the contingencies involved are often enough to help the manager select which decision process to use.[50]

We can use the sample decision tree in Figure 15.7 to better understand the mechanics of Vroom's model. This particular decision tree is suitable for group problem-solving situations with limited time for a decision. (The other three decision trees involve time-driven individual problems and development-driven group or individual problems.) For our problem, let's imagine you are the director of accounting at Microsoft and the executive committee has given you a month to decide whether to switch to an entirely new budgeting process. The new system would require extensive updating of the firm's computerized financial control system, thus meaning lots of work for all your key people. The likely answers to the eight diagnostic questions follow: *QR* = high; *CR* = high;

LI = no; ST = yes; CP = no; GC = yes; CO = no; SI = no. This particular sequence in the decision tree in Figure 15.7 recommends a CII style. (Refer to Figure 15.6 for a summary of the CII decision-making style.) In sum, you should involve your people in this important decision because you need their collective expertise and research capabilities. And later, if the change is made, you will need their support. They will tend to support a change they fully understand and had a direct hand in selecting.

Vroom's model may appear overly complex at first glance, but a closer look reveals a good deal of practical significance. For example, it reminds managers to ask such important questions as: "Is time a critical factor?" "Who has the needed information?" "How will my people respond?" "Do I need their support during implementation?" "Will this decision cause conflict?" By cross-checking pending decisions with a trip through Vroom's diagnostic questions, leaders can sharpen their decision skills.

Transformational Leadership Theory

In his 1978 book, *Leadership*, James McGregor Burns drew a distinction between transactional and transformational leadership. Burns characterized **transformational leaders** as visionaries who challenge people to achieve exceptionally high levels of morality, motivation, and performance.[51] Only transformational leaders, Burns argued, are capable of charting necessary new courses for modern organizations. Why? Because they are masters of change.[52] They can envision a better future, effectively communicate that vision, and get others to willingly make it a reality.

transformational leaders
visionaries who challenge people to do exceptional things

Transactional Versus Transformational Leaders.   Extending the work of Burns, Bernard Bass more recently emphasized the importance of charisma in transformational leadership. Transformational leaders rely heavily on referent power.

He's been called the smartest guy in Silicon Valley and the "Edison of the Internet." And although he is not as widely known as Microsoft's Bill Gates, Bill Joy is the equivalent of a rock legend among computer programmers. Thanks to a 20-year string of programming innovations, the cofounder of Sun Microsystems is a transformational leader in the truest meaning of the term. His odd-sounding breakthroughs—SPARC, Java, and Jini—enabled Sun to be a key player in bringing the World Wide Web to its present state. Like many transformational leaders, Bill Joy thinks "outside the box" and clearly envisions futures others can't even imagine.

Table 15.4

Transactional Versus Transformational Leaders			
Transactional leader		**Transformational leader**	
Contingent reward	Contracts exchange of rewards for effort, promises rewards for good performance, recognizes accomplishments.	**Charisma**	Provides vision and sense of mission, instills pride, gains respect and trust.
Management by exception (active)	Watches and searches for deviations from rules and standards, takes corrective action.	**Inspiration**	Communicates high expectations, uses symbols to focus efforts, expresses important purposes in simple ways.
Management by exception (passive)	Intervenes only if standards are not met.	**Intellectual stimulation**	Promotes intelligence, rationality, and careful problem solving.
Laissez-faire	Abdicates responsibilities, avoids making decisions.	**Individualized consideration**	Gives personal attention, treats each employee individually, coaches, advises.

Source: Bernard M. Bass et al., "From Transactional to Transformational Leadership: Learning to Share the Vision." Reprinted from *Organizational Dynamics* (Winter 1990), © 1990 American Management Association International. Reprinted by permission of American Management Association International, New York, NY. All rights reserved. **http://www.amanet.org**

Chrysler's Lee Iacocca and GE's Jack Welch exemplify charismatic leaders who engineered bold changes at their respective companies.[53] While acknowledging how transformational leaders exhibit widely different styles and tend to stir their fair share of controversy, Bass rounded out Burns's distinction between transactional and transformational leaders (see Table 15.4). Transactional leaders monitor people so they do the expected, according to plan. In contrast, transformational leaders inspire people to do the unexpected, above and beyond the plan. This distinction can mean the difference between maintaining the status quo and fostering creative and productive growth.

Positive Evidence.   It is important to note that the distinction in Table 15.4 is not between bad and good leaders—both types are needed today. This is where transformational leadership theory effectively combines the behavioral styles and situational approaches just discussed. To the traditional behavioral patterns of initiating structure and consideration have been added charismatic and other behaviors.[54] Transformational leadership also needs to be situationally appropriate. Specifically, transformational leadership is needed in rapidly changing situations; transactional leaders can best handle stable situations.

Available laboratory and field research evidence generally supports the transformational leadership pattern. Followers of transformational leaders tend to perform better and to report greater satisfaction than those of transactional leaders.[55]

A Moral Compass for Leaders   15G

Frances Hesselbein, the woman responsible for revitalizing the Girl Scouts of the USA:

Leadership is not a basket of tricks or skills. It is the quality and character and courage of the person who is the leader. It's a matter of ethics and moral compass, the willingness to remain highly vulnerable.

Source: As quoted in Ani Hadjian, "Follow the Leader," *Fortune* (November 27, 1995): 96.

Questions: *How well does Hesselbein's description tie in with the concept of transformational leadership? Explain. Is she really describing a servant leader? Explain.*

Servant Leaders: Putting to Work What You've Learned

Finding ways to practice leadership both on and off the job can help present and future managers develop their abilities. Serving in campus, community, or religious organizations, for example, will give you an opportunity to experiment with different leadership styles in a variety of situations. Leading effectively, like riding a bike, is learned only by doing.

In addition to a working knowledge of the various leadership theories we have just discussed, aspiring leaders need an integrative model to tie everything together. This is where Robert K. Greenleaf's philosophy of the *servant leader* enters the picture as an instructive and inspiring springboard. The servant leader is an ethical person who puts *others*—not herself or himself—in the foreground (see Management Ethics). As a devout Quaker, Greenleaf wove humility and a genuine concern for the whole person into his philosophy of leadership.[56] One person who embodies the servant leader philosophy is John Wooden, who coached the UCLA men's basketball team to an astounding ten national championships: "The great thing about Coach Wooden is that he is what he is," [former player Bill] Walton says. "This is a man with no pretensions. He is a humble, giving person who wants nothing in return but to see other people succeed."[57]

6 Explain Greenleaf's philosophy of the servant leader.

Mentoring

In spite of mountains of leadership research, much remains to be learned about why some people are good leaders whereas many others are not.[58] One thing is clear, though: mentors can make an important difference. Let us explore this interesting process whereby leadership skills are acquired by exposure to role models.

Learning from a Mentor

The many obstacles and barriers blocking the way to successful leadership make it easy to understand why there is no simple formula for developing leaders. Abraham Zaleznik, a respected sociologist, insists that leaders must be nurtured under the wise tutelage of a mentor. A **mentor** is an individual who systematically develops another person's abilities through intensive tutoring, coaching, and guidance.[59] Zaleznik explains the nature of this special relationship:

> Mentors take risks with people. They bet initially on talent they perceive in [junior] people. Mentors also risk emotional involvement in working closely with their juniors. The risks do not always pay off, but the willingness to take them appears crucial in developing leaders.[60]

A survey of 246 health care industry managers found higher satisfaction, greater recognition, and more promotion opportunities among managers with mentors than among those without.[61] Other research suggests that *informal* relationships that arise naturally work better than formally structured pairings.[62] Wal-Mart prefers the structured approach. In the following example, notice how the world's number one retailer has integrated formal mentors into a comprehensive human resources program:

> . . . the company has modified its human resources philosophy from "getting, keeping, and growing" employees to "keeping, growing, and getting" them. The shift isn't just semantics,

mentor *someone who develops another person through tutoring, coaching, and guidance*

Management Ethics

The Servant Leader

The unifying strand that meanders through much of the recent writing and thinking about spirit in the workplace is the concept of "servant leadership." Most credit Robert K. Greenleaf, onetime management researcher at AT&T and life-long philosopher, with introducing the idea in a 1970 essay called "The Servant as Leader."

No, the concept of servant leader is not meant to be an oxymoron, but it's certainly a paradox in a Zen sort of way. Yes, it does stand the traditional view of the leader—the CEO at the peak of the pyramid, the captain at the helm of the ship—on its head. That's intentional. Greenleaf built his philosophy on the idea that the leader exists only to serve his followers; they grant him their allegiance in response to his servant nature.

Greenleaf credits Herman Hesse's *Journey to the East* with providing his inspiration (although an earlier source, the gospel of Luke, also defines a leader as one who serves). In the novel, a group of men on a mythical journey are accompanied by the servant Leo. He performs menial chores for the travelers, but also sustains them with his spirit and song. When Leo disappears, the travelers find they cannot continue without him, and the group falls apart. Writes Greenleaf, "The narrator, one of the party, after some years of wandering, finds Leo and is taken into the Order that had sponsored the journey. There he discovers that Leo, whom he had known first as a *servant*, was in fact the titular head of the Order, its guiding spirit, a great and noble *leader*."

On this foundation, Greenleaf builds his philosophy. According to his essay, servant leaders embody these characteristics:

- *They are servants first.* Like Leo, servant leaders are motivated by a natural desire to serve, not to lead. They must make a conscious choice to *aspire* to lead. People who are leaders first are responding to an innate drive to acquire power or material possessions.
- *They articulate goals.* A servant leader gives certainty and purpose to others by clearly articulating a goal or, in today's leadership parlance, a vision.
- *They inspire trust.* Followers are confident of the leader's values, competence, and judgment. He has a sustaining spirit (*entheos*) that supports the tenacious pursuit of a goal.
- *They know how to listen.* The true, natural servant leader responds to any problem by listening first. You can discipline yourself to learn to listen first, and thus

become a natural servant. Here, Greenleaf draws on the prayer of St. Francis, "Lord, grant that I may not seek so much to be understood as to understand."

- *They are masters of positive feedback.* The servant leader always offers unqualified acceptance of the person, although she doesn't necessarily accept the person's effort or performance.
- *They rely on foresight.* No leader ever has all the information necessary to make major decisions. But servant leaders have an intuitive sense that they use to bridge information gaps. Their ability to detach from day-to-day events allows their conscious and unconscious to work together to "better foresee the unforeseeable."
- *They emphasize personal development.* A servant leader views every problem as originating inside, rather than outside, himself. To remedy any "flaw in the world," the process of change starts in the servant, not "out there." Notes Greenleaf, "This is a difficult concept for that busybody, modern man."

Greenleaf apparently sowed a potent—if slow-growing—seed with this original work. He expanded on the concept in a series of essays and two books, *Servant Leadership* and *Teacher as Servant* (Paulist Press). After retiring from AT&T in 1964, he founded the Center for Applied Ethics, a nonprofit educational organization in Indianapolis, which became the Robert K. Greenleaf Center in 1985.

Why has the servant-leadership model gathered steam in recent years? Certainly our unrelenting fascination with leaders makes the idea at least as pertinent today as it was 23 years ago. Larry Spears, executive director of the Greenleaf Center, offers another explanation. Close to 500,000 copies of Greenleaf's essays and books have been sold since 1970, he says, so perhaps the idea has reached a certain critical mass of people.

The center itself has changed as well. After Greenleaf's death in 1990, it became a membership organization committed to spreading the servant-leadership philosophy. Today, it sponsors an annual conference, conducts workshops, and sells essays, books, and videotapes that carry the servant-leadership message.

With the help of mentors, Bernadette Williams founded her $1.5-million-a-year company, i-stragegy.com, while still a student at UCLA in the early 1990s. As she built her Culver City, California consulting business by creating specialized data-bases, she observed the scarcity of women in high tech. Women of color were practically nonexistent. This prompted her to help create the Women's New Media Alliance (**www.wnma.org**) dedicated to fostering mentor–protégé relationships between successful women in high tech and girls interested in technical fields. Some of these relationships are "virtual" and globe-spanning, thanks to e-mail and the Internet.

says Coleman Peterson, senior vice president of Wal-Mart's people division. It indicates an increased emphasis on retaining and developing the talent Wal-Mart already has, rather than the "hire, hire, hire" strategy Peterson says characterized the company in the past.

To that end, Wal-Mart focuses intensively on how employees adapt during their first 90 days with the company. To make sure new hires don't feel lost at the mammoth company, they are assigned veteran employees as mentors. They are also assessed on their progress at the 30-, 60-, and 90-day marks. These efforts have helped reduce attrition rates by 25 percent. Wal-Mart employees who exhibit leadership potential are sent for training to the Sam Walton Development Center, at company head-quarters in Bentonville, Arkansas.[63]

Dynamics of Mentoring

According to Kathy Kram, who conducted intensive biographical interviews with both members in 18 different senior manager–junior manager mentor rela-tionships, mentoring fulfills two important functions:

Building a Mentor Mosaic   15H

Carol Bartz, CEO of Autodesk, a California software firm:

The assumption behind mentoring—"I'll tether myself to one person who will take care of me"—is bankrupt. A better way is to build what I call a "personal mosaic" of influences, experts, and guides. Personal-mosaic building is about breaking mentoring down: What specific skill do I need? What's my next challenge? For each issue, you seek out an individual—someone who can deal with crises in a certain way, someone who has an excellent time-management system, someone who seems good at handling office politics—for advice, information, and models.

Source: Polly LaBarre, "Carol Bartz," *Fast Company*, no. 21 (January 1999): 75.

Questions: *Is this good advice for today's professionals? Why or why not? What is the main problem with having just one mentor?*

Table 15.5

Mentors Serve Two Important Functions

Career functions*	Psychosocial functions**
Sponsorship	Role modeling
Exposure and visibility	Acceptance and confirmation
Coaching	Counseling
Protection	Friendship
Challenging assignments	

* Career functions are those aspects of the relationship that primarily enhance career advancement.

** Psychosocial functions are those aspects of the relationship that primarily enhance a sense of competence, clarity of identity, and effectiveness in the managerial role.

Source: Kathy E. Kram, "Phases of the Mentor Relationship," *Academy of Management Journal,* 26 (December 1983): 614 (Exhibit 1). Reprinted by permission.

7 **Identify the two key functions that mentors perform and explain how a mentor can develop a junior manager's leadership skills.**

(1) a career enhancement function and (2) a psychological support function (see Table 15.5). Mentor relationships were found to average about five years in length.[64] Thus a manager might have a series of mentors during the course of an organizational career.

Interestingly, the junior member of a mentor relationship is not the only one to benefit. Mentors often derive great intrinsic pleasure from seeing their protégés move up through the ranks and conquer difficult challenges. Moreover, by passing along their values and technical and leadership skills to promising junior managers, mentors can wield considerable power. Mentor relationships do sometimes turn sour. A mentor can become threatened by a protégé who surpasses him or her. Also, cross-gender[65] and cross-racial mentor relationships can be victimized by bias and social pressures.[66]

Behavior Modification

This last approach to influencing behavior can be traced to two psychologists, John B. Watson and Edward L. Thorndike, who did their work in the early twentieth century. From Watson came the advice to concentrate on observable behavior. Accordingly, the philosophy of **behaviorism** holds that observable behavior is more important than hypothetical inner states such as needs, motives, or expectations. From Thorndike came an appreciation of the way in which consequences control behavior. According to Thorndike's classic law of effect, favorable consequences encourage behavior, whereas unfavorable consequences discourage behavior.[67] However, it remained for B. F. Skinner, the late Harvard psychologist, to integrate Watson's and Thorndike's contributions into a precise technology of behavior change.

behaviorism *belief that observable behavior is more important than inner states*

What Is Behavior Modification?

Skinner was the father of *operant conditioning*, the study of how behavior is controlled by the surrounding environment.[68] Although some find Skinner's substitution of environmental control for self-control repulsive and dehumanizing,[69] few deny that operant conditioning actually occurs. Indeed, much of our behavior is the product of environmental shaping. Rather, the debate centers on whether or not natural shaping processes should be systematically managed to alter the course of everyday behavior.[70] Advocates of behavior modification in the workplace believe they should be.[71]

Behavior modification is the practical application of Skinnerian operant-conditioning techniques to everyday behavior problems. **Behavior modification** (B. Mod.) involves systematically managing environmental factors to get people to do the right things more often and the wrong things less often. This is accomplished by managing the antecedents and/or consequences of observable behavior.

behavior modification *systematic management of the antecedents and consequences of behavior*

Managing Antecedents

An **antecedent** is an environmental cue that prompts an individual to behave in a given manner. Antecedents do not automatically *cause* an individual to behave in a predictable manner, as a hot stove causes you to withdraw your hand reflexively when you touch it. Rather, we learn through experience to interpret antecedents as signals that tell us it is time to behave in a certain way if we are to get what we want or to avoid what we do not want. This process is sometimes referred to as cue control. Domino's Pizza Inc. makes effective use of cue control for maintaining product quality.

antecedent *an environmental cue for a specific behavior*

> *[Every Domino's] features a myriad of strategically placed, visually appealing posters displaying helpful, job-related tips and reminders. . . .*
>
> *Centrally located, particularly for the benefit of the oven tender who slices and boxes the just-baked pizza, are two photos, one of "The Perfect Pepperoni" pizza, the other showing a pizza with ten common flaws, one per slice.[72]*

Although often overlooked, the management of antecedents is a practical and simple way of encouraging good performance. As Table 15.6 indicates, there are two ways to manage antecedents. Barriers can be removed, and helpful aids can be offered. These steps ensure that the path to good performance is clearly marked and free of obstacles (which meshes with the path-goal theory of leadership).

8 **Explain the management of antecedents and consequences in behavior modification.**

Barriers: remove barriers that prevent or hinder the completion of a good job. For example:	Aids: provide helpful aids that enhance the opportunity to do a good job. For example:
Unrealistic objectives, plans, schedules, or deadlines	Challenging yet attainable objectives
Uncooperative or distracting coworkers	Clear and realistic plans
Training deficiencies	Understandable instructions
Contradictory or confusing rules	Constructive suggestions, hints, or tips
Inadequate or inappropriate tools	Clear and generally acceptable work rules
Conflicting orders from two or more managers	Realistic schedules and deadlines
	Friendly reminders
	Posters or signs with helpful tips
	Easy-to-use forms
	Nonthreatening questions about progress

Table 15.6

Managing Antecedents

Managing Consequences

Managing the consequences of job performance is more complex than dealing strictly with antecedents because there are four different classes of consequences. Each type of consequence involves a different process. Positive reinforcement and negative reinforcement both encourage behavior, but they do so in different ways. Extinction and punishment discourage behavior, but again, in different ways. These four terms have precise meanings that are often confused by casual observers.

positive reinforcement
encouraging a behavior with a pleasing consequence

Positive Reinforcement.   **Positive reinforcement** encourages a specific behavior by immediately following it with a consequence that the individual finds pleasing. For example, a machine operator who maintains a clean work area because he or she is praised for doing so has responded to positive reinforcement. As the term implies, positive reinforcement reinforces or builds behavior in a positive way.

Negative Reinforcement.   *Negative reinforcement* encourages a specific behavior by immediately withdrawing or terminating something that particular person finds displeasing. Children learn the power of negative reinforcement early in life when they discover that the quickest way to get something is to cry and scream until their parents give them what they want. In effect, the parents are negatively reinforced for complying with the child's demand by the termination of the crying and screaming. In other words, the termination or withdrawal of an undesirable state of affairs (for example, the threat of being fired) has an incentive effect. In a social context, negative reinforcement amounts to blackmail. "Do what I want, or I will continue to make your life miserable" are the bywords of the person who relies on negative reinforcement to influence behavior.

Extinction.   Through *extinction*, a specific behavior is discouraged by ignoring it. For example, managers sometimes find that the best way to keep employees from asking redundant questions is simply not to answer them. Just as a plant will wither and die without water, behavior will fade away without occasional reinforcement.

15I

I Love My Computer, and My Computer Loves Me!

Clifford Nass, Stanford University researcher:

We set up an experiment in which one group of people worked with a computer application that was programmed to offer words of praise every now and then while another group worked with one that didn't. The people who worked on the praise-giving machine developed a greater sense of working in partnership with the computer, which in turn led to a whole host of positive effects, such as a willingness to work longer, enjoyment of the experience, and the confidence to try new things.

Source: As quoted in David Stamps, "The Person Inside the Box," *Training*, 35 (September 1998): 45.

Question: *From a behavior modification standpoint, how do you interpret these results?*

Punishment.   *Punishment* discourages a specific behavior by the immediate presentation of an undesirable consequence or the immediate removal of something desirable. For example, a manager may punish a tardy employee by either assigning the individual to a dirty job or docking the individual's pay.

It is important to remember that positive and negative reinforcement, extinction, and punishment all entail the manipulation of the *immediate* or *direct* consequences of a desired or undesired behavior. If action is taken before the behavior, behavior control is unlikely. For instance, if a manager gives an employee a cash bonus *before* a difficult task is completed, the probability of the task being completed declines because the incentive effect has been removed. In regard to managing consequences, behavior modification works only when there is a contingent ("if . . . then") relationship between a specific behavior and a given consequence.

Positively Reinforce What Is Right About Job Performance

Behavior modification proponents prefer to build up desirable behaviors rather than tear down undesirable ones. Every undesirable behavior has a desirable counterpart that can be reinforced. For example, someone who comes in late once a week actually comes in on time four days a week. To encourage productive behaviors, managers are advised to focus on the positive aspects of job performance when managing consequences. Thus, positive reinforcement is the preferred consequence strategy.[73] This positive approach was effectively taken to heart by Preston Trucking, a Maryland shipping company:

> Preston, years ago, had terrible relations between management and labor. Then, one day, top management resolved to bury the hatchet. All sorts of reforms were announced, including the Four-to-One Rule: For every criticism a manager made about a driver's performance, he had to give him four compliments. You can imagine how this went over. "It was like a . . . like a marriage encounter," says Teamster Nick Costa, rolling his eyes. Eventually, though, drivers discovered that the rule really did reflect a change of heart.[74]

This positive approach to modifying behavior is the central theme in the best-selling book *The One Minute Manager,* which extols the virtues of "catching people doing something *right!*"[75]

Schedule Positive Reinforcement Appropriately

Both the type and the timing of consequences are important in successful B. Mod. When a productive behavior is first tried out by an employee, a continuous schedule of reinforcement is appropriate. Under **continuous reinforcement** every instance of the desired behavior is reinforced. For example, a bank manager who is training a new loan officer to handle a difficult type of account should praise the loan officer after every successful transaction until the behavior is firmly established. After the loan officer seems able to handle the transaction, the bank manager can switch to a schedule of intermittent reinforcement. As the term implies, **intermittent reinforcement** calls for reinforcing some, rather than all, of the desired responses.

The more unpredictable the payoff schedule is, the better the results will be. One way to appreciate the power of intermittent reinforcement is to think of the enthusiasm with which people play slot machines; these gambling devices pay off on an unpredictable intermittent schedule. In the same way, occasional reinforcement of established productive behaviors with meaningful positive consequences is an extremely effective management technique.[76]

continuous reinforcement
every instance of a behavior is rewarded

intermittent reinforcement
rewarding some, but not all, instances of a behavior

Summary

1. Influence is fundamental to management because individuals must be influenced to pursue collective objectives. In addition to motivation, important influence processes include power, leadership, mentoring, and behavior modification. Recent research has identified eight generic influence tactics used on the job: consultation, rational persuasion, inspirational appeals, ingratiating tactics, coalition tactics, pressure tactics, upward appeals, and exchange tactics.

2. The five bases of power are reward, coercive, legitimate, referent, and expert. Empowerment cannot work without a supporting situation such as a skilled individual, an organizational culture of empowerment, an emotionally mature individual with a well-developed character, and empowerment opportunities such as delegation, participation, and self-managed teams.

3. Formal leadership is influencing relevant others to voluntarily pursue organizational objectives. Informal leadership can work for or against the organization. Leadership theory has evolved through four major stages: trait theory, behavioral styles theory, situational theory, and transformational theory. Trait theory is limited in that personal traits generally have poor predictive value. Researchers who differentiated authoritarian, democratic, and laissez-faire styles concentrated on leader behavior rather than personality traits. Leadership studies at Ohio State University isolated four styles of leadership based on two categories of leader behavior: initiating structure and consideration. According to Blake and his colleagues, a 9,9 style (high concern for both production and people) is the best overall style.

4. Situational-leadership theorists believe there is no single best leadership style; rather, different situations require different styles. Many years of study led Fiedler to conclude that task-motivated leaders are more effective in either very favorable or very unfavorable situations, whereas relationship-motivated leaders are better suited to moderately favorable situations. The favorableness of a situation is dictated by the degree of the leader's control and influence in getting the job done. Path-goal leadership theory, an expectancy perspective, assumes that leaders are effective to the extent that they can motivate followers by clarifying goals and clearing the paths to achieving those goals and valued rewards. Unlike Fiedler, path-goal theorists believe that managers can and should adapt their leadership style to the situation.

5. A third situational-leadership model has been put forth by Vroom, Yetton, and Jago. It helps managers select one of five decision-making styles by asking a series of diagnostic questions about the situation. The Vroom model calls for subordinate participation in situations where the manager has incomplete information and requires subordinate support for implementation. In contrast to transactional leaders who maintain the status quo, transformational leaders are visionary, charismatic leaders dedicated to change.

6. Greenleaf's philosophy of the servant leader helps aspiring leaders integrate what they have learned about leadership. The servant leader is motivated to serve rather than lead. Clear goals, trust, good listening skills, positive feedback, foresight, and self-development are the characteristics of a servant leader.

7. Mentors help develop less experienced people by fulfilling career and psychosocial functions. Mentors engage in intensive tutoring, coaching, and guiding. Mentors are role models for aspiring leaders.

8. Behavior modification (B. Mod.) is the practical application of Skinner's operant conditioning principles. B. Mod. involves managing antecedents and consequences to strengthen desirable behavior and weaken undesirable behavior. Proponents of B. Mod. prefer to shape behavior positively through positive reinforcement in lieu of negative reinforcement, extinction, and punishment. Continuous reinforcement is recommended for new behavior and intermittent reinforcement for established behavior.

Putting the Empowerment Puzzle Together

Skills & Tools

1. Individual's skill base

- Technical skills
- Team and communication skills
- Self-management skills

2. Culture of empowerment

- Mutual trust
- Win-win relationships
- Open communication
- Access to key information
- Rewards for initiative and cooperation

4. Empowerment opportunities

- Delegation
- Participative goal setting
- Self-managed teams
- Self-management
- Freedom to experiment

3. Individual's character development and emotional maturity

- Honesty
- Trustworthiness
- Commitment to team/ organizational success
- Desire to learn and grow
- Willingness to adapt and change
- Personal responsibility and accountability

Source: Adapted in part from discussion in Stephen R. Covey, *Principle-Centered Leadership* (New York: Simon & Schuster, 1991), pp. 212–216.

Internet Exercises

1. **Everything you ever wanted to know about social influence (and then some):** Robert B. Cialdini—professor, researcher, and author of the widely used book *Influence: The Science of Persuasion*—says we are exposed to countless good and evil influence tactics every day of our lives. As a researcher, he knows the power of social influence and fears that power is often abused. He and his former doctoral student, Kelton Rhoads, want to tip the scale in your favor by increasing your understanding of social influence. You'll be less apt to be unfairly manipulated if you know what's going on. Their Web site (**www.influenceatwork.com**) not only promotes their consulting business, it also provides an extensive free introduction to the science of influence. At the home page, click on "The Authors" in the main menu to establish the credibility of the Web site. Go back to the home page and click on the "What's Your Influence Quotient (NQ)?" to take a short quiz that raises your awareness of day-to-day social influence attempts. Next, from the main menu, select the category "Introduction to Influence." Among the extensive list of topics, recommended ones include the first six topics plus "6 Principles" and "Framing I."

   Learning Points: 1. Are you surprised at how pervasive influence is in modern life? 2. Generally speaking, do you view social influence as a positive or negative aspect of modern life? Explain. 3. What useful lessons did you learn from this tutorial? 4. Are you better equipped to handle unwanted influence attempts after reading this tutorial? Explain. 5. How can and should managers use influence ethically?

2. **Leadership self-assessment:** Go to **www.queendom.com,** as we have recommended in other chapters, for a free and insightful self-awareness exercise. Select the category "Tests, Tests, Tests. . ." from the home page menu and then scroll down to the "Leadership Test" in the Career/Job section. The 30-question multiple choice test will take 15 to 20 minutes to complete. Read the instructions carefully; then take the test, score it, and read the interpretation.

   Learning Points: 1. Relative to what portion of your life are you assessing your leadership abilities? 2. How would you characterize your leadership style? 3. What are the strong points of your leadership style? 4. What aspects of your leadership style need improvement? What do you need to do to improve?

3. **Check it out:** The Women's Organization for Mentoring Education and Networking, sponsored by WOMEN Unlimited Inc., is dedicated to enhancing diversity and achieving gender parity in the workplace. For instructive full-text articles on mentoring and related topics, go to the organization's home page at **www.women-unlimited.com** and click on "News & Articles." Both women and men can pick up useful career tips from this Web site.

   For updates to these exercises, visit our Web site (**www.hmco.com/college**).

Closing Case

Empowerment Has a Full-time Job at This Temporary Staffing Company

Anthony J. Balsamo, CEO of TAC Worldwide, Newton, Massachusetts (2,000 employees; $1 billion in annual revenues):

In March of 1998, I summoned my senior staff for what I believed would be a defining moment for our company. As a rapidly growing business with $1 billion in revenues and sales offices spread throughout the world, we had become a very large and complex enterprise.

The biggest problem we faced was the need to reengineer our various parallel business units for contract labor, temporary help, and staffing. Over the years, these product lines had become gray and our business units had begun competing with each other, causing strife within the company and confusion among our customers.

My challenge to the management team that morning was to deliver in one year a plan that would break down the old corporate paradigms, eliminate management parochialism, set aside personal agendas, realign the business units, and do what was best for our customers and our company. Many on the team initially felt that these problems were far too ingrained in the fabric of the company to be eliminated. The stain, they said, went too deep.

I had thought a great deal about the need for change, the price we would pay if we failed, and the toll it would take on those of my staff who would be unwilling or unable to accept that change. The most difficult part of the entire process for me was the knowledge that success could mean the loss of some talented executives.

If real change was to occur, I believed that it had to come through the management team, not by fiat from the CEO. Following the meeting, I wondered how my experiment in "collaborative problem solving" would play out. Would the team step up to the challenge? Would they work together to overcome long-entrenched territorial issues? Would they learn to share responsibility and risk at an entirely new level? And, ultimately, would they deliver a plan that would allow us to move forward, or would it turn out that we had lost a year and were no closer to solving the problem?

I had already devised a solution of my own, but I put it in my desk drawer and waited. This March, the team came back with a comprehensive set of recommendations, solutions, and transition programs. This was not the solution I had come up with a year earlier. It was far better. That reality is both humbling and the part of the collaborative process that makes it most exciting. I believe that if I had demanded my own solution I would have gotten back a year's worth of reasons why it wouldn't work, not a year's worth of work to make it work.

Using the team's plan as a guide, we redefined charters and agreed on the transition of millions of dollars of business within our business units. Two vertical business units were also born from the plan. The team even came up with a process for policing their recommendations and verifying that everyone in the company was onboard. I couldn't possibly have thought of all the barriers and roadblocks ahead of us. But the team members did. They solved every one of them.

Source: Anthony J. Balsamo, "The Power of Empowerment." Reprinted from *Management Review*, November 1999. © 1999 American Management Association International. Reprinted by permission of American Management Association International, New York, NY. All rights reserved. http://www.amanet.org

Our company has undergone a paradigm shift. What began as a collaborative effort to help us deal more effectively with one particularly difficult business decision is rapidly becoming a way of life throughout all levels of our company. We are in the midst of changing our entire corporate culture. The principle of collaborative problem solving has been added to our corporate charter, and we now evaluate candidates for promotion by how effectively they put these principles into practice.

In our company's intensely competitive market space, we need to attract and retain highly qualified and imaginative people. We are only as good as our employees, and our employees are only as good as we allow them to be. Collaborative decision making gives bright, creative employees at all levels the opportunity to contribute in ways not available to them in more traditionally managed settings. It's truly amazing to see what happens when you empower people to take ownership of problems and opportunities. Since we implemented this collaborative process, I find that I make far fewer legislative decisions. I now spend a great deal of time confirming the decisions of others.

Certainly, a CEO can dictate and legislate, but he or she can't get people to rally behind a plan without buy-in. When you create an environment where your executive team and the team that supports it believe in the process and have an opportunity to participate, you've just enabled an army of talented people to march toward the goal you've set.

FOR DISCUSSION

1. Using the model in the Skills & Tools box at the end of this chapter as a guide, explain why empowerment works at TAC Worldwide.

2. What influence tactics and power bases did CEO Balsamo rely on in this case?

3. What power base(s) did the empowered management team rely upon?

4. Where would you plot the CEO's leadership style on Blake and McCanse's Leadership Grid®? Explain.

5. Which path-goal leadership style did the CEO exhibit in this case? Explain.

6. What was the single most important key to success in this case?

CHANGE, CONFLICT, and NEGOTIATION

CHAPTER OBJECTIVES

When you finish studying this chapter, you should be able to

1 Identify and describe four types of organizational change according to the Nadler-Tushman model.

2 Explain how people tend to respond differently to changes they like and those they dislike.

3 List at least six reasons why employees resist change and discuss what management can do about resistance to change.

4 Describe how the unfreezing-change-refreezing analogy applies to organization development (OD).

5 Identify and highlight the 5Ps in the checklist for change agents.

6 Contrast the competitive and cooperative conflict styles.

7 Identify and describe five conflict resolution techniques.

8 Identify and describe the elements of effective negotiation and explain the advantage of added value negotiating (AVN).

"CHANGE BEGETS CONFLICT,
CONFLICT BEGETS CHANGE."
dean tjosvold

Trust for a Change

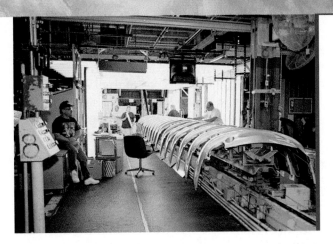

How do you get people who are suspicious of each other—if not downright hostile—to work together on change? David Berdish, 42, an organizational-learning manager, has spent the past eight years wrestling with that question at Ford Motor Co.

In his role as a change agent at Visteon Automotive Systems, Ford's parts-manufacturing company, Berdish helped usher in production and manufacturing changes that helped turn the division around—from $50 million in losses to $175 million in profits. But it took five years. And he didn't do it alone. He had to get engineers and accountants, and union and nonunion factory workers, to stop flinging accusations at each other and start solving problems. He had to get them to start trusting each other.

"Trust equals speed," Berdish says. "Once people have stopped worrying about what the other guy's agenda is, you can make changes much more quickly. But building trust takes time, especially in a company as big as Ford, where there are a gazillion years of baggage associated with where you're from, what you look like, or what you do."

Here are four of Berdish's test-driven tactics for building trust.

Figure Out Where Trust Breaks Down

We had a program to encourage our suppliers to help us save money. If they came up with a design or process idea that cut our production costs, we applied 50 percent of the savings to their next bid. But we didn't get any suggestions, and we couldn't figure out why. So we got the suppliers together during a three-day learning conference, and we asked them why they weren't contributing.

And guess what? We were wrong—they had come up with plenty of ways to realize savings. But our engineers were ignoring them—our people thought the suppliers were trying to show them up. So we dug a little further.

We tracked the average time it took us to execute a change, once we'd made the decision to move on it. The answer just floored us: It took us 89 weeks! We calculated that 39 of those weeks were a direct result of distrust—of people sitting on information or refusing to share ideas. So the problem really wasn't the suppliers, or even the engineers. It was a whole chain of events in which people

were driven by their own agendas and politics, instead of concern for the customer.

Listen, Then Listen Some More

You have to listen to where people are coming from, regardless of whether they're UAW workers or skilled tradespeople or engineers.

On my very first change effort, I went to talk with a veteran production supervisor about some process-improvement issues. He took one look at me and said, "You can take your *Fifth Discipline* and shove it up your ass. I've got to make parts back here." Not such a great beginning.

He had this notion that just because I wasn't part of the production team, I didn't know a thing about the real work that goes on in a factory. But he lightened up when I told him that for my first job, I worked as a production supervisor—just like he did. He shared some ideas about what he thought was wrong with the process. It helped that I had a production background, but it helped even more that I heard him out and showed him some respect. If I go into any effort thinking that I know the system and that other people's views are unimportant, I'm going to fail.

Challenge Assumptions

One of my biggest concerns is figuring out people's assumptions and how those get in the way of the work that needs to get done.

I worked with a group of engineers and production people to try to improve our production launches. Our biggest problem, on an operational level, was dealing with unreliable machinery. Among the engineers, there was a perception that the machines tended to break down at the end of a shift, so the skilled trade workers who ran them could get some extra overtime. Meanwhile inside the factory, there was a perception that the machines broke down because our engineers weren't ordering the right parts.

There may have been a kernel of truth on both sides. But people were so busy pointing fingers that they never talked about how to solve the problem. Once they realized that they were jumping to their own personal conclusions, we could start to figure out how to fix things.

Show Them the Big Picture

A large number of misunderstandings come from people who do not have an overall view of how their role—and other people's roles—fit within the organization.

I've worked with engineers on getting them to do a better job of pitching their projects to the finance guys.

We discuss how getting the go-ahead depends on showing how your effort will cut costs or deliver returns. But some engineers didn't even know what the word "returns" means. Out of that discussion, the engineers finally understood why the finance department asked for projections. Then they stopped thinking of the finance people as enemies—and started seeing them as critical allies.

From there, we were able to stop the cycle in which engineers submitted inflated project budgets because they feared finance was going to cut funds, and finance would automatically cut funds because they assumed the numbers were inflated. Now, project budgets come in and they're either approved or denied. But the numbers are real, and both groups realize that they're part of the same team.

Ford Motor Co., like other big companies around the world, is undergoing revolutionary change to become more competitive. Its past formula for success is inadequate in today's global economy. Downsizing, reorganizations, team structure, speed, and new technology are the orders of the day. Such wrenching changes typically run into resistance among employees who fear change. That's where both external and internal change agents need to understand the dynamics of change, conflict, and negotiation—the topics discussed in this chapter. Ford's Visteon automotive systems can succeed only if skeptics are turned into advocates and potentially destructive conflict channeled into constructive effort.

The purpose of this chapter is to explore the dynamics of organizational change and its natural byproduct, conflict. We discuss change from organizational and individual perspectives, address resistance to change, and examine how to make change happen. We then consider the nature and management of conflict and conclude with a discussion of negotiation.

Change: Organizational and Individual Perspectives

Change is inevitable. How often have we heard this? So often it may appear to be a cliché. But it is the plain truth. Larry Bossidy, for example, saw his fair share of changes prior to his recent retirement. Having learned his craft under Jack Welch at General Electric, Bossidy became CEO of an underachieving AlliedSignal in 1991. By 2000, when AlliedSignal had merged with Honeywell and Bossidy retired, AlliedSignal was a profit machine with a reputation for top-notch quality. Bossidy had this to say about nonstop change: "One of the wonderful things about business: You have to work hard to forget what you know. If I like the business model now, I am not going to like it in five years."[1] Let us tackle this major challenge for managers by looking at four types of organizational change and also at how individuals tend to respond to significant changes. These twin perspectives are important because organizational changes unavoidably have personal impacts.

Types of Organizational Change

Consultant David A. Nadler and management professor Michael L. Tushman together developed an instructive typology of organizational change (see Figure 16.1). On the vertical axis of their model, change is characterized as either anticipatory or reactive. **Anticipatory changes** are any systematically planned changes intended to take advantage of expected situations. Oppositely, **reactive changes** are those necessitated by unexpected environmental events or pressures. The horizontal axis deals with the scope of a particular change, either incremental or strategic. **Incremental changes** involve subsystem adjustments needed to keep the organization on its chosen path. **Strategic changes** alter the overall shape or direction of the organization. For instance, adding a night shift to meet unexpectedly high demand for the company's product is an incremental change. Switching from building houses to building high-rise apartment complexes would be a strategic change. Four resulting types of organizational change in the Nadler-Tushman model are tuning, adaptation, reorientation, and re-creation.[2] These types of organizational changes, listed in order of increasing complexity, intensity, and risk, require a closer look.

Tuning.   This is the most common, least intense, and least risky type of change. Other names for it include preventive maintenance and the Japanese concept of *kaizen* (continuous improvement). The key to effective tuning is to actively anticipate and avoid problems rather than passively waiting for things to go wrong before taking action. For example, Du Pont tuned its marketing efforts by developing an Adopt-a-Customer program. The program "encourages blue-collar workers to visit a customer once a month, learn his needs, and be his representative on the factory floor."[3] This is a refreshing alternative to the traditional practice of waiting for customer complaints and only then trying to figure out how to fix them.

---

1 **Identify and describe four types of organizational change according to the Nadler-Tushman model.**

anticipatory changes *planned changes based on expected situations*

reactive changes *changes made in response to unexpected situations*

incremental changes *subsystem adjustments required to keep the organization on course*

strategic changes *altering the overall shape or direction of the organization*

Figure 16.1

Four Types of Organizational Change

Source: David A. Nadler and Michael L. Tushman, "Beyond the Charismatic Leader: Leadership and Organizational Change." Copyright 1990 by the Regents of the University of California. Reprinted from the *California Management Review*, vol. 32, no. 2. By permission of the Regents.

Sometimes it takes bad times to make us appreciate the good times. Just ask the Irish, who have taken many hard knocks through the years. Things have dramatically changed for the better in Ireland today, as evidenced here by the biggest construction boom in Dublin's history. A young, well-educated population and benefits from European economic unification promise more good times ahead. This sort of systemic change has major implications for organizations and individuals alike.

Adaptation.   Like tuning, adaptation involves incremental changes.[4] But this time, the changes are in reaction to external problems, events, or pressures. For example, after Ford had great success with its aerodynamic styling, General Motors and Chrysler followed suit. In turn, Ford and GM broadened their product lines to compete with Chrysler's trend-setting minivans.

Reorientation.   This type of change is anticipatory and strategic in scope. Nadler and Tushman call reorientation "frame bending" because the organization is significantly redirected. Importantly, there is not a complete break with the organization's past. As *Business Week* reported in 1997, German automaker Mercedes-Benz has gone through some serious frame bending to remain globally competitive:

> *In Alabama, Mercedes is not simply building its first sport-utility vehicle. It's building its first SUV in its first foreign plant, with its first non-German workforce. Even though the auto maker took a big gamble relying on workers who have never built an automobile—let alone a Mercedes—it had little choice.*
>
> *To keep growing, Mercedes executives know they must broaden their customer base to include younger, less affluent buyers. That means sportier, cheaper models—and an escape from the trap of high-priced labor at home.[5]*

Yes, Mercedes-Benz is still in the motor vehicle business. But management is rethinking virtually every aspect of that business, especially since the DaimlerChrysler merger.

Re-Creation.   Competitive pressures normally trigger this most intense and risky type of organizational change. Nadler and Tushman say it amounts to "frame breaking." A stunning example of frame breaking is the software giant Microsoft. Cofounder and CEO Bill Gates tied his company's future to the Internet after initially dismissing it as a passing fad. According to observers at the time:

> *Indeed, in just six months, Gates has done what few executives have dared. He has taken a thriving, $8 billion, 20,000-employee company and done a massive about-face. "I can't think of one corporation that has had this kind of success and after 20 years, just stopped*

and decided to reinvent itself from the ground up," says Jeffrey Katzenberg, a principal of DreamWorks SKG, which has a joint venture with Microsoft. "What they're doing is decisive, quick, breathtaking."[6]

Frame breaking helped Bill Gates to re-create Microsoft's strategy and products around the Internet.

Individual Reactions to Change

Ultimately, workplace changes of all types become a *personal* matter for employees. A merger, for example, means a new job assignment for one person and a new boss for another. The first person may look forward to the challenge of a new assignment, while the second may dread the prospect of adjusting to a new boss. Researchers tell us these two people will tend to exhibit distinctly different response patterns.[7] Specifically, people tend to respond to changes they *like* differently than they do to changes they *dislike*. Let us explore these two response patterns with the goal of developing a contingency model for managers. Importantly, both models are generic, that is, they apply equally to on- and off-the-job changes.

How People Respond to Changes They Like.   According to Figure 16.2, a three-stage adjustment is typical when people encounter a change they like. New college graduates, for instance, often see their unrealistic optimism (stage A) give way to the reality shock (stage B) of earning a living before getting their life and career on track (stage C). Key personal factors—including attitude, morale, and desire to make the change work—dip during stage B. Sometimes the dip is so severe or prolonged the person gives up as, say, when newlyweds head for the divorce court. Stage B is thus a critical juncture where leadership can make a difference.[8]

How People Respond to Changes They Fear and Dislike.   Although exact statistics are not available, the situation in Figure 16.3 probably is more common in the workplace than the one in Figure 16.2. In other words, on-the-job change generally is

> **2** Explain how people tend to respond differently to changes they like and those they dislike.

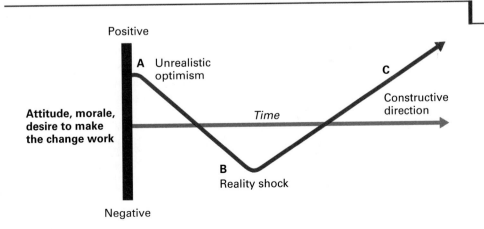

Figure 16.2

How People Tend to Respond to Changes They *Like*

Figure 16.3

How People Tend to Respond to Changes They *Fear* and *Dislike*

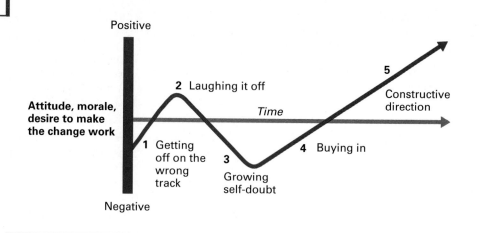

more feared than welcomed. Changes, particularly sudden ones, represent the unknown. Most of us fear the unknown. We can bring the model in Figure 16.3 to life by walking through it with Maria, a production supervisor at a dairy products cooperative. She and her coworkers face a major reorganization involving a switch to team-based production.

In stage 1, Maria feels a bit unsure and somewhat overwhelmed by the sudden switch to teams. She needs a lot more information to decide whether she really likes the idea. She feels twinges of fear. Stage 2 finds Maria joking with the other supervisors about how upper management's enthusiasm for teams will blow over in a few days, so there's no need to worry. Her attitude, mood, and desire for change improve a bit. After an initial training session on team-based management and participation, Maria begins to worry about her job security. Even if she keeps her job, she wonders if she is up to the new way of doing things. Her morale drops sharply in stage 3. In stage 4, after a stern but supportive lecture from her boss about being a team player, Maria comes to grips with her resistance to the team approach. She resolves to stop criticizing management's "fad of the week" and help make the switch to teams a success. Her attitude turns positive, and her morale takes an upswing in stage 5, as she tries participative management techniques and gets positive results. Additional training and some personal research and reading on team-based management convince Maria this approach is the wave of the future.

Six months after the switch to teams was announced, Maria has become an outspoken advocate for teams and participative management. Her job security is strengthened by a pending promotion to the training department, where she will coordinate all team training for supervisors. Unknown to upper management, Maria has even toyed with the idea of starting her own consulting business, specializing in team management. Maria's transition from fear to full adaptation has taken months and has not been easy. But the experience has been normal and positive, including a timely boost from her manager between stages 3 and 4.

A Contingency Model for Getting Employees Through Changes.   Contingency managers, once again, adapt their techniques to the situation. The response patterns in Figures 16.2 and 16.3 call for different managerial actions. Managerial action steps for both situations are listed in Table 16.1. When employees understand that stages B and 3 are normal and expected responses, they will be less apt to panic and more likely to respond favorably to managerial guidance through action steps C and 4 and 5.[9]

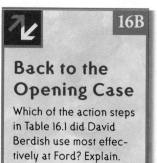

16B

Back to the Opening Case

Which of the action steps in Table 16.1 did David Berdish use most effectively at Ford? Explain.

Situation: The person *likes* the change.

Stage	Managerial Action Steps
A. Unrealistic optimism "What a great idea! It will solve all our problems."	Encourage enthusiasm while directing attention to potential problems and the cooperation and work necessary to get the job done.
B. Reality shock "This is going to be a lot harder than it seemed."	Listen supportively to negative feelings and neutralize unreasonable fears. Set realistic short-term goals. Build self-confidence. Recognize and reward positive comments and progress.
C. Constructive direction "This won't be easy, but we can do it."	Set broader and longer-term goals. Encourage involvement. Emphasize group problem solving and learning. Celebrate individual and group achievements. Prepare for bigger and better things.

Situation: The person *fears* and *dislikes* the change.

Stage	Managerial Action Steps
1. Getting off on the wrong track "What a dumb idea!"	Be a positive role model for the vision of a better way. Be a supportive listener and correct any misunderstanding.
2. Laughing it off "Just another wild idea that won't go anywhere. Don't worry about it."	Same as action step A above.
3. Growing self-doubt "I don't think I have what it takes."	Same as action step B above.
4. Buying in "Okay, I'll give this thing a try."	Encourage the person to let go of the past and look forward to a better future. Build personal commitment. Recognize and reward positive words and actions.
5. Constructive direction "This won't be easy, but we can do it."	Same as action step C above.

Overcoming Resistance to Change

Dealing with change is an integral part of modern management.[10] Change expert Ichak Adizes puts it this way:

> *Living means solving problems, and growing up means being able to solve bigger problems. The purpose of management, leadership, parenting, or governing is exactly that: to solve today's problems and get ready to deal with tomorrow's problems. This is necessary because there is change. No management is needed when there are no problems, and there are no*

Put yourself in the place of Carlos Gutierrez, CEO of Kellogg. Cold cereals account for 80 percent of revenues, but sales are flat in that market because people tend to skip breakfast these days. Upon taking his new position, Gutierrez pledged to raise profits 10 percent a year—time for some big changes and new products. Among the "frame bending" initiatives at Kellogg are cross-functional teams, more free-wheeling creativity, and a renewed commitment to diversity to fight narrow thinking. *Voila!* In just one recent month 65 new product ideas were served up.

problems only when we are dead. To manage is to be alive, and to be alive means to experience change with the accompanying problems it brings.[11]

Within the change typology just discussed, organizational change comes in all sizes and shapes. Often it's new and unfamiliar technology, such as the Internet. It could be a reorganization, a merger, a new pay plan, or perhaps a new performance-appraisal program. Whatever its form, change is like a stone tossed into a still pond. The initial impact causes ripples to radiate in all directions, often with unpredictable consequences. A common consequence of change in organizations is resistance from those whose jobs are directly affected. Both rational and irrational resistance can bring the wheels of progress to a halt. Management faces the challenge of foreseeing and neutralizing resistance to change. The question is, how? To answer that question, we must examine why employees resist change.

Why Do Employees Resist Change?

Employees resist change for many reasons.[12] The following are the most common:

3 List at least six reasons why employees resist change and discuss what management can do about resistance to change.

Surprise.   Significant changes that are introduced on the spur of the moment or with no warning can create a threatening sense of imbalance in the workplace. Regarding this problem, an executive task force at J. C. Penney Co., the well-known retailer, recommended: "Schedule changes in measurable, comfortable stages. Too much, too soon can be counterproductive."[13]

Inertia.   Many members of the typical organization desire to maintain a safe, secure, and predictable status quo. The bywords of this group are, "But we don't do things that way here." Technological inertia also is a common problem. Consider, for example, the history of the standard typewriter keyboard (referred to as the Qwerty keyboard because *Q, W, E, R, T,* and *Y* are the first six letters in the upper left-hand corner).

> *The ungainly layout of the Qwerty keyboard was introduced in 1873 to slow down typists so they wouldn't jam keys. That design imperative quickly disappeared, yet Qwerty has turned back all attempts—including one by its own inventor—to replace it with something faster. The productive cost? Undoubtedly billions of dollars.*[14]

Thanks to resistance to change, the latest high-tech marvels in personal computing come out of the box today complete with an 1873-style keyboard! Supervisors and middle managers who fall victim to unthinking inertia can effectively kill change programs.[15]

Misunderstanding/Ignorance/Lack of Skills.   Without adequate introductory or remedial training, an otherwise positive change may be perceived in a negative light.

Emotional Side Effects.   Those who are forced to accept on-the-job changes commonly experience a sense of loss over past ways of doing things. For example, consider the following chain of events at Japan's Nissan Motor Company:

> *To consolidate the company's brands worldwide, a headquarters edict jettisoned the high-profile Datsun brand from the U.S. market in favor of the corporate moniker. The changeover dragged on for five years, as frustrated dealers stonewalled the change by refusing to pay for new signs. Once drawn to Datsun for performance and sportiness, customers became confused. Many thought Nissan was a Toyota subsidiary. "Unfortunately, the Nissan name is still weak," Chairman Yutaka Kume concedes.*[16]

Lack of Trust.   Promises of improvement are likely to fall on deaf ears when employees do not trust management. Conversely, managers are unlikely to permit necessary participation if they do not trust their people.

Fear of Failure.   Just as most college freshmen have doubts about their chances of ever graduating, challenges presented by significant on-the-job changes can also be intimidating.

Personality Conflicts.   Managers who are disliked by their people are poor conduits for change.

Poor Timing.   In every work setting, internal and/or external events can conspire to create resentment about a particular change. For example, Intel's across-the-board salary cut, in response to an electronics industry slump during the 1980s, generated greater-than-expected resentment because "the salary cuts were timed to come just as taxes for Social Security were reimposed."[17]

Lack of Tact.   As we all know, it is not necessarily what is said that shapes our attitude toward people and events. *How* it is said is often more important. Tactful and sensitive handling of changes is essential.

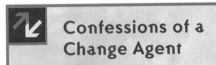

16C

Confessions of a Change Agent

Hi. My name is Seth, and I have a problem: I'm a change junkie. If the world around me isn't changing, I get bored and become inefficient.

On second thought, that's not really my problem. My problem is that while I'm busy advocating change, insisting on change, and teaching change, deep down inside, I hate change. Change is inconvenient, painful, and frightening.

Source: Seth Godin, "Change Agent," *Fast Company,* no. 29 (November 1999): 356.

Questions: *How often are you caught in this revolving door of loving and hating change? Explain the circumstances. How do you deal with such mixed emotions about change in yourself and in others?*

Threat to Job Status/Security.   Because employment fulfills basic needs, employees can be expected to resist changes with real or imaginary impacts on job status or job security.

Breakup of Work Group.   Significant changes can tear the fabric of on-the-job social relationships. Accordingly, members of cohesive work groups often exert peer pressure on one another to resist changes that threaten to break up the group.[18]

These reasons for resisting change help demonstrate that participation is not a panacea. For example, imagine the futility of trying to gain the enthusiastic support of a team of auto assembly line welders for a robot that will eventually take over their jobs. In extreme form, each reason for resisting change can become an insurmountable barrier to genuine participation. Therefore, managers need a broad array of methods for dealing with resistance to change.

Strategies for Overcoming Resistance to Change

Only in recent years have management theorists begun to give serious attention to alternative ways of overcoming resistance to change.[19] At least six options, including participation, are available in this area:

1. *Education and communication.* This strategy is appealing because it advocates prevention rather than cure. The idea here is to help employees understand the true need for a change as well as the logic behind it. Various media may be used, including face-to-face discussions, formal group presentations, or special reports or publications.
2. *Participation and involvement.* Once again, personal involvement through participation tends to defuse both rational and irrational fears about a workplace change. By participating in both the design and implementation of a change, one acquires a personal stake in its success.
3. *Facilitation and support.* When fear and anxiety are responsible for resistance to doing things in a new and different way, support from management in the form of special training, job stress counseling, and compensatory time off can be helpful.
4. *Negotiation and agreement.* Sometimes management can neutralize potential or actual resistance by exchanging something of value for cooperation. An hourly clerical employee may, for instance, be put on a salary in return for learning how to operate a new Internet workstation.
5. *Manipulation and co-optation.* Manipulation occurs when managers selectively withhold or dispense information and consciously arrange events to increase the chance that a change will be successful. Co-optation normally involves token participation. Those who are co-opted with token participation cannot claim they have not been consulted, yet the ultimate impact of their input is negligible.
6. *Explicit and implicit coercion.* Managers who cannot or will not invest the time required for the other strategies can force employees to go along with a change by threatening them with termination, loss of pay raises or promotions, transfer, and the like.

As shown in Table 16.2, each of these strategies for overcoming resistance to change has advantages and drawbacks. Situational appropriateness is the key to success.

Now we turn our attention to implementing changes in organizations.

16D

Back to the Opening Case

"People don't resist change, they resist the unknown."

Source: Consultant Peter Giuliano, as quoted in Stephanie Armour, "Failure to Communicate Costly for Companies," *USA Today* (September 30, 1998): 1B.

Questions: *What key lessons does this statement teach us about avoiding and managing resistance to change? Explain. Did Berdish do a good job with this problem at Ford's Visteon? Explain.*

Table 16.2	**Dealing with Resistance to Change**		
Approach	**Commonly used in situations**	**Advantages**	**Drawbacks**
1. Education + communication	Where there is a lack of information or inaccurate information and analysis	Once persuaded, people will often help with the implementation of the change	Can be very time-consuming if lots of people are involved
2. Participation + involvement	Where the initiators do not have all the information they need to design the change, and where others have considerable power to resist	People who participate will be committed to implementing change, and any relevant information they have will be integrated into the change plan	Can be very time-consuming if participators design an inappropriate change
3. Facilitation + support	Where people are resisting because of adjustment problems	No other approach works as well with adjustment problems	Can be time-consuming, expensive, and still fail
4. Negotiation + agreement	Where someone or some group will clearly lose out in a change, and where that group has considerable power to resist	Sometimes it is a relatively easy way to avoid major resistance	Can be too expensive in many cases if it alerts others to negotiate for compliance
5. Manipulation + co-optation	Where other tactics will not work or are too expensive	It can be a relatively quick and inexpensive solution to resistance problems	Can lead to future problems if people feel manipulated
6. Explicit + implicit coercion	Where speed is essential, and the change initiators possess considerable power	It is speedy, and can overcome any kind of resistance	Can be risky if it leaves people mad at the initiators

Source: Reprinted by permission of the *Harvard Business Review*. An exhibit from "Choosing Strategies for Change," by John P. Kotter and Leonard A. Schlesinger (March–April 1979, p. 111). Copyright © 1979 by the President and Fellows of Harvard College; all rights reserved.

Making Change Happen

In these fast-paced times, managers need to be active agents of change rather than passive observers or, worse, victims of circumstances beyond their control. This active role requires foresight, responsiveness, flexibility, and adaptability. Management author and professor Oren Harari recently offered this perspective:

> We can't deny or delay upheavals that are coming around the corner in every sector of the economy. All we can do is mobilize our company to search for them, seize them as they emerge, and use them to reinvent our business and create new value for customers and investors.[20]

This section focuses on two approaches to making change happen: (1) organization development, typically a formal top-down approach, and (2) a checklist for change agents at all levels, with an emphasis on unofficial change initiatives.

To the casual observer, venerable Ford Motor Company and Internet powerhouse Yahoo! probably have very little in common. But Yahoo!'s cofounder Jerry Yang (right) had the rapt attention of Ford's CEO, Jacques Nasser (center), when the two recently announced a sweeping new business alliance. While the final result won't exactly be Ford.com, Nasser calls the effort a "total reinvention" of the automaker. The idea is to exploit Internet efficiencies throughout the product design/supply chain/assembly/marketing cycle. Success of this bold vision hinges on Nasser's ability to conquer resistance to change within Ford.

Planned Change Through Organization Development (OD)

Organization development has become a convenient label for a host of techniques and processes aimed at making sick organizations healthy and healthy organizations healthier.[21] According to experts in the field:

organization development (OD) *planned change programs intended to help people and organizations function more effectively*

> ***Organization development (OD)*** *consists of planned efforts to help persons work and live together more effectively, over time, in their organizations. These goals are achieved by applying behavioral science principles, methods, and theories adapted from the fields of psychology, sociology, education, and management.*[22]

Others simply call OD *planned change*. Regarding the degree of change involved, OD consultant and writer Warner Burke contends:

> *Organization development is a process of fundamental change in an organization's culture. By fundamental change, as opposed to fixing a problem or improving a procedure, I mean that some significant aspect of the organization's culture will never be the same.*[23]

OD programs generally are facilitated by hired consultants,[24] although inside OD specialists also can be found.

The Objectives of OD.   OD programs vary because they are tailored to unique situations. What is appropriate for one organization may be totally out of place in another. In spite of this variation, certain objectives are common to most OD programs. In general, OD programs develop social processes such as trust, problem solving, communication, and cooperation to facilitate organizational change and enhance personal and organizational effectiveness. More specifically, the typical OD program tries to achieve the following seven objectives:

1. Deepen the sense of organizational purpose (or vision) and align individuals with that purpose.
2. Strengthen interpersonal trust, communication, cooperation, and support.
3. Encourage a problem-solving rather than problem-avoiding approach to organizational problems.
4. Develop a satisfying work experience capable of building enthusiasm.
5. Supplement formal authority with authority based on personal knowledge and skill.
6. Increase personal responsibility for planning and implementing.
7. Encourage personal willingness to change.[25]

Critics of OD are quick to point out that there is nothing really new in this list of objectives. Directly or indirectly, each of these objectives is addressed by one or another general management technique. OD advocates respond by noting that general management lacks a systematic approach. They feel that the usual practice of teaching managers how to plan, solve problems, make decisions, organize, motivate, lead, and control leads to a haphazard, bits-and-pieces management style. According to OD thinking, organization development gives managers a vehicle for systematically introducing change by applying a broad selection of management techniques as a unified and consistent package. This, they claim, leads to greater personal, group, and organizational effectiveness.

The OD Process.   A simple metaphor helps introduce the three major components of OD.[26] Suppose someone hands you a coffee cup filled with clear, solid ice. You look down through the ice and see a penny lying tails up on the bottom of the cup. Now suppose for some reason you want the penny to be frozen in place in a heads-up position. What can you do? There is really only one practical solution. You let the ice in the cup thaw, reach in and flip the penny over, and then refreeze the cup of water. This is precisely how social psychologist Kurt Lewin recommended that change be handled in social systems. Specifically, Lewin recommended that change agents unfreeze, change, and then refreeze social systems.[27]

Unfreezing prepares the members of a social system for change and then helps neutralize initial resistance. Sudden, unexpected change, according to Lewin, is socially disruptive. When the change has been introduced, **refreezing** is necessary to follow up on problems, complaints, unanticipated side effects, and any lingering resistance. This seemingly simple approach to change spells the difference between systematic and haphazard change.

The OD model introduced here is based on Lewin's approach to handling change (see Figure 16.4). Diagnosis is carried out during the unfreezing phase. Change is then carefully introduced through tailor-made intervention. Finally, a systematic follow-up refreezes the situation. Each phase is critical to successful organizational change and development. Still, it takes continual recycling through this three-phase sequence to make OD an ongoing system of planned change.

> **4** Describe how the unfreezing-change-refreezing analogy applies to organization development (OD).

> **unfreezing** *neutralizing resistance by preparing people for change*

> **refreezing** *systematically following up a change program for lasting results*

5P Checklist for Change Agents

OD is rationally planned, formal, systematic, and initiated by top management. As a sign of the times, many of today's organizations cannot be described in those terms.

Figure 16.4 | A General Model of OD

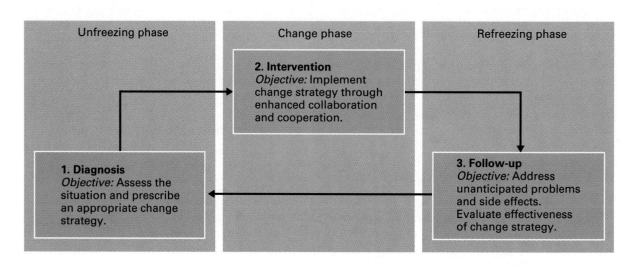

They tend to be spontaneous, informal, experimental, and driven from within. (Interestingly, employees in some of these modern organizations were empowered by earlier OD programs.)[28] Unusual things can happen when empowered employees start to take the initiative. Consider the unconventional language in this recent description of change:

> *Change starts with finding a backer—someone who can sell your plan to the senior team. Change dies without a fighter—someone smart enough and skilled enough to win over the opposition. Change kicks in when people start to trust—in the plan and in one another. Trust is the glue that invariably holds a change effort together. Change just might work when people are focused—on the goal, and on each step that's necessary to achieve it.*
>
> *Getting the buy-in. Overcoming resistance. Building trust. Zeroing in on the objective. These are the critical skills that every change team must leverage if it is to have any hope of succeeding.*[29]

This is not top-down change in the tradition of OD. Rather, it involves change from inside the organization. The 5P checklist gives change agents *at all levels* a road map for turning ideas into action.

The 5P model consists of an easy-to-remember list for anyone interested in organizational change: *preparation, purpose, participation, progress,* and *persistence* (see Figure 16.5). The model is generic, meaning it applies to profit and nonprofit organizations of all sizes. Let us examine each item more closely.

↗↙ The Power of Symbolism   16E

Situation: As discussed in Chapter 7, David Pottruck, co-CEO of discount stockbroker Charles Schwab, decided in 1998 to let e.Schwab's low price cannibalize the firm's main business. The risky move was a smashing success.

To prepare staffers for this particular plunge, Pottruck staged an odd little ceremony in which he walked across the Golden Gate Bridge with 100 or so of Schwab's top managers in tow. He called the event Crossing the Chasm—symbolism intended to suggest leaving one business model behind and embracing a new one based on the Internet.

Source: Jerry Useem, "Internet Defense Strategy: Cannibalize Yourself," *Fortune* (September 6, 1999): 126.

Questions: *What phase of the OD process does this represent? Explain. Why is it important for change agents to know how to use symbolism?*

Figure 16.5

The 5P Checklist for Change Agents

Key action steps

✓	**P**reparation	Develop concept; test assumptions; weigh costs and benefits; identify champion or driver.
✓	**P**urpose	Specify measurable objectives, milestones, deadlines.
✓	**P**articipation	Refine concept while building broad and powerful support.
✓	**P**rogress	Keep things moving forward despite roadblocks.
✓	**P**ersistence	Foster realistic expectations and a sense of urgency while avoiding impatience.

■ *Preparation:* Is the concept or problem clearly defined? Has adequate problem *finding* taken place? Are underlying assumptions sound? Will the end result be worth the collective time, effort, and expense? Can the change initiative be harnessed to another change effort with a high probability of success, or should it stand alone? Does the proposed change have a *champion* or a *driver* who has the passion and persistence to see the process through to completion?

5 **Identify and highlight the 5Ps in the checklist for change agents.**

Corporate mergers aren't just for the big guys anymore. When Eileen Gittins, CEO of Personify, a small San Francisco e-commerce firm, had a growing list of customers clamoring for a broader range of services, she decided to buy a Bay area company, 30-employee Anubis Solutions. Wisely, Gittins and Anubis's cofounders, Adeeb Shana'a and Amit Desai, didn't rush things. In line with what OD experts recommend, they took the time to get comfortable with the "feel" of each other's operations. This unfreezing phase included "cultural ambassadors" who helped employees from both companies get acquainted.

Change Takes Time   **16F**

Barbara Reinhold, career development director, Smith College, Northampton, Massachusetts:

Change is not a process for the impatient. It takes time—a simple truth that many of us fail to realize. First, understand that the metabolism rate—the tolerance for change—of your boss or of your organization might be dramatically different from your own. Then look around. Find other people who are willing to take the journey of change with you. Never go it alone. Undoubtedly, others in your company feel as you do. Your task is to find them.

Source: "Barbara Reinhold," *Fast Company*, no. 23 (April 1999): 94.

Questions: *Which of the 5Ps are evident in this bit of practical advice? What is your "metabolism rate" for change? Does impatience ever cause you problems?*

- *Purpose:* Can the objective or goal of the change initiative be expressed in clear, measurable terms? Can it be described quickly to busy people? What are the specific progress milestones and critical deadlines?
- *Participation:* Have key people been involved in refining the change initiative to the extent of having personal ownership and willingness to fight for it? Have potential or actual opponents been offered a chance to participate? Have powerful people in the organization been recruited as advocates and defenders?
- *Progress:* Are performance milestones and intermediate deadlines being met? If not, why? Is support for the initiative weakening? Why? Have unexpected roadblocks been encountered? How can they be removed or avoided?
- *Persistence:* Has a reasonable sense of urgency been communicated to all involved? (Note: extreme impatience can fray relationships and be stressful.) Has the change team drifted away from the original objective as time passed? Does everyone on the team have realistic expectations about how long the change process will take?

With situational adjustments for unique personalities and circumstances, the 5P approach can help ordinary employees create extraordinary change.[30] So sharpen your concept and take your best shot!

Managing Conflict

Conflict is intimately related to change and interpersonal dealings.[31] Harvard's Abraham Zaleznik offered this perspective:

Because people come together to satisfy a wide array of psychological needs, social relations in general are awash with conflict. In the course of their interactions, people must deal with differences as well as similarities, with aversions as well as affinities. Indeed, in social relations, Sigmund Freud's parallel of humans and porcupines is apt: like porcupines, people prick and injure one another if they get too close; they will feel cold if they get too far apart.[32]

The term *conflict* has a strong negative connotation, evoking words such as opposition, anger, and aggression. But conflict does not have to be a negative experience. Based on research evidence that most organizational conflict occurs within a cooperative context, Dean Tjosvold recently offered this more positive definition: "**Conflict** involves incompatible behaviors; one person interfering, disrupting, or in some other way making another's actions less effective."[33] This definition paves the way for an important distinction between *competitive* (or destructive) conflict and *cooperative* (or constructive) conflict. Cooperative conflict is based on the win-win negotiating attitude discussed later in this chapter. Also, recall our discussion of cooperative conflict in Chapter 14 as a tool for avoiding groupthink.

conflict *incompatible behaviors that make another person less effective*

Dealing with the Two Faces of Conflict

Tjosvold contrasts competitive and cooperative conflict as follows:

> The assumption that conflict is based on opposing interests leads to viewing conflict as a struggle to see whose strength and interests will dominate and whose will be subordinated. We must fight to win, or at least not lose. The assumption that you have largely cooperative goals leads to viewing the conflict as a common problem to be solved for mutual benefit, which in turn makes it more likely that the conflict will be constructive and that people will improve their abilities to deal with conflict.[34]

6 Contrast the competitive and cooperative conflict styles.

Figure 16.6 graphically illustrates the difference between competitive and cooperative conflict. In the competitive mode, the parties pursue directly opposite goals. Each mistrusts the other's intentions and disbelieves what the other party says. Both parties actively avoid constructive dialogue and have a win-lose attitude. Unavoidably, the disagreement persists and they go their separate ways.[35] Does this self-defeating cycle sound familiar? Probably, because most of us at one time or another have suffered through a broken relationship or destructive conflict with the boss.

In sharp contrast, the *cooperative* conflict cycle in Figure 16.6 is a mutually reinforcing experience serving the best interests of both parties. Cooperative conflict is standard practice at Anheuser-Busch, brewer of Budweiser beer:

> When the policy committee of that company considers a major move—getting into or out of a business, or making a big capital expenditure—it sometimes assigns teams to make the case for each side of the question. There may be two teams or even three. Each is knowledgeable about the subject; each has access to the same information. Occasionally someone in favor of the project is chosen to lead the dissent, and an opponent to argue for it. Pat Stokes, who heads the company's beer empire, describes the result: "We end up with decisions and alternatives we hadn't thought of previously," sometimes representing a synthesis of the opposing views. "You become a lot more anticipatory, better able to see what might happen, because you have thought through the process."[36]

As a skill-building exercise, you might want to use the cooperative conflict model in Figure 16.6 to salvage a personal relationship mired in competitive conflict. Show the cooperative model to the other party and suggest starting over with a new set of ground rules. Cooperative goals are the necessary starting point. This process can be difficult, yet very rewarding. Win-win conflict is not just a good idea; it is one of the keys to a better world. (See Skills & Tools at the end of this chapter for tips on how to express anger.)

Figure 16.6 | Competitive Versus Cooperative Conflict

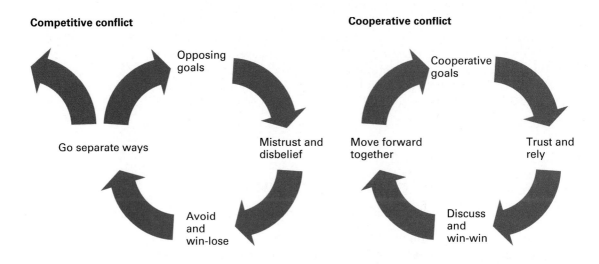

Competitive conflict

Opposing goals → Mistrust and disbelief → Avoid and win-lose → Go separate ways

Cooperative conflict

Cooperative goals → Trust and rely → Discuss and win-win → Move forward together

Source (right figure): Reprinted from *Learning to Manage Conflict: Getting People to Work Together Productively* by Dean Tjosvold. Copyright © 1993 by Dean Tjosvold. First published by Lexington Books. All rights reserved. All correspondence should be sent to Lexington Books, 4720 Boston Way, Lanham, Md. 20706.

16G

Greenpeace Disagrees Without Being Disagreeable

Rick Hind, legislative director, Greenpeace Toxics Campaign:

At Greenpeace, we are often in conflict with PVC manufacturers. The big users of plastics don't need to use PVC—but they don't know that yet. We start out by being reasonable. For example, we met with the whole toy industry before we made a public campaign against vinyl toys. When two meetings resulted in foot-dragging and stonewalling, we began to publicize toy additives. After two years of such publicity, companies became interested in talking with us privately.

Source: As quoted in "Disagree—Without Being Disagreeable," *Fast Company*, no. 29 (November 1999): 58.

Questions: *Why is it so difficult for people to avoid competitive and destructive conflict? Why is it important for environmentalists at Greenpeace to engage in cooperative conflict?*

There are two sets of tools available for managing conflict.[37] The first we call conflict triggers, which stimulate conflict; the second involves conflict resolution techniques, which are used when constructive conflict deteriorates into destructive conflict.

Conflict Triggers

A **conflict trigger** is a circumstance that increases the chances of intergroup or interpersonal conflict. As long as a conflict trigger appears to stimulate constructive conflict,[38] it can be allowed to continue. But as soon as the symptoms of destructive conflict[39] become apparent, steps need to be taken to remove or correct the offending conflict trigger. Major conflict triggers include the following:

- *Ambiguous or overlapping jurisdictions.* Unclear job boundaries often create competition for resources and control. Reorganization can help to clarify job boundaries if destructive conflict becomes a problem (refer to the organization design alternatives discussed in Chapter 10).

conflict trigger *any factor that increases the chances of conflict*

- *Competition for scarce resources.* As the term is used here, *resources* include funds, personnel, authority, power, and valuable information. In other words, anything of value in an organizational setting can become a competitively sought-after scarce resource. Sometimes, as in the case of money and people, destructive competition for scarce resources can be avoided by enlarging the resource base (such as increasing competing managers' budgets or hiring additional personnel).[40]

- *Communication breakdowns.* Because communication is a complex process beset by many barriers, these barriers often provoke conflict. It is easy to misunderstand another person or group of people if two-way communication is hampered in some way. The battle for clear communication never ends.

- *Time pressure.* Deadlines and other forms of time pressure can stimulate prompt performance or trigger destructive emotional reactions. When imposing deadlines, managers should consider individuals' ability to cope.

- *Unreasonable standards, rules, policies, or procedures.* These triggers generally lead to dysfunctional conflict between managers and the people they manage. The best remedy is for the manager to tune into employees' perceptions of fair play and correct extremely unpopular situations before they mushroom.

- *Personality clashes.* It is very difficult to change one's personality on the job. Therefore the practical remedy for serious personality clashes is to separate the antagonistic parties by reassigning one or both to a new job.[41]

- *Status differentials.* As long as productive organizations continue to be arranged hierarchically, this trigger is unavoidable. But managers can minimize dysfunctional conflict by showing a genuine concern for the ideas, feelings, and values of subordinates.

- *Unrealized expectations.* Dissatisfaction grows when expectations are not met. Conflict is another byproduct of unrealized expectations. Destructive conflict can be avoided in this area by taking time to discover, through frank discussion, what people expect from their employment. Unrealistic expectations can be countered before they become a trigger for dysfunctional conflict.[42]

Managers who understand these conflict triggers will be in a much better position to manage conflict in a systematic and rational fashion. Those who passively wait for things to explode before reacting will find conflict managing them (see Management Ethics).

Curbing Workplace Incivility: Let's Start with "Please" and "Thank You" 16H

Rude, obnoxious, boorish behavior. It may not be illegal, but it's all too familiar. You know what I'm talking about . . . [for example,] the guy in the urban assault vehicle who cut you off in traffic.

You race into the office just in time for a meeting with the boss, which starts late and gets interrupted half a dozen times in the hour you've managed to schedule with him because he answers his phone while you sit and wait, inwardly steaming. You return to the semi-haven of your cubicle and begin sorting through 47 e-mails and 11 voice messages. It's not easy to concentrate because the gang from marketing is replaying last night's basketball game just outside your walls. You go to fetch a cup of coffee from the community pot, and find it empty—whoever took the last cup didn't start a new pot brewing . . . and so your day goes.

Source: Chris Lee, "The Death of Civility," *Training*, 36 (July 1999): 25.

Questions: *Do you think standards of social conduct have declined in recent years? Explain. Is incivility a conflict trigger in the workplace? Explain. What can managers do to improve the situation?*

Management Ethics

Good Fun or a Really Bad Idea? You Decide.

Remember your last Truly Great Idea? What if, while you teetered on the cusp of it, the director of marketing slowly, silently, crept into your cubicle and unloaded his clip—of rubber bands, mind you—on the back of your hard-working head? Would you curse and draft a brusque letter to his supervisor, or with lightning speed lunge for your own trusty shooter, 'cause now it's payback time? Your gut response says a lot about whether you belong in some Silicon Valley companies.

Guns that shoot plastic disks, foam arrows, rubber bands, Ping-Pong balls, and even water can be found in startups all over the Valley. . . .

Fans of toy guns point to their ability to puncture seriousness, level hierarchy, strengthen community, and reduce stress in the workplace. Right. Yes. Of course. But what they're really thinking about is the gee-whiz thrill of diving into a cubicle to pop a cap in a coworker's butt. Like short pants or the dog under the desk, the toy gun has become a trapping of the wacky workplace culture that no self-respecting tech firm can do without.

Perhaps because gunplay could strike outsiders as unprofessional—or worse—many companies are reluctant to confirm or deny reports of interoffice warfare.

Officials may be skittish, but sidle up to an employee and you'll hear war stories—often told with an unabashed enthusiasm that borders on glee. Most gunplay occurs among friends. "It's actually an affectionate act. You can shoot me, I'll shoot you, and we'll run around and have a little war," says one engineer. Less frequent—but all the more prized—are all-out battles between departments. To welcome the technical-support division into the fold, the engineers at one company staged a raid. "There was a bunch of them, and they came to our area," remembers one victim, "and they converged on us and kind of spread out and started shooting. It was great!" . . .

Like most things in life, what's fun for some can be hell for the rest. If you don't feel like playing with a gun, say the experts, then don't shoot back, and after a round or two the shooter will desist. But if you never feel like playing, you might have problems in a gun-lovin' company. An engineer at an East Bay company notes, "You have to participate in whatever culture your workplace is providing; otherwise you're seen to be a bad egg." In some companies the bad eggs include a disproportionate number of women. One woman who treasures her gun admits nonetheless, "It's very much a boy culture. What do a bunch of girls do to be playful? We wouldn't say, 'Oh, how fun! Let's shoot each other, hit each other, throw things at each other!' "

Those who don't relish such shenanigans should take heart—gunplay eventually tapers off as a company grows in size and stature or is acquired by a larger firm with a more conventional culture. Those who do relish shenanigans should also take heart—for every company that outgrows the Nerf rocket launcher, another one is born. And it just might be the place to try out your new Super Soaker XP 90 with pulsating nozzle.

Source: Excerpted from Sue Wilson, "Let's Shoot Foam Arrows at Each Other!" *Fortune* (November 22, 1999). © 1999 Time Inc. Reprinted by permission.

Resolving Conflict

7 **Identify and describe five conflict resolution techniques.**

Even the best managers sometimes find themselves in the middle of destructive conflict, whether it is due to inattention or to circumstances beyond their control. In such situations, they may choose to do nothing, called an *avoidance* strategy by some, or try one or more of the following conflict resolution techniques.[43]

Problem Solving.   When conflicting parties take the time to identify and correct the source of their conflict, they are engaging in problem solving. This approach is based on the assumption that causes must be rooted out and attacked if anything is really to change. Problem solving (refer to our discussion of creative problem solving in Chapter 8) encourages managers to focus their attention on causes, factual information, and promising alternatives rather than on personalities or scapegoats. The major shortcoming of the problem-solving approach is that it takes time, but the investment of extra time can pay off handsomely when the problem is corrected instead of ignored and allowed to worsen.

Superordinate Goals.   "Superordinate goals are highly valued, unattainable by any one group [or individual] alone, and commonly sought."[44] When a manager relies on superordinate goals to resolve destructive conflict, he or she brings the conflicting parties together and, in effect, says, "Look, we're all in this together. Let's forget our differences so we can get the job done." For example, a company president might remind the production and marketing department heads who have been arguing about product design that the competition is breathing down their necks. Although this technique often works in the short run, the underlying problem tends to crop up later to cause friction once again.

Compromise.   This technique generally appeals to those living in a democracy. Advocates of compromise say everyone wins because it is based on negotiation, on give and take.[45] However, as discussed in the next section, most people do not have good negotiating skills. They approach compromise situations with a win-lose attitude. So compromises tend to be disappointing, leaving one or both parties feeling cheated. Conflict is only temporarily suppressed when people feel cheated. Successful compromise requires skillful negotiation.

Forcing.   Sometimes, especially when time is important, management must simply step into a conflict and order the conflicting parties to handle the situation in a

Sometimes, as the saying goes, the best man for the job is a *woman*. When Loretta T. DeGrazia got into the male-dominated heating oil business in Boston in 1985, she heard the usual macho response: "What are you doing in this business?" Not one to shy away from conflict, her company, East Coast Petroleum Corp., has since established itself with a list of about 2,400 customers. A background in the business combined with plenty of grit and determination helped DeGrazia overcome both business and personal setbacks. Turmoil and conflict only strengthened this businesswoman.

certain manner. Reliance on formal authority and power of superior position is at the heart of forcing. As one might suspect, forcing does not resolve the conflict and, in fact, may serve to compound it by hurting feelings and/or fostering resentment and mistrust.

Smoothing.   A manager who relies on smoothing says to the conflicting parties something like, "Settle down. Don't rock the boat. Things will work out by themselves." This approach may tone down conflict in the short run, but it does not solve the underlying problem. As with each of the other conflict resolution techniques, smoothing has its place. It can be useful when management is attempting to hold things together until a critical project is completed or when there is no time for problem solving or compromise and forcing is deemed inappropriate.[46]

Problem solving and skillfully negotiated compromises are the only approaches that remove the actual sources of conflict. They are the only resolution techniques that help improve things in the long run. The other approaches amount to short-run, stopgap measures. And managers who fall back on an avoidance strategy are simply running away from the problem. Nonetheless, as mentioned, problem solving and full negotiation sessions can take up valuable time, time that management may not be willing or able to spend at that particular moment. When this is the case, management may choose to fall back on superordinate goals, forcing, or smoothing, whichever seems most suitable.[47]

Negotiating

Negotiating is a fact of everyday life. Our negotiating skills are tested when we begin a new job, rent an apartment, live with a roommate, buy a house, buy or lease a car, ask for a raise or promotion, live with a spouse, divorce a spouse, or fight for custody of a child. Managers have even more opportunities to negotiate. Salespeople, employees, labor unions, other managers, and customers all have wishes the organization may not be able to grant without some give and take. Sadly, most of us are rather poor negotiators. Negotiating skills, like any other crucial communication skill, need to be developed through diligent study and regular practice.[48] In fact, subjects in a recent study who had been trained in negotiating tactics negotiated more favorable outcomes than did those with no such training.[49]

negotiation *decision-making process among interdependent parties with different preferences*

Experts from Northwestern University have defined **negotiation** as "a decision-making process among interdependent parties who do not share identical preferences." They go on to say, "It is through negotiation that the parties decide what each will give and take in their relationship."[50] The scope of negotiations spans all levels of human interaction, from individuals to organizations to nations.[51] Two common types of negotiation are *two-party* and *third-party*. This distinction is evident in common real estate transactions. If you sell your home directly to a buyer after settling on a mutually agreeable price, that is a two-party negotiation. It becomes a third-party negotiation when a real estate agent acts as a go-between for seller and buyer. Regardless of the type of negotiation, the same basic negotiating concepts apply. This final section examines three elements of effective negotiation and introduces a useful technique called *added value negotiating*.

Elements of Effective Negotiation

A good way to learn about proper negotiation is to start from zero. This means confronting and neutralizing one's biases and faulty assumptions. Sports and military metaphors, for example, are usually inappropriate. Why? Because effective negotiators are not bent on beating the opposition or wiping out the enemy.[52] They have a much broader agenda. For instance, effective negotiators not only satisfy their own needs, they also enhance the other party's readiness to negotiate again. Trust is important in this regard. Using this "clean slate" approach to learning, let us explore three common elements of effective negotiation.

8 Identify and describe the elements of effective negotiation and explain the advantage of added value negotiating (AVN).

Adopting a Win-Win Attitude. Culture, as discussed in Chapter 4, has a powerful influence on individual behavior. In America, for example, the prevailing culture places a high value on winning and shames losing. You can be number one or be a loser, with nothing in between. America's cultural preoccupation with winning, while sometimes an admirable trait, can be a major barrier to effective negotiation.[53] A win-win attitude is preferable.

Stephen R. Covey, in his best-selling book, *The Seven Habits of Highly Effective People*, offered this instructive perspective:

> *Win/Win is a frame of mind and heart that constantly seeks mutual benefit in all human interactions. Win/Win means that agreements or solutions are mutually beneficial, mutually satisfying. With a Win/Win solution, all parties feel good about the decision and feel committed to the action plan. Win/Win sees life as a cooperative, not a competitive arena. Most people tend to think in terms of dichotomies: strong or weak, hardball or softball, win or lose. But that kind of thinking is basically flawed. It's based on power and position rather than on principle. Win/Win is based on the paradigm that there is plenty for everybody, that one person's success is not achieved at the expense or exclusion of the success of others.*
>
> *Win/Win is a belief in the Third Alternative. It's not your way or my way; it's a better way, a higher way.*[54]

Replacing a culturally based win-lose attitude with a win-win attitude is quite difficult; deeply ingrained habits are hard to change. But change they must if American managers are to be more effective negotiators in the global marketplace.[55]

Knowing Your BATNA. This odd-sounding label represents the anchor point of effective negotiations. It is an acronym for *Best Alternative to a Negotiated Agreement*. In other words, what will you settle for if negotiations do not produce your desired outcome(s)? Members of the Harvard Negotiation Project, responsible for the concept, call BATNA "the standard against which any proposed agreement should be measured. That is the only standard which can protect you both from accepting terms that are too unfavorable and from rejecting terms it would be in your interest to accept."[56] In today's popular language, it adds up to, "What is your bottom line?" For example, a business seller's BATNA becomes the measuring stick for accepting or rejecting offers.

A realistic BATNA is good insurance against the three decision-making traps discussed in Chapter 8—framing

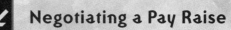

16I Negotiating a Pay Raise

Negotiate your position, not your paycheck. Most bosses don't like to talk about money any more than you do. No matter how much you think you're being underpaid, don't kvetch about it. Instead, talk about what you've achieved for the company and offer to slay even bigger dragons in the future. Says [employment lawyer Lee] Miller: "There's no free lunch. You're unlikely to get a big raise unless you take on more responsibility."

Source: Ronald Henkoff, "Are You (More than) Ready for a Pay Raise?" *Fortune* (December 8, 1997): 236.

Questions: *Do you dislike asking for a pay raise? Why? How well would this negotiating tactic work for you? Explain.*

Figure 16.7

The Bargaining Zone for Negotiators

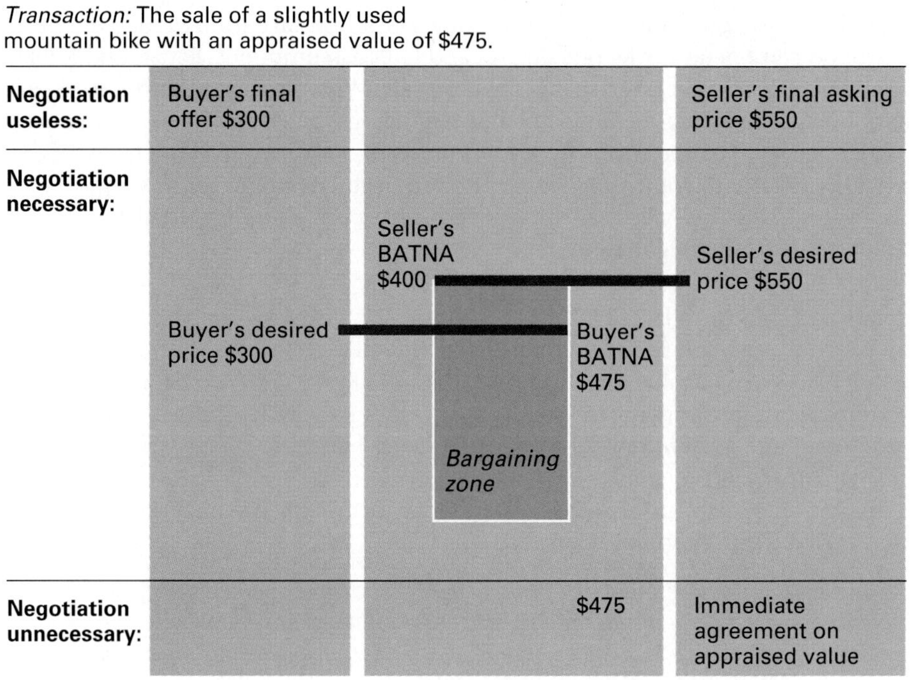

Transaction: The sale of a slightly used mountain bike with an appraised value of $475.

Negotiation useless:	Buyer's final offer $300		Seller's final asking price $550
Negotiation necessary:		Seller's BATNA $400 ▬▬▬▬	Seller's desired price $550
	Buyer's desired price $300 ▬▬▬	Buyer's BATNA $475	
		Bargaining zone	
Negotiation unnecessary:		$475	Immediate agreement on appraised value

error, escalation of commitment, and overconfidence.[57] To negotiate without a BATNA is to stumble along aimlessly in the dark.

Identifying the Bargaining Zone.   Negotiation is useless if the parties involved have no common ground (see top portion of Figure 16.7). At the other extreme, negotiation is unnecessary if both parties are satisfied with the same outcome. Midway, negotiation is necessary when there is a degree of overlap in the ranges of acceptable outcomes. Hence, the **bargaining zone** can be defined as the gap between the two BATNAs; the area of overlapping interests where agreement is possible[58] (see middle portion of Figure 16.7). Since negotiators keep their BATNAs secret, each party needs to *estimate* the other's BATNA when identifying the likely bargaining zone.

bargaining zone *the gap between two parties' BATNAs*

Added Value Negotiating

Win-win negotiation[59] is a great idea that can be difficult to implement on a daily basis. Managers and others tend to stumble when they discover that a win-win attitude is necessary but not enough to get through a tough round of negotiations. A step-by-step process is needed. Karl and Steve Albrecht's recently developed added value negotiating process bridges the gap between win-win theory and practice. **Added value negotiating (AVN)** is a five-step process involving the development of *multiple deals* that add value to the negotiating process.[60] This approach is quite different from traditional "single outcome" negotiating involving "taking something" from the other party. AVN comprises the following five steps:

added value negotiating *five-step process involving development of multiple deals*

This isn't rocket science, but it's close. It's biotech. Steven Holtzman, a brainy guy who studied philosophy at Oxford on a Rhodes Scholarship, works for Millennium Pharmaceuticals. The company specializes in genomics, mapping the human gene structure, and aspires to be a leading drugmaker some day. In the meantime, Holtzman's job is to negotiate complex, book-length partnerships with major drug companies such as Eli Lilly and Bayer. A Bayer aspirin might come in handy with that sort of negotiation headache.

1. *Clarify interests.* Both subjective (judgmental) and objective (observable and measurable) interests are jointly identified and clarified by the two parties. The goal is to find some *common ground* as a basis for negotiation.
2. *Identify options.* What sorts of value—in terms of money, property, actions, rights, and risk reduction—can each party offer the other? This step creates a *marketplace of value* for the negotiators.
3. *Design alternative deal packages.* Rather than tying the success of the negotiation to a single win-win offer, create a number of alternatives from various combinations of value items. This vital step, which distinguishes AVN from other negotiation strategies, fosters *creative agreement.*
4. *Select a deal.* Each party tests the various deal packages for value, balance, and fit. Feasible deals are then discussed jointly and a *mutually acceptable deal* selected.
5. *Perfect the deal.* Unresolved details are hammered out by the negotiators. Agreements are put in writing. *Relationships* are strengthened for future negotiations. According to the Albrechts, "AVN is based on openness, flexibility, and a mutual search for the successful exchange of value. It allows you to build strong relationships with people over time."[61]

Summary

1. Managers need to do a much better job of managing the process of change. Nadler and Tushman's model identifies four types of organizational change by cross-referencing anticipatory and reactive change with incremental and strategic change. Four resulting types of change are tuning, adaptation, reorientation, and re-creation.

2. People who like a change tend to go through three stages: unrealistic optimism, reality shock, and constructive direction. When someone fears or dislikes a change, a more complex process involving five stages tends to occur: getting off on the wrong track, laughing it off, experiencing growing self-doubt, buying in, and moving in a constructive direction. Managers are challenged to help employees deal effectively with reality shock and self-doubt.

3. Inevitable resistance to change must be overcome if the organization is to succeed. Employees resist change for many different reasons, including (but not limited to) inertia, lack of trust, and fear of failure. Modern managers facing resistance to change can select from several strategies, including education and communication, participation and involvement, facilitation and support, negotiation and agreement, manipulation and co-optation, and explicit and implicit coercion.

4. Organization development (OD) is a systematic approach to planned organizational change. The principal objectives of OD are increased trust, better problem solving, more effective communication, improved cooperation, and greater willingness to change. The typical OD program is a three-phase process of unfreezing, change, and refreezing.

5. The 5P checklist for change agents—*preparation, purpose, participation, progress,* and *persistence*—is a generic model for people at all levels in all organizations. Ordinary employees can achieve extraordinary changes by having a clear purpose, a champion or driver for the change initiative, a measurable objective, broad and powerful support achieved through participation, an ability to overcome roadblocks, and a persistent sense of urgency.

6. Competitive conflict is characterized by a destructive cycle of opposing goals, mistrust and disbelief, and avoidance and a win-lose attitude. Oppositely, cooperative conflict involves a constructive cycle of cooperative goals, trust and reliance, and discussion and a win-win attitude.

7. Conflict triggers can cause either constructive or destructive conflict. Destructive conflict can be resolved through problem solving, superordinate goals, compromise, forcing, or smoothing.

8. Three basic elements of effective negotiations are a win-win attitude, a BATNA (Best Alternative to a Negotiated Agreement) to serve as a negotiating standard, and the calculation of a bargaining zone to identify overlapping interests. Added value negotiating (AVN) improves upon standard negotiation strategies by fostering a creative range of possible solutions.

Terms to Understand

Anticipatory changes (p. 491)

Reactive changes (p. 491)

Incremental changes (p. 491)

Strategic changes (p. 491)

Organization development (OD) (p. 500)

Unfreezing (p. 501)

Refreezing (p. 501)

Conflict (p. 505)

Conflict trigger (p. 506)

Negotiation (p. 510)

Bargaining zone (p. 512)

Added value negotiating (p. 512)

How to Express Anger

Although not every angry feeling should be expressed to the person held accountable, this approach is direct and has the most potential to initiate a productive conflict. There are several rules to keep in mind when expressing anger.

- **Check assumptions.** No matter how convinced employees are that someone has deliberately interfered and tried to harm them, they may be mistaken. People can ask questions and probe. It may be that the other person had no intention and was unaware that others were frustrated. The incident may just dissolve into a misunderstanding.
- **Be specific.** People find being the target of anger stressful and anxiety provoking. They fear insults and rejection. The more specific the angry person can be, the less threatening and less of an attack on self-esteem the anger is. Knowing what angered the other can give the target of the anger concrete ways to make amends.
- **Be consistent.** Verbal and nonverbal messages should both express anger. Smiling and verbally expressing anger confuses the issue.
- **Take responsibility for anger.** Persons expressing anger should let the target know that they are angry and the reasoning and steps they took that made them feel unjustly frustrated.
- **Avoid provoking anger.** Expressing anger through unfair, insinuating remarks ("I can't believe someone can be as stupid as you!") can make the target of the anger angry too. Such situations can quickly deteriorate.
- **Watch for impulsivity.** Anger agitates and people say things they later regret.
- **Be wary of self-righteousness.** People can feel powerful, superior, and right; angry people can play, "Now I got 'ya and you will pay." But anger should be used to get to the heart of the matter and solve problems, not for flouting moral superiority.
- **Be sensitive.** People typically underestimate the impact their anger has on others. Targets of anger often feel defensive, anxious, and worried. It is not usually necessary to repeat one's anger to get people's attention.
- **Make the expression cathartic.** Anger generates energy. Telling people releases that energy rather than submerges it. Anger is a feeling to get over, not to hang on to.
- **Express positive feelings.** Angry people depend upon and usually like people they are angry with. People expect help from people who have proved trustworthy, and are angry when it is not forthcoming.
- **Move to constructive conflict management.** Feeling affronted, personally attacked, and self-righteous should not side-track you from solving the underlying problems. Use the anger to create positive conflict.
- **Celebrate joint success.** Anger tests people's skills and their relationship. Be sure to celebrate the mutual achievement of expressing and responding to anger successfully.

Source: Dean Tjosvold, *The Conflict-Positive Organization* (pp. 133–134). © 1991 by Addison-Wesley Publishing Company, Inc. Reprinted by permission of Addison Wesley Longman, Inc.

Internet Exercises

1. **Ready, set, change:** This practical application exercise has three parts: (a) Think of an organizational change you would like to champion at your present or past place of work; (b) draw up an action plan based on the 5P checklist in Figure 16.5; and (c) search the Internet for good ideas about being an effective change agent. (*Note:* an alternative approach in step 1 is to "borrow" a change proposal from a manager you know.) To jump-start your Internet search, go to **www.fastcompany.com** and click on the heading "Archives." From there, scroll down to issue number 5 (October–November 1996) and read Nicholas Morgan's short article "9 Tips for Change Agents." Return to the archives page, scroll up to recent issues of *Fast Company* magazine, and find and read two or three more articles dealing with change.

   Learning Points: 1. Is your proposed change realistic? What do others think about it? 2. What sort of "unfreezing" will need to be done? 3. What sort of resistance will likely be encountered? From whom? 4. How can the resistance to your change be avoided or neutralized? 5. Which powerful people do you need to recruit for your change team? How will you recruit them? 6. What helpful tips and guidelines about being a change agent did you acquire from your Internet search?

2. **Building your tool kit for handling conflict:** Thanks to the Briefings Publishing Group's Web site, lots of free practical tips for dealing with workplace conflict are available online. On the home page (**www.briefings.com**), select the tab "Team Management." On the Team Management Briefings page, read the material under the categories "Conflict" and "Increasing Participation." The other categories may include useful information as well.

   Learning Points: 1. What was the best piece of advice you acquired? 2. What was the most unusual bit of advice you read? 3. What proportion of the material you read dealt with cooperative, as opposed to competitive, conflict (refer back to Figure 16.6)? 4. How would you rate your ability to handle interpersonal conflict between yourself and someone else? Between two other people? 5. What do you need to do to improve your conflict-handling skills?

3. **Check it out:** In discussing the political implications for managers back in Chapter 3, we introduced the practice of *alternative dispute resolution* (ADR). Two common forms of ADR are arbitration and mediation. In arbitration, a third party gathers information from disputing parties and renders a binding decision, much like an informal court. Mediation, on the other hand, occurs when a third party facilitates a constructive dialogue between conflicting parties, who then create their own settlement. Both approaches can save time and money and avoid further clogging the court system. Being an effective mediator is a key conflict-handling skill for managers. To learn more about mediation, visit the Web site sponsored by Stephen R. Marsh (**www.adrr.com**), a lawyer and mediator from Dallas, Texas. In the section "Mediation Essays" (volume one), be sure to read the material under the headings "What Is Mediation?" and "Negotiation in Mediation."

   For updates to these exercises, visit our Web site (**www.hmco.com/college**).

Closing Case | The Unstoppable Entrepreneur

"We've never done it that way before." In these hypercompetitive times, it's hard to believe people utter such words. Yet Bob Schmonsees hears that excuse with maddening frequency.

His small software firm, WisdomWare Inc. has devel-

Source: Republished with permission of *The Wall Street Journal* from "Bob Schmonsees Has a Tool for Better Sales, and It Ignores Excuses," by Thomas Petzinger Jr., *The Wall Street Journal* (March 26, 1999). Permission conveyed through Copyright Clearance Center, Inc.

oped a slick tool that makes salespeople better informed and more efficient. But it requires them—and their bosses—to do things just a little bit differently, and the wall of resistance looms high. "The good news is we've got something that's truly visionary," he says. "That's also the bad news."

But Mr. Schmonsees, 51 years old, as you'll soon see, has plenty of experience scaling huge obstacles. And although his story is intensely personal, it holds lessons for anyone facing an uphill climb in business.

As a high-tech sales manager in the 1970s, Mr. Schmonsees made a priority of protecting salespeople from the endless white papers, binders, and other epistles churned out by marketing types. Each quarter, he condensed a mountain of documents into a pocket-sized booklet that crisply summarized what a sales rep needed to know about the product, the market, and the competition.

Then came disaster. A contender in mixed-doubles tennis and a former football star, Mr. Schmonsees was standing near a ski lift when an out-of-control skier rammed him. His legs were paralyzed. He would spend the rest of his life in a wheelchair.

Fortunately, he discovered a formula for his different world: figure out the new rules for any activity, then take as many small steps as necessary to master those rules. After learning the physics of a tennis swing on wheels and the geometry of playing a second bounce (standard rules), he became the world's top wheelchair player over age 40.

No number of steps, however, could change the behavior of others. The sudden wariness of his former colleagues drove him from the company he loved. Then came many crushing job rejections. But after landing in a junior supervisory position in software sales, he climbed to top marketing management. Later, switching to software vendor Legent Corp., he became global sales chief. "Finally, I was back to where I should have been," he says, though once again it had taken many small steps.

As always, he worked to keep his sales staff informed but not inundated. This was a losing battle by the 1990s, with electronic libraries of marketing material growing like digital kudzu. Pondering this problem one day in the shower, he thought back to those little leatherbound digests he used to hand out.

Why not put something like that online? Even more important, why not enable every piece of information to link with any other piece? That way, salespeople could assemble just the right combination of facts necessary for the task of the moment.

Moving forward with an engineering team, Mr. Schmonsees created the interactive equivalent of Cliffs Notes. While planning a call, a sales rep makes a few menu choices to identify the customer, the product, and the like. One click creates the most up-to-date qualifying questions, another reveals how the competition stacks up, another reports the most common objections, still another suggests an "elevator speech" for precisely those circumstances. Though only a few concise sentences pop on the screen, detailed reports are just a click away.

Mr. Schmonsees left Legent in late 1995. But in his own effort at selling the new product, he ran smack into a powerful objection.

The issue wasn't training; that takes five minutes. Nor was it compatibility; WisdomWare works seamlessly with other front-office software. Neither has any customer winced at the price of $500 and up per user.

The problem was culture. WisdomWare requires marketing managers to write snappy summaries in addition to (or instead of) their beloved white papers. "We've never done it that way!" came the reply.

"When this becomes part of your culture, it's a real competitive advantage," says Dan Gillis, president of SAGA Software, which embraces WisdomWare. "But it takes a real commitment."

The culture of the field force is another hurdle. Users love the encapsulated, up-to-date information that comes to the screen. But WisdomWare depends on those same users to provide intelligence from the field: what the competition is up to, for instance, and which pitches are getting the best and worst results. Sharing information? "We've never had to do *that* before!" came the cry.

Platinum Technology, for one, equipped its sales force of 1,000 with WisdomWare in January [1999]. And although efficiencies are already evident, too few salespeople are giving back information. Platinum's Glenn Shimkus is now searching for ways to reward contributors. "We have to change the culture so that power and rewards come from sharing information, not from hoarding it," he says.

With 20 employees, Mr. Schmonsees is grinding out orders one at a time, counting 10 customers to date. And despite the slow takeoff, the company's venture-capital backers are about to step up for another round. Eventually, the product will run on a hand-held, wireless device that sales reps will consult on their way into sales calls—then use to submit feedback on their way out.

Mr. Schmonsees concedes that the business, for now, is behind his expectations. "It's going to take some time to change the world," he says. But as a metaphor for business, his personal life encourages him. "I take pride in taking a lot of little steps toward a long-term vision," he says.

FOR DISCUSSION

1. Why is Schmonsees uniquely qualified to fight resistance to change?

2. Which of the reasons discussed in this chapter that account for employees' resistance to change are evident in this case? Explain.

3. Using Table 16.2 as a guide, which strategy (or strategies) should Schmonsees use to overcome resistance to WisdomWare? Explain.

4. What lessons from OD apply to this case? Explain.

5. What lessons from the 5P checklist for change agents apply to this case? Explain.

VIDEO SKILL BUILDERS

World Book International, a publisher of educational materials including encyclopedias, videos, and CDs, in many ways typifies today's global organization. It must motivate a diverse array of employees from many different cultures to do their very best. A unique combination of rewards and recognition gets the job done.

4A Motivation at World Book Publishing

Learning objective: To learn how to motivate a diverse workforce in a global company.

Links to textual material: *Chapter 13:* Maslow's needs hierarchy; Herzberg's two-factor theory; Expectancy theory; Goal-setting theory; Extrinsic versus intrinsic rewards; Reward equity; Participation *Chapter 15:* Empowerment; Behavior modification

Discussion questions

1. In terms of Maslow's hierarchy of needs and Herzberg's two-factor theory, how does the annual International Achievement Conference (IAC) motivate the firm's sales representatives?
2. Why does World Book have to be concerned about reward equity?
3. Why do World Book's managers need to know about expectancy motivation theory?
4. What role do intrinsic rewards play in this video case?
5. What evidence of empowerment and behavior modification can you detect?

This inspiring 11-minute video introduces Jayson Goltz, president of Artist's Frame Service, based in Chicago, Illinois, and documents how an entrepreneur's leadership style must grow with the business.

4B Entrepreneurial Leadership

Learning objectives: To demonstrate how modern leaders need to constantly learn and adapt to meet new challenges. To illustrate why successful inspirational leaders are not cookie-cutter imitations, but unique individuals who dare to be different.

Links to textual material: *Chapter 1:* Entrepreneurship *Chapter 12:* Communication *Chapter 13:* Motivating *Chapter 15:* Influence tactics; Power; Leadership *Chapter 16:* Managing change *Chapter 17:* Product/service quality

Discussion questions

1. How well does Jayson Goltz fit the entrepreneur trait profile in Table 1.5? Explain.
2. What influence tactics (see page 459) are evident in this case?
3. Which path-goal leadership style (see pages 470–472) does Goltz seem to rely on the most?
4. Would you label Goltz a transactional or transformational leader (see Table 15.4)? Explain.
5. Is Goltz a good leader? Explain. Would you like to work for him? Why or why not?

Part Five

ORGANIZATIONAL CONTROL
PROCESSES

CHAPTER 17

Organizational Control and
Quality Improvement

ORGANIZATIONAL CONTROL and QUALITY IMPROVEMENT

CHAPTER OBJECTIVES

When you finish studying this chapter, you should be able to

1 Identify three types of control and the components common to all control systems.

2 Discuss organizational control from a strategic perspective.

3 Identify the four key elements of a crisis management program.

4 Identify five types of product quality.

5 Explain how providing a service differs from manufacturing a product and list the five service-quality dimensions.

6 Define *total quality management* (TQM) and discuss the basic TQM principles.

7 Describe at least three of the seven TQM process improvement tools.

8 Explain how Deming's PDCA cycle can improve the overall management process.

9 Specify and discuss at least four of Deming's famous 14 points.

> "MAKE NO MISTAKE:
> CUSTOMERS ARE
> IN CONTROL TODAY."
> anne busquet

Quality Is a Way of Life at Harley-Davidson

It was his first day on the job, two years ago, and Ken Sutton was at a vending machine getting a cup of coffee. Behind him, a machinist he had never met asked, "You're new here, aren't you?"

Sutton allowed that he was.

"Well, let me buy you a cup of coffee," the machinist offered.

It was a simple gesture, but two years later, as vice president and general manager at Harley-Davidson's power train plant in suburban Milwaukee, Sutton remembers what it was like to be welcomed to the family. He learned quickly that "relationships" were an important—maybe the most important—component of Harley-Davidson's corporate culture.

Relationships? Isn't that a bit warm and fuzzy for a workforce full of hard-core bikers building power trains for motorcycles? Here's a factory full of tough-looking, tattooed, and (except for the women) bearded workers. They're producing the most infamous icon of go-to-hell individualism in America, and it turns out they're all worked up about relationships?

Well, yes, says Margaret Crawford, corporate director of training and employee development. "We are very much a relationship-based company." Building strong working relationships—between coworkers, between unions and management, between supervisors and the supervised, between executives and machinists—is a core concern at Harley-Davidson.

That doesn't mean you'll hear phrases like "I hear what you're saying" or "Thanks for sharing" from Harley workers. They are a little more *direct* than that. Harley-Davidson's idea of a healthy working relationship is embedded in five formal values that fit easily on a 3-by-5-inch laminated card and constitute a code of behavior for everyone. Most workers at the power train plant seem to know them verbatim:

- Tell the truth.
- Be fair.
- Keep your promises.
- Respect the individual.
- Encourage intellectual curiosity.

Oil Puddles

You can't get so much as a shoeshine anymore without receiving a card engraved with somebody's mission or vision or values, of course, and all of this would be neither here nor there except that Harley-Davidson is something of a special case.

Not to put too fine a point on it, Harley was at death's door in the early 1980s. The company had a reputation for poor quality, it had lost most of its market share to the Japanese, it was beset with debt, and it was generally going the way of many American manufacturing businesses that are no longer with us. The period from 1969 to 1981 is still referred to as the "AMF years" when Harley was owned by American Machine & Foundry. The history of the AMF years, and the subsequent resurrection of the company, is documented in the book *Well Made in America* by Peter C. Reid.

Reid doesn't attribute Harley's troubles solely to AMF as many observers have, and in fact argues that much of Harley's current success is due to investments made by AMF. But while the bike's reputation for reliability was far from unsullied even before AMF bought the company—bikers took perverse joy in pointing to any oil puddle in the street and speculating that a Harley must have been parked there—the quality of Harley-Davidson's products indisputably suffered during the AMF years.

Reid describes how AMF began to turn this around during the last years of its stewardship with a triad of quality techniques learned from the Japanese: just-in-time inventory (JIT), statistical process control (SPC), and employee involvement. Even so, when AMF put the company up for sale in 1981, it looked to be a death sentence for Harley. Only a last-minute leveraged buyout by 13 of Harley's top managers saved the business. Company veterans still talk about how current CEO Rich Teerlink scrambled from investor to investor on December 31, just hours before Harley would be forced to declare Chapter 11 bankruptcy.

The rest of the tale is now famous as a classic American turnaround, a Cinderella story. Harley survived constant setbacks to reclaim its market share, eliminate its long-term debt, and regain the respect of its customers. It did so by producing bikes of the highest quality and reliability. . . . It owns about 56 percent of the U.S. super-heavyweight motorcycle market—and the only reason its share isn't higher is because the company can't produce enough motorcycles to meet demand. Depending on which bike you order, you'll wait six to 18 months to get a new Harley.

Part of the reason for Harley's success is, of course, a uniquely fanatical brand of customer loyalty. Even during the AMF years, Harley riders kept the faith—though it was sorely tested—and kept buying the company's motorcycles. Employees like to remind people that their company logo may be the only corporate symbol that customers actually tattoo on their bodies. It's also a testimony to the Harley mystique that more than half of all employees own a bike. Most of the executives, including Teerlink, are Harley riders. Workers know that the machine they are currently building might turn out to be their own . . . or the CEO's.

Living Quality

Because Harley-Davidson was one of the first victories of the American quality movement, and perhaps the most dramatic, the company has become a poster child for total quality management (TQM). But you don't hear many people at Harley talking about quality anymore; it's so ingrained in the culture that it has become a way of life.

Many employees have been around long enough to remember the AMF years, however, and there is a palpable sense that nobody wants to take his eyes off the ball ever again. Lest anyone forget that poor quality almost destroyed the company, the other side of the laminated values card presents a list of "issues" or continuing concerns:

- Quality.
- Participation.
- Productivity.
- Flexibility.
- Cash flow.

The one TQM phrase that seems to have survived in the vocabulary of employees is "continuous improvement." It has come to mean not just process improvement on the factory floor, but a more personal improvement of the relationships between people. That's where the "values" kick in. And when people agree to tell the truth, be fair to each other, keep promises, respect each other and encourage curiosity, there is nothing necessarily "soft" about their ensuing interpersonal dealings. As Curt Kapugia, senior quality engineer, puts it, "I could hate your guts, but I still have to respect you as an individual at work so that we can work together.". . .

Stakeholders

This is a word that comes up often in conversations with Harley workers. The corporate values aren't intended solely for interactions between coworkers but are meant to include all the stakeholders of the company. That means workers, managers, unions, the community, the environment, the government and, most importantly, the extended family of Harley-Davidson: its zealous customers. Employees are encouraged to attend some of the rallies the company sponsors (major annual events include gatherings in Sturgis, South Dakota, and Daytona, Florida), to talk to customers and find out what they want. And like its employees, Harley-Davidson's customers aren't shy about expressing their opinions.

Source: Bob Filipczak, "The Soul of the Hog." Reprinted with permission from the February 1996 issue of *Training* magazine. Copyright 1996. Lakewood Publications, Minneapolis, Minn. All rights reserved. Not for resale.

Harley-Davidson's inspiring story teaches us a couple of important management lessons. First, strategies and plans, no matter how well conceived, are no guarantee of organizational success. Those plans need to be carried out by skilled and motivated employees amid changing circumstances and an occasional crisis. Adjustments and corrective action are inevitable. Second, product quality deserves *every* employee's full-time attention; poor quality can doom an organization. This chapter helps present and future managers put these lessons to work by introducing fundamentals of organizational control, discussing crisis management, and exploring product and service quality.

Fundamentals of Organizational Control

The word *control* suggests the operations of checking, testing, regulation, verification, or adjustment. As a management function, **control** is the process of taking the necessary preventive or corrective actions to ensure that the organization's mission and objectives are accomplished as effectively and efficiently as possible. Objectives are yardsticks against which actual performance can be measured. If actual performance is consistent with the appropriate objective, things will proceed as planned. If not, changes must be made. Successful managers detect (and even anticipate) deviations from desirable standards and make appropriate adjustments. Those adjustments can range from ordering more raw materials to overhauling a production line; from discarding an unnecessary procedure to hiring additional personnel; from containing an unexpected crisis to firing a defrauder. Although the possible adjustments exercised as part of the control function are countless, the purpose of the control function is always the same: *get the job done despite environmental, organizational, and behavioral obstacles and uncertainties.*

control *taking preventive or corrective actions to keep things on track*

The United States is famous for many things, but until recently high-speed electric passenger train service was not one of them. Control processes and product quality need to be finely tuned if this Amtrak Acela train, being tested in Colorado, delivers on the promise of a 150-mile-per-hour trip between Boston and New York City. The French and Canadian builders want to cut 48 minutes from the standard train trip between the two cities.

Types of Control

Every open system processes inputs from the surrounding environment to produce a unique set of outputs. Natural open systems, such as the human body, are kept in life-sustaining balance through automatic feedback mechanisms. In contrast, artificial open systems, such as organizations, do not have automatic controls. Instead, they require constant monitoring and adjustment to control for deviations from standards. Figure 17.1 illustrates the control function. Notice the three different types of control: feedforward, concurrent, and feedback.

Feedforward Control. According to two early proponents of feedforward control, "the only way [managers] can exercise control effectively is to see the problems coming in time to do something about them."[1] **Feedforward control** is the active anticipation of problems and their timely prevention, rather than after-the-fact reaction. Carpenters have their own instructive version of feedforward control: "Measure twice, cut once." It is important to note that planning and feedforward control are two related but different processes. Planning answers the question, "Where are we going and how will we get there?" Feedforward control addresses the issue, "What can we do ahead of time to help our plan succeed?" *Preventive maintenance* qualifies as feedforward control. New York City's bridge system illustrates the importance of prevention. According to one study, "the city could save $250 million a year in emergency repair and reconstruction costs by spending $36 million a year to maintain its bridges."[2] Indeed, an ounce of prevention is better than a pound of cure.

feedforward control *active anticipation and prevention of problems, rather than passive reaction*

Of the three types of control, American managers tend to do the poorest job with feedforward control. Longer-term thinking and better cross-functional communication could remedy this situation.

Concurrent Control. This second type of control might well be called real-time control because it deals with the present rather than the future or past.[3] **Concurrent control** involves monitoring and adjusting ongoing activities and processes to ensure compliance with standards. When you are using a bread toaster, for instance, you can

concurrent control *monitoring and adjusting ongoing activities and processes*

Figure 17.1

Three Types of Control

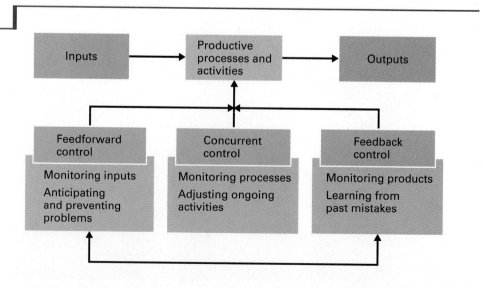

"Now where did I leave my clipboard and favorite pen?" This huge KBkids.com warehouse is no place for forgetful people. If the online retailer of toys is to be profitable, feedforward control will need to be precise. The goal is to have the right toys in stock and in their proper places for easy retrieval at shipping time. When KBkids.com was swamped with nearly one-quarter million hits per day during its first Christmas rush season, it became clear that the information superhighway still has some serious speed bumps to iron out.

set the automatic control mechanism and run the risk of ending up with a piece of charcoal. Because toaster control mechanisms are rather primitive, they are not a very reliable form of feedforward control. To compensate, you can exercise concurrent control by keeping an eye on the toasting process and ejecting your toast by hand when it reaches the right shade. So, too, construction supervisors engage in concurrent control when they help carpenters and plumbers with difficult tasks at the building site.

Feedback Control.   **Feedback control** is gathering information about a completed activity, evaluating that information, and taking steps to improve similar activities in the future. Feedback control permits managers to use information on past performance to bring future performance in line with planned objectives and acceptable standards. For example, by monitoring the complaints from discharged patients about billing errors, a hospital's comptroller learns that the performance of its billing

feedback control *checking a completed activity and learning from mistakes*

NASA Gets an Expensive Math Lesson   17A

In 1999, NASA lost a $125 million Mars Climate Orbiter when it crashed into the red planet after a nine-month trip. At fault was poor communication and a miscalculation. Engineers at Lockheed Martin, builder of the spacecraft, worked in feet and pounds, whereas the Jet Propulsion Laboratory team that guided the flight worked in meters and kilograms. The spacecraft flew 50 miles closer to Mars than intended, making a crash inevitable. "People sometimes make errors," said NASA's space science chief. "The problem here was not the error, it was the failure of . . . the checks and balances in our processes to detect the error."

Source: Paul Hoverstan, "Bad Math Added Up to Doomed Mars Craft," *USA Today* (October 1, 1999): 4A.

Questions: *Which type of control was most needed in this situation? Why?*

For further information about the interactive annotations in this chapter, visit our Web site (**www.hmco.com/college**).

clerks requires attention. Critics of feedback control complain that it is like closing the gate after the horse is gone. Because corrective action is taken after the fact, costs tend to pile up quickly, and problems and deviations persist.

On the positive side, feedback control tests the quality and validity of objectives and standards. Objectives that prove impossible to attain should be made more reasonable. Those that prove too easy need to be toughened. A bank's loan officer, for example, may discover that too much potentially profitable business is being turned away because the criteria for granting credit are too strict. By exercising feedback control—loosening the credit standards that loan applicants must meet—the bank's lending operation can be made more profitable. Of course, if this adjustment leads to a default rate that eats up the additional profits, the credit criteria may need yet another round of feedback control.

In summary, a successful manager must exercise all three types of control in today's complex organizations. Feedforward control helps managers avoid mistakes in the first place; concurrent control enables them to catch mistakes as they are being made; feedback control keeps them from repeating past mistakes. A workable balance among the three types of control is desirable.

Components of Organizational Control Systems

The owner-manager of a small business such as a dry-cleaning establishment can keep things under control by personally overseeing operations and making necessary adjustments. An electrician can be called in to fix a broken pressing machine, poor workmanship can be improved through coaching, a customer's complaint can be handled immediately, or a shortage of change in the cash register can be remedied. A small organization directed by a single, highly motivated individual with expert knowledge of all aspects of the operation represents the ideal control situation.[4] Unfortunately, the size and complexity of most productive organizations have made first-hand control by a single person obsolete. Consequently, multilevel, multidimensional organizational control systems have evolved.[5]

A study of nine large companies in different industries sheds some needed light on the mechanics of complex organizational control systems.[6] After interviewing dozens of key managers, the researchers identified six distinct control subsystems:

1. *Strategic plans:* Qualitative analyses of the company's position within the industry.
2. *Long-range plans:* Typically, five-year financial projections.
3. *Annual operating budgets:* Annual estimates of profit, expenses, and financial indicators.
4. *Statistical reports:* Quarterly, monthly, or weekly nonfinancial statistical summaries of key indicators such as orders received and personnel surpluses or shortages.
5. *Performance appraisals:* Evaluation of employees through the use of management by objectives (MBO) or rating scales.
6. *Policies and procedures:* Organizational and departmental standard operating procedures referred to on an as-needed basis.

A seventh organizational control subsystem is *cultural control.*[7] As discussed in Chapter 9, stories and company legends have a profound impact on how things are done in specific organizations. Employees who deviate from cultural norms are promptly straightened out with glances, remarks, or ridicule.

Complex organizational control systems such as these help keep things on the right track because they embrace three basic components, common to all organizational control systems: objectives, standards, and an evaluation-reward system.[8]

Objectives.   In Chapter 6, we defined an *objective* as a target signifying what should be accomplished and when. Objectives are an indispensable part of any control system because they provide measurable reference points for corrective action. To help Chrysler get back on the road to profitability, former chairman Lee Iacocca set the objective of committing his company in 1990 to cutting $3 billion in costs by July 1991. That particular objective served as a focal point and measuring stick for wide-ranging cost reductions, including layoffs and smaller buyer rebates.[9]

Standards.   Whereas objectives serve as measurable targets, standards serve as guideposts on the way to reaching those targets. Standards provide feedforward control by warning people when they are off the track.[10] Golfers use par as a standard for gauging the quality of their game. When the objective is to shoot par, a golfer who exceeds par on a hole is warned that he or she must improve on later holes to achieve the objective. Universities exercise a degree of feedforward control over student performance by establishing and following admission standards for grades and test scores. Businesses rely on many different kinds of standards, including those in purchasing, engineering, time, safety, accounting, and quality.

A proven technique for establishing challenging standards is **benchmarking,** that is, identifying, studying, and imitating the *best practices* of market leaders.[11] The central idea in benchmarking is to be competitive by striving to be as good as or better than the *best* in the business. The search for benchmarks is not restricted to one's own industry. Consider, for example, United Airlines' recent benchmarking efforts in Marina Del Rey, California:

> *In a bid to boost the quality of its overseas service, United Airlines is bringing some of its attendants to the best hotels, such as the Ritz-Carlton here, to learn the fine points of catering to the needs of the well-heeled.*
>
> *"They are very much recognized name-wise for a higher level of service," explains United trainer Christine Swanstrom. "The clientele we're trying to attract in international is the clientele that would stay at a Ritz."*[12]

benchmarking *identifying, studying, and building upon the best practices of organizational role models*

An Evaluation-Reward System.   Because employees do not get equal results, some sort of performance review is required to document individual contributions to organizational objectives. Extrinsic rewards need to be tied equitably to documented results and improvement. A carefully conceived and clearly communicated evaluation-reward scheme can shape favorable effort-reward expectancies, hence motivating better performance.

When integrated systematically, objectives, standards, and an equitable evaluation-reward system constitute an invaluable control mechanism.

Strategic Control

Managers who fail to complement their strategic planning with strategic control, as recommended in Chapter 7, will find themselves winning some battles but losing the war.[13] The performance pyramid in Figure 17.2 illustrates the necessarily tight linkage between planning and control. It is a strategic model because everything is oriented toward the strategic peak of the pyramid. Objectives based on the corporate vision (or mission) are translated downward during planning. As plans become reality, control measures of activities and results are translated up the pyramid. The flow of objectives and measures requires a good information system.

2 **Discuss organizational control from a strategic perspective.**

Figure 17.2

The Performance Pyramid for Strategic Control

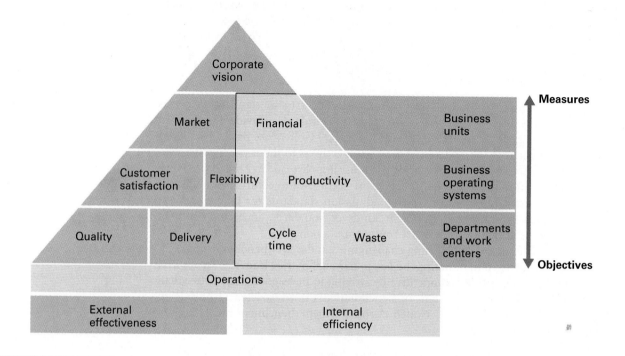

Source: C. J. McNair, Richard L. Lynch, and Kelvin F. Cross, "Do Financial and Nonfinancial Performance Measures Have to Agree?" *Management Accounting* published by the Institute of Management Accountants, Montvale, N.J., 72 (November 1990): 30. Copyright by Institute of Management Accountants. Reprinted by permission.

External effectiveness and internal efficiency criteria are distinguished in Figure 17.2 by color coding. Significantly, all of the external effectiveness areas are focused on the marketplace in general and on the *customer* in particular. According to the performance pyramid, control measures are needed for cycle time, waste, flexibility, productivity, and financial results. *Cycle time* is the time it takes for a product to be transformed from raw materials or parts into a finished good. Notice how *flexibility* relates to both effectiveness and efficiency. A garden tractor manufacturer, for example, needs to be externally flexible in adapting to changing customer demands and internally flexible in training employees to handle new technology.

Identifying Control Problems

Control problems have a way of quietly snowballing into overwhelming proportions. Progressive managers can take constructive steps to keep today's complex operations under control.[14] Two very different approaches are executive reality checks and internal auditing.

Who's in Charge Here? 17B

Avram Miller, high-tech consultant and former Intel Corp. strategist, offers this advice for doing business at Internet speed:

Give up control. Or the illusion of control. Companies no longer determine the success of products and markets—if they ever did. Customers do. Control is an illusion, and the Internet has completely shattered that illusion. Nobody is in charge anymore.

Source: As quoted in Katharine Mieszkowski, "The Power of the Internet Is That You Can Experiment," *Fast Company*, no. 30 (December 1999): 160.

Questions: *What does Miller mean? Does he think managers should throw up their hands and abandon all forms of organizational control? Explain.*

Executive Reality Check. The **executive reality check** occurs when top-level managers periodically work in the trenches to increase their awareness of operations. It is a variation of Peters and Waterman's "management by wandering around," discussed in Chapter 2. Southwest Airlines goes about it this way:

executive reality check *top managers periodically working at lower-level jobs to become more aware of operations*

> The officers of Southwest Airlines, [CEO Herb] Kelleher included, work at least once every quarter as baggage handlers, ticket agents, and flight attendants. "We're trying to create an understanding of the difficulties every person has on his job," explains Kelleher. "When you're actually dealing with customers, and you've done the job yourself, you're in a better position to appraise the effect of some new program or policy."[15]

This approach not only alerts top managers to control problems but also fosters empathy for lower-level employees' problems and concerns.[16] In addition to firsthand reality checks, an internal audit can identify weak spots and problems in the organizational control system.

Internal Audits. There are two general types of auditing, external and internal. External auditing, generally performed by certified public accountants (CPAs), is the verification of an organization's financial records and reports. In the United States, the protection of stockholders' interests is the primary rationale for objective external audits. Of course, the Internal Revenue Service (IRS) and the Securities and Exchange Commission (SEC) also benefit from external auditors' watchdog function. That is, external auditors help keep organizations honest by double-checking to see if reported financial results are derived through generally accepted accounting principles and are based on material fact, not fiction.[17]

internal auditing *independent appraisal of organizational operations and systems to assess effectiveness and efficiency*

Internal auditing differs from external auditing in a number of ways. First, and most obviously, it is performed by an organization's staff rather than by outsiders. Second, internal auditing is intended to serve the interests of the organization as a whole. Also, as the following definition illustrates, internal auditing tends to be more encompassing than the external variety: "**Internal auditing** is the independent appraisal of the various operations and systems control within an organization to determine whether acceptable policies and procedures are followed, established standards are met, resources are used efficiently and economically, planned missions are accomplished effectively, and the organization's objectives are being achieved."[18]

The product of internal auditing is called a *process audit* by some and a *management audit* by others.[19] To strengthen the objectivity of internal auditing, experts recommend that internal auditors report directly to the top person in the organization. In organization development terms, some "unfreezing" needs to be done to quiet the common complaint that internal auditing is a ploy used by top management for snooping and meddling. Timely and valid internal audits are a primary safeguard against organizational decline, as discussed in Chapter 9.

Symptoms of Inadequate Control. When a comprehensive internal audit is not available, a general checklist of symptoms of inadequate control can be a

Not a Clue at the Internal Revenue Service

It has attempted the same gargantuan task of modernizing its computers for 25 years running and failed every time, at a cost in the past decade alone of nearly $4 billion. Thirteen years ago some minor tinkering by the IRS's Philadelphia service center led to "the filing season from hell.". . . Clerks shoved dozens of unprocessed returns into ceiling ducts and wastebaskets just to get them off their desks. Afterward, a consulting firm concluded that it was no surprise the IRS had trouble working on its computers; the surprise was that they worked at all. Here's another surprise: many of the same machines still process your returns today. The system is a tangle of 80 mainframes, 1,335 minicomputers, and 130,000 desktop boxes that are largely unable to communicate with each other.

Source: Jeffrey H. Birnbaum, "Unbelievable! The Mess at the IRS Is Worse Than You Think," *Fortune* (April 13, 1998): 98.

Questions: *If you were appointed commissioner of the IRS, how would you go about getting the $7 billion agency under control? What would be your top priority? Explain.*

useful diagnostic tool. While every situation has some unusual problems, certain symptoms are common:

- An unexplained decline in revenues or profits.
- A degradation of service (customer complaints).
- Employee dissatisfaction (complaints, grievances, turnover).
- Cash shortages caused by bloated inventories or delinquent accounts receivable.
- Idle facilities or personnel.
- Disorganized operations (workflow bottlenecks, excessive paperwork).
- Excessive costs.
- Evidence of waste and inefficiency (scrap, rework).[20]

Problems in one or more of these areas may be a signal that things are getting out of control.

Crisis Management

One need only read the newspaper or watch the nightly news to find abundant evidence of organizational crises. Notable ones in recent history were the near meltdown of the Three Mile Island nuclear power plant in Pennsylvania in 1979; the poisoning of Johnson & Johnson's Tylenol capsules with cyanide in 1982 and 1986; Union Carbide's Bhopal, India, gas leak that reportedly killed more than 3,000 local residents in 1984 (Indian officials say more than 13,000 died);[21] Exxon's Alaskan oil spill in 1989; the 1993

Selling sugary water in bottles and cans doesn't seem like a complicated business at first glance. Yet it is a rigorous science to global giant Coca-Cola. Here a chemist performs exacting tests on product samples from Germany after a product-contamination scare in Europe (see chapter-closing case for details). The handling of this particular crisis ultimately led to the premature retirement of the company's CEO. When public health and safety are involved, companies need a crisis-management program in place to respond quickly and effectively.

bombing of New York's World Trade Center that cost six lives and over $500 million in lost business and property damage;[22] the domestic terrorist bombing that left 168 people dead in Oklahoma City in 1995,[23] and the catastrophic fuel-tank explosion aboard TWA flight 800 in 1996 that staggered both the airline and aircraft maker Boeing.

As you can see, the diversity and scope of organizational crises stretch the imagination. A pair of experts on the subject recently offered this definition of an *organizational crisis:*

> *An organizational crisis is a low-probability, high-impact event that threatens the viability of the organization and is characterized by ambiguity of cause, effect, and means of resolution, as well as by belief that decisions must be made swiftly.*[24]

Clearly, managers need to "manage the unthinkable" in a foresighted, systematic, and timely manner.[25] Enter the emerging discipline known as *crisis management.*

Crisis Management Defined

Traditionally, crisis management was viewed negatively, as "managerial firefighting"— waiting for things to go wrong and then scurrying to limit the damage. More recently, the term has taken on a more precise and proactive meaning. In fact, a body of theory and practice is evolving around the idea that managers should think about the unthinkable and expect the unexpected.[26] **Crisis management** is the systematic anticipation of and preparation for internal and external problems that seriously threaten an organization's reputation, profitability, or survival. Importantly, crisis management involves much more than an expedient public relations ploy or so-called spin control to make the organization look good amid bad circumstances. This new discipline is intertwined with strategic control.

crisis management *anticipating and preparing for events that could damage the organization*

Developing a Crisis Management Program

As illustrated in Figure 17.3, a crisis management program is made up of four elements. Disasters need to be anticipated, contingency plans need to be formulated, and crisis management teams need to be staffed and trained. Finally, the program needs to be perfected through realistic practice. Let us examine each of these elements.

3 Identify the four key elements of a crisis management program.

Conducting a Crisis Audit.   A crisis audit is a systematic way of seeking out trouble spots and vulnerabilities. Disaster scenarios become the topic of discussion as managers ask a series of "What if?" questions. Lists such as the one in Table 17.1 can be useful during this stage. Some crises, such as the untimely death of a key executive, are universal and hence readily identified. Others are industry-specific. For example, crashes are an all-too-real disaster scenario for passenger airline companies.[27]

Figure 17.3 | Key Elements in a Crisis Management Program

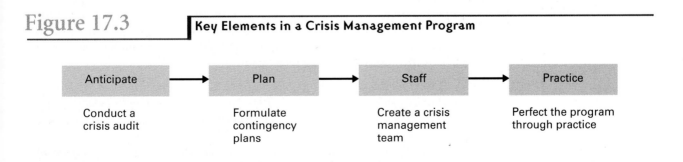

Anticipate → Plan → Staff → Practice

Anticipate	Plan	Staff	Practice
Conduct a crisis audit	Formulate contingency plans	Create a crisis management team	Perfect the program through practice

Table 17.1

An Organizational Crisis Can Come in Many Different Forms

■ Extortion	■ Bribery
■ Hostile takeover	■ Information sabotage
■ Product tampering	■ Workplace bombing
■ Vehicular fatality	■ Terrorist attack
■ Copyright infringement	■ Plant explosion
■ Environmental spill	■ Sexual harassment
■ Computer tampering	■ Escape of hazardous materials
■ Security breach	■ Personnel assault
■ Executive kidnapping	■ Assault of customers
■ Product/service boycott	■ Product recall
■ Work-related homicide	■ Counterfeiting
■ Malicious rumor	■ Natural disaster that destroys corporate headquarters
■ Natural disaster that disrupts a major product or service	■ Natural disaster that eliminates key stakeholders
■ Natural disaster that destroys organizational information base	

Source: Republished with permission of *Academy of Management Review,* from "Reframing Crisis Management," by Christine M. Pearson and Judith A. Clair, 23 (January 1998): Table 1, p. 60. Permission conveyed through Copyright Clearance Center, Inc.

contingency plan *a backup plan for emergencies*

Formulating Contingency Plans.   A **contingency plan** is a backup plan that can be put into effect when things go wrong.[28] Whenever possible, each contingency plan should specify early warning signals, actions to be taken, and expected consequences of those actions.

> *Attention to detail is a crucial component of most contingency plans. Dow has produced a 20-page program for communicating with the public during a disaster, right down to such particulars as who is going to run the copy machines. Many companies designate a single corporate spokes[person] to field all inquiries from the press. A list may be drawn up of those executives to be notified in emergency situations, and the late-night phone numbers of local radio and television stations may be kept posted on office walls.[29]*

Both crisis audits and related contingency plans need to be updated at least annually and, if changing conditions dictate, more often.

Creating a Crisis Management Team.   Organizational crisis management teams have been likened to SWAT teams that police departments use for extraordinary situations such as hostage takings. Crisis management teams necessarily represent different specialties, depending on the likely crisis. For example, an electrical utility company might have a crisis management team made up of a media relations expert, an electrical engineer, a consumer affairs specialist, and a lawyer. As the case of Dow Chemical Canada illustrates, quick response and effective communication are the hallmarks of an effective crisis management team:

> *Dow Chemical Canada decided to improve its crisis plans after a railroad car carrying a Dow chemical derailed near Toronto in 1979, forcing the evacuation of 250,000 residents. Since then, Dow Canada has prepared information kits on the hazards of its products and trained executives in interview techniques.*
>
> *. . . Another accident [years later] spilled toxic chemicals into a river that supplies water for several towns. Almost immediately, Dow Canada's emergency-response team arrived at*

the site and set up a press center to distribute information about the chemicals. They also recruited a neutral expert—the regional public health officer—to speak about the hazards and how to deal with them. The result: officials praised Dow's response.[30]

Although an exact figure is not available, many companies have crisis management teams in place today.

Perfecting the Program Through Practice.   Like athletic teams, crisis management teams can gain the necessary teamwork, effectiveness, and speed of response only through diligent practice. Simulations, drills, and mock disasters provide this invaluable practice. Top-management support of such exercises is essential to provide good role models and create a sense of importance. Moreover, reinforcing employee efforts in this area with an effective reward system can encourage serious practice.[31]

Experts say management's two biggest mistakes regarding organizational crises are (1) ignoring early warning signs and (2) denying the existence of a problem when disaster strikes. A good crisis management program effectively eliminates these self-defeating mistakes.[32]

Back to the Opening Case

Using Table 17.1 as a guide, and making reasonable assumptions, imagine some potential crises that could occur at Harley-Davidson's Milwaukee motorcycle factory. (*Note:* rank the items on your list in order of priority.) Which of the "low-probability, high-impact events" warrant a detailed contingency plan?

The Quality Challenge

Not long ago, North American industry was roundly criticized for paying inadequate attention to the quality of goods and services. Today, as demonstrated by Harley-Davidson in the chapter-opening case, some organizations have achieved a dramatic turnaround.[33] There is even a national trophy for quality in the United States that means prestige and lots of free media exposure for winners: the Malcolm Baldrige National Quality Award. Named for a former U.S. Secretary of Commerce, it was launched by Congress in 1987 to encourage and reward world-class quality.[34] Some observers claim the drive for quality was a passing fad. Tom Peters, the well-known management writer and consultant, offered this instructive perspective in a recent question-and-answer session:

> *Q: Do you think the bloom is off the quality movement?*
>
> *A: I think it's in the genes. The quality movement has gone from hype to something people do. The average American manager, whether she or he is in accounting or purchasing or engineering, takes for granted that quality is a major thing you think about in life. You can't compete with shabby products.*[35]

The balance of this chapter builds a foundation of understanding about quality. The following questions will be answered: How are product and service quality defined? What does total quality management (TQM) involve? What is Deming management?

Defining Quality

According to quality expert Philip Crosby, the basic definition of **quality** is "conformance to requirements."[36] But whose requirements? The sound quality of a CD player may seem flawless to its new owner, adequate to the engineer who helped design it, and terrible to an accomplished musician. In regard to *service* quality, being

quality   *conformance to requirements*

put on hold for 30 seconds when calling a computer company's hotline may be acceptable for one person but very irritating for another. Because quality is much more than a simple either/or proposition, both product and service quality need to be analyzed. To do this, we will explore five types of product quality, the unique challenges faced by service organizations, and the ways in which consumers judge service quality.

Five Types of Product Quality

4 Identify five types of product quality.

Other specialists in the field have refined Crosby's general perspective by identifying at least five different types of product quality: transcendent, product-based, user-based, manufacturing-based, and value-based.[37] Each represents a unique and useful perspective on product quality.

Transcendent Quality.   Inherent value or innate excellence is apparent to the individual. Observing people's varied reactions to pieces of art in a museum is a good way to appreciate the subjectiveness of this type of quality. Beauty, as they say, is in the eye of the beholder.

Product-Based Quality.   The presence or absence of a given product attribute is the primary determinant of this type of quality. Soft tissues, rough sandpaper, flawless glass, sweet candy, and crunchy granola signify product-based quality in very different ways.

These Lexmark laser printers getting their final quality check from Kristine Davis at the firm's Lexington, Kentucky, plant may appear to be look-alike clones. A closer look reveals incredible product diversity. Thanks to manufacturing innovations such as mass customization and just-in-time production, each of the 2,000 printers rolling off Lexmark's assembly line every day could be configured uniquely, depending on the customer's needs. Lexmark's motto is: "Any model, any quantity, any day, without notice." This type of speedy build-to-order operation requires a passionate commitment to quality from *every* employee.

User-Based Quality.   Here, the quality of a product is determined by its ability to meet the user's expectations. Does it get the job done? Is it reliable? Customer satisfaction surveys conducted by *Consumer Reports* magazine give smart shoppers valuable input about user-based quality.

Manufacturing-Based Quality.   How well does the product conform to its design specifications or blueprint? The closer the match between the intended product and the actual one, the higher the quality. Car doors designed to close easily, quietly, and snugly are high quality if they do so. This category corresponds to Crosby's "conformance to requirements" definition of quality.

Value-Based Quality.   When you hear someone say, "I got a lot for my money," the speaker is describing value-based quality. Cost-benefit relationships are very subjective because they derive from human perception and personal preferences. About value," *Fortune* magazine observed: "The concept can be nebulous because each buyer assesses value individually. In the end, value is simply giving customers what they want at a price they consider fair."[38] Wal-Mart's "everyday low price" strategy very successfully exploits this important type of product quality.

> ↗↙ **Do You Take Quality for Granted?**   **17E**
>
> The dramatic improvement in the quality of most products over the past decade or so helped create the new psychology of value. As manufacturers everywhere have improved goods, buyers' expectations have soared. The Japanese call this *atarimae hinshitsu*, which means "quality taken for granted."
>
> *Source:* Stratford Sherman, "How to Prosper in the Value Decade," *Fortune* (November 30, 1992): 91.
>
> **Questions:** *Think of three or four products and/or services you have regularly purchased during the last five years. Has the quality of any of these goods or services gradually improved to the point where you now take for granted certain characteristics that once were in doubt? Which characteristics? What has this done to your expectations for the quality of these same goods or services in the future?*

Unique Challenges for Service Providers

Services are a rapidly growing and increasingly important part of today's global economy. Startling evidence of this appeared in 1999 when *Fortune* magazine published its Global 500 list of the largest companies in the world. General Motors was still number one in terms of sales. But Wal-Mart Stores, ranked number four in sales, had 910,000 employees, far eclipsing GM's payroll of 594,000 employees.[39] Indeed, the vast majority of the U.S labor force now works in the service sector.

Because services are customer-driven, pleasing the customer is more important than ever.[40] Experts say it costs five times more to win a new customer than it does to keep an existing one.[41] Still, U.S. companies lose an average of about 20 percent of their customers each year.[42] Service-quality strategists emphasize that it is no longer enough simply to satisfy the customer. The strategic service challenge today is to *anticipate* and *exceed* the customer's expectations. Many managers of service operations, following the lead of the legendary founder of L. L. Bean Inc., regard customer satisfaction as an ethical responsibility (see Management Ethics).

To varying extents, virtually every organization is a service organization. Pure service organizations such as day-care centers and manufacturers providing delivery and installation services face similar challenges. Specifically, they need to understand and manage five distinctive service characteristics:[43]

5 Explain how providing a service differs from manufacturing a product and list the five service-quality dimensions.

1. *Customers participate directly in the production process.* Although people do not go to the factory to help build the cars and refrigerators they eventually buy, they do need to be present when their hair is styled or a broken bone is set.
2. *Services are consumed immediately and cannot be stored.* Hairstylists cannot store up a supply of haircuts in the same way that electronics manufacturer Intel can amass an inventory of computer chips.

Management Ethics

Leon Leonwood Bean Wrote the Book on Good Service

The first product Leon Bean ever sold was a disaster. It was 1912, and Bean, a 40-year-old hunter and fisherman, had concocted for his own use a hybrid hunting boot with a leather top and a rubber bottom. He liked his invention so much he started selling the boots through the mail to fellow sportsmen, promising refunds if customers weren't satisfied. They weren't—90 of his first 100 pairs fell apart and were returned.

What did Leon do? Yes, he kept his word and refunded the full price, but then what? Did he stop promising refunds? No. Bean went in the other direction: He borrowed $400—a lot of money for a partner in a small-town clothing store in Maine—and used it to perfect the boot. Then he perfected the guarantee. His credo: "No sale is really complete until the product is worn out, and the customer is satisfied."

That kind of service set the tone for one of retailing's most unique enterprises, L. L. Bean. Today the [$1.2 billion a year] mail-order company continues to replace or repair faulty goods, sometimes years after they were sold. . . .

With his own savings, [Bean] paid his way through private high school. He then joined his older brother,

Otho, who ran a clothing store near Freeport, Maine, the current home of L. L. Bean. . . .

He started selling his boots the same year the U.S. Post Office began parcel post service. To tap the big out-of-state market, he acquired the names and addresses of sportsmen who weren't residents but who held Maine hunting licenses, and mailed his catalogue to them. When his brother, Guy, became postmaster, Leon set up his factory on the second floor over the post office and connected the two with a series of chutes and elevators.

He never lost his touch. Knowing that hunters from out of state often drove through Freeport in the middle of the night on their way to some hunting camp in the far wilds, Bean opened for business 24 hours a day. Night customers found a doorbell and a sign that read: "Push once a minute until clerk appears."

Leon Bean ran the company until his death in 1967. He was 94.

Source: Excerpted from Peter Nulty, "The National Business Hall of Fame," *Fortune*, April 5, 1993, 112, 114. © 1993 Time Inc. All rights reserved.

3. *Services are provided where and when the customer desires.* McDonald's does more business by building thousands of restaurants in convenient locations than it would if everyone had to travel to its Oakbrook, Illinois, headquarters to get a Big Mac and fries. Accommodating customers' sometimes odd schedules is a fact of life for service providers. Insurance salespersons generally work evenings and weekends during their clients' leisure periods.

4. *Services tend to be labor-intensive.* Although skilled labor has been replaced by machines such as automatic bank tellers in some service jobs, most services are provided by people to customers face to face. Consequently, the morale and social skills of service employees are vitally important. In fact, customer service has been called a *performing art* requiring a good deal of "emotional labor."[44] It isn't easy to look happy and work hard for an angry customer when you're having a bad day; but good customer service demands it.

5. *Services are intangible.* Objectively measuring an intangible service is more difficult than measuring a tangible good, but nonetheless necessary. AMP Inc., the electrical connector manufacturer headquartered in Harrisburg, Pennsylvania, measures key services. During one observation period, the company reportedly shipped 93 percent of its orders on time and averaged a delay of 3.5 seconds in answering phone calls from customers.[45]

Because customers are more intimately involved in the service-delivery process than in the manufacturing process, we need to go directly to the customer for service-quality criteria. As service-quality experts tell us:

Quality control of a service entails watching a process unfold and evaluating it against the consumer's judgment. The only completely valid standard of comparison is the customer's level of satisfaction. That's a perception—something appreciably more slippery to measure than the physical dimensions of a product.[46]

So how do consumers judge service quality?

Defining Service Quality

Researchers at Texas A&M University uncovered valuable insights about customer perceptions of service quality.[47] They surveyed hundreds of customers of various types of service organizations. The following five service-quality dimensions emerged: *reliability, assurance, tangibles, empathy,* and *responsiveness* (*Learning tip:* remember them with the acronym RATER).[48] Customers apparently judge the quality of each service transaction in terms of these five dimensions. (To better understand each dimension and to gauge your own service-quality satisfaction, take a moment now to complete the short questionnaire in Table 17.2.)

Table 17.2 | What Kind of Service Have You Been Getting Lately?

Think of the kind of treatment you have received in service establishments recently. Pick a specific restaurant, hairstyling salon, bank, airline, hospital, government agency, auto repair shop, department store, bookstore, or other service organization and rate the kind of customer service you received, using the following five RATER factors. Circle one response for each factor and total them.

R   1. *Reliability:* ability to perform the desired service dependably, accurately, and consistently.

Very poor								Very good	
1	2	3	4	5	6	7	8	9	10

A   2. *Assurance:* employees' knowledge, courtesy, and ability to convey trust and confidence.

Very poor								Very good	
1	2	3	4	5	6	7	8	9	10

T   3. *Tangibles:* physical facilities, equipment, appearance of personnel.

Very poor								Very good	
1	2	3	4	5	6	7	8	9	10

E   4. *Empathy:* provision of caring, individualized attention to customers.

Very poor								Very good	
1	2	3	4	5	6	7	8	9	10

R   5. *Responsiveness:* willingness to provide prompt service and help customers.

Very poor								Very good	
1	2	3	4	5	6	7	8	9	10

Total score =

Scoring Key
5-10 Cruel and unusual punishment.
11–20 You call this service?
21–30 Average, but who wants average service?
31–40 Close only counts in horseshoes.
41–50 Service hall-of-fame candidate.

Which of the five RATER dimensions is most important to you? In the Texas A&M study, *reliability* was the most important dimension of service quality, regardless of the type of service involved. Anyone who has waited impatiently for an overdue airplane knows firsthand the central importance of service reliability.

Specific ways to improve product and service quality are presented throughout the balance of this chapter.

An Introduction to Total Quality Management (TQM)

6 Define *total quality management* (TQM) and discuss the basic TQM principles.

total quality management (TQM) *creating an organizational culture committed to continuous improvement in every regard*

Definitions of TQM are many and varied, which is not surprising for an area subject to intense discussion and debate in recent years.[49] For our present purposes, **total quality management (TQM)** is defined as creating an organizational culture committed to the continuous improvement of skills, teamwork, processes, product and service quality, and customer satisfaction.[50] Consultant Richard Schonberger's shorthand definition calls TQM "continuous, customer-centered, employee-driven improvement."[51]

Our definition of TQM is anchored to *organizational culture* because successful TQM is deeply embedded in virtually every aspect of organizational life. As discussed in detail in Chapter 9, an organization's culture encompasses all the assumptions its employees take for granted about how people should think and act. In other words, personal commitment to systematic continuous improvement needs to become an everyday matter of "that's just the way we do things here." For example, Dr. Frank P. Carrubba, chief technical officer at Philips, the huge Dutch electronics firm, believes it is never too early to get people thinking about quality:

"It is not good enough to invent something new," he says. "An elegant result that is not strategic or reproducible in a reliable, high-quality way is not worth much to the customer. Quality has to begin in research. We have to invent in an environment that reflects the same quality we want to achieve throughout the company." [52]

As might be expected with a topic that received so much attention in a relatively short period of time, some unrealistic expectations were created. Unrealistic expectations inevitably lead to disappointment and the need for a new quick fix.[53] However, managers with realistic expectations about the deep and long-term commitment necessary for successful TQM can make it work. TQM can have a positive impact if managers understand and enact these four principles of TQM:

1. Do it right the first time.
2. Be customer-centered.
3. Make continuous improvement a way of life.
4. Build teamwork and empowerment.[54]

Let us examine each of these TQM principles.

17F

Do Airlines Have a Flying Chance of Improving Service Quality?

How a sample of 3,000 frequent fliers ranked factors that determine their satisfaction with an airline:

- On-time performance — 17%
- Aircraft/attendants — 16%
- Convenient flight schedule — 14%
- Airport check-in — 13%
- Frequent flier program — 9%
- Food service — 9%
- Seat comfort — 8%

Source: Data from "Which Airline Is Best? Survey Methods Vary," *USA Today* (June 20, 1995): 4B.

Questions: *How would your ranking of the seven airline service factors differ from the results reported here? Which airline is your favorite? Why? How do your most favorite and least favorite airlines score on the quiz in Table 17.2?*

I. Do It Right the First Time

As mentioned in Chapter 1, the trend in quality has been toward designing and building quality into the product. This approach is much less costly than fixing or throwing away substandard products. Schonberger, who has studied many Japanese and U.S. factories firsthand, contends that "errors, if any, should be caught and corrected at the source, i.e., where the work is performed."[55] Former Motorola Chairman Robert W. Galvin offered this perspective:

> *Our institutions, our companies have had quality departments. And the old testament was that quality is a company, a department, and an institutional responsibility.*
>
> *The new truth is radically different. Quality is a very personal obligation. If you can't talk about quality in the first person . . . then you have not moved to the level of involvement of quality that is absolutely essential.*[56]

Comprehensive training in TQM tools and statistical process control is essential if employees are to accept personal responsibility for quality improvement.

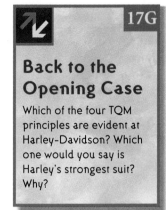

17G

Back to the Opening Case

Which of the four TQM principles are evident at Harley-Davidson? Which one would you say is Harley's strongest suit? Why?

2. Be Customer-Centered

Everyone has one or more customers in a TQM organization. They may be internal or external customers. **Internal customers** are other members of the organization who rely on *your* work to get *their* job done.[57] For example, a corporate lawyer employed by Marriott does not directly serve the hotel chain's customers by changing beds, serving meals, or carrying luggage. But that lawyer has an internal customer when a Marriott manager needs to be defended in court. Walt Disney Company serves its internal customers by providing "employees round-the-clock referrals for medical care and housing, discounts at restaurants and a video-rental service."[58]

Regarding external customers, TQM requires all employees who deal directly with outsiders to be customer-centered. Being **customer-centered** means: (1) anticipating the customer's needs, (2) listening to the customer, (3) learning how to satisfy the customer, and (4) responding appropriately to the customer. Listening to the customer is a major stumbling block for many companies. But at profitable Southwest Airlines, listening to the customer is practically a religion. "Frequent fliers sit in with personnel managers to interview and evaluate prospective flight attendants. They also participate in focus groups to help gauge response to new services or solicit ideas for improving old ones."[59] Appropriate responses depend upon the specific nature of the business.[60] For example, Table 17.3 lists good and bad customer service behaviors at an eastern U.S. supermarket chain. Notice how service-quality training led to very different patterns of behavior for the different jobs.

Vague requests to "be nice to the customer" are useless in TQM organizations. *Behavior,* not good intentions, is what really matters. As discussed in Chapter 15 in relation to behavior modification, desirable behavior needs to be strengthened with *positive reinforcement.* A good role model in this regard is Internet equipment giant Cisco Systems. CEO John T. Chambers sets the tone by giving his personal telephone number to *all* customers and taking calls in the middle of the night. As for the positive reinforcement, "all the company's top execs have their bonuses tied to customer-satisfaction ratings."[61] No surprise, then, that Cisco Systems gets high marks for customer service.

internal customer *anyone in your organization who cannot do a good job unless you do a good job*

customer-centered *satisfying the customer's needs by anticipating, listening, and responding*

Table 17.3

Turning a Supermarket into a Customer-Centered Organization

Employees	Behaviors before the change	Behaviors after the change
Bag packers	Ignore customers Lack of packing standards	Greet customers Respond to customers Ask for customers' preference
Cashiers	Ignore customers Lack of eye contact	Greet customers Respond to customers Assist customers Speak clearly Call customers by name
Shelf stockers	Ignore customers Don't know store	Respond to customers Help customers with correct product location information Knowledgeable about product location
Department workers	Ignore customers Limited knowledge	Respond to customers Know products Know store
Department managers	Ignore customers Ignore workers	Respond to customers Reward employees for responding to customers
Store managers	Ignore customers Stay in booth	Respond to customers Reward employees for service Appraise employees on customer service

Source: Randall S. Schuler, "Strategic Human Resource Management: Linking the People with the Strategic Needs of the Business." Reprinted from *Organizational Dynamics* (Summer 1992): Exhibit 4, p. 29. © 1992 American Management Association International. Reprinted by permission of American Management Association International, New York, NY. All rights reserved. **http://www.amanet.org**

3. Make Continuous Improvement a Way of Life

kaizen *a Japanese word meaning continuous improvement*

The Japanese word for continuous improvement is **kaizen,** which means improving the overall system by constantly improving the little details. TQM managers dedicated to *kaizen* are never totally happy with things. *Kaizen* practitioners view quality as an endless journey, not a final destination. They are always experimenting, measuring, adjusting, and improving. Rather than naively assuming that zero defects means perfection, they search for potential and actual trouble spots.

There are four general avenues for continuous improvement:

- Improved and more consistent product and service *quality*.
- Faster *cycle times* (in cycles ranging from product development to order processing to payroll processing).
- Greater *flexibility* (for example, faster response to changing customer demands and new technology).
- Lower *costs* and less *waste* (for example, eliminating needless steps, scrap, rework, and non–value-adding activities).[62]

Significantly, these are not trade-offs, as traditionally believed. In other words, TQM advocates reject the notion that a gain on one front necessitates a loss on another. Greater quality, speed, and flexibility have to be achieved at lower cost and with less waste. This is an "all things are possible" approach to management. It requires diligent effort and creativity.[63]

4. Build Teamwork and Empowerment

Earlier, we referred to TQM as employee-driven. In other words, it empowers employees at all levels in order to tap their full creativity, motivation, and commitment. *Empowerment*, as defined in Chapter 15, occurs when employees are adequately trained, provided with all relevant information and the best possible tools, fully involved in key decisions, and fairly rewarded for results.[64] TQM advocates prefer to reorganize the typical hierarchy into teams of people from different specialties. For a prime example, consider how Chrysler Corporation reinvented itself prior to becoming part of DaimlerChrysler:

> *Gone are the days when the development of a new vehicle plodded through a rigid set of sequential "chimneys"—from design to engineering to procurement and supply to manufacturing to marketing and sales—until, seven or eight years later, the new model turned up in the customer's driveway. Today Chrysler is organized into four streamlined platform teams: large car, small car, minivan, and Jeep/truck. Each team is composed of product and manufacturing engineers, planners and buyers, marketers, designers, financial analysts, and outside suppliers, and each is responsible for getting their vehicles to market.*
>
> *"It's not the old way: an engineer finishing his piece of the car and tossing the plan over the fence to the next guy up the line," says [retired] chairman Lee A. Iacocca. "Platform teams are about everybody working together. The result is better quality, lower cost, and a reduction in the time it takes to get a product to market."*[65]

In earlier chapters you encountered many ways to promote teamwork and employee involvement: suggestion systems (Chapter 12), quality control circles and self-managed teams (Chapter 13), teamwork and cross-functional teams (Chapter 14), and participative leadership (Chapter 15). Each can be a valuable component of TQM.

Taking TQM to Heart   17H

Medtronic pacemakers are implanted in about 250,000 people every year, and the technology has proved remarkably able to evolve with the times. The basic idea is still to supplement the body's electrical system, yet just about everything else about the product has changed. It has shrunk to the size of a small stopwatch—and packs uncanny intelligence, which lets it sense when your heart is doing fine on its own and when it needs help. It can be fully implanted in the body yet does not require major surgery. A surgeon cuts a four-inch slit under the clavicle bone, creating a pocket for the pacemaker. Then an insulated wire with a silicon tip is fed through the subclavian vein to the inner wall of the heart.

Source: Bethany McLean, "How Smart Is Medtronic Really?" *Fortune* (October 25, 1999): 176.

Question: *Why is it appropriate to call TQM a quality-of-life issue, not only for pacemaker patients, but for every one of us?*

The Seven Basic TQM Process Improvement Tools

Continuous improvement of productive processes in factories, offices, stores, hospitals, hotels, and banks requires lots of measurement. Skilled TQM managers have a large repertoire of graphical and statistical tools at their disposal. The beginner's set consists of the seven tools displayed in Figure 17.4. A brief overview of each will help promote awareness and a foundation for further study.

> **7** Describe at least three of the seven TQM process improvement tools.

Flow Chart.   A **flow chart** is a graphic representation of a sequence of activities and decisions. Standard flow-charting symbols include boxes for events or activities,

flow chart *graphic display of a sequence of activities and decisions*

Figure 17.4

Seven Basic TQM Tools

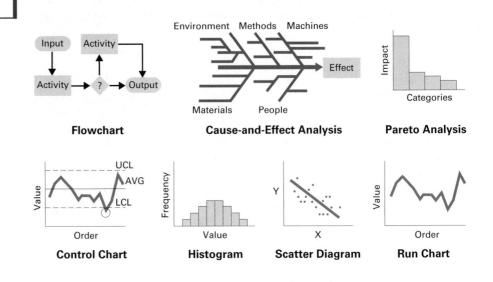

Source: Arthur R. Tenner and Irving J. DeToro, *Total Quality Management* (Figure 9.2, p. 113). © 1992 by Addison-Wesley Publishing Company, Inc. Reprinted by permission of Addison Wesley Longman.

diamonds for key decisions, and ovals for start and stop points. Flow charts show, for instance, how a property damage claim moves through an insurance company. By knowing who does what to the claim, and in which sequence, management can streamline the process by eliminating unnecessary steps or delays. Chapter 6 shows a sample flow chart as a planning and control tool. TQM teams have found flowcharting to be a valuable tool for increasing efficiency, reducing costs, and eliminating waste.

fishbone diagram *a cause-and-effect diagram*

Cause-and-Effect Analysis. The **fishbone diagram,** named for its rough resemblance to a fish skeleton, helps TQM teams visualize important cause-and-effect relationships. (Some refer to fishbone diagrams as Ishikawa diagrams, in tribute to the Japanese quality pioneer mentioned in Chapter 2.) For example, did a computer crash because of an operator error, an equipment failure, a power surge, or a software problem? A TQM team can systematically track down a likely cause by constructing a fishbone diagram. An illustrative fishbone diagram is presented in Skills & Tools at the end of Chapter 8.

Pareto analysis *bar chart indicating which problem needs the most attention*

Pareto Analysis. This technique, popularized by quality expert Joseph M. Juran and also mentioned in Chapter 2, is named for the Italian economist Vilfredo Pareto (1848–1923). Pareto detected the so-called 80/20 pattern in many worldly situations: relatively few people or events (about 20 percent) account for most of the results or impacts (about 80 percent). It is thus most efficient to focus on the few things (or people) that make the biggest difference. The next time you are in class, for example, notice how relatively few students offer the great majority of the comments in class. Likewise, a few students account for most of the absenteeism during the semester. In TQM, a **Pareto analysis** involves constructing a bar chart by counting and tallying the number of times significant quality problems occur. The tallest bar on the chart, representing the most common problem, demands prompt attention. In a newspaper printing operation, for example, the most common cause of printing press stoppages for the week might turn out to be poor-quality paper. A quick glance at a Pareto chart would tell management to demand better quality from the paper supplier.

Control Chart.   *Statistical process control* of repetitive operations helps employees keep key quality measurements within an acceptable range. A **control chart** is used to monitor actual versus desired quality measurements during repetitive operations. Consider the job of drilling a 2-centimeter hole in 1,000 pieces of metal. According to design specifications, the hole should have an inside diameter no larger than 2.1 centimeters and no smaller than 1.9 centimeters. These measurements are the upper control limit (UCL) and the lower control limit (LCL). Any hole diameters within these limits are acceptable quality. Random measurements of the hole diameters need to be taken during the drilling operation to monitor quality. When these random measurements are plotted on a control chart, like the one in Figure 17.4, the operator has a handy visual aid that flags control limit violations and signals the need for corrective action. Perhaps the drill needs to be cleaned, sharpened, or replaced. This sort of statistical process control is less expensive than having to scrap 1,000 pieces of metal with wrong-sized holes.

control chart *visual aid showing acceptable and unacceptable variations from the norm for repetitive operations*

Histogram.   A **histogram** is a bar chart showing whether repeated measurements of a given quality characteristic conform to a standard bell-shaped curve. Deviations from the standard signal the need for corrective action. The controversial practice of teachers "curving" grades when there is an abnormally high or low grade distribution can be implemented with a histogram.

histogram *bar chart indicating deviations from a standard bell-shaped curve*

Scatter Diagram.   A **scatter diagram** is used to plot the correlation between two variables. The one illustrated in Figure 17.4 indicates a negative correlation. In other words, as the value of variable X increases, the value of variable Y tends to decrease. A design engineer for a sporting goods company would find this particular type of correlation while testing the relationship between various thicknesses of fishing rods and flexibility. The thicker the rod, the lower the flexibility.

scatter diagram *diagram that plots relationships between two variables*

Run Chart.   Also called a time series or trend chart, a **run chart** tracks the frequency or amount of a given variable over time. Significant deviations from the norm signal the need for corrective action. Hospitals monitor vital body signs such as temperature and blood pressure with daily logs, actually run charts. TQM teams can use them to spot "bad days." For example, automobiles made in U.S. factories on a Friday or Monday historically have had more quality defects than those assembled on a Tuesday, Wednesday, or Thursday.

run chart *a trend chart for tracking a variable over time*

Before we move on to Deming management, an important point needs to be made. As experts on the subject remind us, "Tools are necessary but not sufficient for TQM."[66] Successful TQM requires a long-term, organizationwide drive for continuous improvement. The appropriate time frame is *years*, not days or months. Tools such as benchmarking and control charts are just one visible feature of that process. Invisible factors—such as values, learning, attitudes, motivation, and personal commitment—dictate the ultimate success of TQM.

> **↗↙ Which TQM Tool?**   17I
>
> **Situation:** A mutual fund company raised its minimum initial investment from zero to $2,500. Why? Smaller accounts are just too expensive. "About 41 percent of all our phone calls were from people with account balances of less than $1,000," said a company official.
>
> *Source:* John Waggoner, "Twentieth Century Plans for Millennium," *USA Today* (August 11, 1994): 8B.
>
> **Question:** *This line of thinking is best explained by which of the seven basic TQM tools? Explain your reasoning.*

Deming Management

It is hard to overstate the worldwide impact of W. Edwards Deming's revolutionary ideas about management. His ideas have directly and indirectly created better and more productive work environments for countless millions of people. This section builds upon the historical sketches in Chapter 2 by examining basic principles of Deming management and Deming's famous 14 points.

Principles of Deming Management

Deming management
application of W. Edwards Deming's ideas for more responsive, more democratic, and less wasteful organizations

Deming management is the application of W. Edwards Deming's ideas to revitalize productive systems by making them more responsive to the customer, more democratic, and more efficient. This approach qualifies as a revolution because, when first proposed by Deming in the 1950s, it directly challenged the legacy of Taylor's scientific management.[67] Scientific management led to rigid and autocratic organizations unresponsive to customers and employees alike. Deming management proposed essentially the opposite. Some of the principles discussed below may not seem revolutionary today because Deming management is becoming ingrained in everyday *good* management.

Quality Improvement Drives the Entire Economy.   Higher quality eventually means more jobs. Deming's simple yet convincing logic is presented in Figure 17.5. Quality improvement is a powerful engine driving out waste and inefficiency. Quality also powers higher productivity, greater market share, and new business and employment opportunities. In short, everybody wins when quality improves.[68]

The Customer Always Comes First.   In his influential 1986 text, *Out of the Crisis*, Deming wrote: "The consumer is the most important part of the production line. Quality should be aimed at the needs of the consumer, present and future."[69] Of course, these are just inspirational words until they are enacted faithfully by individ-

Figure 17.5

Everyone Benefits from Improved Quality

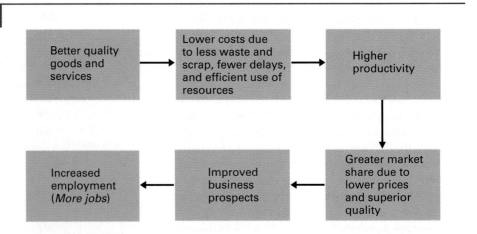

Source: Adapted from W. Edwards Deming, *Out of the Crisis* (Cambridge, Mass.: MIT, 1986), p. 3.

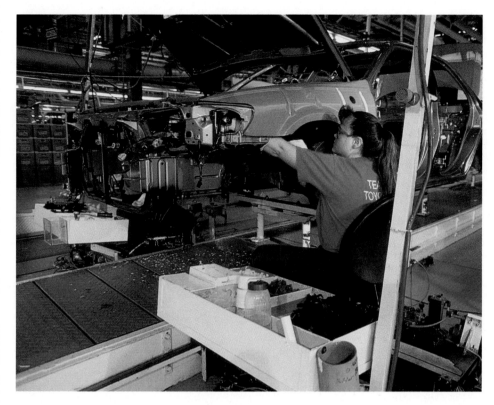

Why duck walk alongside this partly-assembled Toyota Camry when you can ride? Thanks to coworker Mike Lane's suggestion and a *kaizen* team's purchase of a bass boat seat at the local Wal-Mart, Annetta Dawson now comfortably rides alongside Toyota's assembly line in Georgetown, Kentucky, when performing her job. Before, she had to squat and duck walk alongside the moving chassis as she threaded wires through the front wheel wells. Deming would have liked this "bottom-up, fix the system" approach to quality improvement.

uals on the job. Skip Tobey, who joined America West Airlines when it started flying on August 1, 1983, embodies the Deming management spirit:

> *"I'm not just an aircraft cleaner," the 36-year-old Phoenix native said. "That's my title, but that's not the end of my job."*
>
> *Tobey said he looks for ways to help passengers, lending a hand to young families maneuvering strollers through narrow aircraft aisles and assisting elderly travelers.*
>
> *"My satisfaction is tied into quality, helping the passengers," he said. "No matter what it takes, if it means going to the furthest extreme, I'll do it."*[70]

Casual observers might dismiss the importance of Tobey's job, but his contribution was critical as America West fought its way out of bankruptcy in the mid-1990s.

Don't Blame the Person, Fix the System.   Deming management chides U.S. managers for their preoccupation with finding someone to blame rather than fixing problems. His research convinced him that "the system"—meaning management, work rules, technology, and the organization's structure and culture—typically is responsible for upwards of 85 percent of substandard quality. People can and will turn out superior quality, *if* the system is redesigned to permit them to do so. Deming management urges managers to treat employees as internal customers, listening and responding to their ideas and suggestions for improvement. After all, who knows more about a particular job—the person who performs it for 2,000 hours a year or a manager who stops by now and again?

Plan-Do-Check-Act.   Deming's approach calls for making informed decisions on the basis of hard data. His recommended tool for this process is what is popularly known as the **PDCA cycle (plan-do-check-act).** Deming preferred the term *Shewhart cycle,*[71] in recognition of the father of statistical quality control, Walter A. Shewhart,

8 **Explain how Deming's PDCA cycle can improve the overall management process.**

PDCA cycle *Deming's plan-do-check-act cycle that relies on observed data for continuous improvement of operations*

Figure 17.6

Deming's PDCA Cycle

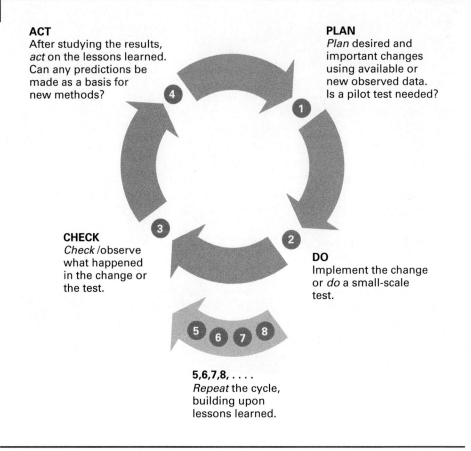

ACT
After studying the results, *act* on the lessons learned. Can any predictions be made as a basis for new methods?

PLAN
Plan desired and important changes using available or new observed data. Is a pilot test needed?

CHECK
Check/observe what happened in the change or the test.

DO
Implement the change or *do* a small-scale test.

5,6,7,8, ...
Repeat the cycle, building upon lessons learned.

Source: Adapted from W. Edwards Deming, *Out of the Crisis* (Cambridge, Mass.: MIT, 1986), p. 88.

mentioned in Chapter 2. (Japanese managers call it the Deming cycle.) Whatever the label, the PDCA cycle reminds managers to focus on what is really important, use observed data, start small and build upon accumulated knowledge, and be research-oriented in observing changes and results (see Figure 17.6).

Deming's 14 Points

Deming formulated his 14 points to transform U.S. industry from what he considered to be its backward ways. Here is a summary of the 14 points that constitute the heart and soul of Deming management:[72]

9 Specify and discuss at least four of Deming's famous 14 points.

1. *Constant purpose.* Strive for continuous improvement in products and services to remain competitive.
2. *New philosophy.* Western management needs to awaken to the realities of a new economic age by demanding wiser use of all resources.
3. *Give up on quality by inspection.* Inspecting for faulty products is unnecessary if quality is built in from the very beginning (see The Global Manager).

The Global Manager

Will Bugs Eat Up the U.S. Lead in Software?

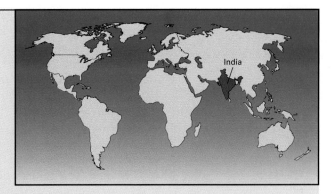

India

If U.S. software companies don't get with it in terms of quality, they could kiss big chunks of business good-bye. Both India and Brazil are mounting intensive campaigns to nurture a world-class software industry. Their competitive advantage will be quality—the virtual extermination of software bugs that infest most U.S.-made packaged software. And their mentors in this quest will be U.S. quality gurus whose voices, mysteriously, are still not widely heeded in their own country.

Already, of the world's 12 software houses that have earned the highest rating from the Software Engineering Institute (SEI) at Carnegie Mellon University, seven are in India. That's largely because Indian programmers are snapping up new methodologies shunned by America's cowboy programmers.

The software scene today is uncomfortably familiar to anyone who followed earlier crises in hardware manufacturing. For decades, quality gurus W. Edwards Deming and J. M. Juran had urged manufacturers to change. The message was: Design in quality at the beginning of the development process, instead of "testing in" pseudo-quality at the end of the production line.

Not Cheap

The quality call to arms mainly fell on deaf ears in the United States—but not in Japan. By the 1970s and 1980s, Japan was grabbing market share with better, cheaper products. They used Deming's and Juran's ideas to slash the cost of good quality to as little as 5 percent of total production costs. In U.S. factories back then, the cost of quality was 10 times as high: 50 percent. In software, it still is.

Watts S. Humphrey knows about the high cost of "testing in" quality. Now 72, he spent 27 years at IBM heading up software production and then quality assurance. "We had two acres of computers just running tests," he recalls, cringing at the thought of all that nonproductive cost. After retiring from IBM in 1986, Humphrey joined the then-fledgling SEI as a fellow. He has since emerged as the Deming of software.

In 1987, he unveiled a system for assessing and improving software quality. Called the capability maturity model (CMM), it has proved its value time and again. For example, in 1990 the cost of quality at Raytheon Electronics Systems was almost 60 percent of total software-production costs. It fell to 15 percent in 1996, thanks to CMM, and has since dipped below 10 percent.

Humdrum

Humphrey has devised two new tools for individual programmers and software teams. They include guidelines for such things as rigorous time management and compiling records of the lessons learned from each project.

That may sound humdrum, but the software tools deliver results. The first user was Advanced Information Services Corp. (AIS), a small contract-software house in Chennai, India, and Peoria, Illinois. When managers adopted Humphrey's new process methods in 1996, profits doubled, and defects nose-dived 98 percent, to a mere 0.05 bugs per 1,000 lines of code.

Like Deming and Juran, Humphrey seems to be winning more plaudits overseas than at home. The Indian government and several companies, including AIS, have just founded the Watts Humphrey Software Quality Institute at the Software Technology Park in Chennai. In hardware, U.S. manufacturers eventually grasped the quality imperative and rejoined the ranks of the world's most admired manufacturers. Let's hope U.S. software makers don't procrastinate over quality as long as their hardware cousins did.

Source: Otis Port, "Will Bugs Eat Up the U.S. Lead in Software?" Reprinted from the December 6, 1999 issue of *Business Week* by special permission. Copyright © 1999 by McGraw-Hill, Inc.

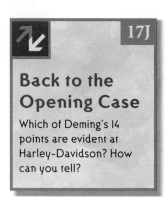

Back to the Opening Case

Which of Deming's 14 points are evident at Harley-Davidson? How can you tell?

4. *Avoid the constant search for lowest-cost suppliers.* Build long-term, loyal, and trusting relationships with single suppliers.

5. *Seek continuous improvement.* Constantly improve production processes for greater productivity and lower costs.

6. *Train everyone.* Make sure people have a clear idea of how to do their job. Informally learning a new job from coworkers entrenches bad work habits.

7. *Provide real leadership.* Leading is more than telling. It involves providing individualized help.

8. *Drive fear out of the workplace.* Employees continue to do things the wrong way when they are afraid to ask questions about why and how. According to Deming, "No one can put in his best performance unless he feels secure. *Se* comes from the Latin, meaning without, *cure* means fear or care. *Secure* means without fear, not afraid to express ideas, not afraid to ask questions."[73] Lack of job security is a major stumbling block for quality improvement in America.

9. *Promote teamwork.* Bureaucratic barriers between departments and functional specialists need to be broken down. Customer satisfaction is the common goal.

10. *Avoid slogans and targets.* Because the *system* is largely responsible for product quality, putting pressure on individuals who feel they do not control the system breeds resentment. Posters with slogans such as "zero defects" and "take pride in quality" do nothing to help the individual measure and improve productive processes. Control charts and other process-control tools, in contrast, give employees direction and encouragement. Deming's approach tells managers that if they provide leadership and continually improve the system, the scoreboard will take care of itself.

11. *Get rid of numerical quotas.* When employees aggressively pursue numerical goals or quotas, they too often take their eyes off quality, continuous improvement, and costs. Hence, Deming management strongly rejects the practice of management by objectives (MBO),[74] discussed in Chapter 6.

12. *Remove barriers that stifle pride in workmanship.* Poor management, inadequate instruction, faulty equipment, and pressure to achieve a numerical goal get in the way of continuous improvement.

13. *Education and self-improvement are key.* Greater knowledge means greater opportunity. Continuous improvement should be the number-one career objective for everyone in the organization.

14. *"The transformation is everyone's job."*[75] Virtually *everyone* in the organization plays a key role in implementing Deming management.

Summary

1. Feedforward control is preventive in nature, whereas feedback control is based on the evaluation of past performance. Managers engage in concurrent control when they monitor and adjust ongoing operations to keep them performing to standard. The three basic components of organizational control systems are objectives, standards, and an evaluation-reward system.

2. According to the performance pyramid, strategic control involves the downward translation of objectives and upward translation of performance measures. Both external effectiveness and internal efficiency criteria need to be achieved.

3. The four elements of a crisis management program are: (a) *anticipate* (conduct a crisis audit), (b) *plan* (formulate contingency plans), (c) *staff* (create a crisis management team), and (d) *practice* (perfect the program through practice).

4. Product quality involves much more than the basic idea of "conformance to requirements." Five types of product quality are transcendent, product-based, user-based, manufacturing-based, and value-based.

5. Service providers face a unique set of challenges that distinguish them from manufacturers. Because we live in a predominantly service economy, it is important to recognize these challenges: (1) direct customer participation, (2) immediate consumption of services, (3) provision of services at customers' convenience, (4) tendency of services to be more labor-intensive than manufacturing, and (5) intangibility of services, making them harder to measure. Consumer research uncovered five service-quality dimensions: reliability, assurance, tangibles, empathy, and responsiveness (RATER). Consumers consistently rank *reliability* number one.

6. Total quality management (TQM) involves creating a culture dedicated to customer-centered, employee-driven continuous improvement. The four TQM principles are

   - Do it right the first time.
   - Be customer-centered.
   - Make continuous improvement a way of life.
   - Build teamwork and empowerment.

7. Seven basic TQM process improvement tools are flow charts, fishbone diagrams, Pareto analysis, control charts, histograms, scatter diagrams, and run charts.

8. Deming's plan-do-check-act (PDCA) cycle forces managers to make decisions and take actions on the basis of observed and carefully measured data. This procedure removes quality-threatening guesswork. The PDCA cycle also helps managers focus on what is really important. PDCA work never ends, because lessons learned from one cycle are incorporated into the next.

9. Deming's famous 14 points seek to revolutionize Western management practices. In summary, they urge managers to seek continuous improvement through extensive training, leadership, teamwork, and self-improvement. The points call for *doing away with* mass quality inspections, selecting suppliers only on the basis of low cost, fear, slogans and numerical quotas, and barriers to pride in workmanship. The transformation, according to Deming, is *everyone's* job.

Terms to Understand

Pros and Cons of ISO 9000[76]

What is ISO 9000—dial-a-horoscope? A foreign sports car? A new galaxy? No, try again: ISO 9000 is a standard of quality management, hugely popular in Europe, that is rapidly taking hold in the United States—and around the globe. If, like many business people, you don't know the first thing about ISO 9000, or if you think this is just another trendy program with a goofy acronym, then listen up. Your customers are calling.

Du Pont, General Electric, Eastman Kodak, British Telecom, and Philips Electronics are among the big-name companies that are urging—or even coercing—suppliers to adopt ISO 9000 (say it ICE-o nine thousand). GE's plastics business, for instance, commanded 340 vendors to meet the standard by June. Declares John Yates, general manager of global sourcing: "There is absolutely no negotiation. If you want to work with us, you have to get it."

"It" is a certificate, awarded by one of many independent auditors, attesting that your factory, laboratory, or office has met quality management requirements determined by the International Organization for Standardization. In the United States the number of certificates issued has more than quintupled in just the past 14 months. . . .

The ISO 9000 standards, spelled out in a slender paperback volume (available in the United States for $235 from the American National Standards Institute, 11 West 42nd Street, New York, New York, 10036; 212-642-4900), do not tell you how to design a more efficient washing machine or build a more reliable nuclear missile. But they provide a framework for showing customers how you test products, train employees, keep records, and fix defects. Think of ISO 9000 not as another variant of total quality management but as a set of generally accepted accounting principles for documenting quality procedures. With certificates issued worldwide estimated at more than 30,000, the standard is rapidly becoming an internationally recognized system, comprehensible to buyers and sellers.

Says Richard Thompson, vice president and general manager of Caterpillar's engine division, whose Mossville, Illinois, plant was among the first American diesel engine factories to win the certificate: "Today, having ISO 9000 is a competitive advantage. Tomorrow, it will be the ante to the global poker game.". . .

ISO is not an acronym—not in any language. It is an official nickname, derived from *isos*, a Greek word meaning equal, as in isobar, isometrics, and isosceles triangle. ISO 9000, published in 1987, is actually a series of five related standards (numbered 9000 through 9004) that has been adopted by 60 countries—including the United States, Japan, Canada, and the [15] members of the EC.

Businessmen, not bureaucrats, are the force driving ISO 9000. Purchasing agents like the certification because it helps them cut through the worldwide clangor of competing quality plans, gurus, audits, and awards. Says Jim Holz, director of suppliers quality assurance at Bell Canada, that country's largest telephone operating company: "Saying you have a total quality management program doesn't mean a lot to me unless you have a way of benchmarking it to a standard that I can understand."

But ISO 9000's biggest virtue, its universality, is also its greatest vice. By setting norms that are attainable across a broad range of industries and cultures, ISO 9000 falls far short of the quality that world-class corporations demand of themselves and their suppliers. . . .

ISO 9000 makes no demands or assurances about the quality of a company's *products*. And the standard virtually ignores the mantra of modern quality management, continuous improvement. Companies don't have to show that they know how to reduce cycle time, cut inventories, or speed up delivery. Nor do they have to demonstrate that their customers are happier than they used to be, or even that their customers are happy at all.

Complains Richard Buetow, director of corporate quality at Motorola: "With ISO 9000 you can still have terrible processes and products. You can certify a manufacturer that makes life jackets from concrete, as long as those jackets are made according to the documented procedures and the company provides the next of kin with instructions on how to complain about defects. That's absurd."

Source: Excerpted from Ronald Henkoff, "The Hot New Seal of Quality," *Fortune* (June 28, 1993): 116–117. © 1993 Time Inc. All rights reserved.

Internet Exercises

1. **An Internet search for higher-quality customer service:** For the vast majority of today's employees who work in the service sector, service quality has two faces: *providing* services and *paying for and receiving* services. Hence, learning more about service quality can have a double benefit as we become better both as service providers and as consumers. Customer service expert John Tschohl's Web site (**www.customer-service.com**) for the Service Quality Institute he founded and heads is an excellent resource. On the home page, click on "Media." Next, select the navigation menu item "Featured Articles!" Under the heading "Past Articles," select and read at least three of the brief tutorials. (*Note:* The third reading, "Want Better Service?," offers great tips on how to complain about bad service.)

   Learning Points: 1. What was the most useful thing you learned about customer service? Explain. 2. If you presently have a service job, what did Tschohl teach you about providing better service? 3. What did Tschohl teach you about demanding and getting better customer service?

2. **Check it out:** To learn more about the work of W. Edwards Deming, go to the Massachusetts Institute of Technology's Center for Advanced Educational Services Internet site (**www.caes.mit.edu**) and click on "Products." On the Products page, select "W. Edwards Deming" and explore the various options. Be sure to read the preface to his classic book, *Out of the Crisis*.

   For updates to these exercises, visit our Web site (**www.hmco.com/college**).

When Coca-Cola's Control Systems Fizzled in Europe

> Closing Case

How could it happen?

That's been the question facing Anton Amon, chief scientist of Coca-Cola Co. and the man responsible for protecting the integrity of the world's best-known brand. Starting ... [in mid-1999] hundreds of consumers of Coke products in Europe began turning up sick, prompting governments to pull Coke from shelves and European newspapers to speculate that Coke cans were contaminated with rat poison.

Now Mr. Amon acknowledges that Coke, a company famed for its attention to quality control, brand protection, and public relations, blundered badly. The result was one of the most serious crises in Coca-Cola's 113-year history.

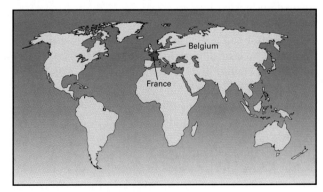

In an interview, the Austrian-born Mr. Amon says that a major culprit was lapses at Coke's bottling plants in Antwerp, Belgium, and Dunkirk, France. The plants are run by Coca-Cola Enterprises Inc., a giant bottler 40 percent-owned by Coca-Cola. The Coke plant in Antwerp failed to follow crucial quality-control procedures. "That's where the accident happened," Mr. Amon says, adding that these lapses allowed contaminated carbon dioxide, the gas that puts the fizz in soft drinks, to slip into Coke's products and make people feel sick.

At almost the same time that things were breaking down in Antwerp, trouble was brewing at a Coke plant in Dunkirk, France. Mr. Amon believes a fungicide that had been sprayed on wooden pallets rubbed off onto the bottom of some cans, creating a "medicinal" smell. While Mr. Amon says those bad odors could have made some sensitive people feel ill, scientists in Belgium and France have been unable to confirm this theory and some remain skeptical.

Carbon dioxide comes from a variety of sources and can be a byproduct of numerous processes, such as alcohol fermentation, the milling of corn and the making of fertilizer. In this case, the CO_2 at the Antwerp plant was contaminated with trace amounts of carbonyl sulfide and hydrogen sulfide, according to Mr. Amon. Neither should have been present. Both are highly toxic. Hydrogen sulfide gives off a rotten-egg smell even if it's present in small amounts. The hydrogen sulfide is hard to detect because it evaporates once the bottle is open.

Mr. Amon says the bottling plant didn't detect the contaminants. Contrary to Coke procedure, the plant wasn't receiving certificates of analysis from the supplier of the gas, Aga Gas AB of Sweden. This certificate vouches for the purity of the CO_2. Mr. Amon also acknowledges that contaminants could have entered the CO_2 after it was delivered to the plant.

Beyond that, Mr. Amon says, workers at the Antwerp plant failed to perform a routine test, required by Coke, after the CO_2 had been pumped into the holding tank at the plant, to confirm that the batch of carbon dioxide smelled and tasted fine.

A CCE spokesman . . . confirmed that the company didn't test the CO_2 batch at the Antwerp plant, and failed to request a certificate of analysis from Aga, supplier of the gas. Officials at Aga say it retained samples of the gas it shipped to CCE, and subsequent tests have shown no impurities. Coke officials say it's possible the gas could have been contaminated after it left Aga. Aga also says CCE has never asked the company to provide a certificate of analysis for each shipment.

The fiasco, which resulted in 14 million cases of Coke products being recalled in five European countries, seems to be subsiding now. No deaths have been reported. Health authorities in Belgium, France, the Netherlands, and Luxembourg have lifted sales restric-

tions on Coke products. Coke said . . . that production at the Antwerp plant will resume. . . . It said it has installed additional quality-assurance personnel in Antwerp and other plants. It isn't clear how much the mess will cost Coca-Cola, but CCE has said it will take about $60 million in second-quarter charges because of the problems. Analysts expect CCE's second-quarter operating profit to be shaved by about $35 million.

Beyond the breakdown in quality control, public-relations failures and other miscalculations worsened Coke's problems. Coke may have missed an early warning in mid-May when the owner of a pub in Herentals, near Antwerp, complained that four people at his bar had become sick after drinking bad-smelling Coca-Cola from glass bottles. Coke says it investigated his complaints, but found no problems at the plant.

Even after more evidence of trouble popped up, the company didn't sense big trouble. Mr. Amon, the company's quality-control czar, wasn't brought into the crisis-control team until June 11, three days after children at a middle school in Bornem, Belgium, began throwing up after drinking Cokes. "They don't come to Atlanta if it's nothing serious," Mr. Amon says of his far-flung colleagues. "The local folks do their own thing."

The children in Bornem had noticed that the Cokes they bought in the school cafeteria on June 8 smelled bad. At about 1 P.M., an administrator called in a complaint to the CCE bottling plant in nearby Antwerp, which had delivered 20 cases of soda to the school that morning. By 1:30 P.M., some had begun feeling ill. By the next day, there were 39 sick kids from 10 different classrooms. Many of the children were rushed to the hospital, where blood and other tests were normal.

CCE employees picked up two cases from the school for testing. Some of the drinks, says CCE official Ben Laubrecht, had "an acid type of odor." That night, CCE officials decided to recall the drinks that were made on June 2 through June 4.

Mr. Amon says that by the time the Bornem school made its complaint, the supply of gas used on June 4, the production date for Coke sent to that school, was used up. So, figuring out what went wrong with the gas might be impossible. "That gas was long gone," he says, and a subsequent batch of gas received at the plant was "clean like a whistle." Since they couldn't test the original gas supply, they started testing soft drinks. It was only a few days after the Bornem incident that Coca-Cola determined the problem was caused by sulfur compounds that had polluted the gas used June 4.

While technicians at the bottling plant struggled to figure out what had gone wrong, other CCE executives were trying to get a grip on what seemed like a little local problem. On June 9, the day after the Bornem children fell ill, the bottler faxed a letter to the school, apologizing for any inconvenience and offering to pay for all medical expenses. In Flemish, it said the company had launched an investigation and that an analysis "we have in our possession at this moment shows that it is about a deviation in taste and color" that might cause headaches and other symptoms but "does not threaten the health of your child."

In reality, officials at the bottling plant still didn't know for sure what was wrong with the drinks. They were anxiously awaiting analyses from Coca-Cola's more sophisticated labs in Atlanta. . . .

On June 15, France banned sales of soft drinks from the Dunkirk plant. Hundreds of people in France were reporting illnesses that they blamed on Coke. French officials complained that Coca-Cola had not provided enough information for them to be certain that there was no health risk.

With the crisis escalating, the company pushed its damage-control machine into high gear. At a chaotic press conference in the Brussels Hilton on the evening of June 15, CCE finally provided an explanation for all the illnesses, blaming bad carbon dioxide and the fungicide problems.

Few were convinced. CCE's explanation was vague, and different officials used different terms to describe the problems. For instance, various CCE and Coca-Cola executives called the chemical on the pallets fungicide, wood preservative, antiseptic, phenol, and creosote. Government officials and politicians in both Belgium and France were baffled. "That a company so very expert in advertising and marketing should be so poor in communicating on this matter is astonishing," says Bernard Kouchner, France's health minister.

Asked about the company's communications, Randal Donaldson, Coca-Cola's chief spokesman, says that "with hindsight, you can certainly do things differently and better, and that certainly applies in this case." He won't elaborate.

The sales bans stayed in place. Coca-Cola scrambled to find experts willing to work fast, and turned to Robert Kroes, a silver-haired professor of toxicology at Utrecht University in the Netherlands. He arrived at Coke's Brussels headquarters June 19. There would be no time for any lab work. Instead, Mr. Kroes says, Coke supplied him with data from its own labs and from other independent laboratories on contaminants found on or in containers. Mr. Kroes's conclusion: There was no health risk. In all,

he spent about eight hours in a Coke office and wrote his report before leaving. While doing his work, he says, he sipped on a can of Coke Light supplied by his hosts.

Soon, Coke was providing to the media Mr. Kroes's report as proof that the levels of impurities were too small to be a health risk. Other reports from hired consultants echoed this, and some suggested that many of the illnesses were psychosomatic. Coke refused to publicly release the results of the independent lab work, and is still denying access to those reports and technicians. A spokesman says he doesn't want the technicians to be asked a lot of "could it be this" questions.

Some government officials remain skeptical of Coke's claims. Bernard Medina, who heads the French government's lab in Bordeaux, says his lab oversaw the testing of 100 samples, including cans, contents of cans, pallets from Dunkirk, and Coke concentrate. They found absolutely no impurities, including the fungicide.

"If there was something, we should have found it," says Mr. Medina. "Still, we wonder."

Mr. Amon, Coke's top scientist, says it's no mystery that others couldn't find the fungicide. He says it probably rubbed off on only 500 to 1,000 cans and that the French lab may not have picked up any of those tainted packages. He also says that the foul odor could dissipate quickly, making it hard to detect.

Belgium and France agreed . . . after personal lobbying by Coke Chairman Douglas Ivester and other Coke officials, to let the company resume normal sales and production. Mr. Amon says he has given strict instructions to never let in a batch of CO_2 without a certificate of analysis and that each plant must do its own test on every incoming shipment of gas.

As for the wooden pallets, "I made it very clear to the CCE folks that those suspect pallets must be destroyed." In the future, pallets cannot be treated with a fungicide, he says. He vows that the slipshod testing "will not happen again."

Case update: Chairman and CEO Douglas Ivester, in a surprise move, resigned in December 1999 after only two years at the top of Coca-Cola.[77]

FOR DISCUSSION

1. What role did feedforward control play in this case?

2. From a crisis management standpoint, what should Coca-Cola have done differently? Explain.

3. What does this case tell us about TQM?

4. How would Deming probably have assessed this situation?

Source: Republished with permission of *The Wall Street Journal* from "Anatomy of a Recall: How Coke's Controls Fizzled Out in Europe," by Nikhil Deogun, James R. Hagerty, Steve Steklow, and Laura Johannes, *The Wall Street Journal* (June 29, 1999). Permission conveyed through Copyright Clearance Center, Inc.

VIDEO SKILL BUILDER

Quality is king at Gulfstream Aircraft Company, where customers' lives are on the line with each of its $30-million corporate jets. Gulfstream's success formula combines a strong customer focus with cross-functional teamwork and a dedication to world-class quality.

5 Gulfstream Aircraft Flies on Quality

Learning objective: To demonstrate how to achieve world-class product quality.

Links to textual material: *Chapter 14:* Cross-functional teamwork *Chapter 17:* Feedforward control; Total quality management; Deming management

Discussion questions

1. Why is cross-functional teamwork a key part of Gulfstream's success?
2. How does Gulfstream achieve feedforward control over product quality and customer satisfaction?
3. Which of the four principles of total quality management (TQM) are evident in this video case?
4. Which of Deming's 14 points are evident in this video case?

Chapter 1

Opening Quotation   As quoted in "Fast Pack 1999," *Fast Company*, No. 22 (February–March 1999): 139.

Opening Case   Bill Meyers, "Umbrellas Make Skies Brighter," *USA Today* (January 14, 1999): 8B. Copyright 1999, USA Today. Reprinted with permission.

Closing Case   Republished with permission of *The Wall Street Journal*, from Jonathan Kaufman, "For Latter-Day CEO, 'All in a Day's Work' Often Means Just That," (May 3, 1999). Permission conveyed through Copyright Clearance Center, Inc.

1. Anne B. Fisher, "Morale Crisis," *Fortune* (November 18, 1991): 76, 80.

2. Alan Farnham, "Who Beats Stress Best—And How," *Fortune* (October 7, 1991): 76. Also see Lauren M. Bernardi, "How to Be a Bad Boss," *Canadian Manager* (Summer 1998): 11–12.

3. Ellen Van Velsor and Jean Brittain Leslie, "Why Executives Derail: Perspectives Across Time and Cultures," *Academy of Management Executive*, 9 (November 1995): 63.

4. For more on dealing with a bad boss, see Anne Fisher, "I'm Being Tortured by a Toxic Colleague . . . I Think My Boss May Be Losing His Mind," *Fortune* (December 8, 1997): 252; Stanley Bing, "Oh, Sure, *Now* You Want to Talk About It," *Fortune* (January 12, 1998): 57–58; and "Busting Bullies," *Training* (April 1999): 16.

5. Linda Grant, "Rambos in Pinstripes: Why So Many CEOs Are Lousy Leaders," *Fortune* (June 24, 1996): 147.

6. Wendy Zellner, "Peace, Love, and the Bottom Line," *Business Week* (December 7, 1998): 83.

7. Ronald Henkoff, "Boeing's BIG Problem," *Fortune* (January 12, 1998). © 1998 Time Inc. Reprinted by permission. For an update, see Janet Rae-Dupree, "Can Boeing Get Lean Enough?" *Business Week* (August 30, 1999): 182.

8. Data from Evelyn L. Wright, "Cracks in the Greenhouse?" *Business Week* (July 26, 1999): 74, 76.

9. Data from "6,000,000,000 People Today," *USA Today* (July 16, 1999): 1A. For good background reading, see Lester R. Brown, Gary Gardner, and Brian Halweil, "16 Impacts of Growth," *The Futurist*, 33 (February 1999): 36–41; and Peter Coy, "The 'Little Emperors' Can Save the World's Aging Population," *Business Week* (August 30, 1999): 140, 142.

10. "Growing World," *USA Today* (August 25, 1998): 1A.

11. David Lamb, "Class of 1993 Faces Up to a New Corporate America," *Los Angeles Times* (June 1, 1993): A13.

12. For the "big picture," see Toby J. Tetenbaum, "Shifting Paradigms: From Newton to Chaos," *Organizational Dynamics*, 26 (Spring 1998): 21–32; and Richard W. Oliver, *The Shape of Things to Come: Seven Imperatives for Winning in the New World of Business* (New York: McGraw-Hill, 1999).

13. Data from Michael Sivy, "Seeking Safety? Coke Isn't It," *Money*, 27 (October 1998): 43–44.

14. Data from "AMA Global Survey on Key Business Issues," *Management Review*, 87 (December 1998): 27–38.

15. James Sloan Allen, "Capitalism Globe Trots with Jordan," *USA Today* (August 16, 1999): 6B. Also see J. Orstrom Moller, "The Growing Challenge to Internationalism," *The Futurist*, 33 (March 1999): 22–27.

16. Sue Zesiger, "Jac Nasser Is Car Crazy," *Fortune* (June 22, 1998): 80.

17. A good historical overview of the quality movement can be found in R. Ray Gehani, "Quality Value-Chain: A Meta-Synthesis of Frontiers of Quality Movement," *Academy of Management Executive*, 7 (May 1993): 29–42.

18. For more, see Kee Young Kim, Jeffrey G. Miller, and Janelle Heineke, "Mastering the Quality Staircase, Step by Step," *Business Horizons*, 40 (January–February 1997): 17–21.

19. See Kenneth R. Thompson, "Confronting the Paradoxes in a Total Quality Environment," *Organizational Dynamics*, 26 (Winter 1998): 62–74.

20. See Gail Dutton, "The Green Bottom Line," *Management Review*, 87 (October 1998): 59–63; and Shaker A. Zahra, "The Changing Rules of Global Competitiveness in the 21st Century," *Academy of Management Executive*, 13 (February 1999): 36–42.

21. For example, see Michael A. Berry and Dennis A. Rondinelli, "Proactive Corporate Environmental Management: A New Industrial Revolution," *Academy of Management Executive*, 12 (May 1998): 38–50; Steve Lerner, "The New Environmentalists," *The Futurist*, 32 (May 1998): 35–39; "Hot World, Cooler Growth," *The Christian Science Monitor* (August 13, 1998): 12; Karen Pennar, "Gordon Conway, Green Revolutionary," *Business Week* (November 16, 1998): 191, 194; and Gary Gardner and Payal Sampat, "Making Things Last: Reinventing Our Material Culture," *The Futurist*, 33 (May 1999): 24–28.

22. See Murray Weidenbaum, Christopher Douglass, and Michael Orlando, "How to Achieve a Healthier Environment *and* a Stronger Economy," *Business Horizons*, 40 (January–February 1997): 9–16; John Carey, "Look Who's Thawing on Global Warming," *Business Week* (November 9, 1998): 103–104; and Al Gore, "Finding a Third Way," *Newsweek* (November 23, 1998): 58.

23. Data from James K. Kouzes and Barry Z. Posner, "The Credibility Factor: What Followers Expect from Their Leaders," *Management Review*, 79 (January 1990): 29–33.

24. Julie Amparano, "As Ethics Crisis Grows, Businesses Take Action," *The Arizona Republic* (November 24, 1996): D9.

25. Robert D. Hof, "What Every CEO Needs to Know About Electronic Business: A Survival Guide," *Business Week* E.BIZ (March 22, 1999): EB 12. A brief history of the Internet/Web can be found

in Matthew Fordahl, "History Not Watching Day of Internet's Birth," *The Arizona Republic* (September 6, 1999): E1, E3.

26. Bernard Wysocki Jr., "Corporate Caveat: Dell or Be Delled," *The Wall Street Journal* (May 10, 1999): A1. Also see Andrew Urbaczewski, Leonard M. Jessup, and Bradley C. Wheeler, "A Manager's Primer in Electronic Commerce," *Business Horizons*, 41 (September–October 1998): 5–16.

27. Richard Wolf, "Billions of Dollars Hang over Internet Tax Debate," *USA Today* (June 22, 1999): 2A.

28. Nanette Byrnes and Paul C. Judge, "Internet Anxiety," *Business Week* (June 28, 1999): 80. Also see Eryn Brown, "9 Ways to Win on the Web," *Fortune* (May 24, 1999): 112–125; Robert D. Hof and Linda Himelstein, "eBay vs. Amazon.com," *Business Week* (May 31, 1999): 128–132; David Dorsey, "The People Behind the People Behind E-Commerce," *Fast Company*, no. 25 (June 1999): 184–198; and Jenny C. McCune, "Boon or Burden?" *Management Review*, 88 (June 1999): 53–57.

29. For related research, see Frank Shipper, "A Study of the Psychometric Properties of the Managerial Skill Scales of the Survey of Management Practices," *Educational and Psychological Measurement*, 55 (June 1995): 468–479; and Frank Shipper and Charles S. White, "Mastery, Frequency, and Interaction of Managerial Behaviors Relative to Subunit Effectiveness," *Human Relations*, 52 (January 1999): 49–66.

30. See Henri Fayol, *General and Industrial Management*, trans. Constance Storrs (London: Isaac Pitman & Sons, 1949).

31. Henry Mintzberg, "The Manager's Job: Folklore and Fact," *Harvard Business Review*, 53 (July–August 1975): 49.

32. Ibid., p. 54.

33. Alan Deutschman, "The CEO's Secret of Managing Time," *Fortune* (June 1, 1992): 136. Also see Steve Kaye, "How to Handle Interruptions that Steal Your Time," *Canadian Manager*, 24 (Summer 1999): 25–26.

34. See Henry Mintzberg, "Managerial Work: Analysis from Observation," *Management Science*, 18 (October 1971): B97–B110.

35. See Scott Adams, *The Dilbert Principle* (New York: HarperBusiness, 1996); and Lisa A. Burke and Jo Ellen Moore, "Contemporary Satire of Corporate Managers: Time to Cut the Boss Some Slack?" *Business Horizons*, 42 (July–August 1999): 63–67.

36. "AMA Research," *Management Review*, 85 (July 1996): 10. Also see Jenny C. McCune, "Brave New World," *Management Review*, 86 October 1997): 11–14; and Robert J. Samuelson, "Why I Am Not a Manager," *Newsweek* (March 22, 1999): 47.

37. Adapted from Earnest R. Archer, "Things You Lose the Right to Do When You Become a Manager," *Supervisory Management*, 35 (July 1990): 8–9. Also see Michael Kaplan, "How to Overcome Your Strengths," *Fast Company*, no. 24 (May 1999): 225–234; and Ram Charan and Geoffrey Colvin, "Why CEOs Fail," *Fortune* (June 21, 1999): 68–78.

38. For specific skills and competencies, see Paul J. Kauffmann Jr., and Thomas L. Long, "Defining High-Performance Workplace Skills—And How Community Colleges Can Help Achieve Them," *National Productivity Review*, 14 (Autumn 1995): 123–131; Scott B. Parry, "The Quest for Competencies," *Training*, 33 (July 1996): 48–56; and Scott B. Parry, "Just What Is a Competency? (And Why Should You Care?)," *Training*, 35 (June 1998): 58–64.

39. Excerpted and adapted from Robert Albanese, "Competency-Based Management Education," *Journal of Management Development*, 8, no. 2 (1989): 69.

40. Excerpt from Susan Caminiti, "America's Most Successful Businesswoman," *Fortune* (June 15, 1992): 106. © 1992 Time Inc. All rights reserved.

41. More detailed accounts of Miner's motivation-to-manage research may be found in John B. Miner, *The Human Constraint: The Coming Shortage of Managerial Talent* (Washington, D.C.: Bureau of National Affairs, 1974), pp. 6–7; John B. Miner and Norman R. Smith, "Decline and Stabilization of Managerial Motivation over a 20-Year Period," *Journal of Applied Psychology*, 67 (June 1982): 297–305.

42. Miner and Smith, "Decline and Stabilization," 1982.

43. See Stephanie Armour, "Management Loses Its Allure," *USA Today* (October 15, 1997): 1B–2B; Nancy Hatch Woodward, "The Coming of the X Managers," *HRMagazine*, 44 (March 1999): 74–80; and Stuart Crainer and Des Dearlove, "Death of Executive Talent," *Management Review*, 88 (July–August 1999): 16–23.

44. See John B. Miner, Jeffrey M. Wachtel, and Bahman Ebrahimi "The Managerial Motivation of Potential Managers in the United States and Other Countries of the World: Implications for National Competitiveness and the Productivity Problem," in *Advances in International Comparative Management*, vol. 4, ed. S. Benjamin Prasad (Greenwich, Conn.: JAI Press, 1989), pp. 147–170; John B. Miner, Chao-Chuan Chen, and K. C. Yu, "Theory Testing Under Adverse Conditions: Motivation to Manage in the People's Republic of China," *Journal of Applied Psychology*, 76 (June 1991): 343–349; and John B. Miner, Bahman Ebrahimi, and Jeffrey M. Wachtel, "How Deficiencies in Motivation to Manage Contribute to the United States' Competitiveness Problem (and What Can Be Done About It)," *Human Resource Management*, 34 (Fall 1995): 363–387.

45. Based on data from Gene Koretz, "Will Downsizing Stymie Clinton's Job-Creating Plans?" *Business Week* (December 28, 1992): 26.

46. See Alan M. Webber, "Fighting to Be Noticed? Brand Yourself," *USA Today* (March 3, 1998): 11A; Catherine Kirchmeyer, "Determinants of Managerial Career Success: Evidence and Explanation of Male/Female Differences," *Journal of Management*, 24, no. 6 (1998): 673–692; Ron Lieber, "Wanna Move Up? Act Up!" *Fast Company*, no. 21 (January 1999): 60, 62; and Del Jones, "Grove Advises Keeping an Eye on Big Picture," *USA Today* (April 28, 1999): 7B.

47. Trends in higher education are discussed in Keith H. Hammonds and Susan Jackson, "The New U," *Business Week* (December 22, 1997): 96–102; Heath Row, "Go to the Head of the Class!" *Fast Company*, no. 24 (May 1999): 261–270; "Online Universities Court a Wary Market," *Training*, 36 (August 1999): 22–23; and Kathleen Morris, "Wiring the Ivory Tower," *Business Week* (August 9, 1999): 90–92.

48. See Ron Zemke, "The Honeywell Studies: How Managers Learn to Manage," *Training*, 22 (August 1985): 46–51.

49. Adapted from Robin Snell, "Graduating from the School of Hard Knocks?" *Journal of Management Development*, 8, no. 5 (1989): 23–30. For a humorous view of the school of hard knocks, see Ray W. Cooksey, G. Richard Gates, and Hilary Pollock, "'Unsafe' Business Acts and Outcomes: A Management Lexicon," *Business Horizons*, 41 (May–June 1998): 41–49.

50. Five dimensions of managerial learning—openness, systematic thinking, creativity, a sense of efficacy, and empathy—are discussed in Michael E. McGill, John W. Slocum Jr., and David Lei, "Management Practices in Learning Organizations," *Organizational Dynamics*, 21 (Summer 1992): 5–17. Also see Marilyn Wood Daudelin, "Learning from Experience Through Reflection," *Organizational Dynamics*, 24 (Winter 1996): 36–48; Martin M. Broadwell, "The Case for Pre-Supervisory Training," *Training*, 33 (October 1996): 103–108; M. Ronald Buckley, Gerald R. Ferris,

H. John Bernardin, and Michael G. Harvey, "The Disconnect Between the Science and Practice of Management," *Business Horizons*, 41 (March–April 1998): 31–38; and John Beeson, "Succession Planning: Building the Management Corps," *Business Horizons*, 41 (September–October 1998): 61–66.

51. Gene Koretz, "Cycles of Death and Rebirth," *Business Week* (November 16, 1998): 26.

52. Data from Bill Meyers, "Worker Shortage Forces Small Businesses into Creative Hiring," *USA Today* (October 30, 1998): 1B–2B. Good primers on small business management are Kathleen R. Allen, *Launching New Ventures: An Entrepreneurial Approach*, 2nd ed. (Boston: Houghton Mifflin, 1999); and Kathleen R. Allen, *Growing and Managing an Entrepreneurial Business* (Boston: Houghton Mifflin, 1999).

53. See David R. Francis, "Spiking Stereotypes About Small Firms," *The Christian Science Monitor* (May 7, 1993): 9; Gene Koretz, "A Surprising Finding on New-Business Mortality Rates," *Business Week* (June 14, 1993): 22; and James Aley, "Debunking the Failure Fallacy," *Fortune* (September 6, 1993): 21. For related reading, see Dean A. Shepherd, "Venture Capitalists' Assessment of New Venture Survival," *Management Science*, 45 (May 1999): 621–632.

54. Data from Larry Light, "Small Business: The Job Engine Needs Fuel," *Business Week* (March 1, 1993): 78.

55. Data from Charles Burck, "Where Good Jobs Grow," *Fortune* (June 14, 1993): 22. Also see Gene Koretz, "Where the New Jobs Are," *Business Week* (March 20, 1995): 24.

56. For more on Birch's research, see Alan Webber, "Business Race Isn't Always to the Swift, but Bet That Way," *USA Today* (February 3, 1998): 15A.

57. For recent data on pay in big companies versus small companies, see Michael Mandel, "Big Players Offer Better Pay," *Business Week* (August 30, 1999): 30.

58. See Conrad S. Ciccotello and C. Terry Grant, "LLCs and LLPs: Organizing to Deliver Professional Services," *Business Horizons*, 42 (March–April 1999): 85–91.

59. See Surinder Tikoo, "Assessing the Franchise Option," *Business Horizons*, 39 (May–June 1996): 78–82; James G. Combs and David J. Ketchen Jr., "Can Capital Scarcity Help Agency Theory Explain Franchising? Revisiting the Capital Scarcity Hypothesis," *Academy of Management Journal*, 42 (April 1999): 196–207; and Josh Martin, "Franchising in the Middle East," *Management Review*, 88 (June 1999): 38–42.

60. See Nelson D. Schwartz, "Secrets of *Fortune*'s Fastest-Growing Companies," *Fortune* (September 6, 1999): 72–86.

61. Howard H. Stevenson and J. Carlos Jarillo, "A Paradigm of Entrepreneurship: Entrepreneurial Management," *Strategic Management Journal*, 11 (Summer 1990): 23 (emphasis added). For interesting and inspiring entrepreneur stories, see Jim Ansara and Michael Hopkins, "Out of Thin Air," *Inc.*: 20th Anniversary Issue, 21 (May 18, 1999): 116–136; and Erik Calonius, "Their Wildest Dreams," *Fortune* (August 16, 1999): 142–153.

62. Stephanie Armour, "Start-Ups Face More Grind than Glamour," *USA Today* (July 12, 1999): 1B.

63. See Robert McNatt, "Startups Grow at an Escargot's Pace," *Business Week* (July 19, 1999): 6.

64. See Gene Koretz, "What Makes an Entrepreneur," *Business Week* (December 9, 1996): 32; and John B. Miner, "The Expanded Horizon for Achieving Entrepreneurial Success," *Organizational Dynamics*, 25 (Winter 1997): 54–67; Gail Dutton, "Wanted: A Practical Visionary," *Management Review*, 87 (March 1998):

33–36; Curtis Hartman, "The Entrepreneur in My Bed," *Inc.*: 20th Anniversary Issue, 21 (May 18, 1999): 91–92; and Norm Brodsky, "The Right Stuff," *Inc.*, 21 (July 1999): 29–30.

65. Geoffrey Smith and Lisa Driscoll, "Victor Kiam, the Self-Sacking Quarterback," *Business Week* (February 25, 1991): 46.

66. Data from ibid.

67. For instructive reading, see Eric G. Flamholtz, *How to Make the Transition from an Entrepreneurship to a Professionally Managed Firm* (San Francisco: Jossey-Bass, 1986); Richard L. Osborne, "Second Phase Entrepreneurship: Breaking Through the Growth Wall," *Business Horizons*, 37 (January–February 1994): 80–86; and Rita Gunther McGrath, "Falling Forward: Real Options Reasoning and Entrepreneurial Failure," *Academy of Management Review*, 24 (January 1999): 13–30.

Chapter 2

Opening Quotation John W. Gardner, *Self-Renewal: The Individual and the Innovative Society* (New York: Harper & Row, 1964), chap. 11.

Opening Case Erik Calonius, "Berry Gordy Jr.," *Fortune* (August 16, 1999): 149. © 1999 Time Inc. Reprinted by permission.

Closing Case Bill Montague, "Russia's New Management Style," *USA Today* (August 12, 1996): 7B. Copyright 1996, USA Today. Reprinted with permission.

1. Alonzo L. McDonald, as quoted in Alan M. Kantrow, ed., "Why History Matters to Managers," *Harvard Business Review*, 64 (January–February 1986): 82.

2. Barbara S. Lawrence, "Historical Perspective: Using the Past to Study the Present," *Academy of Management Review*, 9 (April 1984): 307.

3. For a discussion in this area, see "How Business Schools Began," *Business Week* (October 19, 1963): 114–116. Also see John Trinkaus, "Urwick on the Business Academy," *Business Horizons*, 35 (September–October 1992): 25–29.

4. See Marian M. Extejt and Jonathan E. Smith, "The Behavioral Sciences and Management: An Evaluation of Relevant Journals," *Journal of Management*, 16 (September 1990): 539–551. For a list of forty management-oriented periodicals, see Jonathan L. Johnson and Philip M. Podsakoff, "Journal Influence in the Field of Management: An Analysis Using Salancik's Index in a Dependency Network," *Academy of Management Journal*, 37 (October 1994): 1392–1407.

5. See the instructive time line in "Management Ideas Through Time," *Management Review*, 87 (January 1998): 16–19. Also see Daniel A. Wren and Ronald G. Greenwood, *Management Innovators: The People and Ideas That Shaped Modern Business* (New York: Oxford University Press, 1998).

6. An interesting call for the reintegration of management theory may be found in Max S. Wortman Jr., "Reintegrating and Reconceptualizing Management: A Challenge for the Future," *Review of Business and Economic Research*, 18 (Spring 1983): 1–8.

7. See Henri Fayol, *General and Industrial Management*, trans. Constance Storrs (London: Isaac Pitman & Sons, 1949). An interesting review by Nancy M. Carter of Fayol's book can be found in Allen C. Bluedorn, ed., "Special Book Review Section on the Classics of Management," *Academy of Management Review*, 11 (April 1986): 454–456.

8. Stephen J. Carroll and Dennis J. Gillen, "Are the Classical Management Functions Useful in Describing Managerial Work?" *Academy of Management Review*, 12 (January 1987): 48.

9. Frank B. Copley, *Frederick W. Taylor: Father of Scientific Management* (New York: Harper & Brothers, 1923), I: 3. See the brief profile of Taylor in "Taylorism," *Business Week*: 100 Years of Innovation (Summer 1999): 16.

10. For expanded treatment, see Frank B. Copley, *Frederick W. Taylor: The Principles of Scientific Management* (New York: Harper & Brothers, 1911). A good retrospective review of Taylor's classic writings may be found in Allen C. Bluedorn, ed., "Special Book Review Section on the Classics of Management," *Academy of Management Review*, 11 (April 1986): 443–447. Robert Kanigel's *One Best Way*, a modern biography of Taylor, is reviewed in Alan Farnham, "The Man Who Changed Work Forever," *Fortune* (July 21, 1997): 114.

11. For an interesting update on Taylor, see Christopher Farrell, "Micromanaging from the Grave," *Business Week* (May 15, 1995): 34.

12. George D. Babcock, *The Taylor System in Franklin Management*, 2nd ed. (New York: Engineering Magazine Company, 1917), p. 31.

13. Frederick W. Taylor, *Shop Management* (New York: Harper & Brothers, 1911), p. 22.

14. Frank B. Gilbreth and Lillian M. Gilbreth, *Applied Motion Study* (New York: Sturgis & Walton, 1917), p. 42. A retrospective review of the Gilbreths' writings, by Daniel J. Brass, can be found in Allen C. Bluedorn, ed., "Special Book Review Section on the Classics of Management," *Academy of Management Review*, 11 (April 1986): 448–451.

15. See Frank B. Gilbreth Jr., and Ernestine Gilbreth Carey, *Cheaper by the Dozen* (New York: Thomas Y. Crowell, 1948).

16. For example, see the Gantt chart on p. 64 of Tom D. Conkright, "So You're Going to Manage a Project," *Training*, 35 (January 1998): 62–67.

17. For detailed coverage of Gantt's contributions, see H. L. Gantt, *Work, Wages, and Profits*, 2nd ed. (New York: Engineering Magazine Company, 1913). An interesting update on Gantt's contributions can be found in Peter B. Peterson, "Training and Development: The Views of Henry L. Gantt (1861–1919)," *SAM Advanced Management Journal*, 52 (Winter 1987): 20–23.

18. Good historical overviews of the quality movement are Ron Zemke, "A Bluffer's Guide to TQM," *Training*, 30 (April 1993): 48–55; R. Ray Gehani, "Quality Value-Chain: A Meta-Synthesis of Frontiers of Quality Movement," *Academy of Management Executive*, 7 (May 1993): 29–42; and Sangit Chatterjee and Mustafa Yilmaz, "Quality Confusion: Too Many Gurus, Not Enough Disciples," *Business Horizons*, 36 (May–June 1993): 15–18.

19. Mary Walton, *Deming Management at Work* (New York: Putnam, 1990), p. 13. See John Hillkirk, "World-Famous Quality Expert Dead at 93," *USA Today* (December 21, 1993): 1B–2B; Peter Nulty, "The National Business Hall of Fame: W. Edwards Deming," *Fortune* (April 4, 1994): 124; Keki R. Bhote, "Dr. W. Edwards Deming—A Prophet with Belated Honor in His Own Country," *National Productivity Review*, 13 (Spring 1994): 153–159; Anne Willette, "Deming Legacy Gives Firms Quality Challenge," *USA Today* (October 19, 1994): 2B; and M. R. Yilmaz and Sangit Chatterjee, "Deming and the Quality of Software Development," *Business Horizons*, 40 (November–December 1997): 51–58.

20. See Jack Gordon, "An Interview with Joseph M. Juran," *Training*, 31 (May 1994): 35–41.

21. Zemke, "A Bluffer's Guide to TQM," p. 51. Also see Joseph M. Juran, "Made in U.S.A.: A Renaissance in Quality," *Harvard Business Review*, 71 (July–August 1993): 42–50.

22. See Armand V. Feigenbaum, "How Total Quality Counters Three Forces of International Competitiveness," *National Productivity Review*, 13 (Summer 1994): 327–330. More Feigenbaum ideas can be found in Del Jones, "Employers Going for Quality Hires, Not Quantity," *USA Today* (December 11, 1997): 1B.

23. Crosby's more recent ideas may be found in Philip B. Crosby, *Completeness: Quality for the 21st Century* (New York: Dutton, 1992).

24. Edwin A. Locke, "The Ideas of Frederick W. Taylor: An Evaluation," *Academy of Management Review*, 7 (January 1982): 22–23. Also see David H. Freedman, "Is Management Still a Science?" *Harvard Business Review*, 70 (November–December 1992): 26–38.

25. See Donald W. Fogarty, Thomas R. Hoffman, and Peter W. Stonebraker, *Production and Operations Management* (Cincinnati: South-Western Publishing Co., 1989), pp. 7–8; and Vincent A. Mabert, "Operations in the American Economy: Liability or Asset," *Business Horizons*, 35 (July–August 1992): 3–5.

26. The Hawthorne studies are discussed in detail in F. J. Roethlisberger and William J. Dickson, *Management and the Worker* (Cambridge, Mass.: Harvard University Press, 1939). Dennis W. Organ's review of this classic book, in which he criticizes the usual textbook treatment of it, can be found in Allen C. Bluedorn, ed., "Special Book Review Section on the Classics of Management," *Academy of Management Review*, 11 (April 1986): 459–463.

27. See Ellen S. O'Connor, "The Politics of Management Thought: A Case Study of the Harvard Business School and the Human Relations School," *Academy of Management Review*, 24 (January 1999): 117–131.

28. See Henry C. Metcalf and L. Urwick, *Dynamic Administration: The Collected Papers of Mary Parker Follett* (New York: Harper & Brothers, 1942); Mary Parker Follett, *Freedom and Coordination* (London: Management Publications Trust, 1949). A review by Diane L. Ferry of *Dynamic Administration* can be found in Allen C. Bluedorn, ed., "Special Book Review Section on the Classics of Management," *Academy of Management Review*, 11 (April 1986): 451–454.

29. See L. D. Parker, "Control in Organizational Life: The Contribution of Mary Parker Follett," *Academy of Management Review*, 9 (October 1984): 736–745; Albie M. Davis, "An Interview with Mary Parker Follett," *Negotiation Journal*, 5 (July 1989): 223–225; and Dana Wechsler Linden, "The Mother of Them All," *Forbes* (January 16, 1995): 75–76.

30. An interesting and instructive time line of human resource milestones can be found in "Training and Development in the 20th Century," *Training*, 35 (September 1998): 49–56.

31. For a statistical interpretation of the Hawthorne studies, see Richard Herbert Franke and James D. Kaul, "The Hawthorne Experiments: First Statistical Interpretation," *American Sociological Review*, 43 (October 1978): 623–643. Also see Stephen R. G. Jones, "Worker Interdependence and Output: The Hawthorne Studies Reevaluated," *American Sociological Review*, 55 (April 1990): 176–190.

32. Russell L. Ackoff, "Science in the Systems Age: Beyond IE, OR, and MS," *Operations Research*, 21 (May–June 1973): 664.

33. Charles J. Coleman and David D. Palmer, "Organizational Application of System Theory," *Business Horizons*, 16 (December 1973): 77.

34. Chester I. Barnard, *The Functions of the Executive* (Cambridge, Mass.: Harvard University Press, 1938), p. 65.

35. Ibid., p. 82. A retrospective review, by Thomas L. Keon, of Barnard's *The Functions of the Executive* can be found in Allen C. Bluedorn, ed., "Special Book Review Section on the Classics of Management," *Academy of Management Review*, 11 (April 1986): 456–459.

36. For details, see Lori Verstegen Ryan and William G. Scott, "Ethics and Organizational Reflection: The Rockefeller Foundation and Postwar 'Moral Deficits,' 1942–1954," *Academy of Management Review*, 20 (April 1995): 438–461.

37. Ludwig von Bertalanffy, "The History and Status of General Systems Theory," *Academy of Management Journal*, 15 (December 1972): 411.

38. For an example of an economic/industrial hierarchy of organizations, see Figure 2 (p. 774) in Philip Rich, "The Organizational Taxonomy: Definition and Design," *Academy of Management Review*, 17 (October 1992): 758–781.

39. Susan Albers Mohrman and Allan M. Mohrman Jr., "Organizational Change and Learning," in *Organizing for the Future: The New Logic for Managing Complex Organizations*, eds. Jay R. Galbraith, Edward E. Lawler III, and Associates (San Francisco: Jossey-Bass, 1993), p. 89. For an excellent overview of organizational learning, see David A. Garvin, "Building a Learning Organization," *Harvard Business Review*, 71 (July–August 1993): 78–91. Also see Robert Aubrey and Paul M. Cohen, *Working Wisdom: Timeless Skills and Vanguard Strategies for Learning Organizations* (San Francisco: Jossey-Bass, 1995).

40. For example, see Gary Weiss, "Chaos Hits Wall Street—The Theory, That Is," *Business Week* (November 2, 1992): 138–140.

41. Margaret Wheatley, "Searching for Order in an Orderly World: A Poetic for Post-Machine-Age Managers," *Journal of Management Inquiry*, 1 (December 1992): 340. Also see Margaret J. Wheatley, *Leadership and the New Science: Learning About Organization from an Orderly Universe* (San Francisco: Berrett-Koehler, 1994); John Carey, "Can the Complexity Gurus Explain It All?" *Business Week* (November 6, 1995): 21, 24; Toby J. Tetenbaum, "Shifting Paradigms: From Newton to Chaos," *Organizational Dynamics*, 26 (Spring 1998): 21–32; and Louisa Wah, "Welcome to the Edge," *Management Review*, 87 (November 1998): 24–29.

42. Fremont E. Kast and James E. Rosenzweig, *Organization and Management: A Systems Approach*, 4th ed. (New York: McGraw-Hill, 1985), p. 108.

43. For example, see Joseph A. Maciariello, Jeffrey W. Burke, and Donald Tilley, "Improving American Competitiveness: A Management Systems Perspective," *Academy of Management Executive*, 3 (November 1989): 294–303.

44. Fred Luthans, *Introduction to Management: A Contingency Approach* (New York: McGraw-Hill, 1976), p. 28. Also see Henry L. Tosi Jr. and John W. Slocum Jr., "Contingency Theory: Some Suggested Directions," *Journal of Management*, 10 (Spring 1984): 9–26.

45. Y. K. Shetty, "Contingency Management: Current Perspective for Managing Organizations," *Management International Review*, 14, no. 6 (1974): 27.

46. See Joseph W. McGuire, "Management Theory: Retreat to the Academy," *Business Horizons*, 25 (July–August 1982): 37.

47. Data from John A. Byrne, "How the Best Get Better," *Business Week* (September 14, 1987): 98–99. For an interesting update on Tom Peters, see John A. Byrne, "Ever in Search of a New Take on Excellence," *Business Week* (August 31, 1992): 50–51.

48. *Business Week* listed *In Search of Excellence* among ten indispensable business books. See John A. Byrne, "A Classic Business Bookshelf," *Business Week* (March 5, 1990): 10, 12.

49. Information about the sample in this study may be found in Thomas J. Peters and Robert H. Waterman Jr., *In Search of Excellence* (New York: Harper & Row, 1982), pp. 19–26.

50. Ibid., pp. 16–17.

51. Daniel T. Carroll, "A Disappointing Search for Excellence," *Harvard Business Review*, 61 (November–December 1983): 88.

52. "Who's Excellent Now?" *Business Week* (November 5, 1984): 76–78. 3M Company's troubles since being an "excellent" company are chronicled in De'Ann Weimer, "3M: The Heat Is on the Boss," *Business Week* (March 15, 1999): 82–84.

53. See Michael A. Hitt and R. Duane Ireland, "Peters and Waterman Revisited: The Unended Quest for Excellence," *Academy of Management Executive*, 1 (May 1987): 91–98. Also see James N. Vedder, "How Much Can We Learn from Success?" *Academy of Management Executive*, 6 (February 1992): 56–66.

54. See John A. Byrne, "Management Theory—Or Fad of the Month?" *Business Week* (June 23, 1997): 47; Lex Donaldson and Frederick G. Hilmer, "Management Redeemed: The Case Against Fads That Harm Management," *Organizational Dynamics*, 26 (Spring 1998): 7–20; and Darrell K. Rigby, "What's Today's Special at the Consultants' Café?" *Fortune* (September 7, 1998): 162–163.

55. Peters and Waterman, *In Search of Excellence*, p. 13.

56. For some of Tom Peters's recent ideas, see Tom Peters, "Of Things Fundamental," *Forbes ASAP* (February 26, 1996): 122, 124; Tom Peters, "We Hold These Truths to Be Self-Evident (More or Less)," *Organizational Dynamics*, 25 (Summer 1996): 27–32; and Anne Fisher, "Tom Peters, Professional Loudmouth," *Fortune* (December 29, 1997): 273–276.

57. An instructive look back at *In Search of Excellence* can be found in Michael Hopkins and Joshua Hyatt, "When Everyone Was Excellent," *Inc.*, 21 (May 18, 1999): 111–113.

Chapter 3

Opening Quotation Maureen Minehan, "Future Focus," *HRMagazine*, 43 (1998/SHRM 50th Anniversary): 88.

Opening Case Michael Meyer, "In a League of Her Own," from *Newsweek* (August 2, 1999). Copyright 1999 Newsweek Inc. All rights reserved. Reprinted by permission.

Closing Case Excerpted from Stephanie Armour, "The Challenge: Mix Energy, Experience," *USA Today* (April 20, 1999): 1A–2A. Copyright 1999, USA Today. Reprinted with permission.

1. For more on Fiorina, see Del Jones, "What Glass Ceiling?" *USA Today* (July 20, 1999): 1B–2B.

2. This section adapted from Robert Barner, "The New Millennium Workplace: Seven Changes That Will Challenge Managers—and Workers," *The Futurist*, 30 (March–April 1996): 14–18. Also see George B. Weathersby, "Management May Never Be the Same," *Management Review*, 88 (February 1999): 5; Maureen Minehan, "Forecasting Future Trends for the Workplace," *HRMagazine*, 44 (February 1999): 176; Robert Costanza, "Four Visions of the Century Ahead: Will It Be Star Trek, Ecotopia, Big Government, or Mad Max?" *The Futurist*, 33 (February 1999): 23–28; and Allen Hammond, "3 Global Scenarios: Choosing the World We Want," *The Futurist*, 33 (April 1999): 38–43.

3. Barner, "The New Millennium Workplace," p. 15.

4. Ibid., p. 16.

5. Ibid., p. 18.

6. Data from *1998–1999 Occupational Outlook Handbook*, September 1999 (stats.bls.gov/oco/oco2003.htm). Also see Marc Adams, "The Stream of Labor Slows to a Trickle," *HRMagazine*, 43 (October 1998): 84–89.

7. David Leonhardt, "The Economy's Rising Tide, "*Business Week* (April 26, 1999): 30. Also see David Stamps, "Blue-Collar Blues," *Training*, 35 (May 1998): 32–40; and Maureen Minehan, "A

Critical Need to Build Math and Science Skills of Future Workers," *HRMagazine*, 43 (June 1998): 304.

8. Data from Troy Segal, "When Johnny's Whole Family Can't Read," *Business Week* (July 20, 1992): 68–70. Also see Harold Olmos, "Brazil Sees Education as Good Business," *USA Today* (December 8, 1998): 6B; and Sandra Chereb, "Beyond Words: Businessman's Feat Awarded," *USA Today* (June 9, 1999): 5A.

9. For good background material, see Valerie Frazee, "Workers Learn to Walk So They Can Run," *Personnel Journal*, 75 (May 1996): 115–120; David Stamps, "Will School-to-Work Work?" *Training*, 33 (June 1996): 72–81; Robert Kuttner, "Is Worker Training Really the Answer?" *Business Week* (June 17, 1996): 26; and Kathryn Tyler, "Tips for Structuring Workplace Literacy Programs," *HRMagazine*, 41 (October 1996): 112–116.

10. Data from "1996 Industry Report: The Three R's," *Training*, 33 (October 1996): 65. Also see Peter Troiano, "Challenges for Tomorrow's Company," *Management Review*, 87 (December 1998): 7–8.

11. For an instructive overview, see Jennifer Reingold, "Brain Drain," *Business Week* (September 20, 1999): 112–126.

12. Mark Clements, "What We Say About Aging," *Parade Magazine* (December 12, 1993): 4. Also see "Don't Trust Anyone over 79?" *Business Week* (April 1, 1996): 8.

13. For good discussions, see Ellen Neuborne, "Generation Y," *Business Week* (February 15, 1999): 80–88; and Alison Wellner, "Get Ready for Generation NEXT," *Training*, 36 (February 1999): 42–48.

14. Excerpted from Paul Mayrand, "Older Workers: A Problem or the Solution?" *Proceedings: Textbook Authors' Conference* (AARP: Washington, D.C., October 21, 1992), pp. 28–29. © Reprinted by permission of AARP 1994. For more, see Sherry E. Sullivan and Edward A. Duplaga, "Recruiting and Retaining Older Workers for the New Millennium," *Business Horizons*, 40 (November–December 1997): 65–69; Douglas H. Powell, "Aging Baby Boomers: Stretching Your Workforce Options," *HRMagazine*, 43 (July 1998): 82–85; Allison Kindelan, "Older Workers Can Alleviate Labor Shortages," *HRMagazine*, 43 (September 1998): 200; and Alison Stein Wellner, "Workplace 2018: Retirement Boom or Bust?" *Training*, 36 (August 1999): 54–59.

15. Data from Bill Montague, "Restructuring, and Layoffs, Here to Stay," *USA Today* (February 19, 1996): 1A–2A.

16. Robert Aubrey and Paul M. Cohen, *Working Wisdom: Timeless Skills and Vanguard Strategies for Learning Organizations* (San Francisco: Jossey-Bass, 1995), p. 29.

17. See Eric Rolfe Greenberg, "The Compleat Manager, 21st Century Style," *Management Review*, 87 (January 1998): 9; Nina Munk, "Finished at Forty," *Fortune* (February 1, 1999): 50–66; and Barbara E. Bellesi, "The Changing American Workforce," *Management Review*, 88 (March 1999): 9.

18. John Huey, "Where Managers Will Go," *Fortune* (January 27, 1992): 51.

19. For evidence, see Ellen Ernst Kossek, Melissa Huber-Yoder, Domini Castellino, and Jacqueline Lerner, "The Working Poor: Locked Out of Careers and the Organizational Mainstream?" *Academy of Management Executive*, 11 (February 1997): 76–92; Gene Koretz, "Immigrants' Economic Woes," *Business Week* (June 7, 1999): 26; Gene Koretz, "Illness and Economic Status," *Business Week* (June 14, 1999): 34; and Roger O. Crockett, "Jesse's New Target: Silicon Valley," *Business Week* (July 12, 1999): 111–112.

20. Data from U.S. Bureau of Labor Statistics (**stats.bls.gov/news.release/wkyeng.t03.htm**). Also see Teresa Brady, "How EQUAL Is

Equal Pay?" *Management Review*, 87 (March 1998): 59–61; Joan Oleck, "Colleges Flunk in Pay Equity," *Business Week* (March 1, 1999): 6; and Timothy S. Bland, "Equal Pay Enforcement Heats Up," *HRMagazine*, 44 (July 1999): 138–145.

21. Black managers' experiences with the glass ceiling are discussed in Elizabeth Lesly, "Inside the Black Business Network," *Business Week* (November 29, 1993): 70–81.

22. Ann M. Morrison and Mary Ann Von Glinow, "Women and Minorities in Management," *American Psychologist*, 45 (February 1990): 200 (emphasis added). Also see Belle Rose Ragins, Bickley Townsend, and Mary Mattis, "Gender Gap in the Executive Suite: CEOs and Female Executives Report on Breaking Glass Ceiling," *Academy of Management Executive*, 12 (February 1998): 28–42; Patricia Sellers, "The 50 Most Powerful Women in American Business," *Fortune* (October 12, 1998): 76–98; and Marc Ballon, "The New Girls' Club," *Inc.*, 21 (March 1999): 88.

23. Data from Del Jones, "African-Americans Take Reins at 'Fortune' Firms," *USA Today* (April 27, 1999): 2B. See Roy S. Johnson, "The 500's First Black CEO," *Fortune* (May 11, 1998): 32; Keith H. Hammonds, "Invisible in the Executive Suite," *Business Week* (December 21, 1998): 68; and David Leonhardt, "The Saga of Lloyd Ward," *Business Week* (August 9, 1999): 58–70.

24. Haidee E. Allerton, "News You Can Use," *Training & Development*, 53 (March 1999): 12. Also see Stephanie Armour, "Corporate Women Perform Balancing Act," *USA Today* (December 9, 1997): 3B; and Roy Furchgott, "You've Come a Short Way, Baby," *Business Week* (November 23, 1998): 82–91.

25. Janet Guyon, "Global Glass Ceiling," *Fortune* (October 12, 1998): 102–103.

26. Rhonda Richards, "More Women Poised for Role as CEO," *USA Today* (March 26, 1996): 2B.

27. Data from Bill Meyers, "Women Increase Standing as Business Owners," *USA Today* (June 29, 1999): 1B. Also see Carol Memmott, "Economic Balance of Power Shifting to Women," *USA Today* (June 7, 1999): 8B.

28. Bobby Clay, "It *Is* the Shoes . . . ," *Black Enterprise*, 23 (March 1993): 80. Also see Nina Munk, "Hello Corporate America!" *Fortune* (July 6, 1998): 136–146; Judith C. Holder and Alan Vaux, "African American Professionals: Coping with Occupational Stress in Predominantly White Work Environments," *Journal of Vocational Behavior*, 53 (December 1998): 315–333; Ellis Cose, "The Good News About Black America," *Newsweek* (June 7, 1999): 28–40; and Doug Levy, "Colorblind Commerce?" *USA Today* (August 17, 1999): 1B–2B.

29. Data from Aaron Bernstein, "A Leg Up for the Lowly Temp," *Business Week* (June 21, 1999): 102–103.

30. Gene Koretz, "Taking Stock of the Flexible Work Force," *Business Week* (July 24, 1989): 12. Also see Julie Cohen Mason, "A Temp-ting Staffing Strategy," *Management Review*, 85 (February 1996): 33–36.

31. These research results drawn from Robert P. Vecchio, "Demographic and Attitudinal Differences Between Part-Time and Full-Time Employees," *Journal of Occupational Behaviour*, 5 (July 1984): 213–218. Also see Daniel C. Feldman, Helen I. Doerpinghaus, and William H. Turnley, "Employee Reactions to Temporary Jobs," *Journal of Managerial Issues*, 7 (Summer 1995): 127–141.

32. See Michael M. Phillips, "Part-Time Work Issue Is Greatly Overworked," *The Wall Street Journal* (August 11, 1997): A1; Michael Mandel, "Nonstandard Jobs: A New Look," *Business Week* (September 15, 1997): 28; "Did Someone Say 'Benefits'?" *Training*, 35 (February 1998): 25–26; Kent Blake, " 'She's Just a Temporary,' "

HRMagazine, 43 (August 1998): 45–52; and Gene Koretz, "Employers Pare Health Benefits," *Business Week* (November 30, 1998): 30.

33. Beverly Geber, "The Flexible Work Force," *Training*, 30 (December 1993): 27.

34. For more, see Courtney von Hippel, Stephen L. Mangum, David B. Greenberger, Robert L. Heneman, and Jeffrey D. Skoglind, "Temporary Employment: Can Organizations and Employees Both Win?" *Academy of Management Executive*, 11 (February 1997): 93–104; Bill Leonard, "Part-Time Jobs a Dead End for Some," *HRMagazine*, 43 (November 1998): 24; and Aaron Bernstein, "When Is a Temp Not a Temp?" *Business Week* (December 7, 1998): 90, 92.

35. Data from Maria Puente, "Birth Rate in U.S. at a Record Low," *USA Today* (February 10, 1998): 4A.

36. Brook Larmer, "Latino America," *Newsweek* (July 12, 1999): 48–51.

37. Carlos Fuentes, "The Blending, and Clashing, of Cultures," *The Christian Science Monitor* (June 1, 1992): 19.

38. Data from Del Jones, "Setting Diversity's Foundation in the Bottom Line," *USA Today* (October 15, 1996): 4B.

39. See Jerry Adler, "Sweet Land of Liberties," *Newsweek* (July 10, 1995): 18–23; and Robert J. Samuelson, "Immigration and Poverty," *Newsweek* (July 15, 1996): 43.

40. For good background information, see R. Roosevelt Thomas Jr., "From Affirmative Action to Affirming Diversity," *Harvard Business Review*, 68 (March–April 1990): 107–117; Marc Adams, "Building a Rainbow, One Stripe at a Time," *HRMagazine*, 43 (August 1998): 72–79; Patricia Digh, "Coming to Terms with Diversity," *HRMagazine*, 43 (November 1998): 117–120; and Louisa Wah, "Diversity at Allstate: A Competitive Weapon," *Management Review*, 88 (July–August 1999): 24–30.

41. For example, see Roy S. Johnson, "The 50 Best Companies for Asians, Blacks, and Hispanics," *Fortune* (August 3, 1998): 94–97.

42. Jack McDevitt, "Are We Becoming a Country of Haters?" *USA Today* (September 2, 1992): 9A.

43. Adapted from Sheryl Hilliard Tucker and Kevin D. Thompson, "Will Diversity = Opportunity + Advancement for Blacks?" *Black Enterprise*, 21 (November 1990): 50–60. Also see Jennifer Reingold, "B-Schools That Look Like America," *Business Week* (June 21, 1999): 92, 94.

44. For example, see Dottie Enrico, "Not Just a Policy: A Personal Commitment," *USA Today* (April 27, 1998): 8B.

45. Research support can be found in Joseph J. Martocchio, "Age-Related Differences in Employee Absenteeism: A Meta-Analysis," *Psychology and Aging*, 4 (December 1989): 409–414.

46. Douglas T. Hall and Victoria A. Parker, "The Role of Workplace Flexibility in Managing Diversity," *Organizational Dynamics*, 22 (Summer 1993): 8.

47. Based on Jack Kelley, "Russian Radical Threatens 'New Hiroshimas,'" *USA Today* (December 15, 1993): 8A.

48. For example, see Bill Vlasic, "Amway II: The Kids Take Over," *Business Week* (February 16, 1998): 60–70; Gail Dutton, "Caught in the Middle," *Management Review*, 87 (April 1998): 54–58; "Top Execs Rate Their Legal Counsel," *Management Review*, 88 (March 1999): 39; and William C. Symonds, Lorraine Woellert, and Susan Garland, "Under Fire," *Business Week* (August 16, 1999): 62–68.

49. See Michael D. Eisner, "Critics of Disney's America on Wrong Track," *USA Today* (July 12, 1994): 10A; and Steve Marshall and Carrie Dowling, "Disney Abandons Va. Site," *USA Today* (September 29, 1994): 1A.

50. Julie Schmit, "Baptists Threaten to Boycott Disney," *USA Today* (June 13, 1996): 1A.

51. Ibid.

52. Steven L. Wartick and Robert E. Rude, "Issues Management: Corporate Fad or Corporate Function?" *California Management Review*, 29 (Fall 1986): 124–140. Also see Andrew J. Hoffman, "Institutional Evolution and Change: Environmentalism and the U.S. Chemical Industry," *Academy of Management Journal*, 42 (August 1999): 351–371.

53. David Kirkpatrick, "Environmentalism: The New Crusade," *Fortune* (February 12, 1990): 47. Also see Thomas A. Hemphill, "The New Era of Business Regulation," *Business Horizons*, 39 (July–August 1996): 26–30.

54. Drawn from S. Prakash Sethi, "Serving the Public Interest: Corporate Political Action for the 1980s," *Management Review*, 70 (March 1981): 8–11.

55. See Mary Beth Regan and Stephen H. Wildstrom, "PACs Cross the Street," *Business Week* (April 10, 1995): 94–97; Mary Beth Regan, "What a Difference a Sweep Makes," *Business Week* (September 25, 1995): 6; and Jill Lawrence and Jessica Lee, "Gingrich's Triumph and Debacle: GOPAC," *USA Today* (January 16, 1997): 8A–9A.

56. See David A. Andelman, "Capital Crises," *Management Review*, 87 (May 1998): 49–51; Jeffrey H. Birnbaum, "Capitol Clout: A Buyer's Guide," *Fortune* (October 26, 1998): 177–184; Jeffrey H. Birnbaum, "The Influence Merchants," *Fortune* (December 7, 1998): 134–152; and Mica Schneider, "The Color of Clout," *Business Week* (April 12, 1999): 6.

57. An instructive historical perspective of advocacy advertising may be found in Roland Marchand, "The Fitful Career of Advocacy Advertising: Political Protection, Client Cultivation, and Corporate Morale," *California Management Review*, 29 (Winter 1987): 128–156.

58. Jayne O'Donnell, "White-Collar Crooks Getting More Jail Time," *USA Today* (November 10, 1997): 1B. Also see Paul E. Fiorelli, "Why Comply? Directors Face Heightened Personal Liability After Caremark," *Business Horizons*, 41 (July–August 1998): 49–52; Carol J. Loomis, "Lies, Damned Lies, and Management Earnings: The Crackdown Is Here," *Fortune* (August 2, 1999): 74–92.

59. For example, see David J. Lynch, "Industry Now Must Plug In to Political Game," *USA Today* (January 16, 1996): 1B–2B; and David A. Andelman, "Taking Regulators to Court," *Management Review*, 87 (July–August 1998): 30–32.

60. Data from John R. Allison, "Five Ways to Keep Disputes Out of Court," *Harvard Business Review*, 68 (January–February 1990): 166–177. Also see David Frum, "Piecework," *Forbes* (February 15, 1993): 132, 136; and David Israel, "Learn to Manage the Legal Process," *HRMagazine*, 38 (July 1993): 83–86. Computer software that can cut managers' legal costs is discussed in Walter S. Mossberg, "Put This Counsel on Retainer," *Smart Money*, 4 (March 1995): 135–136, 138.

61. Marianne M. Jennings and Frank Shipper, *Avoiding and Surviving Lawsuits* (San Francisco: Jossey-Bass, 1989), p. 118. Also see David Silverstein, "The Litigation Audit: Preventive Legal Maintenance for Management," *Business Horizons*, 31 (November–December 1988): 34–42; Paul J. H. Schoemaker and Joyce A. Schoemaker, "Estimating Environmental Liability: Quantifying the Unknown," *California Management Review*, 37 (Spring 1995): 29–61; and Milton Bordwin, "Twice Burned: Premises Liability," *Management Review*, 84 (December 1995): 9–11.

62. John R. Allison, "Easing the Pain of Legal Disputes: The Evolution and Future of Reform," *Business Horizons*, 33 (September–October 1990): 15. Also see Kay O. Wilburn, "Employment

Disputes: Solving Them out of Court," *Management Review*, 87 (March 1998): 17–21; Deborah L. Jacobs, "First, Fire the Lawyers," *Inc.*, 21 (January 1999): 84–85; and Milton Bordwin, "Do-It-Yourself-Justice," *Management Review*, 88 (January 1999): 56–58.

63. Daniel McGinn and John McCormick, "Your Next Job," *Newsweek* (February 1, 1999): 45.

64. Data from 1998–1999 *Occupational Outlook Handbook*, September 1999 (**stats.bls.gov/oco/oco2003.htm**). Also see Louisa Wah, "'Hot' Jobs: And the Companies Defining Them," *Management Review*, 88 (January 1999): 37–41; and Kim Kiser, "Move Over, Nerds," *Training*, 36 (January 1999): 54–58.

65. Paul A. Samuelson, *Economics*, 10th ed. (New York: McGraw-Hill, 1976), p. 253. Also see Geoffrey Colvin, "Let the Tough Times Roll," *Fortune* (December 21, 1998): 243–244; Michael J. Panzner, "Are You Ready for Deflationary Decline?" *Management Review*, 88 (January 1999): 23–27; and Norm Brodsky, "How to Profit in the Coming Recession," *Inc.*, 21 (January 1999): 31–35.

66. Brian Dumaine, "How to Manage in a Recession," *Fortune* (November 5, 1990): 60.

67. Data from Gene Koretz, "A D+ for Dismal Scientists," *Business Week* (September 25, 1995): 25.

68. See Martha T. Moore, "Forecasting Is a Tough Job in a Changing World," *USA Today* (November 13, 1995): 1B–2B; Kim Clark, "The Old Man and the Economic Sea," *Fortune* (May 13, 1996): 28–29; and Kim Clark, "A Near-Perfect Tool for Economic Forecasting," *Fortune* (July 22, 1996): 24–26.

69. For an informative discussion of the value of economic forecasting, see Peter L. Bernstein and Theodore H. Silbert, "Are Economic Forecasters Worth Listening To?" *Harvard Business Review*, 62 (September–October 1984): 32–40. Also see "Managing Through Turbulent Times," *Inc.*, 21 (January 1999): 36–40.

70. Lawrence S. Davidson, "Knowing the Unknowable," *Business Horizons*, 32 (September–October 1989): 7. Other forward-looking material can be found in Michael J. Mandel, "The 21st Century Economy," *Business Week* (August 31, 1998): 58–63.

71. Data from Gene Koretz, "Peering into a New Millennium," *Business Week* (January 26, 1998): 22. Also see Marlene Piturro, "What Are You Doing About the New Global Realities?" *Management Review*, 88 (March 1999): 16–22.

72. John Naisbitt and Patricia Aburdene, *Megatrends 2000* (New York: William Morrow, 1990), p. 21.

73. Thomas A. Stewart, "Welcome to the Revolution," *Fortune* (December 13, 1993): 67.

74. Data from Tom Martin and Deborah Greenwood, "The World Economy in Charts," *Fortune* (July 26, 1993): 88–94.

75. G. Pascal Zachary, "Like Factory Workers, Professionals Face Loss of Jobs to Foreigners," *The Wall Street Journal* (March 17, 1993): A9.

76. Michael Mandel, "Foreign Owners Pay Nice Bucks," *Business Week* (July 17, 1995): 26.

77. Marc Levinson, "The Trashing of Free Trade," *Newsweek* (July 12, 1993): 43.

78. See Stephen Millett and William Kopp, "The Top 10 Innovative Products for 2006: Technology with a Human Touch," *The Futurist*, 30 (July–August 1996): 16–20.

79. Jerome B. Wiesner, "Technology and Innovation," in *Technological Innovation and Society*, ed. Dean Morse and Aaron W. Warner (New York: Columbia University Press, 1966), p. 11. Also see Rebecca Ganzel, "Feeling Squeezed by Technology?" *Training*, 35 (April 1998): 62–70; Jenny C. McCune, "The Technology Tread-mill," *Management Review*, 87 (December 1998): 10–12; and Jenny C. McCune, "The Call for Tech-Savvy Employees," *Management Review*, 88 (June 1999): 10–12.

80. Walter Kiechel III, "How We Will Work in the Year 2000," *Fortune* (May 17, 1993): 39. Also see Willem F. G. Mastenbroek, "Organizational Innovation in Historical Perspective: Change as Duality Management," *Business Horizons*, 39 (July–August 1996): 5–14.

81. Catherine Arnst, "Wiring Small Business," *Business Week* (November 25, 1996): 164. For more, see Otis Port, "Machines Will Be Smarter Than We Are," *Business Week* (August 30, 1999): 117, 120; and the Special Report "The Dawn of E-Life," *Newsweek* (September 20, 1999): 42–44, 49.

82. Data from Andy Reinhardt, "Meet Mr. Internet," *Business Week* (September 13, 1999): 128–140.

83. See Linda Yates and Peter Skarzynski, "How Do Companies Get to the Future First?" *Management Review*, 88 (January 1999): 16–22.

84. Brian Dumaine, "Closing the Innovation Gap," *Fortune* (December 2, 1991): 57.

85. Based on Stratford Sherman, "When Laws of Physics Meet Laws of the Jungle," *Fortune* (May 15, 1995): 193–194.

86. Joseph Weber, "Quick, Save the Ozone," *Business Week* (May 17, 1993): 78. For a graphic snapshot of how long it takes consumers to adopt new electronic technologies, see "New Technologies Take Time," *Business Week* (April 19, 1999): 8.

87. See Kevin Kelly, "The Drought Is Over at 3M," *Business Week* (November 7, 1994): 140–141.

88. See Morgan L. Swink, J. Christopher Sandvig, and Vincent A. Mabert, "Adding 'Zip' to Product Development: Concurrent Engineering Methods and Tools," *Business Horizons*, 39 (March–April 1996): 41–49; and Bob Filipczak, "Concurrent Engineering: A Team by Any Other Name?" *Training*, 33 (August 1996): 54–59.

89. See, for example, Erik Calonius, "Garage," *Fortune* (March 4, 1996): 150–161.

90. See Timothy D. Schellhardt, "David and Goliath," *The Wall Street Journal* (May 23, 1996): R14; and Saj-Nicole A. Joni, C. Gordon Bell, and Heidi Mason, "Innovations from the Inside," *Management Review*, 86 (September 1997): 49–53.

91. See Gifford Pinchot III, *Intrapreneuring* (New York: Harper & Row, 1985), p. xvii.

92. Tim Smart, "Kathleen Synnott: Shaping the Mailrooms of Tomorrow," *Business Week* (November 16, 1992): 66.

93. Vince Luchsinger and D. Ray Bagby, "Entrepreneurship and Intrapreneurship: Behaviors, Comparisons, and Contrasts," *SAM Advanced Management Journal*, 52 (Summer 1987): 12. Also see related articles on intrapreneurship in the same issue.

Chapter 4

Opening Quotation   Dean C. Barnlund, "Public and Private Self in Communicating with Japan," *Business Horizons*, 32 (March–April 1989): 40.

Opening Case   Excerpted from Micheline Maynard, "Detroit Gears Up on Its German," *USA Today* (November 30, 1998): 3B. Copyright 1998, USA Today. Reprinted with permission.

Closing Case   Republished with permission of *The Wall Street Journal*, from Joann S. Lublin, "Companies Use Cross-Cultural Training to Help Their Employees Adjust Abroad," (August 4, 1992): B1, B6. Permission conveyed through Copyright Clearance Center, Inc.

1. For more, see Alex Taylor III, "The Germans Take Charge," *Fortune* (January 11, 1999): 92–96; and Micheline Maynard, "Daimler-Chrysler Rides High," *USA Today* (April 28, 1999): 3B.

2. Republished with permission of *The Wall Street Journal*, from Marcus W. Brauchli, "Echoes of the Past," (September 26, 1996): R24. Permission conveyed through Copyright Clearance Center, Inc. Also see Lance Eliot Brouthers, David G. McCalman, and Timothy J. Wilkinson, "The Global Confederation: Lessons from 1783," *Business Horizons*, 41 (March–April 1998): 23–30.

3. Data from Emily Thornton and Kathleen Kerwin, "Can Honda Go It Alone?" *Business Week* (July 5, 1999): 42–45.

4. Geri Smith, "Mexican Makeover," *Business Week* (December 21, 1998): 50.

5. James Cox, "Punitive Actions by U.S. Felt Worldwide," *USA Today* (March 11, 1999): 3B.

6. Based on "Russia Set to Launch U.S.-Built Satellite for the First Time," *International Herald Tribune* (April 9, 1996): 13.

7. Mark Starr, "Kiss That Baby Goodbye," *Newsweek* (May 10, 1993): 72.

8. Data from "Snapshots of the Next Century," *Business Week:* 21st Century Capitalism (Special Issue, 1994): 194. A critical look at economic globalization can be found in Michael Elliott, "International Globalization: Going Home," *Newsweek* (January 6, 1997): 38–42.

9. Data from "Chip Licensing Deal," *USA Today* (November 27, 1996): 1B. *Note:* This six-step sequence is based on Alan M. Rugman, "A New Theory of the Multinational Enterprise: Internationalization Versus Internalization," *Columbia Journal of World Business,* 15 (Spring 1980): 23–29. Also see Lawrence S. Welch and Reijo Luostarinen, "Internationalization: Evolution of a Concept," *Journal of General Management,* 14 (Winter 1988): 34–55.

10. See William J. Burpitt and Dennis A. Rondinelli, "Export Decision-Making in Small Firms: The Role of Organizational Learning," *Journal of World Business,* 33 (Spring 1998): 51–68. Also see Table 2 in Nigel F. Piercy, Anna Kaleka, and Constantine S. Katsikeas, "Sources of Competitive Advantage in High Performing Exporting Companies," *Journal of World Business,* 33 (Winter 1998): 384.

11. For related discussion, see A. B. Sim and Yunus Ali, "Performance of International Joint Ventures from Developing and Developed Countries: An Empirical Study in a Developing Country Context," *Journal of World Business,* 33 (Winter 1998): 357–377; Linda M. Randall and Lori A. Coakley, "Building Successful Partnerships in Russia and Belarus: The Impact of Culture on Strategy," *Business Horizons,* 41 (March–April 1998): 15–22; Andrew C. Inkpen and Kou-Qing Li, "Joint Venture Formation: Planning and Knowledge-Gathering for Success," *Organizational Dynamics,* 27 (Spring 1999): 33–47; and Dianne Cyr, "High Tech, High Impact: Creating Canada's Competitive Advantage Through Technology Alliances," *Academy of Management Executive,* 13 (May 1999): 17–26.

12. David P. Hamilton, "United It Stands," *The Wall Street Journal* (September 26, 1996): R19.

13. Jeremy Main, "Making Global Alliances Work," *Fortune* (December 17, 1990): 121–126.

14. Adapted from ibid. and David Lei and John W. Slocum Jr., "Global Strategic Alliances: Payoffs and Pitfalls," *Organizational Dynamics,* 19 (Winter 1991): 44–62. Also see Andrew C. Inkpen, "Learning and Knowledge Acquisition Through International Strategic Alliances," *Academy of Management Executive,* 12 (November 1998): 69–80; Arvind Parkhe, "Building Trust in International Alliances," *Journal of World Business,* 33 (Winter 1998): 417–437; Steven X. Si and Garry D. Bruton, "Knowledge Transfer in International Joint Ventures in Transitional Economies: The China Experience," *Academy of Management Executive,* 13 (February 1999): 83–90; and Eric W. K. Tsang, "Internationalization as a Learning Process: Singapore MNCs in China," *Academy of Management Executive,* 13 (February 1999): 91–101.

15. See David A. Andelman, "Merging Across Borders," *Management Review,* 87 (June 1998): 44–46.

16. Data from Debra Sparks and Leah Nathans, "Europe's 'Buy American' Policy," *Business Week* (March 8, 1999): 35.

17. Joan Warner, "The World Is Not Always Your Oyster," *Business Week* (October 30, 1995): 132.

18. For example, see Michael Hickins, "Creating a Global Team," *Management Review,* 87 (September 1998): 6; Bruce Kogut, "What Makes a Company Global?" *Harvard Business Review,* 77 (January–February 1999): 165–170; and Thomas A. Stewart, "Getting Real About Going Global," *Fortune* (February 15, 1999): 170, 172.

19. See Bethany McLean, "Coke Stock: Half Full," *Fortune* (May 10, 1999): 168–169.

20. Based on Fons Trompenaars and Charles Hampden-Turner, *Riding the Waves of Culture: Understanding Cultural Diversity in Global Business,* 2nd ed. (New York: McGraw-Hill, 1998), pp. 191–192; Marie-Claude Boudreau, Karen D. Loch, Daniel Robey, and Detmar Straud, "Going Global: Using Information Technology to Advance the Competitiveness of the Virtual Transnational Organization," *Academy of Management Executive,* 12 (November 1998): 120–128; and Michael Hickins, "Reconcilable Differences," *Management Review,* 87 (November 1998): 54–58.

21. Stanley Reed, "Busting Up Sweden Inc.," *Business Week* (February 22, 1999): 52, 54.

22. For example, see Louisa Wah, "Treading the Sacred Ground," *Management Review,* 87 (July–August 1998): 18–22; and Tatiana Kostova and Srilata Zaheer, "Organizational Legitimacy Under Conditions of Complexity: The Case of the Multinational Enterprise," *Academy of Management Review,* 24 (January 1999): 64–81.

23. "Amidst Stiffer International Competition, U.S. Managers Need a Broader Perspective," *Management Review,* 69 (March 1980): 34.

24. C. Bremmer, "The Global Manager—Insights in Succeeding the Challenge," unpublished paper, 1994, as quoted in Philip R. Harris and Robert T. Moran, *Managing Cultural Differences,* 4th ed. (Houston: Gulf Publishing, 1996), pp. 4–5.

25. Howard V. Perlmutter, "The Tortuous Evolution of the Multinational Corporation," *Columbia Journal of World Business,* 4 (January–February 1969): 11.

26. Perlmutter and a colleague later added "regiocentric attitude" to their typology. Such an attitude centers on a regional identification (North America, Europe, and Asia, for example). See David A. Heenan and Howard V. Perlmutter, *Multinational Organization Development* (Reading, Mass.: Addison-Wesley, 1979).

27. Drawn from Brian Dumaine, "The New Turnaround Champs," *Fortune* (July 16, 1990): 36–44.

28. See Amy Borrus, "Can Japan's Giants Cut the Apron Strings?" *Business Week* (May 14, 1990): 105–106.

29. Data from Brook Larmer, "Latino America," *Newsweek* (July 12, 1999): 48–51.

30. Julia Lieblich, "If You Want a Big, New Market . . ." *Fortune* (November 21, 1988): 181. Population update from Larmer, "Latino America."

31. Perlmutter, "The Tortuous Evolution of the Multinational Corporation," p. 16.

32. Gail Dutton, "Building a Global Brain," *Management Review*, 88 (May 1999): 34–38.

33. Rahul Jacob, "Trust the Locals, Win Worldwide," *Fortune* (May 4, 1992): 76.

34. Ibid.

35. Arvind V. Phatak and Mohammed M. Habib, "The Dynamics of International Business Negotiations," *Business Horizons*, 39 (May–June 1996): 34.

36. For more, see Nancy J. Adler, *International Dimensions of Organizational Behavior*, 2nd ed. (Boston: PWS-Kent, 1991), pp. 14–33; Dragan Z. Milosevic, "Echoes of the Silent Language of Project Management," *Project Management Journal*, 30 (March 1999): 27–39; and Andrew Rosenbaum, "Testing Cultural Waters," *Management Review*, 88 (July–August 1999): 41–43.

37. "How Cultures Collide," *Psychology Today*, 10 (July 1976): 69.

38. Trompenaars and Hampden-Turner, *Riding the Waves of Culture*, p. 3.

39. Based on Ashok Nimgade, "American Management as Viewed by International Professionals," *Business Horizons*, 32 (November–December 1989): 98–105.

40. Contrasting Chinese and American traits are presented in Jack Scarborough, "Comparing Chinese and Western Cultural Roots: Why 'East Is East and . . . ,'" *Business Horizons*, 41 (November–December 1998): 15–24. Also see Christopher B. Meek, "*Ganbatte*: Understanding the Japanese Employee," *Business Horizons*, 42 (January–February 1999): 27–36; and Tibbett L. Speer, "Avoid Gift-Giving and Cultural Blunders in Asian Locales," *USA Today* (March 16, 1999): 3E.

41. See "How Cultures Collide," pp. 66–74, 97; Edward T. Hall, *The Hidden Dimension* (Garden City, N.Y.: Doubleday, 1996); and Mary Munter, "Cross-Cultural Communication for Managers," *Business Horizons*, 36 (May–June 1993): 69–78.

42. Ronald E. Dulek, John S. Fielden, and John S. Hill, "International Communication: An Executive Primer," *Business Horizons*, 34 (January–February 1991): 21.

43. This list is based on Edward T. Hall, "The Silent Language in Overseas Business," *Harvard Business Review*, 38 (May–June 1960): 87–96; and Rose Knotts, "Cross-Cultural Management: Transformations and Adaptations," *Business Horizons*, 32 (January–February 1989): 29–33.

44. For detailed discussion, see Allen C. Bluedorn, Carol Felker Kaufman, and Paul M. Lane, "How Many Things Do You Like to Do at Once? An Introduction to Monochronic and Polychronic Time," *Academy of Management Executive*, 6 (November 1992): 17–26. For interesting reading on *time*, see Paul Hellman, "Eating the Desk," *Management Review*, 87 (May 1998): 64; and Diane Brady, "The Clocks Ahead Will Have Our Own Faces," *Business Week* (August 30, 1999): 94, 96.

45. See Gregory K. Stephens and Charles R. Greer, "Doing Business in Mexico: Understanding Cultural Differences," *Organizational Dynamics*, 24 (Summer 1995): 39–55; Mike Johnson, "Untapped Latin America," *Management Review*, 85 (July 1996): 31–34; and Yongsun Paik and J. H. Derick Sohn, "Confucius in Mexico: Korean MNCs and the Maquiladoras," *Business Horizons*, 41 (November–December 1998): 25–33.

46. See Karl Albrecht, "Lost in the Translation," *Training*, 33 (June 1996): 66–70; and Daniel Pianko, "Smooth Translations," *Management Review*, 85 (July 1996): 10. Internet translation services are discussed and critiqued in Andrea Petersen, "Prodigy Plans Internet Service for Spanish Speakers in the U.S.," *The Wall Street Journal* (April 6, 1999): B3; Heath Row, "Road Warrior," *Fast*

Company, no. 23 (April 1999): 82; and Rebecca Ganzel, "Universal Translator? Not Quite," *Training*, 36 (April 1999): 22, 24.

47. Jerry Shine, "More US Students Tackle Japanese," *The Christian Science Monitor* (November 25, 1991): 14.

48. Based on Kathryn Tyler, "Targeted Language Training Is Best Bargain," *HRMagazine*, 43 (January 1998): 61–64; and "When in Rio . . . ," *Training*, 35 (December 1998): 25.

49. Based on Figure 2 in Gary Bonvillian and William A. Nowlin, "Cultural Awareness: An Essential Element of Doing Business Abroad," *Business Horizons*, 37 (November–December 1994): 44–50.

50. "Burger Boost," *USA Today* (October 11, 1995): 1B.

51. See P. Christopher Earley and Harbir Singh, "International and Intercultural Management Research: What's Next?" *Academy of Management Journal*, 38 (April 1995): 327–340; Mary B. Teagarden et al., "Toward a Theory of Comparative Management Research: An Idiographic Case Study of the Best International Human Resources Management Project," *Academy of Management Journal*, 38 (October 1995): 1261–1287; Abraham Sagie and Dov Elizur, "Taking Another Look at Cross-Cultural Research: Rejoinder to Lachman (1997)," *Journal of Organizational Behavior*, 19 (July 1998): 421–427; and Mark Easterby-Smith and Danusia Malina, "Cross-Cultural Collaborative Research: Toward Reflexivity," *Academy of Management Journal*, 42 (February 1999): 76–86.

52. See Geert Hofstede, *Culture's Consequences: International Differences in Work-Related Values*, abridged edition (Newbury Park, Calif.: Sage Publications, 1984); and Geert Hofstede, "Motivation, Leadership, and Organization: Do American Theories Apply Abroad?" *Organizational Dynamics*, 9 (Summer 1980): 42–63. Also see Geert Hofstede, "Cultural Constraints in Management Theories," *Academy of Management Executive*, 7 (February 1993): 81–94; and Richard Hodgetts, "A Conversation with Geert Hofstede," *Organizational Dynamics*, 21 (Spring 1993): 53–61.

53. An extension of Hofstede's original work can be found in Geert Hofstede and Michael Harris Bond, "The Confucius Connection: From Cultural Roots to Economic Growth," *Organizational Dynamics*, 16 (Spring 1988): 4–21. Also see Peter B. Smith, Shaun Dugan, and Fons Trompenaars, "National Culture and the Values of Organizational Employees: A Dimensional Analysis Across 43 Nations," *Journal of Cross-Cultural Psychology*, 27 (March 1996): 231–264; James P. Johnson and Tomasz Lenartowicz, "Culture, Freedom and Economic Growth: Do Cultural Values Explain Economic Growth?" *Journal of World Business*, 33 (Winter 1998): 332–356; and Geert Hofstede, "Problems Remain, but Theories Will Change: The Universal and the Specific in 21st-Century Global Management," *Organizational Dynamics*, 28 (Summer 1999): 34–44.

54. See William G. Ouchi, *Theory Z: How American Business Can Meet the Japanese Challenge* (Reading, Mass.: Addison-Wesley, 1981). Also see David M. Hunt and Donald S. Bolon, "A Review of Five Versions of Theory Z: Does Z Have a Future?" in *Advances in International Comparative Management*, vol. 4, ed. S. Benjamin Prasad (Greenwich, Conn.: JAI Press, 1989), pp. 201–220; and William G. Ouchi and Raymond L. Price, "Hierarchies, Clans, and Theory Z: A New Perspective on Organization Development," *Organizational Dynamics*, 21 (Spring 1993): 62–70.

55. See Richard J. Schmidt, "Japanese Management, Recession Style," *Business Horizons*, 39 (March–April 1996): 70–76; and P. C. Chu, Eric E. Spires, and Toshiyuki Sueyoshi, "Cross-Cultural Differences in Choice Behavior and Use of Decision Aids: A Comparison of

Japan and the United States," *Organizational Behavior and Human Decision Processes*, 77 (February 1999): 147–170.

56. Brian Bremner, "The President Has a Will—But No Way," *Business Week* (March 15, 1999): 92.

57. See Itzhak Harpaz, "The Importance of Work Goals: An International Perspective," *Journal of International Business Studies*, 21 (First Quarter 1990): 75–93. Also see David A. Ralston, David J. Gustafson, Priscilla M. Elsass, Fanny Cheung, and Robert H. Terpstra, "Eastern Values: A Comparison of Managers in the United States, Hong Kong, and the People's Republic of China," *Journal of Applied Psychology*, 77 (October 1992): 664–671.

58. See Bodil Jones, "What Future European Recruits Want," *Management Review*, 87 (January 1998): 6; Bill Leonard, "Workers' Attitudes Similar Worldwide," *HRMagazine*, 43 (December 1998): 28, 30; and Cheryl Comeau Kirschner, "It's a Small World," *Management Review*, 88 (March 1999): 8.

59. Data from Dianne H. B. Welsh, Fred Luthans, and Steven M. Sommer, "Managing Russian Factory Workers: The Impact of U.S.-Based Behavioral and Participative Techniques," *Academy of Management Journal*, 36 (February 1993): 58–79. For related reading, see Dong I. Jung and Bruce J. Avolio, "Effects of Leadership Style and Followers' Cultural Orientation on Performance in Group and Individual Task Conditions," *Academy of Management Journal*, 42 (April 1999): 208–218.

60. Kristin Dunlap Godsey, "Thread by Thread," *Success*, 43 (April 1996): 8.

61. See Cristina B. Gibson and George A. Marcoulides, "The Invariance of Leadership Styles Across Four Countries," *Journal of Managerial Issues*, 7 (Summer 1995): 176–193; and Mary Gowan, Santiago Ibarreche, and Charles Lackey, "Doing the Right Things in Mexico," *Academy of Management Executive*, 10 (February 1996): 74–81.

62. Marshall Loeb, "The Real Fast Track Is Overseas," *Fortune* (August 21, 1995): 129. For more, see "International Assignments: Implications and Practices," *Canadian Manager*, 23 (Spring 1998): 19–20; Karen Roberts, Ellen Ernst Kossek, and Cynthia Ozeki, "Managing the Global Workforce: Challenges and Strategies," *Academy of Management Executive*, 12 (November 1998): 93–106; and "Badgers Abroad: College Gets Global," *Training*, 35 (November 1998): 18.

63. An excellent background article is J. Stewart Black and Hal B. Gregersen, "The Right Way to Manage Expats," *Harvard Business Review*, 77 (March–April 1999): 52–63.

64. "Don't Be an Ugly-American Manager," *Fortune* (October 16, 1995): 225.

65. John R. Engen, "Coming Home," *Training*, 32 (March 1995): 37.

66. See Ceel Pasternak, "Constraints on Expatriate Spouse Employment," *HRMagazine*, 38 (February 1993): 22; Reyer A. Swaak, "Today's Expatriate Family: Dual Careers and Other Obstacles," *Compensation & Benefits Review*, 27 (January–February 1995): 21–26; Marshall Loeb, "How to Help Your Trailing Spouse," *Fortune* (April 15, 1996): 206; and Marilyn Richey, "Global Families: Surviving an Overseas Move," *Management Review*, 85 (June 1996): 57–61.

67. Gene Koretz, ". . . But It Could Be Cold Comfort for U.S. Companies There," *Business Week* (January 22, 1990): 20.

68. See Alan Weiss, "Global Doesn't Mean 'Foreign' Anymore," *Training*, 35 (July 1998): 50–55.

69. For instructive practical applications, see Joann S. Lublin, "Younger Managers Learn Global Skills," *The Wall Street Journal* (March 31, 1992): B1; and Bob Hagerty, "Trainers Help Expatriate Employees Build Bridges to Difficult Cultures," *The Wall Street Journal* (June 14, 1993): B1, B3. Also see Carla Joinson, "Cultural Sensitivity Adds Up to Good Business Sense," *HRMagazine*, 40 (November 1995): 82–85.

70. Robert Moran, "Children of Bilingualism," *International Management*, 45 (November 1990): 93. Also see Wayne T. Price, "Learning the Language Is Critical," *USA Today*, (September 14, 1993): 6E.

71. Based on Joann S. Lublin, "An Overseas Stint Can Be a Ticket to the Top," *The Wall Street Journal* (January 29, 1996): B1, B5.

72. Adapted from Rosalie L. Tung, "Selection and Training of Personnel for Overseas Assignments," *Columbia Journal of World Business*, 16 (Spring 1981): 68–78.

73. See P. Christopher Earley, "Intercultural Training for Managers: A Comparison of Documentary and Interpersonal Methods," *Academy of Management Journal*, 30 (December 1987): 685–698. Also see J. Stewart Black and Mark Mendenhall, "Cross-Cultural Training Effectiveness: A Review and a Theoretical Framework for Future Research," *Academy of Management Review*, 15 (January 1990): 113–136.

74. Data from Joann S. Lublin, "Companies Use Cross-Cultural Training to Help Their Employees Adjust Abroad," *The Wall Street Journal* (August 4, 1992): B1, B6.

75. An excellent resource book is J. Stewart Black, Hal B. Gregersen, and Mark E. Mendenhall, *Global Assignments: Successfully Expatriating and Repatriating International Managers* (San Francisco: Jossey-Bass, 1992). Also see Leigh Ann Collins Allard, "Managing Globe-Trotting Expats," *Management Review*, 85 (May 1996): 39–43; and Linda K. Stroh and Paula M. Caligiuri, "Increasing Global Competitiveness Through Effective People Management," *Journal of World Business*, 33 (Spring 1998): 1–16.

76. See Engen, "Coming Home," pp. 37–40; Barry Newman, "For Ira Caplan, Re-Entry Has Been Strange," *The Wall Street Journal* (December 12, 1995): A12; Timothy Pasquarelli, "Dealing with Discomfort and Danger," *HRMagazine*, 41 (October 1996): 104–110; Evelyn Tan Powers, "Overseas Workers Are Overlooked at Home," *USA Today* (December 4, 1996): 9B; and Martha H. Peak, "Darned Expensive to Take for Granted," *Management Review*, 86 (January 1997): 9.

77. Data from Rosalie L. Tung, "American Expatriates Abroad: From Neophytes to Cosmopolitans," *Journal of World Business*, 33 (Summer 1998): 125–144.

78. David Stauffer, "No Need for Inter-American Culture Clash," *Management Review*, 87 (January 1998): 8.

79. See Louisa Wah, "Surfing the Rough Sea," *Management Review*, 87 (September 1998): 25–29; Paula M. Caligiuri and Wayne F. Cascio, "Can We Send Her There? Maximizing the Success of Western Women on Global Assignments," *Journal of World Business*, 33 (Winter 1998): 394–416.

80. See Lynette Clemetson, "Soul and Sushi," *Newsweek* (May 4, 1998): 38–41.

81. For more, see Jennifer Smith, "Southeast Asia's Search for Managers," *Management Review*, 87 (June 1998): 9; and Brock Stout, "Interviewing in Japan," *HRMagazine*, 43 (June 1998): 71–77.

82. For more, see "Tips for the Harried Business Traveler," *Training*, 36 (August 1999): 16.

Chapter 5

Opening Quotation Stephen R. Covey, *Principle-Centered Leadership* (New York: Simon & Schuster, 1991), p. 95.

Opening Case Excerpted from Ruth Walker, "Seeing the Forest to Save the Trees." This article first appeared in *The Christian Science Monitor* July 31, 1998 and is reproduced with permission. Copyright 1998, The Christian Science Publishing Society. All rights reserved. Also see **www.weyerhaeuser.com.**

Closing Case Excerpted from Samantha Miller and Johnny Dodd, "Net Benefit," *People Weekly* (March 29, 1999): 105–106. © 1999 Time Inc.

1. For example, see John A. Byrne, "The Shredder," *Business Week* (January 15, 1996): 56–61.

2. For an interesting look back at Rockefeller, see Jerry Useem, "Entrepreneur of the Century," *Inc.* Twentieth anniversary issue, 21 (May 18, 1999): 159–173.

3. Susan Gaines, "Growing Pains," *Business Ethics*, 10 (January–February 1996): 20.

4. Thomas M. Jones, "Corporate Social Responsibility Revisited, Redefined," *California Management Review*, 22 (Spring 1980): 59–60. Also see Marc T. Jones, "Missing the Forest for the Trees: A Critique of the Social Responsibility Concept and Discourse," *Business & Society*, 35 (March 1996): 7–41; and David Stamps, "Social Capital," *Training*, 35 (November 1998): 44–52.

5. Michael Ryan, "They Call Their Boss a Hero," *Parade Magazine* (September 8, 1996): 5. Also see Thomas Teal, "Not a Fool, Not a Saint," *Fortune* (November 11, 1996): 201–204.

6. Chris Welles, "What Led Beech-Nut Down the Road to Disgrace," *Business Week* (February 22, 1988): 128. For a good update on Nestlé, see Greg Steinmetz and Tara Parker-Pope, "All over the Map," *The Wall Street Journal* (September 26, 1996): R4, R6.

7. See Joe Queenan, "Juice Men," *Barron's* (June 20, 1988): 37–38.

8. Jones, "Corporate Social Responsibility Revisited," p. 65.

9. This distinction between the economic and the socioeconomic models is based partly on discussion in Courtney C. Brown, *Beyond the Bottom Line* (New York: Macmillan, 1979), pp. 82–83.

10. See the discussion in Art Wolfe, "We've Had Enough Business Ethics," *Business Horizons*, 36 (May–June 1993): 1–3. Also see Robert J. Samuelson, "The Spirit of Adam Smith," *Newsweek* (December 2, 1996): 63.

11. As quoted in Keith H. Hammonds, "Writing a New Social Contract," *Business Week* (March 11, 1996): 60.

12. For example, see Thomas Petzinger Jr., "A Humanist Executive Leads by Thinking in Broader Terms," *The Wall Street Journal* (April 16, 1999): B1; and Gwen Kinkead, "In the Future, People like Me Will Go to Jail," *Fortune* (May 24, 1999): 190–200.

13. For example, see Nancy C. Roberts and Paula J. King, "The Stakeholder Audit Goes Public," *Organizational Dynamics*, 17 (Winter 1989): 63–79. Also see Ronald K. Mitchell, Bradley R. Agle, and Donna J. Wood, "Toward a Theory of Stakeholder Identification and Salience: Defining the Principle of Who and What Really Counts," *Academy of Management Review*, 22 (October 1997): 853–886; Irene Henriques and Perry Sadorsky, "The Relationship Between Environmental Commitment and Managerial Perceptions of Stakeholder Importance," *Academy of Management Journal*, 42 (February 1999): 87–99; William Beaver, "Is the Stakeholder Model Dead?" *Business Horizons*, 42 (March–April 1999): 8–12; and see the collection of articles on stakeholder theory in the April 1999 issue of *Academy of Management Review*.

14. These arguments have been adapted in part from Jones, "Corporate Social Responsibility Revisited," p. 61; and Keith Davis and William C. Frederick, *Business and Society: Management, Public Policy, and Ethics*, 5th ed. (New York: McGraw-Hill, 1984), pp. 28–41.

15. Mark N. Vamos and Stuart Jackson, "The Public Is Willing to Take Business On," *Business Week* (May 29, 1989): 29.

16. Davis and Frederick, *Business and Society*, p. 34.

17. Data from Vamos and Jackson, "The Public Is Willing to Take Business On."

18. Drawn from Ian Wilson, "What One Company Is Doing About Today's Demands on Business," in *Changing Business-Society Interrelationships*, ed. George A. Steiner (Los Angeles: UCLA Graduate School of Management, 1975).

19. Gary Boulard, "Combating Environmental Racism," *The Christian Science Monitor* (March 17, 1993): 8. For updates, see Dennis Cauchon, "Racial, Economic Divide in La.," *USA Today* (September 9, 1997): 3A; Paul Hoversten, "EPA Puts Plant on Hold in Racism Case," *USA Today* (September 11, 1997): 3A; Traci Watson, "La. Town Successful in Stopping Plastics Plant," *USA Today* (September 18, 1998): 7A; and Lynette Clemetson, "A Green Bottom Line," *Newsweek* (November 2, 1998): 53.

20. Mike France, "The World War on Tobacco," *Business Week* (November 11, 1996): 100. Also see David Greising and Linda Himelstein, "Does Tobacco Pay Its Way?" *Business Week* (February 19, 1996): 89–90; and Marc Levinson, "Smoke and Fire," *Newsweek* (March 25, 1996): 38–39.

21. The pressure exerted on Nike is discussed in Aaron Bernstein, "Nike Finally Does It," *Business Week* (May 25, 1998): 46; and Aaron Bernstein, "A Floor Under Foreign Factories?" *Business Week* (November 2, 1998) 126, 130.

22. Based on Mike France and Tim Smart, "The Ugly Talk on the Texaco Tape," *Business Week* (November 18, 1996): 58; Del Jones and Ellen Neuborne, "Texaco Settles Bias Lawsuit," *USA Today* (November 18, 1996): 1B; and "Texaco Sets Goals for Minority Hiring," *USA Today* (December 19, 1996): 2B.

23. Susan Caminiti, "The Payoff from a Good Reputation," *Fortune* (February 10, 1992): 75.

24. See Thomas S. Bateman, and J. Michael Crant, "Proactive Behavior: Meaning, Impact, Recommendations," *Business Horizons*, 42 (May–June 1999): 63–70.

25. See Vincent Jeffries, "Virtue and the Altruistic Personality," *Sociological Perspectives*, 41, no. 1 (1998): 151–166.

26. Data from Louis Uchitelle, "'Mench' Spawns Movement," *The Arizona Republic* (July 7, 1996): D2.

27. Data from Michael V. Russo and Paul A. Fouts, "A Resource-Based Perspective on Corporate Environmental Performance and Profitability," *Academy of Management Journal*, 40 (June 1997): 534–559.

28. Based on Daniel B. Turban and Daniel W. Greening, "Corporate Social Performance and Organizational Attractiveness to Prospective Employees," *Academy of Management Journal*, 40 (June 1996): 658–672.

29. For example, see Marc Ballon, "All Business Is Local," *Inc.*, 21 (June 1999): 109; and Rich Miller, "Greenspan Says Dealing Fairly in Business Pays Dividends," *USA Today* (August 16, 1999): 3B. British management scholar Charles Handy discusses "proper selfishness" in Chapter 5 of Charles Handy, *The Hungry Spirit* (New York: Broadway Books, 1998).

30. Data from Thomas A. Hemphill, "Corporate Governance, Strategic Philanthropy, and Public Policy," *Business Horizons*, 42 (May–June 1999): 57–62.

31. Louis W. Fry, Gerald D. Keim, and Roger E. Meiners, "Corporate Contributions: Altruistic or For-Profit?" *Academy of Management Journal*, 25 (March 1982): 105.

32. For complete details, see Richard E. Wokutch and Barbara A. Spencer, "Corporate Saints and Sinners: The Effects of Philan-

thropic and Illegal Activity on Organizational Performance," *California Management Review*, 29 (Winter 1987): 62–77. Also see Kimberly D. Elsbach and Robert I. Sutton, "Acquiring Organizational Legitimacy Through Illegitimate Actions: A Marriage of Institutional and Impression Management Theories," *Academy of Management Journal*, 35 (October 1992): 699–738.

33. Thomas A. Fogarty, "Corporations Use Causes for Effect," *USA Today* (November 10, 1997): 7B.

34. For example, see Dale Kurschner, "5 Ways Ethical Business Creates Fatter Profits," *Business Ethics*, 10 (March–April 1996): 20–23; Michael A. Verespej, "The Education Difference," *Industry Week* (May 6, 1996): 11–14; Bill Leonard, "Supporting Volunteerism," *HRMagazine*, 43 (June 1998): 84–93; and "Companies Dispatch Vitamin A to Help Malnourished Kids Thrive," *USA Today* (March 15, 1999): 6D.

35. See Mark N. Vamos and Christopher Power, "A Kinder, Gentler Generation of Executives?" *Business Week* (April 23, 1990): 86–87.

36. Mary Beth Marklein, "Taking the Pulse of America's Freshman," *USA Today* (January 25, 1999): 6D.

37. Data from "Judgment at Cash Register," *USA Today* (March 24, 1999): 1B.

38. Data from David A. Andelman, "Honest Profits," *Management Review*, 86 (January 1997): 30–32.

39. Data from John Dillin, "Congress Takes On Task of Mending Its Ways," *The Christian Science Monitor* (February 9, 1993): 1, 4. Also see Louisa Wah, "Workplace Conscience Needs a Boost," *Management Review*, 87 (July–August 1998): 6; and John Dunkelberg and Donald P. Robin, "The Anatomy of Fraudulent Behavior," *Business Horizons*, 41 (November–December 1998): 77–82.

40. Louisa Wah, "Lies in the Executive Wing," *Management Review*, 88 (May 1999): 9.

41. An excellent resource book is LaRue Tone Hosmer, *Moral Leadership in Business* (Burr Ridge, Ill.: Irwin, 1994).

42. See Rushworth M. Kidder, "Tough Choices: Why It's Getting Harder to Be Ethical," *The Futurist*, 29 (September–October 1995): 29–32.

43. See W. Edward Stead, Dan L. Worrell, and Jean Garner Stead, "An Integrative Model for Understanding and Managing Ethical Behavior in Business Organizations," *Journal of Business Ethics*, 9 (March 1990): 233–242; Robert Elliott Allinson, "A Call for Ethically-Centered Management," *Academy of Management Executive*, 9 (February 1995): 73–76; and Dawn-Marie Driscoll, "Don't Confuse Legal and Ethical Standards," *Business Ethics*, 10 (July–August 1996): 44.

44. O. C. Ferrell and John Fraedrich, *Business Ethics: Ethical Decision Making and Cases* (Boston: Houghton Mifflin, 1991), pp. 10–11. Also see Barbara Ettorre, "Temptation of Big Money," *Management Review*, 85 (February 1996): 13–17; and "The Ethical Dilemma," *Selling Power* (March 1996): 32, 34.

45. Business ethics research findings are reviewed in Phillip V. Lewis, "Defining 'Business Ethics': Like Nailing Jell-O to a Wall," *Journal of Business Ethics*, 4 (October 1985): 377–383. Also see William A. Kahn, "Toward an Agenda for Business Ethics Research," *Academy of Management Review*, 15 (April 1990): 311–328; and Gene R. Laczniak, Marvin W. Berkowitz, Russell G. Brooker, and James P. Hale, "The Ethics of Business: Improving or Deteriorating?" *Business Horizons*, 38 (January–February 1995): 39–47.

46. Del Jones, "48% of Workers Admit to Unethical or Illegal Acts," *USA Today* (April 4, 1997): 1A.

47. Ibid., p. 2A.

48. Julia Flynn, "Did Sears Take Other Customers for a Ride?" *Business Week* (August 3, 1992): 24.

49. Based on Kelley Holland, "Sears Settles Up with the Feds," *Business Week* (February 22, 1999): 45; and John McCormick, "The Sorry Side of Sears," *Newsweek* (February 22, 1999): 36–39.

50. For related reading and case studies, see William M. Welch, "IRS Self-Review Finds Unjust Practices," *USA Today* (January 14, 1998): 8A; Thor Valdmanis, "Cooking the Books Proves Common Trick of the Trade," *USA Today* (August 11, 1998): 1B–2B; Lin Grensing-Pophal, "Walking the Tightrope, Balancing Risks and Gains," *HRMagazine*, 43 (October 1998): 112–119; Paula Dwyer and Steven Solomon, "The Citi That Slept?" *Business Week* (November 2, 1998): 94–100; and Joseph Weber, "The Doctor vs. the Drugmaker," *Business Week* (November 30, 1998): 87–88.

51. William Rudelius and Rogene A. Buchholz, "Ethical Problems of Purchasing Managers," *Harvard Business Review*, 57 (March–April 1979): 12. Also see Alan J. Dubinsky, Eric N. Berkowitz, and William Rudelius, "Ethical Problems of Field Sales Personnel," *MSU Business Topics*, 28 (Summer 1980): 11–16; and James R. Davis, "Ambiguity, Ethics, and the Bottom Line," *Business Horizons*, 32 (May–June 1989): 65–70.

52. Thomas R. Horton, "The Ethics Crisis Continues: What to Do?" *Management Review*, 75 (November 1986): 3. Derek Bok, former president of Harvard University, calls for greater civic mindedness in Derek Bok, "A Great Need of the 90s," *The Christian Science Monitor* (May 22, 1992): 18.

53. For details, see Richard F. Beltramini, Robert A. Peterson, and George Kozmetsky, "Concerns of College Students Regarding Business Ethics," *Journal of Business Ethics*, 3 (August 1984): 195–200. Also see Robert A. Peterson, Richard F. Beltramini, and George Kozmetsky, "Concerns of College Students Regarding Business Ethics: A Replication," *Journal of Business Ethics*, 10 (October 1991): 733–738; and Leslie M. Dawson, "Women and Men, Morality and Ethics," *Business Horizons*, 38 (July–August 1995): 61–68.

54. For good management-oriented discussions of values, see Barry Z. Posner and Warren H. Schmidt, "Values and the American Manager: An Update Updated," *California Management Review*, 34 (Spring 1992): 80–94.

55. As quoted in Frank Rose, "A New Age for Business?" *Fortune* (October 8, 1990): 164. Also see E. Thomas Behr, "Acting from the Center," *Management Review*, 87 (March 1998): 51–55; John D. Beckett, "NOBLE Ideas for Business," *Management Review*, 88 (March 1999): 62; and Mark Boardman, "The Corrosion of Character," *HRMagazine*, 44 (July 1999): 224.

56. For excellent treatment of values, see Milton Rokeach, *Beliefs, Attitudes, and Values* (San Francisco: Jossey-Bass, 1968), p. 124; and Milton Rokeach and Sandra J. Ball-Rokeach, "Stability and Change in American Value Priorities, 1968–1981," *American Psychologist*, 44 (May 1989): 775–784. Also see Gregory R. Maio and James M. Olson, "Values as Truisms: Evidence and Implications," *Journal of Personality and Social Psychology*, 74 (February 1998): 294–311.

57. Rokeach, *Beliefs, Attitudes, and Values*, p. 124.

58. See Rick Wartzman, "Nature or Nurture? Study Blames Ethical Lapses on Corporate Goals," *The Wall Street Journal* (October 9, 1987): 27. Two other Rokeach scale studies are reported in Maris G. Martinsons and Aelita Brivins Martinsons, "Conquering Cultural Constraints to Cultivate Chinese Management Creativity and Innovation," *Journal of Management Development*, 15, no. 9 (1996): 18–35; and Ralph A. Rodriguez, "Challenging Demographic Reductionism: A Pilot Study Investigating Diversity in Group Composition," *Small Group Research*, 29 (December 1998): 744–759.

59. Excerpted from Hosmer, *Moral Leadership in Business*, pp. 39–41. © 1994, McGraw-Hill. Reprinted with the permission of the McGraw-Hill Companies.

60. See Archie B. Carroll, "In Search of the Moral Manager," *Business Horizons*, 30 (March–April 1987): 7–15.

61. Data from Brad Lee Thompson, "Ethics Training Enters the Real World," *Training*, 27 (October 1990): 82–94; and "1997 Industry Report: Specific Types of Training," *Training*, 34 (October 1997): 55.

62. For example, see Andrew Stark, "What's the Matter with Business Ethics?" *Harvard Business Review*, 71 (May–June 1993): 38–48; and Dawn Blalock, "Study Shows Many Execs Are Quick to Write Off Ethics," *The Wall Street Journal* (March 26, 1996): C1, C22.

63. For details, see John A. Byrne, "The Best-Laid Ethics Programs . . ." *Business Week* (March 9, 1992): 67–69.

64. See Paul C. Judge, "Ethics for Hire," *Business Week* (July 15, 1996): 26–28; and Louisa Wah, "Lip-Service Ethics Programs Prove Ineffective," *Management Review*, 88 (June 1999): 9.

65. Based on discussion in Thompson, "Ethics Training Enters the Real World." For reasons why ethics programs fail, see Judge, "Ethics for Hire."

66. For informative reading on ethical advocates, see Theodore V. Purcell, "Electing an 'Angel's Advocate' to the Board," *Management Review*, 65 (May 1976): 4–11; Theodore V. Purcell, "Institutionalizing Ethics into Top Management Decisions," *Public Relations Quarterly*, 22 (Summer 1977): 15–20; Beverly Geber, "The Right and Wrong of Ethics Offices," *Training*, 32 (October 1995): 102–109; and Susan Gaines, "Who Are These Ethics Experts Anyway?" *Business Ethics*, 10 (March–April 1996): 26–30.

67. Data from "Social Issues at Work," *Training*, 29 (October 1992): 50; and "1996 Industry Report: Social Issues at Work," *Training*, 33 (October 1996): 71.

68. See Dale Kurschner, "Ethics Programs and Personal Values Are Still Not Enough," *Business Ethics*, 10 (May–June 1996): 12; Gary R. Weaver, Linda Klebe Treviño, and Philip L. Cochran, "Corporate Ethics Programs as Control Systems: Influences of Executive Commitment and Environmental Factors," *Academy of Management Journal*, 42 (February 1999): 41–57; and Louisa Wah, "Ethics Linked to Financial Performance," *Management Review*, 88 (July–August 1999): 7.

69. "Business' Big Morality Play," *Dun's Review* (August 1980): 56.

70. The importance of top-management support, ethical codes, and compliance monitoring are discussed in John A. Byrne, "Businesses Are Signing Up for Ethics 101," *Business Week* (February 15, 1988): 56, 57. Also see Patrick E. Murphy, "Improving Your Ethics Code," *Business Ethics*, 8 (March–April 1994): 23.

71. See Ruth E. Thaler-Carter, "Social Accountability 8000," *HRMagazine*, 44 (June 1999): 106–112.

72. See Richard P. Nielsen, "Changing Unethical Organizational Behavior," *Academy of Management Executive*, 3 (May 1989): 123–130.

73. See Barbara Ettorre, "Whistleblowers: Who's the Real Bad Guy?" *Management Review*, 83 (May 1994): 18–23; and Ellen Neuborne, "Whistle-Blowers Pipe Up More Frequently," *USA Today* (July 22, 1996): 2B.

74. Ralph Nader, "An Anatomy of Whistle Blowing," in *Whistle Blowing*, ed. Ralph Nader, Peter Petkas, and Kate Blackwell (New York: Bantam, 1972), p. 7. For interesting case studies of whistleblowers, see William McGowan, "The Whistleblowers Hall of Fame," *Business and Society Review*, 52 (Winter 1985): 31–36.

75. The federal Whistleblowers Protection Act of 1989 is discussed in David Israel and Anita Lechner, "Protection for Whistleblowers," *Personnel Administrator*, 34 (July 1989): 106. Also see Marshall Loeb, "When to Rat on the Boss," *Fortune* (October 2, 1995): 183; Tom Lowry, "Whistle-Blower Now Fighting Former Allies," *USA Today* (November 9, 1998): 15B; and "The Gadfly of Trinity Place," *Business Week* (April 26, 1999): 110, 112.

76. Adapted from Kenneth D. Walters, "Your Employees' Right to Blow the Whistle," *Harvard Business Review*, 53 (July–August 1975): 26–34, 161–162. Also see Janet P. Near and Marcia P. Miceli, "Effective Whistle-Blowing," *Academy of Management Review*, 20 (July 1995): 679–708; and Kate Walter, "Ethics Hot Lines Tap into More than Wrongdoing," *HRMagazine*, 40 (September 1995): 79–85.

Chapter 6

Opening Quotation As quoted in Brent Schlender, "Peter Drucker Takes the Long View," *Fortune* (September 28, 1998): 170.

Opening Case Excerpted from Cheryl Comeau-Kirschner and Louisa Wah, "Who Has Time to Think?" *Management Review*, 89 (January 2000): 16–23. Reprinted from *Management Review*, January 2000. Copyright © 2000 American Management Association International. Reprinted by permission of American Management Association International, New York, NY. All rights reserved. **http://www.amanet.org.**

Closing Case Adapted by permission of *Harvard Business Review*. Excerpts from "Emerson Electric: Consistent Profits, Consistently," by Charles F. Knight, *Harvard Business Review*, 70 (January–February 1992). Copyright © 1992 by the President and Fellows of Harvard College; all rights reserved.

1. As quoted in Linda Himelstein, "Timothy A. Koogle," *Business Week E.BIZ* (September 27, 1999): EB 26.

2. See Toby Tetenbaum, "To Plan or Not to Plan," *Management Review*, 87 (October 1998): 70; and Andrew Campbell, "Tailored, Not Benchmarked: A Fresh Look at Corporate Planning," *Harvard Business Review*, 77 (March–April 1999): 41–50.

3. Based on discussion in Frances J. Milliken, "Three Types of Perceived Uncertainty About the Environment: State, Effect, and Response Uncertainty," *Academy of Management Review*, 12 (January 1987): 133–143.

4. See Raymond E. Miles and Charles C. Snow, *Organizational Strategy, Structure, and Process* (New York: McGraw-Hill, 1978), p. 29. A validation of the Miles and Snow model can be found in Stephen M. Shortell and Edward J. Zajak, "Perceptual and Archival Measures of Miles and Snow's Strategic Types: A Comprehensive Assessment of Reliability and Validity," *Academy of Management Journal*, 33 (December 1990): 817–832.

5. Sandra Block, "Harley Cycles out of RV Business," *USA Today* (January 23, 1996): 3B. Another "defender" is profiled in Jim Cross, "Back to the Future," *Management Review*, 88 (February 1999): 50–54.

6. "What's the Hard Part? Innovation Never Ends," *Fast Company*, no. 24 (May 1999): 212.

7. Donald C. Hambrick, "Some Tests of the Effectiveness and Functional Attributes of Miles and Snow's Strategic Types," *Academy of Management Journal*, 26 (March 1983): 24. Also see Eli Segev, "Strategy, Strategy Making, and Performance—An Empirical Investigation," *Management Science*, 33 (February 1987): 258–269.

8. See John B. Miner, "The Expanded Horizon for Achieving Entrepreneurial Success," *Organizational Dynamics*, 25 (Winter 1997): 54–66.

9. Joseph Weber, "Just Get It to the Store on Time," *Business Week* (March 6, 1995): 66. For more on VF, see Minda Zetlin, "When It's Smarter to Be Second to Market," *Management Review*, 88 (March 1999): 30–34.

10. For a positive view of analyzers, see Michele Kremen Bolton, "Imitation Versus Innovation: Lessons to Be Learned from the Japanese," *Organizational Dynamics*, 21 (Winter 1993): 30–45.

11. See "How Seagram Is Scrambling to Survive 'The Sobering of America,'" *Business Week* (September 3, 1984): 94–95; Andrea Rothman, "The Maverick Boss at Seagram," *Business Week* (December 18, 1989): 90–98; and Laura Zinn, "Edgar Jr.'s Not So Excellent Ventures," *Business Week* (January 16, 1995): 78–79.

12. For details, see Jeffrey S. Conant, Michael P. Mokwa, and P. Rajan Varadarajan, "Strategic Types, Distinctive Marketing Competencies and Organizational Performance: A Multiple Measures Based Study," *Strategic Management Journal*, 11 (September 1990): 365–383. Also see Shaker A. Zahra and John A. Pearce II, "Research Evidence on the Miles-Snow Typology," *Journal of Management*, 16 (December 1990): 751–768.

13. Based on Mary M. Crossan, Henry W. Lane, Roderick E. White, and Leo Klus, "The Improvising Organization: Where Planning Meets Opportunity," *Organizational Dynamics*, 24 (Spring 1996): 20–35.

14. Scott Adams, "Dilbert's Management Handbook," *Fortune* (May 13, 1996): 104.

15. Based on R. Duane Ireland and Michael A. Hitt, "Mission Statements: Importance, Challenge, and Recommendations for Development," *Business Horizons*, 35 (May–June 1992): 34–42. Also see Christopher K. Bart, "Sex, Lies, and Mission Statements," *Business Horizons*, 40 (December 1997): 9–18; James R. Lucas, "Anatomy of a Vision Statement," *Management Review*, 87 (February 1998): 22–26; and Jeffrey Pfeffer and Robert I. Sutton, "The Smart-Talk Trap," *Harvard Business Review*, 77 (May–June 1999): 135–142.

16. Bill Saporito, "PPG: Shiny, Not Dull," *Fortune* (July 17, 1989): 107.

17. Dan Sullivan, "The Reality Gap," *Inc.*, 21 (March 1999): 119.

18. Anthony P. Raia, *Managing by Objectives* (Glenview, Ill.: Scott, Foresman, 1974), p. 24.

19. For an excellent and comprehensive treatment of goal setting, see Edwin A. Locke and Gary P. Latham, *Goal Setting: A Motivational Technique That Works!* (Englewood Cliffs, N.J.: Prentice-Hall, 1984). Also see Robert D. Pritchard, Philip L. Roth, Steven D. Jones, Patricia J. Galgay, and Margaret D. Watson, "Designing a Goal-Setting System to Enhance Performance: A Practical Guide," *Organizational Dynamics*, 17 (Summer 1988): 69–78.

20. Practical advice on setting priorities may be found in Gerald Williams, "Setting Up Priorities—and Sticking to Them," *Supervisory Management*, 37 (December 1992): 11. Also see David Barry, Catherine Durnell Cramton, and Stephen J. Carroll, "Navigating the Garbage Can: How Agendas Help Managers Cope with Job Realities," *Academy of Management Executive*, 11 (May 1997): 26–42.

21. For example, see Edward C. Baig, "Secretaries for the Rest of Us," *Business Week* (November 16, 1998): 146; Ed Brown, "Stephen Covey's New One-Day Seminar," *Fortune* (February 1, 1999): 138, 140; and Donna J. Abernathy, "A Get-Real Guide to Time Management," *Training & Development*, 53 (June 1999): 22–26.

22. Raia, *Managing by Objectives*, p. 54.

23. See Barbara Moses, "The Busyness Trap," *Training*, 35 (November 1998): 38–42; and Stephen Bertman, "Hyper Culture," *The Futurist*, 32 (December 1998): 18–23.

24. See Peter F. Drucker, *The Practice of Management* (New York: Harper & Row, 1954).

25. As an indication of the widespread interest in MBO, more than 700 books, articles, and technical papers had been written on the subject by the late 1970s. For a brief history of MBO, see George S. Odiorne, "MBO: A Backward Glance," *Business Horizons*, 21 (October 1978): 14–24. An excellent collection of readings on MBO may be found in George Odiorne, Heinz Weihrich, and Jack Mendleson, *Executive Skills: A Management by Objectives Approach* (Dubuque, Iowa: Wm. C. Brown, 1980). Also see Henry H. Beam, "George Odiorne," *Business Horizons*, 39 (November–December 1996): 73–76.

26. T. J. Rodgers, "No Excuses Management," *Harvard Business Review*, 68 (July–August 1990): 87, 89.

27. Problems and solutions in the MBO/performance appraisal linkage are discussed in Jeffrey S. Kane and Kimberly A. Freeman, "MBO and Performance Appraisal: A Mixture That's Not a Solution, Part 1," *Personnel*, 63 (December 1986): 26–36; and Jeffrey S. Kane and Kimberly A. Freeman, "MBO and Performance Appraisal: A Mixture That's Not a Solution, Part 2," *Personnel*, 64 (February 1987): 26–32.

28. For example, see Jan P. Muczyk and Bernard C. Reimann, "MBO as a Complement to Effective Leadership," *Academy of Management Executive*, 3 (May 1989): 131–139.

29. An interesting study of the positive and negative aspects of MBO may be found in Robert C. Ford and Frank S. McLaughlin, "Avoiding Disappointment in MBO Programs," *Human Resource Management*, 21 (Summer 1982): 44–49. Positive research evidence is summarized in Robert Rodgers and John E. Hunter, "Impact on Management by Objectives on Organizational Productivity," *Human Resource Management*, 76 (April 1991): 322–336.

30. For a critical appraisal of MBO core assumptions, see David Halpern and Stephen Osofsky, "A Dissenting View of MBO," *Public Personnel Management*, 19 (Fall 1990): 321–330. Deming's critical comments may be found in W. Edwards Deming, *Out of the Crisis* (Cambridge, Mass.: MIT, 1986), pp. 23–96. Dennis W. Organ, "The Editor's Chair," *Business Horizons*, 39 (November–December 1996): 1.

31. See Richard Babcock and Peter F. Sorensen Jr., "An MBO Check-List: Are Conditions Right for Implementation?" *Management Review*, 68 (June 1979): 59–62.

32. Robert Rodgers and John E. Hunter, "Impact of Management by Objectives on Organizational Productivity," *Journal of Applied Psychology*, 76 (April 1991): 322.

33. See Robert Rodgers, John E. Hunter, and Deborah L. Rogers, "Influence of Top Management Commitment on Management Program Success," *Journal of Applied Psychology*, 78 (February 1993): 151–155.

34. See Jeffrey K. Pinto and Om P. Kharbanda, "Lessons for an Accidental Profession," *Business Horizons*, 38 (March–April 1995): 41–50. For an excellent resource book, see Jeffrey K. Pinto and O. P. Kharbanda, *Successful Project Managers: Leading Your Team to Success* (New York: Van Nostrand Reinhold, 1995).

35. See Tom D. Conkright, "So You're Going to Manage a Project," *Training*, 35 (January 1998): 62–67.

36. Stratford Sherman, "Secrets of HP's 'Muddled' Team," *Fortune* (March 18, 1996): 116. For a good update on HP, see Peter Burrows, "The Boss," *Business Week* (August 2, 1999): 76–84.

37. Louisa Wah, "Most IT Projects Prove Inefficient," *Management Review*, 88 (January 1999): 7.

38. For more, see Susan G. Turner, Dawn R. Utley, and Jerry D. Westbrook, "Project Managers and Functional Managers: A Case Study

of Job Satisfaction in a Matrix Organization," *Project Management Journal*, 29 (September 1998): 11–19; Peg Thoms and Jeffrey K. Pinto, "Project Leadership: A Question of Timing," *Project Management Journal*, 30 (March 1999): 19–26; Gerben van der Vegt, Ben Emans, and Evert van de Vliert, "Effects of Interdependencies in Project Teams," *The Journal of Social Psychology*, 139 (April 1999): 202–214; and Timothy J. Kloppenborg and Joseph A. Petrick, "Leadership in Project Life Cycle and Team Character Development," *Project Management Journal*, 30 (June 1999): 8–13.

39. See Jennifer E. Jenkins, "Moving Beyond a Project's Implementation Phase," *Nursing Management*, 27 (January 1996): 48B, 48D.

40. Based partly on discussion in Pinto and Kharbanda, *Successful Project Managers*, p. 147.

41. For more on project planning and management, see Jan Bottcher, Andreas Drexl, Rainer Kolisch, and Frank Salewski, "Project Scheduling Under Partially Renewable Resource Constraints," *Management Science*, 45 (April 1999): 543–559; Tom Peters, "The WOW Project," *Fast Company*, no. 24 (May 1999): 116–128; and Michael Schrage, "The Proto Project," *Fast Company*, no. 24 (May 1999): 138–144.

42. One example of a flow-chart application is Sharon M. McKinnon, "How Important Are Those Foreign Operations? A Flow-Chart Approach to Loan Analysis," *Financial Analysts Journal*, 41 (January–February 1985): 75–78.

43. See Wilton Woods, "Desktop Reengineering," *Fortune* (June 13, 1994): 147.

44. For examples of early Gantt charts, see H. L. Gantt, *Organizing for Work* (New York: Harcourt, Brace and Howe, 1919), chap. 8.

45. Gantt chart applications can be found in Conkright, "So You're Going to Manage a Project," p. 64; and Andrew Raskin, "Task Masters," *Inc.* Tech 1999, no. 1 (1999): 62–72.

46. Ivars Avots, "The Management Side of PERT," *California Management Review*, 4 (Winter 1962): 16–27.

47. Additional information on PERT can be found in Nancy Madlin, "Streamlining the PERT Chart," *Management Review*, 75 (September 1986): 67–68; Eric C. Silverberg, "Predicting Project Completion," *Research Technology Review*, 34 (May–June 1991): 46–49; Robert L. Armacost and Rohne L. Jauernig, "Planning and Managing a Major Recruiting Project," *Public Personnel Management*, 20 (Summer 1991): 115–126; T. M. Williams, "Practical Use of Distributions in Network Analysis," *Journal of the Operational Research Society*, 43 (March 1992): 265–270; and Hooshang Kuklan, "Effective Project Management: An Expanded Network Approach," *Journal of Systems Management*, 44 (March 1993): 12–16.

48. Adapted in part from John Fertakis and John Moss, "An Introduction to PERT and PERT/Cost Systems," *Managerial Planning*, 19 (January–February 1971): 24–31.

49. Micheline Maynard, "Chrysler Posts Best Earnings Ever," *USA Today* (January 18, 1995): 1B.

50. Data from John Rossant, "De Benedetti at the Brink," *Business Week* (February 12, 1996): 48.

51. Data from Carl Quintanilla, "Emerson Electric Co.'s No. 2 Executive, George Tamke, Moves Closer to No. 1," *The Wall Street Journal* (May 5, 1999): B4.

52. Data from Jeremy Kahn, "The *Fortune* Global 5 Hundred: The World's Largest Corporations," *Fortune* (August 2, 1999): F-7. Also see Justin Martin, "Building Profits the Old-Fashioned Way," *Fortune* (April 13, 1998): 178–182; and Carl Quintanilla, "For Its Profit Streak, Emerson's Reward Is a Laggard Share Price," *The Wall Street Journal* (May 11, 1999): A1, A8.

Chapter 7

Opening Quotation Laurel Cutler is vice chairman of FCB/Leber Katz Partners, an advertising agency in New York City. Quoted in Susan Caminiti, "The Payoff from a Good Reputation," *Fortune* (February 10, 1992): 74.

Opening Case Republished with permission of *The Wall Street Journal*, from Richard Gibson, "Burger King Seeks New Sizzle" (April 14, 1999). Permission conveyed through Copyright Clearance Center, Inc.

Closing Case Excerpted from Neel Chowdhury, "Dell Cracks China," *Fortune* (June 21, 1999): 120–124. © 1999 Time Inc. Reprinted by permission.

1. Data from Lois Therrien, "McRisky," *Business Week* (October 21, 1991): 114–122. For an update on McDonald's, see Bruce Horovitz and Gary Strauss, "Fast-Food Icon Wants Shine Restored to Golden Arches," *USA Today* (May 1, 1998): 1B–2B.

2. See Bryan W. Barry, "A Beginner's Guide to Strategic Planning," *The Futurist*, 32 (April 1998): 33–36; R. Duane Ireland and Michael A. Hitt, "Achieving and Maintaining Strategic Competitiveness in the 21st Century: The Role of Strategic Leadership," *Academy of Management Executive*, 13 (February 1999): 43–57; and Danny Miller and John O. Whitney, "Beyond Strategy: Configuration as a Pillar of Competitive Advantage," *Business Horizons*, 42 (May–June 1999): 5–17.

3. Data from C. Chet Miller and Laura B. Cardinal, "Strategic Planning and Firm Performance: A Synthesis of More than Two Decades of Research," *Academy of Management Journal*, 37 (December 1994): 1649–1665.

4. For related discussion, see Gary Hamel and C. K. Prahalad, "Competing for the Future," *Harvard Business Review*, 72 (July–August 1994): 122–128; Rosabeth Moss Kanter, "Managing for Long-Term Success," *The Futurist*, 32 (August–September 1998): 43–45; and Sheila M. Puffer, "Global Executive: Intel's Andrew Grove on Competitiveness," *Academy of Management Executive*, 13 (February 1999): 15–24.

5. For more, see Stuart L. Hart, "An Integrative Framework for Strategy-Making Processes," *Academy of Management Review*, 17 (April 1992): 327–351. Also see Cheryl Comeau-Kirschner, "Strategic Planners' Expanded Roles," *Management Review*, 88 (June 1999): 7.

6. John A. Byrne, "Strategic Planning," *Business Week* (August 26, 1996): 52.

7. Based on a definitional framework found in David J. Teece, "Economic Analysis and Strategic Management," *California Management Review*, 26 (Spring 1984): 87. An alternative view calls for supplementing the notion of "fit" with the concept of "stretch," thus better accommodating situations where a company's aspirations exceed its present resource capabilities. See Gary Hamel and C. K. Prahalad, "Strategy as Stretch and Leverage," *Harvard Business Review*, 71 (March–April 1993): 75–84.

8. Arnoldo C. Hax, "Redefining the Concept of Strategy and the Strategy Formation Process," *Planning Review*, 18 (May/June 1990): 35.

9. See Michael A. Hitt, Barbara W. Keats, and Samuel M. DeMarie, "Navigating in the New Competitive Landscape: Building Strategic Flexibility and Competitive Advantage in the 21st Century," *Academy of Management Executive*, 12 (November 1998): 22–42.

10. Ronald Henkoff, "How to Plan for 1995," *Fortune* (December 31, 1990): 70.

11. For example, see Takashi Kiuchi, "Business Lessons from the Rain Forest," *The Futurist*, 32 (January–February 1998): 50–53; Jenny C. McCune, "The Game of Business," *Management Review*, 87 (February 1998): 56–58; and Louisa Wah, "The Dear Cost of 'Scut Work,'" *Management Review*, 88 (June 1999): 27–31.

12. Linda Yates and Peter Skarzynski, "How Do Companies Get to the Future First?" *Management Review*, 88 (January 1999): 18. Also see Joseph C. Picken and Gregory G. Dess, "Right Strategy—Wrong Problem," *Organizational Dynamics*, 27 (Summer 1998): 35–49; and Adrian J. Slywotzky, Kevin A. Mundt, and James A. Quella, "Pattern Thinking," *Management Review*, 88 (June 1999): 32–37.

13. See William R. King and David I. Cleland, *Strategic Planning and Policy* (New York: Van Nostrand Reinhold, 1978), pp. 180–183; and Laura Landro, "Giants Talk Synergy but Few Make It Work," *The Wall Street Journal* (September 25, 1995): B1–B2.

14. Bill Vlasic, "The First Global Car Colossus," *Business Week* (May 18, 1998): 40.

15. Based on Matt Krantz, "Amazon Kicks Off Sales of Toys, Electronics," *USA Today* (July 13, 1999): 1B.

16. Based on discussion in Jared Sandberg, "She's Baaack!" *Newsweek* (February 15, 1999): 44–46.

17. "Hotels Developing Multiple Personalities," *USA Today* (September 10, 1996): 4B.

18. Based on Ruth Coxeter, "Hope for Oil Spills Is a Thing with Feathers," *Business Week* (July 18, 1994): 76.

19. Otis Port, "Innovations," *Business Week* (March 29, 1999): 63. Also see Ellen Licking, "Turning a Gooey Mess into Gobs of Cash," *Business Week* (February 1, 1999): 67.

20. "Alfa-Laval: Updating Its Knowhow for the Biotechnology Era," *Business Week* (September 19, 1983): 80.

21. Based on Amy Barrett, "We Have to Be Prime Time," *Business Week* (April 15, 1996): 87.

22. See Michael E. Porter, *Competitive Strategy* (New York: Free Press, 1980), p. 35; and Michael E. Porter, *The Competitive Advantage of Nations* (New York: The Free Press, 1990), p. 39. For updates, see James Surowiecki, "The Return of Michael Porter," *Fortune* (February 1, 1999): 135–138; and Richard M. Hodgetts, "A Conversation with Michael E. Porter: A 'Significant Extension' Toward Operational Improvement and Positioning," *Organizational Dynamics*, 28 (Summer 1999): 24–33.

23. Porter, *The Competitive Advantage of Nations*, p. 37.

24. See Vicki R. Lane, "Brand Leverage Power: The Critical Role of Brand Balance," *Business Horizons*, 41 (January–February 1998): 75–84; Scott Ward, Larry Light, and Jonathan Goldstine, "What High-Tech Managers Need to Know About Brands," *Harvard Business Review*, 77 (July–August 1999): 85–95; and Karen S. Cravens and Chris Guilding, "Strategic Brand Valuation: A Cross-Functional Perspective," *Business Horizons*, 42 (July–August 1999): 53–62.

25. Ron Zemke and Dick Schaaf, *The Service Edge* (New York: New American Library, 1989), p. 360.

26. See Shelly Branch, "The Brand Builders," *Fortune* (May 10, 1999): 132–134.

27. Data from Mark Ivey, "Does Compaq's Formula Still Compute?" *Business Week* (May 13, 1991): 100, 104.

28. See Ronald Grover, "Lod Cook: Mixing Oil and PR," *Business Week* (October 8, 1990): 110–116.

29. See Glen Creno, "Can ARCO Keep Prices Low?" *The Arizona Republic* (April 3, 1999): E1–E2.

30. For details, see Luis Ma. R. Calingo, "Environmental Determinants of Generic Competitive Strategies: Preliminary Evidence from Structured Content Analysis of *Fortune* and *Business Week* Articles (1983–1984)," *Human Relations*, 42 (April 1989): 353–369. For related research, see Praveen R. Nayyar, "Performance Effects of Three Foci in Service Firms," *Academy of Management Journal*, 35 (December 1992): 985–1009.

31. James F. Moore, *The Death of Competition: Leadership and Strategy in the Age of Business Ecosystems* (New York: HarperBusiness, 1996), p. 25. For relevant background material, see Warren Boeker, "Organizational Strategy: An Ecological Perspective," *Academy of Management Journal*, 34 (September 1991): 613–635; and James F. Moore, "Predators and Prey: A New Ecology of Competition," *Harvard Business Review*, 71 (May–June 1993): 75–86.

32. See Courtney Shelton Hunt and Howard E. Aldrich, "The Second Ecology: Creation and Evolution of Organizational Communities," in *Research in Organizational Behavior*, vol. 20, eds. Barry M. Staw and L. L. Cummings (Greenwich, Conn.: JAI Press, 1998), pp. 267–301.

33. For more, see Andy Reinhardt, "The Wintel of Their Discontent," *Business Week* (November 23, 1998): 57.

34. Moore, *The Death of Competition*, p. 228. Also see Kathy Rebello, "Inside Microsoft," *Business Week* (July 15, 1996): 56–67. For an update, see Mark Frankel, "Ellison Gives Gates Another Rap," *Business Week* (October 18, 1999): 60.

35. For interesting reading, see Peter Burrows, "Beyond the PC," *Business Week* (March 8, 1999): 78–88; Bill Gates, "Why the PC Will Not Die," *Newsweek* (May 31, 1999): 64; and Joel Dreyfuss, "Death to the Personal Computer," *Fortune* (July 19, 1999): 138[N].

36. For example, see James A. Belohlav, "The Evolving Competitive Paradigm," *Business Horizons*, 39 (March–April 1996): 11–19; and Raymond W. Smith, "Business as War Game: A Report from the Battlefront," *Fortune* (September 30, 1996): 190–193.

37. Moore, *The Death of Competition*, p. 61. For more on strategic collaboration, see Richard J. Schonberger, "Strategic Collaboration: Breaching the Castle Walls," *Business Horizons*, 39 (March–April 1996): 20–26; Henry Mintzberg, Deborah Dougherty, Jan Jorgensen, and Frances Westley, "Some Surprising Things About Collaboration—Knowing How People Connect Makes It Work Better," *Organizational Dynamics*, 25 (Spring 1996): 60–71; Jeanne M. Liedtka, "Collaborating Across Lines of Business for Competitive Advantage," *Academy of Management Executive*, 10 (May 1996): 20–34; and Jeffrey H. Dyer and Harbir Singh, "The Relational View: Cooperative Strategy and Sources of Interorganizational Competitive Advantage," *Academy of Management Review*, 23 (October 1998): 660–679.

38. See Roger O. Crockett, "Warp Speed Ahead," *Business Week* (February 16, 1998): 80–83.

39. See the section on James Moore in John A. Byrne, "Three of the Busiest New Strategists," *Business Week* (August 26, 1996): 50–51. Moore's book is reviewed in Ira Sager, "The New Biology of Big Business," *Business Week* (April 15, 1996): 19.

40. Robert D. Hof, "A New Era of Bright Hopes and Terrible Fears," *Business Week* (October 4, 1999): 84.

41. Data from ibid., p. 90.

42. Based on Heather Green, "Throw Out Your Old Business Model," *Business Week* E.BIZ (March 22, 1999): EB 22–EB 23.

43. See Beverly Goldberg and John G. Sifonis, "Focusing Your E-Commerce Vision," *Management Review*, 87 (September 1998): 48–51; and David A. Griffith and Jonathan W. Palmer, "Leveraging the Web for Corporate Success," *Business Horizons*, 42 (January–February 1999): 3–10.

44. Based on Leyland Pitt, Pierre Berthon, and Richard T. Watson, "Cyberservice: Taming Service Marketing Problems with the World Wide Web," *Business Horizons*, 42 (January–February 1999): 11–18; and Chris Charuhas, "How to Train Web-Site Builders," *Training*, 36 (August 1999): 48–53.

45. Jane Hodges, "Winning and Keeping Web Surfers: Yahoo," *Fortune* (May 24, 1999): 121.

46. Adapted from ibid., pp. 121–122. Also see Pierre M. Loewe and Mark S. Bonchek, "Branding in the Information Age," *Management Review*, 88 (April 1999): 42.

47. Eryn Brown, "9 Ways to Win on the Web," *Fortune* (May 24, 1999): 114.

48. Louise Lee, "'Clicks and Mortar' at Gap.Com," *Business Week* (October 18, 1999): 152.

49. See Ann Harrington, "Customer Service: FedEx," *Fortune* (May 24, 1999): 124.

50. Jerry Usem, "Internet Defense Strategy: Cannibalize Yourself," *Fortune* (September 6, 1999): 124, 126. © 1999 Time Inc. Reprinted by permission.

51. See Jeffrey L. Seglin, "It's Not That Easy Going Green," *Inc.*, 21 (May 1999): 28–32; Aaron Bernstein, "Sweatshop Reform: How to Solve the Standoff," *Business Week* (May 3, 1999): 186, 188, 190; "Helping the Private Sector Embrace Human Rights," *Business Ethics*, 13 (May–June 1999): 16; and William Echikson, "It's Europe's Turn to Sweat About Sweatshops," *Business Week* (July 19, 1999): 96.

52. As quoted in Brent Schlender, "Why Andy Grove Can't Stop," *Fortune* (July 10, 1995): 91.

53. Henry Mintzberg, "The Design School: Reconsidering the Basic Premises of Strategic Management," *Strategic Management Journal*, 11 (March–April 1990): 192.

54. See Gail Dutton, "What Business Are We In?" *Management Review*, 86 (September 1997): 54–57; and Eric M. Olson, Rachael Cooper, and Stanley F. Slater, "Design Strategy and Competitive Advantage," *Business Horizons*, 41 (March–April 1998): 55–61.

55. See Thomas L. Wheelen and J. David Hunger, "Using the Strategic Audit," *SAM Advanced Management Journal*, 52 (Winter 1987): 4–12; Shaker A. Zahra and Sherry S. Chaples, "Blind Spots in Competitive Analysis," *Academy of Management Executive*, 7 (May 1993): 7–28; Leigh Buchanan, "The Smartest Little Company in America," *Inc.*, 21 (January 1999): 42–54; and John M. Usher, "Specialists, Generalists, and Polymorphs: Spatial Advantages of Multiunit Organization in a Single Industry," *Academy of Management Review*, 24 (January 1999): 143–150.

56. Richard F. Vancil, "Strategy Formulation in Complex Organizations," *Sloan Management Review*, 17 (Winter 1976): 18. Also see Robert E. Linneman and John L. Stanton Jr., "Mining for Niches," *Business Horizons*, 35 (May–June 1992): 43–51.

57. Pete Engardio, "For Citibank, There's No Place like Asia," *Business Week* (March 30, 1992): 66. Population update data from Steve Sternberg, "Earth Welcomes 6 Billionth Baby with Trepidation," *USA Today* (October 11, 1999): 5D.

58. "Is Your Company an Extrovert?" *Management Review*, 85 (March 1996): 7.

59. For example, see Len J. Trevino, "Strategic Responses of Mexican Managers to Economic Reform," *Business Horizons*, 41 (May–June 1998): 73–80; Oren Harari, "Lessons from the Swoosh," *Management Review*, 87 (July–August 1998): 39–42; and Andrew Dietrick, "Charging Forth in Deregulated Turf," *Management Review*, 88 (July–August 1999): 62.

60. See Jay B. Barney, "Looking Inside for Competitive Advantage," *Academy of Management Executive*, 9 (November 1995): 49–61; and W. Jack Duncan, Peter M. Ginter, and Linda E. Swayne, "Competitive Advantage and Internal Organizational Assessment," *Academy of Management Executive*, 12 (August 1998): 6–16.

61. Adapted from Andrew Bartmess and Keith Cerny, "Building Competitive Advantage Through a Global Network of Capabilities," *California Management Review*, 35 (Winter 1993): 78–103. Also see Kenneth E. Marino, "Developing Consensus on Firm Competencies and Capabilities," *Academy of Management Executive*, 10 (August 1996): 40–51; Peter Cappelli and Anne Crocker-Hefter, "Distinctive Human Resources Are Firms' Core Competencies," *Organizational Dynamics*, 24 (Winter 1996): 7–22; David A. Nadler and Michael L. Tushman, "The Organization of the Future: Strategic Imperatives and Core Competencies for the 21st Century," *Organizational Dynamics*, 28 (Summer 1999): 45–60; and Louisa Wah, "Thriving on Diversification," *Management Review*, 88 (July–August 1999): 8.

62. "GE Goal: Keep It Simple," *USA Today* (February 28, 1995): 6B. Also see Alan M. Webber, "Are You on Digital Time?" *Fast Company*, no. 22 (March 1999): 114–118.

63. See Raymond L. Manganelli and Mark M. Klein, "A Framework for Reengineering," *Management Review*, 83 (June 1994): 10–16; J. Robb Dixon, Peter Arnold, Janelle Heineke, Jay S. Kim, and Paul Mulligan, "Business Process Reengineering: Improving in New Strategic Directions," *California Management Review*, 36 (Summer 1994): 93–108; Rahul Jacob, "The Struggle to Create an Organization for the 21st Century," *Fortune* (April 3, 1995): 90–99; Dutch Holland and Sanjiv Kumar, "Getting Past the Obstacles to Successful Reengineering," *Business Horizons*, 38 (May–June 1995): 79–85; and David Stamps, "Over the Line?" *Training*, 33 (January 1996): 57–64.

64. According to Henry Mintzberg, there are four reasons why organizations need strategies: (1) to set direction; (2) to focus effort of contributors; (3) to define the organization; and (4) to provide consistency. For more, see Henry Mintzberg, "The Strategy Concept II: Another Look at Why Organizations Need Strategies," *California Management Review*, 30 (Fall 1987): 25–32.

65. Waldron Berry, "Beyond Strategic Planning," *Managerial Planning*, 29 (March–April 1981): 14.

66. Charles H. Roush Jr., and Ben C. Ball Jr., "Controlling the Implementation of Strategy," *Managerial Planning*, 29 (November–December 1980): 4.

67. Donald C. Hambrick and Albert A. Cannella Jr., "Strategy Implementation as Substance and Selling," *Academy of Management Executive*, 3 (November 1989): 282–283. Another good discussion of strategic implementation may be found in Dale D. McConkey, "Planning in a Changing Environment," *Business Horizons*, 31 (September–October 1988): 64–72.

68. William D. Guth and Ian C. Macmillian, "Strategy Implementation Versus Middle Management Self-Interest," *Strategic Management Journal*, 7 (July–August 1986): 321.

69. See Steven W. Floyd and Bill Wooldridge, "Managing Strategic Consensus: The Foundation of Effective Implementation," *Academy of Management Executive*, 6 (November 1992): 27–39; Steven W. Floyd and Bill Wooldridge, "Dinosaurs or Dynamos? Recognizing Middle Management's Strategic Role," *Academy of Management Executive*, 8 (November 1994): 47–57; and Christopher McDermott and Kenneth K. Boyer, "Strategic Consensus: Marching to the Beat of a Different Drummer?" *Business Horizons*, 42 (July–August 1999): 21–28.

70. See Michael Goold and John J. Quinn, "The Paradox of Strategic Controls," *Strategic Management Journal*, 11 (January 1990): 43–57; and Georg Kellinghusen and Klaus Wubbenhorst,

"Strategic Control for Improved Performance," *Long Range Planning*, 23 (June 1990): 30–40.

71. See Vasudevan Ramanujan and N. Venkatraman, "Planning and Performance: A New Look at an Old Question," *Business Horizons*, 30 (May–June 1987): 19–25.

72. See Andy Hines, "A Checklist for Evaluating Forecasts," *The Futurist*, 29 (November–December 1995): 20–24.

73. See Peter Bishop, "Thinking like a Futurist," *The Futurist*, 32 (June–July 1998): 39–42; and Mark A. Moon, John T. Mentzer, Carlo D. Smith, and Michael S. Garver, "Seven Keys to Better Forecasting," *Business Horizons*, 41 (September–October 1998): 44–52.

74. An excellent overview of forecasting techniques may be found in David M. Georgoff and Robert G. Murdick, "Manager's Guide to Forecasting," *Harvard Business Review*, 64 (January–February 1986): 110–120.

75. Based on C. W. J. Granger, *Forecasting in Business and Economics* (New York: Academic Press, 1980), pp. 6–10.

76. See John T. Mentzer, Carol C. Bienstock, and Kenneth B. Kahn, "Benchmarking Sales Forecasting Management," *Business Horizons*, 42 (May–June 1999): 48–56.

77. "Pokémon Patriarch," *Business Week* (January 10, 2000): 70.

78. Steven P. Schnaars, "How to Develop and Use Scenarios," *Long Range Planning*, 20 (February 1987): 106.

79. For example, see Kathy Moyer, "Scenario Planning at British Airways—A Case Study," *Long Range Planning*, 29 (April 1996): 172–181. Interesting scenarios for the U.S. Social Security system are presented in Aaron Bernstein, "Social Security: Is the Sky Really Falling?" *Business Week* (February 10, 1997): 92.

80. Peter Coy and Neil Gross, "21 Ideas for the 21st Century," *Business Week* (August 30, 1999): 82.

81. For more, see Charles M. Perrottet, "Scenarios for the Future," *Management Review*, 85 (January 1996): 43–46; Michel Godet and Fabrice Roubelat, "Creating the Future: The Use and Misuse of Scenarios," *Long Range Planning*, 29 (April 1996): 164–171; James M. Kouzes and Barry Z. Posner, "Envisioning Your Future: Imagining Ideal Scenarios," *The Futurist*, 30 (May–June 1996): 14–19; and Robert Baldock, "5 Futures," *Management Review*, 88 (October 1999): 52–55.

82. For interesting reading about Internet surveys, see Bruce Horovitz, "High Level of Comfort Leads to Truthful Research Worth a Mint," *USA Today* (May 17, 1999): 1A–2A. Also see "Do Americans Trust Media Polls?" *USA Today* (May 18, 1999): 1A.

83. See Nancy Chambers, "The Really Long View," *Management Review*, 87 (January 1998): 10–15; Karen Thomas, "Fashion Understatement: That's So 5 Minutes Ago," *USA Today* (March 23, 1999): 1D–2D; and H. Donald Hopkins, "Using History for Strategic Problem-Solving: The Harley-Davidson Effect," *Business Horizons*, 42 (March–April 1999): 52–60.

84. See Wendy Zellner, "Chrysler's Next Generation," *Business Week* (December 19, 1988): 52–57.

Chapter 8

Opening Quotation "Ruthann Quindlen," *Fast Company*, no. 25 (June 1999): 104.

Opening Case Excerpted from Eryn Brown, "Scaling a Vertical Learning Curve," *Fortune* (January 24, 2000): 96–98. © 2000 Time Inc. Reprinted by permission.

Closing Case "Caring Enough," *Selling Power*, 19 (June 1999): 18. Copyright 1999–2000 by *Selling Power*. Reprinted by permission of the publisher.

1. Steve Rosenbush, "AT&T Boss Cables the Future," *USA Today* (November 2, 1998): 2B. For more, see Andy Reinhardt, "The Main Event: Bernie vs. Mike," *Business Week* (October 18, 1999): 34–35.

2. Morgan W. McCall Jr. and Robert E. Kaplan, *Whatever It Takes: The Realities of Managerial Decision Making*, 2nd ed. (Englewood Cliffs, N.J.: Prentice-Hall, 1990), p. 5.

3. Paul Hoversten, "Backers Hope Amenities Will Quiet Critics," *USA Today* (February 22, 1995): 2A.

4. Michael Parrish, "Former Arco Chief Still Gambling on Oil Strikes," *Los Angeles Times* (September 21, 1993): D1.

5. See Irwin Ross, "Chrysler on the Brink," *Fortune* (February 9, 1981): 38–42.

6. Justin Martin, "Tomorrow's CEOs," *Fortune* (June 24, 1996): 90.

7. See, for example, Thomas F. O'Boyle, "Profit at Any Cost," *Business Ethics*, 13 (March–April 1999): 13–16.

8. Mark Clayton, "The Ink Is Red at Canadian Mills," *The Christian Science Monitor* (March 11, 1992): 7.

9. See Elke U. Weber, Christopher K. Hsee, and Joanna Sokolowska, "What Folklore Tells Us About Risk and Risk Taking: Cross-Cultural Comparisons of American, German, and Chinese Proverbs," *Organizational Behavior and Human Decision Processes*, 75 (August 1998): 170–186; Robert Simons, "How Risky Is Your Company?" *Harvard Business Review*, 77 (May–June 1999): 85–94; and Gerry McNamara and Philip Bromiley, "Risk and Return in Organizational Decision Making," *Academy of Management Journal*, 42 (June 1999): 330–339.

10. Game theory is discussed in Rob Norton, "Winning the Game of Business," *Fortune* (February 6, 1995): 36. Also see Kevin Maney, "Higher Math Delivers Formula for Success," *USA Today* (December 31, 1997): 1B–2B.

11. Based on Keith H. Hammonds, "Cranberries Rot, So Does the Stock," *Business Week* (December 19, 1994): 42.

12. Coping with uncertainty is discussed in Michael J. Mandel, "The High-Risk Society," *Business Week* (October 28, 1996): 86–94.

13. For an informative discussion see Weston H. Agor, "Managing Brain Skills: The Last Frontier," *Personnel Administrator*, 32 (October 1987): 54–60.

14. See Thomas Petzinger Jr., "Gary Klein Studies How Our Minds Dictate Those 'Gut Feelings,'" *The Wall Street Journal* (August 7, 1998): B1; Vikas Anand, Charles C. Manz, and William H. Glick, "An Organizational Memory Approach to Information Management," *Academy of Management Review*, 23 (October 1998): 796–809; Kent W. Seibert, "Reflection-in-Action: Tools for Cultivating On-the-Job Learning Conditions," *Organizational Dynamics*, 27 (Winter 1999): 54–65; and Lane Jennings, "Intuition in Decision Making," *The Futurist*, 33 (March 1999): 44.

15. For research on decision styles, see Susanne G. Scott and Reginald A. Bruce, "Decision-Making Style: The Development and Assessment of a New Measure," *Educational and Psychological Measurement*, 55 (October 1995): 818–831; and Stacey M. Whitecotton, D. Elaine Sanders, and Kathleen B. Norris, "Improving Predictive Accuracy with a Combination of Human Intuition and Mechanical Decision Aids," *Organizational Behavior and Human Decision Processes*, 76 (December 1998): 325–348.

16. See Bevery Geber, "A Quick Course in Decision Science," *Training*, 25 (April 1988): 54–55; Alan E. Singer, Steven Lysonski, Ming Singer, and David Hayes, "Ethical Myopia: The Case of 'Framing' by Framing," *Journal of Business Ethics*, 10 (January 1991): 29–36; and Glen Whyte, "Decision Failures: Why They Occur and How to

Prevent Them," *Academy of Management Executive*, 5 (August 1991): 23–31.

17. Irwin P. Levin, Sara K. Schnittjer, and Shannon L. Thee, "Information Framing Effects in Social and Personal Decisions," *Journal of Experimental Social Psychology*, 24 (November 1988): 527. For additional research evidence, see Michael J. Zickar and Scott Highhouse, "Looking Closer at the Effects of Framing on Risky Choice: An Item Response Theory Analysis," *Organizational Behavior and Human Decision Processes*, 75 (July 1998): 75–91; and Vikas Mittal and William T. Ross Jr., "The Impact of Positive and Negative Affect and Issue Framing on Issue Interpretation and Risk Taking," *Organizational Behavior and Human Decision Processes*, 76 (December 1998): 298–324.

18. For good background reading, see Barry M. Staw and Jerry Ross, "Knowing When to Pull the Plug," *Harvard Business Review*, 65 (March–April 1987): 68–74; and Barry M. Staw and Jerry Ross, "Understanding Behavior in Escalation Situations," *Science*, 246 (October 13, 1989): 216–220. Also see William S. Silver and Terence R. Mitchell, "The Status Quo Tendency in Decision Making," *Organizational Dynamics*, 18 (Spring 1990): 34–46.

19. See Joel Brockner, "The Escalation of Commitment to a Failing Course of Action: Toward Theoretical Progress," *Academy of Management Review*, 17 (January 1992): 39–61; Beth Dietz-Uhler, "The Escalation of Commitment in Political Decision-Making Groups: A Social Identity Approach," *European Journal of Social Psychology*, 26 (July–August 1996): 611–629; Jennifer L. DeNicolis and Donald A. Hantula, "Sinking Shots and Sinking Costs? Or, How Long Can I Play in the NBA?" *Academy of Management Executive*, 10 (August 1996): 66–67; and Marc D. Street and William P. Anthony, "A Conceptual Framework Establishing the Relationship Between Groupthink and Escalating Commitment Behavior," *Small Group Research*, 28 (May 1997): 267–293.

20. For related research evidence, see Itamar Simonson and Barry M. Staw, "Deescalation Strategies: A Comparison of Techniques for Reducing Commitment to Losing Courses of Action," *Journal of Applied Psychology*, 77 (August 1992): 419–426.

21. "Navy Cancels Contract for Attack Planes," *The Christian Science Monitor* (January 9, 1991): 3. Also see Russell Mitchell, "Desperately Seeking an Attack Bomber," *Business Week* (January 21, 1991): 35. Another good case study of escalation can be found in Jerry Ross and Barry M. Staw, "Organizational Escalation and Exit: Lessons from the Shoreham Nuclear Power Plant," *Academy of Management Journal*, 36 (August 1993): 701–732.

22. For an eye-opening story of one investor doomed by escalation of commitment, see Sarah Mahoney, "All the Wrong Moves," *Smart Money* (January 1995): 114–122. Also see Roger O. Crockett, "Why Motorola Should Hang Up on Iridium," *Business Week* (August 30, 1999): 46.

23. Andy Reinhardt, "A Space Venture That's Sputtering," *Business Week* (November 9, 1998): 156.

24. For an interesting exercise, see J. Edward Russo and Paul J. H. Schoemaker, "The Overconfidence Quiz," *Harvard Business Review*, 68 (September–October 1990): 236–237.

25. Decision traps and personal investing are instructively covered in Gary Belsky, "Why Smart People Make Major Money Mistakes," *Money* (July 1995): 76–85; Jason Zweig, "When the Stock Market Plunges . . . Will You Be Brave or Will You Cave?" *Money* (January 1997): 104–113; Brian O'Reilly, "Why Johnny Can't Invest," *Fortune* (November 9, 1998): 173–178; and Jane Bryant Quinn, "Dumb Luck on Wall Street," *Newsweek* (July 5, 1999): 45.

26. An excellent resource book is James G. March, *A Primer on Decision Making: How Decisions Happen* (New York: The Free Press,

1994). Also see Gwen Ortmeyer, "Making Better Decisions Faster," *Management Review*, 85 (June 1996): 53–56.

27. For example, see Herbert A. Simon, *The New Science of Management Decision*, rev. ed. (Englewood Cliffs, N.J.: Prentice-Hall, 1977), p. 40. Also see James W. Dean Jr. and Mark P. Sharfman, "Does Decision Process Matter? A Study of Strategic Decision-Making Effectiveness," *Academy of Management Journal*, 39 (April 1996): 368–396; Jerre L. Stead, "Whose Decision Is It, Anyway?" *Management Review*, 88 (January 1999): 13; Anna Muoio, "All the Right Moves," *Fast Company*, no. 24 (May 1999): 192–200; and Brian Palmer, "Click Here for Decisions," *Fortune* (May 10, 1999): 153–156.

28. Andrew S. Grove, *High Output Management* (New York: Random House, 1983), p. 98.

29. Simon, *The New Science of Management Decision*, p. 46.

30. See David R. A. Skidd, "Revisiting Bounded Rationality," *Journal of Management Inquiry*, 1 (December 1992): 343–347; and March, *A Primer on Decision Making*, pp. 8–9.

31. See Charles R. Schwenk, "The Use of Participant Recollection in the Modeling of Organizational Decision Processes," *Academy of Management Review*, 10 (July 1985): 496–503. Also see the discussion of "adaptive decision making" in Amitai Etzioni, "Humble Decision Making," *Harvard Business Review*, 67 (July–August 1989): 122–126; and Janet Barnard, "Successful CEOs Talk About Decision Making," *Business Horizons*, 35 (September–October 1992): 70–74.

32. Chester I. Barnard, *The Functions of the Executive* (Cambridge, Mass.: Harvard University Press, 1938), p. 190. Also see Susan S. Kirschenbaum, "Influence of Experience on Information-Gathering Strategies," *Journal of Applied Psychology*, 77 (June 1992): 343–352.

33. Jeffrey Hsu and Tony Lockwood, "Collaborative Computing," *Byte*, 18 (March 1993): 113. Also see Anthony M. Townsend, Michael E. Whitman, and Anthony R. Hendrickson, "Computer Support System Adds Power to Group Processes," *HRMagazine*, 40 (September 1995): 87–91.

34. Catherine Romano, "The Power of Collaboration: Untapped," *Management Review*, 86 (January 1997): 7. See Jennifer Hedlund, Daniel R. Ilgen, and John R. Hollenbeck, "Decision Accuracy in Computer-Mediated Versus Face-to-Face Decision-Making Teams," *Organizational Behavior and Human Decision Processes*, 76 (October 1998): 30–47.

35. George P. Huber, *Managerial Decision Making* (Glenview, Ill.: Scott, Foresman, 1980), pp. 141–142. Also see Michael Pacanowsky, "Team Tools for Wicked Problems," *Organizational Dynamics*, 23 (Winter 1995): 36–51.

36. Ronald Henkoff, "A Whole New Set of Glitches for Digital's Robert Palmer," *Fortune* (August 19, 1996): 193.

37. See Steven G. Rogelberg, Janet L. Barnes-Farrell, and Charles A. Lowe, "The Stepladder Technique: An Alternative Group Structure Facilitating Effective Group Decision Making," *Journal of Applied Psychology*, 77 (October 1992): 730–737; Steven W. Floyd and Bill Wooldridge, "Managing Strategic Consensus: The Foundation of Effective Implementation," *Academy of Management Executive*, 6 (November 1992): 27–39; James R. Larson Jr., Caryn Christensen, Timothy M. Franz, and Ann S. Abbott, "Diagnosing Groups: The Pooling, Management, and Impact of Shared and Unshared Case Information in Team-Based Medical Decision Making," *Journal of Personality and Social Psychology*, 75 (July 1998): 93–108; and Daniel P. Forbes and Francis J. Milliken, "Cognition and Corporate Governance: Understanding Boards of Directors as Strategic Decision-Making Groups," *Academy of Management Review*, 24 (July 1999): 489–505.

38. See Priscilla M. Elsass and Laura M. Graves, "Demographic Diversity in Decision-Making Groups: The Experiences of Women and People of Color," *Academy of Management Review*, 22 (October 1997): 946–973; and Katherine Hawkins and Christopher B. Power, "Gender Differences in Questions Asked During Small Decision-Making Group Discussions," *Small Group Research*, (April 1999): 235–256.

39. See Gayle W. Hill, "Group Versus Individual Performance: Are N + 1 Heads Better than One?" *Psychological Bulletin*, 91 (May 1982): 517–539. Also see John P. Wanous and Margaret A. Youtz, "Solution Diversity and the Quality of Group Decisions," *Academy of Management Journal*, 29 (March 1986): 149–158; and Warren Watson, Larry K. Michaelsen, and Walt Sharp, "Member Competence, Group Interaction, and Group Decision Making: A Longitudinal Study," *Journal of Applied Psychology*, 76 (December 1991): 803–809.

40. A good historical perspective of creativity can be found in Michael Michalko, "Thinking like a Genius," *The Futurist*, 32 (May 1998): 21–25.

41. Based on discussion in N. R. F. Maier, Mara Julius, and James Thurber, "Studies in Creativity: Individual Differences in the Storing and Utilization of Information," *The American Journal of Psychology*, 80 (December 1967): 492–519. Also see Robert Drazin, Mary Ann Glynn, and Robert K. Kazanjian, "Multilevel Theorizing About Creativity in Organizations: A Sensemaking Perspective," *Academy of Management Review*, 24 (April 1999): 286–307; Jack Gordon, "John Cleese on Creativity," *Training*, 36 (April 1999): 34–41; and Marlene Piturro, "Mindshift," *Management Review*, 88 (May 1999): 46–51.

42. Sidney J. Parnes, "Learning Creative Behavior," *The Futurist*, 18 (August 1984): 30–31 (emphasis added). Additional informative reading on creativity may be found in Curtis Sittenfeld, "What's the Big Idea?" *Fast Company*, no. 23 (April 1999): 44–46; Bill Costello, "Make Money by Thinking the Unthinkable," *The Futurist*, 33 (May 1999): 30–34; Kim Kiser, "Lessons from Leonardo," *Training*, 36 (June 1999): 34–40; and Tina DeSalvo, "Unleash the Creativity in Your Organization," *HRMagazine*, 44 (June 1999): 154–164.

43. See Arthur Koestler, *The Act of Creation* (London: Hutchinson, 1969), p. 27.

44. See James L. Adams, *Conceptual Blockbusting* (San Francisco: Freeman, 1974), p. 35.

45. See Charles R. Day Jr., "What a Dumb Idea," *Industry Week* (January 2, 1989): 27–28; and "In Search of Oink," *Management Review*, 88 (January 1999): 32–36.

46. Minda Zetlin, "Nurturing Nonconformists," *Management Review*, 88 (October 1999): 30.

47. John Byrne, "The Search for the Young and Gifted," *Business Week* (October 4, 1999): 108. Also see Ronald Grover, "Disney's Mickey Mensa Club," *Business Week* (March 8, 1999): 108, 110; and Chuck Salter, "We're Not Blue, and We're Not Red. We're Purple. We're the Best of Both Worlds," *Fast Company*, no. 23 (April 1999): 130–144.

48. See Ken Lizotte, "A Creative State of Mind," *Management Review*, 87 (May 1998): 15–17; Alexander Hiam, "Obstacles to Creativity—And How You Can Remove Them," *The Futurist*, 32 (October 1998): 30–34; and "Basil Fawlty, Manager" *Newsweek* (February 15, 1999): 47.

49. For example, see Pat Dillon, "Failure IS an Option," *Fast Company*, no. 22 (February–March 1999): 154–171.

50. Joseph V. Anderson, "Creativity and Play: A Systematic Approach to Managing Innovation," *Business Horizons*, 37 (March–April 1994): 80–85; and Frank Boruch and Monica Boruch, "Your Work Can Be Child's Play," *HRMagazine*, 40 (August 1995): 60–64.

51. List adapted from Roger von Oech, *A Whack on the Side of the Head* (N. P.: Warner Books, 1983). Reprinted by permission.

52. Huber, *Managerial Decision Making*, p. 12.

53. Peter F. Drucker, *The Practice of Management* (New York: Harper & Row, 1954), p. 531.

54. A good typology of business problems is discussed in Tom Kramlinger, "A Trainer's Guide to Business Problems," *Training*, 30 (March 1993): 47–50.

55. Louis S. Richman, "How to Get Ahead in America," *Fortune* (May 16, 1994): 48.

56. For an empirical classification of organizational problems, see David A. Cowan, "Developing a Classification Structure of Organizational Problems: An Empirical Investigation," *Academy of Management Journal*, 33 (June 1990): 366–390.

57. Adapted from Huber, *Managerial Decision Making*, pp. 13–15.

58. Marshall Sashkin and Kenneth J. Kiser, *Total Quality Management* (Seabrook, Md.: Ducochon Press, 1991), p. 153.

59. Adams, *Conceptual Blockbusting*, p. 7.

60. See Bob Filipczak, "Are We Having Fun Yet?" *Training*, 32 (April 1995): 48–56.

61. A good update on brainstorming is Ron Zemke, "In Search of . . . Good Ideas," *Training*, 30 (January 1993): 46–52. Also see Michael W. Kramer, Chao Lan Kuo, and John C. Dailey, "The Impact of Brainstorming Techniques on Subsequent Group Processes: Beyond Generating Ideas," *Small Group Research*, 28 (May 1997): 218–242; Paul Lukas, "The Ultimate Company Town," *Fortune* (February 15, 1999): 48; Janet Kornblum, "Idealab Forecast: Brainstormy," *USA Today* (June 8, 1999): 1B–2B; and Christopher Caggiano, "The Right Way to Brainstorm," *Inc.*, 21 (July 1999): 94.

62. For related research, see John J. Sosik, Bruce J. Avolio, and Surinder S. Kahai, "Inspiring Group Creativity: Comparing Anonymous and Identified Electronic Brainstorming," *Small Group Research*, 29 (February 1998): 3–31.

63. See Bill Meyers, "Inventive Artist Sculpts in Water," *USA Today* (May 14, 1999): 10B; Chris Woodyard, "Automakers' Creative Teams Have Designs on Outside Work," *USA Today* (August 18, 1999): 14B; and Jim Holt, "Creative Togetherness," *Management Review*, 88 (October 1999): 15.

64. See Russell L. Ackoff, "The Art and Science of Mess Management," *Interfaces*, 11 (February 1981): 20–26. Also see Russell L. Ackoff, *Management in Small Doses* (New York: Wiley, 1986), pp. 102–103.

65. See March, *A Primer on Decision Making*, p. 18; and Gina Imperato, "When Is 'Good Enough' Good Enough?" *Fast Company*, no. 26 (July–August 1999): 52.

66. March, *A Primer on Decision Making*, p. 22.

67. James B. Treece, "Shaking Up Detroit," *Business Week* (August 14, 1989): 78.

68. Paul Hawken, "Problems, Problems," *Inc.*, 9 (September 1987): 24.

Chapter 9

Opening Quotation Kevin Freiberg and Jackie Freiberg, *Nuts! Southwest Airlines' Crazy Recipe for Business and Personal Success* (Austin, Texas: Bard Press, 1996), p. 155.

Opening Case Bob Filipczak, "The CEO and the 'Learning Organization.'" Reprinted with permission from the June 1996 issue of *Training* magazine. Copyright 1996. Lakewood Publications, Minneapolis, Minn. All rights reserved. Not for resale.

Closing Case   Republished with permission of *The Wall Street Journal* from "A Software Star Sees Its 'Family' Culture Turn Dysfunctional," by Quentin Hardy, *The Wall Street Journal* (May 5, 1999). Permission conveyed through Copyright Clearance Center, Inc.

1. See B. J. Hodge, William P. Anthony, and Lawrence M. Gales, *Organization Theory: A Strategic Approach*, 5th ed. (Upper Saddle River, N.J.: Prentice-Hall, 1996), p. 10.

2. Adapted from Edgar H. Schein, *Organizational Psychology*, 3rd ed. (Englewood Cliffs, N.J.: Prentice-Hall, 1980), pp. 12–15.

3. See Adam Smith, *The Wealth of Nations* (New York: Modern Library, 1937), p. 7.

4. For example, see Jay R. Galbraith and Edward E. Lawler III, "Effective Organizations: Using the New Logic of Organizing," in *Organizing for the Future: The New Logic for Managing Complex Organizations*, eds. Jay R. Galbraith, Edward E. Lawler III, and Associates (San Francisco: Jossey-Bass, 1993), pp. 293–294. Related research is reported in Kees van den Bos, Henk A. M. Wilke, and E. Allan Lind, "When Do We Need Procedural Fairness? The Role of Trust in Authority," *Journal of Personality and Social Psychology*, 75 (December 1998): 1449–1458.

5. Elliot Jaques, "In Praise of Hierarchy," *Harvard Business Review*, 68 (January–February 1990): 127.

6. For an interesting biography of Henry Ford, see Ann Jardim, *The First Henry Ford: A Study in Personality and Business Leadership* (Cambridge, Mass.: MIT Press, 1970), p. 40.

7. This classification scheme is adapted from Peter M. Blau and William R. Scott, *Formal Organizations* (San Francisco: Chandler, 1962).

8. Nonprofit service organizations are profiled in Bernard A. Nagel and Perry Pascarella, "The Service-Profit Paradox," *Management Review*, 86 (December 1997): 16–19; and Cheryl Dahle, "Do-Gooders Need Not Apply," *Fast Company*, no. 25 (June 1999): 50, 52.

9. David Stamps, "Knights of the Hook and Ladder," *Training*, 35 (June 1998): 46. Also see "Reuben Greenberg," *Fast Company*, no. 24 (May 1999): 104–105.

10. For a real-life version of this story, see Lynn Henning, "Catau Still Enjoys Tying One On," *The Detroit News* (July 4, 1999): 8D.

11. James G. March, *Handbook of Organizations* (Chicago: Rand McNally, 1965), p. ix.

12. For recent research, see Sydney Finkelstein and Richard A. D'Aveni, "CEO Duality as a Double-Edged Sword: How Boards of Directors Balance Entrenchment Avoidance and Unity of Command," *Academy of Management Journal*, 37 (October 1994): 1079–1108.

13. Drawn from Max Weber, *The Theory of Social and Economic Organization*, trans. A. M. Henderson and Talcott Parsons (New York: Oxford University Press, 1947). A critique based on the claim that Weber's work was mistranslated can be found in Richard M. Weiss, "Weber on Bureaucracy: Management Consultant or Political Theorist?" *Academy of Management Review*, 8 (April 1983): 242–248.

14. For a more detailed discussion, consult Warren G. Bennis, *Changing Organizations* (New York: McGraw-Hill, 1966), pp. 4–5.

15. For an excellent critique of modern bureaucracies, see Ralph P. Hummel, *The Bureaucratic Experience*, 3rd ed. (New York: St. Martin's, 1987).

16. See Paul Jarley, Jack Fiorito, and John Thomas Delaney, "A Structural Contingency Approach to Bureaucracy and Democracy in U.S. National Unions," *Academy of Management Journal*, 40 (August 1997): 831–861.

17. See, for example, Brian Dumaine, "The Bureaucracy Busters," *Fortune* (June 17, 1991): 36–50. Also see Craig J. Cantoni, "Eliminating

Bureaucracy—Roots and All," *Management Review*, 82 (December 1993): 30–33; Gifford Pinchot and Elizabeth Pinchot, "Beyond Bureaucracy," *Business Ethics*, 8 (March–April 1994): 26–29; and Oren Harari, "Let the Computers Be the Bureaucrats," *Management Review*, 85 (September 1996): 57–60.

18. Chester I. Barnard, *The Functions of the Executive* (Cambridge, Mass.: Harvard University Press, 1938), p. 165.

19. Charles Perrow, "The Short and Glorious History of Organizational Theory," *Organizational Dynamics*, 2 (Summer 1973): 4.

20. See Alan P. Brache and Geary A. Rummler, "Managing an Organization as a System," *Training*, 34 (February 1997): 68–74; Toby J. Tetenbaum, "Shifting Paradigms: From Newton to Chaos," *Organizational Dynamics*, 26 (Spring 1998): 21–32; and Rosabeth Moss Kanter, "Managing for Long-Term Success," *The Futurist*, 32 (August–September 1998): 43–45.

21. Stratford Sherman, "Andy Grove: How Intel Makes Spending Pay Off," *Fortune* (February 22, 1993): 58. Also see Julia Flynn, "The Biology of Business," *Business Week* (July 14, 1997): 11.

22. Fremont E. Kast and James E. Rosenzweig, *Organization and Management: A Systems and Contingency Approach*, 3rd ed. (New York: McGraw-Hill, 1979), p. 103. An excellent glossary of open-system terms can be found on page 102 of this source.

23. See Stephen Baker, "The Minimill That Acts like a Biggie," *Business Week* (September 30, 1996): 100, 104; and Dean Foust, "Nucor: Meltdown in the Corner Office," *Business Week* (June 21, 1999): 37.

24. See Chris Argyris, "The Executive Mind and Double-Loop Learning," *Organizational Dynamics*, 11 (Autumn 1982): 4–22; and Chris Argyris, "Teaching Smart People How to Learn," *Harvard Business Review*, 69 (May–June 1991): 99–109.

25. See Peter M. Senge, *The Fifth Discipline: The Art and Practice of the Learning Organization* (New York: Doubleday, 1990); Donna J. Abernathy, "Leading Edge Learning: Two Views," *Training & Development*, 53 (March 1999): 40–42; Louisa Wah, "Making Knowledge Stick," *Management Review*, 88 (May 1999): 24–29; and Robert J. Flanagan, "Knowledge Management in Global Organizations in the 21st Century," *HRMagazine*, HR in the 21st Century, 44, no. 11 (1999): 54–55.

26. David A. Garvin, "Building a Learning Organization," *Harvard Business Review*, 71 (July–August 1993): 78–91. For an extension, see Mary Berry, "Learning 'Next Practices' Generates Revenue," *HRMagazine*, 43 (June 1998): 146–152.

27. David Lei, John W. Slocum, and Robert A. Pitts, "Designing Organizations for Competitive Advantage: The Power of Unlearning and Learning," *Organizational Dynamics*, 27 (Winter 1999): 30. For a different perspective, see "Dee W. Hock," *Fast Company*, no. 26 (July–August 1999): 90.

28. See David Stamps, "Is Knowledge Management a Fad?" *Training*, 36 (March 1999): 36–42; Louisa Wah, "Behind the Buzz," *Management Review*, 88 (April 1999): 16–19, 24–26; Eliezer Geisler, "Harnessing the Value of Experience in the Knowledge-Driven Firm," *Business Horizons*, 42 (May–June 1999): 18–26; and Mary M. Crossan, Henry W. Lane, and Roderick E. White, "An Organizational Learning Framework: From Intuition to Institution," *Academy of Management Review*, 24 (July 1999): 522–537.

29. Kim Cameron, "Critical Questions in Assessing Organizational Effectiveness," *Organizational Dynamics*, 9 (Autumn 1980): 70.

30. Regarding profitability, the concept of long-term return on investment is discussed in Ricardo Ernst and Douglas N. Ross, "The Delta Force Approach to Balancing Long-Run Performance," *Business Horizons*, 36 (May–June 1993): 4–10.

31. Winslow Buxton, "Growth from Top to Bottom," *Management Review*, 88 (July–August 1999): 11.

32. Detailed discussions of alternative models of organizational effectiveness may be found in Kishore Gawande and Timothy Wheeler, "Measures of Effectiveness for Governmental Organizations," *Management Science*, 45 (January 1999): 42–58; and Edward V. McIntyre, "Accounting Choices and EVA," *Business Horizons*, 42 (January–February 1999): 66–72.

33. See Jeffrey Pfeffer, "When It Comes to 'Best Practices'—Why Do Smart Organizations Occasionally Do Dumb Things?" *Organizational Dynamics*, 25 (Summer 1996): 33–44.

34. It is instructive to ponder why companies fall from grace over the years. One tracking device is *Fortune* magazine's annual list of "America's Most Admired Corporations." For example, see Thomas A. Stewart, "America's Most Admired Companies," *Fortune* (March 2, 1998): 70–82.

35. Data from Gene Koretz, "Downsizing's Economic Spin," *Business Week* (December 28, 1998): 30. Also see Gene Koretz, "Will Downsizing Ever Let Up?" *Business Week* (February 16, 1998): 26; Kelley Holland, "Smithkline Pulls Way Back," *Business Week* (February 22, 1999): 45; Gene Koretz, "Quick to Fire and Quick to Hire," *Business Week* (May 31, 1999): 34; and Louisa Wah, "To Downsize or Share the Burden?" *Management Review*, 88 (July–August 1999): 10.

36. Peter Lorange and Robert T. Nelson, "How to Recognize—and Avoid—Organizational Decline," *Sloan Management Review*, 28 (Spring 1987): 41.

37. See Robert I. Sutton and Thomas D'Aunno, "Decreasing Organizational Size: Untangling the Effects of Money and People," *Academy of Management Review*, 14 (April 1989): 194–212.

38. See Kim S. Cameron, David A. Whetten, and Myung U. Kim, "Organizational Dysfunctions of Decline," *Academy of Management Journal*, 30 (March 1987): 126–138.

39. See Thane Peterson, "An Exodus at Apple," *Business Week* (February 24, 1997): 46.

40. See Mark A. Mone, William McKinley, and Vincent L. Barker III, "Organizational Decline and Innovation: A Contingency Framework," *Academy of Management Review*, 23 (January 1998): 115–132; Arthur G. Bedeian and Achilles A. Armenakis, "The Cesspool Syndrome: How Dreck Floats to the Top of Declining Organizations," *Academy of Management Executive*, 12 (February 1998): 58–63; Donald N. Sull, "Why Good Companies Go Bad," *Harvard Business Review*, 77 (July–August 1999): 42–52; and Walter J. Ferrier, Ken G. Smith, and Curtis M. Grimm, "The Role of Competitive Action in Market Share Erosion and Industry Dethronement: A Study of Industry Leaders and Challengers," *Academy of Management Journal*, 42 (August 1999): 372–388.

41. Peter F. Drucker, *Managing the Non-Profit Organization* (New York: HarperCollins, 1990), p. 66.

42. The battle against complacency is discussed in Tim Smart, "GE's Welch: 'Fighting Like Hell to Be No. 1,'" *Business Week* (July 8, 1996): 48; and John P. Kotter, "Kill Complacency," *Fortune* (August 5, 1996): 168–170. Also see Ronald Henkoff, "Growing Your Company: Five Ways to Do It Right!" *Fortune* (November 25, 1996): 78–88.

43. Dori Jones Yang and Andrea Rothman, "Reinventing Boeing," *Business Week* (March 1, 1993): 61.

44. For an update, see David Field, "Finance Chief Turning Profits and Heads at Boeing," *USA Today* (August 12, 1999): 5B.

45. Wayne F. Cascio, "Downsizing: What Do We Know? What Have We Learned?" *Academy of Management Executive*, 7 (February 1993): 95. Three downsizing strategies are discussed in Kim S. Cameron, Sarah J. Freeman, and Aneil K. Mishra, "Best Practices in White-Collar Downsizing: Managing Contradictions," *Academy of Management Executive*, 5 (August 1991): 57–73. Also see Charles R. Eitel, "The Ten Disciplines of Business Turnaround," *Management Review*, 87 (December 1998): 13; James R. Morris, Wayne F. Cascio, and Clifford E. Young, "Downsizing After All These Years: Questions and Answers About Who Did It, How Many Did It, and Who Benefited from It," *Organizational Dynamics*, 27 (Winter 1999): 78–87; and Sherry Kuczynski, "Help! I Shrunk the Company," *HRMagazine*, 44 (June 1999): 40–45.

46. Gene Koretz, ". . . And How It Is Paying Off," *Business Week* (November 25, 1996): 30. For an alternative view, see Gene Koretz, "Big Payoffs from Layoffs," *Business Week* (February 24, 1997): 30.

47. Elizabeth Lesly and Larry Light, "When Layoffs Alone Don't Turn the Tide," *Business Week* (December 7, 1992): 100–101. Also see Ronald Henkoff, "Getting Beyond Downsizing," *Fortune* (January 10, 1994): 58–64.

48. See Janina C. Latack, Angelo J. Kinicki, and Gregory E. Prussia, "An Integrative Process Model of Coping with Job Loss," *Academy of Management Review*, 20 (April 1995): 311–342.

49. For example, see Darcey Spears, "Layoff Ethics," *Business Ethics*, 10 (January–February 1996): 62–65; Barbara Ettorre, "Constructive Downsizing?" *Management Review*, 85 (September 1996): 8; Rick Maurer, "Stop! Downsizing Doesn't Work," *Canadian Manager*, 24 (Spring 1999): 11–13, 25; and Marlene Piturro, "Alternatives to Downsizing," *Management Review*, 88 (October 1999): 37–41.

50. See Jay Stuller, "Why Not 'Inplacement'?" *Training*, 30 (June 1993): 37–41.

51. Michelle Neely Martinez, "To Have and to Hold," *HRMagazine*, 43 (September 1998): 130–139.

52. Eric Schine, "Take the Money and Run—Or Take Your Chances," *Business Week* (August 16, 1993): 28. Also see Pat Wechsler, "AT&T Managers Rush out the Door," *Business Week* (June 15, 1998): 53.

53. Plant-closing legislation and programs are discussed in Angelo Kinicki, Jeffrey Bracker, Robert Kreitner, Chris Lockwood, and David Lemak, "Socially Responsible Plant Closings," *Personnel Administrator*, 32 (June 1987): 116–128.

54. For a good overview, see "Closing Law's Key Provisions," *Nation's Business* (January 1989): 58, 60. Also see Richard A. Starkweather and Cheryl L. Steinbacher, "Job Satisfaction Affects the Bottom Line," *HRMagazine*, 43 (September 1998): 110–112.

55. See Joan Szabo, "Severance Plans Shift Away from Cash," *HRMagazine*, 41 (July 1996): 104–108; and Carolyn Hirschman, "Time for a Change," *HRMagazine*, 43 (August 1998): 81–87.

56. See Shari Caudron, "Teach Downsizing Survivors How to Thrive," *Personnel Journal*, 75 (January 1996): 38–48; and Marc Adams, "Training Employees as Partners," *HRMagazine*, 44 (February 1999): 64–70.

57. See David M. Slipy, "Anthropologist Uncovers Real Workplace Attitudes," *HRMagazine*, 35 (October 1990): 76–79; and David A. Kaplan, "Studying the Gearheads," *Newsweek* (August 3, 1998): 62.

58. This definition is based in part on Linda Smircich, "Concepts of Culture and Organizational Analysis," *Administrative Science Quarterly*, 28 (September 1983): 339–358. For excellent discussions of organizational cultures, see Daniel R. Denison, "What *Is* the Difference Between Organizational Culture and Organizational Climate? A Native's Point of View on a Decade of Paradigm Wars," *Academy of Management Review*, 21 (July 1996): 619–654; Byron Sebastian, "Integrating Local and Corporate Cultures," *HRMagazine*, 41 (September 1996): 114–121; Majken Schultz and

Mary Jo Hatch, "Living with Multiple Paradigms: The Case of Paradigm Interplay in Organizational Culture Studies," *Academy of Management Review*, 21 (April 1996): 529–557; and Michael Hopkins and Tom Richman, "The Culture Wars," *Inc.* Twentieth Anniversary Issue, 21 (May 18, 1999): 107–108.

59. Data from John E. Sheridan, "Organizational Culture and Employee Retention," *Academy of Management Journal*, 35 (December 1992): 1036–1056. For parallel findings, see Shelly Branch, "The 100 Best Companies to Work for in America," *Fortune* (January 11, 1999): 118–144.

60. Peter C. Reynolds, "Imposing a Corporate Culture," *Psychology Today*, 21 (March 1987): 38.

61. Based on Harrison M. Trice and Janice M. Beyer, *The Cultures of Work Organizations* (Englewood Cliffs, N.J.: Prentice-Hall, 1993), pp. 5–8.

62. See, for example, Beverly Geber, "100 Days of Training," *Training*, 36 (January 1999): 62–66; Peter Troiano, "Post-Merger Challenges," *Management Review*, 88 (January 1999): 6; and Robert J. Grossman, "Irreconcilable Differences," *HRMagazine*, 44 (April 1999): 42–48.

63. Thomas A. Stewart, "Company Values that Add Value," *Fortune* (July 8, 1996): 145. © 1996 Time Inc. All rights reserved.

64. See David Dorsey, "The New Spirit of Work," *Fast Company*, no. 16 (August 1998): 125–134; and Jim Collins, "When Good Managers Manage Too Much," *Inc.*, 21 (April 1999): 31–32.

65. Gina Imperato, "MindSpring Does a Mind-Flip," *Fast Company*, no. 22 (February–March 1999): 40. The complete list of nine values can be found in Brad Grimes, "Lessons from MindSpring," *Fortune* (June 21, 1999): 186[C]–186[H].

66. See Steve Rosenbush, "Braced to Best Microsoft, Others," *USA Today* (February 17, 1999): 3B; Ron Lieber, "First Jobs Aren't Child's Play," *Fast Company*, no. 25 (June 1999): 155–171; and Tammy D. Allen, Stacy E. McManus, and Joyce E. A. Russell, "Newcomer Socialization and Stress: Formal Peer Relationships as a Source of Support," *Journal of Vocational Behavior*, 54 (June 1999): 453–470.

67. Alan L. Wilkins, "The Culture Audit: A Tool for Understanding Organizations," *Organizational Dynamics*, 12 (Autumn 1983): 34–35.

68. Rebecca Ganzel, "Putting Out the Welcome Mat," *Training*, 35 (March 1998): 54. Also see Marc Belaiche, "A Well Planned Orientation Makes a Difference," *Canadian Manager*, 24 (Spring 1999): 23–24.

69. For the full *story*, see Robert F. Dennehy, "The Executive as Storyteller," *Management Review*, 88 (March 1999): 40–43; Beverly Kaye and Betsy Jacobson, "True Tales and Tall Tales: The Power of Organizational Storytelling," *Training & Development*, 53 (March 1999): 45–50; and Cathy Olofson, "To Transform Culture, Tap Emotion," *Fast Company*, no. 23 (April 1999): 54.

70. Alan L. Wilkins, "The Creation of Company Cultures: The Role of Stories and Human Resource Systems," *Human Resource Management*, 23 (Spring 1984): 43.

71. Adapted from Terrence E. Deal and Allan A. Kennedy, *Corporate Cultures: The Rites and Rituals of Corporate Life* (Reading, Mass.: Addison-Wesley, 1982), pp. 136–139. Also see Haidee E. Allerton, "Dysfunctional Checklist," *Training & Development*, 53 (June 1999): 10; and Jenny C. McCune, "Sorry, Wrong Executive," *Management Review*, 88 (October 1999): 16–21.

72. Eight tips for maintaining the strength of an organization's culture are presented in Trice and Beyer, *Cultures of Work Organizations*, pp. 378–391. Also see Frank J. Barrett, "Creating Appreciative Learning Cultures," *Organizational Dynamics*, 24 (Autumn 1995): 36–49; and Benjamin Schneider, Arthur P. Brief, and Richard A. Guzzo, "Creating a Climate and Culture for Sustainable Organiza-

tional Change," *Organizational Dynamics*, 24 (Spring 1996): 7–19; and Steve Kaye, "Maximize on Cultural Shifts," *Canadian Manager*, 23 (Winter 1998): 13–15.

Chapter 10

Opening Quotation "Sam Walton in His Own Words," *Fortune* (June 29, 1992): 104.

Opening Case Steve Hamm, "'I'm Trying to Let Other People Dive in Before I Do.'" Reprinted from the May 17, 1999 issue of *Business Week* by special permission. Copyright © 1999 by McGraw-Hill, Inc.

Closing Case Republished with permission of *Inc., The Magazine for Growing Companies* from "Tear Down the Walls" by Nancy K. Austin, *Inc.*, 21 (April 1999). Permission conveyed through Copyright Clearance Center, Inc.

1. See Mark Frankel, "A Clearer View of Windows 2000," *Business Week* (November 8, 1999): 46.

2. For research support, see Terry L. Amburgey and Tina Dacin, "As the Left Foot Follows the Right? The Dynamics of Strategic and Structural Change," *Academy of Management Journal*, 37 (December 1994): 1427–1452.

3. John Hoerr, "Sharpening Minds for a Competitive Edge," *Business Week* (December 17, 1990): 72. Also see Henry Mintzberg, "The Effective Organization: Forces and Forms," *Sloan Management Review*, 32 (Winter 1991): 54–67.

4. An interesting overview is Robert W. Keidel, "Rethinking Organizational Design," *Academy of Management Executive*, 8 (November 1994): 12–30. Also see D. Harold Doty, William H. Glick, and George P. Huber, "Fit, Equifinality, and Organizational Effectiveness: A Test of Two Configurational Theories," *Academy of Management Journal*, 36 (December 1993): 1196–1250.

5. See Tom Burns and G. M. Stalker, *The Management of Innovation* (London: Tavistock, 1961), chap. 5.

6. For a related discussion, see Homa Bahrami, "The Emerging Flexible Organization: Perspectives from Silicon Valley," *California Management Review*, 34 (Summer 1992): 33–52.

7. See John A. Courtright, Gail T. Fairhurst, and L. Edna Rogers, "Interaction Patterns in Organic and Mechanistic Systems," *Academy of Management Journal*, 32 (December 1989): 773–802.

8. Lois Therrien, "McRisky," *Business Week* (October 21, 1991): 115.

9. For example, see Thomas A. Stewart, "3M Fights Back," *Fortune* (February 5, 1996): 94–99.

10. Jenny C. McCune, "The Change Makers," *Management Review*, 88 (May 1999): 17. Also see Peter F. Drucker, "Change Leaders," *Inc.*, 21 (June 1999): 65–72.

11. Additional discussion may be found in Barbara Buell, "For Aldus, Being No. 1 Isn't Enough Anymore," *Business Week* (June 11, 1990): 76–77.

12. For a complete summary of Woodward's findings, see Joan Woodward, *Industrial Organization: Theory and Practice* (London: Oxford University Press, 1965), chap. 4.

13. Adapted from Paul R. Lawrence and Jay W. Lorsch, *Organization and Environment* (Homewood, Ill.: Irwin, 1967), p. 11. One new approach to organizational integration is presented in Eileen M. Van Aken, Dominic J. Monetta, and D. Scott Sink, "Affinity Groups: The Missing Link in Employee Involvement," *Organizational Dynamics*, 22 (Spring 1994): 38–54. Also see Anthony Lee Patti and James Patrick Gilbert, "Collocating New Product Development Teams: Why, When, Where, and How?" *Business Horizons*, 40 (November–December 1997): 59–64; and Gail Edmondson, "Where Science Is More than Skin Deep," *Business Week* (June 28, 1999): 75.

14. Ibid., p. 157.

15. A good update on integration is Susan Albers Mohrman, "Integrating Roles and Structure in the Lateral Organization," in *Organizing for the Future: The New Logic for Managing Complex Organizations*, eds. Jay R. Galbraith, Edward E. Lawler III, and Associates (San Francisco: Jossey-Bass, 1993), pp. 109–141.

16. Cheryl Comeau-Kirschner, "The Push for Profits," *Management Review*, 88 (February 1999): 7.

17. For details, see John E. Ettlie and Ernesto M. Reza, "Organizational Integration and Process Innovation," *Academy of Management Journal* (October 1992): 759–827.

18. See Marco Iansiti, "Shooting the Rapids: Managing Product Development in Turbulent Environments," *California Management Review*, 38 (Fall 1995): 37–58; and David A. Morand, "The Role of Behavioral Formality and Informality in the Enactment of Bureaucratic Versus Organic Organizations," *Academy of Management Review*, 20 (October 1995): 831–872.

19. James D. Thompson, *Organizations in Action* (New York: McGraw-Hill, 1967), p. 59.

20. Based in part on Jay R. Galbraith, *Designing Organizations: An Executive Briefing on Strategy, Structure, and Process* (San Francisco: Jossey-Bass, 1995): pp. 24–37.

21. See, for example, Figure 1 in Steven J. Heyer and Reginald Van Lee, "Rewiring the Corporation," *Business Horizons*, 35 (May–June 1992): 13–22.

22. Catherine Arnst, "A Freewheeling Youngster Named IBM," *Business Week* (May 3, 1993): 136.

23. IBM's turnaround is honored in Stuart Crainer, "The 50 Best Management Saves," *Management Review*, 88 (November 1999): 16–23.

24. Drawn from David W. Myers, "Hilton Shifts Focus to Gaming Operations," *Los Angeles Times* (May 12, 1993): D2.

25. Based on Roger O. Crockett, "Motorola Girds for a Shakeup," *Business Week* (April 13, 1998): 33.

26. Adapted from "Dial 800, Talk to Omaha," *Fortune* (January 29, 1990): 16; Rhonda Richards, "Technology Makes Omaha Hotel-Booking Capital," *USA Today* (April 7, 1994): 4B; and Robert D. Kaplan, *An Empire Wilderness: Travels into America's Future* (New York: Random House, 1998), p. 59.

27. Based on Andy Reinhardt and Seanna Browder, "Fly, Damn It, Fly," *Business Week* (November 9, 1998): 150–156. Also see Wim G. Biemans, "Marketing in the Twilight Zone," *Business Horizons*, 41 (November–December 1998): 69–76.

28. For more, see Michael Hammer and James Champy, *Reengineering the Corporation: A Manifesto for Business Revolution* (New York: HarperCollins, 1993); James Champy, *Reengineering Management: The Mandate for New Leadership* (New York: HarperBusiness, 1995); Dutch Holland and Sanjiv Kumar, "Getting Past the Obstacles to Successful Reengineering," *Business Horizons*, 38 (May–June 1995): 79–85; and Rob Duboff and Craig Carter, "Reengineering from the Outside In," *Management Review*, 84 (November 1995): 42–46.

29. See John A. Byrne, "The Horizontal Corporation," *Business Week* (December 20, 1993): 76–81; and Susan Sonnesyn Brooks, "Managing a Horizontal Revolution," *HRMagazine*, 40 (June 1995): 52–58.

30. Rahul Jacob, "The Struggle to Create an Organization for the 21st Century," *Fortune* (April 3, 1995): 91. For related reading, see Michael H. Martin, "Smart Managing," *Fortune* (February 2, 1998): 149–151; and David Stamps, "Enterprise Training: This Changes *Everything*," *Training*, 36 (January 1999): 40–48.

31. Barbara Buell and Robert D. Hof, "Hewlett-Packard Rethinks Itself," *Business Week* (April 1, 1991): 77.

32. A sample of contingency design research is Richard A. D'Aveni and Anne Y. Ilinitch, "Complex Patterns of Vertical Integration in the Forest Products Industry: Systematic and Bankruptcy Risks," *Academy of Management Journal*, 35 (August 1992): 596–625.

33. For an extensive bibliography on this subject, see David D. Van Fleet and Arthur G. Bedeian, "A History of the Span of Management," *Academy of Management Review*, 2 (July 1977): 356–372.

34. L. Urwick, *The Elements of Administration* (New York: Harper & Row, 1944), pp. 52–53.

35. For details of this study, see James C. Worthy, "Organizational Structure and Employee Morale," *American Sociological Review*, 15 (April 1950): 169–179.

36. Drawn from C. W. Barkdull, "Span of Control—A Method of Evaluation," *Michigan Business Review*, 15 (May 1963): 25–32.

37. William H. Wagel, "Keeping the Organization Lean at Federal Express," *Personnel*, 64 (March 1987): 4–12.

38. Paul Kaestle, "A New Rationale for Organizational Structure," *Planning Review*, 18 (July–August 1990): 22. Also see Robert W. Keidel, "Triangular Design: A New Organizational Geometry," *Academy of Management Executive*, 4 (November 1990): 21–37.

39. Joseph Weber, "A Big Company That Works," *Business Week* (May 4, 1992): 126–127.

40. For an update, see Amy Barrett, "J&J Stops Babying Itself," *Business Week* (September 13, 1999): 95–97.

41. For example, see Jeffrey Schmidt, "Breaking Down Fiefdoms," *Management Review*, 86 (January 1997): 45–49.

42. For a comprehensive research summary on centralization and organizational effectiveness, see George P. Huber, C. Chet Miller, and William H. Glick, "Developing More Encompassing Theories About Organizations: The Centralization-Effectiveness Relationship as an Example," *Organization Science*, 1 (1990): 11–40.

43. Based on William E. Rothschild, "How to Ensure the Continued Growth of Strategic Planning," *Journal of Business Strategy*, 1 (Summer 1980): 11–18.

44. Thomas A. Stewart, "The Search for the Organization of Tomorrow," *Fortune* (May 18, 1992): 97. SBUs at a Korean company are discussed in Laxmi Nakarmi, "Goldstar Is Burning Bright," *Business Week* (September 26, 1994): 129–130.

45. For complete details, see Anil K. Gupta, "SBU Strategies, Corporate-SBU Relations, and SBU Effectiveness in Strategy Implementation," *Academy of Management Journal*, 30 (September 1987): 477–500. Also see V. Govindarajan and Joseph Fisher, "Strategy, Control Systems, and Resource Sharing: Effects on Business-Unit Performance," *Academy of Management Journal*, 33 (June 1990): 259–285.

46. For details, see Meni Koslowsky, "Staff/Line Distinctions in Job and Organizational Commitment," *Journal of Occupational Psychology*, 63 (June 1990): 167–173. Also see Hillel Schmid, "Staff and Line Relationships Revisited: The Case of Community Service Agencies," *Public Personnel Management*, 19 (Spring 1990): 71–83.

47. Jay R. Galbraith and Edward E. Lawler III, "Challenges to the Established Order," in *Organizing for the Future: The New Logic for Managing Complex Organizations*, ed. Jay R. Galbraith, Edward E. Lawler III, and Associates (San Francisco: Jossey-Bass, 1993): p. 6. Also see Thomas A. Stewart, "Yikes! Deadwood Is Creeping Back," *Fortune* (August 18, 1997): 221–222; and "Are You a Partner with Line Management?" *Training*, 36 (January 1999): 26–27.

48. See Louis A. Allen, "The Line-Staff Relationship," *Management Record*, 17 (September 1955): 346–349, 374–376.

49. Ibid., p. 348.

50. For additional suggestions for making the best use of staff, see Edward C. Schleh, "Using Central Staff to Boost Line Initiative," *Management Review*, 65 (May 1976): 17–23.

51. See David I. Cleland, "Why Project Management?" *Business Horizons*, 7 (Winter 1964): 81–88. For a discussion of how project management has evolved into matrix management, see David I. Cleland, "The Cultural Ambience of the Matrix Organization," *Management Review*, 70 (November 1981): 24–28, 37–39; and David I. Cleland, "Matrix Management (Part II): A Kaleidoscope of Organizational Systems," *Management Review*, 70 (December 1981): 48–56.

52. See Thomas A. Stewart, "The Corporate Jungle Spawns a New Species: The Project Manager," *Fortune*, (July 10, 1995): 179–180.

53. For a good update, see Christopher A. Bartlett and Sumantra Ghoshal, "Matrix Management: Not a Structure, a Frame of Mind," *Harvard Business Review*, 68 (July–August 1990): 138–145.

54. An informative description of a successful matrix organization may be found in Ellen Kolton, "Team Players," *Inc.* (September 1984): 140–144.

55. See William F. Joyce, "Matrix Organization: A Social Experiment," *Academy of Management Journal*, 29 (September 1986): 536–561.

56. Drawn from Richard M. Hodgetts, "Leadership Techniques in the Project Organization," *Academy of Management Journal*, 11 (June 1968): 211–219. Also see Jeffrey K. Pinto and O. P. Kharbanda, *Successful Project Management: Leading Your Team to Success* (New York: Van Nostrand Reinhold, 1995).

57. Drawn from Susan G. Turner, Dawn R. Utley, and Jerry D. Westbrook, "Project Managers and Functional Managers: A Case Study of Job Satisfaction in a Matrix Organization," *Project Management Journal*, 29 (September 1998): 11–19.

58. See "An About-Face in TI's Culture," *Business Week* (July 5, 1982): 77.

59. Data from Erik W. Larson and David H. Gobeli, "Matrix Management: Contradictions and Insights," *California Management Review*, 29 (Summer 1987): 126–138. Also see Lawton R. Burns and Douglas R. Wholey, "Adoption and Abandonment of Matrix Management Programs: Effects of Organizational Characteristics and Interorganizational Networks," *Academy of Management Journal*, 36 (February 1993): 106–138; and Richard E. Anderson, "Matrix Redux," *Business Horizons*, 37 (November–December 1994): 6–10.

60. For an interesting distinction between delegation and participation, see Carrie R. Leana, "Power Relinquishment Versus Power Sharing: Theoretical Clarification and Empirical Comparison of Delegation and Participation," *Journal of Applied Psychology*, 72 (May 1987): 228–233. Also see Stephen McIntosh, "Buying Time by Delegating," *HRMagazine*, 36 (October 1991): 47–48.

61. Adapted from Marion E. Haynes, "Delegation: There's More to It than Letting Someone Else Do It!" *Supervisory Management*, 25 (January 1980): 9–15. Three types of delegation—incremental, sequential, and functional—are discussed in William R. Tracey, "Deft Delegation: Multiplying Your Effectiveness," *Personnel*, 65 (February 1988): 36–42. Also see Pinto and Kharbanda, *Successful Project Management*, pp. 103–107.

62. Delegation styles of selected U.S. presidents are examined in Edward J. Mayo and Lance P. Jarvis, "Delegation 101: Lessons from the White House," *Business Horizons*, 31 (September–October 1988): 2–12.

63. Alex Taylor III, "Iacocca's Time of Trouble," *Fortune* (March 14, 1988): 79, 81.

64. Andrew S. Grove, *High Output Management* (New York: Random House, 1983), p. 60. Also see Wilson Harrell, "Your Biggest Mistake," *Success*, 43 (March 1996): 88.

65. A good entrepreneur role model who delegates is profiled in Peter Elstrom, "Casey Coswell's Modem Operandi," *Business Week* (November 11, 1996): 104, 107.

66. For interesting facts about delegating, see "Top Dogs," *Fortune* (September 30, 1996): 189; and Bill Leonard, "Good Assistants Make Managers More Efficient," *HRMagazine*, 44 (February 1999): 12.

67. "How Conservatism Wins in the Hottest Market," *Business Week* (January 17, 1977): 43.

68. Adapted from William H. Newman, "Overcoming Obstacles to Effective Delegation," *Management Review*, 45 (January 1956): 36–41; and from Eugene Raudsepp, "Why Supervisors Don't Delegate," *Supervision*, 41 (May 1979): 12–15. Also see Gary Yukl and Ping Ping Fu, "Determinants of Delegation and Consultation by Managers," *Journal of Organizational Behavior*, 20 (March 1999): 219–232.

69. Practical tips on delegation can be found in Douglas Anderson, "Supervisors and the Hesitate to Delegate Syndrome," *Supervision*, 53 (November 1992): 9–11; and Michael C. Dennis, "Only Superman Didn't Delegate," *Business Credit*, 95 (February 1993): 41.

70. For more on initiative, see Michael Frese, Wolfgang Kring, Andrea Soose, and Jeanette Zempel, "Personal Initiative at Work: Differences between East and West Germany," *Academy of Management Journal*, 39 (February 1996): 37–63; and Alan L. Frohman, "Igniting Organizational Change from Below: The Power of Personal Initiative," *Organizational Dynamics*, 25 (Winter 1997): 39–53.

71. Peter F. Drucker, *Managing the Non-Profit Organization* (New York: HarperCollins, 1990), p. 117. Also see Jim Holt, "Management Master," *Management Review*, 88 (November 1999): 15.

72. See, for example, Warren G. Bennis, *Changing Organizations* (New York: McGraw-Hill, 1966).

73. Quoted in Noel M. Tichy and Stratford Sherman, *Control Your Destiny or Someone Else Will: How Jack Welch Is Making General Electric the World's Most Competitive Corporation* (New York: Doubleday, 1993), p. 21. Also see John A. Byrne, "The Corporation of the Future," *Business Week* (August 31, 1998): 102–106; Robert B. Reich, "The Company of the Future," *Fast Company*, no. 19 (November 1998): 124–150; David A. Nadler and Michael L. Tushman, "The Organization of the Future: Strategic Imperatives and Core Competencies for the 21st Century," *Organizational Dynamics*, 28 (Summer 1999): 45–60; and Ron Ashkenas, "Creating the Boundaryless Organization," *Business Horizons*, 42 (September–October 1999): 5–10.

74. Brian Dumaine, "The New Non-Manager Managers," *Fortune* (February 22, 1993): 80. Also see Leonard R. Sayles, "Doing Things Right: A New Imperative for Middle Managers," *Organizational Dynamics*, 21 (Spring 1993): 5–14.

75. Data from Joseph Weber, "Farewell, Fast Track," *Business Week* (December 10, 1990): 192–200.

76. Data from Alan Farnham, "Straight Talk from a New Boss," *Fortune* (April 19, 1993): 85–86.

77. Data from Ricardo Sookdeo, "Why to Buy Big in Bad Times," *Fortune* (July 27, 1992): 96.

78. Edward E. Lawler III, "Substitutes for Hierarchy," *Organizational Dynamics*, 17 (Summer 1988): 15. For a good critique of hierarchy and teams, see "The Team Troubles That Won't Go Away," *Training*, 31 (August 1994): 25–34.

79. Data from David Woodruff, "Ford Has a Better Idea: Let Someone Else Have the Idea," *Business Week* (April 30, 1990): 116–117. Also see Wendy Zellner, "Go-Go Goliaths," *Business Week* (February 13, 1995): 64–70.

80. See Peter F. Drucker, "The Coming of the New Organization," *Harvard Business Review*, 66 (January–February 1988): 45–53. Teams are also discussed in Lynda McDermott, Bill Waite, and Nolan Brawley, "Putting Together a World-Class Team," *Training & Development*, 53 (January 1999): 47–51; Kim Kiser, "Building a Virtual Team," *Training*, 36 (March 1999): 34; and Donald Gerwin, "Team Empowerment in New Product Development," *Business Horizons*, 42 (July–August 1999): 29–36.

81. See Richard Z. Gooding and John A. Wagner III, "A Meta-Analytic Review of the Relationship Between Size and Performance: The Productivity and Efficiency of Organizations and Their Subunits," *Administrative Science Quarterly*, 30 (December 1985): 462–481; Edward E. Lawler III, "Rethinking Organization Size," *Organizational Dynamics*, 26 (Autumn 1997): 24–35; Charles Handy, *The Hungry Spirit* (New York: Broadway Books, 1998), pp. 107–108; and Oren Harari, "Too Big for Your Own Good?" *Management Review*, 87 (November 1998): 30–32.

82. John A. Byrne, "Is Your Company Too Big?" *Business Week* (March 27, 1989): 92. For more on Parker Hannifin, see Christopher Palmeri, "A Process That Never Ends," *Forbes* (December 21, 1992): 52–55. Small units with Dell Computer Corp. are discussed in Carla Joinson, "Moving at the Speed of Dell," *HRMagazine*, 44 (April 1999): 50–56.

83. Marshall Loeb, "Jack Welch Lets Fly on Budgets, Bonuses, and Buddy Boards," *Fortune* (May 29, 1995): 145.

84. See Gregory G. Dess, Abdul M. A. Rasheed, Kevin J. McLaughlin, and Richard L. Priem, "The New Corporate Architecture," *Academy of Management Executive*, 9 (August 1995): 7–20; Alan Hurwitz, "Organizational Structures for the 'New World Order,'" *Business Horizons*, 39 (May–June 1996): 5–14; and James Brian Quinn, Philip Anderson, and Sydney Finkelstein, "Leveraging Intellect," *Academy of Management Executive*, 10 (August 1996): 7–27.

85. Rosabeth Moss Kanter, "The New Managerial Work," *Harvard Business Review*, 67 (November–December 1989): 92. Also see Anthony M. Townsend, Samuel M. DeMarie, and Anthony R. Hendrickson, "Virtual Teams: Technology and the Workplace of the Future," *Academy of Management Executive*, 12 (August 1998); 17–29; and Russ Forrester and Allan B. Drexler, "A Model for Team-Based Organization Performance," *Academy of Management Executive*, 13 (August 1999): 36–49.

86. A good resource book is William G. Dyer, *Team Building: Current Issues and New Alternatives*, 3rd ed. (Reading, Mass.: Addison-Wesley, 1995).

87. See Gary Hamel and Jeff Sampler, "The E-Corporation," *Fortune* (December 7, 1998): 80–92; Randall J. Alford, "Going Virtual, Getting Real," *Training & Development*, 53 (January 1999): 34–44; William B. Werther Jr., "Structure-Driven Strategy and Virtual Organization Design," *Business Horizons*, 42 (March–April 1999): 13–18; Peter Burrows, "Fast, Cheap, and Ahead of the Pack," *Business Week* (April 5, 1999): 36–37; and C. Bruce Kavan, Carol Stoak Saunders, and Reed E. Nelson, "virtual@virtual.org," *Business Horizons*, 42 (September–October 1999): 73–82.

88. Otis Port, "Customers Move into the Driver's Seat," *Business Week* (October 4, 1999): 104, 106.

89. Data from Jeremy Kahn, "The Fortune Global 500," *Fortune* (August 2, 1999): F-1.

Chapter 11

Opening Quotation John Kenneth Galbraith, "Economic Development," in M. R. Rosenberg, ed., *Quotations for the New Age* (Secaucus, N.J.: Citadel Press, 1978), p. 120.

Opening Case Excerpted from Kenneth Labich, "No More Crude at Texaco," *Fortune* (September 6, 1999): 205–212. © 1999 Time Inc. Reprinted by permission.

Closing Case Republished with permission of *The Wall Street Journal*, from "How Amazon.com Staffs a Juggernaut: It's Not About Résumés," by Carol Hymowitz, *The Wall Street Journal* (May 4, 1999). Permission conveyed through Copyright Clearance Center, Inc.

1. For trends in HR, see Bill Leonard, "What CEOs Want from HR?" *HRMagazine*, 43 (November 1998): 80–86; David P. Lepak and Scott A. Snell, "The Human Resource Architecture: Toward a Theory of Human Capital Allocation and Development," *Academy of Management Review*, 24 (January 1999): 31–48; "HR Departments Gaining Respect," *HRMagazine*, 44 (February 1999): 30; Carla Joinson, "Changing Shapes," *HRMagazine*, 44 (March 1999): 41–48; Martin J. Gannon, Patrick C. Flood, and Jaap Paauwe, "Managing Human Resources in the Third Era: Economic Perspectives," *Business Horizons*, 42 (May–June 1999): 41–47; and Joe Dysart, "Kick Your System Outside," *HRMagazine*, 44 (August 1999): 114–122.

2. Drawn from "Peterson Thrives on HR Challenges," *HRMagazine*, 43 (September 1998): 98, 100.

3. See Fred Luthans, Paul A. Marsnik, and Kyle W. Luthans, "A Contingency Matrix Approach to IHRM," *Human Resource Management*, 36 (Summer 1997): 183–199; and Karen Roberts, Ellen Ernst Kossek, and Cynthia Ozeki, "Managing the Global Workforce: Challenges and Strategies," *Academy of Management Executive*, 12 (November 1998): 93–106.

4. Dean Foust, "Why Federal Express Has Overnight Anxiety," *Business Week* (November 9, 1987): 62–66.

5. Jeffrey B. Arthur, "Effects of Human Resource Systems on Manufacturing Performance and Turnover," *Academy of Management Journal*, 37 (June 1994): 670. Also see Mark A. Huselid, "The Impact of Human Resource Management Practices on Turnover, Productivity, and Corporate Financial Performance," *Academy of Management Journal*, 38 (June 1995): 635–672; Brian Becker and Barry Gerhart, "The Impact of Human Resource Management on Organizational Performance: Progress and Prospects," *Academy of Management Journal*, 39 (August 1996): 779–801; and Mark A. Youndt, Scott A. Snell, James W. Dean Jr., and David P. Lepak, "Human Resource Management, Manufacturing Strategy, and Firm Performance," *Academy of Management Journal*, 39 (August 1996): 836–866.

6. Gerald R. Ferris, ed., *Research in Personnel and Human Resources Management: Strategic Human Resources Management in the Twenty-First Century* (Stamford, Conn.: JAI Press, 1999); and Denise M. Rousseau and Michael B. Arthur, "The Boundaryless Human Resource Function: Building Agency and Community in the New Economic Era," *Organizational Dynamics*, 27 (Spring 1999): 7–18.

7. Stephanie Lawrence, "Voices of HR Experience," *Personnel Journal*, 68 (April 1989): 69.

8. Data from Lin Grensing-Pophal, "Taking Your Seat 'At the Table,'" *HRMagazine*, 44 (March 1999): 90–96.

9. A good overview is Susan E. Jackson and Randall S. Schuler, "Human Resource Planning," *American Psychologist*, 45 (February 1990): 223–239.

10. James W. Walker, "Developing Human Resource Strategies," in *Human Resource Forecasting and Strategy Development*, ed.

Manuel London, Emily S. Bassman, and John P. Fernandez (New York: Quorum Books, 1990), p. 82.

11. See Richard J. Mirabile, "The Power of Job Analysis," *Training*, 27 (April 1990): 70–74.

12. For practical tips on writing good job descriptions, see Stephen F. Mona, "The Job Description," *Association Management*, 43 (February 1991): 33–37. Also see Michael P. Cronin, "Choosing Job Description Software," *Inc.*, 15 (February 1993): 30.

13. Human resource information systems are discussed in James F. LeTart, "A Look at Virtual HR: How Far Behind Am I?" *HRMagazine*, 43 (June 1998): 33–42; and Gary Meyer, "Adaptability and Efficiency Are Key Elements of New HR Systems," *HRMagazine*, 43 (September 1998): 38–44.

14. Jo-Ann C. Dixon, "Tomorrow: No Longer a Day Away," *Management Review*, 86 (February 1997): 6.

15. For excellent material on human resource forecasting, see Manuel London, Emily S. Bassman, and John P. Fernandez, eds., *Human Resource Forecasting and Strategy Development* (New York: Quorum Books, 1990).

16. For example, see Elizabeth J. Hawk and Garrett J. Sheridan, "The Right Staff," *Management Review*, 88 (June 1999): 43–48.

17. For more, see Timothy S. Bland and Sue S. Stalcup, "Build a Legal Employment Application," *HRMagazine*, 44 (March 1999): 129–133. For an update on EEO in Japan, see Emily Thornton, "Make Way for Women with Welding Guns," *Business Week* (April 19, 1999): 54.

18. David A. Brookmire and Amy A. Burton, "A Format for Packaging Your Affirmative Action Program," *Personnel Journal*, 57 (June 1978): 294; William Scheibal, "When Cultures Clash: Applying Title VII Abroad," *Business Horizons*, 38 (September–October 1995): 4–8; and Robert M. Gault and Anne M. Kinnane, "Navigating the Maze of Employment Law," *Management Review*, 85 (February 1996): 9–11.

19. See Marc Hequet, "Out at Work," *Training*, 32 (June 1995): 53–58; Dale Kurschner, "The Right to Be Oneself," *Business Ethics*, 10 (May–June 1996): 29; and Kenneth A. Kovach and Peter E. Millspaugh, "Employment Nondiscrimination Act: On the Cutting Edge of Public Policy," *Business Horizons*, 39 (July–August 1996): 65–73.

20. See Charlene Marmer Solomon, "Frequently Asked Questions About Affirmative Action," *Personnel Journal*, 74 (August 1995): 61; and Catherine Yang and Mike McNamee, "A Hand Up, but Not a Handout," *Business Week* (March 27, 1995): 70, 72.

21. For instructive reading on EEO/AAP, see Jere W. Morehead and Peter J. Shedd, "Civil Rights and Affirmative Action: Revolution or Fine-Tuning?" *Business Horizons*, 33 (September–October 1990): 53–60; James P. Pinkerton, "Why Affirmative Action Won't Die," *Fortune* (November 13, 1995): 191–198; and Teresa Brady, "A New Twist on the 'Old' Age Discrimination Act," *Management Review*, 85 (December 1996): 38–39.

22. For related discussion, see Reginald D. Dickson, "The Business of Equal Opportunity," *Harvard Business Review*, 70 (January–February 1992): 46–53; "Debate: Can Equal Opportunity Be Made More Equal?" *Harvard Business Review*, 70 (March–April 1992): 138–158; Jonathan Alter, "Affirmative Ambivalence," *Newsweek* (March 27, 1995): 26; and Joanne D. Leck, David M. Saunders, and Micheline Charbonneau, "Affirmative Action Programs: An Organizational Justice Perspective," *Journal of Organizational Behavior*, 17 (January 1996): 79–89.

23. Julia Lawlor, "Study: Affirmative-Action Hires' Abilities Doubted," *USA Today* (August 31, 1992): 3B. The complete study is reported in Madeline E. Heilman, Caryn J. Block, and Jonathan A. Lucas,

"Presumed Incompetent? Stigmatization and Affirmative Action Efforts," *Journal of Applied Psychology*, 77 (August 1992): 536–554. Also see Beverly L. Little, William D. Murry, and James C. Wimbush, "Perceptions of Workplace Affirmative Action Plans," *Group & Organization Management*, 23 (March 1998): 27–47.

24. Yehouda Shenhav, "Entrance of Blacks and Women into Managerial Positions in Scientific and Engineering Occupations: A Longitudinal Analysis," *Academy of Management Journal*, 35 (October 1992): 897. Also see Mike McNamee, "The Proof Is in Performance," *Business Week* (July 15, 1996): 22. A female executive's view can be found in "Helayne Spivak," *Fast Company*, no. 27 (September 1999): 113.

25. For example, see Jonathan Kaufman, "White Men Shake Off That Losing Feeling on Affirmative Action," *The Wall Street Journal* (September 5, 1996): A1, A4.

26. R. Roosevelt Thomas Jr., "From Affirmative Action to Affirming Diversity," *Harvard Business Review*, 68 (March–April 1990): 114. For an interview with R. Roosevelt Thomas, see Ellen Neuborne, "Diversity Challenges Many Companies," *USA Today* (November 18, 1996): 10B.

27. For more on diversity, see Marc Adams, "Building a Rainbow, One Stripe at a Time," *HRMagazine*, 43 (August 1998): 72–79; Robert W. Thompson, "Diversity Among Managers Translates into Profitability," *HRMagazine*, 44 (April 1999): 10; Parshotam Dass and Barbara Parker, "Strategies for Managing Human Resource Diversity: From Resistance to Learning," *Academy of Management Executive*, 13 (May 1999): 68–80; Joan Crockett, "Diversity as a Business Strategy," *Management Review*, 88 (May 1999): 62; and Patricia Digh, "Getting People in the Pool: Diversity Recruitment That Works," *HRMagazine*, 44 (October 1999): 94–98.

28. Carol Kleiman, "'New Diversity' Is Nothing New to Chicago Advertising Firm," *The Arizona Republic* (May 16, 1993): F2.

29. Data from Kevin Dobbs, "Who's Leading the Blind?" *Training*, 36 (October 1999): 96–108.

30. For an inspiring case study of a blind sports reporter, see Robert Davis, "Friends 'Know of Nothing He Can't Do,'" *USA Today* (October 25, 1999): 10A.

31. For more, see Cheryl Comeau-Kirschner, "New ADA Guidelines," *Management Review*, 88 (April 1999): 6; Peter J. Petesch, "Are the Newest ADA Guidelines 'Reasonable?'" *HRMagazine*, 44 (June 1999): 54–58; Kelley Holland, "Who's Disabled? The Court Rules," *Business Week* (July 5, 1999): 36; and Carole O'Blenes, "ADA Lessons from the Front Lines," *Management Review*, 88 (September 1999): 58–60.

32. Gene Koretz, "Dubious Aid for the Disabled," *Business Week* (November 9, 1998): 30.

33. Catherine Yang, "Business Has to Find a New Meaning for 'Fairness,'" *Business Week* (April 12, 1993): 72.

34. Susan B. Garland, "Protecting the Disabled Won't Cripple Business," *Business Week* (April 26, 1999): 73.

35. See Bob Filipczak, "Adaptive Technology for the Disabled," *Training*, 30 (March 1993): 23–29; and Drew King, "A Comprehensive Approach to Disability Management," *HRMagazine*, 41 (October 1996): 97–102.

36. See Michael P. Cronin, "This Is a Test," *Inc.*, 15 (August 1993): 64–68.

37. See Scott B. Parry, "How to Validate an Assessment Tool," *Training*, 30 (April 1993): 37–42.

38. See Deniz S. Ones, Chockalingam Viswesvaran, and Frank L. Schmidt, "Comprehensive Meta-Analysis of Integrity Test Validities: Findings and Implications for Personnel Selection and Theories of Job Performance," *Journal of Applied Psychology*, 78 (August

1993): 679–703; Kevin R. Murphy, "Why Pre-Employment Alcohol Testing Is Such a Bad Idea," *Business Horizons*, 38 (September–October 1995): 69–74; and Jenny C. McCune, "Testing, Testing 1—2—3," *Management Review*, 85 (January 1996): 50–52; Deniz S. Ones and Chockalingam Viswesvaran, "Gender, Age, and Race Differences on Overt Integrity Tests: Results Across Four Large-Scale Job Applicant Data Sets," *Journal of Applied Psychology*, 83 (February 1998): 35–42; Kevin Johnson, "Government Agencies See Truth in Polygraphs," *USA Today* (April 5, 1999): 11A; and Stephanie Armour, "Could Your Genes Hold You Back?" *USA Today* (May 5, 1999): 1B–2B.

39. For example, see Larry Reibstein, "Spotting the Write Stuff," *Newsweek* (February 17, 1992): 44; and Bill Leonard, "Reading Employees," *HRMagazine*, 44 (April 1999): 67–73.

40. Data from Efrat Neter and Gershon Ben-Shakhar, "The Predictive Validity of Graphological Inferences: A Meta-Analytic Approach," *Personality and Individual Differences*, 10 (1989): 737–745.

41. See David A. Price, "Good References Pave Road to Court," *USA Today* (February 13, 1997): 11A; and David W. Arnesen, C. Patrick Fleenor, and Martin Blizinsky, "Name, Rank, and Serial Number? The Dilemma of Reference Checks," *Business Horizons*, 41 (July–August 1998): 71–78.

42. For details, see Barbara Solomon, "Too Good to Be True?" *Management Review*, 87 (1998): 27–31.

43. Based on discussion in Mark S. Van Clieaf, "In Search of Competence: Structured Behavior Interviews," *Business Horizons*, 34 (March–April 1991): 51–55. Also see Laura M. Graves and Ronald J. Karren, "The Employee Selection Interview: A Fresh Look at an Old Problem," *Human Resource Management*, 35 (Summer 1996): 163–180; and Gary N. Powell and Laurel R. Goulet, "Recruiters' and Applicants' Reactions to Campus Interviews and Employment Decisions," *Academy of Management Journal*, 39 (December 1996): 1619–1640.

44. "Structured Interviewing: Avoiding Selection Problems," by Elliott D. Pursell, Michael A. Campion, and Sarah R. Gaylord, copyright November 1980. Reprinted with permission of *Personnel Journal*, Costa Mesa, Calif.; all rights reserved.

45. Barbara Whitaker Shimko, "New Breed Workers Need New Yardsticks," *Business Horizons*, 33 (November–December 1990): 35–36. For related research, see Allen I. Huffcutt and Philip L. Roth, "Racial Group Differences in Employment Interview Evaluations," *Journal of Applied Psychology*, 83 (April 1998): 179–189.

46. Practical tips on interviewing can be found in "12 Ways to Keep Good People," *Training*, 36 (April 1999): 19; Claudio Fernandez-Araoz, "Hiring Without Firing," *Harvard Business Review*, 77 (July–August 1999): 109–120; and Jim Kennedy, "What to Do When Job Applicants Tell . . . Tales of Invented Lives," *Training*, 36 (October 1999): 110–114.

47. Based on Pursell et al., "Structured Interviewing." Also see Gary Meyer, "*SmartHire* Eases Computer-Guided Interview Preparation," *HRMagazine*, 41 (July 1996): 38–46.

48. See David Stamps, "Cyberinterviews Combat Turnover," *Training*, 32 (April 1995): 43–47.

49. Based on Bruce Bloom, "Behavioral Interviewing: The Future Direction and Focus of the Employment Interview." Paper presented to the Midwest Business Administration Association, Chicago (March 27, 1998).

50. Data from David Stamps, "Performance Appraisals: Out of Sync and as Unpopular as Ever," *Training*, 32 (August 1995): 16.

51. William S. Swan and Philip Margulies, *How to Do a Superior Performance Appraisal* (New York: Wiley, 1991), p. 8. Also see William S. Hubbart, "Bring Performance Appraisal Training to Life," *HRMagazine*, 40 (May 1995): 168 ff., 166.

52. Data from "What to Do with an Egg-Sucking Dog?" *Training*, 33 (October 1996): 17–21.

53. See "Ten Tips: Creating a Terrific Appraisal System," *HRMagazine*, 43 (October 1998): 56; Roger C. Mayer and James H. Davis, "The Effect of the Performance Appraisal System on Trust for Management: A Field Quasi-Experiment," *Journal of Applied Psychology*, 84 (February 1999): 123–136; and James H. Dulebohn and Gerald R. Ferris, "The Role of Influence Tactics in Perceptions of Performance Evaluations' Fairness," *Academy of Management Journal*, 42 (June 1999): 288–303.

54. For EEOC guidelines during performance appraisal, see Swan and Margulies, *How to Do a Superior Performance Appraisal.*

55. Adapted from Hubert S. Field and William H. Holley, "The Relationship of Performance Appraisal System Characteristics to Verdicts in Selected Employment Discrimination Cases," *Academy of Management Journal*, 25 (June 1982): 392–406. A more recent analysis of fifty-one cases that derived similar criteria can be found in Gerald V. Barrett and Mary C. Kernan, "Performance Appraisal and Terminations: A Review of Court Decisions Since *Brito* v. *Zia* with Implications for Personnel Practices," *Personnel Psychology*, 40 (Autumn 1987): 489–503.

56. For more, see Dick Grote, "Painless Performance Appraisals Focus on Results, Behaviors," *HRMagazine*, 43 (October 1998): 52–58.

57. For example, see Jenny C. McCune, "Employee Appraisals, the Electronic Way," *Management Review*, 86 (October 1997): 44–46.

58. For related research, see Todd J. Maurer, Jerry K. Palmer, and Donna K. Ashe, "Diaries, Checklists, Evaluations, and Contrast Effects in Measurement of Behavior," *Journal of Applied Psychology*, 78 (April 1993): 226–231.

59. See Kevin R. Murphy and Virginia A. Pardaffy, "Bias in Behaviorally Anchored Rating Scales: Global or Scale-Specific?" *Journal of Applied Psychology*, 74 (April 1989): 343–346.

60. See Francis Yammarino and Leanne E. Atwater, "Do Managers See Themselves As Others See Them? Implications of Self-Other Rating Agreement for Human Resources Management," *Organizational Dynamics*, 25 (Spring 1997): 35–44; Keith E. Morical, "A Product Review: 360 Assessments," *Training & Development*, 53 (April 1999): 43–47; G. Douglas Huet-Cox, Tjai M. Nielsen, and Eric Sundstrom, "Get the Most from 360-Degree Feedback: Put It on the Internet," *HRMagazine*, 44 (May 1999): 92–103; and Jim Meade, "*Visual 360:* A Performance Appraisal System That's 'Fun,'" *HRMagazine*, 44 (July 1999): 118–122.

61. See David A. Waldman, Leanne E. Atwater, and David Antonioni, "Has 360 Degree Feedback Gone Amok?" *Academy of Management Executive*, 12 (May 1998): 86–94; and Dennis E. Coates, "Don't Tie 360 Feedback to Pay," *Training*, 35 (September 1998): 68–78.

62. For helpful advice, see David Antonioni, "Designing an Effective 360-Degree Appraisal Feedback Process," *Organizational Dynamics*, 25 (Autumn 1996): 24–38; Kenneth M. Nowack, Jeanne Hartley, and William Bradley, "How to Evaluate Your 360 Feedback Efforts," *Training & Development*, 53 (April 1999): 48–53; and Susan J. Wells, "A New Road: Traveling Beyond 360-Degree Evaluation," *HRMagazine*, 44 (September 1999): 82–91.

63. Data from "Industry Report 1999," *Training*, 36 (October 1999): 40.

64. Frederick Kuri, "Basic-Skills Training Boosts Productivity," *HRMagazine*, 41 (September 1996): 77.

65. Data from a U.S. Department of Education literacy study of 13,600 people sixteen and older, as cited in Anna Mulrine, "Can

You Read This Story? Half of All U.S. Adults Can't," *The Christian Science Monitor* (September 10, 1993): 2.

66. Data from "Industry Report 1999," *Training*, 36 (October 1999): 37–81.

67. Training trends are discussed in Richard C. Wells, "Back to the (Internet) Classroom," *Training*, 36 (March 1999): 50–54; Sarah Fister, "CBT Fun and Games," *Training*, 36 (May 1999): 68–78; Margaret Kaeter, "The Automatic Training Tracker," *Training*, 36 (May 1999): ET22–ET30; "Web-Based Training Boom Ahead," *Training*, 36 (August 1999): 16; and David Stamps, "Wired Wired World," *Training*, 36 (August 1999): 40–46.

68. For instructive background reading, see Thomas D. Conkright, "Choosing the Right Training Solution," *Training*, 30 (August 1993): 41–42.

69. Kenneth N. Wexley and Gary P. Latham, *Developing and Training Human Resources in Organizations* (Glenview, Ill.: Scott, Foresman, 1981): 75–77.

70. Ibid., p. 77.

71. Training program evaluation is covered in "Why Training Doesn't Work," *Training*, 35 (February 1998): 24; Donna J. Abernathy, "Thinking Outside the Evaluation Box," *Training & Development*, 53 (February 1999): 19–23; and Dean R. Spitzer, "Embracing Evaluation," *Training*, 36 (June 1999): 42–47.

72. Data from Del Jones, "Legacy Hangs on the Line," *USA Today* (August 15, 1997): 1B–2B; Del Jones, "UAW Faces Cloudy Future," *USA Today* (June 17, 1998): 1B–2B; and David Whitford, "Labor's Lost Chance," *Fortune* (September 28, 1998): 177–182.

73. Justin Fox, "Big Labor Flexes Its Muscles," *Fortune* (June 10, 1996): 26.

74. See Joann Muller, "Workers—and Bosses—Unite?" *Business Week* (April 19, 1999): 66–71; Aaron Bernstein, "Making Nice in Detroit," *Business Week* (June 21, 1999): 46; and Bill Leonard, "The New Face of Organized Labor," *HRMagazine*, 44 (July 1999): 54–65.

75. See Bob Filipczak, "Unions in the '90s: Cooperation or Capitulation?" *Training*, 30 (May 1993): 25–34. Also see Kathleen Kerwin, "Bumps in a Brand-New Road," *Business Week* (March 8, 1999): 36; and Aaron Bernstein, "All's Not Fair in Labor Wars," *Business Week* (July 19, 1999): 43.

76. Adapted from discussion in Filipczak, "Unions in the '90s: Cooperation or Capitulation?"

77. For example, see David G. Epstein and Miles Z. Epstein, "Hand in Hand," *HRMagazine*, 43 (July 1998): 103–108; and Joann Muller, "Delphi Pushes a Peace Program," *Business Week* (February 1, 1999): 122.

78. See Jonathan A. Segal, "Sexual Harassment: Where Are We Now?" *HRMagazine*, 41 (October 1996): 69–73; Debbie Rodman Sandler, "Sexual Harassment Rulings: Less Than Meets the Eye," *HRMagazine*, 43 (October 1998): 136–143; and Carole O'Blenes, "Harassment Grows More Complex," *Management Review*, 88 (June 1999): 49–51.

79. See Susan Crawford, "A Brief History of Sexual Harassment Law," *Training*, 31 (August 1994): 46–49; and Kenneth M. Jarin and Ellen K. Pomfret, "New Rules for Same Sex Harassment," *HRMagazine*, 43 (June 1998): 114–123.

80. "Sex by the Numbers," *Time* (March 8, 1993): 21.

81. See "Beware What You E-Mail," *The Wall Street Journal* (July 2, 1996): A1; and Carole O'Blenes, "Tangling with Technology," *Management Review*, 88 (April 1999): 52–55.

82. Data from Tamara Henry, "Sexual Harassment Pervades Schools, Study Says," *USA Today* (July 23, 1996): 8B.

83. For a list of verbal and nonverbal forms of general harassment, see R. Bruce McAfee and Diana L. Deadrick, "Teach Employees to Just Say 'No!'" *HRMagazine*, 41 (February 1996): 86–89.

84. For details, see David E. Terpstra and Douglas D. Baker, "Outcomes of Federal Court Decisions on Sexual Harassment," *Academy of Management Journal*, 35 (March 1992): 181–190. Also see Leslie Kaufman, "A Report from the Front," *Newsweek* (January 13, 1997): 32.

85. For more, see John Montoya, "Who Should Investigate Sexual Harassment Complaints?" *HRMagazine*, 43 (January 1998): 113–118; Rebecca Ganzel, "What Sexual Harassment Training Really Prevents," *Training*, 35 (October 1998): 86–94; Jonathan A. Segal, "Prevent Now or Pay Later," *HRMagazine*, 43 (October 1998): 145–149; and Joann Muller, "Keeping an Investigation on the Right Track," *Business Week* (July 5, 1999): 84.

86. Data from Brian O'Reilly, "In a Dry Era You Can Still Be Trapped by Drinking," *Fortune* (March 6, 1995): 167–177; and Marilyn Chase, "Finding Ways to Reach an Alcoholic Who Has Elaborate Defenses," *The Wall Street Journal* (October 23, 1995): B1.

87. For informative reading on the physiological effects of alcohol, see Boyce Rensberger, "How Alcohol Noodles with the Brain," *The Washington Post National Weekly Edition* (January 6–12, 1992): 38. Also see Michael Marriott, "Half Steps vs. 12 Steps," *Newsweek* (March 27, 1995): 62; and Michele Turk, "For Problem Drinkers, A Moderate Proposal," *Business Week* (October 23, 1995): 136.

88. James A. Belohlav and Paul O. Popp, "Employee Substance Abuse: Epidemic of the Eighties," *Business Horizons*, 26 (July–August 1983): 29. Also see Tom Lowry, "Professionals Succumb to Drug's Allure," *USA Today* (August 9, 1996): 1B–2B.

89. Data from Robert Davis, "Demands, Isolation of Dentistry Open Gates to Drug Addiction," *USA Today* (April 15, 1999): 1A–2A; and Laura Meckler, "Seven in Ten Drug Users Work Full-Time," **womenconnect.com** (September 9, 1999).

90. Based on Janice Castro, "Battling the Enemy Within," *Time* (March 17, 1986): 52–61; and Peter Corbett, "Bush on Drug War: 'Failure Not Option,'" *The Arizona Republic* (April 9, 1999): E1, E3.

91. Data from Aja Whitaker, "Tight Labor Market Could Mean More Drug Abuse," *Management Review*, 88 (October 1999): 8.

92. See Jonathan A. Segal, "Drugs, Alcohol and the ADA," *HRMagazine*, 37 (December 1992): 73–76.

93. Janet Deming, "Drug-Free Workplace Is Good Business," *HRMagazine*, 35 (April 1990): 61.

94. See Louisa Wah, "Treatment vs. Termination," *Management Review*, 87 (April 1998): 8.

95. Ruby M. Yandrick, "The EAP Struggle: Counselors or Referrers?" *HRMagazine*, 43 (August 1998): 90–96; and Jane Easter Bahls, "Handle with Care," *HRMagazine*, 44 (March 1999): 60–66.

96. Stuart Feldman, "Today's EAPs Make the Grade," *Personnel*, 68 (February 1991): 3.

Chapter 12

Opening Quotation Laurence J. Peter, *Peter's Quotations* (New York: Bantam, 1977), p. 100.

Opening Case See Wendy Zellner, "Southwest's New Direction," *Business Week* (February 8, 1999): 58–59; Del Jones, "Southwest CEO Tops This Year, Magazine Says," *USA Today* (July 12, 1999): 5B; Wendy Zellner, "Earth to Herb: Pick a Co-Pilot," *Business Week* (August 16, 1999): 70–71; Mark Frankel, "Illness Won't Stop Southwest's CEO," *Business Week* (August 30, 1999): 52; and **www.southwest.com**.

Closing Case   Robert I. Stevens, "The Case of the Errant Messenger," *Journal of Systems Management*, 35 (July 1984): 42. Reprinted by permission of the author, Robert I. Stevens.

1. Richard Woodbury, "Prince of Midair," *Time* (January 25, 1993): 55.
2. Ibid.
3. For example, see Robert A. Snyder and James H. Morris, "Organizational Communication and Performance," *Journal of Applied Psychology*, 69 (August 1984): 461–465; Elmore R. Alexander, Marilyn M. Helms, and Ronnie D. Wilkins, "The Relationship Between Supervisory Communication and Subordinate Performance and Satisfaction Among Professionals," *Public Personnel Management*, 18 (Winter 1989): 415–429; and Mary Young and James E. Post, "Managing to Communicate, Communicating to Manage: How Leading Companies Communicate with Employees," *Organizational Dynamics*, 22 (Summer 1993): 31–43.
4. See Anthony Bastardi and Eldar Shafir, "On the Pursuit and Misuse of Useless Information," *Journal of Personality and Social Psychology*, 75 (July 1998): 19–32; Jenny C. McCune, "Data, Data, Everywhere," *Management Review*, 87 (November 1998): 10–12; and Joshua Macht, "Confessions of an Information Sinner," *Inc.*, 21 (January 1999): 73–76.
5. Stephanie Armour, "Failure to Communicate Costly for Companies," *USA Today* (September 30, 1998): 1B.
6. Keith Davis, *Human Behavior at Work: Organizational Behavior*, 6th ed. (New York: McGraw-Hill, 1981), p. 399.
7. For an instructive distinction between one-way (the arrow model) and two-way (the circuit model) communication, see Phillip G. Clampitt, *Communicating for Managerial Effectiveness* (Newbury Park, Calif.: Sage, 1991), pp. 1–24.
8. For interesting reading, see Harriet Rubin, "The Power of Words," *Fast Company*, no. 21 (January 1999): 142–151.
9. Trudy Milburn, "Bridging Cultural Gaps," *Management Review*, 86 (January 1997): 27. Also see Linda Kathryn Larkey, "Toward a Theory of Communicative Interactions in Culturally Diverse Workgroups," *Academy of Management Review*, 21 (April 1996): 463–491; and Jack L. Mendleson and C. Dianne Mendleson, "An Action Plan to Improve Difficult Communication," *HRMagazine*, 41 (October 1996): 118–126.
10. Ernest Gundling, "How to Communicate Globally," *Training & Development*, 53 (June 1999): 30.
11. See Robert H. Lengel and Richard L. Daft, "The Selection of Communication Media as an Executive Skill," *Academy of Management Executive*, 2 (August 1988): 225–232. For a research update, see John R. Carlson and Robert W. Zmud, "Channel Expansion Theory and the Experiential Nature of Media Richness Perceptions," *Academy of Management Journal*, 42 (April 1999): 153–170.
12. See Louisa Wah, "Getting Your Vision Across—in Words," *Management Review*, 87 (March 1998): 6.
13. See Karl Albrecht, "Lost in the Translation," *Training*, 33 (June 1996): 66–70; and Jean-Anne Jordon, "Clear Speaking Improves Career Prospects," *HRMagazine*, 41 (June 1996): 75–82.
14. Drawn from Manjeet Kripalani, "Investing in India: Not for the Fainthearted," *Business Week* (August 11, 1997): 46–47.
15. Data from Louisa Wah, "An Ounce of Prevention," *Management Review*, 87 (October 1998): 9. Also see "Worker Retention Presents Challenge to U.S. Employers," *HRMagazine*, 43 (September 1998): 22; Stephanie Armour, "Cash or Critiques: Which Is Best?" *USA Today* (December 16, 1998): 6B; and Ronda Roberts Callister, Michael W. Kramer, and Daniel B. Turban, "Feedback Seeking Following Career Transitions," *Academy of Management Journal*, 42 (August 1999): 429–438.

16. See Bella M. DePaulo, Deborah A. Kashy, Susan E. Kirkendol, Melissa M. Wyer, and Jennifer A. Epstein, "Lying in Everyday Life," *Journal of Personality and Social Psychology*, 70 (May 1996): 979–995; and Deborah A. Kashy and Bella M. DePaulo, "Who Lies?" *Journal of Personality and Social Psychology*, 70 (May 1996): 1037–1051.
17. "Backward, Chopped-Up Speech Can't Trip Up the Brain," *USA Today* (April 29, 1999): 10D.
18. For discussion of the communication process in modern organizations, see Nick Durutta, *IABC Communication World*, 12 (October 1995): 15–19.
19. Frank Snowden Hopkins, "Communication: The Civilizing Force," *The Futurist*, 15 (April 1981): 39.
20. See "Communications Patterns," *Management Review*, 66 (August 1977).
21. Peter Lowry and Byron Reimus, "Ready, Aim, Communicate!" *Management Review*, 85 (July 1996): 40.
22. Barbara Ettorre, "Communications Breakdown," *Management Review*, 85 (June 1996): 10.
23. Ibid. Also see Barbara Ettorre, "Loose Lips Sink Companies," *Management Review*, 88 (February 1999): 1; and Stephanie Armour, "Laptops, Cell Phones Can Leak Secrets," *USA Today* (August 16, 1999): 4B.
24. Keith Davis, "Grapevine Communication Among Lower and Middle Managers," *Personnel Journal*, 48 (April 1969): 269.
25. See Barbara Ettorre, "Hellooo. Anybody Listening?" *Management Review*, 86 (November 1997): 9; and Prashant Bordia, Nicholas DiFonzo, and Artemis Chang, "Rumor as Group Problem Solving: Development Patterns in Informal Computer-Mediated Groups," *Small Group Research*, 30 (February 1999): 8–28.
26. For more extensive discussion, see the classic article: Keith Davis, "Management Communication and the Grapevine," *Harvard Business Review*, 31 (September–October 1953): 43–49.
27. Hugh B. Vickery III, "Tapping into the Employee Grapevine," *Association Management*, 36 (January 1984): 59–60.
28. John W. Newstrom, Robert E. Monczka, and William E. Reif, "Perceptions of the Grapevine: Its Value and Influence," *Journal of Business Communication*, 11 (Spring 1974): 12–20.
29. See Roy Rowan, "Where Did *That* Rumor Come From?" *Fortune* (August 13, 1979): 130–137.
30. See Nicholas Difonzo, Prashant Bordia, and Ralph L. Rosnow, "Reining in Rumors," *Organizational Dynamics*, 23 (Summer 1994): 47–62.
31. Patricia Sellers, "Lessons from TV's New Bosses," *Fortune* (March 14, 1988): 115, 118.
32. See Alan Zaremba, "Working with the Organizational Grapevine," *Personnel Journal*, 67 (July 1988): 38–41.
33. "Executives Favor Plucking the Fruits from Employee Grapevine," *Association Management*, 36 (April 1984): 105.
34. A comprehensive discussion of rumors and rumor control can be found in Ralph L. Rosnow, "Inside Rumor: A Personal Journey," *American Psychologist*, 46 (May 1991): 484–496.
35. See Albert Mehrabian, "Communication Without Words," *Psychology Today*, 2 (September 1968): 53–55. For a discussion of the nonverbal origins of language, see Sharon Begley, "Talking from Hand to Mouth," *Newsweek* (March 15, 1999): 56–58.
36. For a scholarly discussion of organizational dress, see Anat Rafaeli and Michael G. Pratt, "Tailored Meanings: On the Meaning and Impact of Organizational Dress," *Academy of Management Review*, 18 (January 1993): 32–55. Also see Linda Himelstein, "Levi's vs. the Dress Code," *Business Week* (April 1, 1996): 57–58; and Bodil Jones, "Unsuitable for the Job?" *Management Review*, 85 (July 1996): 51.

37. Excerpt from Brian Hickey, "People Packaging," *America West Airlines Magazine*, 5 (September 1990): 61. Reprinted by permission of the author. Also see Linda Himelstein, "How Do You Get the Boys to Pass You the Ball?" *Business Week* (February 17, 1997): 70; and David Stauffer, "Making an Impact," *Harvard Management Communication Letter*, 2 (August 1999): 4–6.

38. This three-way breakdown comes from Dale G. Leathers, *Nonverbal Communication Systems* (Boston: Allyn & Bacon, 1976), chap. 2. Also see James M. Carroll and James A. Russell, "Facial Expressions in Hollywood's Portrayal of Emotion," *Journal of Personality and Social Psychology*, 72 (January 1997): 164–176.

39. Paul C. Judge, "High Tech Star," *Business Week* (March 15, 1999): 75.

40. Based on A. Keenan, "Effects of the Non-Verbal Behaviour of Interviewers on Candidates' Performance," *Journal of Occupational Psychology*, 49, No. 3 (1976): 171–175. Also see Stanford W. Gregory Jr. and Stephen Webster, "Nonverbal Signal in Voices of Interview Partners Effectively Predicts Communication Accommodation and Social Status Perceptions," *Journal of Personality and Social Psychology*, 70 (June 1996): 1231–1240.

41. See Linda L. Carli, Suzanne J. LaFleur, and Christopher C. Loeber, "Nonverbal Behavior, Gender, and Influence," *Journal of Personality and Social Psychology*, 68 (June 1995): 1030–1041.

42. For details, see Dore Butler and Florence L. Geis, "Nonverbal Affect Responses to Male and Female Leaders: Implications for Leadership Evaluations," *Journal of Personality and Social Psychology*, 58 (January 1990): 48–59.

43. Based on Ben Brown, "Atlanta Out to Mind Its Manners," *USA Today* (March 14, 1996): 7C.

44. See Craig Wilson, "Job Hungry College Seniors Learn to Mind Table Manners," *USA Today* (November 6, 1996): 3D.

45. See David Lewin and Daniel J. B. Mitchell, "Systems of Employee Voice: Theoretical and Empirical Perspectives," *California Management Review*, 34 (Spring 1992): 95–111; and Milan Moravec, Herman Gyr, and Lisa Friedman, "A 21st-Century Communication Tool," *HRMagazine*, 38 (July 1993): 77–81.

46. Shelly Branch, "The 100 Best Companies to Work for in America," *Fortune* (January 11, 1999): 130.

47. See Bruce Fortado, "The Accumulation of Grievance Conflict," *Journal of Management Inquiry*, 1 (December 1992): 288–303; Debra J. Mesch and Dan R. Dalton, "Unexpected Consequences of Improving Workplace Justice: A Six-Year Time Series Assessment," *Academy of Management Journal*, 35 (December 1992): 1099–1114; and George W. Bohlander, "Public Sector Grievance Arbitration: Structure and Administration," *Journal of Collective Negotiations in the Public Sector*, 21, no. 4 (1992): 271–286.

48. For details, see Dick Grote and Jim Wimberly, "Peer Review," *Training*, 30 (March 1993): 51–55.

49. For example, see Jim Meade, "*Inquisite 1.2* Builds Employee Surveys Quickly, Easily," *HRMagazine*, 44 (September 1999): 122–126; and Joe Dysart, "*The Survey System 7.0:* A Tool for Novices, Experts," *HRMagazine*, 44 (September 1999): 128–132.

50. Brian Dumaine, "Creating a New Company Culture," *Fortune* (January 15, 1990): 130.

51. See Brad Fishel, "A New Perspective: How to Get the Real Story from Attitude Surveys," *Training*, 35 (February 1998): 91–94.

52. Wendy Zellner, "Blue Crew at American," *Business Week* (February 22, 1999): 8.

53. See Robert J. Aiello, "Employee Attitude Surveys: Impact on Corporate Decisions," *Public Relations Journal* (March 1983): 21.

54. Michael E. Trunko, "Open to Suggestions," *HRMagazine*, 38 (February 1993): 85.

55. Data from Ceel Pasternak, "HRM Update," *HRMagazine*, 37 (December 1992): 21. The case *against* big monetary rewards for suggestions is presented in Michael P. Cronin, "Small Ideas Are Big Hits," *Inc.*, 15 (August 1993): 28.

56. Michael H. Martin, "Kinko's," *Fortune* (July 8, 1996): 102. For a good suggestion system case study, see Robert Rose, "Kentucky Plant Workers Are Cranking Out Good Ideas," *The Wall Street Journal* (August 13, 1996): B1–B2.

57. See James S. Larson, "Employee Participation in Federal Management," *Public Personnel Management*, 18 (Winter 1989): 404–414. Also see John Tschohl, "Be Bad," *Canadian Manager*, 23 (Winter 1998): 23–24; Stephanie Armour, "Firms Tap Employees for Cost-Saving Suggestions," *USA Today* (January 26, 1999): 1B; and Dale K. DuPont, "Eureka! Tools for Encouraging Employee Suggestions," *HRMagazine*, 44 (September 1999): 134–143.

58. An informative overview may be found in Everett T. Suters, "Hazards of an Open-Door Policy," *Inc.*, 9 (January 1987): 99–101.

59. An example of this problem is reported on p. 118 of Alex Taylor III, "Toyota's Boss Stands Out in a Crowd," *Fortune* (November 25, 1996): 116–122.

60. See Michael Warshaw, "Open Mouth. Lose Career?" *Fast Company*, no. 20 (December 1998): 240–251.

61. As quoted in Sheila M. Puffer, "CompUSA's CEO James Halpin on Technology, Rewards, and Commitment," *Academy of Management Executive*, 13 (May 1999): 31.

62. Curtis Sittenfeld, "Here's How GSA Changed Its Ways," *Fast Company*, no. 25 (June 1999): 88.

63. For more, see Bill Leonard, "Cyberventing," *HRMagazine*, 44 (November 1999): 34–39.

64. For more, see Paul W. Barada, "Before You Go . . . ," *HRMagazine*, 43 (December 1998): 99–102; and "Questions for Exiting Employees," *Training*, 36 (October 1999): 28.

65. Charles F. Knight, "Emerson Electric: Consistent Profits, Consistently," *Harvard Business Review*, 70 (January–February 1992): 60.

66. Catherine Yang, "Low-Wage Lessons," *Business Week* (November 11, 1996): 114.

67. Phil Patton, "There's No Place like Home at Work, Designers Say," *The Arizona Republic* (September 13, 1992): S5.

68. See Bob Filipczak, "Obfuscation Resounding: Corporate Communication in America," *Training*, 32 (July 1995): 29–36.

69. See, for example, Bill Daily and Miriam Finch, "Benefiting from Nonsexist Language in the Workplace," *Business Horizons*, 36 (March–April 1993): 30–34.

70. For a brief discussion of male versus female communication styles, see Cynthia Berryman-Fink, "Changing Sex-Role Stereotypes," *Personnel Journal*, 62 (June 1983): 502, 504. For related reading, see Julia Lawlor, "Tannen Eavesdrops on Office Talk," *USA Today* (October 10, 1994): 3B; and Deborah Tannen, "The Power of Talk: Who Gets Heard and Why," *Harvard Business Review*, 73 (September–October 1995): 138–148.

71. Wendy Martyna, "What Does 'He' Mean? Use of the Generic Masculine," *Journal of Communication*, 28 (Winter 1978): 138. A later study with similar results is Janet A. Sniezek and Christine H. Jazwinski, "Gender Bias in English: In Search of Fair Language," *Journal of Applied Social Psychology*, 16, no. 7 (1986): 642–662. Also see Patricia C. Kelley, "Can Feminist Language Change Organizational Behavior? Some Research Questions," *Business & Society*, 35 (March 1996): 84–88.

72. Del Jones, "'Code Words' Cloud Issue of Discrimination at Work," *USA Today* (October 1, 1996): 1B–2B.

73. Data from Andrew Leonard, "We've Got Mail—Always," *Newsweek* (September 20, 1999): 58–61.

74. For a good overview, see Joan O'C. Hamilton, "Like It or Not, You've Got Mail," *Business Week* (October 4, 1999): 178–184.

75. Jenny C. McCune, "Technology Giveth and Taketh Away," *Management Review*, 88 (September 1999): 7. Also see "You've Got Junk," *Training*, 36 (June 1999): 18.

76. Stephanie Armour, "You Have (Too Much) E-mail," *USA Today* (March 2, 1999): 3B.

77. Drawn from Eryn Brown, "You've Got Mail. :-o," *Fortune* (December 7, 1998): 36, 40; Jenny C. McCune, "Do You Speak Computerese?" *Management Review*, 88 (February 1999): 10–12; "Etiquette with Office Gadgets," *Training*, 36 (January 1999): 24; Joan Tunstall, *Better, Faster Email: Getting the Most Out of Email* (St. Leonards, Australia: Allen & Unwin, 1999); and Donna J. Abernathy, "You've Got Email," *Training & Development*, 53 (April 1999): 18.

78. For more, see Jenny C. McCune, "Working Together, but Apart," *Management Review*, 87 (September 1998): 45–47; and Frank Jossi, "Videoconferencing on the Cheap," *Training*, Special Report: Distance Learning, 35 (October 1998): DL10–DL20.

79. Data from Andrew Kupfer, "Prime Time for Videoconferences," *Fortune* (December 28, 1992): 90–95.

80. Erick Schonfeld, "Desktop Boardroom," *Fortune* (September 9, 1996): 195. Also see Stephen H. Wildstrom, "Make Way for MMX Computers," *Business Week* (February 3, 1997): 22.

81. Tips adapted in part from Michael Emery and Margaret Schubert, "A Trainer's Guide to Videoconferencing," *Training*, 30 (June 1993): 59–63. Also see "Tips for the Photophobic," *Training*, 35 (October 1998): 26.

82. Data from Robert Barker, "Work à la Modem," *Business Week* (October 4, 1999): 170–176.

83. For more information on telecommuting, see Marc Hequet, "Virtually Working: Dispatches from the Home Front," *Training*, 33 (August 1996): 29–35; Melanie Warner, "Working at Home—the Right Way to Be a Star in Your Bunny Slippers," *Fortune* (March 3, 1997): 165–166; Lauren M. Bernardi, "Telecommuting: Legal and Management Issues," *Canadian Manager*, 23 (Fall 1998): 18–19, 28; Lin Grensing-Pophal, "Training Supervisors to Manage Teleworkers," *HRMagazine*, 44 (January 1999): 67–72; Sarah Fister, "A Lure for Labor," *Training*, 36 (February 1999): 56–62; and Nancy B. Kurland and Diane E. Bailey, "Telework: The Advantages and Challenges of Working Here, There, Anywhere, and Anytime," *Organizational Dynamics*, 28 (Autumn 1999): 53–68.

84. Stratford P. Sherman, "America Won't Win Till It Reads More," *Fortune* (November 18, 1991): 202. For useful communication tips, see Jo Condrill and Bennie Bough, *101 Ways to Improve Your Communication Skills Instantly* (Palmdale, Calif.: GoalMinds, 1999).

85. Data from Judi Brownell, "Perceptions of Effective Listeners: A Management Study," *Journal of Business Communication*, 27 (Fall 1990): 401–415.

86. Cynthia Hamilton and Brian H. Kleiner, "Steps to Better Listening," *Personnel Journal*, 66 (February 1987): 20–21.

87. This list has been adapted from John F. Kikoski, "Communication: Understanding It, Improving It," *Personnel Journal*, 59 (February 1980): 126–131; John L. DiGaetani, "The Business of Listening," *Business Horizons*, 23 (October 1980): 40–46; Dick Schaaf, "Listening to Get By," *Training*, 29 (May 1992): 62–67; P. Slizewski, "Tips for Active Listening," *HR Focus* (May 1995): 7; and Dana Ray, "Are You Listening?" *Selling Power*, 19 (June 1999): 28–30.

88. See Wendy Zellner, "O.K., So He's Not Sam Walton," *Business Week* (March 16, 1992): 56–58.

89. See "Wanted: Great Communicators," *The Christian Science Monitor* (June 22, 1990): 8.

90. See Larry R. Smeltzer and Jeanette W. Gilsdorf, "How to Use Your Time Efficiently When Writing," *Business Horizons*, 33 (November–December 1990): 61–64; and Tom Ehrenfeld, "A Ghost Speaks," *Harvard Management Communication Letter*, 2 (August 1999): 10–11.

91. Robert F. DeGise, "Writing: Don't Let the Mechanics Obscure the Message," *Supervisory Management*, 21 (April 1976): 26–28. Also see Don M. Ricks, "Why Your Business-Writing Courses Don't Work," *Training*, 31 (March 1994): 49–52; Kenneth W. Davis, "What Writing Training Can—and Can't—Do," *Training*, 32 (August 1995): 60–63; David A. Bates, "When Good Writing Goes Bad," *Internal Auditor*, 53 (February 1996): 36–38; and Jeffrey Marshall, "How to Write a Perfectly Good Memo," *Harvard Management Communication Letter*, 2 (July 1999): 4–6.

92. See "Give the Boot to Hackneyed Phrases," *Training*, 27 (August 1990): 10. Also see Herschell Gordon Lewis, "100 of the Easiest Ways to Begin an Effective Sales Letter," *Direct Marketing*, 56 (February 1994): 32–34.

93. See "Who to Scratch Off Your Meeting Guest List," *Training*, 35 (July 1998): 17; and Gina Imperato, "You Have to Start Meeting like This!" *Fast Company*, no. 23 (April 1999): 204–210.

94. "Meeting 'Mania' Squanders Time and Money," *HRMagazine*, 43 (August 1998): 24, 26.

95. Stephanie Armour, "Team Efforts, Technology Add New Reasons to Meet," *USA Today* (December 8, 1997): 2A. Copyright 1997, USA Today. Reprinted with permission. Also see Kevin Maney, "Armed with PowerPoint, Speakers Make Pests of Themselves," *USA Today* (May 12, 1999): 3B; and Fred Niederman and Roger J. Volkema, "The Effects of Facilitator Characteristics on Meeting Preparation, Set Up, and Implementation," *Small Group Research*, 30 (June 1999): 330–360.

Chapter 13

Opening Quotation Keith Davis, *Human Behavior at Work: Organizational Behavior*, 6th ed. (New York: McGraw-Hill, 1981), p. 2.

Opening Case Excerpted from Charles Fishman, "The Way to Enough," *Fast Company*, no. 26 (July–August 1999): 160–174. Reprinted from the July–August issue of *Fast Company* magazine. All rights reserved. To subscribe, please call (800) 688-1545.

Closing Case Chuck Hawkins, "Sharon Allred Decker: 'We Had to Recognize that People Have Lives.'" Reprinted from the June 28, 1993 edition of *Business Week* by special permission, copyright © 1993 by McGraw-Hill, Inc.

1. Data from Jeffrey Pfeffer, *The Human Equation: Building Profits by Putting People First* (Boston: Harvard Business School Press, 1998); and Jeffrey Pfeffer and John F. Veiga, "Putting People First for Organizational Success," *Academy of Management Executive*, 13 (May 1999): 37–48.

2. For an excellent historical and conceptual treatment of basic motivation theory, see the collection of readings in Chapter 2 of Richard M. Steers, Lyman W. Porter, and Gregory A. Bigley, *Motivation and Leadership at Work*, 6th ed. (New York: McGraw-Hill, 1996).

3. See Bob Nelson, Lael Good, and Tom Hill, "Motivate Employees According to Temperament," *HRMagazine*, 42 (March 1997): 51–56; Gail Dutton, "The Re-enchantment of Work," *Management Review*, 87 (February 1998): 51–54; Theodore Kinni, "Why We Work," *Training*, 35 (August 1998): 34–39; and Jon R. Katzenbach

and Jason A. Santamaria, "Firing Up the Front Line," *Harvard Business Review*, 77 (May–June 1999): 107–117.

4. See A. H. Maslow, "A Theory of Human Motivation," *Psychological Review*, 50 (July 1943): 370–396; and Ron Zemke, "Maslow for a New Millennium," *Training*, 35 (December 1998): 54–58.

5. Maslow, "A Theory of Human Motivation," p. 375.

6. Dean Foust, "Man on the Spot," *Business Week* (May 3, 1999): 142–143.

7. For more, see Gene Koretz, "The Vital Role of Self-Esteem," *Business Week* (February 2, 1998): 26; Donald G. Gardner and Jon L. Pierce, "Self-Esteem and Self-Efficacy Within the Organizational Context: An Empirical Investigation," *Group & Organization Management*, 23 (March 1998): 48–70; and Perry Pascarella, "It All Begins with Self-Esteem," *Management Review*, 88 (February 1999): 60–61.

8. Maslow, "A Theory of Human Motivation," p. 382.

9. George W. Cherry, "The Serendipity of the Fully Functioning Manager," *Sloan Management Review*, 17 (Spring 1976): 73.

10. Vance F. Mitchell and Pravin Moudgill, "Measurement of Maslow's Need Hierarchy," *Organizational Behavior and Human Performance*, 16 (August 1976): 348. Self-actualizing executives are profiled in Keith H. Hammonds, "The Mission," *Business Week* (March 22, 1999): 97–107; and Micheline Maynard, "Luts Gets a Charge out of New Career," *USA Today* (June 1, 1999): 12B.

11. For example, see Ellen L. Betz, "Two Tests of Maslow's Theory of Need Fulfillment," *Journal of Vocational Behavior*, 24 (April 1984): 204–220.

12. Edward E. Lawler, *Motivation in Work Organizations* (Monterey, Calif.: Brooks/Cole, 1973), p. 34.

13. See Frederick Herzberg, Bernard Mausner, and Barbara Bloch Snyderman, *The Motivation to Work*, 2nd ed. (New York: Wiley, 1959). For a marketing application of Herzberg's theory, see Earl Naumann and Donald W. Jackson Jr., "One More Time: How Do You Satisfy Customers?" *Business Horizons*, 42 (May–June 1999): 71–76.

14. Frederick Herzberg, "One More Time: How Do You Motivate Employees?" *Harvard Business Review*, 46 (January–February 1968): 56. For another view, see Dennis W. Organ, "The Happy Curve," *Business Horizons*, 38 (May–June 1995): 1–3. Herzberg's methodology is replicated in Susan G. Turner, Dawn R. Utley, and Jerry D. Westbrook, "Project Managers and Functional Managers: A Case Study of Job Satisfaction in a Matrix Organization," *Project Management Journal*, 29 (September 1998): 11–19.

15. For details, see Victor H. Vroom, *Work and Motivation* (New York: Wiley, 1964), p. 186. A positive correlation between job satisfaction and job level is reported in Chet Robie, Ann Marie Ryan, Robert A. Schmieder, Luis Fernando Parra, and Patricia C. Smith, "The Relation Between Job Level and Job Satisfaction," *Group & Organization Management*, 23 (December 1998): 470–495.

16. See Robert J. House and Lawrence A. Wigdor, "Herzberg's Dual-Factor Theory of Job Satisfaction and Motivation: A Review of the Evidence and a Criticism," *Personnel Psychology*, 20 (1967): 369–389.

17. For example, see Peter W. Hom, "Expectancy Prediction of Reenlistment in the National Guard," *Journal of Vocational Behavior*, 16 (April 1980): 235–248; John P. Wanous, Thomas L. Keon, and Janina C. Latack, "Expectancy Theory and Occupational/Organizational Choices: A Review and Test," *Organizational Behavior and Human Performance*, 32 (August 1983): 66–86; Alan W. Stacy, Keith F. Widaman, and G. Alan Marlatt, "Expectancy Models of Alcohol Use," *Journal of Personality and Social Psychology*, 58 (May 1990): 918–928; and Anne S. Tsui, Susan J. Ashford, Lynda St. Clair, and Katherine R. Xin, "Dealing with Discrepant Expectations: Response Strategies and Managerial Effectiveness," *Academy of Management Journal*, 38 (December 1995): 1515–1543.

18. For example, see Jim Collins, "Turning Goals into Results: The Power of Catalytic Mechanisms," *Harvard Business Review*, 77 (July–August 1999): 71–82.

19. See, for example, Edwin A. Locke and Gary P. Latham, *Goal Setting: A Motivational Technique That Works!* (Englewood Cliffs, N.J.: Prentice-Hall, 1984).

20. See, for example, Edwin A. Locke, Keryll N. Shaw, Lise M. Saari, and Gary P. Latham, "Goal Setting and Task Performance: 1969–1980," *Psychological Bulletin*, 90 (July 1981): 125–152; Anthony J. Mento, Robert P. Steel, and Ronald J. Karren, "A Meta-Analytic Study of the Effects of Goal Setting on Task Performance: 1966–1984," *Organizational Behavior and Human Decision Processes*, 39 (February 1987): 52–83; and Don VandeWalle, Steven P. Brown, William L. Cron, and John W. Slocum Jr., "The Influence of Goal Orientation and Self-Regulation Tactics on Sales Performance: A Longitudinal Field Test," *Journal of Applied Psychology*, 84 (April 1999): 249–259.

21. "Stretch goals" are discussed in Shawn Tully, "Why Go for Stretch Targets," *Fortune* (November 14, 1994): 145–158; Strat Sherman, "Stretch Goals: The Dark Side of Asking for Miracles," *Fortune* (November 13, 1995): 231–232; and Kenneth R. Thompson, Wayne A. Hochwarter, and Nicholas J. Mathys, "Stretch Targets: What Makes Them Effective?" *Academy of Management Executive*, 11 (August 1997): 48–60.

22. See Christopher Earley, Gregory B. Northcraft, Cynthia Lee, and Terri R. Lituchy, "Impact of Process and Outcome Feedback on the Relation of Goal Setting to Task Performance," *Academy of Management Journal*, 33 (March 1990): 87–105.

23. John Huey, "America's Most Successful Merchant," *Fortune* (September 23, 1991): 50.

24. Stephen Phillips and Amy Dunkin, "King Customer," *Business Week* (March 12, 1990): 91.

25. Lewis Carroll, *Alice's Adventures in Wonderland* (Philadelphia: The John C. Winston Company, 1923), p. 57.

26. See Cynthia D. Fisher, "Boredom at Work: A Neglected Concept," *Human Relations*, 46 (March 1993): 395–417; Marilyn Elias, "Routine Job May Take Toll on Heart," *USA Today* (September 25, 1995): 1D; Jia Lin Xie and Gary Johns, "Job Scope and Stress: Can Job Scope Be Too High?" *Academy of Management Journal*, 38 (October 1995): 1288–1309; and "Stranger in Blue-Collar Land," *Training*, 36 (August 1999): 20.

27. Adapted from J. Richard Hackman, "The Design of Work in the 1980s," *Organizational Dynamics*, 7 (Summer 1978): 3–17. An instructive four-way analysis of job design may be found in Michael A. Campion and Paul W. Thayer, "Job Design: Approaches, Outcomes, and Trade-Offs," *Organizational Dynamics*, 15 (Winter 1987): 66–79.

28. Rick Wartzman, "Houston Turns Out to Be the Capital of the Egg Roll," *The Wall Street Journal* (December 7, 1995): A1. Also see Bob Filipczak, "I, Telemarketus," *Training*, 33 (March 1996): 48–56.

29. For an interesting discussion of people who do society's "dirty work," see Blake E. Ashforth and Glen E. Kreiner, " 'How Can You Do It?' Dirty Work and the Challenge of Constructing a Positive Identity," *Academy of Management Review*, 24 (July 1999): 413–434.

30. Jean M. Phillips, "Effects of Realistic Job Previews on Multiple Organizational Outcomes: A Meta-Analysis," *Academy of Management*

Journal, 41 (December 1998): 686. Also see Peter W. Hom, Roger W. Griffeth, Leslie E. Palich, and Jeffrey S. Bracker, "Revisiting Met Expectations as a Reason Why Realistic Job Previews Work," *Personnel Psychology*, 52 (Spring 1999): 97–112.

31. See Kathryn Tyler, "Sit Up Straight," *HRMagazine*, 43 (September 1998): 123–128.

32. See Lee Smith, "The FBI Is a Tough Outfit to Run," *Fortune* (October 9, 1989): 133–140. Also see Michael A. Campion, Lisa Cheraskin, and Michael J. Stevens, "Career-Related Antecedents and Outcomes of Job Rotation," *Academy of Management Journal*, 37 (December 1994): 1518–1542. For a condensed version of the foregoing study, see Susan Stites-Doe, "The New Story About Job Rotation," *Academy of Management Executive*, 10 (February 1996): 86–87.

33. See M. A. Howell, "Time Off as a Reward for Productivity," *Personnel Administration*, 34 (November–December 1971): 48–51.

34. Fred Luthans and Robert Kreitner, *Organizational Behavior Modification and Beyond: An Operant and Social Learning Approach* (Glenview, Ill.: Scott, Foresman, 1985), p. 192. Also see Diane L. Lockwood and Fred Luthans, "Contingent Time Off: A Nonfinancial Incentive for Improving Productivity," *Management Review*, 73 (July 1984): 48–52. The case for a six-hour workweek is presented in "That's Why They Call It 'Work,' " *Fast Company*, no. 29 (November 1999): 194.

35. Data from Carla O'Dell and Jerry McAdams, "The Revolution in Employee Rewards," *Management Review*, 76 (March 1987): 30–33. For a recent example of CTO in action, see Thomas Petzinger Jr., "They Keep Workers Motivated to Make Annoying Phone Calls," *The Wall Street Journal* (September 20, 1996): B1.

36. J. Richard Hackman and Greg R. Oldham, *Work Redesign* (Reading, Mass.: Addison-Wesley, 1980), p. 20. Also see Michael A. Campion and Michael J. Stevens, "Neglected Questions in Job Design: How People Design Jobs, Task-Job Predictability, and Influence of Training," *Journal of Business and Psychology*, 6 (Winter 1991): 169–191; and Gary Johns, Jia Lin Xie, and Yongqing Fang, "Mediating and Moderating Effects in Job Design," *Journal of Management*, 18 (December 1992): 657–676.

37. David Kirkpatrick, "How Safe Are Video Terminals?" *Fortune* (August 29, 1988): 71. For related research, see Michael A. Campion and Carol L. McClelland, "Interdisciplinary Examination of the Costs and Benefits of Enlarged Jobs: A Job Design Quasi-Experiment," *Journal of Applied Psychology*, 76 (April 1991): 186–198.

38. See J. Barton Cunningham and Ted Eberle, "A Guide to Job Enrichment and Redesign," *Personnel*, 67 (February 1990): 56–61; Roger E. Herman and Joyce L. Gioia, "Making Work Meaningful: Secrets of the Future-Focused Corporation," *The Futurist*, 32 (December 1998): 24–38; and Donna Fenn, "Redesign Work," *Inc.*, 21 (June 1999): 74–84.

39. Phillips and Dunkin, "King Customer," p. 91.

40. Hackman and Oldham, *Work Redesign*, pp. 78–80. Also see John W. Medcof, "The Job Characteristics of Computing and Non-Computing Work Activities," *Journal of Occupational and Organizational Psychology*, 69 (June 1996): 199–212; and Joan R. Rentsch and Robert P. Steel, "Testing the Durability of Job Characteristics as Predictors of Absenteeism over a Six-Year Period," *Personnel Psychology*, 51 (Spring 1998): 165–190.

41. See Ricky W. Griffin, "Effects of Work Redesign on Employee Perceptions, Attitudes, and Behaviors: A Long-Term Investigation," *Academy of Management Journal*, 34 (June 1991): 425–435.

42. See Bob Nelson, *1001 Ways to Reward Employees* (New York: Workman, 1994).

43. See Sheena S. Iyengar and Mark R. Lepper, "Rethinking the Value of Choice: A Cultural Perspective on Intrinsic Motivation," *Journal of Personality and Social Psychology*, 76 (March 1999): 349–366; and Bob Urichuck, "Employee Recognition and Praise," *Canadian Manager*, 24 (Summer 1999): 27–29.

44. See Pamela Kruger, "Money—Is That What You Want?" *Fast Company*, no. 24 (May 1999): 48–50.

45. See George L. Stelluto and Deborah P. Klein, "Compensation Trends into the 21st Century," *Monthly Labor Review*, 113 (February 1990): 38–45. Also see Patricia K. Zingheim and Jay R. Schuster, "Introduction: How Are the New Pay Tools Being Deployed?" *Compensation & Benefits Review*, 27 (July–August 1995): 10–13; and Edward E. Lawler III, "The New Pay: A Strategic Approach," *Compensation & Benefits Review*, 27 (July–August 1995): 14–22; and Stephen Kerr, "Organizational Rewards: Practical, Cost-Neutral Alternatives That You May Know, but Don't Practice," *Organizational Dynamics*, 28 (Summer 1999): 61–70.

46. See Bill Leonard, "Perks Give Way to Life-Cycle Benefits Plans," *HRMagazine*, 40 (March 1995): 45–48.

47. See Lesley Alderman with Jeanhee Kim, "Get the Most from Your Company Benefits," *Money*, 25 (January 1996): 102–106.

48. "Companies Offer Benefits Cafeteria-Style," *Business Week* (November 13, 1978): 116. Also see Michael Hickins, "Creative 'Get-a-Life' Benefits," *Management Review*, 88 (April 1999): 7.

49. See Betty A. Iseri and Robert R. Cangemi, "Flexible Benefits: A Growing Option," *Personnel*, 67 (March 1990): 30–32; Eric T. Wilt, "Cafeteria Plans Help Meet Needs & Control Costs," *Management Review*, 79 (September 1990): 43–46; and Richard Gisonny and Steven Fein, "Better Benefits Emerge from Tax-Wise Choices," *HRMagazine*, 36 (February 1991): 36–39.

50. For complete details, see Alison E. Barber, Randall B. Dunham, and Roger A. Formisano, "The Impact of Flexible Benefits on Employee Satisfaction: A Field Study," *Personnel Psychology*, 45 (Spring 1992): 55–75.

51. See Robert Ford and John W. Newstrom, "Dues-Paying: Managing the Cost of Recognition," *Business Horizons*, 42 (July–August 1999): 14–20; Stephanie Armour, "Watching the Stock Clock," *USA Today* (July 23, 1999): 1B–2B; and "Employers Expanding Stock Options to All," *HR Magazine*, 44 (October 1999): 30.

52. For more, see David A. Bowen, Stephen W. Gilliland, and Robert Folger, "HRM and Service Fairness: How Being Fair with Employees Spills Over to Customers," *Organizational Dynamics*, 27 (Winter 1999): 7–23; and Matt Bloom, "The Performance Effects of Pay Dispersion on Individuals and Organizations," *Academy of Management Journal*, 42 (February 1999): 25–40.

53. A good overview of equity theory can be found in Robert P. Vecchio, "Models of Psychological Inequity," *Organizational Behavior and Human Performance*, 34 (October 1984): 266–282.

54. See J. Stacy Adams and Patricia R. Jacobsen, "Effects of Wage Inequities on Work Quality," *Journal of Abnormal and Social Psychology*, 69 (1964): 19–25; Jerald Greenberg and Suzyn Ornstein, "High Status Job Title as Compensation for Underpayment: A Test of Equity Theory," *Journal of Applied Psychology*, 68 (May 1983): 285–297.

55. For examples, see Thomas A. Stewart, "CEO Pay: Mom Wouldn't Approve," *Fortune* (March 31, 1997): 119–120; and Jennifer Reingold, "Executive Pay," *Business Week* (April 19, 1999): 72–90.

56. See Nina Gupta and Jason D. Shaw, "Let the Evidence Speak: Financial Incentives *Are* Effective!!" *Compensation & Benefits Review*, 30 (March–April 1998): 26–32; Alfred Rappaport, "New Thinking on How to Link Executive Pay with Performance,"

Harvard Business Review, 77 (March–April 1999): 91–101; and Roger Plachy and Sandra Plachy, "Rewarding Employees Who Truly Make a Difference," *Compensation & Benefits Review*, 31 (May–June 1999): 34–39.

57. See Peter V. LeBlanc and Paul W. Mulvey, "How American Workers See the Rewards of Work," *Compensation & Benefits Review*, 30 (January–February 1998): 24–28; and Louisa Wah, "Rewarding Efficient Teamwork," *Management Review*, 88 (February 1999): 7.

58. George Gendron, "Steel Man: Ken Iverson," *Inc.* (April 1986): 47–48.

59. The case *against* incentives is presented in Alfie Kohn, "Why Incentive Plans Cannot Work," *Harvard Business Review*, 71 (September–October 1993): 54–63. Also see Peter Nulty, "Incentive Pay Can Be Crippling," *Fortune* (November 13, 1995): 23; Robert Eisenberger and Judy Cameron, "Detrimental Effects of Reward," *American Psychologist*, 51 (November 1996): 1153–1166; and Alfie Kohn, "Challenging Behaviorist Dogma: Myths About Money and Motivation," *Compensation & Benefits Review*, 30 (March–April 1998): 27, 33–37.

60. Employee involvement is thoughtfully discussed in Jay R. Galbraith, Edward E. Lawler III, and Associates, *Organizing for the Future: The New Logic for Managing Complex Organizations* (San Francisco: Jossey-Bass, 1993), chaps. 6 and 7. Also see William G. Lee, "The Society Builders," *Management Review*, 88 (September 1999): 52–57.

61. See W. Alan Randolph, "Navigating the Journey to Empowerment," *Organizational Dynamics*, 23 (Spring 1995): 19–32; Robert C. Ford and Myron D. Fottler, "Empowerment: A Matter of Degree," *Academy of Management Executive*, 9 (August 1995): 21–31; Gretchen M. Spreitzer, "Social Structural Characteristics of Psychological Empowerment," *Academy of Management Journal*, 39 (April 1996): 483–504. Another view is presented in Martin M. Broadwell, "Why Command & Control Won't Go Away," *Training*, 32 (September 1995): 62–68.

62. Tim R. V. Davis, "Open-Book Management: Its Promise and Pitfalls," *Organizational Dynamics*, 25 (Winter 1997): 7–20. Also see John Case, "HR Learns How to Open the Books," *HRMagazine*, 43 (May 1998): 70–76; Perry Pascarella, "Open the Books to Unleash Your People," *Management Review*, 87 (May 1998): 58–60; and "July Poll Results: Open-Book Management," *HRMagazine*, 43 (September 1998): 18.

63. See Edward E. Lawler III and Susan A. Mohrman, "Quality Circles: After the Honeymoon," *Organizational Dynamics*, 15 (Spring 1987): 42–54; and Gerald E. Ledford Jr., Edward E. Lawler III, and Susan A. Mohrman, "The Quality Circle and Its Variations," in *Productivity in Organizations*, eds. John P. Campbell, Richard J. Campbell, and Associates (San Francisco: Jossey-Bass, 1988), pp. 255–294.

64. Evidence of a positive long-term impact on productivity may be found in Mitchell L. Marks, Philip H. Mirvis, Edward J. Hackett, and James F. Grady Jr., "Employee Participation in a Quality Circle Program: Impact on Quality of Work Life, Productivity, and Absenteeism," *Journal of Applied Psychology*, 71 (February 1986): 61–69. Also see Everett E. Adam Jr., "Quality Circle Performance," *Journal of Management*, 17 (March 1991): 25–39.

65. Charles G. Burck, "What Happens When Workers Manage Themselves," *Fortune* (July 27, 1981): 64.

66. Frank Shipper, "Tapping Creativity," *Quality Circles Journal*, 4 (August 1981): 12. Also see Amal Kumar Naj, "Some Manufacturers Drop Effort to Adopt Japanese Techniques," *The Wall Street Journal* (May 7, 1993): A1.

67. For more, see Ruth Wageman, "Critical Success Factors for Creating Superb Self-Managing Teams," *Organizational Dynamics*, 26 (Summer 1997): 49–61; Milan Moravec, Odd Jan Johannessen, and Thor A. Hjelmas, "The Well-Managed SMT," *Management Review*, 87 (June 1998): 56–58; Bradley L. Kirkman and Benson Rosen, "Beyond Self-Management: Antecedents and Consequences of Team Empowerment," *Academy of Management Journal*, 42 (February 1999): 58–74; Gary Dessler, "How to Earn Your Employees' Commitment," *Academy of Management Executive*, 13 (May 1999): 58–67; and Carla Joinson, "Teams at Work," *HRMagazine*, 44 (May 1999): 30–36.

68. See Susan Caminiti, "What Team Leaders Need to Know," *Fortune* (February 20, 1995): 93–100.

69. "1996 Industry Report: What Self-Managing Teams Manage," *Training*, 33 (October 1996): 69.

70. Brian Dumaine, "Who Needs a Boss?" *Fortune* (May 7, 1990): 52.

71. John Hoerr, "The Payoff from Teamwork," *Business Week* (July 10, 1989): 57.

72. See John Hoerr, "Work Teams Can Rev Up Paper-Pushers, Too," *Business Week* (November 28, 1988): 64–72; and Beverly Geber, "Can TQM Cure Health Care?" *Training*, 29 (August 1992): 25–34.

73. Adapted from David I. Levine, "Participation, Productivity, and the Firm's Environment," *California Management Review*, 32 (Summer 1990): 86–100.

74. For good advice, see Robert C. Liden, Sandy J. Wayne, and Lisa Bradway, "Connections Make the Difference," *HRMagazine*, 41 (February 1996): 73–79; and Michael Donovan, "The First Step to Self-Direction is NOT Empowerment," *Journal for Quality and Participation*, 19 (June 1996): 64–66.

75. Katherine I. Miller and Peter R. Monge, "Participation, Satisfaction, and Productivity: A Meta-Analytic Review," *Academy of Management Journal*, 29 (December 1986): 748.

76. For example, see Adolph Haasen, "Opel Eisenach GMBH— Creating a High-Productivity Workplace," *Organizational Dynamics*, 24 (Spring 1996): 80–85.

77. See Karen S. Kush and Linda K. Stroh, "Flextime: Myth or Reality?" *Business Horizons*, 37 (September–October 1994): 51–55; David Stamps, "Taming Time with Flexible Work," *Training*, 32 (May 1995): 60–66; Elizabeth Sheley, "Flexible Work Options: Beyond 9 to 5," *HRMagazine*, 41 (February 1996): 52–58; and Genevieve Capowski, "The Joy of Flex," *Management Review*, 85 (March 1996): 12–18.

78. Data from "Fourth of Full-Timers Enjoy Flexible Hours," *HRMagazine*, 43 (June 1998): 26, 28.

79. Data from "Valued Benefits for Families," *USA Today* (September 16, 1998): 1B. Also see "Royal Bank's Workers Laud Flexibility," *HRMagazine*, 43 (December 1998): 31–31.

80. Data from V. K. Narayanan and Raghu Nath, "A Field Test of Some Attitudinal and Behavioral Consequences of Flextime," *Journal of Applied Psychology*, 67 (April 1982): 214–218; David A. Ralston, William P. Anthony, and David J. Gustafson, "Employees May Love Flextime, but What Does It Do to the Organization's Productivity?" *Journal of Applied Psychology*, 70 (May 1985): 272–279; and Charles S. Rodgers, "The Flexible Workplace: What Have We Learned?" *Human Resources Management*, 31 (Fall 1992): 183–199.

81. See Jon L. Pierce and Randall B. Dunham, "The 12-Hour Work Day: A 48-Hour, Eight-Day Week," *Academy of Management Journal*, 35 (December 1992): 1086–1098; and Dominic Bencivenga, "Compressed Weeks Fill an HR Niche," *HRMagazine*, 40 (June 1995): 71–74.

82. Jane Easter Bahls, "Two for One: A Working Idea," *Nation's Business* (June 1989): 28. Also see Elizabeth Sheley, "Job Sharing Offers Unique Challenges," *HRMagazine*, 41 (January 1996): 46–49; Carla Joinson, "Time Share," *HRMagazine*, 43 (December 1998): 104–112; and "Is It Nature or Nurture?" *Inc.*, 21 (April 1999): 103.

83. Data from M. F. J. Martens, F. J. N. Nijhuis, M. P. J. Van Boxtel, and J. A. Knottnerus, "Flexible Work Schedules and Mental and Physical Health. A Study of a Working Population with Non-Traditional Working Hours," *Journal of Organizational Behavior*, 20 (January 1999): 35–46.

84. For more, see Gene Koretz, "Parental Leave: Healthier Kids," *Business Week* (January 18, 1999): 30; Bill Leonard, "British Lawmakers Plan to Expand Family Leave Rights," *HRMagazine*, 44 (April 1999): 26; Bill Leonard, "Relieving FMLA Headaches," *HR Magazine*, 44 (July 1999): 40–44; and Eric Paltell, "FMLA: After Six Years, a Bit More Clarity," *HR Magazine*, 44 (September 1999): 144–150.

85. See Michele Galen, "Sure, 'Unpaid Leave' Sounds Simple, but . . ." *Business Week* (August 9, 1993): 32–33.

86. Data from Ann Therese Palmer, "Who's Minding the Baby? The Company," *Business Week* (April 26, 1999): 32. Also see Stephanie Armour, "Watching the Kids on the Boss' Dime," *USA Today* (August 25, 1999): 3B; and Nancy Hatch Woodward, "Child Care to the Rescue," *HRMagazine*, 44 (August 1999): 82–88.

87. See Jerry Goodstein, "Employer Involvement in Eldercare: An Organizational Adaptation Perspective," *Academy of Management Journal*, 38 (December 1995): 1657–1671; and Kate Walter, "Elder Care Obligations Challenge the Next Generation," *HRMagazine*, 41 (July 1996): 98–103.

88. For background information, see Richard S. DeFrank and John M. Ivancevich, "Stress on the Job: An Executive Update," *Academy of Management Executive*, 12 (August 1998): 55–66; Lin Grensing-Pophal, "HR, Heal Thyself," *HRMagazine*, 44 (March 1999): 82–88; and Stephanie Armour, "Employers Urge Workers to Chill Out Before Burning Out," *USA Today* (June 22, 1999): 5B.

89. See Phaedra Brotherton, "Paybacks Are Healthy," *HRMagazine: Focus*, 43 (August 1998): 2–6; Nancy Hatch Woodward, "Add a Refreshing Touch to Benefit Programs," *HRMagazine*, 43 (October 1998): 106–110; Michael Hickins, "Mental Wellness in the Workplace," *Management Review*, 88 (January 1999): 9; and "Employers Promote Healthy Habits," *HRMagazine*, 44 (February 1999): 32, 34.

90. Data from Shelly Branch, "The 100 Best Companies to Work for in America," *Fortune* (January 11, 1999): 134.

91. See Hal Lancaster, "Sabbaticals Can Help You Improve Your Job or Spur a New Career," *The Wall Street Journal* (February 13, 1996): B1; and Stephanie Armour, "Workers View Sabbaticals as Two-Edged Sword," *USA Today* (September 8, 1997): 3B.

Chapter 14

Opening Quotation Gareth R. Jones and Jennifer M. George, "The Experience and Evolution of Trust: Implications for Cooperation and Teamwork," *Academy of Management Review*, 23 (July 1998): 543.

Opening Case Earle Eldridge, "After Spotting Paint Glitch, Lear Workers Eliminate It," *USA Today* (May 7, 1999): 6B. Copyright 1999, USA Today. Reprinted with permission.

Closing Case Republished with permission of *The Wall Street Journal* from "With the Stakes High, a Lucent Duo Conquers Distance and Culture," by Thomas Petzinger Jr., *The Wall Street Journal* (April 23, 1999). Permission conveyed through Copyright Clearance Center, Inc.

1. James P. Masciarelli, "Are You Managing Your Relationships?" *Management Review*, 87 (April 1998): 41. Also see Charles Ehin, "Fostering Both Sides of Human Nature—The Foundation for Collaborative Relationships," *Business Horizons*, 41 (May–June 1998): 15–25.

2. Joseph A. Litterer, *The Analysis of Organizations*, 2nd ed. (New York: Wiley, 1973), p. 231. Also see Deborah F. Crown and Joseph G. Rosse, "Yours, Mine, and Ours: Facilitating Group Productivity Through the Integration of Individual and Group Goals," *Organizational Behavior and Human Decision Processes*, 64 (November 1995): 138–150; and Glenn R. Carroll and Albert C. Teo, "On the Social Networks of Managers," *Academy of Management Journal*, 39 (April 1996): 421–440.

3. For an excellent elaboration of this definition, see David Horton Smith, "A Parsimonious Definition of 'Group': Toward Conceptual Clarity and Scientific Utility," *Sociological Inquiry*, 37 (Spring 1967): 141–167. The importance of social skills in today's diverse workplace is discussed in Carla Joinson, "A Return to Good Manners," *HRMagazine*, 42 (February 1997): 85–89.

4. For related research, see Priti Pradhan Shah, "Who Are Employees' Social Referents? Using a Network Perspective to Determine Referent Others," *Academy of Management Journal*, 41 (June 1998): 249–268; and Ajay Mehra, Martin Kilduff, and Daniel J. Brass, "At the Margins: A Distinctiveness Approach to the Social Identity and Social Networks of Underrepresented Groups," *Academy of Management Journal*, 41 (August 1998): 441–452.

5. For example, see Del Jones, "Employees Rally 'Round the Copier," *USA Today*, (November 16, 1995): 4B; and Thomas A. Stewart, "The Invisible Key to Success," *Fortune* (August 5, 1996): 173–176.

6. David Krackhardt and Jeffrey R. Hanson, "Informal Networks: The Company Behind the Chart," *Harvard Business Review*, 71 (July–August 1993): 104.

7. For a review of small group research, see John M. Levine and Richard L. Moreland, "Progress in Small Group Research," in *Annual Review of Psychology*, vol. 41, ed. Mark R. Rosenzweig and Lyman W. Porter (Palo Alto, Calif.: Annual Reviews Inc., 1990), pp. 139–155.

8. See Cathy Olofson, "Let Outsiders In, Turn Your Insiders Out," *Fast Company*, no. 22 (February–March 1999): 46.

9. For more, see Naomi Ellemers, Russell Spears, and Bertjan Doosje, "Sticking Together or Falling Apart: In-Group Identification as a Psychological Determinant of Group Commitment Versus Individual Mobility," *Journal of Personality and Social Psychology*, 72 (March 1997): 617–626; Hank Rothgerber, "External Intergroup Threat as an Antecedent to Perceptions of In-Group and Out-Group Homogeneity," *Journal of Personality and Social Psychology*, 73 (December 1997): 1206–1212; and Bertjan Doosje, Nyla R. Branscombe, Russell Spears, and Antony S. R. Manstead, "Guilty by Association: When One's Group Has a Negative History," *Journal of Personality and Social Psychology*, 75 (October 1998): 872–886.

10. Peter Nulty, "Cool Heads Are Trying to Keep Commodore Hot," *Fortune* (July 23, 1984): 38, 40.

11. Albert A. Harrison, *Individuals and Groups: Understanding Social Behavior* (Monterey, Calif.: Brooks/Cole, 1976), p. 16. Also see Elizabeth Wolfe Morrison, "Role Definitions and Organizational Citizenship Behavior: The Importance of the Employee's Perspective," *Academy of Management Journal*, 37 (December 1994): 1543–1567; Richard G. Netemeyer, Scott Burton, and Mark W. Johnston, "A Nested Comparison of Four Models of the Consequences of Role Perception Variables," *Organizational Behavior*

and Human Decision Processes, 61 (January 1995): 77–93; and Linn Van Dyne and Jeffrey A. LePine, "Helping and Voice Extra-Role Behaviors: Evidence of Construct and Predictive Validity," *Academy of Management Journal*, 41 (February 1998): 108–119.

12. See, for example, Jo Ellen Moore, "Are You Burning Out Valuable Resources?" *HRMagazine*, 44 (January 1999): 93–97.

13. Harrison, *Individuals and Groups*, p. 401.

14. For example, see Gary Blau, "Influence of Group Lateness on Individual Lateness: A Cross-Level Examination," *Academy of Management Journal*, 38 (October 1995): 1483–1496.

15. Adapted from Daniel C. Feldman, "The Development and Enforcement of Group Norms," *Academy of Management Review*, 9 (January 1984): 47–53. Also see Jose M. Marques, Dominic Abrams, Dario Paez, and Cristina Martinez-Taboada, "The Role of Categorization and In-Group Norms in Judgments of Groups and Their Members," *Journal of Personality and Social Psychology*, 75 (October 1998): 976–988.

16. See Kenneth J. Bettenhausen and Keith J. Murnigham, "The Development of an Intragroup Norm and the Effects of Interpersonal and Structural Challenges," *Administrative Science Quarterly*, 36 (March 1991): 20–35.

17. Gwendolyn Kelly, "Why This Med Student Is Sticking with Primary Care," *Business Week* (November 2, 1992): 125.

18. For related research, see Linda Klebe Trevino and Bart Victor, "Peer Reporting of Unethical Behavior: A Social Context Perspective," *Academy of Management Journal*, 35 (March 1992): 38–64.

19. From *Group Effectiveness in Organizations* by L. N. Jewell and H. J. Reitz (Scott, Foresman, 1981). Reprinted by permission of the authors. Also see Ronald J. Deluga, "Can Work Groups Be Made More Effective? YES!" *Academy of Management Executive*, 8 (August 1994): 105–106; and Jean Lipman-Blumen and Harold J. Leavitt, "Hot Groups 'with Attitude': A New Organizational State of Mind," *Organizational Dynamics*, 27 (Spring 1999): 63–73.

20. Susan A. Wheelan and Felice Tilin, "The Relationship Between Faculty Group Development and School Productivity," *Small Group Research*, 30 (February 1999): 59.

21. For more, see Chao C. Chen, Xiao-Ping Chen, and James R. Meindl, "How Can Cooperation Be Fostered? The Cultural Effects of Individualism-Collectivism," *Academy of Management Review*, 23 (April 1998): 285–304.

22. The following discussion of the six stages of group development is adapted from *Group Effectiveness in Organizations* by Linda N. Jewell and H. Joseph Reitz. Copyright 1981, Scott, Foresman and Company, pp. 15–20. Reprinted by permission. For groundbreaking research in this area, see Warren G. Bennis and Herbert A. Shepard, "A Theory of Group Development," *Human Relations*, 9 (1956); 415–437; Bruce W. Tuckman and Mary Ann C. Jensen, "Stages of Small-Group Development Revisited," *Group & Organization Studies*, 2 (December 1977): 419–427; and John F. McGrew, John G. Bilotta, and Janet M. Deeney, "Software Team Formation and Decay: Extending the Standard Model for Small Groups," *Small Group Research*, 30 (April 1999): 209–234.

23. For a cross-cultural perspective, see Cristina B. Gibson, "Do They Do What They Believe They Can? Group Efficacy and Group Effectiveness Across Tasks and Cultures," *Academy of Management Journal*, 42 (April 1999): 138–152.

24. For example, see Mark C. Bolino, "Citizenship and Impression Management: Good Soldiers or Good Actors?" *Academy of Management Review*, 24 (January 1999): 82–98; Marjorie L. Randall, Russell Cropanzano, Carol A. Bormann, and Andrej Birjulin, "Organizational Politics and Organizational Support as Predictors of Work Attitudes, Job Performance, and Organizational Citizenship Behavior," *Journal of Organizational Behavior*, 20 (March 1999): 159–174; and Barry R. Schlenker and Thomas W. Britt, "Beneficial Impression Management: Strategically Controlling Information to Help Friends," *Journal of Personality and Social Psychology*, 76 (April 1999): 559–573.

25. David E. Hall, "Winning at Office Politics," *Credit & Financial Management*, 86 (April 1984): 20.

26. Marcia Stepanek, "How Fast Is Net Fast?" *Business Week* E.BIZ (November 1, 1999): EB 54.

27. Data from "9-to-5 Not for Everyone," *USA Today* (October 13, 1999): 1B.

28. See Anne Fisher, "Do I Have to Kiss Up?" *Fortune* (March 31, 1997): 123; and Louisa Wah, "Managing—Manipulating?—Your Reputation," *Management Review*, 87 (October 1998): 46–50.

29. See Andrew J. DuBrin, *Winning Office Politics: DuBrin's Guide for the '90s* (Englewood Cliffs, N.J.: Prentice-Hall, 1990); Ken Myers, "Games Companies Play (and How to Stop Them)," *Training*, 29 (June 1992): 68–70; and Stanley Bing, "Are You a Master of (In)Sincerity?" *Fortune* (November 13, 1995): 63.

30. Ethical implications are discussed in Erik W. Larson and Jonathan B. King, "The Systematic Distortion of Information: An Ongoing Challenge to Management," *Organizational Dynamics*, 24 (Winter 1996): 49–61; and Peter Troiano, "Nice Guys Finish First," *Management Review*, 87 (December 1998): 8.

31. Victor Murray and Jeffrey Gandz, "Games Executives Play: Politics at Work," *Business Horizons*, 23 (December 1980): 16.

32. Andrew J. DuBrin, *Fundamentals of Organizational Behavior: An Applied Perspective*, 2nd ed. (Elmsford, N.Y.: Pergamon Press, 1978): p. 154.

33. Dan Farrell and James C. Petersen, "Patterns of Political Behavior in Organizations," *Academy of Management Review*, 7 (July 1982): 407. Also see Andrea Nierenberg, "Masterful Networking," *Training & Development*, 53 (February 1999): 51–53.

34. James R. Healey, "Covert Activity Saved Sports Car," *USA Today* (March 19, 1997): 1B. Also see Denis Collins, "Case Study: 15 Lessons Learned from the Death of a Gainsharing Plan," *Compensation & Benefits Review*, 28 (March–April 1996): 31–40.

35. Adapted from Dan L. Madison, Robert W. Allen, Lyman W. Porter, Patricia A. Renwick, and Bronston T. Mayes, "Organizational Politics: An Exploration of Managers' Perceptions," *Human Relations*, 33 (February 1980): 79–100. Also see Andrew J. DuBrin, "Career Maturity, Organizational Rank, and Political Behavioral Tendencies: A Correlational Analysis of Organizational Politics and Career Experience," *Psychological Reports*, 63 (October 1988): 531–537.

36. Madison et al., "Organizational Politics," p. 97.

37. These political tactics have been adapted from a more extensive list found in DuBrin, *Fundamentals of Organizational Behavior*, pp. 158–170. Also see Jean Mannhelmer Forray, "A Good Relationship with the Boss Pays Off," *Academy of Management Executive*, 9 (February 1995): 79; Arthur G. Bedeian, "Workplace Envy," *Organizational Dynamics*, 23 (Spring 1995): 49–56; Hal Lancaster, "Standing Tall (but Not Too Tall) When You're No. 2," *The Wall Street Journal* (May 21, 1996): B1; Roos Vonk, "The Slime Effect: Suspicion and Dislike of Likeable Behavior Toward Superiors," *Journal of Personality and Social Psychology*, 74 (April 1998): 849–864; and Carol Memmott, "How to Play Cutthroat Office Politics and Win," *USA Today* (July 13, 1998): 2B.

38. For more, see L. A. Witt, "Enhancing Organizational Goal Congruence: A Solution to Organizational Politics," *Journal of Applied Psychology*, 83 (August 1998): 666–674.

39. Adapted from DuBrin, *Fundamentals of Organizational Behavior*, pp. 179–182.

40. See Solomon E. Asch, *Social Psychology* (Englewood Cliffs, N.J.: Prentice-Hall, 1952), chap. 16.

41. For details, see Taha Amir, "The Asch Conformity Effect: A Study in Kuwait," *Social Behavior and Personality*, 12, no. 2 (1984): 187–190; Timothy P. Williams and Shunya Sogon, "Group Composition and Conforming Behavior in Japanese Students," *Japanese Psychological Research*, 26, no. 4 (1984): 231–234.

42. Data from Rod Bond and Peter B. Smith, "Culture and Conformity: A Meta-Analysis of Studies Using Asch's (1952b, 1956) Line Judgment Task," *Psychological Bulletin*, 119 (January 1996): 111–137. Also see Sandra L. Robinson and Anne M. O'Leary-Kelly, "Monkey See, Monkey Do: The Influence of Work Groups on the Antisocial Behavior of Employees," *Academy of Management Journal*, 41 (December 1998): 658–672.

43. Irving L. Janis, *Groupthink*, 2nd ed. (Boston: Houghton Mifflin, 1982), p. 9. See also A. Amin Mohamed and Frank A. Wiebe, "Toward a Process Theory of Groupthink," *Small Group Research*, 27 (August 1996): 416–430; Kjell Granstrom and Dan Stiwne, "A Bipolar Model of Groupthink: An Expansion of Janis's Concept," *Small Group Research*, 29 (February 1998): 32–56; the entire February–March 1998 issue of *Organizational Behavior and Human Decision Processes;* Annette R. Flippen, "Understanding Groupthink from a Self-Regulatory Perspective," *Small Group Research*, 30 (April 1999): 139–165; and Jin Nam Choi and Myung Un Kim, "The Organizational Application of Groupthink and Its Limitations in Organizations," *Journal of Applied Psychology*, 84 (April 1999): 297–306.

44. Adapted from a list in Janis, *Groupthink*, pp. 174–175.

45. Ibid., p. 275.

46. See Rob Norton, "New Thinking on the Causes—and Costs—of Yes Men (and Women)," *Fortune* (November 28, 1994): 31.

47. For excellent discussions of the devil's advocate role, see Charles R. Schwenk, "Devil's Advocacy in Managerial Decision Making," *Journal of Management Studies*, 21 (April 1984): 153–168; and Richard A. Cosier and Charles R. Schwenk, "Agreement and Thinking Alike: Ingredients for Poor Decisions," *Academy of Management Executive*, 4 (February 1990): 69–74.

48. Adapted from a list in Janis, *Groupthink*, pp. 262–271.

49. Julia Flynn, "Giving the Board More Clout," *Business Week*, Bonus Issue: Reinventing America (1992): 74. Also see Richard A. Melcher, "The Best & Worst Boards," *Business Week* (November 25, 1996): 82–98; John A. Byrne, "Listen Up," *Business Week* (November 25, 1996): 100–106; Anthony Bianco and John A. Byrne, "The Rush to Quality on Corporate Boards," *Business Week* (March 3, 1997): 34–35; James D. Westphal, "Collaboration in the Boardroom: Behavioral and Performance Consequences of CEO-Board Social Ties," *Academy of Management Journal*, 42 (February 1999): 7–24; and Gene Koretz, "Friendly Boards Are Not All Bad," *Business Week* (June 14, 1999): 34.

50. As quoted in Sheila M. Puffer, "Continental Airlines' CEO Gordon Bethune on Teams and New Product Development," *Academy of Management Executive*, 13 (August 1999): 28.

51. See Lynda McDermott, Bill Waite, and Nolan Brawley, "Putting Together a World-Class Team," *Training & Development*, 53 (January 1999): 47–51; Donald Gerwin, "Team Empowerment in New Product Development," *Business Horizons*, 42 (July–August 1999): 29–36; and Cheryl Dahle, "Xtreme Teams," *Fast Company*, no. 29 (November 1999): 310–326.

52. An instructive distinction between work groups and teams is presented in Jon R. Katzenbach and Douglas K. Smith, "The Discipline of Teams," *Harvard Business Review*, 71 (March–April 1993): 111–120. Also see Jon R. Katzenbach and Douglas K. Smith, *The Wisdom of Teams: Creating the High-Performance Organization* (New York: HarperCollins, 1999); Paul W. Mulvey, John F. Veiga, and Priscilla M. Elsass, "When Teammates Raise a White Flag," *Academy of Management Executive*, 10 (February 1996): 40–49; and Thomas A. Stewart, "The Great Conundrum—You vs. the Team," *Fortune* (November 25, 1996): 165–166.

53. See Daniel R. Denison, Stuart L. Hart, and Joel A. Kahn, "From Chimneys to Cross-Functional Teams: Developing and Validating a Diagnostic Model," *Academy of Management Journal*, 39 (August 1996): 1005–1023; and Bob Filipczak, "Concurrent Engineering: A Team by Any Other Name?" *Training*, 33 (August 1996): 54–59; Mary Uhl-Bien and George B. Graen, "Individual Self-Management: Analysis of Professionals' Self-Managing Activities in Functional and Cross-Functional Work Teams," *Academy of Management Journal*, 41 (June 1998): 340–350; and Avan R. Jassawalla and Hemant C. Sashittal, "Building Collaborative Cross-Functional New Product Teams," *Academy of Management Executive*, 13 (August 1999): 50–63.

54. Dori Jones Yang, "Grace Robertson: Piloting a Superfast Rollout at Boeing," *Business Week* (August 30, 1993): 77.

55. See Nancy B. Kurland and Diane E. Bailey, "Telework: The Advantages and Challenges of Working Here, There, Anywhere, and Anytime," *Organizational Dynamics*, 28 (Autumn 1999): 53–68.

56. See Kim Kiser, "Working on World Time," *Training*, 36 (March 1999): 28–34.

57. See Jack Gordon, "The Team Troubles That Won't Go Away," *Training*, 31 (August 1994): 25–34; Brian Dumaine, "The Trouble with Teams," *Fortune* (September 5, 1994): 86–92; Lawrence Holpp and Robert Phillips, "When Is a Team Its Own Worst Enemy?" *Training*, 32 (September 1995): 71–82; Steven R. Rayner, "Team Traps: What They Are, How to Avoid Them," *National Productivity Review*, 15 (Summer 1996): 101–115; James Wallace Bishop and K. Dow Scott, "How Commitment Affects Team Performance," *HRMagazine*, 42 (February 1997): 107–111; and Ellen Neuborne, "Companies Save, but Workers Pay," *USA Today* (February 25, 1997): 1B–2B.

58. See Hans J. Thamhain, "Managing Technologically Innovative Team Efforts Toward New Product Success," *Journal of Product Innovation Management*, 7 (March 1990): 5–18. Also see the following study of team effectiveness: Richard J. Magjuka and Timothy T. Baldwin, "Team-Based Employee Involvement Programs: Effects of Design and Administration," *Personnel Psychology*, 44 (Winter 1991): 793–812.

59. See Mark R. Edwards, "Symbiotic Leadership: A Creative Partnership for Managing Organizational Effectiveness," *Business Horizons*, 35 (May–June 1992): 28–33; Richard Rapaport, "To Build a Winning Team: An Interview with Head Coach Bill Walsh," *Harvard Business Review*, 71 (January–February 1993): 111–120; and William G. Dyer, *Team Building: Current Issues and New Alternatives*, 3rd ed. (Reading, Mass.: Addison-Wesley, 1995).

60. See Mark E. Haskins, Jeanne Liedtka, and John Rosenblum, "Beyond Teams: Toward an Ethic of Collaboration," *Organizational Dynamics*, 26 (Spring 1998): 34–50; and Allan B. Drexler and Russ Forrester, "Interdependence: The Crux of Teamwork," *HRMagazine*, 43 (September 1998): 52–62.

61. See Roger C. Mayer, James H. Davis, and F. David Schoorman, "An Integrative Model of Organizational Trust," *Academy of Management*

Review, 20 (July 1995): 709–734; Barbara Ettorre, "The Trust Factor," *Management Review*, 85 (July 1996): 19; and William Cohen, "The Critical Importance of Integrity," *Canadian Manager*, 24 (Spring 1999): 20, 28.

62. See Gerald Andrews, "Mistrust, the Hidden Obstacle to Empowerment," *HRMagazine*, 39 (September 1994): 66–70; and Gretchen M. Spreitzer and Aneil K. Mishra, "Giving Up Control Without Losing Control," *Group & Organization Management*, 24 (June 1999): 155–187.

63. Data from Robert J. Samuelson, "Great Expectations," *Newsweek* (January 8, 1996): 24–33.

64. Tom Davis and Michael J. Landa, "The Trust Deficit," *Canadian Manager*, 24 (Spring 1999): 10.

65. See Dale E. Zand, "Trust and Managerial Problem Solving," *Administrative Science Quarterly*, 17 (June 1972): 229–239.

66. Thomas J. Peters and Robert H. Waterman Jr., *In Search of Excellence* (New York: Harper & Row, 1982), p. 245.

67. Trustworthiness is discussed in Stephen R. Covey, *Principle-Centered Leadership* (New York: Simon & Schuster, 1991), pp. 171–172. Also see the entire July 1998 issue of *Academy of Management Review;* Andrew C. Wicks, Shawn L. Berman, and Thomas M. Jones, "The Structure of Optimal Trust: Moral and Strategic Implications," *Academy of Management Review*, 24 (January 1999): 99–116; Oren Harari, "The Trust Factor," *Management Review*, 88 (January 1999): 28–31; and John K. Butler Jr., "Trust Expectations, Information Sharing, Climate of Trust, and Negotiation Effectiveness and Efficiency," *Group & Organization Management*, 24 (June 1999): 217–238.

68. Adapted from Fernando Bartolomé, "Nobody Trusts the Boss Completely—Now What?" *Harvard Business Review*, 67 (March–April 1989): 137–139.

69. See Ranjay Gulati, "Does Familiarity Breed Trust? The Implications of Repeated Ties for Contractual Choice in Alliances," *Academy of Management Journal*, 38 (February 1995): 85–112; Arvind Parkhe, "Understanding Trust in International Alliances," *Journal of World Business*, 33 (Fall 1998): 219–240; Manfred F. R. Kets De Vries, "High-Performance Teams: Lessons from the Pygmies," *Organizational Dynamics*, 27 (Winter 1999): 66–77; and Prithviraj Chattopadhyay, "Beyond Direct and Symmetrical Effects: The Influence of Demographic Dissimilarity on Organizational Citizenship Behavior," *Academy of Management Journal*, 42 (June 1999): 273–287.

Chapter 15

Opening Quotation As quoted in Keith H. Hammonds, "The Monroe Doctrine," *Fast Company*, no. 28 (October 1999): 232.

Opening Case Micheline Maynard, "She's Jump-Starting Saturn," *USA Today* (February 9, 1999): 3B. Copyright 1999, USA Today. Reprinted with permission.

Closing Case Anthony J. Balsamo, "The Power of Empowerment." Reprinted from *Management Review*, 88 (November 1999): 11. © 1999 American Management Association International. Reprinted by permission of American Management Association International, New York, NY. All rights reserved. **http://www.amanet.org.**

1. Influence tips are offered in Mary Lippitt, "How to Influence Leaders," *Training & Development*, 53 (March 1999): 18–22; "Stephen Covey," *Fast Company*, no. 23 (April 1999): 96; and Lyle Sussman, "How to Frame a Message: The Art of Persuasion and Negotiation," *Business Horizons*, 42 (July–August 1999): 2–6.

2. See Gary Yukl and Cecilia M. Falbe, "Influence Tactics and Objectives in Upward, Downward, and Lateral Influence Attempts," *Journal of Applied Psychology*, 75 (April 1990); 132–140. Also see David Kipnis, Stuart M. Schmidt, and Ian Wilkinson, "Intraorganizational Influence Tactics: Explorations in Getting One's Way," *Journal of Applied Psychology*, 64 (August 1980): 440–452; and Chester A. Schriesheim and Timothy R. Hinkin, "Influence Tactics Used by Subordinates: A Theoretical and Empirical Analysis of the Kipnis, Schmidt, and Wilkinson Subscales," *Journal of Applied Psychology*, 75 (June 1990): 246–257.

3. Adapted from Yukl and Falbe, "Influence Tactics and Objectives in Upward, Downward, and Lateral Influence Attempts." Also see Gary Yukl, Cecilia M. Falbe, and Joo Young Youn, "Patterns of Influence Behavior for Managers," *Group & Organization Management*, 18 (March 1993): 5–28; Randall A. Gordon, "Impact of Ingratiation on Judgments and Evaluations: A Meta-Analytic Investigation," *Journal of Personality and Social Psychology*, 71 (July 1996): 54–70; Bennett J. Tepper, Regina J. Eisenbach, Susan L. Kirby, and Paula W. Potter, "Test of a Justice-Based Model of Subordinates' Resistance to Downward Influence Attempts," *Group & Organization Management*, 23 (June 1998): 144–160; William D. Crano and Xin Chen, "The Leniency Contract and Persistence of Majority and Minority Influence," *Journal of Personality and Social Psychology*, 74 (June 1998): 1437–1450; and Barbara Price Davis and Eric S. Knowles, "A Disrupt-Then-Reframe Technique of Social Influence," *Journal of Personality and Social Psychology*, 76 (February 1999): 192–199.

4. See George F. Dreher, Thomas W. Dougherty, and William Whitely, "Influence Tactics and Salary Attainment: A Gender-Specific Analysis," *Sex Roles*, 20 (May 1989): 535–550; and Herman Aguinis and Susan K. R. Adams, "Social-Role Versus Structural Models of Gender and Influence Use in Organizations," *Group & Organization Studies*, 23 (December 1998): 414–446.

5. See Mahfooz A. Ansari and Alka Kapoor, "Organizational Context and Upward Influence Tactics," *Organizational Behavior and Human Decision Processes*, 40 (August 1987): 39–49.

6. Dean Tjosvold, "The Dynamics of Positive Power," *Training and Development Journal*, 38 (June 1984): 72.

7. See Patricia Sellers, "Women, Sex & Power," *Fortune* (August 5, 1996): 42–56; and Thomas A. Stewart, "Get with the *New* Power Game," *Fortune* (January 13, 1997): 58–62. Also see Geoffrey Colvin, "Naked Power: The Scorecard," *Fortune* (April 27, 1998): 449, 451; and Craig Wilson, "'48 Laws' on Winning Whatever the Stakes," *USA Today* (September 30, 1998): 1D–2D.

8. Morgan McCall Jr., "Power, Influence, and Authority: The Hazards of Carrying a Sword," *Technical Report*, 10 (Greensboro, N.C.: Center for Creative Leadership, 1978), p. 5.

9. For more on these three effects of power, see Anthony T. Cobb, "An Episodic Model of Power: Toward an Integration of Theory and Research," *Academy of Management Review*, 9 (July 1984): 482–493. On power coalitions, both inside and outside the organization, see Henry Mintzberg, "Power and Organization Life Cycles," *Academy of Management Review*, 9 (April 1984): 207–224.

10. Based on Edwin P. Hollander and Lynn R. Offermann, "Power and Leadership in Organizations: Relationships in Transition," *American Psychologist*, 45 (February 1990): 179–189.

11. See William A. Kahn and Kathy E. Kram, "Authority at Work: Internal Models and Their Organizational Consequences," *Academy of Management Review*, 19 (January 1994): 17–50.

12. "There Is No State Here Anymore," *Newsweek* (February 24, 1997): 42.

13. For related discussion, see Allan R. Cohen and David L. Bradford, "Influence Without Authority: The Use of Alliances, Reciprocity,

and Exchange to Accomplish Work," *Organizational Dynamics*, 17 (Winter 1989): 4–17; and Allan R. Cohen and David L. Bradford, *Influence Without Authority* (New York: John Wiley & Sons, 1990).

14. See John R. P. French Jr. and Bertram Raven, "The Bases of Social Power," *Studies in Social Power*, ed. Dorwin Cartwright (Ann Arbor: University of Michigan Press, 1959), pp. 150–167. Eight different sources of power are discussed in Hugh R. Taylor, "Power at Work," *Personnel Journal*, 65 (April 1986): 42–49. Also see H. Eugene Baker III, "'Wax On—Wax Off': French and Raven at the Movies," *Journal of Management Education*, 17 (November 1993): 517–519.

15. John P. Kotter, "Power, Dependence, and Effective Management," *Harvard Business Review*, 55 (July–August 1977): 128. For related research, see Sydney Finkelstein, "Power in Top Management Teams: Dimensions, Measurement, and Validation," *Academy of Management Journal*, 35 (August 1992): 505–538; and Herminia Ibarra, "Network Centrality, Power, and Innovation Involvement: Determinants of Technical and Administrative Roles," *Academy of Management Journal*, 36 (June 1993): 471–501.

16. For a revealing case study, see John A. Byrne, "Chainsaw," *Business Week* (October 18, 1999): 128–147.

17. Patricia Sellers, "What Exactly Is Charisma?" *Fortune* (January 15, 1996): 68. Also see Daniel Sankowsky, "The Charismatic Leader as Narcissist: Understanding the Abuse of Power," *Organizational Dynamics*, 23 (Spring 1995): 57–71.

18. For an instructive review of research, see Philip M. Podsakoff and Chester A. Schriesheim, "Field Studies of French and Raven's Bases of Power: Critique, Reanalysis, and Suggestions for Future Research," *Psychological Bulletin*, 97 (May 1985): 387–411. Also see Chester A. Schriesheim, Timothy R. Hinkin, and Philip M. Podsakoff, "Can Ipsative and Single-Item Measures Produce Erroneous Results in Field Studies of French and Raven's (1959) Five Bases of Power? An Empirical Investigation," *Journal of Applied Psychology*, 76 (February 1991): 106–114; Daniel J. Brass and Marlene E. Burkhardt, "Potential Power and Power Use: An Investigation of Structure and Behavior," *Academy of Management Journal*, 36 (June 1993): 441–470; and Kevin W. Mossholder, Nathan Bennett, Edward R. Kemery, and Mark A. Wesolowski, "Relationships Between Bases of Power and Work Reactions: The Mediational Role of Procedural Justice," *Journal of Management*, 24, no. 4 (1998): 553–552.

19. See Mark R. Story, "The Secrets of Successful Empowerment," *National Productivity Review*, 14 (Summer 1995): 81–90; Gretchen M. Spreitzer, "Psychological Empowerment in the Workplace: Dimensions, Measurement, and Validation," *Academy of Management Journal*, 38 (October 1995): 1442–1465; Mark G. Becker, "Lessons in Empowerment," *Training*, 33 (September 1996): 35–42; Robert E. Quinn and Gretchen M. Spreitzer, "The Road to Empowerment: Seven Questions Every Leader Should Consider," *Organizational Dynamics*, 26 (Autumn 1997): 37–49; Bradley L. Kirkman and Benson Rosen, "Beyond Self-Management: Antecedents and Consequences of Team Empowerment," *Academy of Management Journal*, 42 (February 1999): 58–74; and Christine S. Koberg, R. Wayne Boss, Jason C. Senjem, and Eric A. Goodman, "Antecedents and Outcomes of Empowerment: Empirical Evidence from the Health Care Industry," *Group & Organization Management*, 24 (March 1999): 71–91.

20. Laurel Shaper Walters, "A Leader Redefines Management," *The Christian Science Monitor* (September 22, 1992): 14; and Ani Hadjian, "Follow the Leader," *Fortune* (November 27, 1995): 96. Also see Howard Rothman, "The Power of Empowerment," *Nation's Business* (June 1993): 49, 52.

21. Based on discussion in Covey, *Principle-Centered Leadership*, pp. 214–216. Also see W. Alan Randolph, "Navigating the Journey to Empowerment," *Organizational Dynamics*, 23 (Spring 1995): 19–32; and Alan J. H. Thorlakson and Robert P. Murray, "An Empirical Study of Empowerment in the Workplace," *Group & Organization Management*, 21 (March 1996): 67–83; Kyle Dover, "Avoiding Empowerment Traps," *Management Review*, 88 (January 1999): 51–55; and Richard A. Shafer, "Only the Agile Will Survive," *HRMagazine*, HR in the 21st Century, 44, no. 11 (1999): 50–51.

22. For a recent sampling, see Joseph A. Petrick, Robert F. Scherer, James D. Brodzinski, John F. Quinn, and M. Fall Ainina, "Global Leadership Skills and Reputational Capital: Intangible Resources for Sustainable Competitive Advantage," *Academy of Management Executive*, 13 (February 1999): 58–69; Robert M. Fulmer and Stacey Wagner, "Leadership: Lessons from the Best," *Training & Development*, 53 (March 1999): 29–32; and Harriet Rubin, "How Do We Understand Leadership? Badly. No, Stupidly," *Fast Company*, no. 29 (November 1999): 374–378.

23. See Jonathan E. Smith, Kenneth P. Carson, and Ralph A. Alexander, "Leadership: It Can Make a Difference," *Academy of Management Journal*, 27 (December 1984): 765–776; and Janet M. Dukerich, Mary Lippitt Nichols, Dawn R. Elm, and David A. Vollrath, "Moral Reasoning in Groups: Leaders Make a Difference," *Human Relations*, 43 (May 1990): 473–493.

24. Inspired by the definition in Andrew J. DuBrin, *Leadership: Research Findings, Practice and Skills*, 2nd ed. (Boston: Houghton Mifflin, 1998), p. 2.

25. See Gary Yukl, "Managerial Leadership: A Review of Theory and Research," *Journal of Management*, 15 (June 1989): 251–289; Gary A. Yukl, *Leadership in Organizations*, 2nd ed. (Englewood Cliffs, N.J.: Prentice-Hall, 1989); and Karl O. Magnusen, "The Legacy of Leadership Revisited," *Business Horizons*, 38 (November–December 1995): 3–7.

26. See David L. Cawthon, "Leadership: The Great Man Theory Revisited," *Business Horizons*, 39 (May–June 1996): 1–4; Nathan A. Forney, "Rommel in the Boardroom," *Business Horizons*, 42 (July–August 1999): 37–42; and Thomas A. Stewart, Alex Taylor III, Peter Petre, and Brent Schlender, "Henry Ford, Alfred P. Sloan, Tom Watson Jr., Bill Gates: The Businessman of the Century," *Fortune* (November 22, 1999): 109–128.

27. Fred Luthans, *Organizational Behavior*, 3rd ed. (New York: McGraw-Hill, 1981), p. 419. Also see Gail Dutton, "Leadership in a Post-Heroic Age," *Management Review*, 85 (October 1996): 7.

28. Ralph M. Stogdill, "Personal Factors Associated with Leadership: A Survey of the Literature," *Journal of Psychology*, 25 (1948): 63.

29. Data from James M. Kouzes and Barry Z. Posner, "The Credibility Factor: What Followers Expect from Their Leaders," *Business Credit*, 92 (July–August 1990): 24–28. Also see James M. Kouzes and Barry Z. Posner, *The Leadership Challenge: How to Get Extraordinary Things Done in Organizations* (San Francisco: Jossey-Bass, 1987); and Jennifer Reingold, "In Search of Leadership," *Business Week* (November 15, 1999): 172, 176.

30. Data from Judy B. Rosener, "Ways Women Lead," *Harvard Business Review*, 68 (November–December 1990): 119–125. Also see Chris Lee, "The Feminization of Management," *Training*, 31 (November 1994): 25–31.

31. See "Ways Women and Men Lead," *Harvard Business Review*, 69 (January–February 1991): 150–160.

32. Data from Alice H. Eagly and Blair T. Johnson, "Gender and Leadership Style: A Meta-Analysis," *Psychological Bulletin*, 108 (September 1990): 233–256. Also see Judith A. Kolb, "Are We Still

Stereotyping Leadership? A Look at Gender and Other Predictors of Leader Emergence," *Small Group Research*, 28 (August 1997): 370–393; Virginia W. Cooper, "Homophily or the Queen Bee Syndrome: Female Evaluation of Female Leadership," *Small Group Research*, 28 (November 1997): 483–499; and Robert K. Shelly and Paul T. Munroe, "Do Women Engage in Less Task Behavior Than Men?" *Sociological Perspectives*, 42 (Spring 1999): 49–67.

33. Kurt Lewin, Ronald Lippitt, and Ralph K. White, "Patterns of Aggressive Behavior in Experimentally Created 'Social Climates,'" *Journal of Social Psychology*, 10 (May 1939): 271–299.

34. The risks of shifting styles are discussed in Thomas L. Brown, "Managerial Waffling: In Politics—or in Business—Waffling Suggests Bad Leadership," *Industry Week* (January 18, 1993): 34. Also see Oren Harari, "Leadership vs. Autocracy: They Just Don't Get It!" *Management Review*, 85 (August 1996): 42–45.

35. For an informative summary of this research, see Edwin A. Fleishman, "Twenty Years of Consideration and Structure," in *Current Developments in the Study of Leadership*, ed. Edwin A. Fleishman and James G. Hunt (Carbondale, Ill.: Southern Illinois University Press, 1973), pp. 1–40. Also see Vishwanath V. Baba and Merle E. Ace, "Serendipity in Leadership: Initiating Structure and Consideration in the Classroom," *Human Relations*, 42 (June 1989): 509–525.

36. Three popular extensions of the Ohio State leadership studies may be found in Robert R. Blake and Anne McCanse, *Leadership Dilemmas—Grid Solutions* (Houston: Gulf Publishing, 1990); William J. Reddin, *Managerial Effectiveness* (New York: McGraw-Hill, 1970); and Paul Hersey and Kenneth H. Blanchard, *Management of Organizational Behavior: Utilizing Human Resources*, 5th ed. (Englewood Cliffs, N.J.: Prentice-Hall, 1988), p. 171. Empirical lack of support for Hersey and Blanchard's situational leadership theory is reported in Jane R. Goodson, Gail W. McGee, and James F. Cashman, "Situational Leadership Theory: A Test of Leadership Prescriptions," *Group & Organization Studies*, 14 (December 1989): 446–461.

37. See Abraham K. Korman, "Consideration, 'Initiating Structure,' and Organizational Criteria—A Review," *Personnel Psychology*, 19 (Winter 1966): 349–361.

38. See Blake and McCanse, *Leadership Dilemmas—Grid Solutions*.

39. See Tom Lester, "Taking Guard on the Grid," *Management Today* (March 1991): 93–94.

40. For details of this study, see Robert R. Blake and Jane Srygley Mouton, "Management by Grid® Principles or Situationalism: Which?" *Group & Organization Studies*, 6 (December 1981): 439–455. Also see Robert R. Blake and Jane Srygley Mouton, "A Comparative Analysis of Situationalism and 9,9 Management by Principle," *Organizational Dynamics*, 10 (Spring 1982): 20–43. For another view of leader behavior, see Susan A. Tynan, "Best Behaviors," *Management Review*, 88 (November 1999): 58–61.

41. Fred E. Fiedler, "Job Engineering for Effective Leadership: A New Approach," *Management Review*, 66 (September 1977): 29.

42. For an excellent comprehensive validation study, see Michael J. Strube and Joseph E. Garcia, "A Meta-Analytic Investigation of Fiedler's Contingency Model of Leadership Effectiveness," *Psychological Bulletin*, 90 (September 1981): 307–321.

43. Fred E. Fiedler and Martin M. Chemers, *Leadership and Effective Management* (Glenview, Ill.: Scott, Foresman, 1974), p. 91.

44. Robert J. House and Terence R. Mitchell, "Path-Goal Theory of Leadership," *Journal of Contemporary Business*, 3 (Autumn 1974): 85. The entire Autumn 1974 issue is devoted to an instructive review of contrasting theories of leadership.

45. See Jan P. Muczyk and Bernard C. Reimann, "The Case for Directive Leadership," *Academy of Management Executive*, 1 (November 1987): 301–311.

46. Adapted from House and Mitchell , "Path-Goal Theory of Leadership," p. 83.

47. For path-goal research, see Abduhl-Rahim A. Al-Gattan, "Test of the Path-Goal Theory of Leadership in the Multinational Domain," *Group & Organization Studies*, 10 (December 1985): 429–445; Robert T. Keller, "A Test of the Path-Goal Theory of Leadership with Need for Clarity as a Moderator in Research and Development Organizations," *Journal of Applied Psychology*, 74 (April 1989): 208–212; John E. Mathieu, "A Test of Subordinates' Achievement and Affiliation Needs as Moderators of Leader Path-Goal Relationships," *Basic and Applied Social Psychology*, 11 (June 1990): 179–189; and Retha A. Price, "An Investigation of Path-Goal Leadership Theory in Marketing Channels," *Journal of Retailing*, 67 (Fall 1991): 339–361.

48. See Victor H. Vroom and Philip W. Yetton, *Leadership and Decision-Making* (Pittsburgh: University of Pittsburgh Press, 1973); Victor H. Vroom, "A New Look at Managerial Decision Making," *Organizational Dynamics*, 1 (Spring 1973): 66–80; and Victor H. Vroom and Arthur G. Jago, *The New Leadership: Managing Participation in Organizations* (Englewood Cliffs, N.J.: Prentice-Hall, 1988).

49. The computer program is called MPO (Managing Participation in Organizations). It is available through Leadership Software, Inc., P. O. Box 271848, Houston, TX 77277-1848.

50. Vroom and Jago, *The New Leadership*, p. 182.

51. See J. McGregor Burns, *Leadership* (New York: HarperCollins, 1978). Also see Chris Lee and Ron Zemke, "The Search for Spirit in the Workplace," *Training*, 30 (June 1993): 21–28. Also see Brian S. Moskal, "Running with the Bulls," *Industry Week* (January 8, 1996): 26–34; and Thomas R. Horton, "Selecting the Best for the Top," *Management Review*, 85 (January 1996): 20–23.

52. See David A. Nadler and Michael L. Tushman, "Beyond the Charismatic Leader: Leadership and Organizational Change," *California Management Review*, 32 (Winter 1990): 77–97; and Noel Tichy, "Simultaneous Transformation and CEO Succession: Key to Global Competitiveness," *Organizational Dynamics*, 25 (Spring 1996): 45–59. For more on "vision," see Laurie Larwood, Cecilia M. Falbe, Mark P. Kriger, and Paul Miesing, "Structure and Meaning of Organizational Vision," *Academy of Management Journal*, 38 (June 1995): 740–769; Maria L. Nathan, "What Is Organizational Vision? Ask Chief Executives," *Academy of Management Executive*, 10 (February 1996): 82–83; and Burt Nanus, "Leading the Vision Team," *The Futurist*, 30 (May–June 1996): 21–23.

53. For the negative side of visionary and charismatic leaders, see Jay A. Conger, "The Dark Side of Leadership," *Organizational Dynamics*, 19 (Autumn 1990): 44–55; John B. Judis, "Myth vs. Manager," *Business Month*, 136 (July 1990): 24–33; and Jane M. Howell and Bruce J. Avolio, "The Ethics of Charismatic Leadership: Submission or Liberation?" *Academy of Management Executive*, 6 (May 1992): 43–54. For a tribute to Welch, see Geoffrey Colvin, "The Ultimate Manager," *Fortune* (November 22, 1999): 185–187.

54. See Joseph Seltzer and Bernard M. Bass, "Transformational Leadership: Beyond Initiation and Consideration," *Journal of Management*, 16 (December 1990): 693–703.

55. For example, see Jane M. Howell and Peter J. Frost, "A Laboratory Study of Charismatic Leadership," *Organizational Behavior and*

Human Decision Processes, 43 (April 1989): 243–269; Bernard M. Bass, "From Transactional to Transformational Leadership: Learning to Share the Vision," *Organizational Dynamics*, 18 (Winter 1990): 19–31; Ronald J. Deluga, "The Effects of Transformational, Transactional, and Laissez-Faire Leadership Characteristics on Subordinate-Influencing Behavior," *Basic and Applied Social Psychology*, 11 (June 1990): 191–203; Robert T. Keller, "Transformational Leadership and the Performance of Research and Development Project Groups," *Journal of Management*, 18 (September 1992): 489–501; Philip M. Podsakoff, Scott B. MacKenzie, and William H. Bommer, "Transformational Leader Behaviors and Substitutes for Leadership as Determinants of Employee Satisfaction, Commitment, Trust, and Organizational Citizenship Behaviors," *Journal of Management*, 22, no. 2 (1996): 259–298; J. Bruce Tracey and Timothy R. Hinkin, "Transformational Leadership or Effective Managerial Practices?" *Group & Organization Management*, 23 (September 1998): 220–236; David A. Waldman and Francis J. Yammarino, "CEO Charismatic Leadership: Levels-of-Management and Levels-of-Analysis Effects," *Academy of Management Review*, 24 (April 1999): 266–285; and Warren Bennis, "The End of Leadership: Exemplary Leadership Is Impossible Without Full Inclusion, Initiatives, and Cooperation of Followers," *Organizational Dynamics*, 28 (Summer 1999): 71–80.

56. For more on the servant leader philosophy, see Robert K. Greenleaf, *Servant Leadership: A Journey into the Nature of Legitimate Power and Greatness* (New York: Paulist Press, 1977); and Walter Kiechel III, "The Leader as Servant," *Fortune* (May 4, 1992): 121–122.

57. David Leon Moore, "Wooden's Wizardry Wears Well," *USA Today* (March 29, 1995): 1C–2C. Also see "Jim Stuart," *Fast Company*, no. 27 (September 1999): 114.

58. For good ideas about developing tomorrow's leaders, see Oren Harari, "Quotations from Chairman Powell: A Leadership Primer," *Management Review*, 85 (December 1996): 34–37; Polly LaBarre, "How to Be a Real Leader," *Fast Company*, no. 24 (May 1999): 62, 64; Geoffrey Colvin, "How to Be a Great eCEO," *Fortune* (May 24, 1999): 104–110; Randal Ford, "HH&A: How Leaders Learn from Failure," *Business Horizons*, 42 (September–October 1999): 17–22; and Jon P. Briscoe and Douglas T. Hall, "Grooming and Picking Leaders Using Competency Frameworks: Do They Really Work? An Alternative Approach and New Guidelines for Practice," *Organizational Dynamics*, 28 (Autumn 1999): 37–52.

59. For more, see Lyle Sussman and Richard Finnegan, "Coaching the Star: Rationale and Strategies," *Business Horizons*, 41 (March–April 1998): 47–54; Liz Thach, "14 Ways to Groom Executives," *Training*, 35 (August 1998): 52–55; William C. Byham, "Grooming Next-Millennium Leaders," *HRMagazine*, 44 (February 1999): 46–50; and Liz Thach and Tom Heinselman, "Executive Coaching Defined," *Training & Development*, 53 (March 1999): 35–39.

60. Abraham Zaleznik, "Managers and Leaders: Are They Different?" *Harvard Business Review*, 55 (May–June 1977): 76. For more on mentorship, see Judith G. Lindenberger and Lois J. Zachary, "Play '20 Questions' to Develop a Successful Mentoring Program," *Training & Development*, 53 (February 1999): 12, 14; and Ellen J. Mullen and Raymond A. Noe, "The Mentoring Information Exchange: When Do Mentors Seek Information from Their Proteges?" *Journal of Organizational Behavior*, 20 (March 1999): 233–242.

61. For details, see Ellen A. Fagenson, "The Mentor Advantage: Perceived Career/Job Experiences of Protégés Versus Non-Protégés," *Journal of Organizational Behavior*, 10 (October 1989): 309–320. More mentoring research findings are reported in Belle Rose Ragins and Terri A. Scandura, "Gender Differences in Expected Outcomes of Mentoring Relationships," *Academy of Management Journal*, 37 (August 1994): 957–971; Bennett J. Tepper, "Upward Maintenance Tactics in Supervisory Mentoring and Nonmentoring Relationships," *Academy of Management Journal*, 38 (August 1995): 1191–1205; and Samuel Aryee, Yue Wah Chay, and Juniper Chew, "The Motivation to Mentor Among Managerial Employees: An Interactionist Approach," *Group & Organization Management*, 21 (September 1996): 261–277.

62. See Erik Gunn, "Mentoring: The Democratic Version," *Training*, 32 (August 1995): 64–67; and Ian Cunningham and Linda Honold, "Everyone Can Be a Coach," *HRMagazine*, 43 (June 1998): 63–66.

63. Jeremy Kahn, "The World's Most Admired Companies," *Fortune* (October 11, 1999): 275. Also see Frank Jossi, "Mentoring in Changing Times," *Training*, 34 (August 1997): 50–54.

64. For more, see Kathy E. Kram, "Phases of the Mentor Relationship," *Academy of Management Journal*, 26 (December 1983): 608–625.

65. Good discussions of women and mentoring can be found in R. J. Burke and C. A. McKeen, "Mentoring in Organizations: Implications for Women," *Journal of Business Ethics*, 9 (April–May 1990): 317–332; Belle Rose Ragins and John L. Cotton, "Easier Said Than Done: Gender Differences in Perceived Barriers to Gaining a Mentor," *Academy of Management Journal*, 34 (December 1991): 939–951; and Victoria A. Parker and Kathy E. Kram, "Women Mentoring Women: Creating Conditions for Connection," *Business Horizons*, 36 (March–April 1993): 42–51.

66. For more, see Eileen Kaplan, "Confronting the Issue of Race in Developmental Relationships: Does Open Discussion Enhance or Suppress the Mentor-Protege Bond?" *Academy of Management Executive*, 8 (May 1994): 79–80; Hal Lancaster, "Two Women Hire Help to Smash the Glass Ceiling," *The Wall Street Journal* (November 14, 1995): B1; Linda Himelstein, "How Do You Get the Boys to Pass You the Ball?" *Business Week* (February 17, 1997): 70; Terri A. Scandura, "Dysfunctional Mentoring Relationships and Outcomes," *Journal of Management*, 24, no. 3 (1998): 449–467; and George F. Dreher and Josephine A. Chargois, "Gender, Mentoring Experiences, and Salary Attainment Among Graduates of an Historically Black University," *Journal of Vocational Behavior*, 53 (December 1998): 401–416.

67. See Edward L. Thorndike, *Educational Psychology: The Psychology of Learning* (New York: Columbia University Press, 1913), II, 4.

68. For an instructive account of operant conditioning applied to human behavior, see B. F. Skinner, *Science and Human Behavior* (New York: Free Press, 1953), pp. 62–66. A good update is B. F. Skinner, "What Is Wrong with Daily Life in the Western World," *American Psychologist*, 41 (May 1986): 568–574. Also see Marilyn B. Gilbert and Thomas F. Gilbert, "What Skinner Gave Us," *Training*, 28 (September 1991): 42–48.

69. For example, see Tom Kramlinger and Tom Huberty, "Behaviorism Versus Humanism," *Training & Development Journal*, 44 (December 1990): 41–45; and Alfie Kohn, "Challenging Behaviorist Dogma: Myths About Money and Motivation," *Compensation & Benefits Review*, 30 (March–April 1998): 27, 33–37.

70. For example, see Bob Filipczak, "Why No One Likes Your Incentive Program," *Training*, 30 (August 1993): 19–25; and Alfie Kohn, "Why Incentive Plans Cannot Work," *Harvard Business Review*, 71 (September–October 1993): 54–63.

71. For positive evidence and background, see Alexander D. Stajkovic and Fred Luthans, "A Meta-Analysis of the Effects of Organizational Behavior Modification on Task Performance,"

1975–95," *Academy of Management Journal*, 40 (October 1997): 1122–1149; Fred Luthans and Alexander D. Stajkovic, "Reinforce for Performance: The Need to Go Beyond Pay and Even Rewards," *Academy of Management Executive*, 13 (May 1999): 49–57; and Cheryl Comeau-Kirschner, "Improving Productivity Doesn't Cost a Dime," *Management Review*, 88 (January 1999): 7.

72. Dale Feuer, "Training for Fast Times," *Training*, 24 (July 1987): 28.

73. The use of positive reinforcement in self-managed teams is discussed in "Making Self-Managed Teams Work," *Training*, 30 (April 1993): 8–11. Also see Gary M. Ritzky, "Turner Bros. Wins Safety Game with Behavioral Incentives," *HRMagazine*, 43 (June 1998): 79–83; and Paul Falcone, "Letters of Clarification: A Disciplinary Alternative," *HRMagazine* 44 (August 1999): 134–140.

74. Alan Farnham, "The Trust Gap," *Fortune* (December 4, 1989): 74.

75. Kenneth Blanchard and Spencer Johnson, *The One Minute Manager* (New York: Berkley, 1982), p. 45 (emphasis added). Also see Kenneth Blanchard and Robert Lorber, *Putting the One Minute Manager to Work* (New York: Berkley, 1984).

76. For detailed treatment of B. Mod. in the workplace, see Fred Luthans and Robert Kreitner, *Organizational Behavior Modification and Beyond: An Operant and Social Learning Approach* (Glenview, Ill.: Scott, Foresman, 1985); and Gerald A. Merwin Jr., John A. Thomason, and Eleanor E. Sanford, "A Methodology and Content Review of Organizational Behavior Management in the Private Sector: 1978–1986," *Journal of Organizational Behavior Management*, 10, no. 1 (1989): 39–57. Also see Mark A. Friend and James P. Kohn, "A Behavioral Approach to Accident Prevention," *Occupational Hazards*, 54 (October 1992): 112–115; Thomas K. Connellan and Ron Zemke, *Sustaining Knock Your Socks Off Service* (New York: Amacom, 1993), chap. 13; and Mark E. Furman, "Reverse the 80–20 Rule," *Management Review*, 86 (January 1997): 18–21.

Chapter 16

Opening Quotation Dean Tjosvold, *Learning to Manage Conflict: Getting People to Work Together Productively* (New York: Lexington, 1993), p. xi.

Opening Case "Trust for a Change," *Fast Company*, no. 30 (December 1999): 398, 400. Reprinted from the December 1999 issue of *Fast Company* magazine. All rights reserved. To subscribe, please call (800) 688-1545.

Closing Case Republished with permission of *The Wall Street Journal* from "Bob Schmonsees Has a Tool for Better Sales, and It Ignores Excuses," by Thomas Petzinger Jr., *The Wall Street Journal* (March 26, 1999). Permission conveyed through Copyright Clearance Center, Inc.

1. As quoted in Thomas A. Stewart, "How to Leave It All Behind," *Fortune* (December 6, 1999): 348.

2. Adapted from discussion in David A. Nadler and Michael L. Tushman, "Organizational Frame Bending: Principles for Managing Reorientation," *Academy of Management Executive*, 3 (August 1989): 194–204. Also see Chung-Ming Lau and Richard W. Woodman, "Understanding Organizational Change: A Schematic Perspective," *Academy of Management Journal*, 38 (April 1995): 537–554; Andrew H. Van De Ven and Marshall Scott Poole, "Explaining Development and Change in Organizations," *Academy of Management Review*, 20 (July 1995): 510–540; and Nandini Rajagopalan and Gretchen M. Spreitzer, "Toward a Theory of Strategic Change: A Multi-Lens Perspective and Integrative Framework," *Academy of Management Review*, 22 (January 1996): 48–79.

3. See Brian Dumaine, "Creating a New Company Culture," *Fortune* (January 15, 1990): 127–131.

4. See Tom Duening, "Our Turbulent Times? The Case for Evolutionary Organizational Change," *Business Horizons*, 40 (January–February 1997): 2–8.

5. Bill Vlasic, "In Alabama, the Soul of a New Mercedes?" *Business Week* (March 31, 1997): 70.

6. Kathy Rebello, "Inside Microsoft," *Business Week* (July 15, 1996): 57. Also see Thomas A. Stewart, "When Change Is Total, Exciting—and Scary," *Fortune* (March 3, 1997): 169–170. A nonprofit organization in need of frame breaking is profiled in Monica Langley, "The Lung Association, Its Donations Waning, Casts About for a Cause," *The Wall Street Journal* (April 14, 1999): A1, A10.

7. See Russ Vince and Michael Broussine, "Paradox, Defense and Attachment: Accessing and Working with Emotions and Relations Underlying Organizational Change," *Organization Studies*, 17, no. 1 (1996): 1–21.

8. For interesting profiles of personal/career changes, see Ron Lieber, "Re-invent Yourself," *Fast Company*, no. 29 (November 1999): 228–243.

9. See Timothy A. Judge, Carl J. Thoresen, Vladimir Pucik, and Theresa M. Welbourne, "Managerial Coping with Organizational Change: A Dispositional Perspective," *Journal of Applied Psychology*, 84 (February 1999): 107–122; Quy Nguyen Huy, "Emotional Capability, Emotional Intelligence, and Radical Change," *Academy of Management Review*, 24 (April 1999): 325–345; and Cheryl Dahle, "Big Learning, Fast Futures," *Fast Company*, no. 25 (June 1999): 46, 48.

10. Four instructive case studies are reported in Brent Schlender, "Larry Ellison: Oracle at Web Speed," *Fortune* (May 24, 1999): 128–136; Peter Elkind, "Flying for Fun & Profit," *Fortune* (October 25, 1999): 36–37; Joseph Weber, "Racing Ahead at Nortel," *Business Week* (November 8, 1999): 93–99; and Leah Nathans Spiro, "Merrill's e-Battle," *Business Week* (November 15, 1999): 256–266.

11. Ichak Adizes, *Mastering Change: The Power of Mutual Trust and Respect in Personal Life, Family Life, Business and Society* (Santa Monica, Calif.: Adizes Institute, 1991), p. 6.

12. See Thomas A. Stewart, "Rate Your Readiness to Change," *Fortune* (February 7, 1994): 106–110; and Cheryl Dahle, "Don't Get Mad—Get over It," *Fast Company*, no. 22 (March 1999): 190–201.

13. J. Alan Ofner, "Managing Change," *Personnel Administrator*, 29 (September 1984): 20.

14. Peter Coy, "The Perils of Picking the Wrong Standard," *Business Week* (October 8, 1990): 145. Also see Louis Woo, "Speech Technology Can Shrink World," *USA Today* (June 22, 1999): 6E.

15. For useful tips, see Michael Hickins, "Managing Transitions," *Management Review*, 87 (October 1998): 7.

16. Karen Lowry Miller and Larry Armstrong, "Will Nissan Get It Right This Time?" *Business Week* (April 20, 1992): 84. Also see G. Pascal Zachary, "Smashing Computers: Digital Age Sparks Neo-Luddite Backlash," *The Wall Street Journal Europe* (April 19–20, 1996): 1, 5.

17. "Why They're Jumping Ship at Intel," *Business Week* (February 14, 1983): 108.

18. This list is based in part on John P. Kotter and Leonard A. Schlesinger, "Choosing Strategies for Change," *Harvard Business Review*, 57 (March–April 1979): 106–114; and Joseph Stanislao and Bettie C. Stanislao, "Dealing with Resistance to Change," *Business Horizons*, 26 (July–August 1983): 74–78.

19. For example, see Arnon E. Reichers, John P. Wanous, and James T. Austin, "Understanding and Managing Cynicism About Organizational Change," *Academy of Management Executive*, 11 (February 1997): 48–59; Jack Gordon, "Change Resistance," *Training*, 35 (June 1998): 8, 10; Kenneth E. Hultman, "Let's Stop the Change Game," *Training*, 35 (November 1998): 120; Oren Harari, "Why Do Leaders Avoid Change?" *Management Review*, 88 (March 1999): 35–38; and "Resistance Fighter," *Fast Company*, no. 30 (December 1999): 390–396.

20. Oren Harari, "Eat Change for Breakfast," *Management Review*, 87 (February 1998): 42. Also see Peter F. Drucker, "Change Leaders," *Inc.*, 21 (June 1999): 64–72; and Patricia Hunt Dirlam, "Taking Charge of Change," *Management Review*, 88 (September 1999): 61.

21. See Allison Rossett, "Training & Organization Development: Separated at Birth?" *Training*, 33 (April 1996): 53–59; and Joseph A. Raelin, "Action Learning and Action Science: Are They Different?" *Organizational Dynamics*, 26 (Summer 1997): 21–34.

22. Philip G. Hanson and Bernard Lubin, "Answers to Questions Frequently Asked About Organization Development," in *The Emerging Practice of Organization Development*, ed. Walter Sikes, Allan Drexler, and Jack Grant (Alexandria, Va.: NTL Institute, 1989), p. 16 (emphasis added). For good background information of current OD practices, see W. Warner Burke, "The New Agenda for Organization Development," *Organizational Dynamics*, 26 (Summer 1997): 7–20; Chuck McVinney, "Dream Weaver," *Training & Development* 53 (April 1999): 39–42; and Ron Zemke, "Don't Fix That Company!" *Training*, 36 (June 1999): 26–33.

23. W. Warner Burke, *Organization Development: A Normative View* (Reading, Mass.: Addison-Wesley, 1987), p. 9. Also see Benjamin Schneider, Arthur P. Brief, and Richard A. Guzzo, "Creating a Climate and Culture for Sustainable Organizational Change," *Organizational Dynamics*, 24 (Spring 1996): 7–19.

24. See Allan H. Church, Janine Waclawski, and W. Warner Burke, "OD Practitioners as Facilitators of Change: An Analysis of Survey Results," *Group & Organization Management*, 21 (March 1996): 22–66; Bodil Jones, "Inside-Out Advice," *Management Review*, 85 (December 1996): 8; Barbara Solomon, "The New Rules of Consulting," *Management Review*, 87 (February 1998): 59–61; and Robert H. Schaffer, "Overcome the Fatal Flaws of Consulting: Close the Results Gap," *Business Horizons*, 41 (September–October 1998): 53–60.

25. This list is based on Wendell French, "Organization Development Objectives, Assumptions, and Strategies," *California Management Review*, 12 (Winter 1969): 23–34; and Charles Kiefer and Peter Stroh, "A New Paradigm for Organization Development," *Training and Development Journal*, 37 (April 1983): 26–35.

26. See Robert J. Marshak, "Managing the Metaphors of Change," *Organizational Dynamics*, 22 (Summer 1993): 44–56; Craig L. Pearce and Charles P. Osmond, "Metaphors for Change: The ALPs Model of Change Management," *Organizational Dynamics*, 24 (Winter 1996): 23–35; and Ian Palmer and Richard Dunford, "Conflicting Uses of Metaphors: Reconceptualizing Their Use in the Field of Organizational Change," *Academy of Management Review*, 21 (July 1996): 691–717.

27. A successful application of Lewin's model at British Airways is discussed in Leonard D. Goodstein and W. Warner Burke, "Creating Successful Organization Change," *Organizational Dynamics*, 19 (Spring 1991): 4–17.

28. For example, see Anita Lienart, "Drawing on the Pioneer Spirit," *Management Review*, 87 (December 1998): 19.

29. Bill Breen and Cheryl Dahl, "Field Guide for Change," *Fast Company*, no. 30 (December 1999): 384. Also see Oren Harari, "Leading Change from the Middle," *Management Review*, 88 (February 1999): 29–32.

30. For practical insights on organizational change, see Christian M. Ellis and E. Michael Norman, "Real Change in Real Time," *Management Review*, 88 (February 1999): 33–38; Suzy Wetlaufer, "Driving Change: An Interview with Ford Motor Company's Jacques Nasser," *Harvard Business Review*, 77 (March–April 1999): 77–88; Phil Waga, "IBM Exec Perfects 'Gentle, Important Balancing Act,'" *USA Today* (November 15, 1999): 18B; and Geoffrey Colvin, "Behold the Power of Cheese," *Fortune* (November 22, 1999): 363, 366.

31. For example, see Robert J. Grossman, "Trying to Heal the Wounds," *HRMagazine*, 43 (September 1998): 84–92; Howard M. Guttman, "Conflict at the Top," *Management Review*, 88 (November 1999): 49–53; and Ronald Grover, "Gurus Who Failed Their Own Course," *Business Week* (November 8, 1999): 125–126.

32. Abraham Zaleznik, "Real Work," *Harvard Business Review*, 67 (January–February 1989): 59–60.

33. Dean Tjosvold, *Learning to Manage Conflict: Getting People to Work Together Productively* (New York: Lexington, 1993), p. 8.

34. Ibid. Also see Allen C. Amason, "Distinguishing the Effects of Functional and Dysfunctional Conflict on Strategic Decision Making: Resolving a Paradox for Top Management Teams," *Academy of Management Journal*, 39 (February 1996): 123–148; and Samuel S. Corl, "Agreeing to Disagree," *Purchasing Today*, 7 (February 1996): 10–11.

35. For a case study of problems associated with competitive conflict, see John A. Byrne, "Chainsaw," *Business Week* (October 18, 1999): 128–147.

36. Walter Kiechel III, "How to Escape the Echo Chamber," *Fortune* (June 18, 1990): 130. For other good material on constructive conflict, see Steve Alper, Dean Tjosvold, and Kenneth S. Law, "Interdependence and Controversy in Group Decision Making: Antecedents to Effective Self-Managing Teams," *Organizational Behavior and Human Decision Processes*, 74 (April 1998): 33–52; and William K. Hengen Jr., "Managing Moments of Truth," *Management Review*, 87 (September 1998): 56–60.

37. For good updates on conflict, see James A. Wall Jr. and Ronda Roberts Callister, "Conflict and Its Management," *Journal of Management*, 21, no. 3 (1995): 515–558; Catherine Tinsley, "Models of Conflict Resolution in Japanese, German, and American Cultures," *Journal of Applied Psychology*, 83 (April 1998): 316–323; Patricia Ruzich, "Triangles: Tools for Untangling Interpersonal Messes," *HRMagazine*, 44 (July 1999): 129–136; and Erik J. Van Slyke, "Resolve Conflict, Boost Creativity," *HRMagazine*, 44 (November 1999): 132–137.

38. For example, see Alex Taylor III, "Young in an Olds World," *Fortune* (October 11, 1999): 315–318.

39. See Anne M. O'Leary-Kelly, Ricky W. Griffin, and David J. Glew, "Organization-Motivated Aggression: A Research Framework," *Academy of Management Review*, 21 (January 1996): 225–253; "Aggressive Behavior Bullies into Workplace," *HRMagazine*, 44 (February 1999): 30; and Rudy M. Yandrick, "Lurking in the Shadows," *HRMagazine*, 44 (October 1999): 61–68.

40. See Dean Tjosvold and Margaret Poon, "Dealing with Scarce Resources," *Group & Organization Management*, 23 (September 1998): 237–255.

41. See Lynne M. Andersson and Christine M. Pearson, "Tit for Tat? The Spiraling Effect of Incivility in the Workplace," *Academy of*

Management Review, 24 (July 1999): 452–471; and "Those Annoying Co-Workers," *Training*, 36 (October 1999): 24.

42. For an alternative list of conditions that tend to precipitate conflict, see Alan C. Filley, *Interpersonal Conflict Resolution* (Glenview, Ill.: Scott, Foresman, 1975): pp. 9–12.

43. For related research, see Steven M. Farmer and Jonelle Roth, "Conflict-Handling Behavior in Work Groups: Effects of Group Structure, Decision Processes, and Time," *Small Group Research*, 29 (December 1998): 669–713; and Russell Cropanzano, Herman Aguinis, Marshall Schminke, and Dina L. Denham, "Disputant Reactions to Managerial Conflict Resolution Tactics: A Comparison Among Argentina, the Dominican Republic, Mexico, and the United States," *Group & Organization Management*, 24 (June 1999): 124–154.

44. Stephen P. Robbins, *Managing Organizational Conflict: A Nontraditional Approach* (Englewood Cliffs, N.J.: Prentice-Hall, 1974), p. 62.

45. See Roger Fisher and William Ury, *Getting to Yes: Negotiating Agreement Without Giving In* (Boston: Houghton Mifflin, 1981); Robin L. Pinkley and Gregory B. Northcraft, "Conflict Frames of Reference: Implications for Dispute Processes and Outcomes," *Academy of Management Journal*, 37 (February 1994): 193–205; and A. R. Elangovan, "Managerial Third-Party Dispute Intervention: A Prescriptive Model of Strategy Selection," *Academy of Management Review*, 20 (October 1995): 800–830.

46. See Carla Joinson, "Controlling Hostility," *HRMagazine*, 43 (August 1998): 65–70.

47. See M. Afzalur Rahim, "A Measure of Styles of Handling Conflict," *Academy of Management Journal*, 26 (June 1983): 368–376; Erich Brockmann, "Removing the Paradox of Conflict from Group Decisions," *Academy of Management Executive*, 10 (May 1996): 61–62; and Donald E. Conlon and Daniel P. Sullivan, "Examining the Actions of Organizations in Conflict: Evidence from the Delaware Court of Chancery," *Academy of Management Journal*, 42 (June 1999): 319–329.

48. See Lyle Sussman, "How to Frame a Message: The Art of Persuasion and Negotiation," *Business Horizons*, 42 (July–August 1999): 2–6; and G. Richard Shell, "Negotiator, Know Thyself," *Inc.*, 21 (May 1999): 106–107.

49. Data from Laurie R. Weingart, Elaine B. Hyder, and Michael J. Prietula, "Knowledge Matters: The Effects of Tactical Descriptions on Negotiation Behavior and Outcome," *Journal of Personality and Social Psychology*, 70 (June 1996): 1205–1217. Also see Brad Lee Thompson, "Negotiation Training: Win-Win or What?" *Training*, 28 (June 1991): 31–35.

50. Margaret A. Neale and Max H. Bazerman, "Negotiating Rationally: The Power and Impact of the Negotiator's Frame," *Academy of Management Executive*, 6 (August 1992): 42–51. Also see Terry Anderson, "Step into My Parlor: A Survey of Strategies and Techniques for Effective Negotiation," *Business Horizons*, 35 (May–June 1992): 71–76.

51. For more, see Alan M. Webber, "How to Get Them to Show You the Money," *Fast Company*, no. 19 (November 1998): 198–208; and Kim Kiser, "The New Deal," *Training*, 36 (October 1999): 116–126.

52. See "Powers of Persuasion," *Fortune* (October 12, 1998): 160–164.

53. For a cross-cultural study, see Jeanne M. Brett and Tetsushi Okumura, "Inter- and Intracultural Negotiation: U.S. and Japanese Negotiators," *Academy of Management Journal*, 41 (October 1998): 495–510.

54. Stephen R. Covey, *The Seven Habits of Highly Effective People* (New York: Simon & Schuster, 1989), p. 207. Also see H. Joseph Reitz, James A. Wall Jr., and Mary Sue Love, "Ethics in Negotiation: Oil

and Water or Good Lubrication?" *Business Horizons*, 41 (May–June 1998): 5–14.

55. A good resource book is Roger Fisher and Danny Ertel, *Getting Ready to Negotiate: The Getting to Yes Workbook* (New York: Penguin, 1995). Also see John L. Graham, Alma T. Mintu, and Raymond Rodgers, "Explorations of Negotiation Behaviors in Ten Foreign Cultures Using a Model Developed in the United States," *Management Science*, 40 (January 1994): 72–95; Kathleen Kelley Reardon and Robert E. Spekman, "Starting Out Right: Negotiation Lessons for Domestic and Cross-Cultural Business Alliances," *Business Horizons*, 37 (January–February 1994): 71–79; and Thomas Leung and L. L. Yeung, "Negotiation in the People's Republic of China: Results of a Survey of Small Businesses in Hong Kong," *Journal of Small Business Management*, 33 (January 1995): 70–77.

56. Fisher and Ury, *Getting to Yes: Negotiating Agreement Without Giving In*, p. 104.

57. For an instructive discussion of negotiating biases, see Neale and Bazerman, "Negotiating Rationally: The Power and Impact of the Negotiator's Frame," pp. 42–51.

58. See Chapter 9 in Max H. Bazerman and Margaret A. Neale, *Negotiating Rationally* (New York: The Free Press, 1992), pp. 67–76. Also see Joan F. Brett, Gregory B. Northcraft, and Robin L. Pinkley, "Stairways to Heaven: An Interlocking Self-Regulation Model of Negotiation," *Academy of Management Review*, 24 (July 1999): 435–451.

59. An informative and entertaining introduction to a four-step win-win model can be found in Ross R. Reck and Brian G. Long, *The Win-Win Negotiator: How to Negotiate Favorable Agreements That Last* (New York: Pocket Books, 1987).

60. Based on discussion in Karl Albrecht and Steve Albrecht, "Added Value Negotiating," *Training*, 30 (April 1993): 26–29. Also see Karen M. Kroll, "Successful Negotiating," *Industry Week* (April 1, 1996): 17–18.

61. Ibid., p. 29.

Chapter 17

Opening Quotation "Anne Busquet," *Fast Company*, no. 27 (September 1999): 146.

Opening Case Bob Filipczak, "The Soul of the Hog." Reprinted with permission from the February 1996 issue of *Training* magazine. Copyright 1996. Lakewood Publications, Minneapolis, Minn. All rights reserved. Not for resale.

Closing Case Republished with permission of *The Wall Street Journal* from "Anatomy of a Recall: How Coke's Controls Fizzled Out in Europe," Nikhil Deogun, James R. Hagerty, Steve Steklow, and Laura Johannes, *The Wall Street Journal* (June 29, 1999). Permission conveyed through Copyright Clearance Center, Inc. For more, see William Echikson, "Things Aren't Going Better with Coke," *Business Week* (June 28, 1999): 49.

1. Harold Koontz and Robert W. Bradspies, "Managing Through Feedforward Control," *Business Horizons*, 15 (June 1972): 27.

2. Lucia Mouat, "Crumbling Bridges, Constructive Budgets," *The Christian Science Monitor* (February 26, 1991): 9. Also see Jonathan D. Salant, "States Say Money Lacking to Fix Backlog of Worn Bridges," *USA Today* (November 3, 1997): 18A.

3. For example, see Oren Harari, "Margin Killers," *Management Review*, 88 (December 1999): 33–36.

4. For discussion of a small business that got out of control, see D. M. Osborne, "Fast-Paced Rivals Silence Talking-Beeper Service," *Inc.*, 21 (December 1999): 40.

5. See, for example, Michel Lebas and Jane Weigenstein, "Management Control: The Roles of Rules, Markets, and Culture," *Journal of Management Studies*, 23 (May 1986): 259–272; and Jeffrey A. Alexander, "Adaptive Change in Corporate Control Practices," *Academy of Management Journal*, 34 (March 1991): 162–193.

6. See Richard L. Daft and Norman B. Macintosh, "The Nature and Use of Formal Control Systems for Management Control and Strategy Implementation," *Journal of Management*, 10 (Spring 1984): 43–66.

7. See Harrison M. Trice and Janice M. Beyer, *The Cultures of Work Organizations* (Englewood Cliffs, N.J.: Prentice-Hall, 1993).

8. Based on Eric Flamholtz, "Organizational Control Systems as a Managerial Tool," *California Management Review*, 22 (Winter 1979): 50–59.

9. Data from James B. Treece and David Woodruff, "Crunch Time Again for Chrysler," *Business Week* (March 25, 1991): 92–94.

10. See Stanley F. Slater, Eric M. Olson, and Venkateshwar K. Reddy, "Strategy-Based Performance Measurement," *Business Horizons*, 40 (July–August 1997): 37–44.

11. For more, see Leon Mann, Danny Samson, and Douglas Dow, "A Field Experiment on the Effects of Benchmarking and Goal Setting on Company Sales Performance," *Journal of Management*, 24, no. 1 (1998): 73–96; Andrew Campbell, "Tailored, Not Benchmarked: A Fresh Look at Corporate Planning," *Harvard Business Review*, 77 (March–April 1999): 41–50; and Curtis Sittenfeld, "Here's How GSA Changed Its Ways," *Fast Company*, no. 25 (June 1999): 86, 88.

12. Chris Woodyard, "United Polishes Its First-Class Act," *USA Today* (March 2, 1999): 10B.

13. For more on strategic control, see David Asch, "Strategic Control: A Problem Looking for a Solution," *Long Range Planning*, 25 (April 1992): 105–110; "Strategic Quality Management," *Management International Review*, 33, Special Issue (1993): 3–120; Scott A. Snell, "Control Theory in Strategic Human Resource Management: The Mediating Effect of Administrative Information," *Academy of Management Journal*, 35 (June 1992): 292–327; Irene M. Herremans and John K. Ryans Jr., "The Case for Better Measurement and Reporting of Marketing Performance," *Business Horizons*, 38 (September–October 1995): 51–60; and John H. Lingle and William A. Schiemann, "From Balanced Scorecard to Strategic Gauges: Is Measurement Worth It?" *Management Review*, 85 (March 1996): 56–61; and Joseph C. Picken and Gregory G. Dess, "Out of (Strategic) Control," *Organizational Dynamics*, 26 (Summer 1997): 35–48.

14. See Susan Chandler, "If It's on the Fritz, Take It to Jane," *Business Week* (January 27, 1997): 74, 76; and Trevor Merriden, "The Challenges of Hypergrowth," *Management Review*, 88 (November 1999): 34–38.

15. Alan Farnham, "The Trust Gap," *Fortune* (December 4, 1989): 78. Other forms of executive reality checks are discussed in Brent Schlender, "The New Man Inside Intel," *Fortune* (May 11, 1998): 161–163; and Marcia Stepanek, "How Fast Is Net Fast?" *Business Week* E.BIZ (November 1, 1999): EB 52–EB 54.

16. See A. Richard Krachenberg, John W. Henke Jr., and Thomas F. Lyons, "The Isolation of Upper Management," *Business Horizons*, 36 (July–August 1993): 41–47.

17. For interesting reading, see Cynthia Williams, "Making Social Disclosure as Routine as Financial Disclosure," *Business Ethics*, 13 (November–December 1999): 6.

18. Lawrence B. Sawyer, "Internal Auditing: Yesterday, Today, and Tomorrow," *The Internal Auditor*, 36 (December 1979): 26 (emphasis added). Also see Joseph F. Berardino and Gregory J. Jonas, "Power to the Audit Committee People," *Financial Executive*, 15 (November–December 1999): 36–38.

19. For more, see David G. Coderre, "Computer Assisted Audit Tools and Techniques," *The Internal Auditor*, 50 (February 1993): 24–27; and Albert A. Vondra and Dennis R. Schueler, "Can You Innovate Your Internal Audit?" *Financial Executive*, 9 (March–April 1993): 34–39.

20. This list is based in part on Donald W. Murr, Harry B. Bracey Jr., and William K. Hill, "How to Improve Your Organization's Management Controls," *Management Review*, 69 (October 1980): 56–63. For more on the out-of-control IRS, see Michael Hirsh, "Infernal Revenue Service," *Newsweek* (October 13, 1997): 33–39.

21. Data from "India Protest Marks '84 Bhopal Disaster," *The Arizona Republic* (December 4, 1999): A29.

22. Crisis management lessons from the World Trade Center bombing are discussed in William D. Harrel and John S. DeMott, "Business Lessons from a Disaster," *Nation's Business*, 81 (May 1993): 38–40.

23. Data from "Nation in Brief," *Washington Post* (November 23, 1999): A12 (**www.washingtonpost.com**).

24. Christine M. Pearson and Judith A. Clair, "Reframing Crisis Management," *Academy of Management Review*, 23 (January 1998): 60.

25. See Christine M. Pearson, Judith A. Clair, Sarah Kovoor-Misra, and Ian I. Mitroff, "Managing the Unthinkable," *Organizational Dynamics*, 26 (Autumn 1997): 51–64.

26. See Christine M. Pearson and Ian I. Mitroff, "From Crisis Prone to Crisis Prepared: A Framework for Crisis Management," *Academy of Management Executive*, 7 (February 1993): 48–59; Stephenie Overman, "Be Prepared Should Be Your Motto," *HRMagazine*, 38 (July 1993): 46–49; Christine M. Pearson and Dennis A. Rondinelli, "Crisis Management in Central European Firms," *Business Horizons*, 41 (May–June 1998): 50–60; and Milton Bordwin, "Plan B . . . or Is It Plan C for Crisis?" *Management Review*, 88 (July–August 1999): 53–55.

27. Product boycotts are discussed in Janice E. Jackson and William T. Schantz, "Crisis Management Lessons: When Push Shoved Nike," *Business Horizons*, 36 (January–February 1993): 27–35. Also see Thierry C. Pauchant, Ian I. Mitroff, and Gerald F. Ventolo, "The Dial Tone Does Not Come from God! How a Crisis Can Challenge Dangerous Strategic Assumptions Made About High Technologies: The Case of the Hinsdale Telecommunication Outage," *Academy of Management Executive*, 6 (August 1992): 66–79.

28. See Dale D. McConkey, "Planning for Uncertainty," *Business Horizons*, 30 (January–February 1987): 40–45; and Brahim Herbane, Dominic Elliot, and Ethne Swartz, "Contingency and Continua: Achieving Excellence Through Business Continuity Planning," *Business Horizons*, 40 (November–December 1997): 19–25.

29. Barbara Rudolph, "Coping with Catastrophe," *Time* (February 24, 1986): 53.

30. William C. Symonds, "How Companies Are Learning to Prepare for the Worst," *Business Week* (December 23, 1985): 76.

31. See Lillian Gorman and Kathryn D. McKee, "Disaster and Its Aftermath," *HRMagazine*, 35 (March 1990): 54–58; and William Briggs, "Taking Control After a Crisis," *HRMagazine*, 35 (March 1990): 60–61, 80.

32. For case studies of poor responses, see Russell Mokhiber, "See No Evil," *Business Ethics*, 13 (May–June 1999): 14–15.

33. See Woodruff Imberman, "The American Quest for Quality," *Business Horizons*, 42 (September–October 1999): 11–16.

34. See David A. Garvin, "How the Baldrige Award Really Works," *Harvard Business Review*, 69 (November–December 1991): 80–93; and Robert Bell and Bernard Keys, "A Conversation with Curt W.

Reimann on the Background and Future of the Baldrige Award," *Organizational Dynamics*, 26 (Spring 1998): 51–61.

35. Chris Woodyard, Bruce Horovitz, Gary Strauss, and Anne Willette, "Quality Guru Now Plugs Innovation," *USA Today* (February 27, 1998): 8B.

36. Philip B. Crosby, *Quality Without Tears: The Art of Hassle-Free Management* (New York: Plume, 1984), p. 64. Also see Philip B. Crosby, *Completeness: Quality for the 21st Century* (New York: Dutton, 1992), p. 116.

37. Adapted in part from Ron Zemke, "A Bluffer's Guide to TQM," *Training*, 30 (April 1993): 48–55.

38. Stratford Sherman, "How to Prosper in the Value Decade," *Fortune* (November 30, 1992): 91. Also see Gerald E. Smith and Thomas T. Nagle, "Frames of Reference and Buyers' Perception of Price and Value," *California Management Review*, 38 (Fall 1995): 98–116.

39. Data from Jeremy Kahn, "The *Fortune* Global 5 Hundred: The World's Largest Corporations," *Fortune* (August 2, 1999): F-1, F-2.

40. For example, see David H. Freedman, "Intensive Care," *Inc.*, 21 (February 1999): 72–80; Daniel H. Pink, "Is Your Business a Show Business?" *Fast Company*, no. 23 (April 1999): 84, 86; Paco Underhill, "What Shoppers Want," *Inc.*, 21 (July 1999): 72–82; Michael J. Mandel, "The Internet Economy: The World's Next Growth Engine," *Business Week* (October 4, 1999): 72–77; and Stewart Alsop, "My Trip on America West, or Why Customer Service Still Matters," *Fortune* (November 22, 1999): 359–360.

41. Data from Patricia Sellers, "Getting Customers to Love You," *Fortune* (March 13, 1989): 38–49.

42. Data from Patricia Sellers, "What Customers Really Want," *Fortune* (June 4, 1990): 58–68.

43. Based on discussions in M. Jill Austin, "Planning in Service Organizations," *SAM Advanced Management Journal*, 55 (Summer 1990): 7–12; Everett E. Adam Jr. and Paul M. Swamidass, "Assessing Operations Management from a Strategic Perspective," *Journal of Management*, 15 (June 1989): 181–203; and Ron Zemke, "The Emerging Art of Service Management," *Training*, 29 (January 1992): 37–42.

44. See, for example, Ron Zemke, "Customer Service as a Performing Art," *Training*, 30 (March 1993): 40–44; and Blake E. Ashforth and Ronald H. Humphrey, "Emotional Labor in Service Roles: The Influence of Identity," *Academy of Management Review*, 18 (January 1993): 88–115.

45. Data from Andrew Erdman, "Staying Ahead of 800 Competitors," *Fortune* (June 1, 1992): 111–112.

46. Ron Zemke and Dick Schaaf, *The Service Edge: 101 Companies That Profit from Customer Care* (New York: New American Library, 1989), p. 14. Also see Bob Smith, "Lily Tomlin's Take on Customer Service," *Management Review*, 83 (July 1994): 17–20; and Keki R. Bhote, "What Do Customers Want, Anyway?" *Management Review*, 86 (March 1997): 36–40.

47. See Leonard L. Berry, A. Parasuraman, and Valarie A. Zeithaml, "The Service-Quality Puzzle," *Business Horizons*, 31 (September–October 1988): 35–43; Leonard L. Berry, A. Parasuraman, and Valarie A. Zeithaml, "Improving Service Quality in America: Lessons Learned," *Academy of Management Executive*, 8 (May 1994): 32–45; Leonard L. Berry, Kathleen Seiders, and Larry G. Gresham, "For Love and Money: The Common Traits of Successful Retailers," *Organizational Dynamics*, 26 (Autumn 1997): 7–23; and Kathleen Seiders and Leonard L. Berry, "Service Fairness: What It Is and Why It Matters," *Academy of Management Executive*, 12 (May 1998): 8–20.

48. Based on Paul Hellman, "Rating Your Dentist," *Management Review*, 87 (July–August 1998): 64.

49. For example, see Robert T. Amsden, Thomas W. Ferratt, and Davida M. Amsden, "TQM: Core Paradigm Changes," *Business Horizons*, 39 (November–December 1996): 6–14; Oren Harari, "Ten Reasons TQM Doesn't Work," *Management Review*, 86 (January 1997): 38–44; Thomas Y. Choi and Orlando C. Behling, "Top Managers and TQM Success: One More Look After All These Years," *Academy of Management Executive*, 11 (February 1997): 37–47; and Kenneth R. Thompson, "Confronting the Paradoxes in a Total Quality Environment," *Organizational Dynamics*, 26 (Winter 1998): 62–74.

50. Inspired by a more lengthy definition in Marshall Sashkin and Kenneth J. Kiser, *Total Quality Management* (Seabrook, Md.: Ducochon Press, 1991), p. 25. Another good introduction to TQM is Arthur R. Tenner and Irving J. DeToro, *Total Quality Management: Three Steps to Continuous Improvement* (Reading, Mass.: Addison-Wesley, 1992). Also see the entire July 1994 issue of *Academy of Management Review*.

51. Richard J. Schonberger, "Total Quality Management Cuts a Broad Swath—Through Manufacturing and Beyond," *Organizational Dynamics*, 20 (Spring 1992): 18.

52. "Aiming for the Stars at Philips," Special Advertising Section, Quality '92: Leading the World-Class Company, *Time* (September 21, 1992): 26.

53. See John Shea and David Gobeli, "TQM: The Experiences of Ten Small Businesses," *Business Horizons*, 38 (January–February 1995): 71–77; Loyd Eskildson, "TQM's Role in Corporate Success: Analyzing the Evidence," *National Productivity Review*, 14 (Autumn 1995): 25–38; Richard Reed, David J. Lemak, and Joseph C. Montgomery, "Beyond Process: TQM Content and Firm Performance," *Academy of Management Review*, 21 (January 1996): 173–202; and William A. Hubiak and Susan Jones O'Donnell, "Do Americans Have Their Minds Set Against TQM?" *National Productivity Review*, 15 (Summer 1996): 19–32.

54. Adapted and condensed from David E. Bowen and Edward E. Lawler III, "Total Quality-Oriented Human Resources Management," *Organizational Dynamics*, 20 (Spring 1992): Exhibit 1, 29–41.

55. Richard J. Schonberger, *Japanese Manufacturing Techniques: Nine Hidden Lessons in Simplicity* (New York: Free Press, 1982), p. 35. Also see Barry Berman, "Planning for the Inevitable Product Recall," *Business Horizons*, 42 (March–April 1999): 69–78.

56. Quoted in Harry V. Roberts and Bernard F. Sergesketter, *Quality Is Personal: A Foundation for Total Quality Management* (New York: Free Press, 1993), p. xiii.

57. For contrasting views, see Christopher W. L. Hart, "The Power of Internal Guarantees," *Harvard Business Review*, 73 (January–February 1995): 64–73; and Thomas A. Stewart, "Another Fad Worth Killing," *Fortune* (February 3, 1997): 119–120.

58. Andrew H. Szpekman, "Quality Service Sets You Apart," *HRMagazine*, 37 (September 1992): 74.

59. Richard S. Teitelbaum, "Where Service Flies Right," *Fortune* (August 24, 1992): 115. For another example, see Cathy Olofson, "Rough Seas, Tough Customers," *Fast Company*, no. 25 (June 1999): 56.

60. See Wayne Wilhelm and Bill Rossello, "The Care and Feeding of Customers," *Management Review*, 86 (March 1997): 19–23; Louisa Wah, "The Almighty Customer," *Management Review*, 88 (February 1999): 16–22; and George B. Weathersby, "The Buyer's Point of View," *Management Review*, 88 (May 1999): 5.

61. Andy Reinhardt, "Meet Mr. Internet," *Business Week* (September 13, 1999): 136.

62. Based on discussion in Richard J. Schonberger, "Is Strategy Strategic? Impact of Total Quality Management on Strategy," *Academy of Management Executive*, 6 (August 1992): 80–87.

63. See D. Keith Denton, "Creating a System for Continuous Improvement," *Business Horizons*, 38 (January–February 1995): 16–21; and Thomas Y. Choi, Manus Rungtusanatham, and Ji-Sung Kim, "Continuous Improvement on the Shop Floor: Lessons from Small to Midsize Firms," *Business Horizons*, 40 (November–December 1997): 45–50.

64. Edward E. Lawler III, "Total Quality Management and Employee Involvement: Are They Compatible?" *Academy of Management Executive*, 8 (February 1994): 68–76.

65. "Reinventing Chrysler," Special Advertising Section, Quality '92: Leading the World-Class Company, *Time* (September 21, 1992): 20.

66. Sashkin and Kiser, *Total Quality Management*, p. 42.

67. Based on discussion in Mary Walton, *Deming Management at Work* (New York: Perigee, 1990), p. 16.

68. See Marta Mooney, "Deming's Real Legacy: An Easier Way to Manage Knowledge," *National Productivity Review*, 15 (Summer 1996): 1–8; and Pamela J. Kidder and Bobbie Ryan, "How the Deming Philosophy Transformed the Department of the Navy," *National Productivity Review*, 15 (Summer 1996): 55–63.

69. W. Edwards Deming, *Out of the Crisis* (Cambridge, Mass.: MIT, 1986): p. 5. Also see Oren Harari, "Beyond Zero Defects," *Management Review*, 88 (October 1999): 34–36.

70. Ken Western, "No Matter What It Takes, I'll Do It," *The Arizona Republic* (August 1, 1993): F1.

71. See Figure 5 in Deming, *Out of the Crisis*, p. 88.

72. Adapted from discussion in Deming, *Out of the Crisis*, pp. 23–96; and Howard S. Gitlow and Shelly J. Gitlow, *The Deming Guide to Quality and Competitive Position* (Englewood Cliffs, N.J.: Prentice-Hall, 1987). Also see M. R. Yilmaz and Sangit Chatterjee, "Deming and the Quality of Software Development," *Business Horizons*, 40 (November–December 1997): 51–58.

73. Deming, *Out of the Crisis*, p. 59.

74. The debate is framed in Paula Phillips Carson and Kerry D. Carson, "Deming Versus Traditional Management Theorists on Goal Setting: Can Both Be Right?" *Business Horizons*, 36 (September–October 1993): 79–84.

75. Deming, *Out of the Crisis*, p. 24.

76. For more, see H. Michael Hayes, "ISO 9000: The New Strategic Consideration," *Business Horizons*, 37 (May–June 1994): 52–60; Lisa Sanders, "Going Green with Less Red Tape," *Business Week* (September 23, 1996): 75–76; Stuart F. Brown, "Detroit to Suppliers: Quality or Else," *Fortune* (September 30, 1996): 134[C]–134[H]; Amy Zuckerman, "The Economic Arsenal of the Global Economy," *Management Review*, 86 (January 1997): 57–61; Mustafa V. Uzumeri, "ISO 9000 and Other Metastandards: Principles for Management Practice?" *Academy of Management Executive*, 11 (February 1997): 21–36; and Olivier Boiral and Jean-Marie Sala, "Environmental Management: Should Industry Adopt ISO 14001?" *Business Horizons*, 41 (January–February 1998): 57–64.

77. For details, see Greg Farrell and Michael McCarthy, "Has Coke Lost Its Fizz?" *USA Today* (December 7, 1999): 1B–2B.

Acceptance theory of authority   Barnard's theory that authority is determined by subordinates' willingness to comply (Ch. 9)

Accommodative social responsibility strategy   assuming additional responsibilities in response to pressure (Ch. 5)

Added value negotiating   five-step process involving development of multiple deals (Ch. 16)

Advocacy advertising   promoting a point of view along with a product or service (Ch. 3)

Affirmative action program   making up for past discrimination by actively seeking and employing minorities (Ch. 11)

Alcoholism   a disease in which alcohol abuse disrupts one's normal life (Ch. 11)

Alternative dispute resolution   avoiding courtroom battles by settling disputes with less costly methods, including arbitration and mediation (Ch. 3)

Altruism   unselfish devotion to the interests of others (Ch. 5)

Amoral managers   managers who are neither moral nor immoral, but ethically lazy (Ch. 5)

Antecedent   an environmental cue for a specific behavior (Ch. 15)

Anticipatory changes   planned changes based on expected situations (Ch. 16)

Authority   right to direct the actions of others (Ch. 9)

Bargaining zone   the gap between two parties' BATNAs (Ch. 16)

Behavior modification   systematic management of the antecedents and consequences of behavior (Ch. 15)

Behaviorally anchored rating scales   performance appraisal scales with notations about observable behavior (Ch. 11)

Behaviorism   belief that observable behavior is more important than inner states (Ch. 15)

Benchmarking   identifying, studying, and building upon the best practices of organizational role models (Ch. 17)

Body language   nonverbal communication based on facial expressions, posture, and appearance (Ch. 12)

Break-even point   level of sales at which there is no loss or profit (Ch. 6)

Bureaucracy   Weber's model of a rationally efficient organization (Ch. 9)

Business cycle   the up-and-down movement of an economy's ability to generate wealth (Ch. 3)

Business ecosystem   economic community of organizations and all their stakeholders (Ch. 7)

Cafeteria compensation   plan that allows employees to select their own mix of benefits (Ch. 13)

Capability profile   identifying the organization's strengths and weaknesses (Ch. 7)

Causes   variables responsible for the difference between actual and desired conditions (Ch. 8)

Centralization   the retention of decision-making authority by top management (Ch. 10)

Closed system   a self-sufficient entity (Ch. 2)

Cluster organization   collaborative structure in which teams are the primary unit (Ch. 10)

Coercive power   gaining compliance through threats or punishment (Ch. 15)

Cohesiveness   tendency of group to stick together (Ch. 14)

Collaborative computing   teaming up to make decisions via a computer network programmed with groupware (Ch. 8)

Commonweal organization   nonprofit organization serving all members of a given population (Ch. 9)

Communication   interpersonal transfer of information and understanding (Ch. 12)

Comparative management   study of how organizational behavior and management practices differ across cultures (Ch. 4)

Concurrent control   monitoring and adjusting ongoing activities and processes (Ch. 17)

Concurrent engineering   team approach to product design involving specialists from all functional areas including research, production, and marketing (Ch. 3)

Condition of certainty   solid factual basis allows accurate prediction of decision's outcome (Ch. 8)

Condition of risk   decision made on basis of incomplete but reliable information (Ch. 8)

Condition of uncertainty   no reliable factual information available (Ch. 8)

Conflict   incompatible behaviors that make another person less effective (Ch. 16)

Conflict trigger   any factor that increases the chances of conflict (Ch. 16)

Conformity   complying with prevailing role expectations and norms (Ch. 14)

Contingency approach   research effort to determine which managerial practices and techniques are appropriate in specific situations (Ch. 2)

Contingency design   fitting the organization to its environment (Ch. 10)

Contingency plan   a backup plan for emergencies (Ch. 17)

Contingent time off   rewarding people with early time off when they get the job done (Ch. 13)

Contingent workers   part-timers and other employees who do not have a long-term implicit contract with their ultimate employers (Ch. 3)

Continuous reinforcement   every instance of a behavior is rewarded (Ch. 15)

Contribution margin   selling price per unit minus variable costs per unit (Ch. 6)

Control   taking preventive or corrective actions to keep things on track (Ch. 17)

Control chart   visual aid showing acceptable and unacceptable variations from the norm for repetitive operations (Ch. 17)

Corporate philanthropy   charitable donation of company resources (Ch. 5)

Corporate social responsibility   idea that business has social obligations above and beyond making a profit (Ch. 5)

Creativity   the reorganization of experience into new configurations (Ch. 8)

Crisis management   anticipating and preparing for events that could damage the organization (Ch. 17)

Critical path   most time-consuming route through a PERT network (Ch. 6)

Cross-cultural training   guided experience that helps people live and work in foreign cultures (Ch. 4)

Cross-functional team   task group staffed with a mix of specialists pursuing a common objective (Ch. 14)

Cross-sectional scenarios   describing future situations at a given point in time (Ch. 7)

Culture   a population's taken-for-granted assumptions, values, beliefs, and symbols that foster patterned behavior (Ch. 4)

Customer-centered   satisfying the customer's needs by anticipating, listening, and responding (Ch. 17)

Decentralization   management shares decision-making authority with lower-level employees (Ch. 10)

Decision making   identifying and choosing alternative courses of action (Ch. 8)

Decision rule   tells when and how programmed decisions should be made (Ch. 8)

Defensive social responsibility strategy   resisting additional responsibilities with legal and public relations tactics (Ch. 5)

360-degree review   pooled, anonymous evaluation by one's boss, peers, and subordinates (Ch. 11)

Delegation   assigning various degrees of decision-making authority to lower-level employees (Ch. 10)

Deming management   application of W. Edwards Deming's ideas for more responsive, more democratic, and less wasteful organizations (Ch. 17)

Demographics   statistical profiles of population changes (Ch. 3)

Departmentalization   grouping related jobs or processes into major organizational subunits (Ch. 10)

Differentiation (organizational)   tendency of specialists to think and act in restricted ways (Ch. 10)

Differentiation (strategic)   buyer perceives unique and superior value in a product (Ch. 7)

Downsizing   planned elimination of positions or jobs (Ch. 9)

Dynamic equilibrium   process whereby an open system maintains its own internal balances with help from its environment (Ch. 9)

Effect uncertainty   impacts of environmental changes are unpredictable (Ch. 6)

Effectiveness   a central element in the process of management that entails achieving a stated organizational objective (Ch. 1)

Efficiency   a central element in the process of management that balances the amount of resources used to achieve an objective against what was actually accomplished (Ch. 1)

Employment selection test   any procedure used in the employment decision process (Ch. 11)

Empowerment   making employees *full* partners in the decision-making process and giving them the necessary tools and rewards (Ch. 15)

Enlightened self-interest   a business ultimately helping itself by helping to solve societal problems (Ch. 5)

Entrepreneurship   process of pursuing opportunities without regard to resources currently under one's control (Ch. 1)

Equifinality   open systems can achieve similar ends through different means (Ch. 9)

Escalation of commitment   people get locked into losing courses of action to avoid embarrassment of quitting or admitting error (Ch. 8)

Ethical advocate   ethics specialist who plays a role in top-management decision making (Ch. 5)

Ethics   study of moral obligation involving right versus wrong (Ch. 5)

Ethnocentric attitude   view that assumes the home country's personnel and ways of doing things are best (Ch. 4)

Event outcome forecasts   predictions of the outcome of highly probable future events (Ch. 7)

Event timing forecasts   predictions of when a given event will occur (Ch. 7)

Executive reality check   top managers periodically working at lower-level jobs to become more aware of operations (Ch. 17)

Exit interview   brief structured interview with a departing employee (Ch. 12)

Expectancy   one's belief or expectation that one thing will lead to another (Ch. 13)

Expectancy theory   model that assumes motivational strength is determined by perceived probabilities of success (Ch. 13)

Expert power   compliance based on ability to dispense valued information (Ch. 15)

Extrinsic rewards   payoffs, such as money, that are granted by others (Ch. 13)

Feedback control   checking a completed activity and learning from mistakes (Ch. 17)

Feedforward control   active anticipation and prevention of problems, rather than passive reaction (Ch. 17)

Fishbone diagram   a cause-and-effect diagram (Ch. 17)

Fixed costs   contractual costs that must be paid regardless of output or sales (Ch. 6)

Flextime   allows employees to choose their own arrival and departure times within specified limits (Ch. 13)

Flow chart   graphic display of a sequence of activities and decisions (Ch. 17)

Forecasts   predictions, projections, or estimates of future situations (Ch. 7)

Formal group   collection of people created to do something productive (Ch. 14)

Formal leadership   the process of influencing others to pursue official objectives (Ch. 15)

Framing error   how information is presented influences one's interpretation of it (Ch. 8)

Functional authority   gives staff temporary and limited authority for specified tasks (Ch. 10)

Gantt chart   graphic scheduling technique (Ch. 6)

General systems theory   an area of study based on the assumption that everything is part of a larger, interdependent arrangement (Ch. 2)

Geocentric attitude   world-oriented view that draws upon the best talent from around the globe (Ch. 4)

Glass ceiling   the transparent but strong barrier keeping women and minorities from moving up the management ladder (Ch. 3)

Global company   a multinational venture centrally managed from a specific country (Ch. 4)

Goal setting   process of improving performance with objectives, deadlines, or quality standards (Ch. 13)

Grand strategy   how the organization's mission will be accomplished (Ch. 7)

Grapevine   unofficial and informal communication system (Ch. 12)

Group   two or more freely interacting individuals with a common identity and purpose (Ch. 14)

Groupthink   Janis's term for blind conformity in cohesive in-groups (Ch. 14)

High-context cultures   cultures in which nonverbal and situational messages convey primary meaning (Ch. 4)

Histogram   bar chart indicating deviations from a standard bell-shaped curve (Ch. 17)

Hourglass organization   a three-layer structure with a constricted middle layer (Ch. 10)

Human relations movement   an effort to make managers more sensitive to their employees' needs (Ch. 2)

Human resource management   planning, acquisition, and development of human resources (Ch. 11)

Human resource planning   meeting future human resource needs with a comprehensive staffing strategy (Ch. 11)

Idealize   changing the nature of a problem's situation (Ch. 8)

Incremental changes   subsystem adjustments required to keep the organization on course (Ch. 16)

Influence   any attempt to change another's behavior (Ch. 15)

Informal group   collection of people seeking friendship (Ch. 14)

Informal leadership   the process of influencing others to pursue unofficial objectives (Ch. 15)

Innovation lag   time it takes for a new idea to be translated into satisfied demand (Ch. 3)

Innovation process   the systematic development and practical application of a new idea (Ch. 3)

Instrumental value   enduring belief in a certain way of behaving (Ch. 5)

Integration   collaboration needed to achieve a common purpose (Ch. 10)

Intermediate planning   determining subunit's contributions with allocated resources (Ch. 6)

Intermittent reinforcement   rewarding some, but not all, instances of a behavior (Ch. 15)

Internal auditing   independent appraisal of organizational operations and systems to assess effectiveness and efficiency (Ch. 17)

Internal customer   anyone in your organization who cannot do a good job unless you do a good job (Ch. 17)

International management   pursuing organizational objectives in international and intercultural settings (Ch. 4)

Internet   global network of servers and personal and organizational computers (Ch. 1)

Intrapreneur   an employee who takes personal responsibility for pushing an innovative idea through a large organization (Ch. 3)

Intrinsic rewards   self-granted and internally experienced payoffs, such as a feeling of accomplishment (Ch. 13)

Iron law of responsibility   those who do not use power in a socially responsible way will eventually lose it (Ch. 5)

Issues management   ongoing process of identifying, evaluating, and responding to important social and political issues (Ch. 3)

Job analysis   determining fundamental elements of jobs through systematic observation (Ch. 11)

Job description   summary of duties and qualifications for a specific position (Ch. 11)

Job design   creating task responsibilities based upon strategy, technology, and structure (Ch. 13)

Job enlargement   combining two or more specialized tasks to increase motivation (Ch. 13)

Job enrichment   redesigning jobs to increase their motivational potential (Ch. 13)

Job rotation   moving people from one specialized job to another (Ch. 13)

Kaizen   a Japanese word meaning continuous improvement (Ch. 17)

Leadership   social influence process of inspiring and guiding others in a common effort (Ch. 15)

Learning organization   one that turns new ideas into improved performance (Ch. 9)

Legal audit   review of all operations to pinpoint possible legal liabilities or problems (Ch. 3)

Legitimate power   compliance based on one's formal position (Ch. 15)

Line and staff organization   organization in which line managers make decisions and staff personnel provide advice and support (Ch. 10)

Longitudinal scenarios   describing how the future will evolve from the present (Ch. 7)

Low-context cultures   cultures in which words convey primary meaning (Ch. 4)

Management   the process of working with and through others to achieve organizational objectives in a changing environment (Ch. 1)

Management by objectives (MBO)   comprehensive management system based on measurable and participatively set objectives (Ch. 6)

Managerial ability   the demonstrated capacity to achieve organizational objectives with specific skills and competencies (Ch. 1)

Managerial functions   general administrative duties that need to be carried out in virtually all productive organizations to achieve desired outcomes (Ch. 1)

Managerial roles   specific categories of managerial behavior (Ch. 1)

Managing diversity   process of helping all employees, including women and minorities, reach their full potential (Ch. 3)

Matrix organization   a structure with both vertical and horizontal lines of authority (Ch. 10)

Mechanistic organizations   rigid bureaucracies (Ch. 10)

Media richness   a medium's capacity to convey information and promote learning (Ch. 12)

Mentor someone who develops another person through tutoring, coaching, and guidance (Ch. 15)

Monochronic time a perception of time as a straight line broken into standard units (Ch. 4)

Motivation psychological process giving behavior purpose and direction (Ch. 13)

Motivation to manage desire to succeed in performing managerial functions and roles; one of the three elements of the basic formula for managerial success (Ch. 1)

Multivariate analysis research technique used to determine how a combination of variables interacts to cause a particular outcome (Ch. 2)

Negotiation decision-making process among interdependent parties with different preferences (Ch. 16)

New social contract assumption that employer-employee relationship will be a shorter-term one based on convenience and mutual benefit, rather than for life (Ch. 3)

Noise any interference with normal flow of communication (Ch. 12)

Nonprogrammed decisions decisions made in complex and nonroutine situations (Ch. 8)

Norms general standards of conduct for various social settings (Ch. 14)

Objective commitment to achieve a measurable result within a specified period (Ch. 6)

Objective probabilities odds derived mathematically from reliable data (Ch. 8)

Open system something that depends on its surrounding environment for survival (Ch. 2)

Operational approach production-oriented field of management dedicated to improving efficiency and cutting waste (Ch. 2)

Operational planning determining how to accomplish specific tasks with available resources (Ch. 6)

Operations management the process of transforming material and human resources into useful goods and services (Ch. 2)

Optimize systematically identifying the solution with the best combination of benefits (Ch. 8)

Organic organizations flexible, adaptive organization structures (Ch. 10)

Organization cooperative and coordinated social system of two or more people with a common purpose (Ch. 9)

Organization chart visual display of organization's positions and lines of authority (Ch. 9)

Organization development (OD) planned change programs intended to help people and organizations function more effectively (Ch. 16)

Organizational behavior a modern approach seeking to discover the causes of work behavior and develop better management techniques (Ch. 2)

Organizational culture shared values, beliefs, and language that create a common identity and sense of community (Ch. 9)

Organizational decline organization is weakened by resource or demand restrictions and/or mismanagement (Ch. 9)

Organizational effectiveness being effective, efficient, satisfying, adaptive and developing, and ultimately surviving (Ch. 9)

Organizational politics the pursuit of self-interest in response to real or imagined opposition (Ch. 14)

Organizational socialization process of transforming outsiders into accepted insiders (Ch. 9)

Organizational values shared beliefs about what the organization stands for (Ch. 9)

Organizing creating a coordinated authority and task structure (Ch. 10)

Ostracism rejection from a group (Ch. 14)

Outplacement the ethical practice of helping displaced employees find new jobs (Ch. 9)

Pareto analysis bar chart indicating which problem needs the most attention (Ch. 17)

Participative management empowering employees to assume greater control of the workplace (Ch. 13)

PDCA cycle Deming's plan-do-check-act cycle that relies on observed data for continuous improvement of operations (Ch. 17)

Performance appraisal evaluating job performance as a basis for personnel decisions (Ch. 11)

PERT (Program Evaluation and Review Technique) graphic sequencing and scheduling tool for complex projects (Ch. 6)

PERT activity work in process (Ch. 6)

PERT event performance milestone; start or finish of an activity (Ch. 6)

PERT times weighted time estimates for completion of PERT activities (Ch. 6)

Plan an objective plus an action statement (Ch. 6)

Planning coping with uncertainty by formulating courses of action to achieve specified results (Ch. 6)

Planning horizon elapsed time between planning and execution (Ch. 6)

Polycentric attitude view that assumes local managers in host countries know best how to run their own operations (Ch. 4)

Polychronic time a perception of time as flexible, elastic, and multidimensional (Ch. 4)

Positive reinforcement encouraging a behavior with a pleasing consequence (Ch. 15)

Power ability to marshal resources to get something done (Ch. 15)

Priorities ranking goals, objectives, or activities in order of importance (Ch. 6)

Proactive social responsibility strategy taking the initiative with new programs that serve as models for the industry (Ch. 5)

Problem the difference between actual and desired states of affairs (Ch. 8)

Problem solving conscious process of closing the gap between actual and desired situations (Ch. 8)

Product technology second stage of innovation process involving the creation of a working prototype (Ch. 3)

Production technology third stage of innovation process involving the development of a profitable production process (Ch. 3)

Programmed decisions repetitive and routine decisions (Ch. 8)

Quality conformance to requirements (Ch. 17)

Quality control circles voluntary problem-solving groups committed to improving quality and reducing costs (Ch. 13)

Reactive changes changes made in response to unexpected situations (Ch. 16)

Reactive social responsibility strategy denying responsibility and resisting change (Ch. 5)

Realistic job previews honest explanations of what a job actually entails (Ch. 13)

Reengineering radically redesigning the entire business cycle for greater strategic speed (Ch. 7)

Referent power compliance based on charisma or personal identification (Ch. 15)

Refreezing systematically following up a change program for lasting results (Ch. 16)

Response uncertainty consequences of decisions are unpredictable (Ch. 6)

Reward power gaining compliance through rewards (Ch. 15)

Rewards material and psychological payoffs for working (Ch. 13)

Role socially determined way of behaving in a specific position (Ch. 14)

Run chart a trend chart for tracking a variable over time (Ch. 17)

Satisfice settling for a solution that is good enough (Ch. 8)

Scatter diagram diagram that plots relationships between two variables (Ch. 17)

Scenario analysis preparing written descriptions of equally likely future situations (Ch. 7)

Scientific management developing performance standards on the basis of systematic observation and experimentation (Ch. 2)

Self-managed teams high-performance teams that assume traditional managerial duties such as staffing and planning (Ch. 13)

Semantics study of the meaning of words (Ch. 12)

Sexual harassment unwanted sexual attention that creates an offensive or intimidating work environment (Ch. 11)

Situational analysis finding the organization's niche by performing a SWOT analysis (Ch. 7)

Small business an independently owned and managed profit-seeking enterprise with fewer than 100 employees (Ch. 1)

Span of control number of people who report directly to a given manager (Ch. 10)

Stakeholder audit identifying all parties possibly impacted by the organization (Ch. 5)

State uncertainty unpredictable environment (Ch. 6)

Strategic business unit organizational subunit that acts like an independent business (Ch. 10)

Strategic changes altering the overall shape or direction of the organization (Ch. 16)

Strategic management seeking a competitively superior organization-environment fit (Ch. 7)

Strategic planning determining how to pursue long-term goals with available resources (Ch. 6)

Strategy the pattern of decisions a firm makes (Ch. 7)

Structured interview a set of job-related questions with standardized answers (Ch. 11)

Subjective probabilities odds based on judgment (Ch. 8)

Synergy the concept that the whole is greater than the sum of its parts (Ch. 7)

System a collection of parts that operate interdependently to achieve a common purpose (Ch. 2)

Technology all the tools and ideas available for extending the natural physical and mental reach of humankind (Ch. 3)

Telecommuting sending work to and from one's office via computer modem while working at home (Ch. 12)

Terminal value enduring belief in the attainment of a certain end-state (Ch. 5)

Theory Y McGregor's optimistic assumptions about working people (Ch. 2)

Time series forecasts estimates of future values in a statistical sequence (Ch. 7)

Total quality management (TQM) creating an organizational culture committed to continuous improvement in every regard (Ch. 17)

Training using guided experience to change employee behavior/attitudes (Ch. 11)

Transformational leaders visionaries who challenge people to do exceptional things (Ch. 15)

Transnational company a futuristic model of a global, decentralized network with no distinct national identity (Ch. 4)

Trend analysis hypothetical extension of a past series of events into the future (Ch. 7)

Trust belief in the integrity, character, or ability of others (Ch. 14)

Unfreezing neutralizing resistance by preparing people for change (Ch. 16)

Universal process approach assumes all organizations require the same rational management process (Ch. 2)

Upward communication encouraging employees to share their feelings and ideas (Ch. 12)

Values abstract ideals that shape one's thinking and behavior (Ch. 5)

Variable costs costs that vary directly with production and sales (Ch. 6)

Videoconference live television exchange between people in different locations (Ch. 12)

Virtual organizations Internet-linked networks of value-adding subcontractors (Ch. 10)

Virtual team task group members from dispersed locations who are electronically linked (Ch. 14)

Whistle-blowing reporting perceived unethical organizational practices to outside authorities (Ch. 5)

Photo Credits

Chapter 1 p. 3, Reprinted by permission of Umbrellas Plus; p. 11, Eric O'Connell; p. 18, Cindy Charles; p. 21, DILBERT reprinted by permission of United Feature Syndicate, Inc.; p. 24, Gail Albert Halaban/SABA; p. 27, Brian Smith.

Chapter 2 p. 39, AP Photo; p. 45, Corbis-Bettmann; p. 47 (top), UPI/Corbis-Bettmann; p. 47 (bottom), Stock Montage; p. 48, Aldo Mauro; p. 51 (top), Baker Library/Harvard Business School; p. 51 (bottom), Joan C. Tonn & Urwick Management Center; p. 52, Corbis-Bettmann; p. 61 (left), Reprinted with permission from The Tom Peters Group; p. 61 (right), Reprinted with permission from The Waterman Group.

Chapter 3 p. 70, AP Photo; p. 72, Bernd Auers; p. 74, Rick Solomon/One Digital Day/Against All Odds Productions; p. 82, AP/Wide World Photos; p. 86, Hosea Johnson; p. 93, John Abbott.

Chapter 4 p. 101, AP Photo; p. 105, Black/Toby; p. 108, AP/Wide World Photos; p. 111, AP/Wide World Photos; p. 115, David Lopez Espada; p. 118, Les Stone/Sygma; p. 126, Joanne Chan.

Chapter 5 p. 135, Gary Braasch/Woodfin Camp & Associates; p. 138, Gregory Foster; p. 144, Archive Photos; p. 149, Kenneth Jarecke/Contact; p. 156, Brian Smale.

Chapter 6 p. 165, Image Copyright 2000 PhotoDisk, Inc.; p. 169, Mark A. Wilson; p. 171, Mark Richards; p. 179, Catrina Genovese; p. 190, Sammy Davis.

Chapter 7 p. 198, AP Photos; p. 202, Thomas Sandberg; p. 204, AP/Wide World Photos; p. 208, © Michael Grecco; p. 213, Robert Azzi/Woodfin Camp & Associates; p. 219, Peter Gregoire; p. 220, Copyright Tribune Media Services, Inc. All rights reserved. Reprinted with permission.

Chapter 8 p. 227, Courtesy of Della.com; p. 229, AP/Wide World Photos; p. 231, Mathew Jordan Smith/Corbis-Outline; p. 239, Greg Foster; p. 245, Mark Richards.

Chapter 9 p. 259, Photo courtesy of The Neenan Company; p. 261, Tom Wagner/SABA; p. 264, Bob Pennell/Mail Tribune-Oregon; p. 273, Courtesy of Golden Gate Fields; p. 275, Ted Thai for Time; p. 283, Mojgan B. Azimi.

Chapter 10 p. 293, AP/Wide World Photos; p. 297, Karen Halverson; p. 303, Walter Smith; p. 308, Marc Joseph; p. 319, Alan Levenson.

Chapter 11 p. 327, Chuck Nacke/Woodfin Camp & Associates; p. 331, James Schnepf; p. 335, Greg Miller; p. 345, Webb Chappel; p. 348, Kristine Larsen.

Chapter 12 p. 358, Pam Francis/Gamma Liaison; p. 363, Nina Berman/SIPA; p. 370, Anna Curtis; p. 377, Bob Sacha; p. 380, The New Yorker Collection 1993—Peter Steiner from cartoonbank.com. All rights reserved; p. 382, Michael Greenlar/The Image Works.

Chapter 13 p. 393, Reprinted with permission of Norsk Hydro; p. 397, William Campbell/Time Life Syndications; p. 401, Eric Millette; p. 406, Arnee Adler; p. 410, Tova Baruch; p. 420, David Harbaugh.

Chapter 14 p. 428, © 2000 Eric Haase; p. 431, Franz Lanting/Aurora and Quanta Productions; p. 434, Sports Illustrated; p. 438, Israeli Army/SIPA Press; p. 446, Stefano Hunyady; p. 447, Will McIntyre.

Chapter 15 p. 457, Associated Press/The Tennessean; p. 460, Sammy Davis; p. 464, Nathaniel Welch/SABA; p. 466, Michael T. Keza; p. 475, David Strick/Corbis-Outline; p. 479, Lara Jo Regan/Liaison Agency.

Chapter 16 p. 489, AP/Wide World Photos; p. 492, Gideon Mendel/Network-SABA; p. 496, Tom Maday; p. 500, Jonathan Saunders; p. 503, Andy Freeberg; p. 509, Richard Howard; p. 513, Andrew Garn.

Chapter 17 p. 521, The Terry Wilde Studio; p. 523, AP/Wide World Photos; p. 525, Jeffrey McMillan for USN & WR; p. 530, Jean Claude Ernst/AP/Wide World Photos; p. 534, Ted Rice; p. 545, William Strode.